Oracle Press™

Oracle Database 12*c* PL/SQL Programming

Michael McLaughlin

New York Chicago San Francisco
Athens London Madrid Mexico City
Milan New Delhi Singapore Sydney Toronto

Library of Congress Cataloging-in-Publication Data

McLaughlin, Michael (Michael J.)
Oracle Database 12c PL/SQL programming / Michael McLaughlin.
pages cm
ISBN-13: 978-0-07-181243-6 (paperback : alkaline paper)
ISBN-10: 0-07-181243-1 (paperback : alkaline paper)
1. Oracle (Computer file) 2. PL/SQL (Computer program language) 3. Database design. 4. Database management. 5. Debugging in computer science. I. Title. II. Title: PL/SQL programming.
QA76.9.D3M39544 2014
005.75'85—dc23

2013047485

Oracle Database 12*c* PL/SQL Programming

1 2 3 4 5 6 7 8 9 0 DOC DOC 1 0 9 8 7 6 5 4

ISBN 978-0-07-181243-6
MHID 0-07-181243-1

Sponsoring Editor
Paul Carlstroem

Editorial Supervisor
Janet Walden

Project Manager
Hardik Popli,
Cenveo® Publisher Services

Acquisitions Coordinator
Amanda Russell

Technical Editor
Joseph McLaughlin

Copy Editor
Bill McManus

Proofreader
Amethyst Johannes

Indexer
Jack Lewis

Production Supervisor
Jean Bodeaux

Composition
Cenveo Publisher Services

Illustration
Cenveo Publisher Services

Art Director, Cover
Jeff Weeks

To Lisa, my eternal companion, inspiration, wife, and best friend; and to Sarah, Joseph, Elise, Ian, Ariel, Callie, Nathan, Spencer, and Christianne—our terrific, heaven-sent children. Thank you for your constant support, patience, and sacrifice that made writing yet another book possible.

About the Author

Michael McLaughlin is a professor at BYU–Idaho in the Computer Information Technology Department of the Business and Communication College. He is also the founder of McLaughlin Software, LLC, and is active in the Utah Oracle User's Group. He is the author of eight other Oracle Press books, such as *Oracle Database 11g & MySQL 5.6 Developer Handbook, Oracle Database 11g PL/SQL Programming*, and *Oracle Database 11g PL/SQL Workbook*.

Michael has been writing PL/SQL since it was an *add-on product* for Oracle 6. He also writes C, C++, Java, Perl, PHP, and Python.

Michael worked at Oracle Corporation for over eight years in consulting, development, and support. While at Oracle, he led the release engineering efforts for the direct path CRM upgrade of Oracle Applications 11*i* (11.5.8 and 11.5.9) and led PL/SQL forward compatibility testing for Oracle Applications 11*i* with Oracle Database 9*i*. He is the inventor of the ATOMS transaction architecture (U.S. Patents #7,206,805 and #7,290,056). The patents are assigned to Oracle Corporation.

Prior to his tenure at Oracle Corporation, Michael worked as an Oracle developer, systems and business analyst, and DBA beginning with Oracle 6. His blog is at http://blog.mclaughlinsoftware.com.

Michael lives in eastern Idaho within a two-hour drive to Caribou-Targhee National Forest, Grand Teton National Park, and Yellowstone National Park. He enjoys outdoor activities with his wife and children (six of nine of whom still live at home).

About the Contributing Author

John Harper currently works for the Church of Jesus Christ of Latter-day Saints as a principal database engineer. He greatly enjoys working with the data warehousing, business intelligence, and database engineers there.

John's mentors include Michael McLaughlin, Robert Freeman, Danette McGilvary, and many others who have spent considerable time becoming the experts in their industry. He is both awed and inspired by their abilities and feels lucky to be associated with them.

Recently, John has had the opportunity to work closely with some of the top-notch minds in database security. He hopes to produce a series of publications focused on Oracle products such as Oracle Audit Vault and Database Firewall, and Oracle Data Redaction.

John enjoys Japanese martial arts. During his teenage years and early adulthood, he took jujitsu, karate, judo, and aikido. He loves aikido and hopes to teach it one day. He would also love to learn kyudo if he can find any spare time.

John lives with his wife of over 23 years in Northern Utah County, Utah. They have one adopted daughter, whom they cherish and thoroughly spoil. He has been working with databases for the past 14 years, specializing in Oracle administration, database architecture, database programming, database security, and information quality.

About the Technical Editor

Joseph McLaughlin is an iPhone and Ruby web developer at Deseret Book in Salt Lake City, Utah. He has extensive backend database development experience with Oracle, MySQL, and PostgreSQL. His favorite development languages are Objective-C and Ruby.

Joseph is a recent graduate of BYU–Idaho with a degree in Computer Information Technology. While a college student and independent consultant, Joseph designed, developed, and deployed four mobile applications for the iPhone or iPod Touch.

Aside from programming, Joseph enjoys playing basketball and watching the Boston Red Sox win, especially when they win the World Series.

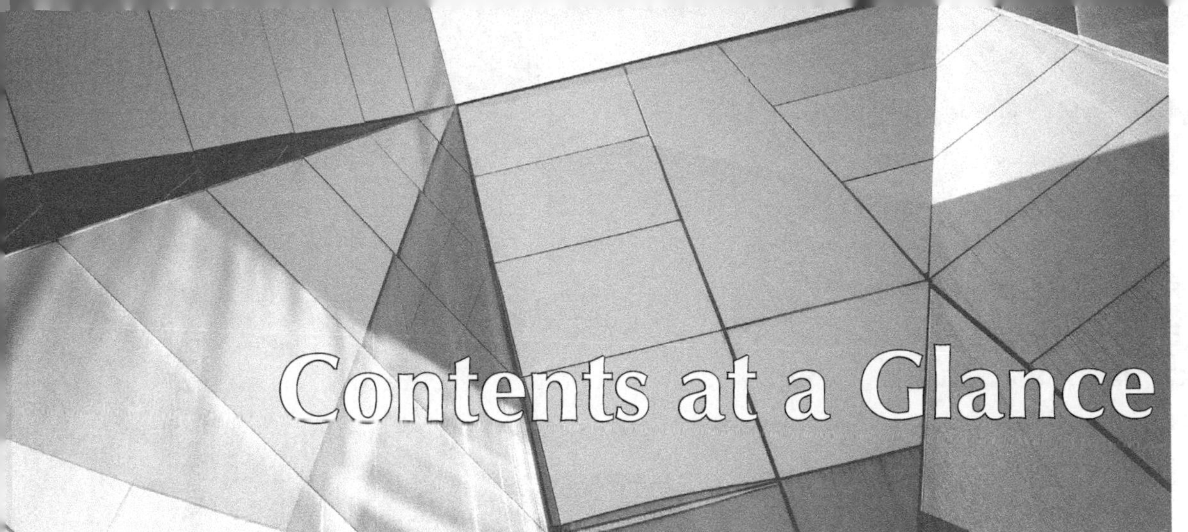

Contents at a Glance

PART I
Oracle PL/SQL

PART II
PL/SQL Programming

PART III
Appendixes and Glossary

Contents

PART III
Appendixes and Glossary

Acknowledgments

Many thanks go to Paul Carlstroem, Amanda Russell, Harry Popli, and the production team that made this book a possibility. There are many unsung heroes and heroines in the production department because they're behind the scenes. The production department typesets, proofreads, and gives their all to make books real, and while I don't know all their names, they deserve acknowledgment for their meticulous work.

Special thanks goes to Bill McManus, the copy editor. He gave an awesome effort to keep the book consistent, well written, and well organized! Special thanks for moral and project support to Paul Carlstroem and Amanda Russell because they were critical to my success, especially as the project went beyond a year. Thanks to Sheila Cepero, who manages the Oracle Publishers Program, for her help with the Oracle Database 12*c* beta testing cycle, and to Lynn Snyder, who managed the Oracle Database 12*c* program.

Thanks to John Harper who contributed elements of Appendix A and wrote Appendix D. John also acted as a second technical editor for the rest of the book, and his great eye for detail certainly contributed to the quality of the book.

Thanks to Pablo Ribaldi for his contributions to Appendix A on data governance. As the Information Governance Manager, he led the LDS Church's Information Communication Services team that won the Data Governance Best Practice Award from DebTech International LLC.

Thanks to the many students and lab tutors who took an interest in this project, like Craig Christensen, Jeremy Heiner, Matthew Mason, Alan Pynes, and Jordan Smith. Also, thanks to Kent Jackson for reading elements of the book and providing suggestions for improvements, and to Steve Rigby, my department chair, for his support in the project.

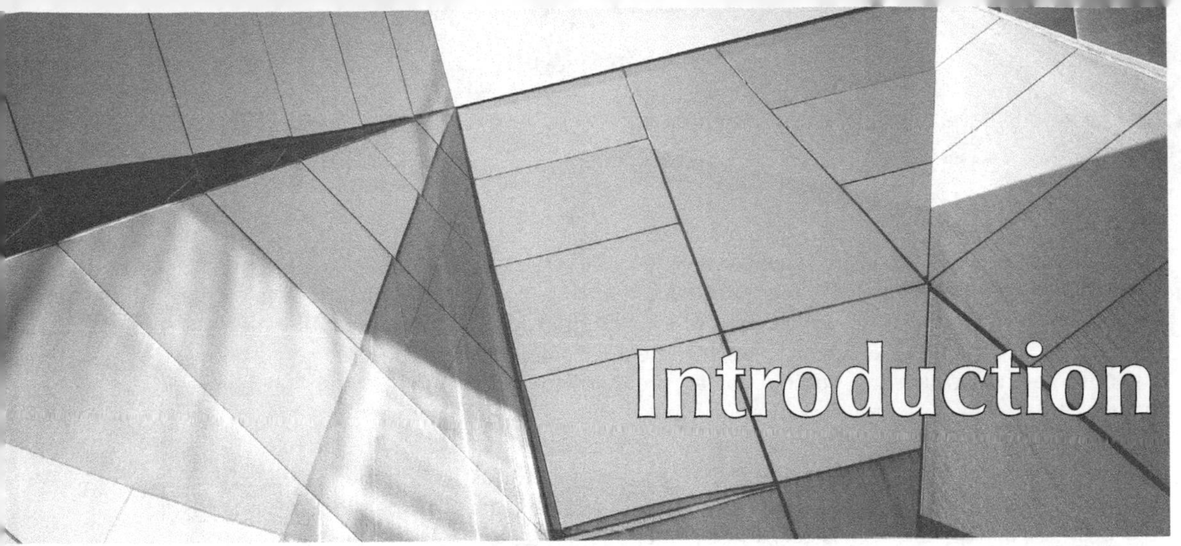

Introduction

This book shows you how to use the PL/SQL programming language. It is full of examples and techniques that can help you build robust database-centric applications. Appendix A shows you the basics of what you should know as an Applications DBA or developer, like starting and stopping the Oracle database and listener, using SQL*Plus as the command-line interface, SQL Developer as the free cross-platform GUI interface, and techniques for SQL tuning. Appendixes B, C, and D show you how to write SQL, use SQL built-in functions, and use PL/SQL built-in packages. The remaining appendixes show you how to use regular expression functions, obfuscate your PL/SQL code through wrapping it, use the hierarchical profiler for PL/SQL, and discover reserved and keywords.

As an author, the Introduction typically is either the last thing you write or the first thing you write. Unlike my strategy for the previous edition, this time I drafted the introduction before writing anything else, and that helped me to make sure I stayed true to a planned course. As indicated in my Acknowledgments page, the production staff also helps clear up what I write, and their talent is critical to bringing a quality book into print.

The introduction covers the following:

- The "Book Outline" section summarizes each chapter in a sentence or two, and should be worth a quick look to give you an overview of how this book is structured.
- The "Lexicon" section gives you the rationale for variable naming conventions in the book and provides recommended time-saving techniques you can use when debugging your code.
- The "Data Model and Source Code to Download" section describes the basis for the examples and tells you where to find the code that creates and seeds the sample video store database.

Book Outline

The book has three parts: "PL/SQL Fundamentals," "PL/SQL Programming," and "Appendixes and Glossary." In the first two parts of the book, each major section of each chapter ends with a "Review Section" that lists the key points presented in that section. Also, each of the chapters in the first two parts concludes with a "Mastery Check," containing ten true-or-false questions and five multiple-choice questions to help you ensure that you understand the material covered in the chapter. The answers are provided in Appendix I.

The third part, "Appendixes and Glossary," contains primers on Oracle Database 12*c*, SQL, SQL built-in functions, PL/SQL built-in packages, regular expressions, wrapping PL/SQL code, the PL/SQL hierarchical profiler, and reserved word and keywords. As mentioned, Appendix I provides the answers to the "Mastery Check" sections. A glossary follows the last appendix.

Part I: PL/SQL Fundamentals

- Chapter 1, "Oracle PL/SQL Development Overview," explains the history and background of PL/SQL and describes the Oracle development architecture. The history and background section explains how SQL is the primary interface, and how PL/SQL extends the behavior of SQL with a built-in imperative programming language, enables the implementation of object-relational features, and allows DBAs and developers to exploit the power of the Oracle 12*c* Database. The Oracle development architecture section covers how the SQL interface works as an interactive and call command-line interface (CLI), and how two-tier and n-tier models work with the Oracle Database 12*c* database.
- Chapter 2, "New Features," introduces the Oracle Database 12*c* SQL and PL/SQL new features. This chapter assumes you have a background in the Oracle Database 11*g* features. The new SQL features cover invisible and identity columns, expanded length of the `VARCHAR2` data type, and enhanced outer join operations. The new PL/SQL features cover invoker rights result cache functions, white listing PL/SQL callers, new error stack management features, embedding functions in the SQL `WITH` clause, and using local PL/SQL data types in embedded SQL statements.
- Chapter 3, "PL/SQL Basics," explains and provides examples of basic features of the PL/SQL programming languages. This chapter covers PL/SQL block structures, behaviors of variables in blocks, basic scalar and composite data types, control structures, exceptions, bulk operations, functions, procedures, packages, transaction scopes, and database triggers. You will find examples of all basic elements of PL/SQL syntax in Chapter 3. It's also the best place to start if you would need a review or introduction to the basics of how you write PL/SQL programs.
- Chapter 4, "Language Fundamentals," covers lexical units (delimiters, identifiers, literals, and comments) and variable and data types. In Chapter 4, you learn the basic building blocks of PL/SQL program units. You also learn what data types are available and how you declare variables of these data types. The subsequent chapters assume you know what data types are available and how to declare them in anonymous and named PL/SQL blocks, which makes it an important chapter to read or pursue before digging into the core features of the PL/SQL language.

- Chapter 5, "Control Structures," describes the conditional statements, iterative statements, cursor structures, and bulk statements. This chapter takes a complete look at `IF` statements and loops. Oracle implements the `IF` statement or `CASE` statement to manage conditional logic, and simple, `FOR`, and `WHILE` loops to manage iterative statements. The discussion of loops qualifies guard and sentinel values, and safeguards for dynamic sentinel values. This chapter covers how you manage cursors in loops and how you manage bulk processing DML statements.
- Chapter 6, "Collections," shows how you can work with SQL varray and table collections, as well as PL/SQL associative arrays (previously known as PL/SQL tables or index-by tables). This chapter's discussion of varray and table collections explains how you can work with both Attribute Data Types (ADTs) and user-defined types (UDT). It also describes the differences between how to use and work with ADT and UDT variables. This chapter also covers how to work with PL/SQL-only associative arrays that use scalar data types or composite data types, which may be record types or object types. This chapter also qualifies the functions and procedures of the Oracle Collection API, and provides examples of using these functions and procedures.
- Chapter 7, "Error Management," explains how you use exceptions in PL/SQL. This chapter covers exception type and scope, exception management built-in functions, user-defined exceptions, and exception stack functions. This chapter shows you how to find and solve the typical errors that can occur when writing PL/SQL programs. This chapter also shows you how to write exception handlers that manage unexpected runtime exceptions. You also learn how to manage exception stacks.

Part II: PL/SQL Programming

- Chapter 8, "Functions and Procedures," explains the architecture of PL/SQL functions and procedures, transaction scope, function options and implementations, and procedure implementations. The architecture section covers how pass-by-value and pass-by-reference functions and procedures work, including how to white list stand-alone functions and procedures in the Oracle Database 12*c*. This chapter also covers SQL positional, named, mixed, and exclusionary call notation. It also describes the various ways you can define functions, like deterministic, parallel-enabled, pipelined, and result cache functions. It shows you how to object table functions that return collections of user-defined types. This chapter also covers how you write recursive and autonomous functions.
- Chapter 9, "Packages," explores how you can work with and use packages. This chapter covers package architecture, specifications, and bodies. It also compares definer rights and invoker rights mechanics, and describes how the database catalog manages the status and validity of package specifications and bodies. This chapter reviews the concepts of how to write forward-referencing stubs and how to overload functions and procedures. It also shows you how to white list package specifications.
- Chapter 10, "Large Objects," shows you how to work with the `BLOB`, `CLOB`, and `NCLOB` internally managed data types and the `BFILE` externally managed data type. This chapter shows you how to create and work with character and binary large object that are internally managed, and how to work with externally managed binary files.

- Chapter 11, "Object Types," covers how you work with object types. This chapter shows you how to declare, implement, and white list object types, as well as how to implement getters, setters, and object comparison functions. After covering those basics, this chapter covers inheritance and polymorphism before implementing object type collections.
- Chapter 12, "Triggers," provides an introduction to database triggers and then shows you how to understand and implement various types of triggers, including DDL, DML, compound, instead-of, and system and database event triggers. It also introduces trigger restrictions.
- Chapter 13, "Dynamic SQL" explains the basics of dynamic SQL statements. This chapter covers Native Dynamic SQL (NDS) and the `dbms_sql` package. All four methods of dynamic SQL statements are covered, such as static DDL and DML statements, dynamic DML statements, dynamic `SELECT` statements with static `SELECT`-lists, and dynamic `SELECT` statements with dynamic `SELECT`-lists.

Part III: Appendixes and Glossary

- Appendix A, "Oracle Database Primer," explains the Oracle Database 12*c* architecture, how to start and stop the Oracle Database 12*c* server and the Oracle listener, Multiversion Concurrency Control, definer rights and invoker rights, SQL interactive and batch processing, database administration, SQL tuning, and SQL tracing.
- Appendix B, "SQL Primer," describes how to use SQL in Oracle Database 12*c*. This appendix covers SQL data types, DDL statements, DML statements, TCL statements, `SELECT` statements, and collection `SET` statements. This appendix also shows you how to unnest queries and how to work with persistent object types.
- Appendix C, "SQL Built-in Functions," provides code complete samples that show you how to use key SQL built-in functions of Oracle Database 12*c*. This appendix covers character functions, data type conversion functions, datetime functions, collection management functions, collection `SET` operators, number functions, error handling functions, and miscellaneous functions.
- Appendix D, "PL/SQL Built-in Packages and Types," explains how to use SQL the Oracle Database 12*c*. This appendix provides an introduction to new PL/SQL built-in packages and provides some examples of key packages.
- Appendix E, "Regular Expression Primer," describes how to use regular expressions in SQL and PL/SQL.
- Appendix F, "Wrapping PL/SQL Code Primer," shows you how to use the `create_wrapped` or `wrap` procedures of the `dbms_ddl` package.
- Appendix G, "PL/SQL Hierarchical Profiler Primer," describes how to use the PL/SQL Hierarchical Profiler. This chapter shows you how to configure the schema, collect profile data, understand profiler output, and use the `plshprof` command-line utility.
- Appendix H, "PL/SQL Reserved Words and Keywords," identifies which reserved words and keywords exist in Oracle Database 12*c*.
- Appendix I, "Mastery Check Answers," provides the answers to all the "Mastery Check" sections of the chapters.
- The Glossary provides definitions of the key concepts identified in the book.

Lexicon

There are many ways to write programs, and they generally differ between programming languages. SQL and PL/SQL code share that commonality: they are different languages and require different approaches. The three subsections cover, respectively, SQL lexicon, PL/SQL stored programs, and other conventions in syntax.

SQL Lexicon

My recommendation on SQL statements is that you align your keywords on the left. That means placing `SELECT` list commas and `WHERE` clause logical `AND [NOT]` or `OR [NOT]` syntax on the left, because it allows you to sight read your code for errors. That recommendation is easy to follow, but my recommendations on how to write *join syntax* are more complex, because you may write joins that use ANSI SQL-89 or ANSI SQL-92. Whereas ANSI SQL-89 lets you organize tables as comma-delimited lists, ANSI SQL-92 has you specify the type of join using keywords.

These are my suggestions on join syntax:

- Always use table aliases, because they ensure you won't run into an ambiguous column error when the `SELECT` list can return two or more columns with the same name. This can happen when you join tables that share the same column name. It's also a good practice to use aliases when you write a query from a single table, because you may subsequently add another table through a join. Appendix B covers the `SELECT` statement and syntax that supports this recommendation.
- When using ANSI SQL-89 and comma-delimited tables, place each table on its own line and the separating columns on the left, like `SELECT` list columns. This lets you sight read your programs. This doesn't apply to multiple-table `UPDATE` and `DELETE` statements found in Appendix B, and you should refer to those chapters for examples.
- When using ANSI SQL-92, you put the join conditions inside the `FROM` clause by using either the `ON` subclause or the `USING` subclause. Two common approaches seem to work best for most developers inside the `FROM` clause with the `ON` or `USING` subclause. In small (two or at maximum three) table joins, place the `ON` or `USING` subclause after the join on the same line. In large joins (three or more), place the `ON` or `USING` subclause on the line below the joining statement. When joins involve multiple columns, left-align logical `AND [NOT]` or `OR [NOT]` syntax to allow you to sight read your code. This is the same recommendation as I made for the `WHERE` clause at the beginning of the section, and it really works well generally.
- ANSI SQL-92 lets you use fully descriptive keywords or use only required keywords. While most of us would like to type the least amount of words possible, ultimately, our code goes to support staff, and its clarity can help avoid frivolous bug reports. Therefore, consider using `INNER JOIN` instead of `JOIN`, `LEFT OUTER JOIN` or `RIGHT OUTER JOIN` instead of `LEFT JOIN` and `RIGHT JOIN`, and `FULL OUTER JOIN` instead of `FULL JOIN`. I've shortened syntax in the book solely because the page-width constraints put a 70-character limit on code lines (or require shrinking the font, which make it less readable).

Now that I've written that, let me share my experience at *not* following syntax advice. The advice was given to me by my instructor at IBM's Santa Teresa Lab (now IBM's Silicon Valley Lab) when he taught me how to write SQL (actually SQL/DS [Structured Query Language/Data System])

A Word on Tools

This book focuses on writing SQL at the command line, because that's how it'll work inside your C++, C#, Java, or PHP programs, but CASE (Computer-Aided Software Engineering) tools are nice. They help you discover syntax and possibilities, provided you don't use them as a crutch.

The best developers aren't those business users who know how to talk a great game, use all the catchwords properly, and market themselves. The best developers are folks who learn how to solve business problems by understanding which technology truly provides the best solution.

Those who apply good engineering skills aren't members of an exclusive club when they lock themselves into only using what a CASE tool provides them. That's true because CASE tools generally only solve the general problems through a drag-and-drop interface. Those folks who advocate *NoSQL* solutions are typically those who never understood how to use a database or how databases help meet critical day-to-day transactional business needs.

In short, use a tool to learn; don't become a slave to it. Always ask why something works and how it might work better. If you do, you'll find that CASE tools are a blessing for getting your job done, not a potentially career-limiting curse (as many have found over the past few years).

in 1985. He told me to put the commas on the left and save myself hours of hunting for missing commas. I ignored the advice and put them on the right, at the end of the line, for a couple of months before realizing he was right. He repeated this maxim to me often that week: "Good programming follows simple principles."

At school now, I emphasize this advice term after term. Some students accept it and use it, and some don't. Those students who don't accept it struggle with the syntax throughout the course because they're always trying to find that missing comma or component in their SQL statement. SQL is not an easy thing to learn because it requires creating a spatial map of data, which isn't a skill all developers possess immediately. Sometimes it takes quite a while to sort through seeing the relationships between data in a relational database. It becomes easier with practice, provided you strive to maintain the clarity of your statements, the consistencies of your approach, and consistent choice of using portable SQL syntax.

PL/SQL Stored Programs

PL/SQL is a fully fledged programming language. It allows you to write programs stored in the database that manage collections of SQL statements as a complete transaction.

Variable naming conventions can be controversial in some organizations, because many developers believe variables should be semantically meaningful. The argument against naming conventions is that the conventions, such as prefixes, decrease code readability. This controversy is simply a conflict of ideas. Both sides have merit, and there are always situations in which choosing one practice over the other is logical. From my perspective, the key is finding balance between what adds stability to the company or corporate enterprise while providing meaningful variable names.

Here in the book, I've tried to be consistent and use prefixes. In some places, I've opted for semantic clarity in variable names (such as the Oracle session or bind variable `:whom` in Chapter 2). I believe that using prefixes increases readability in your code, and I suggest using the prefixes in Table 1.

Some advanced variable data types, known as composite variables, require both prefixes and suffixes. The suffix identifies the type of composite variable. These requirements are unique to the Oracle database. Table 2 qualifies my recommended suffixes (with a lead-in underscore) for Oracle composite data types. Table 2 shows you long and short name versions for the suffixes.

Using suffixes for composite data types is a generally accepted practice because they are UDTs. However, it isn't a rule or requirement in the PL/SQL programming language.

PL/SQL is a strongly typed language with declaration, execution, and exception blocks. Blocked programs use keywords to start and end program units, as opposed to the use of curly braces in C++, C#, Java, and PHP. As found in the GeSHi (Generic Syntax Highlighter) libraries, PL/SQL block keywords are in uppercase letters, and I've adopted that convention throughout the book.

Other Conventions

Sometimes code blocks need clarity. Line numbers are provided throughout the PL/SQL and SQL examples for Oracle because they're a display feature of the SQL*Plus environment.

The text conventions for the book cover highlighting, italicizing, and separating syntax. They are qualified in Table 3.

Hopefully, these conventions make reading the book easier. You'll also find that sidebars appear in gray-shaded boxes throughout the book.

Prefix	Example	Description
`cv`	`cv_input_var`	Represents cursor parameter variables. These are pass-by-value input parameters to cursors in PL/SQL stored programs.
`lv`	`lv_target_var`	Represents local variables defined inside PL/SQL stored programs.
`pv`	`pv_exchange_var`	Represents parameters to PL/SQL stored functions and procedures. They're not exclusively input parameters because PL/SQL supports input and output parameters in both stored functions and procedures.
`sv`	`sv_global_var`	Represents session variables. They act as global variables for the duration of a client connection to the database. Oracle lets you share the values in these variables between anonymous blocks by using a colon before the variable name (`:sv_global_var`) inside the block. Also known as *bind* variables.

TABLE 1. *PL/SQL Variable Prefixes*

Suffix		Description
Long	**Short**	
_ATABLE _AARRAY	_ATAB _AA	_ATABLE, _AARRAY, _ATAB, and _AA are used to describe associative arrays in PL/SQL. My preference is the _ATABLE or _ATAB suffix because the other suffixes aren't intuitively obvious and require documentation in your code.
_CURSOR	_CUR _C	_CURSOR, _CUR, and _C are used to describe variables based on a cursor structure defined in a local declaration block or a package specification in PL/SQL. My preference is the _CURSOR or _C suffix.
_EXCEPTION	_EXCEPT _EX _E	_EXCEPTION, _EXCEPT, _EX, and _E are used to describe user-defined exceptions in PL/SQL. My preference is the _EXCEPTION or _E suffix.
_OBJECT	_OBJ _O	_OBJECT, _OBJ, and _O are used to describe user-defined types (UDTs) in both SQL and PL/SQL. Object types can act like PL/SQL RECORD data types, which are record data structures. They differ because they're schema-level SQL UDTs and not exclusively PL/SQL UDTs. Object types can also be instantiable objects such as C++, C#, and Java classes. My preference is the _OBJECT or _O suffix.
_NTABLE _TABLE	_NTAB _TAB	_NTABLE, _TABLE, _NTAB, and _TAB are used to describe nested tables, which are collection types in SQL and PL/SQL. They act like lists because they have no upward limit on how many elements can be in the collection. My preference is the _TABLE or _TAB suffix because a nested table is the collection most like a list in other programming languages.
_RECORD	_REC _R	_RECORD, _REC, and _R are used to describe UDTs exclusively in PL/SQL. They are a PL/SQL implementation of a record data structure. They can be elements of PL/SQL collections but not of SQL collections. My preference is the _RECORD or _R suffix because they're fully descriptive or shorthand, but many developers opt for _REC.
_TYPE	_T	_TYPE and _T are used to describe UDTs, like subtypes of normal scalar data types described in Chapter 4. Either suffix works for me, but _TYPE seems more frequent in code repositories.
_VARRAY	_VARR _VA	_VARRAY, _VARR, and _VA are used to describe the VARRAY (my mnemonic for this Oracle data type is *virtual array*). The VARRAY collection is the collection most like a standard array in programming languages, because it has a maximum size and must always have sequential index values. It can be used to define SQL and PL/SQL collections. My preference is the _VARRAY or _VA suffix because _VARR too closely resembles generic variable shorthand.

TABLE 2. *PL/SQL Variable Suffixes*

Convention	Meaning
Boldface	Focuses attention on specific lines of code in sample programs.
Italics	Focuses attention on new words or concepts.
`Monospaced`	All code blocks are `monospaced`.
`UPPERCASE COURIER`	Denotes keywords used in SQL and PL/SQL, and SQL built-in function names.
`lowercase courier`	Denotes the names of user-defined tables, views, columns, functions, procedures, packages, and types.
[]	Designates optional syntax and appears in the prototypes.
{}	Groups lists of options, which are separated by a single pipe symbol (|).
|	Indicates a logical OR operator between option lists.
...	Indicates that content repeats or was removed for space conservation.

TABLE 3. *Text Conventions*

Data Model and Source Code to Download

The data model is a small video store. The source code to create and seed the data model for Oracle is found on the publisher's web site for the book:

www.OraclePressBooks.com

Figure 1 shows the basic, or core, tables used in the example programs.

One table in the model may require some explanation, and that's the `common_lookup` table. The `common_lookup` table is a table of tables, as shown in Figure 2.

A set of attributes (columns) that uniquely identify rows is the natural key. It consists of the table and column names plus the type. Types are uppercase strings joined by underscores that make querying these lookup sets easier. The `common_lookup_meaning` column provides the information that you'd provide to an end user making a choice in a drop-down list box.

The primary key of the `common_lookup` table is a surrogate key column, `common_lookup_id` (following the practice of using the table name and an `_id` suffix for primary key column names). A copy of this value is stored in the table and column, such as `item` and `item_type`. With this type of design, you can change the display value of *XBOX* to *Xbox* in a single location, and all code modules and table values would be unchanged. It's a powerful modeling device because it prevents placing components like gender, race, or yes/no answers in web forms (embedded options), and it reduces management costs of your application after deployment.

Let's examine an approach to leveraging common lookup tables in a web-based application. The explanation starts with data stored in a join between two tables—the `member` and `contact`

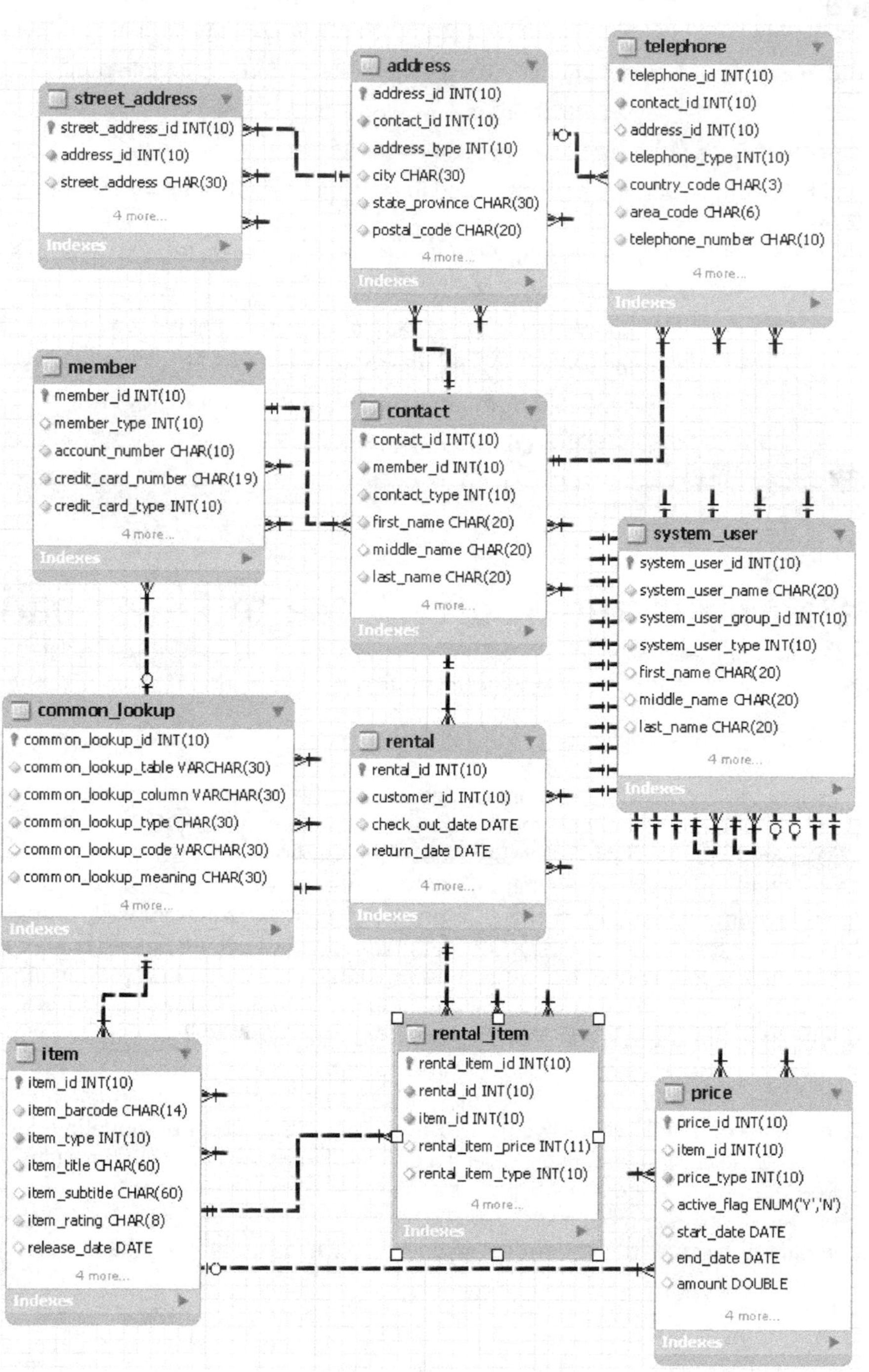

FIGURE 1. *Video Store entity-relationship diagram (ERD)*

common_lookup_id	common_lookup_table	common_lookup_column	common_lookup_type	common_lookup_meaning
1	SYSTEM_USER	system_user_id	SYSTEM_ADMIN	System Administrator
2	SYSTEM_USER	system_user_id	DBA	Database Administrator
3	CONTACT	CONTACT_TYPE	EMPLOYEE	Employee
4	CONTACT	CONTACT_TYPE	CUSTOMER	Customer
5	MEMBER	MEMBER_TYPE	INDIVIDUAL	Individual Membership
6	MEMBER	MEMBER_TYPE	GROUP	Group Membership
7	MEMBER	CREDIT_CARD_TYPE	DISCOVER_CARD	Discover Card
8	MEMBER	CREDIT_CARD_TYPE	MASTER_CARD	Master Card
9	MEMBER	CREDIT_CARD_TYPE	VISA_CARD	VISA Card
10	ADDRESS	ADDRESS_TYPE	HOME	Home
11	ADDRESS	ADDRESS_TYPE	WORK	Work
12	ITEM	ITEM_TYPE	DVD_FULL_SCREEN	DVD: Full Screen
13	ITEM	ITEM_TYPE	DVD_WIDE_SCREEN	DVD: Wide Screen
14	ITEM	ITEM_TYPE	NINTENDO_GAMECUBE	Nintendo GameCube
15	ITEM	ITEM_TYPE	PLAYSTATION2	PlayStation2
16	ITEM	ITEM_TYPE	XBOX	XBOX
17	ITEM	ITEM_TYPE	VHS_SINGLE_TAPE	VHS: Single Tape
18	ITEM	ITEM_TYPE	VHS_DOUBLE_TAPE	VHS: Double Tape
19	TELEPHONE	TELEPHONE_TYPE	HOME	Home
20	TELEPHONE	TELEPHONE_TYPE	WORK	Work
21	PRICE	ACTIVE_FLAG	YES	Yes
22	PRICE	ACTIVE_FLAG	NO	NO

FIGURE 2. *The common_lookup table (table of tables)*

tables. The internal lookup uses the customer's name (the natural key) from the `contact` table to find the membership account information in the `member` table.

```
SELECT   m.account_number
,        m.member_type          -- A fk to common_lookup table.
,        m.credit_card_number
,        m.credit_card_type     -- A fk to common_lookup table.
,        c.first_name
,        c.middle_name
,        c.last_name
,        c.contact_type         -- A fk to common_lookup table.
FROM     member m INNER JOIN contact c
ON       m.member_id = c.member_id
WHERE    c.first_name = 'Harry'
AND      c.middle_name = 'James'
AND      c.last_name = 'Potter';
```

The preceding query returns the following display when you run it through the `dbms_sql` Method 4 code example from Chapter 13, which displays column names on the left and column values on the right. You should note that the `member_type`, `credit_card_type`, and contact_type columns hold foreign key values based on the common_lookup_id surrogate key column.

```
   account_number: SLC-000006
      member_type: 6
credit_card_number: 6011-0000-0000-0086
 credit_card_type: 7
       first_name: Harry
      middle_name: James
        last_name: Potter
     contact_type: 4
```

You have the option of using these values to connect the data through a join or through function calls to the common_lookup table. The common_lookup table contains values that are frequently displayed in application software forms.

The following join connects all three foreign keys to three separate rows in the common_lookup table:

```
SELECT m.account_number
,      cl1.common_lookup_meaning -- Customer friendly display.
,      m.credit_card_number
,      cl2.common_lookup_meaning -- Customer friendly display.
,      c.first_name
,      c.middle_name
,      c.last_name
,      cl3.common_lookup_meaning -- Customer friendly display.
FROM   member m INNER JOIN contact c
ON     m.member_id = c.member_id JOIN common_lookup cl1
ON     cl1.common_lookup_id = m.member_type JOIN common_lookup cl2
ON     cl2.common_lookup_id = m.credit_card_type JOIN common_lookup cl3
ON     cl3.common_lookup_id = c.contact_type
WHERE  c.first_name = 'Harry'
AND    c.middle_name = 'James'
AND    c.last_name = 'Potter';
```

The preceding join yields the following meaningful business information:

```
       account_number: SLC-000006
common_lookup_meaning: Group
   credit_card_number: 6011-0000-0000-0086
common_lookup_meaning: Discover Card
           first_name: Harry
          middle_name: James
            last_name: Potter
common_lookup_meaning: Customer
```

The data returned from any query is symmetrical, which means all columns return the same number of rows. The results of the preceding query are the business results from three lookup activities, and they return the previously chosen values by a business user. However, the results are not what you'd want to display in a web form that presents the ability to change values, such as the member, credit card, or contact types. The reason they're not the correct values to display is that you need the currently selected values and the list of alternative values that an end user can choose when working in an application software form (as shown in Figure 3). Queries don't deliver that capability because result sets are limited to symmetrical data, like that shown from the last query.

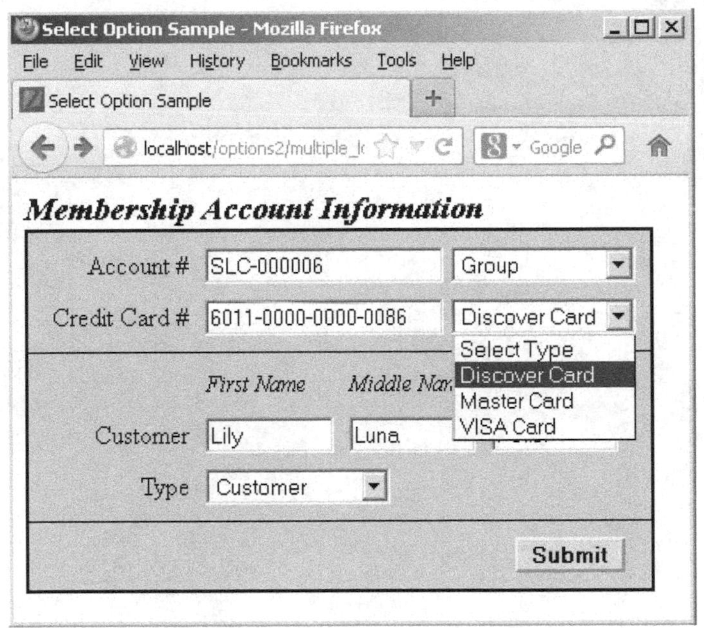

FIGURE 3. *Web form selectivity fields*

You need to get the current and possible values by using the foreign key as a parameter to a function call, and in this example you actually need to make a call by using the table name, column name, and current value. In an HTML web form, the function would return a set of HTML `option` tags to embed within an HTML `select` tag. The currently selected value from the lookups would be the selected HTML `option` tag, and the other possible values would be the unselected HTML `option` tags. This approach would return an asymmetrical result set like the following:

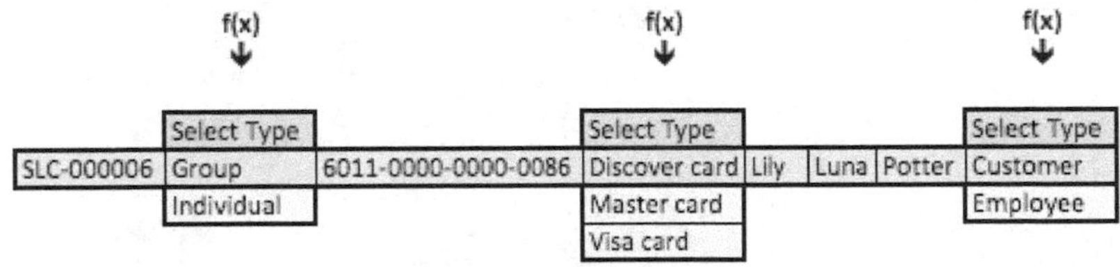

Taking this type of approach to commonly referenced values lets your application code leverage reusable modules more readily. Naturally, this type of function would be more ideally suited to a PL/SQL result cache function in an Oracle Database 12*c* application.

PART I

Oracle PL/SQL

CHAPTER 1

Oracle PL/SQL Development Overview

This chapter introduces you to Oracle PL/SQL development. Understanding the how, what, and why of a programming language provides a strong foundation for learning how to use the programming language effectively to solve problems.

This chapter covers the following:

- PL/SQL's history and background
- Oracle development architecture

The development examples in this book are presented using the SQL*Plus tool because it's the lowest common denominator when it comes to Oracle development. Although development tools such as Dell's Toad and Oracle SQL Developer are great in many ways, they also have a few weaknesses. Their greatness lies in simplifying tasks and disclosing metadata that otherwise might be hidden for months or years. Their weaknesses are more subtle. Tools provide opportunities to solve problems without requiring that you understand either the problem or the solution. Occasionally, this may lead you to choose a suggested solution that is suboptimal or incorrect. Relying on tools also stymies the learning process for new developers. While SQL*Plus is also a tool, it's the foundational tool upon which all other integrated development environments (IDEs) are based. A solid understanding of Oracle basics and SQL*Plus lets you use IDE tools more effectively.

PL/SQL's History and Background

This is the short version of how Oracle Corporation came to exist in its present form. In the 1970s, Larry Ellison recognized a business opportunity in the idea of relational database management systems (RDBMSs). Along with a few friends, Ellison formed the company Software Development Laboratories (SDL) in 1977. A few years later, the founders changed the company name to Relational Software, Inc. (RSI), and subsequently changed it first to Oracle Systems Corporation and finally to Oracle Corporation. Through a combination of its own internal development and the acquisition of multiple companies over the past three and a half decades, Oracle, as it is commonly called, has captured the majority of the RDBMS market.

The concept of an RDBMS is complex. More or less, the idea is to (a) store information about how data is stored or structured, (b) store the data, and (c) access and manage both the structure and data through a common language. Structured Query Language (SQL) is that language (pronounced "sequel" in this book).

Oracle innovated beyond the original specification of SQL and created its own SQL dialect, Procedural Language/Structured Query Language (PL/SQL). While many of the new features of PL/SQL were adopted by the ANSI 92 SQL standard, some remain proprietary to Oracle Database. Those proprietary features give Oracle a competitive edge. Unlike some companies, Oracle isn't content to simply be the leader. It maintains its lead and competitive edge because it continues to innovate. Likewise, Oracle currently sets the industry standard for relational and object-relational databases.

Oracle created PL/SQL in the late 1980s, recognizing the need for a procedural extension to SQL. PL/SQL was and remains an innovative imperative language that supports both event-driven and object-oriented programming. Perhaps the most important aspect of PL/SQL is that you can call SQL statements from inside it, and call PL/SQL from SQL. People still shy away from PL/SQL because they want to remain *database agnostic*, which is a fancy way to say they want SQL solutions that are easily portable to other platforms. Although major competitors have added stored procedures to their competing database products, they've failed to deliver the same power and capability of PL/SQL. The single exception is IBM, which simply implemented PL/SQL very similarly to how it works in Oracle Database. Unfortunately for IBM, the collections of Oracle SQL and PL/SQL built-ins and proprietary SQL extensions leave Oracle in the RDBMS technology lead.

In the late 1990s, Oracle saw the need for an object-relational extension to SQL. In response, it introduced object types in the Oracle 8 database and transformed the Oracle database server. It went from a *relational* database management system (RDBMS) to an *object-relational* database management system (ORDBMS). Oracle continued to improve how object types work in the Oracle 8*i*, 9*i*, 10*g*, 11*g*, and 12*c* releases. PL/SQL is a natural gateway to both creating and using these object types. Clearly, PL/SQL enabled the deployment and evolution of object-relational technologies in the Oracle database.

NOTE
The term object-relational model is interchangeable with the term extended-relational model, but Oracle prefers the former term over the latter.

Oracle also recognized, in 1998, the importance of implementing a Java Virtual Machine (JVM) inside the database. Oracle introduced a JVM in Oracle 9*i* Database. Oracle made improvements in the implementation of the JVM in Oracle Database 10*g*, 11*g*, and 12*c*. PL/SQL interfaces are used to access internal Java libraries that run in the JVM and to access external libraries in C-callable languages. The full functionality of an ORDBMS is possible because of the powerful combination of PL/SQL and an embedded JVM. In fact, PL/SQL has made possible the object-relational model we know as the Oracle database.

Figure 1-1 shows a timeline that covers the evolution of PL/SQL in the Oracle database. Interestingly, Oracle has provided 12 major feature upgrades during the 28-year history of the language. You'll note that Pascal is all but dead and gone, and Ada has had only four upgrades in the past 30+ years. The only language other than PL/SQL showing such feature investment is Java, which Oracle now owns.

From my years of experience with the product and other databases, I conclude that Oracle made the right call by adding PL/SQL to the Oracle database. PL/SQL is an extremely valuable and powerful tool for leveraging the database server. The ability to exploit the Oracle Database 12*c* server is critical to developing dynamic and effective database-centric applications.

Review Section

This section has presented the following details about the history and background of Oracle database:

- Oracle evolved from Relational Software, Inc. (RSI), which evolved from Software Development Laboratories (SDL).
- The SQL language is the interface to the Oracle Database 12*c* database engine, and Oracle extensions provide a competitive advantage.
- The PL/SQL language extends the behavior of SQL and has enabled the evolution of object-relational technologies.
- PL/SQL wraps access to embedded Java libraries.
- PL/SQL makes possible the implementation of an object-relational Oracle database.
- PL/SQL enables developers to exploit the Oracle Database 12*c* server.

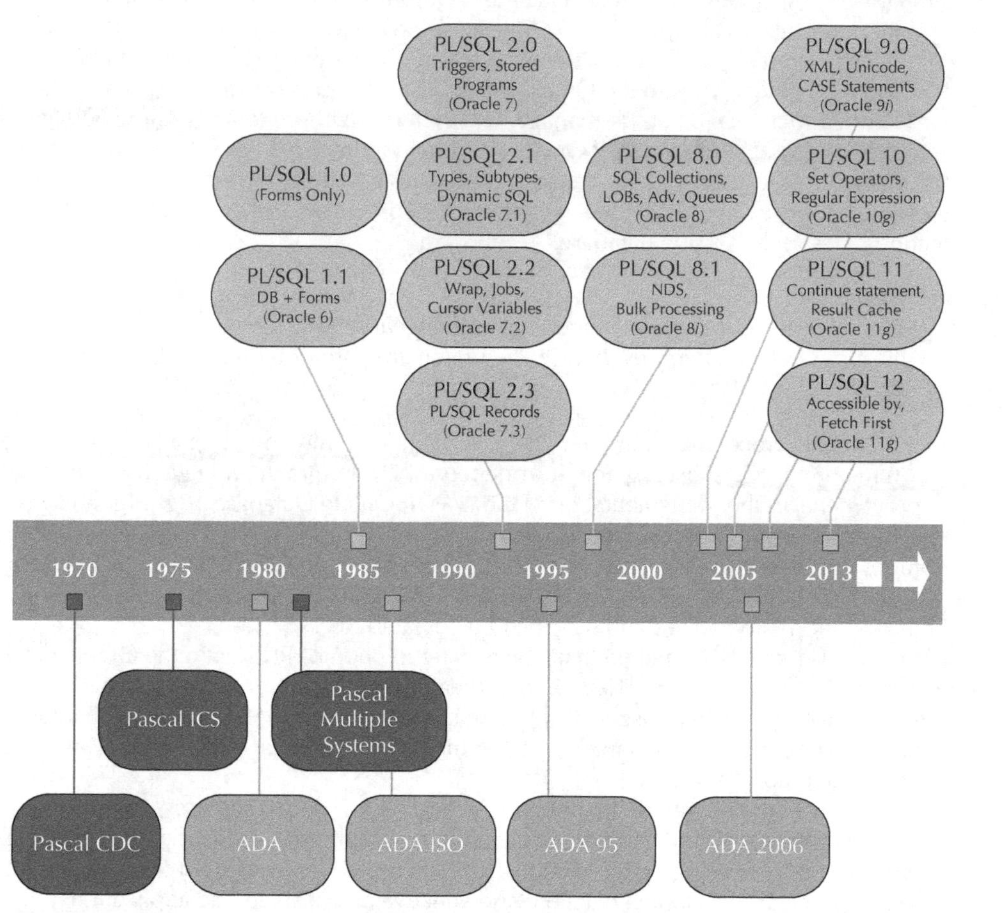

FIGURE 1-1. *PL/SQL language timeline*

Oracle Development Architecture

The architecture of a database has many levels. At the core of Oracle Database 12*c* is SQL. SQL is the interface to the Oracle Database 12*c* database engine, analogous to the steering wheel, brakes, and dashboard of a car. Analogous to the car engine is the server software, which includes an "engine" that stores and processes data, a "transmission" that governs transactions, and an enhanced "odometer" that logs what the system does to files. The server software also includes support programs that manage the system's content integrity, which are analogous to tires, body components, seat cushions, and bumpers. You can find much more about the Oracle Database 12*c* architecture in Appendix A.

Good mechanics must be aware of all the components that make up the vehicle. Likewise, database administrators (DBAs) must be aware of the many components related to an Oracle database system. The DBA is the primary mechanic who works with the engine, with the database developer getting involved from time to time. The rest of the time, the database developer drives the car, which means they focus mostly on the data and working with SQL.

Just as a mechanic maintains and tunes a car's engine to optimize its performance and longevity, a DBA works with the numerous details of the database engine to get the most value from an Oracle database. Many of the details related to RDBMS management don't involve developers. That's because developers focus on interacting with the data, much like how a racecar driver who reports performance problems as they arise. While developers do worry about performance, they often defer resolution of performance problems to DBAs. Those developers who don't take the work to the mechanic (DBA) all the time often cross the line between the DBA and developer roles. By crossing that line, developers often learn new diagnostic skills. Developers who frequently cross that line between DBA and developer roles often become known as *application DBAs*.

Driving a car requires skill handling the steering wheel, accelerator, and brakes, and driving the "Oracle car" requires skill with SQL statements. While some SQL statements let you build database instances (cars), like a factory, others let you maintain, repair, and tune the database. Still other SQL statements let you interact with data, allowing you to insert, update, delete, and query database data. SQL statements that let you interact with data are sometimes called *CRUD functions*, representing create, read, update, and delete (check Appendix B for more details).

Developers who drive the Oracle car often work on small to medium-sized projects, and they're only exposed to the necessary tables, views, and stored programs that support a business application. Application developers like this only work with a small subset of the SQL interface, similar to how drivers of real cars focus on the steering wheel, accelerator, brakes, and fuel gauge.

The following section explains how DBAs can use PL/SQL to maintain and tune the engine and how developers can use PL/SQL to optimize performance. While the details of how you maintain and tune the engine are interesting on their own, this book is targeted at showing you how to use SQL and PL/SQL to solve database-centric application programming problems.

NOTE

*Appendix A describes the database environment, the database components, and the primary interface points—the SQL*Plus command-line interface (CLI) and the Oracle SQL Developer graphical user interface (GUI). Appendix B describes Oracle's implementation of SQL, which is the most complete in the industry.*

Before I explain how to drive the "Oracle car," I need to give you a quick tour of the engine that runs the car. First, you need to understand some terminology if you're new to the Oracle database. Second, the same SQL that manufactures the database lets you "drive" the database. Likewise, SQL actually runs beneath the wizards that Oracle provides.

The Database

An Oracle database is composed of a series of files, a set of processes, and a single database catalog. You create a database by using a tool, such as the Oracle Database Configuration Assistant (whose executable name is `dbca` in all operating systems). The Database Configuration Assistant is one of the programs that you install on the server tier when you install the Oracle product. Collectively, these programs are called a relational database management system (RDBMS). The Database Configuration Assistant is a wizard that simplifies how you create an Oracle database.

When you use a wizard to create a database, it creates the necessary files, processes, and database catalog. The database catalog is a set of tables that knows everything about the structures and algorithms of the database. You probably have heard the database catalog or dictionary called *metadata*, or data about data. Metadata is nothing more than a bunch of tables that define what you can store, manipulate, and access in a database. An Oracle database is also known as a *database instance*. More or less, the RDBMS creates databases like a factory creates cars. Oracle Database 12*c* can create more than one database instance on any server, provided the server has enough memory and disk space. With Oracle Database 12*c*'s *multitenant architecture*, you also have the ability to create *container databases (CDBs)* and *pluggable databases (PDBs)*.

The easiest analogy for an RDBMS would be a word-processing program, such as Microsoft Word, Corel WordPerfect, or Apple Pages. After installing one of these programs on your computer, it becomes a factory that lets you produce documents. Another name that might fit these programs is document management system (DMS), but they're not quite that capable. In short, they provide a user interface (UI) that lets you create and edit documents. This UI is like the steering wheel, accelerator, brakes, and dashboard that enable you to drive a car, but the dashboard probably promotes the UI to a graphical user interface (GUI).

Oracle also provides you with a UI, known as SQL*Plus. Oracle actually originally called its SQL*Plus command-line interface the *Advanced Friendly Interface (AFI)*, as still evidenced by the default temporary file buffer, `afiedt.buf`. As an experienced user, I can testify that it isn't that advanced by today's standards, nor is it that friendly. At least that's true until you try the CLIs of MySQL and SQL Server. After using either, you'd probably conclude, as I have, that SQL*Plus is both advanced and friendly by comparison.

The CLI is the basic UI, but most users adopt GUI tools, such as Dell's Toad (expensive) or Oracle SQL Developer (free). (Appendix A provides guidance on installing, configuring, and working with SQL*Plus and SQL Developer.) Neither the SQL*Plus CLI nor the SQL Developer GUI is difficult to use once you understand the basics of how connections work (also covered in

Multitenant Architecture

Oracle Database 12*c* introduces the multitenant architecture, which is like an apartment complex for Oracle Database instances. While apartment complexes can be located in a single building or in multiple buildings, they generally have one location that manages the complex. Very large apartment complexes may have a centralized management office and local management offices in each of the buildings.

Oracle's multitentant architecture isn't too different from a large, multiple-building apartment complex with a centralized management office. The container database (CDB) is the centralized management office, and pluggable databases (PDBs) are the apartment buildings with local management offices.

Like an apartment complex's centralized management office, the CDB holds the master `sys` and `system` schemas. Individual PDBs hold an `ADMIN` user that enjoys `sysdba` privileges for the PDB, like the `sys` schema does in the CDB. PDBs also hold a `system` schema that works discretely with an individual PDB. The local PDB `ADMIN` user's `sys` and `system` schemas are like the local building manager in a very large apartment complex. Appendix A describes how you configure a PDB.

Appendix A). You need to understand how to use at least one of these tools to operate the Oracle database more effectively.

The command line is an essential tool when you write production code. Production code must be rerunnable, which means you can run the command when it has already been run before. To make production code rerunnable, you package together a set of related SQL and/or PL/SQL commands that you previously typed into a console interactively, and then put them into a file. The file, also known as a *script file*, could, for instance, drop a table before trying to re-create it. Dropping the table before re-creating it differently avoids an `ORA-00955` error, which tells you that you're trying to reuse a name already stored in the data catalog.

You run the script file from the command line, or from another script that calls scripts, which is why I'll show you how to use the command line in the "Two-Tier Model" section later in the chapter.

The PL/SQL Language

The PL/SQL language is a robust tool with many options. PL/SQL lets you write code once and deploy it in the database nearest the data. PL/SQL can simplify application development, optimize execution, and improve resource utilization in the database. PL/SQL isn't a replacement for SQL, which is a set-based declarative language that lets you interact with data and the database. As mentioned, PL/SQL is a powerful imperative language with both event-driven and object-oriented features.

Is PL/SQL Programming a Black Art?

Early on, PL/SQL 1.0 was little more than a reporting tool. Now the `CASE` statement in SQL delivers most of that original functionality. In the mid-1990s, developers described PL/SQL 2.*x* programming as a "black art." This label was appropriate then: there was little written about the language, and the availability of code samples on the Web was limited because the Web didn't really exist as you know it today.

Today, there are still some who see PL/SQL as a black art. They also are passionate about writing database-neutral code in Java or other languages. This is *politically correct speak for avoiding PL/SQL solutions* notwithstanding their advantages. Why is Oracle PL/SQL still considered a black art to these people when there are so many PL/SQL books published today?

Perhaps the reason is the cursors, but the cursors exist in any program that connects through the Oracle Call Interface (OCI) or Java Database Connectivity (JDBC). If not cursors, perhaps it's the syntax, user-defined types, or nuances of functions and procedures. Are those really that much different from their equivalents in other programming languages? If you answer "no" to this question, you've been initiated into the world of PL/SQL. If you answer "yes" or think there's some other magic to the language, you haven't been initiated.

How do you become initiated? The cute answer is to read this book. The real answer is to disambiguate the Oracle jargon that shrouds the PL/SQL language. For example, a variable is always a variable of some type, and a function or procedure is always a subroutine that manages formal parameters by reference or by value and the subroutine may or may not return a result as a right operand. These types of simple rules hold true for every component in the PL/SQL language.

The language is a case-insensitive programming language, like SQL. This has led to numerous formatting best practice directions. Rather than repeat those arguments for one style or another, it seems best to recommend that you find a style consistent with your organization's standards and consistently apply it. *The PL/SQL code in this book uses all uppercase letters for command words and all lowercase letters for variables, column names, and stored program calls.*

PL/SQL was developed by modeling concepts of structured programming, static data typing, modularity, exception management, and parallel (concurrent) processing found in the Ada programming language. The Ada programming language, developed for the United States Department of Defense, was designed to support military real-time and safety-critical embedded systems, such as those in airplanes and missiles. The Ada programming language borrowed significant syntax from the Pascal programming language, including the assignment and comparison operators and the single-quote delimiters.

These choices also enabled the direct inclusion of SQL statements in PL/SQL code blocks. They were important because SQL adopted the same Pascal operators, string delimiters, and declarative scalar data types. Both Pascal and Ada have declarative scalar data types. Declarative data types do not change at runtime and are known as *strong* data types. Strong data types are critical to tightly integrating the Oracle SQL and PL/SQL languages. PL/SQL supports dynamic data types by mapping them at runtime against types defined in the Oracle Database 12*c* database catalog. Matching operators and string delimiters means simplified parsing because SQL statements are natively embedded in PL/SQL programming units.

NOTE
Primitives in the Java programming language describe scalar variables, which hold only one thing at a time.

The original PL/SQL development team made these choices carefully. The Oracle database has been rewarded over the years because of those choices. One choice that stands out as an awesome decision is letting you link PL/SQL variables to the database catalog or cursor. This is a form of runtime type inheritance, and is best implemented when you inherit from a cursor rather than from a table or column.

You use the `%TYPE` and `%ROWTYPE` pseudo types to inherit from the strongly typed variables defined in the database catalog. Oracle calls this type of inheritance *anchoring*, and you can read a complete treatment in the "Attribute and Table Anchoring" section of Chapter 3.

Anchoring PL/SQL variables to database catalog objects is an effective form of structural coupling. It can minimize the number of changes you need to make to your PL/SQL programs. At least, it limits how often you recode when a table's column changes size. However, structural coupling like this is expensive because it causes context switches inside the database server.

Oracle also made another strategic decision when it limited the number of SQL base types and allowed users to subtype base types in the database catalog, enabling them to create a multiple-hierarchy object tree. This type of object tree can continue to grow and mature over time. These types of changes increase the object-oriented features of the Oracle database.

The PL/SQL runtime engine exists as a resource inside the SQL*Plus environment. The SQL*Plus environment has both an interactive mode and a callable server mode. Every time you connect to the Oracle Database 12*c* database, the database creates a new session. Calls from the server's CLI or a remote client's CLI may open an interactive session, while calls from external programs open a server mode session. In either type of session, you can run SQL or PL/SQL statements from the SQL*Plus environment. PL/SQL program units can then run SQL statements or external procedures, as shown in Figure 1-2. SQL statements may also call PL/SQL stored functions or procedures. SQL statements interact directly with the actual data.

Calls directly to PL/SQL can be made through the Oracle Call Interface (OCI) or Java Database Connectivity (JDBC). This lets you leverage PL/SQL directly in your database applications. This is important because it lets you manage transaction scope in your stored PL/SQL program units. This tremendously simplifies the myriad tasks often placed in the data abstraction layer of applications.

PL/SQL also supports building SQL statements at runtime. Runtime SQL statements are dynamic SQL. You can use two approaches for dynamic SQL: one is Native Dynamic SQL (NDS), and the other is the `DBMS_SQL` package. Chapter 13 demonstrates dynamic SQL and covers both NDS and the `DBMS_SQL` package.

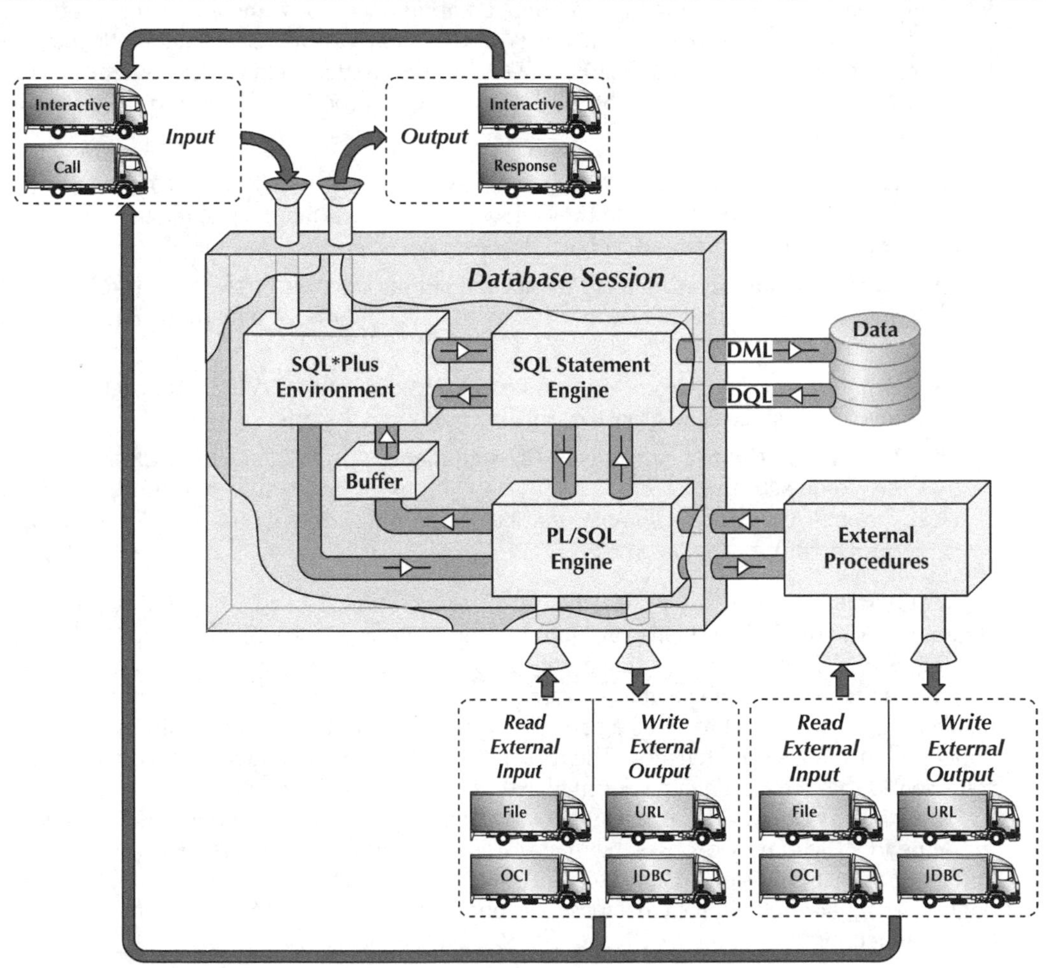

FIGURE 1-2. *Database processing architecture*

You now have a high-level view of the PL/SQL language. Chapter 3 provides an overview of PL/SQL block structures and programming basics.

The Oracle Processing Architecture

Figure 1-2 shows the Oracle processing architecture, or how you "operate the car." Notice that all input goes in through the SQL*Plus environment and all results or notifications return through the same environment. That means you're interfacing with the SQL*Plus CLI when you're working in the SQL Developer GUI, or through an external programming language such as PHP or Java. The only difference between external programming languages and PL/SQL is that you lose access to the interactive features of SQL*Plus when working through external calls in PHP or Java. You access the *call mode* of SQL*Plus when you call it through the Open Database Connectivity (ODBC) interface or JDBC interface.

As you can see in Figure 1-2, PL/SQL serves as the interface between the database and internally deployed Java libraries, file I/O (input/output) operations, and external procedures. SQL is the only point of access to the physical data, and as such it serves as an "automatic transmission" to the many processes that keep the Oracle Database 12*c* database running smoothly.

As covered in Appendix B, the SQL statement engine processes *all* types of SQL statements, which includes the following:

- **Data Definition Language (DDL) statements** `CREATE`, `ALTER`, `DROP`, `RENAME`, `TRUNCATE`, and `COMMENT`. They allow you to create, alter, drop, rename, truncate, and comment tables and other objects.
- **Data Manipulation Language (DML) statements** `SELECT`, `INSERT`, `UPDATE`, `DELETE`, and `MERGE`. They let you query, insert, change, and merge data in the database and remove data from the database.
- **Data Control Language (DCL) statements** `GRANT` and `REVOKE`. They let you grant and revoke privileges and groups of privileges (known as *roles*).
- **Transaction Control Language (TCL) statements** `COMMIT`, `ROLLBACK`, and `SAVEPOINT`. They let you control when to make data permanent or undo temporary changes. They enable you to control all-or-nothing behavior that's *ACID compliant* (check Appendix A for the details).

A SQL statement can call a named PL/SQL program unit, and a PL/SQL block can call a SQL statement. A named PL/SQL program unit is a function or procedure stored in the database catalog. A PL/SQL call to a SQL statement can only include SQL data types and named PL/SQL program units stored in the database catalog. That means it can't call a locally defined function inside a SQL statement. Procedures can't be called inside a SQL statement directly; they must be contained inside a stored function. The reason that you can't call a local function inside a SQL statement is that the SQL engine doesn't have access to a local function.

A complete book would be required to cover all the features in the Oracle SQL implementation, but Appendix B certainly exposes the majority of core features that any reader will use to develop applications or administer a database. SQL is like the automatic transmission to all the complex engine parts that run the Oracle database. Beyond an introduction to SQL, Appendix C covers SQL built-in functions and Appendix D covers PL/SQL built-in packages.

The next two sections discuss the connection mechanism for Oracle databases. The basics of the *two-tier* computing model are described first, followed by a discussion of the more complex *three-tier* model, which is really an *n*-tier model. Understanding these models is essential to understanding how you can use SQL or PL/SQL.

Two-Tier Model

All databases adopt a two-tier model: the engine and the interface. The server is the database engine and a database listener. A *listener* implements the object-oriented analysis and design *observer* pattern. The observer pattern is mainly used to implement distributed event-handling systems. Oracle's listener is a program that listens for incoming requests on an ephemeral (or short-lived) port, and forwards them to a SQL*Plus session. The client is the interface that lets you issue SQL commands and, in Oracle, lets you call PL/SQL blocks.

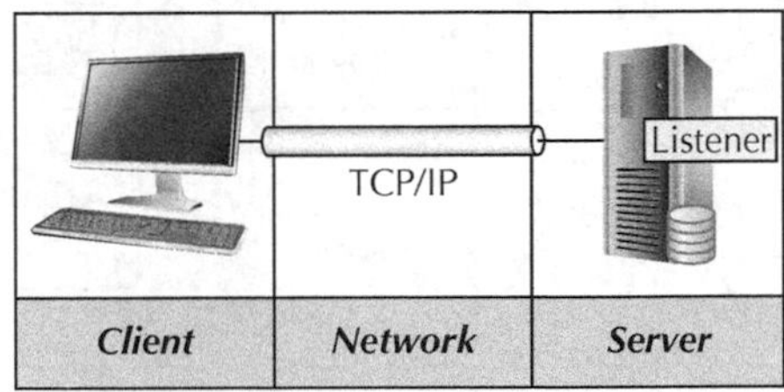

A typical installation of the Oracle database installs both the client and the server on the database server. That's because the mechanic (or DBA) who maintains the engine uses the same interface to manage many of the parts. Other server-side utilities let the DBA manage part replacement when the server is shut down. (Similar to how you'd replace parts in an engine, you'd shut off the engine before taking it apart to replace something.)

Our focus in this book is the interface to the running engine. We use the database server copy of the client software when we drive the database from the local server. Sometimes we want to drive the database remotely from a laptop. We have several ways to accomplish that process. One is to install a copy of the Oracle Client software on a remote machine. Another is to use a tool, such as SQL Developer, to connect across the network.

N-Tier Model

All databases support a three-tier model, because it's really just a middleware solution. As you can see in Figure 1-3, the middle tier of a three-tier model may have many moving parts, and they work like tiers. That's why the industry adopted the *n*-tier model over the original three-tier model. An *n*-tier model more aptly describes what's actually happening in web-based applications. The middleware

- Can have a multithreaded JServlet, Apache module, or general software appliance
- Can have a metric server layer to balance load across multiple devices
- Creates a pool of connections to the Oracle database and shares the connections with requests made by other clients

Typically in an *n*-tier model, the client-to-middleware communication doesn't enjoy a state-aware connection (see Figure 1-3). In fact, it's often stateless through the HTTP/HTTPS protocols.

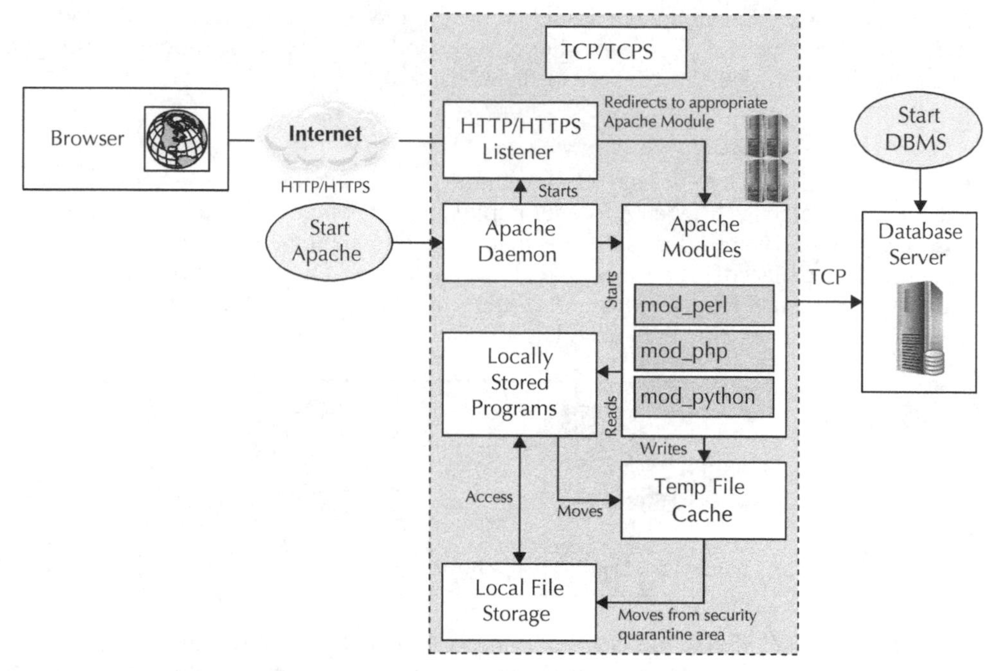

FIGURE 1-3. *N-tier computing model*

This shift in communication semantics means changes are automatic and permanent when they occur. If you submit a data change via an `INSERT`, `UPDATE`, or `DELETE` statement across HTTP/HTTPS and receive acknowledgement of success, that change is permanent. This is known as an *optimistic processing model*. It alone is a reason for stored procedures that manage transactions across multiple tables in any database.

The exception to an optimistic process occurs when the middleware maintains a lock on the data and manages your transaction scope for you. This type of implementation is done for you by default in Oracle Enterprise Manager (OEM) or Oracle Application Express (APEX). Describing the mechanics of how this works would require a chapter of its own. Suffice it to say, this is a possible architecture for your internally developed applications.

Review Section

This section has described the following points about Oracle database architecture:

- SQL is the interface that lets you manage, maintain, and use the Oracle Database 12*c* database engine.
- Oracle provides a SQL*Plus CLI and several GUIs that all interact with SQL and PL/SQL.

- The SQL language is the "automatic transmission" to the data and many processes that keep the Oracle Database 12c database running smoothly. SQL replaces imperative languages as the interface to relational data and RDBMS management.
- The two-tier model represents how SQL works with the data, with the SQL*Plus CLI or SQL GUI acting as the client and the database engine acting as the server.
- The *n*-tier model represents how web-based applications engage the data through a middle tier, which can be three or more tiers in depth.

Summary

This chapter has provided a tour of the Oracle development environment for client- and server-side PL/SQL development. In conjunction with Appendixes A and B, you should be positioned to understand, work with, and experiment with the examples in the subsequent chapters.

Mastery Check

The mastery check is a series of true-or-false and multiple-choice questions that let you confirm how well you understand the material in the chapter. You may check Appendix I for answers to these questions.

True or False:

1. ___Relational Software, Inc. became Oracle Corporation.
2. ___Relational databases store information about how data is stored.
3. ___Relational databases store data.
4. ___SQL is an imperative language that lets you work in the Oracle database.
5. ___The relational database model evolved from the object-relational database model.
6. ___PL/SQL is the procedural extension of SQL.
7. ___PL/SQL is an imperative language that is both event-driven and object-oriented.
8. ___The Oracle database relies on an external Java Virtual Machine to run stored Java libraries.
9. ___A two-tier model works between a browser and a database server.
10. ___A three-tier model is a specialized form of an *n*-tier model.

Multiple Choice:

11. Which of the following describes the roles of the Oracle listener? (Multiple answers possible)

    A. Listen for incoming client requests

    B. Send outgoing requests to client software

    C. Forward requests to the PL/SQL engine

    D. Forward requests to a SQL*Plus session

    E. Forward requests to the SQL engine

12. Which of the following converts a relational model to an object-relational model? (Multiple answers possible)
    A. A data catalog
    B. A set of tables
    C. An object data type
    D. An imperative language that lets you build native object types
    E. A JVM inside the database
13. SQL*Plus provides which of the following? (Multiple answers possible)
    A. An interactive mode
    B. A call mode
    C. A server mode
    D. A client mode
    E. All of the above
14. Which of the following is a capability of PL/SQL?
    A. Call SQL
    B. Implement object types
    C. Wrap C-callable programs
    D. Wrap Java programs
    E. All of the above
15. Which of the following are types of SQL statements? (Multiple answers possible)
    A. Data Definition Language (DDL) statements
    B. Data Manipulation Language (DML) statements
    C. Data Control Language (DCL) statements
    D. Create, replace, update, and delete (CRUD) statements
    E. Transaction Control Language (TCL) statements

CHAPTER 2

New Features

This chapter covers the new SQL and PL/SQL features that directly affect how you write and manage Oracle PL/SQL programs. At the time of writing, I can't guarantee that an additional new feature or two won't get added late in this release cycle or in the next release cycle, so check the *Oracle Database New Features Guide* for the latest updates.

Coverage of the new features in this chapter is divided into the two languages:

- New SQL features
- New PL/SQL features

Some of the features lend themselves to multiple-page descriptions with examples, while others require only a brief introduction because they are described elsewhere in the book—in which case you are referred to the chapter in which the feature is covered. If you're new to PL/SQL, you may want to skip directly to Chapter 3 to read about PL/SQL basics and then return to this chapter.

New SQL Features

Oracle offers a number of new features in Oracle Database 12*c*. The SQL syntax changes are fairly numerous, so we'll concentrate here on the changes that have an impact of functionality.

- Oracle Database 12*c* enables you to use virtual directories in the `LIBRARY` path for external procedures.
- Flashback technology improves with the introduction of valid-time (VT) dimensions.
- The functionality of Oracle's ANSI 92 join syntax grew in Oracle Database 12*c*. You can now perform a `LEFT OUTER JOIN` against two or more tables on the left side of the join.
- Default column values can now hold references to the `.nextval` and `.currval` pseudocolumns, which is a neat feature.
- Oracle Database 12*c* introduces identity columns that maintain auto-incrementing sequences for surrogate keys.
- Oracle Database 12*c* adds the `ON NULL` clause to default values, which closes the door to explicit overrides with a null in the list of values.
- Oracle Database 12*c* increases the size of `VARCHAR2`, `NVARCHAR2`, and `RAW` data types, at least when you set a database parameter correctly.
- Like Microsoft SQL Server, Oracle Database 12*c* enables you to pass the results of queries directly to external programs.
- Oracle Database 12*c* provides native SQL support for query row limits and offsets.
- Oracle Database 12*c* adds a new driver as a drop-in replacement for the MySQL 5.5 client library.
- SQL has gained `CROSS APPLY`, `OUTER APPLY`, and `LATERAL` syntax for when you work with nested tables.
- You can now create views with either definer rights—the old way and current default—or with invoker rights. The only difference is the syntax: the definer rights model uses `BEQUEATH DEFINER` and the invoker rights model uses `BEQUEATH INVOKER`.

Data Catalog DIRECTORY Qualifies a LIBRARY Object

`LIBRARY` objects are repositories for external libraries. External libraries are written in C or a C-callable programming language. They require you to put the physical files in a directory and then specify the name of that directory in the `listener.ora` file and the `CREATE LIBRARY` statement.

Oracle Database 12*c* adds the capability to replace a physical directory with a virtual directory. The following syntax shows you how to create a library with a physical directory:

```
SQL> CREATE OR REPLACE LIBRARY demo IS
  '<oracle_home_directory>/<custom_library>/<file_name>.<file_ext>';
/
```

You can create a `LIBRARY` object by using this new syntax against a virtual directory:

```
SQL> CREATE OR REPLACE LIBRARY demo IS '<library_name.so>' IN
  virtual_directory_name;
```

The second argument is a virtual directory. You can learn how to create virtual directories in the "Virtual Directories" section of Appendix B. That process remains unchanged with the Oracle Database 12*c* release.

Define Tables with Valid-Time (VT) Support

A valid-time (VT) support dimension is now available in Oracle Database 12*c*. Valid time differs from transaction time (TT). VT maps the effective date of a business event, such as a hiring, promotion, or termination. TT maps to the physical point at which a row is inserted or updated.

Oracle Database 11*g* introduced Flashback Data Archive, which uses TT. Flashback lets you look back in time to see query trends, report differences, and audit trails. These are flashback dimensions because they segment data by time intervals.

Oracle Database 12*c* introduces a VT support dimension by formalizing two approaches in table definitions. One defines periods with explicit column assignments. The other defines periods with implicit columns. The new SQL phrase for VT is `PERIOD FOR`, as qualified in the `CREATE TABLE` examples presented in the following subsections.

It's important to note that VT rather than TT drives flashback operations. You use VT to manage your Information Lifecycle Management (ILM) process.

Table with Explicit VT Columns

Let's examine an example `rental` table. It has both `check_out_date` and `return_date` columns. Prior to Oracle Database 12*c*, these columns were managed by your application programming interface (API). They contain important business logic for how a video store, like Redbox, bills customers. The VT feature can now identify these critical columns explicitly, like this:

```
SQL> CREATE TABLE rental
  ( rental_id          NUMBER   GENERATED ALWAYS AS IDENTITY
  , customer_id        NUMBER   CONSTRAINT nn_rental_01 NOT NULL
  , check_out_date     DATE     CONSTRAINT nn_rental_02 NOT NULL
  , return_date        DATE
  , created_by         NUMBER   CONSTRAINT nn_rental_03 NOT NULL
  , creation_date      DATE     CONSTRAINT nn_rental_04 NOT NULL
  , last_updated_by    NUMBER   CONSTRAINT nn_rental_05 NOT NULL
```

```
 9  , last_update_date  DATE     CONSTRAINT nn_rental_06 NOT NULL
10  , PERIOD FOR rental_event (check_out_date, return_date)
11  , CONSTRAINT pk_rental PRIMARY KEY(rental_id)
12  , CONSTRAINT fk_rental_01   FOREIGN KEY(customer_id)
13    REFERENCES contact(contact_id)
14  , CONSTRAINT fk_rental_02   FOREIGN KEY(created_by)
15    REFERENCES system_user(system_user_id)
16  , CONSTRAINT fk_rental_03   FOREIGN KEY(last_updated_by)
17    REFERENCES system_user(system_user_id));
```

Lines 4 and 5 hold the business logic VT columns. Line 10 explicitly assigns an identifier to the period matching the business rule. This enables flashback queries against the period.

An example query with VT logic is

```
SQL> SELECT *
  rental AS OF PERIOD FOR rental_event
                TO_TIMESTAMP('04-AUG-2013 12:00:00 AM');
```

You also have options to use the `AS OF` field against VT intervals when you're using the `dbms_flashback_archive` package. I recommend the explicit VT column approach.

Table with Implicit VT Columns

Options are always available when Oracle introduces features. VT columns aren't an exception. You can define a table with implicit columns by removing any reference to columns in the table. In our preceding `rental` table example, that would mean changing line 10, like this:

```
10  , PERIOD FOR rental_event
```

Line 10 omits the columns from the `CREATE TABLE` statement.

Enhanced Oracle Native LEFT OUTER JOIN Syntax

The Oracle Database 12*c* database now supports `LEFT OUTER JOIN` syntax, which enables you to have two or more tables on the left side of the join. Prior to the new release, you were limited to a single table on the left side of a join. Any attempt to use two tables in Oracle Database 11*g* release raised an `ORA-01417` error.

The benefits are this new feature include the following:

- Merging joins on the left side of the join allows more reordering, which also improves possible execution plans.
- Supporting multiple views simplifies the effort of developers writing outer join operations.

The downside of the enhanced Oracle native `LEFT OUTER JOIN` statement is that it's not portable. The upside is that you get more effective outer join operations.

Default Values for Columns Based on Sequences

Oracle Database 12*c* provides the capability to associate sequences directly with tables. There are two alternatives. One lets you create a sequence and directly map it to a column of a table. The other lets you leverage identity columns (another new feature). While the latter approach doesn't benefit well from default independent sequence values, the former does.

Let's examine an example `customer` table, which, to keep it simple, has only two columns. The first column is a surrogate key column, and it holds a sequence value. Sequence values are unrelated to the data of any table, and should have a one-to-one mapping to the table's natural key. Natural keys are one or more (generally more) not-null columns that uniquely identify each row in table. The `customer_name` column is our natural key in the example. While it's clearly unlikely that a single `customer_name` column could ever be a legitimate natural key, it simplifies our example and lets us focus on the default column values.

Before we create the table, we need to create the sequence for this example. That's a departure from what we've done historically in the Oracle database, but this is our brave new world of Oracle Database 12*c*. We create a generic sequence that starts with the number 1 like

```
SQL> CREATE SEQUENCE customer_s;
```

The sequence needs to be created first because we reference it when we create the table with a default column value:

```
SQL> CREATE TABLE customer
  ( customer_id     NUMBER   DEFAULT customer_s.nextval
  , customer_name   VARCHAR2(20));
```

Since we want to demonstrate how to manage primary and foreign key values in the scope of a transaction, we need to create another sequence and table. The example creates the `preference_s` sequence and `preference` table.

Rather than separate it, like we did before, the code is combined:

```
SQL> CREATE SEQUENCE preference_s;
SQL> CREATE TABLE preference
  ( preference_id     NUMBER   DEFAULT preference_s.nextval
  , customer_id       NUMBER   DEFAULT customer_s.currval
  , preference_name   VARCHAR2(20));
```

The `DEFAULT` sequence values eliminate the need to write `ON INSERT` triggers. They also avoid requiring us to explicitly reference the `.nextval` and `.currval` pseudocolumns in sequenced `INSERT` statements. However, it's critical to understand that the dependency between `.nextval` and `.currval` hasn't changed. *You must call `.nextval` for a sequence before you call `.currval` for the same sequence in a session.*

NOTE
I recommend caution when deciding whether to adopt this technique, because of the dependency between the two sequence pseudocolumns.

We can now insert rows into both tables by using override signatures. Override signatures are lists of all mandatory and desired optional columns that we want to insert into a table. The inserts into these two tables should ensure that the `customer_id` columns hold values that match. That way, they support equijoins between the `customer` and `preference` tables.

```
SQL> INSERT INTO customer (customer_name) VALUES ('Mr. Scott');
SQL> INSERT INTO preference (preference_name) VALUES ('Romulan Ale');
```

Having inserted both rows without any explicit surrogate key values, let's check to see if Oracle Database 12*c* got it right. Using a simple query joining the result, like

```
SQL> SELECT   *
  2  FROM     customer c INNER JOIN preference p USING(customer_id);
```

should return

```
CUSTOMER_ID CUSTOMER_NAME PREFERENCE_ID PREFERENCE_NAME
----------- ------------- ------------- --------------------
          1 Mr. Scott                 1 Romulan Ale
```

The results show that this approach works. The upcoming "Identity Columns" section shows how to use those columns.

Default Values for Explicit Null Insertion

Oracle Database has long allowed you to enter default values for any column. Although you could override that behavior, it required you to explicitly provide a null value during an `INSERT` statement. Oracle Database 12*c* now lets you assign a default value when you opt to provide an explicit null value:

```
SQL> CREATE TABLE essay
  2  ( essay_name    VARCHAR2(30) DEFAULT essay_s.nextval
  3  , essayist      VARCHAR2(30)
  4  , published     DATE DEFAULT TRUNC(SYSDATE)
  5  , text          CLOB
  6  , CONSTRAINT essay_pk
  7    PRIMARY KEY (essay_name, essayist, published));
```

Line 4 guarantees that any attempt to exclude a `published` date results in the insertion of the current date. As qualified in Appendix C on SQL built-in functions, the `TRUNC` function shaves off the hours and minutes of any date-time data type. All `DATE` data types are date-time stamps in an Oracle database.

The following `INSERT` statement adds a row to the `essay` table. It works the same way in Oracle Database 11*g* as it does in Oracle Database 12*c*. It inserts the current date minus the hours, minutes, and seconds into the `published` column. It does so because the `published` column isn't in the list of columns in the override signature.

```
INSERT INTO essay
( essay_name
, essayist
, text )
VALUES
('Why Would I Want to be Superman'
,'21-SEP-2011'
,'At one point or another, everyone has wanted to be someone ...');
```

If you add the `published` column to the override signature, then you can insert an explicit null value. That explicit null value overrides the standard default value. Prior to Oracle Database 12*c*, there was no way to prevent that overriding value. Oracle Database 12*c* provides the `ON NULL` phrase to enable you to prevent an explicit null from being inserted in the column.

You change the value by making this change to line 4 of the `CREATE TABLE` statement:

```
4  , published    DATE DEFAULT ON NULL TRUNC(SYSDATE)
```

The `ON NULL` phrase ensures that you can't insert a null value into the `published` column. This type of change eliminates the need for a database trigger, which would prevent the insertion of a null value in an Oracle Database 11*g* database.

Identity Columns

The database community at large (competitors) has maligned Oracle because they didn't have identity columns. An identity column supports automatic numbering of rows. This type of column typically holds a surrogate key, which is an artificial numbering sequence.

Oracle Database 12*c* delivers an identity operator. Perhaps the better news is that Oracle Database 12*c* provides options for how you generate identity values. The basic identity column typically uses `id` as its label, and Oracle supports that convention unless you change the column name.

TIP

Using the table name with the `_id` suffix rather than the `id` suffix as the identity column name is a better practice.

The following creates a table with two columns, an identity column and a text column:

```
SQL> CREATE TABLE identity
  2  ( id     NUMBER GENERATED ALWAYS AS IDENTITY
  3  , text   VARCHAR2(10));
```

The sample table allows us to exclude the `id` column from an `INSERT` statement. If we only had one column, we'd have to provide a value for the `id` column. It's simpler to write an override signature, which is a form of *named notation*. An override signature adds a *column-list* between the table name and `VALUES` or subquery clauses.

The present `identity` table example is as barebones as it gets because the default identity behavior is `ALWAYS`, which means you can't manually enter an identity value in the `id` column and, since there are no other columns in the table, you can't enter a row. You can only insert rows into a table with an identity column when the table has two or more columns in it, like we've done in the example.

The correct way to work with an `INSERT` statement excludes the `id` identity column from the column-list, like this:

```
SQL> INSERT INTO identity (text) VALUES ('One');
```

Why did Oracle choose `ALWAYS` as the default? The Oracle documentation doesn't explain, but let me venture a guess: If you use `BY DEFAULT` and enter a number higher than the current generated sequence value, you can duplicate a column value without a primary key or unique constraint and cause an insert into the table to fail when it has a primary key or unique constraint.

Appendix B has an "Identity Columns" section that describes how to work with identity columns. The short version is that you will become familiar with the `RETURNING INTO` clause of an `INSERT` statement, because the identity column's sequence is a system-generated sequence that you can't readily access. You can check the "Mapping Identity Columns to Sequences" sidebar in Appendix B for the details.

Identity columns change how we can work in the Oracle database. At least, they change how we can work when we're not supporting legacy code, such as the Oracle E-Business Suite's code base. Oracle Database 12*c*'s identity approach should mean we stop using `sequence.nextval` and `sequence.currval`. That model let us manage the surrogate primary and foreign key values in the scope of a transaction.

Identity columns require that we use the `RETURNING INTO` clause of the `INSERT` statement. It lets us capture the last sequence value from an `INSERT` statement in a local variable. Then, we can reuse the local variable and assign it as the foreign key to a dependent table. Naturally, this assumes that we're managing the insert to these tables in a transaction unit within a PL/SQL block.

Increased Size Limits of String and Raw Types

The maximum size of `VARCHAR2`, `NVARCHAR2`, and `RAW` data types is now configurable in SQL. You can let it remain 4,000 bytes when the `max_string_size` parameter is set to `STANDARD`. Alternatively, you can set the `max_string_size` parameter to `EXTENDED` and the maximum size becomes 32,767 bytes.

The positive aspect of this increased size limit should be clear to developers upgrading from Oracle Database 11*g*. There you could have a PL/SQL `VARCHAR2`, `NVARCHAR2`, or `RAW` that was 32,767 bytes, but you couldn't store it in a column of the same data type. Now you can do that.

Pass Results from SQL Statements to External Programs

Prior to Oracle Database 12*c*, you had to return a `SELECT` statement into a SQL or PL/SQL data type. That meant you had more steps to get to embedded queries in your PL/SQL programs. External programs had to access the results by using a matching scalar or composite data type. The composite data types were typically SQL tables, PL/SQL system reference cursors, or SQL result sets from pipelined table functions.

Oracle Database 12*c* provides you with a new `return_results` procedure in the `dbms_sql` package. This section contains an example that shows you how to use this procedure and package.

The functionality mirrors Microsoft's Shared Source Common Language Infrastructure (CLI). According to a March 2002 article by David Stutz, "The Microsoft Shared Source CLI Implementation," posted on the Microsoft Developer Network (MSDN), "Microsoft has built the Shared Source CLI so that researchers, students, professors, and other interested developers can teach, learn, and experiment with advanced computer language infrastructure." The same article indicates that Microsoft licenses the Shared Source CLI Implementation to anyone who agrees to modify its CLI code for noncommercial purposes only. However, in 2009, Microsoft added C# and CLI to the list of specifications that the Community Promise applies to. That should mean (though I'm not an attorney) that anyone could safely implement it without fearing a patent lawsuit from Microsoft.

Wikipedia has a nice article on CLI at this URL:

http://en.wikipedia.org/wiki/Common_Language_Infrastructure

While Oracle's documentation doesn't cover any licensing issue, it appears Oracle must rely on the Community Promise or have resolved any issue with using it. You can parameterize a function in CLI, like this example:

```
CREATE FUNCTION mydb.getConquistador
(@nationality AS VARCHAR(30))
RETURNS TABLE
RETURN SELECT * FROM mydb.conquistador WHERE nationality = @nationality;
```

The Shared Source CLI function passes a reference to a result set as the return value of a function. Oracle's approach differs. Oracle uses the pass-by-reference `get_next_result` and `return_results` procedures from the `dbms_sql` package. The specification for the `get_next_result` and `return_results` procedures are covered in Table 2-1.

The following is an anonymous block program that shows you how to return an implicit cursor result:

```
SQL> COLUMN item_title FORMAT A30
SQL> COLUMN item_subtitle FORMAT A40
SQL> DECLARE
       /* Declare a cursor. */
       lv_cursor   SYS_REFCURSOR;
     BEGIN
       /* Open a static cursor. */
       OPEN lv_cursor FOR
         SELECT    i.item_title
```

Procedure	**Description**
`get_next_result`	The `get_next_result` procedure has two parameters. The first parameter is an `IN` mode pass-by-value parameter, and it is a reference to a `dbms_sql` cursor reference. The second parameter is an overloaded `OUT` mode pass-by-reference parameter. It retrieves either a single PL/SQL system reference cursor or a reference to a PL/SQL system reference cursor. You are disallowed from referring explicitly to the `OUT` mode `rc` parameter. It has the following prototypes: `GET_NEXT_RESULT( c, rc )` `GET_NEXT_RESULT( c, rc )`
`return_results`	The `return_results` procedure has two parameters. The first parameter is an `IN OUT` mode pass-by-reference overloaded parameter. The `rc` parameter is either a single or collection of PL/SQL system reference cursors or a reference to a single or collection of PL/SQL system reference cursors. The second parameter is a Boolean pass-by-value parameter with a default `TRUE` value. It has the following prototypes: `RETURN_RESULTS( rc, to_client [DEFAULT TRUE] )` `RETURN_RESULTS( rc, to_client [DEFAULT TRUE] )`

TABLE 2-1. *Procedures of the dbms_sql Package that Pass Implicit Result Sets*

```
 8      ,        i.item_subtitle
 9      FROM     item i
10      WHERE    REGEXP_LIKE(i.item_title,'^Star.*');
11
12    /* Call the dbms_sql.return_result procedure. */
13    dbms_sql.return_result(lv_cursor);
14  END;
15  /
```

Line 3 declares a PL/SQL system reference cursor. Lines 6 through 10 open a static query into the local PL/SQL system reference cursor. Line 13 takes the local PL/SQL system reference cursor and returns it a client scope.

The anonymous block prints the following because the results of the cursor are passed back to the calling scope by reference implicitly:

```
ITEM_TITLE                      ITEM_SUBTITLE
------------------------------  ----------------------
Star Wars I                     Phantom Menace
Star Wars II                    Attack of the Clones
Star Wars III                   Revenge of the Sith
```

You actually return two or more result sets when the anonymous block holds two or more local system reference cursors and you have made two or more calls to the `return_results` procedure of the `dbms_sql` package. The `get_next_result` procedure returns a single result set.

New external library functions have been added to work with implicit result sets (IRSs). For example, the OCI8 2.0 library added the `oci_get_implicit_resultset()` function call. You can use it with all of the `oci_fecth_*` functions.

This presents interesting alternatives to the use of system reference cursors and either pipelined table or object table functions. Again, for newbies, Oracle Database 10*g* forward lets you create object table functions, and use the `TABLE` function to return scalar and composite collections from the Oracle database as a relational result set.

Native SQL Support for Query Row Limits and Offsets

Prior to Oracle Database 12*c*, you could only limit the number of rows returned by using a less-than row number (`ROWNUM`) operation. That changes with the new `FETCH FIRST` and `OFFSET` clauses. Oracle Database 12*c* now gives you an expanded set of options to perform a top-n query.

You limit the query to one row with the following:

```
SQL> SELECT    i.item_title
  2  FROM      item i
  3  FETCH FIRST 1 ROWS ONLY;
```

Line 3 shows how the `FETCH FIRST` clause works to return a single row. The funniest thing, if "funny" is the right word, is that you must use the plural `ROWS ONLY` keywords.

As you might imagine you return the first five rows by changing line 3 to this:

```
3 FETCH FIRST 5 ROWS ONLY;
```

Let's say you didn't know how many rows would be returned, and you didn't want to limit the number to 20, 50, 100, or 500 (the most common breaking points). Oracle has also provided you with syntax to return a portion of the total rows. That's accomplished by adding the `PERCENT` keyword to the `FETCH FIRST` clause, like this replacement to line 3:

```
  3  FETCH FIRST 20 PERCENT ROWS ONLY;
```

Oracle Database 12*c* also enables you to skip rows before reading a limited set of records. It's a top-n query from someplace in the midst of the return set. The syntax is for a modified line 3:

```
  3  OFFSET 20 ROWS FETCH FIRST 20 ROWS ONLY;
```

The minimum valid `OFFSET` value is 0. That's important to know when you parameterize a top-n query.

You can parameterize the statement by using bind variables, like this:

```
  3  OFFSET :bv_offset ROWS FETCH FIRST :bv_rows ROWS ONLY;
```

You should always use the `OFFSET` clause when you want to parameterize a top-n query because it lets you write a single statement for two purposes. One lets you read from the beginning of the record set when you provide a zero `OFFSET` value to the statement. The other lets you read from any point other than the beginning of the set. You only read to the end of actual rows when the `:bv_rows` value exceeds the remaining records.

It's also possible to use the `FETCH FIRST` and `OFFSET` clauses inside PL/SQL blocks as implicit. You can use them in a `SELECT-INTO` statement or as the definition of a static cursor. You can also use bind variables inside an anonymous PL/SQL block.

The following shows how to use a `SELECT-INTO` query:

```
SQL> DECLARE
  2    /* Declare a local variable. */
  3    lv_item_title  VARCHAR2(60);
  4  BEGIN
  5    /* Select the variable into a local variable. */
  6    SELECT   i.item_title
  7    INTO     lv_item_title
  8    FROM     item i
  9    FETCH FIRST 1 ROWS ONLY;
 10    dbms_output.put_line('['||lv_item_title||']');
 11  END;
 12  /
```

Line 9 fetches only the first row from the query. It's also possible to include the `OFFSET` clause on line 9, like

```
  9    OFFSET 5 ROWS FETCH FIRST 1 ROWS ONLY;
```

As mentioned, you can embed bind variables inside an anonymous PL/SQL block. You would use the following, provided the value of `:bv_size` is 1:

```
  9    OFFSET :bv_offset ROWS FETCH FIRST :bv_size ROWS ONLY;
```

The limitation of 1 on the value of the `:bv_rows` variable exists because a `SELECT-INTO` statement can only return one row. If the `:bv_rows` value was greater than 1, you'd return an `ORA-01422` exception, which tells you that the row returns too many rows.

You can eliminate the risk of too many rows being returned by embedding a dynamic query in an external program. You can do this by using Open Database Connectivity (ODBC) or Java Database Connectivity (JDBC) libraries.

The following demonstrates the technique of a dynamic top-n query in PHP:

```
// Declare a SQL statement.
$sql = "SELECT   i.item_title "
     . "FROM     item i "
     . "OFFSET :bv_offset ROWS FETCH FIRST :bv_rows ROWS ONLY";

// Prepare the statement and bind the two strings.
$stmt = oci_parse($c,$sql);

// Bind local variables into PHP statement.
oci_bind_by_name($stmt, ":bv_offset", $offset);
oci_bind_by_name($stmt, ":bv_rows", $rows);

// Execute the PL/SQL statement.
if (oci_execute($stmt)) {
```

The next example shows an offset top-n query in a static cursor:

```
SQL> DECLARE
  2    /* Declare a local variable. */
  3    lv_item_title  VARCHAR2(60);
  4    /* Declare a static cursor. */
  5    CURSOR c IS
  6      SELECT   i.item_title
  7      FROM     item i
  8      OFFSET 10 ROWS FETCH FIRST 1 ROWS ONLY;
  9  BEGIN
 10    /* Open, fetch, print, and close the cursor. */
 11    OPEN c;
 12    FETCH c INTO lv_item_title;
 13    dbms_output.put_line('['||lv_item_title||']');
 14    CLOSE c;
 15  END;
 16  /
```

Line 8 uses literal values to set the `OFFSET` value and number of rows returned. You can't substitute variables for the literal values—at least, you can't substitute them in the production version of Oracle Database 12*c* Release 1.

Here's an attempt to use a dynamic cursor:

```
SQL> DECLARE
    /* Declare a local variable. */
    lv_item_title  VARCHAR2(60);
    /* Declare a static cursor. */
    CURSOR c
    ( cv_offset  NUMBER
    , cv_size    NUMBER ) IS
      SELECT   i.item_title
```

```
 9       FROM      item i
10       OFFSET cv_offset ROWS FETCH FIRST cv_size ROWS ONLY;
11   BEGIN
12     NULL;
13   END;
14   /
```

Line 10 sets the top-n query limits with the `cv_offset` and `cv_size` cursor parameters. Line 12 prevents a parsing error by providing a statement within the execution block. The block fails to parse, raises an exception, and disconnects from the active session with this error stack:

```
ERROR:
ORA-03114: not connected to ORACLE

DECLARE
*
ERROR at line 1:
ORA-03113: end-of-file on communication channel
Process ID: 4148
Session ID: 31 Serial number: 3187
```

This type of exception is an unhandled exception. They don't exist very often for long. This type of error gives me the impression that it'll be fixed in due course by Oracle. Although, it's possible that it could be simply documented as a limitation. At any rate, it should be resolved by the time this book publishes.

Oracle Database Driver for MySQL Applications

Oracle Database 12*c* provides a database driver for MySQL applications. It is a drop-in replacement for the MySQL 5.5 client library. It enables applications and tools built on languages that leverage the MySQL C API, like PHP, Ruby, Perl, and Python. The benefit is that users can reuse their MySQL applications against both MySQL and Oracle databases. This improves cross portability of these scripting language solutions.

SQL CROSS APPLY, OUTER APPLY, and LATERAL

The `APPLY` SQL syntax lets you invoke a table-valued function for each row returned by a query's outer table expression. The join treats the table-valued function as the right operand and the outer table expression as the left operand. The join evaluates each row from the right for each row on the left, and the results are combined for the final result set.

There are two variations of this type of operation. The `CROSS APPLY` performs a variation of an inner join. It returns rows from the table or set of tables on the left side of the `CROSS APPLY` operation with rows that match on the left side that are found to match a `WHERE` clause inside the inline view on the right.

This is an example that implements a `CROSS APPLY` join:

```
SQL> SELECT   i.item_title
     FROM     item i CROSS APPLY
                       (SELECT *
                        FROM   rental_item ri
                        WHERE  i.item_id = ri.item_id
                        OFFSET 0 ROWS FETCH FIRST 1 ROWS ONLY);
```

The OUTER APPLY is a variation of a left join operation. The OUTER APPLY works to create an outer join between a table or set of joined tables and an inline view. The inline view must contain a WHERE clause that resolves the relationship between the result set on the left and the inline view on the right. All rows from the table on the left side of the join are returned with matching results from the collection or null values.

This is an example that implements an OUTER APPLY join:

```
SQL> SELECT   i.item_title
     FROM     item i OUTER APPLY
                      (SELECT *
                       FROM    rental_item ri
                       WHERE   i.item_id = ri.item_id
                       OFFSET 0 ROWS FETCH FIRST 1 ROWS ONLY);
```

The LATERAL clause designates a subquery as a lateral inline view. You can specify the tables that appear to the left of the lateral inline view within the FROM clause of a query. You encounter some restrictions when you use a lateral inline view, such as:

- You can't use the PIVOT clause, UNPIVOT clause, or table reference clause.
- You can't use a left correlation when a lateral inline view contains a query partition clause and appears on the right side of a join clause.
- You can't use a left correlation to the first table in a right outer join or full outer join within a lateral view.

The LATERAL clause, part of the ANSI SQL standard, extends Oracle's inline view syntax. While the following query could easily be rewritten as an INNER JOIN, it demonstrates the limitation fixed by Oracle Database 12*c*'s LATERAL clause:

```
SQL> SELECT   *
     FROM     contact c CROSS JOIN
               (SELECT   *
                FROM     member m
                WHERE    c.member_id = m.member_id);
```

The previous query attempts to write an inline view that contains a correlated subquery. It generates the following error message:

```
         WHERE      c.member_id = m.member_id)
                    *
ERROR at line 5:
ORA-00904: "C"."MEMBER_ID": invalid identifier
```

The error means that it can't find the contact table's alias c. The inline view can't find the table's alias because it's unavailable until after the FROM clause is completely parsed. That's why Oracle raises the invalid identifier error (check Chapter 4 for details on identifiers if they're new to you). This same type of error can occur with the CROSS APPLY or OUTER APPLY join operations.

The LATERAL clause lets an inline view resolve tables on the left side of a CROSS JOIN operation. It does this by parsing everything before the LATERAL keyword separately. Separating the parsing operation into two pieces lets an inline view on the right side of the LATERAL keyword resolve the identifier. That means an inline view can now include correlated behaviors, as shown here:

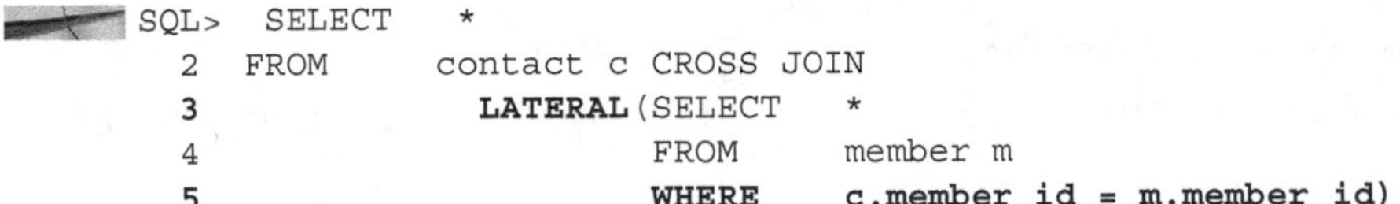

```
SQL> SELECT   *
  2  FROM     contact c CROSS JOIN
  3             LATERAL(SELECT    *
  4                     FROM      member m
  5                     WHERE     c.member_id = m.member_id);
```

The LATERAL keyword on line 3 lets the subquery find any table on the left side of the CROSS JOIN operation. It doesn't work when the unresolved identifier is on the right because the order of operation for lateral operations is left to right.

Bequeath CURRENT_USER Views

Prior to Oracle Database 12*c*, views always behaved like definer rights units. The definer rights privilege is the default for functions, procedures, packages, and types. While not required because it's the default, you would use the AUTHID DEFINER clause when defining stored program units.

Oracle Database 12*c* adds the ability to define the behavior privileges of views. The default behavior is BEQUEATH DEFINER, and it acts like AUTHID DEFINER for stored program units. You override the default privileges by creating views with the BEQUEATH CURRENT user privilege.

Review Section

This section has described the following points about Oracle Database 12*c* new SQL features:

- Oracle Database 12*c* goes beyond simply referring to environment variables in LIBRARY path statements, and lets you use a virtual DIRECTORY.
- Oracle Database 12*c* lets you define explicit and implicit valid-time (VT) dimensions to improve flashback controls for the DBA.
- Oracle Database 12*c* expands the role of the LEFT OUTER JOIN to include multiple tables on the left side of the join.
- Oracle Database 12*c* introduces the CROSS APPLY, OUTER APPLY, and LATERAL syntax for working with nested tables.
- Oracle Database 12*c* supports default columns that can hold the .nextval and .currval pseudocolumns for named sequences.
- Oracle Database 12*c* introduces identity columns that maintain auto-incrementing sequences for surrogate keys.
- Oracle Database 12*c* adds the ON NULL clause to default values, which eliminates manual overrides with explicit null values when inserting or updating tables.
- Oracle Database 12*c* lets you set a parameter to increase the length of VARCHAR2, NVARCHAR2, and RAW data types to 32,767 bytes, which is equivalent to their size in PL/SQL.
- Oracle Database 12*c* enables definer or invoker rights models for views through the BEQUEATH keyword.

New PL/SQL Features

PL/SQL gains a number of new features in Oracle Database 12*c*:

- It lets you cache invoker rights functions.
- A key new enhancement lets you white list callers to stored functions, procedures, packages, and types.
- It provides native support for binding PL/SQL package and Boolean data types as parameters. It also provides native client API support for PL/SQL data types.
- It adds the `utl_call_stack` package.
- It adds a new `expand_sql_text` procedure to the `dbms_utility` package.
- The `parse` procedure has a new formal schema to resolve unqualified object names.
- You can now add PL/SQL functions in a SQL `WITH` clause.
- It's now possible to define local PL/SQL types and use them in embedded SQL statements.
- Oracle Data Provider for .NET (ODP.NET) can now bind `REF CURSOR` parameters for stored procedures.

The following sections cover each of these new PL/SQL features in turn.

Caching of Invoker Rights Functions

Oracle Database 12*c* lets you cache the results of invoker rights functions. It supports this capability by adding the current user identity to the cached results. By so doing, it stores different results from a single invoker rights program. That means you can cache deterministic invoker rights functions, which are those that rely on values in the `CURRENT_USER` database.

The introduction of invoker rights functions changes how you can approach problems. It lets you achieve improved throughput with invoker rights functions in a distributed environment, like pluggable databases.

Ability to White List PL/SQL Program Unit Callers

Oracle Database 12*c* enables you maintain a white list of users who have permission to call your function, procedure, package, or object type. White listing a user authorizes that user to call a stored routine. It supplements your security options. A user granted privileges to execute a stored routine in a schema must also be on the authorized user list.

Oracle Database 12*c* documentation introduces a new way of describing stored routines. It uses the generic `unit_kind` to describe functions, procedures, packages, and object types. The `ACCESSIBLE BY` clause is the key to white listing stored programs when you create or replace them.

The Oracle documentation provides this type of prototype:

```
[ACCESSIBLE BY (unit_kind [schema.]unit_name
[,              unit_kind [schema.]unit_name]
[,... ]]))
```

It's direct and short, but an expanded prototype might provide better clarity, because the keyword for the `unit_kind` must precede the stored program's name:

```
[ACCESSIBLE BY
( [{FUNCTION | PROCEDURE | PACKAGE | TYPE}] [schema.]unit_name)
[,[{FUNCTION | PROCEDURE | PACKAGE | TYPE}] [schema.]unit_name)]
[,... ]]]
```

The following short example shows how to write a white-listing function. It white lists functions, procedures, packages, and types to provide a complete description.

```
SQL> CREATE OR REPLACE FUNCTION library
  2  ( pv_message  VARCHAR2 ) RETURN VARCHAR2
  3  ACCESSIBLE BY
  4  ( FUNCTION  video.gateway
  5  , PROCEDURE video.backdoor
  6  , PACKAGE   video.api
  7  , TYPE      video.hobbit ) IS
  8    lv_message  VARCHAR2(20) := 'Hello ';
  9  BEGIN
 10    lv_message := lv_message || pv_message || '!';
 11    RETURN lv_message;
 12  END;
 13  /
```

Lines 3 through 7 declare the white list of authorized callers. Any of these can call the library function successfully, while no other function, procedure, package, or type can call it. An attempt to create a new function that calls the white-listed function, like this,

```
SQL> CREATE OR REPLACE FUNCTION black_knight
( pv_message  VARCHAR2 ) RETURN VARCHAR2 IS
BEGIN
  RETURN library(pv_message);
END;
/
```

raises a compilation error, which means you need to show the error stack:

```
SQL> show errors
Errors for FUNCTION BLACK_KNIGHT:
LINE/COL ERROR
-------- -------------------------------------------------------------
4/3      PL/SQL: Statement ignored
4/10     PLS-00904: insufficient privilege to access object LIBRARY
```

White listing callers is a prudent and long-overdue enhancement, one that no other database currently implements.

Native Client API Support for PL/SQL Types

This feature enables the Oracle client APIs to describe and bind PL/SQL package types and Boolean types. You use the OCI and JDBC APIs to bind these. You can also use any C-based applications to bind and execute PL/SQL functions or procedures.

New PL/SQL Package UTL_CALL_STACK

Oracle Database 12*c* introduces the `utl_call_stack` package. It provides a number of features that improve error stack handling. An *error stack* is the sequence of exceptions raised and passed up the chain of a programming call. Chapter 6 covers what's in the `utl_call_stack` package, and how to use it.

DBMS_UTILITY Adds EXPAND_SQL_TEXT Subprogram

Oracle Database 12*c* adds an `expand_sql_text` procedure to the `dbms_utility` package. The new procedure lets you expand a view that depends on other views into a single query. It's very useful when you want to see the complete picture of how the code works.

It appears that you should leverage the `expand_sql_text` procedure to discover how views built on views resolve to tables. At least it's the simplest solution available short of you manually refactoring the code one view at a time. The problem with Oracle's `expand_sql_text` function is that it takes an inbound `CLOB` and returns an outbound `CLOB`, while views are stored in `LONG` data type columns. Converting a `LONG` data type to a `CLOB` isn't a trivial task. That's why I wrote a function to do it for you. You can find the `long_to_clob` function in Chapter 10.

Even with the `long_to_clob` function, effectively using the `expand_sql_text` procedure requires some other steps, as shown in the following function:

```
SQL> CREATE OR REPLACE FUNCTION expand_view
( pv_view_name     VARCHAR2 ) RETURN CLOB IS

  /* Declare containers for views. */
  lv_input_view   CLOB;
  lv_output_view  CLOB;

  /* Declare a target variable,  because of the limit of SELECT-INTO. */
  lv_long_view     LONG;

  /* Declare a dynamic cursor. */
  CURSOR c (cv_view_name VARCHAR2) IS
    SELECT   text
    FROM     user_views
    WHERE    view_name = cv_view_name;

BEGIN
  /* Open, fetch, and close cursor to capture view text. */
  OPEN c(pv_view_name);
  FETCH c INTO lv_long_view;
  CLOSE c;

```

```
23     /* Convert a LONG return type to a CLOB. */
24     lv_input_view := long_to_clob(pv_view_name, LENGTH(lv_long_view));
25
26     /* Send in the view text and receive the complete text. */
27     dbms_utility.expand_sql_text(lv_input_view, lv_output_view);
28
29     /* Return the output CLOB value. */
30     RETURN lv_output_view;
31   END;
32   /
```

While it pains me to use LONG data types (true dinosaurs in the Oracle database), doing so is necessary to show you how to use this cool feature. Line 9 declares a lv_long_view variable that uses the LONG data type. Although the parameterized cursor is overkill, good practices should be consistently reinforced. A SELECT-INTO statement can't replace it because you can't use a SELECT-INTO statement with a LONG data type. The FETCH INTO clause does support the assignment of a LONG data type, and that's why we make that left-to-right assignment on line 20.

Next, we call our long_to_clob function with a view_name and the length of the view's text column. Although this is a double query to the catalog, because our long_to_clob remakes the query, the double query is necessary to avoid a character-by-character assignment from the LONG data type to a CLOB data type. Oracle doesn't provide many options when working with LONG data types. For example, the to_clob function doesn't accept a LONG data type as a call parameter.

Check the full details of the long_to_clob function in Chapter 10. The short version is that it leverages the dbms_sql and dbms_lob packages to convert a LONG to a CLOB data type. You can find more about the dbms_sql package in Chapter 13. Chapter 10 covers the dbms_lob package and how you work with large objects.

Line 27 calls the expand_sql_text procedure, and line 30 returns the outbound CLOB from the expand_sql_text procedure. The result of the function gives you a CLOB, which contains the full query based on tables. Once you have it, you need to analyze its performance.

DBMS_SQL Adds a New Formal Schema to the PARSE Procedure

The dbms_sql package adds a new formal schema to the parse procedure. The parse procedure now resolves unqualified object names. This lets a definer rights program unit control the name resolution of dynamic SQL statements that it runs. For example, it now lets you issue a DROP TABLE statement from within a stored procedure when you use the dbms_sql.parse procedure.

PL/SQL Functions in SQL WITH Clause

Oracle Database 12*c* introduces PL/SQL functions inside the WITH clause. The only catch comes when you try to run them, because they have embedded semicolons. Let's say you run the command from inside SQL*Plus. You would first disable the default SQL terminator, a semicolon (;), with this SQL*Plus command:

```
SET SQLTERMINATOR OFF
```

Then, you would create a local function in your `WITH` statement, like

```
SQL> COLUMN person FORMAT A18
SQL> WITH
  2    FUNCTION glue
  3    ( pv_first_name VARCHAR2
  4    , pv_last_name  VARCHAR2) RETURN VARCHAR2 IS
  5      lv_full_name  VARCHAR2(100);
  6    BEGIN
  7      lv_full_name := pv_first_name || ' ' || pv_last_name;
  8      RETURN lv_full_name;
  9    END;
 10    SELECT  glue(a.first_name,a.last_name) AS person
 11    FROM    actor a
 12  /
```

The function on lines 2 through 9 simply concatenates two strings with a single-character white space between them. The semicolons are treated as ordinary characters in the query since the default SQL terminator is disabled. You should also note that the SQL statement is run by the SQL*Plus forward slash and that the complete statement doesn't have a terminating semicolon on line 11.

In this simple example, the `actor` table contains two actors' names (from the *Iron Man* movie franchise), and the query returns

```
PERSON
------------------
Robert Downey
Gwyneth Paltrow
```

You will encounter some parsing difficulty running queries like this when you submit them through tools like Oracle SQL Developer. The easiest fix to those problems is to wrap the query in a view because a view eliminates the need to change the `SQLTERMINATOR` value at runtime. This creates a view based on an embedded PL/SQL function within a `WITH` statement:

```
SQL> CREATE OR REPLACE VIEW actor_v AS
  2  WITH
  3    FUNCTION glue
  4    ( pv_first_name VARCHAR2
  5    , pv_last_name  VARCHAR2) RETURN VARCHAR2 IS
  6    BEGIN
  7      RETURN pv_first_name || ' ' || pv_last_name;
  8    END;
  9    SELECT  glue(a.first_name,a.last_name) AS person
 10    FROM    actor a
 11  /
```

As you know, a view is nothing more than a stored query. The `actor_v` view shrinks the `glue` function by two lines. It removes the declaration of `lv_full_name`, and replaces the assignment of the concatenated values with a direct return of the result on line 7.

If you want to run ordinary SQL commands with the default semicolon, you should reenable the default SQL terminator:

```
SET SQLTERMINATOR ON
```

The obvious benefit of the WITH clause is that it runs once and can be used multiple times in the scope of the query. Likewise, you can embed functions that have a local scope to a single query. Why use a WITH clause when you can use the global temporary table? Tom Kyte has answered that question in his Ask Tom column (http://asktom.oracle.com), explaining more or less that the optimizer can merge a WITH clause with the rest of the statement, while a global temporary table can't.

PL/SQL-Specific Data Types Allowed in SQL

The ability to pass Oracle-specific PL/SQL data types is a great feature in Oracle Database 12*c*. There is one trick to making it work: you have to declare the local variable inside the stored program and then use the local variable in an embedded SQL statement.

Let's demonstrate this feature with a PL/SQL collection and both a named PL/SQL block and an unnamed PL/SQL block. Demonstrating how it works is a five-step process. A sixth step shows you how to fail, which should save you time and explain why pipelined table functions are still needed in Oracle Database 12*c*.

The first step creates a bodiless type_defs package. A *bodiless package* has only type and cursor definitions in a package specification. You set up a bodiless package when you want to share types and cursors among other program units.

The following package specification creates only a single PL/SQL-only associative array, which is a sparsely indexed collection:

```
SQL> CREATE OR REPLACE PACKAGE type_defs IS
       TYPE plsql_table IS TABLE OF VARCHAR2(20)
         INDEX BY BINARY_INTEGER;
     END type_defs;
     /
```

The second step creates a honeymooner table with an identity column and a person column. The person column matches the scalar data type of the associative array, and we'll use the data from the table to populate the PL/SQL associative array.

The definition of the table is

```
SQL> CREATE TABLE honeymooner
     ( honeymooner_id  NUMBER GENERATED ALWAYS AS IDENTITY
     , person          VARCHAR2(20));
```

The third step inserts four rows into the honeymooner table:

```
SQL> INSERT INTO honeymooner (person) VALUES ('Ralph Kramden');
SQL> INSERT INTO honeymooner (person) VALUES ('Alice Kramden');
SQL> INSERT INTO honeymooner (person) VALUES ('Edward Norton');
SQL> INSERT INTO honeymooner (person) VALUES ('Thelma Norton');
```

The first three steps create a bodiless plsql_table package, create a honeymooner table, and seed the honeymooner table with four rows. The fourth step creates an implicit_convert function that reads the four rows from the table and puts them into a PL/SQL associative array. It then returns the PL/SQL associative array, as shown here:

```
SQL> CREATE OR REPLACE FUNCTION implicit_convert
  2    RETURN type_defs.plsql_table IS
  3    lv_index  NUMBER := 1;              -- Counter variable.
  4    lv_list   TYPE_DEFS.PLSQL_TABLE; -- Collection variable.
  5    CURSOR c IS SELECT person FROM honeymooners;
  6  BEGIN
  7    FOR i IN c LOOP
  8      lv_list(lv_index) := i.person;
  9      lv_index := lv_index + 1;
 10    END LOOP;
 11    RETURN lv_list;  -- Return locally scope PL/SQL collection.
 12  END;
 13  /
```

Line 2 defines the `RETURN` type as a PL/SQL associative array. Line 4 declares a local variable of the same PL/SQL associative array as the return type. The loop populates the local variable, and line 11 returns the local variable as a PL/SQL associative array.

The fifth step implements an anonymous block that calls the `implicit_convert` function. Inside the execution block, the *local* PL/SQL associative array is passed to a SQL statement, which reads it successfully with the `TABLE` function.

The unnamed block follows:

```
SQL> DECLARE
  2    list    TYPE_DEFS.PLSQL_TABLE;
  3  BEGIN
  4    list := implicit_convert;
  5    FOR i IN (SELECT    column_value
  6              FROM      TABLE(list)) LOOP
  7      dbms_output.put_line(i.column_value);
  8    END LOOP;
  9  END;
 10  /
```

Line 2 declares a variable by using the `plsql_table` type from the `type_defs` package. Line 4 calls the `implicit_convert` function and assigns the returned PL/SQL associative array to the local variable. Lines 5 and 6 hold a `SELECT` statement that uses the locally declared PL/SQL variable inside the `TABLE` function.

Prior to Oracle Database 12*c*, the `TABLE` function can only translate a *varray* or *table* collection into a SQL result set. The `TABLE` function can now translate a local PL/SQL associative array variable in a SQL scope.

The program fails when you comment out the assignment to the *local* variable on line 4, and replace the local variable with a call to the `implicit_convert` function on line 6. The changes follow:

```
  4  --list := implicit_convert;
  5    FOR i IN (SELECT    column_value
  6              FROM      TABLE(implicit_convert)) LOOP
```

These changes raise the following error stack:

```
            FROM     TABLE(implicit_convert)) LOOP
                           *
ERROR at line 6:
ORA-06550: line 6, column 28:
PLS-00382: expression is of wrong type
ORA-06550: line 6, column 22:
PL/SQL: ORA-22905: cannot access rows from a non-nested table item
ORA-06550: line 5, column 13:
PL/SQL: SQL Statement ignored
ORA-06550: line 7, column 26:
PLS-00364: loop index variable 'I' use is invalid
ORA-06550: line 7, column 5:
PL/SQL: Statement ignored
```

There's good news about this type of failure. You can convert the PL/SQL associative array by wrapping it in a pipelined table function. Yes, pipelined table functions still have a key purpose in our PL/SQL world. Let's say you want to eliminate the bodiless package in which you've defined the PL/SQL associative array. To do so, you would refactor the code into an anonymous block unit, like

```
SQL> DECLARE
  TYPE local_table IS TABLE OF VARCHAR2(20)
    INDEX BY BINARY_INTEGER;
  lv_index  NUMBER := 1;           -- Counter variable.
  lv_list   LOCAL_TABLE; -- Local PL/SQL collection.
  CURSOR c IS SELECT person FROM honeymooners;
BEGIN
  FOR i IN c LOOP
    lv_list(lv_index) := i.person;
    lv_index := lv_index + 1;
  END LOOP;
  FOR i IN (SELECT   column_value
            FROM     TABLE(lv_list)) LOOP
    dbms_output.put_line(i.column_value);
  END LOOP;
END;
/
```

This block unit fails, but not for the same reason that trying to process the associative array as a return value from a PL/SQL function fails, although the error stack might lead you to conclude they fail for the same reason. This one fails because the PL/SQL type isn't defined in the database catalog, and Oracle Database has no way to look it up. That means Oracle Database doesn't know what it's translating to an equivalent SQL data type.

Although Oracle doesn't explain how it performs magic like this conversion, I can venture a guess. Right or wrong, my guess is that Oracle maps the implicit PL/SQL collection to an explicit SQL table collection. If that's too technical for you at this early point in the book, don't be concerned. Chapter 6 explains these composite data types (collections) in great depth.

In short, you can assign a *local* PL/SQL variable to a local SQL context. You can't, at present, assign a *non-local* PL/SQL associative array result from a function.

Implicit REF CURSOR Parameter Binding

Oracle Data Provider for .NET (ODP.NET) can now bind `REF CURSOR` parameters for stored procedures without binding them explicitly. ODP.NET accomplishes this when you provide metadata as part of the .NET configuration files.

> **Review Section**
>
> This section has described the following points about Oracle Database 12*c* new PL/SQL features:
>
> - Oracle Database 12*c* enables you to cache results from invoker rights functions.
> - Oracle Database 12*c* lets you white list the callers of stored functions, procedures, packages, and object types.
> - Oracle Database 12*c* provides native client API support for PL/SQL data types.
> - Oracle Database 12*c* provides new error stack management through the `utl_call_stack` package.
> - Oracle Database 12*c* lets you expand the full text of views that depend on views with the new `expand_sql_text` procedure in the `dbms_utility` package.
> - The `dbms_sql` package adds a new formal schema, which lets it resolve unqualified object names.
> - Oracle Database 12*c* supports embedding PL/SQL functions inside SQL `WITH` clause statements.
> - Oracle Database 12*c* adds the ability to use local PL/SQL data types in local SQL statements.
> - Oracle Database 12*c* supports implicit binding of the PL/SQL `REF CURSOR` data type in ODP.NET.

Supporting Scripts

This section describes programs placed on the McGraw-Hill Professional website to support the book.

- The `dynamic_topnquery.php` program contains the fully functional example excerpted in this chapter.
- The `white_list.sql` program contains all functions, procedures, packages, and types to support the white-listing examples for this chapter.
- The `expanding_view.sql` program contains the functions necessary to convert a `LONG` to a `CLOB` and successfully call the `dbms_utility.expand_sql_text` procedure shown in this chapter.

Summary

This chapter has given you insight into new features unique to Oracle Database 12*c* databases. Throughout the book, you'll also be given insights into the differences between the current and older versions of the Oracle Database and Oracle Database 12*c*.

Mastery Check

The mastery check is a series of true-or-false and multiple-choice questions that let you confirm how well you understand the material in the chapter. You may check Appendix I for answers to these questions.

True or False:

1. ___Valid-time (VT) indicates the point at which transactions commit.
2. ___It is possible to define a default column that uses the `.nextval` pseudocolumn for a sequence.
3. ___It is possible to define a default column that uses the `.currval` pseudocolumn for a sequence.
4. ___The `.currval` pseudocolumn no longer has a dependency on a preceding `.nextval` pseudocolumn call in a session.
5. ___Oracle Database 12*c* doesn't provide a means to prevent the entry of an explicit null in an `INSERT` statement, which means you can still override a `DEFAULT` column value.
6. ___Identity columns let you automatically number the values of a surrogate key column.
7. ___`VARCHAR2`, `NVARCHAR2`, and `RAW` data types are now always 32,767 bytes in the Oracle Database 12*c* database.
8. ___A PL/SQL function can return a PL/SQL associative array directly into a SQL statement with the changes introduced in Oracle Database 12*c*.
9. ___Oracle Database 12*c* now supports top-n query results without an offset value.
10. ___You can embed a PL/SQL function inside a query's `WITH` clause and call it from external programs.

Multiple Choice:

11. Which of the following keywords work when you define a view? (Multiple answers possible)
    - **A.** The `AUTHID DEFINER` keywords
    - **B.** The `BEQUEATH INVOKER` keywords
    - **C.** The `AUTHID CURRENT_USER` keywords
    - **D.** The `BEQUEATH DEFINER` keywords
    - **E.** All of the above

12. Which of the following are correct about caching invoker rights functions? (Multiple answers possible)
    - **A.** A different result set exists for each invoker.
    - **B.** The same result set exists for each invoker.
    - **C.** A cached invoker rights function must be deterministic.
    - **D.** A cached invoker rights function may be non-deterministic.
    - **E.** All of the above.
13. Which of the following support expanding the SQL text of `LONG` columns into `CLOB` columns when working with the `CDB_`, `DBA_`, `ALL_`, and `USER_VIEWS` in the Oracle Database 12*c* database? (Multiple answers possible)
    - **A.** You can use the `to_lob` built-in function to convert `LONG` data types to `CLOB` data types.
    - **B.** You can use the `to_clob` built-in function to convert `LONG` data types to `CLOB` data types.
    - **C.** You can use the `dbms_sql` package to convert `LONG` data types to `VARCHAR2` data types.
    - **D.** You can use the `length` built-in function to discover the size of a `LONG` data type.
    - **E.** You can use the `dbms_lob` package to create a temporary `CLOB` data type.
14. Which of the following is true about which PL/SQL data types you can access in an embedded SQL statement? (Multiple answers possible)
    - **A.** The PL/SQL data type must be declared in a package.
    - **B.** The SQL statement needs to be embedded in the PL/SQL block where the type is defined.
    - **C.** The PL/SQL data type must be locally defined.
    - **D.** The PL/SQL data type may be a return from a PL/SQL function.
    - **E.** All of the above.
15. Which of the following lets you access a surrogate primary key from an identity column for use in a subsequent `INSERT` statement as a foreign key value?
    - **A.** `RETURN INTO`
    - **B.** `RETURNING INTO`
    - **C.** `.nextval`
    - **D.** `.currval`
    - **E.** None of the above

CHAPTER 3

PL/SQL Basics

To learn how to program with PL/SQL in Oracle Database 12*c*, you first need to understand the basic language components of PL/SQL. This chapter introduces you to those components. Subsequent chapters develop details of the components and explain why the PL/SQL language is a robust tool with many options.

As an introduction to PL/SQL basics, this chapter introduces and discusses

- Block structure
- Behavior of variables in blocks
- Basic scalar and composite data types
- Control structures
- Exceptions
- Bulk operations
- Functions, procedures, and packages
- Transaction scope
- Database triggers

PL/SQL is a case-insensitive programming language, like SQL. That means programmers can choose their own conventions to apply when writing code. No standard approach exists. Most programmers choose to differentiate language components by using various combinations of uppercase, lowercase, title case, or mixed case.

Block Structure

PL/SQL was developed by modeling concepts of structured programming, static data typing, modularity, and exception management. It extends the ADA programming language. ADA extended the Pascal programming language, including the assignment and comparison operators and single-quote string delimiters.

Unlike many other modern programming languages that use curly braces ({}) to define programming blocks, PL/SQL uses keywords to define program blocks. The basic prototype for both anonymous and named block PL/SQL programs is shown in Figure 3-1. An anonymous block has limited use and no prior definition in the data catalog. Named programs are stored in the database catalog and they are the reusable subroutines of the database.

Execution Block

As shown in the Figure 3-1 prototype, PL/SQL requires only the execution section for an anonymous block program. The execution section starts with a `BEGIN` keyword and stops at the beginning of the optional exception block or the `END` keyword. *A semicolon ends the anonymous PL/SQL block and the forward slash executes the block.*

PL/SQL Standard Usage for this Book

The PL/SQL code in this book uses all uppercase letters for command words and all lowercase letters for variables, column names, and stored program calls.

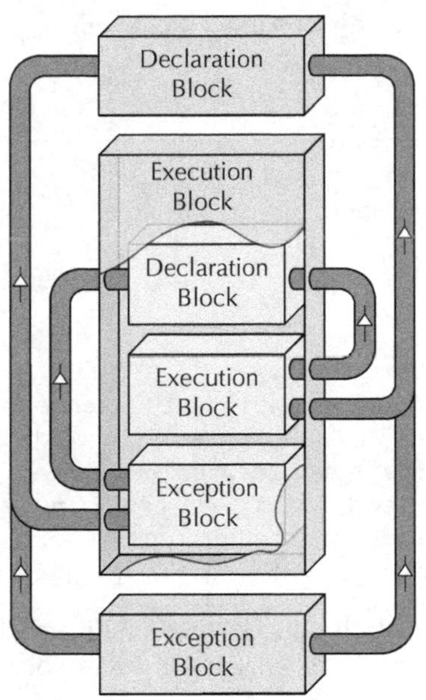

FIGURE 3-1. *Anonymous block structure*

Declaration sections can contain variable definitions and declarations, user-defined PL/SQL type definitions, cursor definitions, reference cursor definitions, local function or local procedure definitions. *Execution* sections can contain variable assignments, object initializations, conditional structures, iterative structures, nested anonymous PL/SQL blocks, or calls to local or stored named PL/SQL blocks. *Exception* sections can contain error handling phrases that can use all of the same items as the execution section. All statements end with a semicolon regardless of which block you put them in.

Basic Block Structure

The simplest PL/SQL block does nothing. You must have a minimum of one statement inside any execution block, even if it's a `NULL` statement. As mentioned, the forward slash executes an anonymous PL/SQL block. The following illustrates the most basic anonymous block program, which does absolutely nothing other than run without an error:

```
SQL> BEGIN
       NULL;
     END;
     /
```

A block without an execution statement raises an exception because PL/SQL doesn't support an empty block. For example, this unnamed block fails:

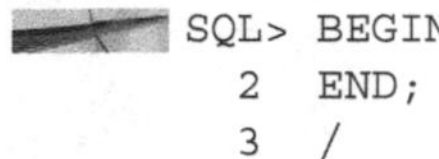

```
SQL> BEGIN
  END;
  /
```

It raises the following exception:

```
END;
*
ERROR at line 2:
ORA-06550: line 2, column 1:
PLS-00103: Encountered the symbol "END" when expecting one of the following:
( begin case declare exit for goto if loop mod null pragma
raise return select update while with <an identifier>
<a double-quoted delimited-identifier> <a bind variable> <<
continue close current delete fetch lock insert open rollback
savepoint set sql execute commit forall merge pipe purge
```

The asterisk (`*`) underneath the `END` keyword indicates that the block ending with the `END` keyword is empty or malformed. It's a parsing error and occurs before the PL/SQL block can run.

NOTE
Every PL/SQL block must contain something, at least a `NULL` *statement, or it will fail runtime compilation, also known as parsing.*

You must enable the SQL*Plus `SERVEROUTPUT` environment variable to print content to the console. The `SERVEROUTPUT` environment variable can take a physical size or the `UNLIMITED` keyword, but it's recommended that you use the `UNLIMITED` keyword.

Let's say you put the following in a `hello_world.sql` script file:

```
SQL> SET SERVEROUTPUT ON SIZE UNLIMITED
SQL> BEGIN
       dbms_output.put_line('Hello World.');
     END;
     /
```

The SQL*Plus `SERVEROUTPUT` environment variable opens an output buffer, and the `dbms_output.put_line` function prints a line of output. All declarations, statements, and blocks are terminated by a semicolon.

You run anonymous blocks by calling them from Oracle SQL*Plus. The `@` symbol in Oracle SQL*Plus loads and executes a script file. The default file extension is `.sql`, but you can override it with another extension. This means you can call a filename without its `.sql` extension. (If these processes are new to you, Appendix A provides a SQL*Plus and SQL Developer tutorial that explains them.)

Then, you call the program from the current working directory where you entered the SQL*Plus environment:

```
@hello_world.sql
```

It would print this message to console:

```
Hello World.
```

You can enter single- or multiple-line comments in PL/SQL. Use two dashes to enter a single-line comment:

```
-- This is a single-line comment.
```

Use the /* and */ delimiters to enter a multiple-line comment:

```
/* This is a multiple-line comment.
   Style and indentation should follow your company standards. */
```

PL/SQL supports two types of programs: anonymous (or unnamed) block programs and named block programs. Both types of programs have *declaration*, *execution*, and *exception handling* blocks. Anonymous blocks support *batch scripting*, which is a collection of SQL statements and anonymous PL/SQL blocks that are run as a program unit. Named blocks are stored programming units that act similarly to shared libraries in other programming languages.

You can use anonymous block programs in scripts or nested inside other named program units. They have scope only in the context of the program unit or script where you put them. You can't call anonymous blocks by name from other blocks because, as the term *anonymous* indicates, anonymous blocks don't have names. All variables are passed to these local blocks by reference, except substitution variables. Substitution variables are typically numeric or string literals, and as such they don't have memory allocation as do variables. You can pass substitution variables to anonymous blocks only when calling them from the SQL*Plus environment.

Figure 3-1 shows you the basic flow of anonymous block programs.

An anonymous block with a substitution variable would look like this:

```
SQL> BEGIN
       dbms_output.put_line('['||'&input'||']');
     END;
     /
```

The ampersand (&) is the default value for the SQL*Plus DEFINE environment variable. It signifies that whatever follows is the name of a substitution variable unless you disable it in SQL*Plus. That means SQL*Plus displays the following when you run the dynamic anonymous block:

```
Enter value for input:
```

The anonymous block prints the following when you enter a *"Hello Linux World."* text string:

```
[Hello Linux World.]
```

Inside the call to the dbms_output.put_line function, piped concatenation glues the closed brackets together with the input text string. Note that the input value can have intervening white space without wrapping the text in quotes.

Whatever you type at the SQL*Plus prompt becomes the value of the &input substitution variable. Substitution variables are assumed to be numeric, and you must enclose string substitution values with single quotes. You see the following exception when you forget to provide the single quotes and enter *"Goodbye"*:

```
  dbms_output.put_line('['||Goodbye||']');
                                      *
ERROR at line 2:
ORA-06550: line 2, column 29:
PLS-00201: identifier 'GOODBYE' must be declared
ORA-06550: line 2, column 3:
PL/SQL: Statement ignored
```

The `PLS-00201` error isn't too meaningful unless you know what an identifier is in your program. The error means the case-insensitive string `GOODBYE` isn't an identifier. Chapter 4 covers identifiers in depth, but for now you simply need to know that they're reserved words, predefined identifiers, quoted identifiers, user-defined variables, subroutines, or user-defined types.

Oracle also lets you use session (or bind) variables, which are similar to substitution variables in anonymous PL/SQL blocks. Session variables differ from substitution variables because they have a memory scope in the context of any connection or database session.

You declare a bind variable in a SQL*Plus session like this:

```
VARIABLE bind_variable VARCHAR2(20)
```

The assignment operator in PL/SQL is a colon plus an equal sign (`:=`). PL/SQL string literals are delimited by single quotes. (Date, numeric, and string literals are covered in Chapter 4.) You assign a value to a bind (or session) variable inside a PL/SQL block by placing a colon before the bind variable name, like this:

```
SQL> BEGIN
  2    :bind_variable := 'Hello Krypton.';
  3    dbms_output.put_line('['||:bind_variable||']');
  4  END;
  5  /
```

Line 2 assigns a *"Hello Krypton."* text string to the session-level bind variable, and line 3 prints it. After assigning a value to the `:bind_variable` session variable, you can query it by prefacing the session variable's name with a colon:

```
SELECT :bind_variable FROM dual;
```

You can declare a bind variable in the session, assign values in PL/SQL blocks, and then access the bind variable in SQL statements or other PL/SQL blocks. You can find more details on using session variables in the Appendix A section "Setting a Session Variable Inside PL/SQL."

Declaration Block

The optional *declaration* block starts with the `DECLARE` keyword and ends with the `BEGIN` keyword for anonymous blocks. The declaration block starts with the name of a subroutine, such as a function or procedure, its lists of formal parameters, and a return type (for a function). Unlike functions, procedures don't return a value; instead, procedures mimic functions or methods that return a `void` data type in C, C++, C#, and Java. You can find more information on subroutines later in this chapter, in the "Functions, Procedures, and Packages" section.

The following anonymous block declares an `lv_input` local variable in the declaration section and assigns the value of the `:bind_variable` to that local variable. That means you need to run the prior program first to set the bind variable before you run the next program.

```
SQL> DECLARE
  2    lv_input   VARCHAR2(30);
  3  BEGIN
  4    lv_input := :bind_variable;
  5    dbms_output.put_line('['||lv_input||']');
  6  END;
  7  /
```

Line 2 defines the local `lv_input` variable as a variable-length string. Line 4 assigns the previously initialized `:bind_variable` to the local `lv_input` variable, and then it prints the local variable's value on line 5.

Exception Block

The last block to introduce is the optional *exception* block. Exception blocks manage raised runtime errors, and a generic exception handler manages any raised error. You use a `WHEN` block to catch an error, and you use a `WHEN OTHERS` block to catch any error raised in the program unit.

The following program demonstrates how an exception block manages an error, such as when an identifier isn't previously declared:

```
SQL> BEGIN
  2    dbms_output.put_line('['||&input||']');
  3  EXCEPTION
  4    WHEN OTHERS THEN
  5      dbms_output.put_line(SQLERRM);
  6  END;
  7  /
```

Line 2 places the `&input` substitution variable in a piped concatenation string without delimiting single quotes (or apostrophes). Even with the exception block, the program still raises an error, because the error is a parsing problem and the exception block only captures runtime exceptions. The only way to fix the problem is to replace `&input` with `'&input'` between the concatenation pipes.

Review Section

This section has described the following points about block structures:

- PL/SQL has one mandatory block, the execution block. Instead of being enclosed in curly braces, as required in other modern programming languages, the execution block starts with a `BEGIN` keyword and ends with an `EXCEPTION` keyword.
- There are two optional blocks—the declaration block and the exception block.

(continued)

- The declaration block starts with a `DECLARE` keyword in an anonymous block and with the subroutine signature in a named block (shown later in this chapter's "Functions, Procedures, and Packages" section) and ends with a `BEGIN` keyword.
- The exception block starts with an `EXCEPTION` keyword and ends with an `END` keyword.
- PL/SQL supports single- and multiple-line comments, which are assumed to be numeric unless enclosed in single quotes.
- Anonymous blocks support substitution variables, and substitution variables are assumed to be numeric unless enclosed in single quotes.
- Anonymous blocks support session-level bind variables, which have a data type after they're defined in SQL*Plus (see Appendix A for a primer on SQL*Plus).

The next section discusses variable scope and assignments. It takes the preceding small example to a new level and shows you how to manage runtime errors.

Behavior of Variables in Blocks

PL/SQL also supports scalar and composite variables. Scalar variables hold only one thing, while composite variables hold more than one thing.

This section covers the scope and behavior of variables in anonymous blocks, nested anonymous blocks, local named blocks, and stored named blocks.

Anonymous Blocks

Variable names begin with letters and can contain alphabetical characters, ordinal numbers (0 to 9), and the $, _, and # symbols. Variables have *local scope* only, which means they're available only in the scope of a given PL/SQL block. The exceptions to that rule are nested anonymous blocks. Nested anonymous blocks operate inside the defining block. This lets them access variables from the containing block. Unfortunately, you can't access variables from the containing block when you've declared variables that share the same name in both the containing and nested anonymous block. Two example anonymous blocks are provided a bit later in the "Nested Anonymous Blocks" section, and those two examples demonstrate the concepts of variable scope in PL/SQL programs.

Scalar and Composite Variables

Scalar variables hold only one thing at a time and are frequently labeled as primitives; these include numbers, strings, and timestamps. Oracle timestamps are dates precise to one thousandth of a second. You can also define compound variables, alternatively labeled composite variables. There's not much difference in the words, but Oracle Database 12c documentation uses the term composite variables. So, this book uses "composite variables" to describe arrays, structures, and objects. Composite variables are variables built from primitives in a programming language.

Declaring a number variable without explicitly assigning the variable causes the initial value to be null. That's because the declaration block does two things:

- Defines the variable by giving it a name and data type
- Assigns an implicit null value to the variable

As a strongly typed programming language, PL/SQL assigns a null value implicitly to any variable that you haven't assigned a value to. All variables must be defined in the language, which means you declare them by giving them a name and type and by assigning them a value.

The following prototype of an anonymous block shows that you can assign a value later in the execution block:

```
SQL> DECLARE
  2    lv_sample NUMBER;
  3  BEGIN
  4    dbms_output.put_line('Value is ['||lv_sample||']');
  5  END;
  6  /
```

This would print the string literal information with nothing between the square brackets. Note on line 4 that a locally declared variable no longer requires delimiting single quotes because it has a declared data type. The output from the program is

```
Value is []
```

You can define a variable with something other than a null value by explicitly assigning a value. The declaration block lets you assign default values by using an assignment operator or the `DEFAULT` reserved word (which are interchangeable) after the data type. Alternatively, you can declare the variable with a null value and assign a new value in the execution block.

The following shows a prototype:

```
DECLARE
  lv_sample [CONSTANT] NUMBER [:= | DEFAULT ] 1;
BEGIN
  ...
END;
/
```

You don't need to assign values in the declaration block, and typically you would only do so when they're constants or act like constants. Variables act like constants when you do two things:

- Declare the variable with a static value in the declaration block
- Opt not to reassign a value in the execution block or the exception block

Assigning an unchanging (or constant) value to a variable is known as a *static assignment*. Static assignments aren't as common as *dynamic assignments*, in which values are assigned at runtime and can change during execution.

As a critical note, you should never assign dynamic values in a declaration block, because any errors that occur as the result of the assignment won't be caught by the local exception block.

The local exception block handles runtime exceptions only in the execution and exception blocks, not in the declaration block.

Let's look at a quick example of a badly designed dynamic assignment. It uses our now familiar `'&input'` (quote delimited) substitution variable run in SQL*Plus:

```
SQL> DECLARE
  2    lv_input  VARCHAR2(10) := '&input';
  3  BEGIN
  4    dbms_output.put_line('['||lv_input||']');
  5  EXCEPTION
  6    WHEN OTHERS THEN
  7      dbms_output.put_line(SQLERRM);
  8  END;
  9  /
```

When prompted for the input value, we enter a value that is too large for our variable-length string data type:

```
Enter value for input: James Tiberius Kirk
```

The program passes the parsing phase because we enclosed the substitution variable in delimiting single quotes. It displays the substitution of our entered value for the substitution variable:

```
old   2:    lv_input  VARCHAR2(10) := '&input';
new   2:    lv_input  VARCHAR2(10) := 'James Tiberius Kirk';
```

Then, it throws a runtime error back to the calling scope:

```
DECLARE
*
ERROR at line 1:
ORA-06502: PL/SQL: numeric or value error: character string buffer too small
ORA-06512: at line 2
```

This error means that our exception handler was ignored. That's because assignments in a declaration block aren't managed as runtime errors. Moving the dynamic assignment from line 2 of the previous declaration block to line 4 of the following execution block puts the assignment into the program's runtime scope. That simple change enables our exception handler to catch and handle the error.

```
SQL> DECLARE
  2    lv_input  VARCHAR2(10);
  3  BEGIN
  4    lv_input := '&input';
  5    dbms_output.put_line('['||lv_input||']');
  6  EXCEPTION
  7    WHEN OTHERS THEN
  8      dbms_output.put_line(SQLERRM);
  9  END;
 10  /
```

Entering the full name of Captain Kirk (from *Star Trek*'s fictional universe) now raises our handled exception rather than the full error stack (Chapter 7 covers error stacks):

```
ORA-06502: PL/SQL: numeric or value error: character string buffer too small
```

The SQLERRM function returns only the assignment error, not the complete stack of errors that aborted execution to the calling scope. Chapter 7 and Appendix C explain the SQLERRM function. What you should learn here is that you should *never* make dynamic assignments a declaration block! This rule also applies to the declaration block of stored functions and procedures. Dynamic assignments in declaration blocks are harder to manage because every calling program must anticipate and manage their outcomes.

The Assignment Model and Language

All programming languages assign values to variables. They typically assign a value to a variable on the left. That's why we've positioned the truck on the left and the cargo being loaded from the right. The truck is our variable, or a location in memory. The cargo or freight is the value we assign to the variable. The assignment process loads the freight into the truck, or assigns the value to the variable.

The prototype for generic assignment in any programming language is

```
left_operand assignment_operator right_operand statement_terminator
```

This assigns the right operand to the left operand. You implement it in PL/SQL as follows:

```
left_operand := right_operand;
```

The left operand must always be a variable. The right operand can be a value, a variable, or a function. Functions must return a variable when they're right operands. This is convenient in PL/SQL because all functions return values. That's the treat. The trick is that only functions returning a SQL data type can be called in SQL statements. Functions returning a PL/SQL data type only work inside PL/SQL blocks.

Right-to-left assignment is possible with the SELECT-INTO statement. The prototype for it is

```
SELECT [ literal_value | column_value ]
INTO     local_variable
FROM   [ table_name | pseudo_table_name ]
WHERE    comparison_statements;
```

(continued)

The following assigns a string literal to a local variable:

```
SQL> VARIABLE sv_reader VARCHAR2(20)
SQL> SELECT 'Hello reader.' AS "Output"
     INTO   :sv_reader
     FROM   dual;
```

It prints

```
Output
-------------
Hello reader.
```

While the right-to-left assignment differs from the routine, it does present you with a valuable option. It's most frequently used when returning a single scalar value or set of columns in a single row from a SQL cursor. A SQL *cursor* is a PL/SQL structure that lets you access the result of a query row by row or as a bulk operation.

Dynamic assignments also have other behaviors that we need to manage in our programs. For example, suppose you attempt to assign a real number of 4.67 to a variable with a `NUMBER` data type, like this:

```
SQL> DECLARE
  2    lv_input  INTEGER;
  3  BEGIN
  4    lv_input := 4.67;
  5    dbms_output.put_line('['||lv_input||']');
  6  EXCEPTION
  7    WHEN OTHERS THEN
  8      dbms_output.put_line('['||SQLERRM||']');
  9  END;
 10  /
```

It doesn't trigger an exception even though the value is equivalent to a `DOUBLE`, `FLOAT`, or `NUMBER` data type while the assignment target (left operand) variable's data type is an `INTEGER`. The program simply prints

```
Value is [5]
```

This happens because Oracle Database 12*c* and its predecessors implicitly cast the value between the two data types. The assignment on line 4 inherits the data type of the target variable on the left of the assignment, and because integers don't have decimals, the assignment rounds the value up. This process is known as casting, and the value suffers a loss of precision when you cast from a decimal number to an integer. Oracle Database 12*c* would round down if we were to rewrite the program and assign a value of 4.49.

Oracle Database 12*c* performs many implicit casting operations. They fail to follow the common rule of programming: *implicitly cast only when there is no loss of precision*. This means you can assign a complex number like 4.67 to an integer and lose the .67 portion of the number.

Likewise, Oracle Database 12*c* offers a series of functions to let you *explicitly* cast when there is greater risk of losing precision. You should choose carefully when you *explicitly* downcast variables. Appendix C covers explicit casting functions.

There are also several product-specific data types. They support various Oracle Database 12*c* products. You can find these data types in the *Oracle Database PL/SQL Packages and Types Reference*.

The assignment operator is not the lone operator in the PL/SQL programming language. Chapter 4 covers all the comparison, concatenation, logical, and mathematical operators. In short, you use

- The equal sign (=) to check for matching values
- The standard greater than symbol or less than symbol with or without an equal sign (>, >=, <, or <=) as a comparison operator to check for inequalities
- The negation (<>, !=, ~=, or ^=) comparison operators to check for nonmatching values

You define `CURSOR` statements in the declaration section. `CURSOR` statements let you bring data from tables and views into your PL/SQL programs. A `CURSOR` statement can have zero or many formal parameters. `CURSOR` parameters are *pass-by-value*, or `IN`-only mode only variables. Chapter 5 covers `CURSOR` statements.

In addition to anonymous block programs, you can also have the following:

- Nested anonymous block programs in the *execution* section of anonymous blocks
- Local named block programs in the *declaration* section, which in turn can contain anonymous and nested blocks of its own
- Calls to stored named block programs

The following subsections examine each one of these in turn.

Nested Anonymous Blocks

Nested anonymous blocks act like the blocks in the example in the preceding section. That's because any program that contains an anonymous block program assumes the SQL*Plus environment's role for a stand-alone anonymous block PL/SQL program.

Here's an example of an anonymous block with a nested anonymous block:

```
SQL> DECLARE
       -- Declare local variable.
       lv_input  VARCHAR2(30) DEFAULT 'OUTER';
     BEGIN
       -- Print the value before the inner block.
       dbms_output.put_line('Outer block ['||lv_input||']');

       -- Nested block.
       BEGIN
         -- Print the value before the assignment.
         dbms_output.put_line('Inner block ['||lv_input||']');

         -- Assign new value to variable.
         lv_input := 'INNER';

         -- Print the value after the assignment.
```

```
17       dbms_output.put_line('Inner block ['||lv_input||']');
18     END;
19
20     -- Print the value after the nested block.
21     dbms_output.put_line('Outer block ['||lv_input||']');
22   EXCEPTION
23     WHEN OTHERS THEN
24       dbms_output.put_line('Exception  ['||SQLERRM||']');
25   END;
26   /
```

Line 3 declares the `lv_input` variable with an initial value of *"Set in the outer block."* The scope of the variable is the outer block of the anonymous block, which means you can assign it new values in the outer or inner blocks. Line 14 in the inner block assigns to the `lv_input` variable a new value, *"Set in the inner block."* The program prints the `lv_input` variable's original value before the inner block assignment:

```
Outer block [OUTER]
Inner block [OUTER]
```

And it prints the altered value *after* the inner block assignment:

```
Inner block [INNER]
Outer block [INNER]
```

This illustrates that nested anonymous blocks have read and write privileges to variables defined in the outer scope. The `lv_outer` variable keeps the value assigned inside the nested block because there's really only one variable, and its scope is set in the outer block. There is an exception to this variable scope rule for anonymous blocks, and it only occurs when you define two variables that share the same name in both the outer and inner blocks.

The next example renames the `lv_input` variable to `lv_outer` and creates a new `lv_active` variable in the outer and nested inner scopes. I chose `lv_active` for the variable name because there are actually two `lv_active` variables when this program runs. One `lv_active` variable is accessible only from the outer block or any nested blocks, while the other `lv_active` variable is accessible only from the inner block.

```
SQL> DECLARE
       -- Declare local variable.
       lv_outer   VARCHAR2(30) DEFAULT 'OUTER';
       lv_active  VARCHAR2(30) DEFAULT 'OUTER';
     BEGIN
       -- Print the value before the inner block.
       dbms_output.put_line('Outer ['||lv_outer||']['||lv_active||']');

       -- Nested block.
       DECLARE
         -- Declare local variable.
         lv_active  VARCHAR2(30) DEFAULT 'INNER';

       BEGIN
         -- Print the value before the assignment.
```

```
16      dbms_output.put_line('Inner ['||lv_outer||']['||lv_active||']');
17
18      -- Assign new value to variable.
19      lv_outer := 'INNER';
20
21      -- Print the value after the assignment.
22      dbms_output.put_line('Inner ['||lv_outer||']['||lv_active||']');
23    END;
24
25    -- Print the value after the nested block.
26    dbms_output.put_line('Outer ['||lv_outer||']['||lv_active||']');
27  EXCEPTION
28    WHEN OTHERS THEN
29      dbms_output.put_line('Exception '||SQLERRM||']');
30  END;
31  /
```

Lines 3 and 4 declare `lv_outer` and `lv_active` variables in the outer block with an `OUTER` string value as their default values. Line 12 declares an `lv_active` variable for the inner block with an `INNER` string value. Line 19 assigns the `INNER` string value to the `lv_outer` variable.

The program prints the following:

```
Outer [OUTER][OUTER]
Inner [OUTER][INNER]
Inner [INNER][INNER]
Outer [INNER][OUTER]
```

The program prints the initial values of the `lv_outer` and `lv_active` variables before entering the anonymous nested block. Next, the program prints the variable values after the nested block's declaration section. Notice that only the `lv_active` value has changed because its scope uses the value from the declaration block of the nested anonymous block. After the assignment of `INNER` to the `lv_outer` variable, both `lv_outer` and `lv_active` hold the `INNER` string value. The `lv_active` variable changes back to `OUTER` after exiting the nested anonymous block because it now refers to the outer anonymous block program.

This section has shown you how variable scope works with nested anonymous block programs. While the example uses an anonymous block program as the outer program unit, the logic and access are the same when you embed nested anonymous blocks in stored subroutines, such as functions, procedures, packages, or object types.

Local Named Blocks

You have a choice between two named block programs (subroutines)—functions and procedures. Functions return a value and are typically used as the right operand in right-to-left variable assignments. Procedures are functions that don't return a value, which would be equivalent to a method in Java that returns a void data type.

Local functions and procedures are only useful in the scope of the program unit where they're embedded. You can implement local functions and procedures in the declaration section of an anonymous block or named block. It's also possible to implement local functions in the member functions and procedures of object types. This is done when you implement the object type in what's known as an object body, as described in Chapter 11.

The following sample program has a local procedure inside an anonymous or unnamed PL/SQL block. It transforms the logic of the nested block program presented in the preceding section into a procedure and lets you explore variable scope for local procedures. The sample program uses the `lv_outer` and `lv_active` variables in the same role as they were used in the previous section. It does make an unavoidable forward reference to function and procedure basics, which are covered later in this chapter.

```
SQL> DECLARE
  2    -- Declare local variable.
  3    lv_outer   VARCHAR2(30) DEFAULT 'OUTER';
  4    lv_active  VARCHAR2(30) DEFAULT 'OUTER';
  5    -- A local procedure without any formal parameters.
  6    PROCEDURE local_named IS
  7      -- Declare local variable.
  8      lv_active  VARCHAR2(30) DEFAULT 'INNER';
  9    BEGIN
 10      -- Print the value before the assignment.
 11      dbms_output.put_line(
 12        'Inner ['||lv_outer||']['||lv_active||']');
 13
 14      -- Assign new value to variable.
 15      lv_local := 'INNER';
 16
 17      -- Print the value after the assignment.
 18      dbms_output.put_line(
 19        'Inner ['||lv_outer||']['||lv_active||']');
 20    END local_named;
 21
 22  BEGIN
 23    -- Print the value before the inner block.
 24    dbms_output.put_line(
 25      'Outer '||lv_outer||']['||lv_active||']');
 26
 27    -- Call to the locally declared named procedure.
 28    local_named;
 29
 30    -- Print the value after the nested block.
 31    dbms_output.put_line(
 32      'Outer ['||lv_outer||']['||lv_active||']');
 33  EXCEPTION
 34    WHEN OTHERS THEN
 35      dbms_output.put_line('Exception  ['||SQLERRM||']');
 36  END;
 37  /
```

Lines 6 through 20 contain the locally defined `local_named` procedure. The `local_named` procedure has no formal parameters and simply implements the same logic found in the earlier nested block. It prints the `lv_outer` and `lv_active` variable values before and after an assignment to the `lv_outer` variable. Note that the local procedure doesn't declare an `lv_outer` variable, which means the assignment is to the `lv_outer` variable defined in the calling scope, or the outer anonymous block program.

Line 27 calls the local procedure, and you get the following output when you run the program:

```
Outer [OUTER][OUTER]
Inner [OUTER][INNER]
Inner [INNER][INNER]
Outer [INNER][OUTER]
```

As you can see, you get the same output as when you ran the nested block in the previous section. That's true because local functions and procedures have access to variables declared in the calling block where they're defined.

The difference between a local procedure and a nested block may appear to be small, but defining a local procedure lets you call the logic multiple times in the same program from a single code base. This approach of putting code logic into a named program is often labeled *modularity*, and it typically improves the clarity of your programming code.

The problem with nested named blocks, however, is that they're not published blocks. This means that one function or procedure may call another before it's defined. This type of design problem is known as a *scope error*, and it raises a compile-time `PLS-00313` exception.

Scope errors typically occur because PL/SQL is a *single-run parse* operation, meaning that the compiler reads through the source once, from top to bottom. That means any identifiers, such as function and procedure names, must be defined before they're called or they'll raise a runtime error.

The following code generates a compile-time `PLS-00313` error because the `jack` procedure refers to the `hector` function before its defined:

```
SQL> DECLARE
  2    PROCEDURE jack IS
  3    BEGIN
  4      dbms_output.put_line(hector||' World!');
  5    END jack;
  6    FUNCTION hector RETURN VARCHAR2 IS
  7    BEGIN
  8      RETURN 'Hello';
  9    END hector;
 10  BEGIN
 11    jack;
 12  END;
 13  /
```

Lines 2 through 5 define a local procedure, `jack`. Inside procedure `jack` is a call on line 4 to the function `hector`. The function isn't defined at this point in the anonymous block, and it raises an out-of-scope error:

```
    dbms_output.put_line(hector||' World!');
                         *
ERROR at line 4:
ORA-06550: line 4, column 26:
PLS-00313: 'B' not declared in this scope
ORA-06550: line 4, column 5:
PL/SQL: Statement ignored
```

As mentioned, this is a compile-time error because all anonymous block programs are parsed before they're executed, and parsing is a compile-time process. Parsing is a process that recognizes identifiers. *Identifiers* are reserved words, predefined identifiers, quoted identifiers, user-defined variables, subroutines, or UDTs. Named blocks are also identifiers.

Function `hector` isn't recognized as an identifier because PL/SQL reads identifiers into memory from top to bottom only once. Under a single-pass parser, function `hector` isn't defined before it's called in procedure `jack`. You can fix this by adding *forward references*. A forward reference to a function or procedure requires only the signature of the function or procedure, rather than its signature and implementation. A forward reference is equivalent to the concept of an *interface* in Java. These prototypes are *stubs* in PL/SQL. Stubs put the name of the future subroutine into the namespace (list of identifiers) so that the compiler accepts the identifier name before parsing its implementation.

The following example provides forward references for all local functions and procedures. I recommend that you always provide these stubs in your programs when you implement local scope named blocks.

```
SQL> DECLARE
  2    PROCEDURE jack;
  3    FUNCTION hector RETURN VARCHAR2;
  4    PROCEDURE jack IS
  5    BEGIN
  6      dbms_output.put_line(b||' World!');
  7    END jack;
  8    FUNCTION hector RETURN VARCHAR2 IS
  9    BEGIN
 10      RETURN 'Hello';
 11    END hector;
 12  BEGIN
 13    jack;
 14  END;
 15  /
```

Lines 2 and 3 provide the stubs to procedure `jack` and function `hector`, respectively, and the modified program parses correctly because it's able to resolve all symbols from the top to the bottom of the anonymous block in one pass.

NOTE
Please remember that, while nested named blocks are very useful, they also require you to implement stubs when they cross reference one another.

The biggest risk of locally named PL/SQL blocks is that they replace schema-level named functions and procedures when they shouldn't. The rule of thumb on whether or not a subroutine should be local is simple: there is virtually no chance that other modules will require the behavior provided by the local subroutine.

Stored Named Blocks

Stored named blocks are subroutines, like functions and procedures, and are often called schema-level functions or procedures. Stored functions return a value and are typically used as the right operand in right-to-left variable assignment; stored procedures are functions that don't return a value. You define a function or procedure in the database by compiling it as a schema object, which makes it a stand-alone component.

Unlike the local procedure in the anonymous block in the previous section, a stored procedure has access only to parameter values passed to it at call time. Any attempt to embed a variable not declared in scope, like the `lv_outer` variable, causes a compilation failure. You must declare a local `lv_outer` variable inside the function, which has the same impact on scope as declaring a local variable in a nested block.

The following example shows how to define a stand-alone stored procedure. This schema-level version of the `local_named` procedure implements the same logic as the embedded version of the procedure introduced in the previous section. (Stored procedures are covered in depth in the "Functions, Procedures, and Packages" section later in this chapter.)

```
SQL> CREATE OR REPLACE PROCEDURE local_named IS
  2    -- Declare local variable.
  3    lv_active  VARCHAR2(30) DEFAULT 'INNER';
  4    lv_outer   VARCHAR2(30) DEFAULT '     ';
  5  BEGIN
  6    -- Print the value before the assignment.
  7    dbms_output.put_line(
  8      'Inner ['||lv_outer||']['||lv_active||']');
  9
 10    -- Assign new value to variable.
 11    lv_outer := 'INNER';
 12
 13    -- Print the value after the assignment.
 14    dbms_output.put_line(
 15      'Inner ['||lv_outer||']['||lv_active||']');
 16  END local_named;
 17  /
```

Line 4 declares a local `lv_outer` variable as a five-character string of white spaces. Line 11 assigns a new value to the local `lv_outer` variable and replaces the string of white spaces.

You can find more on how to create and replace syntax for stored programs in the "Executing a Named Block Program" section of Appendix A. You should note the local definition of the `lv_outer` variable on line 4. The following anonymous block calls the stored procedure because there's no competing local procedure of the same name:

```
SQL> DECLARE
    -- Declare local variable.
    lv_outer   VARCHAR2(30) DEFAULT 'OUTER';
    lv_active  VARCHAR2(30) DEFAULT 'OUTER';

  BEGIN
    -- Print the value before the inner block.
    dbms_output.put_line('Outer ['||lv_outer||']['||lv_active||']');

    -- Call to the locally declared named procedure.
    local_named;

    -- Print the value after the nested block.
```

```
14     dbms_output.put_line('Outer ['||lv_outer||']['||lv_active||']');
15   EXCEPTION
16     WHEN OTHERS THEN
17       dbms_output.put_line('Exception  ['||SQLERRM||']');
18   END;
19   /
```

Line 11 calls the `local_named` stored procedure and prints the following:

```
Outer [OUTER][OUTER]
Inner [     ][INNER]
Inner [INNER][INNER]
Outer [OUTER][OUTER]
```

The first line prints the values from the anonymous block. The second line prints the local variable values before the assignment of the `INNER` string. The third line prints the local procedure's variable values after the assignment. The last line prints the original values from the anonymous block.

By adding parameters to the procedure, you can pass the values from the external scope to the procedure's inner scope or you can pass a reference from the external scope to the procedure's inner scope and return the changed values to the calling outer scope. That's covered in the "Functions, Procedures, and Packages" section later in this chapter.

You have now reviewed how to assign values to variables and how variable scopes work in anonymous and named blocks. The next section explains some basics about string, date, and number scalar data types and composite data types.

Review Section

This section has described the following points about variables, assignments, and scopes:

- Variable names begin with letters and can contain alphabetical characters, ordinal numbers (0 to 9), and the $, _, and # symbols.
- Variables are available in the anonymous or named blocks where they're declared, and in nested anonymous and named blocks defined inside those containing blocks.
- A variable name is unique in an anonymous or named block, and a variable name in a nested anonymous or named block overrides access to a duplicate variable name in an outer block that contains the definition of the anonymous or named block.
- A variable name in a schema-level subroutine (either a function or procedure named block) must be defined inside the named block's declaration block.
- Schema-level subroutines can't access calling scope blocks because they are independently defined blocks.
- Oracle uses a single-pass parsing process for PL/SQL blocks, which means you should use forward-referencing stubs for local functions and procedures.

Basic Scalar and Composite Data Types

This section introduces the basics about the three most common scalar data types, attribute and table anchoring, and four generic composite data types. The common scalar data types are characters, dates, and numbers. Composite data types include SQL UDTs, PL/SQL record types, collections of SQL data types, and collections of PL/SQL data types. Scalar data types hold only one thing, while composite data types hold more than one thing, such as a structure or collection of data.

NOTE

You can find complete coverage of PL/SQL fundamentals and scalar data types in Chapter 4. PL/SQL also uses SQL data types, which are covered in Appendix B.

The next subsection introduces string, date, and number data types as the basic scalar data types, laying a foundation for the subsequent coverage of composite data types. Together they support the subsequent major sections on control structures, exceptions, bulk operations, functions, procedures, packages, transaction scope, and database triggers.

Scalar Data Types

As mentioned, Chapter 4 provides complete coverage of PL/SQL data types. The purpose of this section is to introduce you to basic scalar data types. How you qualify scalar data types is often a byproduct of what you've done in your career but it should be clarified in this section.

More or less, a scalar data type contains one and only one thing, where a "thing" is a single element. The most common way of describing an element asks us to look at it like a number or character, and consider it a primitive data type. Adopting that standard of a primitive type, we would consider a string to be a composite data type because it is ultimately an array of characters. However, that's not the way we view things in a database, and several modern programming languages support that view. For example, Java, C#, and PL/SQL view strings as scalar data types, and they allow strings to be words, sentences, paragraphs, chapters, and books.

The following subsections introduce the three basic and most commonly managed data types, which are strings, dates, and numbers. As mentioned, Chapter 4 contains more complete coverage of these types.

Strings

Strings come in two principal varieties in the Oracle 12*c* database: fixed-length strings and dynamically sized strings. You create a fixed-length string by assigning it a size based on the number of bytes or characters. When you measure size by characters, which is the recommended approach, the number of bytes is determined by the character set. By the way, the default character set is established when you create a database instance (see Appendix A for more details on database instances).

Fixed-length strings use the `CHAR` and Unicode `NCHAR` data types, while dynamically sized strings use the `VARCHAR2` (or alias `VARCHAR`) and Unicode `NVARCHAR2` data types. As a rule, you use the `VARCHAR2` and `NVARCHAR2` data types for most strings because you don't want to allocate unnecessary space for fixed length strings.

This sample program shows you the assignment and subsequent space allocation for both fixed-length and dynamically sized data types:

```
SQL> DECLARE
  lv_fixed     CHAR(40)     := 'Something not quite long.';
  lv_variable  VARCHAR2(40) := 'Something not quite long.';
BEGIN
  dbms_output.put_line('Fixed Length   ['||LENGTH(lv_fixed)||']');
  dbms_output.put_line('Varying Length ['||LENGTH(lv_variable)||']');
END;
/
```

It prints the space allocation sizes:

```
Fixed Length   [40]
Varying Length [25]
```

Strings are useful as primitive data types. Note, however, that the storage space required for fixed-length strings generally exceeds the storage space required for variable-length strings. That typically means variable-length strings are better solutions for most problems, other than strings beyond 32 kilobytes in length. Very large strings should be stored in a `CLOB` data type rather than in a `LONG` data type.

Dates

Dates are always complex in programming languages. The `DATE` data type is the base type for dates, times, and intervals.

Oracle has two default date masks, and both support implicit casting to `DATE` data types. One default date mask is a two-digit day, three-character month, two-digit year (`DD-MON-RR`) format, and the other is a two-digit day, three-character month, four-digit year (`DD-MON-YYYY`) format. Any other string literal requires an overriding format mask with the `TO_DATE` built-in SQL function.

The next example shows you how to assign variables with implicit and explicit casting from conforming and nonconforming strings. Nonconforming strings rely on format masks and SQL built-ins, which you can find more information about in Appendix C.

```
SQL> DECLARE
  lv_date_1  DATE  := '28-APR-75';
  lv_date_2  DATE  := '29-APR-1975';
  lv_date_3  DATE  := TO_DATE('19750430','YYYYMMDD');
BEGIN
  dbms_output.put_line('Implicit ['||lv_date_1||']');
  dbms_output.put_line('Implicit ['||lv_date_2||']');
  dbms_output.put_line('Explicit ['||lv_date_3||']');
END;
/
```

It prints the following:

```
Implicit [28-APR-75]
Implicit [29-APR-75]
Explicit [30-APR-75]
```

When you want to see the four-digit year, use the `TO_CHAR` built-in function with the appropriate format mask. You can also perform date math, as explained in Appendix B.

Numbers

Numbers are straightforward in PL/SQL. You assign integer and complex numbers in the same way to all but the new IEEE 754-format data types. Chapter 4 covers how to use the IEEE-754 format numbers.

The basic number data type is NUMBER. You can define a variable either as an unconstrained NUMBER data type or as a constrained NUMBER data type by qualifying the *precision* or *scale*. Precision constraints prevent the assignment of larger precision numbers to target variables. Scale limitations shave off part of the decimal value but allow assignment while you lose part of the remaining value.

You can assign an unconstrained `NUMBER` data type to a constrained `NUMBER` data type as follows:

```
SQL> DECLARE
       lv_number1  NUMBER;
       lv_number2  NUMBER(4,2)  := 99.99;
     BEGIN
       lv_number1 := lv_number2;
       dbms_output.put_line(lv_number1);
     END;
     /
```

This prints the following when you've enabled the `SERVEROUTPUT` environment variable:

```
99.99
```

The value assigned to `lv_number2` is unchanged because its data type is unconstrained. You can find much more information on numbers in Chapter 4.

Attribute and Table Anchoring

Oracle Database 12*c* and prior versions of the database support attribute and table anchoring. Attribute anchoring lets you anchor the data type in a program to a column in a table. Table anchoring lets you anchor a composite variable, like a `RECORD` type, to a table or cursor structure.

- **`%TYPE`** Anchors a variable to a column in a table or cursor
- **`%ROWTYPE`** Anchors a composite variable to a table or cursor structure

As an example of attribute anchoring, the following shows how you would declare an `lv_dwarf_name` variable anchored to the `name` column of the `dwarf` table:

```
  lv_dwarf_name  dwarf.name%TYPE := 'Bofur';
```

Anchoring couples the local variable to a schema-level table. It is handy when only the size of a variable-length string changes or only the precision and scale of a numeric data type change. It's a potential failure point when the base data type can change over time, such as from number to date or from date to string.

The `%ROWTYPE` attribute offers three possibilities for anchoring composite data types. One option lets you assign the *record* structure of a table as a data type of a variable. The other options lets you assign the record structure of a *cursor* or *system cursor variable* as a data type of a variable.

As an example of table anchoring, you would declare an `lv_dwarf` variable of the `dwarf` table structure with a statement like this:

```
lv_dwarf_record  dwarf%ROWTYPE;
```

The same syntax works to anchor the `lv_dwarf_record` variable to a `dwarf` table, a `dwarf_cursor` cursor, or `dwarf_cursor` system reference cursor variable. Alternatively, you can create a `dwarf_table` associative array collection (covered in the next section) of the `dwarf` table's structure with the following syntax:

```
TYPE dwarf_table IS TABLE OF DWARF%ROWTYPE
  INDEX BY PLS_INTEGER;
```

Where possible, you should use a `%ROWTYPE` anchor with a local cursor. I recommend that because changes to a cursor in the same block typically drives like changes to the program's other components. Anchoring to tables can present problems because a table's structure may evolve differently from the program relying on anchored structures. Table anchoring also creates context switches in your code, which you could find by tracing performance. You can check in the "SQL Tracing" section of Appendix A for instructions on tracing performance.

Oracle Database12*c* introduces another factor when deciding whether or not to anchor to tables. The record structure of an anchored type contains only visible columns. That means you must anchor to explicit cursors when you want to access visible and invisible columns. Clearly, it's a choice you need to make when designing the program.

Visible and Invisible Column Anchoring

Oracle Database 12*c* supports both visible and invisible columns, but now when you use an asterisk (*) to select all columns, you get all visible columns only. You must write an explicit `SELECT` list to get both visible and invisible columns. Please read the "Invisible Columns" section in Appendix B if the concept is new to you.

A quick example shows this best. Let's create a table (adopting J. R. R. Tolkien's lingo):

```
SQL> CREATE TABLE dwarves
  2  ( dwarves_id  NUMBER GENERATED AS IDENTITY
  3  , name        VARCHAR2(20)
  4  , allegiance  VARCHAR2(20) INVISIBLE);
```

Line 2 creates an identity column. An identity column automatically auto increments surrogate key values from an indirect sequence value. (Check the "Identity Columns" section in Appendix B for information about how you can best use identity columns.) Line 4 marks the `allegiance` column as invisible. Therefore, you won't see the `allegiance` column when you describe the table or select columns with an asterisk (*).

As an example, a program that works with table anchoring when all columns are visible, like this

```
SQL> DECLARE
  /* Anchor to a table with an invisible column. */
  dwarf  dwarves%ROWTYPE;
```

```
  4  BEGIN
  5    /* Select all columns into a local variable. */
  6    SELECT * INTO dwarf FROM dwarves FETCH FIRST 1 ROWS ONLY;
  7
  8    /* Print the invisible column. */
  9    dbms_output.put_line(
 10      '['||dwarf.name||'] ['||dwarf.allegiance||']');
 11  END;
 12  /
```

fails with this (shortened) error message:

```
    '['||dwarf.name||'] ['||dwarf.allegiance||']');
                                  *
ERROR at line 10:
ORA-06550: line 10, column 34:
PLS-00302: component 'ALLEGIANCE' must be declared
```

The new *top-n query* syntax on line 6 guarantees that the `SELECT-INTO` only returns a single row. Refactoring the program by adding an explicit cursor and a `SELECT` list that enumerates all columns makes the program successful:

```
SQL> DECLARE
  2    /* Create a cursor to unhide an invisible column. */
  3    CURSOR dwarf_cursor IS
  4      SELECT   dwarves_id
  5      ,        name
  6      ,        allegiance
  7      FROM     dwarves;
  8
  9    /* Anchor to a table with an invisible column. */
 10    dwarf  dwarf_cursor%ROWTYPE;
 11  BEGIN
 12    /* Select all columns into a local variable. */
 13    SELECT dwarves_id, name, allegiance INTO dwarf
 14    FROM dwarves FETCH FIRST 1 ROWS ONLY;
 15
 16    /* Print the invisible column. */
 17    dbms_output.put_line(
 18      '['||dwarf.name||'] ['||dwarf.allegiance||']');
 19  END;
 20  /
```

Basically, anchoring record structures to tables in Oracle Database 12*c* is great if you only want to work with the visible columns, but it's bad if you want to work with all columns. Also, the asterisk now maps to the list of visible columns only, not to the list of all columns (visible and invisible).

Although anchoring variables and data types to other structures in the Oracle Database 12*c* database has benefits, it also has costs. Programs that anchor variables and types to other structures make context switches. These context switches read the referenced data types and apply them to the anchored variables and data types. Context switches present a hidden resource cost to any program that uses anchoring.

Composite Data Types

Composite data types differ from scalar data types because they hold copies of more than one thing. Composite data types can hold a structure of data, which is more or less like a row of data. Alternatively, composite data types can hold collections of data. Beginning with Oracle Database 9*i* Release 2, the following types of composite data types are available:

- **SQL UDT** This can hold a data structure. Two implementations are possible: an object type only implementation, which supports a SQL-level record structure, and both an object type and body implementation, which supports a class instance.
- **PL/SQL record type** This can hold a structure of data, like its SQL UDT cousin. You can implement it by anchoring the data type of elements to columns in tables and views, or you can explicitly define it. You should consider explicit declarations, because nesting these types doesn't work well. An explicitly declared record type is much easier for developers to understand than types that anchor to tables with nested data types.
- **SQL collection** This can hold a list of any scalar SQL data type. SQL collections of scalar variables are Attribute Data Types (ADTs) and have different behaviors than collections of UDTs. You have two possibilities with SQL collections: A *varray* behaves virtually like a standard array in any procedure or object-oriented programming language. It has a fixed number of elements in the list when you define it as a UDT. The other possibility, a *nested table*, behaves like a list in standard programming languages. It doesn't have a fixed number of elements at definition and can scale to meet your runtime needs within your PGA memory constraints.
- **PL/SQL collection** This can hold a list of any scalar SQL data type or record type, and it can also hold a list of any PL/SQL record type. Unlike with the other collections, you're not limited to a numeric index value. You can also use a string as the index value. This is aptly named for that duality of character as an *associative* array. Many experienced programmers still call this a PL/SQL table, as established in the Oracle 8 Database documentation.

The next four subsections describe the various composite data types of Oracle databases from Oracle 9*i* Database forward. As a historical note, associative arrays became available in Oracle 7, and included collections of record structures in the terminal Oracle 7.3 release. Generic tables and varray data types were introduced in Oracle 8 Database.

SQL UDT

A SQL UDT is an object type. Like packages, object types have a specification and a body. The specification is the type and includes a list of attributes (or fields) and methods. Methods can be static or instance functions or procedures, or they can be specialized constructor functions. Constructor functions let you instantiate an object following the instructions in the constructor function logic. Chapter 11 and Appendix B contain much more detail about object types.

Object types publish the blueprint of the object to the schema and guarantee what the object body will implement. You can define an object type to be final, but more often than not you will define them as not final so that others can extend their behaviors by subclassing them. Most objects are instantiable, because there isn't much call for objects with only static methods—you can accomplish that with a package.

The following is a sample `hobbit` object type; it includes a default (no parameter) constructor, an override constructor, and instance methods.

```
SQL> CREATE OR REPLACE TYPE hobbit IS OBJECT
  2  ( name   VARCHAR2(20)
  3  , CONSTRUCTOR FUNCTION hobbit  RETURN SELF AS RESULT
  4  , CONSTRUCTOR FUNCTION hobbit
  5    ( name   VARCHAR2 ) RETURN SELF AS RESULT
  6  , MEMBER FUNCTION get_name RETURN VARCHAR2
  7  , MEMBER FUNCTION set_name (name VARCHAR2)
  8    RETURN hobbit
  9  , MEMBER FUNCTION to_string RETURN VARCHAR2 )
 10    INSTANTIABLE NOT FINAL;
 11  /
```

Line 2 publishes the one `name` attribute of the `hobbit` object type. Line 3 publishes the default (no parameter) constructor. Lines 4 and 5 publish the override constructor that takes a single parameter, and lines 6 and 7 publish instance methods.

It's possible to use object types as parameters and return types in PL/SQL programs, and as column data types or as object tables in the database. Appendix B contains details on the nature of object columns and tables, and how Oracle supports type evolution to allow you to change objects with dependencies.

Object types become more useful after you implement them. The implementation of the object occurs when you define the object body. It's important to ensure that any formal parameters in constructor functions match the name and data type of attributes in the object type (failure to adhere to this rule raises a `PLS-00307` error at compile time).

The following implements the object type:

```
SQL> CREATE OR REPLACE TYPE BODY hobbit IS
       /* Default (no parameter) constructor. */
       CONSTRUCTOR FUNCTION hobbit RETURN SELF AS RESULT IS
         lv_hobbit HOBBIT := hobbit('Sam Gamgee');
       BEGIN
         self := lv_hobbit;
         RETURN;
       END hobbit;
       /* Override signature. */
       CONSTRUCTOR FUNCTION hobbit
       (name   VARCHAR2) RETURN self AS RESULT IS
       BEGIN
         self.name := name;
         RETURN;
       END hobbit;
       /* Getter for the single attribute of the object type. */
       MEMBER FUNCTION get_name RETURN VARCHAR2 IS
       BEGIN
```

```
19        RETURN self.name;
20      END get_name;
21      /* Setter for a new copy of the object type. */
22      MEMBER FUNCTION set_name (name VARCHAR2)
23      RETURN hobbit IS
24        lv_hobbit HOBBIT;
25      BEGIN
26        lv_hobbit := hobbit(name);
27        RETURN lv_hobbit;
28      END set_name;
29      /* Prints a salutation of the object type's attribute. */
30      MEMBER FUNCTION to_string RETURN VARCHAR2 IS
31      BEGIN
32        RETURN 'Hello '||self.name||'!';
33      END to_string;
34
35    END;
36    /
```

Lines 3 through 8 define the default (or no parameter) constructor for the `hobbit` object. Note on line 4 how a local instance of the `hobbit` object is created and assigned to a local variable. Line 6 then assigns the local instance of the `hobbit` object (the `lv_hobbit` variable) to `self`, which is the Oracle equivalent of `this` in Java and means the object instance. That's why the return statement of *constructor functions* differs from the return statement of other functions. Constructor functions return instances of the object, not a local variable or literal value.

You may have noticed that the default constructor calls the override constructor with a default *"Sam Gamgee"* string when creating the local `hobbit` object instance. The override constructor allows the user to provide the name for the object instance, like the `set_name` function (a *setter* method, which sets attributes of the object instance) that returns a new instance of the `hobbit` object. The `hobbit` object type also has a `get_name` function (or a *getter* method, which gets the value of attributes of the object instance). Lastly, the `hobbit` class provides a `to_string` method that prints the value of the object instance with a salutation.

You can now call the object like so with the default constructor and print a salutation to the object instance's `hobbit`:

```
SQL> COLUMN salutation FORMAT A20
SQL> SELECT hobbit().to_string() AS "Salutation"
  2  FROM   dual;
```

The `SELECT` list contains a call to the overriding constructor function of the `hobbit` object type, and it passes the object instance to the `to_string` instance method, which prints the default salutation. This is called *chaining component calls* and is made possible by the component selector (or period) that lets you call any method of the object instance.

It prints

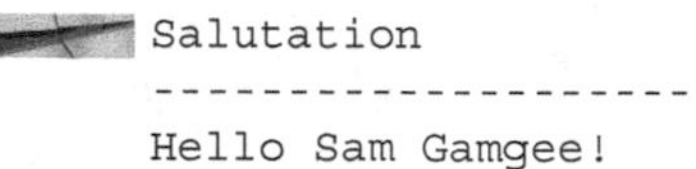

```
Salutation
--------------------
Hello Sam Gamgee!
```

Changing the constructor is done by providing a name, like this:

```
SQL> SELECT hobbit('Bilbo Baggins').to_string() AS "Salutation"
FROM   dual;
```

The preceding code produces the same outcome as calling the `set_name` function:

```
SQL> SELECT  hobbit().set_name('Bilbo Baggins').to_string() AS "Salutation"
FROM    dual;
```

Both print the following:

```
Salutation
--------------------
Hello Bilbo Baggins!
```

After implementing object bodies, you can store objects in tables or pass objects from one named PL/SQL program unit to another (that includes from one object to another object). Chapter 11 goes into more depth on using objects in the Oracle database.

PL/SQL Record Type

A PL/SQL record type is a record data structure, which means it is a row of data across two or more fields of data. The following program creates a PL/SQL record type, assigns values to it, and prints the output:

```
SQL> DECLARE
  2    -- Declare a local user-defined record structure.
  3    TYPE title_record IS RECORD
  4    ( title     VARCHAR2(60)
  5    , subtitle  VARCHAR2(60));
  6
  7    -- Declare a variable that uses the record structure.
  8    lv_title_record  TITLE_RECORD;
  9  BEGIN
 10    -- Assign values to the record structure.
 11    lv_title_record.title := 'Star Trek';
 12    lv_title_record.subtitle := 'Into Darkness';
 13    -- Print the elements of the structure.
 14    dbms_output.put_line('['||lv_title_record.title||']'||
 15                         '['||lv_title_record.subtitle||']');
 16  END;
 17  /
```

Lines 3 through 5 define the PL/SQL record structure, and line 8 declares a variable using the PL/SQL locally scoped `title_record` record type. Lines 11 and 12 support field-level assignments, and lines 14 and 15 print the now populated fields of the string.

Record structures are useful when you write PL/SQL-only solutions, but object types are more useful and portable. You must assign values to any PL/SQL structure at the field level because, unlike Oracle object types, PL/SQL structures don't support constructors.

SQL Collection

SQL collections can exist for scalar data types or SQL UDT elements. Oracle calls SQL collections of scalar columns Attribute Data Types (ADTs). While there are some differences between how ADTs and UDTs are used in the Oracle Call Interface (OCI), the distinct names appears to disambiguate collections of native data types from collections of UDTs.

Creating these collections differs slightly because you don't need to create a UDT for ADT collections. The two subsections that follow examine how you create and work with ADT collections and UDT collections in SQL, respectively, but you should keep in mind that both of these data types also can be PL/SQL collections. The sole difference between SQL and PL/SQL collections is where you can use and construct them.

SQL collections may be tables (or lists) of values or varrays (or arrays in traditional programming languages). Tables have no upward limit on the number of elements in the collection, which is why they act like lists. Varrays have a maximum number of elements set when you define their types.

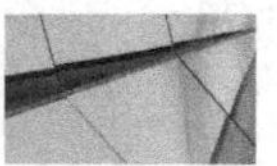

NOTE
Table collections are also called nested tables *when they're embedded inside database tables.*

You must construct tables and varrays by calling the type name, or default constructor, with a list of members. New members are added at the end of either type of collection in the same way. You add new members to a collection by using a two-step process that extends space and assigns a value to an indexed location. Varrays only allow you to extend space within their limit (that's their maximum number of members), and you receive an out-of-bounds error when you attempt to add more than the maximum number of members.

Chapter 6 contains a full treatment of collections, including a review of the application programming interface (API) that supports them. At this point, you need to understand that collections are final types, which means you can't subclass them (you can find more information on subclassing UDTs in Chapter 11). This introduces you to the basics to support subsequent discussions of collections.

ADT Collections An ADT collection in SQL requires that you define a collection of a SQL base data type, such as a string data type. Not to confuse matters, but the syntax is the same as when you create any object type collection in the database.

Presenting the basic similarities and differences between table collections and varray collections seems to be the best approach when introducing ADT collections, so the following examples show how to create each type of ADT collection. If you need more details on the syntax in these examples, Appendix B covers nested tables and varrays in tables and the SQL syntax for creating them.

The syntax for our sample ADT table is

```
SQL> CREATE OR REPLACE
  2    TYPE string_table IS TABLE OF VARCHAR2(30);
  3  /
```

`CREATE OR REPLACE` on line 1 is standard Oracle SQL syntax to create or replace an object of the same name and type. Line 2 defines the ADT of variable-length strings up to 30 characters in length, and is the same as what you would embed in a PL/SQL block. Line 3 uses the SQL forward slash (/) to run or execute the SQL statement.

The syntax for our sample ADT varray is

```
SQL> CREATE OR REPLACE
    TYPE string_varray IS VARRAY(3) OF VARCHAR2(30);
  /
```

The parenthetical number sets the limit or maximum number of members in the varray. After creating a schema-level type, you can describe its definition like this:

```
SQL> DESCRIBE collection_varray
 collection_varray VARRAY(3) OF VARCHAR2(30)
```

The next program shows how to declare a SQL collection in an anonymous block program:

```
SSQL> DECLARE
  2     -- Declare and initialize a collection of grains.
  3     lv_string_list  STRING_TABLE := string_table('Corn','Wheat');
  4   BEGIN
  5     -- Print the first item in the array.
  6     FOR i IN 1..2 LOOP
  7       dbms_output.put_line('['||i||']['||lv_string_list(i)||']');
  8     END LOOP;
  9   END;
 10   /
```

Line 3 declares `lv_string_list` as an instance of the SQL `string_table` collection. It does so by defining the variable with a name and data type and initializing the collection with two values. You initialize a collection by using the type name and by providing a list of the base element of the collection, which is a string. An initialization with a fixed list of values creates a static collection, but you can add members to it because a list has no upward bound.

NOTE
As line 3 shows, a common and recommended convention is to display the data type in uppercase and the constructor call to the type in lowercase.

The range *for* loop (described in detail in the "Iterative Structures" section later in this chapter) reads through the first two, and only, members of the collection. The *for* loop uses a range of 1 to 2, inclusive, and uses the index value (`i`) to keep its place as it iterates across the collection.

The `string_varray` SQL collection type is interchangeable in this sample program, and only one change to the program is required for you to use it. Change line 3 to the following:

```
  3     lv_string_list  STRING_VARRAY := string_varray('Corn','Wheat');
```

In both cases, the program would print

```
[1][Corn]
[2][Wheat]
```

You have the option of allocating space with the `EXTEND` keyword (part of the Oracle Collections API covered in Chapter 6). After allocating space to the collection, you may add elements to either of these ADT collections. While the `string_table` data type has no limit to the space or number of elements you can add, the `string_varray` variable has a limit of three elements.

The next example creates two collections. One is an ADT table of strings with four members, and the other is an ADT varray of strings without initial members. The program reads through the list of members in the ADT table collection and attempts to dynamically, row by row, initialize the ADT varray collection. The program fails while trying to authorize space for the fourth member of the table ADT collection because the ADT varray is limited to three members.

The program code is

```
SQL> DECLARE
  2    -- Declare and initialize a collection of grains.
  3    lv_string_table    STRING_TABLE :=
  4      string_table('Corn','Wheat','Rye','Barley');
  5    lv_string_varray  STRING_VARRAY := string_varray();
  6  BEGIN
  7    -- Print the first item in the array.
  8    FOR i IN 1..lv_string_table.COUNT LOOP
  9      lv_string_varray.EXTEND;
 10      lv_string_varray(i) := lv_string_table(i);
 11    END LOOP;
 12  END;
 13  /
```

Lines 3 and 4 declare the ADT table collection. Line 5 declares the ADT varray collection as an empty collection. Failure to initialize the collection with a call to the collection type causes an uninitialized error like this:

```
DECLARE
*
ERROR at line 1:
ORA-06531: Reference to uninitialized collection
ORA-06512: at line 9
```

The error isn't raised by the definition but rather by the first call to the uninitialized collection, which occurs on line 9. It is a clear best practice to initialize all collections at their definition because, unlike all other variables in the Oracle Database 12c product, collections don't have a natural null state.

Line 8 sets the upper limit of the range *for* loop at the number of members in the `lv_string_table` variable by calling the `COUNT` function. The `COUNT` function is part of the Oracle Collections API, and in this case it returns a value of four.

The first three members of the `lv_string_table` collection are assigned successfully to the `lv_string_varray` collection, but the attempt to extend space for a fourth member raises the following exception:

```
DECLARE
*
ERROR at line 1:
ORA-06532: Subscript outside of limit
ORA-06512: at line 9
```

These examples have covered the basics of using ADT table and varray collections. As a rule, the table collections are easier to work with and generally the preferred solution in most situations.

UDT Collections A UDT collection in SQL requires that you define a collection of a SQL UDT, like the `hobbit` type from earlier in this chapter. After defining the base UDT, you can create a SQL table collection of the `hobbit` type like this:

```
SQL> CREATE OR REPLACE
       TYPE hobbit_table IS TABLE OF HOBBIT;
     /
```

Having created the `hobbit_table` UDT collection, let's define a program that uses it. The following program creates an instance of the collection in the declaration block with two `hobbit` member values, and then it adds two more member values in the execution block:

```
SQL> DECLARE
  2    -- Declare and initialize a collection of grains.
  3    lv_string_table  STRING_TABLE :=
  4      string_table('Drogo Baggins','Frodo Baggins');
  5    lv_hobbit_table  HOBBIT_TABLE := hobbit_table(
  6                                        hobbit('Bungo Baggins')
  7                                      , hobbit('Bilbo Baggins'));
  8  BEGIN
  9    -- Assign the members from one collection to the other.
 10    FOR i IN 1..lv_string_table.COUNT LOOP
 11      lv_hobbit_table.EXTEND;
 12      lv_hobbit_table(lv_hobbit_table.COUNT) :=
 13        hobbit(lv_string_table(i));
 14    END LOOP;
 15
 16    -- Print the members of the hobbit table.
 17    FOR i IN 1..lv_hobbit_table.COUNT LOOP
 18      dbms_output.put_line(
 19        lv_hobbit_table(i).to_string());
 20    END LOOP;
 21  END;
 22  /
```

There are three key things to point out in the preceding example:

- The declaration of `lv_hobbit_table` on lines 5 through 7 includes an initialization of a `hobbit_table` with *comma-delimited instances* of `hobbit` types. This differs from simply listing scalar values like strings, dates, and numbers, and it is a major difference between ADT and UDT collections.
- The assignment of new values on lines 12 and 13 sets the assignment target's index value to the last space allocation, and the assignment is an instance of the `hobbit` type. Note that the index value (`i`) for the value from the `lv_string_table` is inside ordinary parentheses.
- Line 19 prints the `i`th element of the `lv_hobbit_table` and uses the native `to_string` function to print the object type's contents.

The prior example shows how to work with collections of instantiable UDTs, but not how to work with the attributes of object types. A function that returns a collection is also called an *object table function*. You use the `TABLE` function to access members of any collection returned by an object table function.

The following function creates and returns a collection of the `hobbit` type structures:

```
SQL> CREATE OR REPLACE FUNCTION get_hobbits
  2  RETURN HOBBIT_TABLE IS
  3    -- Declare a collection of hobbits.
  4    lv_hobbit_table  HOBBIT_TABLE := hobbit_table(
  5                                         hobbit('Bungo Baggins')
  6                                       , hobbit('Bilbo Baggins')
  7                                       , hobbit('Drogo Baggins')
  8                                       , hobbit('Frodo Baggins'));
  9  BEGIN
 10    RETURN lv_hobbit_table;
 11  END;
 12  /
```

Lines 4 through 8 create a collection of `hobbit` object instances. Line 10 returns a `hobbit_table` collection of `hobbit` instances. You can query the collection by putting the function return value inside a `TABLE` function, like this:

```
SQL> COLUMN hobbit_name FORMAT A14
SQL> SELECT   name AS hobbit_name
  2  FROM     TABLE(get_hobbits())
  3  ORDER BY 1;
```

The `TABLE` function on line 2 takes the result of the `get_hobbits` function and converts the attribute list of nested `hobbit` object instances to an ordinary column result set. The preceding query prints

```
HOBBIT_NAME
--------------
Bilbo Baggins
Bungo Baggins
Drogo Baggins
Frodo Baggins
```

This section has shown you that composite variables are tremendously valuable assets in the PL/SQL and SQL programming environment. They let you define complex logic in named blocks that you can then simply query in C#, Java, PHP, or other external programs. You should take advantage of composite variables where possible.

PL/SQL Collection

This section shows you how to implement the fourth and final composite data type, a PL/SQL-only solution. This is not the most flexible or extensible solution because you have to wrap it in a pipelined function (covered later in this chapter and in Chapter 8) to use it in SQL. The best solution, covered in the previous section, returns a SQL ADT or UDT collection with an object structure and doesn't require wrapping.

ADT Collections The following example follows general practice and shows you how to handle a collection of numbers. You have the option to define a collection of any standard or user-defined scalar PL/SQL data type, such as `DATE`, `INTEGER`, `VARCHAR2`, and so forth. Like a couple of the examples in the previous section, "SQL Collection," this program uses a *for* loop (described in depth in the "Iterative Structures" section later in this chapter), and it prints the members of an initialized PL/SQL collection.

```
SQL> DECLARE
  2    -- Declare a collection data type of numbers.
  3    TYPE number_table IS TABLE OF NUMBER;
  4
  5    -- Declare a variable of thc collcction data types.
  6    lv_collection  NUMBER_TABLE := number_type(1,2,3);
  7  BEGIN
  8    -- Loop through the collection and print values.
  9    FOR i IN 1..lv_collection.COUNT LOOP
 10      dbms_output.put_line(lv_collection(i));
 11    END LOOP;
 12  END;
 13  /
```

Line 3 defines a collection data type, and line 6 declares a variable of the local collection data type and initializes it with three elements. The name of the data type is also the name of the constructor, and the comma-delimited elements comprise the list of values in the collection. Line 9 defines a range *for* loop that navigates from 1 to the count of the three items in the `lv_collection` variable. Like previous examples, you should note that the *for* loop on lines 9 through 11 uses `i` as an iterator and as an index value for navigating the elements of the collection. Index elements are enclosed in ordinary parentheses rather than in square brackets, which is standard in other programming languages.

You can also implement a PL/SQL varray by changing the declaration on line 3, as follows:

```
  3    TYPE number_varray IS VARRAY(3) OF NUMBER;
```

The same rules that apply for interchangeability of tables and varrays also apply to interchangeability of SQL and PL/SQL environments. The only difference between the SQL and PL/SQL environments is how you declare them. They are schema objects in SQL and local data types in PL/SQL.

Associative Arrays of Scalar Variables When implementing a PL/SQL-only solution, you also have the option to use associative arrays of scalar variables, which are the older style of PL/SQL collections. Associative arrays only work inside a PL/SQL scope, and you must use pipelined table functions to convert them for use in a SQL scope. You also can't initialize associative arrays, because you must assign values one at a time to them.

Associative arrays present advantages and disadvantages, but for our introductory discussion, we'll focus on one of the advantages, which is that associative arrays work well as name-value pairs when the index values are strings. Since associative arrays don't require a constructor call or allocation of physical space before assigning values, some developers find that solving collection-related problems is simpler in associative arrays.

Let's convert the SQL ADT example (from the previous section) that raised an uninitialized collection error to a PL/SQL scope associative array indexed by numbers. You declare an associative array by appending either the `INDEX BY BINARY_INTEGER` data type clause or `INDEX BY VARCHAR2` data type clause to the type definition of a table or varray.

The following demonstrates a simple associative array:

```
SQL> DECLARE
  2    -- Declare a collection data type of numbers.
  3    TYPE numbers IS TABLE OF NUMBER INDEX BY BINARY_INTEGER;
  4
  5    -- Declare a variable of the collection data types.
  6    lv_collection  NUMBERS;
  7  BEGIN
  8    -- Assign a value to the collection.
  9    lv_collection(0) := 1;
 10  END;
 11  /
```

Line 3 appends the `INDEX BY BINARY_INTEGER` clause to the definition of the collection type and makes it an associative array collection indexed by integers. Line 9 assigns 1 to the 0 index value, but you can actually use any integer value as the index value of an associative array.

You can redefine this sample program as a name-value pair associative array by changing the definition on line 3 to

```
  3    TYPE numbers IS TABLE OF NUMBER INDEX BY VARCHAR2(10);
```

The index value now requires a string rather than a number, and the assignment of a value on line 9 would change to

```
  9    lv_collection('One') := 1;
```

These examples show you how to declare an associative array indexed by an integer or string. Chapter 6 provides examples that demonstrate when business logic may fit this type of solution.

UDT Collections In addition to creating collections of scalar variables, you can create collections of two types of data structures: the PL/SQL record type and the SQL object type. PL/SQL collections of record types are exclusive to a PL/SQL processing context, which means you can't use them in a query as shown previously with the SQL UDT collection. There are also limits on how you can use SQL object type collections when they're defined inside PL/SQL package specifications, local anonymous blocks, or named blocks—functions or procedures.

The next example implements the `hobbit_table` SQL collection inside the declaration block, which makes it a PL/SQL scoped UDT collection. Defining the `hobbit_table` SQL collection inside an anonymous or named block effectively overrides access to a like-named schema-level SQL UDT collection.

Here's the code to implement a SQL UDT inside an anonymous PL/SQL block:

```
SQL> DECLARE
    -- Declare a local collection of hobbits.
    TYPE hobbit_table IS TABLE OF HOBBIT;

```

```
5    -- Declare and initialize a collection of grains.
6    lv_string_table  STRING_TABLE :=
7      string_table('Drogo Baggins','Frodo Baggins');
8    lv_hobbit_table  HOBBIT_TABLE := hobbit_table(
9                                         hobbit('Bungo Baggins')
10                                      , hobbit('Bilbo Baggins'));
11  BEGIN
12    -- Print the first item in the array.
13    FOR i IN 1..lv_string_table.COUNT LOOP
14      lv_hobbit_table.EXTEND;
15      lv_hobbit_table(lv_hobbit_table.COUNT) :=
16        hobbit(lv_string_table(i));
17    END LOOP;
18    -- Print the members of the hobbit table.
19    FOR i IN 1..lv_hobbit_table.COUNT LOOP
20      dbms_output.put_line(
21        lv_hobbit_table(i).to_string());
22    END LOOP;
23  END;
24  /
```

Line 3 holds the local declaration of the `hobbit_table` SQL UDT. All subsequent references use the locally defined type. Line 16 takes the value from `lv_string_table` ADT collection, and uses it as a call parameter to the `hobbit` constructor function. Then, the instance of a new `hobbit` is assigned as a new element in the `lv_hobbit_table` collection.

Realistically, the only time you would define a SQL UDT inside a PL/SQL block is when you're converting an associative array to a SQL ADT or UDT, and that only happens inside a pipelined table function. You take this path when you're converting legacy associative arrays returned by PL/SQL functions, an example of which is provided in the "Wrapping Legacy Associative Arrays" section of Chapter 6.

Associative Arrays of Composite Variables Like the associative arrays of scalar variables, you can create associative arrays of PL/SQL record types, as shown in the following example. Such collections are limited to use inside PL/SQL programs.

```
SQL> DECLARE
    -- Declare a local user-defined record structure.
    TYPE dwarf_record IS RECORD
    ( dwarf_name  VARCHAR2(20)
    , dwarf_home  VARCHAR2(20));

    -- Declare a local collection of hobbits.
    TYPE dwarf_table IS TABLE OF DWARF_RECORD
      INDEX BY PLS_INTEGER;

    -- Declare and initialize a collection of grains.
    list  DWARF_TABLE;
  BEGIN
     -- Add two elements to the associative array.
```

```
15      list(1).dwarf_name := 'Gloin';
16      list(1).dwarf_home := 'Durin''s Folk';
17      list(2).dwarf_name := 'Gimli';
18      list(2).dwarf_home := 'Durin''s Folk';
19
20    -- Print the first item in the array.
21    FOR i IN 1..list.COUNT LOOP
22      dbms_output.put_line(
23        '['||list(i).dwarf_name||']'||
24        '['||list(i).dwarf_home||']');
25    END LOOP;
26  END;
27  /
```

Line 8 declares a `dwarf_table` associative array of the previous declaration of the `dwarf_record` on lines 3 through 5. You can tell it's a PL/SQL-only associative array because the declaration includes the `INDEX BY PLS_INTEGER` clause on line 9. As mentioned, an associative array doesn't require a constructor call, but it does require you to make direct assignments to rows of the base composite type or member of the base composite type.

If you have a `dwarf` table that mirrors the `dwarf_record` declaration, it's possible to anchor the local variable to a schema-level table. The syntax for that is

```
3    TYPE dwarf_table IS TABLE OF DWARF%ROWTYPE
4      INDEX BY PLS_INTEGER;
```

Coupling an associative array's base data type to a table poses a risk. The risk is that you must remember to synchronize any changes in both the subroutine and table.

Review Section

This section has described the following points about variables, assignments, and scopes:

- A scalar variable holds only one thing, such as a number, string, or date.
- A composite variable holds two or more things, such as a record structure or a collection.
- You can anchor a column with the `%TYPE` attribute and anchor a record structure with the `%ROWTYPE` attribute.
- SQL and PL/SQL support tables and varrays as collections of scalar variables data types, and these collections are Attribute Data Types (ADTs).
- SQL and PL/SQL support tables and varrays as collections of composite variables data types, and these collections are lists or arrays of schema-level user-defined types (UDTs).
- PL/SQL supports associative arrays as collections of scalar variables data types, and these collections are associative arrays of scalar data types.
- PL/SQL supports associative arrays as collections of composite variables data types, and these collections are associative arrays of record structure data types.

Control Structures

Control structures do either of two things: they check a logical condition and branch program execution (in which case they are called *conditional structures*), or they iterate over a condition until it is met or they are instructed to exit (in which case they are called *iterative structures*). The "Conditional Structures" subsection covers *if, elsif, else,* and *case* statements. The "Iterative Structures" subsection covers looping with *for, while,* and *simple loop* structures.

Conditional Structures

As just mentioned, conditional structures check logical conditions and branch program execution. The *if, elsif, else,* and *case* statements are conditional structures.

If, Elsif, and *Else* Statements

The *if* and *elsif* statements work on a concept of Boolean logic. A Boolean variable or an expression, such as a comparison of values, is the only criterion for an *if* or *elsif* statement. While this seems simple, it really isn't, because truth or untruth has a third case in an Oracle database: a Boolean variable or expression can be true, false, or null. This is called *three-valued logic*.

You can manage three-valued logic by using the NVL built-in function. It allows you to impose an embedded check for a null and return the opposite of the logical condition you attempted to validate.

The following example illustrates checking for truth of a Boolean and truth of an expression, ultimately printing the message that neither condition is true:

```
SQL> DECLARE
       lv_boolean BOOLEAN;
       lv_number  NUMBER;
     BEGIN
       IF NVL(lv_boolean,FALSE) THEN
         dbms_output.put_line('Prints when the variable is true.');
       ELSIF NVL((lv_number < 10),FALSE) THEN
         dbms_output.put_line('Prints when the expression is true.');
       ELSE
         dbms_output.put_line('Prints when variables are null values.');
       END IF;
     END;
     /
```

Three-Valued Logic

Three-valued logic means basically that if you find something is true when you look for truth, it is true. By the same token, when you check whether something is false and it is, then it is false. The opposite case isn't proved. That means when something isn't true, you can't assume it is false, and vice versa.

The third case is that if something isn't true, it can be false or null. Likewise, if something isn't false, it can be true or null. Something is null when a Boolean variable is defined but not declared or when an expression compares something against another variable that is null.

This prints

```
Prints because both variables are null values.
```

This always prints the *else* statement because the variables are only defined, not declared. PL/SQL undeclared variables are always null values.

The `NVL` built-in function lets you create programs that guarantee behavior, which is most likely one of the critical things you should do as a developer. The guarantee becomes possible because you're changing the rules and making natural three-valued logic behave as two-valued logic. Sometimes, that's not possible, but oddly enough, when it isn't possible, there's a use case that will compel you to provide code for the null condition.

CASE Statement

The `CASE` statement appears very similar to a switch structure in many programming languages, but it doesn't perform in the same way because it doesn't support fall-through. *Fall-through* is the behavior of finding the first true case and then performing all remaining cases. The *case* statement in PL/SQL performs like an *if-elsif-else* statement.

There are two types of `CASE` statements: the *simple* case and the *searched* case. You can use a `CHAR`, `NCHAR`, or `VARCHAR2` data type in simple *case* statements, and you can use any Boolean expression in searched *case* statements.

The following program shows how to write a simple *case* statement. The *selector* variable (`lv_selector`) is a `VARCHAR2` variable assigned a value through a substitution variable.

```
SQL> DECLARE
  2    lv_selector VARCHAR2(20);
  3  BEGIN
  4    lv_selector := '&input';
  5    CASE lv_selector
  6      WHEN 'Apple' THEN
  7        dbms_output.put_line('Is it a red delicious apple?');
  8      WHEN 'Orange' THEN
  9        dbms_output.put_line('Is it a navel orange?');
 10      ELSE
 11        dbms_output.put_line('It''s a ['||lv_selector||']?');
 12    END CASE;
 13  END;
 14  /
```

The `WHEN` clauses validate their values against the `CASE` selector on line 5. When one `WHEN` clause matches the selector, the program runs the instructions in that `WHEN` clause and exits the `CASE` block. The *break* statement found in languages such as C, C++, C#, and Java is implicitly present.

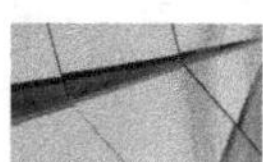

TIP

The `CASE` statement in PL/SQL differs from the `CASE` statement in SQL, because the former ends with `END CASE`, not simply `END`. Don't try the SQL syntax in PL/SQL, because it will raise an exception.

A searched *case* statement works differently from a simple *case* statement because it doesn't limit itself to an equality match of values. You can use a searched *case* statement to validate whether a number is in a range or in a set. The selector for a searched *case* statement is implicitly true and can be excluded unless you want to check for untruth. You provide a false selector value on line 2 if the `WHEN` clauses validate against a false condition, like this:

```
  2     CASE FALSE
```

The following program validates against truth:

```
SQL> BEGIN
  2     CASE
  3       WHEN (1 <> 1) THEN
  4         dbms_output.put_line('Impossible!');
  5       WHEN (3 > 2) THEN
  6         dbms_output.put_line('A valid range comparison.');
  7       ELSE
  8         dbms_output.put_line('Never reached.');
  9     END CASE;
 10   END;
 11   /
```

The range validation on line 5 is met, and it prints this:

```
A valid range comparison.
```

Unlike the *if* and *elsif* statements, you don't need to reduce the natural three-valued logic to two-valued logic. If a searched *case* statement's `WHEN` clause isn't met, the program continues until one is met or the *else* statement is reached.

Iterative Structures

Iterative structures are blocks that let you repeat a statement or a set of statements. These structures come in two varieties: a guard-on-entry loop and a guard-on-exit loop. Figure 3-2 shows the execution logic for these two types of loops.

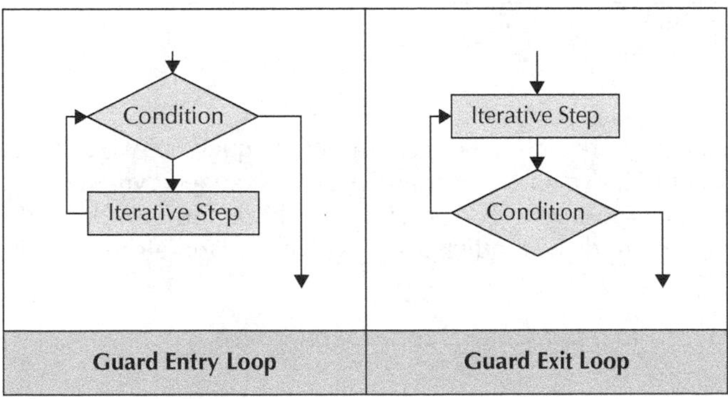

FIGURE 3-2. *Iterative statement logic flows*

Three loop structures in PL/SQL let you implement iteration: the *for*, *while*, and simple loop structures. You can use them either with or without a cursor. A *cursor* is a PL/SQL structure that lets you access the result of a query row by row or as a bulk operation.

For Loop Statements

You can implement the *for* loop as a range loop or as a cursor loop. A range loop moves through a set of sequential numbers, but you need to know the beginning and ending values. It is a guard-on-exit looping structure. You can navigate through a *for* loop forward or backward by using an ascending integer range. Here's an example:

```
SQL> BEGIN
       FOR i IN 0..9 LOOP
         dbms_output.put_line('['||i||']['||TO_CHAR(i+1)||']');
       END LOOP;
     END;
     /
```

The value of the iterator, `i`, is equal to the numbers in the inclusive range values. The iterator has a `PLS_INTEGER` data type. The preceding program prints this:

```
[0][1]
[1][2]
[2][3]
 ...
[8][9]
[9][10]
```

Range *for* loops typically start with 1 and move to a higher number, but you can use 0 (zero) as the low value in the range. Using 0 as a starting point is rare, because arrays and cursors use 1-based numbering. The example shows you how to do it, but you *shouldn't do it*.

The next range *for* loop moves through the sequence from the highest number to the lowest number, and it uses a 1-based number model. Notice that the only evidence of decrementing behavior is the `REVERSE` reserved word.

```
SQL> BEGIN
       FOR i IN REVERSE 1..9 LOOP
         dbms_output.put_line('['||i||']['||TO_CHAR(i+1)||']');
       END LOOP;
     END;
     /
```

Cursor *for* loops work with data sets returned by queries. Two static patterns are possible in addition to an implicit dynamic cursor and a parameterized dynamic cursor. The first example shows you how to write a static cursor without a declaration block. You should write this type of code only when you're doing a quick test program or stand-alone script.

```
SQL> BEGIN
       FOR i IN (SELECT item_title FROM item) LOOP
         dbms_output.put_line(i.item_title);
```

```
4     END LOOP;
5   END;
6   /
```

Line 2 contains the static cursor inside parentheses. At runtime, the query becomes an implicit cursor. Implicit cursors like these should *always be static queries*. You should put queries into formal cursors and then call them in the execution block, like this:

```
SQL> DECLARE
2      CURSOR c IS
3        SELECT item_title FROM item;
4    BEGIN
5      FOR i IN c LOOP
6        dbms_output.put_line(i.item_title);
7      END LOOP;
8    END;
9    /
```

The program declares a formal static cursor on lines 2 and 3. The *for* loop implicitly opens and fetches records from the cursor on line 5. This type or program is more readable than the preceding example. It is also adaptable if your requirements evolve from a static cursor to a dynamic cursor. Whether or not you define cursors with formal parameters, you can include variables in a formal cursor declaration.

The following example shows you how to implement a cursor with a formal parameter. The alternative would be to switch the cursor parameter with a substitution variable on line 6.

```
SQL> DECLARE
 2      lv_search_string VARCHAR2(60);
 3      CURSOR c (cv_search VARCHAR2) IS
 4        SELECT   item_title
 5        FROM     item
 6        WHERE    REGEXP_LIKE(item_title,'^'||cv_search||'*+');
 7    BEGIN
 8      FOR i IN c ('&input') LOOP
 9        dbms_output.put_line(i.item_title);
10      END LOOP;
11    END;
12    /
```

The lines of interest are 3, 6, and 8. Line 3 declares the formal parameter for a dynamic cursor. Line 6 shows the use of the formal parameter in the cursor. Line 8 shows the actual parameter calling the cursor. The actual parameter is a substitution variable because the anonymous block becomes dynamic when you call it. Substitution variable and formal parameters are very similar because they're placeholders for values that arrive when you call your program. You can replace the formal parameter on line 6 with a substitution variable, but that's a very poor coding practice. As a rule, you should always define formal parameters for dynamic cursors.

This concludes the basics of a *for* loop. A twist on the *for* loop involves the `WHERE CURRENT OF` clause, which is discussed next.

WHERE CURRENT OF Clause In my opinion, "a big to-do about nothing" is an appropriate description of the `WHERE CURRENT OF` clause because bulk operations are generally the better solution. However, for completeness, it's important to show a few examples, so I've included two.

The first example shows you how to lock a row with the cursor and then update the same table in a *for* loop:

```
SQL> DECLARE
  2    CURSOR c IS
  3      SELECT * FROM item
  4      WHERE  item_id BETWEEN 1031 AND 1040
  5      FOR UPDATE;
  6  BEGIN
  7    FOR I IN c LOOP
  8      UPDATE item SET last_updated_by = 3
  9      WHERE CURRENT OF c;
 10    END LOOP;
 11  END;
 12  /
```

Line 5 locks the rows with the `FOR UPDATE` clause. Line 9 correlates the update to a row returned by the cursor.

The next example demonstrates how to use the `WHERE CURRENT OF` clause in a bulk operation. (Bulk operations are covered in depth later in this chapter.)

```
SQL> DECLARE
  TYPE update_record IS RECORD
  ( last_updated_by  NUMBER
  , last_update_date DATE );
  TYPE update_table IS TABLE OF UPDATE_RECORD;
  updates UPDATE_TABLE;
  CURSOR c IS
    SELECT last_updated_by, last_update_date
    FROM item
    WHERE  item_id BETWEEN 1031 AND 1040
    FOR UPDATE;
BEGIN
  OPEN c;
  LOOP
    FETCH c BULK COLLECT INTO updates LIMIT 5;
    EXIT WHEN updates.COUNT = 0;
    FORALL i IN updates.FIRST..updates.LAST
      UPDATE item
      SET    last_updated_by = updates(i).last_updated_by
      ,      last_update_date = updates(i).last_update_date
      WHERE CURRENT OF c;
END;
/
```

The `EXIT` statement on line 16 works when the `BULK COLLECT` clause fails to fetch any rows. Like the row-by-row example shown previously, the `FOR UPDATE` clause (on line 11) locks the rows. The `WHERE CURRENT OF` clause on line 21 correlates the update to the rows returned by the bulk-collected cursor.

Now that I've shown you how to use the `WHERE CURRENT OF` clause in a bulk operation, you might wonder why you would want to. After all, the same thing can be accomplished by a correlated `UPDATE` statement, like this:

```
SQL> UPDATE item i1
     SET    last_updated_by = 3
     ,      last_update_date = TRUNC(SYSDATE)
     WHERE  EXISTS (SELECT NULL FROM item i2
                    WHERE  item_id BETWEEN 1031 AND 1040
                    AND    i1.ROWID = i2.ROWID);
```

In fact, Oracle's documentation indicates that it recommends correlated `UDPATE` and `DELETE` statements over the use of the `WHERE CURRENT OF` clause. *I also recommend native SQL solutions when they're available.*

The range and cursor *for* loops are powerful iterative structures. Their beauty lies in their simplicity, and their curse lies in their implicit opening and closing of cursor resources. You should use these structures when access to the data is straightforward and row-by-row auditing isn't required. When you need to perform row-by-row auditing, you should use a *while* or simple loop because they give you more control.

While Loop Statements

A *while* loop is a guard-on-entry loop: you need to manage both the entry and exit criteria of a *while* loop. Unlike the *for* loop, with the *while* loop you don't need an index value because you can use other criteria to control the entry and exit criteria. If you use an index, the Oracle Database 11*g* `CONTINUE` statement can make control more complex, because it allows you to abort an iteration and return to the top of the loop:

```
SQL> DECLARE
       lv_counter NUMBER := 1;
     BEGIN
       WHILE (lv_counter < 5) LOOP
         dbms_output.put('Index at top ['||lv_counter||']');
         IF lv_counter >= 1 THEN
           IF MOD(lv_counter,2) = 0 THEN
             dbms_output.new_line();
             lv_counter := lv_counter + 1;
             CONTINUE;
           END IF;
           dbms_output.put_line('['||lv_counter||']');
         END IF;
         lv_counter := lv_counter + 1;
       END LOOP;
     END;
     /
```

This prints the following:

```
Index at top [1][1]
Index at top [2]
Index at top [3][3]
Index at top [4]
```

Only odd-numbered counter values make it to the bottom of the loop, as illustrated by the second printing of the counter value. That's because the `CONTINUE` statement prints a line return and returns control to the top of the loop. If you replace the `CONTINUE` statement on line 10 with an `EXIT` statement, you will leave the loop rather than skip one iteration through the loop.

You could also do the same thing with the `GOTO` statement and label. You enclose labels inside *guillemets* (a French word pronounced *gee*^{uh} *meys*), also known as double angle brackets. They're available in releases prior to Oracle Database 11*g*, and it pains me to tell you about them because they're only needed when you implement a `GOTO` statement. As a rule, `GOTO` statements aren't good programming solutions. If you must use a `GOTO` statement, here's an example:

```
SQL> DECLARE
  2    lv_counter NUMBER := 1;
  3  BEGIN
  4    WHILE (lv_counter < 5) LOOP
  5      dbms_output.put('Index at top ['||lv_counter||']');
  6      IF lv_counter >= 1 THEN
  7        IF MOD(lv_counter,2) = 0 THEN
  8          dbms_output.new_line();
  9          GOTO skippy;
 10        END IF;
 11        dbms_output.put_line('['||lv_counter||']');
 12      END IF;
 13      << skippy >>
 14      lv_counter := lv_counter + 1;
 15    END LOOP;
 16  END;
 17  /
```

The `GOTO` statement on line 9 skips to the incrementing instruction for the control variable on line 13. It is actually a bit cleaner than the `CONTINUE` statement shown earlier.

The `GOTO` statement should be avoided whenever possible, however. The `CONTINUE` statement should be used minimally and carefully. The *while* loop is powerful but can be tricky if you're not careful when using a `CONTINUE` statement. A poorly coded *while* loop that contains a `CONTINUE` statement can cause an infinite loop.

Simple Loop Statements

The simple loop statement is anything but simple. You use it when you want to control everything that surrounds access to an explicit cursor. Some of these controls are provided through four built-in cursor attributes:

- **`%FOUND`** Returns `TRUE` only when a Data Manipulation Language (DML) statement has changed a row
- **`%ISOPEN`** Always returns `FALSE` for any implicit cursor

- **`%NOTFOUND`** Returns `TRUE` when a DML statement fails to change a row
- **`%ROWCOUNT`** Returns the number of rows changed by a DML statement or the number of rows returned by a `SELECT INTO` statement

These attributes work with cursors or ordinary SQL statements. You access ordinary SQL statements by referring to `SQL` instead of a cursor name. A `SELECT-INTO`, `INSERT`, `UPDATE`, or `DELETE` statement is *found* when it processes rows, and is *not found* when it doesn't. For example, the following anonymous block uses cursor attributes to manage printing log statements to the console:

```
SQL> BEGIN
  2    UPDATE   system_user
  3    SET      last_update_date = SYSDATE;
  4    IF SQL%FOUND THEN
  5      dbms_output.put_line('Updated ['||SQL%ROWCOUNT||']');
  6    ELSE
  7      dbms_output.put_line('Nothing updated!');
  8    END IF;
  9  END;
 10  /
```

`SQL%FOUND` on line 4 checks whether a SQL statement was processed. As you may have surmised, `SQL` isn't just an acronym in Oracle PL/SQL; it is a reserved word that links to an anonymous cursor. If `SQL%FOUND` returns `TRUE`, then line 5 prints the number of rows updated in the table.

A typical simple loop opens a cursor, fetches rows from a cursor, processes rows from a cursor, and closes a cursor. The following program demonstrates those steps and illustrates an anchored data type:

```
SQL> DECLARE
    lv_id    item.item_id%TYPE;   -- This is an anchored type.
    lv_title VARCHAR2(60);
    CURSOR c IS
      SELECT   item_id, item_title
      FROM     item;
  BEGIN
    OPEN c;
    LOOP
      FETCH c INTO lv_id, lv_title;
      EXIT WHEN c%NOTFOUND;
      dbms_output.put_line('Title ['||lv_title||']');
    END LOOP;
    CLOSE c;
  END;
  /
```

This program defines the `lv_id` variable by anchoring the data type to the definition of the `item_id` column in the `item` table. Anchoring ensures that when the definition of the table changes, you don't have to change your program because the anchored data type adjusts automatically. The second `lv_title` variable is explicitly assigned a data type, and any change to the table would require a change to the assigned data type. The first statement after you start a simple loop fetches a row of data, and the second, line 11, checks to make sure a row was fetched. Line 11 also exits the loop when no record is found, which is typically after all rows have been read or no rows were found.

You can extend the preceding model by creating a user-defined record structure and returning the row into a single record structure. Record structures are composite variables. The following example uses a `%ROWTYPE` pseudo column to anchor a catalog table definition to a local variable:

```
SQL> DECLARE
  2    lv_item_record item%ROWTYPE;    -- This is an anchored type.
  3    CURSOR c IS
  4      SELECT   *
  5      FROM     item;
  6  BEGIN
  7    OPEN c;
  8    LOOP
  9      FETCH c INTO lv_item_record;
 10      EXIT WHEN c%NOTFOUND;
 11      dbms_output.put_line('Title ['||lv_item_record.item_title||']');
 12    END LOOP;
 13    CLOSE c;
 14  END;
 15  /
```

On line 11, the `lv_item_record.item_title` statement returns the value of a field in the row of data. The dot between the local variable and the column name is the *component selector*. You actually read this reference from right to left. It means the `item_title` field is selected from the `lv_item_record` component, which is a local variable.

You could also create a record type explicitly. You would do this when you want only a subset of the columns in a table and you don't want to create a view. A local record set variable would be like the following:

```
TYPE item_record IS RECORD
( id    NUMBER
, title VARCHAR2(60));
```

The best approach simply lets you anchor a local variable to the `SELECT` list returned by a cursor, which is a natural record structure. You could rewrite the program like this:

```
SQL> DECLARE
    CURSOR c IS
      SELECT   *
      FROM     item;
    lv_item_record c%ROWTYPE;
  BEGIN
    OPEN c;
    LOOP
      FETCH c INTO lv_item_record;
      EXIT WHEN c%NOTFOUND;
```

```
11       dbms_output.put_line('Title ['||lv_item_record.item_title||']');
12     END LOOP;
13     CLOSE c;
14   END;
15   /
```

Line 5 declares a variable that anchors itself to the definition of a cursor. If you change the cursor, the variable automatically adjusts. This is the most flexible and least coupled way to anchor a variable in PL/SQL. It's also worth mentioning that declaring a variable after a cursor is supported in Oracle Database but not in MySQL.

You'll encounter some glitches down the road with local types like these because they're limited exclusively to a PL/SQL context. The "Composite Data Types" section earlier in this chapter shows the better alternative.

This section has demonstrated how you can use implicit and explicit looping structures. It has also introduced you to the management of the `CURSOR` statement in the execution section of PL/SQL programs.

Review Section

This section has described the following points about conditional and iterative statements:

- PL/SQL supports three-valued logic, which means you must proactively manage potential null states.
- PL/SQL supports the *if*, *elsif*, and *else* conditional logic.
- PL/SQL supports simple and searched *case* statements, and they perform like *if*, *elsif*, and *else* blocks because they don't support fall-through like the C, C++, C#, and Java programming languages.
- PL/SQL supports a *for* loop, which can navigate forward or backward through the data set.
- PL/SQL supports a *while* loop, which can navigate forward through logic based on a condition.
- PL/SQL supports a simple loop, which gives you the most control over the iteration steps and provides features to branch execution on whether or not a condition variable value is set.
- The `EXIT` statement lets you exit a loop or block.
- The `FOR UPDATE` and `WHERE CURRENT OF` clauses synchronize behaviors when locking rows, but you should almost always use a correlated `UPDATE` statement.
- PL/SQL supports a `CONTINUE` statement, which lets you skip over an execution through a loop, and the `GOTO` statement and labels for branching with the `GOTO` statement.
- PL/SQL supports four cursor attributes: `%FOUND`, `%NOTFOUND`, `%ISOPEN`, and `%ROWCOUNT`.

Exceptions

PL/SQL provides an optional block for exception handling, as covered earlier in this chapter. The exception block manages any exceptions that occur while running the execution block. Errors raised in the declaration block are thrown to and managed by the calling scope program. Oracle provides two built-in exception management functions, described next.

- `SQLCODE` returns a negative number that maps to the Oracle predefined exceptions, but one special case, the `NO_DATA_FOUND` exception, returns 100.
- `SQLERRM` is overloaded and provides the following behaviors: returns the actual error as a negative integer, returns a user-defined exception when the number is positive or not found in the predefined Oracle exception list, and returns the actual number parameter as a negative integer with the Oracle-defined message.

The simplest exception handler uses the Oracle keyword `OTHERS` and catches all raised exceptions from the execution block:

```
SQL> DECLARE
  2    lv_letter  VARCHAR2(1);
  3    lv_phrase  VARCHAR2(2) := 'AB';
  4  BEGIN
  5    lv_letter := lv_phrase;
  6  EXCEPTION
  7    WHEN OTHERS THEN
  8      dbms_output.put_line('Error: '||CHR(10)||SQLERRM);
  9  END;
 10  /
```

The assignment of a two-character string to a single-character string on line 5 raises (throws) an exception, which is caught by the exception handler and printed to console:

```
Error:
ORA-06502: PL/SQL: numeric or value error: character string buffer too small
```

Oracle also provides a set of predefined exceptions in the `STANDARD` package. Table 7-2 in Chapter 7 lists and describes these exceptions. Standard error names can replace the `OTHERS` keyword. The `VALUE_ERROR` keyword could do so on line 7, as shown:

```
  7  WHEN VALUE_ERROR THEN
```

This would catch the `ORA-06502` error but not any other exception, which means we would now need two error handlers: one for the specific *"numeric or value error"* and another for everything else, more or less a "catch all" handler. The new exception block would look like this:

```
  6  EXCEPTION
  7    WHEN VALUE_ERROR THEN    -- Specific error handler.
  8      dbms_output.put_line('Error: '||CHR(10)||SQLERRM);
  9    WHEN OTHERS THEN         -- General error handler.
 10      dbms_output.put_line('Error: '||CHR(10)||SQLERRM);
 11  END;
 12  /
```

Many developers use the `OTHERS` keyword as a catch-all handler, but good coding practices recommend using specific exception handlers. You should always place the specific exception handler before the `OTHERS` handler.

PL/SQL also enables us to define user-defined exceptions and write dynamic exceptions. The next two subsections discuss how.

User-Defined Exceptions

You can declare user-defined exceptions in either of two ways: declare an `EXCEPTION` variable only or declare an `EXCEPTION` variable and `EXCEPTION_INIT` compiler directive. The `EXCEPTION` variable by itself lets you catch a user-defined exception with an `OTHERS` exception handler and *if* statement. The *if* statement checks for the user-defined exception number (oddly enough, 1 is that number). The combination of an `EXCEPTION` variable and `EXCEPTION_INIT` compiler directive lets you create a customer exception handler. As you'll see shortly, the `EXCEPTION_INIT` compiler directive maps an exception handler name to a known Oracle error code.

```
SQL> DECLARE
  2    lv_error  EXCEPTION;
  3  BEGIN
  4    RAISE lv_error;
  5    dbms_output.put_line('Can''t get here.');
  6  EXCEPTION
  7    WHEN OTHERS THEN
  8      IF SQLCODE = 1 THEN
  9        dbms_output.put_line('This is ['||SQLERRM||']');
 10      END IF;
 11  END;
 12  /
```

The example declares a user-defined exception of `lv_error` on line 2 and raises it as an exception on line 4. The generic `OTHERS` exception traps the error on line 7, and the *if* statement checks for a user-defined exception on line 8.

The program raises the exception and prints:

```
This is [User-Defined Exception]
```

A two-step declaration process lets you declare an exception and map it to a number. The first step declares the variable and the second step maps the variable to a `PRAGMA, EXCEPTION_INIT` precompiler instruction:

```
SQL> DECLARE
    lv_sys_context  VARCHAR2(20);
    lv_error        EXCEPTION;
    PRAGMA EXCEPTION_INIT(lv_error,-2003);
  BEGIN
    lv_sys_context := SYS_CONTEXT('USERENV','PROXY_PUSHER');
    RAISE lv_error;
    dbms_output.put_line('Can''t get here.');
  EXCEPTION
    WHEN lv_error THEN
```

```
 11       dbms_output.put_line('This is ['||SQLERRM||']');
 12   END;
 13   /
```

Line 3 declares the local exception variable and line 4 maps the Oracle error code to the user-defined exception. Line 6 throws an error because it provides an invalid `PROXY_PUSHER` string as an actual parameter to the `SYS_CONTEXT` function. Line 10 shows the user-defined exception handler that catches the raised exception. The exception block is only capable of managing an `ORA-02003` exception because there's no catchall `OTHERS` exception handler.

The preceding test program raises an exception and prints

```
This is [ORA-02003: invalid USERENV parameter]
```

`ORA-02003` is a real error code found in the `SYS.STANDARD` package. You can read the specification of that package to find a complete list of standard errors.

Dynamic User-Defined Exceptions

Dynamic user-defined exceptions let you raise a customized exception by assigning a number in the range of –20,000 to –20,999. The `RAISE_APPLICATION_ERROR` function provides this ability in PL/SQL. The prototype is

```
RAISE_APPLICATION_ERROR(error_number, error_message [, keep_errors])
```

The following program shows how to raise a dynamic user-defined exception:

```
SQL> DECLARE
  2    lv_error        EXCEPTION;
  3    PRAGMA EXCEPTION_INIT(lv_error,-20001);
  4  BEGIN
  5    RAISE_APPLICATION_ERROR(-20001,'A less original message.');
  6  EXCEPTION
  7    WHEN lv_error THEN
  8      dbms_output.put_line('['||SQLERRM||']');
  9  END;
 10  /
```

Line 2 declares the exception variable and line 3 maps the error to a value in the range of available values. Line 5 throws the exception and line 7 catches the error.

TIP

There are critical errors and noncritical errors in any database-centric application. Critical errors should raise a failure message to the application and customer, while noncritical errors should be recorded and addressed later by support staff. Database triggers are the best place to put programming logic for noncritical errors.

Oracle Database 12c also provides a stack trace management function in the `DMBS_UTILITY` package: the `FORMAT_ERROR_BACKTRACE` function. Handling errors is important, of course, and much more can be said about managing them in exception blocks. Consult Chapter 7 for more information on PL/SQL exception handling.

Review Section

This section has described the following points about exception handling:

- Oracle Database 12*c* provides two custom built-in functions, `SQLCODE` and `SQLERRM`.
- Oracle supports predefined exceptions in the `STANDARD` package and a generic exception handler—`OTHERS`.
- PL/SQL supports user-defined exceptions, which throw a positive 1 as an error value unless you use the precompiler `PRAGMA EXCEPTION_INIT` to set a numeric exception value.
- PL/SQL supports dynamic user-defined exceptions by calling the `RAISE_APPLICATION_ERROR` function, which allows you to define an error message.

Bulk Operations

Oracle Database 10*g* and subsequent releases (that is, all supported releases at the time of writing) provide bulk processing capabilities. These capabilities differ somewhat from the structures presented thus far in the chapter, but they follow the general look and feel. Where possible, bulk processing should be the default in your batch processing and high-volume processing of data.

The following program shows you how to select groups of rows into array structures. You do this with the `BULK COLLECT` clause. I've chosen a limit of 20 rows simply to make it simple with the sample data. Real-world solutions can be hundreds or thousands of records at a time, but I'd recommend *limiting this to a range of 250 to 500 rows*.

```
SQL> DECLARE
  TYPE title_record IS RECORD
  ( title    VARCHAR2(60)
  , subtitle VARCHAR2(60));
  TYPE title_collection IS TABLE OF TITLE_RECORD;
  lv_title_collection TITLE_COLLECTION;
  CURSOR c IS
    SELECT   item_title, item_subtitle
    FROM     item;
BEGIN
  OPEN c;
  LOOP
    FETCH c BULK COLLECT INTO lv_title_collection LIMIT 20;
    EXIT WHEN lv_title_collection.COUNT = 0;
    FOR i IN 1..lv_title_collection.COUNT LOOP
      dbms_output.put_line('['||lv_title_collection(i).title||']');
    END LOOP;
  END LOOP;
  CLOSE c;
END;
/
```

This program is more complex than earlier examples and uses a table collection. After creating a record structure, you create another local collection data type. You then create a variable of the collection type. Line 13 bulk collects the collection of a record structure into a single variable. The range *for* loop on lines 15 through 17 reads the collection and prints only one column value from each record.

After you've selected the data, you should be able to insert or update target tables in the same bulk processing units. You can do so with the FORALL statement. The following lets you perform a bulk update:

```
SQL> DECLARE
  2    TYPE title_record IS RECORD
  3    ( id        NUMBER
  4    , title     VARCHAR2(60)
  5    , subtitle VARCHAR2(60));
  6    TYPE title_collection IS TABLE OF TITLE_RECORD;
  7    lv_title_collection TITLE_COLLECTION;
  8    CURSOR c IS
  9      SELECT   item_id, item_title, item_subtitle
 10      FROM     item;
 11  BEGIN
 12    OPEN c;
 13    LOOP
 14      FETCH c BULK COLLECT INTO lv_title_collection LIMIT 20;
 15      EXIT WHEN lv_title_collection.COUNT = 0;
 16        FORALL i IN lv_title_collection.FIRST..lv_title_collection.LAST
 17          UPDATE   item_temp
 18          SET      item_title = lv_title_collection(i).title
 19          ,        item_subtitle = lv_title_collection(i).subtitle
 20          WHERE    item_id = lv_title_collection(i).id;
 21    END LOOP;
 22  END;
 23  /
```

The FORALL statement on lines 16 through 20 updates 20 rows at a time, but it could easily update more. Bulk processing reduces the context switches in the database and improves online transaction processing application throughput.

Review Section

This section has described the following points about bulk operations:

- The BULK COLLECT INTO clause lets you perform a bulk collect, and it provides you with the LIMIT clause to set the maximum size of rows processed through bulk operations.
- The FORALL statement lets you process a group of rows by managing a collection assignment.

Functions, Procedures, and Packages

PL/SQL stored programming units are typically functions, procedures, packages, and triggers. You can also store object types, but that discussion is reserved for Chapter 11.

Oracle maintains a unique list of stored object names for tables, views, sequences, stored programs, and types. This list is known as a *namespace*. Functions, procedures, packages, and object types are in this namespace. Another namespace stores triggers.

Stored functions, procedures, and packages provide a way to hide implementation details in a program unit. They also let you wrap the implementation from prying eyes on the server tier.

You can group functions and procedures into two types of subroutines based on their formal parameter lists. The first type is a *pass-by-value* program unit, which is where all the parameters use an `IN`-only mode of operation. The second type of subroutine is a pass-by-reference program unit, which has one or more parameters that use `IN OUT` or `OUT`-only mode of operation.

A pass-by-value function or procedure takes inputs, or formal parameters, and returns an output. The formal parameter values are sent into the function, and something completely different is returned to the calling scope. It's like putting ingredients in a bowl and mixing them up to make a cake batter. Once you mix the ingredients into the batter, extracting them individually from the batter is impossible. The cake batter is like the return value from a function.

A pass-by-reference function or procedure takes inputs that can be references to existing variables or values. The contents of `IN OUT` or `OUT`-only variables can change inside a subroutine, which means the contents of pass-by-reference functions or procedures can change.

Pass-by-reference functions and procedures are more coupled with the calling program unit than are pass-by-value functions and procedures. That's because they hold references to formal parameters declared in the external calling scope.

Oracle Database 12*c* adds layering with functions, procedures, and packages by letting you now *white list* which subroutine can call them. You do that with the `ACCESSIBLE BY` clause, which takes one or more functions, procedures, packages, or object types.

Functions

Stored functions are convenient structures because you can call them directly from SQL statements or PL/SQL programs. All stored functions must return a value. You can also use them as right operands because they return a value. Functions are defined in local declaration blocks or the database. You frequently implement them inside stored packages.

The prototype for a stored function is

```
CREATE OR REPLACE [{EDITIONABLE | NONEDITIONABLE}]
[schema.] FUNCTION function_name
( parameter  [IN][OUT] [NOCOPY] {sql_data_type | plsql_data_type}
[,parameter  [IN][OUT] [NOCOPY] {sql_data_type | plsql_data_type}]
[, ... ] )
RETURN {sql_data_type | plsql_data_type}
[ACCESSIBLE BY
( [{FUNCTION | PROCEDURE | PACKAGE | TYPE}] [schema.]unit_name)
[,[{FUNCTION | PROCEDURE | PACKAGE | TYPE}] [schema.]unit_name)]
[,... ]]])
[AUTHID [DEFINER | CURRENT_USER]]
[DETERMINISTIC | PARALLEL_ENABLED]
[PIPELINED]
```

```
[RESULT_CACHE [RELIES ON table_name]] IS
  declaration_statements;
BEGIN
  execution_statements
  RETURN variable;
[EXCEPTION]
  exception_handling_statements
END [function_name];
/
```

Functions can be used as right operands in PL/SQL assignments. You can also call them directly from SQL statements provided they return a SQL data type. Procedures cannot be right operands. Nor can you call them from SQL statements.

Oracle Database 12*c* lets you limit which other program units can call a function, using the new ACCESSIBLE BY clause. You can also define functions with access rights to the same schema or to the calling schema, using the AUTHID value. Choosing the default DEFINER authorized identifier runs the program in the same schema where you defined the function. Choosing the CURRENT authorized identifier runs the program unit in the calling schema.

You can query a function that returns a SQL data type by using the following prototype from the pseudo table DUAL:

```
SELECT    some_function[(actual_parameter [, ...])]
FROM      dual;
```

You are *no longer limited to passing actual parameters by positional order* in SQL statements. This means that you can use PL/SQL named notation in SQL. The "Calling Subroutines" section of Chapter 8 covers how named, positional, and mixed notation work.

The following is a prototype for the same query of a PL/SQL function from the pseudo table DUAL:

```
SELECT    some_function[(formal_parameter => actual_parameter)]
FROM      dual;
```

Named positional calls work best when default values exist for other parameters. There isn't much purpose in calling only some of the parameters when the call would fail. Formal parameters are optional parameters. Named positional calls work best with functions or procedures that have optional parameters.

You can also use the CALL statement to capture a return value from a function into a bind variable. The prototype for the CALL statement follows:

```
SQL> CALL some_function[(actual_parameter [, ...])]
     INTO some_session_bind_variable;
```

The following is a small sample case that concatenates two strings into one:

```
SQL> CREATE OR REPLACE FUNCTION join_strings
     ( string1 VARCHAR2
     , string2 VARCHAR2 ) RETURN VARCHAR2 IS
     BEGIN
       RETURN string1 ||' '|| string2||'.';
     END;
     /
```

You can now query the function from SQL:

```
SQL> SELECT join_strings('Hello','World') FROM dual;
```

Likewise, you can define a session-level bind variable and then use the `CALL` statement to put a variable into a session-level bind variable:

```
SQL> VARIABLE session_var VARCHAR2(30)
SQL> CALL join_strings('Hello','World') INTO :session_var;
```

The `CALL` statement uses an `INTO` clause when working with stored functions. You dispense with the `INTO` clause when working with stored procedures.

If you select the bind variable from the pseudo table `DUAL`, like this:

```
SQL> SELECT :session_var FROM dual;
```

you'll see:

```
Hello World.
```

Functions offer a great deal of power to database developers. They are callable in both SQL statements and PL/SQL blocks.

Procedures

As mentioned in the previous section, procedures cannot be right operands. Nor can you use them in SQL statements. You move data into and out of PL/SQL stored procedures through their formal parameter list. Like stored functions, you can also define local named block programs in the declaration section of procedures.

The prototype for a stored procedure is

```
CREATE OR REPLACE [{EDITIONABLE | NONEDITIONABLE}]
[schema.] PROCEDURE procedure_name
( parameter  [IN] [OUT] [NOCOPY] {sql_data_type | plsql_data_type}
[,parameter  [IN] [OUT] [NOCOPY] {sql_data_type | plsql_data_type}]
[, ... ] )
[ACCESSIBLE BY
( [{FUNCTION | PROCEDURE | PACKAGE | TYPE}] [schema.]unit_name)
[, [{FUNCTION | PROCEDURE | PACKAGE | TYPE}] [schema.]unit_name)]
[,... ]]])
 [ AUTHID DEFINER | CURRENT_USER ] IS
  declaration_statements
BEGIN
  execution_statements;
[EXCEPTION]
  exception_handling_statements
END procedure_name;
/
```

You can define procedures with or without formal parameters. Formal parameters in procedures can be either *pass-by-value* or *pass-by-reference* variables in stored procedures. Pass-by-reference variables have both an `IN` mode and an `OUT` mode. Like functions, when you don't provide a parameter mode, the procedure creation assumes you want the mode to be a pass-by-value variable.

The new ACCESSIBLE BY clause is also available to procedures, and you can define procedures with access rights to the same schema or to the calling schema with the AUTHID value. The AUTHID value works the same way for procedures as it does for functions.

The following implements a stored procedure that encloses a string in square brackets:

```
SQL> CREATE OR REPLACE PROCEDURE format_string
     ( string_in IN OUT VARCHAR2 ) IS
     BEGIN
       string_in := '['||string_in||']';
     END;
     /
```

You can also use the CALL statement to call and pass variables into and out of a procedure. Like the earlier function example, this example uses the CALL statement and bind variable:

```
SQL> VARIABLE session_var VARCHAR2(30)
SQL> CALL join_strings('Hello','World') INTO :session_var;
SQL> CALL format_string(:session_var);
```

You should note that the CALL statement does not use an INTO clause when passing a variable into and out of a stored procedure. This differs from how it works with stored functions.

You also can use the EXECUTE statement with stored procedures. The following works exactly like the CALL statement:

```
SQL> EXECUTE format_string(:session_var);
```

When you select the bind variable from the pseudo table DUAL:

```
SQL> SELECT :session_var FROM dual;
```

you'll see:

```
[Hello World.]
```

Procedures offer you the ability to use pass-by-value or pass-by-reference formal parameters. As you'll see in Chapter 8, stored procedures let you exchange values with external applications.

Packages

Package development starts with planning which shared data types and cursors should be bundled with which functions and procedures. Shared data types let you exchange information using the specifications of scalar, record structure, and collection data types that a package can require. Shared cursors, on the other hand, present the possibility that a query might be reused many times and would be more effectively designed and deployed in one location—in the package specification.

When you deploy packages with shared cursors, you must guarantee their integrity by using the following compiler directive:

```
PRAGMA SERIALLY_REUSABLE;
```

If you fail to remember this fact, a shared cursor might be read by one program starting at the beginning and read by another program somewhere between the first and last rows. That means shared cursors run the risk of being read inconsistently, which is the *worst* type of error you can introduce to PL/SQL. The simple rule is this: when you deploy shared cursors, the package must be serially reusable (always fresh to anyone that calls it).

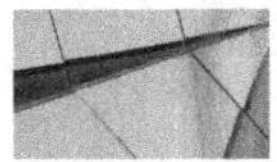

NOTE
Packages that contain shared cursors must be defined as serially reusable code artifacts in the database.

Variables and cursors are declared exactly as they are in other PL/SQL blocks. Functions and procedures are like schema-level objects with one exception: you no longer can use Data Definition Language (DDL) commands to work with them individually. All DDL commands apply to the package specification or body. Likewise, all function and procedure definitions in the package specification must be implemented in the package body the same way—that means names, parameter lists (including default values) for procedures and names, and return types for functions.

Here's the prototype for a package specification:

```
CREATE [OR REPLACE] [{EDITIONABLE | NONEDITIONABLE}]
[schema.] package_name
[ACCESSIBLE BY
( [{FUNCTION | PROCEDURE | PACKAGE | TYPE}] [schema.]unit_name)
[,[{FUNCTION | PROCEDURE | PACKAGE | TYPE}] [schema.]unit_name)]
[,... ]]]) {IS | AS}
[TYPE type_name IS
 {RECORD (column_list) | VARRAY(n) | TABLE [INDEX BY data_type]}]
[variable_name data_type {DEFAULT | :=} value; [ ...]]
[CURSOR cursor_name
 (parameter data_type [, parameter data_type [, ...]) IS
  SELECT statement; [ ...]]
[TYPE reference_cursor IS REF CURSOR
 [ RETURN {catalog_row | cursor_row | record_structure}] [ ...]]
[user_exception EXCEPTION; [ ...]]
[PRAGMA SERIALLY_REUSABLE;]
[FUNCTION public_prototype;] [ ...]
[PROCEURE public_prototype;] [ ...]
END [package_name];
/
```

The new `ACCESSIBLE BY` clause lets you designate which functions, procedures, packages, and object types can call the package. This effectively lets you white list callers of any package structures, types, functions, and procedures.

You can implement a package specification with only data types, variables, cursors, and exceptions, or you can also add functions and procedures. You don't need to define a package body when a package specification has no functions or procedures because there's nothing to implement in the package body. Packages without implementations are called *bodiless packages*. You must provide an implementation of any function or procedure definition from a package specification in the package body.

The data types supported in packages are scalar and PL/SQL composite data types; that means you can't define an object type. You would raise the following compile-time error if you were to attempt to put an object type in a package specification or body:

```
PLS-00540: object not supported in this context.
```

TIP

You cannot implement a user-defined object type in a package.

The sample `overloading` package shows you how to define a serially reusable package. It's done by including a `SERIALLY_REUSABLE` compiler directive in both the package specification and the body. A serially reusable package guarantees all callers of a package function a fresh copy of any shared cursors. The downside of a serially reusable function is that it isn't callable from `SELECT` statements.

The `overloading` package also shows you how to define an overloaded function. It creates a package-level salutation function that takes two or three parameters. Notice that in the package specification, only the function definitions exist, as shown:

```
SQL> CREATE OR REPLACE PACKAGE overloading IS
  2
  3     -- Force fresh copy of shared cursor.
  4     PRAGMA SERIALLY_REUSABLE;
  5
  6     -- Define a default salutation.
  7     FUNCTION salutation
  8     ( pv_long_phrase  VARCHAR2 DEFAULT 'Hello'
  9     , pv_name         VARCHAR2 ) RETURN VARCHAR2;
 10
 11     -- Define an overloaded salutation.
 12     FUNCTION salutation
 13     ( pv_long_phrase  VARCHAR2 DEFAULT 'Hello'
 14     , pv_name         VARCHAR2
 15     , pv_language     VARCHAR2 ) RETURN VARCHAR2;
 16  END;
 17  /
```

Line 4 contains the precompiler instruction that makes this package serially reusable. Lines 8 and 13 contain a parameter with a default value; that same default value must occur for the parameters in the package body. The only difference that can exist between the definition in the package specification and the definition in the package body is that the `DEFAULT` keyword may be interchanged with a colon and equal sign set (`:=`).

After creating the package specification with functions or procedures, you need to create a package body. The following example creates a package body that has a shared cursor and two overloaded functions. The functions both use the shared cursor, and these functions are the only ones that can use the shared cursor. That's because the cursor is declared in the package body rather than in the specification.

The example depends on this table:

```
SQL> CREATE TABLE salutation_translation
( short_salutation  VARCHAR2(4)
, long_salutation   VARCHAR2(12)
, phrase_language   VARCHAR2(12));
```

You would seed it with the following values:

```
SQL> INSERT INTO salutation_translation VALUES ('Hi','HELLO','ENGLISH');
SQL> INSERT INTO salutation_translation VALUES ('Bye','GOODBYE','ENGLISH');
SQL> INSERT INTO salutation_translation VALUES ('Ciao','SALUTE','ITALIAN');
SQL> INSERT INTO salutation_translation VALUES ('Ciao','ADDIO','ITALIAN');
```

A package body prototype differs from the package body because you can implement local functions and procedures in it. The local functions and procedures can be called only from the published functions or procedures that were defined in the package specification. Here's a package body prototype:

```
CREATE [OR REPLACE] package_name BODY {IS | AS}
[TYPE type_name IS
 {RECORD (column_list) | VARRAY(n) | TABLE [INDEX BY data_type]}]
[variable_name data_type {DEFAULT | :=} value; [ ...]]
[CURSOR cursor_name
 (parameter data_type [, parameter data_type [, ...]) IS
  SELECT statement; [ ...]]
[TYPE reference_cursor IS REF CURSOR
 [ RETURN {catalog_row | cursor_row | record_structure}] [ ...]]
[PRAGMA SERIALLY_REUSABLE;]
[FUNCTION local_implementation;] [ ...]
[PROCEURE local_implementation;] [ ...]
[FUNCTION published_body;] [ ...]
[PROCEDURE published_body;] [ ...]
END [package_name];
/
```

Here's the implementation of the package body:

```
SQL> CREATE OR REPLACE PACKAGE BODY overloading IS

    -- Force fresh copy of shared cursor.
    PRAGMA SERIALLY_REUSABLE;
    -- Shared cursor.
    CURSOR c
    ( cv_long_phrase VARCHAR2
    , cv_language VARCHAR2 ) IS
      SELECT    short_salutation
      ,         long_salutation
      FROM      salutation_translation
      WHERE     long_salutation = UPPER(cv_long_phrase)
      AND       phrase_language = UPPER(cv_language);

```

```
  -- Declare a default salutation.
  FUNCTION salutation
  ( pv_long_phrase  VARCHAR2 DEFAULT 'Hello'
  , pv_name         VARCHAR2 ) RETURN VARCHAR2 IS

    -- Local variables.
    lv_short_salutation  VARCHAR2(4) := '';
    lv_language          VARCHAR2(10) DEFAULT 'ENGLISH';

  BEGIN
    -- Read shared cursor and return concatenated result.
    FOR i IN c(pv_long_phrase, lv_language) LOOP
      lv_short_salutation := i.short_salutation;
    END LOOP;
    RETURN lv_short_salutation || ' ' || pv_name || '!';
  END;

  -- Define an overloaded salutation.
  FUNCTION salutation
  ( pv_long_phrase  VARCHAR2 DEFAULT 'Hello'
  , pv_name         VARCHAR2
  , pv_language     VARCHAR2) RETURN VARCHAR2 IS

    -- Local variable.
    lv_short_salutation  VARCHAR2(4) := '';

  BEGIN
    -- Read shared cursor and return concatenated result.
    FOR i IN c(pv_long_phrase, pv_language) LOOP
        lv_short_salutation := i.short_salutation;
    END LOOP;
    RETURN lv_short_salutation || ' ' || pv_name || '!';
  END;
END;
/
```

You can test either of these inside a PL/SQL block or by calling it with the `CALL` statement at the SQL*Plus prompt. It requires a SQL*Plus scope variable to use the `CALL` statement, as covered in the "SQL*Plus Command-line Interface" section of Appendix A. The following declares the variable and calls the function result into the `:message` bind variable:

```
SQL> VARIABLE message VARCHAR2(30)
SQL> CALL overloading.salutation('Hello','Ringo') INTO :message;
```

You can query the result now and see "Hello Ringo!" or you can call the overloaded `salutation` with three parameters like this:

```
SQL> CALL overloading.salutation('Addio','Lennon','Italian')
  2  INTO :message;
```

A query like this

```
SQL> SELECT :message AS "Goodbye Message" FROM dual;
```

yields this:

```
Message
---------------
Ciao Lennon!
```

When you make a package serially reusable, it becomes unavailable in the context of a SELECT statement. By way of example, this query

```
SQL> SELECT overloading.salutation('Addio','Lennon','Italian') AS "Message"
  2  FROM dual;
```

raises this error:

```
SELECT overloading.salutation('Addio','Lennon','Italian') AS "Message"
       *
ERROR at line 1:
ORA-06534: Cannot access Serially Reusable package "STUDENT.OVERLOADING"
ORA-06512: at line 1
```

It is possible to query functions from packages when they're not serially reusable, and the general rule for most commercial packages is that they're not serially reusable. The only time you need to define a package as serially reusable is when it has a shared cursor. Moving the shared cursor into each of the functions would eliminate the need to make this package serially reusable.

Packages are extremely effective for bundling your code into related modules, and this is something you should generally opt for in application design. Now you know how to implement packages.

Review Section

This section has described the following points about packages:

- Functions are local and stand-alone named blocks that return a value and can be used as right operands in assignments.
- Procedures are local and stand-alone named blocks that don't return a value, which means procedures must be called by anonymous blocks, functions, or procedures.
- Functions and procedures are pass-by-value program units when all their parameters use the default IN-only mode of operation.
- Functions and procedures are pass-by-reference program units when one or more of their formal parameters use an IN OUT or OUT-only mode of operation.
- Packages hold related functions, procedures, and data types; they also support overloading of functions and procedures.
- Bodiless packages support data type and shared cursor definitions.

Transaction Scope

Transaction scope is a thread of execution—session. You establish a session when you connect to the Oracle Database 12*c* database. The session lets you set environment variables, such as SERVEROUTPUT, which lets you print from your PL/SQL programs. What you do during your session is visible only to you until you commit any changes to the database. After committing the changes, other sessions can see the changes you've made.

During a session, you can run one or more PL/SQL programs. They execute serially, or in sequence. The first program can alter the data or environment before the second runs, the second program can alter the data or environment before the third runs, and so on. This is true because your session is the main transaction. All activities depend on potentially all the prior activities. You can commit work, which makes all changes permanent, or reject work, which repudiates all or some changes.

PL/SQL program units provide ACID-compliant transactions across more than a single table. As discussed in the "Multiversion Concurrency Control" section of Appendix A, all INSERT, UPDATE, MERGE, and DELETE statements are ACID-compliant. ACID-compliant means an activity is atomic, consistent, isolated, and durable. Oracle's MVCC design guarantees this behavior, and you can read more about it in Appendix A.

The power to control the session rests with the following three commands, which are Transaction Control Language (TCL) commands:

- The COMMIT statement commits all DML changes made from the beginning of the session or since the last ROLLBACK statement.
- The SAVEPOINT statement divides two epochs. An epoch is defined by the transactions between two relative points of time. A SAVEPOINT delimits two epochs.
- The ROLLBACK statement undoes all changes from now to an epoch or named SAVEPOINT, or now to the beginning of a SQL*Plus session.

These commands enable you to control what happens in your session and program routines. The beginning of a session is both the beginning of an epoch and an implicit SAVEPOINT statement. Likewise, the ending of a session is the ending of an epoch and an implicit COMMIT statement.

How you manage transaction scope differs between a single transaction scope and multiple transaction scopes. You create multiple transaction scopes when a function or procedure is designated as an autonomous stored program unit.

Single Transaction Scope

A common business problem involves guaranteeing the sequential behavior of two or more DML statements. The idea is that either they all must succeed or they all must fail, and partial success is not an option. TCL commands let you guarantee the behavior of sequential activities in a single transaction scope.

The following program uses TCL commands to guarantee that both INSERT statements succeed or fail:

```
SQL> BEGIN
    -- Set savepoint.
    SAVEPOINT all_or_nothing;

```

```
5     -- First insert.
6     INSERT INTO member
7     VALUES
8     ( member_s1.nextval    -- Surrogate primary key
      ...
16    , SYSDATE);
17
18    -- Second insert.
19    INSERT INTO contact
20    VALUES
21    ( contact_s1.nextval   -- Surrogate primary key
22    , member_s1.currval    -- Surrogate foreign key
      ...
30    , SYSDATE);
30
31    -- Commit records.
32    COMMIT;
33
34  EXCEPTION
35    -- Rollback to savepoint and raise exception.
36    WHEN others THEN
37      ROLLBACK TO all_or_nothing;
38      dbms_output.put_line(SQLERRM);
39  END;
40  /
```

The entire transaction fails when either the INSERT statement on line 6 or 19 fails because the transaction is an all or nothing affair. The COMMIT statement on line 32 runs only when both INSERT statements succeed. Any failure raises an exception, and any work that did succeed is undone by the ROLLBACK statement on line 37.

Multiple Transaction Scopes

Some business problems require that programs work independently. Independent programs run in discrete transaction scopes. When you call an autonomous program unit, it runs in another transaction scope.

You can build autonomous programs with the AUTONOMOUS_TRANSACTION precompiler instruction or compiler directive. A precompiler instruction is called a PRAGMA and it sets a specific behavior, such as independent transaction scope. Only the following types of programs can be designated as autonomous routines:

- Top-level (not nested) anonymous blocks
- Local, stand-alone, and package subroutines—functions and procedures
- Methods of SQL object type
- Database triggers

The beginning transaction scope is known as the main routine. It calls an autonomous routine, which then spawns its own transaction scope. A failure in the main routine after calling an autonomous program can only roll back changes made in the main transaction scope. The autonomous transaction scope can succeed or fail independently of the main routine. However, the main routine can also fail when an exception is raised in an autonomous transaction.

Multiple transaction scope programs are complex. You should be sure the benefits outweigh the risk when using multiple transaction scope solutions.

Review Section

This section has described the following points about transaction scope:

- Oracle Database is always in transaction mode, which differs from other databases such as MySQL.
- Transaction scope ensures that either all or nothing happens when inserting, updating, or deleting data from two or more tables.
- You should always set a `SAVEPOINT` before attempting to insert, update, or delete data from two or more tables.
- You should always roll back transactions when one part of a multiple-part transaction fails to ensure ACID-compliant transaction (see Appendix A for a more complete description of ACID compliance).

Database Triggers

Database triggers are specialized stored programs that are triggered by events in the database. They run between when you issue an `INSERT`, `UPDATE`, `MERGE`, or `DELETE` statement and commit the change from the SQL DML statement. They use an anonymous block structure, and they're stored inside columns that use the `LONG` data type. The mechanics of passing variables between the SQL DML statement and anonymous block are complex and left for full discussion in Chapter 12.

An SQL statement followed by a COMMIT statement is called a transaction process, or a two-phase commit (2PC) protocol. ACID-compliant transactions use a 2PC to manage one SQL statement or collections of SQL statements. In a 2PC model, the `INSERT`, `UPDATE`, `MERGE`, or a `DELETE` DML statement starts the process and submits changes. These DML statements can also act as events that fire database triggers assigned to the table being changed.

As a result of triggers working between the first and second phase of a two-phase commit (2PC) protocol, you cannot use the following TCL statements in triggers: `SAVEPOINT`, `ROLLBACK`, or `COMMIT`. You can define four types of triggers in the Oracle Database 11*g* family of products:

- **DDL triggers** These triggers fire when you *create*, *alter*, *rename*, or *drop* objects in a database schema. They are useful to monitor poor programming practices, such as when programs create and drop temporary tables rather than use Oracle collections effectively in memory. Temporary tables can fragment disk space and, over time, degrade the database performance.

- **DML or row-level triggers** These triggers fire when you *insert*, *update*, or *delete* data from a table. You can use these types of triggers to audit, check, save, and replace values before they are changed. Automatic numbering of pseudo-numeric *primary keys* is frequently done by using a DML trigger.
- **`INSTEAD OF` triggers** These triggers enable you to stop performance of a DML statement and redirect the DML statement. `INSTEAD OF` triggers are often used to manage how you write to views that disable a direct write because they're not updateable views. The `INSTEAD OF` triggers apply business rules, and directly *insert*, *update*, or *delete* rows in appropriate tables related to these updateable views.
- **System or database event triggers** These triggers fire when a system activity occurs in the database, like the logon and logoff event triggers described in Chapter 12. These triggers enable you to track system events and map them to users.

All four trigger types are covered in depth in Chapter 12. No review section is necessary here because it would simply repeat the preceding list.

Summary

This chapter has reviewed the PL/SQL basics and explained how to jump-start your PL/SQL skills. The coverage should serve to whet your appetite for more exploration of PL/SQL.

Mastery Check

The mastery check is a series of true-or-false and multiple-choice questions that let you confirm how well you understand the material in the chapter. You may check Appendix I for answers to these questions.

True or False:

1. ___A basic block in PL/SQL must have at least a null statement to compile.
2. ___The *elsif* statement lets you branch execution in an *if* statement.
3. ___The `DECLARE` block is where you put all variable, cursor, and local function and procedure implementations.
4. ___An `EXCEPTION` block is where you put handling for errors raised in the declaration block of the same anonymous or named program unit.
5. ___The colon and equal sign set (`:=`) is the only assignment operator in PL/SQL.
6. ___You need to provide forward-referencing stubs for local functions or procedures to avoid a procedure or function "not declared in this scope" error.
7. ___Oracle supports both simple and searched *case* statements.
8. ___Oracle supports SQL and PL/SQL collections as parameter and return value data types.
9. ___Packages let you define overloaded functions and procedures.
10. ___Database triggers run between the first phase of a DML statement and the `COMMIT` statement.

Multiple Choice:

11. Which parameter modes are supported in Oracle PL/SQL? (Multiple answers possible)
    - **A.** `IN`
    - **B.** `INOUT`
    - **C.** `OUT`
    - **D.** `IN OUT`
    - **E.** All of the above
12. Which of the following are valid loop structures in PL/SQL? (Multiple answers possible)
    - **A.** A simple loop
    - **B.** A `FOR` loop
    - **C.** A `WHILE` loop
    - **D.** An `UNTIL` loop
    - **E.** All of the above
13. A simple *case* statement works with which of the following data types? (Multiple answers possible)
    - **A.** A `TEXT` data type
    - **B.** A `VARCHAR2` data type
    - **C.** A `NCHAR` data type
    - **D.** A `CHAR` data type
    - **E.** A `DATE` data type
14. Which of the following isn't a keyword in PL/SQL?
    - **A.** `RECORD`
    - **B.** `REVERSE`
    - **C.** `CURSOR`
    - **D.** `LIMIT`
    - **E.** `STRUCTURE`
15. Which of the following isn't a cursor attribute?
    - **A.** `%FOUND`
    - **B.** `%ISOPEN`
    - **C.** `%TYPE`
    - **D.** `%NOTFOUND`
    - **E.** `%ROWCOUNT`

CHAPTER 4

Language Fundamentals

This chapter builds on the discussion of PL/SQL architecture in Chapter 1 and PL/SQL basics in Chapter 3. It explains scalar and composite variables and how you assign values to these variable types.

The chapter is divided into two sections:

- Lexical units
- Variable and data types

Lexical units are the bricks and mortar that let you build programs. The next two sections cover these fundamentals.

Lexical Units

Lexical units are the building blocks in programming languages. They enable you to build PL/SQL programs. You develop lexical units by combining valid characters and symbols. Lexical units can be delimiters, identifiers, literals, or comments. Delimiters act like the mortar because they provide semantic elements like operators and string literal delimiters. Identifiers are bricks because they include reserved words and keywords as well as both subroutine and variable names. Literals are a convenient way for you to introduce string and numeric constants into your programs. Comments aren't bricks or mortar, but they're important because they help you (or some other future developer) see what you're doing.

Delimiters

Lexical delimiters are symbols or symbol sets. They can act as delimiters or provide other functions in programming languages. Other functions provided by lexical delimiters are assignment, association, concatenation, comparison, math, and statement controls.

The most common example of a delimiter is the character string delimiter. In PL/SQL, you delimit string literals by using a set of single quotes (`' '`). Table 4-1 covers the full set of delimiters and provides some examples of how to use delimiters in the language. The examples include coding techniques and concepts explained in more detail later in this book.

Symbol	Type	Description
`:=`	Assignment	The assignment operator is a colon immediately followed by an equal sign. It is the *only* assignment operator in the language. You assign a right operand to a left operand, like `a := b + c;` This adds the numbers in variables `b` and `c` and then assigns the result to variable `a`. The addition occurs before the assignment due to operator precedence, which is covered later in this chapter.

TABLE 4-1. *PL/SQL Delimiters*

<table>
<tr><th>Symbol</th><th>Type</th><th>Description</th></tr>
<tr><td>:</td><td>Association</td><td>The host variable indicator precedes a valid identifier name and designates that identifier as a session variable. Session variables are also known as bind variables. You use SQL*Plus to define a session variable. Only the CHAR, CLOB, NCHAR, NCLOB, NUMBER, NVARCHAR2, REFCURSOR, and VARCHAR2 data types are available for session variables.
You can define a session variable by using a prototype, like
<code>VARIABLE variable_name data type_name</code>
This implements the prototype by creating a session-level variable-length string:
<code>SQL> VARIABLE my_string VARCHAR2(30)</code>
Then, you can assign a value using an anonymous block PL/SQL program, like
<code>BEGIN
 :my_string := 'A string literal.';
END;
/</code>
You can then query the result from the DUAL pseudo table:
<code>SELECT :my_string FROM dual;</code>
Alternatively, you can reuse the variable in another PL/SQL block program because the variable enjoys a session-level scope. A subsequent anonymous block program in a script could then print the value in the session variable:
<code>BEGIN
 dbms_output.put_line(:my_string);
END;
/</code>
This is a flexible way to exchange variables between multiple statements and PL/SQL blocks in a single script file.</td></tr>
<tr><td>&</td><td>Association</td><td>The substitution indicator lets you pass actual parameters into anonymous block PL/SQL programs. You should never assign substitution variables inside declaration blocks because assignment errors don't raise an error that you can catch in your exception block. You should make substitution variable assignments in the execution block. The following demonstrates the assignment of a string substitution variable to a local variable in an execution block:
<code>a := '&string_in';</code>
(continued)</td></tr>
</table>

TABLE 4-1. *PL/SQL Delimiters*

Symbol	Type	Description
%	Association	The attribute indicator lets you link a database catalog column, row, or cursor attribute. You are anchoring a variable data type when you link a variable to a catalog object, like a table or column. While Chapter 3 introduces type anchoring, the section "Cursor Structures" in Chapter 5 examines how to anchor variables to database catalog items with this operator. This chapter's "System Reference Cursor" section shows how to create strongly typed system reference cursors by anchoring them to tables.
=>	Association	The association operator is a combination of an equal sign and a greater-than symbol. It is used in name notation function and procedure calls. Chapter 8 covers how you use the association operator.

.	Association	The component selector is a period, and it glues references together; for example, a schema and a table, a package and a function, or an object and a member method. Component selectors are also used to link cursors and cursor attributes (columns). The following are some prototype examples:
		`schema_name.table_name`
		`package_name.function_name`
		`object_name.member_method_name`
		`cursor_name.cursor_attr`
		`object_name.nested_object_name.object_attr`
		These are referenced in subsequent chapters throughout this book.

@	Association	The remote access indicator lets you access a remote database through database links.
||	Concatenation	The concatenation operator is formed by combining two perpendicular vertical lines. You use it to glue strings together, as shown: `a := 'Glued'||' '||'together. ';`
=	Comparison	The equal sign is the comparison operator. It tests for equality of value and implicitly does type conversion where possible (see Figure 4-2 for an implicit conversion chart). There is no identity comparison operator because PL/SQL is a strongly typed language. PL/SQL comparison operations are equivalent to identity comparisons because you can only compare like typed values.
-	Comparison	The negation operator symbol is a minus sign. It changes a number from its positive value to its negative value.
<> != ^=	Comparison	There are three not-equal comparison operators. They all perform exactly the same behaviors. You can use whichever suits your organizational needs.

TABLE 4-1. *PL/SQL Delimiters*

Symbol	Type	Description
`>`	Comparison	The greater-than operator is an inequality comparison operator. It compares whether the left operand is greater than the right operand.
`<`	Comparison	The less-than operator is an inequality comparison operator. It compares whether the left operand is less than the right operand.
`>=`	Comparison	The greater-than or equal comparison operator is an inequality comparison operator. It compares whether the left operand is greater than or equal to the right operand.
`<=`	Comparison	The less-than or equal comparison operator is an inequality comparison operator. It compares whether the left operand is less than or equal to the right operand.
`IS NULL`	Comparison	The `IS NULL` comparison operator checks whether the left operand holds a null.
`IS EMPTY`	Comparison	The `IS EMPTY` comparison operator checks whether the left operand holds any elements, and only applies when the left operand is a varray or table collection data type.
`IS SET`	Comparison	The `IS SET` comparison operator checks whether the left operand holds a set of elements, and only applies when the left operand is a varray or table collection data type.
`'`	Delimiter	The character string delimiter is a single quote mark. It lets you define a string literal value. You can assign a string literal to a variable as follows: `a := 'A string literal.';` This creates a string literal from the set of characters between the character string delimiters and assigns it to the variable `a`.
`(` `)`	Delimiter	The opening and closing expressions or list delimiters are an opening parenthesis symbol and closing parenthesis symbol, respectively. You can place a list of comma-delimited numeric or string literals, or *identifiers*, inside a set of parentheses. You use parentheses to enclose formal and actual parameters to subroutines or to produce lists for comparative evaluations.
`,`	Delimiter	The item separator is a comma and delimits items in lists.
`<<` `>>`	Delimiter	The opening and closing guillemets are the opening and closing delimiters, respectively, for labels in PL/SQL. Labels are any valid identifiers in the programming language. Perl and PHP programmers should know these don't work as `HERE` document tags.
`--`	Delimiter	Two adjoining dashes are a single comment operator. Everything to the right of the single comment operator is treated as text and is not parsed as part of a PL/SQL program. An example of a single-line comment is `-- This is a single-line comment.`

(continued)

TABLE 4-1. *PL/SQL Delimiters*

Symbol	Type	Description

/*
*/
	Delimiter	These are the opening and closing multiple-line comment delimiters, respectively. A forward slash followed by an asterisk instructs the parser to ignore as comment text everything until the closing multiple-line comment delimiter. An asterisk followed by a forward slash instructs the parser that the text comment is complete, and everything after it should be parsed as part of the program unit. An example of a multiple-line comment is
		`/* This is line one.`
		` This is line two. */`
		There are many suggestions on how to use multiple-line comments. You should pick one way of doing it that suits your organization's purposes and stick with it.

"	Delimiter	The quoted identifier delimiter is a double quote. It lets you access tables created in case-sensitive fashion from the database catalog. This is required when you have created database catalog objects in case-sensitive fashion. You can do this from Oracle Database 10g forward. For example, you create a case-sensitive table or column by using quoted identifier delimiters:
		`CREATE TABLE "Demo"`
		`("Demo_ID" NUMBER`
		`, demo_value VARCHAR2(10));`
		You insert a row by using the following quote-delimited syntax:
		`INSERT INTO "Demo1" VALUES`
		`(1,'One Line ONLY.');`
		Like the SQL syntax, PL/SQL requires you to use the quoted identifier delimiter to find the database catalog object, like
		`BEGIN`
		` FOR i IN (SELECT "Demo_ID", demo_value`
		`  FROM  "Demo") LOOP`
		` dbms_output.put_line(i."Demo_ID");`
		` dbms_output.put_line(i.demo_value);`
		` END LOOP;`
		`END;`
		`/`
		Beyond the quoted identifier in embedded SQL statements, you must refer to any column names by using quote-delimited syntax. This is done in the first output line, where the loop index (`i`) is followed by the component selector (`.`) and then a quote-delimited identifier (`"Demo_ID"`). You should note that no quotes are required to access the case-insensitive column. If you forget to enclose a case-sensitive column name (identifier), your program returns a `PLS-00302` error that says the identifier is not declared.
		You can also use the quoted identifier delimiter to build identifiers that include reserved symbols, like an `"X+Y"` identifier.

TABLE 4-1. *PL/SQL Delimiters*

Symbol	Type	Description
+	Math	The addition operator lets you add left and right operands and returns a result.
/	Math	The division operator lets you divide a left operand by a right operand and returns a result.

**	Math	The exponential operator raises a left operand to the power designated by a right operand. The operator enjoys the highest precedence for math operators in the language. As a result of that, a fractional exponent must be enclosed in parentheses (also known as expression or list delimiters) to designate order of operation. Without parentheses, the left operand is raised to the power of the numerator and the result is divided by the denominator of a fractional exponent.
		You raise `3` to the third power and assign the result of `27` to variable `a` by using the following syntax:
		`a := 3**3;`
		You raise `8` to the fractional power of `1/3` and assign the result of `2` to variable `a` by using the following syntax:
		`a := 8**(1/3);`
		The parentheses ensures that the division operation occurs first. Exponential operations take precedence on other mathematical operations without parenthetical grouping. Please note that exponential calculations are scientific computing and you should use IEEE-754 data types.

*	Math	The multiplication operator lets you multiply a left operand by a right operand and returns a result.
-	Math	The subtraction operator lets you subtract the right operand from the left operand and returns a result.
;	Statement	The statement terminator is a semicolon. You must close any statement or block unit in PL/SQL with a statement terminator. Oracle Database 12*c* introduces the ability to write functions within the `WITH` clause of a query, and this new feature requires you to disable the semicolon (`;`) while running a query with an embedded function. Chapter 2 and the "In-line Views" section of Appendix B provide more on this behavior.

TABLE 4-1. *PL/SQL Delimiters*

Identifiers

Identifiers are words. They can be reserved words, keywords, predefined identifiers, quoted identifiers, user-defined variables, subroutines, or user-defined types. Reserved words and keywords change from Oracle Database point release to point release, and there's no accurate source for a complete list. You can find reserved words and keywords in Appendix H, built-in SQL functions in Appendix C, and built-in PL/SQL functions in Appendix D.

Reserved Words and Keywords

Both reserved words and keywords are lexical units that provide basic tools for building programs. For example, you use the `NOT` reserved word as a negation in comparison operations, and use the `NULL` keyword to represent a null value or statement. You cannot use these words when defining your own programs and data types.

Predefined Identifiers

Oracle Database 12*c* (and some recent releases prior to it) provides a `STANDARD` package, and it globally grants access to the package through a public grant. The `STANDARD` package defines the built-in functions found in Appendix C. It also contains the definitions for standard data types and errors.

You should be careful to not override any predefined identifiers by creating user-defined identifiers with the same names. This happens any time you define a variable that duplicates a component from the `STANDARD` package, just as you can define a variable in a nested PL/SQL block that overrides the containing block variable name.

Quoted Identifiers

Oracle Database 11*g* forward enables you to use *quoted identifier* delimiters to build identifiers that would otherwise be disallowed because of symbol reuse. Quoted identifiers can include any printable characters, including spaces. However, you cannot embed double quotes inside identifiers. The maximum size of a quoted identifier is 30 characters.

You can also use quoted identifiers to leverage reserved words and keywords. Although this is allowed, it is strongly discouraged by Oracle. For example, the following program creates a quoted identifier "End," which is a case-insensitive reserved word:

```
SQL> DECLARE
       "End" NUMBER := 1;
     BEGIN
       dbms_output.put_line('A quoted identifier End ['||"End"||']');
     END;
     /
```

Again, while this is possible, you should avoid it!

User-Defined Variables, Subroutines, and User-Defined Data Types

You create identifiers when you define program components. User-defined data types can be defined in SQL as schema-level data types, or in PL/SQL blocks. User-defined identifiers must be less than 30 characters and start with a letter; and they can include a `$`, `#`, or `_`. They cannot contain punctuation, spaces, or hyphens.

Anonymous block identifiers are only accessible inside a block or nested block. When you define identifiers in functions and procedures, they are accessible based on their implementation scope. You can access calling scope identifiers from within local functions and procedures but not through schema-level functions and procedures. Package specifications let you define package-level data types that are available in your schema. These package-level data types are also available in other schemas when you grant execute privilege on them to other schemas. Package bodies let you define local data types that are only available to functions and procedures defined within the package body or implementation.

You reference package-level data types by using the component selector to connect the package and data type names. Chapter 9 discusses PL/SQL packages in depth, while Chapter 2 provides a basic introduction.

Literals

A *literal* is an explicit character, string, number, or Boolean value. Literal values are not represented by identifiers. String literals can also represent date or time literals.

Character Literals

Character literals are defined by enclosing any character in a set of single quotes. The literal values are case sensitive, while the programming language is case insensitive. This mirrors the behavior of SQL and data stored in the database as character or string data (the `VARCHAR2` data type is the most commonly used type).

You assign a character literal to a variable using the following syntax:

```
a := 'a';
```

String Literals

String literals are defined like character literals, using single quotes. String literals can contain any number of characters up to the maximum value for the data type. You typically use the `VARCHAR2` data type, or one of its subtypes.

You assign a string literal to a variable using the following syntax:

```
a := 'some string';
```

You can also assign a string literal with double quotes inside it by using the following syntax:

```
a := 'some "quoted" string';
```

The double quotes are treated as normal characters *when embedded in single quotes*.

Numeric Literals

Numeric literals are defined like numbers in most programming languages. The generic numeric literal assignment is done by using the following syntax:

```
a := 2525;
```

You can assign a large number with the following exponent syntax:

```
n := 2525E8; -- This assigns 252,500,000,000 to the variable.
```

You may attempt to assign a number beyond the range of a data type. The numeric overflow or underflow exception is raised when the number is outside the data type's range.

You also can assign a float or a double by using the respective syntax:

```
d := 2.0d; -- This assigns a double of 2.
f := 2.0f; -- This assigns a float of 2
```

These assignments only work with their respective type. A `d` works with a `BINARY_DOUBLE`, while an `f` works with a `BINARY_FLOAT`.

Boolean Literals

Boolean literals can be a Boolean variable or expression and can be true, false, or null. This three-valued state of Boolean variables makes it possible that your program can incorrectly handle a *not true* or *not false* condition any time the variable is null. Chapter 5 covers how to manage conditional statements to secure expected results.

You can make any of the following assignments to a previously declared `BOOLEAN` variable:

```
b := TRUE;  -- This assigns a true state.
b := FALSE; -- This assigns a false state.
b := NULL;  -- This assigns a null or default state.
```

TIP
It is a good practice to assign an initial value of `TRUE` or `FALSE` to all Boolean variables, which means you should always explicitly define their initial state. You should also consider declaring Boolean columns as not null constrained.

Date and Time Literals

Date literals have an implicit conversion from a string literal that maps to the default format mask. The default format masks for dates are `DD-MON-RR` and `DD-MON-YYYY`, where `DD` represents a two-digit day, `MON` represents a three-character month, `RR` represents a two-digit relative year, and `YYYY` represents a four-digit absolute year. Relative years are calculated by counting 50 years forward or backward from the current system clock. You assign a relative or absolute date as follows to previously declared `DATE` data type variables:

```
relative_date := '01-JUN-07';   -- This assigns 01-JUN-2007.
absolute_date := '01-JUN-1907'; -- This assigns 01-JUN-1907.
```

Implicit assignment fails when you attempt other format masks, like `MON-DD-YYYY`. You can explicitly assign date literals by using the `TO_DATE` or `CAST` functions. Only the Oracle proprietary `TO_DATE` function lets you use apply a format mask other than the default. The syntax variations for the `TO_DATE` function are

```
date_1 := TO_DATE('01-JUN-07');              -- Default format mask.
date_2 := TO_DATE('JUN-01-07','MON-DD-YY'); -- Override format mask.
```

The `CAST` function can use either of the default format masks discussed earlier in the section, as shown:

```
date_1 := CAST('01-JUN-07' AS DATE);   -- Relative format mask.
date_2 := CAST('01-JUN-2007' AS DATE); -- Absolute format mask.
```

You can use the `TO_CHAR(date_variable, 'MON-DD-YYYY')` function to view the fully qualified date. These behaviors in PL/SQL mirror the behaviors in Oracle SQL.

Comments

You can enter single- or multiple-line comments in PL/SQL. You use two dashes to enter a single-line comment, and the `/*` and `*/` delimiters to enter a multiple-line comment. A single-line comment is entered as follows:

```
-- This is a single-line comment.
```

A multiple-line comment is entered as follows:

```
/* This is a multiple-line comment.
   Style and indentation should follow your company standards. */
```

Planned comments are straightforward, but you can introduce errors when you comment out code to test or debug your programs. The biggest problem occurs when you comment out all executable statements from a code block. This will raise various parsing errors because every coding block must have at a minimum one statement, as discussed in the "Block Structure" section of Chapter 3.The other problem frequently introduced with single-line comments arises from placing them before either a statement terminator (a semicolon) or an ending block keyword. This also raises a parsing error when you try to run or compile the program unit.

NOTE
Compilation *in PL/SQL programs can mean attempting to run an anonymous block program or creating a stored program unit. In both cases, you are parsing the program into PL/SQL p-code. PL/SQL runs the p-code.*

This section has presented the valid characters and symbols in the language. It has also explained that delimiters, identifiers, literals, and comments are lexical units.

Review Section

This section has described the following points about character and lexical units:

- Lexical units are the basic building blocks in programming languages, and they can be delimiters, identifiers, literals, or comments.
- You can develop lexical units by combining valid characters and symbols.
- Lexical delimiters are symbols or symbol sets that identify string literals and provide assignment, association, concatenation, comparison, math, and statement controls.
- The `STANDARD` package provides predefined identifiers.
- You can create user-defined identifies, such as data type and variable names, that don't conflict with keywords or reserved words.
- You can create quoted identifiers by using double quotes to delimit words that may duplicate keywords and reserved words.
- You can create single- and multiple-line comments.

Variables and Data Types

PL/SQL is a blocked programming language. Program units can be named or unnamed blocks. Unnamed blocks are known as anonymous blocks and are so labeled throughout the book. Named blocks are functions, procedures, and packages with internal functions and procedures, and objects types that include functions and procedures. As Chapter 11 explains, you can have static or instance functions and procedures, and specialized constructor functions that let you create instances of object types.

The PL/SQL coding style differs from that of the C, C++, and Java programming languages. For example, curly braces do not delimit blocks in PL/SQL. The `DECLARE` keyword starts the declaration section in anonymous block programs, and the function or procedure *header*, specification, or signature (name, parameter list, and return type) starts the declaration section in named block programs. The `BEGIN` keyword starts the execution block and ends the declaration block. The `EXCEPTION` keyword starts the exception block. The exception block ends with the `END` keyword, which also ends the program unit. While anonymous block programs are effective in some situations, the more common practice is to develop reusable subroutines—functions, procedures, packages, and object types.

You would typically use anonymous blocks when building scripts to seed data or perform one-time processing activities. Script files are text files that have SQL statements and/or PL/SQL anonymous blocks that perform a set of sequenced steps.

Anonymous blocks are also effective when you want to nest activity in another PL/SQL block's execution section. The basic anonymous block structure must contain an execution section. You can also put *optional* declaration and exception sections in anonymous blocks. Figure 4-1 illustrates both anonymous block (left) and named block (right) prototypes.

The declaration block lets you declare data types, structures, variables, and named functions and procedures. *Declaring* a variable means that you give it a name and a data type. You can also *define* a variable by giving it a name, a data type, and a value. You both declare and assign a value when defining a variable. While you can implement a named block in another program's declaration section, you can't implement named blocks anywhere else in a PL/SQL program. Likewise, anonymous blocks can only be implemented in another program's execution and exception sections. Chapter 3 provides examples of variable scope inside various anonymous and named blocks.

The following two subsections qualify the available PL/SQL data types and their basic use.

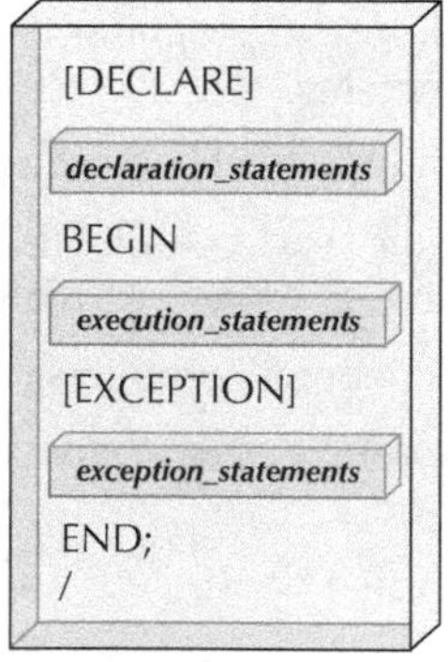

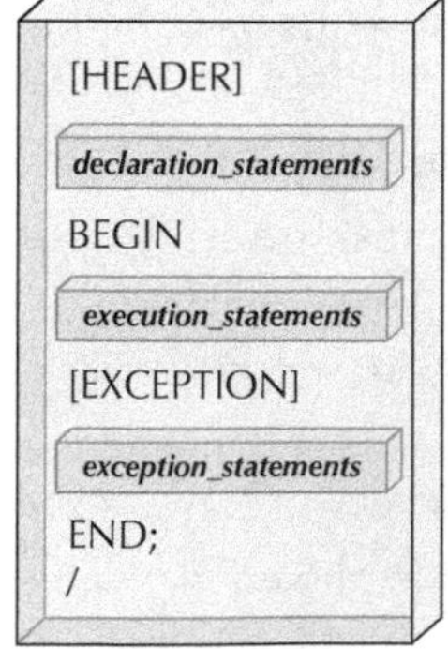

FIGURE 4-1. *PL/SQL block structure*

Variable Data Types

PL/SQL supports two principal variable data types: scalar variables and composite variables. Scalar variables contain only one thing, such as a character, date, or number. Composite variables are variables built from primitives or base types in a programming language. Composite variables in Oracle Database are records (structures), arrays, lists, system reference cursors, and object types. (*System reference cursors* are specialized or *hybrid* PL/SQL-only structures that act like a list of record types and they are discussed in the "System Reference Cursor" section later in this chapter.)

PL/SQL uses all Oracle SQL data types. PL/SQL also introduces a `BOOLEAN` data type and several subtypes derived from the SQL data types. Subtypes inherit the behavior of a data type but also typically have constrained behaviors. An unconstrained subtype doesn't change a base type's behavior. Unconstrained subtypes are also called *aliases*. You can also call any base data type a *supertype*, because it is the model for subtypes. Unconstrained subtypes are interchangeable with their base types, while only qualified values can be assigned to constrained subtypes from base types. You can extend these types by building your own subtypes, as you'll see in the "CHAR and CHARACTER Data Types" section later in this chapter.

Like other programming languages, PL/SQL lets you both define types and declare variables. You label a data type and designate how to manage the data type in memory when you define a type. You define a variable by both declaring the variable and assigning it a value. A variable name is mapped to a known data type and then added to the program's namespace as an identifier when you declare a variable. In some programming languages, no value is assigned to a declared variable. PL/SQL *automatically* assigns most declared variables a null value. This means that variables are generally defined in the language.

You declare variables by *assigning them a type* or by *anchoring their type to a database catalog column*. Anchoring a variable using the `%TYPE` attribute means that your program's variable size automatically adjusts as the size of the column's data type changes. It also means that the data type of your variable can change when the column's data type changes.

While altering a table's column from one data type to another works when there's no data in the table, it doesn't always work when there's data in the table. You only can change a populated column's data type when Oracle knows how to explicitly cast the values from the one data type to the other data type. The lack of an implicit data type conversion means you need to export the column values and manually convert them to the new data type.

Unfortunately, changing a column's data type and converting the data is only the beginning of a conversion process. It's only a beginning because your program is structurally coupled to the column's data type. While it is possible that small changes in size of a string or number may not break your program, it's likely a large change in size might. Likewise, some logic, assignments, and comparisons may fail when the base type changes. Take for example when you convert a column with a string data type to a column with a date data type. There isn't any implicit conversion from a string to date or a string back to a date, and such a *column change may alter logical comparison conditions in your function or procedure*. That's why I'd recommend you only anchor columns with the `%TYPE` when you can guarantee the column's data type won't change over time.

TIP
Altering the column data type does not raise an error but invalidates any stored procedures that misuse the new variable type.

Implicit conversions are determined by the PL/SQL engine. Unlike some programming languages, PL/SQL allows implicit conversions that result in *loss of precision* (or details). If you assign a `BINARY_FLOAT` variable to a `BINARY_INTEGER`, any digits to the right of the decimal place are discarded implicitly. Explicit conversions require you to convert the data, like calling the `TO_CHAR` built-in function to display the timestamp of a `DATE` variable. A list of implicit conversions is found in Figure 4-2.

There is one pseudo exception to the variable declaration rule. Weakly typed system reference cursors are not defined until runtime. A weakly typed system reference cursor takes an assigned cursor number and adopts the record structure of a row assigned to the cursor. A system reference cursor returns a list of its record structure, and you can only assign it to a composite variable. You can also anchor a strongly typed system reference cursor to a catalog table or view. This works much like how you anchor variables to columns, which Chapter 3 covers.

Variable data types can be defined in SQL or PL/SQL. You can use SQL data types in both SQL statements and PL/SQL statements. You can only use PL/SQL data types inside your PL/SQL program units.

FROM \ TO	BINARY_DOUBLE	BINARY_FLOAT	BINARY_INTEGER	BLOB	CHAR	CLOB	DATE	LONG	NCHAR	NCLOB	NUMBER	NVARCHAR2	PLS_INTEGER	RAW	UROWID	VARCHAR2
BINARY_DOUBLE		X	X		X			X	X		X	X	X			X
BINARY_FLOAT	X		X		X				X		X	X	X			X
BINARY_INTEGER	X	X			X				X		X	X	X			X
BLOB														X		
CHAR	X	X	X			X	X	X	X		X	X	X	X	X	X
CLOB					X				X			X				X
DATE					X			X	X			X				X
LONG					X		X		X			X		X		X
NCHAR	X	X	X		X	X	X	X		X	X	X	X	X	X	X
NCLOB					X	X		X	X			X				X
NUMBER	X	X	X		X			X	X			X	X			X
NVARCHAR2	X	X	X		X	X		X		X						X
PLS_INTEGER	X	X	X		X			X	X	X	X	X				X
RAW				X	X			X	X							X
UROWID					X				X	X		X				X
VARCHAR2	X	X	X		X	X	X	X	X	X	X	X	X	X	X	

FIGURE 4-2. *Implicit conversions*

The PL/SQL Buffer and Outputting to the Console

As shown in earlier Figure 1-2 of Chapter 1, there is an output *buffer* between the SQL*Plus and PL/SQL engines. You can open the buffer in SQL*Plus by enabling the `SERVEROUTPUT` environment variable, like

```
SQL> SET SERVEROUTPUT ON SIZE 1000000
```

Once you enable this SQL*Plus environment variable, the output generated by the `PUT_LINE` and `NEW_LINE` procedures of the `DBMS_OUTPUT` package will be displayed in your SQL*Plus environment. It is possible that you may get more output than you expect the first time you run a program after enabling the environment variable. This can happen when you run a program in PL/SQL that enables the buffer from PL/SQL without enabling the environment variable first.

TIP
*SQL*Plus environment variable settings are lost when you change schemas. Don't forget to reset the `SERVEROUTPUT` variable if you change schemas, because the output buffer is effectively closed the minute you change schemas.*

You enable the buffer in PL/SQL by using the following command:

```
dbms_output.enable(1000000);
```

The first write to the buffer after enabling the environment variable will flush all contents to the SQL*Plus environment. You clear the prior contents by disabling any open buffer before enabling it using the following two procedures sequentially:

```
dbms_output.disable;
dbms_output.enable(1000000);
```

The `DISABLE` procedure is recommended to ensure that you don't capture some undesired prior output when running your program. You output to the console using the `PUT_LINE` procedure. The `PUT_LINE` procedure outputs a string and newline character to the buffer. You use the `NEW_LINE` procedure to write a line return.

The following demonstrates how to output information from your PL/SQL program to the SQL*Plus environment:

```
BEGIN
  dbms_output.put_line('Line one.');
  dbms_output.new_line;
  dbms_output.put_line('Line two.');
END;
/
```

This anonymous block program outputs

```
Line one.
Line two.
```

(continued)

This is the technique that you'll use to get output to the console for debugging or to file for reporting. You can also combine the SQL*Plus `SPOOL` command to split standard output to both the console and a file (like the Unix `tee` command). This technique lets you generate text files for reporting.

The first subsection covers scalar data types, the second large objects, the third composite data types, and the fourth reference types. Items are organized for reference and flow. The scalar data types are the primitives of the language and therefore the building blocks for the composite data types. The next section covers these primitive building blocks.

Scalar Data Types

The primitives are grouped into alphabetical sections. Each section describes the data type, demonstrates how to define and/or declare the type or variables of the type, and shows how to assign values to it. Figure 4-3 qualifies the four major types of scalar variables and their implementation base types and subtypes.

You use the following prototype for scalar data types inside the declaration block of your programs:

```
variable_name  data type [NOT NULL] [:= literal_value];
```

Some data types require that you provide a precision when defining a variable. The precision defines the maximum size in bytes or characters for a data type. Similarly, `NUMBER` data types require that you provide the scale. The scale defines the number of decimal places to the right of the decimal point. These conventions mirror the conventions found in SQL for these data types.

Boolean

The `BOOLEAN` data type has three possible values: `TRUE`, `FALSE`, and `NULL`. This three-valued state of Boolean variables makes it possible that your program can incorrectly handle a *not true* or *not false* condition any time the variable is `NULL`. The "Three-valued logic" section of Chapter 3 and the "If-then-else statements" section of Chapter 5 cover how to manage conditional statements to secure expected results.

The following is the prototype for declaring a `BOOLEAN` data type:

```
BOOLEAN [NOT NULL]
```

You can define Boolean variables by implicit null assignment or by explicit assignment of a `TRUE` or `FALSE` value. The following syntax belongs in the declaration block:

```
var1  BOOLEAN;                  -- Implicitly assigned a null value.
var2  BOOLEAN NOT NULL := TRUE;  -- Explicitly assigned a TRUE value.
var3  BOOLEAN NOT NULL := FALSE; -- Explicitly assigned a FALSE value.
```

You should always initialize Boolean variables explicitly in your program units. This practice avoids unexpected behaviors in programs. Using the `NOT NULL` clause during declaration guarantees Boolean variables are never null.

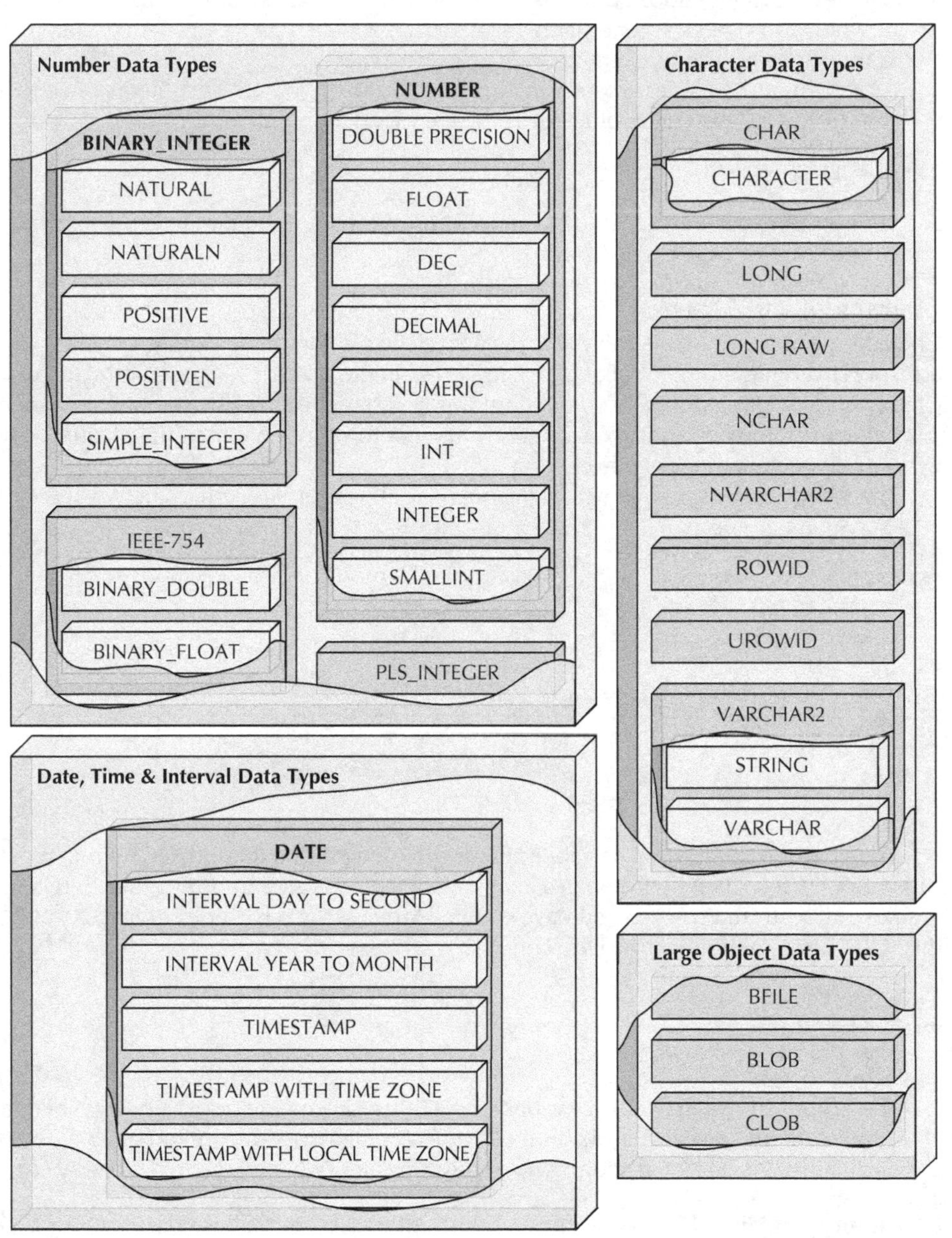

FIGURE 4-3. *Scalar types*

There is little need to subtype a `BOOLEAN` data type, but you can do it. The subtyping syntax is

```
SUBTYPE booked IS BOOLEAN;
```

This creates a subtype BOOKED that is an unconstrained BOOLEAN data type. You may find this useful when you need a second name for a BOOLEAN data type, but generally subtyping a Boolean is not very useful.

As shown in the earlier subsection "Boolean Literals," you assign a literal value to a Boolean variable inside the execution block by using the following syntax:

```
var := TRUE;
```

Unlike strings, the TRUE, FALSE, and NULL values are not delimited by single quotes. All three words are PL/SQL reserved words.

Characters and Strings

Characters and strings work more like the *String* class in the Java programming language. Strings are known as single-dimensional character arrays in the C and C++ programming languages. Character data types store a fixed-length string. You size the string by stating the number of bytes or characters allowed inside the string. Any attempt to store more than the maximum number of bytes or characters throws an exception.

The following program illustrates the memory allocation differences between the CHAR and VARCHAR2 data types:

```
DECLARE
  c CHAR(32767)     := ' ';
  v VARCHAR2(32767) := ' ';
BEGIN
  dbms_output.put_line('c is ['||LENGTH(c)||']');
  dbms_output.put_line('v is ['||LENGTH(v)||']');
  v := v || ' ';
  dbms_output.put_line('v is ['||LENGTH(v)||']');  END;
/
```

The program defines two variables, prints their length (see the PL/SQL built-in functions in Appendix D), and then concatenates another whitespace value to VARCHAR2 to demonstrate memory allocation. Provided you have enabled the SQL*Plus buffer (setting SERVEROUTPUT on), this will output the following to the console:

```
c is [32767]
v is [1]
v is [2]
```

The output shows that a CHAR variable sets the allocated memory size when defined. The allocated memory can exceed what is required to manage the value in the variable. The output also shows that the VARCHAR2 variable dynamically allocates only the required memory to host its value.

CHAR and CHARACTER Data Types The CHAR data type is a base data type for *fixed*-length strings. You can size a CHAR data type up to 32,767 bytes in length, but its default length is 1 byte. Unfortunately, a PL/SQL CHAR is larger than the 4,000-byte maximum allowed in a SQL CHAR column when the MAX_STRING_SIZE parameter is set to STANDARD. Setting the MAX_STRING_SIZE parameter to EXTENDED lets you store up to 32,767 bytes in SQL VARCHAR2 columns. You can store character strings larger than 4,000 bytes inline in CLOB or LONG columns. Oracle recommends that you use the CLOB data type because the LONG and LONG RAW data types are only supported for backward-compatibility purposes.

The following is the prototype for defining a CHAR data type:

```
CHAR[(maximum_size [BYTE | CHAR])] [NOT NULL]
```

The four ways to declare a variable using the CHAR data type and a default null value are

```
var1 CHAR;         -- Implicitly sized at 1 byte.
var2 CHAR(1);      -- Explicitly sized at 1 byte.
var3 CHAR(1 BYTE); -- Explicitly sized at 1 byte.
var4 CHAR(1 CHAR); -- Explicitly sized at 1 character.
```

When you use character space allocation, the maximum size changes depending on the character set of your database. Some character sets use 2 or 3 bytes to store characters. You divide 32,767 by the number of bytes required per character, which means the maximum for a CHAR is 16,383 for a 2-byte character set and 10,922 for a 3-byte character set.

You can use the NOT NULL clause to ensure a value is assigned to a CHAR variable. The general practice is to not restrict CHAR variables without some other compelling business rationale.

The CHARACTER data type is a subtype of the CHAR data type. The CHARACTER data type has the same value range as its base type. It is effectively an alias data type and is formally known as an *unconstrained subtype*. Assignment between variables of CHAR and CHARACTER data types are implicitly converted when the assignment target has the same size.

The size for characters has two factors: the number of units allotted and the type of units allotted. A string of three characters (derived from the character set) cannot fit in a string of three bytes, and, more naturally, a string of three characters cannot fit in a string of two characters. Any attempt to make that type of assignment raises an ORA-06502 error, which means a character string buffer is too small to hold a value.

You can declare a CHAR subtype by using the following prototype:

```
  SUBTYPE subtype_name IS base_type[(maximum_size [BYTE | CHAR])] [NOT NULL];
```

The following example creates and uses a constrained subtype CODE:

```
DECLARE
  SUBTYPE code IS CHAR(1 CHAR);
  c CHAR(1 CHAR) := 'A';
  d CODE;
BEGIN
  d := c;
END;
/
```

Characters and strings cannot specify character ranges. They can only set the maximum size. This differs from the subtyping behaviors of numbers because they can restrict ranges.

Globalization raises a host of issues with how you use variable-length strings. You should consider using NCHAR data types when managing multiple character sets or Unicode.

LONG and LONG RAW Data Types The LONG and LONG RAW data types *are provided only for backward compatibility*. You should use the CLOB or NCLOB data type where you would use the LONG data type, and use the BLOB or BFILE data type instead of the LONG RAW data type. The LONG data type stores character streams, and the LONG RAW data type stores binary streams.

The LONG and LONG RAW data types store variable-length character strings or binary streams up to 32,760 bytes in your PL/SQL programs. This limitation is much smaller than the 2 gigabytes that you can store in LONG or LONG RAW database columns. The LONG and LONG RAW data type maximum size is actually smaller than the maximum for the CHAR, NCHAR, VARCHAR2, and NVARCHAR2 data types, and it is dwarfed by the 8 to 128 terabytes of the LOB data types.

The following are the prototypes for declaring the LONG and LONG RAW data types:

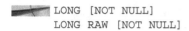

```
LONG [NOT NULL]
LONG RAW [NOT NULL]
```

You can use the NOT NULL clause to ensure a value is assigned to LONG and LONG RAW variables. The general *practice* is to not restrict these data types without some other compelling business rationale.

The LONG and LONG RAW data types can be declared with a default null value as follows:

```
var1 LONG;          -- Implicitly sized at 0 byte.
var2 LONG RAW;      -- Implicitly sized at 0 byte.
```

You can define variables of these types and assign values by using the following syntax:

```
var1 LONG := 'CAR';
var2 LONG RAW := HEXTORAW('43'||'41'||'52'); -- CAR assigned in Hexadecimal.
```

While the LONG data type is easy to use, it is tiny by comparison to the CLOB and NCLOB data types. The CHAR and VARCHAR2 data types also store 7 bytes more of character data than the LONG data type.

TIP

You should consider using variable data types that map to your column data types because over time it is simpler (cheaper) for maintenance programmers to support. It is advisable that you migrate CHAR and LONG column data types to VARCHAR2 and LOB data types, respectively.

You should note that the HEXTORAW function is required to convert hexadecimal streams into raw streams before assignment to LONG RAW data types. An attempt to assign an unconverted character stream raises ORA-06502 as a hexadecimal-to-raw conversion error. Also, you should note that the LONG RAW data stream is not interpreted by PL/SQL.

ROWID and UROWID Data Types The ROWID data type maps to the pseudo column ROWID in any Oracle database table. You can convert it from a ROWID to an 18-character string by using the ROWIDTOCHAR function, or back from a character string using the CHARTOROWID function. Appendix C covers these two SQL built-in functions. An invalid conversion between a string and a ROWID raises a SYS_INVALID_ROWID error.

NOTE

The ROWID data type is now only provided for backward compatibility, and it is recommended that you use the universal rowid *(UROWID) data type.*

The UROWID data type is the *universal rowid*. It works with logical ROWID identifiers stored by an indexed-organized table, whereas the ROWID data type doesn't. You should use the UROWID value for all Oracle ROWID management in PL/SQL programs, and when you are working with non-Oracle ROWID values.

The following are the prototypes for declaring the ROWID and UROWID data types:

```
ROWID
UROWID
```

Implicit conversion works well for both ROWID and UROWID types. There is seldom any need to use either the ROWIDTOCHAR or CHARTOROWID function.

VARCHAR2, STRING, and VARCHAR Data Types The VARCHAR2 data type is a base data type for *variable*-length strings. Beyond that, with a few differences, it behaves more or less like the CHAR data type, as described a bit earlier in the "CHAR and CHARACTER Data Types" section. The content that overlaps is reiterated here for VARCHAR2 in case you are using this book as a reference and haven't already read the description of CHAR. You may notice that the physical size is required for VARCHAR2 data types, whereas it is optional for the CHAR data type and its subtypes.

You can size a VARCHAR2 data type up to 32,767 bytes in length. Unfortunately, a PL/SQL VARCHAR2 data type can be larger than the 4,000-byte maximum stored in a SQL VARCHAR2 column when the MAX_STRING_SIZE parameter is set to STANDARD. Setting the MAX_STRING_SIZE parameter to EXTENDED lets you store up to 32,767 bytes in SQL VARCHAR2 columns. You can also store character strings larger than 4,000 bytes in CLOB or LONG columns. Oracle recommends that you use the CLOB data type because the LONG data type is only supported for backward-compatibility purposes.

The following is the prototype for declaring a VARCHAR2 data type:

```
VARCHAR2(maximum_size [BYTE | CHAR]) [NOT NULL]
```

You can use the NOT NULL clause to ensure a value is assigned to a VARCHAR2 variable. The general practice is to not restrict variable-length strings without some other compelling business rationale. You should consider creating a subtype that enforces the constraint.

You may notice that the physical size is required for VARCHAR2 data types, whereas it is optional for the CHAR data type and its subtypes. Physical size is required because the database needs to know how much space to allocate for a variable using this data type. When you size a VARCHAR2 variable, the PL/SQL engine only allocates enough space to manage the physical data value. This typically optimizes your program runtime.

There are three ways to define a VARCHAR2 variable with a default null value:

```
var1 VARCHAR2(100);      -- Explicitly sized at 100 bytes.
var2 VARCHAR2(100 BYTE); -- Explicitly sized at 100 bytes.
var3 VARCHAR2(100 CHAR); -- Explicitly sized at 100 characters.
```

When you use character space allocation, the maximum size changes, depending on the character set of your database. Some character sets use 2 or 3 bytes to store characters. You divide 32,767 by the number of bytes required per character, which means the maximum for a VARCHAR2 is 16,383 for a 2-byte character set and 10,922 for a 3-byte character set.

The STRING and VARCHAR data types are subtypes of the VARCHAR2 data type. They both have the same value range as the VARCHAR2 base type. They are effectively aliases and are formally known as *unconstrained subtypes*. Assignments between variables of these subtypes are implicitly converted, provided the variables have the same size.

The size for strings has two factors: the number of units allotted and the type of units allotted. A string of three characters (derived from the character set) cannot fit in a string of 3 bytes, and, more naturally, a string of three characters cannot fit in a string of two characters. Any attempt to make that type of assignment raises an ORA-06502 error, which means a character string buffer is too small to hold a value.

You can declare a VARCHAR2 subtype by using the following prototype:

```
SUBTYPE subtype_name IS base_type(maximum_size [BYTE | CHAR]) [NOT NULL];
```

The following example creates a constrained subtype DB_STRING:

```
DECLARE
  SUBTYPE db_string IS VARCHAR2(4000 BYTE);
  c VARCHAR2(1 CHAR) := 'A';
  d DB_STRING;
BEGIN
  d := c;
END;
/
```

The example creates a subtype that cannot exceed the physical limit for a VARCHAR2 column. It works uniformly regardless of the database character set. This can be useful when you want to ensure compliance with physical database limits in PL/SQL code blocks.

Strings cannot specify character ranges the way that number subtypes can specify number ranges. They can only set the maximum size, which can be overridden by declaring the subtype with a new maximum size less than or equal to 32,767 bytes.

Globalization raises a host of issues with how you use variable-length strings. You should consider using NVARCHAR2 data types when managing multiple character sets or Unicode.

Dates, Times, and Intervals

The DATE data type is the base type for dates, times, and intervals. There are two subtypes to manage intervals and three subtypes to manage timestamps. The next three subsections cover dates, intervals, and timestamps.

DATE Data Type The DATE data type in Oracle contains an actual timestamp of activity. The valid range is any date from January 1, 4712 BCE (Before Common Era) to December 31, 9999 CE (Common Era). The most common way to capture a timestamp is to assign the SYSDATE or SYSTIMESTAMP built-in function. They both return fully qualified dates and contain all field elements of a DATE variable or column. The field index for a DATE data type is presented in Table 4-2

The following is the prototype for declaring a DATE data type:

```
DATE [NOT NULL]
```

You can use the NOT NULL clause to ensure a value is assigned to a DATE variable. There are many cases where you will want to restrict DATE variables. If you don't restrict them, then you'll need to wrap them in NVL built-in functions to support logical comparisons.

Field Name	Valid Range	Valid Internal Values
YEAR	–4712 to 9999 (excluding year 0)	Any nonzero integer
MONTH	01 to 12	0 to 11
DAY	01 to 31 (limited by calendar rules)	Any nonzero integer
HOUR	00 to 23	0 to 23
MINUTE	00 to 59	0 to 59
SECOND	00 to 59	0 to 59.9 (where tenths are the fractional interval second)
TIMEZONE_HOUR	–12 to 14 (range adjusts for daylight saving time changes)	Not applicable
TIMEZONE_MINUTE	00 to 59	Not applicable
TIMEZONE_REGION	Value in V$TIMEZONE_NAMES	Not applicable
TIMEZONE_ABBR	Value in V$TIMEZONE_NAMES	Not applicable

TABLE 4-2. *DATE Data Type Field Index*

You can define a DATE variable with a default null or initialized value, as shown:

```
var1 DATE;                  -- Implicitly assigns a null value.
var2 DATE := SYSDATE;       -- Explicitly assigns current server timestamp.
var3 DATE := SYSDATE + 1;   -- Explicitly assigns tomorrow server timestamp.
var4 DATE := '29-FEB-08';   -- Explicitly assigns leap year day for 2008.
```

The TO_DATE function can also convert nonconforming date formats into valid DATE values. Alternatively, the CAST function also works with the default format mask. The default format masks for dates are DD-MON-RR and DD-MON-YYYY.

Use the TRUNC(*date_variable*) function call when you want to extract a date from a timestamp. This is useful when you want to find all transactions that occurred on a particular day. By default the TRUNC built-in function shaves off the time, making a date with 00 hours, 00 minutes, and 00 seconds. The following program demonstrates the concept:

```
DECLARE
  d DATE := SYSDATE;
BEGIN
  dbms_output.put_line(TO_CHAR(TRUNC(d),'DD-MON-YY HH24:MI:SS'));
END;
/
```

Running this script produces

```
12-JUL-13 00:00:00
```

You can't achieve the same thing by using the ROUND(*date_variable*,'*key*') function call. The ROUND function takes an uppercase day, month, or year string instead of an integer as its second parameter. It follows a general pattern of rounding down or rounding up. While it would be great to say everything before noon rounds down to midnight of the current day, that's not the case. When you round with a day value, it can round down to today's or yesterday's morning or round up to the morning of tomorrow or the day after tomorrow. The ROUND function works better with a month value. The month value rounds down the first half of the month to the first day of the current month, and rounds up the second half of the month to the first day of the next month. Likewise, a year value rounds down the first half of the year to the first day of the current year, rounds up the second half of the year to the first day of the next year.

Here's a query to show the inconsistencies:

```
SQL> SELECT TO_CHAR(ROUND(SYSDATE,'DAY'),'DD-MON-YYYY HH24:MI') AS Day
     ,      TO_CHAR(ROUND(SYSDATE,'MONTH'),'DD-MON-YYYY HH24:MI') AS Month
     ,      TO_CHAR(ROUND(SYSDATE,'YEAR'),'DD-MON-YYYY HH24:MI') AS Year
     FROM   dual;
```

It prints the following based on a SYSDATE value the evening of July 15, 2013:

```
DAY               MONTH             YEAR
----------------- ----------------- -----------------
14-JUL-2013 00:00 01-JUL-2013 00:00 01-JAN-2014 00:00
```

My caution is to avoid using the ROUND function to shave off elements of a date-time data type. Use the TRUNC function instead, because its performance is simple and consistent.

The EXTRACT built-in function also lets you capture the numeric month, year, or day from a DATE value. Appendix C lists other functions that let you manipulate DATE data types.

You can declare a DATE subtype by using the following prototype:

```
SUBTYPE subtype_name IS base_type [NOT NULL];
```

You should note that, as when using the character subtypes, you cannot set a date range. Creating a DATE subtype that requires a value is possible. Using DATEN for a null required DATE follows the convention used by the NATURALN and POSITVEN subtypes.

Interval Subtypes You have two DATE subtypes available that let you manage intervals: INTERVAL DAY TO SECOND and INTERVAL YEAR TO MONTH. Their prototypes are

```
INTERVAL DAY[(leading_precision)] TO SECOND[(fractional_second_precision)]
INTERVAL YEAR[(precision)] TO MONTH
```

The default value for the day's leading precision is 2, and the second's fractional second precision is 6. The default value for the year's precision is 2.

You can define an INTERVAL DATE TO SECOND variable with a default null or initialized value, as shown:

```
var1 INTERVAL DAY TO SECOND;       -- Implicitly accept default precisions.
var2 INTERVAL DAY(3) TO SECOND;    -- Explicitly set day precision.
var3 INTERVAL DAY(3) TO SECOND(9); -- Explicitly set day and second precision.
```

You assign a variable value by using the following prototype for an `INTERVAL DAY TO SECOND` data type, where `D` stands for day and `HH:MI:SS` stands for hours, minutes, and seconds, respectively:

```
variable_name := 'D HH:MI:SS';
```

An actual assignment to the same type would look like

```
var1 := '5 08:21:20';  -- Implicit conversion from the string.
```

You can declare an `INTERVAL YEAR TO MONTH` variable with a default null or initialized value, as shown:

```
var1 INTERVAL YEAR TO MONTH;         -- Implicitly accept default precisions.
var2 INTERVAL YEAR(3) TO MONTH;      -- Explicitly set year precision.
```

There are four assignments methods. The following program demonstrates an assignment to `var2`:

```
  DECLARE
  var2 INTERVAL YEAR(3) TO MONTH;
  BEGIN
    -- Shorthand for a 101 year and 3 month interval.
    var2 := '101-3';
    var2 := INTERVAL '101-3' YEAR TO MONTH;
    var2 := INTERVAL '101' YEAR;
    var2 := INTERVAL '3' MONTH;
END;
/
```

This would output the following values, respectively:

```
+101-03
+101-03
+101-00
+000-03
```

Arithmetic operations between the `DATE` data type and interval subtypes follow the rules in Table 4-3. The classic operation is an interval calculation, like subtracting one timestamp from another to get the number of days between dates.

The intervals simplify advanced comparisons but do require a bit of work to master. More information on this SQL and PL/SQL data type is in the *Oracle Database SQL Language Reference* and the *Oracle Database Advanced Application Developer's Guide*.

TIMESTAMP Subtypes The `TIMESTAMP` subtypes extend the `DATE` base type by providing a more precise time. You'll get the same results if the `TIMESTAMP` variable is populated by calling the `SYSDATE` built-in function. The `SYSTIMESTAMP` SQL built-in function provides a more precise time for most platforms.

The following is the prototype for declaring a `TIMESTAMP` data type:

```
TIMESTAMP[(precision)] [NOT NULL]
```

Operand 1 Type	Operator	Operand 2 Type	Result Type
Timestamp	+	Interval	Timestamp
Timestamp	-	Interval	Timestamp
Interval	+	Timestamp	Timestamp
Timestamp	-	Interval	Interval
Interval	+	Interval	Interval
Interval	-	Interval	Interval
Interval	*	Numeric	Interval
Numeric	*	Interval	Interval
Interval	/	Numeric	Interval

TABLE 4-3. *Timestamp and Interval Arithmetic*

You can use the `NOT NULL` clause to ensure a value is assigned to a `TIMESTAMP` variable. There are many cases where you will want to restrict `TIMESTAMP` variables. If you don't restrict them, then you'll need to wrap them in `NVL` built-in functions to support logical comparisons.

You can define a `TIMESTAMP` variable with a default null or initialized value, as shown:

```
var1 TIMESTAMP;                      -- Implicitly assigns a null value.
var2 TIMESTAMP := SYSTIMESTAMP;      -- Explicitly assigns a value.
var3 TIMESTAMP(3);                  -- Explicitly sets precision for null value.
var4 TIMESTAMP(3) := SYSTIMESTAMP; -- Explicitly sets precision and value.
```

The following program demonstrates the difference between the `DATE` and `TIMESTAMP` data types:

```
DECLARE
  d DATE := SYSTIMESTAMP;
  t TIMESTAMP(3) := SYSTIMESTAMP;
BEGIN
  dbms_output.put_line('DATE      ['||d||']');
  dbms_output.put_line('TO_CHAR   ['||TO_CHAR(d,'DD-MON-YY HH24:MI:SS')||']');
  dbms_output.put_line('TIMESTAMP ['||t||']');
END;
/
```

The anonymous block returns

```
DATE      [31-JUL-07]
TO_CHAR   [31-JUL-07 21:27:36]
TIMESTAMP [31-JUL-07 09.27.36.004 PM]
```

The other two TIMESTAMP subtypes demonstrate similar behaviors. Their prototypes are

```
TIMESTAMP[(precision)] WITH TIME ZONE
TIMESTAMP[(precision)] WITH LOCAL TIME ZONE
```

You can declare a TIMESTAMP WITH TIME ZONE variable with a default null or initialized value, as shown:

```
var1 TIMESTAMP WITH LOCAL TIME ZONE;
var2 TIMESTAMP WITH LOCAL TIME ZONE := SYSTIMESTAMP;
var3 TIMESTAMP(3) WITH LOCAL TIME ZONE;
var4 TIMESTAMP(3) WITH LOCAL TIME ZONE := SYSTIMESTAMP;
```

The difference between these timestamps is that those with time zones append the time zone to the timestamp. The TIME ZONE qualifier returns the standard time and an indicator of whether the time zone is using daylight saving time. The LOCAL TIME ZONE qualifier returns the difference between the local time and Greenwich Mean Time (GMT).

Unicode Characters and Strings

Unicode characters and strings exist to support globalization. Globalization is accomplished by using character encoding that supports multiple character sets. AL16UTF16 and UTF8 encoding are provided by the Oracle Database. AL16UTF16 encoding stores all characters in 2 physical bytes, while UTF8 encoding stores all characters in 3 physical bytes.

The NCHAR data type is a Unicode equivalent to the CHAR data type, and the NVARCHAR2 data type is a Unicode equivalent to the VARCHAR2 data type. You should use these data types when building applications that will support multiple character sets in the same database.

NCHAR Data Type The NCHAR data type is a base data type for *fixed*-length Unicode strings and requires you to divide the maximum length of 32,767 by 2 or 3 depending on character set. The NCHAR data type shares the generic behaviors of the CHAR data type covered earlier in this chapter.

Globalization of fixed-length Unicode strings is best suited to the NCHAR data type. You should use these types when the database supports Unicode or may support it in the future.

NVARCHAR2 Data Type The NCHAR data type is a base data type for *variable* Unicode strings and requires you to divide the maximum length of 32,767 by 2 or 3 depending on character set. The NVARCHAR2 data type shares the generic behaviors of the VARCHAR2 data type covered earlier in this chapter.

Globalization of variable-length strings is best suited to the NVARCHAR2 data type. You should use these types when your database instance supports Unicode or may support it in the future.

Numbers

There are four principal number data types: BINARY_INTEGER, IEEE 754–format numbers (BINARY_DOUBLE and BINARY_FLOAT), NUMBER, and PLS_INTEGER. The BINARY_INTEGER and PLS_INTEGER data types are identical, and they both use the native operating system math libraries. Oracle uses PLS_INTEGER to describe both BINARY_INTEGER and PLS_INTEGER as interchangeable, and so does this book in subsequent chapters.

Both IEEE 754–format numbers provide single- and double-precision numbers to support scientific computing. The NUMBER data type uses a custom library provided as part of Oracle Database 11*g* forward. It can store very large fixed-point or floating-point numbers.

BINARY_INTEGER Data Type The BINARY_INTEGER data type is identical to PLS_INTEGER and stores integer numbers from –2,147,483,648 to 2,147,483,647 as 32 bits or 4 bytes. Like the PLS_INTEGER data type, it computes more efficiently within its number range and takes much less space than a NUMBER data type in memory. Math operations using two BINARY_INTEGER variables that yield a result outside of the data type range will raise an ORA-01426 numeric overflow error.

The following is the prototype for declaring a BINARY_INTEGER data type:

```
BINARY_INTEGER
```

You can define a BINARY_INTEGER variable with a null value or initialize the value during declaration. The syntax for both follows:

```
var1 BINARY_INTEGER;
var2 BINARY_INTEGER := 21;
```

The BINARY_INTEGER data type uses native math libraries, and as such, the declaration statement does not allocate memory to store the variable until a value is assigned.

You can define a BINARY_INTEGER subtype by using the following prototype:

```
SUBTYPE subtype_name IS base_type [RANGE low_number..high_number] [NOT NULL];
```

There are several predefined subtypes of the BINARY_INTEGER data type. The NATURAL and POSITIVE subtypes restrict their use to only positive integer values. The NATURALN and POSITIVEN subtypes restrict null assignments. A PLS-00218 error is raised when you attempt to declare a NATURALN or POSITIVEN subtype without initializing the value. They both enforce a not-null constraint on the data type.

The newest subtype is the SIMPLE_INTEGER data type introduced in Oracle Database 11*g*. It truncates overflow and suppresses the raising of any error related to overflow. The performance of the SIMPLE_INTEGER data type is dependent on the value of the PLSQL_CODE_TYPE database parameter. The performance is superior when PLSQL_CODE_TYPE is set to NATIVE because arithmetic operations are performed with the operating system libraries and both overflow and null value checking are disabled. Performance is slower when plsql_code_type is set to INTERPRETED because it prevents overload and performs null value checking.

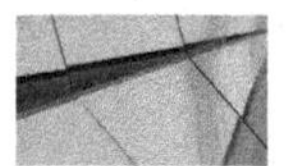

NOTE
Overloading behavior of base types and subtypes in PL/SQL packages is typically disallowed, but the same name or positional formal parameter can be overloaded by using PLS_INTEGER or BINARY_INTEGER *in one signature and SIMPLE_INTEGER in another.*

You should also know that a casting operation from a PLS_INTEGER or BINARY_INTEGER data type to a SIMPLE_INTEGER data type does no conversion unless the value is null. A runtime error is thrown when casting a null value to a SIMPLE_INTEGER variable.

IEEE 754–Format Data Type IEEE 754–format single-precision and double-precision numbers are provided to support scientific computing. They bring with them traditional overflow and infinities problems as part of their definition and implementation. You should use these types of variables for scientific problems, like cube roots and such.

Both the SQL and PL/SQL environments define the `BINARY_FLOAT_NAN` and `BINARY_FLOAT_INFINITY` constants. The PL/SQL environment also defines four other constants. All six constants are listed along with their values in Table 4-4.

NOTE
Oracle Database 12c documentation does not list these constants in the reserved word or keyword lists. They can be found by printing them from a PL/SQL program or querying the `v$reserved_words` *table.*

The following is the prototype for declaring IEEE 754–format data types:

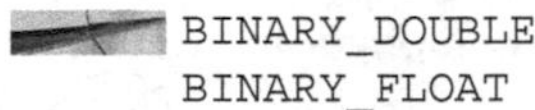

```
BINARY_DOUBLE
BINARY_FLOAT
```

You can define variables of these types with null values or initialize them during declaration. The syntax for both follows:

```
var1 BINARY_DOUBLE;
var2 BINARY_DOUBLE := 21d;
var3 BINARY_FLOAT;
var4 BINARY_FLOAT := 21f;
```

You must always use a `d` for numeric literals assigned to a `BINARY_DOUBLE` and an `f` for numeric literals assigned to a `BINARY_FLOAT`. Oracle Database 12c overloads subroutines that leverage the processing speed of these IEEE 754–format data types.

You can also define a `BINARY_DOUBLE` or `BINARY_FLOAT` subtype by using the following prototype:

```
SUBTYPE subtype_name IS base_type [NOT NULL];
```

Constant Name	Environment	Value
`BINARY_FLOAT_NAN`	SQL & PL/SQL	It contains `Nan`, but comparison operations treat it as a case-insensitive string. NaN in scientific notation means *not a number.*
`BINARY_FLOAT_INFINITY`	SQL & PL/SQL	It contains `Inf`, but comparison operations treat it as a case-insensitive string.
`BINARY_FLOAT_MIN_NORMAL`	PL/SQL	It contains `1.17549435E-038`.
`BINARY_FLOAT_MAX_NORMAL`	PL/SQL	It contains `3.40282347E+038`.
`BINARY_FLOAT_MIN_SUBNORMAL`	PL/SQL	It contains `1.40129846E-045`.
`BINARY_FLOAT_MAX_SUBNORMAL`	PL/SQL	It contains `1.17549421E-038`.

TABLE 4-4. *IEEE 754–Format Data Type Constants*

You should note that, unlike other number data types, these cannot be range constrained. The only constraint that you can impose is that the subtypes disallow null value assignments.

NUMBER Data Type The NUMBER data type uses a custom library provided as part of Oracle Database 12*c*. It can store numbers in the range of 1.0E-130 (1 times 10 raised to the negative 130th power) to 1.0E126 (1 times 10 raised to the 126th power). Oracle recommends using the NUMBER data type only when the use or computation result falls in the range of possible values. The NUMBER data type does not raise a NaN (*not a number*) or infinity error when a literal or computational value is outside the data type range. These exceptions have the following outcomes:

- A literal value below the minimum range value stores a zero in a NUMBER variable.
- A literal value above the maximum range value raises a compilation error.
- A computational outcome above the maximum range value raises a compilation error.

The NUMBER data type supports fixed-point and floating-point numbers. Fixed-point numbers are defined by specifying the number of digits (known as the precision) and the number of digits to the right of the decimal point (known as the scale). The decimal point is not physically stored in the variable because it is calculated by the relationship between the precision and the scale.

The following is the prototype for declaring a fixed-point NUMBER data type:

```
NUMBER[(precision, [scale])] [NOT NULL]
```

Both precision and scale are optional values when you declare a NUMBER variable. The NUMBER data type default size, number of digits, or precision is 38. You can declare a NUMBER variable with only the precision, but you must specify the precision to define the scale.

You can declare fixed-point NUMBER variables with null values or initialize them during declaration. The syntax for NUMBER data type declarations with null values is

```
var1 NUMBER;                 -- A null number with 38 digits.
var2 NUMBER(15);             -- A null number with 15 digits.
var3 NUMBER(15,2);           -- A null number with 15 digits and 2 decimals.
```

The syntax for NUMBER data type declarations with initialized values is

```
var1 NUMBER := 15;           -- A number with 38 digits.
var2 NUMBER(15)  := 15;      -- A number with 15 digits.
var3 NUMBER(15,2) := 15.22;  -- A number with 15 digits and 2 decimals.
```

You can also declare fixed-point numbers by using the DEC, DECIMAL, and NUMER subtypes. Alternatively, you can declare integers using the INTEGER, INT, and SMALLINT subtypes. They all have the same maximum precision of 38.

The following are prototypes for declaring the DOUBLE PRECISION and FLOAT subtypes of the floating-point NUMBER data type:

```
DOUBLE PRECISION[(precision)]
FLOAT[(precision)]
```

Defining the precision of DOUBLE PRECISION or FLOAT variables is optional. You risk losing the natural precision of a floating-point number when you constrain the precision. Both of these variables have a default size, number of digits, or precision of 126. You can define the precision of a FLOAT variable, but not the scale. Any attempt to define the scale of either of these subtypes raises a PLS-00510 error because they cannot have a fixed number of digits to the right of the decimal point.

The syntax for DOUBLE PRECISION and FLOAT declarations with null values is

```
var1 DOUBLE PRECISION;              -- A null number with 126 digits.
var2 FLOAT;                         -- A null number with 15 digits.
var3 DOUBLE PRECISION;              -- A null number with 126 digits.
var4 FLOAT(15);                     -- A null number with 15 digits.
```

The syntax for DOUBLE PRECISION and FLOAT declarations with initialized values is

```
var1 DOUBLE PRECISION := 15;        -- A number with 126 digits.
var2 FLOAT := 15;                   -- A number with 126 digits.
var3 DOUBLE PRECISION(15) := 15;    -- A number with 15 digits.
var4 FLOAT(15) := 15;               -- A number with 15 digits.
```

You also have the REAL subtype of NUMBER that stores floating-point numbers but only uses a precision of 63 digits. The REAL subtype provides 18-digit precision to the right of the decimal point.

PLS_INTEGER Data Type The PLS_INTEGER and BINARY_INTEGER data types are identical and use operating system–specific arithmetic for calculations. They can store integer numbers from –2,147,483,648 to 2,147,483,647 as 32 bits or 4 bytes. The PLS_INTEGER data type takes much less space than a NUMBER data type to store in memory. It also computes more efficiently, provided the numbers and result of the math operation are within its number range. You should note that any math operation that yields a result outside of the range will raise an ORA-01426 numeric overflow error. The error is raised even when you assign the result of the mathematical operation to a NUMBER data type.

The following is the prototype for defining a NVARCHAR2 data type:

```
PLS_INTEGER
```

You can declare a PLS_INTEGER variable with a null value or initialize the value during declaration. The syntax for both follows:

```
var1 PLS_INTEGER;        -- A null value requires no space.
var2 PLS_INTEGER := 11;  -- An integer requires space for each character.
```

The PLS_INTEGER data type uses native math libraries, and as such, the declaration statement doesn't allocate memory to store the variable until a value is assigned. You can test this by using the LENGTH built-in function.

You can declare a PLS_INTEGER subtype by using the following prototype:

```
SUBTYPE subtype_name IS base_type [RANGE low_number..high_number] [NOT NULL];
```

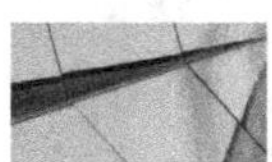

NOTE

Don't confuse a PLS_INTEGER data type with an INTEGER data type. The former uses operating system mathematics libraries, while the latter is a subtype of the NUMBER base type.

The LENGTH Built-in Function

The behavior of the LENGTH built-in function is consistent with what you'll see writing C or C++ programs. When a value is assigned, the LENGTH built-in function returns the number of characters, not the number of bytes required for storage. You also have the LENGTHB, LENGTHC, LENGTH2, and LENGTH4 built-in functions. This means that a PLS_INTEGER data type with five or six numbers would appear to have a character length of 5 or 6, respectively, but actually only takes 4 bytes of space in both cases. This result appears linked to how the NUMBER data type works, where NUMBER column values are stored as C single-dimensional character arrays. The LENGTH function appears to count the positions in all number data types.

Large Objects (LOBs)

Large objects (LOBs) provide you with four data types: BFILE, BLOB, CLOB, and NCLOB. BFILE is a data type that points to an external file, which limits its maximum size to 4GB. BLOB, CLOB, and NCLOB are internally managed types, and their maximum size is 8 to 128 terabytes, depending on the db_block_size parameter value.

LOB columns contain a locator that points to where the actual data is stored. You must access a LOB value in the scope of a transaction. You essentially use the locator as a route to read data from or write data to the LOB column. Chapter 10 provides details of how you access LOB columns and work with LOB data types, including the DBMS_LOB built-in package.

BFILE Data Type

The BFILE data type is a read-only data type *except for setting the virtual directory and file name for the external file.* You use the built-in BFILENAME function to set locator information for a BFILE column. Before you use the BFILENAME function, there are several setup steps. You must create a physical directory on the server, store the file in the directory, create a virtual directory that points to the physical directory, and grant read permissions on the directory to the schema that owns the table or the stored program that accesses the BFILE column.

You retrieve the descriptor (the column name), alias (a virtual directory to the physical directory location), and filename by using the FILEGETNAME procedure from the DBMS_LOB package. The database session_max_open_files parameter sets the maximum number of open BFILE columns. Chapter 10 shows these pieces fit together and provides you with some stored program units to simplify the process.

The following is the prototype for declaring a BFILE data type:

```
BFILE
```

There is one way to define a BFILE variable, and it always contains a null reference by default:

```
var1 BFILE;          -- Declare a null reference to a BFILE.
```

A BFILE data type cannot be defined with a reference unless you write a wrapper to the DBMS_LOB.FILEGETNAME procedure. Chapter 10 provides a wrapper function and explains the limitations that require the wrapper function.

BLOB Data Type

The BLOB data type is a read-write binary large data type. BLOB data types participate in transactions and are recoverable. You can only read and write between BLOB variables and database columns in a transaction scope. BLOB data types are objects and are treated differently than scalar variables. They have three possible states: null, empty, and populated (not empty). They require initialization by the empty_blob function to move from a null reference to an empty state, or a direct hexadecimal assignment to become populated.

BLOBs can store binary files between 8 and 32 terabytes. Unfortunately, you can only access BLOB columns by using the DBMS_LOB package to read and write values after the initial assignment of a value.

PL/SQL lets you declare local BLOB variables in your anonymous and named blocks. However, you must establish an active link between your program and the stored BLOB column to insert, append, or read the column value. Generally, to avoid exhausting your system resources, you'll want to only read or store chunks of large BLOB values.

The following is the prototype for declaring a BLOB data type:

```
BLOB
```

There is one way to declare a BLOB variable with a default null reference:

```
var1 BLOB;                       -- Declare a null reference to a BLOB.
```

There are two ways to define an empty and populated BLOB variable:

```
var1 BLOB := empty_blob();       -- Declare an empty BLOB.
var2 BLOB := '43'||'41'||'52';   -- Declare a hexadecimal BLOB for CAR.
```

BLOB data types are especially useful when you want to store large image files, movies, or other binary files. Their utility depends a great deal on how well you write the interface. Chapter 10 discusses ways to handle interactions between BLOB columns and PL/SQL variables.

CLOB Data Type

The CLOB data type is a read-write character large data type and it performs like a BLOB data type for text strings. CLOBs have the same three possible states: null, empty, or populated (not empty). CLOBs require initialization by the empty_clob() function rather than the empty_blob() function to change from a null reference to an empty state.

Like the BLOB data type, there is one way to define a CLOB variable with a default null reference:

```
var1 CLOB;                 -- Declare a null reference to a CLOB.
```

Other than the initializing function call, you define an empty CLOB variable and a populated one like a BLOB data type:

```
var1 CLOB := empty_clob(); -- Declare an empty CLOB.
var2 CLOB := 'CAR';        -- Declare a CLOB for CAR.
```

CLOB data types are especially useful when you want to store large text files. Examples of large text files are customer notes that support transactions, refunds, or other activities. Large text elements are suited to reading and writing only small chunks at a time. Otherwise, you'll exhaust your system resources. Chapter 10 discusses ways to handle interactions between CLOB columns and PL/SQL variables.

NCLOB Data Type

The NCLOB data type is a read-write Unicode character large data type. NCLOB data types perform like CLOB data types with one exception— more space is allocated to them because they use the Unicode character sets. All other rules are the same, including the `empty_clob()` function call to initialize them.

Composite Data Types

There are three composite generalized data types: records, objects, and collections. Collections can contain a scalar, record, or object data type, and can be implemented as SQL or PL/SQL data types. The latter, once PL/SQL tables, are known as associative arrays from Oracle Database 10*g* forward.

The composite data types are as follows:

- A record data type, also known as a structure, typically contains a collection of related field elements like any row in a table. The code that declares the record data type is like the code that defines a table's structure. Moreover, a record has a structure like a table but is limited to a single row.
- An object data type, also known as a structure, typically contains a collection of related field elements like any row in a table. The code that declares the object data type is typically accompanied by an implementation in an object body, but an object data type without a body acts like a SQL equivalent of a record data type. That means it also defines a structure, like a single row table.
- A collection may be a varray or nested table (Oracle uses the term *nested table* to disambiguate the difference between a programming data type and a physical table) of a scalar or composite data type. A collection of a scalar data type is an Attribute Data Type (ADT), as qualified in Chapter 3, while a collection of a composite data type is a user-defined type (UDT). Collections may use an object data type in a SQL context and a record data type in a PL/SQL context.
- A system reference cursor may return a collection of one to many columns. It is a PL/SQL-only context data type. It has two types—weakly typed and strongly typed. A weakly typed cursor inherits the type at runtime, whereas a strongly typed cursor specifies it at compile time.

Chapter 3 covers composite data types well, so here we only review assignment methods for the composite data types. Refer to Chapter 3 for basic code examples on records, objects, and collections. After the review of assignment methods for records, objects, and collections, we cover PL/SQL system reference cursors.

Nested Table or Table

The idea of nesting falls apart when the collection isn't a persistent object type that defines a column in a table. That's why I chose to use *table* instead of *nested table* in most places in this book.

Records

Records are extremely useful when working with cursors and other exclusively PL/SQL solutions. You can define a stored function that returns a record type, but that limits how you can use the function. *SQL can only access stored functions when they return SQL data types*. The alternative to returning a record type is to return a SQL object type.

The following declares a record with default values, initializes it with overriding values, and prints the values:

```
SQL> DECLARE
  2    -- Declares a default record structure.
  3    TYPE muppet_record IS RECORD
  4    ( salutation  VARCHAR(20)  DEFAULT  'Ms.'
  5    , name        VARCHAR2(10) :=       'Piggy');
  6    -- Declares a variable of the local record structure.
  7    muppet  MUPPET_RECORD;
  8  BEGIN
  9    -- Assignments are by element or field only.
 10    muppet.salutation := 'Mr.';
 11    muppet.name := 'Kermit the frog';
 12    -- Print the record as a pipe concatenated string.
 13    dbms_output.put_line(muppet.salutation||' '||muppet.name);
 14  END;
 15  /
```

It prints

```
Mr. Kermit the frog
```

Lines 3 through 5 declare the local record type. Line 7 declares a variable of the local data type, but actually defines it, because the record structure has default values—Ms. Piggy. Lines 10 and 11 demonstrate that you must assign values field by field. The exception to that rule comes when you assign a cursor return that matches the record structure or the values of a matching record structure. Line 13 shows that the variable name, component selector, and field name are required to print the contents of a record.

Objects

Objects are typically more useful than records, which, from a point of view that leverages object types, are becoming legacy code. That's my view. It appears that Oracle may share my view because it now maps object types to internal and external Java programs. Admittedly, using objects takes more planning and skill upfront, but good design yields great rewards. After all, Oracle Database 12*c* is an object relational database management system.

You can define a stored function that returns an object type and use it in SQL or PL/SQL contexts. The following declares an object in SQL, which makes it a schema-level object:

```
SQL> CREATE OR REPLACE
    TYPE president_record IS OBJECT
    ( salutation  VARCHAR(20)
    , name        VARCHAR2(10));
  /
```

The SQL statement creates a schema-level object type that you can use as a data type in tables or your program units. True objects include an object body that qualifies the implementation of the object type.

Note that the default values no longer exist. That's because object types can't have default values, and an attempt to add them would raise the following compilation error:

```
LINE/COL ERROR
-------- ---------------------------------------------------------
0/0      PL/SQL: Compilation unit analysis terminated
2/5      PLS-00363: expression 'SALUTATION' cannot be used as an
         assignment target
```

It prints

```
Mr. Kermit the frog
```

The following declares an object in SQL, which makes it a schema-level object:

```
SQL> DECLARE
  2    -- Declares a variable of the local record structure.
  3    president  PRESIDENT_OBJECT := president_object('Mr.','Lincoln');
  4  BEGIN
  5    -- Print the record as a pipe concatenated string.
  6    dbms_output.put_line(president.salutation||' '||president.name);
  7  END;
  8  /
```

There's no local declaration of the object type because it exists at the schema level. Line 3 does contain something new, a specialized function call—an object constructor. *Object constructors* are specialized functions that take a list of comma-delimited values and return instances of object types. Failure to construct an object instance raises an uninitialized runtime exception. So, don't forget that instantiation with the constructor.

It prints by using the same approach as the record type:

```
Mr. Lincoln
```

Leveraging your introduction to functions from Chapter 3, let's refactor the logic into a function that returns an instance of the object `president_object`. It's fairly straightforward as long as you remember never to assign dynamic values in the declaration block.

Here's the code:

```
SQL> CREATE OR REPLACE FUNCTION get_president
( pv_salutation VARCHAR2 DEFAULT 'Mr.'
, pv_name       VARCHAR2 ) RETURN president_object IS
  -- Declare a variable of the schema-level object structure.
  president  PRESIDENT_OBJECT := president_object(NULL,NULL);
BEGIN
  -- Assign a value to pre-allocated space.
  president := president_object(pv_salutation,pv_name);
  -- Return the object instance.
  RETURN president;
END;
/
```

Line 5 declares a local variable with a null element, which allocates space for a record. Line 8 assigns the values to the object instance, and line 10 returns the instantiated object with the following query:

```
SQL> COLUMN president FORMAT A40
SQL> SELECT   get_president(pv_name => 'Truman') AS president
  2  FROM     dual;
```

The call to the `get_president` function returns a flattened object, which is the name of the object type and the parenthetical list of values to construct an instance:

```
PRESIDENT(SALUTATION, NAME)
-----------------------------------
PRESIDENT_OBJECT('Mr.', 'Truman')
```

You can convert this to columns by referring to the "Migrate from Objects to a Relational Table" section of Appendix B. Overall, this short section has shown that objects may be consumed in SQL contexts.

Collections

Collections are arrays and lists. Arrays differ from lists in that they use a sequentially numbered index, while lists use a nonsequential numeric or unique string index. Arrays are densely populated lists because they have sequentially numbered indexes. While lists can have densely populated numeric indexes, they can also be sparsely populated, meaning there are gaps in a sequence or the indexes are not sequential.

Oracle supports three types of collections. Two are both SQL and PL/SQL data types, depending on how you define them: varray and nested table (or *table*). The third collection type is a PL/SQL-only data type, called an associative array. The associative array is also known as a PL/SQL table or an index-by table. Refer to Chapter 3 for a full introduction to these three collection types. Flip to Chapter 6 if you're immediately curious about implementing collections.

System Reference Cursors

System reference cursors are pointers to result sets in query work areas. A *query work area* is a memory region (known as a *context area*) in the Oracle Database 12*c* *Program Global Area (PGA)*. The query work area holds information on the query. You'll find the rows returned by a query, the number of rows processed by the query, and a pointer to the parsed query in the query work area. The query work is discrete from the Oracle Shared Pool (see Appendix A).

NOTE
All cursors share the same behaviors whether they are defined as PL/SQL reference cursor data types or ordinary cursors. In fact, every SQL statement is a cursor processed and tracked in a PGA context area.

You use system reference cursors when you want to query data in one program and process it in another, especially when the two programs are in different programming languages. You have the option of implementing a system reference cursor in two ways: one is *strongly typed* and the other is *weakly typed*. System reference cursors are a PL/SQL-only data type. You can define them in anonymous or named blocks. They are most useful when you define them in package specifications, because your programs can share them.

There is one prototype, but how you choose to implement the cursor defines whether it is strongly or weakly typed. The prototype is

```
TYPE reference_cursor_name IS REF CURSOR
  [RETURN catalog_object_name%ROWTYPE];
```

You create a weakly typed system reference cursor by defining it without a return type. A strongly typed system reference cursor has a defined return type. As a rule of thumb, you should use strongly typed system reference cursors when you need to anchor a reference cursor to a catalog object. Weakly typed system reference cursors are ideal when the query returns something other than a catalog object. A generic weakly typed system reference cursor is already defined as `SYS_REFCURSOR`, and it is available anywhere in your PL/SQL programming environment.

The prototype for a best-practice weakly typed system reference cursor is

```
TYPE best_weakly_typed IS REF CURSOR;
```

The prototype for a best-practice strongly typed system reference cursor is

```
TYPE best_strongly_typed IS REF CURSOR RETURN some_table%ROWTYPE;
```

The power of reference cursors becomes more significant when you use them inside stored program units. You can also use reference cursors in anonymous block programs and assign them to a SQL*Plus reference environment variable.

You define a SQL*Plus reference cursor environment variable by defining a variable and pressing ENTER. SQL*Plus statements do not require a semicolon or forward slash to run. The following creates a weakly typed SQL*Plus reference cursor:

```
SQL> VARIABLE sv_refcursor REFCURSOR
```

The following program defines and declares a reference cursor before explicitly opening it and assigning its values to an external session-level variable:

```
SQL> DECLARE
       -- Declare a weakly typed reference cursor.
       TYPE weakly_typed IS REF CURSOR;
       -- Declare a local variable of the weakly typed reference cursor.
       lv_refcursor  WEAKLY_TYPED;
     BEGIN
       -- Open the reference cursor.
       OPEN lv_refcursor FOR
         SELECT   item_title
         ,        COUNT(*)
         FROM     item
         HAVING   (COUNT(*) > 2)
         GROUP BY item_title;

       -- Assign the reference cursor to a SQL*Plus session variable.
       :sv_refcursor := lv_refcursor;
     END;
     /
```

You can query the session-level variable to see the contents of the reference cursor with the following:

```
SQL> SELECT   :sv_refcursor
  2  FROM     dual;
```

The query returns the following, provided you've run the seeding scripts found in the book's introduction:

```
:REFCUR
--------------------
CURSOR STATEMENT : 1
CURSOR STATEMENT : 1
ITEM_TITLE                                                    COUNT(*)
------------------------------------------------------------ ----------
Harry Potter and the Chamber of Secrets                               3
Harry Potter: Goblet of Fire                                          3
Die Another Day                                                       3
Pirates of the Caribbean                                              4
The Lord of the Rings - The Return of the King                        3
  ...

10 rows selected.
```

The SYS_REFCURSOR generic system reference cursor can replace the locally defined reference to a weakly typed cursor. You would make the change by remarking out lines 2 and 3 (to keep the rest of the line numbers intact) and making the following change on line 5:

```
 5    lv_refcursor  SYS_REFCURSOR;
```

Chapter 8 demonstrates how to use a system reference cursor inside functions and procedures. System reference cursors are extremely useful data types when you want to pass a query work area pointer to an external program. You can pass to an external program by using the Oracle Call Interface 8 (OCI8) libraries.

Review Section

This section has described the following points about variables and data types:

- Anonymous blocks use the DECLARE keyword to start the declaration block, while named blocks use the function or procedure header.
- The BEGIN keyword starts the execution block and ends any declaration block.
- The EXCEPTION keyword starts the exception block and the END keyword terminates the program unit.
- You can define data types in local anonymous (unnamed) or named blocks, as well as in nested anonymous blocks.

(continued)

- You can declare scalar and composite variables in the declaration block.
- Scalar variables hold only one thing, such as a number, string, or date.
- You can create subtypes of standard scalar variables in PL/SQL.
- Composite variables hold two or more things, and they can be a record structure of one row and many columns (fields), a collection, or a hybrid collection known as a system reference cursor.
- Some scalar variables implicitly cast while others require programmer intervention with SQL built-in functions.
- SQL composite variables work in both SQL and PL/SQL contexts, while PL/SQL composite variables work only in the PL/SQL context.

Summary

This chapter has explained delimiters; how you define, access, and assign values to variables; and how you work with scalar and composite data types.

Mastery Check

The mastery check is a series of true-or-false and multiple-choice questions that let you confirm how well you understand the material in the chapter. You may check Appendix I for answers to these questions.

True or False:

1. ___A declaration block begins with the function or procedure header, specification, or signature in a named block.
2. ___An execution block can contain a local named block.
3. ___A declaration block can't contain an anonymous block.
4. ___An identifier is a lexical unit.
5. ___The colon and equal sign set (:=) is the only assignment operator in PL/SQL.
6. ___The equal sign and greater than symbol set (=>) is an association operator.
7. ___PL/SQL lets you create subtypes of standard scalar variables.
8. ___A record data type is a SQL data type.
9. ___A system reference cursor is a PL/SQL-only data type.
10. ___The PL/SQL programming language supports arrays and lists as composite data types.

Multiple Choice:

11. Lexical units are the basic building blocks in programming languages, and they can perform which of the following? (Multiple answers possible)

A. A delimiter

B. An identifier

C. A literal

D. A comment

E. An anonymous block

12. Which of the following are valid symbol sets in PL/SQL? (Multiple answers possible)

A. A colon and equal sign set (:=) assignment operator

B. A guillemets or double angle bracket set (<< >>) as delimiters for labels

C. A less than symbol and greater than symbol set (<>) as a comparison operator

D. An exclamation mark and equal sign set (!=) as a comparison operator

E. A opening curly brace and closing curly brace symbol set ({ }) as delimiters for an anonymous block

13. Which of the following are valid scalar data types in PL/SQL? (Multiple answers possible)

A. A `TEXT` data type

B. A `VARCHAR2` data type

C. A `NCHAR` data type

D. A `CHAR` data type

E. A `DATE` data type

14. Which of the following data types are best suited for scientific calculations in PL/SQL? (Multiple answers possible)

A. A `NUMBER` data type

B. A `PLS_INTEGER` data type

C. A `BINARY_DOUBLE` data type

D. A `BINARY_FLOAT` data type

E. A `BINARY_INTEGER` data type

15. Which of the following are reasons for using a system reference cursor?

A. A system reference cursor mimics a table collection

B. An alternative when you want to query data in one program and use it in another

C. A PL/SQL-only solution with the results of composite data type

D. A SQL or PL/SQL solution with the results of a system reference cursor

E. None of the above

CHAPTER 5

Control Structures

This chapter examines the control structures in PL/SQL. Control structures let you make conditional choices, repeat operations, and access data. The `IF` and `CASE` statements let you branch program execution according to one or more conditions. Loop statements let you repeat behavior until conditions are met. Cursors let you access data one row or one set of rows at a time.

This chapter examines the various control structures in the following order:

- Conditional statements
  - `IF` statements
  - `CASE` statements
  - Conditional compilation statements
- Iterative statements
  - Simple loop statements
  - `FOR` loop statements
  - `WHILE` loop statements
- Cursor structures
  - Implicit cursors
  - Explicit cursors
- Bulk statements
  - `BULK COLLECT INTO` statements
  - `FORALL` statements

Conditional Statements

There are three types of conditional statements in programming languages: single-branching statements, multiple-branching statements without fall-through, and multiple-branching statements with fall-through. To *fall through* means to process all subsequent conditions after finding a matching `CASE` statement. Single-branching statements are if-then-else statements. Multiple-branching statements without fall-through are *if-then-elsif-then-else* statements, and with fall-through they are `CASE` statements. Figure 5-1 demonstrates the logical flow of the first two conditional statements. The third is not displayed because PL/SQL *does not* support fall-through, and PL/SQL implements `CASE` statements *like if-then-elsif-then-else* statements.

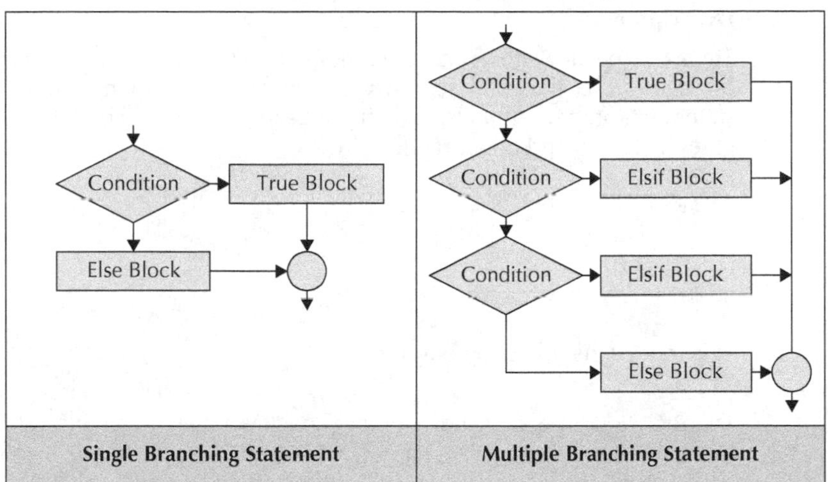

FIGURE 5-1. *Branching statement logical flows*

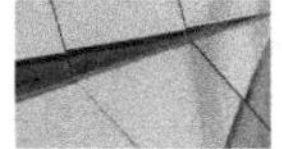

NOTE
PL/SQL uses the `ELSIF` *reserved word in lieu of two separate words—else if. This is a legacy from the Pascal and Ada programming languages.*

The "Condition" diamonds in Figure 5-1 are decision trees. Decision trees represent code branching that happens because of comparison operations. Comparison operations are frequently called *comparison expressions* or *expressions* because they return a true or false value. At least, that's true in a two-valued logic model, where true or false comparisons are straightforward. Not true or not false comparisons are tricky when we change from a two-valued logic model to a three-valued logic model. Three-valued logic occurs where an expression may return true, false, or *null*. Null values are possible anytime a comparison value comes from a database, because scalar data types hold a value or null.

A not true expression is true when the value is false or null in a three-valued logic model, and a not false expression is met when the value is true or null. That's because both a not true expression and a not false expression are true when the condition isn't met or a null makes it unsolvable.

PL/SQL supports lexical symbols, symbol sets, and identifiers as valid comparison operators. Table 5-1 lists and defines symbol comparison operators. Table 5-1 expands the comparison operator list by providing the comparison operators that are identifiers. Identifiers like these are reserved words or keywords, as qualified in Chapter 4.

Operator	Description

`AND`	The `AND` operator allows you to combine two comparisons into one. This operator makes the combination statement true only when both individual statements are true. You also use the `AND` operator with the `BETWEEN` operator to glue the lower- and upper-range values.
	`BEGIN`
	`  IF 1 = 1 AND 2 = 2 THEN`
	`    dbms_output.put_line('True.');`
	`  END IF;`
	`END;`
	`/`
	This returns the following output:
	`True.`

`BETWEEN`	The `BETWEEN` operator allows you to check whether a variable value is between two values of the same data type. The `BETWEEN` operator is also an inclusive operator. *Inclusive* means that a match may include either of the boundary values, which can't be null values. The `BETWEEN` operator also requires that the lower value precede the upper value.
	`BEGIN`
	`  IF 1 BETWEEN 1 AND 3 THEN`
	`    dbms_output.put_line('In the range.');`
	`  END IF;`
	`END;`
	`/`
	This returns the following output:
	`In the range.`

`IN`
`=ANY`
`=SOME`
	The `IN` operator allows you to check whether a variable value is in a set of comma-delimited values and is often called a *lookup value* because it compares a single scalar value against a list of values.
	The `=ANY` and `=SOME` operators perform the same behavior as the `IN` operator. The logic asks if the left operand is found in the set of the right operand, and the logic is an either-or evaluation among a list of values that leverages *short-circuit evaluation,* which stops checking when it finds one match.
	`BEGIN`
	`  IF 1 IN (1,2,3) THEN`
	`    dbms_output.put_line('In the set.');`
	`  END IF;`
	`END;`
	`/`
	This returns the following output:
	`In the set.`

TABLE 5-1. *Comparison Operators*

Operator	Description

`IS EMPTY`	The `IS EMPTY` operator allows you to check whether a *varray* or *table* collection variable is empty. *Empty* means that the collection was constructed without any default elements. This means no space was allocated to the System Global Area (SGA) for elements in the collection. When no element space is allocated, the `IS EMPTY` comparison returns true, and it returns false when at least one element is allocated space. You raise a `PLS-00306` exception when the collection has not been initialized through explicit construction. Chapters 3 and 6 explain how you construct collections.
	
	Note that this only works with collections of scalar SQL data types. An `IS EMPTY` comparison operator implicitly makes an `IS A SET` comparison at the same time, and it's probably more useful than the `IS A SET` comparison operator for that reason.
	`DECLARE`
	`  TYPE list IS TABLE OF INTEGER;`
	`  a LIST := list();`
	`BEGIN`
	`  IF a IS EMPTY THEN`
	`    dbms_output.put_line('"a" is empty.');`
	`  END IF;`
	`END;`
	`/`
	This returns the following output:
	`"a" is empty.`

`IS NULL`	The `IS NULL` operator allows you to check whether a variable value is null. The `NVL` built-in function can enable you to assign any Boolean or expression an explicit true or false value.
	`DECLARE`
	`  var BOOLEAN;`
	`BEGIN`
	`  IF var IS NULL THEN`
	`    dbms_output.put_line('It is null.');`
	`  END IF;`
	`END;`
	`/`
	This returns the following output:
	`It is null.`

(continued)

TABLE 5-1. *Comparison Operators*

Operator	Description

IS A SET	The IS A SET operator allows you to check whether a variable is a *varray* or *table* collection variable, *provided an instance of the variable has been constructed*. It returns true when the variable data type is a varray or table collection and the variable has been constructed. *Constructed* means that an instance of the collection has been created with or without members. Chapter 11 contains more details on the concept of constructing object types.
	The IS A SET comparison operator returns false when the variable data type is an uninitialized (or unconstructed) varray or table collection. You raise a PLS-00306 exception when you use the comparison operator against an associative array. It's important to note that this comparison operator only works with collections of scalar base data types.
	If you forget the "A" in the IS A SET operator and use IS SET, the program would raise a malformed identifier PLS-00103 exception because that's not a valid comparison operator.
	`DECLARE`
	`  TYPE list IS TABLE OF INTEGER;`
	`  a LIST := list();`
	`BEGIN`
	`  IF a IS A SET THEN`
	`    dbms_output.put_line('"a" is a set.');`
	`  END IF;`
	`END;`
	`/`
	This returns the following output:
	`"a" is empty.`

LIKE	The LIKE operator allows you to check whether a variable value is part of another value. The comparison can be made with the SQL lexical underscore (_) for a single-character wildcard, or % for a multiple-character wildcard. The % lexical value inside a string is not equivalent to its use as an anchoring attribute indicator in PL/SQL.
	`BEGIN`
	`  IF 'Str%' LIKE 'String' THEN`
	`    dbms_output.put_line('Match');`
	`  END IF;`
	`END;`
	`/`
	This returns the following output:
	`Match.`

TABLE 5-1. *Comparison Operators*

Operator	Description

MEMBER OF	The MEMBER OF is a logical comparison operator. It lets you find out whether an element is a member of a collection. It only works with collections of scalar SQL data types. It returns true when the element exits in a collection and returns false when it doesn't.
	`DECLARE`
	`  TYPE list IS TABLE OF VARCHAR2(10);`
	`  n VARCHAR2(10) := 'One';`
	`  a LIST := list('One','Two','Three');`
	`BEGIN`
	`  IF n MEMBER OF a THEN`
	`    dbms_output.put_line('"n" is a set.');`
	`  END IF;`
	`END;`
	`/`
	When the left operand element is null, the operator returns false. This means that you should always check for a value before using this comparison operator.
	It prints the following when successful:
	`"n" is empty.`

NOT	NOT is a logical negation operator, and it allows you to check for the opposite of a Boolean state of an expression, provided it isn't null.
	`BEGIN`
	`  IF NOT FALSE THEN`
	`    dbms_output.put_line('True.');`
	`  END IF;`
	`END;`
	`/`
	When the expression or value is null, the NOT operator changes nothing. There is no opposite of null, and *a logical negation of null is also a null*. This returns the following output because FALSE is a Boolean literal and TRUE is the only thing not false when you exclude null values:
	`True.`

OR	The OR operator allows you to combine two comparisons into one. This operator makes the combination statement true when one or the other statement is true. PL/SQL uses short-circuit evaluation, which means it stops evaluating a combination comparison when any one value is false.
	`BEGIN`
	`  IF 1 = 1 OR 1 = 2 THEN`
	`    dbms_output.put_line('True.');`
	`  END IF;`
	`END;`
	`/`
	This returns the following output because of one of the two statements is true:
	`True.`

(continued)

TABLE 5-1. *Comparison Operators*

Operator	Description

`SUBMULTISET`	The `SUBMULTISET` operator lets you check whether a varray or table collection is a subset of a mirrored data type. It returns true if some to all elements in the left set are found in the right set. Note that this operator does not check for a proper subset, which is one item less than the full set or identity set.
	`DECLARE`
	`  TYPE list IS TABLE OF INTEGER;`
	`  a LIST := list(1,2,3);`
	`  b LIST := list(1,2,3,4);`
	`BEGIN`
	`  IF a SUBMULTISET b THEN`
	`    dbms_output.put_line('Valid subset.');`
	`  END IF;`
	`END;`
	`/`
	This prints the following when successful:
	`Valid subset.`

TABLE 5-1. *Comparison Operators*

You also need to know the order of operation for comparison operators. Table 5-2 lists their order of operation. You can override the order of operation by enclosing subordinate expressions in parentheses. PL/SQL compares any expression inside parentheses as a whole result. PL/SQL applies any remaining comparison operators in an expression by their order of operation.

Order	Operator	Definition
1	`**`	Exponentiation
2	`+, -`	Identity and negation
3	`*, /`	Multiplication and division
4	`+, -, ||`	Addition, subtraction, and concatenation

5	`=, <, >, <=, >=, <>, !=, ~=, ^=,`
	`BETWEEN, IN, IS EMPTY, IS NULL,`
	`IS A SET, LIKE, MEMBER OF, SUBMULTISET`
		Comparison

6	`AND`	Conjunction
7	`NOT`	Logical negation
8	OR	Inclusion

TABLE 5-2. *Order of Operations*

X Value	Expression	Result	Negation Expression	Result
True	X is True	True	X is *not* True	False
False	X is True	False	X is *not* True	True
Null	X is True	Null	X is *not* True	True

TABLE 5-3. *Single-Variable Truth Table*

Single-branching expressions return a true, false, or null. Both false and null are not true when you evaluate whether an expression is true. Likewise, both true and null are not false when you evaluate an expression as false. A null expression is never true or false. Table 5-3 maps the possible outcomes in a truth table.

Multiple-branching expressions require two-sided truth tables: one table for the conjunction operator, `AND`, and another for the inclusion operator, `OR`. The conjunction operator creates expressions where you resolve the combination of two expressions, where both are true. The whole statement is not true when one is false or null. Table 5-4 maps the possible outcomes of conjunctive truth—when X and Y expressions are true, false, or null.

Multiple-branching expressions also require a two-sided truth table to examine how the inclusion operator works. *Inclusion* is where two things are true when one or the other is true, but because of null expressions the whole statement can be true, false, or null. Table 5-5 maps the possible outcomes of inclusive truth—when X or Y expressions are true, false, or null.

Inclusive logic performs what's known as short-circuit evaluation, which is known as minimal or McCarthy evaluation (after John McCarthy, a famous computer scientist). The beauty of short-circuit evaluation is that it pares (or eliminates) the need to check other values. That's because you only need one true value for the entire statement to be true.

Tables 5-4 and 5-5 display results from asking whether the values are true. The results change when you ask whether one or both of the values are false. True values become false values. False values become true values. Unfortunately, null values remain false values. The truth tables should help you plan how you will develop your branching logic in `IF` and `CASE` statements. The same logical outcomes extend to three or more expressions, but they don't render in two-dimensional tables.

This section has provided detail to support the following branching subsections, which examine single-branching and multiple-branching statements that use `IF` statements, and multiple-branching statements that use simple and searched `CASE` statements. The subsections are grouped by the `IF` and `CASE` statements.

X and Y	Y is True	Y is False	Y is Null
X is True	True	False	False
X is False	False	False	False
X is Null	False	False	False

TABLE 5-4. *Conjunctive Truth Table—X and Y Expressions are TRUE or FALSE, or NULL*

X or Y	Y is True	Y is False	Y is Null
X is True	True	True	True
X is False	True	False	False
X is Null	True	False	False

TABLE 5-5. *Inclusive Truth Table—X or Y Expressions Are TRUE or FALSE, or NULL*

IF Statements

The `IF` statement supports single-branching and multiple-branching statements. `IF` statements are blocks. They start with a beginning identifier, or reserved word, and end with an ending identifier and a semicolon. All statement blocks require at least one statement, just as anonymous or named blocks do.

`IF` statements evaluate a condition. The condition can be any comparison expression or set of comparison expressions that evaluates to a logical true or false. You can compare two literals or variables of the same type. The variables can actually have different data types, as long as they implicitly or you explicitly convert one of the two types to match the other (see Figure 4-2 in Chapter 4 for the implicit conversion chart). A Boolean variable can replace a comparison operation. You also can compare the results of two function calls as you would two variables or a variable and a single function call, provided the comparison returns a Boolean variable. The valid comparison operators are presented in Table 4-1 and Table 5-1.

If-then-else Statements

The if-then-else statement is a single-branching statement. It evaluates a condition and then runs the code immediately after the condition when the condition is met. The prototype for an if-then-else statement is

```
IF [NOT] [comparison_expression | boolean_value] [AND | OR]
         [comparison_expression | boolean_value] THEN
  true_execution_statements
[ELSE
  unmet_condition_statements ]
END IF;
```

You use the optional `NOT` (the logical negation operator) to check for a false comparison result. While there is only one `[AND | OR]` clause in the `IF` statement, there is no limit to how many conditions you can evaluate. The `ELSE` block is optional. `IF` statements without an `ELSE` block only execute code when a condition is met.

In its simplest form, the following is an if-then statement. It demonstrates an if-then statement comparing two numeric literals:

```
SQL> BEGIN
       IF 1 = 1 THEN
         dbms_output.put_line('Condition met!');
       END IF;
     END;
     /
```

Note that parentheses around the comparison statement on line 2 aren't required. This is a convenience compared to some other programming languages that require them, such as JavaScript and PHP. The equivalent logic using a Boolean variable instead of the comparison operation is

```
SQL> DECLARE
  2    lv_equal BOOLEAN NOT NULL := TRUE;
  3  BEGIN
  4    IF lv_equal THEN
  5      dbms_output.put_line('Condition met!');
  6    END IF;
  7  END;
  9  /
```

Line 4 uses a "lazy" comparison because it evaluates the variable as true. Some developers think it's unwise to use lazy comparisons in PL/SQL, but I disagree. A verbose (or wordy) comparison would change line 4 to the following but not alter the outcome:

```
  4    IF lv_equal = TRUE THEN
```

When you evaluate a Boolean variable or expression that returns a null value, the `IF` statement can't be true and returns a false value. Fortunately, we declare the `lv_equal` variable on line 2 to *disallow a null* value and we assign a `true` value to the variable.

Function Calls as Expressions

When you call a function, you provide values or variables, and the function returns a result. If the function returns a variable-length string, it is called a *string expression* because it yields a string as a result. The result is like a string literal, which is covered in Chapter 4. Alternatively, function definitions can return any other scalar variable data types, and they become expressions that yield values of those data types.

The following example compares a single variable value and an expression return value (or function call return value) on line 16:

```
SQL> DECLARE
  2    -- Declare a local variable.
  3    lv_thing_one  VARCHAR2(5) := 'Three';
  4
  5    -- Declare a local function.
  6    FUNCTION ordinal (n NUMBER) RETURN VARCHAR2 IS
  7      /* Declare a local table collection type. */
  8      TYPE ordinal_type IS TABLE OF VARCHAR2(5);
  9      /* Declare and initialize collection variable. */
 10      lv_ordinal ORDINAL_TYPE :=
 11        ordinal_type('One','Two','Three','Four');
 12    BEGIN
 13      RETURN lv_ordinal(3);
 14    END;
```

(continued)

```
BEGIN
  IF lv_thing_one = ordinal(3) THEN
    dbms_output.put_line('['||ordinal(3)||']');
  END IF;
END;
/
```

Comparisons work with literal values, variable values, and expression return values (or function call return values). The `lv_thing_one` variable value and the expression value returned from the `ordinal` function are found to be equal. The program prints the following (provided the SQL*Plus `SERVEROUTPUT` environment variable is enabled):

```
Three
```

The return value of any function call is an expression or a runtime value that can be compared against the content of a variable value, literal value, or another function call return value. You can also pass a function call return value as a call parameter value to another function or procedure.

You should anticipate runtime behaviors such as receiving a variable or expression result that may be a null value, and use the `NVL` built-in function where possible to resolve them. Doing so avoids unexpected outcomes. The default behavior is fine, provided you want your program to *treat a null value as false*.

Let's assume treating the `lv_equal` variable as a pseudo constant isn't acceptable because the variable is dynamically assigned a value. That means you need to safeguard the behavior of the *if true* comparison operation, and you would do that by using an `NVL` function call on line 4 like

```
4     IF NVL(lv_equal,TRUE) THEN
```

The `NVL` function guarantees that the question answered is true when the `lv_equal` variable's value is null or false. Reversing the question, we would ask a negation question such as *if not false* with the following syntax on line 4:

```
4     IF NOT NVL(lv_equal,FALSE) THEN
```

In single-branching logic, this works well, but in multiple-branching logic, you may need to enclose the `lv_equal` variable in multiple places. Coding solutions in multiple places is a bad idea in any programming language.

You have a better solution when working with dynamic variables. Before you apply the business logic, assign the `lv_equal` variable a default value when it arrives as a null value. The following does that by setting the default value to true:

```
4   IF NOT lv_logic = TRUE AND NOT lv_logic = FALSE THEN
5     lv_logic := TRUE;
6   END IF;
```

Line 4 checks two negation questions, *if not true* and *if not false*. The only time both of those are true is when the variable's value is null. Line 5 assigns true when the variable's value is null, and that guarantees that the comparative logic supporting the business logic resolves correctly.

Having enabled SERVEROUTPUT in SQL*Plus (check Appendix A for instructions), either of these anonymous blocks resolves the comparison as true and prints the following:

```
Condition met!
```

Branching out, you can build an if-then-else statement like

```
SQL> BEGIN
  2    IF 1 = 2 THEN
  3      dbms_output.put_line('Condition met!');
  4    ELSE
  5      dbms_output.put_line('Condition not met!');
  6    END IF;
  7  END;
  8  /
```

The anonymous block resolves the comparison on line 2 as false and prints the ELSE block statement:

```
Condition not met!
```

You can support variables for the literals in these examples or function calls that return matching or convertible data types for comparison. A single function that returns a BOOLEAN data type also works in lieu of the Boolean example.

If-then-elsif-then-else Statements

The *if-then-elsif-then-else* statement is a multiple-branching statement. It evaluates a series of conditions and then runs the code immediately after the first successfully met condition. It exits the block after processing the block and it ignores any subsequently successful evaluations.

The prototype for an *if-then-elsif-then-else* statement is

```
IF     [NOT] {comparison_expression | boolean_value}  [[AND | OR]
             {comparison_expression | boolean_value}] [[AND | OR]
             ... ] THEN
  true_if_execution_statements
[ELSIF [NOT] {comparison_expression | boolean_value}  [[AND | OR]
             {comparison_expression | boolean_value}] [[AND | OR]
             ... ] THEN
  true_elsif_execution_statements ]
[ELSE
  all_unmet_condition_statements ]
END IF;
```

You use the optional NOT operator to check for false comparisons. While there are only two [AND | OR] clauses in the foregoing prototype, the ellipses indicate there isn't a limit on how many conjunction or inclusive conditions you evaluate. While the ELSE block is optional, without it a condition must be met or nothing is done in the conditional block. You should always include an ELSE block even if it only performs a *do-nothing statement*, like a NULL;, because it tells anybody who subsequently supports your code you considered the possibility.

The following demonstrates an *if-then-elsif-then-else* statement where the first two comparisons are true and the third false:

```
SQL> DECLARE
  2    lv_equal BOOLEAN NOT NULL := TRUE;
  3  BEGIN
  4    IF 1 = 1 THEN
  5      dbms_output.put_line('Condition one met!');
  6    ELSIF lv_equal THEN
  7      dbms_output.put_line('Condition two met!');
  8    ELSIF 1 = 2 THEN
  9      dbms_output.put_line('Condition three met!');
 10    END IF;
 11  END;
 12  /
```

The anonymous block resolves the first comparison on line 4 as true and prints the following:

```
Condition one met!
```

As mentioned, the *if-then-elsif-then-else* statement exits after the first comparison is found to be true. That's why the second true comparison on line 6 isn't processed. The default `ELSE` condition runs only when none of the conditions are met.

CASE Statements

There are two types of `CASE` statements in PL/SQL. Both define a selector. A *selector* is a variable, function, or expression that the `CASE` statement attempts to match in `WHEN` blocks. The selector immediately follows the reserved word `CASE`. If you don't provide a selector, PL/SQL adds a Boolean *true* as the selector. You can use any PL/SQL data type as a selector except a `BLOB`, `BFILE`, or composite type. Chapter 4 qualifies composite types as records, objects, collections, and system reference cursors.

The generic `CASE` statement prototype is

```
CASE [{ TRUE | FALSE | selector_variable }]
  WHEN [ criterion | expression ] THEN
    criterion_statements
 [WHEN [ criterion | expression ] THEN
    criterion_statements ]
 [WHEN [ ... ] THEN
    ... ]
  ELSE
    else_block_statements
END CASE;
```

Simple `CASE` statement selectors are variables that use or functions that return valid data types other than Boolean types. Searched `CASE` statement selectors are Boolean variables or functions that return a Boolean variable. The default selector is a Boolean *true*. A searched `CASE` statement can omit the selector when seeking a true expression.

Like the `IF` statement, `CASE` statements have an `ELSE` clause. The `ELSE` clause works like it does in the `IF` statement, but with one twist: you can't omit the `ELSE` block or you will raise a

CASE_NOT_FOUND or PLS-06592 error when the selector is not found. PL/SQL includes this default ELSE condition when you fail to provide one and a runtime execution fails to match a WHEN block.

CASE statements are blocks. They start with a beginning identifier, or reserved word, and end with an ending identifier and a semicolon. All statement blocks require at least one statement, just as anonymous or named blocks do. CASE statements require at least one statement in each WHEN block and in the ELSE block.

Like the *if-then-elsif-then-else* statement, CASE statements evaluate WHEN blocks by sequentially checking for a match against the selector. The first WHEN block that matches the selector runs and exits the CASE block. *There is no fall-through behavior available in PL/SQL.* The ELSE block runs only when no WHEN block matches the selector.

Simple CASE Statements

The simple CASE statement sets a selector that is any PL/SQL data type except a BLOB, BFILE, or composite type. The prototype for a simple CASE statement ignores Boolean selector values and is

```
CASE selector_variable
  WHEN criterion THEN
    criterion_statements
 [WHEN criterion THEN
    criterion_statements
 [WHEN ... THEN
    ... ]]
  ELSE
    all_unmet_condition_statements
END CASE;
```

Simple CASE statements *require that you provide a selector*. You can add many more WHEN blocks than shown, but the more numerous the possibilities, the less effective the CASE statement is as a solution. This is a manageable solution when you typically have ten or fewer choices. Maintainability declines as the list of WHEN blocks grows.

The following example uses a NUMBER data type as the selector:

```
SQL> DECLARE
       lv_selector NUMBER := 0;
     BEGIN
       CASE lv_selector
         WHEN 0 THEN
           dbms_output.put_line('Case 0!');
         WHEN 1 THEN
           dbms_output.put_line('Case 1!');
         ELSE
           dbms_output.put_line('No match!');
       END CASE;
     END;
     /
```

The anonymous block resolves the first comparison as true because the lv_selector variable contains a value of 0. It then prints

```
Case 0!
```

Therefore, the first `WHEN` block matches the selector value. The `CASE` statement ceases evaluation and runs the matching `WHEN` block before exiting the statement. You can substitute other PL/SQL data types for the selector value. The `CHAR`, `NCHAR`, and `VARCHAR2` data types are some possible choices.

Searched CASE Statements

The selector is implicitly set for a searched `CASE` statement unless you want to search for a false condition. *You must explicitly provide a false selector.* Sometimes a searched `CASE` selector value is dynamic based on some runtime logic. When that's the case, you can substitute a function returning a Boolean variable, provided you dynamically set the selector.

Naturally, this is a case where you must *always take precautions to avoid a null value as the selector*. Since the searched `CASE` statement only uses a Boolean selector or comparison expression, you should enclose it in an `NVL` call returning a true or false Boolean value.

The prototype for a simple `CASE` statement is

```
CASE [{ TRUE | FALSE | selector_variable}]
  WHEN {criterion | expression}
  [{AND | OR } {criterion | expression}
  [{AND | OR } ... ]] THEN
    criterion1_statements
 [WHEN {criterion | expression}
  [{AND | OR } {criterion | expression}]
  [{AND | OR } ... ] THEN]
    criterion_statements
 [WHEN { ... } THEN
    ... ]
  ELSE
    block_statements;
END CASE;
```

Like the simple `CASE` statement, you can add many more `WHEN` blocks than shown, but the more numerous the possibilities, the less effective this type of solution is. The following searched `CASE` statement examines searched comparison expressions for truth:

```
SQL> BEGIN
  2    CASE
  3      WHEN 1 = 2 THEN
  4        dbms_output.put_line('Case [1 = 2]');
  5      WHEN 2 = 2 AND 'Something' = 'Something' THEN
  6        dbms_output.put_line('Case [2 = 2]');
  7      ELSE
  8        dbms_output.put_line('No match');
  9    END CASE;
 10  END;
 11  /
```

The single comparison on line 3 fails, while the second conjunctive (a formal and fancy word for two or more comparisons) comparison on line 5 succeeds. It succeeds because it returns true for both comparison operations and returns true. A true result matches the selector's default value of true, which means the program enters that block and prints the result from line 6:

```
Case [2 = 2]
```

If the `CASE` statement searched for a false condition, the selector would match the first `WHEN` block and print that 1 equals 2. You can also use a comparison expression as the selector.

Conditional Compilation Statements

Beginning with Oracle Database 10*g* Release 2, you can use conditional compilation. Conditional compilation lets you include debugging logic or special-purpose logic that runs only when session-level variables are set. The following command sets a PL/SQL compile-time variable `DEBUG` equal to `1`:

```
ALTER SESSION SET PLSQL_CCFLAGS = 'debug:1';
```

Note that the compile-time flag is case insensitive. You can also set compile-time variables to *true* or *false* so they act like Boolean variables. When you want to set more than one conditional compilation flag, you need to use the following syntax:

```
ALTER SESSION SET PLSQL_CCFLAGS = 'name1:value1 [, name(n+1):value(n+1) ]';
```

The conditional compilation parameters are stored as name and value pairs in the `PLSQL_CCFLAG` database parameter. The following program uses the `$IF`, `$THEN`, `$ELSIF`, `$ELSE`, and `$END` reserved preprocessor control tokens to create a conditional compilation code block:

```
SQL> BEGIN
  2    NULL;  -- This is required when the PLSQL_CCFLAGS value is unset.
  3    $IF $$DEBUG = 1 $THEN
  4      dbms_output.put_line('Debug Level 1 Enabled.');
  5    $ELSIF $$DEBUG = 2 $THEN
  6      dbms_output.put_line('Debug Level 2 Enabled.');
  7    $ELSE
  8      dbms_output.put_line('Debug Level other than 1 or 2 Enabled.');
  9    $END
 10  END;
 11  /
```

While lines 3 and 5 compare the `$$DEBUG` value against a numeric literal, this would also work with dynamic variables, like an `&input` substitution variable (check the "Passing Parameters to SQL*Plus Script Files" section in Appendix A for more coverage of substitution variables). When you set `PLSQL_CCFLAGS` equal to 1, this prints

```
Debug Level 1 Enabled.
```

Conditional code blocks differ from normal if-then-else code blocks. Most notably, the `$END` directive closes the block, instead of an `END IF` and semicolon. The `$END` directive ends a conditional statement. An `END IF` closes an `IF` code block. The syntax rules require that closing blocks end with a semicolon or statement terminator. Statement terminators are not conditional lexical units, and their occurrence without a preceding code statement triggers a compile-time error.

The `$$` symbol denotes a PL/SQL conditional compile-time variable. The `ALTER SESSION` statement lets you set conditional compile-time variables. You set them in the `PLSQL_CCFLAGS` session variable. You can set one or many variables in the `PLSQL_CCFLAGS` session variable. All variables are constants until the session ends or they are replaced. You replace these variables by reusing the `ALTER SESSION` statement. All previous conditional compile-time variables cease to exist when you reset the `PLSQL_CCFLAGS` session variable.

The rules governing conditional compilation are set by the SQL parser. You cannot use conditional compilation in SQL object types. This limitation also applies to varray and table collections. Conditional compilation differs in functions and procedures. The behavior changes depending on whether the function or procedure has a formal parameter list. You can use conditional compilation after the opening parenthesis of a formal parameter list, like

```
SQL> CREATE OR REPLACE FUNCTION conditional_type
  ( magic_number $IF $$DEBUG = 1 $THEN SIMPLE_NUMBER $ELSE NUMBER $END )
  RETURN NUMBER IS
  BEGIN
    RETURN magic_number;
  END;
  /
```

Alternatively, you can use conditional compilation after the `AS` or `IS` keyword in no-parameter functions or procedures. Conditional compilation can also be used both inside the formal parameter list and after the `AS` or `IS` in parameter functions or procedures.

Conditional compilation can only occur after the `BEGIN` keyword in triggers and anonymous block program units. Please note that *you cannot encapsulate a placeholder, or bind variable, inside a conditional compilation block.*

You also have predefined inquiry directives with conditional compilation:

- **`$$PLSQL_UNIT`** Returns an empty string for an anonymous block and returns the uppercase name of the function or procedure in a named block.
- **`$$PLSQL_OWNER`** Returns the database user who owns the current program unit, and it is a new predefined inquiry directive with Oracle Database 12*c*.
- **`$$PLSQL_TYPE`** Returns the current program unit's type, and it is also a new predefined inquiry directive with Oracle Database 12*c*.
- **`$$PLSQL_LINE`** Returns an integer for the current line number in the PL/SQL block.

You can test the `$$PLSQL_UNIT` directive in an anonymous block by comparing it against an empty string or null value. The following shows how to use the `$$PLSQL_UNIT` directive in a named block:

```
SQL> CREATE OR REPLACE PROCEDURE running_procedure IS
  BEGIN
    -- Show a predefined inquiry directive.
    IF $$PLSQL_UNIT IS NOT NULL THEN
      dbms_output.put_line(
        'This is line ['||$$PLSQL_LINE||'] of ['||$$PLSQL_UNIT||'].');
    END IF;
  END;
  /
```

Line 4 checks for a not-null `$$PLSQL_UNIT` value and lines 5 and 6 print the `$$PLSQL_LINE` and `$PLSQL_UNIT` directive values. You can run the procedure with the following command:

```
SQL> EXECUTE running_procedure;
```

It prints

```
This is line [6] of [RUNNING_PROCEDURE].
```

Take note that the call to the `PUT_LINE` function of the `DBMS_OUTPUT` package starts on line 5 but the `$$PLSQL_LINE` directive returns its line number even though it's a call parameter to the function call started on line 5.

The last element of conditional compilation is the predefined error directive, which is `$ERROR`. It takes a single variable-length string, which must be a static string literal, and it's terminated by an `$END` reserved preprocessor control token, not by a semicolon. You raise an exception when you terminate the string with a semicolon. Here's an anonymous block to show you how to use it:

```
SQL> BEGIN
  2    NULL;  -- This is required when the PLSQL_CCFLAGS value is unset.
  3    $ERROR 'Conditional User-defined Error' $END
  4  END;
  5  /
```

Line 3 throws an exception whether or not the `PLSQL_CCFLAGS` session variable is set, so use it sparingly. Conditional compilation is best suited to named blocks and lets you turn on debugging in your code without refactoring when a bug occurs in production.

Review Section

This section has described the following points about conditional compilation statements:

- The PL/SQL language supports single-branching and multiple-branching statements without fall-through, and multiple-branching statements use either the `ELSIF` or `CASE` statement.
- You can use conjunction (`AND` logic) or inclusion (`OR` logic) in conditional statements.
- The PL/SQL language implements three-valued logic with the possibility of true, false, and null.
- The `NVL` statement lets you reduce three-valued logic problems to two-valued logic in conditional statements.
- You need to assign default values to dynamic variables when comparison values may fail because they hold null values.
- The PL/SQL language supports both simple and searched `CASE` statements.
- Searched `CASE` statements use a default selector of true but can be configured to use false as the selector value.
- Conditional compilation supports any number of conditional compilation flags, like the `$$DEBUG` example used in this chapter.

Conditional compilation also supports predefined inquiry directives, like `$$PLSQL_LINE` and `$$PLSQL_UNIT`.

Iterative Statements

Iterative statements are blocks that let you repeat a statement or set of statements. There are two types of iterative statements. A guard-on-entry loop guards entry into the loop before running repeatable statements, and a guard-on-exit loop guards exit from the loop. Whether guarding entry or exit, the value controlling the exit from the loop is generally called a *sentinel value*.

The sentinel value can be one or more comparison operations, or the value or values of Boolean variables or expressions that are true or not. Please note that *not* means untrue—and does not mean false—because databases use three-valued logic. If this raises a question in your mind, revisit the three-valued logic discussion in the "If-then-else Statements" section earlier in the chapter.

A loop that only guards exit guarantees that its code block is always run once, and it is commonly called a *repeat-until* or *do-while* loop. Figure 5-2 shows the execution logic for these two iteration statement types.

The PL/SQL language supports simple loops, `FOR` loops, `FORALL` loops, and `WHILE` loops. It does not formally support a repeat-until loop block. You can use the simple loop statement to mimic the behavior of a repeat-until or do-while loop. `WHILE` loops work with arrays and lists, but they are more commonly used with cursors in database programming. Cursors are `SELECT` statements that are processed row by row or by batches of rows from the database. Cursor loops are covered immediately after this introduction to iterative statements, in the "Cursor Structures" section.

Simple Loop Statements

Simple loops are explicit block structures. A simple loop starts with the `LOOP` reserved word and ends with the `END LOOP` reserved words. Simple loops require that you manage any loop index value and their exit criteria. Typically, simple loops are used where easier solutions don't quite fit. Easier solutions are typically reserved for the popular `FOR` loop statement because it manages the loop index and exit criteria for you.

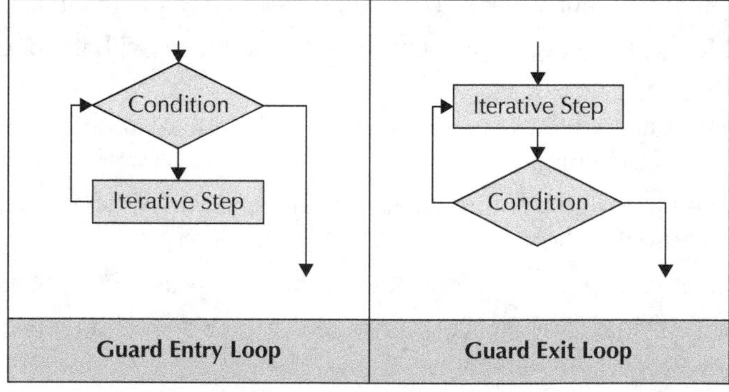

FIGURE 5-2. *Iterative statement logic flows*

There are two prototypes for a simple loop, the difference being that one exits at the top of the loop and the other exits at the end of the loop. Exits are critical in loops unless you want to write an infinite loop, which isn't too often. You exit loops through a credentials process, which is much like presenting your ticket at a theater or concert, as explained shortly. Programs perform this task by checking the results of comparative operations, or Boolean expressions or variables, like *true or false*.

A guard-on-entry loop blocks entry to the loop unless one or more conditions are met (your credentials are validated). To block entry to any loop, you must place conditional statements at the top of the loop. The conditional statements are effectively the guard at your entrance gate. The program's entry guard checks whether the sentinel value allows entry.

Entry guards in programming do one of two things:

- Let you run the operations inside the loop over and over, known as *iteration*, until you fail to meet the entry criteria
- Prevent you from running the operations inside the loop when you fail to have the proper credentials for entry

Sometimes, programmers need to run the code inside the loop at least once before moving on to the next part of their program. In that event, a guard-on-entry loop is a bad choice. You should choose a guard-on-exit loop, which acts like a traditional repeat-until or do-while loop.

A guard-on-exit loop allows you to run the internal logic of the loop at least once. That's like admitting everybody into the theater with or without a ticket until all seats are taken and then asking those without tickets to leave in order to make room for those with tickets. While the theater analogy would most likely be a disaster, a program can apply this logic easily.

A guard-on-exit loop checks the results of comparative operations, or Boolean expressions or variables, at the end of the repeating block of statements. The loop lets you run the logic again while the condition or conditions are met, and you iterate through the loop until the condition or conditions are no longer true. The logic that tests whether you can enter or leave is known as a conditional `EXIT` statement. `EXIT` statements immediately stop code execution and branch you out of the loop statement.

The following examples show techniques for guard-on-entry and guard-on-exit loops:

Guard-on-Entry Loop

```
LOOP
 [counter_management_statements]
  IF NOT entry_condition THEN
    EXIT;
  END IF;
  repeating_statements
END LOOP;
```

Guard-on-Exit Loop

```
LOOP
  repeating_statements
 [counter_management_
statements]
  IF exit_condition THEN
    EXIT;
  END IF;
END LOOP;
```

PL/SQL simplifies writing an `EXIT` statement by providing the `EXIT WHEN` statement, which eliminates the need to write an `IF` statement around the `EXIT` statement.

One of the neat features of PL/SQL is the conditional `EXIT` statement. A conditional `EXIT` statement collapses the `IF` block into a single line of code. The following examples show techniques for guard-on-entry and guard-on-exit loops with conditional `EXIT` statements:

Guard-on-Entry Loop

```
LOOP
 [counter_management_statements;]
  EXIT WHEN NOT entry_condition;
  repeating_statements;
END LOOP;
```

Guard-on-Exit Loop

```
LOOP
  repeating_statements;
 [counter_management_
statements;]
  EXIT WHEN exit_condition;
END LOOP;
```

You should take *careful note* that the counter management logic for guard-on-entry loops must precede the exit management logic. Some developers mistakenly think it belongs below the repeating logic because that's where it goes in a guard-on-exit loop. Any language, like PL/SQL, that supports a `GOTO` or `CONTINUE` statement requires that the counter logic precede the exit management logic in a loop. That's because a `CONTINUE` statement stops an iteration through the loop and restarts at top of the loop. A badly crafted `GOTO` and label combination also could do the same thing. If the counter logic follows the repeating statements, it would be skipped anytime the `CONTINUE` statement runs. Skipping the counter management logic can create an undesired infinite loop.

While the preceding logic seems simple and direct, it often appears to get lost in the process of writing code. That's because databases aren't two-valued logic models. They are three-valued logic models, and that means you must manage the possibility of null values. Null values typically occur when you're writing dynamic loops rather than static ones. Dynamic loops require *safeguarding logic* prior to loop entry, regardless of whether it's a guard-on-entry loop or a guard-on-exit loop.

Static Simple Loops

Let's examine anonymous block programs to demonstrate a guard-on-entry loop and a guard-on-exit loop. Although, you should note that anonymous and named block programs use PL/SQL simple loops. We can identify simple loops based on the starting and ending reserved words—`LOOP` and `END LOOP`.

Guard-on-Entry Loops The loop's entry guard compares the value of the `lv_counter` variable and a numeric constant to see if one is greater than the other. While that condition is true, the program continues to run the statements inside the loop.

The following program is the simplest approach to a guard-on-entry loop because it guarantees both of the operands aren't null values:

```
SQL> DECLARE
    lv_counter NUMBER := 1;
BEGIN
    LOOP
      -- Increment-by-one logic.
      lv_counter := lv_counter + 1;
      -- Entry guard, with a sentinel value of 3.
      IF NOT lv_counter < 3 THEN
        EXIT;
      END IF;
```

```
11        -- Repeatable statements.
12        dbms_output.put_line('Iteration ['||lv_counter||']');
13      END LOOP;
14    END;
15    /
```

It prints the following because it guards *re-entry* (iteration) after running twice:

```
Iteration [1]
Iteration [2]
```

Line 2 declares an `lv_counter` variable with an initial value of 1. Most database collections use 1-based numbering rather than 0-based numbering, which means we generally start with 1 when we iterate through data.

Line 6 is our index counter, and it's the first thing that must happen in the loop. Line 8 is our entry guard, and it's the second thing that must happen in the loop. The entry guard bars entry to all unqualified entrants. The index counter doesn't need to precede the exit guard in this example because the loops aren't interrupted by a `GOTO` or `CONTINUE` statement. However, the index counter *must* precede the exit guard when a `CONTINUE` statement interrupts the loop inside the repeatable statements section. The best practice is to always position the index counter as the first set of instructions at the top of a guard-on-entry loop.

The entry guard asks a negation question, *if not less than 3?*, because we want to exit when that condition isn't met. If we wrote the logic in an affirming statement, it would look like this:

```
 8        IF lv_counter < 3 THEN
 9          NULL; -- A do-nothing statement.
10        ELSE
11          EXIT;
12        END IF;
```

Three lines of code became five lines of code because we move the `EXIT` to the `ELSE` block and include a *do-nothing* `NULL;` statement in the `IF` block. The change also makes the code less readable, and is typically more work than most developers would like to do. However, we can make the entry guard simpler by adopting Oracle's `EXIT WHEN` approach on line 8, as shown:

```
 7      -- Entry guard, with a sentinel value of 3.
 8        EXIT WHEN NOT lv_counter < 3;
```

The `EXIT WHEN` statement takes one line instead of three lines for an if-then statement or five lines for an if-then-else block. With little effort our program becomes shorter and clearer without changing the logic.

NOTE

Unlike C, C++, C#, and Java, the PL/SQL language doesn't support unary operators for index counter logic.

We've covered the basics of static sentinel values for guard-on-entry loops. Please remember that guard-on-entry loops prevent you from running their internal logic once before checking the sentinel value. Next, we look at static guard-on-exit loops.

Guard-on-Exit Loops Guard-on-exit loops let you run the code once before checking whether you should run it again. They're actually more common than guard-on-entry loops and appear as repeat-until and do-while loops in other programming languages. Guard-on-exit loops are popular because their repeatable statement logic is always run at least once (but never more than the sentinel value allows), whereas a guard-on-entry loop prevents running the repeatable statement logic until the sentinel value is met.

Hopefully, you're sold on using the `EXIT WHEN` statement from the previous section. We use only the `EXIT WHEN` statement as the exit condition in this section. That means we won't repeat the earlier demonstration of an if-then or if-then-else exit guard.

The following guard-on-exit loop uses the same basic components as the guard-on-entry loop shown previously:

```
SQL> DECLARE
  2    lv_counter NUMBER := 1;
  3  BEGIN
  4    LOOP
  5      -- Run once for all and then for qualified iterations.
  6      dbms_output.put_line('Iteration ['||lv_counter||']');
  7      -- Increment-by-one logic at least once.
  8      lv_counter := lv_counter + 1;
  9      -- Exit guard, with a static sentinel value of 3.
 10      EXIT WHEN NOT lv_counter < 3;
 11    END LOOP;
 12  END;
 13  /
```

Like the entry guard example in the previous section, the `lv_counter` variable is initialized before entering the loop to avoid problems with null values. The exit guard is the last statement in the loop on line 10 and bars all disqualified entrants from rerunning the repeatable statements of the loop when the value isn't less than the sentinel value of 3.

Static guard values are simple, and the best place to begin understanding how sentinel values work. Assuming you understand them, the next step is to master dynamic guard values.

Dynamic Simple Loops

A simple loop is dynamic when you can't guarantee the loop index or sentinel value at compilation time. Compilation occurs when we create or replace functions, procedures, package specifications or bodies, and (evolve) object types or bodies.

Anytime the index value, sentinel value, or data set arrives dynamically at runtime, we must take additional precautions to guarantee the integrity of our loops. That means adding a *safeguard* at the top of the loop that converts any null values to valid not-null values.

A schema-level procedure can demonstrate dynamic behaviors for both ascending and descending loops. Ascending loops can assume one thing when they traverse a SQL collection in the Oracle database: that the first element has an index value of 1. Descending loops can assume that their start position is the return value from applying the `COUNT` function from Oracle's Collection API against the collection (as covered in Chapter 6).

We need to create a SQL collection before creating the procedure that demonstrates safeguards for a guard-on-entry loop. The following creates an Attribute Data Type (ADT), or list of a scalar data type, of 30 character strings (introduced in Chapter 3):

```
SQL> CREATE OR REPLACE
       TYPE elf_table IS TABLE OF VARCHAR2(30);
     /
```

The ascending procedure has three formal parameters: the `pv_index` parameter takes the starting loop index value, the `pv_sentinel` parameter takes the limit value for the loop, and the `pv_elves` parameter takes an instance of `elves`. Any of these formal parameters can receive null values when you call the procedure, and safeguarding against potential null values is important. Safeguards protect the integrity of the loop within the procedure and avoid runtime errors.

The following procedure includes safeguard logic before the loop and implements a guard-on-entry loop:

```
SQL> CREATE OR REPLACE PROCEDURE ascending
     ( pv_index      NUMBER
     , pv_sentinel   NUMBER
     , pv_elves      ELF_TABLE ) IS

       /* Declare local index and sentinel variables. */
       lv_counter    NUMBER;
       lv_sentinel   NUMBER;

       /* Declare an empty list, which has a size of zero. */
       lv_elves      ELF_TABLE := elf_table();
     BEGIN
       /* Assign the starting index value. */
       lv_counter := NVL(pv_index,1);

       /* Check whether incoming list has elements. */
       IF pv_elves IS NOT EMPTY THEN
         /* Size the sentinel and assign the list to a local clone. */
         lv_sentinel := NVL(pv_sentinel,pv_elves.COUNT);
         lv_elves := pv_elves;
       ELSE
         /* Size the sentinel value. */
         lv_sentinel := 1;
       END IF;

       /* Loop through the list of variables. */
       LOOP
         /* Increment the index counter. */
         lv_counter := lv_counter + 1;

         /* Exit condition. */
         EXIT WHEN lv_counter > lv_sentinel;

```

```
34       /* Repeating statements. */
35       IF lv_elves.COUNT > 0 THEN
36         dbms_output.put_line(
37           '['||lv_counter||'] ['||lv_elves(lv_counter)||']');
38       END IF;
39
40     END LOOP;
41   END;
42   /
```

Line 14 safeguards the loop index counter by assigning a value of 1 when the call parameter is a null value. Lines 17 through 24 safeguard the sentinel value and the local collection. Lines 35 through 38 print the members of the collection when the collection holds one or more members. A call with all null values yields no output, but a call with a null index and sentinel value plus a valid collection, like

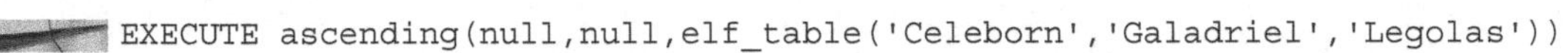

```
EXECUTE ascending(null,null,elf_table('Celeborn','Galadriel','Legolas'));
```

yields the following values because the safeguard provides default values for the index counter and sentinel values:

```
[1] [Celeborn]
[2] [Galadriel]
[3] [Legolas]
```

You've now seen a real example of safeguarding the index, sentinel, and collection for a standard ascending guard-on-entry loop. Space doesn't allow for complete examples of all scenarios, but the logic in the foregoing should allow you to implement safeguarding for descending loops with guard-on-entry or guard-on-exit sentinels.

Skipping Iterations

Skipping iterations in a loop has been possible for many releases of Oracle Database. You would implement skipping logic by using a combination of the `GOTO` statement and a label. While that's still possible, Oracle Database 11*g* introduced the `CONTINUE` and `CONTINUE WHEN` statements. A `CONTINUE` statement differs from the `GOTO` statement because it doesn't direct the program flow to a label. A `CONTINUE` statement stops execution in the midst of a loop and returns control to the top of the loop for the next iteration through the loop.

Although the `CONTINUE` statement provides a neat feature when it meets a requirement, it makes it easier to inadvertently code an infinite loop (typically an undesired behavior). The infinite loop is sometimes harder to see because the code cycles between the top of the loop and the `CONTINUE` statement, and it skips the incrementing or decrementing logic. When you skip the incrementing or decrementing logic, you can't arrive at your sentinel value, resulting in an infinite loop.

We need to safeguard against an inadvertent infinite loop. We do so by remembering the order required for our counter management, repeating statements, and exit condition in a guard-on-exit loop, or inverting them for a guard-on-entry loop.

The following anonymous block illustrates how to avoid an infinite loop while implementing a `CONTINUE` statement in a guard-on-entry simple loop:

```
SQL> DECLARE
       lv_counter NUMBER := 0;
```

```
 3  BEGIN
 4    LOOP
 5      -- Index counter logic.
 6      lv_counter := lv_counter + 1;
 7
 8      -- Guard on entry statement.
 9      EXIT WHEN lv_counter > 5;
10
11      -- Repeatable statement for a continue on odd numbers.
12      IF MOD(lv_counter,2) = 0 THEN
13        CONTINUE;
14      ELSE
15        dbms_output.put_line('Index ['||lv_counter||'].');
16      END IF;
17    END LOOP;
18  END;
19  /
```

This version of the program only prints the even-numbered index value before the sentinel value of 5. That's because the `CONTINUE` statement instructs the program to skip the balance of repeatable statements when the sentinel value is met.

NOTE

The `MOD` function is a SQL built-in function covered in Appendix C.

You can simplify your code by replacing the combination of an `IF` block and `CONTINUE` statement with the `CONTINUE WHEN` statement. The following shows how you would replace the if-then-else statement that starts on line 12 in the foregoing program:

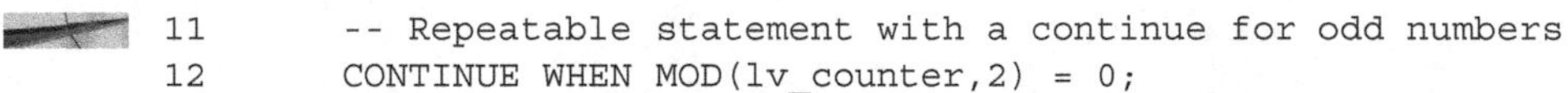

```
11      -- Repeatable statement with a continue for odd numbers.
12      CONTINUE WHEN MOD(lv_counter,2) = 0;
```

The print statement was previously in the `ELSE` block. The `CONTINUE WHEN` statement eliminates the need for the `IF` block.

Either program prints this to the console after five passes through the loop:

```
Iteration [1]
Iteration [3]
Iteration [5]
```

The simple loop becomes much more robust when combined with cursor attributes. That discussion is in the "Cursor Structure" section later in the chapter.

FOR Loop Statements

The `FOR` loop is a favorite of many developers because it is powerful and simple to use. A `FOR` loop manages the loop index and exit for you because it is part of the statement definition.

There are two types of `FOR` loop statements. One is a range `FOR` loop statement and the other is a cursor `FOR` loop statement. The discussion of cursor `FOR` loop statements will be presented later in the chapter, in the context of cursor structures.

Range FOR Loop Statements

A range `FOR` loop statement is ideal when you know the starting and ending points, and the range can be represented in integers. You can also use a `FOR` loop statement to navigate the contents of any varray or table collection or associative array (indexed by an integer) by traversing the number of elements in it. For reference, the `WHILE` loop is a better solution for an associative array indexed by strings.

The prototype for a range `FOR` loop statement is

```
FOR range_index IN [REVERSE] range_bottom..range_top LOOP
  repeating_statements
END LOOP;
```

The *range index* can be any identifier that you prefer. As when writing `FOR` loops in other languages, many developers use `i` as a variable name (after all, `i` stands for iterator). Then, they use `j`, `k`, `l`, and so forth as variable names when nesting loops. The range index for a range `FOR` loop is a `PLS_INTEGER` data type.

You set the starting value when you set the *bottom of the range* to the left of the two dots (or periods), and you set the ending value when you set the *top of the range* to the right of the dots. When you use the `REVERSE` keyword, the `FOR` loop decrements from the top of the range to the bottom of the range. For reference, you can't reverse their position relative to the double dots without causing the program to skip processing the internal logic of the loop.

The `FOR` loop always increments or decrements by 1, and you cannot change that. The following anonymous block program demonstrates an incrementing `FOR` loop statement:

```
SQL> BEGIN
  2    FOR i IN 1..3 LOOP
  3      dbms_output.put_line('Iteration ['||i||']');
  4    END LOOP;
  5  END;
  6  /
```

This code prints

```
Iteration [1]
Iteration [2]
Iteration [3]
```

The range index variable value is printed in the square brackets. You should note that the range limits are inclusive, not exclusive. An exclusive range would have excluded `1` and `3`.

Including the `REVERSE` keyword, we refactor the program by changing line 2 as follows:

```
  2    FOR i IN REVERSE 1..3 LOOP
```

With the `REVERSE` keyword, the program decrements through the range and prints

```
Iteration [3]
Iteration [2]
Iteration [1]
```

There is no EXIT statement in the example because one isn't required. *The EXIT statement is implicitly placed at the top of the loop*. The conditional logic checks whether the range index is less than the top of the range, and it exits when that condition is not met.

If you were to reverse the bottom and top of the range on line 2, like this:

```
2     FOR i IN REVERSE 3..1 LOOP
```

you would exit before processing any statements because the entry guard would find that 3 is not less than 1. Please give it a try to see the embedded logic behind the range FOR loop.

WHILE Loop Statements

WHILE loops are explicit block structures like the simple loops. A WHILE loop starts with a guard-on-entry condition. The WHILE loop requires that you manage the exit criterion (typical) or criteria for the loop, but only requires you to manage a loop index value when you require one. The WHILE loop is a guard-on-entry loop and may exclude a loop index. For example, counter indexes may be excluded when you guard on a data event in a collection or row return. WHILE loops work on truth, and truth may be determined many ways, as you'll see in the examples.

The prototype for the WHILE loop is

```
WHILE { TRUE | NOT FALSE | { condition | condition | ... } } LOOP
    repeating_statements
  [ counter_management_statements ]
END LOOP;
```

The guard-on-entry loop can prevent entry when the guard condition fails to return a Boolean true value when you code it to ask an affirmative question—*while true*. Likewise, if you ask a negation question with the NOT operator—*while not false*—the guard condition can prevent entry when the value returned isn't false. If this sounds familiar, it should, because it is the same issue we worked through with the conditional statement and three-valued logic. Failure can occur because the comparison operation, expression, or Boolean value returns a null value. That's why you need to provide a safeguard before entry to a WHILE loop. Without a safeguard, it's possible your program would never enter a guard-on-entry loop because a null value isn't true or false. The safeguard assigns a default value of true or false to the variable when it contains a runtime null value.

The following example implements a WHILE loop with a comparison condition. The WHILE loop uses a loop index value and a numeric literal as a sentinel value. While the loop index is less than the sentinel value in an ascending index model, the loop continues to manage the repeatable statement logic. Likewise, a WHILE loop manages the repeatable statement logic when the index is greater than the sentinel value in a descending index model.

The following demonstrates a traditional ascending index model:

```
SQL> DECLARE
       lv_counter NUMBER := 1;
     BEGIN
       WHILE (lv_counter < 3) LOOP
         dbms_output.put_line('Index ['||lv_counter||'].');
         lv_counter := lv_counter + 1;
       END LOOP;
     END;
     /
```

Line 2 declares the counter index value, which eliminates the need for writing safeguard logic before the `WHILE` loop. Line 4 compares the loop index against the sentinel value, and line 6 increments the index counter. A descending index model across the same range of values would assign the `lv_counter` variable on line 2 a value of 3, and you would write the exit condition on line 4, like

```
  4     WHILE (lv_counter > 1) LOOP
```

It prints the following:

```
Index [1].
Index [2].
```

The `WHILE` loop performs like a guard-on-entry simple loop. The difference is that you have no way to implement a generic index counter at the top of the loop when you start the counter with a value equal to the first index value. This means using a `CONTINUE` or `CONTINUE WHEN` statement in the `WHILE` loop becomes trickier unless you enter the counter logic as the first instruction in the loop.

The *ugly* version of an indexed-based `WHILE` loop is

```
SQL> DECLARE
  2     /* Initialize at beginning of the range. */
  3     lv_counter NUMBER := 1;
  4   BEGIN
  5     WHILE (lv_counter < 6) LOOP
  6       /* True for all even numbers - print odd results. */
  7       IF MOD(lv_counter,2) = 0 THEN
  8         /* Must increment here to avoid an infinite loop when
  9            the logic for a CONTINUE statement is met. */
 10         lv_counter := lv_counter + 1;
 11         CONTINUE;
 12       ELSE  /* Contains all repeatable statements. */
 13         dbms_output.put_line('Index ['||lv_counter||'].');
 14         /* Increment here for all iterations where the logic
 15            for a CONTINUE statement is unmet. */
 16         lv_counter := lv_counter + 1;
 17       END IF;
 18     END LOOP;
 19   END;
 20   /
```

The counter logic occurs on lines 10 and 16. It should only occur once, and at the top of the `WHILE` loop. The `IF` statement branches the program logic on line 7. It skips even numbers and prints odd numbers. The counter logic on line 10 occurs only for even numbers and must come immediately before the `CONTINUE` instruction (otherwise it would become an infinite loop).

The `ELSE` block also increments the counter when the index value is an odd number. The presence of two incrementing counter instructions in a single loop makes the foregoing program a bad solution. It's also an ugly solution because the counter logic occurs twice and should occur only once. The counter logic should also be the first instruction in the loop. It's not the first instruction because the index value starts with the first value of a densely populated index. A densely populated index typically consists of sequential integers.

You can replace the ugly code with bad (really suboptimal) code by making two changes. Start the loop index counter at 0, or one below the starting index value, and put the counter management logic once at the top of the loop.

The following program implements those two changes:

```
SQL> DECLARE
  2    /* Initialize one below the range. */
  3    lv_counter NUMBER := 0;
  4  BEGIN
  5    WHILE (lv_counter < 6) LOOP
  6      /* Must increment here to avoid an infinite loop when
  7         the logic for a CONTINUE statement is met. */
  8      lv_counter := lv_counter + 1;
  9
 10      /* True for all even numbers - print only odd results. */
 11      IF MOD(lv_counter,2) = 0 THEN
 12        CONTINUE;
 13      ELSE  /* Contains all printable statements. */
 14        dbms_output.put_line('Index ['||lv_counter||'].');
 15      END IF;
 16    END LOOP;
 17  END;
 18  /
```

Line 3 sets the `lv_counter` value to 0, which is one below the first index value. This change makes it possible to place the counter management logic at the top of the loop. You use this type of solution frequently with varray and table collections, and they always have indexes that start with 1.

Line 8 holds the counter logic for the loop in one place. The `CONTINUE` statement on line 12 tells the loop to skip to the top and evaluate the next index value, where it immediately increments the counter. The problem is we have an unnecessary `IF` statement. We can replace it by embracing the `CONTINUE WHEN` statement, as shown in the following good program:

```
SQL> DECLARE
  2    /* Initialize one below the range. */
  3    lv_counter NUMBER := 0;
  4  BEGIN
  5    WHILE (lv_counter < 6) LOOP
  6      /* Must increment here to avoid an infinite loop when
  7         the logic for a CONTINUE statement is met. */
  8      lv_counter := lv_counter + 1;
  9
 10      /* Continue when an even number. */
 11      CONTINUE WHEN MOD(lv_counter,2) = 0;
 12
 13      /* Contains all printable statements. */
 14      dbms_output.put_line('Index ['||lv_counter||'].');
 15    END LOOP;
 16  END;
 17  /
```

The index value is initialized one below the start of the range on line 3. The counter logic occurs once at the top of the loop, on line 8. The `CONTINUE WHEN` statement manages skipping iterations through the loop, and line 14 can only be reached when the index value is an odd number. The good, the bad, and the ugly versions of the `WHILE` loop sample program all print only odd numbers in the following range:

```
Index [1].
Index [3].
Index [5].
```

Although the logic to use a `CONTINUE` statement in a `WHILE` loop works, there's another approach with the `GOTO` statement and a label. Together, they also let us avoid implementing and maintaining the index counter logic in two places. However, the `GOTO` statement requires us to put the counter at the bottom of the loop to work.

The next program demonstrates the `GOTO` and label construct by using a decrementing version of the earlier program:

```
SQL> DECLARE
  2    lv_counter NUMBER := 6;
  3  BEGIN
  4    WHILE (lv_counter > 0) LOOP
  5      /* True for all even numbers. */
  6      IF MOD(lv_counter,2) = 0 THEN
  7        /* Must branch to the index counter logic to avoid
  8           an infinite loop. */
  9        GOTO decrement_index;
 10      ELSE  /* Contains all repeatable statements. */
 11        dbms_output.put_line('Index ['||lv_counter||'].');
 12      END IF;
 13
 14      << decrement_index >>
 15      /* Decrement here for all iterations. */
 16      lv_counter := lv_counter - 1;
 17    END LOOP;
 18  END;
 19  /
```

Line 6 still checks for even numbers, but when the `IF` statement is true, it redirects processing to the `decrement_index` label. The `decrement_index` label on line 14 is where you find the decrementing logic.

As you've seen, the `WHILE` loop is useful when you want to guard entry to a loop. On the downside, the `WHILE` loop can limit how you skip logic with a `CONTINUE` or `CONTINUE WHEN` statement if you don't understand the logic or approach.

The `COUNTINUE` and `CONTINUE WHEN` statements should eliminate any need to ever use a `GOTO` statement. The `GOTO` statement and label should be avoided.

Review Section

This section has described the following points about iterative statements:

- Iterative statements are blocks that let you repeat a statement or set of statements.
- Iterative statements implement an exit guard and a block of repeatable statements.
- The exit guard compares a loop index or variable against a sentinel value to determine when to exit the loop.
- Entry guards and exit guards can work to bar entry to or exit from a loop, and they can be intrinsically linked to index counter and sentinel values.
- To avoid runtime errors, programs should safeguard any dynamic variable values. You do that by checking whether they have null values before your program uses them. This type of checking is necessary because null values don't work properly as index counters because you can't increment them, or as comparison variables because you can't compare them.
- The `CONTINUE`, `CONTINUE WHEN`, and `GOTO` statements let you skip the balance of iteration through a loop, and they require specialized handling with guard-on-entry loops to avoid infinite loops.
- The range `FOR` loop lets you increment or decrement across data by comparing a range of values, and it hides the complexity of its guard-on-entry loop internals.
- The `WHILE` loop is a guard-on-entry loop and requires careful attention to avoid infinite loops when skipping iterations inside of its logic.

Cursor Structures

Cursor structures are the return results from SQL `SELECT` statements. In PL/SQL, you can process `SELECT` statements row by row or as bulk statements. This section covers how you work with row-by-row statement-processing cursors.

There are two types of cursors—implicit and explicit. You create an explicit cursor when you define a cursor inside a declaration block. You create an implicit cursor when you use a `SELECT` statement with an `INTO` clause or `BULK COLLECT INTO` clause, or you embed a `SELECT` statement inside a cursor `FOR` loop statement. Data Manipulation Language (DML) statements inside any execution or exception block are also implicit cursors. These DML statements include `INSERT`, `UPDATE`, `DELETE`, and `MERGE` statements.

The balance of this section discusses implicit and explicit cursors separately. Implicit cursors come first, followed by explicit cursors. The details of bulk processing, which was introduced in Chapter 3, are covered in the last subsection.

Implicit Cursors

Every SQL statement in a PL/SQL block is actually an implicit cursor. You can see how many rows are changed by any statement using the `%ROWCOUNT` attribute after a DML statement. `INSERT`, `UPDATE`, `DELETE`, and `MERGE` statements are DML statements. You can also count the number of rows returned by a SELECT statement or query (regardless of whether you lock rows with the FOR UPDATE clause).

The following example demonstrates the %ROWCOUNT cursor attribute by using a single-row implicit cursor based on the DUAL pseudo table:

```
SQL> DECLARE
  2    lv_number NUMBER;
  3  BEGIN
  4    SELECT 1 INTO lv_number
  5    FROM dual;
  6    dbms_output.put_line('Selected ['||SQL%ROWCOUNT||']');
  7  END;
  8  /
```

The reserved word SQL before the %ROWCOUNT cursor attribute on line 6 stands for any implicit cursor. PL/SQL manages implicit cursors and limits your access to their attributes. Table 5-6 lists the available implicit cursor attributes.

There are five types of implicit cursors. One is an implicit bulk collection cursor, which is covered in the "Bulk Statements" section later in the chapter. The other four implicit cursors are the subject of this section. The first two that are covered are single-row and multiple-row implicit cursors that use a SELECT or DML statement, and the final two are static and dynamic implicit cursors in FOR loops.

Single-Row Implicit Cursors

The SELECT-INTO statement is present in all implicit cursors that query data outside of a loop. It works only when a single row is returned by a SELECT statement. You can select a column or list of columns in the SELECT clause and assign the column(s) to individual variables or collectively to a record data type.

The prototype for a single-row implicit cursor minus standard SQL WHERE, HAVING, GROUP BY, and ORDER BY clauses is

```
SELECT column [, column [, ... ]] INTO  variable [, variable [, ... ]]FROM
table_name;
```

Attribute	Description
%FOUND	Returns TRUE only when a DML statement has changed a row.
%ISOPEN	Always returns FALSE for any implicit cursor.
%NOTFOUND	Returns TRUE when a DML statement fails to change a row.
%ROWCOUNT	Returns the number of rows changed by a DML statement or the number of rows returned by a SELECT INTO statement.

TABLE 5-6. *Implicit Cursor Attributes*

Both of the example programs introduced in this section use the `ITEM` table that is seeded from the code you can download from the McGraw-Hill Professional website. The first example program assigns column values to scalar variables on a one-to-one basis:

```
SQL> DECLARE
  2    id         item.item_id%TYPE;
  3    title      item.item_title%TYPE;
  4    subtitle   item.item_subtitle%TYPE;
  5  BEGIN
  6    SELECT     item_id, item_title, item_subtitle
  7    INTO       id, title, subtitle
  8    FROM       item
  9    WHERE      ROWNUM < 2;
 10    dbms_output.put_line('Selected ['||title||']');
 11  END;
 12  /
```

This example program anchors all variables to the columns of the target table on lines 2 through 4. It also limits the query to one row by using an inequality operator with the Oracle SQL `ROWNUM` pseudocolumn. It prints one row:

```
Selected [Around the World in 80 Days]
```

One-to-one anchoring assignments get very tiresome to type after a while. They also make your code more expensive to maintain over time. The more common convention is to assign the columns as a group through a record data type, or by direct anchoring to a table's definition. The latter approach is available only if you want all the columns in the table; unfortunately, for our example, we only want the same three columns used earlier.

An example with a record data type structure is

```
SQL> DECLARE
  2    TYPE item_record IS RECORD
  3    ( id           item.item_id%TYPE
  4    , title        item.item_title%TYPE
  5    , subtitle     item.item_subtitle%TYPE);
  6    lv_record      ITEM_RECORD;
  7  BEGIN
  8    SELECT    item_id, item_title, item_subtitle
  9    INTO      lv_record
 10    FROM      item
 11    WHERE     rownum < 2;
 12    dbms_output.put_line('Selected ['||dataset.title||']');
 13  END;
 14  /
```

While record data types require explicit construction, columns within the structure can be anchored individually to column data types, as shown on lines 3 through 5. On those lines, the `item` table is glued by the component selector (`.`) to columns from that table and is glued through the columns to their respective data types. The `lv_record` variable on line 6 uses the local `item_record` data type.

Single-row implicit cursors are great quick fixes, but they have a weakness. It is a weakness that many developers attempt to exploit by using it to raise exceptions when cursors return more than one row. They do this because single-row implicit cursors raise an "exact fetch returned too many rows" error (`ORA-01422`) when returning more than one row. Better solutions are available to detect errors before fetching the data. You should explore alternatives when developing your code and, where possible, explicitly handle errors. Explicit cursors are typically better solutions every time.

Multiple-Row Implicit Cursors

There are two ways you can create multiple-row implicit cursors:

- Write any DML statement in a PL/SQL block. DML statements are considered multiple-row implicit cursors, although you can limit them to a single row.
- Write an embedded query in a cursor `FOR` loop rather than define the query in a declaration block. These are `SELECT` statements that have a marvelous feature: all the variables are implicitly provided in the scope of the cursor `FOR` loop.

The following query demonstrates an `implicit` cursor created by a DML statement:

```
SQL> BEGIN
  UPDATE   system_user
  SET      last_update_date = SYSDATE;
  IF SQL%FOUND THEN
    dbms_output.put_line('Updated ['||SQL%ROWCOUNT||']');
  ELSE
    dbms_output.put_line('Nothing updated!');
  END IF;
END;
/
```

As defined in Table 5-6, the `%FOUND` cursor attribute for implicit cursors returns a Boolean true value only when rows are updated. The preceding statement should update five rows and print the following `SQL%ROWCOUNT` result:

```
Updated [5]
```

Cursor FOR Loop Statements

A cursor `FOR` loop statement is ideal when you query a database table or view because it's simple and manages many of the moving parts for you. While you don't generally know how many rows will be returned from a cursor (or query), a `FOR` loop statement manages the opening and closing of the cursor, fetching of records, and exiting of the loop when all records are read.

The examples in this section use static and dynamic implicit cursors. The next section, "Explicit Cursors," demonstrates how to work with explicit cursors. Explicit cursors are defined as a formal cursor structure in the declaration block. As a rule, using explicit cursors is the best practice and using implicit cursors is considered a shortcut that you should avoid in production code.

Static and dynamic implicit cursors are `SELECT` statements defined within parentheses as part of the cursor `FOR` loop statement. Unlike explicit cursors, implicit cursors don't support formal parameter lists. Dynamic implicit cursors rely on local scope access by embedding local variables in their `SELECT` statements.

The prototype for a cursor FOR loop statement is

```
FOR cursor_index IN [cursor_name[(parameter_list)] | (select_statement)] LOOP
  repeating_statements
END LOOP;
```

The *cursor index* can be any identifier that you prefer. As when writing FOR loops in other languages, many developers use i as the cursor index (after all, i stands for iterator). Those same developers also tend to use j, k, l, and so forth as nested cursor index values, but you can use any non-identifier name you want as the cursor index.

Moreover, a cursor index for a cursor FOR loop is a pointer to a result set in a query work area. As described in Chapter 4, a query work area is a memory region (known as a *context area*) in the Oracle Database 12*c* Program Global Area (PGA). The query work area holds information on the query, including the rows returned by a query, the number of rows processed by the query, and a pointer to the parsed query. The query work area resides in the Oracle Shared Pool (see Appendix A).

Static Implicit Cursor This section shows you how to implement a static implicit cursor in a FOR loop. A *static cursor* is composed of SQL keywords, table and column names, and numeric or string literal values. The alternative to a static implicit cursor in this case is a dynamic implicit cursor. The difference between a static implicit cursor and a dynamic implicit cursor is that a dynamic implicit cursor includes locally scoped variable names.

The following example (and many others in the chapter) depends on your having already run the seeding code, as discussed in the Introduction. This particular cursor loop returns the names of Harry Potter films found in the video rental store sample database.

```
SQL> BEGIN
       FOR i IN (SELECT   COUNT(*) AS on_hand
                 ,        item_title AS title
                 ,        item_rating AS rating
                 FROM     item
                 WHERE    item_title LIKE 'Harry Potter%'
                 AND      item_rating_agency = 'MPAA'
                 GROUP BY item_title
                 ,        item_rating) LOOP
         dbms_output.put_line(
           i.on_hand||' '||i.title||' rated '||i.rating);
       END LOOP;
     END;
     /
```

The *cursor index* points to the row, and the component selector (.) links the row pointer to the column name or alias assigned by the implicit cursor. This prints the following from inventory:

```
(3) Harry Potter and the Sorcerer's Stone [PG]
(3) Harry Potter and the Goblet of Fire [PG-13]
(3) Harry Potter and the Chamber of Secrets [PG]
(2) Harry Potter and the Prisoner of Azkaban [PG]
(1) Harry Potter and the Order of the Phoenix [PG-13]
```

There is no `EXIT` statement in the example because one isn't required. The `EXIT` statement is implicitly placed at the top of the loop right after the index counter. The index counter in a cursor loop checks for the presence of another row. The exit condition checks whether all rows have been read and exits when there are no more rows to read.

Dynamic Implicit Cursor As mentioned earlier, the difference between a dynamic implicit cursor and static implicit cursor is that the dynamic one embeds locally scoped variables. The variables act as placeholders and are substituted at runtime with the values from the local variables.

By making only slight changes, we can convert the implicit static cursor from the previous example into a dynamic static cursor. The following program adds a declaration block to declare a local variable and adds a placeholder variable to the `SELECT` statement:

```
SQL> DECLARE
  2    lv_item_title VARCHAR2(60) := 'Harry Potter';
  3  BEGIN
  4    FOR i IN (SELECT   COUNT(*) AS on_hand
  5                ,        item_title AS title
  6                ,        item_rating AS rating
  7                FROM     item
  8                WHERE    item_title LIKE lv_item_title||'%'
  9                AND      item_rating_agency = 'MPAA'
 10                GROUP BY item_title
 11                ,        item_rating) LOOP
 12      dbms_output.put_line(
 13        i.on_hand||' '||i.title||' rated '||i.rating);
 14    END LOOP;
 15  END;
 16  /
```

Line 2 adds a local `lv_item_title` variable and assigns a value of "Harry Potter" to it, and line 8 includes a reference to the local `lv_item_title` variable. The variable in the implicit cursor makes the cursor dynamic rather than static, notwithstanding that it acts like a constant in this program because the value is assigned in the declaration block. Naturally, it returns the same row set.

Explicit Cursors

As discussed earlier in this section, you create an explicit cursor when you define it inside a declaration block. Explicit cursors can be static or dynamic `SELECT` statements. Static `SELECT` statements return the same query each time with potentially different results. The results change as the data changes in the tables or views. Dynamic `SELECT` statements act like parameterized subroutines. They run different queries each time, depending on the actual parameters provided when they're opened.

You open static and dynamic explicit cursors differently, provided they are defined with formal parameters. When they do not have formal parameters, you open them with the same syntax. The actual parameters are then mapped by local variable substitution.

Explicit cursors require you to open, fetch, and close them regardless of whether you're using simple loop statements, `WHILE` loops statements, or cursor `FOR` loop statements. You use the `OPEN` statement to open cursors, the `FETCH` statement to fetch records from cursors, and the `CLOSE` statement to close and release resources of cursors. These statements work with both dynamic and static cursors inside or outside of a looping structure. *Cursor `FOR` loop statements implicitly open, fetch, and close cursors for you.* The `OPEN`, `FETCH`, and `CLOSE` statements are key elements in both of the following subsections, "Static Explicit Cursors" and "Dynamic Explicit Cursors," where the examples use simple loops.

The prototype for the `OPEN` statement is

```
OPEN cursor_name [(parameter [, parameter [, ... ]])];
```

There are two prototypes for the `FETCH` statement. One assigns individual columns to variables, and the other assigns rows to record structure variables.

The prototype for assigning individual columns to matching variables is

```
FETCH cursor_name
INTO  variable [, variable [, ... ]];
```

The prototype for assigning rows to record structure variables is

```
FETCH cursor_name
INTO  record_variable;
```

The prototype for the `CLOSE` statement is

```
CLOSE cursor_name;
```

Table 5-7 lists the explicit cursor attributes, which work the same way for both dynamic and static explicit cursors. Although they have the same names as the implicit cursor attributes, listed in Table 5-6, they work differently. The explicit cursor attributes return different results based on where they are called in reference to the `OPEN`, `FETCH`, and `CLOSE` statements.

The `%FOUND` attribute signals that rows are available to retrieve from the cursor, and the `%NOTFOUND` attribute signals that all rows have been retrieved from the cursor. The `%ISOPEN` attribute lets you know that the cursor is already open, and thus it is something you should consider

Statement	**State**	**%FOUND**	**%NOTFOUND**	**%ISOPEN**	**%ROWCOUNT**
OPEN	Before	Exception	Exception	FALSE	Exception
	After	NULL	NULL	TRUE	0
First FETCH	Before	NULL	NULL	TRUE	0
	After	TRUE	FALSE	TRUE	1
Next FETCH	Before	TRUE	FALSE	TRUE	1
	After	TRUE	FALSE	TRUE	n + 1
Last FETCH	Before	TRUE	FALSE	TRUE	n + 1
	After	FALSE	TRUE	TRUE	n + 1
CLOSE	Before	FALSE	TRUE	TRUE	n + 1
	After	Exception	Exception	FALSE	Exception

TABLE 5-7. *Explicit Cursor Attributes*

running before you attempt to open a cursor. As with implicit cursors, the `%ROWCOUNT` attribute tells you how many rows you've fetched at any given point. Only the `%ISOPEN` attribute works anytime without an error. The other three raise errors when the cursor isn't open. The Table 5-7 matrix captures these changing behaviors.

Static explicit cursors and dynamic explicit cursors are covered next in different subsections to organize the examples and highlight differences. The examples use simple loop statements, but you can also use explicit cursors in `WHILE` loop statements or nested inside range and cursor `FOR` loops.

Static Explicit Cursors

A static explicit cursor is a SQL `SELECT` statement that doesn't change its behavior. An explicit cursor has four components. You define, open, fetch from, and close a cursor. The following example program defines, opens, fetches from, and closes a static cursor into a series of scalar variables:

```
SQL> DECLARE
  2    lv_id        item.item_id%TYPE;
  3    lv_title     VARCHAR2(60);
  4    CURSOR c IS
  5      SELECT   item_id
  6      ,        item_title
  7      FROM     item;
  8  BEGIN
  9    OPEN c;
 10    LOOP
 11      FETCH c
 12      INTO  lv_id
 13      ,     lv_title;
 14      EXIT WHEN c%NOTFOUND;
 15      dbms_output.put_line('Title ['||lv_title||']');
 16    END LOOP;
 17    CLOSE c;
 18  END;
 19  /
```

Line 2 declares a variable by using column anchoring, and line 3 declares a variable by using a static data type (that mirrors the physical column in the `item` table). You should really choose one or the other style, but I wanted you to see both in the same example. The program fetches two columns into two variables on lines 12 and 13. The assignment works because the data types of the local variables on lines 2 and 3 match those for the `SELECT`-list columns on lines 5 and 6 of the cursor definition. The program exits when there are no more records to fetch.

As covered in Chapter 3, cursors offer an alternative to anchoring individual variables to columns of a table, local record structures, and tables. That alternative lets you define a local `lv_record` variable and anchor it to the structure of the cursor, as shown in the next example:

```
SQL> DECLARE
    CURSOR c IS
      SELECT   item_id AS id
      ,        item_title AS title
      FROM     item;
    lv_record  c%ROWTYPE;
  BEGIN
```

```
 8     OPEN c;
 9     LOOP
10       FETCH c
11       INTO  lv_record;
12       EXIT WHEN c%NOTFOUND;
13       dbms_output.put_line('Title ['||lv_record.title||']');
14     END LOOP;
15     CLOSE c;
16   END;
17   /
```

Line 6 declares an `lv_record` variable that inherits a record structure data type from the `SELECT` list of the cursor. Line 13 lets you print the `title` field value from the `lv_record` structure by using the component selector. Using a `FETCH` statement that takes the structure of a cursor and assigns it to a single variable is the best practice.

You should not assign columns to local variables unless you have a compelling reason to do so, and the only reason that seems compelling is that a LOB is being returned as part of the `SELECT` list and requires separate management from the handling of the non-LOB values. Sometimes it is best to handle them in separate cursors. Chapter 6 covers handling nested structures, like varray and table data types.

The PL/SQL-only alternative to coupling the `lv_record` variable to a cursor's row structure is to couple the `lv_record` to a table/view definition or to an explicit record type (check the "Records" section in Chapter 4 for a complete example). If we create an `item_record` record type in the declaration block, we can define the `lv_record` variable on line 9, like this:

```
 6    lv_record  ITEM_RECORD;
```

While this is a valid option in PL/SQL, it isn't as effective as coupling the variable data type to the cursor's row type. I recommend that you always couple variables to a cursor's row structure (over the other alternatives) because it simply makes your code more readable.

To help you avoid going down a dead-end street, you can't `SELECT-INTO` an object type. That means syntax like this will *never* work:

```
SQL> DECLARE
       ...
 6     lv_object  ITEM_OBJECT;
 7   BEGIN
       ...
10       FETCH c
11       INTO  lv_object(lv_id,lv_title);
       ...
16   END;
17   /
```

Line 6 now declares the `lv_object` variable with a SQL `item_object` object type. The `item_object` object type mirrors the cursor's row type. An attempt to assign the values from a cursor structure to an object type constructor raises the following error:

```
     INTO  lv_object(lv_id,lv_title);
           *
ERROR at line 11:
ORA-06550: line 11, column 11:
```

```
PLS-00308: this construct is not allowed as the origin of an assignment
ORA-06550: line 10, column 5:
PL/SQL: SQL Statement ignored
```

While you can't transfer the contents of a cursor's row type to an object type's constructor, you can use a `FOR` loop to transfer a cursor's row type to an object.

The FOR Loop Variant of a Static Cursor A cursor `FOR` loop statement can support direct assignment from any type of variable by implementing a dynamic `SELECT` statement. You embed local variables or cursor parameters in `SELECT` statements to create a dynamic `SELECT` statement. A static `FOR` loop statement uses a static `SELECT` statement in lieu of a dynamic `SELECT` statement.

While you can't call a `FOR` loop with parameters when the cursor is static, you can assign values from the static cursor inside the `FOR` loop statement. It's done by using the `FOR` loop's cursor index. That's because, unlike a range `FOR` loop, where the cursor index is a `PLS_INTEGER` data type, a cursor `FOR` loop's cursor index is an indirect reference to the rows returned from the cursor.

You can assign a record structure to a matching record structure variable. Likewise, you can assign a scalar element of a record structure to a matching scalar variable. The `lv_record` variable can be declared by using either an explicit record type or `%ROWTYPE` anchored to a local or shared cursor variable.

The following demonstrates assigning a record structure from the cursor index:

```
SQL> DECLARE
      ... same as previous example ...
  7  BEGIN
  8    FOR i IN c LOOP
  9      lv_record := i;
 10      dbms_output.put_line('Title ['||lv_record.title||']');
 11    END LOOP;
 12  END;
 13  /
```

Line 9 shows the assignment of the `FOR` loop *iterator* to the `lv_record` variable. As mentioned, this only works for PL/SQL-only record data structures.

You can assign elements from the cursor to scalar variables of a matching type or to fields of the anchored record types. An alternate line 9 assigns a `SELECT`-list element to a field of the `lv_record` data type (an anchored record created by using the `%ROWTYPE` attribute):

```
  9      lv_record.item_title := i.item_title;
```

You also can assign the cursor to a SQL object type constructor. You do that by passing the `SELECT`-list elements as call parameters to the object type constructor. For example, suppose you defined the following object type before running the program:

```
SQL> CREATE OR REPLACE
  TYPE item_object IS OBJECT
  ( id     NUMBER
  , title  VARCHAR2(60));
/
```

Instead of anchoring `lv_record` with the `%ROWTYPE` attribute to the cursor's record structure on line 6, you would assign it your SQL user-defined type (UDT): `item_object`. The modified declaration of `lv_record` is

```
6     lv_record  ITEM_OBJECT;
```

Then, you could assign the cursor's returned record element by element to the `item_object` constructor with the following syntax on line 9:

```
9     lv_record.item_title := item_object(i.item_id, i.item_title);
```

Although the `FOR` loop automates many tasks, unfortunately, it doesn't provide the ability to manage behaviors when it returns or fails to return rows. You need to return to the simple loop to manage those behaviors.

Conditional Return Values It is possible that the cursor may not find any records. When an implicit or explicit cursor runs but doesn't find data, no error is raised. If you want to be notified when the cursor doesn't find any records, you need to add that feature to your code. You can do so by using an `IF` statement and the `%NOTFOUND` and `%ROWCOUNT` cursor attributes in a simple loop (not a `FOR` loop).

The following simple loop example prints a *"No Data Found."* message when the cursor fails to find any records:

```
SQL> DECLARE
  2    CURSOR c IS
  3      SELECT   item_id AS id
  4      ,        item_title AS title
  5      FROM     item
  6      WHERE    item_id = -1;
  7      lv_record  c%ROWTYPE;
  8  BEGIN
  9    OPEN c;
 10    LOOP
 11      FETCH c INTO lv_record;
 12      IF c%NOTFOUND THEN
 13        IF c%ROWCOUNT = 0 THEN  /* No rows returned. */
 14          dbms_output.put_line('No Data Found');
 15        ELSE                   /* One plus rows returned. */
 16          dbms_output.put_line('No More Data Found');
 17        END IF;
 18        EXIT;
 19      ELSE
 20        dbms_output.put_line('Title ['||lv_record.title||']');
 21      END IF;
 22    END LOOP;
 23  END;
 24  /
```

Line 6 adds a `WHERE` clause that ensures the query won't return any rows. No rows are returned by the cursor, and the `c%NOTFOUND` on line 12 returns true. Since the last SQL statement returned no rows, the `c%ROWCOUNT` on line 13 also returns true and prints a *"No Data Found."* message.

When the `c%ROWCOUNT` returns false, the program prints a *"No More Data Found."* message. Line 18 exits the loop after it processes either of the output messages. Unfortunately, you can't replicate this logic inside a cursor `FOR` loop statement.

Dynamic Explicit Cursors

Dynamic explicit cursors are very much like static explicit cursors. They use a SQL `SELECT` statement. Beyond using variables in `SELECT` statements or cursors, you can also embed local variables in `INSERT`, `UPDATE`, `DELETE`, or `MERGE` statements. These variables take the place of what would otherwise be literal values.

Dynamic explicit cursors have the same four components as static cursors: you define, open, fetch from, and close a dynamic cursor. Dynamic explicit cursors also rely on local variable scope access, as do implicit dynamic cursors.

The following example program defines a cursor as a `SELECT` statement that queries the `item` table for a range of values. Both variables are declared as local variables and assigned numeric literal values. The names of the local variables must differ from column names or else the column name values will be substituted in place of the variable values.

```
SQL> DECLARE
  2    lv_lowend   NUMBER := 1010;
  3    lv_highend  NUMBER := 1020;
  4    CURSOR c IS
  5      SELECT    item_id AS id
  6      ,         item_title AS title
  7      FROM      item
  8      WHERE     item_id BETWEEN lv_lowend AND lv_highend;
  9      lv_record  c%ROWTYPE;
 10  BEGIN
 11    OPEN c;
 12    LOOP
 13      FETCH c INTO lv_record;
 14      EXIT WHEN c%NOTFOUND;
 15      dbms_output.put_line('Title ['||lv_record.title||']');
 16    END LOOP;
 17  END;
 18  /
```

Lines 2 and 3 declare the `lv_lowend` and `lv_highend` variables. Line 8 uses the `lv_lowend` and `lv_highend` variables as inclusive boundaries of the `BETWEEN` operator. The values of the local variables are substituted in the `SELECT` statement when you run the program. The same logic works in `FOR` and `WHILE` loops.

You can rely on local variables, but doing so can be confusing and can make the code more difficult to support. While the `INSERT`, `UPDATE`, `DELETE`, and `MERGE` statements limit you to embedding local variables, `SELECT` statements in cursors don't.

Cursors can have formal parameters, like functions and procedures. Moreover, `SELECT` statement cursors should have formal parameters as a best practice. The next example replaces the prior example by altering the cursor definition and the call to the `OPEN` statement:

```
SQL> DECLARE
  2    lv_lowend   NUMBER := 1005;
  3    lv_highend  NUMBER := 1021;
```

```
4     CURSOR c
5     ( cv_low_id NUMBER
6     , cv_high_id NUMBER) IS
7       SELECT   item_id AS id
8       ,        item_title AS title
9       FROM     item
10      WHERE    item_id BETWEEN cv_low_id AND cv_high_id;
11    item_record c%ROWTYPE;
12  BEGIN
13    OPEN c (lv_lowend, lv_highend);
14    LOOP
15      FETCH c INTO item_record;
16      EXIT WHEN c%NOTFOUND;
17      dbms_output.put_line('Title ['||item_record.title||']');
18    END LOOP;
19  END;
20  /
```

Lines 4 through 6 define a cursor with two numeric formal parameters, `cv_low_id` and `cv_high_id`, which are also the inclusive range values of the `BETWEEN` operator on line 10. Line 13 opens the cursor with the `lv_lowend` and `lv_highend` call parameters.

Note that the local variables have physical sizes but the formal parameters don't. That's because formal parameters don't have physical size until runtime or, in this case, until you pass call parameters when you open the cursor on line 13.

Opening a cursor in a `FOR` loop is very much like opening a cursor in a simple loop. You provide a comma-delimited list of call parameters inside parentheses. The following four lines replace the six lines from the preceding example:

```
13    FOR i IN c (lv_lowend, lv_highend) LOOP
14      item := i;
15      dbms_output.put_line('Title ['||item.title||']');
16    END LOOP;
```

So far you've seen how to use cursors, but there's more to see. You have the ability to use cursors inside cursors, as discussed in the next section.

Subcursors

A nested cursor is a subcursor. You create a subcursor by embedding a correlated subquery inside the `SELECT` list of an explicit or dynamic cursor. Correlated subqueries include a join inside the `WHERE` clause that links the subquery to the outer query. You can refer to the "Correlated Subqueries" section of Appendix B for more information on correlated subqueries.

You must explicitly fetch a `SELECT` list into a list of variables when it includes a subcursor. Subcursor results are assigned to variables that use a PL/SQL-only `REF CURSOR` data type. Then, you need to fetch their results inside a nested loop.

You may be asking yourself, "Why would I go to all that trouble?" To answer that question, let's first look at the return set of an ordinary query of three tables. The query uses inner joins to link three tables through their primary and foreign key columns (and some formatting to provide clear output).

```
SQL> COLUMN first_name FORMAT A10
SQL> COLUMN last_name  FORMAT A10
SQL> COLUMN street_address  FORMAT A20
SQL> COLUMN city FORMAT A8
SQL> COLUMN state FORMAT A2
SQL> COLUMN postal_code FORMAT A5
SQL> SELECT   c.first_name
  2  ,        c.last_name
  3  ,        sa.street_address
  4  ,        a.city
  5  ,        a.state_province AS state
  6  ,        a.postal_code
  7  FROM     contact c INNER JOIN address a
  8  ON       c.contact_id = a.contact_id INNER JOIN street_address sa
  9  ON       a.address_id = sa.address_id
 10  WHERE    c.last_name = 'Vizquel';
```

The query returns the following four rows:

```
FIRST_NAME LAST_NAME  STREET_ADDRESS       CITY     ST ZIP
---------- ---------- -------------------- -------- -- -----
Oscar      Vizquel    12 El Camino Real    San Jose CA 95192
Doreen     Vizquel    12 El Camino Real    San Jose CA 95192
Doreen     Vizquel    41277 Roberts Avenue Fremont  CA 94539
Doreen     Vizquel    Apt #14              Fremont  CA 94539
```

The return set is symmetrical, which means you have the same number of rows for each column in the query. Let's look at Doreen Vizquel's results. There are three rows returned for Doreen Vizquel because the bottommost `street_address` table holds three unique results linked to the same `contact` row. Likewise, there are two duplicate rows returned for `city`, `state`, and `zip` because there are two unique `street_address` values linked to the same `address` row. This is known as a symmetrical return set, any one row is duplicated for the related unique rows.

Symmetrical return sets are normal in SQL but generally not too useful in web forms and reports. For example, suppose the program requirements call for an asymmetrical return set, like this:

```
Formatted Address
----------------------------------
1004 Doreen Vizquel
     41277 Roberts Avenue, Apt #14
     Fremont, CA, 94539

     12 El Camino Real
     San Jose, CA, 95192

1003 Oscar Vizquel
     12 El Camino Real
     San Jose, CA, 95192
```

Other than using some fancy SQL*Plus report writing commands, this type of output is not suited to a SQL `SELECT` statement. You can write a function that lets you return a data set like the foregoing by using subcursors.

Since the `format_contact_address` function returns a table collection of `CLOB` data types, we need to define an appropriate SQL table collection. This syntax creates the table collection of `CLOB`s:

```
SQL> CREATE OR REPLACE
       TYPE format_address_table IS TABLE OF CLOB;
     /
```

You now can create a function that uses subqueries to format and return a table collection of formatted contact addresses, like

```
SQL> CREATE OR REPLACE FUNCTION format_contact_address
     ( pv_last_name   VARCHAR2 ) RETURN FORMAT_ADDRESS_TABLE IS

       /* Declare a reference cursor. */
       TYPE ref_cursor IS REF CURSOR;

       /* Declare a nested cursor. */
       CURSOR all_nested_results
       ( cv_last_name   VARCHAR2 ) IS
         SELECT   c.contact_id
         ,        c.first_name
         ||       DECODE(c.middle_name,NULL,' ',' '||c.middle_name||' ')
         ||       c.last_name AS full_name
         ,        CURSOR(SELECT   a.city
                         ,        a.state_province AS state
                         ,        CURSOR(SELECT   sa.street_address
                                         FROM     street_address sa
                                         WHERE    sa.address_id =
                                                    a.address_id)
                         ,        a.postal_code
                         FROM     address a
                         WHERE    a.contact_id = c.contact_id
                         ORDER BY a.start_date DESC)
         FROM     contact c
         WHERE    c.last_name = cv_last_name
         ORDER BY c.last_name
         ,        c.first_name;

         /* Declare a street address counter. */
         lv_street_counter NUMBER := 0;
         lv_index_counter  NUMBER := 1;

         /* Declare two reference cursors. */
         lv_street_cursor  REF_CURSOR;
         lv_address_cursor REF_CURSOR;

         /* Declare local scalar variables. */
```

```
    lv_employee_id    NUMBER;
    lv_full_name      VARCHAR2(62);
    lv_city           VARCHAR2(30);
    lv_state          VARCHAR2(2);
    lv_street_address VARCHAR2(30);
    lv_postal_code    VARCHAR2(10);

    /* Declare a large string as the output target. */
    lv_output_message VARCHAR2(300);
    lv_output_table   FORMAT_ADDRESS_TABLE := format_address_table();

BEGIN

  /* Open the composite cursor. */
  OPEN all_nested_results (pv_last_name);

  /* Read through the cursor result set. */
  LOOP
    FETCH all_nested_results
    INTO  lv_employee_id
    ,     lv_full_name
    ,     lv_address_cursor;
    EXIT WHEN all_nested_results%NOTFOUND;

    /* Set message with base cursor. */
    lv_output_message := lv_employee_id||' '||lv_full_name||CHR(10);

    /* Read through the first-level nested table. */
    LOOP
      FETCH lv_address_cursor
      INTO  lv_city
      ,     lv_state
      ,     lv_street_cursor
      ,     lv_postal_code;
      EXIT WHEN lv_address_cursor%NOTFOUND;

      /* Read through the second-level nested table. */
      LOOP
        FETCH  lv_street_cursor
        INTO   lv_street_address;

        /* Check for all reading all subcursor records. */
        IF lv_street_cursor%NOTFOUND THEN

          /* Append a line return at the end. */
          IF lv_street_counter > 0 THEN
            lv_output_message := lv_output_message||CHR(10);
            lv_street_counter := 0;
          END IF;

          /* Append and print address, then exit subcursor. */
```

```
 89      lv_output_message := lv_output_message||'  '
 90                    || lv_city||', '||lv_state||', '
 91                    || lv_postal_code||CHR(10);
 92
 93      EXIT;
 94    ELSE
 95      /* Append street addresses. */
 96      lv_street_counter := lv_street_counter + 1;
 97
 98      IF lv_street_counter = 1 THEN
 99        lv_output_message := lv_output_message||'  '
100                    || lv_street_address;
101      ELSE
102        lv_output_message := lv_output_message||', '
103                    || lv_street_address;
104      END IF;
105    END IF;
106   END LOOP;
107
108   /* Reset message with base cursor. */
109   lv_output_message := lv_output_message||CHR(10);
110  END LOOP;
111
112  /* Extend space and assign to collection. */
113  lv_output_table.EXTEND;
114  lv_output_table(lv_index_counter) := lv_output_message;
115  lv_index_counter := lv_index_counter + 1;
116 END LOOP;
117
118 /* Close cursor resource. */
119 CLOSE all_nested_results;
120
121 /* Return the formatted address. */
122 RETURN lv_output_table;
123 END;
124 /
```

Line 5 declares a weakly typed system reference cursor, which is used as the target data type for the two subcursors. Lines 14 through 23 contain a subcursor that holds another subcursor. Line 22 contains the correlated subquery's join between the outer cursor and the first-level subcursor. Lines 18 and 19 (actually one line split into two to prevent wrapping in the book) contain the correlated subquery's join between the first- and second-level subcursors.

Lines 34 and 35 declare two target variables for the subcursors. It's possible to eliminate the user-defined and weakly typed `REF_CURSOR` because Oracle provides a generic `SYS_REFCURSOR` data type for this exact purpose. You would change lines 34 and 35 as follows to use the built-in weakly typed cursor data type:

```
 34    lv_street_cursor   SYS_REFCURSOR;
 35    lv_address_cursor  SYS_REFCURSOR;
```

The first-level subcursor is assigned to the system reference cursor on line 59 inside the first-level nested loop, and the second-level subcursor is likewise assigned on line 70. You can then call this function inside the `TABLE` function, like this:

```
SQL> SELECT   column_value AS "Formatted Address"
  2  FROM     TABLE(format_contact_address('Vizquel'));
```

While I try to avoid subcursors, you also can use subcursors when you have tables that hold nested tables. You use cross-joins in lieu of the inner joins between cursor and subcursor, or subcursor and nested subcursor. Leveraging the `employee` table described in the "Nested Collection Types" section of Appendix B, you could substitute this cursor:

```
 9    CURSOR all_nested_results
10    ( cv_start_id  NUMBER
11    , cv_end_id        NUMBER) IS
12      SELECT   e.employee_id
13      ,        e.first_name
14      ||       DECODE(e.middle_name,NULL,' ',' '||e.middle_name||' ')
15      ||       e.last_name AS full_name
16      ,        CURSOR(SELECT   n.city
17                      ,        n.state
18                      ,        CURSOR(SELECT   s.column_value
19                                      FROM     TABLE(n.street_address) s)
20                      ,        n.postal_code
21                      FROM     TABLE(e.home_address) n)
22      FROM     employee e
23      WHERE    e.employee_id BETWEEN cv_start_id AND cv_end_id;
```

Lines 18 and 19 create a subcursor from a nested Attribute Data Type (ADT). Lines 16 through 21 create a subcursor from a nested user-defined type (UDT). Joins between the collections and holding row are unnecessary because the Oracle database implicitly maps their relationships.

This section has explained how to use implicit and explicit cursors in your program units. You've learned that some implicit behaviors are outside of your control. You've also learned that explicit structures provide you with more control.

Review Section

This section has described the following points about cursor structures:

- Cursor structures return row-by-row managed result sets from SQL `SELECT` statements.
- Implicit cursors exist for all DML statements, such as the `INSERT`, `UPDATE`, `DELETE`, and `MERGE` statements.
- PL/SQL supports the `%FOUND`, `%NOTFOUND`, `%ISOPEN`, and `%ROWCOUNT` implicit cursor attributes.
- The `SELECT-INTO` statement is a single-row implicit cursor.

- The INSERT, UPDATE, DELETE, and MERGE statements are multiple-row implicit cursors, although you can limit them to a single row.
- Cursors can be static or dynamic, and dynamic implicit cursors can include placeholders that are references to local variables.
- SELECT statement cursors can have formal parameters, like functions and procedures.
- Cursors support nested cursors, which are called subcursors.

Bulk Statements

Bulk statements let you select, insert, update, or delete large data sets in tables or views. You use the BULK COLLECT statement with SELECT statements and the FORALL statement to insert, update, or delete large data sets.

Table 5-8 lists and describes the two bulk collection attributes. The "INSERT Statements" subsection under the "FORALL Statements" section illustrates how to use the %BULK_ROWCOUNT attribute.

This section explains how to use the BULK COLLECT INTO and FORALL statements. The first subsection discusses the uses of and differences between parallel scalar collections and record collections. The subsequent "FORALL Statements" subsection explains how you can use bulk INSERT, UPDATE, and DELETE statements. While initially shown to you in the "INSERT Statement" section, the last subsection shows you how to use the %BULK_ROWCOUNT(i) and %BULK_EXCEPTIONS(i) bulk collection attributes.

BULK COLLECT INTO Statements

The BULK COLLECT INTO statement lets you select a column of data and insert it into Oracle collection data types. You can use a BULK COLLECT statement inside a SQL statement or as part of a FETCH statement. A SQL statement bulk collection uses an implicit cursor, while a FETCH statement works with an explicit cursor. You cannot limit the number of rows returned when performing bulk collection in an implicit cursor. The FETCH statement lets you append the LIMIT statement to set the maximum number of rows read from the cursor at a time. You can use any standard or user-defined PL/SQL data type as the target of an implicit cursor statement.

Bulk Attribute	Description
%BULK_EXCEPTIONS(i)	Lets you see whether or not a row encountered an error during a bulk INSERT, UPDATE, or DELETE statement. You access these statistics by putting them in range FOR loop statements.
%BULK_ROWCOUNT(i)	Lets you see whether or not an element is altered by a bulk INSERT, UPDATE, or DELETE statement. You access these statistics by putting them in range FOR loop statements.

TABLE 5-8. *Bulk Collection Attributes*

The following is a basic prototype of an implicit bulk collection statement:

```
 SELECT column [, column [, ... ]]
 COLLECT BULK INTO collection [, collection [, ... ]]
 FROM   table_name
[WHERE  where_clause_statements];
```

Bulk collections performed as part of a `FETCH` statement use an explicit cursor. They have the following prototype:

```
 FETCH cursor_name [(parameter [, parameter [, ... ]])]
 BULK COLLECT INTO collection [, collection [, ... ]]
[LIMIT rows_to_return];
```

The number of columns returned by the explicit cursor determines the number of scalar collection targets, or the structure of a record collection target. The `SELECT` statement defines the number and type of columns returned by a cursor.

You can use `BULK COLLECT INTO` statements to insert a series of targets or a single target. A series of targets is a set of collection variables separated by commas. The target comma-delimited collections are known as *parallel collections* because you generally manage them in parallel. A single target is a collection of a record structure. You cannot insert some of the columns into a collection of a record structure and others into scalar collections in the same statement call. Any attempt to do so raises a `PLS-00494` error that disallows coercion into multiple record targets.

The `BULK COLLECT INTO` statement is much faster than a standard cursor because it has one parse, execute, and fetch. Ordinary implicit `INTO` statement cursors or explicit cursors have more parses, executes, and fetches. Bulk operations scale better as the number of rows increases, but very large operations require database configurations to support them.

The "Parallel Collection Targets" and "Record Collection Targets" subsections that follow demonstrate bulk collections using implicit cursors. The last subsection, "LIMIT-Constrained Collection Targets," demonstrates explicit cursors along with the `LIMIT` statement. The `LIMIT` statement lets you constrain the size of bulk selections, but you can only use it with explicit cursors. The last subsection demonstrates how you can work within your database operating constraints, such as the PGA.

Parallel Collection Targets

Scalar collections are the only supported SQL collection data types. When you want to share data with external programs or web applications, you should return your bulk selections into a series of parallel collections. You can exchange these data types with external programs and web applications, using the Oracle Call Interface (OCI).

The following example program uses an implicit `BULK COLLECT INTO` statement cursor and performs a bulk selection into a set of parallel scalar collections:

```
SQL> DECLARE
    -- Declare a collection of a scalar data type.
    TYPE title_collection IS TABLE OF VARCHAR2(60);
    -- Declare two variables that use the scalar collection.
    lv_title     TITLE_COLLECTION;
    lv_subtitle  TITLE_COLLECTION;
  BEGIN
```

```
 8    -- Call an implicit cursor with bulk collection.
 9    SELECT  item_title
10    ,       item_subtitle
11    BULK COLLECT INTO lv_title
12    ,                 lv_subtitle
13    FROM    item;
14    -- Print the output from the bulk collection.
15    FOR i IN 1..lv_title.COUNT LOOP /* Print first element. */
16      dbms_output.put_line('Title ['||lv_title(i)||']');
17    END LOOP;
18  END;
19  /
```

Line 3 defines a collection type that supports both columns that the program needs to capture. Lines 5 and 6 declare variables of the locally defined collection. The `SELECT` statement performs a bulk collection into the `lv_title` and `lv_subtitle` collection variables on lines 11 and 12. Line 15 declares a `FOR` loop that starts at 1 (or the beginning of a table collection) and ends at the count of items in the collection. The repeatable statement in the loop prints only one of the two local variables.

The program demonstrates how you can pass a set of values into two parallel scalar collections. You should ensure that parallel scalar collections remain synchronized or else you'll encounter an error with this coding approach. I don't recommend using this coding approach because it's too expensive to maintain in terms of time and money. You should only choose this direction if you have a key business need to move data around using scalar SQL data types. Otherwise, you should use record collection targets for bulk collection.

Record Collection Targets

The current limitations on building SQL collections limits us to collections of records of *PL/SQL-only structures*. This means that you can only use SQL collections of record structures inside programs that run exclusively in the PL/SQL environment. However, you can wrap these SQL collections inside pipelined table functions (covered in Chapter 8) to convert them to collections of SQL object types.

Although you can declare PL/SQL records and collections of records as data types in PL/SQL bodiless packages (those without package bodies), you can't use them in a SQL context. That's because PL/SQL-only data types can't act as call parameters to functions or procedures when you call them from a SQL statement. Likewise, PL/SQL-only data types can't be return types from PL/SQL functions when you want to call them from a SQL statement.

A better solution is to create a record structure and a collection of the record structure because then you can declare a variable with the record structure collection as its data type. That lets you assign a `SELECT` list directly to a single variable using a `BULK COLLECT INTO` statement, like

```
SQL> DECLARE
    -- Declare a record and collection user-defined type.
    TYPE title_record IS RECORD
    ( title VARCHAR2(60)
    , subtitle VARCHAR2(60));
    TYPE title_table IS TABLE OF TITLE_RECORD;
    -- Declare a variable of the collection data type.
    lv_fulltitle  TITLE_TABLE;
```

```
 9  BEGIN
10    SELECT  item_title
11    ,       item_subtitle
12    BULK COLLECT INTO lv_fulltitle
13    FROM    item;
14    -- Print one element of a structure.
15    FOR i IN 1..lv_fulltitle.COUNT LOOP
16      dbms_output.put_line('Title ['||lv_fulltitle(i).title||']');
17    END LOOP;
18  END;
19  /
```

Lines 3 through 5 define a record structure of two elements. Line 6 defines `title_table` as a collection of the `title_record` record structure. Line 8 declares a variable of the `title_table` collection. Then, the `SELECT` statement assigns the values of two columns through a bulk collection into the `lv_fulltitle` collection on line 12.

LIMIT-Constrained Collection Targets

The `LIMIT` statement lets you set the maximum number of rows returned by a bulk collection. It constrains the bulk collection. You can only constrain the number of rows returned by explicit cursors in a `FETCH` statement.

The downside to this approach is tied to how interactive applications work. Interactive applications generally require all or nothing, not just some of the records. Batch processing programs that manage large transaction processing steps are the best candidates for leveraging this approach. So, the `LIMIT` statement is useful when you're doing batch processing or pulling very large cursors, but not when you're dealing with interactive programs.

Just take note of these words of advice about setting the `LIMIT` value: If your `LIMIT` value is too large, your Oracle RDBMS will spend an inordinate amount of time managing the cursor in memory and too little time doing the work. Make sure the `LIMIT` value is intelligently sized. I find that setting the `LIMIT` value to a number between 500 and 1,000 rows is ample. Anything below 500 isn't worth your time to write the additional code.

The next two subsections demonstrate how to use the `LIMIT` statement with both the parallel collection and record collection approaches.

Parallel Collection Targets As discussed earlier, parallel collections are typically synchronized scalar collection variables. Parallel collections may differ by scalar data type but each must have the same number of rows and matching index values. The prior examples use bulk collection with implicit cursors, but you can also use explicit cursors.

The following program demonstrates how to manage a bulk collection ten rows at a time with an explicit cursor:

```
SQL> DECLARE
      ... same as previous parallel collection example ...
      -- Declare an explicit cursor.
      CURSOR c IS
        SELECT   item_title AS title
        ,        item_subtitle AS subtitle
        FROM     item;
    BEGIN
```

```
13     OPEN c;
14     LOOP
15       -- Fetch explicit cursor into a record collection.
16       FETCH c
17       BULK COLLECT INTO lv_title
18       ,                 lv_subtitle LIMIT 10;
19       EXIT WHEN lv_title.COUNT = 0;
       ... same as previous printing for loop ...
25     END LOOP;
26   END;
27   /
```

Lines 8 through 11 *add* the definition of an explicit cursor. The cursor is opened and fetched by using a bulk collection operation on lines 16 through 18. The fetch retrieves only ten rows at a time because of the appended `LIMIT` clause. The `LIMIT` clause means all iterations through the loop fetch all available rows up to ten rows of data from the open cursor. The last iteration through the loop shouldn't fetch any rows. Please note that line 19 introduces a new type of exit guard. The exit condition in this case checks whether the collection is empty before it exits the loop. More or less, this approach is equivalent exit logic for an ordinary cursor:

```
EXIT WHEN c%NOTFOUND;
```

While ten is a small number, the idea is to limit consumed memory and minimize the number of parses, executes, and fetches. A better number is 250 or 500 because that typically doesn't bottleneck processing or strain computational resources for the database.

Record Collection Targets Over time, if not immediately obvious, you should find that record collection variables are typically better solutions than parallel scalar collections. The next program shows you how to manage bulk collections with an explicit cursor and record collection variable. The example program places a `LIMIT` on how many rows can be processed by the bulk collection. It limits processing to no more than ten rows with each pass through the loop.

The code follows:

```
SQL> DECLARE
       ... same as previous bulk record collection example ...
 9     -- Declare an explicit cursor.
10     CURSOR c IS
11       SELECT   item_title AS title
12       ,        item_subtitle AS subtitle
13       FROM     item;
14   BEGIN
15     OPEN c;
16     LOOP
17       -- Fetch explicit cursor into a record collection.
18       FETCH c
19       BULK COLLECT INTO lv_fulltitle LIMIT 10;
20       EXIT WHEN lv_fulltitle.COUNT = 0;
       ... same as previous printing for loop ...
25     END LOOP;
26   END;
27   /
```

Lines 10 through 13 hold the explicit cursor, and the bulk collect into a record collection occurs on line 19. The `LIMIT` clause ensures ten or fewer rows are processed each time the code traverses the result set from the cursor. Line 20 checks to see when there aren't any more rows to process. That's the only time the `lv_fulltitle` collection should contain zero elements.

FORALL Statements

The `FORALL` loop is designed to work with Oracle collections. It lets you insert, update, and delete bulk data. This section focuses on how to use the `FORALL` statement and build on the introduction of collections in Chapter 3. Chapter 6 covers collections in greater depth.

These examples build on the bulk collection examples from the previous section. They also depend on an `item_temp` table, which serves as the table for `INSERT`, `UPDATE`, and `DELETE` statements. You should create the table by using the following syntax:

```
SQL> CREATE TABLE item_temp
  ( item_id          NUMBER
  , item_title       VARCHAR2(62)
  , item_subtitle    VARCHAR2(60));
```

The following subsections are ordered to support the example code. You insert, update, and delete the data using `FORALL` statements. Then, you can drop the `item_temp` table from the database.

INSERT Statement

Bulk inserts require that you use scalar collections inside the `VALUES` clause. That means you can use parallel collections of scalar variables, or you can use dot notation to supply field elements of a record collection. Any attempt to simply insert the record into the table raises an `ORA-00947` "not enough values" error.

The following example code uses scalar collections to perform a bulk insert:

```
SQL> DECLARE
    -- Define a record type.
    TYPE item_record IS RECORD
    ( id         NUMBER
    , title     VARCHAR2(62)
    , subtitle  VARCHAR2(60));
    -- Define a collection based on the record data type.
    TYPE item_table IS TABLE OF ITEM_RECORD;
    -- Declare a variable of the collection data type.
    lv_fulltitle  ITEM_TABLE;
    -- Declare an explicit cursor.
    CURSOR c IS
      SELECT   item_id AS id
      ,        item_title AS title
      ,        item_subtitle AS subtitle
      FROM     item;
  BEGIN
    OPEN c;
    LOOP
      FETCH c
```

```
21        BULK COLLECT INTO lv_fulltitle LIMIT 10;
22        EXIT WHEN lv_fulltitle.COUNT = 0;
23        FORALL i IN lv_fulltitle.FIRST..lv_fulltitle.LAST
24          INSERT INTO item_temp
25          VALUES
26          ( lv_fulltitle(i).id
27          , lv_fulltitle(i).title
28          , lv_fulltitle(i).subtitle );
29        /* Print the number of rows inserted per iteration. */
30        dbms_output.put_line('['||SQL%ROWCOUNT||'] Inserted.');
31      END LOOP;
32    END;
33    /
```

The FORALL statement on line 23 reads the lv_fulltitle collection but its size is constrained with the BULK COLLECT statement's LIMIT clause. That means the FORALL statement processes only ten or fewer rows when performing the INSERT statement. The record type holds an index value to the collection and a component selector (.) to the field element in the record type. Line 30 shows you how to use the %ROWCOUNT bulk collection attribute on the implicit INSERT statement to the item_temp table. If you've forgotten, the SQL%ROWCOUNT applies to your last processed DML statement.

The real performance advantage comes by placing the COMMIT statement after the end of the loop. Otherwise, you commit for each batch of inserts. There are occasions when the size of data inserted makes it more advantageous to put the COMMIT statement as the last statement in the loop. You should examine the size factors and discuss them with your DBA when you analyze statement performance.

If the value of a LIMIT statement is small, such as 10, I recommend that you *never* commit inside a loop in production. On the other hand, if the value is between 500 and 1,000, I recommend that you commit inside the loop. If you don't write code to commit inside the loop with that type of record set, you will certainly produce code that adversely impacts the database because it forces the database to manage unnecessary redo actions.

UPDATE Statement

Bulk updates require that you use parallel scalar collections or field element references to record collections. As you saw in the previous section, you also must use parallel scalar collections or field element references to a record collection inside the VALUES clause of an INSERT statement.

The following example code uses scalar collections to perform a bulk UPDATE statement:

```
SQL> DECLARE
       ... same as previous bulk insert example ...
        -- Bulk update statement in a FORALL loop.
        FORALL i IN lv_fulltitle.FIRST..lv_fulltitle.LAST
          UPDATE   item_temp
          SET      item_id = lv_fulltitle(i).id
          ,        item_title = lv_fulltitle(i).title
          ,        item_subtitle = lv_fulltitle(i).subtitle
          WHERE    item_id = lv_fulltitle(i).id
          AND NOT (item_title = lv_fulltitle(i).title AND
                   item_subtitle = lv_fulltitle(i).subtitle);
```

```
        ... same as previous bulk insert example ...
END;
/
```

The `FORALL` statement on line 24 reads the `lv_fulltitle` collection and updates rows where the conditions in the `WHERE` clause are met. As with the `INSERT` statement, you should judge where the `COMMIT` statement belongs when updating bulk records.

DELETE Statement

In the scope of a `FORALL` loop, bulk `DELETE` statements work the same way as bulk `INSERT` and `UPDATE` statements. The prior discussion has focused on the use of parallel scalar collections or record collections to perform both bulk inserts and updates. While using record collections is the preferred solution for the `INSERT` and `UPDATE` statements, using record collections is not the best solution for `DELETE` statements. You can safely use a single scalar collection of surrogate keys to identify unique rows in a well-defined table.

The following example code uses a scalar numeric collection to perform bulk delete operations:

```
SQL> DECLARE
  2    -- Define a table of a scalar number data type.
  3    TYPE id_table IS TABLE OF NUMBER;
  4    -- Declare a collection variable.
  5    lv_id  ID_TABLE;
  6    /* Declare an explicit cursor to return the primary key
  7       value from a table. */
  8    CURSOR c IS
  9      SELECT   item_id AS id
 10      FROM     item;
 11  BEGIN
 12    OPEN c;
 13    LOOP
 14      FETCH c
 15      BULK COLLECT INTO lv_id LIMIT 10;
 16      EXIT WHEN lv_id.COUNT = 0;
 17      -- Bulk update statement in a FORALL loop.
 18      FORALL i IN lv_id.FIRST..lv_id.LAST
 19        DELETE
 20        FROM     item_temp
 21        WHERE    item_id = lv_id(i);
 22      /* Print the number of rows inserted per iteration. */
 23      dbms_output.put_line('['||SQL%ROWCOUNT||']');
 24    END LOOP;
 25  END;
 26  /
```

Line 3 defines the `id_table` scalar collection, and line 5 declares a local variable of that data type. Lines 18 through 21 show you how to write bulk `DELETE` statements against an `item_id` primary key column.

This section has demonstrated how to use bulk collections and the `FORALL` statement. Bulk DML statements provide you with significant performance improvements over row-by-row processing. You should look for opportunities to use them where they improve your application throughput.

%BULK_EXCEPTION Handling

Toward the beginning of this "Bulk Statements" section, Table 5-8 introduces the two bulk collection attributes, `%BULK_ROWCOUNT` and `%BULK_EXCEPTION`. You get the number or rows inserted, updated, or deleted by a bulk statement when you couple `SQL` (for the last implicit DML statement) and the `%BULK_ROWCOUNT` bulk collection attribute—`SQL%BULK_ROWCOUNT`. The `%BULK_ROWCOUNT` bulk collection attribute returns the total number, the limit imposed, or the residual number for the last `INSERT`, `UPDATE`, or `DELETE` statement.

`%BULK_EXCEPTION` returns three field values: `COUNT`, `ERROR_INDEX`, and `ERROR_CODE`. The `ERROR_CODE` value is a positive integer, which means you need to multiply any `ERROR_CODE` value by –1 before looking for its error message. You can access the fields by first coupling `SQL` to the `%BULK_EXCEPTION` collection attribute and then using a component selector (`.`) before the field name, like this:

```
SQL%BULK_EXCEPTIONS.COUNT
```

Oracle's exception handling model is like that of most programming languages—straightforward. When a program encounters an error, it raises an exception (in the Java programming language, it throws an exception). The exception block captures and handles thrown exceptions, and exceptions typically stop the program.

Bulk processing has two options. The default option accepts the default exception handling paradigm and stops processing a program's logic with a single error. The override option lets you log errors and continue with the bulk processing until the completion of an `INSERT`, `UPDATE`, or `DELETE` statement. You override the default behavior by appending a `SAVE EXCEPTIONS` clause to the `FORALL` statement. Bulk exceptions raise an `ORA-24381` error code. You need to define a user-defined exception (covered briefly in Chapter 3 and in detail in Chapter 7) to manage bulk exceptions because there isn't a predefined exception for bulk exceptions in the `standard` package.

The following example demonstrates how you handle bulk exceptions. It changes a few things from the prior example. The record type is different, and a unique constraint on the `item_title` and `item_type` columns will raise some errors when the program runs. The errors are important because they show you how to handle bulk exceptions.

```
SQL> DECLARE
    /* Define a record type. */
    TYPE item_record IS RECORD
    ( id      NUMBER
    , title   VARCHAR2(62)
    , type    VARCHAR2(60));
    /* Define a collection based on the record data type. */
    TYPE item_table IS TABLE OF ITEM_RECORD;
    /* Declare a variable of the collection data type. */
    lv_fulltitle  ITEM_TABLE;
    /* Declare an explicit cursor. */
    CURSOR c IS
      SELECT   item_id AS id
      ,        item_title AS title
      ,        item_type AS type
      FROM     item;
    /* Declare a bulk error and map it to Oracle's error code. */
```

```
18    bulk_error  EXCEPTION;
19    PRAGMA  EXCEPTION_INIT(bulk_error, -24381);
20  BEGIN
21    OPEN c;
22    LOOP
23      FETCH c
24      BULK COLLECT INTO lv_fulltitle LIMIT 5;
25      EXIT WHEN lv_fulltitle.COUNT = 0;
26      FORALL i IN lv_fulltitle.FIRST..lv_fulltitle.LAST SAVE EXCEPTIONS
27        INSERT INTO item_temp
28        VALUES
29        ( lv_fulltitle(i).id
30        , lv_fulltitle(i).title
31        , lv_fulltitle(i).type );
32        /* Print the number of rows inserted per iteration. */
33        dbms_output.put_line(
34          '['||SQL%ROWCOUNT||'] Inserted Successfully');
35    END LOOP;
36  EXCEPTION
37    WHEN bulk_error THEN
38      /* Print the count of bulk errors. */
39      dbms_output.put_line(
40        '['||SQL%ROWCOUNT||'] Inserted Successfully');
41      /* Print individual errors. */
42      FOR i IN 1..SQL%BULK_EXCEPTIONS.COUNT LOOP
43        dbms_output.put_line('['
44          || SQL%BULK_EXCEPTIONS(i).ERROR_INDEX ||'] ['
45          || SQLERRM(-1 * SQL%BULK_EXCEPTIONS(i).ERROR_CODE) ||']');
46      END LOOP;
47  END;
48  /
```

Lines 18 and 19 declare a user-defined exception and a precompiler directive that maps the ORA-24381 exception to a bulk_error exception handler. Line 24 sets the LIMIT of bulk inserts at five rows for each call of the FORALL loop. The FORALL statement on line 26 has a SAVE EXCEPTIONS clause at its end, which ensures that exceptions are collected while the FORALL completes the bulk INSERT statement.

Line 45 calls the SQLERRM function with a complex call parameter. While the call parameter should be a negative number, the error_code field of the %BULK_EXCEPTION statement returns a positive integer. That's why we multiply it by a negative inverse (or –1).

It produces the following type of results:

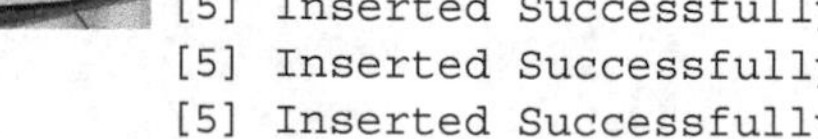

```
[5] Inserted Successfully
[5] Inserted Successfully
[5] Inserted Successfully
[3] Inserted Successfully
[4] [ORA-00001: unique constraint (.) violated]
[5] [ORA-00001: unique constraint (.) violated]
```

The anonymous block processes five rows for each bulk INSERT statement. During the last bulk INSERT statement of five rows, three rows are inserted successfully while two rows are rejected. The two rejected rows violate a UNIQUE database constraint on the combination (covered in Appendix A). The completion of the fourth bulk INSERT statement raises an ORA-24381 exception, and throws control to the exception block.

This section has shown you how to manage bulk DML statements.

Review Section

This section has described the following points about bulk statements:

- Bulk processing can work with parallel collections of scalar data types or collections of record data types.
- The BULK COLLECT statement lets you gather rows from a cursor into a collection, and collections can be single or parallel collections of scalar data types, or collections of records.
- PL/SQL supports the %BULK_EXCEPTIONS(i) and %BULK_ROWCOUNTS(i) bulk collection attributes.
- The FORALL statement lets you take a collection and pass it to an INSERT, UPDATE, or DELETE statement.
- The %ROWCOUNT attribute also works with bulk inserts, updates, and deletes, but in the case of MERGE statements, you're never sure which rows are inserted or updated.
- Record collections work best when FORALL statements work with INSERT or UPDATE statements.
- Single scalar collections work best when FORALL statements work with DELETE statements.
- By default, Oracle's exception handling stops program logic with a single error, which isn't optimal for bulk processing. The %BULK_EXCEPTION collection attribute lets you override the default exception handling process in a FORALL statement, and lets you capture errors for problem rows while successfully processing those rows without errors.

Supporting Scripts

This section describes programs placed on the McGraw-Hill Professional website to support this chapter.

- The conditional_logic.sql program contains small programs that support the "Conditional Statements" section of this chapter.
- The iterative_logic.sql program contains small programs that support the "Iterative Statements" section of this chapter.
- The bulk_processing_logic.sql program contains small programs that support the "Bulk Statements" section of this chapter.

Summary

This chapter has examined the control structures in PL/SQL. You should understand how to effectively use conditional statements and iterative statements. You should also understand how to build and manage cursors in your PL/SQL programs.

Mastery Check

The mastery check is a series of true-or-false and multiple-choice questions that let you confirm how well you understand the material in the chapter. You may check Appendix I for answers to these questions.

True or False:

1. ___Conjunctive logic involves determining when two or more things are true at the same time.
2. ___Inclusion logic involves determining when one or another thing is true at any time.
3. ___Short-circuit logic occurs with inclusion logic.
4. ___Databases always rely on two-valued logic.
5. ___A searched `CASE` statement may use a string or numeric selector.
6. ___A simple `CASE` statement can use a numeric selector.
7. ___Conditional compilation supports conditional compilation flags.
8. ___A `CONTINUE` statement lets you skip the balance of an iteration through a loop.
9. ___A `SELECT-INTO` statement is an example of an explicit cursor.
10. ___The `FORALL` statement lets you perform bulk `INSERT` statements.

Multiple Choice:

11. A conditional statement applied against two operands can evaluate which of the following? (Multiple answers possible)
    - **A.** The truth of a comparison involving only not-null values
    - **B.** The non-truth (or falsity) of a comparison involving only not-null values
    - **C.** The truth of a comparison involving one or more null values
    - **D.** The non-truth (or falsity) of a comparison involving one or more null values
    - **E.** The truth of null values
12. Which of the following are *only* guard-on-entry loops? (Multiple answers possible)
    - **A.** A simple range loop
    - **B.** A range `FOR` loop
    - **C.** A `WHILE` loop
    - **D.** A `DO-UNTIL` loop
    - **E.** A `DO-WHILE` loop

13. Which of the following guards entry and exit to the loop in PL/SQL? (Multiple answers possible)

A. A range `FOR` loop

B. A cursor `FOR` loop

C. A simple loop

D. A `DO-WHILE` loop

E. A `WHILE` loop

14. Which of the following are *only* guard-on-exit loops? (Multiple answers possible)

A. A simple cursor loop

B. A simple range loop

C. A cursor `FOR` loop

D. A `WHILE` loop

E. A range `FOR` loop

15. Which of the following collections work best with a bulk delete operation on a well-defined (or normalized) table with a surrogate key for its single-column primary key? (Multiple answers possible)

A. Parallel scalar collections

B. A single scalar collection

C. A single record collection

D. All of the above

E. None of the above

CHAPTER 6

Collections

Collections are arrays and lists—at least, that's the way they've been labeled since the advent of Java. An *array* is a collection of a fixed number of elements that share the same data type. A *list* is a collection of any number of elements that share the same data type. A list is generally more flexible than an array because you don't have to know before you create a list how many elements belong in the collection

Oracle Database 12*c* provides you with a very powerful collection framework, and the framework lets you create collections in a SQL or PL/SQL context. You can use the collection framework to create the equivalent of arrays, sets, bags, hash tables, and unordered tables.

There are four sections in this chapter. The "Introduction to Collections" section explains the Oracle Database 12*c* collection framework. The "Object Types: Varray and Table Collections" section shows you how to create and work with varrays and table collections. The "Associative Arrays" section shows you how to work with structures that map keys to values. The "Oracle Collection API" section describes and illustrates the application programming interface (API) for Oracle's collection types.

Introduction to Collections

Oracle 8*i* Database forward provides three types of collections. Two are SQL collections and one is a PL/SQL-only collection. Oracle implements a SQL array as a *varray* data type and implements a SQL list as a *table* data type. The PL/SQL-only collection is an *associative array* or an *index-by* table data type and is implemented as a list. While the SQL collections are numerically indexed, you can index an associative array with numbers or strings.

You can implement Oracle SQL collection data types in SQL or PL/SQL. SQL collections are *schema-level* object types. Although you can implement SQL collection data types in PL/SQL, it's best to implement them in SQL, because any SQL data type can be accessed from SQL or PL/SQL. Associative arrays don't enjoy this interchangeable characteristic, and their use is limited to inside a PL/SQL scope.

Oracle Database 12*c* does provide the ability to use a PL/SQL composite data type inside an embedded SQL statement. However, you must declare a local variable of the PL/SQL collection type in the local or containing PL/SQL block first. Then, you embed the SQL statement in the local PL/SQL block. There's a complete example in the "PL/SQL-Specific Data Types Allowed in SQL" section of Chapter 2.

Oracle PL/SQL Tables

The Oracle Database PL/SQL Language Reference 12c Release 1 tells us that associative arrays were previously called *PL/SQL tables* or *index-by tables*. Thus, to be consistent with Oracle's official lingo, you should use the term *associative array* instead. If you frequent Oracle forums, don't be surprised if you still encounter the term *PL/SQL table* or *index-by table* being used in discussions.

	SQL Collections	Associative Arrays
Scope	May be defined in SQL or PL/SQL scope.	Are defined only in PL/SQL scope.
Initialization	Require initialization before their first use.	Don't require initialization.
Assignment	Preallocate space before assigning values. You can preallocate space and assign values for more than one element at a time.	Don't need to allocate space because you manually assign indexes and values one row at a time.
Index	Use a sequential set of integers as index values (at least initially for the table data types), which makes SQL collections densely populated arrays and lists.	Use an integer or string as the index, and the index value may be in any order you like, which makes associative arrays sparsely populated lists.
Base Data Type	Use any SQL scalar data type or UDT object type.	Use any SQL or PL/SQL scalar data type or a PL/SQL record type.

TABLE 6-1. *Differences Between SQL Collections and Associative Arrays*

Beyond the scope limitation, PL/SQL index-by tables differ from the varray and table object types in four key ways: initialization, assignment, index, and base data types. Table 6-1 highlights the differences between how these different collection types work.

Chapter 4 covers the three composite data types: two are the UDT object and PL/SQL record data types, and the third is a collection. The simplest one is a collection of a scalar data type, like a number, string, or date. The scalar data type for this type of collection is the collection's base type. All collections are final data types. That means you can't extend their behavior. The reason that they are final data types isn't explained in Oracle's documentation (the *Oracle Database PL/SQL Language Reference* and *Oracle Object-Relational Developer's Guide*), but Oracle 8*i* forward provides a Collection API to help you work with and manage collections. The Oracle Database PL/SQL Language Reference uses Table 6-2 to qualify how non-PL/SQL composite types map to these PL/SQL composite types.

Non PL/SQL Composite Type	Equivalent PL/SQL Composite Type
Hash table	Associative array
Unordered table	Associative array
Set	Nested table
Bag	Nested table
Array	Varray

TABLE 6-2. *Map of Non PL/SQL to PL/SQL Composite Types*

A record data type generally contains a collection of related field elements, similar to a row in a table. That means a record structure is like a table structure, and a collection of a record structure is like an in-memory PL/SQL-only table.

Object types have both subtle differences and broad differences from record data types. The subtle difference occurs when you define a SQL object type without methods, because it creates a SQL data type that mimics a PL/SQL record type. The subtle difference for assigning data to it requires that you use a constructor function, which is just like a `VALUES` clause of an `INSERT` statement. The values must match by position and data type the list of attributes in the object type. Oracle checks the position and data type of attributes by implicitly inspecting the automatically generated default object constructor (see Chapter 11 for the details).

Before I explain the broad differences, you need to understand how and where you can define and use SQL and PL/SQL object types and PL/SQL record types. You can define object types as schema-level objects in any container or pluggable database or inside any PL/SQL declaration block. You can define record types inside any PL/SQL declaration block.

It's possible to use object and record types in an anonymous or named block that has access to the declaration block where they're defined. Object and record types are locally available when they're defined in the local declaration block. They're also available when defined in an outer declaration block for nested PL/SQL programs. Object and record types are more broadly available when they're defined in package specifications, because any PL/SQL program run by a user that has execute privileges on that package can use them.

Object types can define the data type of a column in a table, the structure of a table, the data type of a parameter in a function or procedure, and the data type of a return type from a function. Record types can also serve as parameters in stored programs or as function return types. Naturally, collections of object and record types inherit the same features and limitations as their base data types.

The broad difference between object types and record types are as follows:

- Object types can define column data types and table structures, while record types can't.
- Object types can serve as parameter data types in functions and procedures called from SQL or PL/SQL, while record types can only work in an exclusively PL/SQL call context.
- Collections of object types can define column data types but not table structures.
- Collections of object types can work in SQL and PL/SQL contexts, while collections of record types are limited to PL/SQL-only contexts.

The similarities and differences of the base data types impact how you work with collections of them. Figure 6-1 shows when you can call collections as parameters and function returns. You should notice that SQL collection data types may be consumed in SQL scope or PL/SQL scope, with one exception: an aggregate table. Aggregate tables occur whenever you return a SQL collection from a function or return a PL/SQL collection from a pipelined table function (see Chapter 8 for more details). Aggregate tables are essentially the same as result sets from `SELECT` statements, and that's why they have an asterisk in Figure 6-1.

Collection Data Type	Scope	SQL Call Parameter	PL/SQL Call Parameter	SQL Function Return	PL/SQL Function Return
Varray	SQL	Yes	Yes	Yes	Yes
Nested Table		Yes	Yes	Yes	Yes
Aggregate Table*				Yes	
Varray	PL/SQL		Yes		Yes
Nested Table			Yes		Yes
Associative Array			Yes		Yes

FIGURE 6-1. *Collection access and return type scopes*

Object Types: Varray and Table Collections

As discussed, collections are programming structures that hold sets of like things, and they fall into two categories, arrays and lists. Arrays typically have a physical size allocated when you define them, while lists have no physical size limit. Oracle implements arrays as the varray data type and lists as the table data type.

Oracle lets you define schema-level object types that hold collections of scalar or object data types. It's also possible that a collection may hold object types that contain other nested varray or table collections. Whether a collection holds a scalar or composite data type, it holds what's known as its *base* data type.

A SQL collection of a scalar data type is an Attribute Data Type (ADT), while a collection of an object type is a user-defined type (UDT). The allocation of space for new members of a SQL collection is essential. Space allocation implicitly increments by one the integer value of the next index. This makes object type collections densely indexed.

The following subsections cover SQL varray and table data types.

Varray Collections

Varray collections are single-dimensional structures that have a maximum number of elements. The elements all have the same data type. As mentioned, the element data type is the base data type of the varray collection.

The prototype for creating a SQL varray collection is

```
TYPE type_name IS {VARRAY | VARYING ARRAY}(size_limit) OF data_type
  [NOT NULL];
```

By default, new elements can be null. You must append the `NOT NULL` clause when you define a collection to preclude null values, although it's generally a good practice to allow null values while ensuring you only add elements that aren't null. You should preclude null values only when you want to raise an exception while trying to assign a null value to a collection.

What's in a Name?

As indicated in the prototype, `VARRAY` and `VARYING ARRAY` can be used interchangeably, but the most common use is `VARRAY`. So, unless you rely on GeSHi (Generic System Highlighter) tools, most of which highlight `VARYING ARRAY` but not `VARRAY`, you should use the term `VARRAY`.

You would define a three-element varray of strings in SQL with the following syntax:

```
SQL> CREATE OR REPLACE
  2    TYPE sql_varray IS VARRAY(3) OF VARCHAR2(20);
  3  /
```

Or, like this:

```
SQL> CREATE OR REPLACE
  2    TYPE sql_varray IS VARYING ARRAY(3) OF VARCHAR2(20);
  3  /
```

In both cases, line 1 uses SQL syntax to create or replace a schema-level object type. Line 2 defines the varray collection, and the syntax on line 2 is how you would define a varray collection in a PL/SQL declaration block. Line 3 executes or compiles the type.

You can actually construct and use object types within a SQL statement without any other components. While it's not too useful, the following example shows how to do it:

```
SQL> SELECT   column_value AS "Three Stooges"
  2  FROM     TABLE(sql_varray('Moe','Larry','Curly'));
```

The `SELECT` list only returns a `column_value` pseudocolumn, which holds the results of any aggregate result returned by an ADT collection. The *"Three Stooges"* column alias just adds a formatting touch. The key to reading the collection is the `TABLE` function, which you can read more about in Appendix C. The query constructs a three-element collection inside the call to the `TABLE` function on line 2.

The results are

```
Three Stooges
---------------
Moe
Larry
Curly
```

You can order the return values by appending an `ORDER BY` clause that references the position of the `column_value` pseudocolumn:

```
  3  ORDER BY 1;
```

You can also override the default sort order with an `ORDER MEMBER` function when you implement an object body (see Chapter 11 for the details). Its ill advised to override the default sort operation of an ADT. The one exception to that rule is when you're using an encrypted scalar data type as the base data type of the collection.

You would define a three-element varray of strings in PL/SQL with the following syntax in any declaration block:

```
SQL> DECLARE
  /* Define a local PL/SQL collection. */
  TYPE sql_varray IS VARRAY(3) OF VARCHAR2(20);
BEGIN
  ...
END;
/
```

The code in the execution and exception blocks would be exactly the same whether you define the varray collection in SQL or PL/SQL. Let's rework the example to construct and consume values from a varray collection in PL/SQL. This time, we declare an `lv_stooges` variable by constructing it with a list of two rather than three string elements. The code follows:

```
SQL> DECLARE
  2    /* Declare a collection variable with a constructor call. */
  3    lv_stooges  SQL_VARRAY := sql_varray('Moe','Larry');
  4  BEGIN
  5    /* Print the number and limit of elements. */
  6    dbms_output.put_line(
  7      'Count ['||lv_stooges.COUNT||'] '||
  8      'Limit ['||lv_stooges.LIMIT||']');
  9
 10    /* Extend space and assign to the new index. */
 11    lv_stooges.EXTEND;
 12
 13    /* Print the number and limit of elements. */
 14    dbms_output.put_line(
 15      'Count ['||lv_stooges.COUNT||'] '||
 16      'Limit ['||lv_stooges.LIMIT||']');
 17
 18    /* Assign a new value. */
 19    lv_collection(lv_stooges.COUNT) := 'Curly';
 20
 21    /* Iterate across the collection to the total number of elements. */
 22    FOR i IN 1..lv_stooges.COUNT LOOP
 23      dbms_output.put_line(lv_stooges(i));
 24    END LOOP;
 25  END;
 26  /
```

Line 3 declares an `lv_stooges` variable of the `sql_varray` collection shown earlier. The call to the `sql_varray` data type with a list of two strings creates an object type collection with two elements. It's possible to construct an empty collection by calling the constructor without any call parameters, like this variation on line 3:

```
  3    lv_stooges  SQL_VARRAY := sql_varray();
```

All varray and table data types have three possible states: null, empty, and populated. A null collection is uninitialized; an empty collection is initialized without any elements; and a populated collection is initialized with at least one element. You use the `IS NULL` comparison operator to check whether a collection is uninitialized before you work with it. The `IS EMPTY` comparison operator lets you find an empty collection, and the `COUNT` function lets you discover how many elements a collection has. The `COUNT` function is part of the Oracle Collection API and is available for all three collection types. The Collection API also includes the `LIMIT` function, which lets you find the maximum number of elements in a varray. You use the `COUNT` and `LIMIT` function by appending them after the component selector (`.`).

Lines 6 through 8 print a `COUNT` value of 2 and a `LIMIT` value of 3 because you have allocated space for two out of three possible elements in the varray. Line 11 extends memory space for a third element, which automatically creates a new index value of 3, and it points to a null element. Lines 14 through 16 print a `COUNT` and `LIMIT` value of 3 because you have now allocated space for all three possible elements. Line 18 assigns a value to the new element of the collection. It identifies the new element by relying on the 1-based numbering of collections and the fact that the `COUNT` function returns a correct index value for the last element in a collection.

Line 23 prints all the elements of the collection, but notice how it identifies the elements of the collection. It uses a parenthetical reference to the index value of the collection, and that's different from other programming languages. Many languages use square brackets to offset index values, but Oracle uses ordinary parentheses.

If you disallow null values by changing the earlier definition of the `sql_varray` data type, the attempt to assign a null value on line 19 would raise the following exception:

```
  lv_collection(lv_collection.COUNT) := NULL;
                                        *
ERROR at line 18:
ORA-06550: line 18, column 41:
PLS-00382: expression is of wrong type
ORA-06550: line 18, column 3:
PL/SQL: Statement ignored
```

The physical size limit guarantees a varray collection can hold only so many elements. This limit is often a key reason for using or avoiding the varray data type. Choosing a varray data type as a developer means you want your program to fail when it attempts to assign a value beyond the limit of possible values. Making that choice is a convenient way to raise an exception when data violates a "no more than" type of rule. It also eliminates writing additional logic to check whether the number of results exceeds a target limit. That's because the varray does that check for you by raising an out-of-bounds error.

We can generate an out-of-bounds error with the prior sample code by making one change. Change the constructor call on line 3 from a list of two elements to a list of three elements (using the original third stooge—*Shemp*, Curly's real-life brother), like

```
  2     lv_collection  SQL_VARRAY := sql_varray('Moe','Larry','Shemp');
```

You would now raise the following exception on line 10 when attempting to add space for an element beyond the physical limit of three elements:

```
DECLARE
*
```

```
ERROR at line 1:
ORA-06532: Subscript outside of limit
ORA-06512: at line 10
```

You would get virtually the same message if you were to attempt to access a varray with an index value of 0. That's because a varray always starts with an index value of 1. You can have a 0 index value in an associative array because it follows different rules.

Since varray and table collections have the same syntax when working with SQL object types and PL/SQL record types, to avoid redundancy, those examples are presented in the next section only.

Table Collections

Table collections are single-dimensional structures that have no limit on the number of elements that they hold—at least, no limit exists other than what's available in the database resources. The key resources that may impose limits are the System Global Area (SGA) and the Program Global Area (PGA). Like a varray collection, the elements of table collections must all have the same data type. The base type of a table collection, like a varray, is the data type of the elements held in the collection. Table collections can hold scalar or composite data types.

The prototype for creating a SQL table collection is

```
TYPE type_name IS TABLE OF data_type [NOT NULL];
```

Unlike the varray collection discussion in the previous section, in this section we work through table collections of scalar and composite data types. We also will look at local and package-level PL/SQL collections.

Scalar Table Collections

Like varray collections, you have the option of allowing or disallowing null values. While the default allows null values, appending a `NOT NULL` clause disallows them. The best practice is to allow null values while ensuring that you only add elements that aren't null (although some programmers disallow null values to ensure null value assignments raise exceptions).

You would define a table of strings in SQL with the following syntax:

```
SQL> CREATE OR REPLACE
  2    TYPE sql_table IS TABLE OF VARCHAR2(20);
  3  /
```

Line 1 uses SQL syntax to create or replace a schema-level object type. Line 2 defines the table collection, and the syntax on line 2 is how you would define a table collection in a PL/SQL declaration block. Line 3 runs or compiles the type.

Like the varray collection example in the previous section, you can query a table collection by using the `TABLE` function in the `FROM` clause of a query. Here's the example of constructing and consuming the collection in a query:

```
SQL> SELECT   column_value AS "Dúnedain"
  2  FROM     TABLE(sql_varray('Aragorn','Faramir','Boromir'))
  3  ORDER BY 1;
```

The `TABLE` function call on line 3 converts the table collection into an aggregate result set. All return sets from queries are formally aggregate result sets. ADTs display their results by using the `column_value` pseudocolumn. The example also uses a column alias, Dúnedain, to format the result set from the query, and returns the following results:

```
Dúnedain
---------
Aragorn
Boromir
Faramir
```

The problem with ADT collections is that you have no way to unnest them when they're used inside a table. That means the only way to add or update an element is through PL/SQL. The "PL/SQL to the Rescue of Updating an ADT Element" sidebar in the "Nested Table Updates" section of Appendix B shows you how to update an embedded ADT element. Therefore, in this section I'll only show you how to add a new element to an ADT by using a PL/SQL function. While an anonymous block could illustrate it, a forward reference to a function seems more effective to use with an `UPDATE` statement.

The code for the `add_element` function is

```
SQL> CREATE OR REPLACE FUNCTION add_element
  2  ( pv_table     SQL_TABLE
  3  , pv_element   VARCHAR2 ) RETURN SQL_TABLE IS
  4
  5    /* Declare a local table collection. */
  6    lv_table     SQL_TABLE := sql_table();
  7  BEGIN
  8
  9    /* Check for an initialized collection parameter. */
 10    IF pv_table.EXISTS(1) THEN  -- A suboptimal comparison.
 11      lv_table := pv_table;
 12    END IF;
 13
 14    /* Check for a not null element before adding it. */
 15    IF pv_element IS NOT NULL THEN
 16      /* Extend space and add an element. */
 17      lv_table.EXTEND;
 18      lv_table(lv_table.COUNT) := pv_element;
 19    END IF;
 20
 21    /* Return the table collection with its new member. */
 22    RETURN lv_table;
 23  END;
 24  /
```

Line 2 declares a formal collection parameter, and line 3 declares a formal collection return type. The logic of the program ensures one of four outcomes:

- Adds an element to a collection with at least one preexisting member
- Adds an element to an empty collection
- Doesn't add a null element to a populated or empty collection
- Initializes an empty collection

Line 6 declares an empty `lv_table` collection because the `pv_table` call parameter may hold a null value. Initializing the `lv_table` collection prevents raising an uninitialized collection error.

Line 10 checks whether the `pv_table` call parameter holds at least one member. It uses the `EXISTS` function with what should be the first index value of the table collection. We make that check because there's no sense assigning an empty collection to the local `lv_table` collection variable. While the `EXISTS` function works by using the first index value as a call parameter, it's a better practice to use an `IS NOT EMPTY` comparison operator, like

```
10    IF pv_table IS NOT EMPTY THEN  -- The BEST PRACTICE always!
```

You ask, "Why is it a better practice?" That's a great question. The answer is tricky, and it is specific to table collections. While varray and table indexes start out at 1, and they are densely populated with sequential integers, it's possible to delete elements. Deleting elements creates gaps in the sequence of index values. That's why checking for the first element may or may not work. All it does is check whether the first element is present. That's not what you want to know in this type of comparison. You want to know whether a table collection is populated. That's why you should *always* use the `IS EMPTY` comparison operator to check whether a table collection is populated.

You can add an element to an ADT that is nested inside a table when you call the `add_an_element` function inside an `UPDATE` statement. The following `UPDATE` statement show you how to add a new element to a nested ADT inside the employee table (the employee table is defined in the "Nested Table Updates" section of Appendix B).

```
SQL> UPDATE TABLE (SELECT  e.home_address
  2                FROM    employee e
  3                WHERE   e.employee_id = 1) e
  4  SET    e.street_address = add_an_element(e.street_address, 'Suite 622')
  5  ,      e.city = 'Oakland'
  6  WHERE e.address_id = 1;
```

Line 4 calls the `add_an_element` function with the original `street_address` ADT column value and a string literal value. Line 4 then assigns the function result to the `street_address` ADT column. You also can write an update function to change an ADT column value (see Appendix B for an example), and a delete function to remove an element from an ADT column.

Line 15 verifies the `pv_element` value isn't null. It extends space for the table collection and assigns the `pv_element` value to the collection on lines 17 and 18. You can test the `add_element` function in a query, like

```
SQL> SELECT   column_value AS "Dúnedain"
     FROM     TABLE(add_element(sql_table('Faramir','Boromir')
                                ,'Aragorn'))
     ORDER BY 1;
```

It prints the ordered set:

```
Dúnedain
----------
Aragorn
Boromir
Faramir
```

The Case of the Missing Index

All varray and table collections start out with numeric index values, and they start with 1 in all cases. While you can't remove an element from a varray, you can remove an element from a table collection. You do it by using the `DELETE` procedure from the Collection API. That means a dense table index may become sparse over the instruction sequence of your program.

A deleted item is a major issue for most developers because they increment across collections by using a `FOR` loop. A `FOR` loop simply iterates to the next member and it can't skip index gaps. However, the best method to illustrate the easy way and the hard way of navigating across a sparsely populated table collection (or at least one at risk of being sparsely populated) is to use a `WHILE` loop, so that's what we'll use in the following sample programs.

The first sample program iterates across the collection without using an increment-by-one logic. This is the easy way to iterate across any collection where the numeric index value may have gaps or the index is a string (more or less a linked list).

```
SQL> DECLARE
  2    /* Declare a meaning-laden variable name and exclude the
  3       lv_ preface from the variable name. */
  4    current  INTEGER;
  5
  6    /* Declare a local table collection. */
  7    lv_table    SQL_TABLE :=
  8                  sql_table('Aragorn','Faramir','Boromir');
  9  BEGIN
 10    /* Remove the lead element of a table collection. */
 11    lv_table.DELETE(1);
 12
 13    /* Set the starting point. */
 14    current := lv_table.FIRST;
 15
 16    /* Check pseudo index value less than last index value. */
 17    WHILE (current <= lv_table.LAST) LOOP
 18      /* Print current value. */
 19      dbms_output.put_line(
 20        'Index ['||current||']['||lv_table(current)||']');
 21
 22      /* Shift the index to the next value. */
 23      current := lv_table.NEXT(current);
 24    END LOOP;
 25  END;
 26  /
```

Note on line 4 that the `current` variable violates the generic rules for naming variables (it lacks the prefix `lv_`). That's because the `current` variable name has special meaning as the *current index value*, and it makes our program more readable. The `current` variable holds the current index value. Line 14 assigns the starting index value, which in this case is 2.

The `WHILE` loop guard on entry checks whether the current value is less than the last value (also the maximum value). Line 23 increments the `current` index to the next available value, which may mean by one, two, or more. The `NEXT` function takes the current index value to find the next index value.

The hard way to iterate across a collection with a sparse index uses increment-by-one logic and a `CONTINUE`, `GOTO`, or `IF` statement to skip over logic when an index value is missing, as shown in the following sample program:

```
SQL> DECLARE
  2    /* Declare a local counter variable. */
  3    lv_counter  INTEGER := 0;
  4
  5    /* Declare a local table collection. */
  6    lv_table    SQL_TABLE :=
  7                  sql_table('Aragorn','Faramir','Boromir');
  8  BEGIN
  9    /* Remove the lead element of a table collection. */
 10    lv_table.DELETE(1);
 11
 12    /* Check pseudo index value less than last index value. */
 13    WHILE (lv_counter <= lv_table.LAST) LOOP
 14      /* Increment the index counter. */
 15      lv_counter := lv_counter + 1;
 16
 17      /* Check whether the index returns a value. */
 18      IF lv_table.EXISTS(lv_counter) THEN
 19        dbms_output.put_line(
 20          'Values ['||lv_counter||'] ['||lv_table(lv_counter)||']');
 21      END IF;
 22    END LOOP;
 23  END;
 24  /
```

Line 3 declares the `lv_counter` variable and sets the initial value to 0, but line 10 deletes that element. Line 13 checks whether the counter value is less than or equal to the last numeric index value before entering the loop. Line 18 checks if an index value references an element in the collection. It only prints output when the element is found.

The first example works best for sparsely populated indexes. The second example, minus the check for a valid index value, works best for densely populated indexes.

Let's look at reimplementing this as an associative array (previously called PL/SQL tables or index-by tables) collection. Recall that we have two options: implement a local table collection or implement a package-level table collection. Any user with execute privileges on the package where you define a table data type can use a package-level variable.

The following uses a local table collection data type:

```
SQL> DECLARE
  2    /* Define a local table collection. */
  3    TYPE plsql_table IS TABLE OF VARCHAR2(20);
  4
  5    /* Declare a local table collection. */
  6    lv_table     PLSQL_TABLE :=
  7                   plsql_table('Aragorn','Faramir','Boromir');
  8  BEGIN
  9    /* Loop through the collection and print the results. */
 10    FOR i IN lv_table.FIRST..lv_table.LAST LOOP
 11      dbms_output.put_line(lv_table(i));
 12    END LOOP;
 13  END;
 14  /
```

Line 3 defines a local table collection. Lines 6 and 7 declare a local variable that uses the local `plsql_table` collection type. A range `FOR` loop lets us navigate through the collection and print results. This local `plsql_table` data type is only available inside the anonymous block program.

A better solution with an associative array collection requires that you implement it in a package specification. While you've only had a brief introduction to packages in Chapter 3, it's necessary to define a package specification to support this example.

You can define PL/SQL-only data types in a package specification. Variables defined in package specifications are package-level data types. Sometimes package specifications only act to define UDTs. When they do so, they don't have accompanying package bodies and are known as *bodiless packages*.

The initial `type_library` defines only a table collection data type:

```
SQL> CREATE OR REPLACE PACKAGE type_library IS
  2    /* Define a local table collection. */
  3    TYPE plsql_table IS TABLE OF VARCHAR2(20);
  4  END;
  5  /
```

Line 3 shows that the definition of a package-level collection type is the same as the definition of a local PL/SQL collection type. The next program mirrors the prior anonymous block program with one exception: it no longer defines a local `plsql_table` collection type. That's because the `lv_table` variable uses the package-level data type.

```
SQL> DECLARE
  2    /* Declare a local table collection. */
  3    lv_table     TYPE_LIBRARY.PLSQL_TABLE :=
  4                   type_library.plsql_table('Aragorn','Faramir','Boromir');
  5  BEGIN
     ...
 10  END;
 11  /
```

Line 3 declares a variable by referring to the package name and data type name. The component selector (`.`) selects the data type from the package specification. You should note that both the data type and table collection constructor must reference the package and data type.

Having shown you the possibilities with scalar collections, the next section shows you how to work with composite collections.

Composite Table Collections

There are two types of composite collections. One is a collection of an object type, and the other is a collection of an object type that holds a nested collection. Collections that hold other collections are *multilevel* collections.

A composite data type or object type that holds only scalar variables is a symmetrical element, which means all elements contain one instance of the composite set of columns. A composite data type that holds scalar and composite data types can still be symmetrical provided that the nested composite data type is like a record structure (or a single row). A composite data type is asymmetrical when it has one member attribute (or field) that is a collection data type.

The subsections that follow show you how to implement symmetrical and asymmetrical composite variables in collections. Appendix B discusses how you work with composite data types in tables. The same appendix also shows you how to write unnested queries and update nested tables.

Symmetrical Composite Table Collections To look at an example of a symmetrical composite table collection, we first need to create a few composite object types. A simple composite object type has two or more columns, and this one has just two attributes (or fields) to keep it manageable. Recall that object types are SQL data types, not PL/SQL data types, and that you must define them as schema-level objects.

The following creates a `prominent_object` composite object type at the schema level:

```
SQL> CREATE OR REPLACE
  TYPE prominent_object IS OBJECT
  ( name      VARCHAR2(20)
  , age       VARCHAR2(10));
/
```

Next, let's create another composite object type that uses the original `prominent_object` composite object type. The `people_object` composite object type holds one copy of the `prominent_object` composite object type, as qualified in the following example:

```
SQL> CREATE OR REPLACE
  2    TYPE people_object IS OBJECT
  3    ( race       VARCHAR2(10)
  4    , exemplar   PROMINENT_OBJECT);
  5  /
```

Line 4 defines a variable of the `prominent_object` composite object type.

The last step creates a table collection of the composite object type:

```
SQL> CREATE OR REPLACE
  TYPE people_table IS TABLE OF people_object;
/
```

Like the varray and table collection examples presented earlier, the primary definition is on line 2. After creating these types, you can query them with the following (albeit complex) syntax:

```
SQL> COLUMN EXEMPLAR FORMAT A40
SQL> SELECT *
  2  FROM   TABLE(
  3           SELECT CAST(COLLECT(
  4                    people_object(
  5                       'Men'
  6                     , prominent_object('Aragorn','3rd Age')
  7                    )
  8                 ) AS people_table
  9           )
 10           FROM dual);
```

The query shows that you need to call the COLLECT function to put the composite object into a runtime collection. Then, you can CAST the runtime collection to a known schema-level collection data type. Finally, you can SELECT the data by using the TABLE function to convert it into an aggregate result set (fancy speak for any result set from a SELECT statement).

It prints the following:

```
RACE       EXEMPLAR(NAME, AGE)
---------- ----------------------------------------
Men        PROMINENT_OBJECT('Aragorn', '3rd Age')
```

The only problem with this output is the constructor versus column values for the nested pseudo (at this point) collection. You can fix that by unnesting the query with a CROSS JOIN, like

```
SQL> SELECT     o.race, n.name, n.age
     ...
 10             FROM  dual) o CROSS JOIN
 11           TABLE(
 12             SELECT CAST(COLLECT(exemplar) AS prominent_table)
 13             FROM dual) n;
```

Line 1 (or the SQL line) shows the SELECT list's three columns. If you were to include an asterisk, the query would return four columns. In addition to the three columns from the SELECT list, it would return the exemplar column, because the cross join simply adds the new columns to the same row of data. The o alias represents the *outer* query, and the n alias represents the nested table, which is based on a prominent_object object type. This returns the nested columns matched against the single row where they're linked. A cross join (or Cartesian product) returns the number of rows found in the nested table because it's always matched against the containing row.

It prints

```
RACE       NAME                 AGE
---------- -------------------- ---------
Men        Aragorn              3rd Age
```

The TABLE function returns an aggregate result set that is compatible with the rest of the query. The SELECT statement and the CAST and COLLECT functions let us work with a single element rather than a real table collection. The exemplar column is returned by the query but filtered out by the `SELECT` list's choice (formally *projection*) of columns. You can check the "Unnesting Queries" section in Appendix B for more information on this approach.

It's actually a much simpler query when you have a real `people_table` collection. The following query fabricates a collection of two elements. The fabricating syntax creates a multilevel `people_table` collection. Here's the code without the `COLLECT` and `CAST` functions:

```
SQL> SELECT  o.race, n.name, n.age
  2  FROM    TABLE(
  3            people_table(
  4                people_object(
  5                   'Men'
  6                 , prominent_object('Aragorn','3rd Age'))
  7            , people_object(
  8                   'Elf'
  9                 , prominent_object('Legolas','3rd Age'))
 10            )) o CROSS JOIN
 11          TABLE(
 12            SELECT CAST(COLLECT(exemplar) AS prominent_table)
 13            FROM dual) n;
```

Lines 3 through 9 (fewer lines would be necessary without the constraints of the printed page) construct a `people_table` collection of two composite elements. Lines 6 and 9 construct the nested `prominent_object` composite type for each element of the collection. Then, the `TABLE` function lets us query the contents of the dynamically created table collection.

It prints

```
RACE       NAME                 AGE
---------- -------------------- ---------
Men        Aragorn              3rd Age
Elf        Legolas              3rd Age
```

Shifting the code from SQL exploration of composite object types, the following creates a local `people_table` instance, and it reads and prints selected contents:

```
SQL> DECLARE
  /* Declare a table collection. */
  lv_tolkien_table  PEOPLE_TABLE :=
                      people_table(
                          people_object(
                             'Men'
                           , prominent_object('Aragorn','3rd Age'))
                        , people_object(
                             'Elf'
                        , prominent_object('Legolas','3rd Age')));
BEGIN
  /* Add a new record to collection. */
  lv_tolkien_table.EXTEND;
  lv_tolkien_table(lv_tolkien_table.COUNT) :=
     people_object('Dwarf'
                  , prominent_object('Gimili','3rd Age'));
```

```
18     /* Read and print values in table collection. */
19     FOR i IN lv_tolkien_table.FIRST..lv_tolkien_table.LAST LOOP
20       dbms_output.put_line(
21         lv_tolkien_table(i).race||': '||lv_tolkien_table(i).exemplar.name);
22     END LOOP;
23   END;
24   /
```

The initial constructor call on lines 3 through 10 is exactly like the one in the preceding query. You allocate space on line 13 and then add a new composite element to the collection on lines 14 through 16.

Line 21 provides the syntax to read the scalar and composite columns of the collection. In both cases, you must first access the `lv_tolkien` collection variable by providing an index value. You read the scalar column by referring to its `race` attribute name. It's more complex to access the nested composite object. After referring to the `lv_tolkien` collection variable with an index value, you access the `exemplar` attribute name. The `exemplar` attribute identifies the nested composite type, and lets you append with a dot (`.`) either of its scalar attributes. The example accesses the nested `name` attribute.

It prints

```
Men: Aragorn
Elf: Legolas
Dwarf: Gimili
```

You can also transfer an object type to a PL/SQL record structure or collection. The `SELECT-INTO` statement from the "Single-Row Implicit Cursors" section of Chapter 5 lets you assign a single object type or one of a collection of object types to a record type. The `BULK COLLECT INTO` statement from the "Record Collection Targets" section of Chapter 5 lets you assign an object collection to a PL/SQL record collection. Rather than write two full examples with a `people_object` and `people_table`, we've got only one that simply limits the number of `people_object` rows returned by the collection:

```
SQL> DECLARE
    /* Declare a PL/SQL record. */
    TYPE tolkien_record IS RECORD
    ( race      VARCHAR2(10)
    , name      VARCHAR2(20)
    , age       VARCHAR2(10));

    /* Declare a table of the record. */
    TYPE tolkien_plsql_table IS TABLE OF TOLKIEN_RECORD;

    /* Declare record and table collection variables. */
    lv_tolkien_record       TOLKIEN_RECORD;
    lv_tolkien_plsql_table  TOLKIEN_PLSQL_TABLE;

    /* Declare a table collection. */
    lv_tolkien_table  PEOPLE_TABLE :=
```

```
17                            people_table(
     ... Same definition as prior example ...
24   BEGIN
25     /* Single-row implicit subquery. */
26     SELECT   o.race, n.name, n.age
27     INTO     lv_tolkien_record
28     FROM     TABLE(lv_tolkien_table) o CROSS JOIN
29              TABLE(
30                SELECT CAST(COLLECT(exemplar) AS prominent_table)
31                FROM   dual) n
32     WHERE    ROWNUM < 2;
33
34     dbms_output.put_line(
35       '['||lv_tolkien_record.race||'] '||
36       '['||lv_tolkien_record.name||'] '||
37       '['||lv_tolkien_record.age ||']');
38   END;
39   /
```

Lines 3 through 6 define the `tolkien_record` structure, and line 9 defines a table of the `tolkien_record` data type. The `SELECT-INTO` query found on lines 26 through 32 returns one row from the `lv_tolkien_table` collection and assigns that row to our local `lv_tolkien_record` variable.

Line 32 limits the table collection to one row with the backward-compatible `ROWNUM` comparison, which prior to Oracle Database 12*c* has always been a pseudo top-n query. Oracle Database 12*c* lets you do better because it provides real top-n query syntax. You can replace line 32 with the following in an Oracle Database 12*c* database:

```
32     FETCH    FIRST 1 ROWS ONLY;
```

From my perspective, the Oracle Database 12*c* top-n query syntax is much clearer than the older syntax. After the `SELECT-INTO` query, the program prints the record's values:

```
[Men] [Aragorn] [3rd Age]
```

Replacing `INTO` with `BULK COLLECT INTO` on line 27 lets the program perform a bulk operation. The bulk operation performed by the following line 27 transfers all rows from the table collection into the local variable of the anonymous block program:

```
27     BULK COLLECT INTO lv_tolkien_plsql_table
```

It's important to note that bulk collections require a table data type of PL/SQL records as their target variables. That's why we created the `lv_tolkien_plsql_table` variable as a collection of records.

Whether or not you replace line 32 (with the `FETCH FIRST 1 ROWS ONLY` clause), the modified program can't print results. That's because it now retrieves one or more rows into a collection. Effectively, with the bulk collect, we changed the target assignment from a composite record structure to a composite collection of the same record structure. The assignment target change breaks our printing logic. We now need to print elements of the collection one at a time, and that means printing them in loop.

The easiest way to accomplish the change is with a `FOR` loop, as shown:

```
33    /* Loop through the result set and print the results. */
34    FOR i IN 1..lv_tolkien_plsql_table.COUNT LOOP
35      dbms_output.put_line(
36        '['||lv_tolkien_plsql_table(i).race||'] '||
37        '['||lv_tolkien_plsql_table(i).name||'] '||
38        '['||lv_tolkien_plsql_table(i).age ||']');
39    END LOOP;
```

You should note that the collection rows are referred to by their index value on lines 36 through 38. The component selector (`.`) then connects the row to a field of the record type. Although I've advocated that you move data to SQL data types, sometimes you do need to move object collection data back to the older (or from the perspective of some, legacy) PL/SQL collection data types. Now you have examples of doing that one row or many rows at a time.

The `SELECT-INTO` or `BULK COLLECT INTO` assignment is generally the most effective way to move data quickly from a table collection of object types into a table collection of PL/SQL records, but there is an alternative way. It requires you to initialize the collection as an empty collection, allocate space, and assign elements one at a time. It's that one at a time assignment in a loop that should alert you to the fact you could create a CPU bottleneck.

NOTE
DBAs who say they hate PL/SQL usually mean that they hate the programs produced by developers who lack the knowledge to write unnesting queries that outperform row-by-row assignments.

While you can construct a table collection without members, you can't construct an instance of a record data type. That's because a record data type doesn't have a default constructor function. The first change to our program occurs on line 13, where we construct an empty collection of records. It requires this change:

```
13    lv_tolkien_plsql_table  TOLKIEN_PLSQL_TABLE := tolkien_plsql_table();
```

If we didn't know any better, we might try to assign the object type directly to the record type. In that scenario, we would rework the execution block to look like the following:

```
SQL> DECLARE
  2    ...
 24  BEGIN
 25    /* Loop through transferring elements one-by-one. */
 26    FOR i IN 1..lv_tolkien_table.COUNT LOOP
 27      lv_tolkien_plsql_table.EXTEND;
 28      lv_tolkien_plsql_table(i) := lv_tolkien_table(i);
 29    END LOOP;
 30    ... never gets here, so no sense in wasting space ...
 38  END;
 39  /
```

Line 27 would work because the collection is an object type. Line 28 would fail because we can't assign an object instance to a PL/SQL RECORD data structure. The attempt generates the following error:

```
    lv_tolkien_plsql_table(i) := lv_tolkien_table(i);
                                 *
ERROR at line 28:
ORA-06550: line 28, column 34:
PLS-00382: expression is of wrong type
ORA-06550: line 28, column 5:
PL/SQL: Statement ignored
```

The error states that you can't assign an object type to a PL/SQL RECORD data type. They're mutually incompatible. You can assign the element values of the object type to the element values of the RECORD data type. The execution block would be rewritten to do the following:

```
SQL> DECLARE
  2    ...
 24  BEGIN
 25    /* Loop through transferring elements one-by-one. */
 26    FOR i IN 1..lv_tolkien_table.COUNT LOOP
 27      lv_tolkien_plsql_table.EXTEND;
 28      lv_tolkien_plsql_table(i).race := lv_tolkien_table(i).race;
 29      lv_tolkien_plsql_table(i).name := lv_tolkien_table(i).exemplar.name;
 30      lv_tolkien_plsql_table(i).age  := lv_tolkien_table(i).exemplar.age;
 31    END LOOP;
 32
 33    /* Loop through the result set and print the results. */
 34    FOR i IN 1..lv_tolkien_plsql_table.COUNT LOOP
 35      dbms_output.put_line(
 36        '['||lv_tolkien_plsql_table(i).race||'] '||
 37        '['||lv_tolkien_plsql_table(i).name||'] '||
 38        '['||lv_tolkien_plsql_table(i).age ||']');
 39    END LOOP;
 40  END;
 41  /
```

Line 28 assigns the race attribute by referring to the object instance by its index value in the collection and its name. Lines 29 and 30 must use the exemplar attribute to access the nested column values of name and age. Once assigned to the record structure, there aren't any nested fields. In this example, the record structure is simple, or absent any nested record structures.

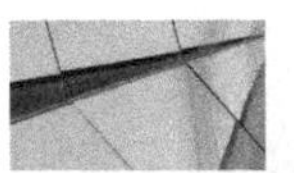

NOTE
You can't assign constructed object instances to PL/SQL RECORD *data types.*

As you may imagine, listing only one *dwarf*, *elf*, or *man* (from the *Lord of the Rings* trilogy) isn't very useful. This type of information would be more natural if the nested composite type were a collection of the people_object composite object type. Such a change makes it an asymmetrical composite data type, and the subject of the next section.

Asymmetrical Composite Table Collections As qualified earlier, an asymmetrical composite varray or table collection holds scalar and collection fields. The former has one row and the latter has one to many rows.

Leveraging our examples from the prior section, let's add a `prominent_table` collection type that has a base type of `prominent_object` composite types. After all, the *Lord of the Rings* trilogy has more than one prominent dwarf, elf, or man, as well as a few prominent women (though unfortunately no female dwarves, females belong to their respective race of dwarves, elves, and men).

```
SQL> CREATE OR REPLACE
       TYPE prominent_table IS TABLE OF prominent_object;
     /
```

Having created a `prominent_table` collection type, let's redefine both the `people_object` and `people_table` composite types. The syntax to create an asymmetrical `people_object` is

```
SQL> CREATE OR REPLACE
  2    TYPE people_object IS OBJECT
  3    ( race       VARCHAR2(10)
  4    , exemplar   PROMINENT_TABLE);
  5  /
```

Line 4 changes from a `prominent_object` data type to a `prominent_table` collection type. There's really no change between the prior and current syntax of the `people_table` because its base type remains unchanged. The base type is the now modified `people_object` composite object, but Oracle Database 12*c* takes care of that change through type evolution.

The last step creates a table collection of the asymmetrical composite data type:

```
SQL> CREATE OR REPLACE
       TYPE people_table IS TABLE OF people_object;
     /
```

While it's nice to see how to do things in SQL (and if you'd like more insight, check the "Unnesting Queries" section in Appendix B), let's implement the new type in an anonymous PL/SQL program. The following program initializes a multilevel collection and then assigns a new element to the collection. The size of this program is large, but that's necessary to give you a complete picture of the moving parts.

```
SQL> DECLARE
       /* Declare a table collection. */
       lv_tolkien  PEOPLE_TABLE :=
                      people_table(
                          people_object(
                             'Men'
                            , prominent_table(
                                  prominent_object('Aragorn','3rd Age')
                                , prominent_object('Boromir','3rd Age')
                                , prominent_object('Faramir','3rd Age')
```

```
11                              , prominent_object('Eowyn','3rd Age')))
12                      , people_object(
13                           'Elves'
14                         , prominent_table(
15                              prominent_object('Legolas','3rd Age')
16                            , prominent_object('Arwen','3rd Age'))));
17  BEGIN
18    /* Add a new record to collection. */
19    lv_tolkien.EXTEND;
20    lv_tolkien(lv_tolkien.COUNT) :=
21       people_object('Dwarves'
22                    , prominent_table(
23                           prominent_object('Gimili','3rd Age')
24                         , prominent_object('Gloin','3rd Age')));
25
26    /* Read and print values in table collection. */
27    FOR i IN lv_tolkien.FIRST..lv_tolkien.LAST LOOP
28      FOR j IN
29        lv_tolkien(i).exemplar.FIRST..lv_tolkien(i).exemplar.LAST LOOP
30        dbms_output.put_line(
31          lv_tolkien(i).race||': '||lv_tolkien(i).exemplar(j).name);
32      END LOOP;
33    END LOOP;
34  END;
35  /
```

Lines 3 through 16 construct a new multilevel table collection. Line 19 allocates space for a new element. Lines 20 through 24 add a new multilevel composite `people_object` variable to the `lv_tolkien` collection.

Line 28 shows how you can perform a nested loop against the multilevel table collection. While the initial `FOR` loop works with the `lv_tolkien` variable, the nested `FOR` loop works with the embedded `exemplar` variable. Moreover, the nested loop reads through the embedded `exemplar` table collection. Line 30 shows how you must use the index value of both collections. You reference the element in `lv_tolkien` collection, then the element in `exemplar` collection, and finally the attribute of the `exemplar` table collection.

It prints

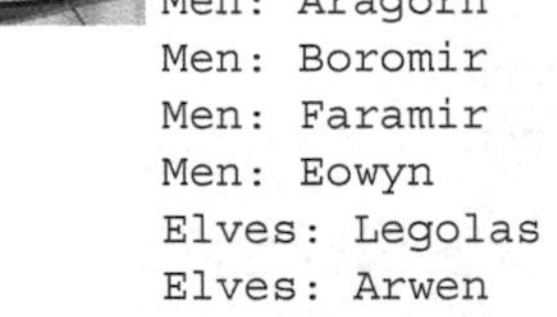

```
Men: Aragorn
Men: Boromir
Men: Faramir
Men: Eowyn
Elves: Legolas
Elves: Arwen
Dwarves: Gimili
Dwarves: Gloin
```

This chaining of operations works no matter how many levels you have in a multilevel collection. While the syntax is verbose, there's not another alternative when working with multilevel collections.

Review Section

This section has described the following points about SQL collection types:

- SQL collections are defined as schema-level object types.
- SQL collections require construction, which you do by calling the type name with a list of actual parameters that map to the definition of the object type's attributes.
- SQL collections with a base scalar data type are Attribute Data Types (ADTs), while collections of object types are user-defined types (UDTs).
- SQL collections have a base type, and it can be either a scalar or composite data type; and a SQL collection is a multilevel collection when its base composite data type is also a collection.
- SQL collections can be function and procedure formal parameters and function return types in both SQL and PL/SQL operating contexts.
- A varray collection is defined with a fixed size, while a table collection is not constrained by a maximum size value.
- The varray always has a sequential or densely populated index.
- The table collection starts with a sequential or densely populated index, but it is possible to delete elements from the collection, which creates gaps in the sequence of index values, potentially making the index sparsely populated.

Associative Arrays

Associative arrays are also single-dimensional structures of an Oracle Database 12*c* database, and they can hold the same base data types as SQL collections. As discussed in the "Oracle PL/SQL Tables" sidebar, they were previously known as PL/SQL tables. This section focuses on single-dimensional structures of the associative array.

Associative arrays are single-dimensional composite data types, and they can hold only a scalar or composite base data type. You can't define a multidimensional collection because collections can't hold multiple copies of a base type across each element (row). While collections can't hold other composite data types, they can hold another copy of the collection in each row. When collections hold other collections, they're called *multilevel* collections.

Associative arrays *cannot* be used as column data types in tables. They may be used only as programming structures. You can only use associative arrays in a PL/SQL context, which means you can't pass a PL/SQL collection as a parameter from within a SQL statement or as a return value from a function.

It is important to note some key issues presented by associative arrays. These issues drive a slightly different approach to illustrating how you use them. Associative arrays

- Do not require initialization and have no constructor syntax. They also do not need to allocate space before assigning values.
- Can be indexed numerically in Oracle Database versions up to and including 12*c*. In Oracle Database 12*c* forward, they can also use unique variable-length strings.
- Can use any integer as the index value, which means any negative, positive, or zero whole numbers.

- Are implicitly converted from equivalent `%ROWTYPE`, record type, and object type return values to associative array structures.
- Require special treatment when using a character string as an index value in any database using globalized settings, such as `NLS_COMP` or `NLS_SORT` initialization parameters.

TIP
Unique strings as indexes can encounter sorting differences when the National Language Support (NLS) character set changes during operation of the database.

The following subsections describe how you can best use associative arrays in your PL/SQL programs.

Defining and Using Associative Arrays

The syntax to define an associative array in PL/SQL has two possibilities. One is

```
CREATE OR REPLACE TYPE type_name AS TABLE OF base_type [ NOT NULL ]
INDEX BY [ PLS_INTEGER | BINARY_INTEGER | VARCHAR2(size) ];
```

The same issues around enabling or disabling null values in nested tables apply to associative arrays. As a rule, you should ensure that data in an array is not null. You can do that either programmatically or by enabling the constraint when defining an associative array. It is a decision that you will need to make on a case-by-case basis.

You can use a negative, positive, or zero number as the index value for associative arrays. Both `PLS_INTEGER` and `BINARY_INTEGER` data types are unconstrained types that map to call specifications in C/C++, C#, and Java in Oracle Database 12*c*.

The other possible syntax to define an associate array in PL/SQL is

```
CREATE OR REPLACE TYPE type_name AS TABLE OF base_type [ NOT NULL ]
INDEX BY key_type;
```

The `key_type` alternative enables you to use `VARCHAR2`, `STRING`, or `LONG` data types in addition to `PLS_INTEGER` and `BINARY_INTEGER`. Both `VARCHAR2` and `STRING` require a size definition. The `LONG` data type does not require a size definition; however, the `LONG` data type is considered deprecated, so avoiding its use is recommended.

As discussed, unlike SQL varray and table collections, associative arrays do not require initialization and can't call a constructor. Other than that, the only major difference between associative arrays and SQL varray and table collections is where you can use them. Associative arrays are limited to an exclusively PL/SQL scope. You can create associative arrays with a base object type, record data type, or scalar data type. Record types also can hold embedded object types.

The following subsections explain how to work with associative arrays of scalar and composite data types, respectively.

Associative Arrays of Scalar Data Types

Working with an associative array of a scalar data type is simpler than working with an associative array of a composite data type. This collection type is an ADT and has some differences from collections of composite data types. One difference is that Oracle Database 12*c* returns the values from an ADT as the `column_value` column, whereas it returns values from composite base types by their field names.

You have the option of using a numeric index or a key (or string) index with associative arrays. The next two subsections present numerically indexed associative arrays and key indexed associative arrays, respectively.

Numerically Indexed Associative Arrays For demonstration purposes, assume that you confused associative arrays with SQL varray or table collections and tried to construct an instance of the associative array in your declaration block, as shown in the following program:

```
SQL> DECLARE
  2    /* Define an associative array of a scalar data type. */
  3    TYPE suit_table IS TABLE OF VARCHAR2(7 CHAR)
  4      INDEX BY BINARY_INTEGER;
  5
  6    /* Declare and attempt to construct an object. */
  7    lv_suit CARD_TABLE := suit_table('Club','Heart','Diamond','Spade');
  8  BEGIN
  9    NULL;
 10  END;
 11  /
```

The associative array definition on lines 3 and 4 is fine. However, the attempt to assign the result of a constructor function on line 7 raises a `PLS-00222` *doesn't exist in scope* error, as shown next, because associative arrays don't have constructor functions that you can call:

```
  lv_suit CARD_TABLE := suit_table('Club','Heart','Diamond','Spade');
                        *
ERROR at line 7:
ORA-06550: line 7, column 25:
PLS-00222: no function with name 'SUIT_TABLE' exists in this scope
ORA-06550: line 7, column 9:
PL/SQL: Item ignored
```

The failure on line 7 occurs because the `INDEX BY` clause makes the collection an associative array, not a nested table. As mentioned, you can't call a constructor with an associative array because one doesn't exist.

The correct way to assign values to an associative array requires that you assign them one at a time in the execution or exception block. Each assignment provides a value and an index value, and the index values may or may not be sequential values. As a rule, they are sequential values, but there's no guarantee that they are sequential when your program reads them (and *that's why you need to be careful about how you read them in your programs*).

The reworked program (which excludes a duplicate declaration block) is

```
SQL> DECLARE
  ...
BEGIN
  /* Assign values to an ADT. */
  lv_suit(1) := 'Club';
  lv_suit(2) := 'Heart';
  lv_suit(3) := 'Diamond';
```

```
13     lv_suit(4) := 'Spade';
14
15     /* Loop through a densely populated indexed collection. */
16     FOR i IN lv_suit.FIRST..lv_suit.LAST LOOP
17       dbms_output.put_line(lv_suit(i));
18     END LOOP;
19   END;
20   /
```

Lines 10 through 13 assign the suits of a deck of cards to the associative array of card suits. Line 17 prints the elements of the `lv_suit` associative array.

Having covered the basics, let's revisit an associative array of an object type. You create the necessary `suit_object` object type like this:

```
SQL> CREATE OR REPLACE
       TYPE suit_object IS OBJECT
       ( suit  VARCHAR2(7));
     /
```

The `suit_object` mimics the scalar data type used in the two previous programs. Staying as close as possible to the preceding two examples, the following shows you how to implement a numerically indexed associative array of an object type:

```
SQL> DECLARE
 2     /* Define an associative array of an object type. */
 3     TYPE suit_table IS TABLE OF suit_object
 4       INDEX BY BINARY_INTEGER;
 5
 6     /* Declare an associative array. */
 7     lv_suit  SUIT_TABLE;
 8   BEGIN
 9     /* Populate elements of the associative array. */
10     lv_suit(1) := suit_object('Club');
11     lv_suit(2) := suit_object('Heart');
12     lv_suit(3) := suit_object('Diamond');
13     lv_suit(4) := suit_object('Spade');
14
15     /* Read the object type contents. */
16     FOR i IN 1..lv_suit.COUNT LOOP
17       dbms_output.put_line(lv_suit(i).suit);
18     END LOOP;
19   END;
20   /
```

Lines 3 and 4 define the local associative array. Line 7 declares the `lv_suit` variable as an associative array. You should note that the declaration of the `lv_suit` variable doesn't use a constructor function. That's because only the elements of the associative array are constructed. Lines 10 through 13 assign constructed instances of the `suit_object` to the numerically indexed elements of the associative array. The "Associative Arrays of Composite Data Types" section later in this chapter covers how you work with elements of composite data types.

Key (or String) Indexed Associative Arrays Having mastered the difference between SQL and PL/SQL associative arrays, you know that you can't call a nonexistent constructor function. You also know that SQL varray and table collections only use numeric indexes. Associative arrays enable you to create collections with key or string indexes, and this section shows you how to implement them.

Instead of creating a collection of cards, as does the previous program, the following program assigns a number to each card. Numbered cards are assigned their respective numbers, aces are assigned 1, and the Jack, Queen, and King face cards map to numbers 11, 12, and 13, respectively.

```
SQL> DECLARE
  2    /* Variable name carries meaning. */
  3    current  VARCHAR2(5);
  4
  5    /* Define an associative array of a scalar data type. */
  6    TYPE card_table IS TABLE OF NUMBER
  7      INDEX BY VARCHAR2(5);
  8
  9    /* Declare and attempt to construct an object. */
 10    lv_card CARD_TABLE;
 11  BEGIN
 12    /* Assign values to an ADT. */
 13    lv_card('One') := 1;
 14    lv_card('Two') := 2;
       ...
 24    lv_card('Queen') := 12;
 25    lv_card('King') := 13;
 26
 27    /* Set the starting point. */
 28    current := lv_card.FIRST;  -- First alphabetical key.
 29
 30    /* Check pseudo index value less than last index value. */
 31    WHILE (current <= lv_card.LAST) LOOP
 32      /* Print current value. */
 33      dbms_output.put_line(
 34        'Values ['||current||']['||lv_card(current)||']');
 35
 36      /* Shift the index to the next value. */
 37      current := lv_card.NEXT(current);
 38    END LOOP;
 39  END;
 40  /
```

Line 7 defines the index as a five-character string. Lines 13 through 25 assign numbers to string index values. Line 28 provides a safeguard to entry of the `WHILE` loop by initializing the first index value. The `WHILE` loop reads through the indexes from lowest to highest, which means alphabetically. That means the program prints

```
Values [Ace][1]
Values [Eight][8]
Values [Five][5]
...
```

The ordering of printed values may surprise you. Associative arrays are always navigated from the lowest to highest value based on the `NLS_COMP` and `NLS_SORT` alphabetical rules. It's probably one of the reasons you don't see too many collections indexed by strings.

Associative Arrays of Composite Data Types

While it's simpler to work with an associative array of scalar data types, most collections are of composite data types. A collection that uses a SQL object type or a PL/SQL record type is an object collection or a record collection, respectively. Oracle Database 12*c* maintains the field or attribute names in the data catalog when you define these types of collections.

The next example reuses the SQL `prominent_object` object type defined in an earlier example of this chapter. Rather than have you flip back a few pages to find it, the type's definition is

```
SQL> CREATE OR REPLACE
  2    TYPE prominent_object IS OBJECT
  3    ( name      VARCHAR2(20)
  4    , age       VARCHAR2(10));
  5  /
```

While you could pull lines 2 through 4 from the SQL object type definition to create a PL/SQL-only version in a declaration block, the pattern of assignment differs between an object data type and a record data type.

The following program defines a `prominent_table` associative array that uses a `prominent_object` object type as its base type. Naturally, the `prominent_table` collection has a local PL/SQL-only scope. You can assign the result of a constructor function to each element in this collection because its base type is an object type. If its base type were a record data type, you would need to make record-to-record or field-level assignments to the collection. The following program also shows you how to assign and retrieve values from an associative array of a composite data type.

```
SQL> DECLARE
  2    /* Declare a local type of a SQL composite data type. */
  3    TYPE prominent_table IS TABLE OF prominent_object
  4      INDEX BY PLS_INTEGER;
  5
  6    /* Declare a local variable of the collection data type. */
  7    lv_array  PROMINENT_TABLE;
  8  BEGIN
  9    /* The initial element uses -100 as an index value. */
 10    lv_array(-100) := prominent_object('Bard the Bowman','3rd Age');
 11
 12    /* Check whether there are any elements to retrieve. */
 13    IF lv_array.EXISTS(-100) THEN
 14      dbms_output.put_line(
 15        '['||lv_array(-100).name||']['||lv_array(-100).age||']');
 16    END IF;
 17  END;
 18  /
```

Line 10 assigns a value to the –100th element of the local `lv_array` variable that is declared on line 7. While it's unconventional to use negative integers as index values, the program uses one to show you that it's possible. You can use any integer value in any order as the index value of an associative array. Please note that the object type requires two string attributes, and that's what we supply in the constructor.

If you were to remark out the assignment on line 10 or change the index value, the references to the element on line 15 would fail. That's because it would reference an unknown index value and then it would raise the following runtime exception:

```
DECLARE
*
ERROR at line 1:
ORA-01403: no data found
ORA-06512: at line 12
```

Line 15 also shows you how to refer to embedded attribute or field values of the object type. You must reference them by using their attribute names. That means you can work with either the whole set of attributes or only one attribute at a time.

You should always take the precaution of evaluating the presence of an associative array's index value, because its absence raises an exception. By so doing, your program only references elements that have valid index values. Line 13 checks whether there is an element with an index value of -100. The program only reaches line 15 when there's a valid element at the specified index value.

Refactoring the prior example, let's examine how a record data type works in an associative array. To properly extend what you've done so far, let's use a composite record data type made up of a scalar data type and object type. The program code follows:

```
SQL> DECLARE
  2    /* Define a symmetrical record data type. */
  3    TYPE prominent_record IS RECORD
  4    ( id        INTEGER
  5    , element   PROMINENT_OBJECT );
  6
  7    /* Declare a local type of a SQL composite data type. */
  8    TYPE prominent_table IS TABLE OF prominent_record
  9      INDEX BY PLS_INTEGER;
 10
 11    /* Declare a local variable of the collection data type. */
 12    lv_array  PROMINENT_TABLE;
 13  BEGIN
 14    /* The initial element uses 1 as an index value. */
 15    lv_array(1).id := 1;
 16    lv_array(1).element := prominent_object('Bilbo Baggins','3rd Age');
 17    /* The initial element uses 1 as an index value. */
 18    lv_array(2).id := 2;
 19    lv_array(2).element := prominent_object('Frodo Baggins','3rd Age');
 20
 21    /* Check whether there are any elements to retrieve. */
 22    FOR i IN 1..lv_array.COUNT LOOP
 23      IF lv_array.EXISTS(i) THEN
 24        dbms_output.put_line('['||lv_array(i).id||']'||
 25                             '['||lv_array(i).element.name||']'||
```

```
26                                    '['||lv_array(i).element.age||']');
27        END IF;
28      END LOOP;
29    END;
30    /
```

Lines 3 through 5 define a composite record data type with a scalar integer and a composite object type. You can access the `id` field name by prefacing it with the `lv_array` variable name with a subscript index value and the component selector (`.`). The other field in the record data type is more complex because it's an embedded object type. As you nest composite data types, you require another component selector to get to the nested fields or attributes.

Lines 15 and 18 assign integer values to the `id` field of the `prominent_record` record data type. The assignments to the two `id` fields are direct assignments. Lines 16 and 19 assign a constructed object instance to the `element` field of the same record data type. The assignments to the two `element` fields are also direct assignments, but the assignments to the `name` and `age` attributes are indirect assignments. That because they are made through the object type's constructor function. Lines 24 through 26 retrieve the `id` field value and the `element` field value's `name` and `age` attributes.

```
10    lv_array(-100) := lv_prominent_record;
```

You have seen in this section how to work with associative arrays. We'll explore the Oracle Collection API next.

Review Section

This section has described the following points about PL/SQL associative arrays:

- Associative arrays are defined as PL/SQL-only data types.
- Associative arrays must be assigned elements one at a time.
- Associative arrays with a base scalar data type are Attribute Data Types (ADTs).
- Associative arrays with a base composite data type are PL/SQL user-defined types (UDTs).
- Composite type associative arrays with a base record type must be assigned one record at a time or one record element at a time, and those with a base object type must be assigned a constructed object type.
- Associative arrays have a sparsely populated index, which may be numeric (negative, positive, or zero integer) values or string index values.

Oracle Collection API

Oracle 8*i* Database introduced the Collection API, which provides simplified access to collections. It works with all three collection types. SQL varray and table collections use integers as indexes. Associative arrays in Oracle Database 11*g* and forward support numeric and string index values.

The Collection API methods are really not "methods" in a truly object-oriented sense. They are functions and procedures. While `EXTEND`, `TRIM`, and `DELETE` are procedures, the rest are functions. Table 6-3 summarizes the Oracle Databases 12*c* Collection API.

Method	Definition
`COUNT`	Returns the number of elements that have been allocated space in varray and table data types, and returns the total of all elements in associative arrays. The return value of the `COUNT` method can be smaller than the return value of `LIMIT` for the `varray` collection. It has the following prototype: `PLS_INTEGER COUNT`

`DELETE`	Lets you remove elements from table collections and associative arrays. It doesn't work with varray collections, and an attempt to remove an element from a varray raises a `PLS-00306` exception.
	The `DELETE` method takes two formal parameters; one is mandatory and the other is optional. Both parameters are index values and must occur in ascending order. The `DELETE` procedure deletes everything from the parameter `n` to `m`, inclusively, when you supply two parameters.
	The prototypes are as follows:
	`void DELETE(n)`
	`void DELETE(n,m)`

`EXISTS`	Checks to find an element with the supplied index in a collection. It returns *true* when the element is found and *null* when an initialized varray or table is empty. It has one mandatory parameter, which is a valid index value. It has the following prototype: `Boolean EXISTS(n)`

`EXTEND`	Allocates space for one or more new elements in a varray or table collection. It has two optional parameters. It adds space for one element by default without a parameter.
	The first parameter designates how many physical spaces should be allocated in memory, the only constraint being the limit (or maximum value) of the varray.
	The second parameter is an index value. When the function receives two parameters, the first determines how many elements to add and the second is an index value. The `EXTEND` procedure uses the index value to copy a value into the newly added space.
	It has the following prototypes:
	`void EXTEND`
	`void EXTEND(n)`
	`void EXTEND(n,i)`

`FIRST`	Returns the lowest subscript value in a collection. It can return a **`PLS_INTEGER`, `VARCHAR2`,** or **`LONG`** type. It has the following prototype: `mixed FIRST`
`LAST`	Returns the highest subscript value in a collection. It can return a **`PLS_INTEGER`, `VARCHAR2`,** or **`LONG`** type. It has the following prototype: `mixed LAST`

TABLE 6-3. *Oracle Database 12c Collection API*

Method	Definition
`LIMIT`	Returns the highest possible subscript value in a collection. It can only return a **`PLS_INTEGER`** type, and can only be used by a `VARRAY` data type. It has the following prototype: `mixed LIMIT`
`NEXT(n)`	Returns the next higher subscript value in a collection when successful; otherwise returns *false*. The return value is a **`PLS_INTEGER`, `VARCHAR2`,** or **`LONG`** type. It requires a valid index value as an actual parameter and raises an exception when the index is invalid. It has the following prototype: `mixed NEXT(n)`
`PRIOR(n)`	Returns the next lower subscript value in a collection when successful; otherwise returns false. The return value is a **`PLS_INTEGER`, `VARCHAR2`,** or **`LONG`** type. It requires a valid index value as an actual parameter and raises an exception when the index is invalid. It has the following prototype: `mixed PRIOR(n)`

`TRIM`	Removes a subscripted value from a collection. It has one optional parameter. Without an actual parameter, it removes the highest element from the array. An actual parameter is interpreted as the number of elements removed from the end of the collection.
	It has the following prototype:
	`void TRIM`
	`void TRIM(n)`

TABLE 6-3. *Oracle Database 12c Collection API*

Note that only the `EXISTS` method fails to raise an exception when a SQL varray or table collection element is null. Instead, it returns true because it checks for an element allocated in memory. Any scalar data type element may contain a null or a value, and any object type element may contain a null, empty, or object instance.

The following tests the limit of the EXISTS method:

```
SQL> DECLARE
  /* Define the table collection. */
  TYPE empty_table IS TABLE OF prominent_object;
  /* Declare a table collection variable */
  lv_array  EMPTY_TABLE := empty_table(null);
BEGIN
  /* Check whether the element is allocated in memory. */
  IF lv_array.EXISTS(1) THEN
    dbms_output.put_line('Valid collection.');
  ELSE
    dbms_output.put_line('Invalid collection.');
  END IF;
END;
/
```

Line 5 declares a local `lv_array` table collection with a single null element value. Line 8 checks whether there's memory allocated for the first element of the collection, and it returns true and prints

```
Valid collection.
```

That's why you should combine it with an evaluation that checks whether the element contains a value. You can modify line 8 like this to check for memory allocation and a value:

```
8     IF lv_array.EXISTS(1) AND lv_array(1) IS NOT NULL THEN
```

The conjunction operator (AND) guarantees that when the `EXISTS` function returns false, the comparison operation stops. Conjunctive operators perform *short-circuit evaluation*, and they pare the evaluation tree when one comparison is false. A short-circuit evaluation guarantees that the second condition is never reached when the first is false.

There are five standard collection exceptions, described in Table 6-4.

The following subsections examine each of the Collection API methods in alphabetical order, with examples to demonstrate each of the methods in action. Some examples include multiple Collection API methods because, like the coverage of the collection types, it is hard to treat the Collection API methods in isolation. Where a single example fully covers multiple methods, it will be cross referenced.

COUNT Method

The `COUNT` method is a function. It has no formal parameter list. It returns the number of elements in the array. The number of elements in an array corresponds to the closing boundary element of a collection because Oracle Database uses 1-based index numbering. The following example program returns the number of items in a collection by using the `COUNT` method:

```
SQL> DECLARE
       /* Define a table collection. */
       TYPE x_table IS TABLE OF INTEGER;
```

Collection Exception	Raised By
`COLLECTION_IS_NULL`	An attempt to use a null collection.
`NO_DATA_FOUND`	An attempt to use a subscript that has been deleted or is nonexistent in an associative array.
`SUBSCRIPT_BEYOND_COUNT`	An attempt to use a numeric index value that is higher than the current maximum number value or an element that has been deleted from a table. The error applies only to varray and table collections.
`SUBSCRIPT_OUTSIDE_LIMIT`	An attempt to use a numeric index value outside of the `LIMIT` return value. The error applies only to a varray collection.
`VALUE_ERROR`	An attempt is made to use a data type that cannot be converted to a `PLS_INTEGER` type.

TABLE 6-4. *Collection Exceptions*

```
 4
 5     /* Declare an initialized table collection. */
 6     lv_table  NUMBER_TABLE := number_table(1,2,3,4,5);
 7   BEGIN
 8     DBMS_OUTPUT.PUT_LINE('How many? ['||lv_table.COUNT||']');
 9   END;
10   /
```

Line 8 prints

```
How many? [5]
```

The best use case for the COUNT function involves checking the number of elements before performing some task with the collection.

DELETE Method

The DELETE method is a procedure. It is an overloaded procedure. (If the concept of overloading is new to you, consult Chapter 9.) One version of the procedure takes a single formal parameter, and the other version takes two formal parameters. You provide the index to delete when you use one parameter. You provide a range of index values when you use two parameters. The lower of the two index values must be the first parameter to delete and the higher of the two must be the last parameter to delete. You would provide the index value twice if you were deleting a single index value with a call to the two-parameter version.

The following anonymous block program shows you how to perform range deletions:

```
SQL> DECLARE
       /* Declare variable with meaningful name. */
       current INTEGER;

       /* Define a table collection. */
       TYPE x_table IS TABLE OF VARCHAR2(6);

       /* Declare an initialized table collection. */
       lv_table  X_TABLE := xtable('One','Two','Three','Four','Five');
     BEGIN
       /* Remove one element with an index of 2. */
       lv_table.DELETE(2,2);

       /* Remove elements for an inclusive range of 4 to 5. */
       lv_table.DELETE(4,5);

       /* Set the starting index. */
       current := lv_table.FIRST;

       /* Read through index values in ascending order. */
       WHILE (current <= lv_table.LAST) LOOP
         dbms_output.put_line(
           'Index ['||current||'] Value ['||lv_table(current)||']');
         /* Shift index to next higher value. */
         current := lv_table.NEXT(current);
```

```
26     END LOOP;
27   END;
28   /
```

Line 12 removes one element from the collection, by using the index of 2. You really don't need to call the inclusive range version of the DELETE procedure to remove a single element. It would be simpler to use the single-element DELETE procedure on line 12, like

```
12     lv_table.DELETE(2);
```

Line 15 removes two elements from the collection, which is the right way to use the inclusive range version of the function. While the program starts with five elements, it has only two when it enters the WHILE loop:

```
Index [1] Value [One]
Index [3] Value [Three]
```

As a rule of thumb, call with a single index when you want to delete one element. Call with two index values when you want to delete two or more elements. While the use case for the DELETE procedure supports removing an element from the collection, you really have to ask yourself why you let the element into the collection. All too often, the DELETE procedure filters out results that you should have removed with a WHERE or HAVING clause from a cursor.

NOTE
The WHERE clause filters in or out rows from a DML statement. The HAVING clause filters out aggregated rows from a DML statement with aggregation functions in the SELECT list.

EXISTS Method

The EXISTS method is a function. It supports only one formal parameter, which should be a valid index value. The index value may be a number or a unique string. A unique string index only works when you use it against an associative array. The EXISTS function returns true or null, and it generally works best inside a conditional IF statement.

As mentioned, the EXISTS function doesn't raise a COLLECTION_IS_NULL exception when it encounters an empty collection. Instead, it returns a null value when a varray or table collection is empty. There are two varieties of null element collections. One is a varray or table that has been initialized without any elements. The other is an associative array without any elements.

The following program demonstrates the best way to use the EXISTS method:

```
SQL> DECLARE
       /* Define table. */
       TYPE x_table IS TABLE OF VARCHAR2(10);

       /* Declare an index counter. */
       lv_index  NUMBER := 1;

       /* Declare a local collection variable. */
       lv_table  X_TABLE := x_table();
     BEGIN
```

```
11     IF lv_table.EXISTS(lv_index) AND NOT lv_table.COUNT = 0 THEN
12       dbms_output.put_line('List ['||lv_table(lv_index)||']');
13     END IF;
14   END;
15   /
```

Line 3 defines a table collection. Line 9 declares the `lv_table` variable as an initialized collection. Line 11 uses the `EXISTS` function to check for the first element. Since one doesn't exist, it returns a null. Conjunctive logic (the `AND` logical operator) uses the `COUNT` function next, and it checks whether there aren't any elements. The logic on line 11 could be rewritten to check whether there are more than zero elements, like

```
11     IF lv_table.EXISTS(lv_index) AND lv_table.COUNT > 0 THEN
```

You need to ask both questions to ensure that you don't attempt to access a nonexistent index value. That's because the `EXISTS` function returns a null when the index isn't found. The function returns nothing because the table collection is empty. If you rework line 9 to create a table collection of one or more elements,

```
09     lv_table  X_TABLE := x_table('Something');
```

the program would print the following string:

```
List [Something]
```

You can avoid runtime errors by using the `EXISTS` function before working with an element of the collection. That's the sole use case for its existence.

EXTEND Method

The `EXTEND` method is a procedure. Like `DELETE`, it's also an overloaded procedure. (Chapter 9 covers overloading, if that's a new concept to you.) There are three overloaded versions of the `EXTEND` procedure:

- One takes no parameters. It allocates space for one element.
- One takes one parameter. It allocates space for the number of elements designated by the parameter.
- One takes two parameters. Like the one-parameter version, it allocates space for the number of elements designated by the first parameter. The second parameter must be a valid index value, and it's used to copy the value from the referenced index into the newly allocated space.

The following program shows how to allocate new space with the `EXTEND` procedure (leveraging the anonymous block from the `DELETE` procedure example):

```
SQL> DECLARE
     ... same as the DELETE procedure ...
  7
  8     /* Declare an initialized table collection. */
  9     lv_table  X_TABLE := x_table('One');
 10   BEGIN
```

```
11    /* Extend space, and assign a value. */
12    lv_table.EXTEND;
13
14    /* Assign a value to the last allocated element. */
15    lv_table(lv_table.COUNT) := 'Two';
16
   ... same as the DELETE procedure ...
27  END;
28  /
```

Line 9 changes from the earlier example by constructing a collection of only one element. Line 12 extends space for one element. Line 15 identifies the last added element by calling the `COUNT` function.

The program prints

```
Index [1] Value [One]
Index [2] Value [Two]
```

The use case for the `EXTEND` method exists when you want to assign an unknown number of elements from a cursor to a varray or table collection. It gives you two principal alternatives. One adds the space one element at a time (as shown in the previous example). The other adds all the space at one time, but it requires that you know how many elements will be added to the collection.

FIRST Method

The `FIRST` method is a function. It returns the lowest index value used in a collection, which is one of the boundary elements of a collection. The `FIRST` function returns a numeric 1 when working with a varray or table collection. It returns the lowest integer value from an associative array indexed numerically. Similarly, it returns the lowest string index value from an associative array; which value is considered lowest depends on how strings are sorted (based on the `NLS_COMP` and `NLS_SORT` alphabetical rules).

While the rule applying to numbers is clear, the rule for strings sometimes isn't. The following example creates a string-indexed associative array and then prints its first value:

```
SQL> DECLARE
       /* Define an associative array. */
       TYPE x_table IS TABLE OF INTEGER
         INDEX BY VARCHAR2(9 CHAR);

       /* Declare an associative array variable. */
       lv_table  X_TABLE;
     BEGIN
       /* Add elements to associative array. */
       lv_table('Seven') := 7;
       lv_table('Eight') := 8;

       /* Print the element returned by the lowest string index. */
       dbms_output.put_line(
         'Index ['||lv_table.FIRST||']['||lv_table(lv_table.FIRST)||']');
     END;
     /
```

Lines 10 and 11 assign two elements to an associative array. The values are entered lowest to highest, but the indexes are ordered highest to lowest when treated as sorted strings. Lines 14 and 15 (for book formatting purposes) print the index and value of the collection for the first element of the associative array:

```
Index [Eight] [8]
```

The `FIRST` function is critical in finding the first index value in any collection, but its importance becomes most evident when searching for the first index value in a sparsely populated index. The use case for the `FIRST` function is to determine definitively where you should start when navigating a collection.

LAST Method

The `LAST` method is a function. Like the `FIRST` function, the `LAST` function returns the index of a boundary element of the collection. The `LAST` function returns the highest index value used in a collection. The `LAST` function also returns the same value as the `COUNT` function in varray and table collections, which isn't always the same value returned by the `LIMIT` function. While the `LAST` function returns the highest integer value from varray and table collections, it returns either the highest integer value or the highest string index value from an associative array. Oracle Database uses the `NLS_COMP` and `NLS_SORT` values to create alphabetical sorting rules, which decide how to sort strings.

If you replace the `FIRST` function call with a `LAST` function call on line 15 from the sample program for the `FIRST` method (presented in the previous section), the program prints the highest alphabetical string index and value:

```
14    dbms_output.put_line(
15      'Index ['||lv_table.LAST||']['||x_list(lv_table.LAST)||']');
```

And, that is

```
Index [Seven] [7]
```

The `LAST` function is critical in finding the last index value in any collection, but its [referring to `LAST` indeed of `FIRST`] importance becomes most evident when searching for the last index value in an associative array and a sparsely populated string index.

LIMIT Method

The `LIMIT` method is a function. It returns the highest possible subscript value for a varray, and you can't use it with any other type of collection.

The example program that follows illustrates the `LIMIT` method:

```
SQL> DECLARE
       /* Define an associative array. */
       TYPE x_varray IS VARRAY(5) OF INTEGER;

       /* Declare an initialized table collection. */
       lv_array  X_VARRAY := x_varray(1,2,3);
     BEGIN
       /* Print the count and limit values. */
```

```
 9     dbms_output.put_line(
10       'Count['||lv_array.COUNT||']: Limit['||lv_array.LIMIT||']');
11   END;
12   /
```

Line 3 defines a five-element varray collection. Line 6 constructs the varray with three elements. Line 10 prints the count and limit of elements in the varray, which are

```
Count[3]: Limit[5]
```

The `LIMIT` function serves the purpose of qualifying the maximum number of elements in a varray. The use case for the `LIMIT` function would be using it as a guard condition to avoid adding more than the maximum number of elements in a varray.

NEXT Method

The `NEXT` method is a function. It returns the next index value by receiving the current index value. Since Oracle collections act like singly linked lists, not rings, when you get to the last index, the `NEXT` method returns a null. While you can increment one at a time with a densely populated index, you can't do the same with a sparsely populated index. The `NEXT` function lets you move from one index to another whether the index is densely or sparsely populated.

The following snippet from an earlier example shows how you use the `NEXT` function:

```
10   BEGIN
11     /* Set the starting index. */
12     current := lv_table.FIRST;
13
14     /* Read through index values in ascending order. */
15     WHILE (current <= lv_table.LAST) LOOP
16       dbms_output.put_line(
17         'Index ['||current||'] Value ['||lv_table(current)||']');
18       /* Shift index to next higher value. */
19       current := lv_table.NEXT(current);
20     END LOOP;
21   END;
22   /
```

Line 12 assigns the lowest index value to a `current` variable. Line 15 evaluates the `current` variable's value against the highest index value. The comparison uses a less-than or equal operator because you want to exit the loop before the `NEXT` function returns a null value. Ultimately, line 19 shifts the index value to the next highest value.

Navigating across a sparsely populated index is the essential use case for the `NEXT` function. You should navigate from the lowest to the highest index value in table collections and associative arrays with the `NEXT` function.

PRIOR Method

The `PRIOR` method is a function. It returns the prior element's index value by using the current index value as an argument to the function. Like the `NEXT` function, the `PRIOR` function lets you move across a collection by skipping missing index values in a sparsely populated index. Unlike the `NEXT` function, which moves from the lowest to the highest index value, the `PRIOR` method traverses the index from the highest to the lowest index value.

Refactoring the `WHILE` loop from the prior section, you would decrement a collection with the `PRIOR` function like this:

```
10  BEGIN
11    /* Set the starting index. */
12    current := lv_table.LAST;
13
14    /* Read through index values in ascending order. */
15    WHILE (current <= lv_table.FIRST) LOOP
16      dbms_output.put_line(
17        'Index ['||current||'] Value ['||lv_table(current)||']');
18      /* Shift index to next higher value. */
19      current := lv_table.PRIOR(current);
20    END LOOP;
21  END;
22  /
```

The change on line 12 requires starting with the return value of the `LAST` function rather than the return value of the `FIRST` function. Line 15 also makes a similar change, and it replaces a call to the `LAST` function with a call to the `FIRST` function. Line 19 replaces the `NEXT` function call with a `PRIOR` function call because it's now decrementing through the collection.

Like the `NEXT` function, the `PRIOR` function's use case is managing a decrementing process across a sparsely populated index list. The `PRIOR` function lets you navigate from the highest to lowest index value without worrying about gaps in the index sequence of values.

TRIM Method

The `TRIM` method is a procedure, and it's an overloaded procedure. (Again, consult Chapter 9 if the concept of overloading is new to you.) The `TRIM` procedure only works with varray and table collections. There are two overloaded versions of the `TRIM` procedure:

- One takes no parameters. It deallocates space for one element.
- One takes one parameter. It deallocates space for the number elements designated by the parameter.

The following program deallocates existing space from a collection:

```
SQL> DECLARE
  /* Declare variable with meaningful name. */
  current INTEGER;

  /* Define a table collection. */
  TYPE x_table IS TABLE OF VARCHAR2(6);

  /* Declare an initialized table collection. */
  lv_table  X_TABLE := x_table('One','Two','Three','Four','Five');
BEGIN
  /* Remove three elements from the end of the table. */
  lv_table.TRIM(3);

  /* Set the starting index. */
```

```
15     current := lv_table.FIRST;
16
17     /* Read through index values in ascending order. */
18     WHILE (current <= lv_table.LAST) LOOP
19       dbms_output.put_line(
20         'Index ['||current||'] Value ['||lv_table(current)||']');
21       /* Shift index to next higher value. */
22       current := lv_table.NEXT(current);
23     END LOOP;
24   END;
25   /
```

Line 9 declares an `lv_table` table collection variable with five elements. Line 12 removes the last three elements by trimming them.

The program prints the first two elements:

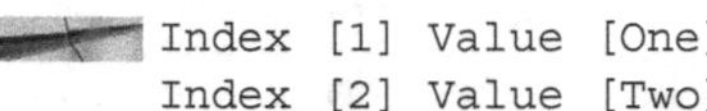

```
Index [1] Value [One]
Index [2] Value [Two]
```

The use case for the `TRIM` procedure is removing elements from the end of a collection. You can remove one element or a set of elements. When you trim the elements, you remove both their values and their space. That means the `COUNT` function would return `2` after the `TRIM` procedure call on line 12 of the preceding program.

You have now gone through the complete Oracle 12c Collection API. It is time to summarize what you have covered in the chapter.

Review Section

This section has described the following points about the Oracle Collection API:

- The Oracle Collection API simplifies working with all three types of Oracle collections.
- The methods of the Oracle Collection API are functions or procedures; some only work with one or two of the collection types, while others perform differently based on the type of collection.
- The `LIMIT` function only works with varray collections, and it captures the maximum number of elements allowed in the collection.
- The overloaded `EXTEND` procedure only works with varray and table collections, and it allocates space before you can assign values.
- The `EXISTS` function lets you check whether an element has been allocated memory.
- The `DELETE` procedure lets you remove an element from a collection.
- The `COUNT` function returns the number of elements in a varray or table collection. The `COUNT` and `LIMIT` function can return the same number for a varray collection, but only when the varray collection is full.
- The `NEXT`, `PRIOR`, `FIRST`, and `LAST` functions let you traverse sparsely populated index lists by painlessly skipping gaps in the sequence.
- The `TRIM` procedure lets you deallocate space from varray and table collections.

Supporting Scripts

This section describes programs placed on the McGraw-Hill Professional website to support this chapter.

- The `sql_collection.sql` program contains small programs that support the "Object Types: Varray and Table Collections" section of this chapter.
- The `symmetrical_composites.sql` program contains fully functional examples for the redacted versions in the chapter.
- The `asymmetrical_composites.sql` program contains fully functional examples for the redacted versions in the chapter.
- The `associative_array.sql` program contains small programs that support the "Associative Arrays" section of this chapter.
- The `collection_api.sql` program contains small programs that support the "Oracle Collection API" section of this chapter.

Summary

This chapter has covered the definition and use of varrays, nested tables, and associative arrays, which are the Oracle Database 12*c* collection types. You have worked through examples in SQL DML and PL/SQL that use Oracle Database 12*c* collections. Finally, you have explored the details of the Oracle Collection API.

Mastery Check

The mastery check is a series of true-or-false and multiple-choice questions that let you confirm how well you understand the material in the chapter. You may check Appendix I for answers to these questions.

True or False:

1. ___SQL varray collections can only be used in a SQL context.
2. ___Table collections can be used in a SQL context or a PL/SQL context.
3. ___Associative arrays can be used only in a PL/SQL context.
4. ___A table collection can hold a record or object type as its composite base data type.
5. ___A varray has a fixed number of elements when you define it.
6. ___A varray or table of a scalar variable is an Attribute Data Type (ADT).
7. ___A varray or table of a composite data type is a user-defined type (UDT).
8. ___A `LIMIT` function from the Oracle Collection API only works with table collections.
9. ___A `BULK COLLECT` statement can work with a table collection of object types.
10. ___The `TABLE` function lets you consume a varray or table collection as an ordinary SQL result set.

Multiple Choice:

11. Which of the following is a densely populated index in an Oracle varray or table collection? (Multiple answers possible)
    - **A.** A sequence of negative integers without any gaps in the sequence of integers
    - **B.** A sequence of positive integers starting at a number of your choosing without any gaps in the sequence of integers
    - **C.** A sequence of positive integers starting at 1 without any gaps in the sequence
    - **D.** A sequence of letters without any gaps in the sequence of integers
    - **E.** A sequence of positive integers starting at 1 with some gaps in the sequence of integers
12. Which of the following support string indexes? (Multiple answers possible)
    - **A.** PL/SQL tables
    - **B.** Table collections
    - **C.** Varray collections
    - **D.** Associative arrays
    - **E.** Java ArrayList classes
13. Which of the following is a sparsely populated index in an Oracle varray or table collection? (Multiple answers possible)
    - **A.** A sequence of negative integers without any gaps in the sequence of integers
    - **B.** A sequence of positive integers starting at a number of your choosing without any gaps in the sequence of integers
    - **C.** A sequence of positive integers starting at 1 without any gaps in the sequence
    - **D.** A sequence of letters without any gaps in the sequence of integers
    - **E.** A sequence of positive integers starting at 1 with some gaps in the sequence of integers
14. Which of the following are boundary elements of collections? (Multiple answers possible)
    - **A.** The index value returned by the `FIRST` function
    - **B.** The index value returned by the `COUNT` function
    - **C.** The index value returned by the `LIMIT` function
    - **D.** The index value returned by the `LAST` function
    - **E.** All of the above
15. Which of the following collections work in SQL and PL/SQL contexts? (Multiple answers possible)
    - **A.** Varray collections of scalar data types
    - **B.** Varray collections of record data types
    - **C.** Table collections of scalar data types
    - **D.** Table collections of object data types
    - **E.** All of the above

CHAPTER 7

Error Management

This chapter covers PL/SQL error management.

Two types of PL/SQL errors exist: those that happen at compilation time (also known as syntax errors or compile-time errors) and those that happen at runtime (also known as semantic errors). You will see compilation errors in both anonymous and named blocks—functions, procedures, packages, or user-defined object types. Compilation errors are easier to find because Oracle immediately alerts you when it comes across syntax errors. Semantic errors occur as a result of bad logic in your program, and they can be very subtle. In some cases, only a keen eye catches them before runtime. You handle semantic errors in the exception blocks of your PL/SQL programs.

As stated, runtime errors are complex and more difficult to solve because they only occur occasionally. Two scenarios exist for runtime errors: they are raised automatically, such as `NO_DATA_FOUND` errors, or they are not raised automatically. The latter are logical errors. You must create user-defined exceptions for logical errors. Moreover, logical errors cannot be managed when they occur inside the declaration block—unless exception assignments are made via static string or numeric literal variables that act like constants.

You will learn about both compilation errors and runtime errors in this chapter. You'll also learn how to capture and manage thrown exceptions.

The following topics are covered in this chapter:

- Exception types and scope
    - Compilation errors
    - Runtime errors
- Exception management built-in functions
- User-defined exceptions
    - Declaring user-defined exceptions
    - Dynamic user-defined exceptions
- Exception Stack Functions

Although this chapter is designed to be read sequentially, you can skim through it first and then quickly dive into almost any section that you are particularly interested in.

Exception Types and Scope

As previously mentioned, two types of errors exist in PL/SQL: compilation errors and runtime errors. A compilation error occurs if you have made an error typing a program, such as forgetting a comma, period, identifier, or semicolon. As defined in Chapter 4, identifiers include reserved words and keywords as well as both subroutine and variable names. These compilation errors are lexical errors. The compiler catches lexical errors when it parses the program's plain text file. Parsing is the process of reading a text file to ensure that it meets the lexical usage rules of a programming language.

Runtime errors occur when actual data fails to meet the rules (or, more precisely, the programming instructions) defined by your program unit.

Chapter 3 explains variable and subroutine scopes. Variable and subroutine scopes have two views. One view is a top-down availability of variables and subroutines, and the other view is bottom-up accessibility to variables and subroutines. Developers who design their code before they write any of it take a top-down view, while those who write code before they design it take a bottom-up view. The first version of your program code should always take a top-down view, while the progressive iterations from prototype to finished product benefit from a bottom-up view.

The amount of time it takes you to write and maintain good code decreases as your ability to understand and manage exceptions increases. That's because when you design first, you add exception handlers. The exception handlers provide you with clues that tell you where the code is broken and what you need to do to fix it.

Compile-time errors are often easy to see because they identify the line number of the exception or the line following the exception. The lines with errors fail to compile and Oracle's exception handling engine keeps track of the line and row numbers where syntax errors occur.

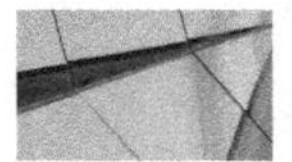

NOTE
Compile-time errors may have incorrect numbers when debugging triggers because the trigger declaration isn't counted by the parsers in the line count of the trigger body, or anonymous block.

Runtime errors aren't quite so easy to see. That's because when runtime exception are thrown and potentially re-thrown by the calling program. The first runtime exception throws (or *raises*, according to Oracle semantics) an exception. Either a local handler or the calling handler catches the exception. Handlers may handle the exception or re-throw it. That process can repeat itself until the exception reaches the point where it all started.

Figure 7-1 shows this exception management process.

The next two subsections cover compilation errors and runtime errors in more depth.

Compilation Errors

Compilation errors are generally typing errors. The parsing of your PL/SQL text file into a set of interpreted instructions, known as p-code, finds lexical errors. Lexical errors occur when you misuse a delimiter, identifier, literal, or comment. You can misuse lexical units by

- Forgetting a semicolon (the statement terminator)
- Using only one delimiter when you should use two, such as failing to enclose a string literal
- Misspelling an identifier (reserved words and keywords)
- Commenting out a lexical value required by the parsing rules

There are three general patterns for error messages:

- **Prior line errors** Point to an error on the prior statement line, which is generally a missing statement terminator.
- **Current line errors** Point to the column of the error or one column after the error. The difference generally means that the parser is looking for a missing lexical unit.
- **Declaration errors** Point to any failure in the declaration block, and generally have the actual error line as the last line of the error message.

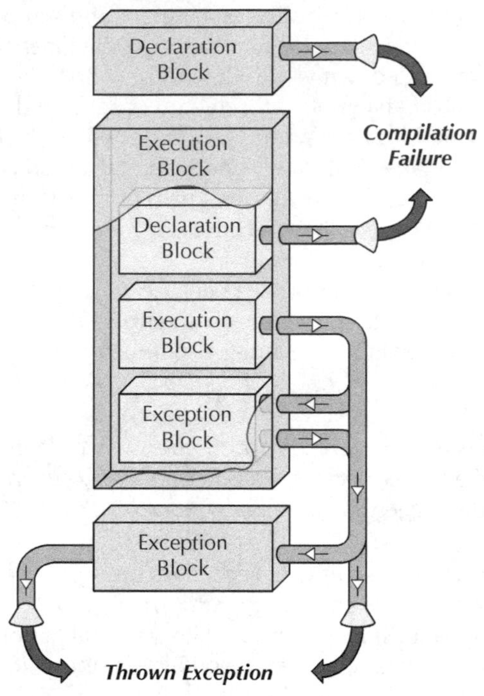

FIGURE 7-1. *Exception scope and routing*

The following program should print a Hello World message, but it fails to compile because it is missing the statement terminator on line 2:

```
SQL> BEGIN
  2    dbms_output.put_line('Hello World.')
  3  END;
  4  /
```

This raises the following error message:

```
END;
*
ERROR at line 3:
ORA-06550: line 3, column 1:
PLS-00103: Encountered the symbol "END" when expecting one of the following:
:= . ( % ;
The symbol ";" was substituted for "END" to continue.
```

This error message may look undecipherable, but it is actually quite informative when you know how to read it. The first line of the error message provides either the line where the error occurred or the line after the error. The second line places an asterisk immediately below the error location or the first column of the line. The `PLS-00103` error message raised by the example says that a lexical unit is missing immediately before the `END` reserved word. This typically means the error occurred one statement line before the echoed error message line. The error message also provides five possible lexical values for a missing symbol. The parser suggests using a semicolon. In this case the semicolon or statement terminator is the missing lexical unit. The semicolon should end the statement on line 2.

The next example shows a compilation error where the error occurs on the same line:

```
SQL> DECLARE
  2    lv_a  NUMBER := 0;
  3    lv_b  NUMBER;
  4    lv_c  NUMBER;
  5  BEGIN
  6    lv_c := lv_a  lv_b;
  7    dbms_output.put_line('['||lv_c||']');
  8  END;
  9  /
```

The error message displayed is

```
  lv_c := lv_a  lv_b;
                *
ERROR at line 6:
ORA-06550: line 6, column 17:
PLS-00103: Encountered the symbol "LV_B" when expecting one of the following:
. ( * @ % & = - + ; < / > at in is mod remainder not rem
<an exponent (**)> <> or != or ~= >= <= <> and or like LIKE2_
LIKE4_ LIKEC_ between || multiset member SUBMULTISET_
The symbol "." was substituted for "LV_B" to continue.
```

The `PLS-00103` error message says that a lexical unit is missing immediately before the variable `lv_b`. The asterisk on the second line below the variable `lv_b` tells you that the error occurs immediately before the variable. You can fix this program by placing any arithmetic operator in between the `lv_a` and `lv_b` variables.

A variation on the prior error message places the asterisk immediately below where the error occurs in a statement line. The following program raises this type of error message:

```
SQL> DECLARE
  2    lv_a  NUMBER;
  3  BEGIN
  4    lv_a = 1;
  5  END;
  6  /
```

Line 4 contains a comparison operator when it should use an assignment operator. The error message points to the comparison operator as the problem:

```
  lv_a = 1;
       *
ERROR at line 4:
ORA-06550: line 4, column 8:
```

```
PLS-00103: Encountered the symbol "=" when expecting one of the following:
:= . ( @ % ;
The symbol ":= was inserted before "=" to continue.
```

The error message points to the incorrect use of a comparison operator. This is an easy type of error message to read and understand.

You receive a less obvious error message when you trigger an error in the declaration block. The following example tries to assign a two-character string to a one-character variable in the declaration block:

```
SQL> DECLARE
  2    lv_a CHAR := 'AB';
  3  BEGIN
  4    dbms_output.put_line('['||lv_a||']');
  5  END;
  6  /
```

The program raises the following error message, which would provide very little information if you were trying to apply the previously discussed rules:

```
DECLARE
*
ERROR at line 1:
ORA-06502: PL/SQL: numeric or value error: character string buffer too small
ORA-06512: at line 2
```

The error points to line 1. Unlike the earlier errors, this does not point to a problem before the `DECLARE` statement. It tells you that the error occurs in the declaration block. The statement following the `ERROR at line 1` message describes the problem, and the following line tells you the line number where it occurs.

It's important to note that the last line is actually the first error written to the exception stack. The `ORA-06512` error on the last line of the error message points to the line number where the problem occurs. The next line put in the stack describes the problem. The third message says the problem occurs in the declaration block.

The error occurs when the program tries to assign a string literal `'AB'` into a single-character-sized variable. The error occurs after parsing the program when it attempts to bind any string and numeric literal values to variables.

Runtime Errors

Runtime errors can happen in declaration, execution, and exception PL/SQL blocks. The easiest to catch and handle are those errors thrown from an execution block because they are caught first by any local exception block and next by any containing block. On the other hand, only an external exception block can catch errors thrown from declaration or exception blocks.

Exception blocks contain `WHEN` blocks, which catch specific errors or general errors. The prototype for the `WHEN` block is

```
WHEN [predefined_exception | user_defined_exception | OTHERS] THEN
[RETURN | EXIT ];
```

The WHEN block can take an Oracle predefined exception name, a user-defined exception, or the catch-all OTHERS keyword. You use the OTHERS reserved word when you want a WHEN clause to catch any exception. Unless you want to skip your specific exception handlers, the WHEN OTHERS exception handler should always be the last exception handler.

Later in the chapter, Table 7-2 lists Oracle predefined exception names. The predefined errors map to known error numbers. They are defined in the sys.standard package. Oracle predefines these errors as follows in the sys.standard package:

```
CURSOR_ALREADY_OPEN exception;
  pragma EXCEPTION_INIT(CURSOR_ALREADY_OPEN, '-6511');
```

Alternatively, you can define your own exceptions, which is a two-step process. First, you assign a variable that uses the EXCEPTION data type. Second, you map your user-defined EXCEPTION variable to a specific error numbers. The PRAGMA (a *precompiler* instruction) lets you map the exception to the error number, as done in the sys.standard package.

The "User-Defined Exceptions" section, later in this chapter, covers the process of creating user-defined exceptions. Oracle also provides two built-in exception handling functions: SQLCODE and SQLERRM. They provide a simplified way to see the raised error code and its message. Table 7-1 explains the SQLCODE and SQLERRM built-in functions.

The following subsections cover execution and exception block errors first and then declaration block errors. They're ordered that way because you need to see how the basic mechanics work before you see how they fail.

Execution and Exception Block Errors

Errors raised in the execution block are thrown to the local exception block where they are caught and managed. *Exception handler* is another name for the exception block in PL/SQL. When the local exception block fails to catch an exception, it throws the exception back to the program that called it. That program may be the SQL*Plus environment, a SQL statement (more on this in Chapter 8), or a PL/SQL block. In fact, the PL/SQL block can simply be an outer block, which is the simplest way to demonstrate the behavior.

Function	Oracle Predefined Error	User-Defined Error
SQLCODE	Returns a negative integer for standard Oracle exceptions, except the NO_DATA_FOUND exception, which returns a positive 100.	Returns a positive 1 if no EXCEPTION_INIT PRAGMA is defined. If an EXCEPTION_INIT PRAGMA is defined, it returns a valid number in the range of –20001 to –20999.
SQLERRM	Returns the error code and message of a standard Oracle exception. SQLERRM is an overloaded function that operates only in the exception block.	Returns a 1 and a "User-Defined Exception" message when the exception is thrown by the RAISE statement. Returns a valid negative integer in the qualified range and a text message when the exception is thrown by the raise_application_info function.

TABLE 7-1. *Oracle Exception Management Built-in Functions*

Oracle Built-in Exception Handling Functions

The `SQLCODE` function returns the error number associated with an exception. The `SQLERRM` function returns the error number and the message associated with an exception. Unfortunately, how they work is not as simple as the preceding sentences suggest, because they work differently under different scenarios. That's why they're qualified next. They're also covered in Appendix C.

The SQLCODE Exception Function The `SQLCODE` function returns one of three values. It returns a negative number for all predefined Oracle exceptions, except the `NO_DATA_FOUND` exception. The `SQLCODE` function returns a positive 100 for a `NO_DATA_FOUND` exception. The `SQLCODE` function also returns a positive 1 when a user-defined exception is raised.

The SQLERRM Exception Function The `SQLERRM` function returns an error code and either an empty string or a message. It returns the following:

- A code and message for any unhandled error code or Oracle predefined exception name.
- A 100 code value and a User-Defined Exception message for a user-defined exception thrown by the following statement:

```
RAISE user_defined_exception;
```

- A –20001 to –20999 code value and a customized message for a user-defined exception thrown by the following function call:

```
RAISE_APPLICATION_ERROR(error_code, customized_message);
```

The `PRAGMA EXCEPTION_INIT` maps a negative integer to an error message. A call to the `RAISE_APPLICATION_ERROR` function throws that error with a customized message. Then, the `SQLERRM` function returns the code and customized message.

You should keep track of user-defined messages, because developers tend to use and reuse the same number for different kinds of errors. This practice of reusing errors for different purposes confuses system users and administrators. It makes it difficult, if not impossible, to understand what specific errors mean. The question is, how can you manage it? I suggest that you create a common lookup table in which to store and maintain the list of defined errors and then require developers to log their use of user-defined messages in that table. Then, whenever a developer needs to know which error numbers are in use, they can check the values in the table. This approach avoids reusing user-defined values and makes identification of errors and maintenance of user-defined messages a snap.

Calling programs should have generic exception handlers to manage any exceptions re-thrown by other program units. The next program shows you how to handle a locally raised exception in a local exception block. The exception block only manages a `value_error` exception. While a number of things can raise a `value_error` exception, the following program raises the error by trying to put a two-character string in a one-character variable:

```
SQL> DECLARE
  2    lv_a VARCHAR2(1);
  3    lv_b VARCHAR2(2) := 'AB';
  4  BEGIN
  5    lv_a := lv_b;
  6  EXCEPTION
  7    WHEN value_error THEN
  8      dbms_output.put_line(
  9        'You can''t put ['||lv_b||'] in a one character string.');
 10  END;
 11  /
```

Line 1 declares a one-character `lv_a` variable. Line 3 declares a two-character `lv_b` variable. Line 5 attempts to assign the two-character variable to the one-character variable; it fails and raises the following error:

```
You can't put [AB] in a one character string.
```

This shows you how a local error is caught and managed by a local exception block. It also uses the `value_error` built-in exception in the `WHEN` clause. The `WHEN` clause becomes a `value_error` exception handler, and it only catches and manages `ORA-06502` errors. Any other exception would be ignored and thrown to the SQL*Plus session.

The following raises a `NO_DATA_FOUND` error inside the inner block. Since the only exception handler only checks for a `value_error` built-in exception, the error isn't caught. Instead, it is re-thrown to the calling block, as shown:

```
SQL> DECLARE
  lv_a  VARCHAR2(1);
BEGIN
  DECLARE
    lv_b VARCHAR2(2);
  BEGIN
    SELECT 1 INTO lv_b
    FROM dual
    WHERE 1 = 2;
    lv_a := lv_b;
  EXCEPTION
    WHEN value_error THEN
      dbms_output.put_line(
        'You can''t put ['||lv_b||'] in a one character string.');
  END;
EXCEPTION
  WHEN others THEN
    dbms_output.put_line(
```

```
19         'Caught in outer block ['||SQLERRM||'].');
20   END;
21   /
```

The `SELECT-INTO` query on lines 7 through 9 fails to select a numeric literal value into a local variable. That's because the `WHERE` clause always returns false (after all, 1 isn't equal to 2). The local `value_error` exception handler is skipped and the error is re-thrown to the calling scope or outer block. The `others` exception handler catches the `NO_DATA_FOUND` exception.

You should always put the `others` exception handler last in a list of exception handlers because it's generic and catches all other exceptions—both those that you anticipate and those that you don't anticipate.

The preceding program's exception handler in the outer block prints the following `SQLERRM` message:

```
Caught in outer block [ORA-01403: no data found].
```

You can manually raise a user-defined exception without encountering one. The `RAISE` statement lets you throw such an error. The following program uses this technique to show you what happens when an error is raised inside an exception block:

```
SQL> DECLARE
  2    lv_a  VARCHAR2(1);
  3    e     EXCEPTION;
  4  BEGIN
  5    DECLARE
  6      lv_b VARCHAR2(2) := 'AB';
  7    BEGIN
  8      RAISE e;
  9    EXCEPTION
 10      WHEN others THEN
 11        lv_a := lv_b;
 12        dbms_output.put_line('Never reaches this line.');
 13    END;
 14  EXCEPTION
 15    WHEN others THEN
 16      dbms_output.put_line(
 17       'Caught in outer block->'||dbms_utility.format_error_backtrace);
 18  END;
 19  /
```

Line 8 calls the `RAISE` statement to throw an error. It passes control to the exception block that starts on line 9. Line 11 attempts to assign a two-character string to a one-character variable-length string. The error passes control from the inner block to the outer block's exception handler.

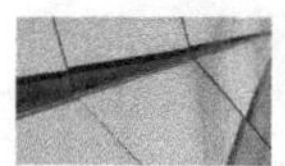

NOTE
Always put the general `others` error handler at the end of any list of exception handlers.

The outer block calls the `format_error_backtrace` function and returns

```
Caught in outer block->ORA-06512: at line 11
```

The ORA-06512 exception identifies the line number where the error occurred. This line number is calculated by parsing the file submitted to run the program. You can find that line number by running the script file from SQL*Plus and then typing **list** (actually, you only need to type the letter **l**). It lists the program with the line numbers that are reported by an ORA-06512 error. You can query the DBA_, ALL_, or USER_SOURCE view when the program is a stored function, procedure, package, or object type.

You can replace the call to format_error_backtrace with two calls to Oracle Database 12c's new utl_call_stack package. One call gets the error number and the other call gets the line number, as qualified later in the chapter in Table 7-3. However, neither of these functions returns the "ORA-" or ": at " substrings, which make the format_error_backtrace output readable.

You return a value from the backtrace_line function with the following call:

```
utl_call_stack.backtrace_line(utl_call_stack.backtrace_depth)
```

and you get the line number for the error with the following function call:

```
utl_call_stack.backtrace_line(utl_call_stack.backtrace_depth)
```

The "Exception Stack Functions" section later in this chapter expands on these types of supporting utilities for exception handling. The utl_call_stack package is also mentioned in Appendix C.

This section has demonstrated the basics of runtime exception management. You should note that when you raise an error in the execution block, it is handled locally, if possible. When the local exception block doesn't manage the error, the error is sent to an outer block or SQL*Plus environment. PL/SQL throws exceptions raised in an exception block to an outer block or the SQL*Plus environment.

Declaration Block Errors

As demonstrated earlier in the chapter, if you attempt to assign a two-character string literal to a one-character variable, an exception is raised at compile time. A runtime exception is raised when you call the program with an inappropriate value for the assignment. Like raised errors in the exception block, you can't catch runtime errors in the local exception block, because the declaration block throws the error back to the calling program's scope.

The next example rewrites an earlier example from the chapter. It assigns the value of a substitution variable to a local variable. (The "Interactive Mode Parameter Passing" section of Appendix A explains the use of substitution variables.) It doesn't raise a compile-time error because substitution variables don't have a physical size until runtime.

```
SQL> DECLARE
       lv_a CHAR := '&input';
     BEGIN
       dbms_output.put_line('['||lv_a||']');
     EXCEPTION
       WHEN OTHERS THEN
         dbms_output.put_line('['||SQLERRM||']'
     END;
     /
```

Line 2 assigns a substitution variable to the local variable. Assigning a value of `'AB'` to the substitution variable raises a runtime exception like the following:

```
DECLARE
*
ERROR at line 1:
ORA-06502: PL/SQL: numeric or value error: character string buffer too small
ORA-06512: at line 2
```

The inner anonymous block raises an unhandled exception because the exception block on lines 5 through 7 can't manage runtime exceptions.

The following program shows you how to capture the raised exception in the outer block:

```
SQL> BEGIN
  2    DECLARE
  3      lv_a CHAR := '&input';
  4    BEGIN
  5      dbms_output.put_line('['||lv_a||']');
  6    END;
  7  EXCEPTION
  8    WHEN OTHERS THEN
  9      dbms_output.put_line('['||SQLERRM||']');
 10  END;
 11  /
```

You capture the exception raised on line 3 by nesting the original program in another program. The container program captures the unhandled exception when the nested program throws it back to its calling program's scope.

This same behavior exists in stored program units, like functions and procedures. While procedures require wrapping their calls, functions don't. If you call a function directly from SQL, it can raise an unhandled exception.

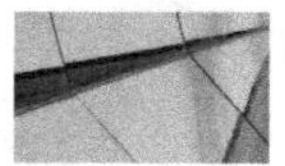

NOTE
You can call stored functions from SQL when they return a native SQL data type.

The following function replicates the dynamic assignment problem, but does so in a stored programming unit:

```
SQL> CREATE OR REPLACE FUNCTION runtime_error
(lv_input  VARCHAR2) RETURN VARCHAR2 IS
  a VARCHAR2(1) := lv_input;
BEGIN
  NULL;
EXCEPTION
  WHEN others THEN
    dbms_output.put_line('Function error.');
END;
/
```

Line 2 takes a single input parameter. A call to the `runtime_error` function passes any valid `VARCHAR2` string (that's up to 32,768 bytes when the `MAX_STRING_SIZE` is set to `EXTENDED`). That's possible because formal parameters of functions or procedures have no physical size limit. Formal `VARCHAR2` parameters inherit their size from the calling parameters.

Inside the function, you assign the formal parameter to a one-character `lv_input` variable. The assignment raises a runtime exception when the input is greater than a one-character string.

You can call this function in SQL by using it as a `SELECT`-list element of a query, like:

```
SQL> SELECT runtime_error ('AB') FROM dual;
```

It generates the following unhandled exception:

```
SELECT runtime_error ('AB') FROM dual;
       *
ERROR at line 1:
ORA-06502: PL/SQL: numeric or value error: character string buffer too small
ORA-06512: at "PLSQL.RUNTIME_ERROR", line 3
```

This section has demonstrated that you should make dynamic assignments in execution blocks because PL/SQL doesn't catch dynamic assignment errors in local exception handlers.

TIP
Good PL/SQL coding practices avoid dynamic assignments in declaration blocks.

Review Section

This section has described the following points about exception types and scope:

- Compile-time errors typically are typing errors, and they occur during the parsing of PL/SQL programs. They can include errors with lexical units, and they can be the misspelling of or misuse of identifiers as variable names. The misspelled or misused identifiers are typically keywords or reserved words in SQL or PL/SQL languages.
- A compile-time error may point to one of three locations: the first character of the next line, when the error occurs as the last element of the preceding line; a character immediately following the error on the same line; or the beginning of the declaration block, for a nonparsing error.
- Runtime errors occur after the program is parsed and literal values are assigned to local variables.
- Runtime errors can occur in the declaration, execution, or exception blocks.
- Runtime errors thrown in the execution block are handled by the local exception block.
- Runtime errors thrown in the declaration or exception block can't be handled by local exception blocks.

Exception Management Built-in Functions

Oracle provides a series of predefined exceptions in the `sys.standard` package. These are useful tools in your debugging of Oracle PL/SQL programs. Most errors raise a negative number as their error number.

You find error codes by using the `SQLCODE` built-in function. The `SQLERRM` built-in function returns both error codes and messages. The earlier "Oracle Built-in Exception Handling Functions" section explains how the `SQLCODE` and `SQLERRM` functions work. You can also find more coverage in Appendix C on these two error handling functions.

The predefined exceptions are noted in Table 7-2.

Exception	Error	When Raised
`ACCESS_INTO_NULL`	ORA-06530	When you attempt to access an uninitialized object.
`CASE_NOT_FOUND`	ORA-06592	When you have defined a `CASE` statement without an `ELSE` clause and none of the `CASE` statements meet the runtime condition.
`COLLECTION_IS_NULL`	ORA-06531	When you attempt to access an uninitialized table or varray collection.
`CURSOR_ALREADY_OPEN`	ORA-06511	When you attempt to open a cursor that is already open.
`DUP_VAL_ON_INDEX`	ORA-00001	When you attempt to insert a duplicate value to a table's column when there is a unique index on it.
`INVALID_CURSOR`	ORA-01001	When you attempt a disallowed operation on a cursor, like closing a closed cursor.
`INVALID_NUMBER`	ORA-01722	When you attempt to assign something other than a number to a number or when the `LIMIT` clause of a bulk fetch returns a non-positive number.
`LOGIN_DENIED`	ORA-01017	When you attempt to log in with a program to an invalid username or password.
`NO_DATA_FOUND`	ORA-01403	When you attempt to use the `SELECT-INTO` structure and the statement returns a null value; when you attempt to access a deleted element in a nested table; or when you attempt to access an uninitialized element in an associative array.

TABLE 7-2. *Predefined Exceptions in the Standard Package*

Exception	Error	When Raised
NO_DATA_NEEDED	ORA-06548	When a caller to a pipelined function signals no need for further rows.
NOT_LOGGED_ON	ORA-01012	When a program issues a database call and is not connected, which is typically after the instance has disconnected your session.
PROGRAM_ERROR	ORA-06501	When an error occurs that Oracle has not yet formally trapped. This happens all too often with a number of the object features of the database.
ROWTYPE_MISMATCH	ORA-06504	When your cursor structure fails to agree with your PL/SQL cursor variable, or an actual cursor parameter differs from a formal cursor parameter.
SELF_IS_NULL	ORA-30625	When you try to call an object type non-static member method in which an instance of the object type has not been initialized.
STORAGE_ERROR	ORA-06500	When the SGA has run out of memory or has been corrupted.
SUBSCRIPT_BEYOND_COUNT	ORA-06533	When the space allocated to a table or varray collection is smaller than the subscript value used.
SUBSCRIPT_OUTSIDE_LIMIT	ORA-06532	When you use an illegal index value to access a varray or table collection, which means a non-positive integer.
SYS_INVALID_ROWID	ORA-01410	When you try to convert a string into an invalid ROWID value.
TIMEOUT_ON_RESOURCE	ORA-00051	When the database is unable to secure a lock to a resource.
TOO_MANY_ROWS	ORA-01422	When using the SELECT-INTO structure and the query returns more than one row.
USERENV_COMMITSCN_ERROR	ORA-01725	You can only use the function userenv('COMMITSCN') as a top-level expression in a VALUES clause of an INSERT statement or as a right operand in the SET clause of an UPDATE statement. It's raised when a system change number (SCN) can't be written to a database file.
VALUE_ERROR	ORA-06502	When you try to assign a variable into another variable that is too small to hold it.
ZERO_DIVIDE	ORA-01476	When you try to divide a number by zero.

TABLE 7-2. *Predefined Exceptions in the Standard Package*

These predefined exceptions are very handy tools for writing exception handlers. You should use these when they meet your exception handling needs. When they don't meet your needs, you should create user-defined exceptions.

User-Defined Exceptions

You can declare user-defined exceptions in the following three ways. This section explains all three and shows you how to implement and throw them.

- Declare an `EXCEPTION` variable in the declaration block, which you can throw by using the `RAISE` statement.
- Declare an `EXCEPTION` variable and map it to a standard Oracle exception with a `PRAGMA` (or precompiler) instruction in the declaration block. This type of error occurs when the code generates the standard Oracle exception.
- Use the `raise_application_error` function to create a dynamic exception. This technique doesn't require you to declare an `EXCEPTION` variable. The function lets you map a user-defined error code to a message. You can call the `raise_application_error` function in the execution or exception blocks. Calling the function throws a dynamic exception. It's important to note that you must use an integer in the range of –20000 to –20999 as the error number.

NOTE
Oracle E-Business Suite and other software applications already use numbers in the –20000 to –20999 range for their exceptions. You should try to avoid conflicts when working with the Oracle E-Business Suite.

The "Declaring User-Defined Exceptions" subsection shows you how to work with the first two types of user-defined exceptions. The subsequent "Dynamic User-Defined Exceptions" subsection shows you how to use the third type of exception.

Declaring User-Defined Exceptions

This section shows you how to declare an exception and raise it. It also shows you how to declare a precompiler instruction or compiler directive that lets you map an exception to an error code. Moreover, it covers the first two types of user-defined exceptions.

You declare an exception like any other variable in PL/SQL. After declaring it, you can raise the exception, but you have no way to catch it in the exception handler. The purpose behind your user-defined exception dictates which way you declare it.

The following program declares and raises an exception:

```
SQL> DECLARE
       e EXCEPTION;
     BEGIN
       RAISE e;
       dbms_output.put_line('Can''t get here.');
     EXCEPTION
```

```
 7     WHEN OTHERS THEN  /* Catch all exceptions. */
 8       /* Check user-defined exception. */
 9       IF SQLCODE = 1 THEN
10         dbms_output.put_line('This is a ['||SQLERRM||'].');
11       END IF;
12   END;
13   /
```

Line 2 declares a local EXCEPTION variable. Line 4 raises the user-defined exception. Since there's no PRAGMA (or precompiler) instruction, it raises an error code of 1. The exception block uses a generic handler to catch all exceptions on line 7, and line 9 checks for a user-defined exception code.

The program raises the exception and prints

```
This is a [User-Defined Exception].
```

A two-step declaration process lets you declare an exception and map it to a number. The first step is to declare an EXCEPTION variable. The second step is to declare a PRAGMA, which is a precompiler instruction or compiler directive. PRAGMA instructions let you direct the compiler to perform something differently than the default behavior.

While PL/SQL supports a number of PRAGMA directives, you use the following compiler directive to map an exception string to an error code:

```
PRAGMA EXCEPTION_INIT(locally_declared_exception, error_code);
```

TIP

You should avoid mapping a user-defined exception to an error code that is already a predefined exception, as qualified in Table 7-2.

The following example program defines an EXCEPTION variable and maps the exception to an error number:

```
SQL> DECLARE
  2    lv_a VARCHAR2(20);
  3    invalid_userenv_parameter EXCEPTION;
  4    PRAGMA EXCEPTION_INIT(invalid_userenv_parameter,-2003);
  5  BEGIN
  6    lv_a := SYS_CONTEXT('USERENV','PROXY_PUSHER');
  7  EXCEPTION
  8    WHEN invalid_userenv_parameter THEN
  9      dbms_output.put_line(SQLERRM);
 10  END;
 11  /
```

Line 3 declares a local EXCEPTION variable. Line 4 provides the compiler directive that maps the exception name to an error number. Line 6 raises a real ORA-02003 error code because proxy_pusher isn't a valid USERENV system context. Line 8 is a specialized exception handler that only catches invalid calls to the sys_context function.

The choice of `invalid_userenv_parameter` also mirrors its actual definition in the `sys.standard` package body. The code prints the standard Oracle error message:

```
ORA-02003: invalid USERENV parameter
```

Our prior example relies on a predefined Oracle exception. Let's examine what happens when we map a user-defined error code to a local exception. Again, it's important to note that you must declare user-defined error codes in the range of –20001 to –20999.

The following maps a local exception to a user-defined error code:

```
SQL> DECLARE
  2    e  EXCEPTION;
  3    PRAGMA EXCEPTION_INIT(e,-20001);
  4  BEGIN
  5    RAISE e;
  6  EXCEPTION
  7    WHEN e THEN
  8    dbms_output.put_line(SQLERRM);
  9  END;
 10  /
```

Line 3 maps the local exception to a valid user-defined error code. Line 5 raises or throws the exception. Line 7 catches our local exception and prints

```
ORA-20001:
```

The `SQLERRM` function returns only the user-defined error code because there's no standard message associated with user-defined error codes. The next section shows you how to fix that deficit with the `RAISE_APPLICATION_ERROR` function.

Dynamic User-Defined Exceptions

This section shows you how to declare an exception, assign it a number, and provide it with a user-defined error message. This is the third type of exception, a dynamic user-defined exception. This section also introduces the idea of an error stack, which is a collection of cascading exceptions.

The `RAISE_APPLICATION_ERROR` function lets you raise an exception and provide a customized error message. The prototype for the dynamic `RAISE_APPLICATION_ERROR` function is

```
RAISE_APPLICATION_ERROR(error_number, error_message [, keep_errors])
```

The function's first formal parameter is an error number, which must be in the range of –20000 to –20999. You raise an `ORA-21000` error when you provide any other value. The second formal parameter is a user-defined error message. You can provide any string message value you'd like, but try to keep it under 68 characters, because `SQLERRM` returns a nine-character error code, a semicolon, and white space before the error message. The last formal parameter is optional. The optional parameter has a default value of `FALSE`. You override it by providing a `TRUE` value, in which case you're instructing the function to add the new error message to any existing error stack.

It's possible to show how to use the dynamic `RAISE_APPLICATION_ERROR` function without declaring an exception or compiler directive. The following raises a dynamic exception without a local exception or compiler directive:

```
SQL> BEGIN
  2    RAISE_APPLICATION_ERROR(-20001,'A not too original message.');
  3  EXCEPTION
  4    WHEN others THEN
  5      dbms_output.put_line(SQLERRM);
  6  END;
  7  /
```

Line 2 raises the dynamic exception. Line 4 catches any exception because it uses the generic `others` keyword. The program prints

```
ORA-20001: A not too original message.
```

The next program combines declaring an `EXCEPTION` variable and a compiler directive with declaring a dynamic exception. It shows you how they work together in a program. Why bother declaring an `EXCEPTION` variable and compiler directive when dynamic exceptions don't need them? Because you can create a custom exception handler when you combine them with a dynamic exception.

The anonymous block code follows:

```
SQL> DECLARE
  2     e EXCEPTION;
  3    PRAGMA EXCEPTION_INIT(e,-20001);
  4  BEGIN
  5    RAISE_APPLICATION_ERROR(-20001,'A less original message.');
  6  EXCEPTION
  7    WHEN e THEN
  8      dbms_output.put_line(SQLERRM);
  9  END;
 10  /
```

Line 2 declares the exception variable. Line 3 declares the compiler directive with a user-defined error code value. Line 5 throws the exception with the same user-defined error code. Line 7 catches the dynamic error because the error code values on lines 3 and 5 couple the behavior of the exception variable and dynamic exception.

The specialized error handler prints the same dynamic error message:

```
ORA-20001: A less original message.
```

Unlike the message files for standard Oracle errors, this message is dynamic to your PL/SQL program units. The `SQLERRM` built-in function does not look up the message in an external file for a dynamic exception. Instead, it uses the string literal value provided as the second parameter to the `RAISE_APPLICATION_ERROR` function.

TIP

*Oracle stores error messages by language in several of the Oracle home directories, and all the error messages have a *.msg file type.*

Building on what you now know, let's add and shift some code from a prior example and then look at how to generate an error stack with the RAISE_APPLICATION_ERROR function.

The following program simply throws and captures a value_error exception:

```
SQL> DECLARE
  2    lv_a         VARCHAR2(1);
  3    lv_b VARCHAR2(2) := 'AB';
  4  BEGIN
  5    lv_a := lv_b;
  6    dbms_output.put_line('Never reaches this line.');
  7  EXCEPTION
  8    WHEN value_error THEN
  9      RAISE_APPLICATION_ERROR(-20001,'A specific message.');
 10    WHEN others THEN
 11      dbms_output.put_line(SQLERRM);
 12  END;
 13  /
```

Line 5 throws a value_error exception by attempting a two-character assignment to a one-character variable. The value_error exception handler raises a dynamic exception on line 9, which suppresses the original exception:

```
DECLARE
*
ERROR at line 1:
ORA-20001: A specific message.
ORA-06512: at line 9
```

This is the default behavior of the RAISE_APPLICATION_ERROR function. The last element of the exception is an ORA-06512 error. It reports the line number that threw the exception, which is line 9, where you raise the application error. You can change the default behavior of the RAISE_APPLICATION_ERROR function by replacing the default value of the optional third parameter.

The modified line 11 would look like this:

```
 11      RAISE_APPLICATION_ERROR(-20001,'A specific message.',TRUE);
```

It would raise the following error stack:

```
DECLARE
*
ERROR at line 1:
ORA-20001: A specific message.
ORA-06512: at line 9
ORA-06502: PL/SQL: numeric or value error: character string buffer too small
```

What's lost in this approach is the original line number of the error. What's gained is a list of all raised exceptions. In real code, the RAISE_APPLICATION_ERROR function would provide a meaningful error to your support personnel, who could then proceed to troubleshoot the problem.

This section has demonstrated how to declare exceptions and use them. You have seen how to map existing Oracle errors and error message definitions to user-defined exceptions. You have also seen how to provide your own error messages dynamically.

Review Section

This section has described the following points about user-defined exceptions:

- You can declare user-defined exceptions in any declaration block.
- You can declare a `PRAGMA`, which is a precompiler instruction or compiler directive that maps an error code to a user-defined exception.
- The `RAISE` statement lets you throw an exception.
- A `RAISE` statement with an Oracle error code lets the `SQLERRM` function return an error code and message.
- A `RAISE` statement with a user-defined error code lets the `SQLERRM` function return only an error code because there's no external message file that supports the error code.
- The `RAISE_APPLICATION_ERROR` function lets you raise a dynamic error code and message with or without an exception stack.

Exception Stack Functions

The exception stack is a first-in, last-out data structure. The first error thrown becomes the last error displayed. This is analogous to a stack of printed paper. The first page printed is at the bottom of the stack, and the last page printed is at the top.

PL/SQL throws an exception in the execution block when a failure occurs. The failure triggers or fires any exception handlers in the local exception block. Program units re-throw exceptions when they're not handled locally. This re-throwing can occur once, twice, or several times. It continues until control returns to the outermost PL/SQL block.

The behavior or re-throwing exceptions creates an error stack. You analyze the error stack to find the root cause. The root cause is always the first error thrown.

There are two approaches to managing errors in PL/SQL. Which approach you should choose depends on your application transaction control requirements. You raise an exception to stop the process when you run into a fatal business logic gap. Such an exception stops the business process and rolls back the transaction to a state where the data is safe and consistent. Alternatively, you log a nonfatal business process error by using an autonomous block of code. The best way to do that is to use a database trigger, which Chapter 12 covers.

Oracle Database 12*c* introduces the `utl_call_stack` package, which contains the functions and procedures listed in Table 7-3. Oracle Database 10*g* forward only has the `format_error_backtrace` function, which you find in the `dbms_utility` package.

We need to create a couple of stored procedures before we use the `utl_call_stack` package. They're kept very short to show a three-level call stack:

```
SQL> CREATE OR REPLACE PROCEDURE pear IS
       /* Declare two variables. */
       lv_one_character  VARCHAR2(1);
```

Package Function	Description
`backtrace_depth`	Returns the number of backtrace items in the backtrace. It returns a `PLS_INTEGER` of 1 or greater, and returns a 0 in the absence of an exception.
`backtrace_line`	Returns the line number of the backtrace unit at the specified backtrace depth. It takes a single input parameter, which is the result from the `backtrace_depth` function. It returns the line number where the error occurred at that particular depth of execution.
`backtrace_unit`	Returns the name of the unit at the specified backtrace depth. It takes a single input parameter, which is the result from the `backtrace_depth` function. It returns a module name or a null value for an anonymous block.
`current_edition`	Returns the current edition name of the unit of the subprogram at the specified dynamic depth. It takes a single input parameter, which is the result from the `backtrace_depth` function. It returns the edition name of the program where the database employs *edition-based redefinition*.
`concatenate_subprogram`	Returns a concatenated form of a unit-qualified name. Takes the qualified name as an input parameter and returns the fully qualified program name.
`dynamic_depth`	Returns the number of subprograms on the call stack.
`error_depth`	Returns the number of errors on the error stack.
`error_msg`	Returns the error message of the error at the specified error depth.
`error_number`	Returns the error number of the error at the specified error depth. It takes a single input parameter, which is the result from the `backtrace_depth` function.
`lexical_depth`	Returns the lexical nesting level of the subprogram at the specified dynamic depth. It takes a single input parameter, which is the result from the `backtrace_depth` function.
`owner`	Returns the owner name of the unit of the subprogram at the specified dynamic depth. It takes a single input parameter, which is the result from the `backtrace_depth` function.
`unit_line`	Returns the line number of the unit of the subprogram at the specified dynamic depth. It takes a single input parameter, which is the result from the `backtrace_depth` function.
`subprogram`	Returns the unit-qualified name of the subprogram at the specified dynamic depth. It takes a single input parameter, which is the result from the `backtrace_depth` function.

TABLE 7-3. *Functions in the utl_call_stack Package*

```
 4     lv_two_character   VARCHAR2(2)  := 'AB';
 5   BEGIN
 6     lv_one_character := lv_two_character;
 7   END pear;
 8   /
```

Staying with the simple example of assigning a two-character string to a one-character variable, the `pear` procedure declares `lv_one_character` and `lv_two_character` variables on lines 3 and 4, respectively. The assignment of the two-character value to the one-character variable on line 6 will throw an error whenever you call the `pear` procedure. The lack of an exception handler in the `pear` procedure means it throws the error back to its caller.

The `orange` procedure is even simpler because it doesn't include any variable declarations:

```
SQL> CREATE OR REPLACE PROCEDURE orange IS
  2  BEGIN
  3    pear();
  4  END orange;
  5  /
```

The call to the `pear` procedure on line 3 causes the `pear` procedure to throw an exception. That exception can't be handled because the `orange` procedure doesn't have any exception handlers for the error.

The `apple` procedure mimics the `orange` procedure. It only calls the `orange` procedure. Like the `orange` procedure, the `apple` procedure doesn't have any exception handlers, which means it re-throws any exception from the `orange` procedure to its calling scope program:

```
SQL> CREATE OR REPLACE PROCEDURE apple IS
     BEGIN
       orange();
     END apple;
     /
```

There's no surprise with the `apple` procedure. Like the preceding `orange` procedure, the `apple` procedure calls the `orange` procedure. The `apple` procedure re-throws the caught exception to its calling scope because it lacks an exception handler. The calling scope is the following anonymous block program:

```
SQL> BEGIN
       apple;
     EXCEPTION
       WHEN others THEN
         FOR i IN REVERSE 1..utl_call_stack.backtrace_depth LOOP
           /* Check for an anonymous block. */
           IF utl_call_stack.backtrace_unit(i) IS NULL THEN
             /* utl_call_stack doesn't show an error, manually override. */
             dbms_output.put_line(
               'ORA-06512: at Anonymous Block, line '||
                utl_call_stack.backtrace_line(i));
           ELSE
              /* utl_call_stack doesn't show an error, manually override. */
             dbms_output.put_line(
```

```
15              'ORA-06512: at '||utl_call_stack.backtrace_unit(i)||
16              ', line '||utl_call_stack.backtrace_line(i));
17          END IF;
18
19          /* The backtrace and error depth are unrelated, and the depth of
20             calls can be and generally is higher than the depth of errors. */
21          IF i = utl_call_stack.error_depth THEN
22            dbms_output.put_line(
23                'ORA-'||LPAD(utl_call_stack.error_number(i),5,0)
24                  ||' '||utl_call_stack.error_msg(i));
25          END IF;
26        END LOOP;
27  END;
28  /
```

Line 2 calls the `apple` procedure, which ultimately returns an exception. The anonymous block program does have an exception handler. The exception handler manages any exception by starting a decrementing loop on line 5 and ending on line 26. Line 7 checks to see if the `backtrace_unit` function returns a null value. It returns a null when the calling program is an anonymous block program and has the qualified name of a stored function or procedure.

Lines 10 and 15 place the traditional `ORA-06512` error code before the program units that raise the exception because it's not captured by the `utl_call_stack` package. You only find the original thrown error in the error stack managed by the `utl_call_stack` package. This can be illustrated when you try to call for the exception at a backtrace depth rather than an error depth. For example, this program has a backtrace depth of 4 and an error depth of 1. That's why line 21 exists.

Line 21 checks whether the error depth is equal to the backtrace depth. If you removed the `IF` block on lines 21 and 25, the program would fail because it would make a call to a nonexistent error depth on line 23, like this:

```
23                'ORA-'||LPAD(utl_call_stack.error_number(i),5,0)
```

It would result in the following exception:

```
BEGIN
*
ERROR at line 1:
ORA-64610: bad depth indicator
ORA-06512: at "SYS.UTL_CALL_STACK", line 130
ORA-06512: at line 21
ORA-06502: PL/SQL: numeric or value error: character string buffer too small
```

Suffice it to say, you always need to differentiate between the backtrace depth and error depth to avoid errors like that. As a rule of thumb, the error depth is always less than the backtrace depth. This is a new feature, so it may evolve between releases.

Let's move back to analyzing the earlier program. Line 22 left-pads the error number with zeros to return a five-digit number because the function returns the number as an integer. Line 22 also puts an `'ORA-'` string in front of the left-padded error code and appends the error message after the error code.

The foregoing program prints

```
ORA-06512: at VIDEO.PEAR, line 6
ORA-06512: at VIDEO.ORANGE, line 3
ORA-06512: at VIDEO.APPLE, line 3
ORA-06512: at Anonymous Block, line 2
ORA-06502 PL/SQL: numeric or value error: character string buffer too small
```

You can raise the same stack trace with a call to the `format_error_backtrace` function, which is found in the `dbms_utility` package. That means switching lines 22 through 24 with the following lines 22 and 23 would replace all the preceding logic for a stack trace:

```
22            dbms_output.put_line(
23              dbms_utility.format_error_backtrace);
```

However, the stack trace from the `format_error_backtrace` function doesn't print well when you call it from inside the `put_line` procedure, because it forces additional line breaks. It takes some effort, but we can get a clean stack trace by making the following changes to our program:

```
SQL> DECLARE
       lv_length   NUMBER;
       lv_counter  NUMBER := 0;
       lv_begin    NUMBER := 1;
       lv_end      NUMBER;
       lv_index    NUMBER := 0;
       lv_trace    VARCHAR2(2000);
     BEGIN
       apple;
     EXCEPTION
       WHEN others THEN
         FOR i IN REVERSE 1..utl_call_stack.backtrace_depth LOOP
           /* The backtrace and error depth are unrelated, and the depth of
              calls can be and generally is higher than the depth of errors. */
           IF i = utl_call_stack.error_depth THEN
             /* Capture the stack trace. */
             lv_trace := dbms_utility.format_error_backtrace;

             /* Count the number of line returns - ASCII 10s. */
             lv_length := REGEXP_COUNT(lv_trace,CHR(10),1);

             /* Read through the stack to remove line returns. */
             WHILE (lv_counter < lv_length) LOOP
               /* Increment the counter at the top. */
               lv_counter := lv_counter + 1;

               /* Get the next line return. */
               lv_end := REGEXP_INSTR(lv_trace,CHR(10),lv_begin,1);

               /* Cut out the first substring from the stack trace. */
               dbms_output.put_line(SUBSTR(lv_trace,lv_begin,lv_end - lv_begin));
```

```
32
33           /* Assign the substring ending to the beginning. */
34           lv_begin := lv_end + 1;
35         END LOOP;
36       END IF;
37     END LOOP;
38
39         /* Print the actual original error message. */
40         dbms_output.put_line(
41             'ORA-'||LPAD(utl_call_stack.error_number(i),5,0)
42              ||': '||utl_call_stack.error_msg(i));
43       END IF;
44     END LOOP;
45 END;
46 /
```

Line 15 ensures that the evaluation process begins with the first item in the error stack. Line 28 marks the index location within the string for line returns. Line 31 prints only the substring from the stack trace. Lines 40 through 42 print the original error.

This prints the following stack trace:

```
ORA-06512: at "VIDEO.PEAR", line 6
ORA-06512: at "VIDEO.ORANGE", line 3
ORA-06512: at "VIDEO.APPLE", line 3
ORA-06512: at line 9
ORA-06502: PL/SQL: numeric or value error: character string buffer too small
```

This knowledge comes in handy when you want to render the stack trace in HTML. You can make a slight modification to replace the line returns with HTML `<br />` tags (which adds line returns enabled for web pages).

The best-practice steps for making such a change require adding a few lines to the preceding program. The following displays the key modifications:

```
SQL> DECLARE
       ...
       lv_break     VARCHAR2(6) := '<br />';
     BEGIN
       apple;
     EXCEPTION
       ...
               /* Replace and cut out the next substring from stack trace. */
               lv_trace := REGEXP_REPLACE(lv_trace,CHR(10),lv_break,lv_end,1);
               lv_end := lv_end + LENGTH(lv_break);
               dbms_output.put_line(
                 SUBSTR(lv_trace,lv_begin,lv_end - lv_begin));
       ...
     END;
     /
```

Line 8 adds a new local variable for an HTML <br /> tag. Line 32 replaces the line return with the HTML line break tag. Line 33 adds the length of the tag to reset the ending point for the current substring and starting point for the next substring.

The modified program prints

```
ORA-06512: at "VIDEO.PEAR", line 6<br />
ORA-06512: at "VIDEO.ORANGE", line 3<br />
ORA-06512: at "VIDEO.APPLE", line 3<br />
ORA-06512: at line 10<br />
ORA-06502: PL/SQL: numeric or value error: character string buffer too small<br />
```

This section has shown you how to use both stack trace tools. It has also given you some ideas for how you can mix and match the tools to get a desired result.

Review Section

This section has described the following points about user-defined exceptions:

- Oracle provides you with the `utl_call_stack` package to manage exception stacks.
- The `dbms_utility` package provides you with the `format_error_backtrace` function, which generates a stack trace.
- The `utl_call_stack` package keeps tabs of the execution stack separately from the error stack.
- It's possible to parse and convert the text output from the `format_error_backtrace` function to HTML output.

Supporting Scripts

This section describes programs placed on the McGraw-Hill Professional website to support the book.

- The `exception_handling.sql` program contains small programs that support the exception types, built-in functions, and user-defined exceptions.
- The `stack_trace_management.sql` program contains programs that support how you manage stack traces as covered in this chapter.

Summary

This chapter has explained how to work with PL/SQL error management. It has qualified the differences between compilation errors and runtime errors. You have also learned about the unhandled behavior of runtime errors that occur in declaration blocks and how to handle raised errors in both the execution and exception blocks.

Mastery Check

The mastery check is a series of true-or-false and multiple-choice questions that let you confirm how well you understand the material in the chapter. You may check Appendix I for answers to these questions.

True or False:

1. ___Oracle PL/SQL programming requires you to understand how to capture and analyze both compile-time errors and runtime errors.
2. ___A compile-time error may occur when you try to run an anonymous block program.
3. ___A runtime error may occur when you try to compile a stored procedure.
4. ___A runtime error may occur when you call a stored procedure.
5. ___A `THROW` command raises a runtime exception.
6. ___It's possible to declare a user-defined `EXCEPTION` variable with the same error code as a predefined exception.
7. ___A `PRAGMA` is a precompiler instruction or compiler directive.
8. ___An `EXCEPTION_INIT` complier directive lets you map a user-defined `EXCEPTION` variable to a message.
9. ___A `raise_application_error` function call lets you map only a user-defined error code to a custom error message.
10. ___A call to the `format_error_backtrace` function from the `utl_call_stack` package creates a stack trace.

Multiple Choice:

11. Which of the following error codes belongs to a predefined exception? (Multiple answers possible)
    - **A.** `ORA-01402`
    - **B.** `ORA-01722`
    - **C.** `ORA-06548`
    - **D.** `ORA-01422`
    - **E.** `ORA-00001`
12. Which of the following is a predefined exception keyword? (Multiple answers possible)
    - **A.** `CURSOR_IS_OPEN`
    - **B.** `INVALID_NUMBER`
    - **C.** `LOGIN_DENIED`
    - **D.** `NO_DATA_FOUND`
    - **E.** `VALUE_INCORRECT`

13. Which of the following lets you raise an exception in PL/SQL? (Multiple answers possible)
    - **A.** A `THROW e;` statement
    - **B.** A `RAISE e;` statement
    - **C.** A `THROW;` statement
    - **D.** A `RAISE;` statement
    - **E.** A `raise_application error` function call
14. Which of the following are functions of the `utl_call_stack` package? (Multiple answers possible)
    - **A.** The `backtrace_error` function
    - **B.** The `backtrace_depth` function
    - **C.** The `error_number` function
    - **D.** The `subprogram_name` function
    - **E.** The `error_depth` function
15. Which of the following displays an HTML-ready stack trace? (Multiple answers possible)
    - **A.** The `utl_call_stack.current_edition` function
    - **B.** The `dbms_utility.format_stack_trace` function
    - **C.** The `dbms_utility.format_error_backtrace` function
    - **D.** All of the above
    - **E.** None of the above

PART II

PL/SQL Programming

CHAPTER 8

Functions and Procedures

As you've seen in previous chapters, there are two types of subroutines: functions and procedures. You use these to build database-tier libraries to encapsulate application functionality, which is then collocated on the database tier for efficiency.

This chapter covers the following subroutine topics:

- Function and procedure architecture
- Transaction scope
- Functions
    - Creation options
    - Pass-by-value functions
    - Pass-by-reference functions
- Procedures
    - Pass-by-value procedures
    - Pass-by-reference functions

Oracle Database 12*c* supports subroutines that are stored as functions and procedures in the database. They are named PL/SQL blocks. You can deploy them as stand-alone subroutines or as components in packages. Packages and object types can contain both functions and procedures. Anonymous blocks can also have local functions and procedures defined in their declaration blocks. You can also nest functions and procedures inside other functions and procedures.

You publish functions and procedures as stand-alone units or within packages and object types. Stand-alone units are also known as schema-level functions or procedures. Publishing functions and procedures within packages and object types means that they are defined in the package specification or object type, not in the package body or object type body. They're local subroutines when you define functions or procedures inside package bodies or object type bodies. Local subroutines aren't published subroutines. Likewise, subroutines defined in the declaration block of anonymous block programs are local subroutines.

You deploy collections of related functions and procedures in packages and object types. Packages and object types serve as library containers in the database. Packages act as primary library containers because you don't have to create instances to use them, whereas some subroutines in object types require you to create instances to use them. Packages also let you overload functions and procedures. Chapter 9 covers packages.

User-defined object types are SQL data types. Inside object types, functions and procedures can be defined as class- or instance-level subroutines. Class functions and procedures are static subroutines, and you can access them the same way you use functions and procedures in packages. Instance-level subroutines are only accessible when you create an instance of an object type. Chapter 11 covers object types.

The sections work sequentially to build a foundation of concepts. If you wish to skip ahead, browsing from the beginning may provide clarity to later sections.

Function and Procedure Architecture

As described in Chapter 4, functions and procedures are named PL/SQL blocks. You can also call them subroutines or subprograms. They have headers in place of the declaration block. The header defines the function or procedure name, a list of formal parameters, and a return data type for functions. Formal parameters define variables that you can send to subroutines when you call them. You use both formal parameters and local variables inside functions and procedures. While functions return a data type, procedures don't. At least, procedures don't formally list a return data type, because they return a void. The void is explicitly defined in other programming languages, like C, C#, Java, and C++. Procedures can return values through their formal parameter list variables when they are passed by reference.

Local functions and procedures don't require, but should have, forward-referencing stubs. While stored functions and procedures define their parameter list and return types in the database catalog, local functions don't. Providing forward-referencing stubs for local functions or procedures avoids a procedure or function "not declared in this scope" error. The "Local Named Blocks" section in Chapter 3 has an example of the best practice.

There are four types of generic subroutines in programming languages. The four types are defined by two behaviors: whether they return a formal value or not and whether their parameter lists are passed by value or by reference.

You set formal parameters when you define subroutines. You call subroutines with actual parameters. Formal parameters define the list of possible variables, and their position and data type. Formal parameters do not assign values other than a default value, which makes a parameter optional. Actual parameters are the values you provide to subroutines when calling them. You can call subroutines without an actual parameter when the formal parameter has a default value. Subroutines may be called without actual parameters if all their formal parameters are defined as optional.

Subroutines are black boxes. They're called that because black boxes hide their implementation details and only publish what you can send into them or receive from them. Table 8-1 describes and illustrates these subroutines.

The "Black Box"

The *black box* (the term comes from engineering lexicon) is part of verification and validation. Verification is a process that examines whether you built something right. Validation checks whether you built the right thing. For example, you validate that the manufacturing line is producing iPod nanos, and then you verify that they are being made to the new specification.

Integration testing validates whether components work as a part. You can't see how the product works. You only know what it should do when you provide input, like a function that should add two numbers. If one plus one equals two, then the function appears to work per expectations. This is black box testing.

Black box testing is the process of validation. Verification requires peering into the black box to inspect how it behaves. This type of testing is *white box* testing because you can see how things actually work—step by step. Unit testing verifies that your function or procedure builds the thing right. An example would be verifying that you're using the right formula to calculate the future value of money using compounding interest.

Subroutine Description	Subroutine Illustration
Pass-by-value functions: They receive copies of values when they are called. These functions return a single output variable upon completion. The output variable can be a scalar or compound variable. This type of function can also perform external operations, like SQL DML statements to the database.	Input Output Black Box
Pass-by-reference functions: They receive references to variables when they are called. The references are actual parameters to the function. Like other functions, they return a single output value, which can be a scalar or compound variable. Unlike functions that work with values, this type of function can change the values of actual parameters. They return their actual parameter references upon completion to the calling program. This type of function can also perform external operations, like SQL DML statements to the database, but only in the context of a PL/SQL block.	Reference Input Output Black Box Reference Output
Pass-by-value procedures: They receive copies of values when they are called. Procedures do not return an output variable. They only perform internal operations on local variables or external operations, like SQL statements to the database.	Input Black Box
Pass-by-reference procedures: They receive references to variables when they are called. Procedures do not return an output variable. This type of procedure can change the value of actual parameters. They return their actual parameter references upon completion to the calling program. They can also perform external operations, like SQL statements to the database.	Reference Input Black Box Reference Output

TABLE 8-1. *List of Subroutine Types*

Subroutines are functions when they return output and are procedures when they don't. Functions return output as values represented as SQL or PL/SQL data types. Chapter 4 qualifies the characteristics of PL/SQL data types, and Appendix B discusses SQL data types. Pass-by-value functions are sometimes called *expressions* because you submit values that are returned as a result. When the return data type is a SQL type, you can call the function inside a SQL statement.

Creating a pass-by-value function is like baking a cake. You put variables inside a black box, mix them up, and you get a result. The original ingredients or variables are consumed by making the cake. Creating a pass-by-reference function is like polishing a gem stone. You put the stone in with a solution and polish it. The solution dissipates but the stone remains; the stone is your pass-by-reference or `IN OUT` mode variable. The remaining case is an `OUT` mode pass-by-reference variable. Consider the analogy of slicing up salami into pieces. Until you complete the process, you don't know how many slices it yields. The number of pieces is the `OUT` mode variable result.

NOTE
Data types are defined in the database catalog two ways. They can be defined as native or user-defined SQL types, or as user-defined PL/SQL types inside package specifications.

You can use functions as right operands in assignments because their result is a value of a data type defined in the database catalog. Both pass-by-value and pass-by-reference functions fill this role equally inside PL/SQL blocks. You can use pass-by-reference functions in SQL statements only when you manage the actual parameters before and after the function call. You can also use the `CALL` statement with the `INTO` clause to return SQL data types from functions.

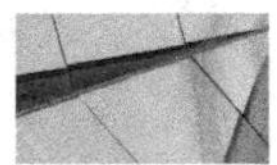

NOTE
Technically, you only need to handle SQL session bind variables before the call to a pass-by-reference function.

Figure 8-1 shows how you can assign the return value from a function in a PL/SQL block. SQL statements typically use pass-by-value functions because they don't manage reference output. Most SQL function calls submit columns or literals as actual parameters and expect a scalar return value. A SQL function call mimics a SQL expression, which is a SQL query that returns only one column and row.

Procedures can't serve as right operands. Procedures also must have runtime scope set inside a calling PL/SQL block. You cannot call procedures in SQL statements. However, you can use the `CALL` statement or `EXECUTE` statement to run procedures in SQL*Plus. Procedures are also self-contained units, whereas functions can only run as part of an assignment, comparative evaluation, or SQL statement.

Generic or default functions and procedures run *inline*, which means that they run in the same process context as their calling program unit. Inline programs exist in the same transaction scope as the calling program. An inline program can't commit without committing any DML statements processed before its call in the transaction scope. Autonomous programs run in a separate process context and have an independent transaction control.

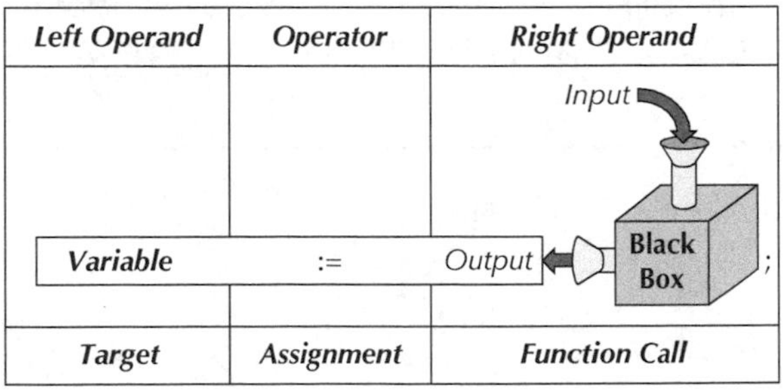

FIGURE 8-1. *Assignment of a function result*

Oracle Database 12*c* adds the ability to white list the callers of any function or procedure. You do that by providing the `ACCESSIBLE BY` clause with a list of functions, procedures, packages, and object types. Once you white list a function or procedure, only those white listed functions, procedures, packages, or object types that are white listed may call the function or procedure.

PL/SQL functions or procedures can also run SQL statements inside their black boxes. These actions are not represented in the previous diagrams. Figure 8-2 shows a modified pass-by-value function that actually updates the database. This gets more complex for pass-by-reference functions because they have an output, reference output, and database action as outcomes of a single function. A function that calls an `INSERT`, `UPDATE`, or `DELETE` statement typically can't run inside a query. It can run inside another PL/SQL block.

NOTE
You can include SQL statements in functions.

You can call a pass-by-value function from inside a `SELECT` statement when it meets one of two conditions. One condition requires that there can't be any embedded DML statements because you can't have a transaction context inside a query. The other condition lets you embed DML statements when a function runs autonomously.

You can't use a pass-by-reference function because there's no way to manage an `IN OUT` or `OUT`-only mode parameter (covered in the upcoming Table 8-2). Autonomous programs run in a different session context from their caller. That means the embedded `INSERT`, `UPDATE`, or `DELETE` statements don't return a direct acknowledgement of their success or failure, unless the function raises an exception.

Any attempt to call a non-autonomous function *inside a query* with an `INSERT`, `UPDATE`, or `DELETE` statement fails with an `ORA-14551` error. Likewise, an attempt to use a pass-by-reference function returns an `ORA-06572` error, which means the function has `IN OUT` or `OUT`-only mode formal parameters.

The benefit of wrapping an `INSERT`, `UPDATE`, or `DELETE` statement in an autonomous function is that you can create a wait-on-completion function. A wait-on-completion function returns one value when successful and another when not. Typically, this is done by returning a 1 for true and a 0 for false, which mimics a Boolean in a SQL context. You can't create a wait-on-completion autonomous procedure without using an `OUT` mode parameter. That means wait-on-completion procedures can't work in SQL statements. Wait-on-completion functions or procedures let you check for completion of a spawned or forked process before continuing with your current program's execution. Wait-on-completion functions are also known as pessimistic functions

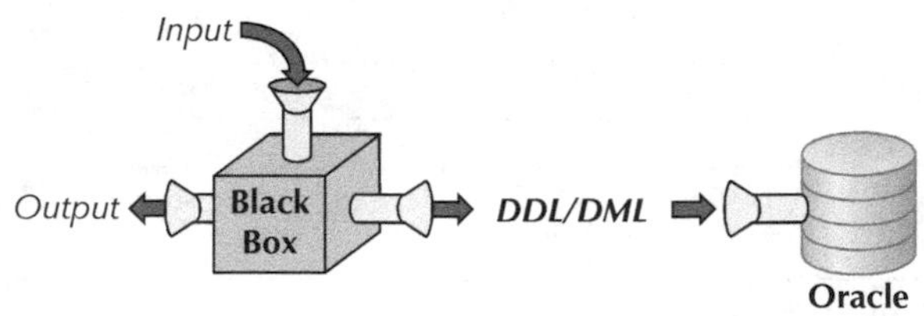

FIGURE 8-2. *Pass-by-value functions with read-write access to the database*

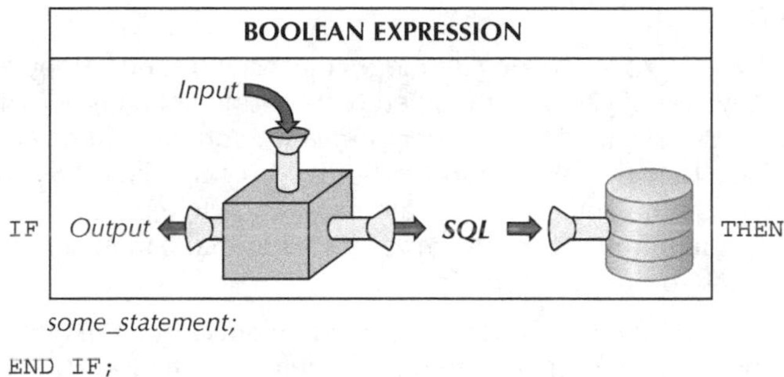

FIGURE 8-3. *Pessimistic functions guarantee outcomes of SQL statements.*

because they verify an event before continuing to process programming logic. Figure 8-3 displays a generic pessimistic function.

PL/SQL qualifies functions and procedures as pass-by-value or pass-by-reference subroutines by the mode of their formal parameter lists. PL/SQL supports three modes—*read-only*, *write-only*, and *read-write*. The `IN` mode is the default and designates a formal parameter as read-only. `OUT` mode designates a write-only parameter, and `IN OUT` mode designates a read-write parameter mode. Table 8-2 presents the details of these available parameter modes.

By default, Oracle Database 12*c* programs send copies of all parameters to subroutines when they call them. Although this may seem strange, because it is contrary to the concept of pass-by-reference subroutines, it is exactly what you'd expect for a pass-by-value subroutine.

When subroutines complete successfully, they copy `OUT` or `IN OUT` mode parameters back into external variables. This approach guarantees the contents of an external variable are unchanged before a subroutine completes successfully. This eliminates the possibility of writing partial result sets because an error terminates a subroutine. When an exception is thrown by a subroutine, you have an opportunity to attempt recovery or write variables to log files.

You can override the default behavior of passing copies of variables when calling functions and procedures for local transactions. This means you use fewer resources and actually pass a reference, not a copy of data. You cannot override that default behavior when calling the program unit via a database link or external procedure call. You override the copy behavior by using the `NOCOPY` hint.

The `NOCOPY` hint doesn't override the copy rule when

- An actual parameter is an element of an associative array. The `NOCOPY` hint works when you pass a complete associative array but not a single element.
- An actual parameter is `NOT NULL` constrained.
- An actual parameter is constrained by scale.
- An actual parameter is an implicitly defined record structure, which means you used either the `%ROWTYPE` or `%TYPE` anchor.
- An actual parameter is an implicitly defined record structure from a `FOR` loop, which fails because the native index has restricted scope to the loop structure.
- An actual parameter requires implicit type casting.

Mode	Description
`IN`	The `IN` mode, the default mode, means you send a copy as the actual parameter. Any formal parameter defined without an explicit mode of operation is implicitly an `IN`-only mode parameter. It means a formal parameter is read-only. When you set a formal parameter as read-only, you can't alter it during the execution of the subroutine. You *can* assign a default value to a parameter, making the parameter optional. You use the `IN` mode for all formal parameters when you want to define a pass-by-value subroutine.
`OUT`	The `OUT` mode means you send a reference, but a *null* as an initial value. A formal parameter is write-only. When you set a formal parameter as write-only, no initial physical size is allocated to the variable. You allocate the physical size and value inside your subroutine. You can't assign a default value, which would make an `OUT` mode formal parameter optional. If you attempt that, you raise a `PLS-00230` error. The error says that an `OUT` or `IN OUT` mode variable cannot have a default value. Likewise, you cannot pass a literal as an actual parameter to an `OUT` mode variable because that would block writing the output variable. If you attempt to send a literal, you'll raise an `ORA-06577` error with a call from SQL*Plus, and a `PLS-00363` error inside a PL/SQL block. The SQL*Plus error message states the output parameter is not a bind variable, which is a SQL*Plus session variable. The PL/SQL error tells you that the expression (or, more clearly, literal) cannot be an assignment target. You use an `OUT` mode with one or more formal parameters when you want a write-only pass-by-reference subroutine.
`IN OUT`	The `IN OUT` mode means you send a reference and starting value. A formal parameter is read-write. When you set a formal parameter as read-write, the actual parameter provides the physical size of the actual parameter. While you can change the contents of the variable inside the subroutine, you can't change or exceed the actual parameter's allocated size. The `IN OUT` mode restrictions on default values and literal values mirror those of the `OUT` mode.

TABLE 8-2. *Subroutine Parameter Modes*

You can define functions, procedures, packages, or object types in either of two ways:

- **Definer rights model** This default model of operation ensures that stored programs work with local data that resides in the same schema. It automatically sets `AUTHID` to `DEFINER`.
- **Invoker rights model** You can define a subroutine to write to the current user's local repository. You do this by defining the `AUTHID` as `CURRENT_USER`. The invoker rights model has a single code repository that allows independent users to act on local data. This type of model requires you to maintain multiple copies of tables or views in different schemas or databases. You then grant the `EXECUTE` privilege to other schemas. The invoker rights model best supports distributed computing models.

What Is Local Data?

Oracle qualifies local data as materialized views, synonyms, tables, or views. Tables and materialized views are physically stored data. Views are runtime queries drawn from tables, materialized views, and other views. Synonyms are pointers to materialized views, synonyms, tables, or views.

You can write to a local materialized view, table, view, or synonym from a stored subprogram collocated in the same schema. Synonyms can point to objects in the same schema or another schema. When the object is defined in another schema, you must have privileges to read or write to them for a synonym to translate correctly to the object. A local synonym can resolve a schema, component selector (the period or dot), and object name into a local schema name.

The examples in this chapter and the book use the definer rights model, which is the more common solution. The differences between the two models are described in detail in Appendix A.

Oracle Database 11*g* introduced changes in how name and positional notation work in both SQL and PL/SQL. With those changes, they actually now work the same way in both SQL and PL/SQL. This fixes a long-standing awkwardness in how you made function and procedure calls in the database.

Review Section

This section has described the following points about the architecture of functions and procedures:

- Pass-by-value functions are black boxes that perform tasks by consuming inputs and returning a completely new result.
- Pass-by-value procedures are black boxes that perform tasks by consuming inputs without returning a result.
- Pass-by-reference functions are black boxes that perform tasks by consuming some inputs and returning other inputs as altered values to the calling variables, and returning a completely new result.
- Pass-by-reference procedures are black boxes that perform tasks by consuming some inputs and returning other inputs as altered values to the calling variables.
- Inline functions and procedures run in the same transaction scope as the calling program unit.
- Autonomous functions and procedures run in a different transaction scope from the calling program unit.
- The `IN` mode is the default mode and is a pass-by-value parameter, and the `IN OUT` and `OUT` modes are pass-by-reference parameters.
- The `ACCESSIBLE BY` clause lets you white list functions and procedures.
- Final control of whether the `NOCOPY` hint passes a copy or a reference to the parameter rests with Oracle's PL/SQL engine.

Transaction Scope

As discussed in the "Data Transactions" section of Appendix A, transaction scope is a thread of execution—a process. You establish a session when you connect to the database. What you do during your session is visible only to you until you commit any changes to the database. After committing the changes, other sessions can see the changes you've made.

During a session, you can run one or more PL/SQL programs. They execute serially, or in sequence. The first program can alter the data or environment before the second runs, and so on. This is true because your session is the main transaction. All activities depend on one or more prior activities. You can commit work, making all changes permanent, or reject work, repudiating all or some changes.

Functions and procedures are the natural way to guarantee ACID compliance when you want to guarantee the ACID compliance across two or more DML statements. Appendix A explains ACID compliance. Oracle Database 12*c* database implements all `INSERT`, `UPDATE`, `DELETE`, and `MERGE` statements as ACID-compliant transactions. However, sometimes you may want to perform two DML statements against the same or different tables, and the only way to guarantee that such behavior is ACID compliant is to use a function or procedure. You enclose the collection of DML statements in a single transaction scope within the stored program unit, as illustrated in Figure 8-4.

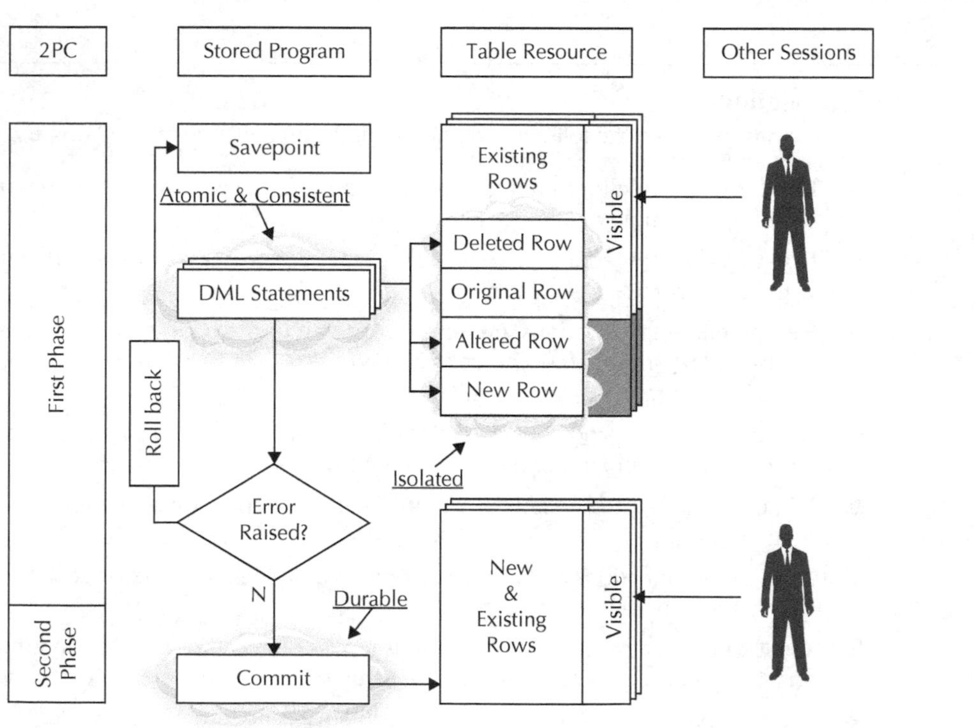

FIGURE 8-4. *Stored program transaction flow*

Guaranteeing the ACID compliance of two or more DML statements when they work against one or more tables is the core purpose of functions and procedures. The other purpose of functions and procedures is to *isolate and modularize* your program logic.

Transaction scope is fairly straightforward when you work within a single context. A context is a process or program scope. Oracle Database 12*c* manages program scope by individual sessions. That means any program that runs inside a single session has one *operational* context. Within that operational context or session, Oracle functions and procedures may call SQL statements, and SQL statements may call named PL/SQL blocks. These internal calls within the scope of an operational transaction are known as *context switches*.

Functions and procedures have one of two types of scope. They are dependently scoped by default, which means that they run inline or in the same transaction scope as the main process. The main process is the calling program. However, you can set functions or procedures to run in their own operational scope by defining them as autonomous transactions. It's always more complex to manage autonomous transactions because they run independently.

NOTE
Don't confuse an inline flow with the compiler trick of inlining subroutines. The latter means taking a copy of a discrete stand-alone program and embedding it as a local routine.

Autonomous transactions can commit their local work independently of the calling program—that is, provided they don't create resource contention, which is where two independent processes try to change the same data. Oracle's MVCC architecture prevents a direct collision, and that's one of the reasons individual autonomous programs must have their own `COMMIT` statement. The `COMMIT` statement makes all changes spawned by autonomous block changes permanent notwithstanding the main program control rules.

Autonomous transactions are great when you want something to happen notwithstanding the success or failure of something else. They're useful when you want to write data in a trigger before raising an exception that causes the main program's failure. However, they're dangerous for the same reason. You can inadvertently write data states when you don't want them written.

You should note that transaction scope is controlled by using the `SAVEPOINT`, `ROLLBACK`, and `COMMIT` commands. Both autonomous functions and procedures *must include their own `COMMIT` statement*. If you fail to provide a minimum of a `COMMIT` statement inside an autonomous program unit, it fails to compile.

Calling Subroutines

Prior to Oracle Database 11*g*, you could use both positional notation and named notation when calling subroutines in PL/SQL program units, but you could not use named notation in SQL calls to functions. Oracle Database 11*g* fixed that shortfall and introduced mixed notation calls too.

Positional notation means that you provide a value for each variable in the formal parameter list. The values must be in sequential order and must also match the data type. *Named notation* means that you pass actual parameters by using their formal parameter name, the association operator (=>), and the value. Named notation lets you only pass values to required parameters, which means you accept the default values for any optional parameters.

The new *mixed notation* means that you can now call subroutines by a combination of positional notation and named notation. This becomes very handy when parameter lists are defined with all mandatory parameters first, and optional parameters next. It lets you avoid naming the mandatory parameters and lets you skip optional parameters where their default values work. It does not solve exclusionary notation problems. Exclusionary problems occur with positional notation when optional parameters are interspersed with mandatory parameters, and when you call some but not all optional parameters.

The following function lets you experiment with these different approaches. The function accepts three optional parameters and returns the sum of three numbers.

```
CREATE OR REPLACE FUNCTION add_three_numbers
( a NUMBER := 0, b NUMBER := 0, c NUMBER := 0 ) RETURN NUMBER IS
BEGIN
  RETURN a + b + c;
END;
/
```

The first three subsections show you how to make positional, named, and mixed notation function calls. The last one demonstrates how to make exclusionary notation calls.

Positional Notation

You use positional notation to call the function as follows:

```
BEGIN
  dbms_output.put_line(add_three_numbers(3,4,5));
END;
/
```

Named Notation

You call the function using named notation as follows:

```
BEGIN
  dbms_output.put_line(add_three_numbers(a => 4,b => 5,c => 3));
END;
/
```

Mixed Notation

You call the function by a mix of both positional and named notation as follows:

```
BEGIN
  dbms_output.put_line(add_three_numbers(3,c => 4,b => 5));
END;
/
```

There is a restriction on mixed notation. All positional notation actual parameters must occur first and in the same order as they are defined by the function signature. *You cannot provide a position value after a named value without raising an exception.*

Exclusionary Notation

As mentioned, you can also exclude one or more of the actual parameters when the formal parameters are defined as optional. All parameters in the `add_three_numbers` function are optional. The following example passes a value to the first parameter by positional reference and to the third parameter by named reference:

```
BEGIN
  dbms_output.put_line(add_three_numbers(3,c => 4));
END;
/
```

When you opt to not provide an actual parameter, it acts as if you're passing a null value. This is known as exclusionary notation. Oracle has recommended for years that you should list optional parameters last in function and procedure signatures. They've also recommended that you sequence optional variables so that you never have to skip an optional parameter in the list. These recommendations exist to circumvent errors when making positional notation calls.

You can't really skip an optional parameter in positional notation call. This is true because all positional calls are in sequence by data type, but you can provide a comma-delimited null value when you want to skip an optional parameter in the list. Oracle supports mixed notation calls from Oracle Database 11*g* forward. You can now use positional notation for your list of mandatory parameters and named notation for optional parameters. This lets you skip optional parameters without naming all parameters explicitly.

SQL Call Notation

Previously, you had only one choice. You had to list all the parameters in their positional order because you couldn't use named references in SQL. This was fixed in Oracle Database 11*g*; *now you can call parameters just as you do from a PL/SQL block*. The following demonstrates mixed notation in a SQL call:

```
SQL> SELECT add_three_numbers(3,c => 4,b => 5)
  2  FROM dual;
```

As in earlier Oracle Database releases, you can only call functions that have `IN`-only mode variables from SQL statements. You cannot call a function from SQL when any of its formal parameters are defined as `IN OUT` mode or `OUT`-only mode variables without handling the actual parameter in SQL*Plus as a session bind variable. This is true because you must pass a variable reference when a parameter has an `OUT` mode.

Review Section

This section has described the following points about the transaction scope of functions and procedures:

- A transaction scope lets you manage multiple DML statements against one or more tables with an ACID-compliant guarantee that all or none of the DML statements work or fail.
- Default transaction scope occurs in a single operational context.
- Autonomous functions and procedures run in their own operational context and require a minimum of a `COMMIT` instruction to compile.
- Oracle supports positional, named, mixed, and exclusionary call notation in SQL and PL/SQL contexts.

Functions

As previously described, PL/SQL has pass-by-value and pass-by-reference functions. Both types of functions return output values. Function output values can be any SQL or PL/SQL data type. You can use functions that return SQL data types inside SQL statements. Functions returning PL/SQL data types work only inside PL/SQL blocks.

One exception to these general rules is that you cannot call a stored function that contains a DML operation from inside a SQL query. If you do, it raises an `ORA-14551` error saying that it can't perform a DML operation inside a query. However, you can call a function that performs a DML operation inside `INSERT`, `UPDATE`, and `DELETE` statements.

Functions can also contain nested named blocks, which are local functions and procedures. You define named blocks in the declaration block of the function. You can likewise nest anonymous blocks in the execution block.

The following illustrates a named block function prototype:

```
[{EDITIONALBE | NONEDITIONALBE}] FUNCTION function_name
(  parameter  [IN][OUT] [NOCOPY] sql_datatype | plsql_datatype
[, parameter  [IN][OUT] [NOCOPY] sql_datatype | plsql_datatype
[, ... ]]) RETURN [ sql_data_type | plsql_data_type ]
[ AUTHID [ DEFINER | CURRENT_USER ]]
[ DETERMINISTIC | PARALLEL_ENABLE ]
[ PIPELINED ]
[ACCESSIBLE BY
( [{FUNCTION | PROCEDURE | PACKAGE | TYPE}] [schema.]unit_name)
[,[{FUNCTION | PROCEDURE | PACKAGE | TYPE}] [schema.]unit_name)]
[,... ]]])
[ RESULT_CACHE [ RELIES ON table_name [, table_name [, ...]]]] IS
  declaration_statements
BEGIN
  execution_statements
  RETURN variable;
[EXCEPTION]
  exception_handling_statements
END [function_name];
/
```

You call functions by providing any required parameters as a list of arguments inside opening and closing parentheses. No parentheses are required when functions aren't defined with required parameters. This differs from most other programming languages. Calls in other languages require an empty set of opening and closing parentheses.

The prototype for a function call with actual parameters from SQL*Plus is

```
CALL function_name(parameter [, parameter [, ...]])
INTO target_variable_name;
```

When there aren't any mandatory formal parameters, the prototype differs, as shown:

```
CALL function_name INTO target_variable_name;
```

Assignments inside PL/SQL blocks with mandatory parameters look like:

```
target_variable_name :=
  function_name(parameter [, parameter [, ...]]);
```

The assignment prototype drops the parentheses when unnecessary:

```
target_variable_name := function_name;
```

Returning a function value as an expression is done by using the following prototype:

```
external_function_name(function_name( parameter
                                      [, parameter [, ...]]));
```

There are several optional configurations that you can use when creating functions. You can define a function to support a definer rights or invoker rights model by including the `AUTHID` clause. You can also guarantee the behavior of a function, which makes it possible to use functions in SQL statements, function-based indexes, and materialized views. You can also configure functions to return pipelined tables and, in Oracle Database 12*c*, shared result sets from the cache in the SGA.

As previously introduced, Oracle Database 12*c* now lets you white list callers of functions, procedures, packages, or object types via the `ACCESSIBLE BY` clause. You should use it anytime you want your security API to validate before calling stored functions. Chapter 2 contains a full example of white listing a `library` function.

As discussed, you can define formal parameters in one of three modes:

- `IN` mode, for read-only parameters
- `OUT` mode, for write-only parameters
- `IN OUT` mode, for read-write parameters.

The parameter modes let you create pass-by-value and pass-by-reference functions. You build a pass-by-value function when you define *all* parameters as `IN` mode. Alternatively, you build a pass-by-reference function when you defined *one or more* parameters as an `IN OUT` mode or `OUT`-only mode parameters.

The next three sections discuss how you can create functions. The first section examines the optional clauses that let you create functions for various purposes. The second section examines pass-by-value functions, and the third discusses pass-by-value functions.

Function Model Choices

What are the rules of thumb with regard to choosing a pass-by-value or pass-by-reference function? They're quite simple, as you'll see.

You should implement a pass-by-value function when you want to produce a result by consuming the input. You also should implement a pass-by-value function when you want to use the function in a SQL statement. A pass-by-value function is ideal when its transaction scope is autonomous. In object-oriented programming terms, you want to use a pass-by-value function when you want the lowest possible coupling—*message coupling*.

When programs are loosely coupled, they're more flexible and reusable in applications. Tightly coupled programs are intrinsically linked to form a processing unit—like root beer and vanilla ice cream are used make a traditional root beer float, so are these programs blended to form a processing unit.

You implement a pass-by-reference function when you need to couple behavior of the calling and called program units (known as *data coupling*). This happens when the function is called in a single threaded execution scope, which is the default in most transactional database applications. Tightly coupled programs such as these let you opt to return values through the `IN OUT` or `OUT` mode formal parameters. When the parameters receive raw and return processed data, the formal return value of the function becomes a signal of success or failure.

PL/SQL functions that use the return type to signal success or failure typically implement either a Boolean or number data type. They use the Boolean when you design them to work exclusively inside PL/SQL blocks and a number when they might need to work in either a SQL or PL/SQL scope.

A pass-by-reference function is ideal when you want to couple client-side interaction with server-side modules. In this context, you should define the function as autonomous. Autonomous functions run in their own transaction scope and are thereby independent of the calling transaction scope. The only way you know whether they succeeded or failed is to capture their return state through the function return type.

A pass-by-reference function is generally a bad idea when you simply want to couple two server-side programs. When the programs are on the same tier and might be called in the same serial transaction scope, you should implement the behavior as a pass-by-reference procedure. A pass-by-reference procedure is a specialized form of a function that returns no value. Procedures are most similar to C, C++, C#, or Java methods that return a *void* rather than a tangible data type.

Creation Options

You create functions for SQL statements, function-based indexes, and materialized views by using the `DETERMINISTIC` clause or the `PARALLEL_ENABLE` clause. The `DETERMINISTIC` and `PARALLEL_ENABLE` clauses replace the older `RESTRICT_REFERENCES` precomplier instructions that limited what functions could do when they were in packages. The new clauses let you assign the same restrictions to functions in packages, and they also let you assign them to stand-alone stored functions.

The `PIPELINED` clause lets you build functions that return pipelined tables. Pipelined tables act like pseudo–reference cursors and are built using modified PL/SQL collection types. They let you work with PL/SQL collections of record structures without defining them as instantiable user-defined object types. You can also read the collections in SQL statements as you would an inline view.

Object table functions let you return a varray or table collection directly to any DML statement. That is, if you remember to wrap the result in a `TABLE` function call. The object table function lets you stop writing pipelined table functions, except for legacy PL/SQL code. You will probably use pipelined table functions to wrap legacy PL/SQL functions that return associative arrays of scalar or record data types.

Oracle Database 11*g* introduced the cross-session result cache for definer rights functions. Oracle Database 12*c* lets you cache the results of invoker rights functions. It does this by adding the current user identity to the cached results. You implement the result cache feature by defining functions with the `RESULT_CACHE` clause. The cross-session result cache stores the actual parameters and result for each call to these functions and, for invoker rights programs, the `CURRENT_USER` value. A second call to the function with the same actual parameters finds the result in the cross-session cache and thereby avoids rerunning the code. The result is stored in the SGA. When the result cache runs out of memory, it ages out the least used function call results.

Backward Compatibility Issues for Functions

Functions were restricted subroutines before Oracle 8*i* Database (8.1.6). You had to define them with a guarantee of performance, which was known as their *level of purity*. The guarantees limited whether functions could read or write to package variables or to the database.

These limits can still be imposed on functions inside packages by using the `RESTRICT_REFERENCES PRAGMA` options listed in the following table. A `PRAGMA` is a precomplier instruction.

Option	Description
`RNDS`	The `RNDS` option guarantees a function *r*eads *n*o *d*ata *s*tate. This means you cannot include a SQL query of any type in the function. It also cannot call any other named block that includes a SQL query. A `PLS-00452` error is raised during compilation if you have a query inside the function's program scope that violates the `PRAGMA` restriction.
`WNDS`	The `WNDS` option guarantees a function *w*rites *n*o *d*ata *s*tate. This means you cannot include SQL statements that insert, update, or delete data. It also cannot call any other named block that includes a SQL query. A `PLS-00452` error is raised during compilation if you have a DML statement inside the function's program scope that violates the `PRAGMA` restriction.
`RNPS`	The `RNPS` option guarantees a function *r*eads *n*o *p*ackage *s*tate, which means that it does not read any package variables. This means you cannot access a package variable in the function. It also cannot call any other named block that reads package variables. A `PLS-00452` error is raised during compilation if you have a query inside the function's program scope that violates the `PRAGMA` restriction.
`WNPS`	The `WNPS` options guarantees a function *w*rites *n*o *p*ackage *s*tate, which means that it does not write any values to package variables. This means you cannot change package variables or call another named block that changes them. A `PLS-00452` error is raised during compilation if you have a statement inside the function's program scope that violates the `PRAGMA` restriction.
`TRUST`	The `TRUST` option instructs the function not to check whether called programs enforce other `RESTRICT_REFERENCES` options. The benefit of this option is that you can slowly migrate code to the new standard. The risks include changing the behavior or performance of SQL statements. For reference, the other options guard conditions necessary to support function-based indexes and parallel query operations.

You should define these `PRAGMA` restrictions in package specifications, not in package bodies. There should be only one `PRAGMA` per function. You can include multiple options in any `RESTRICT_REFERENCES` precomplier instruction. The `TRUST` option can be added to restricting `PRAGMA` instructions when you want to enable a restricted function to call other

(continued)

unrestricted functions. The TRUST option disables auditing whether called functions adhere to the calling program unit's restrictions—level of purity.

NOTE
You should consider replacing these restricting precompiler instructions with the DETERMINISTIC *clause or* PARALLEL_ENABLE *clause to guarantee the behavior of a function.*

Backward compatibility is nice but seldom lasts forever. You should replace these old precompiler instructions by defining functions with the new syntax. This means making functions DETERMINISTIC when they are used by function-based indexes. Likewise, you should define functions as PARALLEL_ENABLE when they may run in parallelized operations.

DETERMINISTIC Clause

The DETERMINISTIC clause lets you guarantee that a function always works the same way with any inputs. This type of guarantee requires that a function doesn't read or write data from external sources, like packages or database tables. Only deterministic functions work in materialized views and function-based indexes. They are also recommended solutions for user-defined functions that you plan to use in SQL statement clauses, like WHERE, ORDER BY, or GROUP BY; or SQL object type methods, like MAP or ORDER.

Deterministic functions typically process parameters in the exact same way. This means that no matter what values you submit, the function works the same way. They should *not* have internal dependencies on package variables or data from the database. The following function is deterministic and calculates the present value of an investment:

```
SQL> CREATE OR REPLACE FUNCTION pv
( future_value  NUMBER
, periods       NUMBER
, interest      NUMBER )
RETURN NUMBER DETERMINISTIC IS
BEGIN
  RETURN future_value / ((1 + interest)**periods);
END pv;
/
```

Assume you want to know how much to put in a 6 percent investment today to have $10,000 in five years. You can test this function by defining a bind variable, using a CALL statement to put the value in the bind variable, and querying the result against the DUAL table, like this:

```
SQL> VARIABLE result NUMBER
SQL> CALL pv(10000,5,6) INTO :result;
SQL> COLUMN money_today FORMAT 9,999.90
SQL> SELECT :result AS money_today
FROM   dual;
```

Materialized Views

Unlike a standard view in a relational database, a materialized view is a cached result set. As a cached result set, it is stored as a concrete table.

Materialized views are more responsive to queries because they don't demand resources to dynamically build the view each time. The trade-off is that materialized views are often slightly out of date because underlying data *may change between when the view is cached versus it is accessed*.

You can use function-based indexes in materialized views provided they use deterministic functions. Deterministic functions always produce the same result value when called with any set of actual parameters. They also guarantee that they don't modify package variables or data in the database.

Consider using materialized views when the underlying table data changes *infrequently* and query speed is important. Materialized views are possible solutions when developing data warehouse fact tables.

The function call uses positional notation but could also use named notation or mixed notation. It prints the formatted present value amount:

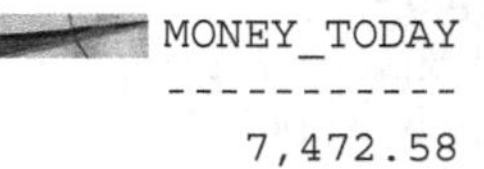

```
MONEY_TODAY
-----------
   7,472.58
```

You use deterministic functions inside materialized views and function-based indexes. Both materialized views and function-based indexes must be rebuilt when you change the internal working of deterministic functions.

PARALLEL_ENABLE Clause

`PARALLEL_ENABLE` lets you designate a function to support parallel query capabilities. This type of guarantee requires that a function doesn't read or write data from external sources, like packages or database tables. You should consider designating functions as safe for parallel operations to improve throughput, but the Oracle Database 12*c* optimizer may run undesignated functions when it believes they are safe for parallel operations. Java methods and external C programs are *never* deemed safe for parallel operations.

The following function supports parallel SQL operations and merges last name, first name, and middle initial into a single string:

```
SQL> CREATE OR REPLACE FUNCTION merge
( last_name      VARCHAR2
, first_name     VARCHAR2
, middle_initial VARCHAR2 )
RETURN VARCHAR2 PARALLEL_ENABLE IS
BEGIN
  RETURN last_name ||', '||first_name||' '||middle_initial;
END;
/
```

You can use the function safely in database queries, like

```
SQL> SELECT   merge(last_name,first_name,middle_initial) AS full_name
  FROM     contact
  ORDER BY last_name, first_name, middle_initial;
```

This query depends on the code discussed in the introduction and returns

```
FULL_NAME
-----------------
Sweeney, Ian M
Sweeney, Irving M
  ...
```

Parallel operations do not always occur when you use the PARALLEL_ENABLE hint. Parallel operations are more expensive with small data sets. The Oracle Database 12*c* optimizer judges when to run operations in parallel mode. Also, sometimes the optimizer runs functions in parallel when they're not marked as parallel enable. It makes this decision after checking whether the function can support the operation. It is a good coding practice to enable functions for parallel operation when they qualify.

PIPELINED Clause

The PIPELINED clause provides improved performance when functions return collections, like varray or table collections. You'll also note performance improvements when returning system reference cursors by using the PIPELINED clause. Pipelined functions also let you return aggregate tables. Aggregate tables act like collections of PL/SQL record structures. They only work in SQL statements.

This section discusses collection concepts. Chapter 6 covers collections for those new to PL/SQL. Collections are arrays and lists of scalar and compound variables. Pipelined functions only work with table or varray collections. These two types of collections are indexed by sequential numbers. You can also build collections of user-defined SQL object types, which are treated like single-dimensional arrays of number, strings, or dates.

The easiest implementation of a pipelined function involves a collection of scalar values defined by a SQL data type. You define a NUMBERS data type as a varray collection of NUMBER by using the following command:

```
SQL> CREATE OR REPLACE
    TYPE numbers AS VARRAY(10) OF NUMBER;
  /
```

The 10 in parentheses after the VARRAY sets the maximum number of elements in the collection, as qualified by Chapter 6. VARRAY data types are very similar to arrays. Arrays in most programming languages are initialized with a fixed size or memory allocation.

After you create the collection data type, you can describe it at the SQL command line:

```
SQL> DESCRIBE NUMBERS
 NUMBERS VARRAY(10) OF NUMBER
```

NOTE

When you create types in the database, the DDL command acts like a PL/SQL block. These commands require a semicolon to end the statement and a forward slash to execute it (or compile it into the database).

A pipelined function depends on available SQL or PL/SQL collection data types. These types are limited to varray or table collections. You can define SQL collection types of scalar variables or user-defined object types.

The following defines a pipelined function that returns a list of numbers:

```
SQL> CREATE OR REPLACE FUNCTION pipelined_numbers
  2  RETURN NUMBERS
  3  PIPELINED IS
  4    list NUMBERS := numbers(0,1,2,3,4,5,6,7,8,9);
  5  BEGIN
  6    FOR i IN 1..list.LAST LOOP
  7      PIPE ROW(list(i));
  8    END LOOP;
  9    RETURN;
 10  END;
 11  /
```

The function returns the `NUMBERS` user-defined SQL data type from the data catalog. That means it's a SQL table collection. The function declares a local table collection of `NUMBERS` on line 4. It also initializes the table collection. As discussed in Chapter 6, you initialize a table collection by calling the user-defined SQL data type name with an empty set of parentheses or with a list of the base type of the collection. In this case, it's a base type of numbers. Line 7 assigns *elements from the collection to the pipe*.

You can then query the results as follows:

```
SQL> SELECT *
FROM TABLE(pipelined_numbers);
```

The output is a single column with the ordinal numbers from 0 to 9.

Pipelined functions can also use PL/SQL collection types. PL/SQL collection types can hold scalar variables or user-defined object types like their SQL equivalents. They can also be collections of record structures. This means they are similar to system reference cursors.

Unlike system reference cursors, PL/SQL collection types cannot be defined as SQL or PL/SQL data types. They can only be defined as PL/SQL data types. In order to return these types in stored functions, they must be defined inside a package specification. Chapter 9 covers packages in depth.

The following package specification declares a record structure, a table collection that uses the `account_record` data structure, and a function that returns the table collection:

```
SQL> CREATE OR REPLACE PACKAGE pipelined IS
  /* Declare a PL/SQL record and collection type. */
  TYPE account_record IS RECORD
  ( account     VARCHAR2(10)
  , full_name   VARCHAR2(42));
```

```
 6     TYPE account_table IS TABLE OF account_record;
 7
 8     /* Declare a pipelined function. */
 9     FUNCTION pf RETURN account_table PIPELINED;
10   END pipelined;
11   /
```

Line 6 declares a collection of the record structure declared above it. Line 9 declares a `pf` function as a pipelined function. You should take careful note that the collection on line 6 is a table collection rather than an associative array. A pipelined table function requires the data to be put in a table or varray collection.

The `pf` function is implemented in the package body:

```
SQL> CREATE OR REPLACE PACKAGE BODY pipelined IS
  2     /* Implement a pipelined function. */
  3     FUNCTION pf
  4     RETURN account_collection
  5     PIPELINED IS
  6       /* Declare a collection control and collection
  7          variable. */
  8       counter NUMBER := 1;
  9       account ACCOUNT_COLLECTION := account_collection();
 10
 11       /* Declare a cursor. */
 12       CURSOR c IS
 13         SELECT   m.account_number
 14         ,        c.last_name || ', '||c.first_name full_name
 15         FROM     member m JOIN contact c
 16         ON       m.member_id = c.member_id
 17         ORDER BY c.last_name, c.first_name;
 18     BEGIN
 19       FOR i IN c LOOP
 20         /* Allot space and add values to collection. */
 21         account.EXTEND;
 22         account(counter).account   := i.account_number;
 23         account(counter).full_name := i.full_name;
 24         /* Assign the record structure to the PIPE. */
 25         PIPE ROW(account(counter));
 26         counter := counter + 1;
 27       END LOOP;
 28       RETURN;
 29     END pf;
 30   END pipelined;
 31   /
```

The package body implements only the `pf` function. Inside the `pf` function, line 8 implements a counter for the `account` table collection. Line 9 declares and initializes the `account` collection. The `account` and `full_name` fields are individually assigned variables from the cursor because a PL/SQL record type doesn't support a constructor call.

There is a more efficient assignment available. You can assign the `iterator` of a cursor `FOR` loop directly to a table collection when the list of data types match. The syntax replaces lines 22 and 23 with this:

```
22        account(counter) := i;
23
```

As you can see, the assignment went from two individual field assignments on lines 22 and 23 to a single record assignment from the cursor on line 22. You'll most likely use the direct cursor assignment any time you're working with a collection of PL/SQL records.

Varray and table collections are internal objects of a package when you implement them in a package. While they require explicit construction when the base type is an object, they can't accept constructed object assignments when the base type is a PL/SQL record structure.

Varray and table collections require you to allocate space before adding elements to a collection. The `EXTEND` method on line 19 allocates space for one element and then values are assigned to components of that indexed element. As discussed, they may be assigned by field element or by record through the cursor pointer, or iterator of a cursor `FOR` loop.

Line 25 assigns the PL/SQL collection to a `PIPE`, which translates the collection into a SQL result set, which you may then display or consume as a result set with the `TABLE` function. The `PIPE` is a simplex (one-way communication channel) FIFO (First In, First Out) translator. Line 28 returns the `PIPE`, which is the table collection as a SQL result set.

You can call the function using the package name, component selector, and function name, as shown:

```
SQL> SELECT *
  FROM TABLE(pipelined.pf);
```

This returns rows from the record structure:

```
ACCOUNT    FULL_NAME
---------- ----------------
B293-71447 Sweeney, Ian
B293-71446 Sweeney, Irving
  ...
```

It may appear that you're limited to packages because that's where you've declared the `account_table` return type. While package varray and table collections aren't directly available in the data dictionary, they are available to other PL/SQL programs because they're implicitly created in the data catalog. The fact that they're declared in a package specification also lets us implement them in stand-alone functions.

The following stand-alone function implements the same logic as the `pf` pipelined function, the difference being that it's a stand-alone schema-level function:

```
SQL> CREATE OR REPLACE FUNCTION pf
  RETURN pipelined.account_collection
  PIPELINED IS
    /* Declare a collection control and collection variable. */
    counter NUMBER := 1;
    account PIPELINED.ACCOUNT_COLLECTION :=
              pipelined.account_collection();

```

```
 9    ... cursor redacted to save space ...
15  BEGIN
17      FOR i IN c LOOP
18        /* Allot space and add values to collection. */
19        account.EXTEND;
20        account(counter) := i;
21
22        /* Assign the record structure to the PIPE. */
23        PIPE ROW(account(counter));
24        counter := counter + 1;
25      END LOOP;
26    RETURN;
27  END pf;
28  /
```

The only difference is how you reference the PL/SQL collection type. Note on lines 6 and 7 that the pipelined package name precedes the table collection type. It does so for the variable's data type on line 6 and the constructor function call on line 7.

You can now call the function by referencing only the function name, like

```
SQL> SELECT *
  FROM   TABLE(pf);
```

You can use pipelined functions to build views, like this:

```
SQL> CREATE OR REPLACE VIEW pipelined_view AS
    SELECT   result.account
    ,        result.full_name
    FROM     TABLE(pf) result;
```

Views built by calls to pipelined functions require `INSTEAD OF` triggers to manage inserts, updates, and deletes. At least, you build the `INSTEAD OF` trigger when you want to allow DML operations.

Pipelined functions are designed to let you use collections of scalar variables or record structures. The previously demonstrated pipelined functions convert the PL/SQL collection into an aggregate table. You cannot reuse the pipelined table in another PL/SQL scope, but you can use it in SQL scope queries.

Prior to Oracle Database 12*c*, a pipelined table function was your only alternative to access a PL/SQL collection in a SQL statement. Now you can access a local PL/SQL associative array in a SQL statement. There's no sense in repeating the full example from Chapter 2, but the following unnamed block shows you how to use a PL/SQL associative array in a query:

```
SQL> DECLARE
    lv_list   TYPE_DEFS.PLSQL_TABLE;
  BEGIN
    list := implicit_convert;
    FOR i IN (SELECT   column_value
              FROM     TABLE(lv_list)) LOOP
      dbms_output.put_line(i.column_value);
    END LOOP;
  END;
  /
```

Pipelined Results Are Limited to SQL Scope

There is a temptation to pass the return value from a pipelined function to another PL/SQL module because it isn't clear that these aggregate tables are designed only for use in SQL statements. You receive a `PLS-00653` error when you try to pass a pipelined function result to another PL/SQL program as an actual parameter. A `PLS-00653` error states that "aggregate/table functions are not allowed in PL/SQL scope." Pipelined table results are only accessible in SQL scope.

The following procedure passes compilation checks because it refers to a valid PL/SQL collection type:

```
SQL> CREATE OR REPLACE PROCEDURE read_pipe
     ( pipe_in pipelined.account_collection ) IS
     BEGIN
       FOR i IN 1..pipe_in.LAST LOOP
         dbms_output.put(pipe_in(i).account);
         dbms_output.put(pipe_in(i).full_name);
       END LOOP;
     END read_pipe;
     /
```

This seems a logical segue to control the reading of a pipelined table. The following demonstrates how you would call the procedure by passing the result set of a call to the pipelined `pf` function:

```
EXECUTE read_pipe(pf);
```

This raises the following error message:

```
BEGIN read_pipe(pf); END;
      *
ERROR at line 1:
ORA-06550: line 1, column 10:
PLS-00653: aggregate/table functions are not allowed in PL/SQL scope
```

The error occurs because the actual data type passed to the procedure is a pipelined aggregate or table with equivalent values but not a PL/SQL collection data type. Fortunately, the error message gives you great feedback when you know that a pipelined aggregate table *isn't* a PL/SQL collection type.

Line 6 refers to the local `lv_list` associative array, which is based on an associative array type defined in the `type_defs` package example. Oracle Database 12*c* knows how to translate the associative array in the context switch between PL/SQL and SQL because `lv_list` is declared in the local block where you call the `SELECT` statement.

You now know how to use pipelined functions and understand their strengths and weaknesses. They're great tools when you want to get data into a query or view that requires procedural logic.

Object Table Functions

Although no clause exists for object table functions, it seems best to discuss them here because they are the new alternative to pipelined table functions. They let you convert SQL collections to a SQL result set. This eliminates the need for using PL/SQL associative arrays in all but a few rare cases. One of those would be when you want a sparsely populated string-based index.

As a rule, SQL table collections perform as well as associative arrays. They also are more flexible to work with when you call them from external languages, like Java.

Creating an object table function is a three-step process: you define the record structure as an object type, then define the collection, and finally define a function to show how to return the collection from a PL/SQL context to a SQL context.

Ultimately, you can simply query the models inside a SQL statement. This makes lists and arrays of SQL object types reusable in the context of external programming languages such as C#, C++, Java, and Hypertext Preprocessor (PHP).

You create the base SQL user-defined type (UDT) like this:

```
SQL> CREATE OR REPLACE TYPE title_structure IS OBJECT
( title varchar2(60)
, subtitle varchar2(60));
/
```

You can create the collection by using a varray or table collection. A table collection is always the more flexible option because it doesn't have a predefined number of elements. You create a SQL table collection of the object type like this:

```
SQL> CREATE OR REPLACE
  TYPE title_table IS TABLE OF title_structure;
/
```

The following function is a rather trivial example but is effective because of its readability and small size (it has one less input parameter than the earlier anonymous block). Naturally, when you write real logic, it will be a bit more complex, because this could easily be solved as an ordinary query:

```
SQL> CREATE OR REPLACE FUNCTION get_full_titles
( pv_title  VARCHAR2 ) RETURN TITLE_TABLE IS

  -- Declare a variable that uses the record structure.
  lv_counter          PLS_INTEGER := 1;

  -- Declare a variable that uses the record structure.
  lv_title_table      TITLE_TABLE := title_table();

  -- Declare dynamic cursor structure.
  CURSOR c ( cv_search VARCHAR2 ) IS
    SELECT   item_title, item_subtitle
    FROM     item
    WHERE    REGEXP_LIKE( item_title
                        , '^.*'||cv_search||'.*','i')
    AND      item_type =
              (SELECT common_lookup_id
               FROM   common_lookup
```

```
19                WHERE  common_lookup_type =
20                         'DVD_WIDE_SCREEN')
21      ORDER BY release_date;
22
23  BEGIN
24    -- Open the cursor and map results to collection.
25    FOR i IN c (pv_title) LOOP
26      lv_title_table.EXTEND;           -- Extends memory.
27
28      /* The assignment pattern for a SQL Collection is
29         incompatible with the cursor return type, and you
30         must construct an instance of the object type
31         before assigning it to collection. */
32      lv_title_table(lv_counter) :=
33        title_structure(i.item_title,i.item_subtitle);
34      lv_counter := lv_counter + 1;    -- Increment counter.
35    END LOOP;
36    RETURN lv_title_table;
37  END;
38  /
```

Line 8 declares the collection variable by instantiating it as a null value collection. Inside the FOR loop, line 26 extends memory space for a new element in the collection. Lines 32 and 33 assign an instance of the title structure to an indexed element of the collection. It is critical that you note that the assignment requires that you explicitly construct an instance of the structure by passing actual parameters of equal type.

You can then query the result as follows:

```
SQL> SELECT  title
  2  FROM    TABLE(get_full_titles('Harry'));
```

The column name is no longer that of the table but is that of the element in the SQL record structure. This differs from the column_value pseudocolumn returned by an Attribute Data Type (ADT) collection, as qualified in Chapter 6. It doesn't appear that they put the Harry Potter movies into moratorium after all. The results from the query are

```
TITLE
--------------------------------------------
Harry Potter and the Sorcerer's Stone
Harry Potter and the Chamber of Secrets
   ...
```

Composite variables are tremendously valuable assets in the PL/SQL and SQL programming environment. They let you define complex logic in named blocks that you can then simply query in C#, Java, or PHP programs. You should take advantage of composite variables where possible.

RESULT_CACHE Clause

The RESULT_CACHE clause was new in Oracle Database 11*g*. Oracle Database 12*c* extends the behaviors of result cache functions to work with invoker rights programs. A result cache function stores the function name, the call parameters, the results, and the CURRENT_USER value in the SGA. Oracle Database 12*c* adds the CURRENT_USER value to the stored results. This is how Oracle Database 12*c* maintains different result sets for different callers of the same function.

The `RESULT_CACHE` clause instructs the PL/SQL engine to check the result cache for function calls with matching actual parameters. A matching function call also stores the result, and the cache returns the result and skips rerunning the function. This means the function only runs when new parameters are sent to it.

NOTE
Cross-session functions only work with `IN` mode formal parameters.

The prototype for the `RESULT_CACHE` clause has an optional `RELIES_ON` clause. The `RELIES_ON` clause is critical because it ensures any change to the underlying table invalidates the result cache. This also means any DML transactions that would change result sets. The `RELIES_ON` clause ensures that the cache is dynamic, representing the current result set. You can list any number of dependent tables in the `RELIES_ON` clause, and they're listed as comma-delimited names.

The next example depends on the downloadable code from the publisher's website. You can find a description of the code in the Introduction. Also, this example builds upon the discussion of table collections in Chapter 6.

This statement lets you build a collection of `VARCHAR2` values:

```
SQL> CREATE OR REPLACE
       TYPE strings AS TABLE OF VARCHAR2(60);
     /
```

This function implements a cross-session result cache with the `RELIES_ON` clause:

```
SQL> CREATE OR REPLACE FUNCTION get_title
     ( pv_partial_title VARCHAR2 ) RETURN STRINGS
     RESULT_CACHE RELIES_ON(item) IS
       /* Declare control and collection variable. */
       counter      NUMBER  := 1;
       return_value STRINGS := strings();

       -- Define a parameterized cursor.
       CURSOR get_title
       ( cv_partial_title VARCHAR2 ) IS
       SELECT   item_title
       FROM     item
       WHERE    UPPER(item_title) LIKE '%'||UPPER(cv_partial_title)||'%';
     BEGIN
       -- Read the data and write it to the collection in a cursor FOR loop.
       FOR i IN get_title(pv_partial_title) LOOP
         return_value.EXTEND;
         return_value(counter) := i.item_title;
         counter := counter + 1;
       END LOOP;
       RETURN return_value;
     END get_title;
     /
```

Line 3 qualifies the `get_title` function as a result cache function. The cached results don't change between calls when the function is deterministic. They do change when the function is nondeterministic. All functions that rely on data in the tables are nondeterministic. You use the `RELIES_ON` clause when working with nondeterministic functions.

Cached values are discarded when there's a change to any table in the `RELIES_ON` list. Oracle discards cached results when there's an `INSERT`, `UPDATE`, or `DELETE` statement against the `item` table in this case.

While it's possible that some table changes may not merit discarding cached results, you should routinely list all tables that are referenced in the result cache function. The `RELIES_ON` clause ensures the integrity of the result set against changes in the source data only when you include all tables in the clause.

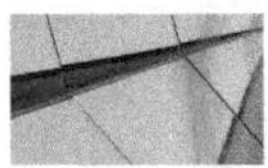

NOTE
The `RELIES_ON` clause can accept one actual parameter or a list of actual parameters.

You can test the `get_title` function with the following anonymous block program:

```
SQL> DECLARE
       lv_list STRINGS;
     BEGIN
       lv_list := get_title('Harry');
       FOR i IN 1..lv_list.LAST LOOP
         dbms_output.put_line('list('||i||') : ['||lv_list(i)||']');
       END LOOP;
     END;
     /
```

Like the earlier examples with a pipelined table function, you can test the `get_title` function inside a query:

```
SQL> SELECT   column_value
     FROM TABLE(get_title('Harry'));
```

After calling the result cache function, you insert, delete or update dependent data. Then, you'll find new result sets are displayed. This change ensures that stale data never misleads the user. The `RELIES_ON` clause ensures the integrity of the result set, but it does cost you some processing overhead.

TIP
You should consider excluding the `RELIES_ON` clause to improve transactional efficiency in data warehouse implementations.

The preceding sections have covered the available options for defining functions. These skills are assumed when discussing pass-by-value functions.

Pass-by-Value Functions

A *pass-by-value* function receives values when they're called. They return a single thing upon completion. The tricky parts with this type of function are the data types of the inputs and outputs. Inputs are formal parameters and have only one mode in pass-by-value programs, and that's an `IN`-only mode. An `IN`-only mode means that you send a copy of either a variable value or a literal value into the function as a raw input. These copies are actual parameters or call parameters. All raw materials (call parameters) are consumed during the production of the finished goods—or the return value of this type of function. The return type value of the function must be assigned to a variable in a PL/SQL block, but it can also be returned as an expression in a SQL query.

Functions return a single output variable. Output variables can be scalar values or composite data types. This means that a single variable can contain many things when it is a composite data type.

As discussed, you can define pass-by-value functions as deterministic or parallel enable when the functions don't alter package variables or database values. You can also define functions to return pipelined tables that mimic SQL or PL/SQL collections. The results of pipelined functions require that you use them in SQL scope. All functions except those created with pipelined results support result caches.

Whether functions interact with the file system or database does not impact how they act inside your PL/SQL code block. You can use a function to assign a result to a variable, or return a variable as an expression. Figure 8-1, earlier in the chapter, illustrates using a function as a right operand in an assignment operation.

A sample `hello_whom` function, a variation on the classic `hello_world` function, demonstrates a pass-by-value function:

```
SQL> CREATE OR REPLACE FUNCTION hello_whom
( pv_name IN VARCHAR2 ) RETURN VARCHAR2 IS
  /* Default name value. */
  lv_name  VARCHAR2(10) := 'World';
BEGIN
  /* Check input name and substitute a valid value. */
  IF pv_name IS NOT NULL THEN
    lv_name := pv_name;
  END IF;
  /* Return the phrase. */
  RETURN 'Hello '||lv_name||'!';
END;
/
```

When you call the `hello_whom` function from a query, like this:

```
SQL> SELECT   hello_whom('Henry') AS "Salutation"
FROM     dual;
```

it prints

```
Salutation
-------------
Hello Henry!
```

Line 2 explicitly qualifies the `IN` mode of operation for the pass-by-value parameter. The default for parameters when none is provided is the `IN` mode. So, omitting from the function's signature doesn't change a pass-by-value parameter's mode of operation.

The following line 2 is functionally equivalent to the previous one:

```
  2  ( pv_name  VARCHAR2 ) RETURN VARCHAR2 IS
```

As a rule, providing the mode of operation adds clarity to your function. However, most programmers leave it out.

Inexperienced programmers sometimes reverse the logic of the `IF` block and check for a null parameter and then try assigning the local variable to the parameter:

```
  7     IF pv_name IS NULL THEN
  8       pv_name := lv_name;
```

It raises the following message:

```
Errors for FUNCTION HELLO_WHOM:
LINE/COL ERROR
---- -----------------------------------------------------------------


8/5  PL/SQL: Statement ignored
8/5  PLS-00363: expression 'PV_NAME' cannot be used as an assignment
     target
```

You can use a function that returns a variable as an expression when you put it inside a call to another PL/SQL built-in function, like this:

```
SQL> EXECUTE dbms_output.put_line(TO_CHAR(pv(10000,5,6),'9,999.90'));
```

The most embedded pass-by-value function runs first in the preceding line. That means the call to the pv function returns a value as a call parameter to the `TO_CHAR` SQL built-in function. The `TO_CHAR` function formats the first call parameter's value with the format mask provided as the second call parameter. It outputs the following when `SERVEROUTPUT` is enabled:

```
7,472.58
```

The preceding example uses the pv function demonstrated earlier in this chapter's "DETERMINISTIC Clause" section. It also uses the `TO_CHAR` built-in function, which you can read more about in Appendix D on SQL built-in functions.

As mentioned, Oracle Database 12*c* introduces white listing as a new feature. You can white list the earlier `hello_whom` function like this:

```
SQL> CREATE OR REPLACE FUNCTION hello_whom
  2  ( pv_name IN VARCHAR2 ) RETURN VARCHAR2
  3  ACCESSIBLE BY
  4  ( FUNCTION  video.gateway
  5  , PROCEDURE video.backdoor
  6  , PACKAGE   video.api
  7  , TYPE      video.hobbit ) IS
  8    /* Default name value. */
```

```
 9    lv_name  VARCHAR2(10) := 'World';
10  BEGIN
11    /* Check input name and substitute a valid value. */
12    IF pv_name IS NOT NULL THEN
13      lv_name := pv_name;
14    END IF;
15    /* Return the phrase. */
16    RETURN 'Hello '||lv_name||'!';
17  END;
18  /
```

Lines 3 through 7 specify the authorized list of callers, which is known as a white list. White lists authorize a list of functions, procedures, packages, and object types to perform some activity. They're the opposite of black lists, which disallow access to a list of functions, procedures, packages, and object types. After you white list the `hello_whom` function, you can attempt to call it from a query, like this:

```
SQL> SELECT   hello_whom('Henry') AS "Salutation"
  2  FROM     dual;
```

It raises the following exception:

```
SELECT   hello_whom('Henry') AS "Salutation"
         *
ERROR at line 1:
ORA-06552: PL/SQL: Statement ignored
ORA-06553: PLS-904: insufficient privilege to access object HELLO_WHOM
```

At present, there doesn't appear to be any way in Oracle Database 12*c* to grant privileges to queries from a schema. That means you'd need to wrap a call to the `hello_world` function in one of the authorized modules, like this `gateway` function:

```
SQL> CREATE OR REPLACE FUNCTION gateway
  2  ( pv_name IN VARCHAR2 ) RETURN VARCHAR2 IS
  3  BEGIN
  4    /* Return the phrase. */
  5    RETURN hello_whom(pv_name);
  6  END;
  7  /
```

When you call the authorized `gateway` function from a query, like this:

```
SQL> SELECT   gateway('Samuel') AS "Salutation"
  2  FROM     dual;
```

it calls the white-listed `hello_whom` function on line 5 and returns the following result:

```
Salutation
-------------
Hello Samuel!
```

PL/SQL pass-by-value functions are defined by the following six rules:

- All formal parameters must be defined as *write-only* variables by using the `IN` mode.
- All formal parameters are locally scoped variables that *cannot* be changed during execution inside the function.
- Any formal parameter can use any valid SQL or PL/SQL data type. Only functions with parameter lists that use SQL data types work in SQL statements.
- Any formal parameter may have a default initial value.
- The formal return variable can use any valid SQL or PL/SQL data type, but pipelined return tables must be used in SQL statements. You can't access pipelined table results in another PL/SQL scope.
- Any system reference cursor cast from a SQL query into a function is not writeable and therefore must be passed through an `IN` mode parameter.

System Reference Cursor Functions

All cursor result sets are static structures stored in the Oracle SGA. Cursor variables are actually references or handles. The handle points to an internally cached result set from a query. You populate cursor variables by fetching records, typically by using

```
OPEN cursor_name FOR select_statement;
```

You access cursors by using a reference or handle that lets you scroll their content. Once you declare an implicit or explicit cursor structure, you can then assign its reference to a SQL cursor data type. You can also return these cursor variables as function return types or as `IN OUT` or `OUT` reference variables in function and procedure signatures. The result sets are *read-only* structures.

The following shows how to return a cursor using a function:

```
SQL> CREATE OR REPLACE FUNCTION get_full_titles
RETURN SYS_REFCURSOR IS
  lv_title_cursor SYS_REFCURSOR;
BEGIN
  OPEN lv_title_cursor FOR
    SELECT  item_title, item_subtitle
    FROM    item;
  RETURN lv_title_cursor;
END;
/
```

The function uses the predefined `SYS_REFCURSOR`, which is a weakly typed system reference cursor. A weakly typed reference cursor can assume any record structure at runtime, whereas a strongly typed reference cursor is anchored to a database catalog object.

The `OPEN` clause creates a reference in the SGA for the cursor. You can then pass the reference to another PL/SQL block as a cursor variable, as shown in the following anonymous block:

```
SQL> DECLARE
  /* Declare a record and collection type. */
  TYPE full_title_record IS RECORD
  ( item_title    item.item_title%TYPE
```

```
    , item_subtitle item.item_subtitle%TYPE);
    lv_full_title_table FULL_TITLE_RECORD;

    /* Declare a system reference cursor variable. */
    lv_title_cursor SYS_REFCURSOR;
  BEGIN
    /* Assign the reference cursor function result. */
    lv_title_cursor := get_full_titles;

    /* Print one element at a time. */
    LOOP
      FETCH lv_title_cursor INTO lv_full_title_table;
      EXIT WHEN titles%NOTFOUND;
      dbms_output.put_line('Title ['||lv_full_title_table.item_title||']');
    END LOOP;
  END;
  /
```

NOTE

There is never an OPEN statement before the loop when a cursor is passed into a subroutine because the cursor is already open. Cursor variables are actually references that point into a specialized cursor work area in the SGA.

The receiving or processing block needs to know what record type is stored in the cursor. Some programmers use this requirement to argue that you should use only strongly typed reference cursors. In PL/SQL-only solutions, they have a point. The other side of the argument can be made for weakly typed reference cursors when you query them through external programs using the OCI libraries. In these external languages, you can dynamically discover the structure of reference cursors and manage them discretely through generic algorithms.

Deterministic Pass-by-Value Functions

Let's examine a deterministic pass-by-value function, calculating the *future value* of a bank deposit. The following builds the `fv` function:

```
SQL> CREATE OR REPLACE FUNCTION fv
  ( current_value   NUMBER := 0
  , periods         NUMBER := 1
  , interest        NUMBER)
  RETURN NUMBER DETERMINISTIC IS
  BEGIN
    /* Compounded Daily Interest. */
    RETURN current_value*(1+((1+((interest/100)/365))**365-1)*periods);
  END fv;
  /
```

The function defines three formal parameters. Two are optional parameters because they have default values. The default values are the current balance of the account and the 365 days of the year (for non-leap years). The third parameter is mandatory because no value is provided. As discussed, the `IN` mode is the default, and you do not have to specify it when defining functions.

As a general practice, mandatory parameters come before optional parameters. This is critical when actual parameters are submitted in positional order. Oracle Database 11*g* supports positional order, named notation order, and mixed notation.

After defining an output variable, you use the `CALL` statement to run the function using named notation:

```
SQL> VARIABLE future_value NUMBER
SQL> CALL fv(current_value => 10000, periods => 5, interest => 4)
     INTO :future_value
     /
```

You can then use the following to select the future value of $10,000 after five years at 4 percent annual interest compounded daily:

```
SQL> SELECT :future_value FROM dual;
```

Alternatively, you can format with SQL*Plus and call the function in SQL with this statement:

```
SQL> COLUMN future_value FORMAT 99,999.90
SQL> SELECT fv(current_value => 10000, periods => 5, interest => 4) FROM dual;
```

Both the `CALL` statement and SQL query return a result of $12,040.42. The compounding of interest yields $40.42 more than an annual rate. There might be an extra penny or two, depending on where leap year falls in the five years, but the function doesn't manage that nuance in the calculation.

As covered in Chapter 2, Oracle Database 12*c* lets you embed functions inside the `WITH` clause of a `SELECT` statement. You need to suppress the SQL terminator value, a semicolon (`;`) by default, before you embed a function inside the `WITH` clause of a `SELECT` statement. The SQL terminator restriction on embedding functions means you must run the `SELECT` statement from a customized SQL*Plus environment. The better alternative is to create a view in the specialized SQL*Plus session, which other programs can then use without specialized rules.

The following deterministic `glue` function and `person` view were introduced in Chapter 2. Together, they show you how to embed a deterministic function in the `WITH` clause of a `SELECT` statement.

```
SQL> WITH
       FUNCTION glue
       ( pv_first_name VARCHAR2
       , pv_last_name  VARCHAR2) RETURN VARCHAR2 IS
         lv_full_name  VARCHAR2(100);
       BEGIN
         lv_full_name := pv_first_name || ' ' || pv_last_name;
         RETURN lv_full_name;
       END;
       SELECT   glue(a.first_name,a.last_name) AS person
       FROM     actor a
     /
```

Pass-by-Value Functions That Wrap Java Libraries

It's possible to write the programming logic for your stored functions and procedures in Java libraries. Then, you write a PL/SQL wrapper that accesses the library.

The following `TwoSignersJava` library checks whether there are two authorized signers on a group account. You would use it to return a 0 (or false flag) when it's fine to add a second authorized signer, or return a 1 (or true flag) when there are already two authorized signers. You can create this library from the SQL*Plus command line:

```
SQL> CREATE OR REPLACE AND COMPILE JAVA SOURCE NAMED "TwoSignersJava" AS

       // Required class libraries.
       import java.sql.*;
       import oracle.jdbc.driver.*;

       // Define class.
       public class TwoSignersJava {

         // Connect and verify new insert would be a duplicate.
         public static int contactTrigger(Integer memberID)
           throws SQLException {
           Boolean duplicateFound = false;  // Control default value.

           // Create a Java 5 and Oracle 11g connection forward.
           Connection conn =
             DriverManager.getConnection("jdbc:default:connection:");

           // Create a prepared statement that accepts binding a number.
           PreparedStatement ps =
              conn.prepareStatement("SELECT   null " +
                                    "FROM     contact c JOIN member m " +
                                    "ON       c.member_id = m.member_id " +
                                    "WHERE    c.member_id = ? " +
                                    "HAVING   COUNT(*) > 1");

           // Bind the local variable to the statement placeholder.
           ps.setInt(1, memberID);

           // Execute query and check if there is a second value.
           ResultSet rs = ps.executeQuery();
           if (rs.next())
             duplicateFound = true;         // Control override value.

           // Clean up resources.
           rs.close();
           ps.close();
           conn.close();

           /* Return 1 (true) when two signers and 0 when they don't. */
           if (duplicateFound) return 1;
           else                return 0; }}
     /
```

Lines 16 and 17 would be on a single line normally but they're split across two lines here to accommodate the formatting of the book's text. The internal connection syntax on line 17 works for Java 5 forward, and you would replace it with the following for an Oracle Database 10*g* database (technically no longer supported with the production release of Oracle Database 12*c*). When you migrate Java libraries from an Oracle Database 10*g* database forward to an Oracle Database 11*g* or 12*c* database, you need to change internal Oracle connection syntax.

```
15        // Create an Oracle 10g JDBC connection.
16        Connection conn = new OracleDriver().defaultConnection();
```

The PL/SQL wrapper for this library is

```
SQL> CREATE OR REPLACE FUNCTION two_signers
  2  ( pv_member_id  NUMBER) RETURN NUMBER IS
  3  LANGUAGE JAVA
  4  NAME 'TwoSingersJava.contactTrigger(java.lang.Integer) return int';
  5  /
```

Line 3 designates that you have implemented the function body in Java for the `two_signers` function. Line 4 maps the Java data types to the native Oracle types.

The following shows you how to test all the moving parts:

```
SQL> SELECT  CASE
               WHEN two_signers(member_id) = 0 THEN 'Only one signer.'
               ELSE 'Already two signers.'
             END AS "Available for Assignment"
     FROM    contact c JOIN member m USING (member_id)
     WHERE   c.last_name = 'Sweeney'
     OFFSET 1 ROWS FETCH FIRST 1 ROWS ONLY;
```

Although, you'd probably call the `two_signers` function from a `WHERE` clause. For example, you'd do so if you wanted your production code to insert data from the `contact` and `member` tables, with a `WHERE` clause checking for a zero value from the `two_signers` function.

The function on lines 2 through 9 simply concatenates two strings with a single-character white space between them. Assuming that you disable the `SQLTERMINATOR` in SQL*Plus, the semicolons are treated as ordinary characters in the query. You should also note that the SQL statement is run by the SQL*Plus forward slash and that the complete statement doesn't have a terminating semicolon on line 11.

Unfortunately, you can't suppress the `SQLTERMINATOR` value when you make calls from other programming languages. The means you need to wrap any query with an embedded function in a WITH clause as a view.

Assuming you create an `actor_v` view by using the preceding query, you could query the result like this:

```
SQL> COLUMN person FORMAT A18
SQL> SELECT   a.person
     FROM     actor_v;
```

And retrieve results, like

```
PERSON
------------------
Nicolas Cage
Diane Kruger
```

Embedding deterministic functions in a view seems a logical thing to do when your business case requires a deterministic function inside a query. After all, views do abstract or hide logic from application programmers.

Nondeterministic Pass-by-Value Functions

The key difference between nondeterministic and deterministic functions is simple: the former relies on inputs and data, while the latter relies only on inputs. That means you may get different results with the same inputs from a nondeterministic function. Naturally, that can't happen in a deterministic function.

In Oracle Database 12*c*, you can now write a *nondeterministic function* by including a cursor that searches for a partial string in a first or last name. The `full_name` function delivers that functionality:

```
SQL> CREATE OR REPLACE FUNCTION full_name
     ( pv_search_name  VARCHAR2) RETURN VARCHAR2 IS
       /* Declare local return variable. */
       lv_retval  VARCHAR2(50);
       /* Declare a dynamic cursor. */
       CURSOR get_names
       ( cv_search_name  VARCHAR2) IS
         SELECT   c.first_name, c.middle_name, c.last_name
         FROM     contact c
         WHERE    REGEXP_LIKE(c.first_name, cv_search_name,'i')
         OR       REGEXP_LIKE(c.last_name, cv_search_name,'i')
         OFFSET 1 ROWS FETCH FIRST 1 ROWS ONLY; -- New Oracle 12c feature.
     BEGIN
       /* Check for a middle name. */
       FOR i IN get_names('^.*'||pv_search_name||'.*$') LOOP
         IF i.middle_name IS NOT NULL THEN
           lv_retval := i.first_name||' '||i.middle_name||' '||i.last_name;
         ELSE
           lv_retval := i.first_name||' '||i.last_name;
         END IF;
       END LOOP;
     END;
     /
```

The call parameter determines the results from a table of data. The function returns only one row because of the use of an Oracle Database 12*c* new *top-n query* restriction. Line 12 guarantees that the function only returns a single row where the first and last names match the search criteria. The result changes when you change the input, but the result of a nondeterministic program also returns when the underlying data changes in the tables.

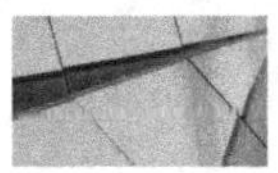

TIP
The any character before (`'^.*'`) and after (`'.*$'`) regular expressions is used in two places within the dynamic cursor but only provided once with the call parameter to the cursor.

The key piece of knowledge about nondeterministic functions is that they depend on two dynamic inputs. One is the call parameters and the other is the data stored in the database.

- Call parameters can't change during execution of the function, which means formal parameters can't be assignment targets inside the function. You raise a `PLS-00363` error that tells you the expression (formal parameter) can't be used as an assignment target.
- Nondeterministic functions may return different results when called with the same parameters because another user can change the data stored in the database between the two calls.

DML-Enabled Pass-by-Value Functions

Functions also let you process DML statements inside them. Some people think that functions shouldn't be used to perform DML statements simply because, historically, procedures were used. The only downside of embedding a DML statement inside a function is that you can't call that function inside a query. At least, you can't call it when it's in the same operational context unless it's an autonomous function. An attempt at calling an inline (or default) function raises an `ORA-14551` error. The error message says that you can't have a DML operation inside a query.

Recall from the discussion of the function and procedure architecture that pessimistic functions return an affirmative result when they succeed and a negative result when they fail. Inside an exclusively PL/SQL scope, you can write a pessimistic function with a Boolean return type. A pessimistic function also must include Transaction Control Language (TCL) statements when it runs in an autonomous context. Let's create a small `avatar` table to look at how a pessimistic function works:

```
SQL> CREATE TABLE avatar
  ( avatar_id    NUMBER GENERATED AS IDENTITY
  , avatar_name  VARCHAR2(30));
```

The following demonstrates a pessimistic function that inserts a row into the `avatar` table when successful:

```
SQL> CREATE OR REPLACE FUNCTION add_avatar
  ( pv_avatar_name   VARCHAR2 ) RETURN BOOLEAN IS
    /* Set function to perform in its own transaction scope. */
    PRAGMA AUTONOMOUS_TRANSACTION;
    /* Set default return value. */
```

```
  6     lv_retval  BOOLEAN := FALSE;
  7   BEGIN
  8     /* Insert row into avatar. */
  9     INSERT INTO avatar (avatar_name)
 10     VALUES (pv_avatar_name);
 11     /* Save change inside its own transaction scope. */
 12     COMMIT;
 13     /* Reset return value to true for complete. */
 14     lv_retval := TRUE;
 15     RETURN lv_retval;
 16   END;
 17   /
```

Line 2 defines a Boolean return type. Line 4 declares a compiler directive that makes the function an autonomous program unit. Line 12 commits the work that occurs only within the function. Line 15 returns a local Boolean variable.

You can test the pessimistic function with the following anonymous block program:

```
SQL> DECLARE
  2     /* Declare local variable. */
  3     lv_avatar  VARCHAR2(30);
  4     /* Declare a local cursor. */
  5     CURSOR capture_result
  6     (cv_avatar_name  VARCHAR2) IS
  7       SELECT   avatar_name
  8       FROM     avatar
  9       WHERE    avatar_name = cv_avatar_name;
 10   BEGIN
 11     IF add_avatar('Earthbender') THEN
 12       dbms_output.put_line('Record Inserted');
 13       ROLLBACK;
 14     ELSE
 15       dbms_output.put_line('No Record Inserted');
 16     END IF;
 17     OPEN capture_result('Earthbender');
 18     FETCH capture_result INTO lv_avatar;
 19     CLOSE capture_result;
 20     dbms_output.put_line('Value ['||lv_avatar||'].');
 21   END;
 22   /
```

Line 11 calls the pessimistic `add_avatar` function and returns true. That means the `add_avatar` autonomous function inserted a row in a discrete transaction scope. The `ROLLBACK` statement on line 13 can't roll back the transaction because it was committed in another transaction scope.

The test program prints the following on line 20, which shows the written row:

```
Value [Earthbender].
```

You can modify the return type of the function with the following changes:

```
SQL> CREATE OR REPLACE FUNCTION add_avatar
  2  ( pv_avatar_name  VARCHAR2 ) RETURN NUMBER IS
       ...
  6    lv_retval  NUMBER := 0;
  7  BEGIN
       ...
 13    /* Reset return value to true for complete. */
 14    lv_retval := 1;
 15    RETURN lv_retval;
 16  END;
 17  /
```

Line 2 changes the return type of the function to a `NUMBER`. Line 6 sets the initial value of the local return variable to 0, which typically indicates a false value. Line 14 resets it to 1, which serves as our true value.

You can now call the altered pessimistic function from a SQL `SELECT` statement, like this:

```
SQL> SELECT   CASE
  2             WHEN add_avatar('Firebender') = 1 THEN 'Success' ELSE 'Failure'
  3           END AS Autonomous
  4  FROM     dual;
```

Line 2 returns the `Success` string after inserting the `Firebender` value. This is a very powerful feature of autonomous functions, and becomes more powerful when you enclose a query like this in a view.

Recursive Functions

Using recursive functions is a useful tool for solving some complex problems, such as advanced parsing. A recursive function calls one or more copies of itself to resolve a problem by converging on a result. Recursive functions look backward in time, whereas nonrecursive functions look forward in time. Recursive functions are a specialized form of pass-by-value functions.

Nonrecursive programs take some parameters and begin processing, often in a loop, until they achieve a result. This means they start with something and work with it until they find a result by applying a set of rules or evaluations. This means nonrecursive programs solve problems moving forward in time.

Recursive functions have a base case and a recursive case. The base case is the anticipated result. The recursive case applies a formula that includes one or more calls back to the same function. One recursive call is known as a *linear* or *straight-line* recursion. Recursive cases that make two or more recursive calls are *nonlinear*. Linear recursion is much faster than nonlinear recursion, and the more recursive calls, the higher the processing costs. Recursive functions use the recursive case only when the base case isn't met. A result is found when a recursive function call returns the base case value. This means recursive program units solve problems moving backward in time, or one recursion after another.

Solving factorial results is a classic problem for linear recursion. The following function returns the factorial value for any number:

```
SQL> CREATE OR REPLACE FUNCTION factorial
( n BINARY_DOUBLE ) RETURN BINARY_DOUBLE IS
BEGIN
  IF n <= 1 THEN
    RETURN 1;
  ELSE
    RETURN n * factorial(n - 1);
  END IF;
END factorial;
/
```

The base case is met when the `IF` statement resolves as true. The recursive case makes only a single call to the same function. Potentially, the recursive case can call many times until it also returns the base case value of 1. Then, it works its way back up the tree of recursive calls until an answer is found by the first call.

Fibonacci numbers are more complex to derive because they require two recursive calls for each level of recursion. A recursive program is nonlinear when it makes two or more calls that are separated by an operator. These are nonlinear for two reasons:

- Mathematical operators have a lower order of precedence than function calls. That means functions are always called first, before other operators perform their respective functions.
- Each recursive call may spawn zero or two recursive function calls. A linear recursion calls one copy at each level of the recursion, and a nonlinear recursion calls more than one copy at any level of recursion.

The following `Fibonacci` function maintains title case in the database thanks to the quoted identifier, which is a specialized delimiter (check Table 4-1 for delimiter details). After all, credit should be given to a great mathematician!

```
SQL> CREATE OR REPLACE FUNCTION "Fibonacci"
  2  ( n BINARY_DOUBLE ) RETURN BINARY_DOUBLE IS
  3  BEGIN
  4    /* Set the base case. */
  5    IF n < 2 THEN
  6      RETURN n;
  7    ELSE
  8      RETURN fibonacci(n - 2) + fibonacci(n - 1);
  9    END IF;
 10  END "Fibonacci";
 11  /
```

Lines 6 and 8 have `RETURN` statements. This really is suboptimal as a coding practice because there should only be one `RETURN` statement in any function. The alternative to this design would be to add a local variable to the function and then assign the results from the base or alternate case to that local variable.

The addition operator on line 8 has a lower order of precedence than a function call. Therefore, the recursive call on the left is processed first until it returns an expression. Then, the recursive call on the right is resolved to an expression. The addition happens after both recursive calls return expressions.

Calling a preserved case function requires a trick, as shown next. The following `FibonacciSequence` function calls the `Fibonacci` function eight times, which gives us the classic *Fibonacci* sequence (the same one left by Jacques Saunière when he's murdered in the Louvre by Silas in Dan Brown's *The Da Vinci Code*):

```
SQL> CREATE OR REPLACE FUNCTION "FibonacciSequence"
  2  RETURN VARCHAR2 IS
  3    /* Declare an output variable. */
  4    lv_output  VARCHAR2(40);
  5  BEGIN
  6    /* Loop through enough for the DaVinci Code myth. */
  7    FOR i IN 1..8 LOOP
  8      IF lv_output IS NOT NULL THEN
  9        lv_output := lv_output||', '||LTRIM(TO_CHAR("Fibonacci"(i),'999'));
 10      ELSE
 11        lv_output := LTRIM(TO_CHAR("Fibonacci"(i),'999'));
 12      END IF;
 13    END LOOP;
 14    RETURN lv_output;
 15  END;
 16  /
```

Lines 9 and 11 take the binary double and format it into a number without any leading white space. Note that the double quotes enclose only the function name and not the parameter list. That's the trick to calling case-preserved function names. Line 11 runs the first call to the `Fibonacci` program, and line 9 runs for all subsequent calls. Line 9 concatenates results to the original string.

You can query the case-preserved `FibonacciSequence` with this syntax:

```
SQL> SELECT   "FibonacciSequence"
     FROM     dual;
```

It produces the following output:

```
FibonacciSequence
-------------------------
1, 1, 2, 3, 5, 8, 13, 21
```

This discussion has demonstrated how you can implement recursion. You should note that recursion lends itself to pass-by-value functions because you only want the base case returned. While you can call recursive functions using pass-by-reference semantics, you shouldn't. Recursive parameters should not be altered during execution because that creates a mutating behavior in the recursive case.

You should explore recursion when you want to parse strings or are checking for syntax rules. It is much more effective than trying to move forward through the string.

This section has explained how to use pass-by-value functions. The next section builds on this information and explores pass-by-reference functions.

Pass-by-Reference Functions

Pass-by-reference functions can exhibit many of the behaviors we've worked through earlier in the chapter. As discussed, they can have `IN`, `IN OUT`, or `OUT` mode parameters. An `IN` mode parameter passes in a value that can change but is consumed wholly. An `IN OUT` mode parameter passes in a reference that can change and be returned in a new state. An `OUT` mode parameter passes in nothing but can return something.

You use pass-by-reference functions when you want to perform an operation, return a value from the function, and alter one or more actual parameters. These functions can only act inside the scope of another program or environment. The SQL*Plus environment lets you define session-level variables (also known as bind variables) that you can use when you call these types of functions. You cannot pass *literals* (like dates, numbers, or strings) into a parameter defined as `OUT` or `IN OUT` mode.

PL/SQL pass-by-reference functions are defined by the following six rules:

- At least one formal parameter must be defined as a *read-only or read-write* variable by using the `OUT` mode or `IN OUT` mode, respectively.
- All formal parameters are locally scoped variables that you can change during operations inside the function.
- Any formal parameter can use any valid SQL or PL/SQL data type. Only functions with parameter lists that use SQL data types work in SQL statements.
- Any `IN` mode formal parameters can have a default initial value.
- The formal return variable can use any valid SQL or PL/SQL data type, but pipelined return tables must be used in SQL statements. You can't access pipelined table results in another PL/SQL scope.
- Any system reference cursor cast from a SQL query into a function is not writeable and therefore must be passed through an `IN` mode parameter.

The following pass-by-reference `counter` function demonstrates returning an altered parameter variable value and a discrete return variable. The `IN OUT` mode `pv_number` variable submits a number that's incremented inside the `counter` function. The `counter` function's formal return type is a `VARCHAR2`, and it holds a message about the incoming and outgoing value of the `pv_number` parameter.

```
SQL> CREATE OR REPLACE FUNCTION counter
  ( pv_number         IN  OUT  INTEGER
  , pv_increment_by   IN       INTEGER  DEFAULT 1)
  RETURN VARCHAR2 IS
    /* Declare a return value. */
    lv_return  VARCHAR2(50) := 'Inbound [';
  BEGIN
    /* Add inbound value. */
    lv_return := lv_return || pv_number ||'] ';

    /* Replace a null value to ensure increment. */
    IF pv_number IS NOT NULL THEN
      pv_number := pv_number + pv_increment_by;
    ELSE
```

```
15        pv_number := 1;
16      END IF;
17
18      /* Add inbound value. */
19      lv_return := lv_return || 'Outbound [' || pv_number ||']';
20
21      /* Return increment_by module. */
22      RETURN lv_return;
23    END;
24    /
```

Line 2 defines the `IN OUT` mode `pv_number` parameter. Line 12 checks whether the `pv_number` isn't null. Line 13 increments the value of `pv_number` by one. Line 15 assigns a value of 1 to `pv_number` when the original number is null. Both lines 13 and 15 assign new values to the `pv_number` parameter. This is possible because a pass-by-reference parameter with either `IN OUT` mode or `OUT` mode is a valid assignment target. That differs from `IN` mode parameters, which can't be assignment targets in the function.

You can test the `counter` function with the following anonymous block:

```
SQL> DECLARE
  /* Declare an increment by value. */
  lv_counter        INTEGER := 0;
  lv_increment_by   INTEGER := 1;
BEGIN
  /* Loop through five times. */
  FOR i IN 1..5 LOOP
    dbms_output.put_line(
      'Counter ['||i||'] {'||counter(lv_counter)||'}');
        END LOOP;
END;
/
```

The output from the anonymous block is

```
Counter [1] {Inbound [0] Outbound [1]}
Counter [2] {Inbound [1] Outbound [2]}
  ...
```

As you can see in the output, the `IN OUT` mode actual parameter is always incremented by one. A read-only (`OUT` mode) formal parameter can't work in this type of call because the new value is never read.

Changing the `IN OUT` mode to `OUT` mode for the `pv_number` parameter gives you a completely different function. With the following change to the parameter list of the `counter` function, every call now holds a null value:

```
  2  ( pv_number             OUT   INTEGER
```

The same anonymous block program yields these results:

```
Counter [1] {Inbound [] Outbound [1]}
Counter [2] {Inbound [] Outbound [1]}
  ...
```

This section has covered how you define and use a pass-by-reference function. You should recognize that there are two types of pass-by-reference parameters. One type has a value on entry and exit: `IN OUT` mode variables. The other always has a null value on entry and should have a value on exit: `OUT` mode parameters.

Review Section

This section has described the following points about the behaviors and characteristics of functions:

- The `DETERMINISITIC` clause designates that a program always returns the same results with the same parameters.
- The `PARALLEL_ENABLE` clause designates that a function supports parallel query capabilities; these are best implemented with both the `DETERMINISTIC` and `PARALLEL_ENABLE` clauses.
- The `PIPELINED` clause lets you create pipelined table functions, which translate PL/SQL associative array collections into SQL aggregate result sets.
- In lieu of the `PIPELINED` clause, you can convert or wrap associative arrays as SQL table collections.
- The `RESULT_CACHE` clause lets you cache result sets from deterministic and nondeterministic functions and, effective with Oracle Database 12*c*, lets you work with invoker rights functions.
- Pass-by-value functions take `IN`-only mode variables and don't let you use the parameters as assignment targets.
- A system reference cursor function returns a PL/SQL system reference cursor.
- The difference between deterministic and nondeterministic functions is that nondeterministic functions have runtime dependencies on internally referenced tables.
- You can embed DML statements inside autonomous pass-by-value functions, which requires that you provide Transaction Control Language (TCL) commands inside the functions. These types of functions are known as pessimistic functions.
- Oracle supports both linear and nonlinear recursive functions.
- Oracle supports `IN OUT` and `OUT` mode parameters in pass-by-reference variables.

Procedures

A *procedure* is essentially a function with a void return type. As such, you can't use it as a right operand because it doesn't have a return value. Procedures, like functions, are black boxes. Procedures provide a named subroutine that you call within the scope of a PL/SQL block. Although the behavior differs slightly whether you pass call parameters by *value* or *reference*, the inputs and outcomes are the only way to exchange values between the calling block and the procedure.

Procedures cannot be right operands or called from SQL statements. They do support using `IN`, `OUT`, and `IN OUT` mode formal parameters.

Like functions, procedures can also contain nested named blocks. Nested named blocks are local functions and procedures that you define in the declaration block. You can likewise nest anonymous blocks in the execution block or procedures.

The following illustrates a named block procedure prototype:

```
[{EDITIONALBE | NONEDITIONALBE}] PROCEDURE procedure_name
( parameter1       [IN][OUT] [NOCOPY] sql_datatype | plsql_datatype
, parameter2       [IN][OUT] [NOCOPY] sql_datatype | plsql_datatype
, parameter(n+1)   [IN][OUT] [NOCOPY] sql_datatype | plsql_datatype )
[ACCESSIBLE BY
( [{FUNCTION | PROCEDURE | PACKAGE | TYPE}] [schema.]unit_name)
[,[{FUNCTION | PROCEDURE | PACKAGE | TYPE}] [schema.]unit_name)]
[,... ]]])
[ AUTHID DEFINER | CURRENT_USER ] IS
  declaration_statements
BEGIN
  execution_statements
[EXCEPTION]
  exception_handling_statements
END [procedure_name];
/
```

You can define procedures with or without formal parameters. Formal parameters in procedures can be either pass-by-value or pass-by-reference variables in stored procedures. *Pass-by-reference* variables have both an IN mode and an OUT mode. Similar to functions, a procedure is created as a *pass-by-value* procedure when you don't specify the parameter mode, because it uses the default IN mode. Compiling (creating or replacing) the procedure implicitly assigns the IN mode phrase when none is provided. Like functions, formal parameters in procedures also support optional default values for IN mode parameters.

The ACCESSIBLE BY clause lets you white list callers of the procedure. You can white list functions, procedures, packages, or object types.

The AUTHID clause sets the execution authority model. The default is definer rights, which means anyone with execution privileges on the procedure acts as if they are the owner of that same schema. Defining the AUTHID as CURRENT_USER overrides the default and sets the execution authority to invoker rights. Invoker rights authority means that you call procedures to act on your local data, and it requires that you replicate data objects in any participating schema.

As in functions, the *declaration* block is between the IS and BEGIN phrases, while other blocks mirror the structure of anonymous block programs. Procedures require an execution environment, which means you must call them from SQL*Plus or another program unit. The calling program unit can be another PL/SQL block or an external program using the OCI or JDBC.

Procedures are used most frequently to perform DML statements and transaction management. You can define procedures to act in the current transaction scope or an independent transaction scope. As with functions, you use the PRAGMA AUTONOMOUS_TRANSACTION to set a procedure so that it runs as an independent transaction.

Pass-by-Value Procedures

A *pass-by-value* procedure receives values when they're called. They return nothing tangible to the calling scope block, but they can interact with the database. Pass-by-value procedures implement a *delegation model*. Procedures are often used to group and control a series of DML statements in the scope of a single transaction.

The mode of all formal parameters is IN-only for pass-by-value procedures. This means they receive a copy of an external variable or a numeric or string literal when you call the procedure. Call parameters can't be changed during the execution of a subroutine. You can transfer the contents from a call parameter to a local variable inside the procedure and then update that calling scope variable.

As discussed, you can define pass-by-value procedures to run autonomously in a separate transaction scope, or you can accept the default and have them run in the current transaction scope. Pass-by-value procedures frequently run in the current transaction scope. They organize database DML statements, such as INSERT statements to multiple tables.

PL/SQL pass-by-value procedures are defined by the following five rules:

- All formal parameters must be defined as *write-only* variable by using the IN mode.
- All formal parameters are locally scoped variables that *cannot* be changed during execution inside the procedure.
- Any formal parameter can use any valid SQL or PL/SQL data type.
- Any formal parameter may have a default initial value.
- Any system reference cursor cast from a SQL query into a function is not writeable and therefore must be passed through an IN mode parameter. This includes those passed as explicit cursor variables and those cast using the CURSOR function. As mentioned in the section "System Reference Cursor" earlier in the chapter, cursor variables are actually references or handles. The handles point to internally cached result sets, which are read-only structures.

Sometimes you'll want to build smaller reusable program units. For example, each INSERT statement could be put into its own stored procedure. You accomplish that by implementing pass-by-reference procedures. These new procedures expand the parameter lists by using both primary and foreign key parameters. The parameter list change makes the procedures capable of exchanging values between programs.

The adding_avatar procedure demonstrates a procedure that inserts values into two tables. The procedure uses two call parameters. The first value goes to the first table, and the second value goes to the second table. I've opted for a small table to demonstrate the concept without losing too much of the SQL syntax. This example relies on the avatar and episode tables. They're defined with Oracle Database 12c identity columns.

The first table is the avatar table:

```
SQL> CREATE TABLE avatar
  2  ( avatar_id     NUMBER GENERATED AS IDENTITY
  3                  CONSTRAINT avatar_pk PRIMARY KEY
  4  , avatar_name   VARCHAR2(30));
```

Line 2 creates the avatar_id column as an identity column with a primary key constraint. It's necessary to define a primary key constraint for the avatar_id column because the episode table refers to that column for its foreign key column.

The following defines the episode table:

```
SQL> CREATE TABLE episode
  2  ( episode_id     NUMBER GENERATED AS IDENTITY
  3                   CONSTRAINT episode_pk PRIMARY KEY
  4  , avatar_id      NUMBER CONSTRAINT episode_nn1 NOT NULL
  5  , episode_name   VARCHAR2(30)
  6  , CONSTRAINT episode_fk1 FOREIGN KEY(avatar_id)
  7    REFERENCES avatar(avatar_id));
```

Line 4 defines a NOT NULL constraint for the avatar_id column. Lines 6 and 7 define an out-of-line foreign key constraint for the same avatar_id column. Together these two constraints mean that it's impossible to insert a row into the episode table without providing a valid value from the list of possible values in the primary key avatar_id column of the avatar table.

The adding_contact procedure shows you how to use a pass-by-value procedure to manage multiple DML statements across a single transaction scope:

```
SQL> CREATE OR REPLACE PROCEDURE adding_avatar
  2  ( pv_avatar_name    VARCHAR2
  3  , pv_episode_name   VARCHAR2 ) IS
  4
  5    /* Declare local variable to manage IDENTITY column
  6       surrogate key. */
  7    lv_avatar_id  NUMBER;
  8  BEGIN
  9    /* Set a Savepoint. */
 10    SAVEPOINT all_or_none;
 11
 12    /* Insert row into avatar. */
 13    INSERT INTO avatar (avatar_name)
 14    VALUES (pv_avatar_name)
 15    RETURNING avatar_id INTO lv_avatar_id;
 16
 17    /* Insert row into avatar. */
 18    INSERT INTO episode (avatar_id, episode_name)
 19    VALUES (lv_avatar_id, pv_episode_name);
 20
 21    /* Save change inside its own transaction scope. */
 22    COMMIT;
 23  EXCEPTION
 24    WHEN OTHERS THEN
 25      ROLLBACK TO all_or_none;
 26  END;
 27  /
```

Lines 2 and 3 define the formal parameters for the adding_avatar procedure. Line 10 sets a SAVEPOINT, which is a beginning point for the transaction. Lines 13 through 15 insert a row into the avatar table. The RETURNING INTO clause returns the value from the identity column into a local variable. Line 19 uses the lv_avatar_id local variable as the foreign key value when it inserts into the episode table. After the INSERT statements to both the avatar and episode tables, the writes to both tables are committed on line 22. If there's an exception, line 25 rolls back any part of the transaction that may have occurred.

This anonymous block program tests the procedure:

```
SQL> BEGIN
       adding_avatar('Airbender','Episode 1');
     END;
     /
```

Unfortunately, the identity columns are not backward compatible with prior editions of the database. Oracle Database 11*g* supports sequence calls in `INSERT` statements with the `.nextval` and `.currval` pseudocolumns. The `.nextval` pseudocolumn supports pseudocolumns for primary key columns. The `.currval` pseudocolumn supports pseudocolumns for foreign key columns, and you must call the `.currval` pseudocolumn in the same session after you call the `.nextval` pseudocolumn.

Here are the equivalent lines in an Oracle Database 11*g* database:

```
    ...
    INSERT INTO avatar (avatar_id, avatar_name)
    VALUES (avatar_s.nextval, pv_avatar_name);
    ...
    INSERT INTO episode (episode_id, avatar_id, episode_name)
    VALUES (episode_s.nextval, avatar_s.currval, pv_episode_name);
    ...
```

Stepping back one release to Oracle Database 10*g*, you must query the `.nextval` result into a local variable before you try to use it in an `INSERT` statement. Here is the code for performing that task:

```
    /* Get the sequence into a local variable. */
    SELECT   avatar_s.nextval
    INTO     lv_avatar_id
    FROM     dual;
```

Pass-by-value procedures let you perform tasks in the database or external resources. When you designate a pass-by-value procedure as an autonomous program unit with a compile directive, the procedure becomes optimistic and a no-wait module. Pass-by-value procedures also let you manage primary and foreign keys in a single program scope.

Pass-by-Reference Procedures

A basic pass-by-reference procedure takes one or more call parameters by reference. Inside the procedure, the values of the reference variables can change. Their scope is defined by the calling program unit, and to some extent they treat variables much like nested anonymous blocks.

As discussed, you can define pass-by-reference procedures to run autonomously. Then, they execute in a separate transaction scope. You can also accept the default and run them in the current transaction scope. They organize database DML statements to move data between the program and database, or they send data to external program units.

PL/SQL pass-by-reference procedures are defined by the following five rules:

- At least one formal parameter must be defined as a *read-only or read-write* variable by using the `OUT` mode or `IN OUT` mode, respectively.
- All formal parameters are locally scoped variables that you can change during operations inside the procedure.

- Any formal parameter can use any valid SQL or PL/SQL data type.
- Any IN mode formal parameters can have a default initial value.
- Any system reference cursor cast from a SQL query into a procedure is not writeable and therefore must be passed through an IN mode parameter.

Pass-by-value procedures let you put sequences of multiple DML statements into a single transaction and program scope. You are able to share values, like primary and foreign keys, inside of the black box when using them. Pass-by-value procedures can function as pessimistic programming blocks. That's accomplished by using an OUT mode parameter to signal success or failure.

The following is a pass-by-reference variation of the adding_avatar procedure:

```
SQL> CREATE OR REPLACE PROCEDURE adding_avatar
  2  ( pv_avatar_name   IN      VARCHAR2
  3  , pv_episode_name  IN      VARCHAR2
  4  , pv_completion        OUT BOOLEAN) IS
  5
  6    /* Declare local variable to manage IDENTITY column
  7       surrogate key. */
  8    lv_avatar_id  NUMBER;
  9  BEGIN
 10    /* Set completion variable. */
 11    pv_completion := FALSE;
 12
 13    /* Set a Savepoint. */
 14    SAVEPOINT all_or_none;
 15
    ...
 24
 25    /* Save change inside its own transaction scope. */
 26    COMMIT;
 27
 28    /* Set completion variable. */
 29    pv_completion := TRUE;
 30  EXCEPTION
 31    WHEN OTHERS THEN
 32      ROLLBACK TO all_or_none;
 33  END;
 34  /
```

Line 4 introduces a pv_completion pass-by-reference variable, and it has OUT mode operation. That means you can't assign a value but can receive a value at the completion of the procedure. Line 11 assigns an initial value to the pv_completion variable. The assignment precedes setting the SAVEPOINT for the transaction. After the COMMIT statement, line 29 assigns TRUE to the pv_completion variable. An exception would stop execution of the transaction and roll back the DML statements to the SAVEPOINT. The pass-by-reference procedure returns false when the transaction doesn't complete and returns true when it does. If you added a compiler directive to make this an autonomous transaction, it would become a wait-on-completion autonomous procedure because the pv_completion parameter must be returned to the calling scope. Removing the pass-by-reference parameter, you get a no-wait pass-by-value procedure.

Inlining Subroutine Calls

Inlining is a compiler behavior that copies an external subroutine into another program. This is done to avoid the overhead of frequently calling an external subroutine. While leaving the decision to the compiler is always an option, you can designate when you would like to suggest an external call is copied inline.

You designate a subroutine call for inlining by using the following prototype:

```
PRAGMA INLINE(subroutine_name, 'YES'|'NO')
```

The compiler ultimately makes the decision whether to inline the subroutine, because precomplier instructions are only hints. There are other factors that make inlining some subroutines undesirable. This `PRAGMA` affects any call to the function or procedure when it precedes the call. It also impacts every call to `CASE`, `CONTINUE-WHEN`, `EXECUTE IMMEDIATE`, `EXIT-WHEN`, `LOOP`, and `RETURN` statements.

The behavior of the `PRAGMA INLINE` precomplier hint changes depending on the setting of the `PLSQL_OPTIMIZE_LEVEL` session variable. Subprograms are inlined when `PLSQL_OPTIMIZE_LEVEL` is set to 2 and are only given a high priority when set to 3. If the `PLSQL_OPTIMIZE_LEVEL` is set to 1, subprograms are only inlined when the compiler views it as necessary.

Smaller units, like pass-by-reference procedures, are more reusable but are harder to manage. They can exist for every table or view in your application. Lager units, like pass-by-value procedures, let you manage complex processes in a single black box. They tend to implement what are sometimes called workflow units. Pass-by-value procedures are generally more process centric than data-centric wrappers and less expensive to maintain. However, you should note that pass-by-reference procedures are ideal for supporting stateless web-based applications.

The best rule of thumb is probably that all procedures should focus on process-centric activities. Then, you can choose which subroutine best suits your task.

Review Section

This section has described the following points about the behaviors and characteristics of procedures:

- You can define procedures as pass-by-value or pass-by-reference modules.
- A pass-by-value procedure is an optimistic program when you make it an autonomous unit with a compiler directive.
- A pass-by-reference procedure is a pessimistic program. Making a procedure an autonomous program unit with a compiler directive doesn't change its status as a pessimistic module.
- Procedures can create ACID-compliant transactions that span multiple tables.
- It is possible to inline program execution with a compiler directive.

Supporting Scripts

This section describes programs placed on the McGraw-Hill Professional website to support the book.

- The `deterministic.sql`, `java_library.sql`, `merging.sql`, `pass_by_reference.sql`, `pipelined.sql`, `recursive.sql`, and `result_cache.sql` programs contain fully functional examples for the redacted versions in the "Functions" section of this chapter.
- The `avatar.sql` program contains small programs that support the "Procedures" section of this chapter.

Summary

You should now have an understanding of transaction scope and how to implement functions and procedures. This should include knowing when to choose a function over a procedure and vice versa.

Mastery Check

The mastery check is a series of true-or-false and multiple-choice questions that let you confirm how well you understand the material in the chapter. You may check Appendix I for answers to these questions.

True or False:

1. ___A pass-by-value function takes parameters that are consumed completely and changed into some outcome-based value.
2. ___An `INLINE` compiler directive lets you include a stand-alone module as part of your compiled program unit.
3. ___A pass-by-reference function takes literal values for any of the call parameters.
4. ___A pass-by-value procedure takes literal values for any of the call parameters.
5. ___The `RETURN` statement must always include a literal or variable for all pass-by-value and pass-by-reference functions.
6. ___You need to provide forward-referencing stubs for local functions or procedures to avoid a procedure or function "not declared in this scope" error.
7. ___You can't assign an `IN` mode parameter a new value inside a stored function or procedure.
8. ___You can't assign an `IN OUT` mode parameter a new value inside a stored function or procedure.
9. You can't embed an `INSERT`, `UPDATE`, or `DELETE` statement in any function that you plan to call from a SQL `SELECT` statement.
10. ___Some functions can only be called from within a PL/SQL scope.

Multiple Choice:

11. Which types of subroutines return a value at completion? (Multiple answers possible)
    - **A.** A pass-by-value function
    - **B.** A pass-by-value procedure
    - **C.** A pass-by-reference function
    - **D.** A pass-by-reference procedure
    - **E.** All of the above
12. Which of the following clauses are supported in PL/SQL? (Multiple answers possible)
    - **A.** An `INLINE` clause
    - **B.** A `PIPELINED` clause
    - **C.** A `DETERMINISTIC` clause
    - **D.** A `NONDETERMINISTIC` clause
    - **E.** A `RESULT_CACHE` clause
13. Which call notations are supported by the Oracle Database 12*c* database? (Multiple answers possible)
    - **A.** Positional notation
    - **B.** Named notation
    - **C.** Mixed notation
    - **D.** Object notation
    - **E.** Exclusionary notation
14. Which of the following isn't possible with a result cache function in the Oracle Database 12*c* database? (Multiple answers possible)
    - **A.** A definer rights deterministic pass-by-value function
    - **B.** An invoker rights deterministic pass-by-value function
    - **C.** A definer rights nondeterministic pass-by-value function
    - **D.** An invoker rights nondeterministic pass-by-value function
    - **E.** A definer rights nondeterministic pass-by-reference function
15. Which of the following is specifically a backward-compatible Oracle 8*i* Database compiler directive?
    - **A.** `RESTRICT_ACCESS`
    - **B.** `INLINE`
    - **C.** `AUTONOMOUS`
    - **D.** `DETERMINISTIC`
    - **E.** `EXCEPTION_INIT`

CHAPTER 9

Packages

Packages are the backbone of Oracle Database 12*c* application development. They let you group functions and procedures as components into libraries. Inside these package libraries you can have shared variables, types, and components. Components are functions and procedures. Unlike stand-alone stored functions and procedures, covered in Chapter 8, stored packages divide their declaration from their implementation. Package specifications publish the declaration, and package bodies implement the declaration.

This chapter explains how to declare, implement, leverage, and manage stored packages. It is written in a way to help the novice user grasp package concepts; however, the ideas contained herein are suitable for even the advanced PL/SQL programmer.

This chapter covers the following package-related topics:

- Package architecture
- Package specification
- Package body
- Definer versus invoker rights mechanics
- Managing packages in the database catalog

While packages aren't object types, they can mimic some features of object types. As you'll see later in this chapter, you can use the `SERIAL_REUSABLE` precompiler directive to make packages state-aware. So, if you're unfamiliar with the concept of object types, you may want to look ahead and glance through Chapter 11 before covering serially reusable packages.

Package Architecture

Packages are stored libraries in the database. They are owned by the user schema where they're created, like tables and views. This ownership makes packages schema-level objects in the database catalog, like stand-alone functions and procedures.

Package specifications declare variables, data types, functions, and procedures, and the package declaration publishes them to the local schema. You use package variables and data types in other PL/SQL blocks, and you call published functions and procedures from PL/SQL blocks inside or outside of the package where they're declared.

Oracle Database 12*c* adds the ability to white list packages, which restricts the callers to a list of functions, procedures, other packages, and object types. While all users, other than the owner, must be granted the `EXECUTE` privilege on a package to call its published components, a white-listed package must also authorize its callers.

Other than the ability to white list, the same rules that apply to tables, views, and SQL data types apply to packages. Stand-alone modules (like stand-alone functions and procedures) also have the ability to white list their callers. Published components have context inside the package, just as stand-alone components have context inside a user's schema.

The Oracle Database 12*c* security model lets you grant the `EXECUTE` privilege on any package to all users (*through a grant to* `PUBLIC`). This effectively makes it possible to grant public access to packages. Alternatively, you can restrict access to packages when you choose to do so. Prior to Oracle Database 12*c*, an invoker rights package always runs with the privilege of its invoker, meaning the invoker rights package might perform operations unintended by or forbidden to its owner when the invoker user holds greater privileges than the owner. Oracle Database 12*c* has also narrowed the scope of invoker rights programs. By default, it now disallows inheritance of user privileges. You must override that default (ill advised) by granting either the `INHERIT PRIVILEGES` or `INHERIT ANY PRIVILEGES` privilege to the caller of the package to replicate the behavior of earlier Oracle Database releases. These Oracle Database security tools let you narrow privileges to targeted audiences.

You define (*declare and implement*) package-only scope functions and procedures in package bodies. Package-only scope functions and procedures can access anything in the package specification. They can also access anything declared before them in the package body. However, they don't know anything declared after them in the package body. This is true because PL/SQL uses a single-pass parser. Parsers place identifiers into a temporary name space as they read through the source code. A parser fails when identifiers are referenced before they are declared. This is why identifiers are declared in a certain order in PL/SQL declaration sections. Typically, you declare identifiers in the following order: data types, variables, exceptions, functions, and procedures.

The sequencing of identifiers solves many but not all problems with forward referencing (see the sidebar). Sometimes a component implementation requires access before another component exists. While you could shift the order of some components to fix this sequencing problem, it is often more effective to declare a forward-referencing stub, which declares a subroutine without implementing it. You can do this in any declaration block.

Forward Referencing

The concept of *forward referencing* is rather straightforward. To use an analogy, after you arrive home from a conference, you can't send a text message to a new acquaintance from that conference if you didn't get their cell phone number. In the same vein, you can't call a function or procedure until you know its name and formal parameter list.

The following example, similar to one in Chapter 3, demonstrates that the local `first` procedure can't call the local `second` procedure until the `second` procedure has been declared, or placed in scope. The example is missing a forward-referencing stub or prototype for the `second` procedure, which means the `first` procedure doesn't know anything about the `second` procedure when it wants to call it.

```
SQL> DECLARE
       -- Placeholder for a forward-referencing stub.
       PROCEDURE first(pv_caller  VARCHAR2) IS
       BEGIN
         dbms_output.put_line('"First" called by ['||pv_caller||']');
         second('First');
       END;
       PROCEDURE second(pv_caller  VARCHAR2) IS
       BEGIN
         dbms_output.put_line('"Second" called by ['||pv_caller||']');
       END;
     BEGIN
       first('Main');
     END;
     /
```

(continued)

The program raises the following exception because it lacks a forward-referencing stub for the local `second` procedure:

```
    second('First');
    *
ERROR at line 6:
ORA-06550: line 6, column 5:
PLS-00313: 'SECOND' not declared in this scope
ORA-06550: line 6, column 5:
PL/SQL: Statement ignored
```

You can fix the error by providing a forward-referencing stub on line 2. It would look like the following:

```
  2    PROCEDURE second(pv_caller  VARCHAR2);
```

This prints

```
"First" called by [Main]
"Second" called by [First]
```

The execution block knows everything in its declaration block or external declaration block(s). The forward-referencing stub lets the PL/SQL single-pass parser put the `second` procedure declaration in its list of identifiers. It is added before the parser reads the `first` procedure because single-pass parsers read from the top down. When the parser reads the `first` procedure, it knows about the `second` procedure. The parser then validates the call to the `second` procedure and looks for the implementation of `second` later in the program to compile the code successfully. The parser raises a `PLS-00328` error if the subprogram is missing after reading the complete source code.

NOTE
Java uses a two-pass parser and lets you avoid forward declarations.

Package specifications exist to declare implementations. Package bodies provide implementations of the declarations found in the package specifications. Package bodies must implement all functions and procedures defined by the package specification. However, local functions and procedures can raise errors when you fail to provide them in the package body.

Figure 9-1 depicts the package specification and body. It shows you that the package specification acts as an interface to the package body. You can declare variables, types, and components inside both the package specification and the body. Those declared in the package specification are published, while those declared only in the package body are private components.

You can use published package-level user-defined types in other programs but you can't use private user-defined types in other programs. Named blocks defined inside component implementations are private modules, or part of the *black box* of local functions or procedures.

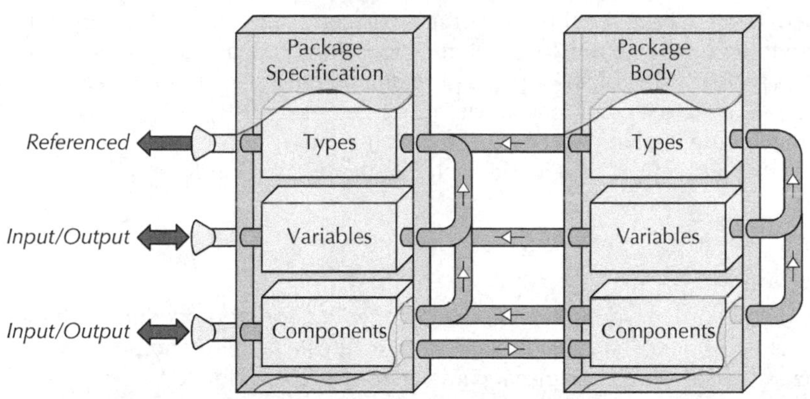

FIGURE 9-1. *PL/SQL package architecture*

(See the sidebar "The 'Black Box'" in Chapter 8 for details about the black box.) The advantage of defining functions in a package body is that they can be shared across all public and private functions and procedures. You need to ensure that forward-referencing stubs or specifications exist at the top of your package bodies because their compilation process includes a single-run parser.

Types can be referenced by external PL/SQL blocks. You can assign values to package variables or use their values. Constants are specialized variables that disallow assignments. You can only use the values of constants as right operands. External PL/SQL blocks call package functions and procedures when they're declared in a package specification. Components declared only in the package body call published components through their package declarations.

Chapter 4 discusses scalar and composite data types that are available in anonymous and named blocks. All of these are available in packages because they're named blocks. You can use any scalar or compound variable available in your package specification or body. You can also create user-defined data types in your package or package body. When user-defined data types are defined in the package specification, they are publicly available to anyone who either has the correct privileges or is white listed. When user-defined data types are defined in the package body, they are available only privately to PL/SQL blocks implemented in the package body.

As with functions and procedures, you can declare variables, types, and components in your package specification or body. Unlike stand-alone functions and procedures, you can access and use data types from your package specification in other PL/SQL blocks. You only need to preface the components with the package name and the component selector (`.`) before the data type, as shown in the following call:

```
EXECUTE some_package.some_procedure('some_string');
```

NOTE

Package types may include shared cursors. Shared cursors are mutually exclusive structures during runtime in Oracle Database 12c, which means they can be run by only a single process at any time.

The way in which you implement variables and data types is the same whether you're declaring them in a package specification or in a package body. You'll also find that, in addition to doing everything described in Chapter 8, functions and procedures also support overloading. Overloading is typically an object-oriented programming language (OOPL) feature, and it lets you define a function name with different signatures (or parameter lists). You can overload functions or procedures that are defined in package specifications. Unfortunately, you can't overload functions or procedures that are defined and implemented in the package body.

Overloading

Overloading means that you create more than one function or procedure with the same identifier (or *component name*) but different signatures. Function and procedure signatures are defined by their respective formal parameter lists. An overloaded component differs in either the number of parameters or the data types of parameters in respective positions. While PL/SQL supports named, mixed, and positional notation (Oracle Database 11*g* forward), formal parameters are *only* unique by position and data type. Parameter names do not make formal parameter lists unique.

For example, you cannot overload the `adding` function that uses two numbers by simply changing the formal parameter names, like this:

```
SQL> CREATE OR REPLACE PACKAGE not_overloading IS
       FUNCTION adding (a NUMBER, b NUMBER) RETURN NUMBER;
       FUNCTION adding (one NUMBER, two NUMBER) RETURN BINARY_INTEGER;
     END not_overloading;
     /
```

NOTE
PL/SQL allows you to overload functions and procedures by simply renaming variables, but at runtime the ambiguity raises a `PLS-00307` exception.

You can compile this package specification and implement its package body without raising a compile-time error. However, you can't call the overloaded function without finding that too many declarations of the function exist. The ambiguity between declarations raises the `PLS-00307` exception. The return data type for functions is not part of their signature. A change in the return data type for functions does not alter their unique signatures because the return type isn't part of the signature.

Redefining the package declaration as follows lets you call either implementation of the `adding` function. The data types now differ between the two declarations.

```
SQL> CREATE OR REPLACE PACKAGE overloading IS
       FUNCTION adding (a NUMBER, b NUMBER) RETURN NUMBER;
       FUNCTION adding (a VARCHAR2, b NUMBER) RETURN NUMBER;
       FUNCTION adding (a NUMBER, b VARCHAR2) RETURN NUMBER;
       FUNCTION adding (a VARCHAR2, b VARCHAR2) RETURN BINARY_INTEGER;
     END not_overloading;
     /
```

The following illustration shows you how overloading works inside the black box. In the first signature, the second parameter is a CLOB and third is a DATE, while their positions are reversed in the second signature. A drawing of the sample adding function would show two round funnels for the VARCHAR2 parameters and two square funnels for the NUMBER parameters.

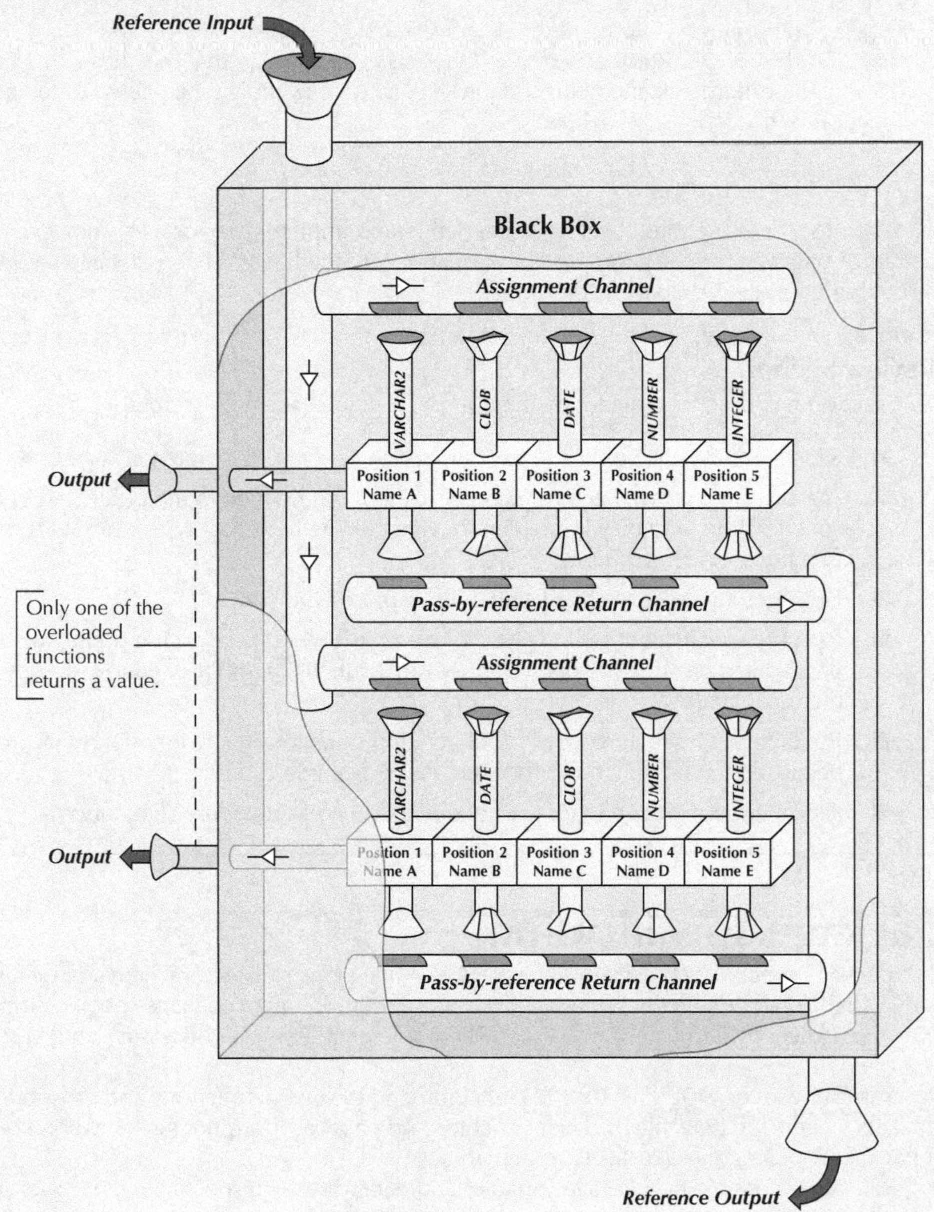

(continued)

You call an overloaded function or procedure name with a list of actual parameters. Inside the black box, the runtime engine identifies the sequence and data types of the actual parameters. It matches the calls against possible candidates. When the runtime engine finds a matching candidate, it sends the actual parameters to that version of the function or procedure.

This information is stored in the database catalog. You can see it in the `CDB_`, `ALL_`, `DBA_`, and `USER_ARGUMENTS` views. If there isn't a signature that matches a function call, the PL/SQL runtime engine returns an `ORA-06576` error, indicating you've called an invalid function or procedure.

The next three sections cover how you define and implement packages. They examine the details of package specifications and bodies, and examine how you can manage packages through the Oracle Database 12*c* catalog.

Review Section

This section has described the following points about package architecture:

- Packages have the published package specification and private package body.
- The private package body implements everything defined in the public package specification, and may implement private user-defined data types, variables, cursors, functions, and procedures.
- Packages can have a white list that limits those who can call it.
- Package specifications eliminate the need for forward-referencing public functions and procedures because the definitions of those functions and procedures are defined in the data catalog.
- Package bodies require forward-referencing stubs for private functions and procedures because their compilation process relies on a single-run parser.
- Packages support overloading public function and procedure signatures.

Package Specification

The package specification declares a package as a black box to a user's schema, but it also publishes the available public functions and procedures. After compiling a package specification, you can create packages and functions that use it. The implementation isn't necessary until you want to test the parts.

You can use the SQL*Plus `DESCRIBE` command to see the functions and procedures inside a package. Unfortunately, the package variables and data types are not visible when you describe a package by using the `DESCRIBE` command.

You can determine the package variables and data types by inspecting the package specification found in the `text` column of the `CDB_`, `ALL_`, `DBA_`, and `USER_SOURCE` administrative views. While the `text` column displays the data catalog information from the package specification, it doesn't necessarily display the implementation because you can wrap your code when you compile it. Wrapping the implementation obfuscates the code by converting it into a meaningless set of characters. Appendix F discusses wrapping your PL/SQL code.

You can query the data catalog information, and sometimes the actual source, from the `USER_SOURCE` view for definer rights programs. To see invoker rights programs, owned by another user typically, you need to have superuser privileges to use the `CDB_`, `ALL_`, or `DBA_SOURCE` administrative view.

From SQL*Plus you can query the `CDB_`, `ALL_`, or `DBA_SOURCE` administrative view by using the following formatting commands and `SELECT` statement:

```
SQL> -- Set page break to maximum SQL*Plus value.
SQL> SET PAGESIZE 49999
SQL> -- Set column formatting for 80-column display.
SQL> COLUMN line FORMAT 99999 HEADING "Line#"
SQL> COLUMN text FORMAT A73   HEADING "Text"
SQL> -- Query any source in the user's account.
SQL> SELECT   line
  2  ,        text
  3  FROM     user_source
  4  WHERE UPPER(name) = UPPER('&input_name');
```

NOTE
*Oracle Database 12*c *and previous releases store all metadata by default in uppercase strings. You can override that default behavior in Oracle Database 12*c*, as described in the sidebar "Case-Sensitive Table and Column Names" of Appendix B. The* `UPPER` *function around the column name ensures you'll always match uppercase strings from the database catalog.*

The next five subsections discuss the prototype features and serially reusable precompiler directive of a package specification and how you work with variables, types, and components. They point out changes in behavior between serially reusable packages and non–serially reusable packages. Non–serially reusable packages are the default. Types are subdivided into structures, cursors, and collections.

Prototype Features

The prototype for a package specification lists all components as optional because it is possible to build a package without any components. The prototype shows the possibilities for package variables, types, and subroutines (*functions and procedures*).

Since the previous edition of this book, the package specification prototype includes two new elements: the optional `EDITIONABLE` clause, introduced in Oracle Database 11*g* Release 2, and the white-listing `ACCESSIBLE BY` clause, introduced in Oracle Database 12*c*. Following is a generic package specification:

```
CREATE [OR REPLACE] PACKAGE package_name
[ EDITIONABLE | NONEDITIONABLE ]
[ AUTHID {DEFINER | CURRENT_USER} ]
[ ACCESSIBLE BY
```

```
  ( FUNCTION  some_schema.function_name
  [, PROCEDURE some_schema.procedure_name
  [, PACKAGE   some_schema.package_name
  [, TYPE      some_schema.object_type_name]]] )]  IS
  [PRAGMA SERIALLY_REUSABLE;]
  [variable_name    [CONSTANT] scalar_data_type [:= value];]
  [collection_name [CONSTANT] collection_data_type [:= constructor];]
  [object_name      [CONSTANT] object_data_type [:= constructor];]

  [TYPE record_structure IS RECORD
   (  field_name  data_type
   [, field_name  data_type
   [, ... ]]);]

  [CURSOR cursor_name
   [(parameter_name  data_type
   [,parameter_name  data_type
   [, ... ]])] IS
     select_statement;]

  [TYPE ref_cursor IS REF CURSOR [RETURN { catalog_row | record_structure }];]
  [user_exception_name EXCEPTION;
  [PRAGMA EXCEPTION_INIT(user_exception_name,-20001);]]

  [FUNCTION function_name
  [( parameter  [IN][OUT] [NOCOPY] sql_data_type | plsql_data_type
  [, parameter  [IN][OUT] [NOCOPY] sql_data_type | plsql_data_type
  [, ... ]])]
  RETURN { sql_data_type | plsql_data_type }
  [ DETERMINISTIC | PARALLEL_ENABLED ]
  [ PIPELINED ]
  [ RESULT_CACHE [ RELIES_ON (table_name) ]];]

  [ PRAGMA RESTRICT_REFERENCES ({ DEFAULT | function_name }
                               , option [, option [, ... ]]); ]

  [PROCEDURE procedure_name
  [( parameter1      [IN][OUT] [NOCOPY] sql_data_type | plsql_data_type
  [, parameter2      [IN][OUT] [NOCOPY] sql_data_type | plsql_data_type
  [, parameter(n+1) [IN][OUT] [NOCOPY] sql_data_type | plsql_data_type])];]
END package_name;
/
```

NOTE
The `OR REPLACE` clause is very important. Without it, you must drop the package specification before attempting to re-declare it.

Definer rights packages use an `AUTHID` value of `DEFINER`, while invoker rights packages use an `AUTHID` value of `CURRENT_USER`. Appendix A describes definer and invoker rights in more detail, and they're touched on in the "Schema-Level Programs" sidebar a bit later in this chapter.

The EDITIONABLE clause lets you create multiple copies of the same package in the database at the same time. These EDITIONABLE packages only apply to certain editions of the database, and they enable virtually zero-downtime upgrades of the database. You should check the *Oracle Database Advanced Application Developer's Guide* for more information on editions in the Oracle Database 11*g* Release 2 and Oracle Database 12*c* release.

The ACCESSIBLE BY clause lets you white list a package. White listing limits those in the list as the only authorized callers of public functions and procedures. White listing also extends itself to public variables and data types. Refer to Chapter 2 for coverage on white listing as a new feature. A package specification is white listed like this:

```
SQL> CREATE OR REPLACE PACKAGE small_one
  2  ACCESSIBLE BY
  3  ( FUNCTION  video.gateway
  4  , PROCEDURE video.backdoor
  5  , PACKAGE   video.api
  6  , TYPE      video.hobbit ) IS
  7    FUNCTION add
  8    ( lv_a  NUMBER
  9    , lv_b  NUMBER ) RETURN NUMBER;
 10  END small_one;
 11  /
```

You use the ACCESSIBLE BY clause only in package specifications, as shown on lines 2 through 6. Waiting until the "Package Body" section to introduce the small_one package body (or implementation) would be a bit disjointed, so here's the package body for the small_one package:

```
SQL> CREATE OR REPLACE PACKAGE BODY small_one IS
    FUNCTION add
    ( lv_a  NUMBER
    , lv_b  NUMBER ) RETURN NUMBER IS
    BEGIN
      RETURN lv_a + lv_b;
    END add;
  END small_one;
  /
```

Note the absence of an ACCESSIBLE BY clause from the package body declaration. You can then create the gateway function to call the small_one.add function. The function compiles because the small_one package specification includes the gateway function on its white list.

The gateway function takes two parameters and passes them through to the white-listed add function, as you can see in the following implementation of the gateway function:

```
SQL> CREATE OR REPLACE FUNCTION gateway
  ( pv_a  NUMBER
  , pv_b  NUMBER ) RETURN NUMBER IS
  BEGIN
    RETURN small_one.add(pv_a, pv_b);
  END;
  /
```

You can test the whole thing with the following anonymous block program:

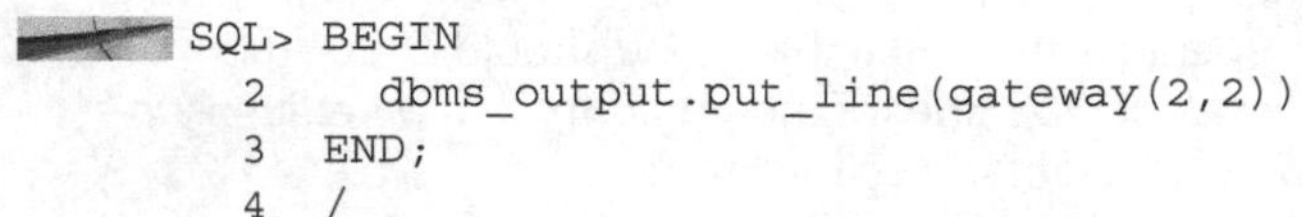

```
SQL> BEGIN
       dbms_output.put_line(gateway(2,2));
     END;
     /
```

The call to the `gateway` function passes in two 2s and gets back a 4.

Serially Reusable Precompiler Directive

The `SERIALLY_REUSABLE PRAGMA` (precompiler directive or instruction) can only be used in a package context. You must use it in both the package specification and the body. This practice differs from the `PRAGMA` instructions covered in previous chapters for exceptions, functions, and procedures. The `SERIALLY_REUSABLE PRAGMA` is important when you want to share variables and cursors because it guarantees their starting state each time they're called.

The `CONSTANT` qualifier lets you designate variables as read-only and static variables. While not mentioned in earlier chapters, you can also designate any variable as a `CONSTANT` in any anonymous or named block. A constant can't be used as an assignment target in any package where it is defined. Constants become more important when you share them through package specifications.

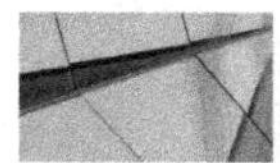

NOTE
You cannot use package variables as assignment targets when they're defined as constants. Any attempt to assign a value to a constant raises a `PLS-00363` exception.

Package exceptions are helpful development tools because they can be referenced by other program units. All you need do to use a package exception in other programs is prepend the package name and component selector to the exception.

For example, you would declare an exception like

```
sample_exception EXCEPTION;
PRAGMA EXCEPTION_INIT(sample_exception,-20003);
```

Chapter 7 demonstrates how you can leverage exceptions. You declare them in packages just as you do in stand-alone functions and procedures, or anonymous blocks.

The section "System Reference Cursors" in Chapter 4 only discusses strongly and weakly typed reference cursors. There, the chapter covers strongly typed reference cursors as data types anchored to a catalog object, like a table or view. Package specifications let you share record type definitions with other PL/SQL blocks. This feature lets you share record types with other PL/SQL blocks and anchor reference cursors to package-defined record types.

The nested function definition also shows the potential for pipelined and cached result sets. You should remember to use a collection as the return type of pipelined functions. If you forget, the compilation cycle raises a `PLS-00630` exception stating that you must return a supported collection.

NOTE
The cached result set *feature works for stand-alone* (schema-level) *functions but doesn't work for functions inside packages.*

Schema-Level Programs

Stored functions, procedures, packages, and objects are schema-level programs. Only schema-level programs can be defined as programs with definer rights or invoker rights. The default model of operation is *definer rights*, which means the code runs with the permissions available to the owner of the schema. You can define a schema-level program as an invoker rights model by including the `AUTHID` as `CURRENT_USER`. An invoker rights model runs with the permissions of the schema that calls the component.

The definer rights model runs with the privileges of the owning schema and is best suited for a centralized computing model. The `AUTHID` as `DEFINER` sets a schema-level program as a definer rights model, but it is unnecessary because that's the default. The invoker rights model requires you to maintain multiple copies of tables or views in different schemas or databases.

Package specifications define packages. The package body only implements the declaration from the package specification. The package specification is the schema-level program. You can define a package as definer rights or invoker rights, but all components of the package inherit a single mode of operation.

You raise a `PLS-00157` exception when try to set the mode of operation for functions and procedures when they're inside packages. Functions and procedures defined inside packages *are not* schema-level programs. They're actually nested components of packages. They inherit the operational mode of the package.

The sidebar "Backward Compatibility Issues for Functions" in Chapter 8 includes a table that covers the precomplier options that restrict function performance. The package specification introduces a `DEFAULT` mode, which means apply the limitations to all functions defined in the package. Again, these precomplier options that restrict function behaviors and the `TRUST` option are intended more for backward compatibility than for new development.

Variables

Packages are non–serially reusable by default. This means that a second user isn't guaranteed the same package after a first user calls a package. The default works well when you don't declare shared variables or cursors in a package specification because the functions and procedures are reusable. At least, they're reusable when they don't depend on package variables. Moreover, you should always make packages serially reusable when they contain shared variables.

You define a package as serially reusable by placing the `SERIALLY_REUSABLE PRAGMA` in the package specification, as shown next. The `PRAGMA` changes the basic behavior of package variables. A serially reusable package creates a new (*fresh*) copy of the package when it is called by another program unit, whereas a default (*non–serially reusable*) package reuses variables.

```
PRAGMA SERIALLY_REUSABLE;
```

While you declare variables like any other anonymous or named block, they are not hidden inside the black box. Package-level variables are publicly accessible from other PL/SQL programs. This means package-level variables are public or shared variables. They are also subject to change by one or more programs. The duration of package-level variables varies in any session. The length of time can extend through the life of a connection or can be shortened when other packages displace it in the SGA. The older and less-used packages can age out of the SGA because of how the least-used algorithm works. The least-used algorithm acts more or less like a garbage collector for the database. It is very similar to the garbage collector in a JVM (Java Virtual Machine).

Enabling other program units to change package-level variables generally isn't a good practice. In fact, it couples the behavior of two or more programs on something that can change state unexpectedly. As a rule of thumb, you should avoid public variables. It's a better coding practice to implement package variables inside the package body, which makes them behave like protected attributes in OOPLs such as C++, C#, or Java.

You can access shared constants or variables from package specifications. Constants have fixed values whether you declare the package as serially reusable or non–serially reusable. Variables don't have a fixed value in either case. A serially reusable package guarantees the initial values of variables because a call to the package always gets a new copy of the package. A non–serially reusable package doesn't guarantee the initial value because it can't. A non–serially reusable package variable returns either the initial value or last value of a variable. The last value is returned when the package still resides in the SGA from a prior call in the same session.

The following example creates a `shared_variables` package specification and demonstrates the behavior of a non–serially reusable package specification. The package defines a constant and a variable. You can use the package specification to test the behavior of shared variables.

```
SQL> CREATE OR REPLACE PACKAGE shared IS
       lv_protected   CONSTANT NUMBER := 1;
       pv_unprotected          NUMBER := 1;
     END shared;
     /
```

The following `change_unprotected` procedure changes the state of the package-level variable and then prints the `lv_unprotected` variable value. It takes one formal parameter, which can be any number.

```
SQL> CREATE OR REPLACE PROCEDURE change_unprotected
     (pv_value  NUMBER) IS
       /* Declare the initial package variable value. */
       lv_package_var  NUMBER := shared.lv_unprotected;
       /* Define the unit to run in a discrete session. */
       PRAGMA AUTONOMOUS_TRANSACTION;
     BEGIN
       shared.lv_unprotected := shared.lv_unprotected + pv_value;
       dbms_output.put_line(
         'Calls ['||pv_value||'] + ['||lv_package_var||']'
         || ' = ['||shared.lv_unprotected||']');
     END change_unprotected;
     /
```

NOTE

You can access package specification variables from PL/SQL blocks but not from SQL commands.

Line 4 captures the value from the package-level variable before reassigning it a value on line 8. Lines 9 through 11 print the output as the *number to add*, the *initial value* of the `lv_unprotected` package-level variable, and the *new value* of the `lv_unprotected` package-level variable. You can test the durability of the shared package-level variable with the following anonymous block program. It calls the `change_unprotected` function four times.

```
SQL> BEGIN
       FOR i IN 1..4 LOOP
         change_unprotected(i);
       END LOOP;
     END;
     /
```

It prints

```
Calls [1] + [1] = [2]
Calls [2] + [2] = [4]
Calls [3] + [4] = [7]
Calls [4] + [7] = [11]
```

You should note that *number to add* increments by one, and the *initial value* starts at 1 and becomes the *new_value* the next time you call the `change_unprotected` function. This type of incrementing continues until the package ages out of the SGA, or you switch connections.

You use the following command to reset the `shared_variables` package to age out of the SGA:

```
SQL> ALTER PACKAGE shared_variables COMPILE SPECIFICATION;
```

The procedure always returns 3 when you redefine it as serially reusable. This is true because each call to the package gets a fresh copy. Serially reusable packages re-initialize the values of shared variables. The only difference between a serially reusable variable and a constant is that a constant can never change its value, while the variable can. The change is lost on any subsequent call to the package when the package is serially reusable. As a rule of thumb, package specification variables *should always be constants*.

Types

There are two generalized types that you can declare in packages: static data types and dynamic data types. Data types are typically PL/SQL structures, collections, reference cursors, and cursors. All of these can be dynamic or static data types. They are dynamic when their declaration anchors their type to a row or column definition. You use the `%ROWTYPE` to anchor to a row and the `%TYPE` to anchor to a column, as qualified in the "Attribute and Table Anchoring" section of Chapter 3. Types are static when they rely on explicitly declared SQL data types, such as `DATE`, `INTEGER`, `NUMBER`, or `VARCHAR2`.

As a general rule, package specifications are independent of other schema-level objects. You build dependencies when you anchor types declared in package specifications to catalog objects, like tables and views. If something changes in the dependent table or view, the package specification becomes invalid. As discussed later in the chapter, in the section "Managing Packages in the Database Catalog," changes in package specifications can create a *cascade reaction* that invalidates numerous package bodies and stand-alone schema-level programs.

Pseudotypes or Attributes

The %ROWTYPE and %TYPE act as pseudotypes because they inherit the base catalog type for a table or column, respectively. More importantly, they implicitly anchor PL/SQL variable data types to the database catalog, shared package cursors, or local cursors. They are also known as attributes because they're preceded by the attribute indicator (the % symbol). The important point to remember is that these attributes inherit a data type and anchor a variable's data type to the database catalog.

Beyond the dynamic or static condition of package types, a shared cursor is a package cursor. Shared cursors are dynamic insofar as they return different data sets over time. Other package data types don't inherit anything beyond the default values that may be assigned during their declaration.

You can use any PL/SQL record type or collection type that you declare in a package specification as a formal parameter or function return data type of a named PL/SQL block. You can't use these PL/SQL data types in SQL statements. PL/SQL blocks that reference package-level record and collection types are dependent on the package. If the package specification becomes invalid, so do the external program units that depend on the package declarations.

Chapter 8 contains an example using this technique in the "PIPELINED Clause" section. There it declares a pipelined package specification that contains a record type and a collection type. The collection type is dependent on the record structure. The stand-alone pf pipelined function returns an *aggregate table* to the SQL environment. The stand-alone function uses the package-level collection type, which implicitly relies on the package-level record structure. This example demonstrates how you can use record and collection types found in package specifications in other PL/SQL blocks.

Declaring shared cursors in the package specification anchors a cursor to the tables or views referenced by its SELECT statement. This makes the package specification dependent on any referenced tables or views. A change to the tables or views can invalidate the package specification and all package bodies that list the invalid specification as a dependent.

Shared cursors can be queried simultaneously by different program units. The first program that opens the cursor gains control of the cursor until it is released by a CLOSE cursor command. *Prior to Oracle Database 11*g, *these shared cursors were not read consistent and required that you declare the package serially reusable to ensure they performed as read-consistent cursors.* Any attempt to fetch from an open shared cursor by another process is denied immediately. An ORA-06511 'cursor already open' exception should be thrown, but the error message can be suppressed when the calling program runs as an autonomous transaction. Autonomous transactions suppress the other error and raise an ORA-06519 exception. Unfortunately, PL/SQL doesn't have a WAIT *n* (*seconds*) command syntax that would allow you to wait on an open cursor. This is probably one reason some developers avoid shared cursors.

The following demonstrates a shared cursor package specification definition:

```
SQL> CREATE OR REPLACE PACKAGE shared_types IS
       CURSOR item_cursor IS
         SELECT   i.item_id
         ,        i.item_title
         FROM     item i;
     END shared_cursors;
     /
```

You can then access the shared cursor in an anonymous or named block, as follows:

```
SQL> BEGIN
  FOR i IN shared_types.item_cursor LOOP
    dbms_output.put_line('['||i.item_id||']['||i.item_title||']');
  END LOOP;
END;
/
```

NOTE
You can also reference any package specification collection type by prepending the package name and component selector.

There's the temptation to use a reference cursor defined by a record structure. You may choose that development direction because you don't want to create a view. The following declares a strongly typed PL/SQL-only reference cursor:

```
SQL> CREATE OR REPLACE PACKAGE shared_types IS
  CURSOR item_cursor IS
    SELECT   i.item_id
    ,        i.item_title
    FROM     item i;
  TYPE item_type IS RECORD
  ( item_id    item.item_id%TYPE       -- Anchored to the data catalog.
  , item_title item.item_title%TYPE); -- Anchored to the data catalog.
END shared_types;
/
```

You can now use the reference cursor but not with the package-level cursor. Reference cursors only support explicit cursors. You can test the shared package-level record structure and cursor by first creating a SQL session-level (or *bind*) variable, like

```
SQL> VARIABLE refcur REFCURSOR
```

Then, you can run the following anonymous block program:

```
SQL> DECLARE
  TYPE package_typed IS REF CURSOR RETURN shared_types.item_type;
  quick PACKAGE_TYPED;
BEGIN
  OPEN quick FOR
    SELECT item_id, item_title FROM item;
 :refcur := quick;
END;
/
```

The `package_typed` variable uses the package specification data type to create a strong reference cursor that is dependent on a package-level data type as opposed to a schema-level table or view. The record structure *is a catalog object declared in the context of the package.*

The anonymous block returns the cursor results into the bind variable. You can query the bind variable reference cursor as follows:

```
SQL> SELECT :refcur FROM dual;
```

The query will return the results from the explicit query in the `FOR` clause. You should note that `OPEN` *`reference cursor`* `FOR` *`sql_statement`*`;` fails if you change the query so that it returns a different set of data types or columns.

NOTE
The substitution of a dynamic reference for a literal query raises a `PLS-00455` exception, which is "cursor such-and-such *cannot be used in a dynamic SQL `OPEN` statement."*

Shared record structures, collections, and reference cursors are the safest types to place in package specifications. They become accessible to anyone with the `EXECUTE` privilege on the package, but they aren't part of the output when you describe a package. As mentioned in the beginning of the "Package Specification" section, you must query the source to find the available package specification types.

Components: Functions and Procedures

The components in package specifications are functions or procedures. They have slightly different behaviors than their respective schema-level peers. Package specification functions and procedures are merely *forward-referencing* stubs. They define the namespace for a function or procedure and their respective signatures. Functions also define their return types.

The package specification information is recorded in the `CDB_`, `ALL_`, `DBA_`, and `USER_ARGUMENTS` catalog views. These catalog views are covered in the "Checking Dependencies" subsection later in this chapter.

You define a function stub as follows:

```
FUNCTION a_function
( a NUMBER := 1
, b NUMBER) RETURNS NUMBER;
```

You define a procedure stub like this:

```
PROCEDURE a_procedure
( a NUMBER := 1
, b NUMBER);
```

The sample declarations assign a default to the first formal parameter, which makes it optional. When there's an optional parameter before mandatory parameters, you need to use named notation.

The package specification is also where you provide any `PRAGMA` instructions for package-level functions and procedures. Two `PRAGMA` instructions can apply to either the whole package or all functions in a package. The `SERIALLY_REUSABLE` precomplier instruction must be placed in both the package specification and the body. The `RESTRICT_REFERENCES` precomplier instruction applies to all functions when you use the keyword `DEFAULT` instead of a function name.

The following precomplier instruction restricts the behavior of all functions in the package and guarantees they can't write any database state:

```
SQL> CREATE OR REPLACE PACKAGE financial IS
       FUNCTION fv
       (current NUMBER, periods NUMBER, interest NUMBER) RETURN NUMBER;
       FUNCTION pv
       (future  NUMBER, periods NUMBER, interest NUMBER) RETURN NUMBER;
       PRAGMA RESTRICT_REFERENCES(DEFAULT, WNDS);
     END financial;
     /
```

Chapter 8 contains the implementation of the `fv` and `pv` functions declared in the package specification. They don't write data states, and their implementations would succeed in a package body.

Review Section

This section has described the following points about the package specification:

- Package specifications publish the public functions and procedures of the package, but package specifications don't publish the package's user-defined public variables and data types.
- Package variables and user-defined data types aren't visible without physically inspecting the package specification stored in the data catalog.
- You can use the `CDB_`, `ALL_`, `DBA_`, and `USER_SOURCE` administrative views to see the source of any package's specification, provided it isn't wrapped (see Appendix F).
- You can restrict package specifications by limiting the package to an edition or by white listing which named blocks can call the package's public functions and procedures.
- Packages are OOPL components. Packages let you overload functions and procedures, and they maintain public variable state during the scope of a session or until they age out of the database's SGA.
- You must use the `SERIALLY_REUSABLE` precompiler instruction to guarantee the state of public variables and data types. (As a word of advice, it's a bad practice in OOPLs to declare public variables.)

Package Body

A package body contains both public and private parts. Public parts are defined in the package specification. Private parts are declared and implemented only in the package body.

You must implement all public functions and procedures in a package body. Public functions and procedures are those declared in the package specification as function and procedure prototypes. When you implement a package body, you must guarantee that public function and procedure signatures match exactly with their prototypes. That means that all the parameters in the parameter list must match the variable name, data type, and any default value found in their respective prototype.

Package bodies also include private variables, data types, functions, and procedures. You're at liberty to implement private functions and procedures as you like.

NOTE
When migrating an obsolete Oracle 9i database, you need to know that formal parameters declared in the specification weren't enforced in the package body in Oracle 9i Database. This means you'll need to provide them manually to migrate old PL/SQL code forward to supported versions of Oracle Database.

The next four subsections discuss the prototype features of a package body and how you can implement variables, types, and components in your package bodies. They point out changes in behavior between serially reusable packages and non–serially reusable packages. As mentioned, packages are non–serially reusable by default. As in the "Package Specification" section earlier, types are subdivided into structures, cursors, and collections.

Prototype Features

The package body prototype is very similar to the package specification prototype. The package body can declare almost everything that the specification sets except two things. You can't reference the new Oracle Database 12*c* `ACCESSIBLY BY` clause inside the package body, because it's only allowed in the package specification. You can't define `PRAGMA` instructions for functions inside a package body. Any attempt raises a `PLS-00708` error that says you must put them in the package specification.

You can use `EXCEPTION_INIT PRAGMA` instructions for package-level exceptions, provided they're unique from those declared in your package specification. You can also override a variable that is declared in the package specification. You do this by declaring the variable again in the package body. When you do this, you make both copies of this variable inaccessible to your package body. Any reference inside a package body to the doubly declared variable raises a `PLS-00371` exception when you attempt to compile the package body. The exception tells you that at most one declaration for the variable is permitted. This exception indicates not only that Oracle didn't intend users to take advantage of this behavior, but that it may actually be a bug.

The prototype for a package body follows:

```
CREATE [OR REPLACE] PACKAGE package_name
  [EDITIONABLE | NONEDITIONABLE] IS
  [PRAGMA SERIALLY_REUSABLE;]
  [variable_name    [CONSTANT] scalar_data_type [:= value];]
  [collection_name  [CONSTANT] collection_data_type [:= constructor];]
  [object_name      [CONSTANT] object_data_type [:= constructor];]

  [TYPE record_structure IS RECORD
   (  field_name  data_type
   [, field_name  data_type
   [, ...]]);]

  [CURSOR cursor_name
   [( parameter_name  data_type
```

```
 [, parameter_name  data_type
 [, ...]])] IS
   select_statement;]

[TYPE ref_cursor IS REF CURSOR [RETURN { catalog_row | record_structure }];]

[user_exception_name EXCEPTION;
[PRAGMA EXCEPTION_INIT(user_exception_name,-20001);]]

-- This is a forward-referencing stub to a function implemented later.
[FUNCTION function_name
[( parameter  [IN][OUT] [NOCOPY] sql_data_type | plsql_data_type
[, parameter  [IN][OUT] [NOCOPY] sql_data_type | plsql_data_type
[, ... )]
RETURN { sql_data_type | plsql_data_type }
[ DETERMINISTIC | PARALLEL_ENABLED ]
[ PIPELINED ]
[ RESULT_CACHE [ RELIES_ON (table_name) ]];]

-- This is a forward-referencing stub to a procedure implemented later.
[PROCEDURE procedure_name
[( parameter  [IN][OUT] [NOCOPY] sql_data_type | plsql_data_type
[, parameter  [IN][OUT] [NOCOPY] sql_data_type | plsql_data_type
[, ... )];]

[FUNCTION function_name
[( parameter  [IN][OUT] [NOCOPY] sql_data_type | plsql_data_type
[, parameter  [IN][OUT] [NOCOPY] sql_data_type | plsql_data_type
[, ... ]])]
RETURN { sql_data_type | plsql_data_type }
[ DETERMINISTIC | PARALLEL_ENABLED ]
[ PIPELINED ]
[ RESULT_CACHE [ RELIES_ON (table_name) ]] IS
[ PRAGMA AUTONOMOUS_TRANSACTION;]       -- Check rules in Chapter 8.
   some_declaration_statement;          -- Check rules in Chapter 8.
 BEGIN
   some_execution_statement;            -- Check rules in Chapter 8.
[EXCEPTION
   WHEN some_exception THEN
   some exception_handling_statement;] -- Check rules in Chapter 7.
 END [function_name];]

[PROCEDURE procedure_name
[( parameter  [IN][OUT] [NOCOPY] sql_data_type | plsql_data_type
[, parameter  [IN][OUT] [NOCOPY] sql_data_type | plsql_data_type
[, ... ]])] IS
[ PRAGMA AUTONOMOUS_TRANSACTION;]       -- Check rules in Chapter 8.
   some_declaration_statement;          -- Check rules in Chapter 8.
 BEGIN
   some_execution_statement;            -- Check rules in Chapter 8.
```

```
  [EXCEPTION
     WHEN some_exception THEN
     some exception_handling_statement;] -- Check rules in Chapter 7.
   END [procedure_name];]
END [package_name];
/
```

You must include the SERIALLY_REUSABLE PRAGMA (precomplier directive) in the package body if the package specification uses it. This practice differs from the PRAGMA instructions covered earlier.

Variables

Package-level variables declared in package bodies differ from those declared in package specifications. You can't access package-level variables outside of the package. That's why they're sometimes called *protected* or *private*. Only functions and procedures published by the package specification can access package-level variables. This makes these variable very much like instance variables in an OOPL like Java, which would make them private variables. At least, package-level variables retain their state from the point of the first call to the package until the end of the session or they age out of the SGA.

Packages act like classes, and package functions and procedures act like methods in OOPL classes. In that vein, published functions and procedures are public, package-level functions and procedures are protected (or limited to the package scope), and local functions and procedures are private. Package-level variables are called *protected* and *private* interchangeably by developers, but they should be considered private to the package and protected to the functions and procedures of the package.

The following package specification creates a function and a procedure. The get function returns the value of a package body variable. The set procedure lets you reset a package body variable's value. This package is non–serially reusable, so it retains its variable values until the package ages out of the SGA.

```
SQL> CREATE OR REPLACE PACKAGE package_variables IS
       /* Declare package components. */
       PROCEDURE set(value VARCHAR2);
       FUNCTION get RETURN VARCHAR2;
     END package_variables;
     /
```

Package specifications don't know which private components exist in package bodies. The implementation details of private components are not visible outside of the package body. Public functions and procedures can access any private component, such as private variables, data types, functions, and procedures. Other PL/SQL programs can also call any of the public functions and procedures. At least, other programs can call them if the programs are granted the EXECUTE privilege on the package or are included in the white list of authorized callers.

Package bodies declare private variables, data types, functions, and procedures. Any public function or procedure can access and use any of the private components because they share the same implementation scope. Private functions and procedures also can call other private functions and procedures. In both cases, functions and procedures in a package body can call other functions and procedures without prepending the package name and component selector (`.`). However, in some circles, it's considered a good practice to include the package name before calls to private functions and procedures. From my perspective, it certainly avoids ambiguity. Likewise, you can use the package name and component selector to qualify local or private variables and data types.

The package body implements the previous package specification as follows:

```
SQL> CREATE OR REPLACE PACKAGE BODY package_variables IS
       /* Declare package scope variable. */
       variable VARCHAR2(20) := 'Initial Value';
       /* Implement a public function. */
       FUNCTION get RETURN VARCHAR2 IS
       BEGIN
         RETURN variable;
       END get;
       /* Implement a public procedure. */
       PROCEDURE set(value VARCHAR2) IS
       BEGIN
         variable := value;
       END set;
     END package_variables;
     /
```

The `get` function returns the package-level variable. The `set` procedure resets the package-level variable. After you compile the program, you can test the behavior by declaring a session-level (bind) variable. Call the `get` function to return a value into the bind variable. You can then query the bind variable:

```
SQL> VARIABLE outcome VARCHAR2(20)
SQL> CALL package_variables.get() INTO :outcome;
SQL> SELECT :outcome AS outcome FROM dual;
```

The output is

```
OUTCOME
--------------
Initial Value
```

Execute the `set` procedure to reset the variable's value. Call the `get` function again before you requery the bind variable. The test results are

```
SQL> EXECUTE package_variables.set('New Value');
SQL> CALL package_variables.get() INTO :outcome;
SQL> SELECT :outcome AS outcome FROM dual;
```

The output is

```
OUTCOME
--------------
New Value
```

If you rerun the `package_variables get` function in the same session, it works differently. You would print "New Value" first, not "Initial Value," because the package hasn't aged out of the SGA.

A `CREATE OR REPLACE` DDL command replaces a package specification only when there's a change between the original package specification and the new package specification. Otherwise, the DDL command simply skips the process. You can change the package body's implementation without altering the status or definition of the package specification.

You can force a change and refresh variables by changing sessions, or by running an `ALTER` command to recompile the package specification. After recompilation, all variables are returned to their initial values. You can alter the package before rerunning the script and see the same results shown previously.

The syntax to recompile only a package specification is

```
ALTER PACKAGE package_variables COMPILE SPECIFICATION;
```

Only local variables, those declared in functions and procedures, have a fresh value each time you call them. That's because they don't retain their values in between calls.

If you change the package from non–serially reusable to serially reusable, the test results change. Each call to a serially reusable package body gets a new copy of both the package specification and the body. The package-level variable is always the same.

NOTE
You can't call a serially reusable package from a `SELECT` statement.

As a rule, you should consider declaring packages as non–serially reusable libraries. If you adopt that rule, you should avoid public variables. When you declare public variables, you invite other programs to couple their behavior by using them.

If you *must* declare public variables (and I'd love to see the use case that supports this), you should declare them only as constants in the package specification. If you want to make your packages cohesive (independent) and avoid coupling (dependency), you should declare package variables in the package body. Alternatively, you can declare local variables inside both public and private functions and procedures.

Ultimately, all package variables should have protected or private access in packages. Although PL/SQL doesn't have formal access modifiers like those in C++, C#, and Java, variable access is set by the following rules:

- Variables declared in a package specification are public access, which means any other PL/SQL code module may use them.
- Variables declared in the package body are protected access, which means you limit the scope of access to subroutines of the package.
- Variables declared in the declaration block of the subroutines are local or private to the subroutine where they're declared, which means only that subroutine can access them.

Some developers who come from a business perspective of "let's get it done quickly" don't adhere to these guidelines. Unfortunately, packages that don't maximize cohesion and minimize coupling are no better than stand-alone functions and procedures.

Singleton Design Pattern

A Singleton design pattern lets you construct only one instance of an object. It guarantees any subsequent attempt to construct an instance fails until the original object instance is discarded. This pattern is widely used in OOPLs, such as C++, C#, and Java.

You can guarantee a single instance of a package in any session, too. To do so, you simply embed a call to a locally scoped function or procedure as the first step in *all published* functions and procedures. The locally scoped function or procedure holds a local variable that should match a package-level control variable. If the values match, the local function or procedure changes the package-level variable to lock the package.

You also need another locally scoped function or procedure as the last step in all published functions and procedures. The last step resets all package variables to their initial state. The easiest way to accomplish this is to write a procedure that resets the default values for package variables. You call the resetting procedure as the last statement in your published function or procedure.

Don't forget to reset the control variable with the other variables. If you forget to reset the control variable, the package will be locked until the end of the session or until it ages out of the SGA.

Types

As with the package specification, you can declare dynamic or static data types in package bodies. Data types are typically PL/SQL structures, collections, reference cursors, and cursors. You can declare dynamic data types by anchoring them to row or column declarations, as outlined in the "Attribute and Table Anchoring" section of Chapter 3. You declare static data types when types are explicitly declared as SQL data types.

Package bodies are dependent on their package specification. They are also dependent on other schema-level objects that they use in their implementation of components. The behaviors of types in the package body are consistent with those of the package specification, with one exception: PL/SQL blocks outside of the package body can't access elements declared in the package body.

Components: Functions and Procedures

Components are implementations of published functions or procedures or they are declarations or definitions of package-only functions or procedures. You can also declare local components inside published or package-only functions or procedures.

Declaring something before the implementation is called forward referencing (or a prototype), a complete example of which is provided in the sidebar "Forward Referencing" earlier in this chapter. When you define local components, you provide both their declaration and their implementation. Sometimes you need to declare a component before you're ready to implement it. You do this by providing a forward-referencing stub for a function or procedure.

Components can only specify whether they are autonomous transactions or local transactions. Local transactions run inside a pre-existing transaction scope. Autonomous transactions run discretely in their own transaction scope. By default, all functions and procedures are local transactions unless you declare them as autonomous transactions. The `AUTONOMOUS_TRANSACTION` precompiler directive declares a function or procedure as autonomous.

Only published functions or procedures can be called from PL/SQL blocks that are external to the package. Package-level functions can be called from three types of components: published components, package-level components, or local components. Local components are declared and implemented (*or defined*) inside a published or package-level component. Another option is to define a local component inside another local component. Chapter 8 covers the rules governing how you declare and implement functions and procedures.

The `components` package specification declares only a *getter* function and a *setter* procedure. A *getter* component simply gets something from the black box, while a *setter* component sets an initial value or resets an existing value inside the black box. These are stock terms in OOP. As you've discovered earlier in this chapter, they also apply well to PL/SQL packages that are declared as non–serially reusable.

The `components` package specification is

```
SQL> CREATE OR REPLACE PACKAGE components IS
       PROCEDURE set (value VARCHAR2); -- Declare published procedure.
       FUNCTION get RETURN VARCHAR2;   -- Declare published function.
     END components;
     /
```

Functions are almost always declared before procedures in PL/SQL, but their sequencing is meaningless inside a package specification. It is meaningful when you declare them as local functions and procedures because of forward-referencing possibilities.

The `components` package body adds a package-level function, a package-level procedure, and two shared variables. One variable is provided to demonstrate how you would implement a Singleton pattern in a PL/SQL package. The other variable contains a value that should always have an initial value.

The `components` package body is

```
SQL> CREATE OR REPLACE PACKAGE BODY components IS
       -- Declare package scoped shared variables.
       key NUMBER := 0;
       variable VARCHAR2(20) := 'Initial Value';
       -- Define package-only function and procedure.
       FUNCTION locked RETURN BOOLEAN IS
         key NUMBER := 0;
       BEGIN
         IF components.key = key THEN
           components.key := 1;
           RETURN FALSE;
         ELSE
           RETURN TRUE;
         END IF;
       END locked;
       PROCEDURE unlock IS
         key NUMBER := 1;
       BEGIN
         IF components.key = key THEN
           components.key := 0;          -- Reset the key.
           variable := 'Initial Value'; -- Reset initial value of shared variable.
         END IF;
       END unlock;
```

```
  -- Define published function and procedure.
  FUNCTION get RETURN VARCHAR2 IS
  BEGIN
    RETURN variable;
  END get;
  PROCEDURE set (value VARCHAR2) IS
  BEGIN
    IF NOT locked THEN
      variable := value;
      dbms_output.put_line('The new value until release is ['||get||'].');
      unlock;
    END IF;
  END set;
END components;
/
```

The key action occurs in the set procedure. It locks the package to change, changes a shared variable, gets a copy of the temporary value (also known as a *transitive value*) of the shared variable, and unlocks the package. The unlock procedure resets the control key and resets the shared package variable.

You can test this by first creating a session or bind variable:

```
SQL> VARIABLE current_content VARCHAR2(20)
```

After setting the bind variable, you call the function and return the value into the bind variable. A SELECT statement lets you see the initial package value, as shown:

```
SQL> CALL components.get() INTO :current_content;
SQL> SELECT :current_content AS contents FROM dual;
```

It returns the following:

```
CONTENTS
------------------
Initial Value
```

The temporary value is printed to console when you call the set procedure. At least, it is printed when you've enabled SERVEROUTPUT first.

```
SQL> SET SERVEROUTPUT ON SIZE UNLIMITED
SQL> EXECUTE components.set('New Value');
```

The output should look like this:

```
The new value until release is [New Value].
```

A subsequent call to the get function returns the original value of the package variable. The components package implements a Singleton pattern for shared package variables.

The locked function and unlock procedure ensure that the package state is always the same. You are able to call the set procedure to change a variable, and then see the change with a call to the get function. This is not possible when the package is serially reusable. A call to the get function inside the set function always grabs a new copy of the package when the package is declared serially reusable.

The `components` package demonstrates an approach to managing shared package variables between calls. In this example, the shared package variable behaves like an instance variable in a user-defined object. As mentioned earlier in this chapter, Chapter 11 covers user-defined objects. Clearly, this is a lot of work to share a variable and guarantee that the next call to the package finds the same initial value.

You can add a package-level log procedure and make it autonomous by adding the following at the bottom of the `components` package body:

```
37     PROCEDURE log (value VARCHAR2) IS
38       PRAGMA AUTONOMOUS_TRANSACTION; -- Set autonomous behavior.
39     BEGIN
40       /* Write the value in the log. */
41       INSERT INTO logger VALUES (value);
42       /* Commit the record in the autonomous session. */
43       COMMIT;
44     END;
45   END components;
```

Line 38 designates the `log` procedure of the `components` package as an autonomous transaction. That means its state is outside the rest of the package. After writing to the `logger` table, the autonomous `log` procedure must commit its work on line 43 because its transaction scope is outside of any other call to the `components` package.

Aside from showing you how to implement the Singleton pattern, this code demonstrates how you call package-level components through published components. It also shows you how to implement an autonomous procedure in a package. The package-level components are hidden package-level components.

Review Section

This section has described the following points about the package body:

- Package bodies implement public functions and procedures.
- Package bodies can't set the `AUTHID` and `ACCESSIBLE BY` clauses, which are only set in the package specifications.
- Private functions and procedures are only accessible through public functions and procedures from external callers, or from other package functions and procedures.
- Public and private package variables maintain state while the package remains in the SGA.
- Public and private functions and procedures may be designated to run in the local session, the default, or in a separate session. You must add an `AUTONOMOUS_TRANSACTION` precompiler directive to make a function or procedure within the package run in a separate session.
- You can implement a package as a Singleton design pattern, but it would be better to use an object type because that's really the purpose of an object type in an ORDBMS database.
- Protected variables are declared at the package level, and private variables are declared as local variables in individual functions and procedures.
- Serially reusable packages can't be called from a `SELECT` statement.

Definer vs. Invoker Rights Mechanics

Earlier references have touched on the concepts of definer rights and invoker rights. These are models of operation. The default model of operation for stored programs is definer rights. Definer rights programs act on catalog objects that are declared in the same schema. They perform with all the privileges of the schema owner.

A definer rights model does not dictate that all declared catalog objects must be owned by the same schema as the package owner. Synonyms may point to catalog objects owned by another user if that other user has granted privileges to their catalog objects. Catalog objects can be functions, packages, procedures, materialized views, sequences, tables, or views. Figure 9-2 shows you a visual representation of a definer rights model where all the catalog objects are owned by the same user.

A schema is a container of stored programs. The schema grants access to stored programs, or *black boxes*, through privileges. External users may create synonyms to simplify call statements to external programs. Synonyms only translate (*resolve*) when grants, stored programs, and catalog objects are valid in the owning schema. The combination of synonyms and grants lets external users call programs with inputs and retrieve output from stored program in another schema.

The definer rights model is ideal when you want to deploy a single set of stored programs that act on local catalog objects. Alternatively, it also works when you want to have all access centralized in a single schema. The centralized access model is a bit more complex because the access schema may contain synonyms that point to stored programs in other schemas. The stored programs in turn have definer rights on catalog objects in their own schema.

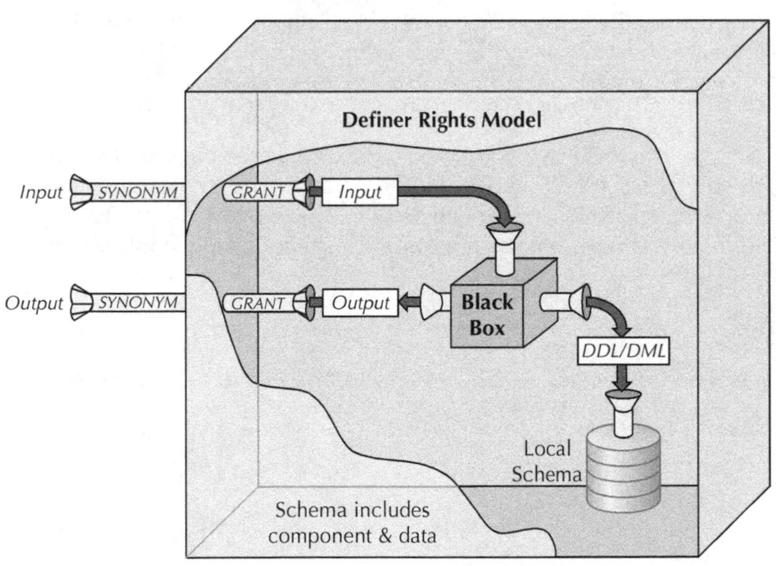

FIGURE 9-2. *Definer rights model of operation with local catalog objects*

Grants and Synonyms

Assume you have a package named manage_items declared and implemented as a definer rights program in your video PDB schema. You want to create a second schema called purchasing and let the purchasing user access the manage_items package. There are two steps required to make access seamless to the manage_items package.

The first step requires you to connect as the video user and grant the EXECUTE privilege on the manage_items package to the new purchasing schema. The following command grants that privilege:

```
GRANT EXECUTE ON manage_items TO purchasing;
```

After you grant the EXECUTE privilege on the package, the purchasing user can access the package. However, the purchasing user must prepend the video schema name and a component selector to see the package, as follows:

```
SQL> DESCRIBE video.manage_items
```

TIP
You have limited privileges when grants are made through roles. Functions and procedures that contain SQL statements may fail at runtime when grants are not explicit privileges.

You can dispense with the schema name and component selector by creating a SYNONYM in the purchasing schema. A SYNONYM translates an alias to a fully qualified reference, like video.manage_items. You create a synonym using the same name as the package as follows:

```
CREATE SYNONYM manage_items FOR video.manage_items;
```

After you create the synonym, you can describe the package by using the SYNONYM. This lets you dispense with prepending the schema name and component selector to packages or any other catalog object. You can grant the EXECUTE privilege to all other users by substituting the schema name with PUBLIC. The following grants permissions to all other database users:

```
GRANT EXECUTE ON manage_items TO PUBLIC;
```

Grants and synonyms are powerful tools. You can find GRANT definitions in the USER_TAB_PRIVS administrative view. SYNONYM values are in the USER_SYNONYMS view.

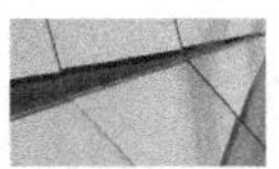

NOTE
A centralized access schema is exactly how the Oracle E-Business Suite runs.

More or less, the definer rights model lets individual users act on subsets of data that are stored in a common repository. You implement the definer rights model by having your stored programs control access and authentication by using the `dbms_application_info` package to set the `client_info` column in `V$SESSION`. The stored programs stripe the data by adding a column that ties to the user's organization or business entity.

The invoker rights model requires you to set the `AUTHID` value to `CURRENT_USER` in any schema-level program. This approach requires that you identify all catalog objects that are dependencies of invoker rights programs. After identifying the dependencies, you must replicate those catalog objects to any schema that wants to call the invoker rights programs. This requirement is due to the fact that *invoker rights models resolve by using the caller's privileges, not the definer's privileges*.

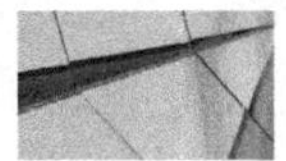

NOTE
Database triggers and functions called from within views are always executed with definer rights and run with the privileges of the user that owns the triggering table or view.

You choose an invoker rights mode of operation to support distributed data repositories. A single code repository can use grants and synonyms to bridge transactions across a network by using a `DB_LINK`. A `DB_LINK` lets you resolve a network alias through the `tnsnames.ora` file to find another Oracle database. Appendix A describes how to configure and use the `tnsnames.ora` file.

The invoker rights model best supports data that is stored in a separate user schema. It is also ideal for distributed database solutions when they're running in the same instance. There are significant limitations to remote calls when making remote procedure calls that use database links.

Review Section

This section has described the following points about the comparison of definer vs. invoker rights mechanics:

- Definer rights programs work with the data in their own schema generally, while invoker rights programs work with local data.
- Definer rights programs run in their own schema, and you must grant the `EXECUTE` privilege to other users that you would like to allow to use a definer rights program.
- A `GRANT` gives the privilege to run a definer rights package.
- A `SYNONYM` puts the schema name and component selector in the data catalog and gives the package a name in the context of another user's schema.

Remote Calls

Remote calls are made from one database instance to another. You make remote calls through database links (DB_LINK). A user must have the CREATE DATABASE LINK privilege to create a database link. You grant the privilege, as the SYSTEM user, by using the following syntax:

```
GRANT CREATE DATABASE LINK TO schema_name;
```

After granting this to a schema, you can create a database link to another schema. The prototype to create a DB_LINK is

```
CREATE DATABASE LINK db_link_name
CONNECT TO schema_name IDENTIFIED BY schema_password
USING 'tns_names_alias'
```

A database link is a static object in the database. It stores the schema name and password to resolve a remote connection. You must update database links whenever the remote database changes its schema's password. Database links can reference other database instances or a different schema of the same database.

The examples in this sidebar use a DB_LINK named loopback, which allows you to reconnect to the same instance. You don't need to change anything in the tnsnames.ora file to make a loopback database link work. However, there are some rules on the calls that you can make using a remote connection. You can call schema-level components provided that they don't require arguments.

For example, you call a remote status function by using the following syntax when using the loopback database link:

SQL:

```
SELECT status@loopback FROM dual;
```

PL/SQL:

```
BEGIN
  dbms_output.put_line('Status ['||status@loopback||']');
END;
/
```

The remote schema-level component can contain DDL or DML statements. You cannot return a handle to a LOB. Any attempt to do so raises an ORA-22992 exception that says you can't use a LOB locator selected from a remote table.

Managing Packages in the Database Catalog

As databases grow, so do the stored programs that support them. Whether you choose to implement a definer or invoker rights solution, understanding what you've added to your schema is very important. The next three sections show you how to find, validate, and describe packages, check their dependencies, and choose a validation method in the Oracle Database 12c database.

Finding, Validating, and Describing Packages

The CDB_, ALL_, DBA_, and USER_OBJECTS administrative views let you find packages. They also let you validate whether a package specification or body is valid or invalid. Rather than create new code artifacts, the example in this section uses the pipelined package and pf function created in the "PIPELINED Clause" section of Chapter 8.

The following query lets you check whether package specifications and bodies have been created and are valid. The SQL*Plus column formatting ensures the output is readable in one 80-column screen.

```
COLUMN object_name FORMAT A10
SELECT   object_name
,        object_type
,        last_ddl_time
,        timestamp
,        status
FROM     user_objects
WHERE    object_name IN ('PIPELINED','PF');
```

This query should return data like this:

```
OBJECT_NAME OBJECT_TYPE          LAST_DDL_ TIMESTAMP           STATUS
----------- ------------------- --------- ------------------- ------
PF          FUNCTION             03-JAN-08 2008-01-03:22:50:23 VALID
PIPELINED   PACKAGE              03-JAN-08 2008-01-03:22:50:19 VALID
PIPELINED   PACKAGE BODY         03-JAN-08 2008-01-03:22:50:20 VALID
```

If you put an extraneous character in the pipelined package body, it will fail when you run it. After attempting to compile an incorrect package body, requery the data and you should see something like this:

```
OBJECT_NAME OBJECT_TYPE          LAST_DDL_ TIMESTAMP           STATUS
----------- ------------------- --------- ------------------- -------
PF          FUNCTION             03-JAN-08 2008-01-03:22:50:23 VALID
PIPELINED  PACKAGE              03-JAN-08 2008-01-03:22:50:19 VALID
PIPELINED  PACKAGE BODY         03-JAN-08 2008-01-03:22:53:34 INVALID
```

The invalid package body does not invalidate the pf function because the pf function is dependent on the package specification, not the package body. You should fix the pipelined package body and recompile it before attempting the next step.

If you now put an extraneous character in the pipelined package specification, it fails when you try to compile it. Requerying the data from the USER_SOURCE view tells you that the dependent package body and pf function are also invalid:

```
OBJECT_NAME OBJECT_TYPE          LAST_DDL_ TIMESTAMP           STATUS
----------- ------------------- --------- ------------------- -------
PF          FUNCTION             03-JAN-08 2008-01-03:22:50:23 INVALID
PIPELINED   PACKAGE              03-JAN-08 2008-01-03:23:06:10 INVALID
PIPELINED   PACKAGE BODY         03-JAN-08 2008-01-03:22:53:34 INVALID
```

You can rebuild the pipelined package by running the pipelined.sql script located on the McGraw-Hill Professional website. You will find that the pf function is still invalid in the database catalog after you recompile the package specification and body (which would not be the case if you reran the script).

You can validate the pf function by an explicit compilation statement like

```
ALTER FUNCTION pf COMPILE;
```

Or, you can simply call the function as follows, which validates that its dependent objects are valid before running the statement. This is known as a *lazy compile* but is actually called automatic recompilation.

```
SELECT * FROM TABLE(pf);
```

You can describe the package like you would a table or view from SQL*Plus:

```
SQL> DESCRIBE pipelined
```

It returns the following:

```
FUNCTION PF RETURNS ACCOUNT_COLLECTION
```

You may notice that the record and collection type declared in the package specification aren't displayed. This is normal. As stated in the "Package Specification" section earlier in the chapter, you must query the CDB_, ALL_, DBA_, or USER_SOURCE administrative view to find the complete package declaration. Wrapped package bodies will be returned from that query as gibberish that you should discard.

This section has shown you how to find, validate, and describe packages. The next section explores checking dependencies.

Checking Dependencies

The CDB_, ALL_, DBA_, and USER_DEPENDENCIES administrative views let you examine dependencies between stored programs. As done in the previous section, the example here uses the pipelined package and pf function created in the "PIPELINED Clause" section of Chapter 8.

The following query lets you see the dependencies for the pf function. The SQL*Plus column formatting ensures that the output is readable in one 80-column screen.

```
COLUMN name FORMAT A10
COLUMN type FORMAT A8
COLUMN referenced_name FORMAT A30
COLUMN referenced_type FORMAT A10
COLUMN dependency_type FORMAT A4
SELECT  name
,       type
,       referenced_name
,       referenced_type
,       dependency_type
FROM    user_dependencies
WHERE   name = 'PF';
```

The analyzed output from the returned `user_dependencies` table is displayed in the following illustration. The `pf` function has a direct hard dependency on the `pipelined` package and two direct hard dependencies on the `contact` and `member` tables. The two tables are referenced in the `FROM` clause of the `CURSOR` declared in the `pf` function.

```
NAME        TYPE     REFERENCED_NAME                 REFERENCED DEPE
----------------------------------------------------------------
PF          FUNCTION STANDARD                        PACKAGE    HARD
PF          FUNCTION SYS_STUB_FOR_PURITY_ANALYSIS    PACKAGE    HARD
PF          FUNCTION PLITBLM                         SYNONYM    HARD
PF          FUNCTION CONTACT                         TABLE      HARD
PF          FUNCTION MEMBER                          TABLE      HARD
PF          FUNCTION PIPELINED                       PACKAGE    HARD

6 rows selected.
```

These dependencies are set because of the cursor in the function.

This dependency is on record type found in the package specification.

This section has shown you how to find the dependencies between stored programs. The combination of the two sources should enable you to determine what your dependencies are and their respective frequency.

Comparing Validation Methods: Timestamp vs. Signature

Stored programs are validated or invalidated by using a timestamp or signature method. The timestamp method is the default for most Oracle databases. The timestamp method compares the `last_ddl_time` column, which you can check in the `CDB_`, `ALL_`, `DBA_`, or `USER_OBJECT` view. When the base object has a newer timestamp than that of the dependent object, the dependent object will be recompiled.

Dates and timestamps always provide some interesting twists and turns. When you are working in a distributed situation and the two database instances are in different time zones, the comparison may be invalid. You may also encounter unnecessary recompilations when distributed servers are in the same time zone. Dependent objects are compiled even when the change in the `last_ddl_time` column didn't result in a change of the base object.

Another complication with timestamp validation occurs when PL/SQL is distributed between the server and Oracle Forms. In this case, a change in the base code can't trigger recompilation because it isn't included in the runtime version of the Oracle Form.

The alternative to timestamp validation is the signature method. This method works by comparing the signature of schema-level and package-level functions and procedures. You must alter the database as a privileged user to convert the database to signature method validation. You would use the following command syntax:

```
ALTER SYSTEM SET REMOTE_DEPENDENCIES_MODE = SIGNATURE;
```

NOTE
You must hold the `ALTER SYSTEM` privilege to issue this command.

This command changes the `remote_dependencies_mode` parameter in your `spfile.ora` or `pfile.ora` configuration file. If you want the change to be permanent, you should change it in your configuration file.

Signature method works by checking whether the base object signature changes between compilation events. If there is a change, it will force compilation of dependent packages. You can find the signature information in the `CDB_`, `ALL_`, `DBA_`, and `USER_ARGUMENTS` views.

NOTE
Remote procedure calls may raise an `ORA-04062` exception when a remote database uses timestamp mode rather than signature mode.

The timestamp method is ideal for centralized environments. The signature method is sometimes more effective for centralized development environments but generally is a preferred solution in distributed database applications.

Review Section

This section has described the following points about how you can manage packages in the database catalog:

- You can use the database catalog to discover the presence and status of functions, procedures, and packages.
- The `DESCRIBE` command lets you see the published functions and procedures of both stand-alone packages and package units.
- Oracle supports two validation methods for functions, procedures, and packages: the timestamp method and the signature method.
- The timestamp method of validation doesn't work well when the servers use different time zones, and you should switch to the signature method of validation when working in a distributed situation.

Summary

This chapter has shown you why packages are the backbone of Oracle Database 12c application development. You've learned how to group functions and procedures into libraries that include overloading. You've also learned the difference between package and local variables, types, and components, and you've seen how to plan and manage these features.

Mastery Check

The mastery check is a series of true-or-false and multiple-choice questions that let you confirm how well you understand the material in the chapter. You may check Appendix I for answers to these questions.

True or False:

1. ___Package specifications can define only functions and procedures.
2. ___Package bodies can define variables, data types, functions, and procedures.
3. ___You define functions or procedures in package specifications and implement them in package bodies.
4. ___You define function stubs and provide their implementations in package bodies.
5. ___A forward reference is required for any function or procedure to avoid inadvertent use before its implementation in the package body.
6. ___A grant of `EXECUTE` on a package lets a user in another schema run a definer rights package against the definer's local data.
7. ___A `SYNONYM` provides an alias for a privilege.
8. ___A package must contain all autonomous and non-autonomous functions and procedures.
9. ___A package maintains a variable's value until it's aged out of the SGA or you issue a `FLUSH VARIABLE` *`variable_name`* statement.
10. ___You can query a serially reusable package from a `SELECT` statement.

Multiple Choice:

11. Which of the following is a `PRAGMA` (precompiler directive) reserved to packages? (Multiple answers possible)
    - **A.** `AUTONOMOUS_TRANSACTION`
    - **B.** `AUTO_TRANSACTION`
    - **C.** `SERIALLY_REUSABLE`
    - **D.** `EXCEPTION_INIT`
    - **E.** `ACCESSIBLE_BY`
12. Which of the following can be defined in a package specification? (Multiple answers possible)
    - **A.** An object type
    - **B.** A record type
    - **C.** A function
    - **D.** A procedure
    - **E.** An autonomous function
13. Which of the following is a publically accessible variable? (Multiple answers possible)
    - **A.** A variable declared in a function of a package
    - **B.** A variable declared in a procedure of a package
    - **C.** A variable declared in a package specification
    - **D.** A variable declared in a package body outside of a function or procedure
    - **E.** All of the above

14. Which of the following support overloading? (Multiple answers possible)
    - A. Stand-alone functions
    - B. Stand-alone procedures
    - C. Functions declared in the package specification
    - D. Procedures declared in the package specification
    - E. Functions declared in the package body
15. Which of the following guarantees variables are fresh each time you call a package? (Multiple answers possible)
    - A. A declaring the variables in an autonomous function
    - B. A declaring the variables in a local procedure
    - C. A declaring the variables in a local function
    - D. A declaring the variables outside a function or procedure in a package body
    - E. A declaring the variables outside a function or procedure in a package specification

CHAPTER 10

Large Objects

Large objects (LOBs) are powerful data structures that let you store text, images, music, and video in the database. Oracle Database 11*g* dramatically changed the LOB landscape by reengineering how large objects work. Oracle Database 12*c* builds upon those changes by optimizing the engines that support LOBs. They're now faster and more secure (*SecureFiles*). You can now define Binary LOB (BLOB), Character LOB (CLOB), or National Character LOB (NCLOB) columns in SecureFiles when you create a table or alter it.

LOBs can hold up to a maximum of 8 to 128 terabytes, depending on how you configure your database's db_block_size parameter. Oracle Database 12*c* lets you set db_block_size to a value of 2KB to 32KB. The values are multiples of two—2KB, 4KB, 8KB, 16KB, and 32KB. The default value for db_block_size is 8KB. This formula sets the maximum size of large objects in an instance:

*Maximum size = (4GB – 1) * db_block_size*

You can find your database instance's maximum LOB size with a call to the dbms_lob package's get_storage_limit function. You can store these LOBs in BLOB or CLOB variables or columns, or you can store them outside the database as BFILE (binary file) columns. BFILE columns actually store a locator that points to the physical location of an external file. The "Large Strings" section in Appendix B covers the storage syntax for LOBs. LOBs are stored in segments within the database, which are effectively rows in specialized tables.

Oracle Database 11*g*, Release 2, added new methods to the dbms_lob package to support SecureFiles. While this chapter focuses on LOB management, it limits the coverage of SecureFiles to only the new methods in the dbms_lob package. You can read more about SecureFiles by consulting the *Oracle Database SecureFiles and Large Objects Developer's Guide 12c Release*.

This chapter explains how to use PL/SQL to work with the different LOB data types. It covers these topics:

- Working with internally stored large object types
- Reading files into internally stored columns
- Working with binary files (BFILEs)
- Understanding the dbms_lob package

The concepts governing how you use BLOB, CLOB, and NCLOB data types are very similar. That's why you'll examine how to work with internally stored large object types first. Then, you'll work with reading large files into internally stored CLOB and BLOB data types. CLOB and NCLOB data types are covered first since they let you focus on managing transactions with large blocks of text. The BLOB data type comes second because the concepts build on those presented for character large objects. BLOBs store binary documents, like Adobe PDF (Portable Document Format) files, images, and movies, inside the database. Access and display of the BLOB files is supplemented by using the PHP programming language to render images in web pages.

After your introduction to internally managed LOBs, you'll learn how to set up, configure, read, and maintain BFILE data types. They require more effort in some ways because the catalog only stores locator data, and you have to guarantee their physical presence in the file system. The dbms_lob package is discussed last because not all the functions are necessary to show how to use large objects. Each section builds on the former, but you should be able to use each section as a quick reference, too.

Working with Internally Stored LOB Types

The CLOB, NCLOB, and BLOB data types can define a column in a table or nested table. As described, they have a maximum physical size between 8 and 128 terabytes, which is stored in segments defined by the table's STORAGE clause. The "Large Strings" section in Appendix B covers the LOB storage clause.

The CLOB and NCLOB data types let you store large text files. The difference between them is that the NCLOB must qualify the character set of the text. Large text data types serve many purposes, such as holding a chapter in a book, a book in a library, or an XML fragment. The BLOB data type lets you store large binary files, like images, music tracks, movies, or PDF files.

This section examines how you work with these LOB data types. XML types, a CLOB subclass, aren't covered here. You can refer to the *Oracle XML DB Developer's Guide 12c Release* for direction on using these types to support XML.

LOB Assignments Under 32K

CLOB, NCLOB, and BLOB columns are usually stored separately from the rest of the row in a table. Only the descriptor or locator is physically stored in the column. The locator points to where the physical contents of a LOB are stored and provides a reference to a private work area in the SGA. This work area allows us to scroll through the content and write new chunks of data. Some of the Oracle documentation for earlier versions of Oracle Database use *descriptor* to refer to the CLOB, NCLOB, and BLOB locator, and use *locator* when referring to working with external BFILEs. Oracle Database 12*c* documentation begins to consistently label both as locators.

The CLOB, NCLOB, and BLOB data types are object types. They require implicit or explicit construction. Both SQL and PL/SQL support implicit and explicit construction of CLOB and NCLOB data types from VARCHAR2 data types, NVARCHAR2 data types, or string literals. They also support implicit and explicit construction of BLOB data types from hexadecimal string literals. Neither SQL nor PL/SQL supports implicit assignment from a LONG data type to a CLOB or NCLOB data type. For reference, the TO_CHAR function and SELECT-INTO statement also can't convert a LONG column value into a long string or convert a LONG RAW column value into a long binary string. The "Converting a LONG to a CLOB" sidebar later in this chapter shows you how to use the dbms_sql package to make the conversion from a LONG data type to a CLOB data type.

You can implicitly construct a CLOB or NCLOB variable by assigning a number or character type. When assigning a number, the number is first cast to a character type and then converted to a CLOB data type. Character conversion for CHAR, NCHAR, NVARCHAR2, and VARCHAR2 data types is constrained by the SQL or PL/SQL environments. *SQL restricts you to a 4,000-byte conversion when the max_string_size parameter is set to STANDARD, whereas SQL with a max_string_size parameter set to EXTENDED and PL/SQL let you convert 32,767 bytes of character data.*

While there is no direct constructor that lets you create a new CLOB instance with a physical size greater than the 32,767-byte environment limit, you can use the dbms_lob package to do so. The dbms_lob package provides two approaches to writing CLOB, NCLOB, and BLOB data types. One approach writes the whole LOB at one time, and the other writes it piece by piece. For example, you can initialize a new instance through the write procedure of the dbms_lob built-in package, and then use the append procedure to add data. The package is available within PL/SQL, Java, or any C-callable language. Java accesses the dbms_lob package through the JDBC (Java Database Connectivity) library and accesses C-callable programs through the OCI (Oracle Call Interface) libraries.

Small LOB Assignments

The next two subsections show you how to assign values to BLOB, CLOB, and NCLOB data types. For the latter two data types, I've opted to show only the assignment to a CLOB because the assignment to a CLOB and the assignment to an NCLOB work the same way.

CLOB or NCLOB PL/SQL Assignments The following anonymous block shows you how to declare a CLOB variable in a PL/SQL program block, a refresher from material in Chapter 4:

```
SQL> DECLARE
  2    var1 CLOB;                        -- Declare a null reference to a CLOB.
  3    var2 CLOB := empty_clob();        -- Declare an empty CLOB.
  4    var3 CLOB := 'some_string';       -- Declare a CLOB with a string literal.
  5  BEGIN
  6    ...
  7  END;
  8  /
```

In a PL/SQL context, it's possible to declare a CLOB with a null value, an initialized empty CLOB, or with a string value in a SQL or PL/SQL scope. Line 2 assigns a null value to var1, line 3 assigns an empty CLOB object type to var2, and line 4 assigns a string literal to var3. It's also possible to make a left-to-right assignment with the SELECT-INTO statement in PL/SQL, or to read a file directly into a LOB with the dbms_lob package. As mentioned earlier, the SELECT-INTO statement doesn't support the assignment of a LONG data type to a CLOB or NCLOB data type.

Unfortunately, only the dbms_lob package lets you assign strings that are longer than 32,767 bytes. You can assign very large strings (greater than 32,767 bytes) by using the manipulation procedures of the dbms_lob package. The "Manipulation Methods" section later in this chapter describes how you can write very large strings.

You also have the ability to read an external file and assign its contents to a CLOB or NCLOB data type. The loadfromfile and loadclobfromfile procedures in the dbms_lob package support a direct assignment from external files. Flip forward to the "Reading Files into Internally Stored Columns" section of this chapter for more information on how to assign files to CLOB and NCLOB data types.

Unfortunately, the SQL context isn't as flexible. SQL doesn't support a SELECT-INTO statement, and SQL can't work with the dbms_lob package's manipulation procedures. That's because SQL can't support a call to a *pass-by-reference* procedure, which only works in a PL/SQL, ODBC, OCI, or JDBC context. In SQL, you have three options:

- You can assign a string literal that is less than 32,767 bytes in length in the VALUES clause of an INSERT statement or as a column value of a SELECT-list in an INSERT statement.
- You can assign an empty_clob constructor function call in the VALUES clause of an INSERT statement or as a column value of a SELECT-list in an INSERT statement.
- You can assign an initialized CLOB data type through a *pass-by-value* PL/SQL function or PL/SQL function wrapper of a C-callable program in the VALUES clause of an INSERT statement or as a column value of a SELECT-list in an INSERT statement.

BLOB PL/SQL Assignments As with the CLOB and NCLOB data types, you have three ways to declare a BLOB data type in a PL/SQL context. The following anonymous block shows you how to declare a BLOB:

```
SQL> DECLARE
  2    var1 BLOB;                      -- Declare a null reference to a BLOB.
  3    var2 BLOB := empty_blob();      -- Declare an empty BLOB.
  4    var3 BLOB := '43'||'41'||'52'; -- Declare with hexadecimal values.
  5  BEGIN
  6    ...
  7  END;
  8  /
```

Declaring a BLOB with a null reference on line 2 mirrors the syntax for a CLOB or NCLOB. Line 2 declares an empty BLOB with an empty_blob function call, rather than an empty_clob function call. Although you can assign hexadecimal values to a BLOB, you're unlikely to encounter a scenario in which that's called for. It's also possible to assign a value from a RAW column, but RAW columns are deprecated. RAW columns are small, at no more than 32,760 bytes, which is generally too small for real binary streams.

SQL provides you three options that are similar to those you have when assigning very large strings to CLOB and NCLOB data types. You can use a hexadecimal string sequence when the binary stream is smaller than 32,767 bytes. You can use an empty_blob function call to initialize a column or variable. You also can use a pass-by-value PL/SQL function when the binary stream is larger than 32,767 bytes, provided that the function returns an initialized large binary stream.

It's much more likely that you'll assign binary files to BLOB columns. That's done with the loadblobfromfile procedure in the dbms_lob package. This chapter covers that process in the "Reading Local Files into BLOB Columns" section.

LOB Assignments over 32K

This section covers how you assign large strings and binary streams to CLOB, NCLOB, and BLOB data types. The mechanics differ from those used for LOB assignments under 32K because the limits of SQL*Plus restrict how you can insert or update them. The dbms_lob package makes it possible for you to assign an initial chunk of data and then append other chunks data until you have loaded all chunks of data for a long string or binary stream.

Initializing an Object

You declare a scalar variable by assigning a type and value. You call a function by passing actual parameters. However, you declare an object instance by calling a specialized function that initializes an object type. Initialized object types are objects or object instances.

The process of initializing an object type is known as *constructing an object*. Construction occurs by calling a specialized function that typically shares the name of the object type. This specialized function is called a *constructor*. Object-oriented programming lingo uses the terms *initializing* and *constructing* interchangeably. They both mean giving life to an object type.

State	Description
NULL	The column in a table row contains a null value.
Empty	The column contains a LOB locator (or descriptor) that is an empty instance. You can verify an empty LOB by calling the dbms_lob.getlength function. The function returns a 0 value for an empty BLOB, CLOB, or NCLOB column.
Populated	The column contains a LOB locator, and a call to dbms_lob.getlength returns a positive integer value for a BLOB, CLOB, or NCLOB column.

TABLE 10-1. *Possible CLOB, NCLOB, and BLOB Data States*

The CLOB, NCLOB, and BLOB columns differ from columns of scalar data types because they're not limited to NULL or NOT NULL states. CLOB, NCLOB, and BLOB data types are either NULL, *empty*, or *populated*, as qualified in Table 10-1.

LOB Construction for Assignments Greater Than 32,767 Bytes

Inserting a string longer than 32,767 bytes directly into an uninitialized CLOB, NCLOB, or BLOB column isn't supported by the INSERT or UPDATE statement. As discussed, you can insert a very large string into a CLOB or an NCLOB or insert a very large binary stream into a BLOB column (or update the string or the stream). However, you need a PL/SQL function or procedure to insert a very large string or a very large binary stream.

Writing a PL/SQL function is the easiest solution to this type of problem. You could write and use a custom pass-by-value PL/SQL function to create a CLOB or NCLOB. The function would take a table collection of 32,767-byte strings or binary streams and return an appropriate LOB data type. Inside the function, you would use the RETURNING INTO clause with an INSERT or UPDATE statement.

The RETURNING INTO clause has the following prototype (which is illustrated in Figure 10-1):

```
RETURNING call_locator INTO return_locator
```

The *call locator* identifies the LOB column, and the *return locator* provides a duplex (two-way) pipe to write a very large string or binary stream in segments (or parts). Initially, you insert or update with the empty_blob function for a BLOB and the empty_clob function for a CLOB or NCLOB. The empty_blob or empty_clob function ensures the initial value is a LOB, and the RETURNING INTO clause gives you a duplex pipe to write and append data to the LOB column.

You can write very large strings directly to CLOB or NCLOB columns with this approach with the INSERT statement or UPDATE statement when the statement is enclosed in a transaction scope. The INSERT or UPDATE statement starts a transaction, and a COMMIT or ROLLBACK statement ends the transaction scope.

The following INSERT and UPDATE statement prototypes demonstrate a specialized approach to managing LOB data types. They work inside PL/SQL functions or external programming languages, like C, C++, C#, and Java. The RETURNING keyword of the RETURNING INTO clause is awkward at first, but it means *channeling out the column reference into a local variable.*

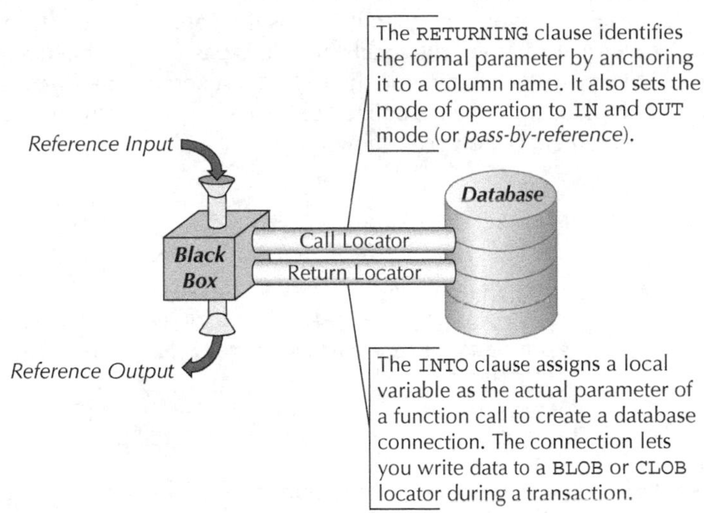

FIGURE 10-1. *The implicit LOB locator function architecture*

INSERT Statement for CLOBs or NCLOBs The `INSERT` statement initializes a `CLOB` column, and then it returns the locator through the `RETURNING INTO` clause into a local variable. The local variable is passed by reference and has an `OUT` mode of operation. You can check Chapter 3 for details on the `OUT` mode of operation, but essentially it disallows the submission of a value to a formal parameter in a function signature. In the `INSERT` statement, the assignment inside the `VALUES` clause acts as part of an `IN` mode operation. As mentioned, the `INSERT` statement starts a transaction scope. You can add to or replace the contents pointed to by the locator during the scope of this transaction.

The `INSERT` statement prototype is shown here:

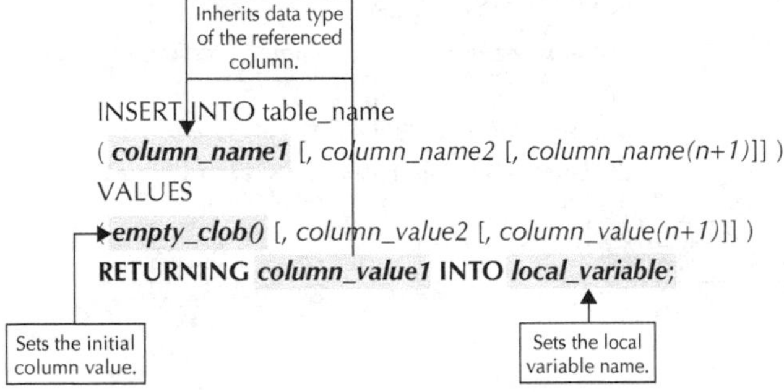

UPDATE Statement for CLOBs or NCLOBs The `UPDATE` statement sets a `CLOB` column value with the `empty_clob` function, and then it returns the column locator through the `RETURNING INTO` clause into a local variable. The local variable is passed by reference and has an `OUT` mode of operation. Like the `INSERT` statement, the `UPDATE` statement also starts a transaction scope. You can add to or replace the contents pointed to by the locator during the scope of this transaction.

The `UPDATE` statement prototype is shown here:

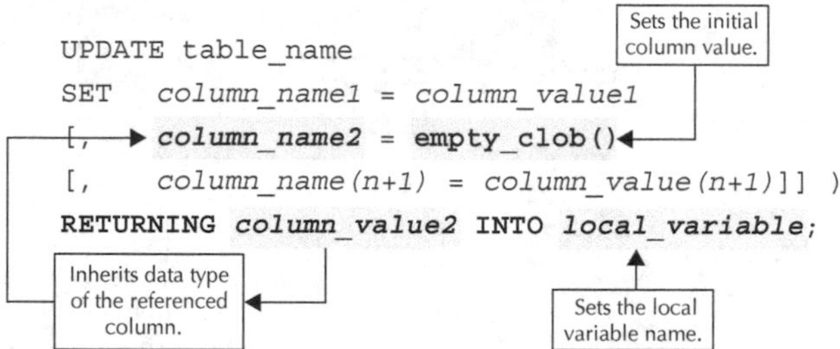

The alternative for the `BLOB` data type is a mirror to what you've just seen with the `CLOB` and `NCLOB` data types. The following sections show you prototypes for an `INSERT` statement and an `UPDATE` statement.

INSERT Statement for BLOBs The `INSERT` statement initializes a `BLOB` column and then it returns the locator through the `RETURNING INTO` clause into a local variable. The local variable is passed by reference and has an `OUT` mode of operation. You can check Chapter 3 for details on the `OUT` mode of operation, but essentially it disallows the submission of a value to a formal parameter in a function signature. In the `INSERT` statement, the assignment inside the `VALUES` clause acts as part of an `IN` mode operation. The `INSERT` statement also starts a transaction scope. You can add to or replace the contents pointed to by the locator during the scope of this transaction.

The `INSERT` statement prototype is shown here:

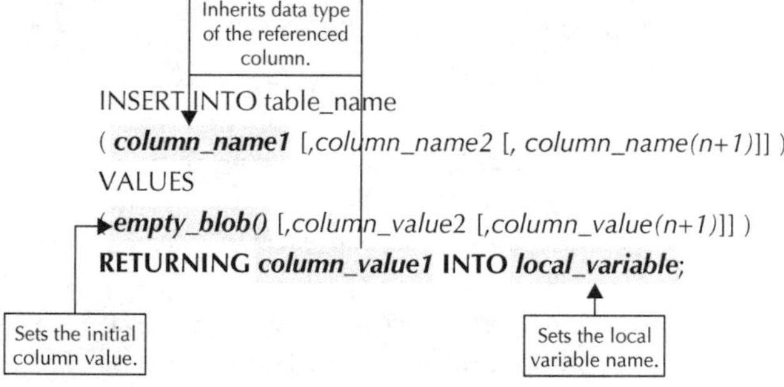

UPDATE Statement for BLOBs The UPDATE statement assumes `column_name2` is a BLOB data type. It sets the BLOB column's value, and then it returns the locator through the RETURNING INTO clause to a local variable. The local variable is passed by reference and has an OUT mode of operation. Like the INSERT statement, the UPDATE statement starts a transaction scope. You can add to or replace the contents pointed to by the locator during the scope of this transaction.

The UPDATE statement prototype is shown here:

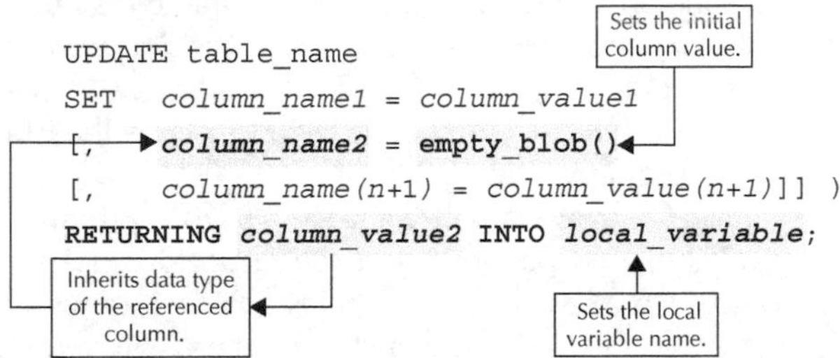

The initial assignment of an `empty_blob` or `empty_clob` function call is generally the most effective way to manage inserting truly large LOB values. It's the suggested approach made in the *Oracle Database Large Objects Developer's Guide*.

The following SQL INSERT statement inserts an `empty_clob` constructor in the `item_desc` column of the `item` table:

```
SQL> INSERT INTO item VALUES
  2  ( item_s1.nextval
  3  ,'ASIN: B00003CXI1'
     ...
  7  ,'Harry Potter and the Sorcerer''s Stone'
  8  ,'Two-Disc Special Edition'
  9  , empty_clob()   -- item_desc column
 10  , empty_blob()   -- item_blob column
 11  ,'PG'
 12  ,'MPAA'
     ...
```

Line 9 inserts an empty CLOB into the `item_desc` column, and line 10 inserts an empty BLOB into the `item_blob` column. Once you've inserted an empty CLOB and BLOB, you can update the columns with the `dbms_lob` package.

A basic UPDATE statement limits you to updating the CLOB or NCLOB column with a string up to 4,000 or 32,767 bytes (depending on the value of the `max_string_size` parameter). At least, it's the limit if you try to assign the result of a VARCHAR2 or NVARCHAR2. The limit decreases when you update a CLOB column with a LONG variable or a BLOB column with a LONG RAW variable. That's because they both have a limit of 32,760 bytes. You can eliminate the maximum limit by writing a stored function that creates a CLOB, NCLOB, or BLOB variable and returns it as its function result.

Converting a LONG to a CLOB

Converting a LONG data type column to a CLOB data type requires several steps. Converting a LONG isn't done too frequently because LONG columns exist only in Oracle tables. LONG columns typically support view text and database trigger bodies.

Oracle has been warning through several releases of the database that LONG columns will be deprecated. Although LONG columns exist in Oracle Database 12*c*, Oracle new features don't provide new tools for converting them. The to_char function doesn't support a call parameter of a LONG data type. The SELECT-INTO statement can't assign the value of a LONG column to a local variable. You still must use the dbms_sql package to convert LONG values to ordinary strings.

A complete solution for converting a LONG to a CLOB is provided next. It wraps the dbms_utility package's new pass-by-reference expand_sql_text procedure, which Oracle designed to take a view with dependencies on other views and return a query based only on tables. Oracle's design of the expand_sql_text procedure poses a hurdle because views are currently stored in LONG columns, which are difficult to convert to other string data types. Only the dbms_sql package (see Chapter 13) supports converting LONG data types to VARCHAR2, CLOB, or NCLOB data types. The wrapping procedure takes a view name, converts the LONG to a CLOB, calls the new procedure, and returns a CLOB data type with final results.

The solution is a pass-by-value function, which means it can be embedded in a query. It uses a local function to verify a *view* name because the dbms_assert package only lets you verify a table or view name. There are several advanced tricks in this solution, and the comments should help illustrate them for you. As mentioned, the function contains a forward reference to dbms_sql material that's covered in Chapter 13. Key code lines using dbms_sql appear in bold text. Please check that material if you have any questions on the use of dbms_sql to generate dynamic SQL statements.

```
SQL> CREATE OR REPLACE FUNCTION expand_sql_text
( pv_view_name      VARCHAR2 )
RETURN CLOB AS

  /* Declare containers for views. */
  lv_input_view   CLOB;
  lv_output_view  CLOB;

  /* Declare a variable, because of the limit of SELECT-INTO. */
  lv_long_view  LONG;

  /* Declare local variables for dynamic SQL. */
  lv_cursor     INTEGER := dbms_sql.open_cursor;
  lv_feedback   INTEGER;          -- Acknowledgement of dynamic execution
  lv_length     INTEGER;          -- Length of string
  lv_return     CLOB;             -- Function output
  lv_stmt       VARCHAR2(2000);   -- Dynamic SQL statement
  lv_string     VARCHAR2(32760); -- Maximum length of LONG data type

  /* Declare user-defined exception. */
  invalid_view_name  EXCEPTION;
```

```
  PRAGMA EXCEPTION_INIT(invalid_view_name, -20001);

  /* Declare a dynamic cursor. */
  CURSOR c (cv_view_name VARCHAR2) IS
    SELECT   text
    FROM     user_views
    WHERE    view_name = cv_view_name;

  FUNCTION verify_view_name
  ( pv_view_name      VARCHAR2 )
  RETURN BOOLEAN AS
    /* Default return value. */
    lv_return_result  BOOLEAN := FALSE;

    /* Declare cursor to check view name. */
    CURSOR c (cv_view_name  VARCHAR2) IS
      SELECT   NULL
      FROM     user_views
      WHERE    view_name = cv_view_name;
  BEGIN
    FOR i IN c (pv_view_name) LOOP
      lv_return_result := TRUE;
    END LOOP;

    RETURN lv_return_result;
  END verify_view_name;
BEGIN
  /* Throw exception when invalid view name. */
  IF NOT verify_view_name(pv_view_name) THEN
     RAISE invalid_view_name;
  END IF;

  /* Open, fetch, and close cursor to capture view text. */
  OPEN c(pv_view_name);
  FETCH c INTO lv_long_view; -- Fetched into a LONG variable.
  CLOSE c;

  /* Create dynamic statement. */
  lv_stmt := 'SELECT text'||CHR(10)
          || 'FROM user_views'||CHR(10)
          || 'WHERE view_name = '''||pv_view_name||'''';

  /* Parse and define a LONG column. */
  dbms_sql.parse(lv_cursor, lv_stmt, dbms_sql.native);
  dbms_sql.define_column_long(lv_cursor,1);

  /* Only attempt to process the return value when fetched. */
  IF dbms_sql.execute_and_fetch(lv_cursor) = 1 THEN
    dbms_sql.column_value_long(
        lv_cursor
      , 1
      , LENGTH(lv_long_view)  -- Size a LONG variable.
      , 0
      , lv_string             -- Output the VARCHAR2 string.
```

(continued)

```
 76         , lv_length);
 77     END IF;
 78
 79     /* Check for an open cursor. */
 80     IF dbms_sql.is_open(lv_cursor) THEN
 81       dbms_sql.close_cursor(lv_cursor);
 82     END IF;
 83
 84     /* Create a local temporary CLOB in memory:
 85        - It returns a constructed lv_return_result.
 86        - It disables a cached version.
 87        - It sets the duration to 12 (the value of the dbms_lob.call
 88          package-level variable) when the default is 10. */
 89     dbms_lob.createtemporary(lv_input_view, FALSE, dbms_lob.CALL);
 90
 91     /* Append the LONG to the empty temporary CLOB. */
 92     dbms_lob.WRITE(lv_input_view, LENGTH(lv_long_view), 1, lv_string);
 93
 94     /* Send in the view text and receive the complete text. */
 95     dbms_utility.expand_sql_text(lv_input_view, lv_output_view);
 96
 97     /* Return the output CLOB value. */
 98     RETURN lv_output_view;
 99   EXCEPTION
100     WHEN invalid_view_name THEN
101       RAISE_APPLICATION_ERROR(-20001,'Invalid View Name.');
102     WHEN OTHERS THEN
103       RETURN NULL;
104   END expand_sql_text;
105   /
```

Lines 55 through 57 open, fetch, and close a cursor against the view. The fetch on line 56 puts the `LONG` column's value into a local `LONG` variable. While you can't directly read the `LONG` variable's value, the SQL `LENGTH` built-in lets us capture the length of the variable. By knowing the *length* of the variable, we're able to read the contents of the `LONG` variable directly into a `CLOB` variable with only one call to the `dbms_sql.column_value_long` procedure on lines 70 through 76.

Line 89 lets us create a temporary `CLOB` variable and is like using the `empty_clob` function. The difference is that it opens a handle that lets us write directly into the local `CLOB` variable, which we do on line 92. Line 95 holds the call to the new `dbms_utility` procedure. The `expand_sql_text` procedure takes a view dependent on views and transforms it to a query based on tables only.

If you wanted just the text of a view returned as a `CLOB`, you could change line 95 from a call to the `expand_sql_text` procedure to a simple assignment between `CLOB` variables:

```
 95     lv_output_view := lv_input_view;
```

Since views are limited by the 32,760 maximum size of a `LONG` data type, you can also rewrite this function to return a `VARCHAR2` data type.

The unfortunate reality of any function wrapping the creation of a LOB is that it will also be limited by the available memory in the Oracle Database 12*c* SGA. While an `UPDATE` statement by itself isn't the optimal solution, here is how one would look updating the `item_desc` column with a string literal value:

```
SQL> UPDATE item
  2  SET    item_desc = 'Harry Potter is seemingly an ordinary eleven-year'
  3  WHERE  item_title = 'Harry Potter and the Sorcerer''s Stone'
  4  AND    item_type IN
     ...
```

This `UPDATE` statement sets the `item_desc` column on line 2 equal to a string value less than 32,767 bytes. When LOBs are larger, you must use the `writeappend` procedure from the `dbms_lob` package to append additional data after an initial write. The upcoming section "Reading Local Files into CLOB or NCLOB Columns" demonstrates this approach.

It's important to note that you can also assign values to a `CLOB` column through the `VALUES` clause of an `INSERT` statement. That's possible when you write that user-defined function mentioned earlier. The next section covers how you can write such a function.

Using a PL/SQL Function to Assign a CLOB PL/SQL also provides you with a second choice on how you can insert a string in a `CLOB` column. At least, you have a second choice when the string is 32,767 or less bytes in length. While you only have one way to successfully assign a string larger than 32,767 bytes, it's nice to have options with smaller strings.

This option lets you insert a string into a `CLOB` column directly without first initializing the column with a call to the `empty_clob` function. You can accomplish this by writing a pass-by-value wrapper function. It would take any `VARCHAR2` string with a value of 32,767 or less bytes.

A `create_clob` function takes a string as an input value. It then calls two pass-by-reference procedures from the `dbms_lob` package to convert the string to a `CLOB` value. You implement a `create_clob` function as shown:

```
SQL> CREATE OR REPLACE FUNCTION create_clob
( pv_input_string  VARCHAR2 )
RETURN CLOB AS
  /* Declare a local CLOB variable. */
  lv_return  CLOB;
BEGIN
  /* Create a temporary CLOB in memory for the scope of the call. */
  dbms_lob.createtemporary(lv_return, FALSE, dbms_lob.CALL);

  /* Write the string to the empty temporary CLOB. */
  dbms_lob.WRITE(lv_return, LENGTH(pv_input_string), 1, pv_input_string);

  /* Return a CLOB value. */
  RETURN lv_return;
END create_clob;
/
```

Line 8 creates a temporary CLOB variable. Line 11 evaluates the length of the string and converts it to a CLOB variable. Line 14 returns the temporary CLOB and lets you embed it as a function call in a VALUES clause. It works because it's an assignment of an initialized CLOB to a CLOB column. That means it requires no casting operation.

Review Section

This section has described the following points about working with LOBs:

- Character Large Objects (CLOBs), National Character Large Objects (NCLOBs), and Binary Large Objects (BLOBs) support character strings of 8 to 128 terabytes. Oracle Database 12*c* lets you set `db_block_size` to a value of 2KB to 32KB.
- The CLOB, NCLOB, and BLOB data types are object types, and Oracle doesn't provide a convenient SQL built-in function to construct a LOB.
- The `dbms_lob` package contains functions and procedures that let you read, write, and append data to CLOB variables and columns.
- The terms *descriptor* and *locator* are sometimes used interchangeably, but Oracle prefers *locator* to describe the pointer to the location of CLOBs stored in the database.
- You have NULL, empty, or populated CLOB variables and columns.
- Oracle supports direct writes of strings in a PL/SQL context but not in a SQL context. This means you need to write a function that takes a string and returns a CLOB to pass a string to the VALUES clause of an INSERT statement.
- When inserting or updating data larger than 32,767 bytes, you need to initialize a CLOB with a call to the `empty_clob` function. You pass the segments of data through the locator in chunks no larger than 32,768 bytes.

Reading Files into Internally Stored Columns

The `dbms_lob` package provides all the tools required to load large objects directly when they exceed the byte stream limitations of SQL or PL/SQL. The first step requires that you define a *virtual directory*, an internal directory alias that points to a canonical or fully qualified path.

In this example, you create a virtual directory that points to your local temporary directory. You must connect as the `system` user to define virtual directories. The following commands work on your specific operating system:

Linux or Unix

```
SQL> CREATE DIRECTORY generic AS '/tmp';
```

Windows

```
SQL> CREATE DIRECTORY generic AS 'C:\Windows\temp';
```

After you create the virtual directory, you need to grant read permissions on the directory to the `student` CDB or PDB user. The syntax is

```
SQL> GRANT READ ON DIRECTORY generic TO student;
```

You have two available approaches to loading files, which the next two subsections discuss. One runs as a PL/SQL stored procedure on the server, and the other uses an external programming language. I've chosen PHP to demonstrate the external programming language.

Reading Local Files into CLOB or NCLOB Columns

The next steps are reading the file and writing the data to the `CLOB` column. While a couple of small snippets could show the concepts adequately, a single working code example is provided so that you can cut and paste it right into your applications. The example uses NDS (Native Dynamic SQL). Check Chapter 13 if you're curious about the mechanics of NDS.

The following `load_clob_from_file` procedure demonstrates how you do this:

```
SQL> CREATE OR REPLACE PROCEDURE load_clob_from_file
( src_file_name     IN VARCHAR2
, table_name        IN VARCHAR2
, column_name       IN VARCHAR2
, primary_key_name  IN VARCHAR2
, primary_key_value IN VARCHAR2 ) IS

  /* Declare local variables for DBMS_LOB.LOADCLOBFROMFILE procedure. */
  des_clob   CLOB;
  src_clob   BFILE := BFILENAME('GENERIC',src_file_name);
  des_offset NUMBER := 1;
  src_offset NUMBER := 1;
  src_size   INTEGER;
  ctx_lang   NUMBER := dbms_lob.default_lang_ctx;
  warning    NUMBER;

  /* Define local variable for Native Dynamic SQL. */
  stmt VARCHAR2(2000);
BEGIN
  /* Opening source file is a mandatory operation. */
  IF dbms_lob.fileexists(src_clob) = 1 AND NOT
     dbms_lob.isopen(src_clob) = 1 THEN
    src_size := dbms_lob.getlength(src_clob);
    dbms_lob.open(src_clob,DBMS_LOB.LOB_READONLY);
  END IF;

  /* Assign dynamic string to statement. */
  stmt := 'UPDATE '||table_name||' '
       || 'SET    '||column_name||' = empty_clob() '
       || 'WHERE  '||primary_key_name||' = '||''''||primary_key_value||''' '
       || 'RETURNING '||column_name||' INTO :locator';

  /* Run dynamic statement. */
  EXECUTE IMMEDIATE stmt USING OUT des_clob;
```

```
35
36     /* Read and write file to CLOB and close source file. */
37     dbms_lob.loadclobfromfile( dest_lob     => des_clob
38                              , src_bfile    => src_clob
39                              , amount       => dbms_lob.getlength(src_clob)
40                              , dest_offset  => des_offset
41                              , src_offset   => src_offset
42                              , bfile_csid   => dbms_lob.default_csid
43                              , lang_context => ctx_lang
44                              , warning      => warning );
45     dbms_lob.close(src_clob);
46
47     /* Test the exit criteria before committing the work. */
48     IF src_size = dbms_lob.getlength(des_clob) THEN
49       $IF $$DEBUG = 1 $THEN
50         dbms_output.put_line('Success!');
51       $END
52       COMMIT;
53     ELSE
54       $IF $$DEBUG = 1 $THEN
55         dbms_output.put_line('Failure.');
56       $END
57       RAISE dbms_lob.operation_failed;
58     END IF;
59   END load_clob_from_file;
60   /
```

The procedure takes arguments that let you use it against any table that has a single CLOB column and a one-column primary key. The bfilename function on line 10 returns the canonical directory path from the database catalog and appends the filename. The open procedure call on line 24 opens the external file and reads it into a BFILE data type. The dynamic UPDATE statement sets the CLOB column to an empty_clob constructor. Then, the UPDATE statement returns the designated column into an output variable. The :locator bind variable is the output variable in the NDS statement. You assign the CLOB locator to the des_clob variable when the NDS statement runs.

NOTE

An UPDATE statement that uses a RETURNING INTO clause changes the target column value for all updated rows.

All the preceding actions read the source file and thread a CLOB column locator into the program scope. With these two resource handlers, the call to the loadclobfromfile procedure on lines 37 through 44 transfers the contents of the open file to the CLOB locator. This read-and-write operation is not subject to the 32,767-byte handling limit of VARCHAR2 data types.

While this example loads the entire file in one operation, it's likely that you may read only chunks of large files directly into CLOB columns. The source file offset (src_offset) and destination CLOB column offset (dest_offset) values let you parse chunks out of the file and place them in the CLOB column. Adding the logic for a loop lets you load large files by chunks, as opposed to a single read.

You can test this stored procedure by running the following anonymous block program:

```
SQL> BEGIN
  2    FOR i IN (SELECT item_id
  3              FROM   item
  4              WHERE  item_title = 'The Lord of the Rings - Fellowship ...'
  5              AND    item_type IN
  6                      (SELECT common_lookup_id
  7                       FROM   common_lookup
  8                       WHERE  common_lookup_table = 'ITEM'
  9                       AND    common_lookup_column = 'ITEM_TYPE'
 10                       AND    REGEXP_LIKE( common_lookup_type
 11                                         ,'^(DVD|VHS)*'))) LOOP
 12
 13      -- Call reading and writing CLOB procedure.
 14      load_clob_from_file( src_file_name     => 'LOTRFellowship.txt'
 15                         , table_name        => 'ITEM'
 16                         , column_name       => 'ITEM_DESC'
 17                         , primary_key_name  => 'ITEM_ID'
 18                         , primary_key_value =>  TO_CHAR(i.item_id));
 19    END LOOP;
 20  END;
 21  /
```

The call to the `load_clob_from_file` procedure on lines 14 through 18 loads the same value into every row where the surrogate primary key value, `item_id`, meets the business rule. The business rule uses a regular expression search. The regular expression gets all DVD and VHS rows where the `item_title` is "The Lord of the Rings – Fellowship of the Ring" and `item_type` maps to a string value starting with a `DVD` or `VHS` substring. Appendix E explains further how you can leverage regular expressions in your Oracle Database 12*c* PL/SQL code.

You can run the following formatting and query to confirm that the three rows now have `CLOB` columns with data streams that are longer than 4,000 bytes:

```
SQL> -- Format column for output.
SQL> COL item_id    FORMAT 9999
SQL> COL item_title FORMAT A50
SQL> COL size       FORMAT 9,999,990
SQL> -- Query column size.
SQL> SELECT item_id
,      item_title
,      dbms_lob.getlength(item_desc) AS "SIZE"
FROM   item
WHERE  dbms_lob.getlength(item_desc) > 0;
```

It yields the following three rows:

```
  ITEM_ID ITEM_TITLE                                           SIZE
--------- -------------------------------------------------- ------
     1037 The Lord of the Rings - Fellowship of the Ring       5,072
     1038 The Lord of the Rings - Fellowship of the Ring       5,072
     1039 The Lord of the Rings - Fellowship of the Ring       5,072
```

This section has shown you how to load directly from files into CLOB columns. The same rules apply for NCLOBs. There's a slight difference in how you handle BLOB columns. The difference is covered in the next section. You have also learned how to use the dbms_lob package to read external files. You should note that there are fewer security restrictions than those required to process utl_file or external Java file I/O operations.

Reading Local Files into BLOB Columns

In this section you learn how to read the file and write its contents to a BLOB column. As in the previous section, while a couple of small snippets could show the concepts adequately, a single working code example is provided so that you can cut and paste it right into your applications. The example uses NDS, which makes a forward reference to material covered in Chapter 13.

The following load_blob_from_file procedure demonstrates how you do this:

```
SQL> CREATE OR REPLACE PROCEDURE load_blob_from_file
  ( src_file_name     IN VARCHAR2
  , table_name        IN VARCHAR2
  , column_name       IN VARCHAR2
  , primary_key_name  IN VARCHAR2
  , primary_key_value IN VARCHAR2 ) IS
    /* Declare variables for DBMS_LOB.LOADBLOBFROMFILE procedure. */
    des_blob   BLOB;
    src_blob   BFILE := BFILENAME('GENERIC',src_file_name);
    des_offset NUMBER := 1;
    src_offset NUMBER := 1;
    /* Declare a pre-reading size. */
    src_blob_size NUMBER;
    /* Declare local variable for Native Dynamic SQL. */
    stmt VARCHAR2(2000);
  BEGIN
    /* Opening source file is a mandatory operation. */
    IF dbms_lob.fileexists(src_blob) = 1 AND NOT
       dbms_lob.isopen(src_blob) = 1 THEN
      src_blob_size := dbms_lob.getlength(src_blob);
      dbms_lob.open(src_blob,DBMS_LOB.LOB_READONLY);
    END IF;
    /* Assign dynamic string to statement. */
    stmt := 'UPDATE '||table_name||' '
         || 'SET    '||column_name||' = empty_blob() '
         || 'WHERE  '||primary_key_name||' = '||''''||primary_key_value||''' '
         || 'RETURNING '||column_name||' INTO :locator';
    /* Run dynamic statement. */
    EXECUTE IMMEDIATE stmt USING OUT des_blob;
    /* Read and write file to BLOB. */
    dbms_lob.loadblobfromfile( dest_lob    => des_blob
                             , src_bfile   => src_blob
                             , amount      => dbms_lob.getlength(src_blob)
                             , dest_offset => des_offset
                             , src_offset  => src_offset );
    /* Close open source file. */
    dbms_lob.close(src_blob);
```

```
38     /* Commit write. */
39     IF src_blob_size = dbms_lob.getlength(des_blob) THEN
40       $IF $$DEBUG = 1 $THEN
41         dbms_output.put_line('Success!');
42       $END
43       COMMIT;
44     ELSE
45       $IF $$DEBUG = 1 $THEN
46         dbms_output.put_line('Failure.');
47       $END
48       RAISE dbms_lob.operation_failed;
49     END IF;
50   END load_blob_from_file;
51   /
```

The procedure takes five arguments on lines 2 through 6 that let you use it against any table that has a single BLOB column and a one-column surrogate primary key. The bfilename function returns a canonical filename on line 9. After validating that the file exists and isn't open on lines 18 and 19, the dbms_lob.open procedure call opens the external file on line 21. The dynamic UPDATE statement on lines 24 through 27 sets the BLOB column to an empty_blob and then returns the column into an output variable. The :locator bind variable is the output variable in the NDS statement. The program returns a BLOB locator and assigns it to the des_blob variable when the NDS statement runs. The loadblobfromfile procedure call on lines 31 through 35 reads it into a BFILE data type. Line 39 compares the external file size against the uploaded BLOB column before committing the transaction on line 43. When the external file size isn't the same as the BLOB column, the load_blob_from_file procedure raises an exception on line 48. Conditional code blocks signal successful or unsuccessful completion of the procedure when you test the procedure. Naturally, you need to set the PLSQL_CCFLAGS option earlier in the session when you test the procedure, as qualified in Chapter 5.

All the preceding actions read the source file and destination BLOB column locator into the program scope. With these two resource handlers, the call to loadblobfromfile procedure transfers the contents of the open file to the BLOB locator. This read-and-write operation lets you put large chunks of files directly into BLOB columns. The source file offset (src_offset) and destination BLOB column offset (dest_offset) values let you parse chunks out of the file and place them in the BLOB column. You can add a loop to approach the upload a chunk at a time for very large binary files, like movies.

You can test this stored procedure by running the following anonymous block program:

```
SQL> BEGIN
       FOR i IN (SELECT item_id
                 FROM   item
                 WHERE  item_title = 'Harry Potter and the Sorcerer''s Stone'
                 AND    item_type IN
                  (SELECT common_lookup_id
                   FROM   common_lookup
                   WHERE  common_lookup_table = 'ITEM'
                   AND    common_lookup_column = 'ITEM_TYPE'
                   AND    REGEXP_LIKE(common_lookup_type,'^(dvd|vhs)*','i'))) LOOP
         /* Call procedure for matching rows. */
         load_blob_from_file( src_file_name     => 'HarryPotter1.png'
```

```
                              , table_name        => 'ITEM'
                              , column_name       => 'ITEM_BLOB'
                              , primary_key_name  => 'ITEM_ID'
                              , primary_key_value => TO_CHAR(i.item_id) );
  END LOOP;
END;
/
```

The call to the `load_blob_from_file` procedure is made for every `item_id` value that meets the business rule, which is defined by the regular expression search. The regular expression gets all DVD and VHS rows where the `item_title` is "Harry Potter and the Sorcerer's Stone" and the apostrophe is back-quoted to treat the embedded single quote as an embedded apostrophe. The `item_type` maps to a string value starting with a `DVD` or `VHS` substring, which means that images are loaded into all the target columns for any matching rows. Appendix E explains further how regular expressions work in Oracle Database 12*c*.

You can run the following formatting and query to confirm that the two rows now have `BLOB` columns with binary data streams:

```
SQL> -- Format column for output.
SQL> COL item_id    FORMAT 9999
SQL> COL item_title FORMAT A50
SQL> COL size       FORMAT 9,999,990
SQL> -- Query column size.
SQL> SELECT item_id
  2  ,      item_title
  3  ,      dbms_lob.getlength(item_blob) AS "SIZE"
  4  FROM   item
  5  WHERE  dbms_lob.getlength(item_blob) > 0;
```

It yields the following three rows:

```
   ITEM_ID ITEM_TITLE                                            SIZE
---------- -------------------------------------------------- -------
      1021 Harry Potter and the Sorcerer's Stone              121,624
      1022 Harry Potter and the Sorcerer's Stone              121,624
```

This section has shown you how to load directly from files into `BLOB` columns. You have also revisited how to use the `dbms_lob` package to read external files. You should note that there is less security restriction than that required to perform `utl_file` or external Java file I/O operations.

Working with LOBs Through Web Pages

Like PL/SQL, external programming languages work with the same limitations for uploading and writing `CLOB` or `NCLOB` columns. You must choose whether you enter small chunks (32,767 bytes) or large chunks of 1MB or beyond. This section assumes you want to upload and write large chunks.

The PHP solution is a bit easier than deploying EJBs (Enterprise JavaBeans) because it has fewer noticeably moving parts. You should note that this type of solution builds a PL/SQL procedure that can support any external web programming language that works with the Oracle JDBC or OCI8 libraries.

PHP introduces you to the issue of uploading a file to the server. In the previous PL/SQL solution, the file is already in the `/tmp` directory (magically done by the Oracle DBA). This program example assumes you have a background in PHP. If you don't have that background, you can refer to *Oracle Database 10*g *Express Edition PHP Web Programming* (Oracle Press, 2006), Oracle's *The Underground PHP and Oracle Manual*, or Oracle's *Oracle Database 2 Day + PHP Developer's Guide*. Only the critical components of the PHP code are displayed in the book, but you can download the complete code from the McGraw-Hill Professional website.

NOTE

*The OCI8 version that supports DRCP (Database Resident Connection Pooling) feature in Oracle Database 11*g *or newer.*

The preparation to implement this solution differs from what you did for a PL/SQL-only solution (such as creating a virtual directory and granting read permissions). For the PHP solution, you must install an Apache HTTP Server, Zend Core for Oracle, and then create a physical directory in your `DocumentRoot` directory. You find the canonical directory path for `DocumentRoot` in the Apache `httpd.conf` file.

The `DocumentRoot` canonical paths are typically

Linux or Unix

```
/var/www/html
```

Windows

```
C:\Program Files\Apache Group\Apache2\htdocs
```

After you download the files from the publisher's website, add a `temp` directory in your `DocumentRoot` directory. Then, copy the required files to the `DocumentRoot` directory. You should also put the image and text files in a local client directory where you plan to run your browser sessions.

Procedures to Upload CLOB, NCLOB, or BLOB Columns

This section requires that you create two stored procedures: one that manages `CLOB` or `NCLOB` data types, and another that manages `BLOB` data types. Assuming you're using the `videodb` PDB, compile the following pass-by-reference procedure in that schema. The PHP programs use it to secure a connection for uploading large text and image files.

```
SQL> CREATE OR REPLACE PROCEDURE web_load_clob_from_file
( item_id_in IN      NUMBER
, descriptor IN OUT CLOB ) IS
BEGIN
  /* This a DML transaction.
  UPDATE     item
  SET        item_desc = empty_clob()
  WHERE      item_id = item_id_in
  RETURNING item_desc INTO descriptor;
END web_load_clob_from_file;
/
```

This `web_load_clob_from_file` procedure lets you open a `CLOB` locator and access it from a PHP library file. There are three key features in this procedure. First, the formal parameter on line 3 is a `CLOB` locator with an `IN OUT` mode access. Second, the `RETURNING INTO` clause on line 9 provides a local variable gateway into the `SET` clause's column variable on line 7. Third, the lack of a `COMMIT` in the stored procedure leaves the `CLOB` locked and DML transaction scope open for the external web program.

Now, you need to compile the following stored procedure to manage the upload of `BLOB` columns in the same video schema in your `videodb` PDB:

```
SQL> CREATE OR REPLACE PROCEDURE web_load_blob_from_file
( item_id_in IN     NUMBER
, descriptor IN OUT BLOB ) IS
BEGIN
  -- A FOR UPDATE makes this a DML transaction.
  UPDATE    item
  SET       item_blob = empty_blob()
  WHERE     item_id = item_id_in
  RETURNING item_blob INTO descriptor;
END web_load_blob_from_file;
/
```

The `web_load_blob_from_file` procedure mirrors the `web_load_clob_from_file` procedure with one exception: the `IN OUT` mode variable is a `BLOB`, not a `CLOB`. While it would be awesome if we could define a generic superclass, like `LOB`, for both `BLOB` and `CLOB` data types, it's not currently supported in the Oracle Database 12*c* database.

HTML and PHP Components for CLOB and BLOB Uploads

The first step in PHP is to upload the physical file from the client to the server. This requires an HTML form and PHP script file. There are different HTML forms for the `CLOB` and `BLOB` data types. Both of the HTML files can be found on the McGraw-Hill Professional website.

This is the important part of the `UploadItemDescriptionForm.htm` file:

```
<html>
<body>
<form id="uploadForm" action="UploadItemDesc.php"
      enctype="multipart/form-data" method="post">
    ...
</form>
</body>
</html>
```

The `action` name-value pair instructs the program which PHP file to call when you submit the form. The `CLOB` upload calls the `UploadItemDesc.php` file. You can see the rendered page in Figure 10-2, which helps you know what to expect when you test the code.

Figure 10-2 shows this form rendered with the inputs from Table 10-2. The canonical path starts from a mount point in Linux or Unix. The program starts from a logical drive in Windows, known as the `htdocs` folder. Regardless of your operating system implementation, the Browse button takes you to your GUI file chooser dialog. After you select the file to upload in your file chooser dialog, click the Submit button.

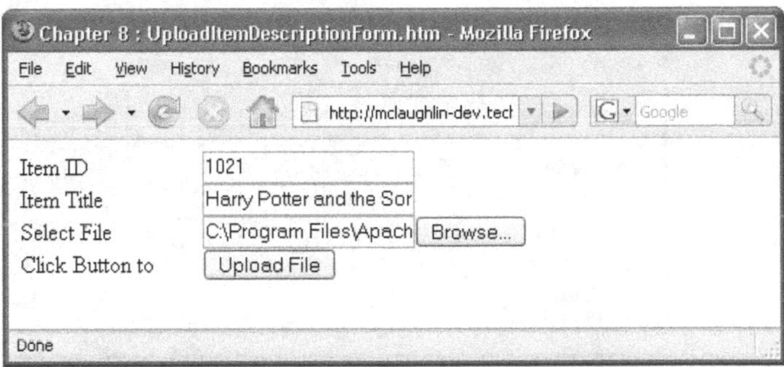

FIGURE 10-2. *UploadItemDescriptionForm.htm*

The only difference between the BLOB and CLOB HTML forms is the action tag, so that's all that is displayed for the BLOB form:

```
<form id="uploadForm" action="UploadItemBlob.php"
      enctype="multipart/form-data" method="post">
```

You can see the rendered page in Figure 10-3, which helps you know what to expect when you test the code.

Figure 10-3 shows the form with the inputs from Table 10-3. The canonical path starts from a mount point in Linux or Unix. The program starts from a logical drive in Windows, known as the htdocs folder. Regardless of your operating system implementation, the Browse button takes you to your GUI file chooser dialog. After you select the file to upload in your file chooser dialog, click the Submit button.

Both the UploadItemDesc.php and UploadItemBlob.php programs first call a PHP process_uploaded_file function. This function stores the temporary file to the default upload location, which is a temp folder you need to create in the htdocs folder.

After the program copies the file to its controlled location, the program then reads the file contents into memory. It then writes the file content to the database.

Prompt	**Input**
Item Number	1021
Item Title	Harry Potter and the Sorcerer's Stone
Select File	{*canonical_path*}HarryPotterSocererStone.txt

TABLE 10-2. *Inputs to UpdateItemDescriptionForm.htm*

FIGURE 10-3. *UploadItemBlobForm.htm*

The PHP `process_uploaded_file` function is

```
// Manage file upload and return file as string.
function process_uploaded_file() {
  // Declare a variable for file contents.
  $contents = "";
  // Define the upload filename for Windows or Linux.
  if (ereg("Win32",$_SERVER["SERVER_SOFTWARE"]))
    $upload_file = getcwd()."\\temp\\".$_FILES['userfile']['name'];
  else
    $upload_file = getcwd()."/temp/".$_FILES['userfile']['name'];
  // Check for and move uploaded file.
  if (is_uploaded_file($_FILES['userfile']['tmp_name']))
    move_uploaded_file($_FILES['userfile']['tmp_name'],$upload_file);
  // Open a file handle and suppress an error for a missing file.
  if ($fp = @fopen($upload_file,"r")) {
    // Read until the end-of-file marker.
    while (!feof($fp))
      $contents .= fgetc($fp);
    // Close an open file handle.
    fclose($fp); }
  // Return file content as string.
  return $contents; }
```

Prompt	Input
Item Number	1021
Item Title	Harry Potter and the Sorcerer's Stone
Select File	{*canonical_path*}HarryPotter1.png

TABLE 10-3. *Inputs to UpdateItemBlobForm.htm*

The function tests whether the server is a Windows machine before finding the target canonical path for the uploaded file. The function puts the uploaded file in the `temp` directory and then it reads the file contents into a string. The function returns the file contents as a string. You should note that PHP strings can be much longer than the 32,767 bytes defined as the maximum PL/SQL string length. In this case, the string is only 6,737 bytes.

After calling the `process_uploaded_file` function, the next step for the `UploadItemDesc.php` is to call the `web_load_clob_from_file` procedure. The program binds the local variables into this anonymous block and then executes the procedure. The `:item_desc` bind (placeholder) variable passes a locator to the PHP program, and through that locator saves the data:

```
$rlob->save($item_desc);
```

A more complete excerpt follows (and the complete code can be found on the McGraw-Hill Professional website):

```
<?php
  ...
    // Declare a PL/SQL execution command.
    $stmt = "BEGIN
               web_load_clob_from_file(:id,:item_desc);
             END;";
    // Strip special characters to avoid ORA-06550 and PLS-00103 errors.
    $stmt = strip_special_characters($stmt);

    // Parse a query through the connection.
    $s = oci_parse($c,$stmt);

    // Define a descriptor for a CLOB.
    $rlob = oci_new_descriptor($c,OCI_D_LOB);

    // Define a variable name to map to CLOB descriptor.
    oci_define_by_name($s,':item_desc',$rlob,SQLT_CLOB);

    // Bind PHP variables to the OCI types.
    oci_bind_by_name($s,':id',$id);
    oci_bind_by_name($s,':item_desc',$rlob,-1,SQLT_CLOB);

    // Execute the PL/SQL statement.
    if (oci_execute($s,OCI_DEFAULT)) {
      $rlob->save($item_desc);
      oci_commit($c);
      query_insert($id,$title); }

    // Disconnect from database.
    oci_close($c); }
  ...
```

The UploadItemBlob.php program differs from UploadItemDesc.php in four places. The first difference is that it calls the web_load_blob_from_file procedure, like this:

```
// Declare a PL/SQL execution command.
$stmt = "BEGIN
           web_load_blob_from_file(:id,:item_blob);
         END;";
```

The next two differences involve binding the IN OUT mode parameter. It's a BLOB in this case, not a CLOB, so you must use this to define the column mapping:

```
oci_define_by_name($s,':item_blob',$rlob,SQLT_BLOB);
```

And, you must use this to bind the column mapping:

```
oci_bind_by_name($s,':item_blob',$rlob,-1,SQLT_BLOB);
```

The final difference deals with the column value being saved in the database:

```
  $rlob->save($item_blob);
```

This section has explained how you can load the CLOB and BLOB to the database. The next section explains how you read them from the database.

HTML and PHP Components for Displaying CLOB and BLOB Columns

The query_insert function call comes after committing the CLOB or BLOB. The UploadItemBlob.php program has the more complete version of the query_insert function. It queries the CLOB value and reuses the surrogate primary item_id key to render the BLOB value.

The full query_insert function follows:

```
function query_insert($id,$title) {
  // Return successful attempt to connect to the database.
  if ($c = @oci_new_connect("video","video","video")) {
    // Declare a SQL SELECT statement returning a CLOB.
    $stmt = "SELECT item_desc FROM item WHERE item_id = :id";
    // Parse a query through the connection.
    $s = oci_parse($c,$stmt);
    // Bind PHP variables to the OCI types.
    oci_bind_by_name($s,':id',$id);
    // Execute the PL/SQL statement.
    if (oci_execute($s)) {
      // Return a LOB descriptor as the value.
      while (oci_fetch($s)) {
        for ($i = 1;$i <= oci_num_fields($s);$i++)
          if (is_object(oci_result($s,$i))) {
            if ($size = oci_result($s,$i)->size()) {
              $data = oci_result($s,$i)->read($size); }
            else
              $data = " "; }
          else {
            if (oci_field_is_null($s,$i))
```

```
          $data = " ";
        else
          $data = oci_result($s,$i); }}
    // Free statement resources.
    oci_free_statement($s);
    // Format HTML table to display BLOB photo and CLOB description.
    $out = '<table border="1" cellpadding="5" cellspacing="0">';
    $out .= '<tr>';
    $out .= '<td align="center" class="e">'.$title.'</td>';
    $out .= '</tr>';
    $out .= '<tr><td class="v">';
    $out .= '<div>';
    $out .= '<div style="margin-right:5px;float:left">';
    $out .= '<img src="ConvertBlobToImage.php?id='.$id.'">';
    $out .= '</div>';
    $out .= '<div style="position=relative;">'.$data.'</div>';
    $out .= '</div>';
    $out .= '</td></tr>';
    $out .= '</table>'; }
    // Print the HTML table.
    print $out;
    // Disconnect from database.
    oci_close($c); }
  else {
    // Assign the OCI error and format double and single quotes.
    $errorMessage = oci_error();
    print htmlentities($errorMessage['message'])."<br />"; }}
```

The `oci_result($s,$i)->read($size)` command lets you read a LOB column value pointed to by a LOB locator. The example reads the entire `CLOB` value. It then displays the value in the web page.

The image (`img`) HTML tag contains a call out to another PHP `ConvertBlobToImage.php` program. It's a specialized program that contains no exposed HTML. It returns only two key lines after reading the content of the `BLOB` into a local variable. These two lines effectively let the browser render the image as if it were a stored PNG (Portable Network Graphics) file on the operating system.

Those lines call the `header` function and then a set of functions to convert the raw binary stream recovered from the `item_blob` column into a resource and then image file, as shown:

```
header('Content-type: image/png');
imagepng(imagecreatefromstring($data));
```

This set of steps creates an image that the browser can read as an image. This graphics format may require some additional configuration of your Apache server. You may need the *exif* and *gd* extensions to work with the PNG images.

The `query_insert` function renders the page shown in Figure 10-4.

This section has demonstrated how you can upload and read large character and binary files across the Web. You've seen how to write a PL/SQL procedure that keeps the transaction state open so that remote programs can directly write `CLOB`, `NCLOB`, and `BLOB` data types.

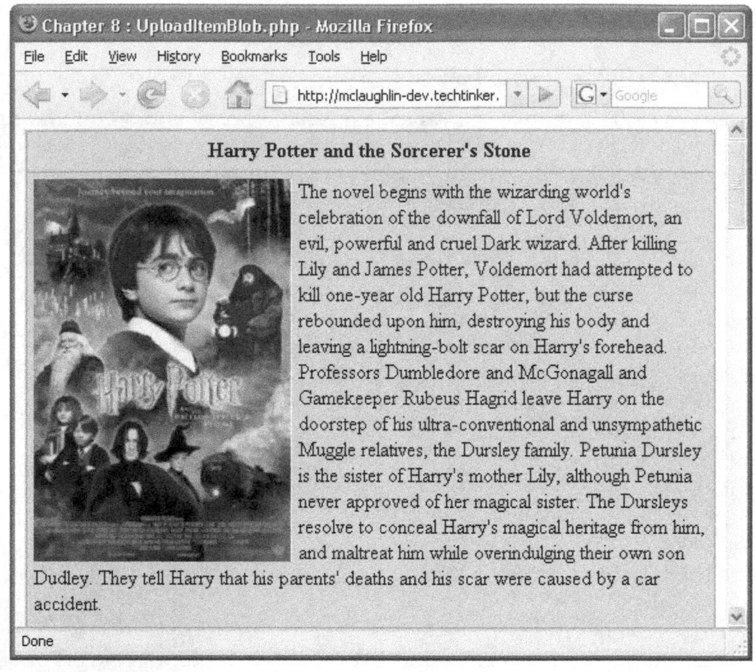

FIGURE 10-4. *Rendered CLOB and BLOB column values*

Review Section

This section has described the following points about how you read and write from local files into `CLOB`, `NCLOB`, and `BLOB` columns:

- Virtual directories support the use of the `bfilename` function, which lets you find external files.
- The `dbms_lob` package's `loadclobfromfile` procedure lets you read a character file in its entirety or in chunks.
- The `dbms_lob` package's `loadblobfromfile` procedure lets you read a binary file in its entirety or in chunks.
- A pass-by-reference procedure enables a web-based program to open a locator value, which lets the program upload large objects through the HTTP protocol. It does so by providing access to a column's locator value.
- External programming languages open, access, and load large objects through pass-by-reference stored procedures.

Working with Binary Files (BFILEs)

The BFILE (binary file) data type works differently than its counterpart BLOB, CLOB, and NCLOB data types. The largest differences are that BFILE values are *read-only* LOB data types and are stored externally from the database. Unlike BLOB, CLOB, and NCLOB data types, the BFILE has a maximum physical size set by the operating system.

The first subsection explores how you configure and use the database to leverage external files that are referenced as BFILE columns. You will set up another virtual directory (like those in the earlier sections), define a BFILE locator, and examine how virtual directories limit your access to the canonical filenames of external BFILE source files. The second subsection shows you how to extend the database catalog and read canonical filenames, which simplifies how you call external files from server-side programs.

Creating and Using Virtual Directories

Virtual directories are like synonyms: they point to another thing—a physical directory on the operating system. The virtual and physical directory names are stored in the database catalog and are viewable in the dba_directories view. Database users can view them when they have been granted the SELECT privilege on the view or the SELECT_CATALOG_ROLE role. By default, the system user accesses the dba_directories view through the SELECT_CATALOG_ROLE role.

You typically create virtual directories as the system user or as another database user that enjoys the DBA role privilege. Alternatively, the system user can grant the CREATE ANY DIRECTORY privilege to a user. This alleviates a burden from the DBA but can lead to a proliferation of virtual directories and potential naming conflicts. You should generally disallow users other than the DBA to create virtual directories.

All virtual directories are actually owned by the sys user for a CDB and the ADMIN user for a PDB. The physical directory is always the canonical path, which means a fully qualified directory path. A Linux or Unix canonical path starts at a mount point and ends at the desired directory. A Windows canonical file path starts at the physical drive letter and, as in Linux or Unix, ends at the desired directory.

You should connect as the system user and define an image virtual directory. The following commands work on your specific operating system:

Linux or Unix

```
CREATE DIRECTORY images AS '/var/www/html/images';
```

Windows

```
SQL> CREATE DIRECTORY images AS
  2     'C:\Program Files\Apache Group\Apache2\htdocs\images';
```

After you create the virtual directory, connect as the videoadm SYSDBA user of the PDB. As that user, grant read permissions on the directory to the video PDB user. The syntax is

```
SQL> GRANT READ ON DIRECTORY images TO video;
```

The next steps typically involve creating a virtual alias and directory in your Apache `httpd.conf` file. If you wish to configure the Apache virtual alias and directory, you can check the "Creating an Apache Virtual Alias and Directory" sidebar. There are very good reasons to set virtual aliases and directories in Apache. As a rule, you must mirror the definition of the Apache alias and virtual directory with the configuration of the Oracle database virtual directory. The rule exists (*rumor has it*) because the `dbms_lob` package `filegetname` procedure provides only the base filename, and doesn't provide a means to find canonical filenames. Canonical filenames are the combination of canonical paths and base filenames.

As previously discussed, you can open a file in your PL/SQL block without knowing the canonical path. This happens because the `open` procedure in the `dbms_lob` package resolves it for you. When you read the file through the virtual directory by using the `open` procedure, you must provide a separate module to render images in web pages. This is required because the file has been converted into a raw byte stream when opened for reading. Whenever you read the file as a byte stream, you must convert the file back into an image when rendering it in a web page.

You should copy the `Raiders3.png` file from the publisher's website and put it in your platform-specific physical directory that maps to your `images` virtual directory in the database.

Creating an Apache Virtual Alias and Directory

Two Apache configuration steps are required when you want to enable a new virtual directory. You need to configure an alias and directory in your `httpd.conf` file, as follows for your respective platform:

Linux or Unix:

```
Alias /images/ "/var/www/html/images"

<Directory "/var/www/html/images">
  Options None
  AllowOverride None
  Order allow,deny
  Allow from all
</Directory>
```

Windows:

```
Alias /images/ "C:/Program Files/Apache Group/Apache2/htdocs/images/"

<Directory "C:/Program Files/Apache Group/Apache2/htdocs/images">
  Options None
  AllowOverride None
  Order allow,deny
  Allow from all
</Directory>
```

After you make these changes in your Apache configuration file, you must stop and start your Apache instance. You use the Apache service on a Windows system and the `apachectl` shell script on a Linux or Unix system.

You can find that physical system directory (or *canonical path*) by writing the following query as the `system` user:

```
SQL> SELECT *
FROM   dba_directories
WHERE  directory_name = 'IMAGES';
```

After you've configured the virtual directory and put the `Raiders3.png` file in the correct directory, you should insert a `BFILE` locator into a database column for testing. You can use the following statement to update a column with a `BFILE` locator:

```
SQL> UPDATE item
SET item_photo = BFILENAME('IMAGES','Raiders3.png')
WHERE  item_id = 1055;
```

You need to commit the update as follows. If you forget that step, later you may get a browser error telling you the image can't be displayed because it contains errors. This is the standard error when the `BFILE` column returns a null or empty stream.

```
SQL> COMMIT;
```

You can verify that the file exists and the virtual directory resolves. Confirming the existence of the file before attempting to open it provides your program with more control. The following anonymous block lets you confirm the file existence and get its file size. Naturally, you must enable `SERVEROUTPUT` in SQL*Plus to see any output.

```
SQL> DECLARE
  file_locator BFILE;
BEGIN
  SELECT item_photo INTO file_locator FROM item WHERE item_id = 1055;
  /* Check for a valid locator. */
  IF dbms_lob.fileexists(file_locator) = 1 THEN
    dbms_output.put_line(
      'File is: ['||dbms_lob.getlength(file_locator)|| ']');
  ELSE
    dbms_output.put_line('No file found.');
  END IF;
END;
/
```

The `dbms_lob.fileexists` function was built to work in both SQL and PL/SQL. Since SQL does not support a native Boolean data type, the function returns a 1 when it finds a file and a 0 when it fails. The anonymous block should return the following:

```
File is: [126860]
```

If you've successfully added both the image alias and the virtual directory to your Apache `httpd.conf` file, you should be able to display the file by using the following URL:

```
http://<hostname>.<domain_name>/images/Raiders3.png
```

Figure 10-5 depicts the image file found by the URL by itself.

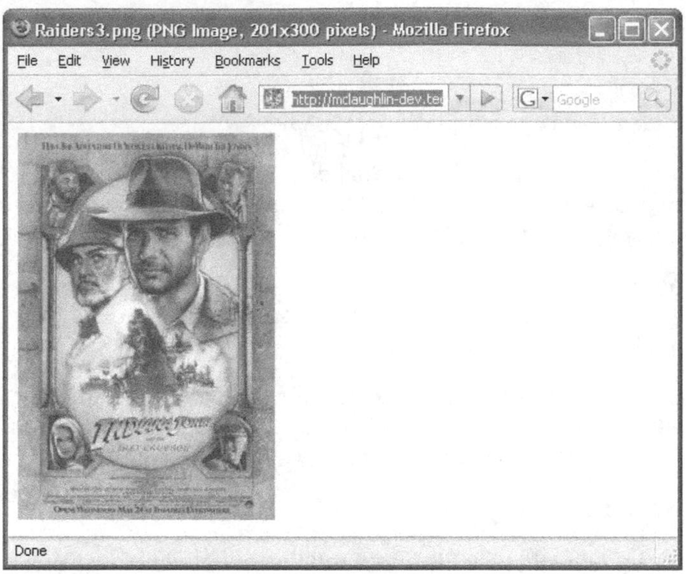

FIGURE 10-5. *PNG file rendered as an image*

While the database can read the file without an Apache alias and virtual directory, the reading process converts it to a byte stream. This puts the complexity of making an image reference on par with reading a `BLOB` column from the database. You will need to convert the byte stream back into a file. This is true whether you're using C, C++, C#, Java, or PHP to accomplish the task.

The `ConvertFileToImage.php` program only changes the column name of the query from `item_blob` to `item_photo`, and that's why it didn't seem worth reprinting here. The program can read a physical file from any virtual database directory because the program leverages the database catalog to resolve the physical file location. It leverage the database catalog through the `BFILE` locator.

Another approach to rending image files involves what's known as *structural coupling* between the virtual Apache and database directories. This means that you define the database virtual directory as *images* when you also define the Apache alias as *images*. This lets you build a relative path to the image file location in the `src` element of the `img` tag. It also avoids the issue of converting a binary stream back into a file.

The first step in accomplishing this type of approach requires a wrapper function around the `filegetname` procedure of the `dbms_lob` package. The `get_bfilename` function delivers that wrapper. You may reuse this program for other tables because it uses NDS to query and return the data. The encapsulation of the `SELECT` statement inside the anonymous block lets you capture the return value easily. You will find more on NDS in Chapter 13.

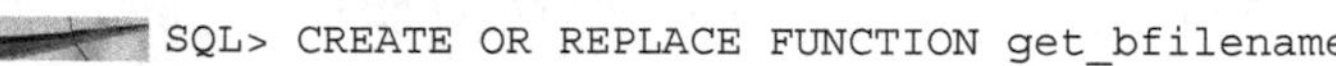

```
SQL> CREATE OR REPLACE FUNCTION get_bfilename
  ( table_name        VARCHAR2
  , column_name       VARCHAR2
  , primary_key_name  VARCHAR2
```

```
5  , primary_key_value VARCHAR2)
6  RETURN VARCHAR2 IS
7    /* Declare a locator. */
8    locator           BFILE;
9    /* Declare alias and filename. */
10   dir_alias VARCHAR2(255);
11   directory VARCHAR2(255);
12   file_name VARCHAR2(255);
13   /* Declare local variable for Native Dynamic SQL. */
14   stmt      VARCHAR2(2000);
15   delimiter VARCHAR2(1) := '/';
16   /* Declare a local exception for size violation. */
17   directory_num EXCEPTION;
18   PRAGMA EXCEPTION_INIT(directory_num,-22285);
19 BEGIN
20   /* Use an anonymous block to create an OUT mode variable. */
21   stmt := 'BEGIN '
22        || 'SELECT '||column_name||' '
23        || 'INTO :locator '
24        || 'FROM '||table_name||' '
25        || 'WHERE '||primary_key_name||' = '||''''||primary_key_value||''';'
26        || 'END;';
27   /* Return a scalar query result from a dynamic SQL statement. */
28   EXECUTE IMMEDIATE stmt USING OUT locator;
29   /* Check for available locator. */
30   IF locator IS NOT NULL THEN
31     dbms_lob.filegetname(locator,dir_alias,file_name);
32   END IF;
33   /* Return filename. */
34   RETURN delimiter||LOWER(dir_alias)||delimiter||file_name;
35 EXCEPTION
36   WHEN directory_num THEN
37   RETURN NULL;
38 END get_bfilename;
39 /
```

The `dir_alias` on line 34 is the virtual database directory name. The function returns the `dir_alias`, a / (forward slash), and base filename. Assuming that you're using the `Raiders3.png` file, it should return

```
/images/Raiders3.png
```

The `QueryRelativeBFILE.php` program uses the `get_bfilename` return value as the `src` element of the `img` tag. This works *only when the Apache alias also points to the same location*. The query inside the PHP program makes a call to the `get_bfilename` function and returns the value as the third element in the query. The PHP program assumes that the virtual path is the only string returned with a leading / (forward slash). You probably want to explore other alternatives when you can have more than one image location in a single row of data.

The `QueryRelativeBFILE.php` program follows:

```
<?php
  // Declare input variables.
  (isset($_GET['id']))    ? $id = (int) $_GET['id'] : $id = 1021;
  // Call the local function.
  query_insert($id);
  // Query results after an insert.
  function query_insert($id) {
    // Return successful attempt to connect to the database.
    if ($c = @oci_connect("video","video","video")) {
      // Declare a SQL SELECT statement returning a CLOB.
      $stmt = "SELECT   item_title
               ,        item_desc
               ,        get_bfilename('ITEM','ITEM_PHOTO','ITEM_ID',:id)
               FROM     item
               WHERE    item_id = :id";
      // Parse a query through the connection.
      $s = oci_parse($c,$stmt);
      // Bind PHP variables to the OCI types.
      oci_bind_by_name($s,':id',$id);
      // Execute the PL/SQL statement.
      if (oci_execute($s)) {
        // Return a LOB descriptor as the value.
        while (oci_fetch($s)) {
          for ($i = 1;$i <= oci_num_fields($s);$i++)
            if (is_object(oci_result($s,$i))) {
              if ($size = oci_result($s,$i)->size())
                if (oci_field_type($s,$i) == 'CLOB')
                  $data = oci_result($s,$i)->read($size);
              else
                $data = " "; }
            else {
              if (oci_field_is_null($s,$i))
                $title = " ";
              else
                if (substr(oci_result($s,$i),0,1) == '/')
                  $photo = oci_result($s,$i);
                else
                  $title = oci_result($s,$i); }
        } // End of the while(oci_fetch($s)) loop.
        // Free statement resources.
        oci_free_statement($s);
        // Format HTML table to display BLOB photo and CLOB description.
        $out = '<table border="1" cellpadding="5" cellspacing="0">';
        $out .= '<tr>';
        $out .= '<td align="center" class="e">'.$title.'</td>';
        $out .= '</tr>';
        $out .= '<tr><td class="v">';
```

```
      $out .= '<div>';
      $out .= '<div style="margin-right:5px;float:left">';
      $out .= '<img src="'.$photo.'">';
      $out .= '</div>';
      $out .= '<div style="position=relative;">'.$data.'</div>';
      $out .= '</div>';
      $out .= '</td></tr>';
      $out .= '</table>'; }
    // Print the HTML table.
    print $out;
    // Disconnect from database.
    oci_close($c); }
  else {
    // Assign the OCI error and format double and single quotes.
    $errorMessage = oci_error();
    print htmlentities($errorMessage['message'])."<br />"; }}
?>
```

While `QueryRelativeBFILE.php` works for web-based solutions, it fails to work for server-side programs that require the canonical filename, which is always an absolute value. It is less expensive in terms of machine resources because it only reads the image file and serves it to the Apache server. The problems with this approach are twofold. First, you have an administrative duty to synchronize the two virtual directories. Second, any user can view the source and determine some information about your physical file structure. As a security precaution, consuming a small amount of overhead to obfuscate (*hide*) the location of files is a good thing. Likewise, eliminating the job of synchronizing Apache and Oracle Database 12*c* virtual directories makes your application less expensive to maintain. Figure 10-6 shows the output of this relative image query.

This section has shown you how to configure and use virtual directories to support external `BFILE` locators. It has also compared the process of using Apache alias and virtual directories to the process of using the database to resolve external file locations. The next section shows you how to remake the rules, and how to access the canonical path and filenames stored in the database catalog.

Reading Canonical Path Names and Filenames

This section demonstrates how you can modify the database catalog and enable your programs to translate a `BFILE` locator to secure both the canonical path name and the canonical filename. You must open permissions to secure the virtual directory information owned by the `sys` user. As a rule of thumb, you should grant access to `sys` objects with care and allow *only* the minimum access required when building your database applications. This generally translates to a two-step process. First, you grant the privilege from `sys` to `system`. Second, you encapsulate the privilege by writing a stored function or procedure (*and don't forget to wrap the source from prying eyes, too*).

The data required for capturing canonical paths is found in the `dba_directories` view. The `system` user for a CDB or the `ADMIN` user for a PDB only has privileges through the `SELECT_CATALOG_ROLE` role, which limits the `system` user access to only viewing the `dba_directories` view. Role privileges disallow a user to build a stored function or procedure that queries the catalog view. Hence, the `system` user can't accesses the `dba_directories` view through only a `SELECT_CATALOG_ROLE` role.

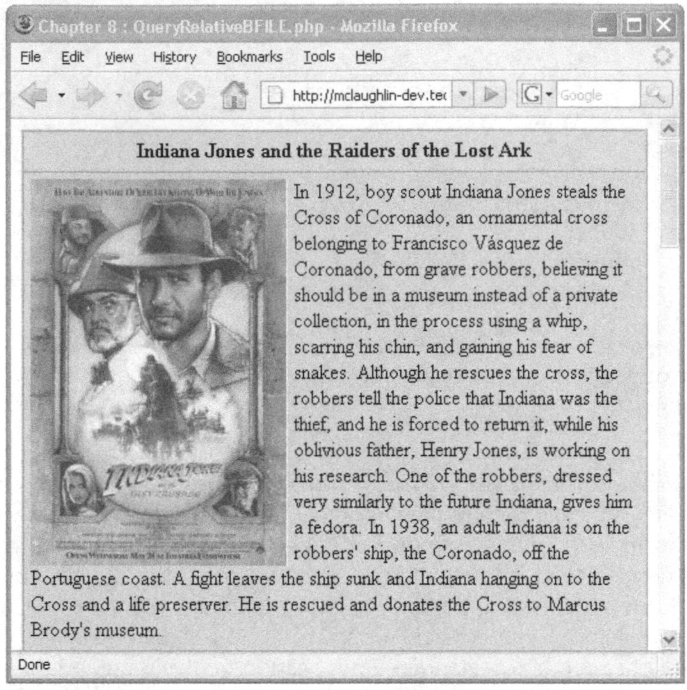

FIGURE 10-6. *Rendered page from the QueryRelativeBFILE.php program*

You need to connect either as the privileged `sys` user for a CDB:

```
SQL> sqlplus '/ as sysdba'
```

or as the `ADMIN` user of the `videodb` PDB:

```
SQL> sqlplus videoadm@video AS SYSDBA
```

This will require the database administrator password. This is typically the same as the `system` password. Sometimes the passwords differ because a company chooses to monitor the gatekeeper more closely as a result of Sarbanes-Oxley compliance. After connecting as the `sys` user, you should grant the minimum necessary privilege, which is `SELECT` on the specific view.

The grant command is this for a CDB:

```
SQL> GRANT select ON dba_directories TO system;
```

The grant command changes for a PDB. You should grant the privilege to the `ADMIN` (`videoadm`) user of the PDB (`videodb`):

```
SQL> GRANT select ON dba_directories TO videoadm;
```

Now, you should connect as the `system` user for a CDB or the `ADMIN` user for a PDB. The `videoadm` user account is the `ADMIN` user for the PDB qualified in this chapter and Appendixes A and B. After connecting, create the `get_directory_path` function, as follows:

```
SQL> CREATE OR REPLACE FUNCTION get_directory_path
  2  ( virtual_directory IN VARCHAR2 )
  3  RETURN VARCHAR2 IS
  4    /* Declare return variable. */
  5    directory_path VARCHAR2(256);
  6    /* Declare dynamic cursor. */
  7    CURSOR get_directory (virtual_directory VARCHAR2) IS
  8      SELECT   directory_path
  9      FROM     sys.dba_directories
 10      WHERE    directory_name = virtual_directory;
 11    /* Declare a local exception for name violation. */
 12    directory_name EXCEPTION;
 13    PRAGMA EXCEPTION_INIT(directory_name,-22284);
 14  BEGIN
 15    OPEN  get_directory (virtual_directory);
 16    FETCH get_directory
 17    INTO  directory_path;
 18    CLOSE get_directory;
 19    /* Return filename. */
 20    RETURN directory_path;
 21  EXCEPTION
 22    WHEN directory_name THEN
 23      RETURN NULL;
 24  END get_directory_path;
 25  /
```

The `get_directory_path` function takes a virtual directory on line 2 as its only formal parameter. It uses the virtual directory to find the canonical path. Lines 8 through 10 declare a dynamic cursor against the `sys.dba_directories` view. That's why you had to grant the `SELECT` privilege earlier. Lines 16 and 17 fetch the canonical path into the local `directory_path` variable. Line 20 returns a valid canonical path or line 23 returns a null value for the canonical path.

The following query lets you test the `get_directory_path` function. You should test it in the `system` schema for a CDB or the `ADMIN` schema for a PDB.

```
SQL> SELECT   get_directory_path('IMAGES')
  2  FROM     dual;
```

You also can use the `filegetname` procedure in the `dbms_lob` package to find the virtual directory. It returns the canonical path and base filename for any `BFILE` locator into a pass-by-reference call parameter. While a pass-by-reference call to the `filegetname` procedure is tightly coupled, the `get_directory_path` function requires a virtual directory name and image filename to be useful. You must discover the virtual directory name and image filename before you can call the `get_directory_path` function.

The `get_canonical_bfilename` function uses NDS to return a `BFILE` column, and the reference to the `BFILE` column provides you with the virtual directory name and image filename. The `get_canonical_bfilename` function wraps (or hides) the virtual directory name and image filename requirement. This way you write one function for any number of possible BFILE columns. The only problem with this example is that it depends on a single-column primary key for all target tables. Also, it is an invoker rights program. That's because the table and data should always exist in the caller's schema.

You should compile the get_canonical_bfilename function in the system schema of a CDB or the ADMIN schema of a PDB after you've compiled the get_directory_path function:

```
SQL> CREATE OR REPLACE FUNCTION get_canonical_bfilename
  ( table_name        IN     VARCHAR2
  , bfile_column_name IN     VARCHAR2
  , primary_key       IN     VARCHAR2
  , primary_key_value IN     VARCHAR2
  , operating_system  IN     VARCHAR2 := 'WINDOWS')
  RETURN VARCHAR2 AUTHID CURRENT_USER IS
    /* Declare default delimiter. */
    delimiter          VARCHAR2(1) := '\';

    /* Declare statement variable. */
    stmt               VARCHAR2(200);

    /* Declare a locator. */
    locator            BFILE;

    /* Declare alias and filename. */
    dir_alias          VARCHAR2(255);
    directory          VARCHAR2(255);
    file_name          VARCHAR2(255);

    /* Declare a local exception for size violation. */
    directory_num EXCEPTION;
    PRAGMA EXCEPTION_INIT(directory_num,-22285);
  BEGIN
    /* Assign dynamic string to statement. */
    stmt := 'BEGIN '
         || ' SELECT '||bfile_column_name||' '
         || ' INTO :column_value '
         || ' FROM  '||table_name||' '
         || ' WHERE '||primary_key||'='
         || ''''||primary_key_value||''''||';'
         || 'END;';

    /* Run dynamic statement. */
    EXECUTE IMMEDIATE stmt USING OUT locator;

    /* Check for available locator. */
    IF locator IS NOT NULL THEN
      dbms_lob.filegetname(locator,dir_alias,file_name);
    END IF;

    /* Check operating system and swap delimiter. */
    IF operating_system <> 'WINDOWS' THEN
```

```
45      delimiter := '/';
46    END IF;
47
48    /* Create a canonical filename. */
49    file_name :=
50      get_directory_path(dir_alias)||delimiter||file_name;
51
52    /* Return filename. */
53    RETURN file_name;
54  EXCEPTION
55    WHEN directory_num THEN
56      RETURN NULL;
57  END get_canonical_bfilename;
58  /
```

The last parameter on line 6 is optional, and it has a default value of `Windows`. It's there to let you designate the function to run on Windows or Linux/Unix operating systems. Line 7 defines the function as an invoker rights program because the internal NDS statement requires local schema access to the table and data. Lines 27 through 33 hold an NDS statement for a PL/SQL anonymous block, which provides one outbound bind variable on line 29. Line 36 manages the `OUT` mode parameter inside the `USING` clause.

Line 40 calls the `filegetname` procedure. The `dir_alias` (*database virtual directory*), `directory` (*canonical directory*), and `file_name` (*base filename*) variables on line 50 must be defined as 255-character strings before calling the `filegetname` procedure from the `dbms_lob` package. The balance of the function concatenates (*glues*) the canonical path and base filename together into a canonical filename.

While you may choose to grant this to only one or a select handful of schemas, you should consider making it a public grant like this:

```
SQL> GRANT EXECUTE ON get_canonical_bfilename TO PUBLIC;
```

Assuming you'll want to build a synonym because that's how the example works, as the `system` user you need to grant the `CREATE SYNONYM` privilege to the `video` user. The syntax is

```
SQL> GRANT CREATE SYNONYM TO video;
```

You also need to create synonyms for the `get_canonical_bfilename` because it's owned by the `system` user in a CDB or the `ADMIN` user in a PDB. Otherwise, you need to prepend the schema name and a component selector before each call to the function.

This synonym can't translate until the reciprocal grant is made, which you'll make in a moment. Reconnect as the `video` user:

```
SQL> connect video@video/video
```

and create the synonym for a CDB:

```
SQL> CREATE SYNONYM get_canonical_bfilename
  2    FOR system.get_canonical_bfilename;
```

or for a `videoadm` `ADMIN` user of a `videodb` PDB:

```
SQL> CREATE SYNONYM get_canonical_bfilename
  2    FOR videoadm.get_canonical_bfilename;
```

Now you can call the `get_canonical_bfilename` function and get the canonical filename for the `Raiders3.png` file:

```
SQL> SELECT   get_canonical_bfilename(
  2                table_name => 'ITEM'
  3              , bfile_column_name => 'ITEM_PHOTO'
  4              , primary_key => 'ITEM_ID'
  5              , primary_key_value => '1021') AS canonical_file_name
  6  FROM     dual;
```

It returns the operating system–specific values (provided you've set it up earlier):

Linux or Unix

```
/var/www/html/images/Raiders3.png
```

Windows

```
C:\Program Files\Apache Group\Apache2\htdocs\images\Raiders3.png
```

This approach avoids configuring the Apache alias and virtual directory. It is also a handy alternative in some organizations where control of virtual paths is strictly regulated and restricted. However, it does still require you to read and convert the binary stream into an image or document. At least this is true for web pages. Other server-side programs can leverage this mechanism to read images directly from their physical location.

Two programs let you implement this type of solution much as you implemented a read of both `CLOB` and `BLOB` columns in the earlier "Working with LOBs Through Web Pages" section in this chapter. Before working through these steps, you should download the `Raiders3.txt` file from the publisher's website, and load it to the database with one of the tools introduced earlier in this chapter.

The file upload is more complex than the previous examples because the file directory is no longer guaranteed to be a subdirectory of the directory containing an uploading web page. Therefore, we'll focus on the two scripts that are required to read and display the externally stored `BFILE` and internally stored `CLOB` description.

The `QueryPhotoBFILE.php` script reads the title and `CLOB` description from the `item` table, and the script calls the `ReadCanonicalFileToImage.php` script inside a `src` element of an `img` tag. The program follows:

```
<?php
  // Declare input variables.
  (isset($_GET['id']))    ? $id = (int) $_GET['id'] : $id = 1021;
  // Call the local function.
  query_insert($id);
  // Query results after an insert.
  function query_insert($id) {
    // Return successful attempt to connect to the database.
    if ($c = @oci_connect("video","video","video")) {
      // Declare a SQL SELECT statement returning a CLOB.
      $stmt = "SELECT item_title, item_desc FROM item WHERE item_id = :id";
      // Parse a query through the connection.
      $s = oci_parse($c,$stmt);
      // Bind PHP variables to the OCI types.
```

```
      oci_bind_by_name($s,':id',$id);
      // Execute the PL/SQL statement.
      if (oci_execute($s)) {
        // Return a LOB descriptor as the value.
        while (oci_fetch($s)) {
          for ($i = 1;$i <= oci_num_fields($s);$i++)
            if (is_object(oci_result($s,$i))) {
              if ($size = oci_result($s,$i)->size())
                $data = oci_result($s,$i)->read($size);
              else
                $data = " "; }
            else {
              if (oci_field_is_null($s,$i))
                $title = " ";
              else
                $title = oci_result($s,$i); }}
        // Free statement resources.
        oci_free_statement($s);
        // Format HTML table to display BLOB photo and CLOB description.
        $out = '<table border="1" cellpadding="5" cellspacing="0">';
        $out .= '<tr>';
        $out .= '<td align="center" class="e">'.$title.'</td>';
        $out .= '</tr>';
        $out .= '<tr><td class="v">';
        $out .= '<div>';
        $out .= '<div style="margin-right:5px;float:left">';
        $out .= '<img src="ReadCanonicalFileToImage.php?id='.$id.'">';
        $out .= '</div>';
        $out .= '<div style="position=relative;">'.$data.'</div>';
        $out .= '</div>';
        $out .= '</td></tr>';
        $out .= '</table>'; }
      // Print the HTML table.
      print $out;
      // Disconnect from database.
      oci_close($c); }
    else {
      // Assign the OCI error and format double and single quotes.
      $errorMessage = oci_error();
      print htmlentities($errorMessage['message'])."<br />"; }}
?>
```

The program reads and assigns the CLOB column to the `$data` variable, and the `item_title` column to the `$title` variable. You should note that there aren't any changes required to the Apache alias or virtual directory configuration for this solution.

The `ReadCanonicalFileToImage.php` program is

```
<?php
  // Return successful attempt to connect to the database.
  if ($c = @oci_new_connect("video","video","video")) {
    // Declare input variables.
```

```
    (isset($_GET['id']))    ? $id = $_GET['id'] : $id = 1021;
    // Declare a SQL SELECT statement returning a CLOB.
    $stmt = "SELECT get_canonical_bfilename('ITEM','ITEM_PHOTO','ITEM_ID',:id)
             FROM   dual";
    // Parse a query through the connection.
    $s = oci_parse($c,$stmt);
    // Bind PHP variables to the OCI types.
    oci_bind_by_name($s,':id',$id);
    // Execute the PL/SQL statement.
    if (oci_execute($s)) {
      // Return a LOB descriptor and free resource as the value.
      while (oci_fetch($s)) {
        for ($i = 1;$i <= oci_num_fields($s);$i++)
          if ((!is_object(oci_result($s,$i))) && (!oci_field_is_null($s,$i)))
            $data = oci_result($s,$i);
          else
            $data = " "; }
      // Print the header first.
      header('Content-type: image/png');
      imagepng(imagecreatefromstring(file_get_contents($data))); }
    // Disconnect from database.
    oci_close($c); }
  else {
    // Assign the OCI error and format double and single quotes.
    $errorMessage = oci_error();
    print htmlentities($errorMessage['message'])."<br />"; }
?>
```

The `ReadCanonicalFileToImage.php` program renders the image by reading the canonical filename. The program then uses the PHP `file_get_contents` function to read the file into a binary string. The `imagecreatefromstring` function coverts the binary stream to a resource, and the `imagepng` function converts the resource into a file. Refer back to Figure 10-6, which shows the displayed image from this program.

In this section you have learned how to work with external files—`BFILE` data types. The examples have taught you how to leverage the locator and extend the database catalog to secure both canonical path names and filenames.

Review Section

This section has described the following points about working with `BFILE` types:

- `BFILE`s are physically stored externally while they hold a reference descriptor or locator that is stored in the column.
- A `BFILE` relies on virtual directories.
- Virtual directories are stored in the database catalog, and they hold the path resolution to find external `BFILE`s.
- You can architect a solution where you can discover the canonical path without hard-coding it, but it requires special grants and synonyms to make it work.

Understanding the DBMS_LOB Package

Discussions earlier in the chapter rely on elements of the `dbms_lob` package. These elements include functions, procedures, and package specification constants. This section summarizes the balance of the features in the `dbms_lob` package, and it is divided into seven subsections, which cover, in order: package constants, package exceptions, opening and closing methods (*a term that encompasses functions and procedures*), manipulation methods, introspection methods, `BFILE` methods, and temporary LOB methods.

Package Constants

There are several package constants that you can use when working with functions and procedures in the `dbms_lob` package. The general, option type, and option value constants for the `dbms_lob` package are qualified in Table 10-4. The Database File System (DBFS) constants are qualified in Table 10-8 in the "Security Link Methods" section at the end of this chapter.

Package Constant	Classification	Type	Value
CALL	General	PLS_INTEGER	12
DEFAULT_CSID	General	INTEGER	0
DEFAULT_LANG_CTX	General	INTEGER	0
FILE_READONLY	General	BINARY_INTEGER	0
LOBMAXSIZE	General	INTEGER	1.84467 e 19
LOB_READONLY	General	BINARY_INTEGER	0
LOB_READWRITE	General	BINARY_INTEGER	1
NO_WARNING	General	INTEGER	0
SESSION	General	PLS_INTEGER	10
TRANSACTION	General	PLS_INTEGER	11
WARN_INCONVERTIBLE_CHAR	General	INTEGER	1
OPT_COMPRESS	Option Type	PLS_INTEGER	1
OPT_DEDUPLICATE	Option Type	PLS_INTEGER	4
OPT_ENCRYPT	Option Type	PLS_INTEGER	2
COMPRESS_OFF	Option Value	PLS_INTEGER	0
COMPRESS_ON	Option Value	PLS_INTEGER	1
ENCRYPT_OFF	Option Value	PLS_INTEGER	0
ENCRYPT_ON	Option Value	PLS_INTEGER	1
DEDUPLICATE_OFF	Option Value	PLS_INTEGER	0
DEDUPLICATE_ON	Option Value	PLS_INTEGER	1

TABLE 10-4. *DBMS_LOB Package Constants*

Position	Field Name	Data Type
1	LOB_OFFSET	INTEGER
2	LEN	INTEGER
3	PRIMARY_LOB	BLOB
4	PRIMARY_LOB_OFFSET	NUMBER
5	MIME_TYPE	VARCHAR2(80)

TABLE 10-5. *Field Map of the BLOB_DEDUPLICATE_REGION Record Structure*

These constants have various uses inside the package. They should be used in lieu of their numeric equivalents because, while unlikely, Oracle reserves the right to change the values.

There are also four package specification types. Two are structures. A structure is a list of variables organized by position and data type. Structures act like rows of data. The other two types are associative arrays of the base structures. Both the types and structures are limited to uses in your PL/SQL blocks. They are covered next in pairs, the base structure and the associative array.

BLOB_DEDUPLICATE_REGION Record Structure

The `BLOB_DEDUPLICATE_REGION` type is a record composed of five fields, as qualified in Table 10-5. The `BLOB_DUPLICATE_REGION_TAB` type is an associative array indexed by `PLS_INTEGER`.

CLOB_DEDUPLICATE_REGION Record Structure

The `CLOB_DEDUPLICATE_REGION` type is a record composed of five fields, as qualified in Table 10-6. The `CLOB_DUPLICATE_REGION_TAB` type is an associative array indexed by `PLS_INTEGER`.

Package Exceptions

There are eight exceptions defined in the `dbms_lob` package. They are covered in Table 10-7. You should try to leverage these exceptions where appropriate in your own code before you create new user-defined exceptions.

Position	Field Name	Data Type
1	LOB_OFFSET	INTEGER
2	LEN	INTEGER
3	PRIMARY_LOB	CLOB
4	PRIMARY_LOB_OFFSET	NUMBER
5	MIME_TYPE	VARCHAR2(80)

TABLE 10-6. *Field Map of the CLOB_DEDUPLICATE_REGION Record Structure*

Exception Name	Error Code	Definition
ACCESS_ERROR	ORA-22925	Occurs when you attempt to write more than the maximum size allowed for a LOB column.
INVALID_ARGVAL	ORA-21560	Occurs when you pass a null value or a value outside of the 1–4GB range.
INVALID_LOCATOR	ORA 22275	Occurs when you pass an invalid LOB locator value.
INVALID_DIRECTORY	ORA-22287	Occurs when you attempt to read or write to a virtual database directory that no longer translates to a valid file system directory.
NOEXIST_DIRECTORY	ORA-22285	Occurs when you attempt to read or write to a virtual database directory that doesn't exist.
NOPRIV_DIRECTORY	ORA-22286	Occurs when you attempt to read or write to a virtual database directory and you have not been granted the appropriate access privilege.
OPEN_TOOMANY	ORA-22290	Occurs when you attempt to open more files than are allowed for the instance.
OPERATION_FAILED	ORA-22288	Occurs when you attempt to access a file that doesn't exist, or a file to which the Oracle user doesn't have read or write privileges.
UNOPENED_FILE	ORA-22289	Occurs when you try to perform operations on an external file before you've opened it.

TABLE 10-7. *DBMS_LOB Package Exceptions*

Opening and Closing Methods

The opening and closing methods apply to all LOB data types. You have a function to check whether a file is already open, and procedures to open and close LOB data types.

CLOSE Procedure

You call the `close` procedure to close a LOB. This is a pass-by-reference procedure for the LOB locator parameter. It requires that you define an appropriate LOB variable in the block where you call the procedure. You can't close a LOB unless it is already opened without raising an `ORA-22289` exception.

The overloaded procedure has the following prototypes:

```
CLOSE(file_loc => bfile_locator)
CLOSE(lob_loc => blob_locator)
CLOSE(lob_loc => clob_locator)
```

You can find examples of the `close` function in the `load_clob_from_file.sql` and `load_blob_from_file.sql` files, which are available on the publisher's website.

ISOPEN Function

You call the isopen function to check if a LOB is already open. You should use this function instead of the fileisopen function because fileisopen only checks for opened files using the input BFILE locator. The function is written to run in both SQL and PL/SQL environments. It returns a 1 when successful and a 0 when unsuccessful because there aren't any Boolean types in SQL.

The overloaded function has the following prototypes:

```
ISOPEN(file_loc => bfile_locator) RETURNS NUMBER
ISOPEN(lob_loc => blob_locator) RETURNS NUMBER
ISOPEN(lob_loc => clob_locator) RETURNS NUMBER
```

You can find examples of the isopen function in the load_clob_from_file.sql and load_blob_from_file.sql files.

OPEN Procedure

You call the open procedure to open a LOB. This is a pass-by-reference procedure for the LOB locator parameter. It requires that you define an appropriate LOB variable in the block where you call the procedure. You can open BLOB, CLOB, or NCLOB files in read-only or read-write mode, and open BFILEs in read-only mode. While you don't have to use the constants, it is safer to do so. You should use the lob_readonly or lob_readwrite constants for read-only or read-write mode, respectively. The open mode uses a default of dbms_lob.lob_readonly, and the actual parameter is optional.

The overloaded procedure has the following prototypes:

```
OPEN(file_loc => bfile_locator
    [,open_mode => open_mode ])
OPEN(lob_loc => blob_locator
    [,open_mode => open_mode ])
OPEN(lob_loc => clob_locator
    [,open_mode => open_mode ])
```

You can find examples of the open function in the sections "Reading Local Files into CLOB or NCLOB Columns" and "Reading Local Files into BLOB Columns" earlier in the chapter. You'll also find them in the load_clob_from_file.sql and load_blob_from_file.sql files.

Manipulation Methods

The manipulation methods are a collection of functions and procedures that allow you to read, write, and alter the content of LOBs. Several new features were added in Oracle Database 11g and carried forward to 12c, including compression, deduplication, and secure file encryption.

Many methods are overloaded to work with all LOB data types, while some only work with BLOB, CLOB, and NCLOB data types. The following subsections cover these manipulation methods and point out when a method is limited in scope.

You must create a transaction context by using an INSERT or UPDATE statement to use these manipulation methods against LOB columns. The RETURNING INTO clause opens the transaction scope and a COMMIT statement closes it. You use the locator returned by these statements as the gateway to copying one LOB to another of equivalent type.

APPEND Procedure

You call the append procedure to append to a BLOB, CLOB, or NCLOB data type. The append procedure is a pass-by-reference procedure for the LOB locator parameter. It allows you to add the contents of *another LOB* at the end of a LOB column. The writeappend procedure does the same thing, except it accepts a RAW or VARCHAR2 stream to append to a BLOB or CLOB column, respectively.

The overloaded procedure has the following prototypes:

```
APPEND(dest_lob => blob_locator
      ,src_lob => new_lob_stream)
APPEND(dest_lob => clob_locator
      ,src_lob => new_lob_stream)
```

CONVERTTOBLOB Procedure

You call the converttoblob procedure to convert a CLOB or NCLOB to a BLOB data type. The converttoblob procedure is a pass-by-reference procedure for the destination_blob_locator, source_blob_locator, destination_offset, source_offset, and language_context parameters.

The procedure has the following prototype:

```
CONVERTTOBLOB(dest_lob => destination_blob_locator
             ,src_blob => source_blob_locator
             ,amount => amount
             ,dest_offset => destination_offset
             ,src_offset => source_offset
             ,blob_csid => blob_csid
             ,lang_context => language_context
             ,warning => warning)
```

CONVERTTOCLOB Procedure

You call the converttoclob procedure to convert a BLOB to a CLOB or NCLOB data type. The converttoclob procedure is a pass-by-reference procedure for the LOB locator, destination and source offset, and language context parameters.

The procedure has the following prototype:

```
CONVERTTOCLOB(dest_lob => destination_blob_locator
             ,src_clob => source_clob_locator
             ,amount => amount
             ,dest_offset => destination_offset
             ,src_offset => source_offset
             ,blob_csid => clob_csid
             ,lang_context => language_context
             ,warning => warning)
```

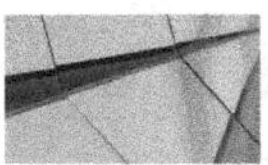

NOTE

The overloaded CONVERTTOCLOB procedure uses a blob_csid parameter name, but it really should be a clob_csid parameter name. While it's been that way for several releases, the name will probably change in a future release.

COPY Procedure

You call the copy procedure to copy a BLOB to another BLOB or a CLOB or NCLOB to another equivalent character LOB data type. The copy procedure is a pass-by-reference procedure for the destination LOB locator parameter.

The overloaded procedure has the following prototypes:

```
COPY(dest_lob => destination_blob_locator
     src_lob => source_blob_locator
     amount => amount
     dest_offset => destination_offset
     src_offset => source_offset)
COPY(dest_lob => destination_clob_locator
     src_lob => source_clob_locator
     amount => amount
     dest_offset => destination_offset
     src_offset => source_offset)
```

ERASE Procedure

You call the erase procedure to erase a chunk of a BLOB, a CLOB, or an NCLOB data type. The erase procedure is a pass-by-reference procedure for the LOB locator and amount parameters. The default offset is 1, and the offset is an optional parameter.

The overloaded procedure has the following prototypes:

```
ERASE(lob_loc => blob_locator
     ,amount => amount
    [,offset => offset ])
ERASE(lob_loc => clob_locator
     ,amount => amount
    [,offset => offset ])
```

FRAGMENT_DELETE Procedure

You call the fragment_delete procedure to delete a chunk of a BLOB, a CLOB, or an NCLOB data type. The fragment_delete procedure is a pass-by-reference procedure for the LOB locator parameter.

The overloaded procedure has the following prototypes:

```
FRAGMENT_DELETE(lob_loc => blob_locator
               ,amount => amount
              [,offset => offset])
FRAGMENT_DELETE(lob_loc => clob_locator
               ,amount => amount
              [,offset => offset])
```

FRAGMENT_INSERT Procedure

You call the fragment_insert procedure to insert a chunk of data (or a stream) to a BLOB, a CLOB, or an NCLOB data type. This procedure is a pass-by-reference procedure for the LOB locator parameter.

The overloaded procedure has the following prototypes:

```
FRAGMENT_INSERT(lob_loc => blob_locator
               ,amount => amount
               ,offset => offset
               ,buffer => raw_buffer)
FRAGMENT_INSERT(lob_loc => clob_locator
               ,amount => amount
               ,offset => offset
               ,buffer => character_buffer)
```

FRAGMENT_MOVE Procedure

You call the `fragment_move` procedure to move a chunk of data (or a stream) to another location in the same LOB. This function only works with `BLOB`, `CLOB`, or `NCLOB` data types. The `fragment_move` procedure is a pass-by-reference procedure for the LOB locator parameter.

The overloaded procedure has the following prototypes:

```
FRAGMENT_MOVE(lob_loc => blob_locator
             ,amount => amount
             ,src_offset => source_offset
             ,dest_offset => destination_offset)
FRAGMENT_MOVE(lob_loc => clob_locator
             ,amount => amount
             ,src_offset => source_offset
             ,dest_offset => destination_offset)
```

FRAGMENT_REPLACE Procedure

You call the `fragment_replace` procedure to move a chunk of data (or a stream) to replace a chunk of data in the same LOB. This function only works with `BLOB`, `CLOB`, or `NCLOB` data types. The `fragment_replace` procedure is a pass-by-reference procedure for the LOB locator parameter.

The overloaded procedure has the following prototypes:

```
FRAGMENT_REPLACE(lob_loc => blob_locator
                ,old_amount => old_amount
                ,new_amount => new_amount
                ,offset => offset
                ,buffer => buffer)
FRAGMENT_REPLACE(lob_loc => clob_locator
                ,old_amount => old_amount
                ,new_amount => new_amount
                ,offset => offset
                ,buffer => buffer)
```

ISSECUREFILE Function

You call the `issecurefile` function in Oracle Database 11*g* or newer to determine if a `BLOB`, `CLOB`, or `NCLOB` is configured as a secure file. This function only works in a PL/SQL scope because it returns a `BOOLEAN` data type, and it is a pass-by-value function.

The overloaded function has the following prototypes:

```
ISSECUREFILE(lob_loc => blob_locator) RETURNS BOOLEAN
ISSECUREFILE(lob_loc => clob_locator) RETURNS BOOLEAN
```

The following anonymous block demonstrates how to use this new function:

```
SQL> DECLARE
       audit_blob BLOB;
       CURSOR c IS
         SELECT NVL(item_blob,empty_blob)
         FROM item
         WHERE item_id = 1021;
     BEGIN
       OPEN c;
       FETCH c INTO audit_blob;
       IF dbms_lob.issecurefile(audit_blob) THEN
         dbms_output.put_line('A secure file.');
       ELSE
         dbms_output.put_line('Not a secure file.');
       END IF;
       CLOSE c;
     END;
     /
```

The `issecurefile` function requires that the `BLOB` column be initialized. If you attempt to apply this function to an invalid LOB locator, it raises an `ORA-22275` error. There is an opportunity to find this error anytime a row leaves the `BLOB` column non-initialized or null. It is a good coding practice to enclose it in an `NVL` function call providing an `empty_blob` or `empty_clob` constructor. By so doing, you evaluate for SecureFiles without the risk of raising a null exception. This approach ensures both nonsecure files and null values are managed by the `ELSE` clause. The approach also lets you suppress runtime errors triggered by an invalid LOB locator exception.

LOADBLOBFROMFILE Procedure

You call the `loadblobfromfile` procedure to copy a physical file, treated as a `BFILE`, to a `BLOB` data type. The `loadblobfromfile` procedure is a pass-by-reference procedure for the destination LOB locator and the destination and source offset parameters. You must always call the open procedure before this file, or you will raise an `ORA-22889` for an unopened file.

The procedure has the following prototype:

```
LOADBLOBFROMFILE(dest_lob => destination_blob_locator
                ,src_bfile => source_bfile
                ,amount => amount
                ,dest_offset => destination_offset
                ,src_offset => source_offset)
```

LOADCLOBFROMFILE Procedure

You call the `loadclobfromfile` procedure to copy a physical file, treated as a `BFILE`, to a `CLOB` data type. The `loadclobfromfile` procedure is a pass-by-reference procedure for the destination LOB locator, the destination and source offset, and language context parameters. You must always call the open procedure before this file, or you will raise an `ORA-22889` for an unopened file.

The procedure has the following prototype:

```
LOADCLOBFROMFILE(dest_lob => destination_clob_locator
                ,src_bfile => source_bfile
                ,amount => amount
                ,dest_offset => destination_offset
                ,src_offset => source_offset
                ,bfile_csid => bfile_csid
                ,lang_context => language_context
                ,warning => warning)
```

LOADFROMFILE Procedure

You call the `loadfromfile` procedure to copy a physical file, treated as a `BFILE`, to a `BLOB`, `CLOB`, or `NCLOB` data type. The `loadfromfile` procedure is a pass-by-reference procedure for the destination LOB locator parameter. You must always call the `open` procedure before this file, or you will raise an `ORA-22889` for an unopened file. The destination and source offset parameters use a default value of 1, and are therefore optional parameters.

The overloaded procedure has the following prototypes:

```
LOADFROMFILE(dest_lob => destination_blob_locator
            ,src_lob => source_bfile
            ,amount => amount
           [,dest_offset => destination_offset
           [,src_offset => source_offset ]])
LOADFROMFILE(dest_lob => destination_clob_locator
            ,src_lob => source_bfile
            ,amount => amount
           [,dest_offset => destination_offset
           [,src_offset => source_offset ]])
```

While this procedure works, you should consider using the `loadblobfromfile` or `loadclobfromfile` procedure first. They provide more control, and you can set language context for `CLOB` columns.

SETOPTIONS Procedure

You call the `setoptions` procedure to override the storage option of SecureFiles, or `BLOB`, `CLOB`, and `NCLOB` data types, in Oracle Database 12*c*. The `setoptions` procedure is a pass-by-reference procedure for the LOB locator parameter. You must always create a transaction to access a specific LOB locator.

The Oracle Database 12*c* documentation says you can change either the default column compression or deduplication settings. The documentation did not say, at time of writing, that you could override the default column encryption. However, encryption is one of three new constants added to the `dbms_lob` package in Oracle Database 12*c*. Full utility of these features may await a bug fix or the second release of Oracle Database 12*c*.

The overloaded procedure has the following prototypes:

```
SETOPTIONS(lob_loc => blob_locator
          ,option_types => option_type
          ,options => options)
SETOPTIONS(lob_loc => blob_locator
```

```
        ,option_types => option_type
        ,options => options)
```

TRIM Procedure

You call the `trim` procedure to trim unwanted content from `CLOB`, `NCLOB`, or `BLOB` data types. The `trim` procedure is a pass-by-reference procedure for the LOB locator parameter and requires a transaction context to change a LOB column value.

The overloaded procedure has the following prototypes:

```
TRIM(lob_loc => blob_locator
    ,newlen => new_length)
TRIM(lob_loc => clob_locator
    ,newlen => new_length)
```

WRITE Procedure

You call the `write` procedure to write data to a `CLOB`, `NCLOB`, or `BLOB` data type beginning at a specified offset. The default offset is 1. Beginning in Oracle Database 11*g*, you should consider using the `fragment_insert` or `fragment_replace` procedure instead of the `write` procedure.

The overloaded procedure has the following prototypes:

```
WRITE(lob_loc => blob_locator
     ,amount => amount
     ,offset => offset
     ,buffer => raw_buffer)
WRITE(lob_loc => clob_locator
     ,amount => amount
     ,offset => offset
     ,buffer => character_buffer)
```

WRITEAPPEND Procedure

You call the `writeappend` procedure to append data to the end of a `CLOB`, `NCLOB`, or `BLOB` data type. The overloaded procedure has the following prototypes:

```
WRITEAPPEND(lob_loc => blob_locator
           ,amount => amount
           ,buffer => raw_buffer)
WRITEAPPEND(lob_loc => clob_locator
           ,amount => amount
           ,buffer => character_buffer)
```

Introspection Methods

Introspection methods let you discover something about the value in the instance of a data type. Some of these methods should look familiar because they're staples in working with strings.

COMPARE Function

You call the `compare` function to check whether two LOBs of the same data type are equal or two LOB *fragments* of the same data type are equal. The function is a pass-by-value module. It works with `BLOB`, `CLOB`, `NCLOB`, or `BFILE` data types. The `compare` function works in both SQL and PL/SQL environments. It returns a 0 when the two LOBs (or LOB fragments) are equal and a 1 when they're not.

The overloaded function has the following prototypes:

```
COMPARE(lob_1 => bfile_locator_1
       ,lob_2 => bfile_locator_2
       ,amount => amount
      [,offset_1 => offset_1
      [,offset_2 => offset_2 ]]) RETURNS NUMBER
COMPARE(lob_1 => blob_locator_1
       ,lob_2 => blob_locator_2
       ,amount => amount
      [,offset_1 => offset_1
      [,offset_2 => offset_2 ]]) RETURNS NUMBER
COMPARE(lob_1 => clob_locator_1
       ,lob_2 => clob_locator_2
       ,amount => amount
      [,offset_1 => offset_1
      [,offset_2 => offset_2 ]]) RETURNS NUMBER
```

You should notice from the prototypes that the size for comparison is optional for BLOB, CLOB, and NCLOB but is required for BFILE data types. The simplest way to compare two values is with a SQL statement, like

```
SQL> SELECT CASE
           WHEN DBMS_LOB.COMPARE(i1.item_blob,i2.item_blob) = 0 THEN
           THEN 'True'
           ELSE 'False'
         END AS compared
  FROM item i1 CROSS JOIN item i2
  WHERE i1.item_id = 1021 AND i2.item_id = 1022;
```

This statement returns true if you've uploaded the same image of Harry Potter to both rows (as done in the load_blob_from_file.sql script). Otherwise, it returns false.

GETCHUNKSIZE Function

You call the getchunksize function to check the read and write chunk size. This is typically the block size (*as determined by the db_block_size database parameter*) minus a handling value. If your db_block_size is set to 8KB (8,192 bytes), then the chunk size will be 8,132 bytes. The function works with BLOB, CLOB, or NCLOB data types.

The overloaded procedure has the following prototypes:

```
GETCHUNKSIZE(lob_loc => blob_locator) RETURNS NUMBER
GETCHUNKSIZE(lob_loc => clob_locator) RETURNS NUMBER
```

The simplest way to call this function is

```
SELECT DBMS_LOB.GETCHUNKSIZE(i1.item_blob)
FROM item i1
WHERE i1.item_id = 1021;
```

In most cases, it returns 8,132 bytes because the default db_block_size parameter value is 8,192 bytes. The query should work provided you inserted the Harry Potter image into the BLOB column for this row.

GET_DEDUPLICATED_REGIONS Procedure

You call the `get_deduplicated_regions` procedure to check for deduplicated regions in Oracle SecureFiles. This is a new procedure as of Oracle Database 11*g*. The function works with `BLOB`, `CLOB`, or `NCLOB` data types. It is a pass-by-reference procedure for the associative array of structures, which are implementations of the record structures covered earlier in the "Package Constants" subsection of this chapter.

The overloaded procedure has the following prototypes:

```
GET_DEDUPLICATED_REGIONS(lob_loc => blob_locator
                        ,region_table => blob_deduplicated_table)
GET_DEDUPLICATED_REGIONS(lob_loc => clob_locator
                        ,region_table => clob_deduplicated_table)
```

GETLENGTH Function

You call the `getlength` function to get the length of a LOB. The function works with `BLOB`, `CLOB`, `NCLOB`, or `BFILE` data types. It is a pass-by-value function and essential in many regards for working with LOB columns.

The overloaded function has the following prototypes:

```
GETLENGTH(file_loc => bfile_locator) RETURNS NUMBER
GETLENGTH(lob_loc => blob_locator) RETURNS NUMBER
GETLENGTH(lob_loc => clob_locator) RETURNS NUMBER
```

GETOPTIONS Function

You call the `getoptions` function to examine the storage options of SecureFiles, which are `BLOB`, `CLOB`, or `NCLOB` data types in Oracle Database 12*c*. This function is a pass-by-reference function for the LOB locator parameter. You must always create a transaction to access a specific LOB locator. Full utility of these features may await a bug fix or the second release of Oracle Database 12*c*.

The overloaded function has the following prototypes:

```
GETOPTIONS(lob_loc => blob_locator
          ,option_types => option_type) RETURNS BINARY_INTEGER
GETOPTIONS(lob_loc => clob_locator
          ,option_types => option_type) RETURNS BINARY_INTEGER
```

GET_STORAGE_LIMIT Function

You call the `get_storage_limit` function to get the maximum storage length of a LOB. The function works with `BLOB`, `CLOB`, or `NCLOB` data types. It is a pass-by-value function.

The overloaded function has the following prototypes:

```
GET_STORAGE_LIMIT(lob_loc => blob_locator) RETURNS NUMBER
GET_STORAGE_LIMIT(lob_loc => clob_locator) RETURNS NUMBER
```

INSTR Function

You call the `instr` function to find the position where a byte pattern begins in a LOB. The function works with `BLOB`, `CLOB`, `NCLOB`, or `BFILE` data types. It is a pass-by-value function. The `offset` and `nth_occurrence` parameters have a default value of 1, which makes them optional.

The overloaded function has the following prototypes:

```
INSTR(file_loc => bfile_locator
     ,option_types => raw_byte_pattern
    [,offset => offset
    [,nth => nth_occurrence ]]) RETURNS NUMBER
INSTR(lob_loc => blob_locator
     ,option_types => raw_byte_pattern
    [,offset => offset
    [,nth => nth_occurrence ]]) RETURNS NUMBER
INSTR(lob_loc => clob_locator
     ,option_types => character_pattern
    [,offset => offset
    [,nth => nth_occurrence ]]) RETURNS NUMBER
```

READ Procedure

You call the `read` procedure to read data from a `CLOB`, `NCLOB`, or `BLOB` data type beginning at a specified offset. There is no default offset value, and it is a mandatory actual parameter.

The procedure is pass-by-reference for the locator and buffer. The overloaded procedure has the following prototypes:

```
READ(file_loc => bfile_locator
    ,amount => amount
    ,offset => offset
    ,buffer => raw_buffer)
READ(lob_loc => blob_locator
    ,amount => amount
    ,offset => offset
    ,buffer => raw_buffer)
READ(lob_loc => blob_locator
    ,amount => amount
    ,offset => offset
    ,buffer => character_buffer)
```

SUBSTR Function

You call the `substr` function to read data from a `CLOB`, `NCLOB`, or `BLOB` data type beginning at a specified offset. The default for the amount and offset is 1. This is a pass-by-value function that returns a `RAW` data type for `BFILE` and `BLOB` data types and a `VARCHAR2` data type for `CLOB` or `NCLOB` data types. The function is subject to the character stream limits of the environment where you use it. This means that the `substr` function can return a 4,000-byte or 32,767-byte string, depending on the `max_string_size` database parameter setting.

The overloaded function has the following prototypes:

```
SUBSTR(file_loc => bfile_locator
      [,amount => amount
      [,offset => offset ]) RETURNS RAW
SUBSTR(lob_loc => blob_locator
      [,amount => amount
      [,offset => offset ]) RETURNS RAW
```

```
SUBSTR(lob_loc => clob_locator
      [,amount => amount
      [,offset => offset ]) RETURNS VARCHAR2
```

You can find an example that uses the `dbms_lob.substr` procedure in the "GETCONTENTTYPE Function" section later in this chapter. The optional `offset` parameter lets you pick a starting point for a substring in the `CLOB`.

BFILE Methods

The `BFILE` methods only support external and read-only `BFILE` data types. Some of the `BFILE` methods have recommended alternatives. Oracle hasn't deprecated any methods in the `dbms_lob` package but has superseded some methods by new `dbms_lob` methods. Recommendations that you call alternative methods are noted in their respective subsections.

FILECLOSE Procedure

You call the `fileclose` procedure to close a `BFILE`. This is a pass-by-reference procedure for the LOB locator parameter. It requires that you define an appropriate LOB variable in the block where you call the procedure. You can't close a LOB unless it is already opened without raising an `ORA-22289` exception. Oracle recommends you use the `close` procedure instead of the `fileclose` procedure.

The procedure has the following prototype:

```
FILECLOSE(file_loc => bfile_locator)
```

FILECLOSEALL Procedure

You call the `filecloseall` procedure to close all open files. This function has no formal parameter.

The procedure has the following prototype:

```
FILECLOSEALL
```

FILEEXISTS Function

You call the `fileexists` function to check if a file exists on the file system. It relies on the virtual database directory translation to a physical directory on the file system. You can use this function in SQL or PL/SQL environments, and it returns a 1 if true and a 0 if false.

The function has the following prototype:

```
FILEEXISTS(file_loc => bfile_locator) RETURNS NUMBER
```

FILEGETNAME Procedure

You call the `filegetname` procedure to finds the base filename in a `BFILE` locator. You must call the procedure only after you initialize all three actual parameter values to `VARCHAR2(255)` strings. The definition of space for declared variables is required because the virtual database directory and base filename formal parameters are `OUT` mode variables, which must be sized before calling a pass-by-reference function or procedure.

The procedure has the following prototype:

```
FILEGETNAME(file_loc => bfile_locator
           ,dir_alias => virtual_database_directory
           ,filename => base_file_name)
```

For details of how to use the filegetname procedure, refer to the example of using get_bfilename as a wrapper function around the filegetname procedure, presented in the section "Creating and Using Virtual Directories" earlier in the chapter.

FILEISOPEN Function

The fileisopen function is used to check if a BFILE is already open. This function is provided only for backward compatibility, so you should not use it. Instead, you should use the isopen function. Like the isopen function, fileisopen is written to run in both SQL and PL/SQL environments. It returns a 1 when successful and a 0 when unsuccessful because there aren't any Boolean types in SQL.

The function has the following prototype:

```
FILEISOPEN(file_loc => bfile_locator) RETURNS NUMBER
```

You can find examples in the load_clob_from_file.sql and load_blob_from_file.sql files on the publisher's website.

FILEOPEN Procedure

You call the fileopen procedure to open a BFILE. This is a pass-by-reference procedure for the LOB locator parameter. It requires that you define an appropriate LOB variable in the block where you call the procedure. Oracle recommends you use the open procedure instead of the fileopen procedure. The optional open mode parameter has a default value of dbms_lob.lob_readonly.

The procedure has the following prototype:

```
FILEOPEN(file_loc => bfile_locator
        [,open_mode => open_mode ])
```

Temporary LOB Methods

Temporary LOB data types are not linked to a physical location in the database. The LOB locator points to a memory location where the temporary LOB is written.

CREATETEMPORARY Procedure

You call the createtemporary procedure to create a temporary BLOB, CLOB, or NCLOB in memory. Temporary LOBs are time-bound entities, and you should constrain their existence to the smallest time slice possible. The optional duration parameter is bound by the dbms_lob.session constant, which is the length of the session.

You must use the createtemporary procedure when you want to assemble a BLOB, CLOB, or NCLOB in memory from a collection of pieces. The pieces are typically in the form of a collection of raw byte or character segments. You typically create a temporary LOB inside a pass-by-value function when you want to do either of the following:

- Use a table collection of raw bytes or characters as the input parameter
- Return the reference to the temporary LOB (generally larger than 32,767 bytes) as the return value of a pass-by-value function inside a SQL statement or PL/SQL block

You also can use a pass-by-reference function or procedure to return a temporary BLOB, CLOB, or NCLOB reference. An IN OUT or OUT-only mode parameter can return the temporary

LOB reference to the calling program's scope. While this type of solution is possible, I don't recommend it. A pass-by-value function is a more portable and cohesive solution to return a LOB. You can find an example of such a pass-by-value function in the "Converting a LONG to a CLOB" sidebar earlier in this chapter.

The overloaded procedure has the following prototypes:

```
CREATETEMPORTY(lob_loc => blob_locator
              ,cache => cache
             [,dur => duration ])
CREATETEMPORTY(lob_loc => clob_locator
              ,cache => cache
             [,dur => duration ])
```

ISTEMPORARY Function

You call the `istemporary` function to free resources that held a temporary `BLOB` or `CLOB` variable. This is an important function and should be used each time you manage a temporary LOB. It works with `BLOB`, `CLOB`, or `NCLOB` data types. The `istemporary` function works in both SQL and PL/SQL environments. It returns a 1 when successful and a 0 when not.

The overloaded function has the following prototypes:

```
ISTEMPORARY(lob_loc => blob_locator) RETURNS NUMBER
ISTEMPORARY(lob_loc => clob_locator) RETURNS NUMBER
```

FREETEMPORARY Procedure

You call the `freetemporary` procedure to free the memory consumed for a temporary `BLOB`, `CLOB`, or `NCLOB` in memory. This is an important procedure and should be used each time you manage a temporary LOB.

The overloaded procedure has the following prototypes:

```
FREETEMPORARY(lob_loc => blob_locator)
FREETEMPORARY(lob_loc => clob_locator)
```

This section has reviewed the methods of the `dbms_lob` package. Several new methods were added in Oracle Database 11*g*, and there may yet be more added to simplify the access and management of LOBs.

Security Link Methods

The security link methods were added in Oracle Database 11g Release 2. They're designed to work with the Database File System (DBFS). DBFS takes advantage of the SecureFiles storage features introduced by Oracle Database 11*g* Release 1. You can find out how to use and configure the DBFS package in Chapter 6 of the *Oracle Database SecureFiles and Large Objects Developer's Guide*.

Chapter 4 of the *Oracle Database SecureFiles and Large Object Developer's Guide* shows you how to use DBFS. Several methods were added to the `dbms_lob` package to support DBFS. It's important to note that Oracle also added (in Oracle Database 11*g* Release 2) seven constants to the `dbms_lob` package to support these new methods, as outlined in Table 10-8. The methods also work with BasicFiles (nonencrypted files).

Understanding the security link methods is critical when working with Oracle SecureFiles. The following subsections describe each in turn.

Package Constant	Classification	Type	Value
DBFS_LINK_NEVER	DBFS	PLS_INTEGER	0
DBFS_LINK_YES	DBFS	PLS_INTEGER	1
DBFS_LINK_NO	DBFS	PLS_INTEGER	2
DBFS_LINK_CACHE	DBFS	PLS_INTEGER	1
DBFS_LINK_NOCACHE	DBFS	PLS_INTEGER	0
DBFS_LINK_PATH_MAX_SIZE	DBFS	PLS_INTEGER	1024
CONTENTTYPE_MAX_SIZE	DBFS	BINARY_INTEGER	128

TABLE 10-8. *Database File System Constants in the dbms_lob Package*

COPY_DBFS_LINK Procedure

You call the `copy_dbfs_link` procedure to copy an existing DBFS link into a new `BLOB`, `CLOB`, or `NCLOB` column. You can use the `dbfs_link_cache` or `dbfs_link_nocache` constant as a `flag` parameter value. The `dbfs_link_nocache` constant is the default and the best choice with large LOBs.

The overloaded procedure has the following prototypes:

```
COPY_DBFS_LINK(lob_loc_det => target_blob_locator
              ,lob_loc_src => source_blob_locator
              ,flags => caching_enabled_or_disabled)
COPY_DBFS_LINK(lob_loc_det => target_clob_locator
              ,lob_loc_src => source_clob_locator
              ,flags => caching_enabled_or_disabled)
```

COPY_FROM_DBFS_LINK Procedure

You call the `copy_from_dbfs_link` procedure to copy a LOB from the DBFS Hardware Security Module (HSM) Store into the database. An HSM Store is a physical or software device that safeguards and manages digital keys for storing authentication. It also provides cryptoprocessing without revealing the decrypted data.

NOTE
Cryptoprocessing means cryptographic operations performed by a computer.

The `copy_from_dbfs_link` procedure lets you copy a `BLOB`, `CLOB`, or `NCLOB` from the HSM Store into the database. The overloaded procedure has the following prototypes:

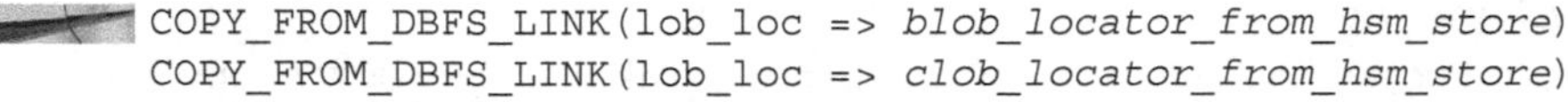

```
COPY_FROM_DBFS_LINK(lob_loc => blob_locator_from_hsm_store)
COPY_FROM_DBFS_LINK(lob_loc => clob_locator_from_hsm_store)
```

DBFS_LINK_GENERATE_PATH Function

The `dbfs_link_generate_path` function returns a globally unique file pathname that you can use for archiving `CLOB`, `NCLOB`, or `BLOB` columns. The globally unique file pathname is guaranteed to be unique across all calls to this function for any `CLOB`, `NCLOB`, or `BLOB` column.

The overloaded procedure has the following prototypes:

```
DBFS_LINK_GENERATE_PATH(lob_loc => blob_locator
                       ,storage_dir => virtual_directory) RETURNS VARCHAR2
DBFS_LINK_GENERATE_PATH(lob_loc => clob_locator
                       ,storage_dir => virtual_directory) RETURNS VARCHAR2
```

GETCONTENTTYPE Function

The `getcontenttype` function returns a content type value previously set by the `setcontenttype` procedure. The `getcontenttype` function returns a null value when no content type has been set inside a `CLOB`, `NCLOB`, or `BLOB` column.

The overloaded procedure has the following prototypes:

```
GETCONTENTTYPE(lob_loc => blob_locator) RETURNS VARCHAR2
GETCONTENTTYPE(lob_loc => clob_locator) RETURNS VARCHAR2
```

The following code shows you how to use the `getcontenttype` function and `setcontenttype` procedure:

```
SQL> DECLARE
  2    /* Declare a CLOB variable. */
  3    lv_clob  CLOB;
  4    /* Declare a cursor. */
  5    CURSOR c
  6    ( cv_weapon_id  NUMBER ) IS
  7      SELECT   weapon_desc
  8      FROM     weapon
  9      WHERE    weapon_id = cv_weapon_id;
 10  BEGIN
 11    /* Open and fetch a cursor. */
 12    OPEN c (2);
 13    FETCH c INTO lv_clob;
 14    /* Set the content type of a CLOB. */
 15    dbms_lob.setcontenttype(lv_clob,'Medieval');
 16    /* Print the content of the CLOB and content type. */
 17    dbms_output.put_line(
 18      'Clob Variable: '||dbms_lob.substr(lv_clob,10)||CHR(10)||
 19      'Content Type:  '||dbms_lob.getcontenttype(lv_clob));
 20  END;
 21  /
```

Line 15 sets the `content` of the local variable, which is actually a reference to a `CLOB` column in the `weapon` table. That means when you set the content type of the local variable, you actually set the content type of the `weapon_desc` column. Line 18 prints a string literal and the first ten characters of a `CLOB` column. Line 19 prints the content type that you set on line 15.

GET_DBFS_LINK Function

The `get_dbfs_link` function links a SecureFile to a specified path name. It doesn't copy the data to the path.

The overloaded procedure has the following prototypes:

```
GET_DBFS_LINK(lob_loc => blob_locator) RETURNS VARCHAR2
GET_DBFS_LINK(lob_loc => clob_locator) RETURNS VARCHAR2
```

GET_DBFS_LINK_STATE Procedure

The get_dbfs_link_state procedure links a SecureFile to a specified path name, and it returns three OUT-only mode parameter values. The pass-by-reference parameters are storage_path, state, and cached. The storage_path parameter returns the storage path where the LOB is stored in the DBFS HSM Store. The state parameter returns one of the following three constant values: DBFS_LINK_NEVER, DBFS_LINK_NO, or DBFS_LINK_YES. The cached parameter returns a Boolean true or false.

The overloaded procedure has the following prototypes:

```
GET_DBFS_LINK_STATE(lob_loc => blob_locator
                   ,storage_path => virtual_directory
                   ,state => state_of_link
                   ,cached => true_or_false)
GET_DBFS_LINK_STATE(lob_loc => clob_locator
                   ,storage_path => virtual_directory
                   ,state => state_of_link
                   ,cached => true_or_false)
```

SETCONTENTTYPE Procedure

The setcontenttype procedure sets the content type for a BLOB, CLOB, or NCLOB column. The "GETCONTENTTYPE Function" section earlier in this chapter has an example of using the setcontenttype procedure.

The overloaded procedure has the following prototypes:

```
SETCONTENTTYPE(lob_loc => blob_locator
              ,contenttype => content_type)
SETCONTENTTYPE(lob_loc => clob_locator
              ,contenttype => content_type)
```

SET_DBFS_LINK Procedure

The set_dbfs_link procedure sets the storage path where the LOB is stored in the DBFS HSM store. The overloaded procedure has the following prototypes:

```
SETCONTENTTYPE(lob_loc => blob_locator
              ,storage_path => virtual_directory)
SETCONTENTTYPE(lob_loc => clob_locator
              ,storage_path => virtual_directory)
```

Review Section

This section has qualified the following points about working with the dbms_lob package.

- To understand how to use the dbms_lob package, you need to understand the key package constants and exceptions.
- Many of the procedures in the dbms_lob package are pass-by-reference, which means you need to carefully wrap their behaviors in other program units.

Supporting Scripts

This section describes programs placed on the McGraw-Hill Professional website to support the book.

The LONG to CLOB Script

The `expanding_view.sql` program contains the stored function to convert a `LONG` column from a view to a `CLOB` variable.

Manage LOBs from the File System

The `load_blob_from_file.sql` and `load_clob_from_file.sql` programs show you how to load large objects from the file system.

Manage CLOB and BLOB LOBs Through the Web

The following SQL, HTML, and PHP files work collectively to show you how to load `CLOB` and `BLOB` data types through web applications.

- `create_web_clob_loading.sql`
- `create_web_blob_loading.sql`
- `UploadItemBlobForm.htm`
- `UploadItemDescriptionForm.htm`
- `ConvertBlobToImage.php`
- `UploadItemBlob.php`
- `UploadItemDescription.php`

Manage BFILE LOBs Through the Web

The following SQL and PHP files work collectively to show you how to load `BFILE` data types through web applications. The SQL files require you to run them under different ownership and with different privileges.

- `get_bfilename.sql`
- `get_canonical_bfilename.sql`
- `get_directory_path.sql`
- `ConvertFileToImage.php`
- `QueryRelativeBFILE.php`
- `ReadCanonicalFileToImage.php`

Summary

This chapter has covered how PL/SQL works with `BLOB`, `CLOB`, and `NCLOB` internally stored large objects, and how to define these base types as SecureFiles. You have also seen how to use and leverage internal locators to external `BFILE` files. Image retrieval has been demonstrated by using the PHP programming language.

Mastery Check

The mastery check is a series of true-or-false and multiple-choice questions that let you confirm how well you understand the material in the chapter. You may check Appendix I for answers to these questions.

True or False:

1. ___CLOB and NCLOB data types are object types and require explicit construction in a SQL context.
2. ___CLOB and NCLOB data types are subclasses to a generic LOB class.
3. ___The BLOB data type holds binary streams.
4. ___You can assign a string literal to a CLOB inside a VALUES clause of an INSERT statement.
5. ___A stored function can convert a LONG data type to a CLOB data type.
6. ___The empty_clob function supports the CLOB, NCLOB, and BLOB data types.
7. ___You can assign strings of hexadecimal values to BLOB variables in a PL/SQL context.
8. ___A BFILE depends on a virtual directory to find the external file.
9. ___A SELECT-INTO statement can assign a string to a CLOB variable.
10. ___A SELECT-INTO statement can assign a LONG column value to a CLOB variable.

Multiple Choice:

11. Which of the following are pass-by-reference procedures in the dbms_lob package? (Multiple answers possible)
    - **A.** lob_readonly
    - **B.** write
    - **C.** lob_readwrite
    - **D.** writeappend
    - **E.** isopen
12. Which of the following are functions in the dbms_lob package? (Multiple answers possible)
    - **A.** open
    - **B.** isopen
    - **C.** converttoblob
    - **D.** unopened_file
    - **E.** issecurefile
13. Which of the following are exceptions in the dbms_lob package? (Multiple answers possible)
    - **A.** OPEN_TOOMANY
    - **B.** NOPRIV_DIR
    - **C.** NOEXIST_DIRECTORY

D. `UNINITIALIZED_BLOB`

E. `GETOPTIONS`

14. Which of the following are LOBs in an Oracle Database 12*c* database? (Multiple answers possible)

A. A `BLOB`

B. A `CLOB`

C. A `NCLOB`

D. A `BFILE`

E. All of the above

15. Which of the following are internally stored LOBs in Oracle Database 12*c*? (Multiple answers possible)

A. A `BLOB`

B. A `CLOB`

C. A `NCLOB`

D. A `BFILE`

E. All of the above

CHAPTER 11

Object Types

This chapter examines how you define, initialize, and use objects. It lays a foundation of what PL/SQL object types are and how object-oriented programming (OOP) works by covering the following topics:

- Object basics
  - Declaring object types
  - Implementing object bodies
  - White listing object types
  - Getters and setters
  - Static member methods
  - Comparing objects
- Inheritance and polymorphism
  - Declaring subclasses
  - Implementing subclasses
  - Type evolution
- Implementing object type collections
  - Declaring object type collections
  - Implementing object type collections

Procedural programming functions perform well-defined tasks, and they hide the details of their operation. A collection of functions can be grouped together to perform a task that requires a set of functions. Organized groups of functions are *modules*, and the process of grouping them together is *modularization*. Modules are stored in PL/SQL packages.

Packages, like functions and procedures, hide their complexity through a predefined *application programming interface (API)*. While you can access global variables and constants that are declared in package specifications, you can't guard against their external change without implementing a Singleton pattern. The sidebar "Singleton Design Pattern" in Chapter 9 explains how you can control access with a Singleton pattern. Functions and procedures present different problems because they control all operations on their runtime variables.

Object-oriented programming solutions fix some of the shortcomings of functions, procedures, and packages because they maintain the operational state of their variables. Object types define how to store data and define API operations, also known as `MEMBER` functions or `MEMBER` procedures. Operations are generally described as methods in OOP languages (OOPLs), but they are implemented as class member functions or procedures in PL/SQL.

Exploring where OOP started helps explain why maintaining object state is important. The idea for OOPLs comes from the Simula language developed in Norway in the 1960s. The concept of an object evolved from the idea that simulated events pass through many small software factories, known as "finite-state" or "state" machines. State machines are miniature applications that simulate real-world events.

An object that moves through a series of state machines in software is analogous to a ball in a physical pinball machine (where the software *"ball"* is the object). The software "ball" isn't really moving in response to mechanical devices but in response to state machines that simulate bumpers, bats, and other physical objects. The velocity, spin, and direction of the software ball are its internal state, which must be known and tracked to determine where it will strike and at what speed and spin. These factors determine how the next bumper, or state machine, will impact the software ball.

The possible characteristics and behaviors of the software ball are its attributes and operations. Since each ball starts with the same characteristics and behaviors, you can define a single piece of code to contain these attributes, as a blueprint would implement them. The blueprint qualifies the name and data types of attributes, and the name, formal parameter lists, and return types of methods. In OOPLs, the blueprint is called an abstract class. The single piece of code implements the blueprint as an object type. Each creation of a runtime unit of this code is an *instantiation*, or creation of an object.

Objects are also state machines. They are defined by variables that have known and unknown values, and these variables enable or constrain the operations of real-time instances. Object type instances are objects, though realistically this formalism seems lost more often than not. Object types and objects are also known as classes in many OOPLs. This book uses the following key terms when describing object types, objects, and object instances:

- *Abstract class* describes an object type because the attributes defined by the object type must be implemented by the object body.
- *Object type* and *class* interchangeably describe the implementation of an object type or an object body.
- *Object* and *class instance* interchangeably describe a runtime instance of an object body or class instance.

NOTE
While an abstract class isn't a prefect corollary, it's the closest available.

To state it in PL/SQL terms, an object type (or abstract class) mirrors the behavior of a package specification, and an object body (or class) implements the object type (or abstract class) much the same as a package body implements a package specification. The difference is that you're guaranteed to get a fresh class instance each time without using a serially reusable precompiler directive, which is an improvement over serially reusable packages covered in Chapter 9.

Inside of these object types and class instances you have hidden data and operations. The process of hiding data storage and operations is described by two words in object-oriented programming. The first is *encapsulation*—the process of hiding the operational details; and the second is *abstraction*—the process of using generalization to mask task complexity. The internal aspects of object types are wrapped, as a birthday present is wrapped by colorful paper. The wrappers access the hidden components through published operations, which is similar to the package architecture described in Chapter 9.

These hidden operations and data plus their wrapper operations require OO programmers to take some time to work out what should be an object and then to define the object type. This analysis and design process is called object-oriented analysis and design (OOAD). OOAD evolved from concepts in systems engineering and business process modeling. It has gone through several variations from the 1960s, including symbolic representation models like Booch and object-modeling technique (OMT). These models were merged into the Unified Modeling Language (UML) in the 1990s.

The current method for visually representing object types is generally done in UML. Object types are represented by a rectangle divided into three rectangular sections. The topmost section contains the object type name. The middle section contains the list of attributes, which are variables used in the object type. The bottom section contains the list of methods that describes the API to the object type or object. Figure 11-1 contains a sample UML diagram describing the `SomeClass` object type.

OOP has two types of APIs in object types: *static* and *instance*. Static methods allow you to access object type variables and methods without creating an instance of a class. Static variables *aren't* available in PL/SQL. You can only implement static methods in PL/SQL, such as package functions and procedures.

Instance methods let you access object variables and methods of an instance of a class. They *are not static* and they are only available after you create an instance of an object type. Then, they are capable of managing class events.

The static area of objects is generally limited to variables and functions that are common features across all class instances. You can use static functions to return a copy of an instantiated class, which implements the OOP Concrete Builder pattern. Likewise, you can use static member functions or procedures to return what would otherwise be an instance variable. The section "Static Member Methods" later in this chapter contains an example of returning an instance as a return type. That example shows you how to implement a Concrete Factory design pattern in PL/SQL.

Oracle Database 12*c*, like its predecessors since Oracle 9*i* Database, lets you create object types and bodies as SQL data types. You can use these object types as SQL data types in four situations: as a column data type when you define a table, as the data type of an object attribute when you declare an object type, as a formal parameter data type in the signature of a function or procedure, and as a return type for a function.

Oracle Database 12*c* qualifies objects as either *persistent* or *transient*. The qualification is made by assessing the lifetime of the objects.

Persistent objects are further qualified by dividing them into stand-alone objects and embedded objects. Stand-alone objects are stored in a database table and have a unique object identifier. Embedded objects *are not stored* in a database table but rather are embedded in another Oracle

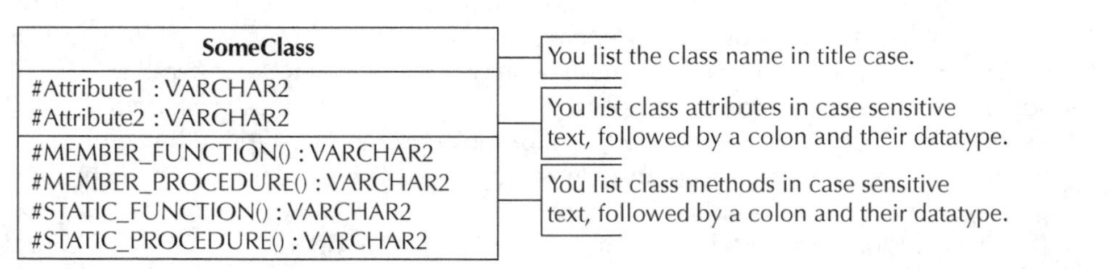

FIGURE 11-1. *UML class diagram*

structure, like another object type, package, function, or procedure. Embedded objects have a lifetime limited to the runtime of the programming unit where they're deployed. You don't have an object identifier for embedded objects, which makes using them through the OCI difficult. Refer to the Appendix B sections "Object Data Type," "Object Types," and "Nested Collection Types" for more information about persistent objects. You can also find more details about persistent objects in the *Oracle Database Object-Relational Developer's Guide 12c Release*. Persistent objects have an indefinite lifetime because they exist as long as they're stored in the database as column values.

Transient objects are instances of objects that aren't stored in the database. They have a lifetime limited to the duration of their use in a PL/SQL block. These are the primary type of objects you'll learn about in this chapter.

You will now learn how to define and implement objects in PL/SQL. While the sections can be read independently for reference purposes, they are positioned to be read sequentially.

Object Basics

The same naming requirements as those used with other objects in the database apply to objects. Object type names in PL/SQL must start with an alphabetical character and consist of only alphabetical characters, numbers, or underscores. *Object names share the same name space as all other objects except database triggers.*

Scope for object types is the same as for other stand-alone functions or procedures, and package functions and procedures. It is also limited to the defining schema. You must grant the `EXECUTE` privilege on an object type if you want another schema to be able to use it.

Classes, unlike functions, cannot have return types. Class instantiation returns a copy or instance of a class. While object construction generally occurs as the source operand on the right side of an assignment operator, you can dynamically construct an object instance as an actual parameter to a function, or as a member of a collection. The existence of object instances is limited to the duration of the call, or its membership as a component of a collection.

You will find that objects are similar to those in many other languages but different enough that you may want to review the PL/SQL object operators at this point. Table 4-1 in Chapter 4 provides you with a list of PL/SQL delimiters that also support example programs in this chapter.

Having met the general concepts, you will now work through the specifics of implementing *transient* object types in PL/SQL. You will begin by learning how to declare, implement, instantiate, and white list objects. Then, you'll examine good OOP techniques, such as using getters, setters, static methods, and comparative class methods.

Declaring Objects Types

PL/SQL object types, like package specifications, have a prototype definition, which includes three specialized functions—`CONSTRUCTOR`, `MAP`, and `ORDER`. A `CONSTRUCTOR` function lets you create an instance of an object. The `MAP` and `ORDER` functions allow you to sort objects inside SQL statements, or sort object instances inside a varray or table collection.

You can implement one or more `CONSTRUCTOR` functions, but the signatures must follow the overloading rules qualified in the "Overloading" sidebar in Chapter 9 plus one additional rule: any parameter name in a `CONSTRUCTOR` function must match an attribute name and data type as declared by the object type's definition. `CONSTRUCTOR` functions return an instance of the object type, which is known in PL/SQL as `SELF`, not the Java *this*. Like other keywords in PL/SQL,

SELF isn't case sensitive like Java's this. CONSTRUCTOR functions can also use PRAGMA instructions to restrict their behaviors. As for the MAP and ORDER functions, you can only implement one or the other in any object type.

You can define functions with a CONSTRUCTOR, MEMBER, or STATIC keyword. A MEMBER function or procedure works with instance data, while a STATIC function or procedure works without instantiating an instance of the object. Parameter lists for MEMBER or STATIC functions and procedures follow the same rules as those for stand-alone functions and procedures, as qualified in Chapter 6.

Attributes (*instance variables*) and methods are listed in a single parameter list that applies to the object type. You can't declare object type variables as you can package variables. All attributes are instance-only variables, which means you can access them only after you construct an object instance.

You need to list elements in the following order: attributes, constructors, functions, procedures, and the MAP or ORDER function. If you try to put an attribute at the end of the list, you'll receive a PLS-00311 error telling you that the declaration of the object type is malformed because you have elements out of sequence.

The prototype for object types is

```
CREATE [OR REPLACE] OBJECT TYPE object_name [UNDER parent_object_type]
[EDITIONABLE | NONEDITIONABLE]
[AUTHID {DEFINER | CURRENT_USER}]
[ACCESSIBLE BY
( {FUNCTION | PROCEDURE | PACKAGE | TYPE} [schema.]unit_name)
[,[{FUNCTION | PROCEDURE | PACKAGE | TYPE}] [schema.]unit_name)]
[,... ]])] IS OBJECT
( [instance_variables {sql_datatype | plsql_datatype}]
, [CONSTRUCTOR FUNCTION constructor_name
  [( parameter_list )] RETURN RESULT AS SELF
, [{[OVERRIDING] MEMBER | STATIC} FUNCTION function_name
  [( parameter_list )] RETURN { sql_data_type | plsql_data_type }
, [{[OVERRIDING] MEMBER | STATIC} PROCEDURE procedure_name
  [( parameter_list)]
,{[MAP FUNCTION map_name RETURN { CHAR | DATE | NUMBER | VARCHAR2 } |
  [ORDER FUNCTION order_name RETURN { sql_data_type | plsql_data_type }}])
[NOT] INSTANTIABLE [NOT] FINAL;
/
```

NOTE
The OR REPLACE clause is very important because without it you must drop the object type before attempting to redeclare it.

Oracle object types are EDITIONABLE from Oracle Database 11*g*, Release 2 forward. The EDITIONABLE clause lets you create concurrent versions of object types. With concurrent versions of object types you can support current and future software requirements. Together, they let you concurrently test and migrate users from the old edition to the new edition by simply switching editions.

The ACCESSIBLE BY clause, which is new to Oracle Database 12*c*, lets you white list the callers of the object type. The "White Listing Object Types" section later in this chapter shows you how to white list your object types.

Any MEMBER or STATIC function can return a scalar or composite data type. The composite data types can be any object type or SQL collection data type. A MEMBER or STATIC function can't return a collection of a PL/SQL record type.

The INSTANTIABLE clause is the default behavior. The INSTANTIABLE clause makes it possible for you to create instances of an object type. You limit an object type to only STATIC functions and STATIC procedures when you make an object type NOT INSTANTIABLE.

Objects also are FINAL by default. You can't subclass a FINAL object type. That's why all the object type examples use a NOT FINAL clause, which makes object types subclassable.

You can build an object type with the following statement:

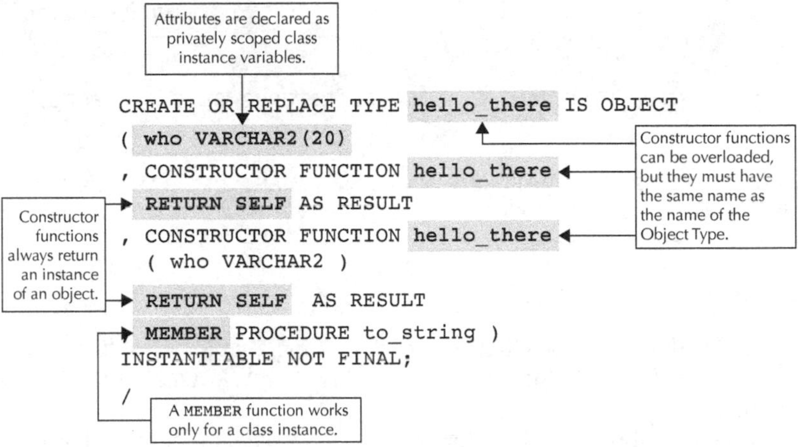

The hello_there basic class has two CONSTRUCTOR functions and only the to_string instance method. CONSTRUCTOR function names must match the object type name, like Java classes. One CONSTRUCTOR function creates an instance of the object without actual call parameters, while the other requires a mandatory parameter to create an instance of the object type. If you changed the mandatory parameter in the CONSTRUCTOR function to an optional parameter, you could trigger a PLS-00307 exception at runtime. This happens because the signature of a no-parameter CONSTRUCTOR function and that of a CONSTRUCTOR function with one optional parameter are equal at runtime when you don't supply a value. A call made with a parameter would resolve and construct an object instance.

NOTE

The compiler raises a PLS-00658 error when you forget to match your CONSTRUCTOR function to the name of the object type.

The MEMBER procedure is only accessible once you've created an object instance. This object is instantiable (*capable of creating an object instance*) and NOT FINAL (*capable of being extended or subtyped*). Subtypes of object types are also called *type dependents* by the Oracle documentation. All object type variables are instance variables. As such, they are not available through static functions and procedures.

After you create an object type, you examine it by using the DESCRIBE command, like

```
SQL> describe HELLO_THERE
```

You get the following back to your console:

```
HELLO_THERE is NOT FINAL
 Name                                      Null?    Type
 ----------------------------------------- -------- -------------------
 WHO                                                VARCHAR2(20)
METHOD
------
 FINAL CONSTRUCTOR FUNCTION HELLO_THERE RETURNS SELF AS RESULT
METHOD
------
 FINAL CONSTRUCTOR FUNCTION HELLO_THERE RETURNS SELF AS RESULT
 Argument Name                  Type                    In/Out Default?
 ------------------------------ ----------------------- ------ --------
 WHO                            VARCHAR2                IN
 MEMBER PROCEDURE TO_STRING
```

The output is different from what you get describing a table, view, function, procedure, or package. You get a list of all instance variables, class CONSTRUCTOR functions, and member functions and procedures.

The next section shows you how to implement this declaration. You'll also see how to construct an instance and use it in a PL/SQL block.

Implementing Object Bodies

PL/SQL object bodies, like package bodies, must implement their declarations exactly. This means you must provide an implementation in the object body for everything you have in the object type. Unlike when implementing declarations for package bodies, you can't add private methods known *only* to the object body. Nor can you add the equivalent of package-level variables inside an object body implementation. The only attributes, functions, and procedures in object bodies are those declared in the object type. This will become clearer later in this chapter when we discuss how you create subtypes or specializations of your object types.

NOTE
Unlike the object types in some OOPLs, Oracle Database 12c object types don't support inner classes.

Inside of functions and procedures, you can define named functions and procedures in the declaration block and define anonymous block programs in the execution block. You address the attributes of object types by prefacing them with SELF, a component selector (.), and the attribute name.

The following is the prototype for implementing an object body:

```
CREATE [OR REPLACE] OBJECT TYPE object_name
[AUTHID {DEFINER | CURRENT_USER}] IS
( [CONSTRUCTOR FUNCTION constructor_name
  [( parameter_list )] RETURN RESULT AS SELF IS
     BEGIN
       execution_statements;
     END [constructor_name];
  [{MEMBER | STATIC} FUNCTION function_name
  [( parameter_list )] RETURN { sql_data_type | plsql_data_type } IS
     BEGIN
       execution_statements;
     END [function_name];
  [{MEMBER | STATIC} PROCEDURE procedure_name IS
  [( parameter_list)]
     BEGIN
       execution_statements;
     END [procedure_name];
 {[MAP FUNCTION map_name RETURN { CHAR | DATE | NUMBER | VARCHAR2 } IS
     BEGIN
       execution_statements;
     END [procedure_name]; |
  [ORDER FUNCTION order_name RETURN { sql_data_type | plsql_data_type } IS
     BEGIN
       execution_statements;
     END [procedure_name];}])
END [object_name];
```

An object body implementation is very similar to a package body implementation, except it excludes local variables and components. As mentioned earlier, the MAP and ORDER functions are specialized units, and you can only implement whichever one was declared in the object type.

TIP
Exclude the object name at the end of the object body, because it sometimes suppresses meaningful errors and causes compilation failure.

There are a few subtle changes between traditional functions and procedures and object bodies. The least subtle is the idea of an object instance. An object instance is represented inside the object body as SELF. SELF is a departure from the traditional *this* keyword from Java and other OOPLs. Object instance attributes are elements of SELF, just as field values are elements of a record structure. The same syntax rules apply for assigning and retrieving values, as shown in the hello_there object body.

```
CREATE OR REPLACE TYPE BODY hello_there IS
  CONSTRUCTOR FUNCTION hello_there  --Default constructor.
  RETURN SELF AS RESULT IS
    hello HELLO_THERE := hello_there('Generic Object');
  BEGIN
    self := hello;
    RETURN;
  END hello_there;
  CONSTRUCTOR FUNCTION hello_there  --Overriding constructor.
  (who VARCHAR2) RETURN SELF AS RESULT IS
  BEGIN
    self.who := who;
    RETURN;
  END hello_there;
  MEMBER PROCEDURE to_string IS
  BEGIN
    dbms_output.put_line('Hello '||self.who||'.');
  END to_string;
END hello_there;
/
```

Construct a class instance by calling the overriding constructor with an actual parameter.
Assign the local class instance to the internal SELF instance.
Assign the actual parameter to the class instance variable.
Read the class instance variable.

The parameter_list element of an object body is deceptively simple. The parameters in the parameter list of an object body must match the attributes in the attribute list of an object type. This means that you can't define a CONSTRUCTOR function in an object body that uses any parameter name that isn't also an attribute name in the object type. If you do so, your object body will fail to parse correctly, and will fail compilation with a PLS-00307 exception. The exception message tells you that *"too many declarations of 'object_type_name' match this call."* The "too many declarations" exception message means that you have at least one CONSTRUCTOR function that uses a parameter value not found in the list of object type attributes.

When you define an object *type*, you can create a CONSTRUCTOR function with a parameter name that is not found in the list of attributes. However, you shouldn't do so, because although the object type parses and compiles successfully, any attempt to implement that design as an object body fails.

Object types should generally provide a default CONSTRUCTOR function. Default CONSTRUCTOR functions typically have no formal parameters. In objects where the formal parameters are required to make instances useful, the default CONSTRUCTOR function calls the CONSTRUCTOR function with default parameters. This is done in an object body by four steps. First, you create a local variable of the object type. Second, you instantiate the local (*internal*) class with default actual parameters. Third, you assign the transient local object to the instance itself. Fourth, you return a handle to the current object. The RETURN statement works differently in an object than it does in a stand-alone function. It *never* takes an argument, because it is returning a copy of the object type.

The behavior of managing a default CONSTRUCTOR function can be tricky, but they simplify the construction of object instances. The default CONSTRUCTOR function hides (*from the eyes of the consuming developer*) the details of creating an object instance. The overriding CONSTRUCTOR function provides the values to build an object instance but hides the details of how to do so.

Object Type Arguments and CONSTRUCTOR Functions Must Agree

As mentioned, the names of CONSTRUCTOR function parameters must match the names and data types defined in the object type's CONSTRUCTOR function prototype. Let's say you violate this rule when you define the object type, like this change to the example shown in the previous illustration:

```
SQL> CREATE OR REPLACE TYPE hello_there IS OBJECT
  2  ( who VARCHAR2(20)
  3  , CONSTRUCTOR FUNCTION hello_there
  4    RETURN SELF AS RESULT
  5  , CONSTRUCTOR FUNCTION hello_there
  6    ( bad VARCHAR2 )
  7    RETURN SELF AS RESULT
     ...
 11  INSTANTIABLE NOT FINAL;
 12  /
```

Line 2 defines who as the only attribute of the hello_there object type. Line 6 violates the rule of name agreement between object type attributes and CONSTRUCTOR function parameter names. Oddly, it compiles without a problem. Personally, I believe this behavior should be considered a bug, but it's been the same through several Oracle Database releases. The hello_there object type compiles successfully.

You get a compilation error when you breach the rule of name agreement between object type attributes and CONSTRUCTOR function parameter names. Let's say you try to write a CONSTRUCTOR function that uses parameter name that violates the rule of name agreement, like:

```
SQL> CREATE OR REPLACE TYPE BODY hello_there IS
  ...
    CONSTRUCTOR FUNCTION hello_there
    (bad VARCHAR2) RETURN SELF AS RESULT IS
    BEGIN
      self.who := bad;
      RETURN;
    END hello_there;
  ...
  END;
  /
```

(continued)

Lines 10 and 11 declare the CONSTRUCTOR function with a bad parameter name, which is also *bad* because it doesn't agree with the one who attribute of the hello_there object type. It raises the following error at compilation time:

```
LINE/COL ERROR
-------- -----------------------------------------------------------------
--
4/11     PL/SQL: Item ignored
4/26     PLS-00307: too many declarations of 'HELLO_THERE' match this
call
6/5      PL/SQL: Statement ignored
6/13     PLS-00320: the declaration of the type of this expression is
         incomplete or malformed
```

The key error occurs on line 11, which is where the bad parameter name occurs. The second meaningful error occurs on line 26. Its meaning is less clear. It's raised when the parsing gets to the end of the list of functions and procedures. The error tells you that there are too many declarations of the hello_there object type's CONSTRUCTOR function. That's true because Oracle Database 11*g* forward creates an implicit CONSTRUCTOR function with the who argument when one isn't found during parsing. Since the code provides one CONSTRUCTOR function with a bad parameter name and Oracle provides another with the who parameter name, there are two CONSTRUCTOR functions with the same signature. Now you can avoid a tedious and less obvious error that can waste developer time.

The to_string procedure lets you see the contents of the constructed class. You can test the class by calling the default CONSTRUCTOR function, as shown

```
SQL> SET SERVEROUTPUT ON SIZE 1000000
SQL> DECLARE
  2    hello HELLO_THERE := hello_there;  -- hello_there() works too!
  3  BEGIN
  4    hello.to_string();
  5  END;
  6  /
```

Line 2 constructs an instance of the hello_there object type by using the default CONSTRUCTOR function. You also can construct an instance with or without empty parentheses, like function and procedure calls in PL/SQL blocks. You call the member procedure just as you would a package procedure.

Line 4 calls a member procedure of a hello_there instance and prints

```
Hello Generic Object.
```

The next anonymous block calls the overriding CONSTRUCTOR function. This provides a non-default parameter to the instance. The code is

```
SQL> DECLARE
  2    hello HELLO_THERE := hello_there('Overriding Object');
  3  BEGIN
  4    hello.to_string();
  5  END;
  6  /
```

Line 2 constructs an instance of the hello_there object type with a static string. As a rule, you shouldn't construct an instance in the declaration block unless it's with a string literal. Line 4 calls the same to_string() member procedure as the prior example. This time it prints

```
Hello Overriding Object.
```

This section has shown you how to implement object bodies. You have also learned how to construct an object instance, and how to distinguish between a default CONSTRUCTOR function and an overriding CONSTRUCTOR function.

White Listing Object Types

As introduced in Chapter 2 and expanded upon in Chapters 8 and 9, *white listing* is a new capability in Oracle Database 12*c* that enables you to qualify who can call a function, procedure, package, or object type.

The following defines a hello_there object type that white lists only a sorter function. Any other caller that attempts to instantiate a hello_there object type fails because they have insufficient privileges.

```
SQL> CREATE OR REPLACE TYPE hello_there
  2  ACCESSIBLE BY (FUNCTION  white_hat) IS OBJECT
  3  ( who VARCHAR2(20)
  4  , CONSTRUCTOR FUNCTION hello_there
  5    RETURN SELF AS RESULT
  6  , CONSTRUCTOR FUNCTION hello_there
  7    ( who VARCHAR2 )
  8    RETURN SELF AS RESULT
  9  , MEMBER FUNCTION get_who RETURN VARCHAR2
 10  , MEMBER PROCEDURE set_who (who VARCHAR2)
 11  , MEMBER FUNCTION to_string RETURN VARCHAR2 )
 12  INSTANTIABLE NOT FINAL;
 13  /
```

Line 2 uses the ACCESSIBLE BY clause to white list the white_hat function. You create only object types with the ACCESSIBLE BY clause because object bodies inherit the behavior from the object type. Line 11 changes a to_string procedure to a to_string function, which I'm doing to support my testing of the object type.

The illustration in the previous section provides the `hello_there` object body, but it doesn't show the new `to_string` function:

```
27     MEMBER FUNCTION to_string RETURN VARCHAR2 IS
28     BEGIN
29       RETURN 'Hello '||self.who;
30     END to_string;
```

Line 27 implements the `to_string` function from the object type. Line 29 returns a "Hello *Whomever*" (italic for the placeholder only) salutation.

The next anonymous block calls the now *white-listed* overriding `CONSTRUCTOR` function, like it did before it was white listed. The block's code is

```
SQL> DECLARE
  2    hello HELLO_THERE := hello_there('Overriding Object');
  3  BEGIN
  4    hello.to_string();
  5  END;
  6  /
```

It fails with the following error:

```
  hello HELLO_THERE := hello_there('Overriding Object');
        *
ERROR at line 2:
ORA-06550: line 2, column 9:
PLS-00904: insufficient privilege to access object HELLO_THERE
```

Line 2 can't construct an instance of the `hello_there` object type because it isn't white listed with privileges. Now, let's create the `white_hat` function, because it's white listed in the `hello_there` object type:

```
SQL> CREATE OR REPLACE FUNCTION white_hat
  2  ( pv_string  VARCHAR2) RETURN VARCHAR2 IS
  3    hello HELLO_THERE;
  4  BEGIN
  5    /* Instantiate a new instance of hello_there. */
  6    hello := hello_there(NVL(pv_string,'Overriding Object'));
  7    RETURN hello.to_string();
  8  EXCEPTION
  9    WHEN OTHERS THEN
 10      RETURN NULL;
 11  END;
 12  /
```

Changing the calling program from an anonymous block to a named block lets us parameterize the `white_hat` function. Line 3 now declares a `hello` variable of the `hello_there` object type, but the declaration line no longer initializes an instance of the `hello_there` object type. That's true because the input parameter to the `CONSTRUCTOR` function is now a dynamic value, and as qualified in the section "Anonymous Blocks" in Chapter 3, the assignment should be made only in an execution block. Line 6 initializes the `hello_there` object type in the execution block and uses an `NVL` built-in as a precaution against a null value input.

Now, you can call the `white_hat` function with the following query:

```
SQL> SELECT white_hat('the Lone Ranger') AS "Result"
     FROM   dual;
```

This time it prints

```
Result
-------------------------
 Hello the Lone Ranger.
```

Let's look at how the `white_hat` function's error handling works for dynamic inputs. We can do that by changing the short string literal of "the Lone Ranger" to one longer than the maximum size of the `hello_there` object type's `who` attribute. Realistically, the object body should have its own exception handling, but the exception blocks were left out to keep the examples as short as possible.

The following query causes an exception in the `CONSTRUCTOR` function of the `hello_there` object type, which is caught by an exception block of the `white_hat` function:

```
SQL> SELECT white_hat('the Long Ranger and Tonto') AS "Result"
     FROM   dual;
```

The query prints a null result because the exception block returns a null value.

This section has shown you how to white list object types. It also has shown you how you can call an object type inside a stored function while passing a dynamic value to the object type's `CONSTRUCTOR` function.

Getters and Setters

Getters and *setters* are common OOP terms indicating that you get or set a class instance variable. In PL/SQL you need to write an individual `get_variable_name()` function and `set_variable_name()` function for each class attribute.

The following modified `hello_there` object type extends the previous `hello_there` object type by adding a `get_who()` member function and a `set_who()` member procedure. There's no magic in choosing a function for the *getter* because you want to take something out of the object instance. Functions return expressions, as you'll find in Chapter 6. The *setter* can be either a function or a procedure, but more often than not it's a procedure. Setter method calls don't generally return a value. In most OOPLs, you implement setters as functions with a void return type.

The modified `hello_there` object type is

```
SQL> CREATE OR REPLACE TYPE hello_there IS OBJECT
     ( who VARCHAR2(20)
     , CONSTRUCTOR FUNCTION hello_there
       RETURN SELF AS RESULT
     , CONSTRUCTOR FUNCTION hello_there
       ( who VARCHAR2 )
       RETURN SELF AS RESULT
```

```
 8  , MEMBER FUNCTION get_who RETURN VARCHAR2
 9  , MEMBER PROCEDURE set_who (pv_who VARCHAR2)
10  , MEMBER PROCEDURE to_string )
11  INSTANTIABLE NOT FINAL;
12  /
```

The implementation of these two member methods is straightforward. The *setter* on line 9 passes a new value for *who*, while the *getter* on line 8 retrieves the current value.

The `hello_there` object body is

```
SQL> CREATE OR REPLACE TYPE BODY hello_there IS
  2    CONSTRUCTOR FUNCTION hello_there RETURN SELF AS RESULT IS
  3      /* Declare an instance if called without a parameter. */
  4      hello HELLO_THERE := hello_there('Generic Object');
  5    BEGIN
  6      /* Instantiate this object type. */
  7      self := hello;
  8      RETURN;
  9    END hello_there;
 10    CONSTRUCTOR FUNCTION hello_there
 11    (who VARCHAR2) RETURN SELF AS RESULT IS
 12    BEGIN
 13      /* Instantiate this object type. */
 14      self.who := who;
 15      RETURN;
 16    END hello_there;
 17    MEMBER FUNCTION get_who RETURN VARCHAR2 IS
 18    BEGIN
 19      /* Return an instance variable. */
 20      RETURN self.who;
 21    END get_who;
 22    MEMBER PROCEDURE set_who (pv_who VARCHAR2) IS
 23    BEGIN
 24      /* Set an instance variable. */
 25      self.who := pv_who;
 26    END set_who;
 27    MEMBER PROCEDURE to_string IS
 28    BEGIN
 29      /* Print an identifying statement. */
 30      dbms_output.put_line('Hello '||self.who||'.');
 31    END to_string;
 32  END;
 33  /
```

The *setter* on lines 22 through 26 assigns a new value from the actual parameter, and the *getter* on lines 17 through 21 grabs the current class instance value. The following anonymous block demonstrates calling these new member methods:

```
SQL> DECLARE
  hello HELLO_THERE := hello_there('Overriding Object');
BEGIN
```

```
4      hello.to_string();
5      hello.set_who('Newbie Object');
6      dbms_output.put_line(hello.get_who);
7      hello.to_string();
8    END;
9    /
```

Line 2 instantiates a local instance of the `hello_there` object type. Line 5 calls the `set_who` setter procedure, and line 6 calls the `get_who` getter function. The anonymous block successfully resets and gets the values as shown:

```
Hello Overriding Object.
Newbie Object.
Hello Newbie Object.
```

This section has shown you how to implement and use getters and setters.

Static Member Methods

The static functions and procedures let you use an object type like a standard package. Static methods can create instances of their object type, but they are limited to working with instances of the object like external PL/SQL blocks.

The nice thing about static methods is that they can provide developers with a standard look and feel of procedural programming. You can write static methods to perform standard programming tasks, or to return an instance of their class. Writing a function that returns a class instance can simplify how you use objects because you don't have to worry about long parameter lists in the `CONSTRUCTOR` functions.

The following declares an object type that includes a static function:

```
SQL> CREATE OR REPLACE TYPE item_object IS OBJECT
  2  ( item_title      VARCHAR2(60)
  3  , item_subtitle   VARCHAR2(60)
  4  , CONSTRUCTOR FUNCTION item_object
  5    RETURN SELF AS RESULT
  6  , CONSTRUCTOR FUNCTION item_object
  7    ( item_title    VARCHAR2
  8    , item_subtitle VARCHAR2) RETURN SELF AS RESULT
  9  , STATIC FUNCTION get_item_object (pv_item_id NUMBER) RETURN ITEM_OBJECT
 10  , MEMBER FUNCTION to_string RETURN VARCHAR2 )
 11  INSTANTIABLE NOT FINAL;
 12  /
```

The static function `get_item_object` on line 9 takes one parameter, `pv_item_id`. The parameter doesn't map to the parameter lists in the `CONSTRUCTOR` functions, but the static function returns an instance of the `item_object` object type. This means that the static function must create an instance of the object type as a local variable before it can return one to a calling program.

External programs create an instance of the object type before they can act on it. The static `get_item_object` function lets you initialize an object instance without calling the `CONSTRUCTOR` function. In fact, you can assign the result from the `get_item_object` function to a variable declared as the same object type. The result is an active transient object instance.

The following implements the object body of the `item_object` class:

```
SQL> CREATE OR REPLACE TYPE BODY item_object IS
  2    CONSTRUCTOR FUNCTION item_object
  3    RETURN SELF AS RESULT IS
  4      /* Declare an instance if called without a parameter. */
  5      item ITEM_OBJECT :=
  6        item_object('Generic Title','Generic Subtitle');
  7    BEGIN
  8      /* Instantiate this object type. */
  9      self := item;
 10      RETURN;
 11    END item_object;
 12    CONSTRUCTOR FUNCTION item_object
 13    ( item_title    VARCHAR2
 14    , item_subtitle VARCHAR2) RETURN SELF AS RESULT IS
 15    BEGIN
 16      /* Instantiate by attribute. */
 17      self.item_title := item_title;
 18      self.item_subtitle := item_subtitle;
 19      RETURN;
 20    END item_object;
 21    STATIC FUNCTION get_item_object
 22    (pv_item_id NUMBER) RETURN ITEM_OBJECT IS
 23      /* Create a local item_object instance. */
 24      item ITEM_OBJECT;
 25      /* Create a dynamic cursor. */
 26      CURSOR c (cv_item_id NUMBER) IS
 27        SELECT i.item_title, i.item_subtitle
 28        FROM   item i
 29        WHERE  i.item_id = cv_item_id;
 30    BEGIN
 31      /* Read one row into the object type. */
 32      FOR i IN c (pv_item_id) LOOP
 33        item := item_object(i.item_title,i.item_subtitle);
 34      END LOOP;
 35      RETURN item;
 36    END get_item_object;
 37    MEMBER FUNCTION to_string RETURN VARCHAR2 IS
 38    BEGIN
 39      /* Print an identifying statement. */
 40      RETURN '['||self.item_title||']['||self.item_subtitle||']';
 41    END to_string;
 42  END;
 43  /
```

Lines 21 through 36 list the implementation of the `get_item_object` `STATIC` function. The `get_item_object` `STATIC` function uses a single formal parameter that finds a unique row in the `item` table. The static function uses the values from the local `c` cursor to construct an instance of the `item_object` object type. It then returns the local `item` instance variable as its return value.

You can test the static method by using the following anonymous block program:

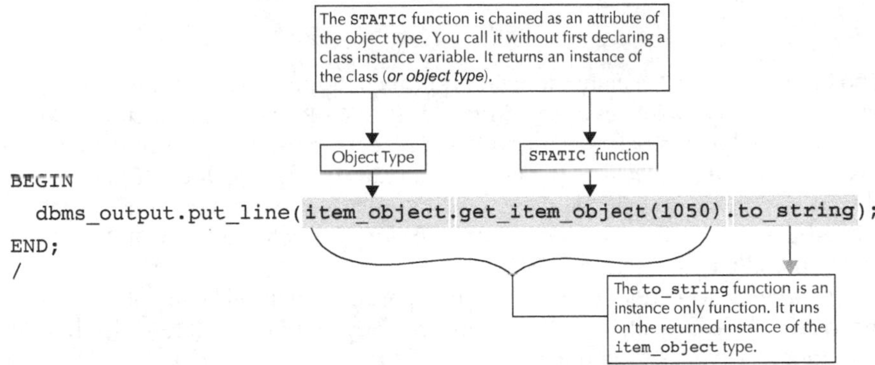
The STATIC function is chained as an attribute of the object type. You call it without first declaring a class instance variable. It returns an instance of the class (*or object type*).
Object Type
STATIC function
The to_string function is an instance only function. It runs on the returned instance of the item_object type.

```
BEGIN
  dbms_output.put_line(item_object.get_item_object(1050).to_string);
END;
/
```

The call to the object involves a couple of component selectors. Oracle refers to this process of connecting multiple pieces together with periods as *attribute chaining*. You call the static `get_item_object` function by referencing the schema-level `item_object` object type. The result of the static function call is a valid instance of the object type. You can then add a period and a call to the `to_string` instance function.

NOTE
The `to_string` function call works with or without parentheses, like ordinary stand-alone and package functions.

It prints

```
[Pirates of the Caribbean][The Curse of the Black Pearl]
```

This section has shown you how to declare and implement a static function. You can use this approach to accomplish building other static methods that let you leverage object types in your database.

Comparing Objects

Comparing object instances is very important in OOP. In the Java programming language, an *equals* method is provided for the root node of its single object hierarchy. Good programming practice dictates that you should override it when you implement your own classes that extend the behavior of a base object type class.

Oracle object types don't have a root node that you extend in the same way as you can extend the Java root node. You have a master template that you implement through SQL DDL syntax. Oracle does provide two predefined member functions, `MAP` and `ORDER`. You can implement only one `MAP` or `ORDER` function in any object type. If you attempt to define both, the object type specification raises a `PLS-00154` error during compilation. The error states that "An object type may have only 1 `MAP` or 1 `ORDER` method." The `MAP` member function doesn't take a formal parameter, and can only return a scalar type of `CHAR`, `DATE`, `NUMBER`, or `VARCHAR2`.

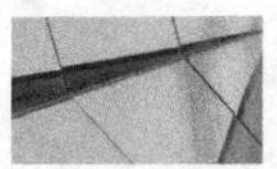

TIP
Subclasses can't override the `MAP` *or* `ORDER` *functions found in a parent class.*

The benefit of a `MAP` member function is limited. It limits you to testing for equality based on a single number that identifies a class instance. The `ORDER` member function is more flexible because it can take parameters of any SQL data type. However, the `ORDER` member function only returns a `NUMBER` data type. The parameter is the advantage, and the return type really isn't a disadvantage. You may recall that many built-in functions return a number so that you can use them in SQL and PL/SQL. If the `ORDER` member function returned a `BOOLEAN` data type, it would only let you compare objects in PL/SQL.

The next two subsections demonstrate comparing objects with `MAP` and `ORDER` member functions. You'll have to choose what works best for you, but the `ORDER` member function is recommended as the better option.

Comparing with the MAP Member Function

As discussed, the `MAP` member function validates against a scalar type of `CHAR`, `DATE`, `NUMBER`, or `VARCHAR2` data type. The `MAP` member function works best when a single attribute value of a class instance determines whether it is equal to or greater than another object instance. When more than one attribute, or a relationship of attributes, determines ordering, the `MAP` member function fails to allow you to sort objects easily.

You can accomplish a barebones example by declaring only `CONSTRUCTOR` and `MAP` member functions. The following declares the `map_comparison` object type:

```
SQL> CREATE OR REPLACE TYPE map_comp IS OBJECT
  2  ( who VARCHAR2(20)
  3  , CONSTRUCTOR FUNCTION map_comp
  4    (who VARCHAR2) RETURN SELF AS RESULT
  5  , MAP MEMBER FUNCTION equals RETURN VARCHAR2 )
  6  INSTANTIABLE NOT FINAL;
  7  /
```

`MAP` is a keyword designating the function for sorting operations. `MAP` precedes the definition of an instance function, as shown on line 5. The implementation of the `map_comp` object type is

```
SQL> CREATE OR REPLACE TYPE BODY map_comp IS
       CONSTRUCTOR FUNCTION map_comp
       (who VARCHAR2) RETURN SELF AS RESULT IS
       BEGIN
         self.who := who;
         RETURN;
       END map_comp;
       MAP MEMBER FUNCTION equals RETURN VARCHAR2 IS
       BEGIN
         RETURN self.who;
       END equals;
     END;
     /
```

Lines 8 through 11 show the `MAP` function, which simply returns the single attribute of the `MAP_COMP` object type. The test program creates a collection of object types in mixed alphabetical order, and then runs the items through a bubble sort operation to put them in ascending order. The code follows:

```
SQL> DECLARE
  2    /* Declare a collection of an object type. */
  3    TYPE object_list IS TABLE OF MAP_COMP;
  4    /* Initialize four objects in mixed alphabetical order. */
  5    lv_obj1 MAP_COMP := map_comp('Ron Weasley');
  6    lv_obj2 MAP_COMP := map_comp('Harry Potter');
  7    lv_obj3 MAP_COMP := map_comp('Luna Lovegood');
  8    lv_obj4 MAP_COMP := map_comp('Hermione Granger');
  9    /* Define a collection of the object type. */
 10    lv_objs OBJECT_LIST := object_list(lv_obj1,lv_obj2,lv_obj3,lv_obj4);
 11    /* A local procedure that swaps A and B. */
 12    PROCEDURE swap (a IN OUT MAP_COMP, b IN OUT MAP_COMP) IS
 13      c MAP_COMP;
 14    BEGIN
 15      c := b;
 16      b := a;
 17      a := c;
 18    END swap;
 19  BEGIN
 20    /* A bubble sort. */
 21    FOR i IN 1..lv_objs.COUNT LOOP
 22      FOR j IN 1..lv_objs.COUNT LOOP
 23        IF lv_objs(i).equals = LEAST(lv_objs(i).equals,lv_objs(j).equals) THEN
 24          swap(lv_objs(i),lv_objs(j));
 25        END IF;
 26      END LOOP;
 27    END LOOP;
 28    /* Print reorderd objects. */
 29    FOR i IN 1..lv_objs.COUNT LOOP
 30      dbms_output.put_line(lv_objs(i).equals);
 31    END LOOP;
 32  END;
 33  /
```

Lines 12 through 18 define a local pass-by-reference `swap` procedure. The `swap` procedure performs a bubble sort. The anonymous block produces the following output:

```
Harry Potter
Hermione Granger
Luna Lovegood
Ron Weasley
```

The `LEAST` function determines whether the outer loop element `MAP` member function result is less than the inner loop element. When the result is less, the `LEAST` function swaps the values until the least of the entire set is the first element in the collection, and the rest are in ascending order. While bubble sorts are inefficient, they're nice tools for demonstrating concepts. Changing the comparison operation on line 23 to not equal (<>) would print a descending list.

This section has demonstrated how you can sort by using the `MAP` member function. As you can see, the logic for the comparison lies largely outside of the object type. This means the sorting isn't hidden and the logic isn't encapsulated.

Trick-or-Treating with Persistent Object Types

While the chapter is about transient objects in the scope of your PL/SQL programs, it seems only fair to not leave you in a lurch regarding persistent object types. You could find some interesting trick or treat behavior when you try *reading objects* from the database.

The following is a quick example that helps you understand how to read your stored objects from the database. The first step is to create a `persistent_object` table and `persistent_object_s1` sequence as follows:

```
SQL> CREATE TABLE persistent_object
     ( persistent_object_id NUMBER
     , mapping_object       MAP_COMP );
SQL> CREATE SEQUENCE persistent_object_s1;
```

Second, you'll insert the nine companions in the Fellowship of the Ring. The syntax is the same for each but you'll need to switch the names in the `CONSTRUCTOR` function:

```
SQL> INSERT INTO persistent_object
     VALUES (persistent_object_s1.nextval,map_comp('Frodo Baggins'));
```

You can select these natively, in which case you'll see return values like

```
MAPPING_OBJECT(WHO)
-------------------------
MAP_COMP('Frodo Baggins')
```

This type of query doesn't let you apply instance methods. You might start to think that these object types have little use. The *trick* is the `TREAT` function. The `TREAT` function takes a column return and *treats* it as the *object type* you designate.

The column formatting ensures it displays well for you. The following query allows you to query the column values as object instances and sort them with their own equals function:

```
SQL> COLUMN primary_key FORMAT 9999999 HEADING "Primary|Key ID"
SQL> COLUMN fellowship  FORMAT A30     HEADING "Fellowship Member"
SQL> SELECT   persistent_object_id AS primary_key
     ,        TREAT(mapping_object AS map_comp).equals() AS fellowship
     FROM     persistent_object
     WHERE    mapping_object IS OF (map_comp)
     ORDER BY 2;
```

The `TREAT` function works with object types or subclasses of object types, as explained in the section "Inheritance and Polymorphism" later in this chapter.

Comparing with the ORDER Member Function

The ORDER member function allows you to pass an object instance into another object and compare whether they're equal. You can also build it to judge whether one object instance is greater or smaller than another. While the MAP member function works best with single-attribute class instances, the ORDER member function supports internal validation when more than one attribute indexes an object instance.

You can accomplish a barebones example by declaring two attributes, a CONSTRUCTOR function and an ORDER member function. The MAP member function required that you implement the matching code externally from the object type. ORDER member functions require that you resolve whether or not to sort into a single number.

The following declares the order_comp object type:

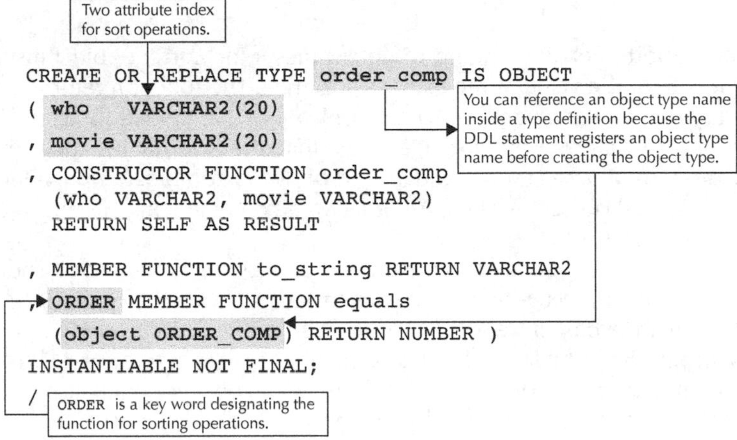

Two attribute index for sort operations.
CREATE OR REPLACE TYPE order_comp IS OBJECT
(who VARCHAR2(20)
, movie VARCHAR2(20)
, CONSTRUCTOR FUNCTION order_comp
(who VARCHAR2, movie VARCHAR2)
RETURN SELF AS RESULT
, MEMBER FUNCTION to_string RETURN VARCHAR2
, ORDER MEMBER FUNCTION equals
(object ORDER_COMP) RETURN NUMBER)
INSTANTIABLE NOT FINAL;
/
You can reference an object type name inside a type definition because the DDL statement registers an object type name before creating the object type.
ORDER is a key word designating the function for sorting operations.

The order_comp function takes a parameter of its own object type. This mimics the equivalent behavior in Java for the *equals* method. The idea is to pass an object instance inside another of the same type because the object type should contain the validation of whether two instances are equal or not. A to_string function is also declared, which will let you examine the contents of object instances.

The following implements the object body:

```
SQL> CREATE OR REPLACE TYPE BODY order_comp IS
       CONSTRUCTOR FUNCTION order_comp
       (who VARCHAR2, movie VARCHAR2) RETURN SELF AS RESULT IS
       BEGIN
         self.who := who;
         self.movie := movie;
         RETURN;
       END order_comp;
       MEMBER FUNCTION to_string RETURN VARCHAR2 IS
       BEGIN
         RETURN '['||self.movie||']['||self.who||']';
       END to_string;
```

```
13     /* Implement ORDER function. */
14     ORDER MEMBER FUNCTION equals
15     (object order_comp) RETURN NUMBER IS
16     BEGIN
17       IF self.movie < object.movie THEN
18         RETURN 1;
19       ELSIF self.movie = object.movie AND self.who < object.who THEN
20         RETURN 1;
21       ELSE
22         RETURN 0;
23       END IF;
24     END equals;
25   END;
26   /
```

The primary sort operation on line 17 determines if the current object instance's `movie` attribute is less than the value of the external instance. The function returns 1 when that's true. The secondary sort operation on line 19 runs only when the first attributes match. It determines if the current object instance's `who` attribute is less than the external instance. The `ORDER` member function also returns 1 when the secondary sort finds the *combination* of values less than the values of the external object instance. All other value comparisons are rejected, and the `ORDER` member function returns 0.

The `equals` function returns 1 as the true outcome, which means you should sort the instance passed as an actual parameter before the base instance. When the `equals` function returns 0 as the false outcome, the base instance should remain in its current position in a list.

The test program is a bit larger for this comparison but straightforward. Like the program that tested the `MAP` member function, this program creates a collection, initializes eight object instances, and initializes the collection. You should notice that the only change to the `swap` procedure is a change of data type in the formal parameters.

Equals or Not Comparison

While the example does more than a standard equals method, you could implement a direct equality comparison by changing the `IF` block to

```
      IF self.movie = object.movie AND self.who = object.who THEN
        RETURN 1;
      ELSE
        RETURN 0;
      END IF;
```

This `IF` block would then return 1 when both objects are equal, and return 0 when they're not. It doesn't provide you with a sorting key, but you could implement another `sorting_hat` method for that.

It follows:

```
SQL> DECLARE
  -- Declare a collection of an object type.
  TYPE object_list IS TABLE OF ORDER_COMP;

  -- Initialize four objects in mixed alphabetical order.
  lv_obj1 ORDER_COMP := order_comp('Ron Weasley','Harry Potter 1');
  lv_obj2 ORDER_COMP := order_comp('Harry Potter','Harry Potter 1');
  lv_obj3 ORDER_COMP := order_comp('Luna Lovegood','Harry Potter 5');
  lv_obj4 ORDER_COMP := order_comp('Hermione Granger','Harry Potter 1');
  lv_obj5 ORDER_COMP := order_comp('Hermione Granger','Harry Potter 2');
  lv_obj6 ORDER_COMP := order_comp('Harry Potter','Harry Potter 5');
  lv_obj7 ORDER_COMP := order_comp('Cedric Diggory','Harry Potter 4');
  lv_obj8 ORDER_COMP := order_comp('Severus Snape','Harry Potter 1');

  -- Define a collection of the object type.
  lv_objs OBJECT_LIST := object_list(lv_obj1,lv_obj2,lv_obj3,lv_obj4
                                    ,lv_obj5,lv_obj6,lv_obj7,lv_obj8);

  -- Swaps A and B.
  PROCEDURE swap (a IN OUT ORDER_COMP, b IN OUT ORDER_COMP) IS
    c ORDER_COMP;
  BEGIN
    c := b;
    b := a;
    a := c;
  END swap;

BEGIN
  -- A bubble sort.
  FOR i IN 1..lv_objs.COUNT LOOP
    FOR j IN 1..lv_objs.COUNT LOOP
      IF lv_objs(i).equals(lv_objs(j)) = 0 THEN
        swap(lv_objs(i),lv_objs(j));
      END IF;
    END LOOP;
  END LOOP;
  -- Print reordered objects.
  FOR i IN 1..lv_objs.COUNT LOOP
    dbms_output.put_line(lv_objs(i).to_string);
  END LOOP;
END;
/
```

You should gain better use of the ORDER member function by consistently labeling it as *equals* because that mimics Java. It is a recommended solution to standardize how you deploy transient objects in your code.

The anonymous block program simply passes a copy of one instance to the other on line 32. This is the preferred approach when you write OO programs. You *swap* them when the `equals` function returns 1 (*which means true*). The function returns true when the actual parameter isn't greater than the base instance. This sorts the instances in ascending order.

You get the following output:

```
[Harry Potter 1] [Harry Potter]
[Harry Potter 1] [Hermione Granger]
[Harry Potter 1] [Ron Weasley]
[Harry Potter 1] [Severus Snape]
[Harry Potter 2] [Hermione Granger]
[Harry Potter 4] [Cedric Diggory]
[Harry Potter 5] [Harry Potter]
[Harry Potter 5] [Luna Lovegood]
```

If you change the `IF` block to check for 0 (*or false*), like this

```
32        IF objects(i).equals(objects(j)) = 0 THEN
33          swap(objects(i),objects(j));
34        END IF;
```

you get a *descending* sort like

```
[Harry Potter 5] [Luna Lovegood]
[Harry Potter 5] [Harry Potter]
[Harry Potter 4] [Cedric Diggory]
[Harry Potter 2] [Hermione Granger]
[Harry Potter 1] [Severus Snape]
[Harry Potter 1] [Ron Weasley]
[Harry Potter 1] [Hermione Granger]
[Harry Potter 1] [Harry Potter]
```

This section has demonstrated how to compare objects by using the `MAP` member function or `ORDER` member function. You've seen how to leverage both while working with transient object instances.

Review Section

This section has described the following points about the basics of using objects.

- Oracle Database 12*c* qualifies object types as persistent objects or transient objects, and further qualifies persistent objects as stand-alone objects or embedded objects. You deploy stand-alone objects in tables, embedded objects in other object types, and transient objects in PL/SQL blocks.
- Only persistent object types have unique object identifiers.
- Object types share the same name space as tables, views, synonyms, functions, procedures, and packages. Only database triggers have a separate name space.

- You declare an object type like a package with prototype functions and procedures, but object types have three specialized functions—CONSTRUCTOR, MAP, and ORDER.
- Object type CONSTRUCTOR functions may have parameters, but they must use both the name and data type of the object type's attributes, and they return an instance of the object type.
- You can create instances of an object type when you append the INSTANTIABLE clause.
- You can create a type dependent of an object type when you append the NOT FINAL clause to it; otherwise, you can't create type dependents or subtypes.
- The current instance is known by the case-insensitive SELF keyword, which is equivalent to case-sensitive *this* in Java.
- Object types can contain only MEMBER (*instance*) and STATIC functions and procedures.
- You can white list object types with Oracle Database 12*c*'s new ACCESSIBLE BY clause.
- You implement an object type with an object body, and an object body can contain only MEMBER and STATIC functions and procedures.
- You should implement *getters* to retrieve attribute values and *setters* to set and/or modify attribute values.
- You can use either a MAP function or an ORDER function for object instance equality comparisons, but the ORDER function is the preferred and most OOPL-like solution.

Inheritance and Polymorphism

Object-oriented programming languages demand a change in thinking, but sometimes you may find yourself asking why they demand a change in thinking. I believe inheritance and polymorphism are the reasons why you need to think differently. The foregoing part of this chapter explains the mechanics of building object types as libraries. You can also build packages by developing a collection of functions and procedures. While building libraries of object types requires more effort and design than building packages, the return on your investment of time is their extensibility.

Objects are extensible because you can add to their capabilities by building subclasses. *Subclasses* inherit the behaviors of other classes, which become known as *superclasses*. Subclasses can also override the behaviors of their superclass by creating methods to replace superclass members. The idea that subclasses extend and change behaviors of their superclasses is termed *morphing*. *Polymorphing* is the process of multiple subclasses inheriting the behaviors of superclasses.

The classic example of polymorphism is a generalized class that defines a vehicle. You can develop specializations of the vehicle class by building car, motorcycle, truck, and van subclasses. These subclasses extend the general attributes and methods provided by the vehicle class and, in some cases, provide overriding methods. The specialized methods manage the differences between driving a car or riding a motorcycle, and they serve as an example of why you develop subclasses. When the vehicle class is subclassed, the vehicle class is promoted and called a superclass.

Objects inherit and polymorph behaviors by extending base behaviors in an organized tree called an object *hierarchy*. Object hierarchies contain libraries of object types, which are reusable programming units (or, in the OOP lexicon, reusable code artifacts).

Reusability has many facets. Using static functions and procedures to exchange information between class instances enables you to position reusable class components. These static structures have general use across all or many class instances and support sharing function and variable states.

Subclasses are created according to two patterns: single inheritance and multiple inheritance. Single-tree OOPLs, such as Java, support the single-inheritance model. C++ supports a multiple-inheritance model. PL/SQL uses a single-inheritance model. Figure 11-2 shows you conceptually what the single-inheritance model looks like.

While the semantics of Java and PL/SQL support only the single-inheritance model, you can use the OOP principle of aggregation to overcome this limitation. Inheritance is a specialized form of aggregation, which you can implement without much effort. Ordinary aggregation is more complex and requires you to

- Declare a class variable of another class
- Instantiate an instance of the embedded other class
- Develop method wrappers that redirect action to the embedded class instance methods

You can implement inheritance and aggregation in the same class. Together, they mimic the multiple-inheritance model.

Inheritance means that you define a class as a child of a parent class—a subclass of a class. When you create an instance of the subclass, you get an instance that has the behaviors of the parent class and subclass. If a subclass provides a method that has the same name as a parent class method, the subclass method overrides the parent class method. This means that when you call the method (*function or procedure*), it will implement the subclass method, not the parent class method.

The power of OOP exists in extending generalized behaviors and organizing variables and functions into real-world object types. You have learned how to build and access object types and instances of objects. In the next sections, you will learn how to extend general classes into subclasses.

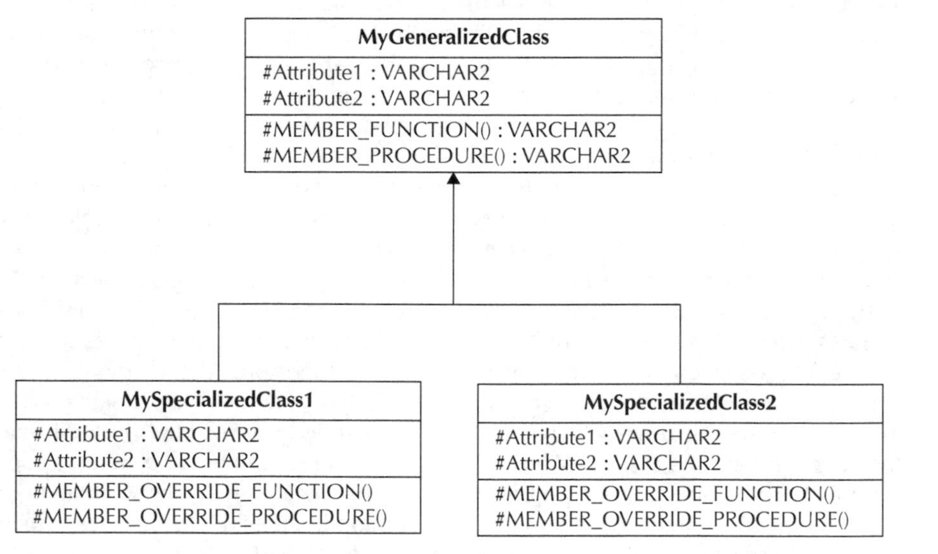

FIGURE 11-2. *Single-inheritance UML model*

Declaring Subclasses

Subclasses require a bit of new and very specific Oracle vocabulary. Unlike the Java programming language, where a subclass *extends* behavior, Oracle object types develop their implementation *under* the superclass. This really means the same thing—subclasses extend behavior. The `UNDER` keyword is consistent with the mental image you may have formed from Figure 11-2.

You must state that a member method is an *overriding behavior* by putting the `OVERRIDING` keyword in front of the `MEMBER` (or instance) function or procedure. While this is also a departure from how you override methods in Java, it does improve the clarity of definition. This is especially true when you inspect the declaration of an object type in the database catalog. If you started with Java, the syntax may require an adjustment.

There are several restrictions that apply to subtypes. You can't override type attributes, which means you don't list them when you declare the subtype. If you forget the rule, the compiler reminds you with a `PLS-00410` error. The `PLS-00410` error is adequate but was really developed for duplication when you create a *record type*. The message is "duplicate fields in RECORD, TABLE or argument list are not permitted." The error means that an object type and all subtypes share a formal parameter list (aka *argument list*). Subtypes can implement the same attributes implemented by sibling subtypes but not the same attributes implemented by the parent class. A *sibling subtype* is one that is directly subclassed from the same parent class.

The `MAP` and `ORDER` member functions are elements of the formal parameter list. They are only implemented in the object type. This limitation means that you must kludge comparative validation of subtypes by implementing another member function for comparisons. Alternatively, you can couple the parent `MAP` or `ORDER` function to all subtypes. This type of coupling requires that you maintain both when changing either. Subtypes call the `MAP` or `ORDER` member function for base object comparison and then the member function performs a supplemental subtype comparison.

The compiler raises a `PLS-00154` error when you attempt to put a `MAP` or `ORDER` function in a subtype where the parent already has one. This error is also triggered because of the shared formal parameter list.

The example shown next extends the behavior of the `order_comp` object presented in the section "Comparing with the ORDER Member Function" earlier in this chapter. It is critical that you confirm that the parent object type is declared and valid in your schema before you try to create a subclass. Next, you will see how to create a subclass and override a method, which in this case is a member function.

You declare the `order_subcomp` object type as follows:

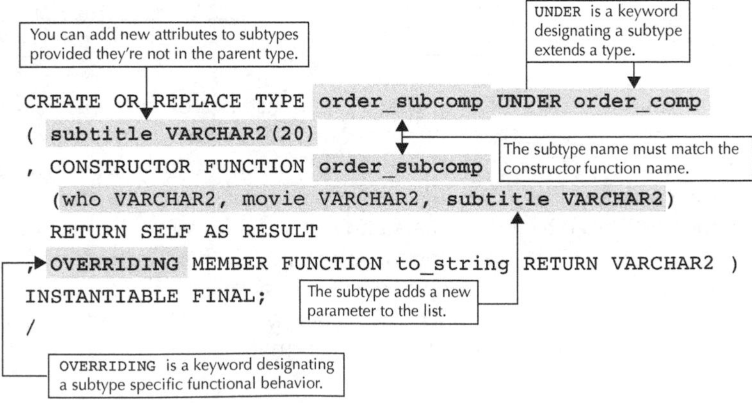

This order_subcomp subtype is deployed under the order_comp subtype. It extends the behavior of the type and inherits all behaviors that are not overridden. The subtype adds a new parameter to the list and reflects the parameter list change in the CONSTRUCTOR function. It also overrides the to_string function of the parent subtype.

After you subtype an object type, the parent type has dependents. You can't replace the object type without invalidating the children and then you can only do it by adding the FORCE clause to the DDL DROP TYPE statement. This means there is some significant linkage that you'll need to account for in your deployment and maintenance scripts. It is known as *type evolution*, and you can find a discussion of it in the section "Type Evolution" later in this chapter.

Implementing Subclasses

The process of implementing subclasses is closer to the generic process for implementing a base object type. Unlike the object type declaration, the object body doesn't actually reference the object type.

You can implement this function by applying the principles covered earlier in this chapter. The implementation of the object body is shown here:

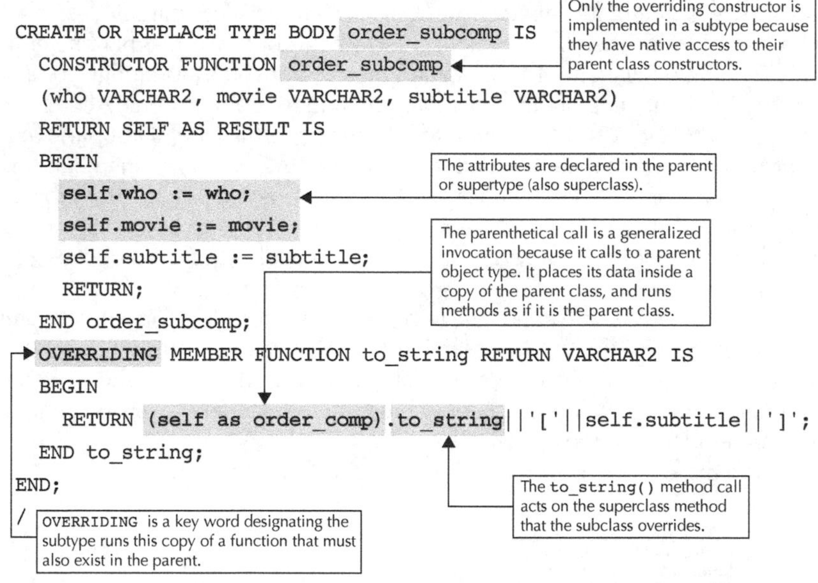

CREATE OR REPLACE TYPE BODY order_subcomp IS
  CONSTRUCTOR FUNCTION order_subcomp
  (who VARCHAR2, movie VARCHAR2, subtitle VARCHAR2)
  RETURN SELF AS RESULT IS
  BEGIN
    self.who := who;
    self.movie := movie;
    self.subtitle := subtitle;
    RETURN;
  END order_subcomp;
  OVERRIDING MEMBER FUNCTION to_string RETURN VARCHAR2 IS
  BEGIN
    RETURN (self as order_comp).to_string||'['||self.subtitle||']';
  END to_string;
END;
/
Only the overriding constructor is implemented in a subtype because they have native access to their parent class constructors.
The attributes are declared in the parent or supertype (also superclass).
The parenthetical call is a generalized invocation because it calls to a parent object type. It places its data inside a copy of the parent class, and runs methods as if it is the parent class.
The to_string() method call acts on the superclass method that the subclass overrides.
OVERRIDING is a key word designating the subtype runs this copy of a function that must also exist in the parent.

The implementation shows that you construct an instance of the subtype with three parameters. You should note that the CONSTRUCTOR function assigns values to the who and movie attributes, which are declared by the base object type. While you can write to those variables inside the constructor, you cannot write to or read them in other methods of the subtype object. If you want to access them, you'll need to write getters and setters in the superclass to make it possible. Any attempt to directly access them in a subclass raises a PLS-00671 error.

The OVERRIDING member function presents a new syntax. The syntax lets you call to the parent class and execute any method. The overriding to_string function calls the superclass to_string function and treats the return value as an expression:

```
(self as order_comp).to_string
```

You cannot gain access to parent class attributes because there aren't any. Your subclass initializes superclass attributes as instance attributes inside the subclass. When you call a superclass function or procedure, it operates on the instance class variables in the subtype. It doesn't matter whether they were declared in the superclass.

The anonymous block that tests this subtype is a modified version of the one in the section "Comparing with the ORDER Member Function." The only change is that one of the eight object instances is now a subtype, and the subtype works in the context of the collection of the *base* object type.

The program is

```
SQL> DECLARE
       /* Declare a collection of an object type. */
       TYPE object_list IS TABLE OF ORDER_COMP;

       /* Initialize one subtype. */
       lv_obj1 ORDER_SUBCOMP := order_subcomp('Ron Weasley','Harry Potter 1'
                                             ,'Sorcerer''s Stone');
       /* Initialize seven types. */
       lv_obj2 ORDER_COMP := order_comp('Harry Potter','Harry Potter 1');
       lv_obj3 ORDER_COMP := order_comp('Luna Lovegood','Harry Potter 5');
       lv_obj4 ORDER_COMP := order_comp('Hermione Granger','Harry Potter 1');
       lv_obj5 ORDER_COMP := order_comp('Hermione Granger','Harry Potter 2');
       lv_obj6 ORDER_COMP := order_comp('Harry Potter','Harry Potter 5');
       lv_obj7 ORDER_COMP := order_comp('Cedric Diggory','Harry Potter 4');
       lv_obj8 ORDER_COMP := order_comp('Severus Snape','Harry Potter 1');

       /* Declare a collection of the object type. */
       lv_objs OBJECT_LIST := object_list(lv_obj1,lv_obj2,lv_obj3,lv_obj4
                                         ,lv_obj5,lv_obj6,lv_obj7,lv_obj8);

       /* Swaps A and B. */
       PROCEDURE swap (a IN OUT ORDER_COMP, b IN OUT ORDER_COMP) IS
         c ORDER_COMP;
       BEGIN
         c := b;
         b := a;
         a := c;
       END swap;

     BEGIN
       -- A bubble sort.
       FOR i IN 1..lv_objs.COUNT LOOP
         FOR j IN 1..lv_objs.COUNT LOOP
           IF lv_objs(i).equals(lv_objs(j)) = 1 THEN
             swap(lv_objs(i),lv_objs(j));
           END IF;
         END LOOP;
       END LOOP;
       /* Print reordered objects. */
       FOR i IN 1..lv_objs.COUNT LOOP
```

```
      dbms_output.put_line(lv_objs(i).to_string);
    END LOOP;
  END;
  /
```

The anonymous block prints the following to console:

```
[Harry Potter 1][Harry Potter]
[Harry Potter 1][Hermione Granger]
[Harry Potter 1][Ron Weasley][Sorcerer's Stone]
[Harry Potter 1][Severus Snape]
[Harry Potter 2][Hermione Granger]
[Harry Potter 4][Cedric Diggory]
[Harry Potter 5][Harry Potter]
[Harry Potter 5][Luna Lovegood]
```

The `object1` instance variable is constructed by calling the subtype. The subtype instance is then added to the collection of the base type. It is also passed as an actual argument to the base type `ORDER` member function and the local `swap` procedure. In both cases the subtype masqueraded as the base object type.

Subtypes are a combination of the base class code and subclass code. The base object body code acts on the subclass attributes when a subclass initializes them. The subclass-specific methods act on the subclass-only components. You can also call any method from your parent class to work with attributes stored there. Together you get the attributes and behaviors of the base class and subclass. You isolate subtypes by using the `IS OF (object)` in an `IF` block.

The anonymous block implicitly *treats* all elements of the nested table as their native type. This is more or less what you accomplish by calling the `TREAT` function in a query. The `TREAT` function constructs a transient object instance from a persistent object `CONSTRUCTOR` function. You create the `CONSTRUCTOR` function when you store the object in a table. Reading the object from the table requires you to create an instance of the object at runtime, as shown in the sidebar "Trick-or-Treating with Persistent Object Types" earlier in the chapter.

Subtypes are implicitly cast at runtime. This means they behave the same as transient object types. The following creates a table using the `ORDER_COMP` supertype:

```
SQL> CREATE TABLE harry_potter
  ( harry_potter_id  NUMBER
  , character_role   ORDER_COMP );
```

You can then insert both a superclass and a subclass into the `harry_potter` table:

```
SQL> INSERT INTO harry_potter VALUES
  ( 1, order_subcomp('Ron Weasley','Harry Potter 1','Sorcerer''s Stone'));
SQL> INSERT INTO harry_potter VALUES
  ( 1, order_comp('Hermione Granger','Harry Potter 1'));
```

These insert the following raw data, which you can query with

```
SQL> COLUMN character_role FORMAT A68
SQL> SELECT character_role
  FROM   harry_potter;
```

It shows

```
CHARACTER_ROLE(WHO, MOVIE)
--------------------------------------------------------------------
ORDER_SUBCOMP('Ron Weasley', 'Harry Potter 1', 'Sorcerer''s Stone')
ORDER_COMP('Hermione Granger', 'Harry Potter 1')
```

The column title for the query appends the CONSTRUCTOR function for the object superclass. One row stores a call to the subclass CONSTRUCTOR function, and the other stores a call to the superclass CONSTRUCTOR function.

You can select the object contents by using the TREAT function. The TREAT function actually constructs an instance of the object by calling recursively for each row the CONSTRUCTOR function stored in the table.

With the SQL*Plus formatting, the query returns the results of the to_string instance function:

```
SQL> COLUMN character_role FORMAT A50
SQL> SELECT TREAT(character_role AS ORDER_COMP).to_string() AS character
  2  FROM   harry_potter;
```

You must include the parentheses when calling the instance method in a SQL statement. This statement returns the following:

```
CHARACTER
---------------------------------------------
[Harry Potter 1][Ron Weasley][Sorcerer's Stone]
[Harry Potter 1][Hermione Granger]
```

As you can see, the TREAT function constructs an instance of the supertype or subtype. It determines which to call by reading the CONSTRUCTOR function call that is stored in the column. You should always declare columns with the supertype. If you forget and declare a column that uses the subtype, the database lets you insert superclass CONSTRUCTOR functions, but they fail at runtime. This behavior should really raise an ORA-00932 error, which explains that inconsistent data types are disallowed. You receive an ORA-00932 error when you attempt to enter another unrelated object type CONSTRUCTOR function.

The rule is simple: always declare object data types with the topmost class in a hierarchy. Leave the subtyping to the database, unless you're querying. Queries use the TREAT function.

This section has shown you how to build subclasses, override methods, and call superclass methods.

Type Evolution

Object *type evolution* refers to changes in object types when they have dependents. This is a concern when using transient objects but is a critical issue when you actually store data in persistent objects in the database. Oracle fixes this in Oracle Database 12*c*, and now object types can readily evolve. I think this is one of the coolest features in the new release! You can read about it in the "Evolving an Object Type" section of Appendix B.

In Oracle Database releases prior to 12*c*, type evolution was a concern when using transient objects and was a critical issue when actually storing data in persistent objects in the database. Therefore, you had to guarantee that you were one hundred percent sure of the requirements before you used object types in database tables, which realistically is never! Your only alternative prior to Oracle Database 12*c* required you to develop a migration strategy to move the contents of older persistent object types into new ones.

Prior to Oracle Database 12*c*, any attempt to add an attribute to a base object type like `order_comp` when `order_subcomp` already existed in the database would raise an `ORA-02303` error, which states that you can't "drop or replace a type with type or table dependents." The *type* refers to transient objects, or programming components only. *Table dependents* are columns that use the object type as their data type. The natural fix to this problem is to upgrade to Oracle Database 12*c*.

NOTE
At the time of writing, type evolution only works in CDB schemas, not in PDB schemas. I imagine this may be fixed by the time this book prints. If not, implement object types in CDB schemas and grant privileges to them.

An all too familiar complaint about Oracle's object types that I hear (principally from Microsoft SQL Server–inclined folks) is, "You can't migrate the data to relational tables once you put the data into object types!" While I understand the inclination to see Oracle's implementation of object types as a lock-in marketing strategy, it isn't. Oracle doesn't do that! Oracle looks for the best of breed, and as a result, it sometimes acquires and integrates technology while throwing out the stuff it had previously. You can implement object types as tables or object columns, and you can migrate the object data through a collection of SQL built-in functions. All you need to know is how to do it, and you can find a complete example in the "Migrate from Objects to a Relational Table" section of Appendix B.

Review Section

This section has described the following points about the basics of inheritance and polymorphism with Oracle object types:

- Oracle Database 12*c* PL/SQL implements a single-hierarchy object tree, which means a subclass can inherit the behaviors of only one other object type.
- You can create a subclass of an object type when the base object type has a `NOT FINAL` clause. The `NOT FINAL` clause means a class can be specialized by a subclass.
- The `UNDER` keyword designates an object subtype of another object type.
- You can override the behavior of a parent class by putting the `OVERRIDING` keyword in front of a `MEMBER` (or instance) function or procedure.
- You can't override the behavior of a `MAP` or `ORDER` function or procedure.
- An object subtype lets you access a `MEMBER` function or procedure of the parent class by using the `(self as` *`object_type_name`*`)` before a function or procedure call. You use the syntax inside any overriding `MEMBER` function or procedure, as qualified in the "Implementing Subclasses" section of this chapter.
- The `TREAT` SQL built-in function lets you instantiate an object instance.
- Oracle Database 12*c* now supports type evolution, which means when you change an object type with object type dependents, the change then cascades through all the object type dependents.

Implementing Object Type Collections

Declaring object type collections is fairly easy because you simply declare a varray or table of the object type. Collections are a specialized object type, as covered in Chapter 6.

Since collections don't inherit any of the behaviors from their base element data type, you must wrap a collection type inside another object type if you want to access those behaviors. The wrapping object type can let you manage a list or array of the base object type. Arrays limit the number of elements to a fixed size, while nested tables are open-ended lists. You should generally implement lists, not arrays, when you build collections of object types.

The next two sections show you how to declare and implement an object type collection. You should read them in sequence because you need to understand the declaration before the implementation.

Declaring Object Type Collections

Object type collections require a base object type and a collection of the base object type. After you create those, you can build an object type collection. This section leverages the `item_object` type created in the section "Static Member Methods" earlier in the chapter.

You create the collection of the `item_object` type with the following syntax:

```
SQL> CREATE OR REPLACE TYPE
  item_table IS TABLE OF item_object;
/
```

The wrapper to the collection should define at least one instance variable. The instance variable should have the `item_table` collection data type. You should provide a default `CONSTRUCTOR` function that creates a collection by querying the database, and provide a `CONSTRUCTOR` function that takes a collection of the base object type.

The declaration of an object type collection of the `item_table` is

```
SQL> CREATE OR REPLACE TYPE items_object IS OBJECT
  2  ( items_table ITEM_TABLE
  3  , CONSTRUCTOR FUNCTION items_object
  4    RETURN SELF AS RESULT
  5  , CONSTRUCTOR FUNCTION items_object
  6    (items_table ITEM_TABLE) RETURN SELF AS RESULT
  7  , MEMBER FUNCTION get_size RETURN NUMBER
  8  , STATIC FUNCTION get_items_table RETURN ITEM_TABLE)
  9  INSTANTIABLE NOT FINAL;
 10  /
```

The `item_table` attribute on line 2 is a nested table of the base `item_object` type variable. Oracle lets you declare user-defined object types with attributes that are any type of scalar or composite data type. You also have a static `get_items_table` function on line 8 that lets you generate and return a collection of the base `item_object` object type.

Implementing Object Type Collections

This section shows you how to implement the object type collection that you have declared. It also implements another concrete factory pattern by constructing a collection through a static function call.

Concrete Factory Pattern

A concrete factory pattern is derived from an abstract factory pattern. It provides a design approach to build object instances. There are many ways to implement this OO design pattern, as is true for most design patterns. The get_item_table function in the "Static Member Methods" section of this chapter uses a static member function as the factory. The static member function creates an instance of `item_object` and returns it to the calling program.

The object type declares the interface for the *factory* and *object type*. The static `get_item_object` function returns an object type. A static function is a factory when it returns an instance of an object.

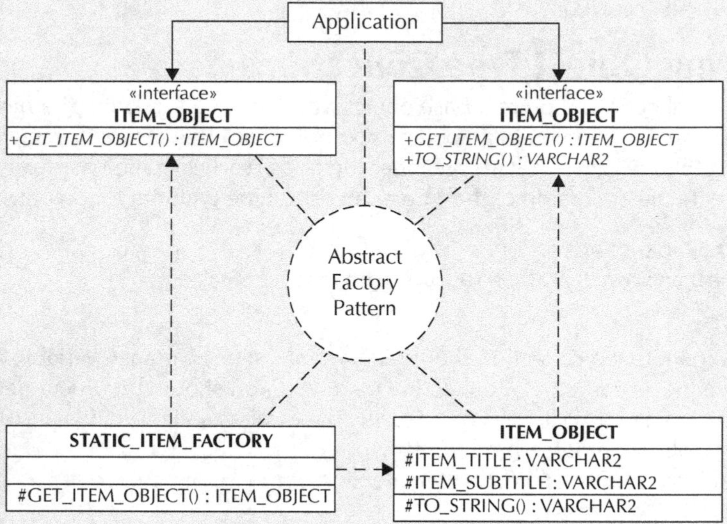

The `item_object` instance in the illustration represents only the instance components. The static component has been abstracted from the instance into a separate class in the drawing. It illustrates the role of the static function as a factory.

The object body implements the following:

```
SQL> CREATE OR REPLACE TYPE BODY items_object IS
    CONSTRUCTOR FUNCTION items_object
    RETURN SELF AS RESULT IS
      /* Declare local constructor variables. */
      c              NUMBER := 1; -- Counter for table index.
      item           ITEM_OBJECT;
      items_table    ITEM_TABLE := item_table();
```

```

    /* Static cursor for table contents. */
    CURSOR get_item IS
      SELECT item_title, item_subtitle FROM item;
  BEGIN
    /* Dynamically read the table contents into an item_object collection. */
    FOR i IN get_item LOOP
      item := item_object(i.item_title,i.item_subtitle);
      items_table.EXTEND;
      items_table(c) := item; /* Must use unrelated index. */
      c := c + 1;             /* Increment index. */
    END LOOP;
    /* Assign the constructed collection to the instance variable. */
    self.items_table := items_table;
    RETURN;
  END items_object;

  CONSTRUCTOR FUNCTION items_object
  (items_table ITEM_TABLE) RETURN SELF AS RESULT IS
  BEGIN
    self.items_table := items_table;
    RETURN;
  END items_object;
  MEMBER FUNCTION get_size RETURN NUMBER IS
  BEGIN
    RETURN self.items_table.COUNT;
  END get_size;
  STATIC FUNCTION get_items_table RETURN ITEM_TABLE IS
    /* Declare local constructor variables. */
    c           NUMBER := 1; -- Counter for table index.
    item        ITEM_OBJECT;
    items_table ITEM_TABLE := item_table();

    /* Static cursor for table contents. */
    CURSOR get_item IS
      SELECT item_title, item_subtitle FROM item;
  BEGIN
    /* Dynamically read the table contents into an item_object collection. */
    FOR i IN get_Item LOOP
      item := item_object(i.item_title,i.item_subtitle);
      items_table.EXTEND;
      items_table(c) := item; /* Must use unrelated index. */
      c := c + 1;             /* Increment index. */
    END LOOP;
    RETURN items_table;
  END get_items_table;
END;
/
```

The default CONSTRUCTOR function on lines 2 through 23 builds a list of all qualifying rows from the item table and assigns the local collection to a nested item_table collection on line 21. The following syntax creates an items_object by calling the default CONSTRUCTOR function:

```
SQL> DECLARE
       lv_items ITEMS_OBJECT;
     BEGIN
       lv_items := items_object();
       dbms_output.put_line(lv_items.get_size);
     END;
     /
```

The overriding CONSTRUCTOR function takes an item_table collection as its only parameter. The local c variable provides the index value because you can't construct object type collections by using the i (*iterator*) of the *for*-loop. You can call the overriding CONSTRUCTOR function with the result of the STATIC get_items_table function.

The get_items_table function does virtually the same thing as the default CONSTRUCTOR function on lines 35 through 53 of the items_object. The difference between the CONSTRUCTOR function and the STATIC get_items_table function is what they return. The CONSTRUCTOR function returns an instance of the items_object object type, which has an attribute that holds a nested collection of item_object instances. The STATIC get_items_table function returns a collection of item_object instances. Any STATIC function can return any type of scalar or composite variable, like a varray or table collection.

You can use results from the static get_items_table function to initialize the items_object collection by calling the overriding CONSTRUCTOR function. The following anonymous block shows you how:

```
SQL> DECLARE
  2    lv_items ITEMS_OBJECT;
  3  BEGIN
  4    /* Call the override CONSTRUCTOR function with the result
  5       from the STATIC get_items_table function. */
  6    lv_items := items_object(items_object.get_items_table);
  7    dbms_output.put_line(lv_items.get_size);
  8  END;
  9  /
```

The overriding items_object CONSTRUCTOR function takes a call from the static function as its actual parameter on line 6. Line 7 calls the get_size instance function to verify how many elements exist in the nested items_table collection.

You can also use the static function to retrieve the collection of item_object instances. Once you construct the instance of a collection of items_object object types, you can print the contents of the individual elements by calling the base object's to_string function.

The following demonstrates this functionality:

```
SQL> DECLARE
       lv_items ITEM_TABLE;
     BEGIN
       lv_items := items_object.get_items_table;
```

```
  FOR i IN 1..lv_items.COUNT LOOP
    dbms_output.put_line(lv_items(i).to_string);
  END LOOP;
END;
/
```

This section has shown you how to declare an object type collection. You have also declared a static method that you can implement as a concrete factory. The static method allows you to grab an instance object type collection without explicitly constructing it in your stand-alone PL/SQL blocks.

Review Section

This section has described the following points about the basics of implementing object type collections:

- You can create an array of any object type, provided you define it as a SQL varray or table collection first and then as an attribute of an object type.
- You can instantiate a varray or table collection as an attribute of an object type inside a `CONSTRUCTOR` function.
- You can instantiate a varray or table collection as an attribute of an object type inside a `STATIC` function that returns the collection type.
- The index value of a collection inside an object type must be a different integer value than the index of a range `FOR` loop.

Supporting Scripts

This section describes programs placed on the McGraw-Hill Professional website to support this chapter.

- The `basic_objects.sql` program contains examples that support the basic `hello_there` object type and the getters and setters examples.
- The `static_methods.sql` program contains examples that support the use of `STATIC` methods.
- The `map_compare.sql` and `order_compare.sql` programs contain examples that use `MAP` and `ORDER` functions and procedures.
- The `overriding_objects.sql` program contains examples that use subtypes and overriding functions and procedures.

Summary

This chapter has examined how you define, initialize, and use objects. You should now have a foundational understanding of what objects are and how you can use them in your PL/SQL applications.

Mastery Check

The mastery check is a series of true-or-false and multiple-choice questions that let you confirm how well you understand the material in the chapter. You may check Appendix I for answers to these questions.

True or False:

1. ___Object types are instantiable by default.
2. ___Object types are extensible by default.
3. ___The *this* keyword references an instance of an object type inside an object body.
4. ___You can have a `MAP` function and an `ORDER` function in the same object type.
5. ___You can have a `MAP` procedure and an `ORDER` procedure in the same object type.
6. ___`CONSTRUCTOR` functions require the name and data type to be the same as the attributes of the object type.
7. ___Getters always should be implemented as `MEMBER` functions.
8. ___Setters always should be implemented as `MEMBER` procedures.
9. ___The `UNDER` clause designates a superclass.
10. ___The `OVERRIDING` clause lets a subtype override a `STATIC` function or procedure.

Multiple Choice:

11. Which of the following are keywords in object types? (Multiple answers possible)
    - **A.** The `MAP` keyword
    - **B.** The `OVERRIDE` keyword
    - **C.** The `OVERRIDING` keyword
    - **D.** The `NONSTATIC` keyword
    - **E.** The `MEMBER` keyword
12. Which of the following are valid types of functions in object types? (Multiple answers possible)
    - **A.** An `ORDER` function
    - **B.** An `OVERRIDE` function
    - **C.** A `MEMBER` function
    - **D.** An `UNDER` function
    - **E.** A `STATIC` function
13. Which of the following are valid types of procedures in object types? (Multiple answers possible)
    - **A.** An `ORDER` procedure
    - **B.** A `MAP` procedure
    - **C.** An `UNDER` procedure

D. A MEMBER procedure

E. A STATIC procedure

14. Which of the following require an instance of the object type? (Multiple answers possible)

A. A STATIC function

B. A STATIC procedure

C. A CONSTRUCTOR function

D. A MEMBER function

E. A MEMBER procedure

15. Which of the following can be a function return type (or normalized table with a surrogate key for its single-column primary key)? (Multiple answers possible)

A. A VARCHAR2 data type

B. A NUMBER data type

C. A varray or table collection data type

D. A RECORD data type

E. An OBJECT data type

CHAPTER 12

Triggers

Database *triggers* are specialized stored programs. They are not called directly but are triggered by events in the database. They run between the time you issue a command and the time you perform the database management system action. This time interval is the transaction lifecycle. You can read more about the transaction lifecycle in the "Data Transactions" section of Appendix A. Appendix A also discusses ACID-compliant transactions and the two-phase commit (2PC) processes, in the section "Data Transactions." Together, they support the Oracle Database implementation of MVCC.

Triggers on `INSERT`, `UPDATE`, and `DELETE` statements run during the first phase of the transaction lifecycle. Other triggers run on immediate events, which occur when you create or change things in the database, or you connect or disconnect from the database.

You can write triggers in PL/SQL or Java. Triggers can capture events that create, modify, or drop objects, and they can capture inserts to, updates of, and deletes from tables or views. They can also monitor changes in the state of the database or schema, and the actions of users.

This chapter covers the following:

- Introduction to triggers
- Database trigger architecture
- Data Definition Language (DDL) triggers
- Data Manipulation Language (DML) triggers
- Compound triggers
- `INSTEAD OF` triggers
- System and database event triggers
- Trigger restrictions

The sections of this chapter lay a foundation and develop ideas sequentially. They should also serve as a quick reference if you want to focus on writing a specific trigger type quickly. For example, you can go to the section "Data Manipulation Language Triggers" to learn how to write triggers for `INSERT`, `UPDATE`, and `DELETE` statements.

Introduction to Triggers

As mentioned, database triggers are specialized stored programs. As such, they are defined by very similar DDL rules. Likewise, triggers can call SQL statements and PL/SQL functions and procedures. You can choose to implement triggers in PL/SQL or Java.

Database triggers differ from stored functions and procedures because you can't call them directly. Database triggers are fired when a triggering event occurs in the database. This makes them very powerful tools in your efforts to manage the database. You are able to limit or redirect actions through triggers.

You can do the following with triggers:

- Control the behavior of DDL statements, such as altering, creating, or renaming objects
- Control the behavior of DML statements, like `INSERT`, `UPDATE`, and `DELETE` statements
- Control the sequence of and synchronize calls to triggers

- Enforce referential integrity, complex business rules, and security policies
- Control and redirect DML statements when they change data in a view
- Audit information of system access and behavior by creating transparent logs

Prior to Oracle Database 11*g*, sequencing and synchronizing calls to triggers wasn't possible. Oracle Database 11*g* introduced the `FOLLOWS` clause, which lets you sequence the execution of DML database triggers. Oracle Database 11*g* also introduced compound triggers to help you manage larger events, like those triggering events that you would sequence.

Using triggers has some risks. The risks are complex because not only do SQL statements fire triggers, triggers call SQL statements. A trigger can call a SQL statement that in turn fires another trigger. The subsequent trigger could repeat the behavior and fire another trigger. This creates *cascading triggers*. Oracle Database 12*c* and earlier releases limit the number of cascading triggers to 32, after which an exception is thrown.

The following is a summary of the five types of triggers and their uses:

- **Data Definition Language (DDL) triggers** These triggers fire when you create, change, or remove objects in a database schema. They are useful to control or monitor DDL statements. An *instead of create table* trigger provides you with a tool to ensure table creation meets your development standards, like including storage or partitioning clauses. You can also use them to monitor poor programming practices, such as when programs *create* and *drop* temporary tables rather than use Oracle collections. Temporary tables can fragment disk space and degrade database performance over time.
- **Data Manipulation Language (DML) triggers** These triggers fire when you insert, update, or delete data in a table. You can fire them once for all changes on a table, or for each row change, using *statement-* or *row-level* trigger types, respectively. DML triggers are useful to control DML statements. You can use these triggers to audit, check, save, and replace values before they are changed. In Oracle Database 11*g* databases, automatic numbering of numeric primary keys is frequently done by using a row-level DML trigger. This is no longer the case in Oracle Database 12*c* because of the introduction of identity columns.
- **Compound triggers** These triggers act as both statement- and row-level triggers when you insert, update, or delete data in a table. You can declare variables in a global trigger state in a compound trigger. The compound trigger also lets you capture information at four timing points: (a) before the firing statement, (b) before each row change from the firing statement, (c) after each row change from the firing statement, and (d) after the firing statement. You can use these types of triggers to audit, check, save, and replace values before they are changed when you need to take action at both the statement and row event levels.
- **`INSTEAD OF` triggers** These triggers enable you to stop performance of a DML statement and redirect the DML statement. `INSTEAD OF` triggers are often used to manage how you write to nonupdatable views. The `INSTEAD OF` triggers apply business rules and directly insert, update, or delete rows in tables that define updatable views. Alternatively, the `INSTEAD OF` triggers insert, update, or delete rows in designated tables unrelated to the view. You also have an *instead of create table* trigger that lets you automate appending storage or partitioning clauses.

- **System event and database event triggers** These triggers fire when a system activity occurs in the database, like the logon and logoff event triggers. They are useful for auditing information of system access. These triggers let you track system events and map them to users.

Triggers have some restrictions that are important to note. The largest one is that the trigger body can be no longer than 32,760 bytes, because trigger bodies are stored in LONG data type columns. This means you should consider keeping your trigger bodies small. You do that by placing the coding logic in other schema-level components, like functions, procedures, and packages. Another advantage of moving the coding logic out of the trigger body is that you can't wrap it when it's in trigger bodies (the process of wrapping code is explained in Appendix F).

You can capture the logic of your database triggers by querying them from the data catalog. Trigger bodies are stored as anonymous blocks. With Oracle Database 12c's new multitenant architecture, you can find the trigger body, or code logic, in four versions of three views. The data catalog views are

- The CDB_, DBA_, ALL_, and USER_TRIGGERS views
- The CDB_, DBA_, ALL_, and USER_TRIGGER_COLS views
- The CDB_, DBA_, ALL_, and USER_TRIGGER_ORDERING views

While displaying the values from LONG columns isn't difficult with SQL*Plus or SQL Developer, converting the logic from a LONG column to a CLOB or VARCHAR2 data type is complex. Converting the LONG data type is complex because you need to perform that by using the dbms_sql package. Chapter 10 provides you with complete code to convert a LONG to a CLOB in the "Converting a LONG to a CLOB" sidebar. You also can learn how to convert a LONG to a VARCHAR2 data type in the "NDS Is the Key to Converting LONG Data Types" section of Chapter 13.

Each of these triggers has a set of rules that govern its use. We will cover all five triggers in their respective sections. The next section describes the architecture of database triggers.

Privileges Required to Use Triggers

You must have the CREATE TRIGGER system privilege to create a trigger on an object that you own. If the object is owned by another user, you'll need that user to grant you the ALTER privilege on the object. Alternatively, the privileged user can grant a power user the ALTER ANY TABLE and CREATE ANY TRIGGER privileges.

You have definer permissions on your own schema-level components, but you must have EXECUTE permission when you call a schema-level component owned by another user. You should document any required privileges during development to streamline subsequent implementation.

Review Section

This section has described the following points in the introduction to Oracle Database 12*c* triggers:

- Oracle Database 12*c* supports five types of database triggers: DDL, DML, compound, `INSTEAD OF`, and system or database event triggers.
- DDL triggers let you capture events that create, modify, or drop objects.
- DML triggers let you capture changes in data caused by `INSERT`, `UPDATE`, and `DELETE` statements. You can write these triggers to run as statement- or row-level triggers before or after the insert, update, or delete event.
- You can sequence the execution of DML triggers by using the `FOLLOWS` clause.
- Compound triggers let you capture changes in data from the perspective of four different timing events for `INSERT`, `UPDATE`, and `DELETE` statements.
- `INSTEAD OF` triggers work on views typically, and let you engineer the logic to insert, update, or delete data in views that may not otherwise be writable. `INSTEAD OF` triggers also let you automate adding storage or partitioning clauses.
- System or database event triggers let you manage the database environment.

Database Trigger Architecture

Database triggers are defined in the database in much the same way as packages are defined. They're composed of two pieces: the database trigger declaration and the body. The declaration states how and when a trigger is called. You can't call a trigger directly. They are triggered *(called)* by a firing event. Firing events are DDL or DML statements or database or system events. Database triggers implement an object-oriented analysis and design (OOAD) *Observer* pattern, which means they listen for an event and then take action when the event occurs. *The trigger body is an anonymous block PL/SQL program unit* and it's stored in a `LONG` column within the data catalog.

Trigger declarations consist of four parts: a trigger name, a statement, a restriction, and an action. The first three define the trigger declaration, and the last defines the trigger body. A trigger name must be unique among triggers but can duplicate the name of any other object in a schema because triggers have their own namespace. A namespace is a list of identifiers, and in this case the namespace of database triggers determines a unique list for database trigger names.

A trigger statement identifies the event or statement type that fires the trigger. A trigger restriction, such as a `WHEN` clause or an `INSTEAD OF` clause, limits when the trigger runs. A trigger action is a trigger body.

NOTE

A namespace is a unique list of identifiers maintained in the database catalog.

A database trigger declaration is valid unless you remove the object that it observes. A database trigger declaration also creates a runtime process when an event fires it. The trigger body is not as simple. A trigger body can depend on other tables, views, or stored programs. This means that you can invalidate a trigger body by removing a dependency. Dependencies are local schema objects, but those include synonyms that may resolve across the network. You invalidate a trigger when the trigger body becomes invalid. Trigger bodies are specialized anonymous block programs. You can call and pass them parameters only through the trigger declaration.

The linkage becomes acute when you define a DDL trigger on the `CREATE` event. As discussed in the next section, "Data Definition Language Triggers," an invalid trigger body for a `CREATE` trigger disables your ability to re-create the missing dependency. Similar behaviors occur for other DDL events, like `ALTER` and `DROP`.

You can recompile triggers after you can replace any missing dependencies. The syntax is

```
ALTER TRIGGER trigger_name COMPILE;
```

Triggering events communicate directly with the trigger. You have no control over or visibility into how that communication occurs, other than what you can access by calling event attribute functions. The "Event Attribute Functions" section later in this chapter shows you how to use them in triggers.

DDL, statement-level DML, and system or database event triggers occur once for an event or for a series of rows that may change. You have no ability to change or access the data changed by these types of database triggers. However, row-level DML triggers do provide you with direct access to the data your `INSERT`, `UPDATE`, or `DELETE` statements touch. You can define database triggers that run inside or outside of the transaction scope of their firing event. The default behavior is to run inside the transaction scope. The alternative runs outside the transaction scope by spawning a separate transaction scope. You create an independent transaction scope by including the `AUTONOMOUS_TRANSACTION` precompiler directive inside the declaration block of the trigger body.

NOTE

A `MERGE` statement is both an `INSERT` statement and an `UPDATE` statement, and you must write `INSERT` and `UPDATE` statement triggers for `MERGE` statements.

You gain access to the data changes in row-level DML triggers through the `new` and `old` pseudo-record types. You also gain the same access to data changes in `INSTEAD OF` triggers. The structure of these types is dynamic and defined at runtime. The trigger declaration inherits the declaration of these values from the DML statement that fires it.

The way in which DML row-level and `INSTEAD OF` triggers call their trigger bodies is different from how statement-level triggers call their trigger bodies. When an event fires this type of trigger, the trigger declaration spawns a runtime program unit, which is the real "trigger" in this process. The trigger makes available `new` and `old` pseudo-record structures by communicating with the DML statement that fired it. The trigger code block can access these pseudo-record structures by calling them as bind variables. The trigger code block is an anonymous PL/SQL block that is only accessible through a trigger declaration.

You also have the ability to replace the `new` and `old` pseudo-record structures with user-defined names of your own choosing. That's done with the following prototype:

```
REFERENCING new AS myNew old AS myOld
```

As discussed in Chapter 4, Table 4-1, under the host variable indicator, bind variables allow you to reach outside of a program's scope. You can access variables defined in the calling program's scope. The `:in` and `:out` variables are bind variables inside trigger bodies, or `:myNew` and `:myOld` user-defined pseudo-record structures. The pseudo-record structure lets your trigger code block communicate with your trigger session. Only row-level triggers can reference these pseudo-record structure bind variables. Row-level trigger code blocks can read and write through these bind variables, as shown in Figure 12-1.

You can also call external stand-alone or package functions and procedures from trigger bodies. When you call programs from the trigger body, the called programs are *black boxes*. This means that external stored programs can't access the `:new` and `:old` bind variables. You do have the option to pass them by value or reference to other stored functions and procedures.

Oracle Database 11*g* introduced compound triggers. The compound trigger changes the landscape of writing triggers by introducing timing blocks and a global trigger state. The timing blocks mimic the four types of DML triggers, but the global trigger state lets you coordinate the exchange of information between the timing events. Inside the global trigger state, you can declare variables, types, and cursors that each of the timing events can read and write to.

Table collections are probably the most useful structure that you can define in the global trigger state. That's because you can write data collected inside the `BEFORE EACH ROW` and `AFTER EACH ROW` timing events. Collections like these let you perform bulk writes to `logging` tables in the `AFTER STATEMENT` timing event.

`BEFORE STATEMENT` The code in this timing event runs before the DML statement. It executes just like a before statement-level trigger. You can collect before statement data and write it to the global trigger state variables.

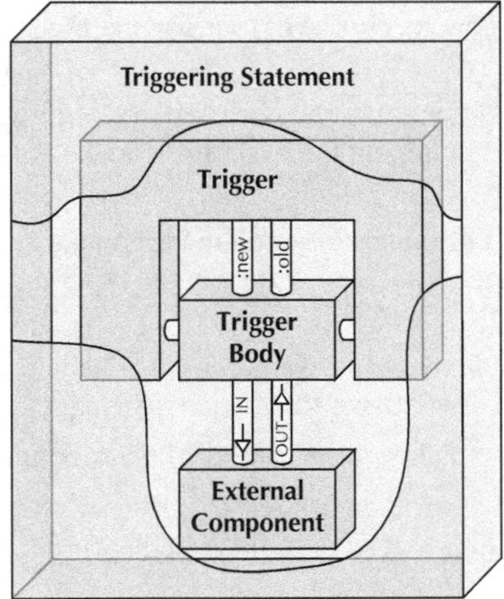

FIGURE 12-1. *Trigger architecture*

`BEFORE EACH ROW` The code in this timing event runs before each row. Here, you capture the before and after state values of any column in the target table. You can also read values set by the before statement timing event and write values to any global trigger state variables.

`AFTER EACH ROW` The after each row timing event lets you capture column values set by the DML statement or overridden by the before each row timing event.

`AFTER STATEMENT` The after statement is the last timing event. It's where you can perform bulk inserts to logging tables…at least that's true when you've gathered data from the before and after each row timing events into table collections. (It's possible to use varray collections, but, as mentioned in Chapter 6, using table collections is more flexible.)

You can define multiple triggers on any object or event. Oracle Database 10*g* and prior releases didn't provide any way to sequence the order of how triggers fired. This limit existed because triggers were *interleaved*, meaning that programs worked independently as discrete processes. Oracle Database 11*g* and forward eliminates this limitation. Oracle Database 11*g* added the `FOLLOWS` clause to trigger definitions. The `FOLLOWS` clause guarantees that a trigger fires following another trigger. A trigger without the `FOLLOWS` clause fires first, provided all other triggers use the `FOLLOWS` clause.

Review Section

This section has described the following points about the Oracle Database 12*c* database trigger architecture:

- Database triggers are like packages because they have a trigger declaration and trigger body.
- The trigger declarations consist of four parts: a trigger name, a statement, a restriction, and an action.
- The trigger body is an anonymous block PL/SQL program unit. As an anonymous block, you must implement the execution block. You may implement a declaration and exception block.
- Database triggers listen for an event and then take action when the event occurs. This is an implementation of the object-oriented analysis and design (OOAD) Observer pattern.
- Database triggers have their own namespace, which means you can have the same name for a table as you have for a database trigger.
- Database triggers may become invalid when dependencies in the trigger body are removed.
- You can use the alter trigger command to recompile a trigger after a dependency of the trigger body has been restored.

- DDL, statement-level DML, and system or database triggers have no access to the data they impact (an exception occurs when you alter or drop a column in a DDL trigger).
- Row-level DML triggers have access to the data they impact through the `new` and `old` pseudo-record structures.
- You can override the `new` and `old` pseudo-record structure names when you define the database trigger.
- DML statement-level triggers have before and after statement timing events.
- DML row-level triggers have before statement, before each row, after each row, and after statement timing events.
- You can synchronize triggers by using the `FOLLOWS` clause when you define database triggers.
- Compound database triggers have a global trigger state and the same four timing events as a DML row-level trigger.

Data Definition Language Triggers

Data Definition Language triggers fire when you create, change, or remove objects in a database schema. They are useful to control or monitor DDL statements. Table 12-1 lists the DDL events that work with DDL triggers. These triggers support both `BEFORE` and `AFTER` event triggers and work at the database or schema level.

You often use DDL triggers to monitor significant events in the database. Sometimes you use them to monitor errant code. Errant code can perform activities that corrupt or destabilize your database. More often, you use DDL triggers in development, test, stage, and production systems to understand and monitor the dynamics of database activities. The following list describes the purpose of each of these different environments and how DDL triggers are used in each:

- **Development systems** Support white box and black box testing of code modules. These tests include letting you or other developers create, alter, and drop different database objects. Concurrent testing of different modules can lead to confusion and errors. DBAs need to use DDL triggers to monitor the code components that developers put into the development system. As a DBA, you use information from DDL triggers to diagnose and fix code components. Without DDL triggers to capture information, it becomes more difficult to find and fix problems with the database instance.
- **Test systems** Support integration testing, which lets you examine how individual modules interact with one another. The development staff and your company's technical business users work on these test systems. The staff performs regression and load testing. They use DDL triggers to check the effectiveness of how modules work with one another.
- **Stage systems** Support alpha and beta testing by technical business users. Stage systems are engineered to mimic production servers. Stage systems use DDL triggers to ensure control rules limit changes on the server.
- **Production systems** Support the operation of small to large corporations. You use DDL triggers to manage business application rules and enforce security protocols. These DDL triggers help you identify, log, and control activities in the production instance.

DDL Event	Description
ALTER	You change something about objects, like their constraints, names, storage clauses, or structure.
ANALYZE	You compute object statistics for the cost optimizer.
ASSOCIATE STATISTICS	You link a statistic type to a column, function, package, type, domain index, or index type.
AUDIT	You enable auditing on an object or system.
COMMENT	You document the purpose of columns or tables.
CREATE	You create objects in the database, like objects, privileges, roles, tables, users, and views.
DDL	You use the DDL event to represent any of the primary DDL events. It effectively represents any DDL event acting on anything.
DISASSOCIATE STATISTICS	You unlink a statistic type to a column, function, package, type, domain index, or index type.
DROP	You remove objects from the database, like objects, privileges, roles, tables, users, and views.
GRANT	You grant privileges or roles to users in the database. The privileges enable a user to act on objects, like objects, privileges, roles, tables, users, and views.
NOAUDIT	You disable auditing on an object or system.
RENAME	You rename objects in the database, like columns, constraints, objects, privileges, roles, synonyms, tables, users, and views.
REVOKE	You revoke privileges or roles from users in the database. The privileges enable a user to act on objects, like objects, privileges, roles, tables, users, and views.
TRUNCATE	You truncate tables, which drops all rows from a table and resets the high-water mark to the original storage clause initial extent value. Unlike the DML DELETE statement, the truncate command can't be reversed by a rollback command. You can use the new flashback to undo the change.

TABLE 12-1. *Available DDL events*

DDL triggers are very useful when you patch your application code. They can let you find potential changes between releases. You can also use the INSTEAD OF CREATE trigger during an upgrade to enforce table creation storage clauses or partitioning rules.

CAUTION
The overhead of these types of triggers should be monitored carefully in production systems.

These triggers can also track the creation and modification of tables by application programs that lead to database fragmentation. They are also effective security tools when you monitor GRANT and REVOKE privilege statements. The following sections list and describe in detail the event attribute functions you can use to supplement your DDL triggers.

Event Attribute Functions

The following is a list of system-defined event attribute functions:

- ORA_CLIENT_IP_ADDRESS
- ORA_DATABASE_NAME
- ORA_DES_ENCRYPTED_PASSWORD
- ORA_DICT_OBJ_NAME
- ORA_DICT_OBJ_NAME_LIST
- ORA_DICT_OBJ_OWNER
- ORA_DICT_OBJ_OWNER_LIST
- ORA_DICT_OBJ_TYPE
- ORA_GRANTEE
- ORA_INSTANCE_NUM
- ORA_IS_ALTER_COLUMN
- ORA_IS_CREATING_NESTED_TABLE
- ORA_IS_DROP_COLUMN
- ORA_IS_SERVERERROR
- ORA_LOGIN_USER
- ORA_PARTITION_POS
- ORA_PRIVILEGE_LIST
- ORA_REVOKEE
- ORA_SERVER_ERROR
- ORA_SERVER_ERROR_DEPTH
- ORA_SERVER_ERROR_MSG
- ORA_SERVER_ERROR_NUM_PARAMS
- ORA_SERVER_ERROR_PARAM
- ORA_SQL_TXT
- ORA_SYSEVENT
- ORA_WITH_GRANT_OPTION
- SPACE_ERROR_INFO

Each of the following subsections has a brief description and basic examples of how to use the specific event attribute function. You should note that these functions are designed to work in the context of a DDL trigger. The event attribute functions return null values outside of a database trigger context. You should recall from the "Database Trigger Architecture" section earlier in this chapter that trigger bodies are anonymous PL/SQL blocks. That's why I show most of the examples that follow without line numbers. There are two exceptions to this rule. One example shows you how to implement a system trigger with an event attribute, and the other shows you how to implement a DDL trigger with an event attribute. The "ORA_CLIENT_IP_ADDRESS" section demonstrates the system trigger, and the "ORA_IS_DROP_COLUMN" section demonstrates the DDL trigger.

Trigger Logging Table

A trigger `logging` table can be many things and serve many purposes. This `logging` table is designed to support DDL triggers that alter or drop a column. It leverages the concept of nested tables of object types, which are discussed in the "Nested Collection Types" section of Appendix B. The `logging` table requires that you create two base object types, which act like SQL record types, and two collections of the base object types.

(continued)

The object types and collections of object types are defined by these SQL statements:

```
SQL> /* Base Object Type for Surrogate Keys. */
SQL> CREATE OR REPLACE
       TYPE who_audit_key IS OBJECT
       ( row_id       CHAR(18) -- Convert to character string.
       , row_value    NUMBER );
     /
SQL> /* Collection of Base Object Type for Surrogate Keys. */
SQL> CREATE OR REPLACE
       TYPE who_audit_key_table IS TABLE OF who_audit_key;
     /
SQL> /* Base Object Type for Surrogate Keys. */
SQL> CREATE OR REPLACE
       TYPE who_audit_value IS OBJECT
       ( row_id       CHAR(18) -- Convert to character string.
       , row_value    DATE );
     /
SQL> /* Collection of Base Object Type for Surrogate Keys. */
SQL> CREATE OR REPLACE
       TYPE who_audit_value_table IS TABLE OF who_audit_value;
     /
```

The `row_id` field value in the `who_audit_key` and `who_audit_value` collections must be explicitly converted to a character string because you can't put a `ROWID` data type in an object type. The `who_audit_key_table` and `who_audit_value_table` collections are table collections. Table collections are effective when you don't know how many rows might exist when you drop or alter a column in a table, which is always.

The following creates the `logging` table to hold information from our database trigger example:

```
SQL> CREATE TABLE logging
  2  ( logging_id         NUMBER GENERATED ALWAYS AS IDENTITY
  3  , message            VARCHAR2(266)
  4  , user_ids           WHO_AUDIT_KEY_TABLE
  5  , user_timestamps    WHO_AUDIT_VALUE_TABLE
  6  , CONSTRAINT logging_pk PRIMARY KEY (logging_id))
  7    NESTED TABLE user_ids STORE AS who_audit_id
  8  , NESTED TABLE user_timestamps STORE AS who_audit_timestamp;
```

The `logging` table implements an identity column on line 2 as a surrogate key. The identity column's name is the table name plus an `_id` suffix. The `message` column stores the trigger's raised error message in the `logging` table. The `user_ids` column and `user_timestamps` columns are nested tables that would hold any data dropped or altered by a DDL statement. Lines 7 and 8 designate two parallel nested tables, which you should know based on the comma delimiting them on line 8.

You would embed a Native Dynamic SQL (NDS) or `dbms_sql` operation to capture the data from a table name discovered at runtime. You could then query the data before altering or dropping a table's column. Both NDS and `dbms_sql` are covered in Chapter 13.

Some examples require full illustration, and a couple of them write results gathered during trigger execution to a `logging` table. You can find the full definition of that table in the "Trigger Logging Table" sidebar in this chapter.

ORA_CLIENT_IP_ADDRESS

The `ORA_CLIENT_IP_ADDRESS` function takes no formal parameters. It returns the client IP address as a `VARCHAR2` data type.

The following is an example of a system trigger using an event attribute function. It requires you to connect as the `system` user of the CDB or the `ADMIN` user of the PDB, and then create the following table.

```
SQL> CREATE TABLE logon_ip
  ( logon_ip_id        NUMBER GENERATED ALWAYS AS IDENTITY
  , logon_ip_address   VARCHAR2(15));
```

Realistically, you'd capture more information, but this shows you how to capture an IP address. IP addresses have at most four three-digit numbers between 0 and 255, and three periods or dots, which is why I sized the `logon_ip_address` column at 15 characters.

You can use it like this in a real system trigger:

```
SQL> CREATE OR REPLACE TRIGGER connecting_trigger
  2    AFTER LOGON ON DATABASE
  3  DECLARE
  4    ip_address VARCHAR2(15);
  5  BEGIN
  6    IF ora_sysevent = 'LOGON' THEN
  7      /* Capture the IP address to a local variable. */
  8      ip_address := ora_client_ip_address;
  9
 10      /* Write the logon IP address to a table. */
 11      INSERT INTO logon_ip
 12      (logon_ip_address)
 13      VALUES
 14      (ip_address); -- Could use ora_client_ip_address function call.
 15    END IF;
 16  END;
 17  /
```

Line 4 declares a local `ip_address` variable. Line 8 captures the value from the `ORA_CLIENT_IP_ADDRESS` function and assigns it to the local variable. The `INSERT` statement uses the local `ip_address` variable in the `VALUES` clause. While you don't really need to create a local variable in this simple trigger, a fine-grain auditing solution could benefit from a local variable. A fine-grain auditing solution would compare the return value against an internal white list of IP addresses and rules.

ORA_DATABASE_NAME

The `ORA_DATABASE_NAME` function takes no formal parameters. It returns the database name as a `VARCHAR2` data type.

You can use it like this:

```
DECLARE
  database VARCHAR2(50);
BEGIN
  database := ora_database_name;
END;
```

ORA_DES_ENCRYPTED_PASSWORD

The ORA_DES_ENCRYPTED_PASSWORD function takes no formal parameters. It returns the DES-encrypted password as a VARCHAR2 data type. This is equivalent to the value in the sys.user$ table password column in Oracle Database 12c. Passwords are no longer accessible in the DBA_USERS or ALL_USERS views.

You can use it like this:

```
DECLARE
  password VARCHAR2(60);
BEGIN
  IF ora_dict_obj_type = 'USER' THEN
    password := ora_des_encrypted_password;
  END IF;
END;
```

ORA_DICT_OBJ_NAME

The ORA_DICT_OBJ_NAME function takes no formal parameters. It returns an object name as a VARCHAR2 data type. The object name represents the target of the DDL statement.

You can use it like this:

```
DECLARE
  database VARCHAR2(50);
BEGIN
  database := ora_dict_obj_name;
END;
```

ORA_DICT_OBJ_NAME_LIST

The ORA_DICT_OBJ_NAME_LIST function takes one formal parameter. The formal parameter is also returned because it is passed by reference as an OUT mode list of VARCHAR2 variables. The formal parameter data type is defined in the dbms_standard package as ora_name_list_t. The ora_name_list_t is a table of VARCHAR2(64) data types. The *function returns the number of elements in the list* as a PLS_INTEGER data type. The name_list contains the list of object names touched by the triggering event.

You can use it like this:

```
DECLARE
  name_list DBMS_STANDARD.ORA_NAME_LIST_T;
  counter    PLS_INTEGER;
BEGIN
  IF ora_sysevent = 'ASSOCIATE_STATISTICS' THEN
    counter := ora_dict_obj_name_list(name_list);
  END IF;
END;
```

ORA_DICT_OBJ_OWNER

The ORA_DICT_OBJ_OWNER function takes no formal parameters. It returns an owner of the object acted upon by the event as a VARCHAR2 data type.

You can use it like this:

```
DECLARE
  owner VARCHAR2(30);
BEGIN
  database := ora_dict_obj_owner;
END;
```

ORA_DICT_OBJ_OWNER_LIST

The ORA_DICT_OBJ_OWNER_LIST function takes one formal parameter. The formal parameter is also returned because it is passed by reference as an OUT mode list of VARCHAR2 variables. The formal parameter data type is defined in the dbms_standard package as ora_name_list_t. The ora_name_list_t is a table of VARCHAR2(64) data types. The *function returns the number of elements in the list* indexed by a PLS_INTEGER data type.

In the example, the owner_list contains the list of object owners where their statistics were analyzed by a triggering event. You can use it like this:

```
DECLARE
  owner_list DBMS_STANDARD.ORA_NAME_LIST_T;
  counter    PLS_INTEGER;
BEGIN
  IF ora_sysevent = 'ASSOCIATE_STATISTICS' THEN
    counter := ora_dict_obj_owner_list(owner_list);
  END IF;
END;
```

ORA_DICT_OBJ_TYPE

The ORA_DICT_OBJ_TYPE function takes no formal parameters. It returns the data type of the dictionary object changed by the event as a VARCHAR2 data type.

You can use it like this:

```
DECLARE
  type VARCHAR2(19);
BEGIN
  database := ora_dict_obj_type;
END;
```

ORA_GRANTEE

The ORA_GRANTEE function takes one formal parameter. The formal parameter is also returned because it is passed by reference as an OUT mode list of VARCHAR2 variables. The formal parameter data type is defined in the dbms_standard package as ora_name_list_t. The ora_name_list_t is a table of VARCHAR2(64) data types. The *function returns the number of elements in the list* indexed by a PLS_INTEGER data type. The user_list contains the list of users granted privileges or roles by the triggering event.

You can use it like this:

```
DECLARE
  user_list dbms_standard.ora_name_list_t;
  counter   PLS_INTEGER;
BEGIN
  IF ora_sysevent = 'GRANT' THEN
    counter := ora_grantee(user_list);
  END IF;
END;
```

ORA_INSTANCE_NUM

The `ORA_INSTANCE_NUM` function takes no formal parameters. It returns the current database instance number as a `NUMBER` data type.

You can use it like this:

```
DECLARE
  instance NUMBER;
BEGIN
  instance := ora_instance_num;
END;
```

ORA_IS_ALTER_COLUMN

The `ORA_IS_ALTER_COLUMN` function takes one formal parameter, which is a column name. The function returns a *true* or *false* value as a `BOOLEAN` data type. It is true when the column has been altered, and it is false when it hasn't been changed. This function worked with the traditional uppercase catalog information, but in Oracle Database 12*c* you need to match the catalog case if you opted to save any tables in a case-sensitive format. The example uses a case-insensitive string as an actual parameter.

You can use it like this:

```
SQL> CREATE OR REPLACE TRIGGER dropping_column
    BEFORE ALTER ON SCHEMA
  DECLARE
    /* Column length has grown in Oracle 12c to 128. */
    TYPE column_table IS TABLE OF VARCHAR2(128);

    /* Identify the list of columns to monitor. */
    lv_column_table COLUMN_TABLE := column_table('CREATED_BY'
                                                ,'CREATION_DATE'
                                                ,'LAST_UPDATED_BY'
                                                ,'LAST_UPDATE_DATE');
  BEGIN
    /* Check for altering a table when you want to capture
       dropping a column. */
    IF ORA_SYSEVENT = 'ALTER' AND ORA_DICT_OBJ_TYPE = 'TABLE' THEN
       /* Read through the list of monitored columns. */
       FOR i IN 1..lv_column_table.COUNT LOOP
         /* Check for a drop of a monitored column and record it. */
```

```
19          IF ORA_IS_ALTER_COLUMN(lv_column_table(i)) OR
20             ORA_IS_DROP_COLUMN(lv_column_table(i)) THEN
21            INSERT INTO logging
22            (message)
23            VALUES
24            (ora_dict_obj_owner||'.'||
25             ora_dict_obj_name||'.'||
26             lv_column_table(i)||' column dropped.');
27          END IF;
28        END LOOP;
29      END IF;
30    END;
31    /
```

Line 2 instructs the trigger to run when an `ALTER` statement runs against the schema. Line 15 checks whether an `ALTER TABLE` statement fired the trigger. Lines 19 and 20 check whether the change touches a column of interest, like the standard *who-audit* columns. The following statement would fire the preceding trigger if a `sample` table exists with a `last_updated_by` column:

```
SQL> ALTER TABLE sample1
  2    DROP COLUMN last_updated_by;
```

Querying the `message` column of the `logging` table, you would find the following message:

```
MESSAGE
----------------------------------------------
VIDEO.SAMPLE1.LAST_UPDATED_BY column dropped.
```

This is very useful if you want to guard against changing standard who-audit columns, like `CREATED_BY`, `CREATION_DATE`, `LAST_UPDATED_BY`, or `LAST_UPDATE_DATE`. These are security columns generally used to identify who last touched the data through the standard application programming interface (API). Any change to columns like these can destabilize an API.

ORA_IS_CREATING_NESTED_TABLE

The `ORA_IS_CREATING_NESTED_TABLE` function takes no formal parameters. It returns a *true* or *false* value as a `BOOLEAN` data type when you create a table with a nested table.

You can use it like this:

```
BEGIN
  IF ora_sysevent = 'CREATE' AND
     ora_dict_obj_type = 'TABLE' AND
     ora_is_creating_nested_table THEN
       INSERT INTO logging_table
       VALUES (ora_dict_obj_name||'.'||' created with nested table.');
  END IF;
END;
```

ORA_IS_DROP_COLUMN

The ORA_IS_DROP_COLUMN function takes one formal parameter, which is a column name. The function returns a *true* or *false* value as a BOOLEAN data type. It is true when the column has been dropped, and it returns false when it hasn't been dropped. This function worked with the traditional uppercase catalog information, but in Oracle Database 12c you need to match the catalog case if you opted to save any tables in a case-sensitive format. The example uses a case-insensitive string as an actual parameter.

You can use it like this:

```
DECLARE
  TYPE column_list IS TABLE OF VARCHAR2(32);
  columns COLUMN_LIST := column_list('CREATED_BY','LAST_UPDATED_BY');
BEGIN
  IF ora_sysevent = 'DROP' AND
     ora_dict_obj_type = 'TABLE' THEN
     FOR i IN 1..columns.COUNT THEN
        IF ora_is_drop_column(columns(i)) THEN
          INSERT INTO logging_table
          VALUES (ora_dict_obj_name||'.'||columns(i)||' changed.');
        END IF;
    END LOOP;
  END IF;
END;
```

This function is very useful if you want to guard against changing standard *who-audit* columns, like those discussed previously for the ORA_IS_ALTER_COLUMN function.

ORA_IS_SERVERERROR

The ORA_IS_SERVERERROR function takes one formal parameter, which is an error number. It returns a *true* or *false* value as a BOOLEAN data type when the error is on the error stack.

You can use it like this:

```
BEGIN
  IF ora_is_servererror(4082) THEN
    INSERT INTO logging_table
    VALUES ('ORA-04082 error thrown.');
  END IF;
END;
```

ORA_LOGIN_USER

The ORA_LOGIN_USER function takes no formal parameters. The function returns the current schema name as a VARCHAR2 data type.

You can use it like this:

```
BEGIN
  INSERT INTO logging_table
  VALUES
  ( ORA_LOGIN_USER ||' is the current user.');
END;
```

ORA_PARTITION_POS

The ORA_PARTITION_POS function takes no formal parameters. The function returns the numeric position with the SQL text where you can insert a partition clause. This is only available in an INSTEAD OF CREATE trigger.

You can use the following, provided you add your own partitioning clause:

```
DECLARE
  sql_text  ORA_NAME_LIST_T;
  sql_stmt  VARCHAR2(32767);
  partition VARCHAR2(32767) := 'partitioning_clause';
BEGIN
  FOR i IN 1..ora_sql_txt(sql_text) LOOP
    sql_stmt := sql_stmt || sql_text(i);
  END LOOP;
  sql_stmt := SUBSTR(sql_text,1,ORA_PARTITION_POS - 1)||' '
          || partition||' '||SUBSTR(sql_text,ORA_PARTITION_POS);
  /* Add logic to prepend schema because it runs under SYSTEM. */
  sql_stmt := REPLACE(UPPER(sql_stmt),'CREATE TABLE '
                     ,'CREATE TABLE '||ora_login_user||'.');
  EXECUTE IMMEDIATE sql_stmt;
END;
```

The coding sample requires that you grant the owner of the trigger the CREATE ANY TRIGGER privilege. You should consider a master privileged user for your application and avoid using the system schema.

ORA_PRIVILEGE_LIST

The ORA_PRIVILEGE_LIST function takes one formal parameter. The formal parameter is also returned because it is passed by reference as an OUT mode list of VARCHAR2 variables. The formal parameter data type is defined in the dbms_standard package as ora_name_list_t. The ora_name_list_t is a table of VARCHAR2(64) data types. The *function returns the number of elements in the list* indexed by a PLS_INTEGER data type. The priv_list contains the list of privileges or roles granted by the triggering event.

You can use it like this:

```
DECLARE
  priv_list DBMS_STANDARD.ORA_NAME_LIST_T;
  counter   PLS_INTEGER;
BEGIN
  IF ORA_SYSEVENT = 'GRANT' OR ORA_SYSEVENT = 'REVOKE' THEN
    counter := ora_privilege_list(priv_list);
  END IF;
END;
```

Line 5 illustrates inclusionary logic from Chapter 5, and many developers write code like this because they feel it's clearer. I'd suggest there's a better way. You can replace line 5 with a lookup operator, like this:

```
  5     IF ORA_SYSEVENT IN ('GRANT','REVOKE') THEN
```

The IN lookup operator ensures you only call the ORA_SYSEVENT event attribute function once. After calling the ORA_SYSEVENT function, you compare its value against the list of values. You can also use the =ANY or =SOME lookup operators in lieu of the IN lookup operator. All three deliver the same functionality. Appendix B discusses lookup operators in server sections.

ORA_REVOKEE

The ORA_REVOKEE function takes one formal parameter. The formal parameter is also returned because it is passed by reference as an OUT mode list of VARCHAR2 variables. The formal parameter data type is defined in the dbms_standard package as ora_name_list_t. The ora_name_list_t is a table of VARCHAR2(64) data types. The *function returns the number of elements in the list* indexed by a PLS_INTEGER data type. The priv_list contains the list of users that had privileges or roles revoked by the triggering event.

You can use it like this:

```
DECLARE
  revokee_list DBMS_STANDARD.ORA_NAME_LIST_T;
  counter      PLS_INTEGER;
BEGIN
  IF ORA_SYSEVENT = 'REVOKE' THEN
    counter := ORA_REVOKEE(priv_list);
  END IF;
END;
```

ORA_SERVER_ERROR

The ORA_SERVER_ERROR function takes one formal parameter, which is the position on the error stack, where 1 is the top of the error stack. It returns an error number as a NUMBER data type.

You can use it like this:

```
DECLARE
  error NUMBER;
BEGIN
  FOR i IN 1..ORA_SERVER_ERROR_DEPTH LOOP
    error := ORA_SERVER_ERROR(i);
  END LOOP;
END;
```

ORA_SERVER_ERROR_DEPTH

The ORA_SERVER_ERROR_DEPTH function takes no formal parameters. The function returns the number of errors on the error stack as a PLS_INTEGER data type. The code samples for the ORA_SERVER_ERROR and ORA_SERVER_ERROR_MSG functions demonstrate how you can use it.

ORA_SERVER_ERROR_MSG

The ORA_SERVER_ERROR_MSG function takes one formal parameter, which is the position on the error stack, where 1 is the top of the error stack. It returns an error message text as a VARCHAR2 data type.

You can use it like this:

```
DECLARE
  error VARCHAR2(64);
BEGIN
  FOR i IN 1..ora_server_error_depth LOOP
    error := ORA_SERVER_ERROR_MSG(i);
  END LOOP;
END;
```

ORA_SERVER_ERROR_NUM_PARAMS

The ORA_SERVER_ERROR_NUM_PARAMS function takes no formal parameters. The function returns the count of any substituted strings from error messages as a PLS_INTEGER data type. For example, an error format could be "Expected %s, found %s." The code sample for the ORA_SERVER_ERROR_PARAM function shows how you can use it.

ORA_SERVER_ERROR_PARAM

The ORA_SERVER_ERROR_PARAM function takes one formal parameter, which is the position in an error message, where 1 is the first occurrence of a string in the error message. It returns an error message text as a VARCHAR2 data type. You can use it like this:

```
DECLARE
  param VARCHAR2(32);
BEGIN
  FOR i IN 1..ora_server_error_depth LOOP
    FOR j IN 1..ora_server_error_num_params(i) LOOP
      param := ORA_SERVER_ERROR_PARAM(j);
    END LOOP;
  END LOOP;
END;
```

ORA_SQL_TXT

The ORA_SQL_TXT function takes one formal parameter. The formal parameter is also returned because it is passed by reference as an OUT mode list of VARCHAR2 variables. The formal parameter data type is defined in the dbms_standard package as ora_name_list_t. The ora_name_list_t is a table of VARCHAR2(64) data types. The function returns the number of elements in the list indexed by a PLS_INTEGER data type. The list contains the substrings of the processed SQL statement that triggered the event. The coding example is shown with the ORA_PARTITION_POS function.

ORA_SYSEVENT

The ORA_SYSEVENT function takes no formal parameters. The function returns the system event that was responsible for firing the trigger as a VARCHAR2 data type. You can use it like this:

```
BEGIN
  INSERT INTO logging_table
  VALUES (ORA_SYSEVENT||' fired the trigger.');
END;
```

ORA_WITH_GRANT_OPTION

The ORA_WITH_GRANT_OPTION function has no formal parameters. The function returns a *true* or *false* value as a BOOLEAN data type. It returns *true* when privileges are granted with *grant option*. You can use it like this:

```
BEGIN
  IF ORA_WITH_GRANT_OPTION THEN
    INSERT INTO logging_table
    VALUES ('ORA-04082 error thrown.');
  END IF;
END;
```

SPACE_ERROR_INFO

The SPACE_ERROR_INFO function uses six formal pass-by-reference parameters. They are all OUT mode parameters. The prototype is

```
SPACE_ERROR_INFO( error_number OUT NUMBER
                , error_type OUT VARCHAR2
                , object_owner OUT VARCHAR2
                , table_space_name OUT VARCHAR2
                , object_name OUT VARCHAR2
                , sub_object_name OUT VARCHAR2)
```

This function returns *true* when the triggering event is related to an *out-of-space* condition, and it fills in all the outbound parameters. You implement this with a logging table that supports at least the six OUT parameters. When the function returns *false*, the OUT mode variables are null.

You can use it like this:

```
DECLARE
  error_number    NUMBER;
  error_type      VARCHAR2(12);
  object_owner    VARCHAR2(30);
  tablespace_name VARCHAR2(30);
  object_name     VARCHAR2(128);
  subobject_name  VARCHAR2(30);
BEGIN
  IF SPACE_ERROR_INFO( error_number, error_type
                     , object_owner, tablespace_name
                     , object_name, subobject_name) THEN
    INSERT INTO logging_table
    VALUES
    ( ... );
  END IF;
END;
```

Building DDL Triggers

The prototype for building DDL triggers is

```
CREATE [OR REPLACE] [EDITIONABLE | NONEDITIONABLE] TRIGGER trigger_name
{BEFORE | AFTER | INSTEAD OF} ddl_event ON {DATABASE | SCHEMA}
[WHEN (logical_expression)]
```

```
[DECLARE]
  declaration_statements
BEGIN
  execution_statements
END [trigger_name];
/
```

You can use the INSTEAD OF clause only when auditing a creation event. BEFORE triggers make sure the contents of the trigger body occur before the triggering DDL command, while AFTER triggers run last. See the section "ORA_PARTITION_POS" earlier in this chapter for an implementation of an INSTEAD OF CREATE trigger that appends a partitioning table.

The DDL example trigger requires that you create the audit_creation table and audit_creations_s1 sequence before the trigger. If you forget to create one or both, you can't create either after you attempt to compile the database trigger. This limitation exists because you have a valid trigger declaration but an invalid trigger body. You must drop or disable the trigger *(declaration)* before you can create anything in the schema.

You should note that the table and trigger share the same name. This is possible because there are two namespaces in Oracle databases, one for triggers and another for everything else.

You create the table and sequence as follows:

```
SQL> CREATE TABLE audit_creation
  2  ( audit_creation_id NUMBER
  3  , audit_owner_name  VARCHAR2(30) CONSTRAINT audit_creation_nn1 NOT NULL
  4  , audit_obj_name    VARCHAR2(30) CONSTRAINT audit_creation_nn2 NOT NULL
  5  , audit_date        DATE         CONSTRAINT audit_creation_nn3 NOT NULL
  6  , CONSTRAINT audit_creation_p1   PRIMARY KEY (audit_creation_id));
SQL> CREATE SEQUENCE audit_creation_s1;
```

Alternatively, Oracle Database 12*c* lets you define identity columns, which eliminate the need for you to manually set surrogate primary key values with manual sequence pseudocolumns. You would change line 2 from the preceding CREATE TABLE statement to use an identity column, like

```
2  ( audit_creation_id NUMBER GENERATED ALWAYS AS IDENTITY
```

ALWAYS is the default (and, yes, you can omit it safely) when you create an identify column. You can read more about the identity column in the "Identity Columns" section of Appendix B.

Now you can create the audit_creation system trigger. This trigger shows you the behavior of a DDL trigger when dependencies become unavailable to the trigger:

```
SQL> CREATE OR REPLACE TRIGGER audit_creation
  2  BEFORE CREATE ON SCHEMA
  3  BEGIN
  4    INSERT INTO audit_creation VALUES
  5    ( audit_creation_s1.nextval
  6    , ORA_DICT_OBJ_OWNER
  7    , ORA_DICT_OBJ_NAME
  8    , SYSDATE);
  9  END audit_creation;
 10  /
```

Lines 6 and 7 use *event attribute functions*, and they simplify writing a DDL trigger. You should use event attribute functions where possible to capture enriched content from your DDL triggers.

The following DDL statement triggers the system trigger, which inserts data from the event attribute functions. It creates a `mythology` synonym that doesn't translate to anything real, but it does create an event that fires the trigger.

The DDL statement is

```
CREATE SYNONYM mythology FOR plsql.some_myth;
```

You can query the results of the `audit_creation` trigger from the `audit_creation` table. While it's possible to use the same name for both the table and the database trigger (as done), doesn't it cause you to wonder, "Is that right?" That's why I'd like to suggest you append a `_T` (underscore and T) at the end of trigger names. It's simply clearer and inexpensive to do. Please remember that just because you can do something doesn't mean you should, like reuse table names for trigger names.

The following SQL*Plus formatting (covered in the "Interactive Mode Parameter Passing" section of Appendix A) helps us see what the trigger logged:

```
SQL> COL audit_creation_id FORMAT 99 HEADING "Audit|Creation|ID #"
SQL> COL audit_owner_name  FORMAT A6 HEADING "Audit|Owner|Name"
SQL> COL audit_obj_name    FORMAT A8 HEADING "Audit|Object|Name"
SQL> COL audit_obj_name    FORMAT A9 HEADING "Audit|Object|Name"
SQL> SELECT * FROM audit_creation;
```

The query returns

```
    Audit Audit  Audit
 Creation Owner  Object    Audit
     ID # Name   Name      Date
--------- ------ --------- ---------
       21 PLSQL  MYTHOLOGY 17-NOV-08
```

You have now seen how to implement a DDL trigger. The next section examines DML triggers.

Review Section

This section has described the following points about the Oracle Database 12*c* DDL database trigger architecture:

- DDL triggers fire when you create, change, or remove objects in a database.
- Oracle Database 12*c*'s event attribute functions provide a readymade set of code you can use in your DDL triggers and system or database event triggers.
- You can create DDL triggers that work against the whole database, editions, or schemas.
- You also can limit a DDL trigger to a single PDB instance in Oracle Database 12*c*'s new multitenant architecture.
- Oracle Database 12*c*'s event attribute functions only return values in the context of a database trigger.
- You can use the `INSTEAD OF CREATE` clause when you want to automate a standard partition storage clause every time you create a table.

Data Manipulation Language Triggers

DML triggers can fire *before* or *after* INSERT, UPDATE, and DELETE statements. DML triggers can be statement- or row-level activities. *Statement-level* triggers fire and perform a statement or set of statements once no matter how many rows are affected by the DML event. *Row-level* triggers fire and perform a statement or set of statements for *each* row changed by a DML statement.

A *principal caveat* of triggers that manage data changes is that you cannot use SQL Data Control Language (DCL) in them, unless you declare the trigger as autonomous. When triggers run inside the scope of a transaction, they disallow setting a SAVEPOINT or performing either a ROLLBACK or COMMIT statement. Likewise, they can't have a DCL statement in the execution path of any function or procedure that they call.

The prototype for building DML triggers is

```
CREATE [OR REPLACE] [EDITIONABLE | NONEDITIONABLE] TRIGGER trigger_name
{BEFORE | AFTER}
{INSERT | UPDATE | UPDATE OF column [, column [, ... ]] | DELETE}
ON table_name
[FOR EACH ROW]
[REFERENCING {old | new} [ROW] AS something_else
            [{old | new} [ROW] AS something_else]]
[ENABLE | DISABLE]
[FOLLOWS table_name]
[WHEN (logical_expression)]
[DECLARE]
  [PRAGMA AUTONOMOUS_TRANSACTION;]
  declaration_statements
BEGIN
  execution_statements
END [trigger_name];
/
```

Oracle Database 11*g* Release 2 added the EDITIONABLE or NONEDITIONABLE feature of DML triggers. It allows different trigger behaviors in various editions of the Oracle database.

The BEFORE or AFTER clause determines whether the trigger fires *before* or *after* the change is written to your local copy of the data. You can define a BEFORE or AFTER clause on tables but not on views. While the prototype shows that you can use either an INSERT, UPDATE, UPDATE OF *(a column)*, or DELETE statement, you can also use an inclusion, OR, operator between the events. Using one OR between two events creates a single trigger that runs for two events. You can create a trigger that supports all four possible events with multiple inclusion operators.

There are two options for DML triggers. You can declare them as *statement-level* triggers, which are also known as *table-level* triggers, or you can declare them as *row-level* triggers.

You have a FOR EACH ROW clause, a WHEN clause, and new and old pseudo-records in row-level triggers. The FOR EACH ROW clause specifies that the trigger should fire for each row, as opposed to once per statement. The WHEN clause acts as a filter specifying when the trigger fires. Unlike when working with other stored program units, you must qualify a DECLARE block when you declare local variables, types, or cursors in a trigger.

Triggers require the DECLARE block in trigger bodies because the declaration of a trigger is separate from the trigger body. Trigger bodies are like anonymous block PL/SQL programs. They are called by the trigger, and the trigger implicitly manages parameter passing. Unlike anonymous blocks, trigger bodies don't support substitution variables. They support *bind* variables, but only in the context of row-level triggers. There is no parameter passing to statement-level triggers.

Statement- and row-level triggers have different purposes and approaches. The trigger types are covered in the next two subsections.

Statement-Level Triggers

Statement-level triggers are also known as table-level triggers because they're triggered by a change to a table. Statement-level triggers capture and process information when a user inserts, updates, or deletes one or more rows in a table. You can also restrict (*filter*) UPDATE statement triggers by constraining them to fire only when a specific column value changes. You can restrict the trigger by using an UPDATE OF clause. The clause can apply to a *column name* or a *comma-delimited list of column names*.

You can't use a WHEN clause in a statement-level trigger. You also can't use the REFERENCING clause (which lets you change the new or old pseudo-records) when creating a statement-level trigger. An attempt to do so raises an ORA-04082 exception, which is a compile-time error telling you that new or old references aren't allowed in statement-level triggers. It's important to note that this same error also can be raised when compiling row-level triggers. The REFERENCING clause triggers this parsing error, but you can safely ignore the error when compiling row-level triggers.

You can implement statement-level triggers on inserting, updating, or deleting events. Statement-level triggers don't let you collect transaction details. You have access to only the type of event and values returned by event attribute functions. The UPDATE OF clause lets you filter the triggering event to a specific column change.

The statement-level example uses an UPDATE OF *column name* event. The trigger depends on your running the create_store.sql script from the publisher's website. You can find a reference to it in the Introduction to this book.

The trigger logs events in the price_type_log table. It must be created before you compile the trigger. The following statement creates the table:

```
SQL> CREATE TABLE price_type_log
( price_id      NUMBER              CONSTRAINT price_type_log_nn1 NOT NULL
, user_id       VARCHAR2(32)        CONSTRAINT price_type_log_nn2 NOT NULL
, action_date   DATE                CONSTRAINT price_type_log_nn3 NOT NULL
, CONSTRAINT    price_type_log_p1 PRIMARY KEY (price_id))
/
```

After creating the table, you can create the trigger. It is possible that the trigger can fail if you've already declared another price_t1 trigger on another table. The REPLACE command only works when the CREATE OR REPLACE TRIGGER command works against the same table. You raise an ORA-04095 exception when a trigger name already exists for another table.

The following trigger works in Oracle Database 11*g* or 12*c*. Oracle 10*g* doesn't support references to sequence .nextval or .currval pseudocolumns in SQL statements when they're inside a PL/SQL block.

Backward Compatibility of .nextval

In prior releases, like Oracle Database 10*g*, you would need to remove the call to the `.nextval` pseudocolumn from the `INSERT` statement. You would need to refactor it like this for the older releases:

```
SQL> CREATE OR REPLACE TRIGGER price_t
  2  AFTER UPDATE OF price_type ON price
  3  DECLARE
  4    lv_price_id NUMBER;
  5  BEGIN
  6    -- Retrieve sequence value and store in local variable.
  7    SELECT price_type_log_s1.nextval
  8    INTO lv_price_id
  9    FROM dual;
 10    -- Insert logging values.
 11    INSERT INTO price_type_log
 12    VALUES
 13    ( lv_price_id
 14    , USER
 15    , SYSDATE);
 16  END price_t1;
 17  /
```

The refactoring requires that you declare a local variable on line 4, then select a value from the sequence on lines 7 to 8, and use the local variable inside the `INSERT` statement on line 13. Relatively, it's a lot of work to move backward, but that's probably why Oracle made it work inside DML statements in the current release.

Oracle Database 11*g* and forward releases *do* support references to sequence `.nextval` and `.currval` pseudocolumns in SQL statements when they're inside PL/SQL blocks. The following is included:

```
SQL> CREATE OR REPLACE TRIGGER price_t1
    AFTER UPDATE OF price_type ON price
  BEGIN
    /* This statement only works in Oracle 11g forward. */
    INSERT INTO price_type_log
    VALUES
    (price_log_s1.nextval,USER,SYSDATE);
  END price_t1;
  /
```

It's fair to assume that code will continue to use the `.nextval` and `.currval` pseudocolumns in SQL statements and transaction management for some time. However, you should consider migrating to the new identity columns, which are discussed in the "Identity Columns" section of Appendix B.

Assuming you redefine the price table with a price_id identity column, the trigger would change to the following override signature for the INSERT statement:

```
SQL> CREATE OR REPLACE TRIGGER price_t1
  2    AFTER UPDATE OF price_type ON price
  3  BEGIN
  4    /* This statement only works in Oracle 11g forward. */
  5    INSERT INTO price_type_log
  6    (user_id, action_date)
  7    VALUES
  8    (USER,SYSDATE);
  9  END price_t1;
 10  /
```

Line 6 provides an override signature. Override signatures qualify which columns of data you'll provide in the VALUES clause. You can check the "Insert Statements" section of Appendix B for more details on INSERT statements. Personally, I think the code is cleaner this way, and it's certainly more portable to other relational databases.

You can trigger this by running the following UPDATE statement that changes nothing because it simply reassigns the current value of the price_type column to itself:

```
SQL> UPDATE price p
SET    p.price_type = p.price_type
WHERE  EXISTS (SELECT NULL
               FROM   price q
               WHERE  q.price_id = p.price_id);
```

The following query shows that the trigger fired and wrote audit information to the price_type_log table:

```
SQL> SELECT *
FROM price_type_log;
```

This subsection has shown you how to use statement-level DML triggers. The next section shows you how to write row-level triggers.

Row-Level Triggers

Row-level triggers let you capture new and prior values from each row. This information can let you audit changes, analyze behavior, and recover prior data without performing a database recovery operation.

There are two *pseudo*-records when you use the FOR EACH ROW clause in a row-level trigger. They both refer to the columns referenced in the DML statement. The pseudo-records are composite variables; new or old are the pseudo-record variable names in the WHEN clause, and :new and :old are the *bind* variables in the trigger body. They differ because the trigger declaration and body are separate PL/SQL blocks. The new and old pseudo-records are declared in scope by the row-level trigger declaration. The trigger declaration is the calling block, and the trigger body is the called block. Bind variables are passed *by reference* between PL/SQL blocks when an event fires a trigger in a database session. The elements of the pseudo-record are pseudo-fields.

The new and old pseudo-records are session-level composite variables. They're implicitly declared in the scope of the triggering event, which is the DML statement. Unlike stand-alone functions and procedures, triggers do not have formal signatures, but they have access to column values changed by DML statements. These column values are the elements of the pseudo-records, or pseudo-fields. Pseudo-field values are those columns inserted by an `INSERT` statement, set by an `UPDATE` statement, or destroyed by a `DELETE` statement.

You access pseudo-fields by referencing the `new` or `old` pseudo-records, a component selector, and a column name in the `WHEN` clause. Inside a trigger body, you preface the pseudo-records with a colon (`:`). The colon lets you reference the externally scoped pseudo-records in the trigger body. The DML statement declares the list of column names *(pseudo-fields)*.

The following example demonstrates a trigger that replaces a white space in a last name with a dash for hyphenated names. It's actually a business rule in some human resource departments to disallow multiple names in a `last_name` column. This practice has always struck me as odd, because there are many names that lead with a preface like *de* or *von* followed by a white space.

```
CREATE OR REPLACE TRIGGER contact_insert_t1
  BEFORE INSERT ON contact
  FOR EACH ROW
  WHEN (REGEXP_LIKE(new.last_name,' '))
BEGIN
  :new.last_name := REGEXP_REPLACE(:new.last_name,' ','-',1,1);
END contact_insert_t1;
/
```


The `WHEN` clause checks whether the value of the pseudo-field for the `last_name` column in the `contact` table contains a white space. If the condition is met, the trigger passes control to the trigger body. The trigger body has one statement; the `REGEXP_REPLACE` function takes a copy of the pseudo-field as an actual parameter. `REGEXP_REPLACE` changes any white space in the string to a dash and returns the modified value as a result. The result is assigned to the pseudo-field and becomes the value in the `INSERT` statement. This is an example of using a DML trigger to enforce a business policy of entering all last names as hyphenated.

The trigger depends on your having run the `create_store.sql` script, as discussed in the Introduction to the book. After compiling the trigger in your test schema, you can test the trigger by running the following `INSERT` statement:

```
SQL> INSERT INTO contact
  ( contact_id
    ...
  , last_update_date )
  VALUES
  ( contact_s1.nextval
    ...
  ,'Catherine'
  ,'Zeta Jones'
    ...
  , SYSDATE );
```

It converts the last name to a hyphenated last name. You query `last_name` from the `contact` table to see the actual inserted value:

```
SQL> SELECT    last_name
     FROM      contact
     WHERE     last_name LIKE 'Zeta%';
```

You should have the following results:

```
LAST_NAME
--------------------
Zeta-Jones
```

Let's add another trigger on the same table and instruct it to follow the execution of the `contact_insert_t1` trigger. The code for this trigger checks for multiple names in the `first_name` column, and accepts only the first one:

```
SQL> CREATE OR REPLACE TRIGGER contact_insert_t2
  2    BEFORE INSERT ON contact
  3    FOR EACH ROW
  4    FOLLOWS contact_insert_t1
  5    WHEN (REGEXP_LIKE(new.first_name,' '))
  6  BEGIN
  7    /* Accept only the first of multiple names. */
  8    :new.first_name :=
  9      SUBSTR(:new.first_name,1,REGEXP_INSTR(:new.first_name,' ',1,1,0,'i')-1);
 10  END contact_insert_t2;
 11  /
```

You should note the `_t1` suffix indicates the first trigger, and the second trigger uses a `_t2` suffix because it follows the first trigger. Line 4 explains that it's the second trigger because it follows the trigger without a `FOLLOWS` clause. Lines 8 and 9 parse the value being inserted as the `first_name` column and insert only the first substring.

A new `INSERT` statement lets us test both triggers. It inserts `first_name` and `last_name` values that meet the criteria of both of the triggers' `WHEN` clauses. That means the triggers fire and run their respective trigger body. The `INSERT` statement is

```
SQL> INSERT INTO contact
     ( contact_id
       ...
     , last_update_date )
     VALUES
     ( contact_s1.nextval
       ...
     ,'John the Actor'
     ,'Rhys Davies'
       ...
     , SYSDATE );
```

While the first trigger converts the last name to a hyphenated last name, the second trigger parses the string and returns only the first value. You query `first_name` and `last_name` from the `contact` table to see the actual inserted values:

```
SQL> SELECT   first_name
     ,        last_name
     FROM     contact
     WHERE    last_name LIKE 'Rhys%';
```

You should have the following results:

```
FIRST_NAME           LAST_NAME
-------------------- --------------------
John                 Rhys-Davies
```

Naturally, you can consolidate these two triggers into a single database trigger. The following `contact_insert_t` trigger does exactly that:

```
SQL> CREATE OR REPLACE TRIGGER contact_insert_t1
  2    BEFORE INSERT ON contact
  3    FOR EACH ROW
  4    WHEN (REGEXP_LIKE(new.last_name,' ') OR REGEXP_LIKE(new.first_name,' '))
  5  BEGIN
  6    /* Enforce hyphenated names. */
  7    :new.last_name := REGEXP_REPLACE(:new.last_name,' ','-',1,1);
  8
  9    /* Enforce one name only. */
 10    :new.first_name :=
 11      SUBSTR(:new.first_name,1,REGEXP_INSTR(:new.first_name,' ',1,1,0,'i')-1);
 12  END contact_insert_t1;
 13  /
```

Line 4 consolidates the two `WHEN` clauses to a single `WHEN` clause. That means the trigger body can then perform both input conversions.

There are two problems with the preceding DML trigger. First, you aren't logging the attempt to violate the business rule when you automate compliance. Failure to capture the attempt means you lose the opportunity to correct data entry practices and educate the business staff of compliance-based rules. Second, you haven't prevented an administrator from saying, "That's not what I want, let me update it" and then updating the column value without a problem, because your trigger only restricts `INSERT` statement behavior.

You can log things in the same transaction context when you don't choose to raise an exception. However, it's a bad idea to capture logging information in the same transaction context, because you lose your logging information when the user performs a rollback. I'd recommend that you write all logging triggers as autonomous transactions.

To show you how to log the data, let's create a small `log_name_change` table for the example. The syntax to create it with an identity column is

```
SQL> CREATE TABLE log_name_changes
     ( log_name_change  NUMBER  GENERATED ALWAYS AS IDENTITY
     , name_submitted   VARCHAR2(20)
     , name_modified    VARCHAR2(20));
```

The new logging version of the trigger is

```
SQL> CREATE OR REPLACE TRIGGER contact_insert_t1
  2    BEFORE INSERT ON contact
  3    FOR EACH ROW
  4    REFERENCING new AS myNew
  5    WHEN (REGEXP_LIKE(myNew.last_name,' '))
  6  DECLARE
  7    /* Declare local variables. */
  8    lv_name_submitted  VARCHAR2(20);
  9    lv_name_modified   VARCHAR2(20);
 10
 11    /* Declare trigger as an autonomous transaction. */
 12    PRAGMA AUTONOMOUS_TRANSACTION;
 13  BEGIN
 14    /* Assign submitted last name. */
 15    lv_name_submitted := :myNew.last_name;
 16
 17    /* Enforce hyphenated names. */
 18    :myNew.last_name := REGEXP_REPLACE(:myNew.last_name,' ','-',1,1);
 19
 20    /* Assign modified last name. */
 21    lv_name_modified := :myNew.last_name;
 22
 23    /* Autonomous transaction writes before and after values. */
 24    INSERT INTO log_name_change
 25    ( name_submitted
 26    , name_modified )
 27    VALUES
 28    ( lv_name_submitted
 29    , lv_name_modified );
 30
 31    /* Commit the write. */
 32    COMMIT;
 33  END contact_insert_t1;
 34  /
```

Line 4 uses the REFERENCING clause to rename the new pseudo-record to myNew, which is actually case insensitive, so :myNew would work as well. Line 5 now checks for the myNew.last_name value, which reflects the renaming of the new pseudo-record.

Line 12 uses the PRAGMA AUTONOMOUS_TRANSACTION (precompiler directive) to make the trigger body an autonomous program unit. That means it runs in its own transaction scope. A ROLLBACK statement after the INSERT statement would only undo the insert into the contact table, not the insert into the log_name_change table. Line 32 commits the write to the log_name_change table, and committing the write is required any time you implement an autonomous trigger body.

You can modify the original or subsequent logging trigger to prevent somebody from updating the `last_name` column with a white space. You actually can prevent that in a single trigger by using the inclusion `OR` operator, like

```
SQL> CREATE OR REPLACE TRIGGER contact_insert_t1
  2    BEFORE INSERT OR UPDATE OF last_name ON contact
  3    FOR EACH ROW
  4    WHEN (REGEXP_LIKE(new.last_name,' '))
  5  BEGIN
  6    :new.last_name := REGEXP_REPLACE(:new.last_name,' ','-',1,1);
  7  END contact_insert_t1;
  8  /
```

Line 2 ensures the trigger is now fired on any `INSERT` statement and *only* for `UPDATE` statements that change the `last_name` column. It is always better to build triggers that work with multiple DML events when you take the same or similar type of action. You also can build single triggers to perform different tasks, and my opinion is that it's generally a better practice to minimize the number of triggers where possible.

Let's say the business case assumes an `INSERT` statement of a multiple-name `first_name` or nonhyphenated `last_name` is an error of omission, and a trigger should correct the error. That means you don't surface the problem to the business user when they make the mistake. A second business rule identifies that any attempt to update the `first_name` column with multiple names or the `last_name` column with a nonhyphenated last name is an error of commission. That means you do want to surface the violation of the business rules directly to the business user attempting the action.

A single trigger can manage these different rules for the `INSERT` and `UPDATE` statements. It accomplishes it by leveraging the `INSERTING` and `UPDATING` functions (covered in Table 12-3 later in the chapter). Here's the trigger implementation to achieve these two behaviors:

```
SQL> CREATE OR REPLACE TRIGGER contact_insert_t
    BEFORE INSERT OR UPDATE OF first_name, last_name ON contact
    FOR EACH ROW
    WHEN (REGEXP_LIKE(new.last_name,' ') OR REGEXP_LIKE(new.first_name,' '))
  BEGIN
    /* Enforce hyphenated names. */
    :new.last_name := REGEXP_REPLACE(:new.last_name,' ','-',1,1);

    /* Selectively evaluate only insert or update actions. */
    IF INSERTING THEN
      :new.first_name :=
        SUBSTR(:new.first_name
              ,1
              ,REGEXP_INSTR(:new.first_name,' ',1,1,0,'i')-1);
    ELSIF UPDATING THEN
      IF REGEXP_LIKE(:new.first_name,' ') THEN
        RAISE_APPLICATION_ERROR(-20099,'Updates can''t use multiple names.');
      ELSIF REGEXP_LIKE(:new.last_name,' ') THEN
        RAISE_APPLICATION_ERROR(-20100,'Inserts non-hyphenated last name..');
```

```
20         END IF;
21       END IF;
22   END contact_insert_t;
23   /
```

Line 2 now manages only insert and updates where the business user changes the `first_name` or `last_name` column value. Line 4 filters which column changes the trigger should fix. Line 10 uses the `INSERTING` function to perform the automatic repair process. Line 15 uses the `UPDATING` function to perform the notification process for an error of commission. Lines 16 through 20 manage the two different kinds of errors.

Repeating the test for an `INSERT` statement isn't necessary because the logic works the same as it does in prior examples. The `UPDATE` statement changes behavior, and here's an example of an `UPDATE` statement that fires the database trigger:

```
SQL> UPDATE contact
     SET first_name = 'John the Actor'
     WHERE last_name LIKE 'Rhys%';
```

It raises the following user-defined exception:

```
UPDATE contact
       *
ERROR at line 1:
ORA-20099: Updates can't use multiple names.
ORA-06512: at "VIDEO.CONTACT_INSERT_T", line 13
ORA-04088: error during execution of trigger 'VIDEO.CONTACT_INSERT_T'
```

The trigger raises the exception on line 13 of the trigger body, which means you must subtract the four lines of trigger declaration to find the right line where the error is thrown.

Another common use for a DML trigger is automatic numbering for a primary key column, although this is no longer necessary because Oracle Database 12*c* now supports identity columns. You still can create this type of trigger with or without a `WHEN` clause. With a `WHEN` clause, the trigger can filter when it should or shouldn't run. For example, a `WHEN` clause lets you *insert* a manual primary key value by suppressing the one generated by a sequence called inside a trigger. This type of solution lets you perform bulk processing without calling the sequence for each row insert. While it's possible to do this, it's a horrible solution. Rather than use a `WHEN` clause for bulk operations, you should use NDS to disable the trigger prior to the bulk operations and re-enable the trigger after the bulk operations. You'll also need to use DNS to drop and re-create the associated sequence, because you can't alter the sequence to reset its starting value.

Rather than build a multiple-table example, we will examine automatic numbering from the perspective of logging new connections to the database and logging disconnections from the database. The balance of the code for this example is in the section "Data Definition Language Triggers" earlier in the chapter. The DDL triggers that monitor login and logout events call a `user_connection` package that logs to a `connection_log` table. The table definition is

```
SQL> CREATE TABLE connection_log
     ( event_id           NUMBER(10)
     , event_user_name    VARCHAR2(30) CONSTRAINT log_event_nn1 NOT NULL
     , event_type         VARCHAR2(30) CONSTRAINT log_event_nn2 NOT NULL
     , event_date         DATE         CONSTRAINT log_event_nn3 NOT NULL
     , CONSTRAINT connection_log_p1    PRIMARY KEY (event_id));
```

The *row-level* trigger connection_log_t1 demonstrates the proper way to write a pseudo-automatic numbering trigger for Oracle Database 10*g* (which becomes obsoleted with the release of Oracle 12*c*):

```
SQL> CREATE OR REPLACE TRIGGER connection_log_t1
    BEFORE INSERT ON connection_log
    FOR EACH ROW
  BEGIN
    SELECT   connection_log_s1.nextval
    INTO     :new.event_id
    FROM     dual;
  END;
  /
```

The connection_log_t1 trigger demonstrates managing a sequence, but it also shows you how to SELECT INTO a pseudo-field variable. You should really modify the trigger when deploying it on an Oracle Database 12*c* database because you no longer have to select a sequence value into a variable from the pseudo-table dual. You can simply assign it directly.

The *row-level* trigger connection_log_t2 demonstrates the proper way to write a pseudo-automatic numbering trigger for Oracle Database 12*c*:

```
SQL> CREATE OR REPLACE TRIGGER connection_log_t1
    BEFORE INSERT ON connection_log
    FOR EACH ROW
  BEGIN
    :new.event_id := connection_log_s1.nextval;
  END;
/
```

The connection_log_t1 and connection_log_t2 triggers fire always, which means they fire even when you don't want them to. You lose the ability to override the sequence-based column values.

These row-level triggers illustrate two processing rules. One rule is that you must reference a pseudo-row column as an *ordinary* variable in the WHEN clause, because the actual trigger fires in the same memory scope as the DML transaction. The other rule is that you must reference a pseudo-row column as a *bind* variable inside the actual trigger scope, where it is running in a different memory space. The pseudo-rows new and old are *pass-by-reference* structures, and they contain your active DML session variable values when arriving at the trigger body. The new and old pseudo-record variables also receive any changes made in the trigger body when they are returned to your active DML session.

All the old pseudo-record columns are null when you execute an INSERT statement, and the new pseudo-record columns are null when you run a DELETE statement. Both new and old pseudo-records are present during UPDATE statements, but only for those columns referenced by the SET clause. Table 12-2 displays the availability of pseudo-records.

This subsection has shown you how to write *row-level* triggers. It demonstrated how to use the new and old pseudo-records in your WHEN clause and trigger body.

	old	new
INSERT	No	Yes
UPDATE	Yes	Yes
DELETE	Yes	No

TABLE 12-2. *Pseudo-Record Availability*

This section has covered how to use DML triggers and has examined both statement- and row-level trigger implementation. You should be able to use DML triggers by drawing on what you have learned in this section.

Review Section

This section has described the following points about the Oracle Database 12*c* DML database trigger architecture:

- DML triggers can fire before or after an `INSERT`, `UPDATE`, or `DELETE` statement.
- DML triggers can be statement-level or row-level triggers.
- DML triggers can run in the same transaction scope as the `INSERT`, `UPDATE`, or `DELETE` statement, or they can run in an autonomous scope.
- You can support the `MERGE` statement by providing a `INSERT` or `UPDATE` database trigger.
- Statement-level DML triggers fire once before and after the `INSERT`, `UPDATE`, or `DELETE` statement.
- Row-level DML triggers can pass the record structure of any `INSERT`, `UPDATE`, or `DELETE` statement, which allows you to evaluate and change old and new column values.
- The `WHEN` clause lets you filter when a trigger fires its trigger body.
- You can sequence database triggers by using the `FOLLOWS` clause from Oracle Database 11*g* forward.
- Oracle Database 11*g* forward supports editioning of database triggers.
- You can use DML triggers to mimic automatic numbering in surrogate key columns. You do so by calling a sequence into the session memory and then using the next value of the sequence as a primary key value.
- A single DML trigger can manage an `INSERT`, `UPDATE`, or `DELETE` event, or it can manage two or more events at the same time.

Compound Triggers

Compound triggers acts as both statement- and row-level triggers when you insert, update, or delete data in a table. As mentioned, compound triggers contain a global trigger state and four timing blocks. You can use a compound trigger to capture information at four timing points: (a) before the firing statement, (b) before each row change from the firing statement, (c) after each row change from the firing statement, and (d) after the firing statement. You can use these types of triggers to audit, check, save, and replace values before they are changed when you need to take action at both the statement and row event levels.

Prior to compound triggers, you had to go to great lengths to mimic this behavior and you ran the risk of a memory leak with the failure of an `AFTER STATEMENT` trigger. A compound trigger functions like a multithreaded process. There is a declaration section for the trigger as a whole, and each *timing point section* has its own local declaration section. Timing point sections are subordinate trigger blocks of the compound trigger.

You can use a compound trigger when you want the behavior of both statement-level and row-level triggers. Compound triggers can be defined on either a table or a view. Compound triggers don't support filtering actions with the `WHEN` clause or the use of the autonomous transaction `PRAGMA`. You can use the `UPDATE OF` *column name* filter as a governing event in updates. Also, the firing order of compound triggers is not guaranteed because they can be interleaved (*mixed between*) with the firing of stand-alone triggers.

TIP
You can always call out to a stored function or procedure that runs autonomously.

Compound triggers don't support an `EXCEPTION` block, but you can implement `EXCEPTION` blocks in any of the subordinate timing point blocks. The `GOTO` command is restricted to a single timing point block, which means you can't call between timing blocks. You can use the `:new` and `:old` pseudo-records in the row-level statement blocks but nowhere else.

The minimum implementation of a compound trigger requires that you implement at least one timing point block. Only DML statements trigger compound triggers. Also, compound triggers don't fire when (a) the DML statement doesn't change any rows and (b) the trigger hasn't implemented at least a `BEFORE STATEMENT` or `AFTER STATEMENT` block. Compound triggers have significant performance advantages when your DML statements use bulk operations.

The prototype for a compound trigger is

```
CREATE [OR REPLACE] [EDITIONABLE | NONEDITIONABLE] TRIGGER trigger_name
FOR {INSERT | UPDATE | UPDATE OF column [, column [, ... ]] | DELETE}
ON table_name
COMPOUND TRIGGER
[BEFORE STATEMENT IS
  [declaration_statement]
 BEGIN
   execution_statement
 END BEFORE STATEMENT;]
[BEFORE EACH ROW IS
```

```
    [declaration_statement]
  BEGIN
    execution_statement
  END BEFORE EACH ROW;]
 [AFTER EACH ROW IS
    [declaration_statement]
  BEGIN
    execution_statement
  END AFTER EACH ROW;]
 [AFTER STATEMENT IS
    [declaration_statement]
  BEGIN
    execution_statement
  END AFTER STATEMENT;]
END [trigger_name];
/
```

The following example rewrites as a compound trigger the insert event row-level trigger from the earlier section "Row-Level Triggers":

```
SQL> CREATE OR REPLACE TRIGGER compound_connection_log_t1
       FOR INSERT ON connection_log
       COMPOUND TRIGGER
       BEFORE EACH ROW IS
     BEGIN
       IF :new.event_id IS NULL THEN
         :new.event_id := connection_log_s1.nextval;
       END IF;
     END BEFORE EACH ROW;
     END;
     /
```

You should note three key elements about compound triggers.

- You can't filter events in this type of trigger by using a `WHEN` clause.
- As mentioned, `:new` and `:old` pseudo-records are only available in the `BEFORE EACH ROW` and `AFTER EACH ROW` timing blocks.
- Variables declared in the global declaration block retain their value through the execution of all timing blocks that you've implemented.

You can collect row-level information in either the `BEFORE EACH ROW` timing point or the `AFTER EACH ROW` timing point and transfer that information to a global collection declared in the trigger body. Then, you can perform bulk operations with the collection contents in the `AFTER STATEMENT` timing point. If you don't write the data to another table, you could raise a "maximum number of recursive calls" error, `ORA-00036`.

The next example demonstrates collecting information in the row-level timing points, transferring it to a global collection, and processing it as a bulk transaction in the `AFTER STATEMENT` timing block. This example depends on your running the `create_store.sql` script, which is described in the Introduction. The first step requires creating a log repository, which is done by creating the following table and sequence:

```
SQL> CREATE TABLE price_event_log
     ( price_log_id     NUMBER
     , price_id         NUMBER
     , created_by       NUMBER
     , creation_date    DATE
     , last_updated_by  NUMBER
     , last_update_date DATE );
SQL> CREATE SEQUENCE price_event_log_s1;
```

The trigger populates `created_by` and `last_updated_by` columns as part of the applications *"who-audit"* information. It assumes that you're striping the data, which means you need to set a `client_info` value for the session. The physical `client_info` section is found in the `V$SESSION` view. You can read more about these concepts in the sidebar "Reading and Writing Session Metadata" later in the chapter.

The following sets the `client_info` value to 3, which is a valid `system_user_id` in the `system_user` table:

```
EXECUTE dbms_application_info.set_client_info('3');
```

The trigger depends on the state of the `CLIENT_INFO` column, but as you might imagine, it can't control it. Therefore, the trigger assigns a –1 when the `CLIENT_INFO` value is missing during its execution.

The following defines the compound trigger with both `BEFORE EACH ROW` and `AFTER STATEMENT` timing blocks:

```
SQL> CREATE OR REPLACE TRIGGER compound_price_update_t1
     FOR UPDATE ON price
     COMPOUND TRIGGER
       /* Declare a global record type. */
       TYPE price_record IS RECORD
       ( price_log_id     price_event_log.price_log_id%TYPE
       , price_id         price_event_log.price_id%TYPE
       , created_by       price_event_log.created_by%TYPE
       , creation_date    price_event_log.creation_date%TYPE
       , last_updated_by  price_event_log.last_updated_by%TYPE
       , last_update_date price_event_log.last_update_date%TYPE );
       /* Declare a global collection type. */
       TYPE price_list IS TABLE OF PRICE_RECORD;
       /* Declare a global collection and initialize it. */
       price_updates  PRICE_LIST := price_list();
     BEFORE EACH ROW IS
       /* Declare or define local timing point variables. */
       c        NUMBER;
       user_id NUMBER :=
         NVL(TO_NUMBER(SYS_CONTEXT('userenv','client_info')),-1);
     BEGIN
       /* Extend space and assign dynamic index value. */
       price_updates.EXTEND;
```

```
    c := price_updates.LAST;
    price_updates(c).price_log_id := price_event_log_s1.nextval;
    price_updates(c).price_id := :old.price_id;
    price_updates(c).created_by := user_id;
    price_updates(c).creation_date := SYSDATE;
    price_updates(c).last_updated_by := user_id;
    price_updates(c).last_update_date := SYSDATE;
  END BEFORE EACH ROW;
  AFTER STATEMENT IS
  BEGIN
    /* Bulk insert statement. */
    FORALL i IN price_updates.FIRST..price_updates.LAST
      INSERT INTO price_event_log
      VALUES
      ( price_updates(i).price_log_id
      , price_updates(i).price_id
      , price_updates(i).created_by
      , price_updates(i).creation_date
      , price_updates(i).last_updated_by
      , price_updates(i).last_update_date );
  END AFTER STATEMENT;
  END;
  /
```

The `BEFORE EACH ROW` timing block collects row-level data and stores it in a global collection, which can then be read from another timing block. The numeric index for the collection is dynamic and leverages the Oracle Collection API `LAST` method. If you'd like to check how that works, please refer to Chapter 6, where it is covered.

The `AFTER STATEMENT` timing block reads the global collection and performs a bulk insert of the data to the log table. The next time the trigger is fired, the global collection is empty because the compound trigger implementation is serialized.

You can test the trigger by running the following `UPDATE` statement:

```
SQL> UPDATE price
  SET    last_updated_by =
    NVL(TO_NUMBER(SYS_CONTEXT('userenv','client_info')),-1);
```

Then, you can query the `price_event_log` table:

```
SQL> SELECT * FROM price_event_log;
```

This example has shown you how to capture row-level data, save it in a global collection, and reuse it in a statement-level statement.

This section has explained compound triggers and shown you how to implement them. They allow you to mix the benefits and operations of statement- and row-level triggers in a single trigger.

Reading and Writing Session Metadata

The process of writing to and reading from the session `client_info` column requires you to use the `dbms_application_info` package. You use the `set_client_info` procedure in the `dbms_application_info` package to write data into the 64-character `client_info` column found in the `V$SESSION` view. The following anonymous PL/SQL block assumes that the `created_by` and `last_updated_by` columns should be 3:

```
SQL> BEGIN
       /* Write value to V$SESSION.CLIENT_INFO column. */
       DBMS_APPLICATION_INFO.SET_CLIENT_INFO('3');
     END;
     /
```

You can now read this value by calling the `read_client_info` procedure. You should enable `SERVEROUTPUT` using SQL*Plus to see the rendered output when you run the following program:

```
SQL> DECLARE
       client_info      VARCHAR2(64);
     BEGIN
       /* Read value from V$SESSION.CLIENT_INTO column. */
       DBMS_APPLICATION_INFO.READ_CLIENT_INFO(client_info);
       DBMS_OUTPUT.PUT_LINE('[ '||client_info||']');
     END;
     /
```

User-defined session columns let you store unique information related to user credentials from your access control list (ACL). You assign a session column value during user authentication. Then, the session `client_info` column allows you to manage multiple user interactions in a single schema. Authenticated users can access rows from tables when their session `client_info` column value matches a striping column value in the table.

Review Section

This section has described the following points about the Oracle Database 12*c* compound database trigger architecture:

- Compound database triggers support a global state that lets you define variables available at any of the four timing points.
- Compound database triggers support DML events at four timing points: `BEFORE STATEMENT`, `BEFORE EACH ROW`, `AFTER EACH ROW`, and `AFTER STATEMENT`.
- Compound database triggers don't support a global exception block, but each of the timing blocks supports exception blocks.

INSTEAD OF Triggers

You can use the INSTEAD OF trigger to intercept INSERT, UPDATE, and DELETE statements and replace those instructions with alternative procedural code. Nonupdatable views generally have INSTEAD OF triggers to accept the output and resolve the issues that make the view nonupdatable. INSTEAD OF triggers are editionable from Oracle Database 11*g* Release 2 forward.

The prototype for building an INSTEAD OF trigger is

```
CREATE [OR REPLACE] [EDITIONABLE | NONEDITIONABLE] TRIGGER trigger_name
INSTEAD OF {dml_statement}
ON {object_name | database | schema}
FOR EACH ROW
[WHEN (logical_expression)]
[DECLARE]
  declaration_statements
BEGIN
  execution_statements
END [trigger_name];
/
```

INSTEAD OF triggers are powerful alternatives that resolve how you use complex and nonupdatable views. When you know how the SELECT statement works, you can write procedural code to update the data not directly accessible through nonupdatable views.

You can only deploy an INSTEAD OF DML trigger against a view. There is no restriction as to whether the view is updatable or nonupdatable, but generally INSTEAD OF triggers are built for nonupdatable views.

The following view is supported by the data model provided on the publisher's website. It is also a nonupdatable view because of the DECODE statement, as shown:

```
SQL> CREATE OR REPLACE VIEW account_list AS
     SELECT   c.member_id
     ,        c.contact_id
     ,        m.account_number
     ,        c.first_name
     ||       DECODE(c.middle_name,NULL,' ',' '||c.middle_name||' ')
     ||       c.last_name FULL_NAME
     FROM     contact c JOIN member m ON c.member_id = m.member_id;
```

Without an INSTEAD OF trigger, a DML statement against this view can raise an ORA-01776 exception that says you're disallowed from modifying more than one base table through a join. You could also raise an ORA-01779 exception that says you're disallowed from modifying a column because it fails to map to a non-key-preserved table.

You can create an INSTEAD OF trigger that would allow you to update or delete from this view. However, the view doesn't have enough information to support INSERT statements to either base table. Without redefining the view, there is also no programmatic way to fix these shortcomings.

The following is an INSTEAD OF INSERT trigger. It raises an exception for any insertion attempt to the nonupdatable view.

```
SQL> CREATE OR REPLACE TRIGGER account_list_insert
     INSTEAD OF INSERT ON account_list
     FOR EACH ROW
     BEGIN
       RAISE_APPLICATION_ERROR(-20000,'Not enough data for insert!');
     END;
     /
```

After compiling the trigger, an INSERT statement run against the view now raises the following exception stack:

```
INSERT INTO account_list
            *
ERROR at line 1:
ORA-20000: Not enough data for insert!
ORA-06512: at "PLSQL.ACCOUNT_LIST_INSERT", line 2
ORA-04088: error during execution of trigger 'PLSQL.ACCOUNT_LIST_INSERT'
```

The question here is, do you want to define three INSTEAD OF event triggers or one? A number of developers opt for multiple INSTEAD OF triggers as opposed to one that does everything. You should consider defining one trigger for inserting, updating, and deleting events. Table 12-3 qualifies the INSERTING, UPDATING, and DELETING functions from the dbms_standard package. These functions let you determine the type of DML event and write one trigger that manages all three DML events.

Certain required fields for an insert to either the member table or contact table are missing from the view. There is also a programmatic way to fix these shortcomings.

Function Name	**Return Data Type**	**Description**
DELETING	BOOLEAN	The DELETING function returns a Boolean true when the DML event is deleting.
INSERTING	BOOLEAN	The INSERTING function returns a Boolean true when the DML is inserting.
UPDATING	BOOLEAN	The UPDATING function returns a Boolean true when the DML is updating.

TABLE 12-3. *Data Manipulation Language Event Functions*

You can build a complete trigger for all DML statements by using the event function from Table 12-3. The following provides an example `INSTEAD OF` trigger:

```
SQL> CREATE OR REPLACE TRIGGER account_list_dml
       INSTEAD OF INSERT OR UPDATE OR DELETE ON account_list
       FOR EACH ROW
     DECLARE
       /* Anchor variable declaration. */
       lv_source  account_list.full_name%TYPE := :new.full_name;

       /* Declare variables. */
       lv_fname  VARCHAR2(43);
       lv_mname  VARCHAR2(1);
       lv_lname  VARCHAR2(43);

       /* Check whether all dependents are gone. */
       FUNCTION get_dependents
       (pv_member_id NUMBER) RETURN BOOLEAN IS
         /* Declare a local variable. */
         lv_rows  NUMBER := 0;

         /* Declare a dynamic cursor. */
         CURSOR c
         (cv_member_id NUMBER) IS
           SELECT   COUNT(*)
           FROM     contact
           WHERE    member_id = pv_member_id;
       BEGIN
         /* Open the cursor with the function input. */
         OPEN c (pv_member_id);
         FETCH c INTO lv_rows;

         /* Return false when there's more than one row. */
         IF lv_rows > 0 THEN
           RETURN FALSE;
         ELSE
           RETURN TRUE;
         END IF;
       END get_dependents;

     BEGIN
       /* Take action inline with scope of DML statement. */
       IF INSERTING THEN    -- On insert event.
         RAISE_APPLICATION_ERROR(-20000,'Not enough data for insert!');
       ELSIF UPDATING THEN  -- On update event.
         /* Assign source variable. */
         lv_source := :new.full_name;

         -- Parse full_name for elements.
         lv_fname := LTRIM(REGEXP_SUBSTR(lv_source,'(^|^ +)([[:alpha:]]+)',1));
         lv_mname := REGEXP_SUBSTR(
```

```
                      REGEXP_SUBSTR(
                          lv_source
                        ,'( +)([[:alpha:]]+)(( +|. +))',1),'([[:alpha:]])',1);
    lv_lname := REGEXP_SUBSTR(
                      REGEXP_SUBSTR(
                          lv_source
                        ,'( +)([[:alpha:]]+)( +$|$)',1),'([[:alpha:]]+)',1);

    /* Update name change in base table. */
    UPDATE contact
    SET    first_name = lv_fname
    ,      middle_name = lv_mname
    ,      last_name = lv_lname
    WHERE  contact_id = :old.contact_id;
  ELSIF DELETING THEN  -- On delete event.
    /* Remove a row. */
    DELETE FROM contact
    WHERE member_id = :old.member_id;

    /* Only delete the parent when there aren't any more children. */
    IF get_dependents(:old.member_id) THEN
      DELETE FROM member WHERE member_id = :old.member_id;
    END IF;
  END IF;
END;
/
```

There are some tricks or risks inherent in this type of trigger. Risks are bad in triggers because triggers should be foolproof. One potential flaw in *this* trigger is the assignment of the pseudo-field `:new.full_name` in the declaration section. The database doesn't check when you compile the trigger if the size of the `source` variable is large enough to handle possible assignments. This is a critical place to use type anchoring, as discussed in the section "Attribute and Table Anchoring" in Chapter 3.

The `account_list_dml` trigger anchors the source variable to the assigned column value, which ensures you won't raise `ORA-06502`, `ORA-06512`, and `ORA-04088` errors. An assignment in the `DECLARE` block of a trigger body does raise a runtime exception, like stand-alone anonymous block programs.

This trigger fires on any DML event against the nonupdatable view, and it handles the insert, update, or deletion to the base tables where appropriate. As mentioned, there wouldn't be enough information to perform `INSERT` statements to the base tables. The trigger raises a user-defined exception when someone attempts to insert a new record through the view. There is enough information to *update* the name, but as you can tell, it isn't a trivial bit of work. You should know that the regular expression for the middle name won't work if you have leading white space before the first name. The `DELETE` statement only touches one table unless all dependent rows in the `contact` table have been deleted first, because you never want to leave orphaned rows in a dependent table.

This section has shown you how to write individual-event and multiple-event `INSTEAD OF` triggers. You should try to write all DML events in a single `INSTEAD OF` trigger because that makes them much easier to maintain.

Nonupdatable Views

Views are nonupdatable when they contain any of the following constructs:

- Set operators
- Aggregate functions
- `CASE` or `DECODE` statements
- `CONNECT BY`, `GROUP BY`, `HAVING`, or `START WITH` clauses
- The `DISTINCT` operator
- Joins (with exceptions when they contain the joining key)

You also cannot reference any pseudo-columns or expressions when you update a view.

Review Section

This section has described the following points about the Oracle Database 12*c* `INSTEAD OF` database trigger architecture:

- You can use the `INSTEAD OF` trigger to intercept `INSERT`, `UPDATE`, and `DELETE` statements and replace those instructions with alternative procedural code. Nonupdatable views generally have `INSTEAD OF` triggers to accept the output and resolve the issues that make the view nonupdatable. `INSTEAD OF` triggers are editionable from Oracle Database 11*g* Release 2 forward.
- The `INSTEAD OF` trigger intercepts `INSERT`, `UPDATE`, and `DELETE` statements against nonupdatable views and enables writing changes to the underlying tables.
- DML event functions support taking different actions based on the firing event.

System and Database Event Triggers

System triggers enable you to audit *server startup* and *shutdown*, *server errors*, and *user logon* and *logoff* activities. They are convenient for tracking the duration of connections per user and the uptime of the database server. They also can use event attribute functions, as shown earlier in this chapter. As auditing devices, system and database event triggers are best suited for logging what they find rather than raising exceptions.

The prototype for building a database system trigger is

```
CREATE [OR REPLACE] TRIGGER trigger_name
{BEFORE | AFTER} database_event ON {database | schema}
[DECLARE]
  declaration_statements
BEGIN
  execution_statements
END [trigger_name];
/
```

The *logon* and *logoff* triggers monitor the duration of connections. The DML statements for these triggers are in the `user_connection` package. The `connecting_trigger` and `disconnecting_trigger` triggers both call procedures in the `user_connection` package to insert logon and logoff information per user.

The `connecting_trigger` provides an example of a system trigger that monitors users' logons to the database, as shown:

```
SQL> CREATE OR REPLACE TRIGGER connecting_trigger
  AFTER LOGON ON DATABASE
BEGIN
  user_connection.connecting(sys.login_user);
END;
/
```

The `disconnecting_trigger` provides an example of a system trigger that monitors users' logoffs from the database, as shown:

```
SQL> CREATE OR REPLACE TRIGGER disconnecting_trigger
  BEFORE LOGOFF ON DATABASE
BEGIN
  user_connection.disconnecting(sys.login_user);
END;
/
```

Both triggers are compact and call methods of the `user_connection` package. This package requires the `connection_log` table, which is

```
SQL> CREATE TABLE connection_log
( event_id           NUMBER
, event_user_name    VARCHAR2(30) CONSTRAINT log_event_nn1 NOT NULL
, event_type         VARCHAR2(14) CONSTRAINT log_event_nn2 NOT NULL
, event_date         DATE         CONSTRAINT log_event_nn3 NOT NULL
, CONSTRAINT connection_log_p1  PRIMARY KEY (event_id));
```

The package body declares two procedures. One supports the *logon* trigger, and the other supports the *logoff* trigger. The package specification is

```
SQL> CREATE OR REPLACE PACKAGE user_connection AS
  PROCEDURE connecting (user_name IN VARCHAR2);
  PROCEDURE disconnecting (user_name IN VARCHAR2);
END user_connection;
/
```

The implementation of the `user_connection` package body is

```
SQL> CREATE OR REPLACE PACKAGE BODY user_connection AS
  PROCEDURE connecting (user_name IN VARCHAR2) IS
  BEGIN
    INSERT INTO connection_log
    (event_user_name, event_type, event_date)
    VALUES (user_name,'CONNECT',SYSDATE);
  END connecting;
  PROCEDURE disconnecting (user_name IN VARCHAR2) IS
```

```
    BEGIN
      INSERT INTO connection_log
      (event_user_name, event_type, event_date)
      VALUES (user_name,'DISCONNECT',SYSDATE);
    END disconnecting;
  END user_connection;
  /
```

You may notice that the `connection_log` table has four columns but the `INSERT` statement only uses three. This is possible because the `connection_log_t1` trigger automatically assigns the next value from the `connection_log_s1` sequence. You can find the source of the `connection_log_t1` trigger in the section "Row-Level Triggers" in this chapter.

This section has demonstrated how you can build system triggers.

Review Section

This section has described the following points about the Oracle Database 12*c* system and database event triggers:

- System and database event triggers let you capture events like logging on or off the system, or connecting to different schemas.
- System and database event triggers are best suited to log activities rather than raise exceptions.

Trigger Restrictions

There are several restrictions on how you implement triggers in Oracle Database 12*c*. They are fairly consistent between releases, but Oracle Database 11*g* forward has relaxed some mutating table restrictions. Restrictions have been covered in earlier sections when they apply to only one type of trigger.

The following subsections cover the remaining restrictions.

Maximum Trigger Size

A trigger body can be no longer than 32,760 bytes, as noted in the section "Introduction to Triggers" at the beginning of this chapter. This size limitation means that you should consider keeping your trigger bodies small in size. You can accomplish this without losing any utility by moving coding logic into other schema-level components, such as functions, procedures, and packages. An advantage of moving the coding logic out of the trigger body is that you can reuse the code. You can also wrap schema-level objects, whereas you can't wrap trigger bodies. Appendix F discusses wrapping your PL/SQL code to hide it from prying eyes.

SQL Statements

Nonsystem trigger bodies can't contain DDL statements. They also can't contain Data Control Language (DCL) or Transaction Control Language (TCL) commands, like `ROLLBACK`, `SAVEPOINT`, or `COMMIT`. This rule holds true for the schema-level components that you call from nonsystem trigger bodies when the trigger runs within the scope of the triggering statement.

If you declare a trigger as autonomous, nonsystem trigger bodies can contain DCL commands because they don't alter the transaction scope. They act outside of it. You enable a trigger to work outside the scope of a triggering statement by putting the following in its `DECLARE` block:

```
PRAGMA AUTONOMOUS_TRANSACTION;
```

A larger problem with SQL statements exists with remote transactions. If you call a remote schema-level function or procedure from a trigger body, it is possible that you may encounter a timestamp or signature mismatch. A mismatch invalidates the trigger and causes the triggering SQL statement to fail.

LONG and LONG RAW Data Types

The `LONG` and `LONG RAW` data types are legacy components. No effort is spent on updating them, and you should migrate to LOBs at your earliest opportunity.

You can't declare a local variable in a trigger with the `LONG` or `LONG RAW` data type. However, you can insert into a `LONG` or `LONG RAW` column when the value can be converted to a constrained data type, like a `CHAR` or `VARCHAR2`. The maximum length is 32,000 bytes.

Row-level triggers cannot use a `:new` or `:old` pseudo-record, or row of data, when the column is declared as a `LONG` or `LONG RAW` data type.

Mutating Tables

A *mutating* table is a table that is undergoing change. Change can come from an `INSERT`, `UPDATE`, or `DELETE` statement, or from a `DELETE CASCADE` constraint. This type of error can only happen on row-level triggers.

You can't query or modify tables when they're changing. This makes sense if you think about it. If a trigger fires because of a change on a table, it can't see the change until it is final. While you can access the `new` and `old` pseudo-records, you can't read the state of the table. Any attempt to do so raises an `ORA-04091` exception.

The following example demonstrates how mutating errors can occur. First create a `mutant` table, as follows:

```
SQL> CREATE TABLE mutant
  ( mutant_id     NUMBER
  , mutant_name   VARCHAR2(20));
```

You can then insert the four primary ninja turtles:

```
SQL> INSERT INTO mutant VALUES (mutant_s1.nextval,'Donatello');
SQL> INSERT INTO mutant VALUES (mutant_s1.nextval,'Leonardo');
SQL> INSERT INTO mutant VALUES (mutant_s1.nextval,'Michelangelo');
SQL> INSERT INTO mutant VALUES (mutant_s1.nextval,'Raphael');
```

After inserting the data, you can build the following trigger:

```
SQL> CREATE OR REPLACE TRIGGER mutator
    AFTER DELETE ON mutant
    FOR EACH ROW
  DECLARE
    lv_rows  NUMBER;
  BEGIN
```

```
    SELECT    COUNT(*)
    INTO      lv_rows
    FROM      mutant;
    dbms_output.put_line('[lv_rows] has '||lv_rows||']');
  END;
  /
```

The trigger body attempts to get the number of rows, but it can't find the number of rows because the record set is not final. This restriction exists to prevent the trigger from seeing inconsistent data.

You can fire the trigger by running the following command to delete Michelangelo from the mutant table:

```
SQL> DELETE FROM mutant
     WHERE  mutant_name = 'Michelangelo';
```

After running that statement, the DELETE statement raises the following error stack:

```
DELETE FROM mutant WHERE mutant_name = 'Michelangelo'
            *
ERROR at line 1:
ORA-04091: table PLSQL.MUTANT is mutating, trigger/function may not see it
ORA-06512: at "PLSQL.MUTATOR", line 4
ORA-04088: error during execution of trigger 'PLSQL.MUTATOR'
```

A trigger rolls back the trigger body instructions and triggering statement when it encounters a mutating table. You should be careful to avoid mutating table errors now that you understand why they can occur.

System Triggers

System triggers can present interesting problems. Most problems relate to limitations or constraints imposed by event attribute functions. Some of the event attribute functions may be undefined for certain DDL events. You should refer to the section "Event Attribute Functions" earlier in this chapter to understand exactly what to expect from event attribute functions.

Event attribute functions are declared and implemented in the Oracle `standard` package. You can also encounter a problem creating objects after a system trigger fails to compile. This occurs for a `CREATE` event trigger when a `CREATE` event fires the trigger and the trigger body is invalid due to a missing object dependency. The missing dependency invalidates the trigger and marks it as invalid. When you try to create the missing object, the `CREATE` event trigger raises an `ORA-04098` error and disallows the DDL statement. To proceed, you must drop the invalid trigger, fix the object dependency, and recompile the trigger.

You can use the `audit_creation` trigger created in the section "Data Definition Language Triggers" to illustrate this restriction. If you drop the `audit_creation` table, the `audit_creation` trigger becomes invalid. Subsequently, you raise an `ORA-04098` error while attempting to create this missing table. You can't proceed until you drop the trigger, or you disable it. You disable the trigger by running the following command:

```
ALTER TRIGGER audit_creations DISABLE;
```

You can now create the table, and the trigger should revalidate when it is called. If the trigger is still invalid, you can compile it with this syntax:

```
ALTER TRIGGER audit_new_stuff COMPILE;
```

This section has covered some trigger restrictions. You should check the individual sections for restrictions that are specific to certain trigger types.

Review Section

This section has described the following points about Oracle Database 12*c* trigger restrictions:

- A trigger body can be no longer than 32,760 bytes, which is the size of a `LONG` data type.
- Nonsystem trigger bodies can't contain DDL statements.
- `LONG` and `LONG RAW` data types are legacy components, and you should avoid implementing solutions with them.
- Mutating tables are tables undergoing change, and you can't query or modify data while they're changing.
- You can encounter problems with DDL statements when system triggers fail to compile.

Supporting Scripts

This section describes programs placed on the McGraw-Hill Professional website to support the chapter.

- The `ddl_triggers.sql` program contains the scripts that support DDL trigger examples.
- The `dml_triggers.sql` program contains the scripts that support DML trigger examples.
- The `compound_triggers.sql` program contains the scripts that support the compound trigger example.
- The `system_triggers.sql` program contains the scripts that support the system and database event trigger example.

Summary

This chapter has reviewed the five types of database triggers. It has explained triggers and their architecture.

Mastery Check

The mastery check is a series of true-or-false and multiple-choice questions that let you confirm how well you understand the material in the chapter. You may check Appendix I for answers to these questions.

True or False:

1. ___Statement-level database triggers can change the `new` pseudo-record column values with the `INSERT` and `UPDATE` statements.
2. ___Oracle Database 12*c* supports triggers on Data Definition Language (DDL) statements.
3. ___Row-level database triggers can change the `new` pseudo-record column values with the `INSERT` and `UPDATE` statements.
4. ___Compound database triggers have four timing points.
5. ___Compound database triggers can implement a global exception handler.
6. ___Event attribute functions are designed for use in triggers and non-trigger PL/SQL program units.
7. ___You can implement event attribute functions in system event triggers.
8. ___You can define a single DML trigger that fires for `INSERT`, `UPDATE`, or `DELETE` statements on the same table.
9. ___You can define a DDL trigger for a `MERGE` statement.
10. ___It's possible to define an autonomous trigger body.

Multiple Choice:

11. Which of the following types of database triggers work in an Oracle database? (Multiple answers possible)
    A. DDL triggers
    B. TCL triggers
    C. DML triggers
    D. `INSTEAD OF` triggers
    E. Compound triggers
12. Which of the following types of database triggers work with a nonupdatable view in an Oracle database? (Multiple answers possible)
    A. DDL triggers
    B. DML triggers
    C. System event triggers
    D. TCL triggers
    E. `INSTEAD OF` triggers
13. You have `new` and `old` pseudo-record structures for which triggers in an Oracle database? (Multiple answers possible)
    A. DML statement-level triggers
    B. DDL row-level triggers
    C. DDL statement-level triggers

D. DML row-level triggers

E. Compound triggers

14. Which of the following are event functions? (Multiple answers possible)

A. A `MERGING` function

B. An `INSERTING` function

C. An `UPDATING` function

D. A `DELETING` function

E. All of the above

15. Oracle requires what syntax to access new column values from an `INSERT` or `UPDATE` statement in the code block? (Multiple answers possible)

A. `new.column_name`

B. `:new.column_name`

C. `old.column_name`

D. `:old.column_name`

E. None of the above

CHAPTER 13

Dynamic SQL

Native Dynamic SQL (NDS), delivered in Oracle 9*i* Database and improved in Oracle Database 10*g*, 11*g*, and 12*c*, provides a replacement for all but two key features of the `dbms_sql` package. So, NDS is the future, but `dbms_sql` isn't quite the past. While you should consider moving appropriate `dbms_sql` code forward at the earliest opportunity, some `dbms_sql` code will remain relevant for awhile. NDS and the `dbms_sql` package let you create and execute SQL at runtime.

The chapter is divided into three principal areas:

- Dynamic SQL architecture
- Native Dynamic SQL (NDS)
  - Dynamic statements
  - Dynamic statements with inputs
  - Dynamic statements with inputs and outputs
  - Dynamic statements with an unknown number of inputs
- DBMS_SQL package
  - Dynamic statements
  - Dynamic statements with input variables
  - Dynamic statements with variable inputs and fixed outputs
  - Dynamic statements with variable inputs and outputs
  - DBMS_SQL package

Dynamic SQL statements are a powerful technology that let you write and execute queries as your programs run. This means the DDL and DML statements can change as your programming needs change.

The architecture of dynamic statements applies to both NDS and `dbms_sql`. The architecture is covered first, and you should at least examine that section instead of going straight to the NDS section or `dbms_sql` section. NDS is covered before `dbms_sql` because you can do everything with NDS except two things:

- Manage dynamic statements when the number and data type of columns are unknown before runtime
- Convert `LONG` and `RAW` columns to variable length strings to either a `VARCHAR2`, `CLOB`, or `NCLOB` data types

You must use the `dbms_sql` package to manage those statements. The `dbms_sql` package is covered in detail, including the features replaced by NDS, because there's often a lot of old code that gets migrated and supported for years.

Dynamic SQL Architecture

Dynamic SQL delivers the flexibility to solve many problems. It allows you to write what are known as lambda-style functions. You declare lambda-style functions like other functions, but they can have an unknown parameter list and return type. Dynamic SQL provides this functionality to the PL/SQL programming language.

While you have two approaches available for building dynamic programs, NDS and the `dbms_sql` package, keep in mind that, as mentioned in the introduction, Oracle Database 12*c* includes the latest improvements to NDS, and `dbms_sql` is provided primarily for backward compatibility.

You have essentially two architectures that apply in both cases. You can concatenate ("glue") strings together, or you can implement placeholders. The gluing of strings is susceptible to SQL injection attacks. SQL injection attacks prey on the issues surrounding quoting strings. While gluing strings is risky, it's unavoidable in certain circumstances. You should use the `dbms_assert` package when you creating dynamic statements by gluing strings together. Implementing placeholders makes your dynamic SQL immune to SQL injection attacks. You probably know these placeholders as bind variables. They act as formal parameters to dynamic statements, but they're not quite as tidy as the signatures of functions and procedures.

At compile time, none of the elements in the dynamic statement are validated against objects in the database. This lets you write statements that will work with future components or work for multiple components. The decision about what these dynamic statements will do rests with how you call them.

The process of running a dynamic statement involves four steps. First, the statement is parsed at runtime. Second, a statement maps call parameters to placeholders in a statement string. Statements map variables to the placeholders by using their relative position in a statement string. When you map variables to placeholders you are binding variables to a statement. Binding mimics calling a function. The only difference is the parameter list is interspersed inside a dynamically built function. Third, the NDS engine parses and runs the statement with any bound variables. Fourth, the statement returns values to the calling statement through one of two methods. One method uses `IN OUT` mode call variables in the `USING` clause, which makes the statement act like a pass-by-reference function. The other method returns values through the `RETURNING INTO` clause. The process for `dbms_sql` is a bit more complex; you can find the process flow chart in the *Oracle Database PL/SQL Packages and Types Reference 12c Release*.

Native Dynamic SQL (NDS)

NDS is a powerful and simple tool. It is easy to use and deploy. It generally meets most needs for lambda-style functions. This section is divided into three parts. First, you cover dynamic statements, which are gluing strings together to make dynamic statements. Second, you learn how to use input bind variables. Third, you learn how to return data from NDS statements.

As you work through the various approaches to writing NDS statements, I'll provide comparisons to the types of `dbms_sql` statements they replace. To do so, it's important to qualify the four methods provided by the `dbms_sql` package. Table 13-1 shows you the four `dbms_sql` methods.

The sections work through the four `dbms_sql` methods by their complexity. Method 1 is the least complex, while Method 4 is the most complex. NDS provides a more efficient approach to Methods 1 through 3, but again there's no NDS equivalent to Method 4.

Method	Description	Functions or Procedures

1	Method 1 supports DML or DDL statements that are static. Static statements have no inputs or outputs when they're defined. Method 1 also does not support `SELECT` statements.	`EXECUTE`
		`OPEN_CURSOR`
		`PARSE`

2	Method 2 supports DML statements that are dynamic, which means they have bind variables. This method requires that you know the number and data type of bind variables at statement definition. Method 2 also does not support `SELECT` statements.	`BIND_ARRAY`
		`BIND_VARIABLE`
		`EXECUTE`
		`OPEN_CURSOR`
		`PARSE`

3	Method 3 supports DML statements that are dynamic, which means they have bind variables. It also supports the `RETURNING INTO` clause, which lets you retrieve columns and LOB locators from DML statements. This method requires that you know the number and data type of bind variables at statement definition. Method 3 supports `SELECT` statements, provided you know the number and data types at statement definition.	`BIND_ARRAY`
		`BIND_VARIABLE`
		`COLUMN_VALUE`
		`DEFINE_COLUMN`
		`EXECUTE`
		`EXECUTE_AND_FETCH`
		`FETCH_ROWS`
		`OPEN_CURSOR`
		`PARSE`
		`VARIABLE_VALUE`

4	Method 4 supports DML statements that are dynamic, which means they have bind variables. It also supports the `RETURNING INTO` clause, which lets you retrieve columns and LOB locators from DML statements. This method does not require advanced knowledge of the number and data type of bind variables at statement definition. Method 4 supports `SELECT` statements without requiring you to know the number and data type of columns at statement definition.	`BIND_ARRAY`
		`BIND_VARIABLE`
		`COLUMN_VALUE`
		`DEFINE_COLUMN`
		`DESCRIBE_COLUMNS`
		`DESCRIBE_COLUMNS2`
		`DESCRIBE_COLUMNS3`
		`EXECUTE`
		`EXECUTE_AND_FETCH`
		`FETCH_ROWS`
		`OPEN_CURSOR`
		`PARSE`
		`VARIABLE_VALUE`

TABLE 13-1. *DBMS_SQL Methods of Operation*

Dynamic Statements

This section shows you how to run dynamic statements. These statements are static shells when you define your programs. They are constructed as statements during runtime. They require dynamic execution for different reasons. These types of statements implement Method 1 from the `dbms_sql` package. Table 13-1 lists these methods.

You write DDL statements in dynamic SQL to avoid failures during compilation. An example would be a statement that should perform only when an object exists. Without dynamic SQL statements, the program unit could fail due to missing objects in the database.

The reasons for using dynamic DML statements differ. More often than not, the purpose is tied to checking something in the current session before you perform a statement. For example, you may read the CLIENT_INFO value from the session to check for authentication, roles, and privileges in an end-user application.

The subsections demonstrate dynamic DDL and DML statements, respectively.

Dynamic DDL Statements

A frequently performed task in stand-alone scripts is to check whether something is in the database before you act on it. You don't want to run a DROP statement on a table or sequence that doesn't exist.

NOTE

Unlike MySQL, Oracle Database 12c doesn't provide an IF EXISTS *clause when creating tables and sequences.*

The following anonymous block shows you how to conditionally drop a sequence. It uses a FOR loop to check whether the sequence exists and then it creates and runs a dynamic DDL statement. You should enable the SQL*Plus SERVEROUTPUT environment variable before testing this code if you want to see a confirmation message. You can run this anonymous block successfully whether there is or isn't a sample_sequence. The sample program creates the sequence, validates that it exists in the user_sequences view, and then runs this anonymous block. After that, it queries the user_sequences view to confirm it's no longer there.

```
SQL> BEGIN
       /* Use a loop to check whether to drop a sequence. */
       FOR i IN (SELECT null
                 FROM   user_objects
                 WHERE  object_name = 'SAMPLE_SEQUENCE') LOOP
         EXECUTE IMMEDIATE 'DROP SEQUENCE sample_sequence';
         dbms_output.put_line('Dropped [sample_sequence].');
       END LOOP;
     END;
     /
```

NDS is simple and direct. You simply query to see if the table is there, and when it's not there, you drop it. The EXECUTE IMMEDIATE statement runs the command.

Dynamic DML Statements

Dynamic DML statements are often simply strings assembled at runtime. They can be inserted as function or procedure parameters. The problem with gluing strings together from inputs is that they're subject to *SQL injection attacks*. The dbms_assert package lets you validate input parameters against SQL injection attacks.

The following procedure lets you dynamically build an INSERT statement to the item table:

```
SQL> CREATE OR REPLACE PROCEDURE insert_item
     ( pv_table_name    VARCHAR2
     , pv_asin          VARCHAR2
     , pv_item_type     VARCHAR2
     , pv_item_title    VARCHAR2
     , pv_item_subtitle VARCHAR2 := ''
     , pv_rating        VARCHAR2
     , pv_agency        VARCHAR2
     , pv_release_date  VARCHAR2 ) IS
```

```
10    stmt VARCHAR2(2000);
11  BEGIN
12    stmt := 'INSERT INTO '||dbms_assert.simple_sql_name(pv_table_name)
13         ||' VALUES '
14         || '( item_s1.nextval '
15         || ','||dbms_assert.enquote_literal('ASIN'||CHR(58)||pv_asin)
16         || ',(SELECT   common_lookup_id '
17         || '  FROM     common_lookup '
18         || '  WHERE    common_lookup_type = '
19         ||                dbms_assert.enquote_literal(pv_item_type)||')'
20         || ','||dbms_assert.enquote_literal(pv_item_title)
21         || ','||dbms_assert.enquote_literal(pv_item_subtitle)
22         || ', empty_clob() '
23         || ', NULL '
24         || ','||dbms_assert.enquote_literal(pv_rating)
25         || ','||dbms_assert.enquote_literal(pv_agency)
26         || ','||dbms_assert.enquote_literal(pv_release_date)
27         || ', 3, SYSDATE, 3, SYSDATE)';
28    /* Run the command. */
29    EXECUTE IMMEDIATE stmt;
30  END insert_item;
31  /
```

The `item` table could be hard-coded in the string, but it is a parameter to highlight the `qualified_sql_name` function. The `qualified_sql_name` function on line 12 compares the string against the namespace value in the schema. It raises an `ORA-44004` error when the actual parameter is incorrect. The `enquote_literal` function puts containing quotes around string literals in SQL statements. This function is superior to the older style where you backquote the quotes like this `'''`*`some_string`*`'''` to get a delimited string literal `'`*`some_string`*`'`.

You can test the program with the following anonymous block:

```
SQL> BEGIN
       insert_item ( table_name => 'ITEM'
                   , asin => 'B00005O3VC'
                   , item_title => 'Monty Python and the Holy Grail'
                   , item_subtitle => 'Special Edition'
                   , rating => 'PG'
                   , agency => 'MPAA'
                   , release_date => '23-OCT-2001');
     END;
     /
```

It successfully enters a new item in the `item` table.

Dynamic Statements with Inputs

A dynamic statement with input variables takes you one step beyond gluing strings together. This lets you write a statement with placeholders. The placeholders act like formal parameters but are interspersed inside the SQL statement. You pass actual parameters by placing them as arguments to the `USING` clause. This NDS approach let's you implement the equivalent of Method 2 operations in the `dbms_sql` package.

SQL Injection Attacks

SQL injection attacks are attempts to gain access to information that should be protected. SQL injection uses unbalanced quotes in SQL statements to alter the behavior of dynamic SQL statements. Dynamic SQL is a place where some hacker might try to exploit your code.

Oracle Database 11*g* forward has the `dbms_assert` package to help you prevent SQL injection attacks. `dbms_assert` has the following functions:

- The `enquote_literal` function takes a string input and adds leading and trailing single quotes to the output string.
- The `enquote_name` function takes a string input and promotes it to uppercase before adding leading and trailing double quotes to the output string. An optional Boolean parameter lets you disable capitalization by setting it to `false`.
- The `noop` function takes a string input and returns the same value as an output without any validation. The `noop` function is overloaded and can manage a `VARCHAR2` or `CLOB` data type.
- The `qualified_sql_name` function validates the input string as a valid schema-object name. This function lets you validate your functions, procedures, packages, and user-defined objects. The actual parameter evaluates in lowercase, mixed case, or uppercase.
- The `schema_name` function takes a string input and validates whether it is a valid schema name. The actual parameter needs to be uppercase for this to work properly. So, you should pass the actual parameter inside a call to the `UPPER` function, which is covered in Appendix C.
- The `simple_sql_name` function validates the input string as a valid schema-object name. This function lets you validate your functions, procedures, packages, and user-defined objects.
- The `sql_object_name` function validates the input string as a valid schema-object name. This function lets you validate your functions, procedures, and packages. At the time of writing it raised an `ORA-44002` error when checking a user-defined object type.

You can find more information about the `dbms_assert` package in the *Oracle Database PL/SQL Packages and Types Reference 12c Release*. Oracle NDS is immune to SQL injection attacks when you use bind variables as opposed to gluing things together.

Placeholders are positional based on their location in the SQL statement, or PL/SQL call parameter. You must have an actual parameter in the `USING` clause for each placeholder. The `USING` clause takes a comma-delimited list of parameters. They are `IN` mode (*pass-by-value*) parameters unless you specify otherwise. You override the default mode of operation by setting any parameter to `IN OUT` mode or `OUT`-only mode.

You use IN mode parameters when executing a SQL statement. The IN OUT or OUT mode requires that you enclose the SQL statement inside an anonymous block, or that you call a PL/SQL function or procedure. The Oracle documentation from Oracle Database 11*g* forward makes the following recommendations regarding placeholder variables:

- If a dynamic SQL SELECT statement returns at most one row, you should return the value through an INTO clause. This requires that you either open the statement as a reference cursor or enclose the SQL statement inside an anonymous block. The former does not use an IN OUT or OUT mode parameter in the USING clause, while the latter requires it.
- If a dynamic SQL SELECT statement returns more than one row, you should return the value through a BULK COLLECT INTO clause. Like the INTO clause, the bulk collection requires that you either (a) open the statement as a reference cursor, or (b) enclose the SQL statement inside an anonymous block. The former does not use an IN OUT or OUT mode parameter in the USING clause, while the latter requires it.
- If a dynamic SQL statement is a DML statement with input only placeholders, you should put them in the USING clause.
- If a dynamic SQL statement is a DML statement and uses a RETURNING INTO clause, you should put the input values in the USING clause and put the output values in the NDS RETURNING INTO clause.
- If the dynamic SQL statement is a PL/SQL anonymous block or CALL statement, then you should put both input and output parameters in the USING clause. All parameters listed in the USING clause are IN-only mode parameters. You must override the default and designate them as IN OUT or OUT.

The examples in this section demonstrate all approaches with SQL statements and calling a PL/SQL anonymous block. As a rule of thumb, you should avoid enclosing an NDS statement in an anonymous block because using the RETURNING INTO clause is superior and simpler.

The following example rewrites the insert_item procedure from the prior section. This one uses bind variables:

```
SQL> CREATE OR REPLACE PROCEDURE insert_item
( pv_asin           VARCHAR2
, pv_item_type      VARCHAR2
, pv_item_title     VARCHAR2
, pv_item_subtitle VARCHAR2 := ''
, pv_rating         VARCHAR2
, pv_agency         VARCHAR2
, pv_release_date   DATE ) IS
  stmt VARCHAR2(2000);
BEGIN
  stmt := 'INSERT INTO item VALUES '
       || '( item_s1.nextval '
       || ',''ASIN''||CHR(58)||:asin '
       || ',(SELECT   common_lookup_id '
       || '  FROM     common_lookup '
       || '  WHERE    common_lookup_type = :item_type)'
```

```
           || ', :item_title '
           || ', :item_subtitle '
           || ', empty_clob() '
           || ', NULL '
           || ', :rating '
           || ', :agency '
           || ', :release_date '
           || ', 3, SYSDATE, 3, SYSDATE)';
  EXECUTE IMMEDIATE stmt
  USING pv_asin, pv_item_type, pv_item_title, pv_item_subtitle
  ,      pv_rating, pv_agency, pv_release_date;
END insert_item;
/
```

You may have noticed a couple of changes. Foremost is that all the `dbms_assert` package calls were removed. Bind variables inherit the data type from the actual parameter passed through the `USING` clause. This is why there are no delimiting quotes around the variables that would otherwise be string literals. The next change you may notice is the removal of the table name substitution. You can't substitute a table name as a bind variable without raising an `ORA-00903` error at runtime. The last change is the data type of the `release_date` parameter; it is now a `DATE` type.

Bind variables in NDS statements are like formal parameters in functions and procedures. While they are scattered throughout a statement, you read them from left to right because the NDS statement is a string. Their occurrence in the NDS statement string maps their position, and the `USING` clause parameter must follow that left-to-right ordering.

The `EXECUTE IMMEDIATE` statement uses all variables passed as actual parameters through the `USING` clause as `IN` mode–only variables. As is the case for formal parameters in functions and procedures, the `IN` mode is the default. You need to specify `OUT` mode when you want variables' results returned to the local program scope by the `USING` clause.

If the number of parameters in the list is fewer than the actual number of placeholders, you raise an `ORA-01008` error, which says that not all variables are bound. The `USING` clause replaces the old `bind_value` and `bind_array` procedures in the `dbms_sql` package.

The following anonymous block lets you test the replacement `insert_item` procedure:

```
SQL> BEGIN
       insert_item (asin => 'B00005O3VC'
                   ,item_type => 'DVD_FULL_SCREEN'
                   ,item_title => 'Monty Python and the Holy Grail'
                   ,item_subtitle => 'Special Edition'
                   ,rating => 'PG'
                   ,agency => 'MPAA'
                   ,release_date => '23-OCT-2001');
     END;
     /
```

Using bind variables is generally preferred over gluing strings together, but both options have their purposes. Using bind variables is preferred because it makes your code immune to SQL injection attacks.

Dynamic Statements with Inputs and Outputs

The ability to bind inputs is powerful and simple using NDS. The terrific thing about getting output variables is that it is *so simple*. This is a refreshing change over the verbose `dbms_sql` approach that you can find in the section "Dynamic Statements with Input and Output Variables" later in the chapter. This approach let's NDS provide the equivalent of the `dbms_sql` package's Method 3.

The following uses a dynamic statement that returns its outbound values through a PL/SQL cursor variable:

```
SQL> DECLARE
  2    /* Define explicit record structure. */
  3    TYPE title_record IS RECORD
  4    ( item_title     VARCHAR2(60)
  5    , item_subtitle  VARCHAR2(60));
  6    /* Define dynamic variables. */
  7    title_cursor  SYS_REFCURSOR;
  8    title_row     TITLE_RECORD;
  9    stmt          VARCHAR2(2000);
 10  BEGIN
 11    /* Set statement. */
 12    stmt := 'SELECT  item_title, item_subtitle '
 13         || 'FROM    item '
 14         || 'WHERE   SUBSTR(item_title,1,12) = :input';
 15    /* Open and read dynamic cursor, then close it. */
 16    OPEN title_cursor FOR stmt USING 'Harry Potter';
 17    LOOP
 18      FETCH title_cursor INTO title_row;
 19      EXIT WHEN title_cursor%NOTFOUND;
 20      dbms_output.put_line(
 21        '['||title_row.item_title||']['||title_row.item_subtitle||']');
 22    END LOOP;
 23    CLOSE title_cursor;
 24  END;
 25  /
```

The NDS statement is dynamic, accepting a single input bind variable on line 14. The `OPEN FOR` statement on line 16 simply appends the `USING` clause to accept filtering criteria. The `USING` clause in this context is `IN` mode only. If you attempt to specify an `OUT` mode operation, the parser raises a `PLS-00254` error.

You output the results of the query as you would any other reference cursor statement. The "System Reference Cursors" section in Chapter 4 covers system reference cursors.

A bulk operation is also possible in NDS. Chapter 3 has a section called "Bulk Statements" that you may cross reference while working through the bulk processing examples. You simply call the `FETCH BULK COLLECT INTO` statement. This is demonstrated in the next query:

```
SQL> DECLARE
    /* Define explicit record structure. */
    TYPE title_record IS RECORD
    ( item_title     VARCHAR2(60)
    , item_subtitle  VARCHAR2(60));
```

```
 6    TYPE title_collection IS TABLE OF TITLE_RECORD;
 7    /* Define dynamic variables. */
 8    title_cursor      SYS_REFCURSOR;
 9    titles            TITLE_COLLECTION;
10    stmt              VARCHAR2(2000);
11  BEGIN
12    /* Set statement. */
13    stmt := 'SELECT  item_title, item_subtitle '
14         || 'FROM    item '
15         || 'WHERE   SUBSTR(item_title,1,12) = :input';
16    /* Open and read dynamic cursor, then close it. */
17    OPEN title_cursor FOR stmt USING 'Harry Potter';
18    FETCH title_cursor BULK COLLECT INTO titles;
19    FOR i IN 1..titles.COUNT LOOP
20      dbms_output.put_line(
21        '['||titles(i).item_title||']['||titles(i).item_subtitle||']');
22    END LOOP;
23    CLOSE title_cursor;
24  END;
25  /
```

The FETCH BULK COLLECT INTO statement on line 18 moves the entire cursor return set into the collection variable. In a larger program scope, you could return the collection record set to another PL/SQL block, or to a pipelined function as described in Chapter 8. You can also reference the section "FORALL Statements" in Chapter 5 to see how you could then use bulk inserts to process the resulting collection.

The last item to cover is how you use NDS to handle input and output variables. You declare actual parameters as OUT mode variables in the USING clause. This approach requires two things: you enclose the SQL statement in an anonymous block PL/SQL program, and you return the variable through a RETURNING INTO clause.

The next two scripts depend on your adding another row to the item table. This anonymous block uses the insert_item procedure that you build by running the create_nds3.sql script (available on the McGraw-Hill Professional website).

```
SQL> BEGIN
       insert_item (asin => 'B000G6BLWE'
                   ,item_type => 'DVD_FULL_SCREEN'
                   ,item_title => 'Young Frankenstein'
                   ,rating => 'PG'
                   ,agency => 'MPAA'
                   ,release_date => '05-SEP-2006');
     END;
     /
```

The following example demonstrates reading and writing through a CLOB locator with a dynamic SQL statement. Oracle Database 12*c* documentation recommends this approach. It has a couple of benefits. First, all input bind variables are passed through the USING clause, and all output bind variables are returned through the RETURNING INTO clause. Second, there is no need to create an enclosing anonymous PL/SQL block for the statement.

The recommended script is

```
SQL> DECLARE
  2    /* Define explicit record structure. */
  3    lv_target  CLOB;
  4    lv_source  VARCHAR2(2000) := 'A Mel Brooks comedy classic!';
  5    lv_movie   VARCHAR2(60) := 'Young Frankenstein';
  6    stmt     VARCHAR2(2000);
  7  BEGIN
  8    /* Set statement. */
  9    stmt := 'UPDATE  item '
 10         || 'SET     item_desc = empty_clob() '
 11         || 'WHERE   item_id = '
 12         || '          (SELECT item_id '
 13         || '           FROM   item '
 14         || '           WHERE  item_title = :input) '
 15         || 'RETURNING item_desc INTO :descriptor';
 16    EXECUTE IMMEDIATE stmt USING lv_movie RETURNING INTO lv_target;
 17    dbms_lob.writeappend(lv_target,LENGTH(lv_source),lv_source);
 18    COMMIT;
 19  END;
 20  /
```

The `:input` placeholder on line 14 receives the local `lv_movie` value from the `USING` clause on line 16. The statement's `RETURNING INTO` clause on line 15 returns the `:descriptor` placeholder to the `lv_target` local variable on line 16. As qualified in Chapter 10, the LOB locator is a special connection to a work area that lets you read from and write to a `CLOB` variable. The locator acts like an `IN OUT` mode variable. This is a very simple and direct approach compared to the alternative. The alternative would have you replace the `RETURNING INTO` clause with an `IN OUT` mode parameter in the `USING` clause, which would require you to enclose the SQL statement in a PL/SQL anonymous block.

You could also write a stand-alone procedure to manage this `UPDATE` statement. The procedure would look like this:

```
SQL> CREATE OR REPLACE PROCEDURE get_clob
( pv_item_title  VARCHAR2, pv_item_desc_out IN OUT CLOB ) IS
BEGIN
  UPDATE  item
  SET     item_desc = empty_clob()
  WHERE   item_id =
            (SELECT item_id
             FROM   item
             WHERE  item_title = pv_item_title)
             RETURNING item_desc INTO pv_item_desc_out;
END get_clob;
/
```

After creating the procedure, you can then use NDS to call the stored procedure. This *works more like a call through the OCI than NDS*. It does provide you with the ability to dynamically marshal call parameters by filtering them through some procedural logic.

The following calls the stored procedure and writes a new string to the `CLOB` column. The actual call semantic is enclosed in an anonymous block, which is required when you want to use `IN OUT` or `OUT` mode placeholders.

```
SQL> DECLARE
       /* Define explicit record structure. */
       lv_target   CLOB;
       lv_source   VARCHAR2(2000)  := 'A Mel Brooks classic movie!';
       lv_movie    VARCHAR2(60)  := 'Young Frankenstein';
       stmt        VARCHAR2(2000);
     BEGIN
       /* Set statement. */
       stmt := 'BEGIN '
            || '  get_clob(:input,:output); '
            || 'END;';
       EXECUTE IMMEDIATE stmt USING lv_movie, IN OUT lv_target;
       dbms_lob.writeappend(lv_target,LENGTH(lv_source),lv_source);
       COMMIT;
     END;
     /
```

The `USING` clause maps the `lv_movie` local variable to the `:input` placeholder, and the `lv_target` local variable to the `:output` placeholder. The call to the stand-alone procedure returns a `CLOB` locator. You use the `CLOB` locator as the first actual parameter to the `dbms_lob.writeappend` procedure. It writes the contents of the `lv_source` local variable to the `CLOB` column *courtesy of the placeholder*.

You can't replace an `IN OUT` mode variable in the `USING` clause with a `RETURNING INTO` clause because it would fail. The attempt raises an `ORA-06547` error for a PL/SQL anonymous block. The error tells you that the `RETURNING INTO` clause can only be used with an `INSERT`, `UPDATE`, or `DELETE` statement. The preferred solution is an `IN OUT` or `OUT`-only mode parameter in the `USING` clause when working with dynamic (or runtime) PL/SQL anonymous blocks.

NOTE

The `get_clob` function fails if you have more than one row in the table that meets the criteria. You should delete any extra copies to test this.

You can confirm any of the writes by running the following query:

```
SQL> SELECT   item_desc
     FROM     item
     WHERE    item_title = 'Young Frankenstein';
```

You'll see

```
ITEM_DESC
--------------------------
A Mel Brooks classic movie!
```

Dynamic Statements with an Unknown Number of Inputs

This section shows you how to create statements that run with an unknown number of placeholders. It demonstrates what is known as `dbms_sql` Method 4 (refer to Table 13-1), which allows you to bind a variable number of placeholders in statements.

The following shows you how to build an unknown number of inputs, while returning a known list of columns. You still need to use Method 4 and `dbms_sql` when you have a variable list of both inputs and outputs.

```
SQL> DECLARE
       /* Declare explicit record structure and table of structure. */
       TYPE title_record IS RECORD
       ( item_title     VARCHAR2(60)
       , item_subtitle  VARCHAR2(60));
       TYPE title_table IS TABLE OF title_record;
       /* Declare dynamic variables. */
       title_cursor  SYS_REFCURSOR;
       title_rows    TITLE_TABLE;
       /* Declare dbms_sql variables. */
       c             INTEGER := dbms_sql.open_cursor;
       fdbk          INTEGER;
       /* Declare local variables. */
       counter       NUMBER := 1;
       column_names  DBMS_SQL.VARCHAR2_TABLE;
       item_ids      DBMS_SQL.NUMBER_TABLE;
       stmt          VARCHAR2(2000);
       substmt       VARCHAR2(2000) := '';
     BEGIN
       /* Find the rows that meet the criteria. */
       FOR i IN (SELECT 'item_ids' AS column_names
                 ,       item_id
                 FROM    item
                 WHERE   REGEXP_LIKE(item_title,'^Harry Potter')) LOOP
         column_names(counter) := counter;
         item_ids(counter) := i.item_id;
         counter := counter + 1;
       END LOOP;
       /* Dynamically create substatement. */
       IF item_ids.COUNT = 1 THEN
         substmt := 'WHERE item_id IN (:item_ids)';
       ELSE
         substmt := 'WHERE item_id IN (';
         FOR i IN 1..item_ids.COUNT LOOP
           IF i = 1 THEN
             substmt := substmt ||':'||i;
           ELSE
             substmt := substmt ||',:'||i;
           END IF;
         END LOOP;
```

```
      substmt := substmt || ')';
    END IF;
    /* Set statement. */
    stmt := 'SELECT  item_title, item_subtitle '
         || 'FROM    item '
         ||  substmt;
    /* Parse the statement with DBMS_SQL. */
    dbms_sql.parse(c,stmt,dbms_sql.native);
    /* Bind the bind variable name and value. */
    FOR i IN 1..item_ids.COUNT LOOP
      dbms_sql.bind_variable(c,column_names(i),item_ids(i));
    END LOOP;
    /* Execute using dbms_sql. */
    fdbk := dbms_sql.execute(c);
    /* Convert the cursor to NDS. */
    title_cursor := dbms_sql.to_refcursor(c);
    /* Open and read dynamic cursor, then close it. */
    FETCH title_cursor BULK COLLECT INTO title_rows;
    FOR i IN 1..title_rows.COUNT LOOP
      dbms_output.put_line('['||title_rows(i).item_title||']['
        ||title_rows(i).item_subtitle||']');
    END LOOP;
    /* Close the System Reference Cursor. */
    CLOSE title_cursor;
  END;
  /
```

The program dynamically builds a SQL `SELECT` statement. The query looks like the following:

```
SQL> SELECT    i.item_title
  ,         i.item_subtitle
  FROM      item i
  WHERE     i.item_id IN (:1,:2,:3,:4,:5,:6,:7,:8,:9,:10,:11,:12,:13,:14);
```

The loop binds the list of numeric placeholders with the values in the `item_ids` associative array. The call to the `dbms_sql.to_refcursor` function converts the `dbms_sql` cursor to a standard weakly typed system reference cursor. It also closes the original `dbms_sql` cursor. If you try to close the `dbms_sql` cursor after conversion, you raise an `ORA-29471` error. The error message says that you're denied access because the package no longer owns the resource.

After converting to the system reference cursor, you simply use the standard NDS features to bulk-fetch the record set. You can also convert back from NDS to `dbms_sql` by using the `to_cursor_number` function.

This section has shown you how to use NDS. You should note two things in particular: NDS is simple to implement and simple to use. The next section describes the older and more complex `dbms_sql`.

Review Section

This section has described the following points about Native Dynamic SQL:

- NDS lets you create dynamic programs at runtime.
- NDS supports concatenating (or gluing) strings together to make a statement.
- NDS statements built through concatenation should use the `dbms_assert` package functions to prevent SQL injection attacks.
- NDS supports bind variables, which are like parameters scattered throughout a statement. If you think of NDS statements as long strings, you refer to bind variables in the order they occur when reading the string from the left to the right.
- The `EXECUTE IMMEDIATE` statement dispatches an NDS statement for execution.
- The `EXECUTE IMMEDIATE` statement support `IN`, `IN OUT`, and `OUT` mode parameters, and is the preferred solution when calling NDS statements that include PL/SQL anonymous blocks.
- The `RETURNING INTO` clause supports `OUT` mode parameters for `INSERT`, `UPDATE`, and `DELETE` statements.
- The `OPEN` *`system_reference_cursor`* `FOR` *`nds_statement`* lets you create dynamic `SELECT` lists easily.

DBMS_SQL Package

Oracle introduced the `dbms_sql` package in Oracle 7. It gave you a way to store object code in the database that would dynamically build SQL statements. It was an innovative solution because it works around the problem of how PL/SQL checks dependencies. Prior to `dbms_sql`, you could not store a SQL statement unless the table existed with the same definition.

`dbms_sql` was enhanced in Oracle 8*i* Database to support collections. The package has grown through successive releases up to Oracle 9*i* Database. As discussed in the section "Native Dynamic SQL (NDS)" earlier in the chapter, the direction shifted to NDS with the release of Oracle 9*i*.

The `dbms_sql` package provides several overloaded procedures. If you were to do run a `describe` command on the `dbms_sql` package, you would find a copy of each of these overloaded procedures for the types listed. The section "DBMS_SQL Package Definition" documents the constants, types, functions, and procedures.

`dbms_sql` still has two major features that are not delivered in NDS. It can manage dynamic statements when the number and data type of columns are unknown before runtime. This feature is possible because of two `dbms_sql` procedures: `describe_columns` and `describe_columns2`. You also have the ability to convert `LONG` and `RAW` columns to strings with the `column_value_long` procedure of the `dbms_sql` package.

Like the NDS approach, `dbms_sql` supports string concatenation and bind variables. If you need a refresher on bind variables, please check Chapter 3. Unlike NDS, the `dbms_sql` package requires explicit grants.

DBMS_SQL Grants and Privileges

The dbms_sql package is owned by the SYS schema. It is sometimes necessary to grant permissions to the SYSTEM user first. Then, you can grant permissions to the individual users rather than provisioning them through roles. You generally need access to the dbms_sql and dbms_sys_sql packages.

You grant permissions from the SYS account to the SYSTEM user with the following two statements:

```
GRANT EXECUTE ON dbms_sys_sql TO system WITH GRANT OPTION;
GRANT EXECUTE ON dbms_sql TO system WITH GRANT OPTION;
```

After granting the proper privileges to the SYSTEM user, you can grant them to your c##plsql CDB or video PDB user to run the sample programs. You grant the following privileges as the system user:

```
GRANT EXECUTE ON sys.dbms_sys_sql TO plsql;
GRANT EXECUTE ON sys.dbms_sql TO plsql;
```

You should now be able to run the scripts in this file, provided you've also installed the video store example discussed in the Introduction to this book.

Oracle qualifies four types of dynamic SQL statements. You use certain functions and procedures with each method type. Table 13-1, introduced in the "Native Dynamic SQL (NDS)" section earlier, lists the methods, their definitions, and the dbms_sql functions and procedures that you use with each.

The next four subsections examine the dbms_sql package. The first three demonstrate the features and use of dynamic SQL with the dbms_sql package. The last section documents the package constants, types, functions, and procedures.

Dynamic Statements

This section shows you how to run dynamic statements. These statements are static when you define your programs. They are constructed at runtime. They require dynamic execution for different reasons. These types of statements implement Method 1 from Table 13-1.

You write DDL statements in dynamic SQL to avoid failures during compilation. An example would be a statement that should perform only when an object exists. Without dynamic SQL statements, the program unit could fail due to missing objects in the database.

The reasons for using dynamic DML statements differ. More often than not, the purpose is tied to checking something in the current session before you perform a statement. For example, you may read the CLIENT_INFO value from the session to check for authentication, roles, and privileges in an end-user application.

The subsections demonstrate dynamic DDL and DML statements, respectively.

Dynamic DDL Statements

A frequently performed task in stand-alone scripts is to check whether something is in the database before you act on it. You don't want to run a DROP statement on a table or sequence that doesn't exist.

The following anonymous block shows you how to conditionally drop a sequence. It uses a FOR loop to check whether the sequence exists and then it creates and runs a dynamic DDL statement. You should enable the SQL*Plus SERVEROUTPUT environment variable before testing this code, if you want to see the confirmation message. The code follows:

```
SQL> DECLARE
  2    /* Define local DBMS_SQL variables, and open cursor. */
  3    c      INTEGER := dbms_sql.open_cursor;
  4    fdbk   INTEGER;
  5    stmt   VARCHAR2(2000);
  6  BEGIN
  7    /* Use a loop to check whether to drop a sequence. */
  8    FOR i IN (SELECT null
  9              FROM   user_objects
 10              WHERE  object_name = 'SAMPLE_SEQUENCE') LOOP
 11      /* Build, parse, and execute SQL statement, then close cursor. */
 12      stmt := 'DROP SEQUENCE sample_sequence';
 13      dbms_sql.parse(c,stmt,DBMS_SQL.NATIVE);
 14      fdbk := dbms_sql.execute(c);
 15      dbms_sql.close_cursor(c);
 16      dbms_output.put_line('Dropped Sequence [SAMPLE_SEQUENCE].');
 17    END LOOP;
 18  END;
 19  /
```

The declaration block defines three variables for dbms_sql statements. Line 3 holds the database cursor number, named c for *cursor* (by tradition more than anything else). You're welcome to change it to something more meaningful to you, but you'll see it as c in all the sample programs. The database cursor variable c is defined, not declared, by calling the dbms_sql.open_cursor function. Line 4 declares fdbk (which stands for *feedback*). It is used to capture the return value from the dbms_sql.execute function. Line 5 declares the third variable, stmt (which stands for *statement*).

The execution block assigns a valid DDL statement to the stmt variable. Then, the dbms_sql.parse procedure ties the cursor number and statement together and runs the statement using the current database version's execution semantics.

You can test the program by creating a sample_sequence with the following syntax:

```
SQL> CREATE SEQUENCE sample_sequence;
```

You can confirm the sequence is there and working by querying the database catalog, or by incrementing the sequence. This verifies the presence of the sequence by incrementing it:

```
SQL> SELECT sample_sequence.nextval FROM dual;
```

Run the conditional DROP statement and you see this message:

```
Dropped Sequence [SAMPLE_SEQUENCE].
```

You have now seen how to implement a dynamic DDL statement using the dbms_sql package. If you check the corresponding "Dynamic DDL Statements" section in the "Native Dynamic SQL (NDS)" section, you'll see that this approach is more typing for little or no return.

Dynamic DML Statements

Dynamic DML statements are often created as strings at runtime. They often audit some state or behavior before deciding how to build the DML statement. This section discusses dbms_sql Method 1, which allows only strings or patchworks of strings.

The example in this section uses a code block that changes the column values for an INSERT statement. Authenticated users enter one type of data, while unauthenticated users enter another.

You could check the value of the CLIENT_INFO variable in the session, and then choose the value to insert into the last_updated_by column of a table. Chapter 12 has a sidebar "Reading and Writing Session Metadata" that explains how you can set and get the CLIENT_INFO value for your session.

The example checks if the value has been set. If not set, it substitutes a –1 for the last_updated_by column. That would be an illegal user, and entering it conditionally lets you track manual SQL entries to a production database. Actually, it should update both the created_by and last_updated_by columns for completeness, but you'll do that in a subsequent example with bind variables.

```
SQL> DECLARE
  /* Declare local DBMS_SQL variables, and open cursor. */
  c       INTEGER := dbms_sql.open_cursor;
  fdbk    INTEGER;
  stmt1   VARCHAR2(2000);
  stmt2   VARCHAR2(20)  := '-1,SYSDATE)';
  /* V$SESSION.CLIENT_INFO variable. */
  client VARCHAR2(64);
BEGIN
  stmt1 := 'INSERT INTO item VALUES '
        || '( item_s1.nextval '
        || ',''ASIN'||CHR(58)||' B000VBJEEG'''
        || ',(SELECT   common_lookup_id '
        || '  FROM     common_lookup '
        || '  WHERE    common_lookup_type = ''DVD_WIDE_SCREEN'') '
        || ',''Ratatouille'''
        || ','''''
        || ', empty_clob() '
        || ', NULL '
        || ',''G'''
        || ',''MPAA'''
        || ',''06-NOV-2007'''
        || ', 3, SYSDATE,';
  /* Get the current CLIENT_INFO value and conditionally append to string. */
  dbms_application_info.read_client_info(client);
  IF client IS NOT NULL THEN
    stmt1 := stmt1 || client || ',SYSDATE)';
  ELSE
    stmt1 := stmt1 || stmt2;
  END IF;
    /* Build, parse, and execute SQL statement, then close cursor. */
  dbms_sql.parse(c,stmt1,dbms_sql.native);
  fdbk := dbms_sql.execute(c);
```

```
34     dbms_sql.close_cursor(c);
35     dbms_output.put_line('Rows Inserted ['||fdbk||']');
36   END;
37   /
```

Unless you set the `CLIENT_INFO` column value, this script should insert one row with a –1 in the `last_updated_by` column. As you tell from the statement, typing SQL statements into a variable is tedious and a backquoting feat when successful. You raise an `ORA-01756` error, which says "quoted string not properly terminated," when you fail to get all the single quotes matched.

Colons inside dynamic SQL statements are indicators of placeholders. When `dbms_sql.parse` parses a statement string, it marks placeholders as bind value targets. If you fail to call either the `bind_array` or `bind_variable` procedure before you execute the parsed statement, it would fail due to the missing bind variable. You bind *scalar* variables by calling the `bind_variable` procedure, and you bind *nested tables* by calling the `bind_array` procedure.

You should use `CHR(58)` in lieu of the colon when you want to insert a colon as text, because the parser doesn't interpret it as a bind variable. That's what I've done on line 12. While the parsed output string contains a colon, the parsing process didn't trigger a substitution.

All the `dbms_sql` command syntax mirrors the syntax in the DDL example in the preceding section. You have now seen how to create and implement dynamic SQL statements by creating and executing conditionally constructed strings.

Dynamic Statements with Input Variables

The prior section demonstrated how you dynamically piece strings together to build a statement. That is a cumbersome process, and as you might guess, there is a better way. This section discusses `dbms_sql` Method 2, which allows you to bind variables into statements.

You generally know the statement structure of your DML statements when you write a PL/SQL block. You can actually write your dynamic statements like a function, with input values. You call these input variables *placeholders* instead of formal parameters. Inside the statements they act as bind variables, and you may find many people calling them that.

Writing a DDL or DML statement that uses placeholders is much easier than gluing strings together through concatenation. `dbms_sql` Method 2 from Table 13-1 provides this feature. Table 13-2 lists some errors that can occur when using placeholders and bind variables.

You should also note that you can implement a PL/SQL block with `dbms_sql`. The only caveat is that you terminate the string with a semicolon. This is a departure from how ordinary SQL statements work. The difference occurs because the closing semicolon terminates the PL/SQL block. A semicolon acts as an execution instruction for a SQL statement. You will see an example of this approach in the next section, "Dynamic Statements with Input and Output Variables."

The following example re-implements the `INSERT` statement from the prior section. This time it uses replacement variables. The anonymous block is rewritten as a stand-alone procedure. After creating the procedure, you can insert new items into the `item` table through the procedure.

The following is the stand-alone procedure that implements `IN` mode placeholders or bind variables:

```
SQL> CREATE OR REPLACE PROCEDURE insert_item
  ( pv_asin      VARCHAR2
  , pv_title     VARCHAR2
  , pv_subtitle  VARCHAR2 := NULL
  , pv_itype     VARCHAR2 := 'DVD_WIDE_SCREEN'
```

Error Code	Description and Fix
ORA-00928	You raise an ORA-00928 error when you put placeholders inside the overriding signature of an INSERT statement. The signature is the formal parameter list between the table name and VALUES clause. The generic "missing SELECT keyword" message can be misleading.
ORA-06502	You raise an ORA-06502 error when an explicit size is required for a CHAR, RAW, or VARCHAR2 variable and you fail to provide one. You need to include the output size when you call the bind_variable_char or bind_variable_raw procedure. The generic "PL/SQL: numeric or value error" message can be misleading.
ORA-01006	You raise an ORA-01006 error when you enclose placeholders for VARCHAR2 data types in quotes. The bind_variable function binds the value and data type to the statement, which eliminates the need for delimiting quotes. The generic "bind variable does not exist" message is a complete misnomer, but now you know how to fix it.
PLS-00049	You raise a PLS-00049 error when a placeholder receives an unexpected data type that can't be implicitly converted to the target data type. You need to ensure any assignments are explicitly made with the correct data type. Don't rely on implicit type conversion and you'll never be disappointed. The "bad bind variable" message isn't clear, but it's spot on because you've sent the wrong data type.

TABLE 13-2. *Errors That Can Occur When Using DBMS_SQL*

```
 , pv_rating   VARCHAR2
 , pv_agency   VARCHAR2
 , pv_release  DATE ) IS
   /* Define local DBMS_SQL variables. */
   c       INTEGER := dbms_sql.open_cursor;
   fdbk    INTEGER;
   stmt    VARCHAR2(2000);
   /* Variable to get OUT parameter value. */
   lv_client VARCHAR2(64);
 BEGIN
   stmt := 'INSERT INTO item VALUES '
        || '( item_s1.nextval '
        || ',''ASIN''||CHR(58)|| :asin'
        || ',(SELECT   common_lookup_id '
        || '  FROM     common_lookup '
        || '  WHERE    common_lookup_type = :itype) '
        || ',:title'
        || ',:subtitle'
        || ', empty_clob() '
        || ', NULL '
        || ',:rating'
```

```
27          || ',:agency'
28          || ',:release'
29          || ',:created_by,SYSDATE,:last_updated_by,SYSDATE)';
30    /* Call and dynamically set the session for the CLIENT_INFO value. */
31    dbms_application_info.read_client_info(client);
32    IF client IS NOT NULL THEN
33      lv_client := TO_NUMBER(lv_client);
34    ELSE
35      lv_client := -1;
36    END IF;
37    /* Parse and execute the statement. */
38    dbms_sql.parse(c,stmt,dbms_sql.native);
39    dbms_sql.bind_variable(c,'asin',pv_asin);
40    dbms_sql.bind_variable(c,'itype',pv_itype);
41    dbms_sql.bind_variable(c,'title',pv_title);
42    dbms_sql.bind_variable(c,'subtitle',pv_subtitle);
43    dbms_sql.bind_variable(c,'rating',pv_rating);
44    dbms_sql.bind_variable(c,'agency',pv_agency);
45    dbms_sql.bind_variable(c,'release',pv_release);
46    dbms_sql.bind_variable(c,'created_by',lv_client);
47    dbms_sql.bind_variable(c,'last_updated_by',lv_client);
48    fdbk := dbms_sql.execute(c);
49    dbms_sql.close_cursor(c);
50    dbms_output.put_line('Rows Inserted ['||fdbk||']');
51  END insert_item;
52  /
```

The placeholders are represented in bold text inside the dynamic `INSERT` statement. They don't have delimiting single quotes around them because the value and data type are bound to the statement, and the delimiters are unnecessary. If you forget and include the delimiting internal quotes in the statement, an `ORA-01006` error is raised at runtime. You need to remove the single quotes or enclose the statement in a PL/SQL block.

Lines 39 through 47 bind either a parameter or a local variable to a placeholder name in the dynamic SQL `stmt` (statement). The order of how you bind parameters or local variables to placeholders is immaterial, which is unlike the restriction on the `USING` clause in NDS.

As the number of bind variables increases, so do the calls to the `bind_variable` procedure. You must call the `dbms_sql` package's `bind_variable` procedure for each placeholder.

This section has shown you how to use Method 2 dynamic SQL, which lets you substitute input variables.

Dynamic Statements with Variable Inputs and Fixed Outputs

This section shows you how to implement placeholders that either input or output data from SQL statements. It demonstrates `dbms_sql` Method 3, which allows you to have `IN` mode bind variables and map `SELECT`-list values to local variables.

Dynamic `SELECT` statements work in Method 3, provided you know at compile time how many columns are retrieved. In this section you work with a set of scalar return values and a single scalar input value, then a set of associative arrays and a range of scalar input values.

NDS Is the Key to Converting LONG Data Types

The legacy of the LONG and LONG RAW data type is that someday you would need to move the data. I'd suggest the day has arrived with Oracle Database 12*c*. After all, Oracle Database 12*c* enables you to store a 32,767-byte string in a VARCHAR2 column, as qualified in the "VARCHAR2, STRING, and VARCHAR Data Types " section of Chapter 4.

The dbms_sql package provides the only way to convert LONG or LONG RAW columns into VARCHAR2 or CLOB data types. You perform the conversion with the dbms_sql package's column_value_long procedure. The "Converting a LONG to a CLOB" section in Chapter 10 shows you how to convert a LONG data type to a CLOB data type. This sidebar shows you how to convert LONG data types to VARCHAR2 data types.

To do the conversion, I've written the following long_to_varchar2 function, which takes a view_name column value from the CDB_, ALL_, DBA_, or USER_VIEWS administrative view and the length of the text column value. The text column is where Oracle stores the view's text in a LONG data type column. Without the length of the LONG, you must read character by character to find the whole LONG column's value.

```
SQL> CREATE OR REPLACE FUNCTION long_to_varchar2
  ( pv_view_name      VARCHAR2
  , pv_column_length  INTEGER )
  RETURN VARCHAR2 AS
    /* Declare local variables. */
    lv_cursor    INTEGER := dbms_sql.open_cursor;
    lv_feedback  INTEGER;          -- Feedback of dynamic execution
    lv_length    INTEGER;          -- Length of string
    lv_return    VARCHAR2(32767);  -- Function output
    lv_stmt      VARCHAR2(2000);   -- Dynamic SQL statement
    lv_string    VARCHAR2(32760);  -- Maximum length of LONG data type
  BEGIN
    /* Create dynamic statement. */
    lv_stmt := 'SELECT text'||CHR(10)
            || 'FROM user_views'||CHR(10)
            || 'WHERE view_name = '''||pv_view_name||'''';
    /* Parse and define a long column. */
    dbms_sql.parse(lv_cursor, lv_stmt, dbms_sql.native);
    dbms_sql.define_column_long(lv_cursor,1);
    /* Only attempt to process the return value when fetched. */
    IF dbms_sql.execute_and_fetch(lv_cursor) = 1 THEN
      dbms_sql.column_value_long(
          lv_cursor
        , 1
        , pv_column_length
        , 0
        , lv_string
        , lv_length);
    END IF;
    /* Check for an open cursor. */
    IF dbms_sql.is_open(lv_cursor) THEN
      dbms_sql.close_cursor(lv_cursor);
    END IF;
```

(continued)

```
34     /* Convert the long length string to a maximum size length. */
35     lv_return := lv_string;
36     RETURN lv_return;
37   END long_to_varchar2;
38   /
```

Lines 25 through 33 hold the logic for transferring the contents of a LONG data type to a VARCHAR2 data type. Internally, the dbms_sql package converts the LONG data type (up to 32,760 bytes) to a VARCHAR2 data type.

The following return_view_text wrapper function queries the USER_VIEWS view, gets the size of the LONG column, and calls the long_to_varchar2 function:

```
SQL> CREATE OR REPLACE FUNCTION return_view_text
  2   ( pv_view_name  VARCHAR2 ) RETURN VARCHAR2 IS
  3     /* Declare a target variable, because of the limit of SELECT-INTO. */
  4     lv_long_view  LONG;
  5     /* Declare a dynamic cursor. */
  6     CURSOR c (cv_view_name VARCHAR2) IS
  7       SELECT   text
  8       FROM     user_views
  9       WHERE    view_name = cv_view_name;
 10   BEGIN
 11     /* Open, fetch, and close cursor to capture view text. */
 12     OPEN c(pv_view_name);
 13     FETCH c INTO lv_long_view;
 14     CLOSE c;
 15
 16     /* Return the output CLOB value. */
 17     RETURN long_to_varchar2(pv_view_name, LENGTH(lv_long_view));
 18   END;
 19   /
```

You can't use the SELECT-INTO with a LONG data type as a target. That's why I've defined a dynamic cursor on lines 6 through 9, and opened, fetched, and closed it on lines 12 and 13. The SQL LENGTH built-in lets me submit the length of the LONG column to the long_to_varchar2 function as the second parameter on line 17.

This sidebar should demonstrate why knowing how to use the dbms_sql package makes you a powerful PL/SQL programmer.

You are performing *row-by-row* queries when you manage scalar output values. The output values of associate arrays are single-dimensional arrays of scalar values. You process *parallel arrays* when you return multiple columns from a SELECT statement into associative arrays through *bulk* processing. You need to be very attentive to managing how you navigate through these to ensure your index values are always equal. Failure to keep the index in synchronization means you're looking at columns from different rows.

Debugging Tips for DBMS_SQL with SELECT Statements

It is critical when working with scalar variable-length strings that you provide a physical size to the `dbms_sql.define_columns` procedure. You must also do so when returning a scalar `RAW` data type. If you forget to provide the physical size, the `dbms_sql` package raises a `PLS-00307` error. The error says too many declarations of `define_column` match this call. The error is actually a bit tricky because it involves how implicit casting works when calling this function.

You can make your life easier by simply providing the fourth parameter, which is the length of a `CHAR`, `RAW`, or `VARCHAR2` data type.

This syntax is probably among the most tedious for the `DBMS_SQL` package, regardless of whether you're returning one value, row-by-row values, or bulk statement values. You should consider the NDS `OPEN FOR` clause for these types of operation because it's simpler.

The *row-by-row* and *bulk* processing examples are covered in separate subsections.

Row-by-Row Statement Processing

The sample program shows you how to process single- and multiple-row returns from a dynamic `SELECT` statement. These examples depend on the `item` table that is built by the `create_store.sql` script discussed in the Introduction of this book.

The single-row statement is

```
SQL> DECLARE
       c                        INTEGER := dbms_sql.open_cursor;
       fdbk                     INTEGER;
       statement                VARCHAR2(2000);
       lv_item_id               NUMBER := 1081;
       lv_item_title            VARCHAR2(60);
       lv_item_subtitle         VARCHAR2(60);
     BEGIN
       /* Build and parse SQL statement. */
       statement := 'SELECT item_title'||CHR(10)
                 || ',       item_subtitle'||CHR(10)
                 || 'FROM    item WHERE item_id = :item_id'||CHR(10)
                 || 'WHERE   item_id = :item_id';
       dbms_sql.parse(c,statement,dbms_sql.native);
       /* Define column mapping, execute statement, and copy results. */
       dbms_sql.define_column(c,1,item_title,60);     -- Define OUT mode variable.
       dbms_sql.define_column(c,2,item_subtitle,60); -- Define OUT mode variable.
       dbms_sql.bind_variable(c,'item_id',item_id);  -- Bind IN mode variable.
       fdbk := dbms_sql.execute_and_fetch(c);
       dbms_sql.column_value(c,1,item_title);     -- Copy query column to variable.
       dbms_sql.column_value(c,2,item_subtitle); -- Copy query column to variable.
       /* Print return value and close cursor. */
       dbms_output.put_line(
         '['||item_title||']['||NVL(item_subtitle,'None')||']');
       dbms_sql.close_cursor(c);
     END;
     /
```

This approach lets you enter the `SELECT` columns natively in the statement because they're `OUT` mode variables. You need to define the columns before executing the statement and then copy the column values to a local variable after fetching them. You reference columns by position and local variables by name. This differs for the `IN` mode variable, which uses a semicolon to identify it as a replacement variable (*or bind variable*).

This query should return

```
[We Were Soldiers] [None]
```

You've now seen how to return a single row, but more often than not you return more than one row. The following example performs a row-by-row query and prints the contents of the returned rows:

```
SQL> DECLARE
  2    c                        INTEGER := dbms_sql.open_cursor;
  3    fdbk                     INTEGER;
  4    statement                VARCHAR2(2000);
  5    lv_item1                 NUMBER := 1003;
  6    lv_item2                 NUMBER := 1013;
  7    lv_item_title            VARCHAR2(60);
  8    lv_item_subtitle         VARCHAR2(60);
  9  BEGIN
 10    /* Build and parse SQL statement. */
 11    statement := 'SELECT item_title'||CHR(10)
 12              || ',      item_subtitle'||CHR(10)
 13              || 'FROM item'||CHR(10)
 14              || 'WHERE item_id BETWEEN :item1 AND :item2'||CHR(10)
 15              || 'AND item_type = 1014';
 16    dbms_sql.parse(c,statement,dbms_sql.native);
 17    /* Define column mapping and execute statement. */
 18    dbms_sql.define_column(c,1,item_title,60);    -- Define OUT mode variable.
 19    dbms_sql.define_column(c,2,item_subtitle,60); -- Define OUT mode variable.
 20    dbms_sql.bind_variable(c,'item1',item1);      -- Bind IN mode variable.
 21    dbms_sql.bind_variable(c,'item2',item2);      -- Bind IN mode variable.
 22    fdbk := dbms_sql.execute(c);
 23    /* Read results. */
 24    LOOP
 25      EXIT WHEN dbms_sql.fetch_rows(c) = 0;       -- No more results.
 26      /* Copy and print. */
 27      dbms_sql.column_value(c,1,item_title);      -- Copy column to variable.
 28      dbms_sql.column_value(c,2,item_subtitle);   -- Copy column to variable.
 29      dbms_output.put_line(
 30        '['||item_title||']['||NVL(item_subtitle,'None')||']');
 31    END LOOP;
 32    dbms_sql.close_cursor(c);
 33  END;
 34  /
```

You define the column mapping once for each column on lines 18 and 19, and you bind variables once on lines 20 and 21, respectively. You also need to copy each row's column values to the local variable to process them, as shown on lines 27 and 28 in the preceding loop.

With the SQL*Plus `SERVEROUTPUT` environment variable set, this should print

```
[Casino Royale] [None]
[Die Another Day] [None]
[Die Another Day] [2-Disc Ultimate Version]
[Golden Eye] [Special Edition]
[Tomorrow Never Dies] [None]
[Tomorrow Never Dies] [Special Edition]
```

You've now seen how to process single- and multiple-row returns from a `SELECT` statement. The next section shows you how to manage bulk `SELECT` operations.

Bulk Statement Processing

Bulk processing is often a better solution then row-by-row statements. You should use NDS for this behavior, not `dbms_sql`. The `BULK COLLECT INTO` clause would only work in the context of a PL/SQL block. The `dbms_sql` binding process isn't designed to support SQL statements inside anonymous blocks. If you attempt that type of unsupported work-around, you'll ultimately raise a `PLS-00497` error.

Dynamic Statements with Variable Inputs and Outputs

This section shows you how to implement placeholders that are inputs and how to work with a variable number of columns returned by a `SELECT` list. It demonstrates `dbms_sql` Method 4, which allows you to use a variable number of `IN` mode bind variables in SQL statements and return a variable number of columns from a `SELECT` statement.

To illustrate this for you, I've picked a feature from MySQL that doesn't exist in Oracle without a user-defined `vertical_query` function. This function takes a table or view name and a `WHERE` clause as formal parameters. It returns a vertical collection of column names and values for each row, and extends an example from Oracle's *Ask Tom* column (by Thomas Kyte) in November 2000.

Before defining the function, you need to create a `query_result` collection of strings. Since the base type is a scalar data type, the following is an Attribute Data Type (ADT).

```
SQL> CREATE OR REPLACE
       TYPE query_result AS TABLE OF VARCHAR2(77);
     /
```

The `vertical_query` function is complex and unfortunately long, but it's a rock-solid example of the `dbms_sql` package's Method 4:

```
SQL> CREATE OR REPLACE FUNCTION vertical_query
     ( table_name VARCHAR2, where_clause VARCHAR2 ) RETURN query_result IS

       /* Open a cursor for a query against all columns in a table. */
       base_stmt INTEGER := dbms_sql.open_cursor;

       /* Open a cursor for a dynamically constructed query, which excludes
          any non-displayable columns with text. */
       stmt      INTEGER := dbms_sql.open_cursor;

       /* Declare local variables, assumes MAX_STRING_LENGTH is STANDARD. */
```

```
  colValue   VARCHAR2(4000);       -- Maximum string length for column values.
  STATUS     INTEGER;              -- Acknowledgement of DBMS_SQL.EXECUTE
  tableDesc dbms_sql.desc_tab2;  -- Hold metadata for the queries.
  colCount   NUMBER;               -- Variable for the column count.
  rowIndex   NUMBER := 0;          -- Row number retrieved from the cursor
  colLength NUMBER := 0;           -- Length of the longest column name

  /* Declare local variable for the dynamically constructed query. */
  dynamic_stmt VARCHAR2(4000) := 'SELECT ';

  /* Declare an index for the return collection. */
  rsIndex NUMBER := 0;

  /* Declare a collection variable and instantiate the collection. */
  result_set QUERY_RESULT := query_result();

  /* Declare an exception for a bad table name, raised by a call to
     the dbms_assert.qualified_sql_name function. */
  table_name_error EXCEPTION;
  PRAGMA EXCEPTION_INIT(table_name_error, -942);

  /* Declare exception handlers for bad WHERE clause statements.
     ------------------------------------------------------------
     Declare an exception for a missing WHERE keyword. */
  missing_keyword EXCEPTION;
  PRAGMA EXCEPTION_INIT(missing_keyword, -933);

  /* Declare an exception for a bad relational operator. */
  invalid_relational_operator EXCEPTION;
  PRAGMA EXCEPTION_INIT(invalid_relational_operator, -920);

  /* Declare an exception for a bad column name. */
  invalid_identifier EXCEPTION;
  PRAGMA EXCEPTION_INIT(invalid_identifier, -904);

  /* Declare an exception for a missing backquoted apostrophe. */
  misquoted_string EXCEPTION;
  PRAGMA EXCEPTION_INIT(misquoted_string, -1756);

  /* ---------------------------------------------------------- */

  /* Declare a function that replaces non-displayable values. */
  FUNCTION check_column( p_name   VARCHAR2
                       , p_type   NUMBER ) RETURN VARCHAR2 IS

    /* Return column name or literal value. */
    retval VARCHAR2(30);

  BEGIN

    /* Find strings, numbers, et cetera and replace non-display values. */
```

```
    IF p_type IN (1,2,8,9,12,69,96,100,101,112,178,179,180,181,231) THEN

      /* Assign the column name for a displayable column value. */
      retval := p_name;

    ELSE

      /* Re-assign string literals for column names where values aren't
         displayable. */
      SELECT DECODE(p_type, 23,'''RAW not displayable.'''
                          ,105,'''MLSLABEL not displayable.'''
                          ,106,'''MLSLABEL not displayable.'''
                          ,113,'''BLOB not displayable.'''
                          ,114,'''BFILE not displayable.'''
                          ,115,'''CFILE not displayable.'''
                          ,'''UNDEFINED not displayable.''')
      INTO retval
      FROM dual;

    END IF;

    -- Return the column name or an apostrophe delimited string literal.
    RETURN retval;
  END check_column;

  /* ------------------------------------------------------- */

BEGIN

    /* Prepare unfiltered display cursor. */
    dbms_sql.parse( base_stmt
                  ,'SELECT * FROM'||CHR(10)
                  ||dbms_assert.simple_sql_name(TABLE_NAME)||CHR(10)
                  ||where_clause, dbms_sql.native);

  /* Describe the table structure:
  || --------------------------------------------------------
  ||  1. Store metadata in tableDesc
  ||  2. Store the number of columns in colCount
  || -------------------------------------------------------- */
  dbms_sql.describe_columns2(base_stmt, colCount, tableDesc);

  -- Define individual columns and assign value to colValue variable.
  FOR i IN 1..colCount LOOP

    -- Define columns for each column returned into tableDesc.
    dbms_sql.define_column(base_stmt, i, colValue, 4000);

    -- Find the length of the longest column name.
    IF LENGTH(tableDesc(i).col_name) > colLength THEN
      colLength := LENGTH(tableDesc(i).col_name);
```

```
  END IF;

  -- Replace non-displayable column values with displayable values.
  IF i < colCount THEN
    dynamic_stmt := dynamic_stmt
                 || check_column(tableDesc(i).col_name
                                ,tableDesc(i).col_type) || ' AS '
                 || tableDesc(i).col_name || ', ';
  ELSE
    dynamic_stmt := dynamic_stmt
                 || check_column(tableDesc(i).col_name
                                ,tableDesc(i).col_type) || ' AS '
                 || tableDesc(i).col_name ||CHR(10)
                 ||'FROM '|| dbms_assert.simple_sql_name(TABLE_NAME)
                 || CHR(10) || where_clause;
  END IF;

END LOOP;

/* Provide conditional debugging instruction. */
$IF $$DEBUG = 1 $THEN
   dbms_output.put_line(dynamic_stmt);
$END

/* Prepare unfiltered display cursor. */
dbms_sql.parse(stmt, dynamic_stmt, dbms_sql.native);

/* Describe the table structure:
|| ------------------------------------------------------------
||  1. Store metadata in tableDesc (reuse of existing variable)
||  2. Store the number of columns in colCount
|| ------------------------------------------------------------ */
dbms_sql.describe_columns2(stmt, colCount, tableDesc);

/* Define individual columns and assign value to colValue variable. */
FOR i IN 1..colCount LOOP
  dbms_sql.define_column(stmt, i, colValue, 4000);
END LOOP;

/* Execute the dynamic cursor. */
STATUS := dbms_sql.EXECUTE(stmt);

/* Fetch the results, row-by-row. */
WHILE dbms_sql.fetch_rows(stmt) > 0 LOOP

  /* Reset row counter for output display purposes. */
  rowIndex := rowIndex + 1;

  /* Increment the counter for the collection and extend space. */
  rsIndex := rsIndex + 1;
  result_set.EXTEND;
```

```
    result_set(rsIndex) := '******************************** '
                        || rowIndex
                        || '. row ********************************';

    /* For each column, print left-aligned column names and values. */
    FOR i IN 1..colCount LOOP

      /* Increment the counter for the collection and extend space. */
      rsIndex := rsIndex + 1;
      result_set.EXTEND;

      /* Limit display of long text. */
      IF tableDesc(i).col_type IN (1,9,96,112) THEN
        /* Display 40 character substrings of long text. */
        dbms_sql.column_value(stmt, i, colValue);
        result_set(rsIndex) := RPAD(tableDesc(i).col_name, colLength,' ')
                            || ' : ' || SUBSTR(colValue, 1,40);
       ELSE
         /* Display full value as character string. */
         dbms_sql.column_value(stmt, i, colValue);
         result_set(rsIndex) := RPAD(tableDesc(i).col_name, colLength,' ')
                             || ' : ' || colValue;
      END IF;
    END LOOP;
  END LOOP;

  /* Increment the counter for the collection and extend space. */
  FOR i IN 1..3 LOOP
    rsIndex := rsIndex + 1;
    result_set.EXTEND;

    CASE i
      WHEN 1 THEN
        result_set(rsIndex) := '************************************'
                            || '************************************';
      WHEN 2 THEN
        result_set(rsIndex) := CHR(10);
      WHEN 3 THEN
        result_set(rsIndex) := rowIndex || ' rows in set';
    END CASE;
  END LOOP;

  /* Return collection. */
  RETURN result_set;
EXCEPTION
  /* Customer error handlers, add specialized text or collapse into one. */
  WHEN table_name_error THEN
    dbms_output.put_line(SQLERRM);
  WHEN invalid_relational_operator THEN
    dbms_output.put_line(SQLERRM);
  WHEN invalid_identifier THEN
    dbms_output.put_line(SQLERRM);
```

```
    WHEN missing_keyword THEN
      dbms_output.put_line(SQLERRM);
    WHEN misquoted_string THEN
      dbms_output.put_line(SQLERRM);
    WHEN OTHERS THEN
      dbms_output.put_line(SQLERRM);
END;
/
```

You can run the function with the following syntax (`column_value` is the standard name returned from a scalar schema-level collection):

```
SQL> SELECT column_value
  2  FROM   TABLE(vertical_query('ITEM','WHERE item_title LIKE ''Star%'''));
```

It produces output like the following:

```
******************************** 1. ROW ********************************
ITEM_ID                : 1002
ITEM_BARCODE           : 24543-02392
ITEM_TYPE              : 1011
ITEM_TITLE             : Star Wars I
ITEM_SUBTITLE          : Phantom Menace
ITEM_RATING            : PG
  ...
******************************** 2. ROW ********************************
ITEM_ID                : 1003
ITEM_BARCODE           : 24543-5615
ITEM_TYPE              : 1010
ITEM_TITLE             : Star Wars II
ITEM_SUBTITLE          : Attack OF the Clones
ITEM_RATING            : PG
  ...
************************************************************************
```

This section has shown you how to implement `dbms_sql`'s Method 4 with an unknown number of inputs and outputs until runtime.

DBMS_SQL Package Definition

The `dbms_sql` package has been in the product since Oracle 7. Changes and fixes have made it a very stable and robust component in the database. It is popular notwithstanding the release of NDS in Oracle 9*i*. In Oracle Database 12*c*, the only thing you can't do in NDS is work with statements that have an unknown set of columns at runtime. The `dbms_sql` package lets you manage these statements.

This section covers the constants, variables, functions, and procedures found in the `dbms_sql` package. You can go to the appropriate subsection to check component definitions.

DBMS_SQL Constants

The `dbms_sql` package has three constants, all of which are designed to support the `dbms_sql.parse` procedure. Table 13-3 defines the constants. As noted, you should use only the `NATIVE` constant from Oracle 8*i* Database forward.

Constant Name	Description	Value
NATIVE	You should use only the NATIVE constant from Oracle 8*i* Database forward. It is an INTEGER data type and indicates the parsing language.	1
V6	You shouldn't use the V6 constant any more.	0
V7	You should use the V7 constant only if you're running the desupported Oracle 7 Database release.	2

TABLE 13-3. *DBMS_SQL Available Constants*

DBMS_SQL Data Types

The dbms_sql package supports associative arrays (*the old PL/SQL tables*) that are indexed by binary integers for the following base scalar types: BFILE, BINARY_DOUBLE, BLOB, CLOB, DATE, INTERVAL_DAY_TO_SECOND, INTERVAL_YEAR_TO_MONTH, NUMBER, TIME, TIMESTAMP, TIMESTAMP_WITH_LTZ, and UROWID. These associative array data types use a naming pattern of <*scalar_type*>_TABLE. They are designated as Data Structures in the *Oracle Database PL/SQL Packages and Types Reference 12*c *Release*.

A dbms_sql.varchar2_table table type is also described in the same reference as a general type. It behaves consistently with the bulk data types.

The dbms_sql package also supports three record types:

- desc_rec supports the describe_columns procedure. The procedure uses it to describe columns for a cursor opened and parsed by the dbms_sql package.

```
TYPE desc_rec IS RECORD ( col_type            BINARY_INTEGER := 0
,                         col_max_len         BINARY_INTEGER := 0
,                         col_name            VARCHAR2(32)   := ''
,                         col_name_len        BINARY_INTEGER := 0
,                         col_schema_name     VARCHAR2(32)   := ''
,                         col_schema_name_len BINARY_INTEGER := 0
,                         col_precision       BINARY_INTEGER := 0
,                         col_scale           BINARY_INTEGER := 0
,                         col_charsetid       BINARY_INTEGER := 0
,                         col_charsetform     BINARY_INTEGER := 0
,                         col_null_ok         BOOLEAN        := TRUE);
```

- desc_rec2 supports the describe_columns2 procedure. The procedure uses it to describe columns for a cursor opened and parsed by the dbms_sql package.

```
TYPE desc_rec2 IS RECORD ( col_type            BINARY_INTEGER := 0
,                          col_max_len         BINARY_INTEGER := 0
,                          col_name            VARCHAR2(32767):= ''
,                          col_name_len        BINARY_INTEGER := 0
,                          col_schema_name     VARCHAR2(32)   := ''
,                          col_schema_name_len BINARY_INTEGER := 0
,                          col_precision       BINARY_INTEGER := 0
,                          col_scale           BINARY_INTEGER := 0
,                          col_charsetid       BINARY_INTEGER := 0
,                          col_charsetform     BINARY_INTEGER := 0
,                          col_null_ok         BOOLEAN        := TRUE);
```

- `desc_rec3` supports the `describe_columns3` procedure. The procedure uses it to describe columns for a cursor opened and parsed by the `dbms_sql` package.

```
TYPE desc_rec3 IS RECORD ( col_type            BINARY_INTEGER := 0
,                          col_max_len         BINARY_INTEGER := 0
,                          col_name            VARCHAR2(32767):= ''
,                          col_name_len        BINARY_INTEGER := 0
,                          col_schema_name     VARCHAR2(32)   := ''
,                          col_schema_name_len BINARY_INTEGER := 0
,                          col_precision       BINARY_INTEGER := 0
,                          col_scale           BINARY_INTEGER := 0
,                          col_charsetid       BINARY_INTEGER := 0
,                          col_charsetform     BINARY_INTEGER := 0
,                          col_null_ok         BOOLEAN        := TRUE
,                          col_type_name       VARCHAR2(32)   := ''
,                          col_type_name_len   BINARY_INTEGER := 0);
```

There are also associative arrays for each of the record types. These record structures and associative arrays are used for Method 4 processing, which involves an unknown set of columns at compile time.

DBMS_SQL Functions and Procedures

The functions and procedures of the `dbms_sql` package have endured over the years. They are still widely used, while virtually everything can run through NDS. Some of the customer reasoning for their continued use is related to backward compatibility or coding standards that try to keep things the same. Clearly, Oracle Database 12*c* continues the trend toward deprecating the `dbms_sql` package somewhere in the future.

Whether you need them for maintenance or want to replace them with NDS, the following synopses should help you quickly check the functions and procedures of the `dbms_sql` package. If you run into permission issues, check the sidebar "DBMS_SQL Grants and Privileges" earlier in this chapter.

BIND_ARRAY Procedure The `bind_array` procedure supports bulk DML operations. The procedure binds a nested table collection into a SQL statement. You can choose a collection from a list of base SQL data types. It is an overloaded procedure. There are two types of signatures, and all parameters use an `IN` mode of operation.

Prototype 1

```
bind_array( cursor_number NUMBER
          , column_name   VARCHAR2
          , collection    <datatype_list> )
```

Prototype 2

```
bind_array( cursor_number NUMBER
          , column_name   VARCHAR2
          , collection    <datatype_list>
          , index1        NUMBER
          , index2        NUMBER )
```

The collection is an associative array, indexed by a BINARY_INTEGER. You can choose the base scalar variable from: BFILE, BLOB, CLOB, DATE, NUMBER, ROWID, TIME, TIMESTAMP, TIME WITH TIME ZONE, or VARCHAR2. This function also supports table and varray collections and user-defined object types through the OCI libraries.

BIND_VARIABLE Procedure The bind_variable procedure supports row-by-row DML operations. The function binds a wide variety of data types into a SQL statement. It is an overloaded procedure with two principal types of signature. One signature take three parameters and the variable_value parameter can be any of the valid datatype_list scalar or composite variables. All parameters in this signature use an IN mode of operation. The other signature takes four parameters and only works with a VARCHAR2 variable_value. The out_value_size parameter is an IN OUT mode, and returns the size of the bound variable.

Prototype 1

```
bind_variable( cursor_number   NUMBER
             , column_name     VARCHAR2
             , variable_value  <datatype_list> )
```

Prototype 2

```
bind_variable( cursor_number   NUMBER
             , column_name     VARCHAR2
          , variable_value     VARCHAR2
          , out_value_size     NUMBER )
```

The datatype_list includes any of these SQL scalar data types: BFILE, BINARY_DOUBLE, BINARY_FLOAT, BLOB, CLOB, DATE, INTERVAL YEAR TO MONTH, INTERVAL YEAR TO SECOND, NUMBER, REF OF STANDARD, ROWID, TIME, TIME WITH TIME ZONE, TIMESTAMP, TIMESTAMP WITH TIME ZONE, or VARCHAR2. The datatype_list also includes an Attribute Data Type (ADT), varray, table, or opaque collection.

BIND_VARIABLE_CHAR Procedure The bind_variable_char procedure supports row-by-row DML operations. The function binds a CHAR data type into a SQL statement. It is an overloaded procedure with two signatures, and all parameters use an IN mode of operation.

Prototype 1

```
bind_variable_char( cursor_number  NUMBER
                  , column_name    VARCHAR2
                  , variable_value CHAR )
```

Prototype 2

```
bind_variable_char( cursor_number  NUMBER
                  , column_name    VARCHAR2
                  , variable_value CHAR
                  , out_value_size NUMBER )
```

The out_value_size parameter captures the size of the CHAR variable_value parameter.

BIND_VARIABLE_RAW Procedure The bind_variable_raw procedure supports row-by-row DML operations. The function binds a RAW data type into a SQL statement. It is an overloaded procedure with two signatures, and all parameters use an IN mode of operation.

Prototype 1

```
bind_variable_raw( cursor_number  NUMBER
                 , column_name    VARCHAR2
                 , variable_value RAW )
```

Prototype 2

```
bind_variable_raw( cursor_number  NUMBER
                 , column_name    VARCHAR2
                 , variable_value RAW
                 , out_value_size NUMBER )
```

The out_value_size parameter captures the size of the RAW variable_value parameter.

BIND_VARIABLE_ROWID Procedure The bind_variable_rowid procedure supports row-by-row DML operations. The function binds a ROWID data type into a SQL statement. It is not an overloaded procedure, with a single signature, and all parameters use an IN mode of operation.

Prototype

```
bind_variable_rowid( cursor_number  NUMBER
                   , column_name    VARCHAR2
                   , variable_value ROWID )
```

CLOSE_CURSOR Procedure The close_cursor procedure closes an open dbms_sql cursor. The cursor number is passed by reference as an IN OUT mode variable.

Prototype

```
close_cursor( cursor_number  NUMBER )
```

COLUMN_VALUE Procedure The column_value procedure supports bulk and row-by-row queries. The function binds the output from a SELECT statement into an OUT mode variable. The variable can be a scalar variable or a nested table of a scalar variable. The cursor_name and position are IN mode variables. On the other hand, the variable_value or collection_value, column_error, and actual_length parameters are OUT mode variables. The procedure has three overloaded signatures.

Prototype 1

```
column_value( cursor_number    NUMBER
            , position         NUMBER
            , variable_value   <datatype_list> )
```

Prototype 2

```
column_value( cursor_number      NUMBER
            , position           NUMBER
            , collection_value   <datatype_list> )
```

Prototype 3

```
column_value( cursor_number      NUMBER
            , position           NUMBER
            , collection_value   <datatype_list>
            , column_error       NUMBER
            , actual_length      NUMBER )
```

The data type can be an ADT (*scalar collection)* or UDT (*associative array*) variable of any of these SQL data types: BFILE, BLOB, CLOB, DATE, NUMBER, ROWID, TIME, TIMESTAMP, TIME WITH TIME ZONE, or VARCHAR2.

The prototype signature five parameters are restricted to an *associative array* of a DATE, NUMBER, or VARCHAR2 scalar data type. This function also supports *associative arrays, table collections, varray collections,* and user-defined object types through the OCI libraries.

COLUMN_VALUE_CHAR Procedure The column_value_char procedure supports row-by-row SELECT statements. The function binds the output from a SELECT statement for a CHAR column into an OUT mode variable. It is an overloaded procedure, and it has two signatures.

Prototype 1

```
column_value_char( cursor_number  NUMBER
                 , position       NUMBER
                 , variable_value CHAR )
```

Prototype 2

```
column_value_char( cursor_number  NUMBER
                 , position       NUMBER
                 , variable_value CHAR
                 , column_error   NUMBER
                 , actual_length  NUMBER )
```

COLUMN_VALUE_LONG Procedure The column_value_long procedure supports row-by-row queries. The function binds the output from a SELECT statement for a LONG column into an OUT mode variable. It is not an overloaded procedure, and it has one signature.

Prototype

```
column_value_long( cursor_number   IN     NUMBER
                 , position        IN     NUMBER
                 , variable_value  IN     LONG
                 , value              OUT VARCHAR2
                 , value_length       OUT NUMBER )
```

COLUMN_VALUE_RAW Procedure The `column_value_raw` procedure supports row-by-row queries. The function binds the output from a `SELECT` statement for a `RAW` column into an `OUT` mode variable. It is an overloaded procedure, and it has two signatures.

Prototype 1

```
column_value_raw( cursor_number    NUMBER
                , position         NUMBER
                , variable_value   RAW )
```

Prototype 2

```
column_value_raw( cursor_number    NUMBER
                , position         NUMBER
                , variable_value   RAW
                , column_error     NUMBER
                , actual_length    NUMBER )
```

COLUMN_VALUE_ROWID Procedure The `column_value_rowid` procedure supports row-by-row queries. The function binds the output from a `SELECT` statement for a `ROWID` column into an `OUT` mode variable. It is an overloaded procedure, and it has two signatures.

Prototype 1

```
column_value_rowid( cursor_number    NUMBER
                  , position         NUMBER
                  , variable_value   ROWID )
```

Prototype 2

```
column_value_rowid( cursor_number  NUMBER
                  , position       NUMBER
                  , variable_value ROWID
                  , column_error   NUMBER
                  , actual_length  NUMBER )
```

DEFINE_ARRAY Procedure The `define_array` procedure supports bulk queries. The function defines (or maps) a nested table to columns of a `SELECT` statement. You must use this before calling the `column_value` procedure. It is an overloaded procedure, and it has one type of signature.

Prototype

```
define_array( cursor_number  NUMBER
            , position       NUMBER
            , collection     <datatype_list>
            , count          NUMBER
            , lower_bound    NUMBER )
```

The `count` parameter sets the maximum number of elements returned. The `lower_bound` parameter sets the starting point, which is typically 1.

The data type can be an *associative array* variable of any of these SQL data types: `BFILE`, `BLOB`, `CLOB`, `DATE`, `NUMBER`, `ROWID`, `TIME`, `TIMESTAMP`, `TIME WITH TIME ZONE`, or `VARCHAR2`.

DEFINE_COLUMN Procedure The `define_column` procedure supports row-by-row queries. The function defines (or maps) column values to columns of a `SELECT` statement. You must use this before calling the `column_value` procedure. It is an overloaded procedure, and it has one type of signature.

Prototype

```
define_column( cursor_number   NUMBER
             , position        NUMBER
             , variable_value  <datatype_list> )
```

The data type can be a *scalar* variable of any of these SQL data types: `BFILE`, `BLOB`, `CLOB`, `DATE`, `NUMBER`, `ROWID`, `TIME`, `TIMESTAMP`, `TIME WITH TIME ZONE`, or `VARCHAR2`.

DEFINE_COLUMN_CHAR Procedure The `define_column_char` procedure supports row-by-row queries. The function defines (or maps) column values to columns of a `SELECT` statement. You must use this before calling the `column_value` procedure. It is not an overloaded procedure, and it has one signature.

Prototype

```
define_column_char( cursor_number  NUMBER
                  , position       NUMBER
                  , variable_value CHAR )
```

DEFINE_COLUMN_LONG Procedure The `define_column_long` procedure supports row-by-row queries. The function defines (or maps) column values to columns of a `SELECT` statement. You must use this before calling the `column_value` procedure. It is not an overloaded procedure, and it has one signature.

Prototype

```
define_column_long( cursor_number   NUMBER
                  , position        NUMBER
                  , variable_value  LONG )
```

DEFINE_COLUMN_RAW Procedure The `define_column_raw` procedure supports row-by-row queries. The function defines (or maps) column values to columns of a `SELECT` statement. You must use this before calling the `column_value` procedure. It is not an overloaded procedure, and it has one signature.

Prototype

```
define_column_raw( cursor_number   NUMBER
                 , position        NUMBER
                 , variable_value  RAW )
```

DEFINE_COLUMN_ROWID Procedure The `define_column_rowid` procedure supports row-by-row queries. The function defines (or maps) column values to columns of a `SELECT` statement. You must use this before calling the `column_value` procedure. It is not an overloaded procedure, and it has one signature.

Prototype

```
define_column_rowid( cursor_number   NUMBER
                   , position        NUMBER
                   , variable_value  ROWID )
```

DESCRIBE_COLUMNS Procedure The `describe_columns` procedure supports bulk and row-by-row queries and DML operations. The function describes columns for a cursor opened and parsed by the `dbms_sql` package. It only works with column names that are 30 characters or smaller in Oracle Database 10*g* but works with 32-character column names in Oracle Database 12*c*. It is not an overloaded procedure, and it has one signature.

Prototype

```
describe_columns( cursor_number      NUMBER
                , column_count       NUMBER
                , record_collection  DBMS_SQL.DESC_TAB )
```

The `dbms_sql.desc_tab` data type is an associative array of the `dbms_sql.desc_rec` record type. The `desc_rec` record type contains the metadata about the column values. The information is a subset of what you would find in the `USER_TABLES` view.

DESCRIBE_COLUMNS2 Procedure The `describe_columns2` procedure supports bulk and row-by-row queries and DML operations. The function describes columns for a cursor opened and parsed by the `dbms_sql` package. It only works with column names that are up to 32,767 bytes in length from Oracle Database 10*g* forward. It is not an overloaded procedure, and it has one signature.

Prototype

```
describe_columns2( cursor_number     NUMBER
                 , column_count      NUMBER
                 , record_collection DBMS_SQL.DESC_TAB2 )
```

The `dbms_sql.desc_tab2` data type is an associative array of the `dbms_sql.desc_rec2` record data type. The `desc_rec2` record data type contains the same metadata about the column values as `desc_rec` but allows for a larger column name. The information is a subset of what you would find in the `USER_TABLES` view.

DESCRIBE_COLUMNS3 Procedure The `describe_columns3` procedure supports bulk and row-by-row queries and DML operations. The function describes columns for a cursor opened and parsed by the `dbms_sql` package. It only works with column names that are up to 32,767 bytes in length from Oracle Database 10*g* forward. It is not an overloaded procedure, and it has one signature.

Prototype

```
describe_columns3( cursor_number     NUMBER
                 , column_count      NUMBER
                 , record_collection DBMS_SQL.DESC_TAB3 )
```

The dbms_sql.desc_tab3 data type is an associative array of the dbms_sql.desc_rec3 record data type. The desc_rec3 record data type contains the same metadata about the column values as desc_rec2, plus it adds the data type name and name length to the record structure. The information is a broader subset of what you would find in the USER_TABLES view.

EXECUTE Function The execute function runs the statement associated with an open dbms_sql cursor. It returns the number of rows touched by DML statements. You should ignore the return value when it runs a DDL statement because it is a meaningless value (*technically, an undefined value*). This function is not overloaded, and it has one signature. The parameter uses an IN mode of operation.

Prototype

```
execute( cursor_number  NUMBER ) RETURN NUMBER
```

EXECUTE_AND_FETCH Function The execute_and_fetch function runs the statement associated with an open dbms_sql cursor and fetches one or more rows from a cursor. The function is more or less like running the execute and fetch_rows functions in tandem. The function returns the number of rows touched by DML statements. You should ignore the return value when it runs a DDL statement because it is a meaningless value (*technically, an undefined value*).

The optional exact_fetch parameter is false by default, which lets you return more than one row. You can return only one row when you override the default value of the exact_fetch parameter. Oracle 7 forward does not support an exact_fetch option for LONG data type columns.

The function is not overloaded. It also has one signature. The parameter uses an IN mode of operation.

Prototype

```
execute_and_fetch( cursor_number  NUMBER
                 , exact_fetch    BOOLEAN DEFAULT FALSE ) RETURN NUMBER
```

FETCH_ROWS Function The fetch_rows function fetches a row or set of rows from a given cursor. You can run the fetch_rows function until all rows are read. The column_value function reads the fetched row or set of rows into a local variable. The local variable can be a *scalar* or *nested table* data type. The cursor number is passed by using an IN mode of operation. The fetch_rows function returns the number of rows fetched, or a –1. The latter means that all rows have been read.

Prototype

```
fetch_rows( cursor_number  NUMBER ) RETURN NUMBER
```

IS_OPEN Function The is_open function checks whether a cursor is open. It returns true when the cursor is open and false when it's not. The function is not overloaded. It also has one signature. The parameter uses an IN mode of operation.

Prototype

```
is_open( cursor_number  NUMBER ) RETURN BOOLEAN
```

LAST_ERROR_POSITION Function The `last_error_position` function returns the byte offset in a SQL statement text where an error occurred. Unlike other things that start with a 1, this checks the string with the first position being 0. You must call this function after the `PARSE` call but before any execution function call.

Prototype

```
last_error_position RETURN NUMBER
```

LAST_ROW_COUNT Function The `last_row_count` function returns the cumulative number of rows fetched from a query. You get the cumulative number when you call the `last_row_count` function after an `execute_and_fetch` or `fetch_rows` call. If you call this function after an `execute` function, you get 0.

Prototype

```
last_row_count RETURN NUMBER
```

LAST_ROW_ID Function The `last_row_id` function returns the `ROWID` value of the last row fetched from a query. You get the `ROWID` when you call the `last_row_id` function after an `execute_and_fetch` or `fetch_rows` call.

Prototype

```
last_row_id RETURN ROWID
```

LAST_SQL_FUNCTION_CODE Function The `last_sql_function_code` function returns SQL function code for the statement. You can find these codes in the *Oracle Call Interface Programmer's Guide 12*c *Release*. This must be called immediately after you run the SQL statement, or the return value is undefined.

Prototype

```
last_sql_function_code RETURN INTEGER
```

OPEN_CURSOR Function The `open_cursor` function opens a cursor in the database, and returns the cursor's number. You must call the `close_cursor` function to close the cursor and release the resource.

Prototype

```
open_cursor RETURN INTEGER
```

PARSE Procedure The `parse` procedure parses a given statement string. All statements are parsed immediately. DML statements queue on a call to `execute` or `execute_and_fetch` functions. DDL statements are run immediately after they're successfully parsed. It is an overloaded procedure, and it has ten types of signatures. Recent changes in Oracle Database 11*g*, Release 2 and Oracle Database 12*c* add overloaded methods to accommodate editioning and pluggable databases.

Prototype 1

```
parse( cursor_number  NUMBER
     , statement      {CLOB | VARCHAR2}
     , language_flag  NUMBER )
```

Prototype 2

```
parse( cursor_number  NUMBER
     , statement      {CLOB | VARCHAR2}
     , language_flag  NUMBER
     , edition        VARCHAR2 )
```

Prototype 3

```
parse( cursor_number  NUMBER
     , statement      {VARCHAR2S | VARCHAR2A}
     , language_flag  NUMBER
     , lower_bound    NUMBER
     , upper_bound    NUMBER
     , language_flag  NUMBER )
```

Prototype 3

```
parse( cursor_number                NUMBER
     , statement                    {VARCHAR2S | VARCHAR2A}
     , language_flag                NUMBER
     , edition                      VARCHAR2
     , apply_crossedition_trigger   NUMBER
     , fire_apply_trigger           NUMBER )
```

Prototype 5

```
parse( cursor_number  NUMBER
     , statement      {VARCHAR2S | VARCHAR2A}
     , language_flag  NUMBER
     , lower_bound    NUMBER
     , upper_bound    NUMBER
     , language_flag  NUMBER
     , edition        VARCHAR2 )
```

Prototype 6

```
parse( cursor_number                NUMBER
     , statement                    {CLOB | VARCHAR2 }
     , language_flag                NUMBER
     , edition                      VARCHAR2
     , apply_crossedition_trigger   VARCHAR2
     , fire_apply_trigger           BOOLEAN
     , schema                       VARCHAR2 )
```

Prototype 7

```
parse( cursor_number                    NUMBER
     , statement                       {VARCHAR2S | VARCHAR2A}
     , language_flag                    NUMBER
     , lower_bound                      NUMBER
     , upper_bound                      NUMBER
     , language_flag                    NUMBER
     , edition                          VARCHAR2
     , apply_crossedition_trigger       VARCHAR2
     , fire_apply_trigger               BOOLEAN )
```

Prototype 8

```
parse( cursor_number                    NUMBER
     , statement                       {VARCHAR2S | VARCHAR2A}
     , language_flag                    NUMBER
     , lower_bound                      NUMBER
     , upper_bound                      NUMBER
     , language_flag                    NUMBER
     , edition                          VARCHAR2
     , apply_crossedition_trigger       VARCHAR2
     , fire_apply_trigger               BOOLEAN
     , schema                           VARCHAR2 )
```

Prototype 9

```
parse( cursor_number                   NUMBER
     , statement                      {CLOB | VARCHAR2}
     , language_flag                   NUMBER
     , edition                         VARCHAR2
     , apply_crossedition_trigger      VARCHAR2
     , fire_apply_trigger              BOOLEAN
     , schema                          VARCHAR2
     , container                       VARCHAR2 )
```

Prototype 10

```
parse( cursor_number                    NUMBER
     , statement                       {VARCHAR2S | VARCHAR2A}
     , language_flag                    NUMBER
     , lower_bound                      NUMBER
     , upper_bound                      NUMBER
     , language_flag                    NUMBER
     , edition                          VARCHAR2
     , apply_crossedition_trigger       VARCHAR2
     , fire_apply_trigger               BOOLEAN
     , schema                           VARCHAR2
     , container                        VARCHAR2 )
```

The VARCHAR2S data type is a nested table collection of 256-byte strings. The VARCHAR2A data type is a nested table collection of 32,767-byte strings.

TO_CURSOR_NUMBER Function The `to_cursor_number` function converts an NDS cursor to a `dbms_sql` cursor. It can be useful when you open a cursor of indefinite columns and want to process it by using the `dbms_sql` package. It takes a single `IN` mode cursor reference, and it returns a generic reference cursor.

Prototype

```
to_cursor_number( reference_cursor REF CURSOR ) RETURNS NUMBER
```

TO_REFCURSOR Function The `to_refcursor` function converts a `dbms_sql` cursor number to an NDS reference cursor. It can be useful when you open a cursor in `dbms_sql` and want to process it by using NDS. It takes a single `IN` mode cursor number, and it returns a cursor number.

Prototype

```
to_refcursor( cursor_number NUMBER ) RETURNS REF CURSOR
```

VARIABLE_VALUE Procedure The `variable_value` procedure supports bulk and row-by-row DML operations. It is used to transfer a variety of data type results back through a `RETURNING INTO` clause. The function binds a wide variety of data types into a SQL statement. It is an overloaded procedure with a single type of signature. The cursor and column name are passed by value as `IN` mode operations. The variable value is returned because it is passed as an `OUT` mode variable.

Prototype

```
variable_value( cursor_number  NUMBER
              , column_name    VARCHAR2
              , variable_value <datatype_list> )
```

The data type list includes *scalar* or *associative arrays* of scalar variables. You can use any of the following scalar data types: `BFILE`, `BINARY_DOUBLE`, `BINARY_FLOAT`, `BLOB`, `CLOB`, `DATE`, `INTERVAL YEAR TO MONTH`, `INTERVAL YEAR TO SECOND`, `NUMBER`, `REF OF STANDARD`, `ROWID`, `TIME`, `TIMESTAMP`, `TIMESTAMP WITH TIME ZONE`, `TIME WITH TIME ZONE`, or `VARCHAR2`. This function also supports associate arrays (PL/SQL tables), varrays, and user-defined object types through the OCI libraries.

VARIABLE_VALUE_CHAR Procedure The `variable_value_char` procedure supports row-by-row DML operations. It is used to transfer `CHAR` data type results back through a `RETURNING INTO` clause. It is an overloaded procedure with two signatures. The cursor and column name are passed by value as `IN` mode operations. The variable value is returned because it is passed as an `OUT` mode variable.

Prototype

```
variable_value_char( cursor_number  NUMBER
                   , column_name    VARCHAR2
                   , variable_value CHAR )
```

VARIABLE_VALUE_RAW Procedure The variable_value_raw procedure supports row-by-row DML operations. It is used to transfer CHAR data type results back through a RETURNING INTO clause. It is an overloaded procedure with two signatures. The cursor and column name are passed by value as IN mode operations. The variable value is returned because it is passed as an OUT mode variable.

Prototype

```
variable_value_raw( cursor_number  NUMBER
                  , column_name    VARCHAR2
                  , variable_value RAW )
```

VARIABLE_VALUE_ROWID Procedure The variable_value_rowid procedure supports row-by-row DML operations. It is used to transfer CHAR data type results back through a RETURNING INTO clause. It is an overloaded procedure with two signatures. The cursor and column name are passed by value as IN mode operations. The variable value is returned because it is passed as an OUT mode variable.

Prototype

```
variable_value_rowid( cursor_number  NUMBER
                    , column_name    VARCHAR2
                    , variable_value ROWID )
```

This section has reviewed the functions and procedures in the dbms_sql package. You should find most of them in the dbms_sql examples

Review Section

This section has described the following points about the dbms_sql package, which supports dynamic SQL statements:

- The dbms_sql package may require grants to access the dbms_sql and dbms_sys_sql packages.
- The dbms_sql package supports static SQL statements that process DDL and DML statements. These dynamic statements are known as Method 1.
- The dbms_sql package supports dynamic SQL statements that process DML statements with bind variables. These dynamic statements are known as Method 2.
- The dbms_sql package supports dynamic SQL statements with a set of known inputs and outputs. They process DML statements with bind variables and a RETURNING INTO clause. These dynamic statements are known as Method 3.
- The dbms_sql package supports dynamic SQL statements with a set of runtime-determined inputs and outputs. They process DML statements with bind variables and a RETURNING INTO clause. These dynamic statements are known as Method 4.
- The dbms_sql package supports converting LONG, LONG RAW, and RAW data types.

Supporting Scripts

This section describes programs placed on the McGraw-Hill Professional website to support this chapter.

- The `create_nds1.sql`, `create_nds2.sql`, `create_nds3.sql`, `create_nds4.sql`, `create_nds5.sql`, `create_nds6.sql`, and `create_nds7.sql` scripts support the "Native Dynamic SQL (NDS)" section of this chapter.
- The `create_dbms_sql1.sql`, `create_dbms_sql2.sql`, `create_dbms_sql3.sql`, `create_dbms_sql4.sql`, `create_dbms_sql5.sql`, and `create_dbms_sql7.sql` scripts support the "DBMS_SQL Package" section of this chapter.

Summary

This chapter has shown you how to leverage NDS and the `dbms_sql` package to create and execute dynamic SQL statements. You should now have a foundation on how you can use them in your PL/SQL applications.

Mastery Check

The mastery check is a series of true-or-false and multiple-choice questions that let you confirm how well you understand the material in the chapter. You may check Appendix I for answers to these questions.

True or False:

1. ___NDS supports dynamic DDL statements with bind variables.
2. ___NDS supports static DDL statements.
3. ___NDS supports dynamic DML statements with bind variables.
4. ___NDS supports dynamic `SELECT` statements with a known set of columns.
5. ___NDS supports dynamic PL/SQL anonymous blocks.
6. ___NDS supports string literals with an embedded colon (`:`).
7. ___NDS statements with an unknown number of inputs rely on the `dbms_sql` package.
8. ___Without NDS, you must explicitly use the `dbms_sql` package to open a cursor.
9. ___With an unknown set of dynamic inputs, you must parse, execute, and fetch results with functions and procedures found in the `dbms_sql` package.
10. ___You only need to define columns and bind variables to retrieve `SELECT`-list values from a dynamic query with the `dbms_sql` package.

Multiple Choice:

11. Which of the following are procedures in the `dbms_sql` package? (Multiple answers possible)
    - **A.** `bind_array`
    - **B.** `bind_variable`
    - **C.** `fetch_rows`
    - **D.** `is_open`
    - **E.** `parse`
12. Which of the following are functions in the `dbms_sql` package? (Multiple answers possible)
    - **A.** `bind_array`
    - **B.** `execute_and_fetch`
    - **C.** `fetch_rows`
    - **D.** `is_open`
    - **E.** `parse`
13. Which of the following are package constants? (Multiple answers possible)
    - **A.** The `NATIVE` constant
    - **B.** The `V6` constant
    - **C.** The `V7` constant
    - **D.** The `V8` constant
    - **E.** All of the above
14. Which of the following are `dbms_sql`-supported base scalar types for collections? (Multiple answers possible)
    - **A.** The `BLOB` data type
    - **B.** The `CLOB` data type
    - **C.** The `BINARY_DOUBLE` data type
    - **D.** The `BINARY_FLOAT` data type
    - **E.** The `TIMESTAMP` data type
15. Which of the following `dbms_sql` functions or procedures execute a query? (Multiple answers possible)
    - **A.** The `parse_and_execute` procedure
    - **B.** The `parse_and_execute` function
    - **C.** The `execute` function
    - **D.** The `execute_and_fetch` function
    - **E.** The `execute_fetch_all` function

PART III

Appendixes and Glossary

APPENDIX A

Oracle Database Primer

This appendix first introduces you to the general concepts of Oracle database architecture. It then describes how to start and stop both the database instance and the database listener, how to work with Oracle SQL*Plus and Oracle SQL Developer, and how to tune and trace SQL. If you are responsible for managing an Oracle database instance, learning these basic skills is critical if you don't already possess some experience as an Oracle database administrator (DBA).

This appendix covers the preceding material in the following sequence:

- Oracle database architecture
- Starting and stopping the Oracle Database 12*c* server
- Starting and stopping the Oracle listener
- Multiversion Concurrency Control
- Definer rights and invoker rights
- SQL interactive and batch processing
- Database administration
- SQL tuning
- SQL tracing

NOTE
For a general introduction to managing the Oracle Database product stack, check out Oracle Database 12c DBA Handbook, *by Bob Bryla (Oracle Press, 2014). In addition, Oracle's online document library offers step-by-step instructions on Oracle Database administration in the* Oracle Database 2 Day DBA 12*c manual, and provides in-depth treatment of Oracle Database administration in the* Oracle Database *Administrator's Guide 12c.*

This appendix assumes that you will read it sequentially, and thus each section may reference material introduced earlier. Naturally, you can skip forward to an area of interest if you already understand the earlier material.

Oracle Database Architecture

The Oracle Database 12*c* database is available in three editions:

- Oracle Database 12*c* Express Edition (XE), a free, limited version of the Standard Edition
- Oracle Database 12*c* Standard Edition (SE), the best-selling edition
- Oracle Database 12*c* Enterprise Edition (EE), the full-featured product

The most significant architectural change in Oracle Database 12*c* is that it divides the database into two parts, a container database (CDB) and one or more pluggable databases (PDBs). The data catalog includes references to the standard catalog, and adding PDBs synchronizes the data catalog through provisioning when using the Oracle Database Configuration Assistant (DBCA) utility.

You can explore the new information about the CDB with this query set:

```
COLUMN db_name    FORMAT A20
COLUMN cdb        FORMAT A3
COLUMN auth_id    FORMAT A10
COLUMN user_id    FORMAT A10
COLUMN container  FORMAT A10
SELECT   sys_context('userenv', 'db_name') AS db_name
,       (SELECT cdb FROM v$database) AS cdb
,        sys_context('userenv', 'authenticated_identity') AS auth_id
,        sys_context('userenv', 'current_user') AS user_id
,        NVL(sys_context('userenv', 'con_Name'), 'NON-CDB') AS container
FROM     dual;
```

It returns the following from a sample Oracle Database 12*c* installation:

```
DB_NAME              CDB AUTH_ID    USER_ID    CONTAINER
-------------------- --- ---------- ---------- ----------
orcl                 YES system     SYSTEM     CDB$ROOT
```

You can gain more insight into the PDBs with this query:

```
COLUMN RESTRICTED FORMAT A10
SELECT   v.name
,        v.open_mode
,        NVL(v.restricted, 'n/a') AS restricted
,        d.status
FROM     v$PDBs v INNER JOIN dba_pdbs d USING(guid)
ORDER BY v.create_scn;
```

It returns the following from a sample Oracle Database 12*c* installation:

```
NAME                           OPEN_MODE  RESTRICTED STATUS
------------------------------ ---------- ---------- -------------
PDB$SEED                       READ ONLY  NO         NORMAL
PDBORCL                        MOUNTED    n/a        NORMAL
```

All three editions of Oracle Database 12*c* contain all the standard relational database management system components, embedded Java, collection types, and PL/SQL runtime engine that set Oracle apart in the database industry. These components enable any of these Oracle database management systems to manage small to large data repositories and consistently access data requested concurrently by multiple users. Oracle Database 12*c* Enterprise Edition also includes many features that empower advanced context and object management.

The components of Oracle database management systems can be divided into two groups of services:

- **Data repositories (aka databases)** Enable a SQL interface that can access any column value in one or more rows of a table or result set. *Result sets* are selected values of a single table or the product of joins between multiple tables (SQL joins are described in Appendix B). *Tables* are persistent, two-dimensional collections that are organized by rows of defined structures. You create these structures when defining and creating tables in a database instance. Databases are *relational* databases when they include a data catalog that tracks the definitions of structures.

- **Programs** Enable you to administer and access the data repository, thereby providing the infrastructure to manage that data repository. The combination of a data repository and enabling programs is known as an *instance* of a database because the programs process and manage the data repository and data catalog. A *data catalog* stores information about data, known as *metadata*. The data catalog also defines how the database management system programs will access and manage user-defined databases. The programs are background processes that manage the physical input and output to physical files and other required processing activities. Opening a relational database instance starts these background processes.

Integrating the data repository and administrative programs requires a relational programming language that (a) has a linear structure, (b) can be accessed interactively or within procedural programs, and (c) supports data definition, manipulation, and query activities. The Structured Query Language (SQL) is the relational programming language used by the Oracle Database and most other relational database products.

Appendix B introduces how to work with Oracle SQL. Like any spoken or written language, SQL has many dialects. The Oracle Database 12c products support two dialects of SQL. One is the Oracle proprietary SQL syntax and the other is the ANSI 1999 SQL standard. The SQL language provides users with high-level *definition*, *set-at-a-time*, *insert*, *update*, and *delete* operations, as well as the ability to *select* data. SQL is considered a high-level language because it enables you to access data without dealing with physical file-access details.

Data catalogs are tables that map data that defines other database tables, views, stored procedures, and structures. Database management systems define frameworks, which qualify what can belong in data catalogs to support database instances. Database management systems also use SQL to define, access, and maintain the data catalog. Beneath the SQL interface and background processes servicing SQL commands, the database management system contains a set of library programs that manage transaction control. These services guarantee that transactions in a multiple user database are ACID-compliant.

ACID-compliant transactions are atomic, consistent, isolated, and durable. *Atomic* means that every part or no part of a transaction completes. *Consistent* means that the same results occur whether the transaction is serially or concurrently run. *Isolated* means that changes are invisible to any other session until made permanent by a commit action. *Durable* means the transaction is written to a permanent store at the conclusion of the transaction.

The architecture of the Oracle database instance is shown in Figure A-1. As you can see, it includes a shared memory segment, known as the System Global Area (SGA), active background processes, and files. The SGA contains various buffered areas of memory that process queries, inserts, updates, and delete statements in databases. The active background processes, described next, support the database instance. The files supporting the database instance are divisible into three segments—files that contain instance variables, files that contain the physical data and data catalog files, and files that contain control files, log files, and archive files.

There are five required Oracle database instance background processes, listed next along with a description of the services they perform:

- *Process Monitor* (PMON) cleans up the instance after failed processes by rolling back transactions, releasing database locks and resources, and restarting deceased processes.
- *System Monitor* (SMON) manages system recovery by opening the database, rolling forward changes from the online redo log files, and rolling back uncommitted transactions. SMON also coalesces free space and deallocates temporary segments.

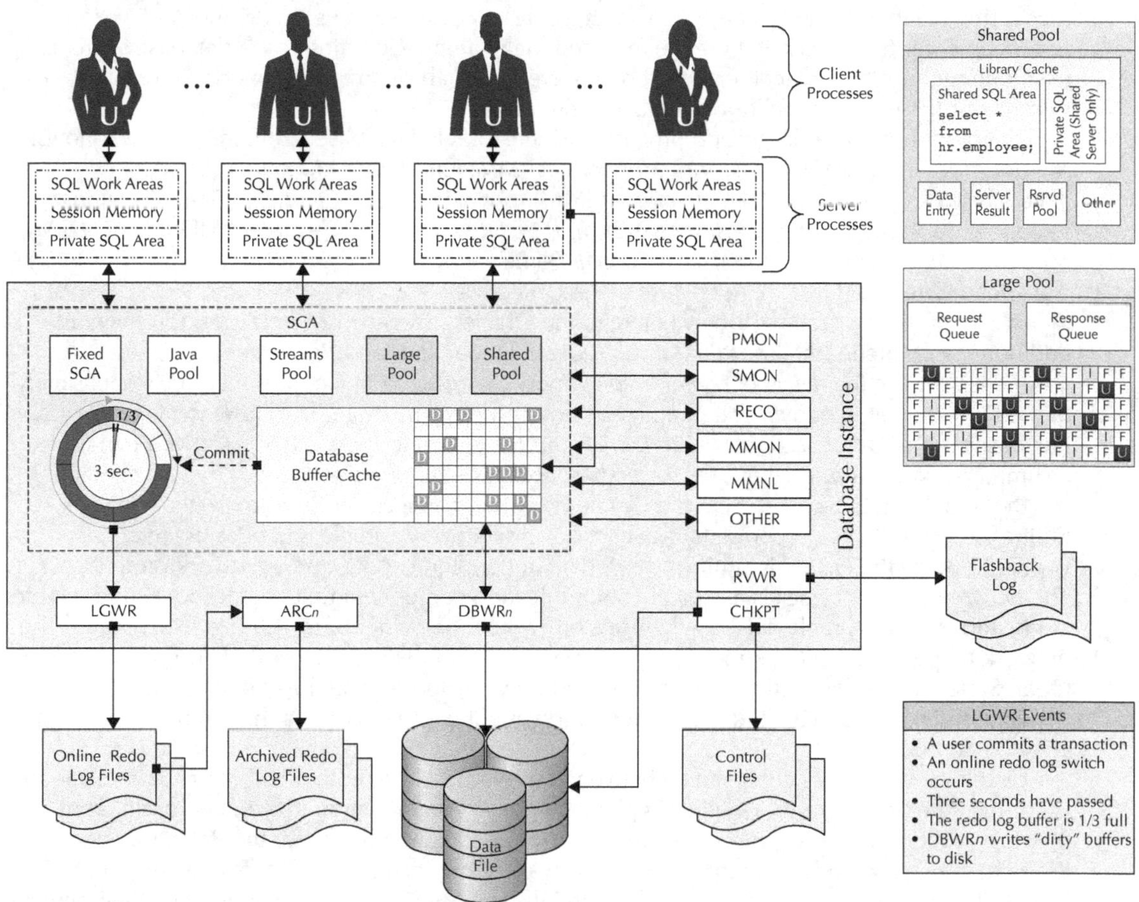

FIGURE A-1. *Oracle database instance architecture diagram*

- *Database Writer* (DBWR*n*) writes data to files when any of the following occur: checkpoints are reached, dirty buffers reach their threshold or no buffers are free, timeouts occur, Oracle Real Application Clusters (RAC) ping requests are made, tablespaces are placed in `OFFLINE` or `READ ONLY` state, tables are dropped or truncated, or tablespaces begin backup processing.
- *Log Writer* (LGWR) writes at user commits or three-second intervals, whichever comes first; when the redo log buffer is one-third full, online redo log switch occurs, or there is 1MB of redo instructions; and before a *Database Writer* writes dirty buffers to disk.
- *Checkpoint* (CKPT) signals the *Database Writer* at checkpoints and updates the file header information for database and control files at checkpoints.

Figure A-1 also shows an optional background process, *Archiver* (ARC*n*), that is critical to recovering databases. When an Oracle database instance is in archive mode, the *Archiver* process's writes to the redo log file are mirrored in the archive log files as the database switches from one redo log file to another. You should have the database in archive mode unless it is a test system and the time to rebuild it is trivial or unimportant.

The other optional background processes for the Oracle Database 12*c* family are as follows: *Memory Monitor* (MMON), *Memory Monitor Lite* (MMNL), *Memory Manager* (MMAN), *Automatic Shared Memory Management* (ASMM), *Coordinator Job Queue* (CJQ0), *Dispatcher* (D*nnn*), *RAC Lock Manager – Instance* (LCK*n*), *RAC DLM Monitor – Remote* (LMD*n*), *RAC DLM Monitor – Global Locks* (LMON), *RAC Global Cache Service* (LMS), *Parallel Query Slaves* (P*nnn*), *Advanced Queuing* (QMN*n*), *Recoverer* (RECO), *Recovery Writer* (RVWR*n*), and *Shared Server* (S*nnn*). All of these processes are available in the Oracle Database 12*c* products. You may only additionally configure the *Coordinator Job Queue*, *Dispatcher*, and *Recoverer* processes.

Understanding the *details* of how shared memory, processes, and files interact is the responsibility of the DBA. As noted earlier, you can find a fairly comprehensive guide to how to manage databases in the *Oracle Database 12c DBA Handbook* (Oracle Press, 2014), and you can find a summary explanation in the *Oracle Database Express Edition 2 Day DBA 12c Release* manual.

Beyond the database instance, the Oracle database management system provides many utilities. These utilities support database backup and recovery, Oracle database file integrity verification (via the DBVerify utility—`dbv`), data import and export, and a network protocol stack. The network protocol stack is a critical communication component that enables local and remote connections to the Oracle database by users other than the owner of the Oracle executables. The networking product stack is known as Net8. Net8 is a complete host layer that conforms to the Open Systems Interconnection (OSI) model and provides the session, presentation, and application layers. You can find more information about the OSI model at http://en.wikipedia.org/wiki/OSI_model.

Oracle Net8 enables connectivity between both local and remote programs and the database instance. Remote programs, whether implemented on the same physical machine or different physical machines, use remote procedure calls (RPCs) to communicate to the database instance. RPCs let one computer call another computer by directing the request to a listener service.

RPCs require software on both the client and the server. The remote client program environment needs to know how to get to the server programming environment, which is found by reading the `tnsnames.ora` file in the Oracle Database 12*c* Client software. The Oracle Database 12*c* Server software provides the implementation for the Oracle listener that receives and handles RPC requests. Net8 provides the packaging and de-packaging of network packets between local and remote programs and a database instance.

The Oracle listener listens for Net8 packaged transmissions on a specific port. The packaged transmissions are Oracle Net8 encoded packages. Packages are received from a network transport layer, such as TCP/IP, at a designated port number. The default port number is 1521. This port is where the Oracle listener hears, receives, and connects the transactions to the local database instance.

As illustrated in Figure A-2, when the package arrives at the listening port, a listener thread hears it and then hands it to the Oracle Call Interface (OCI) thread. Then, the transaction is sent through the Net8 transport layer to remove the packaging and pass the SQL command to a transactional object in a database instance, such as a table, view, or stored procedure.

This process has two variations: thick client and thin client. Thick-client communication, the old model, supports client-server computing, which worked like `telnet` or *secure shell* (`shh`)

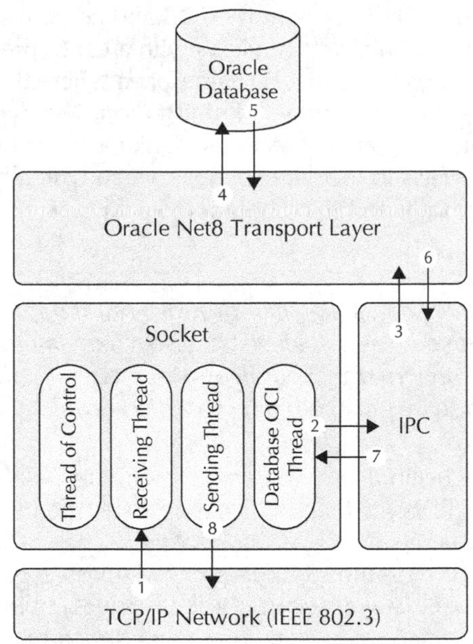

FIGURE A-2. *Oracle listener architecture*

across state-aware network sockets. The thick-client communication model requires that you install an Oracle Database 12*c* Client software application on the client. The Oracle Database 12*c* Client software contains the necessary programs and libraries to effect bidirectional state-aware sockets between a client and the server computer. The newer, thin-client communication supports both state-aware and stateless transaction patterns but it does so differently. All you need is an OCI library that enables you to package the communication into a compatible Net8 packet. Java Database Connectivity (JDBC) programs use an Oracle Java archive, while C, C++, Java, PHP, and other third-party programming languages use the OCI8 libraries to make connections to the Oracle database. The JDBC programs can work with only the Java archive file, while the others require the Oracle Database 12*c* Client installation.

User Account vs. Namespace

Although they have the same name, there is a subtle difference between a user account and its corresponding namespace. A user account by itself represents no more than stored authentication tokens. At the time of account creation, no namespace exists, even if the user is granted rights such as `CONNECT`, `INSERT`, `UPDATE`, `DELETE`, and `SELECT` on a myriad of database objects. The namespace is not created until the user is granted rights to create database objects and actually creates a database object. Oracle chose to label the namespace the same as the user account that owns it, which causes a great deal of confusion for DBAs and users alike.

Inside the database instance, user accounts are called *schemas*. The superuser schemas are known as `sys` and `system`. They support the CDB and contain some elements that map across all PDBs. One example is the administrative views with a `CDB_` prefix. The `sys` schema has rights to all database objects. It also owns a special namespace where the data catalog is stored. The `sys` schema should never be used for routine administration. The `system` schema has a master set of roles and privileges that enables the DBA to use it like a superuser account. The `system` schema contains administrative views to the data catalog, which typically are easier to use than trying to kludge through the physical tables that contain the data catalog.

CAUTION
A small mistake in the data catalog can destroy your database instance and provide you with no way to recover it. Also, changing things in the `sys` schema is not supported by your license agreement unless you are instructed to do so by Oracle to fix a specified problem.

As mentioned at the beginning of this section, Oracle Database 12*c* introduces the concept of Pluggable Databases (PDBs), which in turn introduces the concept of private context data dictionaries. Every PDB has its own `sys` and `system` schemas, and they work like the superuser schemas for the CDB. The `sys` and `system` schemas exist as part of the PDB `ADMIN` schema.

Unix or Linux requires that you set an `$ORACLE_HOME` environment variable that maps to the physical Oracle database management system home directory. Windows does not automatically create an `%ORACLE_HOME%` environment variable because it adds the fully qualified directory path to your `%PATH%` variable.

You set the correct operating environment in Unix or Linux by running the following commands in the Bash or Korn shell as the owner of the Oracle database installation:

```
# export set ORACLE_SID=oracle_sid
# export set ORACLE_ASK=no
```

You can then navigate to the default `/usr/local/bin` directory to find the installed `oraenv` file. You then source it as shown in the Bash or Korn shell:

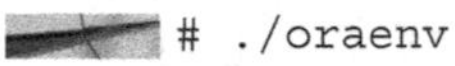

```
# ./oraenv
```

You will find further instructions in the *Oracle Database Installation Guide 12*c *Release*. These are also found on the http://docs.oracle.com web site under documentation for Oracle Database 12*c*.

Microsoft Windows Services

The design of Microsoft Windows compels Oracle to deploy services to start and stop the database and listener. Oracle creates this Microsoft service by using the platform-specific utility `ORADIM`. Fortunately, the Oracle Database 12*c* installation builds these services for you as a post-installation step when you use the DBCA. You should change these services only if you truly understand how to do so. A mistake working with the `ORADIM` facility can force you to refresh your operating system or manually clean up the registry.

This section has provided you with a summary of the Oracle database architecture and pointed you to some additional useful references. You can also review whitepapers and administrative-related database architecture notes posted on http://otn.oracle.com for additional information. In the next sections, you will learn how to start and stop the database and listener, and learn how to access SQL*Plus to run SQL statements.

Starting and Stopping the Oracle Database 12*c* Server

This section demonstrates how to start and stop the Oracle Database 12*c* server. The command-line utility is `sqlplus` and works the same for the Unix, Linux, and Microsoft Windows versions. The only difference is linked to account ownership of the database. This difference exists because of how the file system and ownership models work in Unix, Linux, and Microsoft Windows.

The Oracle database management system can support multiple database instances. Each instance is a separate CDB. This capability makes it necessary to assign each instance a unique System Identifier (SID). The generic database SID value is `orcl` when installing the Oracle Database 12*c* server. The assignment of the SID is the same regardless of platform.

A PDB is a private context, on an instance within an instance. As such, a PDB has its own SID value. The PDB's SID value is the name of the PDB when you provision it. Unlike the CDB's external SID value, there's no environment variable that you set for a PDB because the resolution of PDBs is internally managed by the Oracle Database 12c database. You configure access through the Oracle listener.

After provisioning a `videodb` PDB with a `CREATE PLUGGABLE DATABASE` statement, you must add a `SID_DESC` definition to Oracle's `listener.ora` file, like this:

```
SID_LIST_LISTENER =
  (SID_LIST =
    (SID_DESC =
      (SID_NAME = CLRExtProc)
      (ORACLE_HOME = C:\app\oracle\product\12.1.0\dbhome_1)
      (PROGRAM = extproc)
      (ENVS = "EXTPROC_DLLS=ONLY:<oracle_home_dir>\bin\oraclr12.dll")
    )
    (SID_DESC =
      (SID_NAME = VIDEODB)
      (ORACLE_HOME = <oracle_home>)
    )
  )
```

The `SID_NAME` is assigned the PDB's database name, and the `ORACLE_HOME` variable is assigned the fully qualified path to the physical directory. This configuration is necessary to provide access to the `sysdba` role for the `videodb` PDB. After making these changes to the `listener.ora` file, it's necessary to stop and start the listener to make the changes effective. You can read more about how you start, stop, and status the Oracle listener in the "Starting and Stopping the Oracle Listener" section later in this appendix.

While adding a `SID_DESC` definition to the `listener.ora` file provides access to the database, you also need to configure the `tnsnames.ora` file. The `tnsnames.ora` file acts like a police officer directing traffic, and it maps a TNS alias to an Oracle database SID value. The following `video` TNS alias maps access through a port to the `videodb` PDB:

```
VIDEO =
  (DESCRIPTION =
    (ADDRESS = (PROTOCOL = TCP)(HOST = localhost)(PORT = 1521))
    (CONNECT_DATA =
      (SERVER = DEDICATED)
      (SERVICE_NAME = videodb)
    )
  )
```

Together these changes let you access the `videodb` PDB from the command line. They're necessary to let you start and stop the `videodb` PDB, which can be stopped separately from the CDB.

The following subsections explain how to start and shut down the Oracle Database 12*c* server in the Unix/Linux and Microsoft Windows environments, respectively.

Unix or Linux Operations

Oracle Database 12*c* installs as the `oracle` user in a `dba` group on the Unix or Linux system and is set up to start at boot. When you want to shut down or start the database after the system has booted, use the *substitute user*, `su`, command. The `su` command lets you become another user and inherit that user's environment variables. For example, the following command lets you change from a less privileged user to the `oracle` owner:

```
su - oracle
```

You assume the mantle of `oracle` by providing the correct password to the account. Then, how you start or stop the database depends on which Oracle Database 12*c* edition you are using. As an Oracle Database 12*c* XE user (when it ships after Release 2), you can use the script built during installation to *start, stop, restart, configure,* or check the *status* of the database and all attendant services by typing the following:

```
/etc/init.d/oracle-xe {start|stop|restart|configure|status}
```

Alternatively, with an Oracle Database 12*c* SE or EE installation, you can use the `sqlplus` utility to *start, stop, restart, configure,* or *status* the database or *start* the Oracle listener and then use the Oracle Enterprise Manager (OEM) Database Control utility to *start, stop, restart,* or check the *status* of the database.

You will need to build an environment file and source it into your environment. The following values are the minimum required values for your environment file:

```
export set ORACLE_HOME=/mount_point/12c/product/12.1.0/db_1
export set PATH=$PATH:$ORACLE_HOME/bin:.
export set ORACLE_SID=oracle_sid
export set LD_LIBRARY_PATH=/usr/lib/openwin/lib:$ORACLE_HOME/lib
```

Assuming that you are in the same directory as your environment file, you source your environment in the Bash or Korn shell as follows:

```
. ./12c.env
```

Starting Oracle Enterprise Manager

If the console tells you that the `emctl` program was not found, it most likely was not found in your path statement. You can determine whether the executable is in your current path by using the `which` utility:

```
which -a emctl
```

The `-a` option returns a list of all `emctl` programs in order of their precedence in your `$PATH` environment variable. You fix the `$PATH` environment variable by adding the required directory path where the executable is found. After you fix your `$PATH` environment variable in the environment file, source the environment file again.

Then, you can start the Oracle Enterprise Manager Database Control utility as follows:

```
# emctl start dbconsole
```

You can also issue a `sqlplus` command to connect to the Oracle Database 12*c* instance as the privileged user `sys`, using a specialized role for starting and stopping the database. The connection command to the `sysdba` role is

```
sqlplus '/ as sysdba'
```

NOTE

You can connect directly to the Oracle database only when you are the owner of the Oracle database. This type of connection is a direct connection between the shell process and the database, which means that the communication is not routed through Net8 and the Oracle listener does not need to be running.

After connecting to the `SQL>` prompt, you will need to provide the Oracle superuser password. Once authenticated, you will be the `sys` user in a specialized role known as `sysdba`. The `sysdba` role exists for starting and stopping your database instance and performing other administrative tasks. You can see your current Oracle user name by issuing the following SQL*Plus command:

```
SQL> show user
USER is "SYS"
```

Assuming the database is already started, you can use the following command to see the current SGA values:

```
SQL> show sga

Total System Global Area 1233534976 bytes
Fixed Size                  1297104 bytes
Variable Size             935765296 bytes
Database Buffers          285212672 bytes
Redo Buffers               11259904 bytes
```

You can shut down the database by choosing abort, immediate, transactional, or normal after the shutdown command. Only the abort method fails to secure transaction integrity, which means that database recovery is required when restarting the database. The other three *shut down* methods do not require recovery when restarting the database. The optional arguments perform the following types of *shut down* operations:

- *Shutdown* normal stops any new connections to the database and waits for all connected users to disconnect; then the Oracle instance writes completed database transactions from redo buffers to data files and marks them closed, terminates background processes, closes the database, and dismounts the database.
- *Shutdown* transactional stops any new connections to the database and disconnects users as soon as the current transactions complete; when all transactions complete, the Oracle instance writes database and redo buffers to data files and marks them closed, terminates background processes, closes the database, and dismounts the database.
- *Shutdown* immediate stops all current SQL statements, rolls back all active transactions, and immediately disconnects users from the database; then the Oracle instance writes database and redo buffers to data files and marks them closed, terminates background processes, closes the database, and dismounts the database.
- *Shutdown* abort stops all current SQL statements and immediately shuts down without writing database and redo buffers to data files; the Oracle instance does not roll back uncommitted transactions but terminates running processes without closing physical files and the database, and it leaves the database in a mounted state, requiring recovery when restarted.

The following illustrates using shutdown immediate statement on a database instance:

```
SQL> shutdown immediate
Database closed.
Database dismounted.
ORACLE instance shut down.
```

When you want to start the database, you have three options. You can start the database by using the startup command and either the nomount, mount, or open (default) option. The optional arguments perform the following types of startup operations:

- *Startup* nomount starts the instance by reading the parameter file in the $ORACLE_HOME/dbs directory. This file can be named spfile.ora or pfile.ora. The former can't be read in a text editor but is the default parameter file option beginning with Oracle 9*i* Database. You can create an editable pfile.ora file using SQL as the sys user in the role of sysdba from an open database. This startup option starts the background processes, allocates the SGA shared memory segment, and opens the alertSID.log and trace files. The SID is the name of an Oracle database instance. The value is stored in the data catalog and control files. This type of startup should be done only when creating a new database or rebuilding control files during a backup and recovery operation.
- *Startup* mount does everything the nomount process does, and then it continues by locating, opening, and reading the control files and parameter files to determine the status of the data files and online redo log files, but it performs no checks to verify the existence

or state of the data files. This type of `startup` is useful when you need to rename the data files, change the online redo file archiving process, or perform full database recovery.

- *Startup* `open` does everything the `mount` process does, and then it continues by locating, opening, and reading the online data files and redo log files. This is the default *startup* operation, and you use it when opening the database for user transactions.
- *Startup restrict* lets you start the database completely but prevents users from connecting and using the database.

After reconnecting to the database if you disconnected, you can issue the `startup` command. If you provide a `nomount` or `mount` argument to the `startup` command, only those processes specified in the previous list will occur. When you provide the `startup` command with no argument, the default argument `open` is applied and the database will be immediately available for user transactions. The following demonstrates a standard startup of the database instance:

```
SQL> startup
ORACLE instance started.

Total System Global Area 1720328192 bytes
Fixed Size                  2382680 bytes
Variable Size            1291846824 bytes
Database Buffers          419430400 bytes
Redo Buffers                6668288 bytes
Database mounted.
Database opened.
```

Viewing how the database moves from *shutdown* to *nomount* to *mount* to *open* is helpful. The following syntax demonstrates moving the database one step at a time from a *shutdown* instance to an open database:

```
SQL> startup nomount
ORACLE instance started.

Total System Global Area 1720328192 bytes
Fixed Size                  2382680 bytes
Variable Size            1291846824 bytes
Database Buffers          419430400 bytes
Redo Buffers                6668288 bytes
SQL> ALTER DATABASE MOUNT;

Database altered.

SQL> ALTER DATABASE OPEN;

Database altered.
```

The preceding output demonstrates that the Oracle instance creates the shared memory segment before opening the database, even in a `startup nomount` operation. The memory segment is the first operation because it is the container where you store the open instance. You can use an `ALTER` SQL statement against the database to mount and open the database instance.

You can also use the SQL*Plus executable to start and stop embedded PDBs. The syntax is very similar to what you use to start and stop an Oracle Database 12*c* instance. You have three options to start a PDB.

Option one lets you connect at the `sysdba` role for the CDB and start all PDBs with the following command:

```
SQL> ALTER PLUGGABLE DATABASE ALL OPEN;
```

Option two lets you connect at the `sysdba` role for the CDB and start one pluggable database with this command:

```
SQL> ALTER PLUGGABLE DATABASE OPEN pdb_name;
```

TIP

You also have the option of shutting down the PDB by switching the `OPEN` *keyword with a* `CLOSE` *keyword. When you* `CLOSE` *a PDB, it's like* `SHUTDOWN IMMEDIATE` *for a CDB.*

Option three lets you connect to an embedded `videodb` PDB with the `sysdba` role with the following syntax:

```
sqlplus sys@VIDEO as sysdba
```

The `sys@VIDEO` provides access to the PDB-only data dictionary and discrete `sysdba` role. You can't gain access to the PDB-only data dictionary through any other means, and this access is only available after you've configured the `listener.ora` and `tnsnames.ora` files.

In this next example, we'll take a new security precaution. Connecting to the database on a command line discloses the user name and potentially the password of the user. Oracle recommends that you connect by using the `/NOLOG` option, which prevents disclosing the user name or password while logging into the database. After all, the operating system keeps a log of all user commands, which can be compromised by a hack of the server.

```
# sqlplus /nolog
SQL*Plus: Release 12.1.0.1.0 Production ON Tue Aug 13 01:28:30 2013
Copyright (c) 1982, 2013, Oracle.  ALL rights reserved.

SQL> CONNECT videoadm@VIDEO/Video1
Connected.
SQL> SHOW USER
USER IS "VIDEOADM"
```

A connection made with the `CONNECT` statement isn't recorded in the operating system, and as a result denies information to would-be hackers. It's the Oracle recommended way to connect to the database.

You start the database with the familiar `startup` command, like

```
SQL> STARTUP
Pluggable Database opened.
```

This section has shown you how to shut down and restart your database instance in a Linux or Unix environment. It has also laid a foundation for some insights into routine database administration tasks, which you can explore further in the "Database Administration" section later in this appendix or by referencing the *Oracle Database 12c DBA Handbook* (Oracle Press, 2014).

Microsoft Windows Operations

Oracle Database 12*c* installs as a standard program on the Microsoft Windows system. You have full access from any user account that has Administrator privileges. Oracle Database 12*c* also installs several services using the platform-specific `ORADIM` utility. You can find these services by opening the Control Panel and navigating to the *Services* icon. The navigation path differs depending on whether you are in the *Classic* view or the *Category* view. In the *Classic* view, click *Administrative Tools* and then click *Services*. In the *Category* view, first click *System and Security*, then click *Administrative Tools*, and then you have to double-click *Services*. This opens the *Services* view displayed in the following illustration.

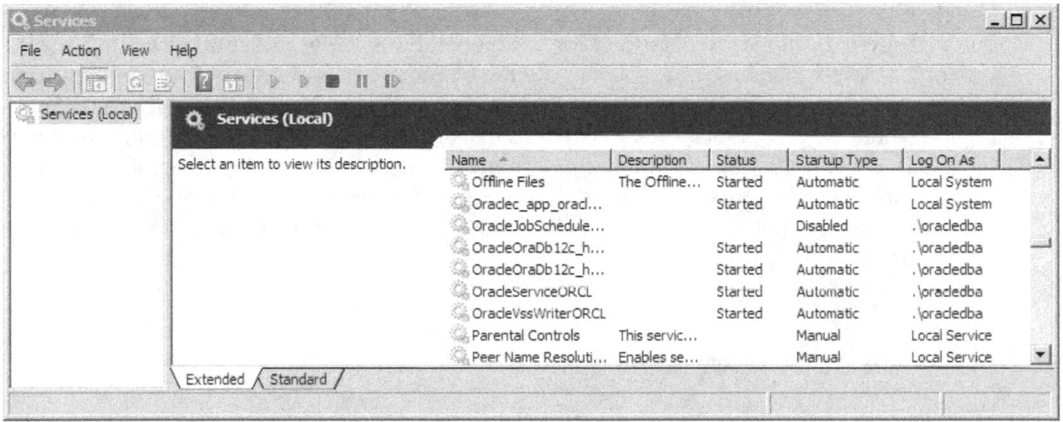

TIP

An easy way to launch Services is to open the Command Prompt utility and enter ***services.msc****.*

As a general rule, you are best served by starting, restarting, and shutting down the services from this GUI view. However, you will need the Command Prompt utility when you want to perform data backup and recovery activities. You can access the `sqlplus` utility from any Command Prompt session to manually *start*, *stop*, *restart*, *configure*, or *status* the database. This is possible because the fully qualified directory path is placed in the generic `%PATH%` environment variable for all *Administrator* accounts during the product installation. Making changes in the database requires that you connect to the Oracle Database 12*c* instance as the privileged user `sys`.

You use the SQL*Plus executable, `sqlplus`. You connect using the following syntax with the Windows user that installed the software:

```
sqlplus '/ as sysdba'
```

After connecting to the SQL> prompt, you have the same access. The only difference is the pattern for environment variables. For example, you can find the spfile.ora file or pfile.ora file in the %ORACLE_HOME%\dbs directory.

You can also use the SQL*Plus executable to access embedded PDB instances. The process mirrors that shown for Unix and Linux earlier in the previous section and thus isn't repeated here, to conserve space and avoid redundancy.

This section has shown you how to shut down and restart your database instance in a Windows environment. It has also laid a foundation for some insight into routine database administration tasks, which you can explore further in in the "Database Administration" section later in this appendix or by referencing the *Oracle Database 12c DBA Handbook* (Oracle Press, 2014).

Starting and Stopping the Oracle Listener

The Oracle lsnrctl utility lets you start the server-side Oracle listener process on a port that you set in the listener.ora configuration file. There are actually three files used in configuring the Oracle Net8 listener: the listener.ora, tnsnames.ora, and sqlnet.ora configuration files. The sqlnet.ora file is not necessary for basic operations and is not configured in the shipped version of Oracle Database 12c. You can use the sqlnet.ora file to set network tracing commands, which are qualified in the *Oracle Database Net Services Administrator's Guide 12c Release* and *Oracle Database Net Services Reference 12c Release* documentation from Oracle. You may browse or download these documents at http://docs.oracle.com/ for supplemental information.

The network configuration files are in the network/admin subdirectory of the Oracle Database 12c product home directory. The following qualifies the default Oracle product home by platform:

Linux or Unix

```
/mount_point/directory_to_oracle_home/
```

Windows

```
C:\directory_to_oracle_home
```

The Oracle product home path is typically set as an environment variable for all user accounts. Environment variables are aliases that point to something else, and they exist in all operating systems. You can set an Oracle product home directory as follows by platform:

Linux or Unix

```
export set ORACLE_HOME=/mount_point/directory_to_oracle_home/
```

Windows

```
C:\directory_to_oracle_home
```

You can then navigate to the Oracle product home by using $ORACLE_HOME in Unix or Linux or %ORACLE_HOME% in Microsoft Windows. These settings are temporary unless you put them in a configuration file that gets sourced when you connect to your system in Unix or Linux. Standard practice is to put these settings in your .bashrc file or have your system administrator put them in the standard .profile account in Linux. You can also configure permanent environment variables in the *System Properties* dialog box in Microsoft Windows. You will find the instructions for setting the environment variables in the *Oracle Database 2 Day DBA 12c Release* manual.

TIP
To set your environment variables in Microsoft Windows 7, open the Control Panel, launch the System *icon (in Classic view), click* Advanced System Settings *to open the* System Properties *dialog box with the* Advanced *tab displayed, and then click the* Environment Variables *button.*

The sample `listener.ora` file is a configuration file. A `listener.ora` file exists after you install Oracle Database 12*c*. You will find that your `listener.ora` file contains the *Oracle product home directory*, your server machine *hostname*, and a *port number*, as shown in the following example. These values are critical pieces of information that enable your listener to find your Oracle database installation. These data components mirror the configuration directives that enable Apache to hand off HTTP requests to appropriate services. The only differences between the Unix or Linux OS version and the Microsoft Windows OS version are the different path statement for the Oracle product home and the case sensitivity or insensitivity of the hostname. The *hostname* is lowercase for a Unix or Linux system and uppercase for Microsoft Windows.

The `listener.ora` file uses bold text to highlight generic components, like the *hostname*, *port_number*, and *oracle_product_home_directory*, and listener name. Generic names allow you to provide specific values. The one exception is the listener name, which is the default `LISTENER` value.

```
-- An example of a default listener.ora file.
LISTENER =
  (DESCRIPTION_LIST =
    (DESCRIPTION =
      (ADDRESS = (PROTOCOL = IPC)(KEY = EXTPROC1))
      (ADDRESS = (PROTOCOL = TCP)(HOST = hostname)(PORT = port_number))
    )
  )

SID_LIST_LISTENER =
  (SID_LIST =
    (SID_DESC =
      (SID_NAME = PLSExtProc)
      (ORACLE_HOME = oracle_product_home_directory)
      (PROGRAM = extproc)
    )
  )
```

The `listener.ora` has two key addressing components. The first is the actual listener name, which by default isn't too original because it is an uppercase string, `LISTENER`. The default listener name is implicitly assumed unless you provide an overriding listener name to any `lsnrctl` command. You must explicitly provide the listener name when you use anything other than the default as your actual listener name.

The listener name is also appended to the `SID_LIST_` descriptor, which registers static maps for external procedures and the Oracle Heterogeneous Server. Oracle Database 12*c* uses one external procedure configuration—`PLSExtProc`. Oracle recommends that you have discrete listeners for IPC and TCP traffic, but in the standard listener configuration file they share a listener. Unless you change the listener file, you will encounter an `ORA-28595` error because user-defined shared libraries (called dynamic-link libraries in Windows) must communicate across an IPC channel.

The `DEFAULT_SERVICE_LISTENER` parameter is set to `orcl` in the `listener.ora` file. `ORCL` also is the global name of the current database instance. The `SERVICE_NAME` parameter defaults to the global database name when one is not specified in the `spfileSID.ora` or `pfileSID.ora` file. The service name for any Oracle database is the database name concatenated to the database domain. Oracle Database 12*c* defines the default database name as `ORCL` and assigns no database domain. You can find this information by connecting as the `sys` user under the `sysdba` role, formatting the return values, and running the following query:

```
COL name FORMAT A30
COL value FORMAT A30

SELECT   name
,        value
FROM     v$parameter
WHERE    name LIKE '%name'
OR       name LIKE '%domain';
```

The query returns the following data:

```
NAME                           VALUE
------------------------------ ------------------------------
db_domain
instance_name                  orcl
db_name                        orcl
db_unique_name                 orcl
```

Net8 is designed to support client load balancing and connect-time failover. The `SERVICE_NAME` parameter replaces the `SID` parameter that previously enabled these features. The `tnsnames.ora` file is a mapping file that enables client requests to find the Oracle listener. The `tnsnames.ora` file contains a network alias that maps to the Oracle `SERVICE_NAME` and connection configurations to facilitate access to external procedures. The *hostname* and *port_number* enable the network alias, `orcl`, to find the Oracle listener. Naturally, there is an assumption that your *hostname* maps through DNS resolution or the local host file to a physical IP address.

TIP

You can add the hostname and IP address to your local host file when you do not resolve to a server through DNS. The `/etc/host` file is the Linux host file, and the `C:\WINDOWS\system32\drivers\etc\hosts` file is the Microsoft Windows host file.

The following is an example of a `tnsnames.ora` file:

```
-- An example of a default tnsnames.ora file.
ORCL =
  (DESCRIPTION =
    (ADDRESS = (PROTOCOL = TCP)(HOST = hostname)(PORT = port_number))
```

```
    (CONNECT_DATA =
      (SERVER = DEDICATED)
      (SERVICE_NAME = ORCL)
    )
  )

EXTPROC_CONNECTION_DATA =
  (DESCRIPTION =
    (ADDRESS_LIST =
      (ADDRESS = (PROTOCOL = IPC)(KEY = EXTPROC1521))
    )
    (CONNECT_DATA =
      (SID = PLSExtProc)
      (PRESENTATION = RO)
    )
  )
```

The HOST and PORT values are replaced by the KEY value when you change the PROTOCOL from TCP to IPC. Some strings in these configuration files are case sensitive, such as the PROGRAM value in the `listener.ora` file and the KEY value in the `tnsnames.ora` file. These must match exactly between files or you will receive an ORA-28576 error when accessing the external procedure.

These files support the `lsnrctl` utility regardless of platform. The `lsnrctl` utility enables you to *start*, *stop*, and *status* the listener process. As discussed in the earlier coverage of how to start and stop the database instance, you need to be the `oracle` user in the Linux environment and an *Administrator* user in the Microsoft Windows environment.

The default installation starts the Oracle listener when the system boots, but you should check whether it is running before you attempt to shut it down. You can use the following to check the status of the Oracle listener:

```
lsnrctl status
```

As discussed, the command implicitly substitutes LISTENER as the default second argument. If you have changed the default listener name, you will need to provide the listener name explicitly when you *start*, *stop*, or check the *status* of the listener. You should see the following on a Windows system (and only slight differences on a Unix system or Windows system) when you check the status of a running Oracle Database 12*c* listener:

```
LSNRCTL for 64-bit Windows: Version 12.1.0.0.2 - Beta on 05-MAY-2013 23:43:34
Copyright (c) 1991, 2012, Oracle.  All rights reserved.

Connecting to (DESCRIPTION=(ADDRESS=(PROTOCOL=IPC)(KEY=EXTPROC1521)))
STATUS of the LISTENER
------------------------
Alias                     LISTENER
Version                   TNSLSNR for 64-bit Windows: Version 12.1.0.0.2 - Beta
Start Date                28-APR-2013 15:25:41
Uptime                    7 days 8 hr. 17 min. 54 sec
Trace Level               off
Security                  ON: Local OS Authentication
```

```
SNMP                      OFF
Listener Parameter File   C:\app\oracledba\product\12.1.0\dbhome_1\network\...
Listener Log File         C:\app\oracledba\diag\tnslsnr\betawin\listener\alert\...
Listening Endpoints Summary...
  (DESCRIPTION=(ADDRESS=(PROTOCOL=ipc)(PIPENAME=\\.\pipe\EXTPROC1521ipc)))
  (DESCRIPTION=(ADDRESS=(PROTOCOL=tcp)(HOST=mclaughlin12c)(PORT=1521)))
  (DESCRIPTION=(ADDRESS=(PROTOCOL=tcp)(HOST=mclaughlin12c)(PORT=5500))
  (Presentation=HTTP)(Session=RAW))
Services Summary...
Service "CLRExtProc" has 1 instance(s).
  Instance "CLRExtProc", status UNKNOWN, has 1 handler(s) for this service...
Service "orcl" has 1 instance(s).
  Instance "orcl", status READY, has 1 handler(s) for this service...
Service "orclXDB" has 1 instance(s).
  Instance "orcl", status READY, has 1 handler(s) for this service...
Service "pdborcl" has 1 instance(s).
  Instance "orcl", status READY, has 1 handler(s) for this service...
Service "video2small" has 1 instance(s).
  Instance "orcl", status READY, has 1 handler(s) for this service...
The command completed successfully
```

You can stop the service by using

```
lsnrctl stop
```

You can restart the service by using

```
lsnrctl start
```

After stopping and starting the listener, you should check if you can make a network connection from your user account to the listener. This is very similar to the idea of a network ping operation, except you are pinging the Oracle Net8 connection layer. You use the `tnsping` utility to verify an Oracle Net8 connection, as follows:

```
tnsping orcl
```

You should see the following type of return message but with a real *hostname* as opposed to the substituted `hostname` value, provided you haven't changed the default network *port number*:

```
C:\>tnsping orcl

TNS Ping Utility for 64-bit Windows: Version 12.1.0.0.2 on 05-MAY-2013
Copyright (c) 1997, 2012, Oracle.  All rights reserved.

Used parameter files:
C:\app\oracledba\product\12.1.0\dbhome_1\network\admin\sqlnet.ora

Used TNSNAMES adapter to resolve the alias
Attempting to contact (DESCRIPTION = (ADDRESS = (PROTOCOL = TCP)
(HOST = hostname) (PORT = 1521)) (CONNECT_DATA = (SERVER = DEDICATED)
(SERVICE_NAME = orcl)))
OK (30 msec)
```

The `tnsping` utility checks the `sqlnet.ora` parameter file for any instructions that it may contain. Net8 connections first check the `sqlnet.ora` file to find any network tracing instructions before proceeding with connection attempts. The Oracle Net8 tracing layers are very powerful tools and can assist you in diagnosing complex connection problems. You will find answers to configuring `sqlnet.ora` in the *Oracle Database Net Services Reference 12c Release*.

You can use a GUI tool to *start, stop*, and *status* the Oracle listener when you are running on Microsoft Windows. To find the GUI tool from the *Control Panel* in the *Classic* view, click *Administrative Tools* and then click *Services*, in the *Category* view, click *System and Security*, click *Administrative Tools*, and then click *Services*. Select ***OracleORCLListener*** in the list of services in the right panel and click *Stop the service*.

This section has explained where the configuration files are located and how they work to enable you to *start, stop*, and check the *status* of the Oracle listener.

Multiversion Concurrency Control

Multiversion Concurrency Control (MVCC) uses database snapshots to provide transactions with memory-persistent copies of the database. This means that users, via their SQL statements, interact with the in-memory copies of data rather than directly with physical data. MVCC systems isolate user transactions from each other and guarantee transaction integrity by preventing *dirty transactions*, writes to the data that shouldn't happen and that make the data inconsistent. Oracle Database 12*c* prevents dirty writes by its MVCC and transaction model.

Transaction models depend on transactions, which are *ACID-compliant* blocks of code. Oracle Database 12*c* provides an MVCC architecture that guarantees that all changes to data are ACID-compliant, which ensures the integrity of concurrent operations on data—transactions.

As described earlier, in the section "Oracle Database Architecture," ACID-compliant transactions meet four conditions:

- **Atomic** They complete or fail while undoing any partial changes.
- **Consistent** They change from one state to another the same way regardless of whether the change is made through parallel actions or serial actions.
- **Isolated** Partial changes are never seen by other users or processes in the concurrent system.
- **Durable** They are written to disk and made permanent when completed.

Oracle Database 12*c* manages ACID-compliant transactions by writing them to disk first, as redo log files only or as both redo log files and archive log files. Then it writes them to the database. This multiple-step process with logs ensures that Oracle database's buffer cache (part of the instance memory) isn't lost from any completed transaction. Log writes occur before the acknowledgement-of-transactions process occurs.

The smallest transaction in a database is a single SQL statement that inserts, updates, or deletes rows. SQL statements can also change values in one or more columns of a row in a table. Each SQL statement is by itself an ACID-compliant and MVCC-enabled transaction when managed by a transaction-capable database engine. The Oracle database is always a transaction-capable system. Transactions are typically a collection of SQL statements that work in close cooperation to accomplish a business objective. They're often grouped into *stored programs*, which are functions, procedures, or triggers. *Triggers* are specialized programs that audit or protect data. They enforce business rules that prevent unauthorized changes to the data.

SQL statements and stored programs are foundational elements for development of business applications. They contain the interaction points between customers and the data and are collectively called the application programming interface (API) to the database. User forms (typically web forms today) access the API to interact with the data. In well-architected business application software, the API is the only interface that the form developer interacts with.

Database developers, such as you and I, create these code components to enforce business rules while providing options to form developers. In doing so, database developers must guard a few things at all cost. For example, some critical business logic and controls must prevent changes to the data in specific tables, even changes in API programs. That type of critical control is often written in database triggers. SQL statements are events that add, modify, or delete data. Triggers guarantee that API code cannot make certain additions, modifications, or deletions to critical resources, such as tables. Triggers can run before or after SQL statements. Their actions, like the SQL statements themselves, are temporary until the calling scope sends an instruction to commit the work performed.

A database trigger can intercept values before they're placed in a column, and it can ensure that only certain values can be inserted into or updated in a column. A trigger overrides an `INSERT` or `UPDATE` statement value that violates a business rule and then it either raises an error and aborts the transaction or changes the value before it can be inserted or updated into the table. Chapter 12 offers examples of both types of triggers in Oracle Database 12*c*.

MVCC determines how to manage transactions. MVCC guarantees how multiple users' SQL statements interact in an ACID compliant manner. The next two sections qualify how data transactions work and how MVCC locks and isolates partial results from data transactions.

Data Transactions

Data Manipulation Language (DML) commands are the SQL statements that transact against the data. They are principally the `INSERT`, `UPDATE`, and `DELETE` statements. The `INSERT` statement adds new rows in a table, the `UPDATE` statement modifies columns in existing rows, and the `DELETE` statement removes a row from a table.

The Oracle `MERGE` statement transacts against data by providing a conditional insert or update feature. The `MERGE` statement lets you add new rows when they don't exist or change column values in rows that do exist. (Appendix B covers merging data from external sources with the `MERGE` statement.) Oracle also provides a conditional `INSERT ALL` statement (also covered in Appendix B) that lets you insert into multiple tables from the same data source.

NOTE
All of these statements are transactions by themselves, like the `INSERT`, `UPDATE`, and `DELETE` statements.

Inserting data seldom encounters a conflict with other SQL statements because the values become a new row or rows in a table. Updates and deletes, on the other hand, can and do encounter conflicts with other `UPDATE` and `DELETE` statements. `INSERT` statements that encounter conflicts occur when columns in a new row match a preexisting row's uniquely constrained columns. The insertion is disallowed because only one row can contain the unique column set.

These individual transactions have two phases in transactional databases such as Oracle. The first phase involves making a change that is visible only to the user in the current session. The user then has the option of committing the change, which makes it permanent, or rolling back the change, which undoes the transaction. Developers use Data Control Language (DCL) commands to confirm or cancel transactions. The `COMMIT` statement confirms or makes permanent any change, and the `ROLLBACK` statement cancels or undoes any change.

A generic transaction lifecycle (see Figure A-3) for a two-table insert process implements a business rule that specifies that neither `INSERT` statement works unless they both work. Moreover, if the first `INSERT` statement fails, the second `INSERT` statement never runs; and if the second `INSERT` statement fails, the first `INSERT` statement is undone by a `ROLLBACK` statement to a `SAVEPOINT`. After a failed transaction is unwritten, good development practice requires that you write the failed event(s) to an error log table. The write succeeds because it occurs after the `ROLLBACK` statement but before the `COMMIT` statement.

A SQL statement followed by a `COMMIT` statement is called a *transaction process*, or a *two-phase commit (2PC)* protocol. ACID-compliant transactions use a 2PC protocol to manage one SQL statement or collections of SQL statements. In a 2PC protocol model, the `INSERT`, `UPDATE`, `MERGE`, or `DELETE` DML statement starts the process and submits changes. These DML statements can also act as events that fire database triggers assigned to the table being changed.

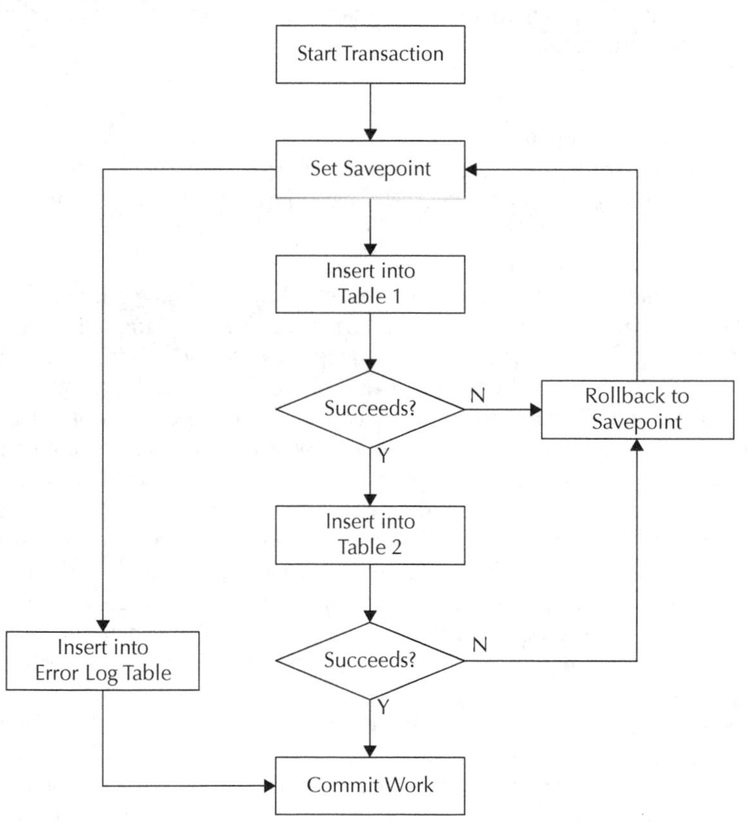

FIGURE A-3. *Transaction lifecycle*

Transactions become more complex when they include database triggers because triggers can inject an entire layer of logic within the transaction scope of a DML statement. For example, database triggers can do the following:

- Run code that verifies, changes, or repudiates submitted changes
- Record additional information after validation in other tables (they can't write to the table being changed—or, in database lexicon, "mutated"
- Throw exceptions to terminate a transaction when the values don't meet business rules

As a general rule, triggers can't contain a `COMMIT` or `ROLLBACK` statement because they run inside the transaction scope of a DML statement. Oracle databases give developers an alternative to this general rule because they support *autonomous transactions*. Autonomous transactions run outside the transaction scope of the triggering DML statement. They can contain a `COMMIT` statement and act independently of the calling scope statement. This means an autonomous trigger can commit a transaction when the calling transaction fails. Chapter 13 covers this advanced behavior.

As independent statements or collections of statements add, modify, and remove rows, one statement transacts against data *only* by locking rows: the `SELECT` statement. A `SELECT` statement typically doesn't lock rows when it acts as a cursor in the scope of a stored program. A *cursor* is a data structure that contains rows of one-to-many columns in a stored program. This is also known as a list of record structures.

NOTE
The ability to lock rows for pending transaction statements is why the `SELECT` statement is considered a DML command. That's generally accomplished by appending a `FOR UPDATE` clause in Oracle SQL or MySQL.

Cursors act like ordinary SQL queries, except they're managed by procedure programs row by row. There are many examples of procedural programming languages. PL/SQL and SQL/PSM programming languages are procedural languages designed to run inside the database. C, C++, C#, Java, Perl, and PHP are procedural languages that interface with the database through well-defined interfaces, such as Java Database Connectivity (JDBC) and Open Database Connectivity (ODBC).

Cursors can query data two ways. One way locks the rows so that they can't be changed until the cursor is closed; closing the cursor releases the lock. The other way doesn't lock the rows, which allows them to be changed while the program is working with the data set from the cursor. The safest practice is to lock the rows when you open the cursor, and that should always be the case when you're inserting, updating, or deleting rows that depend on the values in the cursor not changing until the transaction lifecycle of the program unit completes.

Loops use cursors to process data sets. That means the cursors are generally opened at or near the beginning of program units. Inside the loop the values from the cursor support one to many SQL statements for one to many tables.

Stored and external programs create their *operational scope* inside a database connection when they're called by another program. External programs connect to a database and enjoy their own operational scope, known as a *session scope*. The session defines the programs' operational scope. The operational scope of a stored program or external program defines the *transaction scope*. Inside the transaction scope, the programs interact with data in tables by inserting, updating, or deleting data until the operations complete successfully or encounter a critical failure. These stored program units commit changes when everything completes successfully, or they roll back changes when any critical instruction fails. Sometimes, the programs are written to roll back changes when any instruction fails.

In the Oracle Database, the most common clause to lock rows is the `FOR UPDATE` clause, which is appended to a `SELECT` statement. An Oracle database also supports a `WAIT` *n* seconds or `NOWAIT` option. The `WAIT` option is a blessing when you want to reply to an end user form's request and can't make the change quickly. Without this option, a change could hang around for a long time, which means virtually *indefinitely* to a user trying to run your application. MySQL doesn't support this *wait* or *no wait* feature. The default value in an Oracle database is `NOWAIT`, `WAIT` without a timeout, or *wait indefinitely*. You should avoid this default behavior when developing program units that interact with customers. The Oracle Database also supports a full table lock with the SQL `LOCK TABLE` command, but you would need to embed the command inside a stored or external program's instruction set.

DML Locking and Isolation Control

Oracle's locking and isolation control implement the American National Standards Institute (ANSI)/International Standards Organization (ISO) SQL standards. This leave you with the ANSI SQL:92 possibilities presented in Table A-1.

As indicated, dirty reads are possible when you implement the ANSI read committed level. Dirty reads should never occur—and Oracle prevents them—while nonrepeatable and phantom reads do occur occasionally. Nonrepeatable reads occur in large systems where `UPDATE` or `DELETE` statements change the data between a user's first and subsequent `SELECT` statements from the database. Phantom reads are similar but involve new data, typically from `INSERT` statements.

You can prevent nonrepeatable or phantom reads by setting the database to serializable mode (see Table A-2). Issuing a `SET TRANSACTION READ ONLY` command provides you with read consistency. More can be found on transaction consistency in the *Oracle Database Advanced Application Developer's Guide 12c Release*.

Oracle's automatic table locking is the default because it represents a balance between maximum concurrency and serialization. While automatic table locking is the preferred method, you do have the following explicit commands at your disposal:

- `SELECT * FROM` *`some_table`* **`FOR UPDATE;`**
- `SET TRANSACTION READ ONLY`
- `SET TRANSACTION ISOLATION LEVEL SERIALIZABLE`
- `LOCK TABLE`

Isolation Level	Dirty Read	Nonrepeatable Read	Phantom Read
Read committed	Possible	Possible	Possible
Read uncommitted	Not possible	Possible	Possible
Repeatable read	Not possible	Not possible	Possible
Serializable	Not possible	Not possible	Not possible

TABLE A-1. *ANSI SQL:92 Isolation Levels*

Operation	Read Committed	Serializable
Dirty write	Not possible	Not possible
Dirty read	Not possible	Not possible
Nonrepeatable read	Possible	Not possible
Phantoms	Possible	Not possible
Row-level locking	Yes	Yes
Reads block writes	No	No
Writes block reads	No	No
Row-level blocking writes	Yes	Yes

TABLE A-2. *Oracle Read-Committed vs. Serializable Transactions*

The `FOR UPDATE` clause locks only rows touched by a statement, which differs from the `LOCK TABLE` command, which locks all rows in the table. You also have the `FOR UPDATE WAIT` *n* (seconds), which tells Oracle to wait for *n* seconds when a lock already exists. If the existing lock still exists at the end of the *n* seconds, the connection is lost.

Following are the five valid lock modes:

ROW EXCLUSIVE The least restrictive lock level, allows for row sharing. It also prevents users from locking the entire table for exclusive access. `ROW EXCLUSIVE` locks are automatically obtained by any `INSERT`, `UPDATE`, or `DELETE` statement.

ROW SHARE While like `ROW EXCLUSIVE` mode, it's also known as `SHARE UPDATE` mode. The `ROW SHARE` permits concurrent access to locked tables but prohibits users from locking any table for exclusive access.

SHARE Allows `SELECT` statements but prohibits other updates to a locked table.

SHARE ROW EXCLUSIVE Like `SHARE` mode, it lets you prevent other users from locking tables in `SHARE` mode. It does allow others to look at any rows in the `SHARE ROW EXCLUSIVE` table.

EXCLUSIVE The most restrictive level, prevents all DML activities other than `SELECT` statements.

Definer Rights and Invoker Rights

The definer rights model is the default for Oracle Database 12*c*, but Oracle also supports the invoker rights model. Definer rights approaches are best suited to centralized database architectures, while invoker rights repositories best support distributed database models with a common shared code base.

Definer Rights

A centralized data repository is synonymous with the definer rights model. The definer owns all objects that it creates and holds the right to query them and transact with them. A definer can also grant rights on the tables, views, and stored programs to other users. Stored programs run with the same privileges as the definer. This is the application design pattern that supports Virtual Private Databases (VPDs). Effectively, every table becomes like an apartment building or a multiple-tenancy building: some rows in the table belong to one user or privileged group while others belong to another user.

The definer rights model offers two advantages. The first advantage is that you can stripe your tables and wrap them in views so that only certain rows can be seen by specific users. The second advantage is that you can wrap access to the tables behind a series of stored functions and procedures, which provides an additional security barrier.

Opting to stripe tables requires that you add a column to them that stores a unique ID or name. A view implements a filtering clause that checks whether the current user or database matches the striped column value. This limits access to rows of data to information recorded during the session—the duration of a connection. It's similar to assigning apartment numbers to tenants in a large building.

The strategy of separating tables from connections is powerful. It compels programmers to use your API rather than query and transact directly against the data. You can also set session-level variables with key data. For example, many business applications connect all users to the database with the same user name, password, and database name, but then validate against an access control list (ACL) stored in a table. Heading back to the analogy of an apartment building, every tenant has the same key to unlock the building's external door. Each tenant has a unique key to access his or her apartment. An ACL is analogous to a cabinet where spare keys to all the apartments are stored, indexed by apartment tenant.

When APIs wrap access to tables, they filter queries to a restricted list of rows. The APIs identify requestors by inspecting the ACL, determining their rights of access to rows, and filtering their access to rows. APIs also provide another barrier to wide-open access to data tables. The parameters for the API guarantee access rules. APIs also let you control parameters by using prepared statements, which help minimize the possibility of SQL injection attacks.

Restricting web-based program components from directly accessing tables also provides a way to vet (audit and verify) parameters for SQL injection attacks. Using stored programs also gives you control over the scope and integrity of transactions, which presumes good development always uses transaction databases. Although individual DML statements are individually ACID-compliant and naturally MVCC-safe, stored programs extend those protections to sets of DML statements. This lets a complete business process have the same guarantee provided by individual DML statements.

The definer rights model also gives you control over table and table relationship designs, because the stored programs constitute an additional barrier to your data. They abstract or hide the internal structure of your tables and their relationships. This means that the design of tables, views, and relationships can change independently of web-based or other interfaces.

Overall, the definer rights model offers extremely strong benefits. The model doesn't offer good support for distributed data sets, however. The definer rights model isn't a good fit when the business requires independent database instances and consolidation models at fixed financial periods, such as weekly, monthly, quarterly, or yearly. Those types of models fit better with the invoker rights model, covered next.

Invoker Rights

The invoker rights model uses distributed data repositories and a common code base. This means that all stored programs run with the rights of the invoker, or caller, of the programs. Therefore, the invoker must have access to any tables or views that the stored programs use, or the invoker must have his or her own copies. Typically, this requires that duplicate copies of the tables and views be deployed into every invoker's work area.

Adopting the invoker rights model inherently separates data into discrete work areas. This model is desirable when the business model supports franchisees that operate as separate business entities. In a franchisee model, application software helps the franchises operate the same way and collect critical information for consolidation. It also lets the central franchising operation control the look, feel, and integrity of data over which it doesn't have direct control.

Invoker rights also can parallel the analogy of an apartment building, as discussed in the context of definer rights. It is a decidedly different model, however, because the tenants reside in different buildings in a complex, and each building has its own external door. Tenants in building A hold keys for building A and tenants in building B hold keys for building B, but both have keys to the common area. This is a model of a distributed database.

Years ago, the separate franchisees might operate on separate servers, but today these types of operations exist in virtual clouds. They often share a single deployment but retain control over their data. This type of model is used in many hosting companies around the world.

Invoker rights models don't prevent the striping of data, as discussed earlier, but they may disclose how that security information is managed. Note that the most effective implementations of invoker rights models define key parts of their solutions as definer rights components. Separation is critical in hiding how they manage security. Otherwise, disclosure to one franchisee may expose others to educated and directed hacking exploits. Therefore, the combination of both approaches makes for a stronger security deployment when the security component is implemented in the definer rights model.

SQL Interactive and Batch Processing

SQL*Plus provides an interactive and batch processing environment that dispatches commands to the SQL and PL/SQL engines. You can work either in the interactive SQL*Plus command-line interface (CLI) or in Oracle SQL Developer through a Java-based GUI. This section explains how to use these two primary interfaces to the SQL and PL/SQL engines. There are many other commercial products from other vendors that let you work with Oracle, but coverage of those products is beyond the scope of this book.

SQL*Plus Command-Line Interface

SQL*Plus is the client software for Oracle that runs SQL statements and anonymous block PL/SQL statements in an interactive and batch development environment. The statements are organized in the order that you generally encounter them as you start working with SQL*Plus or the MySQL Monitor.

Although Oracle supports large object types, prior to Oracle Database 10*g* you couldn't display more than 32,767 characters' worth of them in SQL*Plus. That's because the maximum size of a long data type was 32,767, and SQL*Plus displayed large objects using the `LONG` data type. From Oracle Database 10*g* forward, you can set the `LONG` environment variable as high as you want, and it works. The `CLOB` data type is displayed now by SQL*Plus, but the `LONG` environment variable hasn't changed yet. Likewise, you can see a billion bytes of a binary large object in SQL*Plus.

Connecting to and Disconnecting from SQL*Plus

After installing the product on the Windows OS, you access SQL*Plus from the command line. This works when the operating system finds the `sqlplus` executable in its path environment variable (`%PATH%` on Windows and `$PATH` on Linux). Linux installations require that you configure this manually. When `sqlplus` is in the path environment variable, you can access it by typing the following:

```
sqlplus some_username/some_password
```

The preceding connect string uses IPC to connect to the Oracle database. You can connect through the network by specifying a valid net service name, like this:

```
sqlplus some_username/some_password@some_net_service_name
```

While this works, and many people use it, you should simply enter your user name and let the database prompt you for the password. That way, it's not displayed as clear text, as shown in the following illustration.

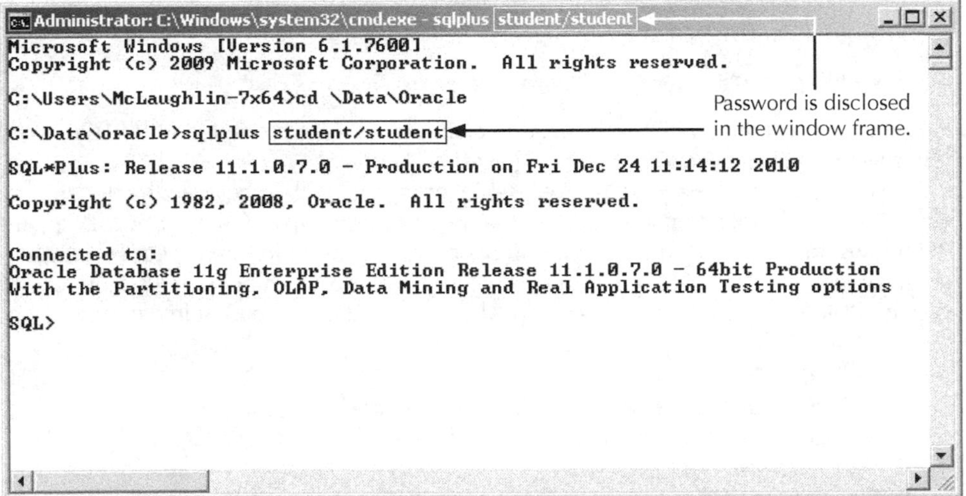

NOTE
Aside from the obvious security risks of the Windows dialog, it is possible for others to snoop for passwords from command histories.

To avoid displaying your password, you should connect in the following way, which uses IPC:

```
sqlplus some_username
```

Or you can connect using the network layer by using a net service name like this:

```
sqlplus some_username@some_tns_alias
```

You'll then see a password prompt. As you type your password, it is masked from prying eyes. The password also won't be visible in the window of the command session.

The problem with either of these approaches is that you've disclosed your user account name at the operating system level. No matter how carefully you've host-hardened your operating system, there's no reason to disclose unnecessary details. The recommended best practice for connecting at the command line is to use `/nolog`, like this:

```
sqlplus /nolog
```

After you're connected as an authenticated user, you can switch to work as another user by using the following syntax, which discloses your password to the screen but not the session window:

```
SQL> CONNECT some_otheruser/some_password
```

Or you can connect through a net service name, like

```
SQL> CONNECT some_otheruser@net_service_name/some_password
```

Alternatively, you can connect with or without a net service name to avoid displaying your password:

```
SQL> CONNECT some_otheruser
```

As with the preceding initial authorization example, you are prompted for the password. Entering it in this way also protects it from prying eyes.

If you try to run the `sqlplus` executable and it fails with a message that it can't find the `sqlplus` executable, you must correct that issue. Check whether the `%ORACLE_HOME%\bin` (Windows) or `$ORACLE_HOME/bin` (Linux or Unix) is found in the respective `%PATH%` or `$PATH` environment variable. Like `PATH`, the `ORACLE_HOME` is also an operating system environment variable. `ORACLE_HOME` should point to where you installed the Oracle database.

NOTE
Make sure your `%PATH%` or `$PATH` variable includes the Oracle executables, which are in the `bin` directory of the `ORACLE_HOME`.

You can use the following commands to check the contents of your path environment variable. Instructions for setting these are in the *Oracle Database Installation Guide* for your platform and release:

- Windows: `echo %PATH%`
- Linux or Unix: `echo $PATH`

When you've connected to SQL*Plus, you will see the `SQL>` prompt.

If you haven't created your own user, you can connect with the `system` user name and password and create one. The Oracle `root` account is the `sys` user, but Oracle recommends that you use the `system` user, which shares most administration rights and privileges. It provides insurance that you won't directly update the data dictionary, which is found in the `SYS` schema.

You set the password for the `sys` and `system` users when installing the Oracle database. If you're new to Oracle, refer to the "Create a Default Oracle User" sidebar later in this appendix for instructions. If you didn't install the database, you can ask whoever did to create a user name for you.

After you create a user, you must grant privileges to the user. Privileges let the user connect to the database and perform runtime tasks. You may also grant privileges as groups. This is done with *roles*, which are collections of privileges. The caveat with roles is that they change between releases.

It is critical that you understand exactly what roles do before you grant privileges through them. For example, you should avoid granting the CONNECT and RESOURCE roles because the Oracle Database 10*g* documentation announced that they will be deprecated in future versions. These roles are still available in Oracle Database 12*c*.

NOTE
Oracle plans to deprecate the CONNECT *and* RESOURCE *roles and began letting customers know of this change in the Oracle Database 10*g *documentation.*

The CONNECT and RESOURCE roles are overused in many sample databases and in some production databases. Legacy roles can create unnecessary vulnerabilities by conveying more than the necessary privileges to user accounts. You should always check which privileges come with any role before granting the role, which you'll learn about in the "Security Privileges" section later in this appendix. Acknowledging that caveat, roles are preferred to grants because they provide a layer of abstraction.

TIP
Granting the RESOURCE *role to a user automatically grants unlimited tablespace to that user, at least up to the physical size limit imposed on a tablespace by its physical files.*

The benefit of abstraction in roles is an added layer of security. Although users should understand what they can and can't do, a hacker shouldn't be able to query an administrative view and discover what they can do as that user. For example, when a hacker gains access to a database user, he will often query well-known views to determine the amount of control he can exert on the system. Granting privileges through roles obstructs a hacker's ability to query privileges from the USER_SYS_PRIVS administrative view in an Oracle database. The hacker would be able to see only the roles he's been granted directly through the USER_ROLE_PRIVS administrative view. That forces a user, or a hacker acting as a non-superuser, to experiment with syntax before he knows what he can or can't do. The delay may limit damage done by a hacker.

Sometimes, privileges convey permission to perform an overloaded behavior. The Oracle CREATE PROCEDURE privilege is an example. It allows you to create a function or procedure. Functions and procedures are stored blocks of executable code that return output to the calling process (see Chapters 8 and 9). Although there are a number of differences between functions and procedures, the significant one is that a function's output can be assigned to a variable, while a procedure's output can't. A procedure doesn't have a result that can serve as an expression or as a right operand in an assignment.

A user can see her privileges in the USER_SYS_PRIVS administrative view. You can learn more about roles and privileges in "Security Privileges" later in this appendix.

Working in the SQL*Plus Environment

Unlike other SQL environments, the SQL*Plus environment isn't limited simply to running SQL statements. Originally, it was written as a SQL report writer. This means SQL*Plus contains a number of features to make it friendlier and more useful. (That's why SQL*Plus was originally known as an Advanced Friendly Interface [AFI]). Examples of these friendlier and useful features include a set of well-designed formatting extensions that enables you to format and aggregate result set data. SQL*Plus also lets you interactively edit files from the command line.

Create a Generic PDB Oracle User

In this sample code, you create a `student` PDB Oracle user/schema with a minimum set of permissions. Before you can make these changes, you need to either connect as the `ADMIN` user for the PDB or use `ALTER SESSION` to change the context to the PDB as the container `sysdba` account.

You change context to the standard sample database `pdborcl` PDB with this syntax:

```
SQL> ALTER SESSION SET container=pdborcl;
```

The following example shows you how to create a `student` Oracle user/schema with a minimum set of permissions. First, create the PDB `student` account (or have your DBA create it):

```
SQL> CREATE USER student IDENTIFIED BY student
  2  DEFAULT TABLESPACE pdb_users QUOTA 50M ON pdb_users
  3  TEMPORARY TABLESPACE temp;
```

This is a limited account because you can consume only up to 50MB of space in the `users` tablespace, which is available in all sample Oracle databases. A *tablespace* is a logical unit that can contain one or more users and one or more physical data files where those users can read and write data. Tablespaces can include one to many physical files, and the size of the tablespaces is constrained by the space available in these files. You can learn more about tablespaces in the *Oracle Database 12*c *DBA Handbook* (Oracle Press, 2014).

Next, you should grant several privileges to the `student` PDB user. The Data Control Language (DCL) provides the `GRANT` command to perform this task. The `GRANT` command enables an authorized user to assign roles and privileges to other users. The following example uses privileges, which are provided as comma-separated lists:

```
SQL> GRANT create cluster, create indextype, create operator
  2  ,     create procedure, create sequence, create session
  3  ,     create table, create trigger, create type
  4  ,     create view, unlimited tablespace TO student;
```

The grant extends the permission to connect to the database through the `CREATE SESSION` privilege.

This section explains how you can dynamically configure your environment to suit your needs for each connection, configure SQL*Plus to remember settings for every connection, discover features through the interactive help menus, and shell out of or exit the SQL*Plus environment.

Configuring SQL*Plus Environment You can configure your SQL*Plus environment in two ways. One requires that you configure it each time that you start a session (dynamically). The other requires that you configure the `glogin.sql` file, which is the first thing that runs after a user authenticates and establishes a connection with the database. The caveat to modifying the `glogin.sql` file is that any changes become universal for all users of the Oracle Database installation. Also, only the owner of the Oracle account can make these changes.

*Dynamically Configuring SQL*Plus*—Every connection to SQL*Plus is configurable. Some developers choose to put these instructions inside their script files, while others prefer to type them as they go. Putting them in the script files means you have to know what options you have first. The SQL*Plus `SHOW` command lets you find *all* of them with the keyword `ALL`, like this:

```
SHOW ALL
```

The SQL*Plus `SHOW` command also lets you see the status of a given environment variable. The following command displays the default value for the `FEEDBACK` environment variable:

```
SHOW FEEDBACK
```

It returns the default value unless you've altered the default by configuring it in the `glogin.sql` file. The `oracle` user has the rights to make any desired changes in this file, but they apply to all users who connect to the database. The default value for `FEEDBACK` is

```
FEEDBACK ON for 6 or more rows
```

By default, an Oracle database shows the number of rows touched by a SQL command only when six or more rows are affected. If you also want to show feedback when five or fewer rows are affected, the following syntax resets the environment variable:

```
SET FEEDBACK ON
```

It returns 0 or the number of rows affected by any SQL statement.

Setting these environment variables inside script files allows you to designate runtime behaviors, but you should also reset them to the default at the conclusion of the script. When they're not reset at the end of a script, they can confuse a user expecting the default behaviors.

*Configuring the Default SQL*Plus Environment File*—The `glogin.sql` file is where you define override values for the environment variables. You might want to put many things beyond environment variable values into your `glogin.sql` configuration file. The most common is a setting for the default editor in Linux or Unix, because it's undefined out of the box. You can set the default editor to the `vi` text editor in Linux by adding the following line to the `glogin.sql` file:

```
DEFINE _EDITOR=vi
```

The `DEFINE` keyword has two specialized uses in SQL*Plus. One lets you define substitution variables (sometimes called user variables) that act as session-level variables. The other lets you enable or disable the ampersand (`&`) symbol as a substitution variable operator. It is enabled by default because the `DEFINE` environment variable is `ON` by default. You disable the specialized role by setting `DEFINE` to `OFF`. SQL*Plus treats the ampersand (`&`) as an ordinary text character when `DEFINE` is `OFF`. You can find more on this use of the `DEFINE` environment variable in the "When to Disable Substitution Variables" sidebar later in this appendix.

Substitution variables are placeholder variables in SQL statements or session-level variables in script files. They are placeholder variables when you precede them with one ampersand and are session-level variables when you precede them with two ampersands. As placeholders, they are discarded after a single use. Including two ampersands (`&&`) makes the assigned value of a substitution variable reusable. You can set a session-level variable either with the `DEFINE` command, as shown previously with the _EDITOR variable, or by using a double ampersand (&&), as in the following:

```
SELECT '&&BART' FROM dual;
```

With two ampersands, the query prompts the user for a value for the BART session-level variable and sets the value as a session-level variable. A single ampersand would simply prompt, use it, and discard it. Assuming you enter *"Cartoon Character"* as the response to the preceding query, you see the value by querying it with a single or double ampersand:

```
SELECT '&BART' AS "Session Variable" FROM dual;
```

This displays the following:

```
Session Variable
-----------------
Cartoon Character
```

Or you can use the DEFINE command like this:

```
DEFINE BART
```

This displays the following:

```
DEFINE BART                = "Cartoon Character" (CHAR)
```

The scope of the session variable lasts throughout the connection unless you undefine it with the following command:

```
UNDEFINE BART
```

Although you can define substitution variables, you can use them only by preceding their name with an ampersand. That's because a single ampersand also lets you read the contents of substitution variables when they're set as session-level variables. Several user variables are reserved for use by Oracle Database. These user variables can contain letters, underscores, or numbers in any order. When reserved for use by Oracle, these variables all start with an underscore, as is the case with the _EDITOR variable. Any reference to these variables is case-insensitive.

SQL*Plus checks the contents of the _EDITOR user variable when you type the EDIT command, often abbreviated as ED. The EDIT command launches the executable stored in the _EDITOR user variable. The Windows version of Oracle Database comes preconfigured with Notepad as the default editor. It finds the Notepad utility because it's in a directory found in the operating system path variable. If you choose another editor, you need to ensure that the executable is in your default path environment. In Windows, you should create a shortcut that points to the physical location of the new editor, and put it in the C:\Windows\System32 directory.

The DEFINE command also lets you display the contents of all session-level variables. There is no all option for the DEFINE command, as there is for the SHOW command. You simply type DEFINE without any arguments to get a list of the default values:

```
DEFINE _DATE               = "12-MAY-13" (CHAR)
DEFINE _CONNECT_IDENTIFIER = "" (CHAR)
DEFINE _USER               = "" (CHAR)
```

```
DEFINE _PRIVILEGE       = "" (CHAR)
DEFINE _SQLPLUS_RELEASE = "1201000002" (CHAR)
DEFINE _EDITOR          = "Notepad" (CHAR)
```

The preceding user variables are set by Oracle during a `/nolog` connection. When you connect as a container or pluggable user, the `DEFINE` command displays a different result. Shown next is the example after having connected as the `student` (a pluggable database user):

```
DEFINE _DATE            = "12-MAY-13" (CHAR)
DEFINE _CONNECT_IDENTIFIER = "orcl" (CHAR)
DEFINE _USER            = "STUDENT" (CHAR)
DEFINE _PRIVILEGE       = "" (CHAR)
DEFINE _SQLPLUS_RELEASE = "1201000002" (CHAR)
DEFINE _EDITOR          = "Notepad" (CHAR)
DEFINE _O_VERSION       = "Oracle Database 12c Enterprise ... " (CHAR)
DEFINE _O_RELEASE       = "1201000002" (CHAR)
```

The last two lines are displayed only when you're connected as a user to the Oracle Database 12*c* database. As previously explained, you can define the contents of other substitution variables.

Although substitution variables have many uses, their primary purpose is to support the SQL*Plus environment. For example, you can use them to reset the `SQL>` prompt. You can reset the default SQL*Plus prompt by using two predefined session-level variables, like this:

```
SET sqlprompt "'SQL:'_user at _connect_identifier>"
```

This would change the default prompt to look like this when the `_user` name is `system` and the `_connect_identifier` is `orcl`:

```
SQL: SYSTEM at orcl>
```

This type of prompt takes more space, but it shows you your current user and schema at a glance. It's a handy prompt to help you avoid making changes in the wrong schema or instance, which occurs too often in daily practice.

A number of possibilities exist for modifying your prompt beyond this example. The preceding example provided the syntax to set the prompt for the duration of the connection. If you want to modify the starting default prompt, you can edit `%ORACLE_HOME%\sqlplus\admin\glogin.sql` in Windows or its equivalent in Linux or Unix.

Using Interactive Help in the SQL*Plus Environment SQL*Plus also provides an interactive help console that contains an index of help commands. You can find the index of commands by typing the following in SQL*Plus:

```
SQL> help index
```

It displays the following:

```
Enter Help [topic] for help.

 @             COPY         PAUSE                    SHUTDOWN
 @@            DEFINE       PRINT                    SPOOL
 /             DEL          PROMPT                   SQLPLUS
```

```
ACCEPT          DESCRIBE      QUIT                          START
APPEND          DISCONNECT    RECOVER                       STARTUP
ARCHIVE LOG     EDIT          REMARK                        STORE
ATTRIBUTE       EXECUTE       REPFOOTER                     TIMING
BREAK           EXIT          REPHEADER                     TTITLE
BTITLE          GET           RESERVED WORDS (SQL)          UNDEFINE
CHANGE          HELP          RESERVED WORDS (PL/SQL)       VARIABLE
CLEAR           HOST          RUN                           WHENEVER OSERROR
COLUMN          INPUT         SAVE                          WHENEVER SQLERROR
COMPUTE         LIST          SET                           XQUERY
CONNECT         PASSWORD      SHOW
```

You can discover more about the commands by typing `help` with one of the index keywords. The following demonstrates the `STORE` command, which lets you store the current buffer contents as a file:

```
SQL> help store
```

It displays the following:

```
STORE
-----
 Saves attributes of the current SQL*Plus environment in a script.

 STORE {SET} file_name[.ext] [CRE[ATE] | REP[LACE] | APP[END]]
```

This is one way to save the contents of your current SQL statement into a file. You'll see another, the `SAVE` command, shortly in this appendix. You might want to take a peek in the "Writing SQL*Plus Log Files" section later in this appendix if you're experimenting with capturing the results of the `HELP` utility by spooling the information to a log file.

As discussed, the duration of any SQL*Plus environment variable is from the beginning to the end of any session. Define environment variables in the `glogin.sql` file when you want them to be available in all SQL*Plus sessions.

Shelling Out of the SQL*Plus Environment In cases where you don't want to exit an interactive session of SQL*Plus, you can leave the session (known as *shelling out*) and run operating system commands. The `HOST` command lets you do that, like so:

```
SQL> HOST
```

Anything that you do inside this operating system session other than modify files is lost when you leave it and return to the SQL*Plus session. The most frequent things that most developers do in a shelled-out session are check the listing of files and rename files. Sometimes, developers make small modifications to files, exit the subshell session, and rerun the file from SQL*Plus.

You exit the operating system shell environment and return to SQL*Plus by typing `EXIT`.

An alternative to shelling out is to run a single operating system command from SQL*Plus. For example, you can type the following in Windows to see the contents of the directory from which you entered SQL*Plus:

```
SQL> HOST dir
```

Linux works with the HOST command, too. In Linux, you also have the option of a shorthand version of the HOST command—the exclamation mark (!). You use it like this:

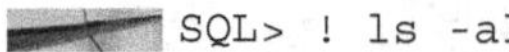

```
SQL> ! ls -al
```

The difference between the ! and HOST commands is that you can't use substitution variables with !. Also, ! doesn't work when you're deployed on a Windows platform.

Exiting SQL*Plus Environment You use QUIT or EXIT to exit a session in the SQL*Plus program. Either command ends a SQL*Plus session and releases any session variables.

The next sections show you how to write, save, edit, rerun, edit, abort, call, run, and pass parameters to SQL statements. Then you'll learn how to call PL/SQL programs and write SQL*Plus log files.

Writing SQL Statements with SQL*Plus

A simple and direct way to demonstrate how to write SQL statements in SQL*Plus is to write a short query. Queries use the SELECT keyword to list columns from a table and use the FROM keyword to designate a table or set of tables. The following query selects a string literal value ("Hello World!") from thin air with the help of the *pseudo table* dual. The dual pseudo table is a structure that lets you query one or more columns of data without accessing a table, view, or stored program. Oracle lets you select any type of column except a large object (LOB) from the dual table. The dual table returns only one row of data.

NOTE
The dual table exists in MySQL and Microsoft SQL Server but is optional in the equivalent syntax.

```
SELECT 'Hello World!' FROM dual;
```

Notice that Oracle requires single quotation marks as delimiters of string literal values. Any attempt to substitute double quotation marks raises an ORA-00904 error message, which means you've attempted to use an invalid identifier. For example, you'd generate the following error if you used double quotes around the string literal in the original statement:

```
SELECT "Hello World!" FROM dual
       *
ERROR at line 1:
ORA-00904: "Hello World!": invalid identifier
```

If you're coming from the MySQL world to work in Oracle databases, this may seem a bit provincial. MySQL works with either single or double quotes as string delimiters, but Oracle doesn't. No quote delimiters are required for numeric literals.

SQL*Plus places a query or other SQL statement in a special buffer when you run it. Sometimes you may want to save these queries in files. The next section shows you how to do that.

Saving SQL Statements with SQL*Plus

Sometimes you'll want to save a SQL statement in a file. That's actually a perfect activity for the SAVE or STORE command (rather than spooling a log file). Using the SAVE or STORE command

Back-Quoting in Oracle

The art of back-quoting is critical in many programming languages. You back-quote a character that has special purpose in a programming language when you want to use the character as ordinary text. The apostrophe (`'`) is a special character in Oracle's implementation of SQL.

When you have a string with an apostrophe, you must back-quote the apostrophe with another apostrophe. Here's an example:

```
SELECT 'Ralph Malph is stealing Fonzie''s bike.' AS Statement
FROM dual;
```

The first apostrophe instructs the parser to treat the next character as an ordinary text character. This means that the second apostrophe is stored in a column or printed from the query. This syntax also works in the MySQL database. Here's the output from the query:

```
Statement
---------------------------------------
Ralph Malph is stealing Fonzie's bike.
```

Beginning with Oracle Database 10g, you have an alternative to back-quoting an apostrophe. You may use the following syntax:

```
SELECT q'(Ralph Malph is stealing Fonzie's bike.)' AS trite
FROM dual;
```

Alternatives are nice. You should use the one that works best for you.

lets you save your current statement to a file. Capturing these ad hoc SQL statements is generally important—after all, SQL statements ultimately get bundled into rerunnable script files before they ever move into production systems.

Use the following syntax to save a statement as a runnable file:

```
SAVE some_new_file_name.sql
```

If the file already exists, you can save the file with this syntax:

```
SAVE some_new_file_name.sql REPLACE
```

CAUTION

Note that `SAVE` and `STORE` commands that include a `REPLACE` option have no undo capability. That means any existing file with the same name is immediately unrecoverable. Use the `REPLACE` option with care.

Editing SQL Statements with SQL*Plus

You can edit your current SQL statements from within SQL*Plus by using `EDIT`. SQL*Plus preconfigures itself to launch Notepad when you type `EDIT` or the shorthand `ED` in any Windows installation of Oracle Database.

Although the `EDIT` command points to Notepad when you're working in Windows, it isn't configured by default in Linux or Unix. You have to set the editor for SQL*Plus when running on Linux or Unix. Refer to the "Working in the SQL*Plus Environment" section earlier in the appendix for details about setting up the editor.

Assuming you've configured the editor, you can edit the last SQL statement by typing `EDIT` like this (or you can use `ED`):

```
SQL> EDIT
```

The temporary contents of any SQL statement are stored in the `afiedt.buf` file by default. After you edit the file, you can save the modified statement into the buffer and rerun the statement. Alternatively, you can save the SQL statement as another file.

Rerunning SQL*Plus SQL Statements from the Buffer

After you edit a SQL statement, SQL*Plus automatically lists it for you and enables you to rerun it. Use a forward slash (/) to run the last SQL statement from the buffer. The semicolon at the end of your original SQL statement isn't stored in the buffer; it's replaced by a forward slash. If you add the semicolon back when you edited the SQL statement, you would see something like the following with the semicolon at the end of the last line of the statement:

```
SQL> EDIT
Wrote file afiedt.buf
  1* SELECT 'Hello World!' AS statement FROM dual;
```

A forward slash can't rerun this from the buffer because the semicolon is an *illegal character*. You would get an error like this:

```
SQL> /
SELECT 'Hello World!' AS statement FROM dual;
                                           *
ERROR at line 1:
ORA-00911: invalid character
```

To fix this error, you should re-edit the buffer contents and remove the semicolon. The forward slash would then run the statement.

Some SQL statements have so many lines that they don't fit on a single page in your terminal or shell session. In these cases, you can use the `LIST` command (or simply a lowercase `l` or uppercase `L`) to see only a portion of the current statement from the buffer. The `LIST` command by itself reads the buffer contents and displays them with line numbers at the SQL prompt.

If you're working with a long PL/SQL block or SQL statement, you can inspect ranges of line numbers with the following syntax:

```
SQL> LIST 23 32
```

This will echo back to the console the inclusive set of lines from the buffer if they exist. Another command-line interface is used to edit line numbers. It's very cumbersome and limited in its utility, so you should simply edit the SQL statement in a text editor.

Aborting Entry of SQL Statements in SQL*Plus

When you're working at the command line, you can't just point the mouse to the prior line and correct an error; instead, if your statement has an error, your must either abort the statement or run it and wait for it to fail. SQL*Plus lets you abort statements with errors.

To abort a SQL statement that you're writing interactively, press ENTER, type a period (.) as the first character on the new line, and then press ENTER again. This aborts the statement but leaves it in the active buffer file in case you went to edit it.

TIP

The period (`.`) aborts the statement only when it's the first character on a line.

After aborting a SQL statement, you can use the instructions in the previous "Editing SQL Statements with SQL*Plus" section to edit the statement with the `ed` utility—that is, if editing the statement is easier than retyping the whole thing.

Calling and Running SQL*Plus Script Files

Script (or *batch*) files are composed of related SQL statements and are the primary tool for implementing new software and patching old software. You use script files when you run installation or update programs in test, stage, and production environments. Quality and assurance departments want script files to ensure code integrity during predeployment testing. If errors are found in the script file, the script file is fixed by a new version. The final version of the script file is the one that a DBA runs when installing or upgrading an application or database system.

NOTE

A batch file is a shell script file containing a series of commands run by the command interpreter in the Microsoft Windows OS and PowerShell Scripting language.

A script is *rerunnable* only if it can manage preexisting conditions in the production database without raising errors. You must eliminate all errors because administrators might not be able to judge which errors can be safely ignored. This means the script must perform conditional drops of tables and data migration processes.

Assuming you have a file named `create_data.sql` in a `C:\Data` directory, you can run it with the @ (*at*) command in SQL*Plus. This script can be run from within SQL*Plus with either a relative filename or an absolute filename. A relative filename contains no path element because it assumes the present working path. An absolute filename requires a fully qualified path (also known as a canonical path) and filename.

The relative filename syntax depends on starting SQL*Plus from the directory where you have saved the script file. Here's the syntax to run the `create_data.sql` file:

```
@create_data.sql
```

Although the relative filename is easy to use, it limits you to starting SQL*Plus from a specific directory, which is not always possible. The absolute filename syntax works regardless of where you start SQL*Plus. Here's an example for Windows:

```
@C:\Data\create_data.sql
```

The @ command is also synonymous with the SQL*Plus START command. This means you can also run a script file based on its relative filename like this:

```
START create_data.sql
```

The @ command reads the script file into the active buffer and then runs the script file. You use two @@ symbols when you call one script file from another script file that exists in the same directory. Combining the @@ symbols instructs SQL*Plus to look in the directory specified by the command that ran the calling script. This means that a call such as the following runs a subordinate script file *from the same directory*:

```
@@some_subordinate.sql
```

If you need to run scripts delivered by Oracle and they reside in the ORACLE_HOME, you can use a handy shortcut: the question mark (?). The question mark maps to the ORACLE_HOME. This means you can run a library script from the \rdbms subdirectory of the ORACLE_HOME with this syntax in Windows:

```
?\rdbms\somescript.sql
```

The shortcuts and relative path syntax are attractive during development but should be avoided in production. Using fully qualified paths from a fixed environment variable such as the %ORACLE_HOME% in Windows or $ORACLE_HOME in Linux is generally the best approach.

Passing Parameters to SQL*Plus Script Files

Understanding how to write and run static SQL statements or script files is important, but understanding how to write and run SQL statements or script files that can solve dynamic problems is even more important. To write dynamic scripts, you use substitution variables, which act like *placeholders* in SQL statements or scripts. As mentioned earlier, SQL*Plus supports two modes of processing: interactive mode and call mode.

Interactive Mode Parameter Passing When you call a script that contains substitution variables, SQL*Plus prompts for values that you want to assign to the substitution variables. The standard prompt is the name of the substitution variable, but you can alter that behavior by using the ACCEPT SQL*Plus command.

For example, assume that you want to write a script that looks for a table with a name that's some partial string, but you know that the search string will change. A static SQL statement wouldn't work, but a dynamic one would. The following dynamic script enables you to query the database catalog for any table based on only the starting part of the table name. The placeholder variable is designated using an ampersand (&) or two. Using a single ampersand instructs SQL*Plus to make the substitution at runtime and forget the value immediately after the substitution. Using two ampersands instructs SQL*Plus to make the substitution, store the variable as a session-level variable, and undefine the substitution variable.

```
SQL> SELECT   table_name
  2  ,        column_id
  3  ,        column_name
  4  FROM     user_tab_columns
  5  WHERE    table_name LIKE UPPER('&input')||'%';
```

The UPPER function on line 5 promotes the input to uppercase letters because Oracle stores all metadata in uppercase and performs case-sensitive comparisons of strings by default. The query prompts as follows when run:

```
Enter value for input: it
```

When you press ENTER, it shows the substitution of the value for the placeholder, like so:

```
old   5: WHERE    table_name LIKE UPPER('&input')||'%'
new   5: WHERE    table_name LIKE UPPER('it')||'%'
```

At least this is the default behavior. The behavior depends on the value of the SQL*Plus VERIFY environment variable, which is set to ON by default. You can suppress that behavior by setting the value of VERIFY to OFF:

```
SET VERIFY OFF
```

You can also configure the default prompt by using SQL*Plus formatting commands, like so:

```
ACCEPT input CHAR PROMPT 'Enter the beginning part of the table name:'
```

This syntax acts like a double ampersand assignment and places the input substitution in memory as a session-level variable.

You can also format output through SQL*Plus. The COL[UMN] command qualifies the column name, the FORMAT command sets formatting to either numeric or alphanumeric string formatting, and the HEADING command lets you replace the column name with a reporting header. The following is an example of formatting for the preceding query:

```
SQL> COLUMN table_name    FORMAT A20   HEADING "Table Name"
SQL> COLUMN column_id     FORMAT 9990  HEADING "Column|ID"
SQL> COLUMN column_name   FORMAT A20   HEADING "Column Name"
```

The table_name column and column_name column now display the first 20 characters before wrapping to the next line because they are set to an alphanumeric size of 20 characters. The column_id column now displays the first four numeric values and would display a 0 when the column_id value is less than 1. Actually, this only illustrates the possibility of printing at least a 0 because a surrogate key value can't have a value less than 1. The column headers for the table_name and column_name columns print in title case with an intervening whitespace, while the column_id column prints "Column" on one line and "ID" on the next.

Advanced Formatting of SQL*Plus Output SQL*Plus enables you to assign column values from queries to object variables and create dynamic titles with these object values. SQL*Plus also lets you perform computations with result sets and set column breaks.

The following gives you an example of advanced SQL*Plus reporting:

```
-- Set prompt message.
ACCEPT INPUT PROMPT "Enter [TABLE | VIEW ] unless you want both: "

-- Set the heading and title.
SET HEADING ON
TTITLE LEFT o1 o2 ' >' SKIP 1 -
'-------------------------------------------------------' SKIP 1

-- Clear column and page breaks.
CLEAR COLUMNS
CLEAR BREAKS

-- Set page breaks.
BREAK ON REPORT
BREAK ON c2 SKIP PAGE

-- Assign columns to SQL*Plus object variables.
COL c1 NEW_VALUE o1 NOPRINT
COL c2 NEW_VALUE o2 NOPRINT

-- Format display columns.
COL c3 FORMAT A32 HEADING "Name"
COL c4 FORMAT A8  HEADING "Null?"
COL c5 FORMAT A33 HEADING "Type"
COL c6 FORMAT A1  HEADING "Default?"

-- Display results from a dynamic query.
SELECT   DECODE(st.object_type,'TABLE','Table Name: < '
,                              'VIEW' ,'View Name: < ') c1
,        st.table_name c2
,        st.column_name c3
,        st.nullable c4
,        st.data_type c5
,        st.data_default c6
FROM     schema_tables st
WHERE    st.table_name LIKE UPPER('&input')||'%'
ORDER BY st.table_name
,        st.column_id;
```

This produces a SQL report with a row break between every table and displays a dynamic title that display a literal like one of the following:

```
Table Name: < table_name >
```

or

```
View Name: < view_name >
```

When to Disable Substitution Variables
Substitution variables are important aspects of the SQL*Plus environment and should generally be enabled. However, you need to disable substitution variables when you create and compile a Java source file. Java code uses the double ampersand (&&) as the *logical and* operator. Before attempting to create and compile a Java source file, you should disable the `DEFINE` environment variable:

```
SET DEFINE OFF
```

After you've created and compiled the Java source file, you should re-enable substitution variables with the `ON` option.

The left angle bracket and string literal are returned as part of `c1`, translated to `o1`. `c2` returns the table or view name to `o2`, and the right angle bracket is defined as a text literal in the SQL*Plus `TTITLE` statement.

You can also perform computations on the result set. You can find details on these features in the *SQL*Plus User's Guide and Reference* from Oracle.

Batch Mode Parameter Passing Batch mode operations typically involve a script file that contains more than a single SQL statement. The following example uses a file that contains a single SQL statement because it successfully shows the concept and conserves space.

The trick to batch submission is the `-s` *option flag*, or the silent option. Script files that run from the command line with this *option flag* are batch programs (those using the SQL*Plus call mode). They suppress a console session from being launched and run much like statements submitted through the JDBC API or ODBC API. Batch programs must include a `QUIT` or `EXIT` statement at the end of the file or they will hang in SQL*Plus. This technique lets you create a file that can run from an operating system script file, also commonly known as a *shell script*.

The following `sample.sql` file shows how you would pass a parameter to a dynamic SQL statement embedded in a script file:

```
-- Disable echoing substitution.
SET VERIFY OFF

-- Open log file.
SPOOL demo.txt

-- Query data based on an externally set parameter.
SELECT   table_name
,        column_id
,        column_name
FROM     user_tab_columns
WHERE    table_name LIKE UPPER('&1')||'%';

-- Close log file.
```

```
SPOOL OFF

-- End session connection.
QUIT;
```

You would call the program from a batch file in Windows or a shell script in Linux. The syntax would include the user name and password, which presents a security risk. Provided you've secured your local server and you routinely purge your command history, you would call a `sample.sql` script from the present working directory like this:

```
sqlplus -s student/student @sample.sql
```

You can also pass the user name and password as connection parameters, which is illustrated in the following sample:

```
SET VERIFY OFF
SPOOL demo.txt
CONNECT &1/&2
SELECT USER FROM dual;
SPOOL OFF
QUIT;
```

The script depends on the `/nolog` option to start SQL*Plus without connecting to a schema. You would call it like this, providing the user name and password:

```
sqlplus -s /nolog @create_data.sql student student
```

As mentioned, there are risks to disclosing user names and passwords, because the information from the command line can be hacked from user history logs. Therefore, you should use anonymous login or operating system user validation when you want to run scripts like these.

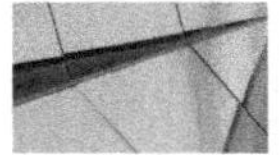

NOTE
Configuring the anonymous user account is a necessary component of working with the Oracle XDB Server. The Oracle Database 12c DBA Handbook *(Oracle Press, 2014) shows you how to configure operating system user account validation in lieu of formal credentials.*

Calling PL/SQL Programs

PL/SQL provides capabilities that don't exist in SQL that are required by some database-centric applications. PL/SQL programs are stored programs that run inside a separate engine from the SQL statement engine. Their principal role is to group SQL statements and procedural logic to support transaction scopes across multiple SQL statements.

PL/SQL supports two types of stored programs: anonymous blocks and named blocks. Anonymous blocks are stored as trigger bodies and named blocks can be either stand-alone functions or procedures. PL/SQL also supports *packages*, which are groups of related functions and procedures. Packages support function and procedure overloading and provide many of the key utilities for Oracle databases. Oracle also supports object types and object bodies with the PL/SQL language. Object types support `MEMBER` and `STATIC` functions and procedures.

Functions and procedures support pass-by-value and pass-by-reference methods available in other procedural programming languages. Functions return a value when they're placed as right operands in an assignment and as calling parameters to other functions or procedures. Procedures don't return a value or reference as a right operand and can't be used as calling parameters to other functions or procedures.

NOTE
You can find more details about functions and procedures in Chapter 8.

Sometimes you'll want to output diagnostic information to your console or formatted output from small PL/SQL programs to log files. This is easy to do in Oracle Database because PL/SQL supports anonymous block program units.

Before you can receive output from a PL/SQL block, you must open the buffer that separates the SQL*Plus environment from the PL/SQL engine. You do so with the following SQL*Plus command:

```
SET SERVEROUTPUT ON SIZE UNLIMITED
```

You enable the buffer stream for display to the console by changing the status of the `SERVEROUTPUT` environment variable to `ON`. Although you can set the `SIZE` parameter to any value, the legacy parameter limit of 1 million bytes no longer exists. That limit made sense in earlier releases because of physical machine limits governing console speed and network bandwidth. Today, there's really no reason to constrain the output size, and you should always use `UNLIMITED` when you open the buffer.

You now know how to call the various types of PL/SQL programs. Whether the programs are yours or built-ins provided by Oracle, much of the logic that supports features of Oracle databases rely on stored programs.

Executing an Anonymous Block Program The following example demonstrates a traditional "Hello World!" program in an anonymous PL/SQL block. It uses a specialized stored program known as a *package*. Packages contain data types, shared variables, and cursors, functions, and procedures. You use the package name, a dot (the *component selector*), and a function or procedure name when you call package components.

You print "Hello World!" with the following anonymous block program unit:

```
SQL> BEGIN
  2    DBMS_OUTPUT.PUT_LINE('Hello World!');
  3  END;
  4  /
```

PL/SQL is a strongly typed language that uses declarative blocks rather than the curly braces you may know best from C, C#, C++, Java, Perl, or PHP. The execution block starts with the `BEGIN` keyword and ends with an `EXCEPTION` or `END` keyword. Since the preceding sample program doesn't employ an exception block, the `END` keyword ends the program. All statements and blocks in PL/SQL end with a semicolon. The forward slash on line 4 executes the anonymous block program because the last semicolon ends the execution block. The program prints "Hello World!" to the console, provided you opened the buffer by enabling the SQL*Plus `SERVEROUTPUT` environment variable.

Anonymous block programs are very useful when you need one-time procedural processing and plan to execute it in the scope of a single batch or script file. Displaying results from the internals of the PL/SQL block is straightforward, as discussed earlier in this section: enable the `SERVEROUTPUT` environment variable.

Setting a Session Variable Inside PL/SQL Oracle databases also support session variables, which are not the same as session-level substitution variables. *Session variables* act like global variables in the scope and duration of your connection, as do session-level substitution variables, but the former differ from substitution variables in two ways. Substitution variables are limited to a string data type, while session variables may have any of the following data types: `BINARY_DOUBLE`, `BINARY_FLOAT`, `CHAR`, `CLOB`, `NCHAR`, `NCLOB`, `NUMBER`, `NVARCHAR2`, `REFCURSOR`, or `VARCHAR2`. Session variables, more commonly referred to as *bind variables*, can't be assigned a value in SQL*Plus or SQL scope. You must assign values to session variables in an anonymous PL/SQL block.

Session variables, like session-level substitution variables, are very useful because you can share them across SQL statements. You must define session variables with the `VARIABLE` keyword, which gives them a name and data type but not a value. As an example, you can define a bind variable as a 20-character-length string like so:

```
VARIABLE whom VARCHAR2(20)
```

You can assign a session variable with an anonymous PL/SQL block or a `CALL` to a stored function. Inside the anonymous block, you reference the variable with a colon preceding the variable name. The colon points to a session-level scope that is external to its local block scope:

```
BEGIN
  :whom := 'Sam';
END;
/
```

After assigning a value to the session variable, you can query it in a SQL statement or reuse it in another PL/SQL anonymous block program. The following query from the `dual` pseudo table concatenates string literals before and after the session variable:

```
SELECT 'Play it again, ' || :whom || '!' FROM dual;
```

The colon appears in SQL statements, too. Both the anonymous block and SQL statement actually run in execution scopes that are equivalent to other subshells in operating system shell scripting. The query prints the following:

```
Play it again, Sam!
```

The `dual` pseudo table is limited to a single row but can return one to many columns. You can actually display 999 columns, which is the same as the number of possible columns for a table.

Executing a Named Block Program Stored functions and procedures are known as *named blocks*, whether they're stand-alone programs or part of a package. You can *call* a named function into a session variable or return the value in a query. Procedures are different because you *execute* them in the scope of a session or block and they have no return value (procedures are like functions that return a `void` data type).

The following is a "Hello World!" function that takes no parameters:

```
SQL> CREATE OR REPLACE FUNCTION hello_function RETURN VARCHAR2 IS
BEGIN
  RETURN 'Hello World!';
END hello_function;
/
```

A query of the function uses the dual pseudo table, like so:

```
SELECT hello_function FROM dual;
```

When you call in a query a function that doesn't have defined parameters, you can omit the parentheses traditionally associated with function calls with no arguments. However, if you use the SQL*Plus CALL syntax, you must provide the opening and closing parentheses or you raise an ORA-06576 error message. Assuming that the return value of the function will be assigned to a bind variable of output, you need to define the session variable before calling the function value into the output variable.

The following defines a session variable as a 12-character, variable-length string:

```
VARIABLE my_output VARCHAR2(12)
```

The following statement calls the function and puts the result in the session variable :my_output. Preceding the session variable with a colon is required to make it accessible from SQL statements or anonymous PL/SQL blocks.

```
CALL hello_world AS INTO :my_output;
```

The lack of parentheses causes this statement to fail and raises an ORA-06576 error message. Adding the parentheses to the CALL statement makes it work:

```
CALL hello_world() AS INTO :my_output;
```

Procedures work differently and are run by the EXECUTE command. The following defines a stored procedure that echoes out the string "Hello World!" Procedures are easier to work with from SQL*Plus because you don't need to define session variables to capture output. All you do is enable the SQL*Plus SERVEROUTPUT environment variable.

```
SQL> CREATE OR REPLACE PROCEDURE hello_procedure IS
BEGIN
  dbms_output.put_line('Hello World!');
END hello_procedure;
/
```

You can execute the procedure successfully like so:

```
EXECUTE hello_procedure;
```

Or you can execute the procedure with parentheses, like so:

```
EXECUTE hello_procedure();
```

You should see "Hello World!" using either form. If it isn't displayed, enable the SQL*Plus SERVEROUTPUT environment variable. Remember that nothing returns to the console without enabling the SERVEROUTPUT environment variable.

All the examples dealing with calls to PL/SQL named blocks use a *pass-by-value* method, which means that values enter the program units, are consumed, and other values are returned. *Pass-by-reference* methods are covered in Chapter 8.

Writing SQL*Plus Log Files

When you're testing the idea of how a query should work and want to capture one that did work, you can write it directly to a file. You can also capture all the activity of a long script by writing it to a log file. You can write log files in either of two ways: capture only the *feedback* messages, such as "four rows updated," or capture the statement executed and then the feedback message. The output of the latter method are called *verbose* log files.

You can write verbose log files by leveraging the SQL*Plus ECHO environment variable in SQL*Plus. You enable it with this command:

```
SET ECHO ON
```

Enabling the ECHO command splits your SQL commands. It dispatches one to run against the server and echoes the other back to your console. This allows you to see statements in your log file before the feedback from their execution.

You open a log file with the following command:

```
SPOOL C:\Data\somefile.txt
```

This logs all output from the script to the file C:\Data\somefile.txt until the SPOOL OFF command runs in the session. The output file's extension is not required but defaults to .lst when not provided explicitly. As an extension, .lst doesn't map to a default application in Windows or Linux environments. It's a convention to use some file extension that maps to an editor as a text file.

You can append to an existing file with the following syntax:

```
SPOOL C:\Data\somefile.txt APPEND
```

Both of the foregoing syntax examples use an absolute filename. You can do the same thing in Linux by substituting a mount point for the logical drive (C:\) and changing the backslashes to forward slashes. You use a relative filename when you omit the qualified path, in which case the file is written to the directory where you launched sqlplus.

When using a relative path, you should know that it looks in the directory where you launched sqlplus. That directory is called the *present working directory* or, by some old csh (C Shell) folks, the *current working directory*. In older Windows versions, a GUI version of SQL*Plus (that's deprecated as of Oracle Database 11*g*) writes to the bin directory of the Oracle home.

You close a log file with the following command:

```
SPOOL OFF
```

No file exists until you close the buffer stream. Only one open buffer stream can exist in any session. This means you can write only to one log file at a time from a given session. Therefore, you should spool only in script files that aren't called by other script files that might also spool to a log file. You shouldn't attempt to log from the topmost script because that makes triaging errors among the programming units more complex.

TIP
When you spool to a log file, make the log file extension something other than `.sql`*, to avoid overwriting your script filename.*

A pragmatic approach to development requires that you log work performed. Failure to log your work can have impacts on the integrity of data and processes.

Oracle SQL Developer Interface

Oracle SQL Developer is a Java-based GUI development and data modeling tool. Oracle produces it and releases it free of charge to any developer that would like to use it. There are other GUI tools available that offer similar functionality, but we'll focus on SQL Developer because it is a natural fit for PL/SQL programming in Oracle Database 12*c*. This section shows you how to launch, configure, and use SQL Developer.

Launching Oracle SQL Developer

SQL Developer is installed as part of the Oracle Database 12*c* installation. It's found in the following platform-specific directories:

Linux or Unix

```
$ORACLE_HOME/sqldeveloper/sqldeveloper/sqldeveloper
```

Windows

```
$ORACLE_HOME\sqldeveloper\sqldeveloper\sqldeveloper
```

After installing and configuring the Oracle Database 12*c* database, you can run SQL Developer by launching the executable. At least, you can when the directory is in your environment path. You should add the path to your environment file in Linux, or in Windows as part of the default `%PATH%` environment.

Configuring Oracle SQL Developer

The first time you launch SQL Developer, you'll see the following dialog box that requests the Java Home.

Oracle SQL Developer
Enter the full pathname for java.exe:
C:\Program Files (x86)\Java\jdk1.6.0_45\bin
Browse...
OK
Cancel

Fixing the SQL Developer JDK

If you accidently enter an incorrect value for the JDK in the dialog box, you can't launch SQL Developer because it's pointed to the wrong location for the JDK. You only have a manual fix to this type of problem.

The fix requires you to edit the `sqldeveloper.conf` file and replace the value for `SetJavaHome`. For a Windows installation, the correct path is as follows:

```
SetJavaHome C:\Program Files (x86)\Java\jdk1.6.0_45
```

The Linux location of Oracle SQL Developer can change based on installation choices. That means you need to locate where you've installed it. For reference, the `sqldeveloper.conf` file is a plain text file that you can edit with any text editor.

After you fix the `SetJavaHome` value, you can launch SQL Developer successfully.

On Linux, you can install Java 6.0 SDK where you want, but on Windows, you install it differently based on whether you have a 32-bit or 64-bit version of the Windows OS. If you have a 32-bit version of Windows, enter the following as the Java Software Development Kit (JDK)'s directory:

```
C:\Program Files\Java\jdk1.6.0_45
```

If you have a 64-bit Windows installation, enter the following Java Software Development Kit (JDK)'s directory:

```
C:\Program Files (x86)\Java\jdk1.6.0_45
```

The last two digits (45) will change as new JDKs are released. The SQL Developer released with Oracle Database 12c, Release 1 doesn't support Java 7 and you'll raise an error dialog unless you've installed and configured Java 6. Click the *OK* button to proceed with launching the SQL Developer software.

The dialog box that appears, shown next, lets you configure file type associations. You shouldn't check any of the boxes because SQL Developer would become the default application for all those file type. Click the *OK* button to proceed with the installation.

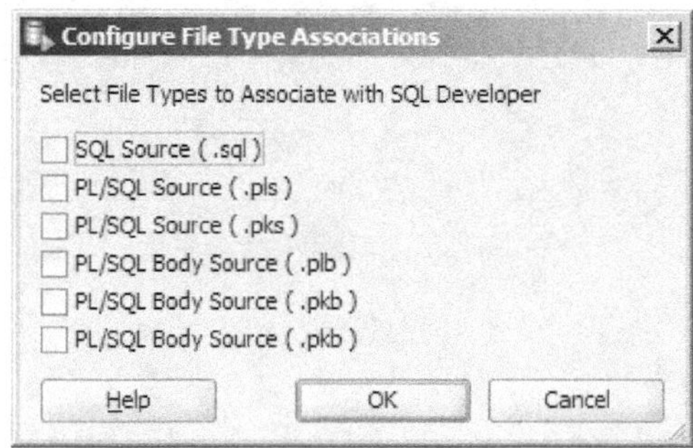

After those simple configuration steps, you see the initial SQL Developer screen. Click the green + (plus symbol) to configure an initial connection to the Oracle Database 12*c* database.

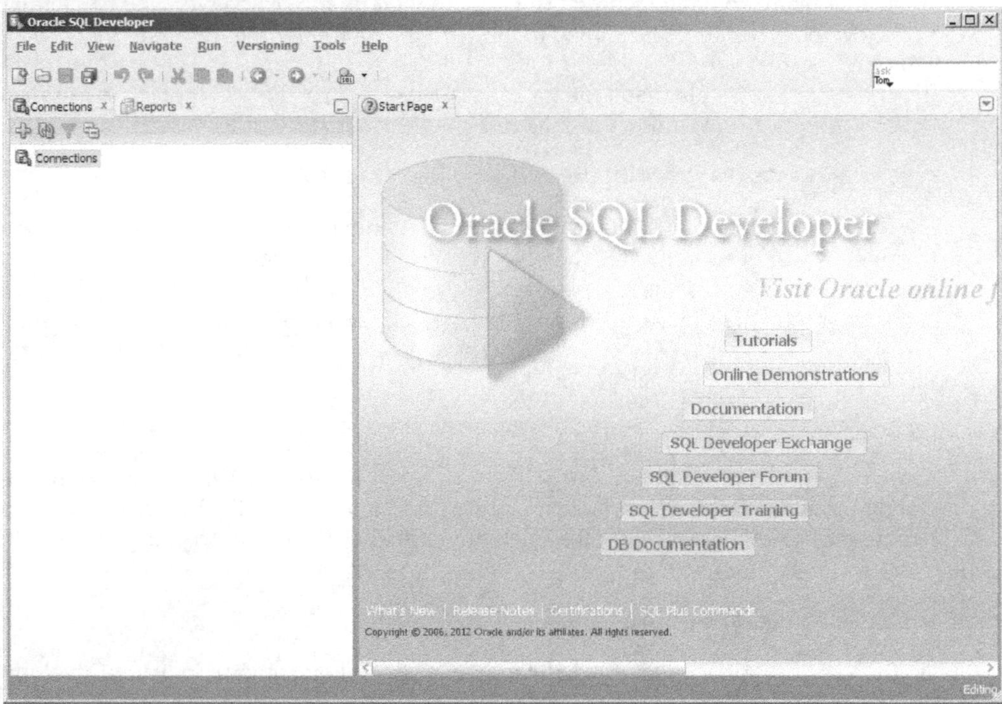

The New/Select Database Connection dialog box launches. As shown next, it initially displays the *Basic* connection type information. Typically, you will configure a *TNS* connection type. To do so, click the *Connection Type* drop-down arrow and choose *TNS*.

New / Select Database Connection
Connection Name | Connection Details
Connection Name
Username
Password
Save Password
Oracle Access
Connection Type Basic Role default
Hostname localhost
Port 1521
SID xe
Service name
OS Authentication Kerberos Authentication Proxy Connection
Status :
Help Save Clear Test Connect Cancel

As shown next, for purposes of demonstration, enter **PluggableUser** in the *Connection Name* field, enter **video** in the *Username* field, and enter a valid password in the *Password* field. Click the Network Alias radio button and choose ORCL from the drop-down list. Click the *Test* button before you create the connection.

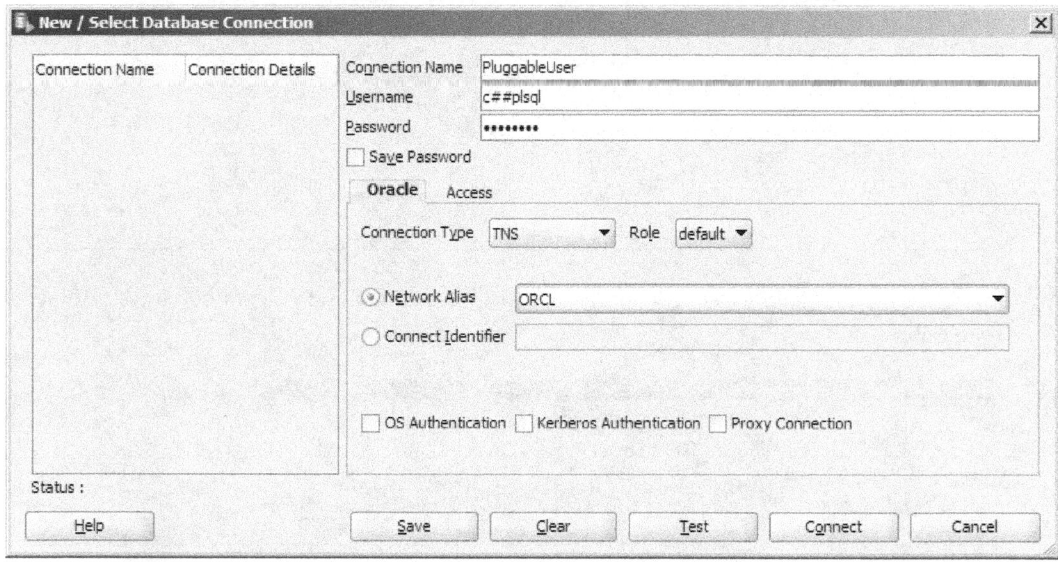

The *Status* field in the bottom-left corner should now indicate *Success*, as shown next. Click the *Connect* button to save the new database connection and exit the configuration dialog box.

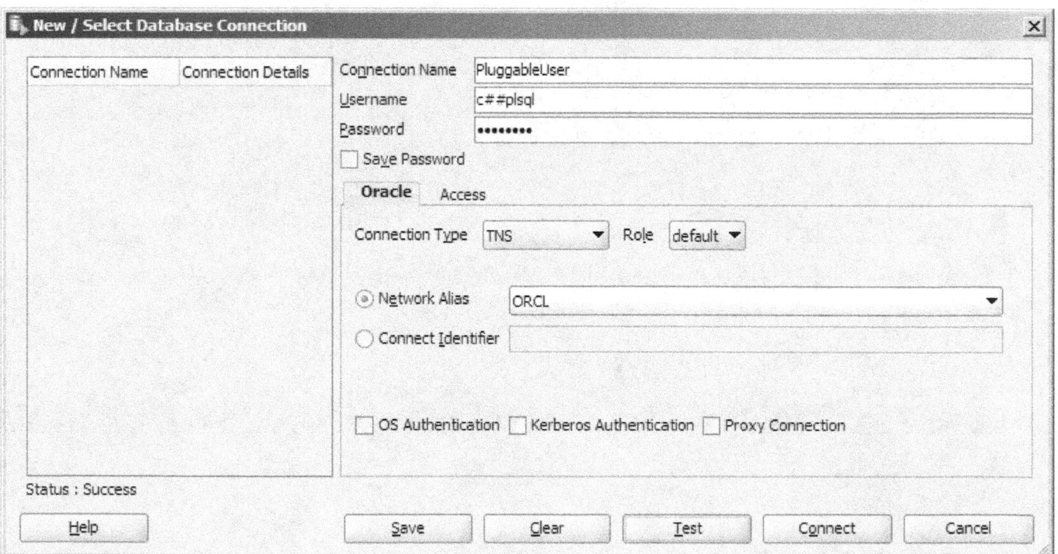

As shown next, the Connections panel on the left side of SQL Developer will list the new *PluggableUser* connection below the generic Connections repository, and you'll have a SQL Worksheet in the right panel.

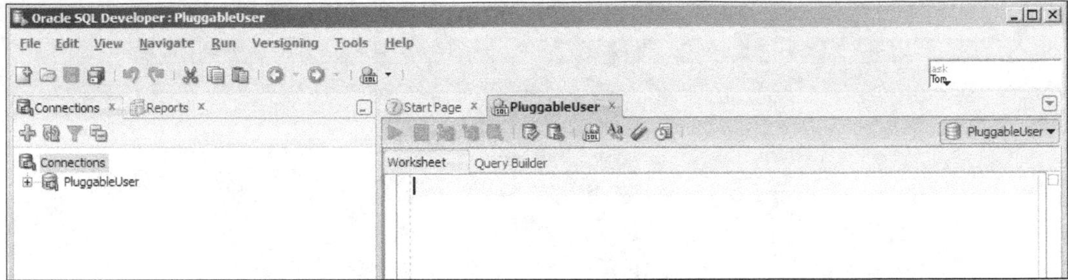

Click the *PluggableUser* connection and you'll see a list of data catalog views displayed below it.

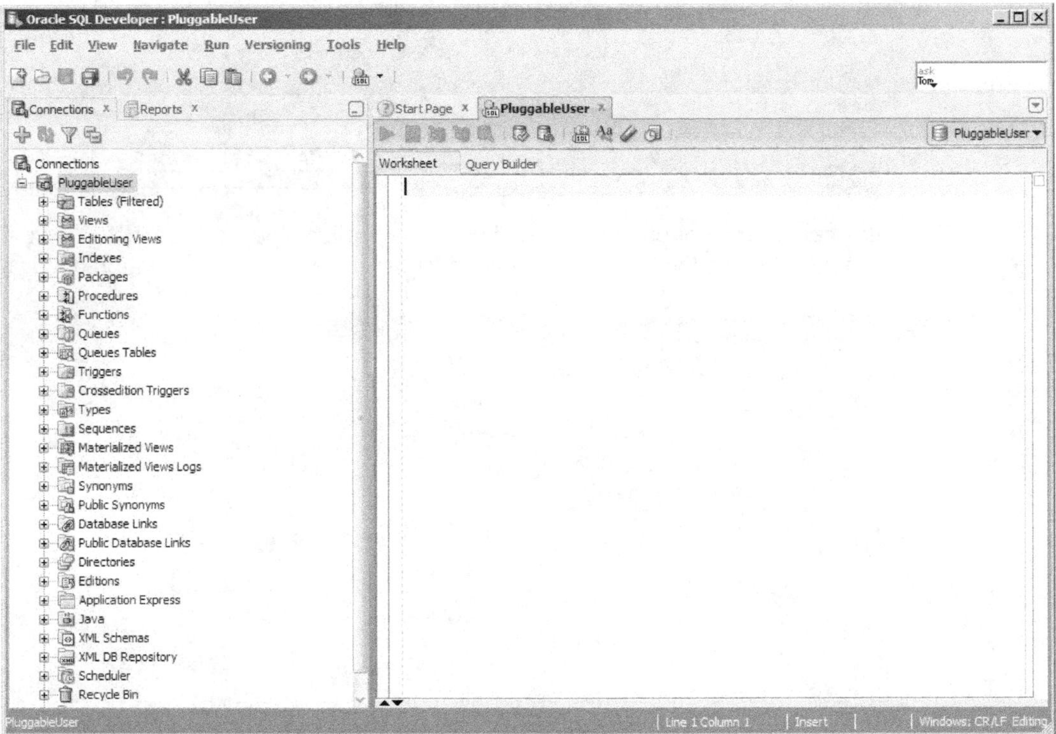

Using Oracle SQL Developer

Enter a query in the Worksheet panel, like this:

```
SELECT user FROM dual;
```

The semicolon isn't needed when you run a statement from SQL Developer, and it is ignored when present. The result should look as follows:

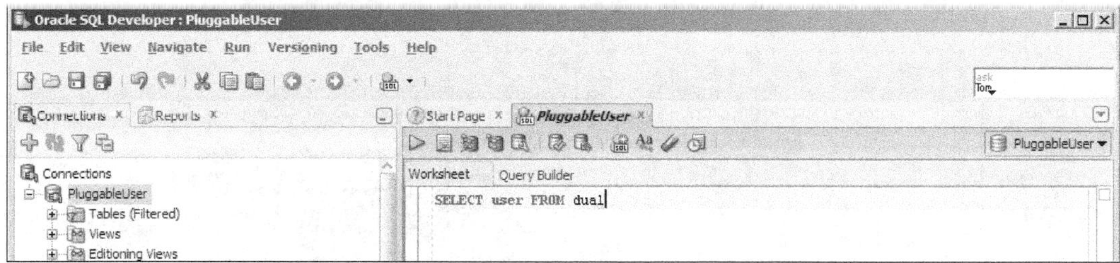

Click the green arrow button in the toolbar, and you should see the query result as shown here:

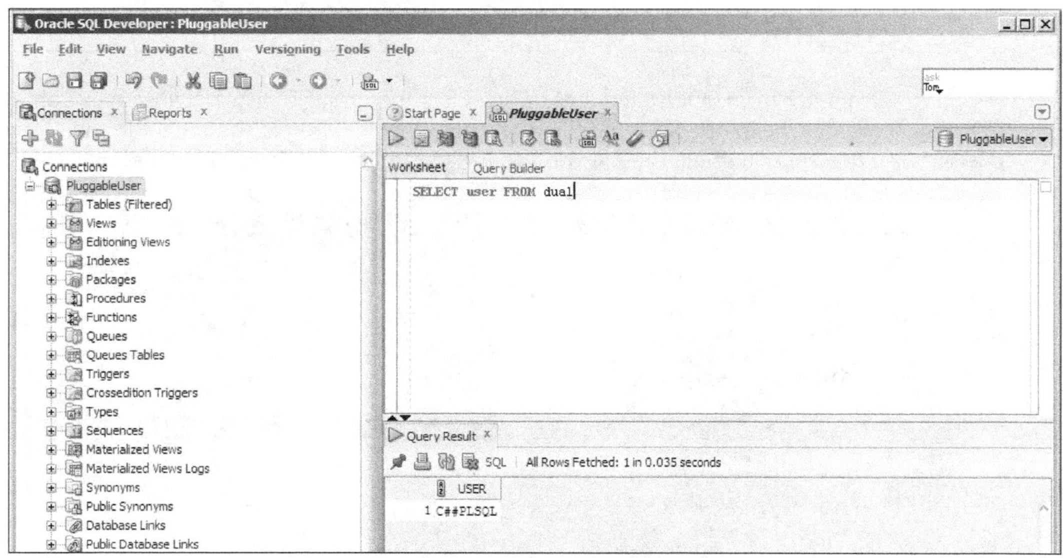

You can also run an anonymous block PL/SQL program unit by entering it in the Worksheet panel. When you click the green arrow button, an acknowledgment of successful execution is displayed, as shown in the following script output.

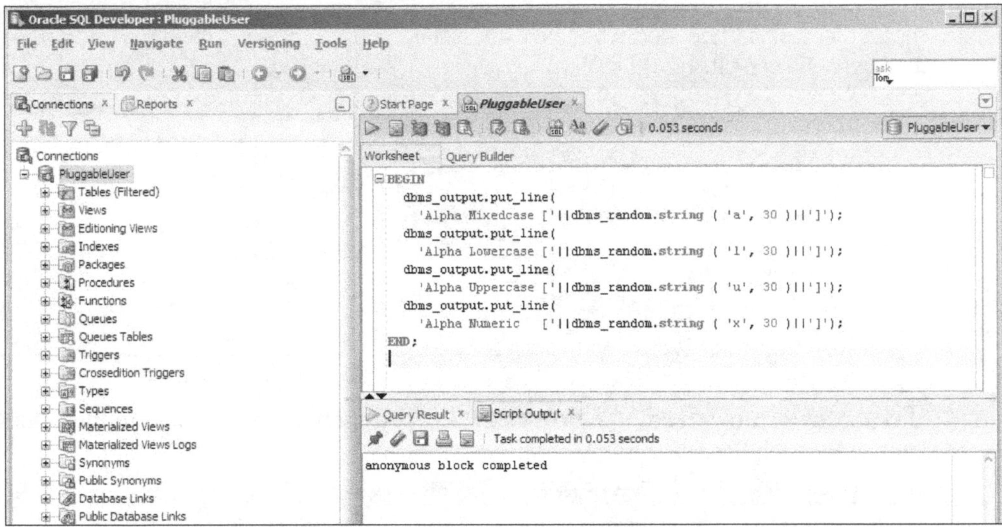

Script files differ from SQL statements or PL/SQL anonymous blocks because they can include SQL*Plus commands. To open a script file, first choose *File | Open* in the menu. In the *Open* dialog box, shown next, select the file you want to load into the *Worksheet* panel.

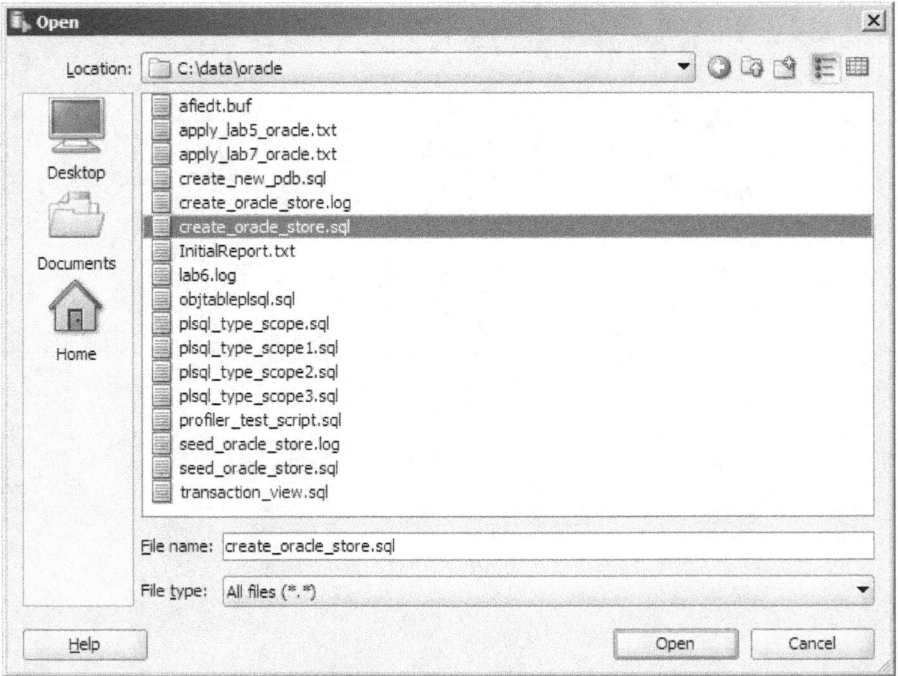

After you choose a file, click the *Open* button to load the file content into the *Worksheet* panel, as shown here:

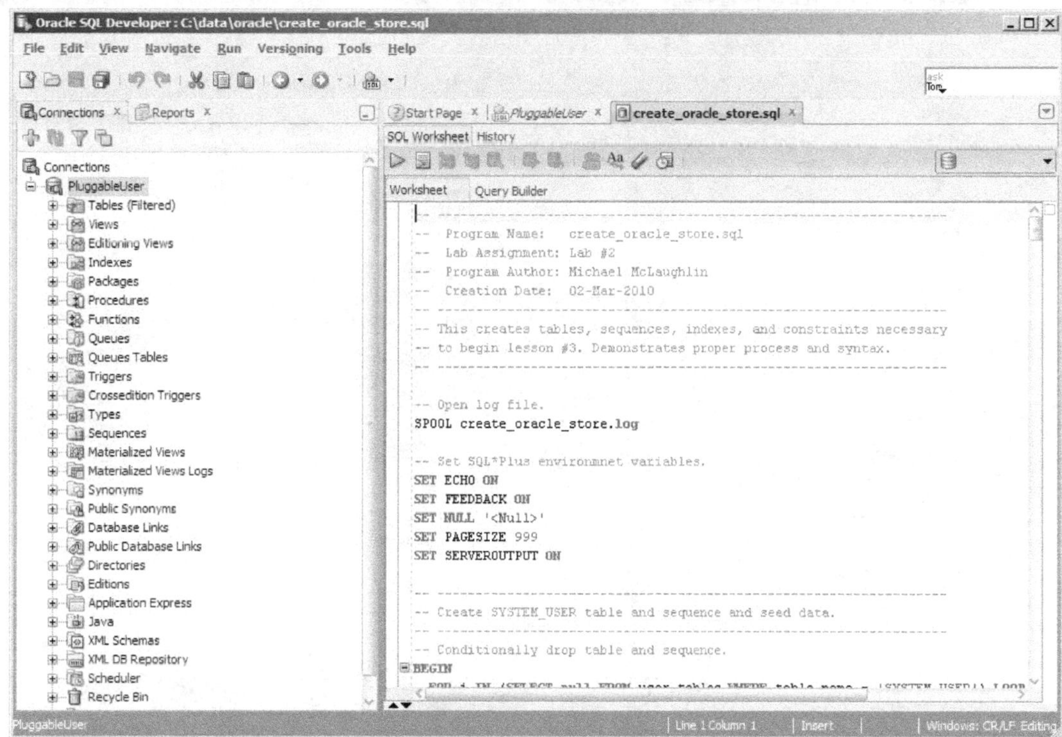

To run a script file, instead of clicking the green arrow button, click the button to its right that shows a document with a small green arrow icon in its lower-left corner. Doing so should display a *Select Connection* dialog box that verifies the connection you want to use, as shown next. Choose the valid *Connection*, and click the *OK* button to continue.

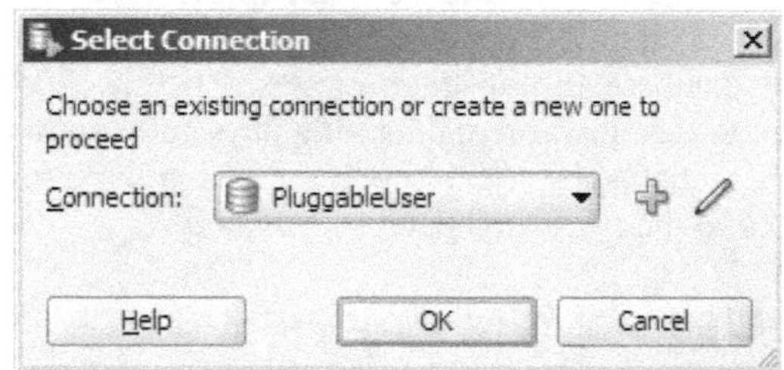

The last screen shows the script output:

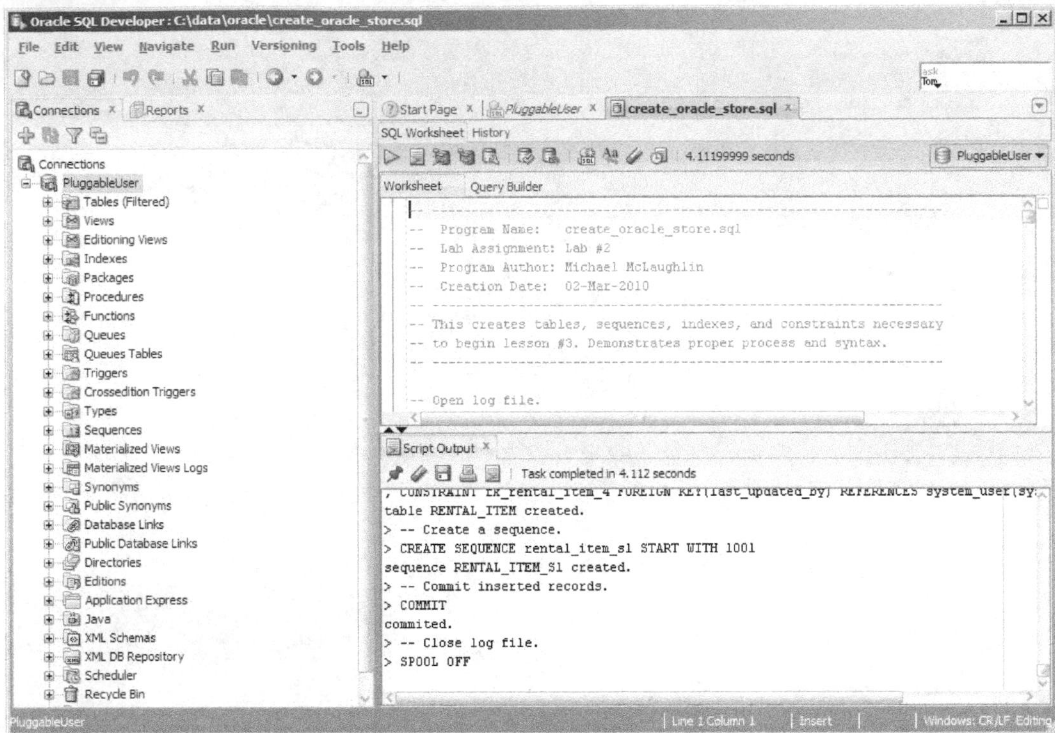

This concludes your introduction to how to configure and work with the basics of Oracle SQL Developer. It's a great tool, so make sure to explore it further on your own.

Database Administration

Database administration is generally divided into two major roles: the physical DBA and the application DBA. Since this book is targeted at developers and application DBAs, this section does not cover all the database administration tasks of the physical DBA, such as creating and maintaining tablespaces, creating and maintaining physical files, and managing the storage aspects of tables. Instead, this section shows you how to provision users, use database constraints, and harden the database, and then explains data governance.

Provisioning Users

Users hold privileges to work in the database. Each database designates at least one default *superuser*. The superuser enjoys *all* privileges in the database.

The Oracle database defines two superusers, `sys` and `system`, and follows the ANSI-SPARC architecture's three-tiered model. This architectural model divides the schema or database into three views: internal, conceptual, and external.

The *internal* view consists of the physical reality of how data is organized, which is specific to any DBMS. The internal view also contains the editable data catalog that maintains all the data about data, or *metadata*. This metadata contains all the definitions of users, databases, tables, indexes, constraints, sequences, data types, and views. Inside the internal view and with the proper credentials, a superuser can alter the contents of the data catalog with DML statements. That means an authorized user could use an `INSERT`, `UPDATE`, or `DELETE` statement to change critical metadata outside the administrative barrier of system privileges and DDL statements.

CAUTION
Never use DML statements to change the data catalog values without the express instruction of Oracle Support.

The *conceptual* view consists of the community view of data. The *community* view is defined by the users with access privileges to the database, and it represents an administrator's view of data from the perspective of SQL. This view of data provides administrator-friendly views of data stored in the data catalog.

It isn't possible to change the contents of the metadata in the community view, except through DDL statements such as `ALTER`, `CREATE`, and `DROP`. Developers can use these DDL statements only against objects or, in the case of the `ALTER` statement, against system and database environment settings. These types of environment settings enable such things as database traces measuring behavior and performance. You can find more details about these types of DDL statements in the *Oracle Database 12*c *DBA Handbook* (Oracle Press, 2014).

Oracle implements the concept of the community view as a collection of *striped views*. Striped views detect the user and allow them to see only things they have rights to access. These views typically start with `CDB_`, `DBA_`, `ALL_`, and `USER_` prefixes, and you access them as you would any other table or view through queries with a `SELECT` statement. The views prefixed with `ALL_` and `DBA_` are accessible only to the Oracle superusers: `sys`, `system`, and user-defined accounts granted superuser privileges.

Every user has access to the striped views prefixed with `USER_`. Those views provide access to structures only in the user's schema or personal work area.

The *external* view consists of access to the user's schema or database, which is a private work area. Users typically have complete control over the resources of their schema or database, but in some advanced architectures, users can have restricted rights. In those models, the user may be able to perform only the following tasks:

- Create tables and sequences
- Create or replace stored program units
- Grant or revoke privileges and synonyms (described later, in the "Granting Oracle Privileges" section)
- Limit access to memory, disk space, or network connections

Oracle's `sys` and `system` users are synonymous with the two schemas for the internal and conceptual views, respectively. The differences between the definition of the internal view and the privileges conveyed when connecting as `sys` aren't immediately visible.

You cannot change things in the `sys` schema when you connect as the `sys` user, unless you connect with the `/ as sysoper` (*system operator*) or `/ as sysdba` (*system DBA*) privilege.

You have full privileges as the system DBA but only a subset of privileges as the system operator. Typically, the only thing you perform with either of these responsibilities is routine maintenance or granting of specialized privileges. Routine maintenance would include starting and stopping the database. Specialized privileges include granting a user wider privileges or revoking privileges already granted, and defining the internal Java permissions though the `dbms_java` package.

Although you can create new users and grant them privileges such as superuser privileges, you shouldn't alter the predefined roles of the superusers. The following sections describe how to create users and how to grant privileges to or revoke privileges from a user.

Creating a CDB Oracle User

Creating a CDB user is synonymous with creating a schema in an Oracle database. Here we'll focus on the aspects of authentication, profile, and account status for an Oracle database user. All user-defined CDB users must use `c##` as a preface to the name from Oracle Database 12*c* forward.

The SQL prototype to create a user allows you to identify the user with a password, an external Secure Sockets Layer (SSL)-authenticated certificate name, or a globally identified user name based on a Lightweight Directory Access Protocol (LDAP) entry.

The following syntax lets you create a `c##plsql` CDB user that is identified by a local database password:

```
CREATE USER c##plsql IDENTIFIED BY Mag1c200;
```

Alternatively, you can create a student PDB user after changing the `CONTAINER` context of the CDB's `sysdba` user. Assuming the PDB is open, you alter the session to change the context to the PDB. The syntax for both statements for a standard Oracle Database 12*c* sample database is

```
ALTER SESSION SET CONTAINER=pdborcl;
CREATE USER student IDENTIFIED BY student;
```

One alternative to a local password is an SSL-authenticated certificate name, which would look like this:

```
CREATE USER c##plsql IDENTIFIED EXTERNALLY AS 'certificate_name';
```

The LDAP alternative would look the same but use a different source:

```
CREATE USER c##plsql IDENTIFIED EXTERNALLY AS 'CN=miles,O=apple,C=US';
```

The certificate is an SSL file. It lets you encrypt your database credentials to support secure data communication.

Any of the three syntax methods can be used to create a private `student` pluggable database work area, which is a traditional schema in a pluggable-enabled database. A number of other options are available for the default and temporary tablespaces of the work area, and quota syntax is available to limit the space authorized for a schema. These clauses are covered in the "Database" section later in the appendix.

Another clause allows you to assign a profile to users when you create them. That clause generally follows any tablespace assignments and quota limits. An example that assumes default assignment of tablespaces and quota limits would look like this with a local password:

```
CREATE USER student IDENTIFIED BY student
PROFILE profile_name;
```

Profiles allow you to restrict the number of concurrent user sessions, amount of CPU per call, and so forth. Profiles also let you impose restrictions or override password functions. The latter allows you to enhance the base security provided by the Oracle database, like surrounding the castle gate with a moat.

You can also set a password as expired. With this setting, when the user signs on with a provided password, he or she will be prompted to change it immediately. This is the best practice for issuing user accounts. Accounts are unlocked by default, but sometimes an account should be locked. For example, you might need to create the schema as a reference for development purposes in another schema before planned use of the schema. These clauses generally follow all of those previously discussed. A sample `CREATE` statement with these clauses would look like this:

```
CREATE USER student IDENTIFIED BY student
PROFILE profile_name
PASSWORD EXPIRE
ACCOUNT LOCK;
```

TIP

For security reasons, you should always use `PASSWORD EXPIRE`.

You can use an `ALTER` statement to unlock the user account when the time comes to activate it. Appendix B shows the `ALTER` statement syntax to unlock an account.

Restricting access through the Oracle Transparent Network Substrate (TNS) is accomplished by configuring the Oracle networking stack. This is different from the authentication model in the MySQL database, where the user's point of access is part of his or her unique identification. For example, you can configure the `sqlnet.ora` file to be used to restrict connections within a domain.

The following example shows how to enable or exclude client machine access (host hardening), which is covered later in the appendix in the "Listener Hardening" section. The parameter lines go into the `sqlnet.ora` file on the server.

```
tcp.validnode_checking = yes
tcp.invited_nodes = (192.168.0.91)
tcp.excluded_nodes = (192.168.0.129)
```

The first parameter allows you to check whether the IP address is authorized. The second line shows you how to authorize a client, and the third line shows you how to prohibit a client from connecting to the Oracle database server.

After the user connects to the database, you can provide fine-grain access control through SQL configuration. For example, you can restrict a user's access down to the column level with the `DBMS_REPCAT` package, as shown in Appendix D. Then, you grant execute privileges on the program only to users who should have limited access privileges.

You can find full documentation on Oracle networking in *Oracle Database Net Services Reference 12c Release*.

This concludes the basics of setting up a new user account. You can explore the topic in more depth online in the *Oracle Database SQL Language Reference 12c Release*.

Oracle Network Tracing

Sometimes you'll need to trace what's happening in the Oracle portion of the network communication stack. You do that by configuring the `sqlnet.ora` file. It is possible to set four levels of tracing: Oracle Worldwide Support (16), Administration (10), User (4), and Tracing Off (0).

When you add the following parameters to the `sqlnet.ora` file, you generate a server-side network trace file:

```
trace_level_server = 10
trace_file_server = server.trc
trace_directory_server = <path_to_trace_dir>
```

The `trace_level_server` value designates the desired level of tracing. The setting shown (`10`) here provides values at the local administrator level.

An alternative to server-side tracing is client-side tracing, which can be accomplished by adding a parameter to the `sqlnet.ora` file, like this:

```
trace_level_client = 10
trace_unique_client = on
trace_file_client = sqlnet.trc
trace_directory_client = <path_to_trace_dir>
```

Network tracing is a valuable tool when you're debugging your application stack. You might likewise need to debug the processing instruction sets, and that is included in the "Conditional Compilation Statements" section in Chapter 5.

Creating a PDB Oracle User

Creating a PDB user is also synonymous with creating a pluggable database or schema. The substantial difference between a container and pluggable database user are

- A CDB user name must start with a `c##` preface. After the `c##` preface, a CDB user name includes letters, underscores, and numbers. Container database users are created in the CDB, which means their information is stored in the container's data catalog. The CDB `sys` or `system` user or a privileged user-defined CDB user can change the password of a CDB user.
- A PDB user name may start with a letter and include letters, underscores, and numbers. A pluggable database user is an `ADMIN` user who is created when you define the PDB. The PDB is the only repository for pluggable database users. The container database `sys` and `system` users can't change pluggable users by default, unless you use the `ALTER SESSION` statement to set the container as a PDB. Only the pluggable `sys`, `system`, and `ADMIN` pluggable users can change the status or password of the pluggable user.

You create an ADMIN user for a PDB when you create it. The syntax to create a video PDB with a videoadm ADMIN user is

```
SQL> CREATE PLUGGABLE DATABASE videodb
  2    ADMIN USER videoadm IDENTIFIED BY Video1
  3    ROLES = (dba)
  4    DEFAULT TABLESPACE videots
  5      DATAFILE '<oracle_home_dir>/VIDEOPDB/VIDEO01.DBF' SIZE 500M ONLINE
  6    FILE_NAME_CONVERT = ('<oracle_home_dir>/PDBSEED/',
  7                         '<oracle_home_dir>/VIDEOPDB/');
```

Line 2 creates the pluggable videoadm user and assigns it a password. Line 3 assigns the user the dba role and enables it to act like an Oracle Database 11*g* system user in the private context of the videodb PDB. You should reuse the pluggable videodb name when converting the filenames for the PDB catalog.

The step on lines 6 and 7 clones the generic catalog from the seed version to an implementation version. It creates three physical files for the pluggable videodb database, pdbseed_temp01.dbf, sysaux01.dbf, and system01.dbf, and nests them in a videopdb directory. The nesting directory separates these files from the CDB files. The last provisioning step creates the default videots tablespace shown on line 5. The physical file location is placed in the videodb subdirectory to keeps its files in the same location.

You raise an exception when you create the DEFAULT TABLESPACE before creating the PDB. The exception raised when you execute CREATE PLUGGABLE DATABASE is

```
CREATE PLUGGABLE DATABASE videodb
*
ERROR at line 1:
ORA-00604: error occurred at recursive SQL level 1
ORA-01537: cannot add file 'C:\APP\ORACLE\ORADATA\ORCL\VIDEO01.DBF' - file
```

You can change the password of the videoadm user by connecting with the sysdba privilege to the PDB, like this:

```
# sqlplus sys@video as sysdba
Enter password: Video1
SQL> ALTER USER videoadm IDENTIFIED BY Video2;
```

Now, you can create users in the PDB. As mentioned earlier, it is also possible to do this as the CDB's sysdba user when you change the default CONTAINER context. The syntax is consistent with prior releases:

```
SQL> CREATE USER student IDENTIFIED BY student;
SQL> GRANT CREATE cluster, CREATE indextype, CREATE operator
  2  ,     CREATE PROCEDURE, CREATE SEQUENCE, CREATE SESSION
  3  ,     CREATE TABLE, CREATE TRIGGER, CREATE TYPE
  4  ,     CREATE VIEW, UNLIMITED TABLESPACE TO student;
```

This section has shown you how to work with PDB users. As with CDB users, you can explore the topic in more depth online in the *Oracle Database SQL Language Reference 12c Release*.

Granting Security Privileges

Security privileges are permissions granted to individual users to work in the database. Some privileges grant wide-ranging permissions while others grant narrowly defined rights. Privileges should be granted to users only after careful consideration and only to support real business needs. Wide-ranging permissions offer more rights, such as `CREATE ANY RESOURCE`, which allows users to create any type of database object in their own schema or others' schemas. That degree of access, however, is probably a bad idea for anybody other than a DBA.

Designing the architecture for database applications requires making design decisions involving technology and security. These decisions must resonate at every level of the development organization to support integration when the pieces of the application product are assembled. Security, a crucial component in application design, manages how users of the application interact with the data.

The superuser account holds all privileges and grants database privileges to other users. Privileges provide permissions to perform a task or a series of tasks. Some databases support the concept of *roles*, or groups of related privileges. A role gives a user a series of bundled privileges. Roles are a convenient tool when you understand what they do. They're dangerous, however, if you lack knowledge about what they do, because you can inadvertently grant privileges that you shouldn't.

There are two types of security privileges: system privileges and object privileges. System privileges don't relate to a specific object or schema/database. Object privileges provide specific permissions to work with individual objects or schemas/databases.

System privileges allow a user to take wide-ranging actions and thus should be restricted to specific administrative user accounts. They allow a user to administer a system, create new privileges, change the behavior of existing privileges, change the behavior of system resources, or manipulate any type of object, such as tables, views, indexes, and so forth. DBAs have system privileges, and these privileges are often provided to developers in small test systems. When developers package their code for integration testing and deployment, DBA system privileges run their code.

Object privileges grant specific access to objects to a single user or set of users. These privileges often allow the user to manipulate data objects such as tables or views: a user can select, insert, update, or delete data. They also grant privileges to run or execute stored programs, such as stored functions, stored procedures, and instantiable object types. Object privileges also are granted to the DBA during implementation (as qualified in Table A-3), but they're key

Object(s)	Object Privilege(s)
COLUMN, INDEX, MATERIALIZED VIEW, TABLE, VIEW	ALTER, CREATE, COMMENT, DROP, SELECT
CLUSTER, DATABASE, LINK	ALTER, CREATE, DROP
DIRECTORY	READ, WRITE
FUNCTION, PROCEUDRE	ALTER, CREATE, DROP, EXECUTE
INDEX	ALTER, CREATE, DROP
TABLE, VIEW	DELETE, INSERT, LOCK, UPDATE
TRIGGER	ALTER, CREATE, DROP
USER	ALTER, CREATE, DROP

TABLE A-3. *Object Privileges*

components of application architectures. They allow the application designer to segment sets of tables and programs into separate schemas. These schemas act like packages in object-oriented programming languages.

Both system and object privileges can be revoked by the grantor or a superuser. Any work the user does to the data while he or she has access to the system remains unaltered when privileges are revoked. Therefore, privileges should be granted only where appropriate, and their use should be monitored.

Granting Oracle Privileges

Creating an account in an Oracle database doesn't automatically enable it for use. First you must grant basic permissions to use the account. The `system` user or an administrator account created with the `CREATE ANY USER` privilege should run these commands.

These are the basic privileges that you would want to extend to a default user. However, privileges don't work when you create a user without a default and temporary tablespace clause, unless you also grant `UNLIMITED TABLESPACE` (but don't), as shown here:

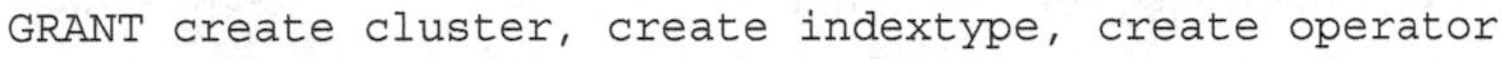

```
GRANT create cluster, create indextype, create operator
,     create procedure, create sequence, create session
,     create table, create trigger, create type
,     create view, unlimited tablespace TO video;
```

This type of `GRANT` statement lets you create a user in a small, developer-only environment, but you shouldn't do this in a production database. It works because you avoid assigning default and temporary tablespaces by granting unlimited space rights. This is never a good thing to do, except on your laptop! Some might say that you shouldn't do it on your laptop either, but that is for you to decide.

The `ALTER` statement also lets you assign a default tablespace and a temporary tablespace after a user is created. Both the `CREATE` and `ALTER` statements let you assign quotas to the default tablespace, but you can no longer assign a quota to the temporary tablespace. Any attempt to do so raises an error. This change became effective with Oracle Database 10*g* Release 2. You can find the syntax for the `ALTER` statement in Appendix B.

NOTE
*Beginning with Oracle Database 10*g *Release 2, you can no longer assign a temporary tablespace quota.*

A sample grant of `SELECT` privileges, typically made by a user for his or her own schema objects, would look like this:

```
GRANT SELECT ON some_tablename TO some_user;
```

Sometimes you may want to grant a privilege to another user along with the privilege to extend those privileges to a third party. This is the infrequent pattern of grants reserved for setting up administrative users. You append a `WITH GRANT OPTION` clause to give another user the right to provide other users with the privileges you've conveyed to them:

```
GRANT SELECT ON some_tablename TO some_user WITH GRANT OPTION;
```

Oracle also supports the concept of a *synonym*, which simplifies how another user can access your object. Without a synonym, the other user would need to put your user name and a dot (.) in front of the object name before accessing it. The dot is called a *component selector*. A synonym creates an alias that maps the user name, component selector, and object name to a synonym (alias) name in the user's work area or schema.

You don't need to use a component selector on objects that you create in your schema. They're natively available to you. The sys superuser has access to every object in the Oracle Database 12c server by simply addressing objects by their fully qualified location—schema name, component selector, and object name. This makes perfect sense when you recall that the user and schema names are synonymous.

You create a synonym like this:

```
CREATE SYNONYM some_tablename FOR some_user.some_tablename;
```

Typically, but not always, the local table name is the same as the table name in the other schema. You can also grant privileges on a table to a PUBLIC account, which gives all other users access to the table. Public synonyms also exist to simplify how those users access the table.

You would grant the SELECT privilege to the PUBLIC account with this syntax:

```
GRANT SELECT ON some_tablename TO PUBLIC;
```

After granting the privilege, you create a public synonym with this syntax:

```
CREATE PUBLIC SYNONYM some_tablename FOR some_user.some_tablename;
```

As a rule of thumb, use the PUBLIC account only when you're granting privileges to stored programs with invoker rights. This appendix previously discussed both the default definer rights model and the invoker rights model.

Revoking Privileges

You can revoke any privilege from a user provided that you or a peer superuser granted that privilege. For example, suppose that while reading the previous section you accidentally granted the UNLIMITED TABLESPACE privilege to the video user, and now you want to revoke it. The command to do so would look like this:

```
REVOKE unlimited tablespace FROM video;
```

The interesting thing about this revocation is that it doesn't immediately disable the user from writing to the tablespace generally. That's because revocation only disallows the allocation of another extent to any table previously created by the user. An *extent* is a contiguous block of space inside a tablespace. Extents are added when an INSERT or UPDATE statement can't add anything more in the allocated space. The number of extents allocated to a table is a measure of the fragmentation of the table on disk.

You can revoke privileges from the PUBLIC account with the same type of syntax:

```
REVOKE SELECT ON some_tablename FROM PUBLIC;
```

When you revoke privileges that included a WITH GRANT OPTION clause, make sure you also revoke the granting option. There should be a routine process in place for validating the grants and privileges to ensure that they comply with your company's governance policy and appropriate laws, such as Sarbanes-Oxley in the United States. You can find more information about hardening in an application context in the book *Oracle E-Business Suite Security*, by John Abel (Oracle Press, 2006).

Using Database Constraints

Constraints are critical components in databases. They *restrict* (constrain) what you can add to, modify in, or delete from tables with `INSERT`, `UPDATE`, and `DELETE` statements. Constraints let you restrict what can be placed in columns, rows, tables, or relationships between tables. That's a tremendously broad statement that requires some qualification. So what are these restrictions and why are they important?

This section covers the following database constraints:

- `NOT NULL`
- `UNIQUE`
- Primary key
- Foreign key
- `CHECK`

A preliminary understanding of constraint capabilities should help you focus on their respective roles as you read this section. Two types of constraints are used: column constraints and table constraints. A *column constraint* applies to a single column. You define it inline by adding it to the same line in which you define the column. Inline constraints don't require an explicit reference to the column because they apply to the column that shares the line. You can also define a column constraint after the definition of all column values in Oracle Database. Constraints that follow the definition of columns are out-of-line constraints because they are not placed on the same line as their column definition. You create tables with the `CREATE` statement, covered in Appendix B.

The generalized definition of a `CREATE TABLE` statement is as follows:

```
CREATE TABLE table_name
( column_name1  data_type1  inline_constraint_definition
, out_of_line_constraint_definition );
```

Some constraints involve more than a single column. Multiple-column constraints are *table constraints*. Table constraints are always defined after the list of columns as you create a table, because they depend on the column definitions. Alternatively, table constraints can be added to a table definition with an `ALTER TABLE` statement. Appendix B covers the syntax for maintenance activities such as the `ALTER TABLE` statement.

Figure A-4 provides a matrix that compares constraints against the behaviors they can restrict: columns, rows, tables, and external relationships between tables.

Column-level constraints let you restrict whether a column can be empty or must contain a value. They also let you restrict the values that can be inserted into a column, such as only a *Yes* or *No* string, and restrict the values to a list of values found in another table (that's the role of a foreign key, as you'll discover later in this section).

Row-level constraints let you restrict the behavior of one or a group of column values based on one or a group of column values in the same row. For example, you could constrain one column's value based on another column's value.

Constraint	Column	Row	Table	External
Not Null	✓	✗	✗	✗
Check	✓	✓	✗	✗
Unique	✗	✗	✓	✗
Primary Key	✓	✗	✓	✗
Foreign Key	✓	✗	✗	✓
Index	✗	✗	✓	✗
Trigger	✓	✓	✓	✓

FIGURE A-4. *Constraint matrix*

Table-level constraints let you restrict the behavior between rows in a table. A unique constraint on one or a group of columns prevents more than one row from having the same value for that column or group of columns.

External constraints are trickier because they involve relationships between tables. They limit the value list of a column or a group of columns (foreign key) to those values already found in another column or group of columns (primary key) in another table. This type of constraint is known as a *referential integrity constraint* because it ensures that a reference in one table can be found in another.

The following subsections describe `NOT NULL`, `UNIQUE`, primary key, foreign key, and `CHECK` constraints.

NOT NULL Constraints

A `NOT NULL` constraint applies to a single column only, as indicated in Figure A-4. It restricts a column by making it mandatory, which means you can't insert a row without a value in the column. Likewise, you can't update a mandatory column's value from something to a null value. Optional columns are nullable or null-allowed. This means you can enter something or nothing, where nothing is a null value. Null values also differ from empty strings.

Oracle requires that you define `NOT NULL` constraints inline. There's no option to add a `NOT NULL` constraint as a table constraint in an Oracle `CREATE TABLE` statement. You can, however, use the `ALTER TABLE` statement to add a `NOT NULL` constraint to an existing table's column. That is, provided the table is empty or you've put data in that column for all existing rows before you alter the table to add a `NOT NULL` constraint.

`NOT NULL` constraints impose a minimum cardinality of 1 on a column, which typically makes the column's cardinality [1..1] (one-to-one). This is a Unified Modeling Language (UML) notation for cardinality. The UML notation assigns the minimum cardinality constraint to the number on the left and the maximum cardinality constraint to the number on the right. The two dots in the middle indicate a range.

Maximum cardinality is always considered 1, because each column has one data type and one value in a relational model. The rule applies to all scalar data types.

The maximum cardinality rule changes in an object relational database management system (ORDBMS), such as Oracle Database 12*c*. That's because it supports collection data types. In an ORDBMS, the maximum cardinality can be one to many, depending on what you measure. It is one when you measure whether or not a column contains a collection data type, and it's many when you measure the number of elements in a collection data type. Another twist is some arbitrary number between one and many, which happens with a varray collection type in an Oracle database. The varray collection has a fixed maximum size, like ordinary arrays in programming languages.

Oracle lets you create `NOT NULL` columns when you create tables and lets you modify a column in an existing table to make it a `NOT NULL` or null-allowed column. You perform the former with the `CREATE TABLE` statement and the latter with the `ALTER TABLE` statement. Appendix B shows you how to use the `CREATE TABLE` and `ALTER TABLE` statements.

All rows must contain data in the target column before you can add a `NOT NULL` constraint. You can remove a `NOT NULL` constraint from a column by using an `ALTER TABLE` statement.

You can mimic the behavior of a `NOT NULL` constraint by adding a `CHECK` constraint after the table is created. `NOT NULL` and `CHECK` constraints are stored exactly alike in the data catalog. Unfortunately, a `NOT NULL` restriction on a `CHECK` constraint isn't displayed when you describe the table. Using a `CHECK` constraint to mimic a `NOT NULL` constraint is not a good idea, because it can be misleading to other developers and disguise business rules.

Cardinality

Cardinality comes from set mathematics and simply means the number of elements in a set. For example, in an arbitrary set of five finite values, a cardinality of [1..5] qualifies the minimum of 1 and the maximum of 5. This set expresses a range of five values.

In databases, cardinality applies to the following:

- The number of values in an unconstrained column within a row has a default cardinality of [0..1] (zero-to-one) for nullable columns. (The minimum cardinality of 0 applies only to nullable columns.)
- The number of values in a `NOT NULL` constrained column within a row has a cardinality of [1..1] (one-to-one).

When there's no upward limit on the number of values in a column, it holds a *collection*. Collections typically contain one-to-many elements and their cardinality is [0..*] (zero-to-many).

Developers often describe the frequency of repeating values in a table as having low or high cardinality. *High cardinality* means the frequency of repeating values is closer to unique, where unique is the highest cardinality. *Low cardinality* means values repeat many times in a table, such as a gender column, where the distribution is often close to half and half. A column that always contains the same value, which shouldn't occur, is in the lowest cardinality possible.

Cardinality also applies to binary relationships between tables. Two principal physical implementations of binary relationships exist: one-to-one and one-to-many. The one-to-many relationship is the most common pattern. In this pattern, the table on the one side of the relationship holds a primary key and the table on the many side holds a foreign key.

NOTE
Although you can use a `CHECK` *constraint like a* `NOT NULL` *constraint, you shouldn't.*

You can also give meaningful names to `NOT NULL` constraints in an Oracle database when you create tables. Using meaningful names helps you to diagnose runtime violations of the constraint more easily than when working with system-generated names. Finding the name of a `NOT NULL` constraint is more difficult if you didn't assign a constraint name.

You can also find the columns of a `NOT NULL` or `CHECK` constraint in the `CDB_`, `DBA_`, `ALL_`, `USER_CONSTRAINTS`, or `USER_CONS_COLUMNS` view. You can use the following query to discover information about the constraint:

```
SQL> COLUMN owner           FORMAT A10
SQL> COLUMN constraint_name FORMAT A20
SQL> COLUMN table_name      FORMAT A20
SQL> COLUMN position        FORMAT 9
SQL> COLUMN column_name     FORMAT A20
SQL> SELECT   ucc.owner
  ,      ucc.constraint_name
  ,      ucc.table_name
  ,      ucc.column_name
  ,      ucc.position
  FROM   user_constraints uc INNER JOIN user_cons_columns ucc
  ON     ucc.owner = uc.owner
  AND    ucc.constraint_name = uc.constraint_name
  WHERE  uc.constraint_type = 'C';
```

The same query works to return `CHECK` constraints, because `NOT NULL` constraints are variations on `CHECK` constraints in the data catalog.

UNIQUE Constraints

A `UNIQUE` constraint is a table-level constraint, as indicated in Figure A-4, because it makes the value in a column or set of columns unique within the table. Table-level constraints apply to relationships between columns, sets of columns, or all columns in one row against the same columns in other rows of the same table. `UNIQUE` constraints are out-of-line constraints that are set after the list of columns in a `CREATE` statement. Alternatively, you can add them through an `ALTER` statement after creating a table.

Every well-designed table should have a minimum of two unique keys: a natural key and a surrogate key. The *natural key* is a column or set of columns that describes the subject of the table and makes each row unique. You can search a table for a specific record by using the natural key in a `WHERE` clause, which makes natural keys internal identifiers within the set of data in a table. Natural keys are rarely a single column.

All *surrogate keys* are uniquely indexed as a single column. Surrogate keys are ID columns. They're generally produced from automatic numbering structures known as *sequences*. Oracle Database 12*c* introduces identity columns, which hide the sequence creation, as qualified in Appendix B. Surrogate keys don't describe anything about the data in the table. They do, however, provide a unique identifier that can be shared with other related tables. Those related tables can then link their data back to the table where the surrogate keys are unique.

The natural and surrogate keys are potential candidates to become the primary key of a data table. As such, they're also *candidate* keys. The primary key uniquely identifies rows in the table and must contain a unique value, as opposed to a null value. As a rule, you should choose the surrogate key as the primary key because all joins will use the single column. This makes writing joins in SQL statements easier and less expensive to maintain over time because surrogate keys shouldn't change or be reused. By itself, a surrogate key, a sequence-generated value, doesn't provide optimal search performance when you have lots of data. That's accomplished by a unique index made up of the surrogate key and the natural key. That type of index helps to optimize databases to find and retrieve rows faster.

A `UNIQUE` constraint can apply to either a single column or a set of columns. You can create a `UNIQUE` constraint in Oracle Database 12*c* when you create or alter a table. The `UNIQUE` constraint automatically creates an index to manage the constraint—after all, it is a table constraint, and when you attempt to add a row that duplicates a unique column or set of columns, there must be a reference against which it can make a comparison to prevent it. Those reference points are *indexes*, and they're organized by a *B-tree*, an inverted tree structure that expedites finding a matching piece of data. A B-tree brackets elements in groups and then subgroups until it arrives at the basic elements of data, which are the column or columns of data qualified as unique.

As mentioned, you can create a table with a `UNIQUE` constraint or alter an existing table to add a `UNIQUE` constraint. Creating a `UNIQUE` constraint implicitly adds a unique index. The `UNIQUE` constraint is visible in the `CDB_`, `DBA_`, `ALL_`, or `USER_CONSTRAINTS` administrative view of the database catalog. You can also find the columns of the `UNIQUE` constraint in the `ALL_`, `DBA_`, `USER_CONSTRAINTS`, or `USER_CONS_COLUMNS` view. Likewise, you can find another entry for the `UNIQUE` constraint in the `CDB_`, `DBA_`, `ALL_`, `USER_INDEXES`, or `USER_IND_COLUMNS` view.

The following query shows you how to check the Oracle database catalog for `UNIQUE` constraints:

```
SQL> COLUMN owner           FORMAT A10
SQL> COLUMN constraint_name FORMAT A20
SQL> COLUMN table_name      FORMAT A20
SQL> COLUMN position        FORMAT 9
SQL> COLUMN column_name     FORMAT A20
SQL> SELECT   ucc.owner
  ,         ucc.constraint_name
  ,         ucc.table_name
  ,         ucc.position
  ,         ucc.column_name
  FROM      user_constraints uc INNER JOIN user_cons_columns ucc
  ON        ucc.owner = uc.owner
  AND       ucc.constraint_name = uc.constraint_name
  WHERE     uc.constraint_type = 'U';
```

The query returns a list of all `UNIQUE` constraints from the data catalog. You cannot drop this implicitly created index because the `UNIQUE` constraint is dependent on it. An attempt to drop an implicitly created unique index results in an `ORA-02429` exception. This exception's error message text aptly says that you cannot drop an index used for enforcement of a unique/primary key. However, you can alter the table and drop the `UNIQUE` constraint. The command also implicitly drops the supporting index.

Oracle Unique Indexes

You can create an index as a stand-alone object in an Oracle database. Indexes behave differently than constraints. For example, there is no `UNIQUE` constraint visible in the `USER_CONSTRAINTS` administrative view of the database catalog or in the superuser views of `ALL_` and `DBA_CONSTRAINTS`. However, you can find entries for unique indexes in the `ALL_`, `DBA_`, `USER_INDEXES`, or `USER_IND_COLUMNS` view.

The following query is similar to the query that finds `UNIQUE` constraints, but it uses different tables. It finds all unique indexes.

```
COLUMN table_owner     FORMAT A10
COLUMN index_name      FORMAT A20
COLUMN table_name      FORMAT A20
COLUMN column_position FORMAT 9
COLUMN column_name     FORMAT A20
SQL> SELECT    ui.table_owner
  2  ,         uic.index_name
  3  ,         ui.uniqueness
  4  ,         uic.table_name
  5  ,         uic.column_position
  6  ,         uic.column_name
  7  FROM      user_indexes ui JOIN user_ind_columns uic
  8  ON        uic.index_name = ui.index_name
  9  AND       uic.table_name = ui.table_name
 10  WHERE     ui.uniqueness = 'UNIQUE';
```

You would find the nonunique indexes with the following change to line 10:

```
10  WHERE    ui.uniqueness = 'NONUNIQUE';
```

You also have the right to drop (or remove) indexes without modifying the table that the indexes organize. This is possible because no `UNIQUE` constraint is dependent on the unique index.

It's important to note that unique constraints create unique indexes and that each index speeds access while slowing inserts, updates, and deletes. Unique constraints should be added for natural keys and a combination of the surrogate and natural key. Using unique constraints for other than the natural key purposes requires careful consideration because it can impact the efficiency of throughput, especially in online transaction processing (OLTP) systems.

Primary Key Constraints

As previously mentioned, primary keys uniquely identify every row in a table. Primary keys are also the published identifier of tables. As such, primary keys are the point of contact between data in one table and data in other tables. Primary keys also contain the values that foreign key columns copy and hold. When using referential integrity, the primary and foreign keys' shared values let you link data from different tables together through join operations.

Primary keys can be column or table constraints. They're column constraints when they apply to a single column, such as a surrogate key. They're generally table constraints when they apply to a natural key, because natural keys usually contain more than one column. Natural keys often contain multiple columns because that is generally how you qualify uniqueness in a set.

A single-column primary key exhibits two behaviors: it is *not null*, and it is *unique*. A multiple-column primary key can have a set of behaviors different from those of a single-column primary key. Although the collection of columns must be not null and unique in the set, it is possible that one or more, but not all, columns can contain a null value. This rule is *not* consistently enforced across relational databases in the industry.

Oracle implements all primary keys as `NOT NULL` and `UNIQUE`. This means all columns in a single- or multiple-column primary key are *mandatory* columns. Any attempt to insert a null value in a column of a primary key generates an `ORA-01400` error. The error message tells you that you cannot insert `NULL` into the primary key.

You can assign a meaningful name to primary key constraints, but Oracle assigns a system-generated name when you don't. It is much more difficult to trace back errors on primary key constraints if you don't give them meaningful names. You can look up the definition of primary keys in the `CDB_`, `DBA_`, `ALL_`, or `USER_CONSTRAINTS` and `USER_CONS_COLUMNS` administrative views. Primary keys always have a `P` in the `CONSTRAINT_TYPE` column.

Here's the syntax for this query:

```
SQL> COLUMN owner           FORMAT A10 HEADING "Owner"
SQL> COLUMN table_name      FORMAT A20 HEADING "Table Name"
SQL> COLUMN constraint_name FORMAT A20 HEADING "Constraint Name"
SQL> COLUMN column_name     FORMAT A20 HEADING "Column Name"
SQL> COLUMN constraint_type FORMAT A1  HEADING "Primary|Key"
SQL> SELECT   ucc.owner
     ,        ucc.constraint_name
     ,        ucc.table_name
     ,        ucc.position
     ,        ucc.column_name
     FROM     user_constraints uc INNER JOIN user_cons_columns ucc
     ON       ucc.owner = uc.owner
     AND      ucc.constraint_name = uc.constraint_name
     WHERE    uc.constraint_type = 'P';
```

Primary key constraints should never be omitted when you create a table. Likewise, you should create a unique constraint that contains the surrogate primary key column and all of the natural key columns. The unique constraint speeds all join resolution because it relies on multiple columns rather than a single column.

Foreign Key Constraints

As indicated in Figure A-4, a foreign key constraint is both a column-level constraint and an external constraint. The column-level constraint restricts the list of values to those found in a primary key column or set of columns. The primary key column(s) generally exists in another table, which is why an external constraint exists. A self-referencing relationship occurs when the foreign key points to a primary key in the same table. In a self-referencing relationship, the primary and foreign keys are different columns or different sets of columns.

A foreign key constraint basically instructs the database to allow only the insertion or update of a column's value to a value found in a referenced primary key. Foreign keys always contain the same number of columns as the primary key, and the data types of all columns must match.

The column and data type matching criteria is the minimum matching criteria. The values in the foreign key column(s) must match the values in the primary key column(s). More or less, foreign keys impose a boundary range of values on foreign column(s).

The matching values in the foreign and primary key columns allow you to join rows found in one table to those found in another table. Joins between primary and foreign keys are made on the basis of equality between column values, and they are *equijoins*, joins that are based on the equality of values in two columns or two sets of columns.

Foreign key constraints make the database responsible for enforcing cross-referencing rules. These rules ensure *referential integrity*, which means that a constraint reference guarantees a foreign key value must be found in the list of valid primary key values. Many commercial database applications don't impose referential integrity through constraints because companies opt to enforce them through stored programs. A collection of stored programs that protects the integrity of relationships is an application programming interface (API). The benefit of an API is that it eliminates the overhead imposed by foreign key constraints. This also means DML statements run faster without database-level constraint validation.

The downside of foreign key constraints is minimal but important to understand. Although foreign key constraints guarantee referential integrity of data, they do so at a cost of decreased performance. A nice compromise position on foreign keys is to deploy them in the stage environment (preproduction) to identify any referential integrity problems with your API.

NOTE
A stage environment *is where stable information technology companies conduct end-user testing and final integration testing.*

Foreign key constraints are useful tools for electronic data processing (EDP) auditors regardless of whether they're deployed to maintain referential integrity. For example, an EDP auditor can attempt to add a foreign key constraint to verify whether the API does actually maintain the integrity of relationships. An EDP auditor knows there's a problem with an API if a foreign key can't be added. That type of failure occurs when the data doesn't meet the necessary referential integrity rules. Likewise, an EDP auditor verifies the referential integrity of an API when foreign key constraints can be added to a primary-to-foreign key relationship. Such experimental foreign key constraints are removed at the conclusion of an EDP audit.

An Oracle foreign key constraint is very robust and can have three possible implementations:

- The default implementation prevents the update or deletion of a primary key value when a foreign key holds a copy of that value.
- Another implementation lets you delete the row but not update the primary key column or set of column values. This is accomplished by appending an `ON DELETE CASCADE` clause when creating or modifying the foreign key constraint.

Mandatory or Optional Foreign Keys

A mistaken belief among some database developers is that a foreign key constraint restricts a column's cardinality such that it must have a value. A foreign key constraint does not implement a `NOT NULL` constraint. You must assign a `NOT NULL` constraint when you want to prevent the insertion or update of a row without a valid foreign key value.

- Another implementation updates the foreign key value to a null value when the row containing the primary key is deleted. Like the other options, you can't update the primary key column value. This doesn't work when a foreign key column has a column-level `NOT NULL` constraint. In that case, any attempt to delete the row holding the primary key raises an `ORA-01407` error, which reports that the foreign key column can't be changed to a null value.

You can disable a foreign key constraint in an Oracle database. This would let a `DELETE` statement remove the row that has a primary key value with dependent foreign key values. Enabling the foreign key constraint after deleting the row with the primary key raises an `ORA-02298` error. The error indicates that the database can't validate the rule that the constraint supports, which is that every foreign key value must be found in the primary key.

The Oracle database also requires that you add foreign key constraints as out-of-line constraints when creating a table. This means that foreign key constraints are treated as table constraints. You can add self-referencing foreign key constraints during table creation, but inserting values requires that the first row insertion validates its foreign key against the primary key value in the same row. This means the first row must have the same value for the primary and foreign key column or set of columns.

You can also find foreign keys in the `CDB_`, `DBA_`, `ALL_`, `USER_CONSTRAINTS`, or `USER_CONS_COLUMNS` administrative views.

```
SQL> COL c_source FORMAT A38 HEADING "Constraint Name:| Table.Column"
SQL> COL r_column FORMAT A38 HEADING "References:| Table.Column"
SQL> SELECT   uc.constraint_name||CHR(10)
  ||        '('||ucc1.TABLE_NAME||'.'||ucc1.column_name||')' c_source
  ,         'REFERENCES'||CHR(10)
  ||        '('||ucc2.TABLE_NAME||'.'||ucc2.column_name||')' r_column
  FROM      user_constraints uc
  ,         user_cons_columns ucc1
  ,         user_cons_columns ucc2
  WHERE     uc.constraint_name = ucc1.constraint_name
  AND       uc.r_constraint_name = ucc2.constraint_name
  AND       ucc1.POSITION = ucc2.POSITION
  AND       uc.constraint_type = 'R'
  ORDER BY ucc1.TABLE_NAME
  ,         uc.constraint_name;
```

This is similar to the other queries against the database catalog. The only difference is that the constraint type value narrows it to referential integrity.

CHECK Constraints

`CHECK` constraints let you verify the value of a column during an insert or update. A `CHECK` constraint can set a boundary, such as the value can't be less than, greater than, or between certain values. This differs from the boundary condition imposed by foreign key constraints because `CHECK` constraints qualify their boundaries rather than map them to dynamic values in an external table.

As mentioned earlier in the `NOT NULL` constraint discussion, you can use a `CHECK` constraint to guarantee `NOT NULL` behaviors, but that is considered a bad practice. Boundary conditions on the value of a column are typically column-level constraints. You also have set membership conditions. This type of validation works against a set of real numbers, characters, or strings.

Beyond the column-level role of a CHECK constraint, there are boundary and set membership conditions where the comparison values are the values of other columns in the same row. When the boundaries are set by the values of other columns in the same row, a CHECK constraint becomes a row-level constraint.

A simple boundary or set element example can also apply to row-level constraints. A row-level CHECK constraint can disallow the insertion of a null value when another column in the same row would also contain a null value. (A business rule that illustrates this type of need would be a menu item table that has separate columns that classify whether an item belongs on the breakfast, lunch, or dinner menu.)

Beyond boundary and set membership CHECK constraints are complex business rule conditions that involve checking multiple other columns for sets of business rules. These complex CHECK constraints are powerful tools, and in some cases are relegated to database triggers because not all databases implement CHECK constraints. Row-level constraints must be implemented in database triggers when CHECK constraints aren't supported in a database management system.

Basketball scoring provides a nice business rule for illustrating a *row-level* CHECK constraint that is complex. When a player scores a field goal from a shooting position beyond the 3-point boundary, the goal is worth 3 points. Any other basket is worth 2 points, unless it is a free throw. Free throws are worth 1 point. Let's assume the table designed to record points during the game contains the following three columns:

- An optional column (that is null allowed) records whether the basket was made from beyond the 3-point boundary; you enter an X when the condition is met: a field goal.
- An optional column (again, null allowed) records whether a basket was a free throw; you enter an X when the condition is met.
- A mandatory column for the number of points is constrained by values in the optional columns for a field goal and a free throw. When the field goal column contains an X, you enter a 3. When the free throw column contains an X, you enter 1. When neither contains an X, you enter 2.

A hidden rule in the foregoing business logic is that an X can be inserted or updated in the 3-point boundary column only when the free throw column is null, and vice versa. It's hidden because it doesn't change the entry of a value for the points scored, only the entry of the Xs in the same row. You would implement CHECK constraints on the field goal and free throw columns that would verify that the other column is null before allowing the insertion of a value in the respective column.

Oracle supports boundary constraints, set membership conditions, and complex logic CHECK constraints. This means you can avoid writing database triggers for many row-level constraints, which makes implementation actions easier.

The query for a NOT NULL constraint works for all CHECK constraints. You can find the rule enforced by a CHECK constraint in the search_condition column of the ALL_, DBA_, or USER_CONSTRAINTS view.

Security Hardening

This section discusses the following methods of hardening your database against attacks:

- Oracle Audit Vault and Database Firewall
- Password hardening
- Listener hardening

NOTE

For an exhaustive discussion of the technical aspects of database security, see Effective Oracle Database 12c Security by Design, *by David Knox (Oracle Press, 2014). David's book is not intended to discuss logistical problems.*

Categories of Attackers

For the past several years, the Verizon RISK Team has been publishing an annual Data Breach Investigations Report (DBIR). This report breaks down major data breaches by identifying the following: who is behind the data breaches, how the breaches occurred, what commonalities exist between the breaches, and where mitigation efforts should be focused. Verizon is not the only publisher of this kind of report, but its report is always very good.

Figure A-5 represents a compilation of the data regarding sources of attack from the past five years of the Verizon DBIR. It is interesting to see that employee and partner attacks have virtually been eliminated. Contrariwise, criminal attacks have grown steadily. This group comprises activists who wish to expose or embarrass whomever their nemesis is, or desire to cripple financial or utility networks for terroristic purposes. Whatever the reason is, they *want* your data and they are spending millions of dollars per year to get at it.

One of the most common reasons attackers are able to breach data is the use of default or weak passwords. Modern hackers typically use malware or brute-force techniques to discover accounts that have weak or well-known passwords.

Database hackers are very sophisticated and professional in their work, spending many hours gaining footholds in your network and researching it. Then, in one fell-swoop, they snatch your most valuable data and cover up their tracks.

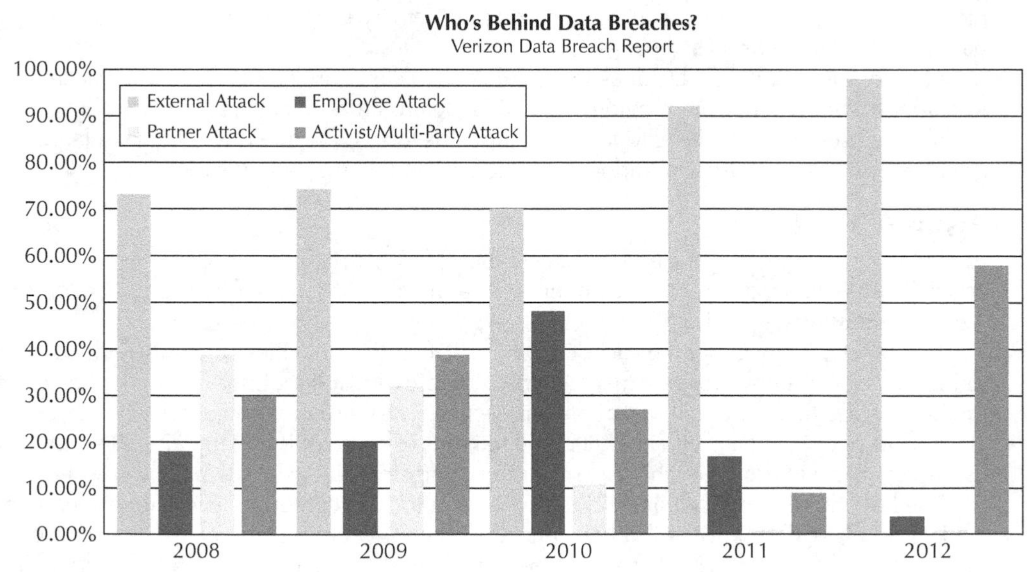

FIGURE A-5. *Identifying the major source of data breaches*

The business of data harvesting is big! Billions of dollars are lost every year as a result of data breaches. Data harvesters are paid per record, especially if those records contain sensitive information such as credit card numbers or tax IDs. What's more, as a DBA you could be facing charges in some jurisdictions if you're negligent in managing the security risks of your company or corporation. Database security skills are likely to become as mainstream and as important as database backup, recovery, and design skills. In the future, you will need database security skills to even land a job as a DBA.

Oracle Audit Vault and Database Firewall

Benjamin Franklin's axiom "an ounce of prevention is worth a pound of cure" applies perfectly to database security—preventing something bad from happening in the first place is much more practical than attempting to fix a problem once it has occurred. However, the preventative activities that you choose may not be the most efficient. In fact, some activities, while well intended, may hinder the business while providing very little protection. For example, system administrators may spend inordinate amounts of time setting up complex, multilayered firewalls in an attempt to protect their servers from hackers, only to discover that their efforts have merely slowed down hackers because no steps were taken to

- Actively listen to network and database traffic
- Alert when anomalies happen
- Intervene in hacking activities when they are in progress

A better approach to database security would be to set up fewer network zones and ramp up proactive measures like honey pots, real-time traffic monitoring/alerting, and production data redaction. This kind of prevention requires a shift in thinking from how you can stop hackers to how you can detect and intervene while the hack is in progress. Luckily, Oracle provides you with tools such as Audit Vault and Database Firewall. This tool provides you with "eyes" and "ears" on database activity. It can alert you when suspicious activity is happening and obscure the data when unauthorized users access it.

Oracle Audit Vault and Database Firewall is not a silver bullet that stops all attackers. It is able to gather traffic patterns and provide you with a clear picture of database activity, but it does not administer itself. You will need to train and tune this tool. It is quite possible that a large organization will require an additional DBA to adequately manage this tool.

Password Hardening

Aside from having eyes, ears, and an intervention plan, you must harden user access. It will do you very little good to purchase detection tools and configure them if your user accounts have weak or default passwords.

Hackers typically go for the easiest target first. Their first activities generally include an attempt to log in via well-known user name/password combinations. If that doesn't work, they create *rainbow tables* that store millions of user name/password/hash combinations. These types of tables are easy to populate. Hackers simply upload millions of passwords and then loop through a targeted list of user names. They alter the user's password and store the resulting hash values.

The last and most difficult method of password cracking attempts to reverse-engineer a password via known algorithms and seed values. Imagine a rainbow table that creates a hash for every letter in a password. Each successful attempt is recorded until the entire password is cracked. Hackers have become extremely sophisticated in these methods. They have recently graduated from standard

CPU-based cracking to GPU-based cracking. Programs such as Whitepixel take advantage of the massive processing power of popular video cards to accelerate brute-force password cracking.

It's not amazing to find that there are large server farms dedicated to password cracking, but sometimes it's amazing to find out how they're put together with inexpensive parts. One site showed a GPU-based farm with 25 high-end ATI graphics cards racked in what looked like HP-DL500 servers. Table A-4 shows how quickly passwords can be cracked using a system like that.

Notice that the new GPU farms are able to crack 13-character passwords in a mere 2.7 months. It isn't until 14 characters are used that the time-to-crack threshold crosses the 6 month mark. Huzzah! It's time to rethink password lifetime and length. Do you have passwords that you haven't changed in the past 6 months? How about longer than 6 months?

User Roles and Profiles DBAs who use Oracle default roles end up in trouble when they try to secure their database. Sometimes they'll drop default roles or users only to discover that they've broken their database. It is much better to create specific roles that address your company's needs. Just like roles, profiles need to be created to meet the needs of your company. For example, you may want to create separate profiles for your human users and your system/computer users as follows:

```
CREATE PROFILE human_analyst...
CREATE PROFILE human_engineer...
CREATE PROFILE human_dba...
CREATE PROFILE comp_application...
CREATE PROFILE comp_dblink...
CREATE PROFILE comp_audit...
```

It is best to audit accounts that are assigned to various profiles separately. Users who are assigned the `human_dba` profile should probably be audited for everything that they do, while a user assigned to the `human_analyst` profile may not need as much auditing.

Password Length	Password	CPU-Time-Seconds	GPU-Time-Seconds
5	Dg(Kv	0.3400	0.0000
6	P?6Z%~	180.0000	0.0000
7	Q(?B@y^	7,200.0000	0.0001
8	^md=?^P5	1,728,000.0000	0.0148
9	6F<DsL].E	31,536,000.0000	0.2704
10	01.?_b.=/(	693,792,000.0000	5.9481
11	H#cKCdrNP6b	126,144,000,000.0000	1,081.4815
12	R2*8cO<rUZu5	126,144,000,000,000.0000	1,081,481.4815
13	lxsiopMi$7570	819,936,000,000,000.0000	7,029,629.6296
14	8p0nBTq:)y$*.u	1,387,584,000,000,000,000.0000	11,896,296,296.2963
15	pt#j\TCaBkK=nZ8	126,144,000,000,000,000,000.0000	1,081,481,481,481.4800
16	sKfHER)!Z)dkX.IE	2,207,520,000,000,000,000,000.0000	18,925,925,925,925.9000

TABLE A-4. *Time-to-Crack Calculations*

For now, we will focus only on the password portions of the profile. Type the following at a SQL prompt:

```
CREATE PROFILE human_analyst
  password_life_time         90
  password_grace_time        7
  password_reuse_max         0
  password_lock_time         unlimited
  failed_login_attempts      6
  password_verify_function   pwvf_12c;
```

Most of these parameters accept the word `unlimited` as input; however, I strongly recommend that you never use the `unlimited` argument, except in the `PASSWORD_LOCK_TIME` parameter. Here is a list of each parameter and the meaning of its input variable:

- `PASSWORD_LIFE_TIME` How long the password will live, in days, without requiring a change
- `PASSWORD_GRACE_TIME` How many extra days the user is given to change a password
- `PASSWORD_REUSE_MAX` How many times a user is allowed to reuse a password
- `PASSWORD_LOCK_TIME` How long, in days, the account will be locked
- `PASSWORD_LOGIN_ATTEMPTS` How many incorrect password attempts are allowed
- `PASSWORD_VERIFY_FUNCTION` The function you use to determine password strength

In the previous example of the `human_dba` and `human_analyst` profiles, users are allowed only 90 days between password changes, plus a 7-day grace period. They cannot reuse a password, and their account will be permanently locked if they fail more than six times to authenticate. Finally, the password verification function named `PWVF_12C` is used to validate password strength.

Generating Random Passwords When establishing password requirements, there's a fine line between locking down users too much and locking them down just enough. You must discover your company's needs and lock down your environment appropriately. You would face a backlash from users if you were to require them to maintain passwords that look like this:

```
UD;_!U{;?44{-SU4WP@/AYB=X_^E[=.
```

However, a password like this one is very strong and would be appropriate for nonhuman accounts.

The following example shows how to put together a simple password verification function. This program is written in workable chunks, which is the approach you should take in all of your programming.

The Oracle-supplied package `dbms_random` supplies pretty good randomization, but its default seed value does not generate truly random strings. Therefore, you need to set the seed value to something unique in order to produce millions of unique strings. Issuing the following query demonstrates a possible seed value:

```
SQL> SELECT   TO_CHAR( systimestamp )
  2  ||       sys_context( 'USERENV', 'SID' )
  3  ||       sys_context( 'USERENV', 'INSTANCE' ) my_seed
  4  FROM     dual;
```

It returns

```
MY_SEED
----------------------------------------
01-MAR-13 09.06.56.634275 AM -07:001251
```

Notice that the `my_seed` variable contains a unique instance number, a session identifier, and a timestamp. This creates enough random bits to allow the `dbms_random.string` function to create passwords that really are random. A test run of 1000 simultaneous threads generated over 6 million passwords in just a few minutes, with no duplicates.

Now that you know how to generate random data, you need to know what the `string` function of the `dbms_random` package is capable of. Issue the following query to test the output:

```
SQL> BEGIN
       dbms_output.put_line(
         'Alpha Mixedcase ['||dbms_random.string ( 'a', 30 )||']');
       dbms_output.put_line(
         'Alpha Lowercase ['||dbms_random.string ( 'l', 30 )||']');
       dbms_output.put_line(
         'Alpha Uppercase ['||dbms_random.string ( 'u', 30 )||']');
       dbms_output.put_line(
         'Alpha Numeric   ['||dbms_random.string ( 'x', 30 )||']');
       dbms_output.put_line(
         'Any Printable   ['||dbms_random.string ( 'p', 30 )||']');
     END;
     /
```

The preceding query returns

```
Alpha Mixedcase [bFcthbTwDWjAaHYMQbrjXwVpnFJRGA]
Alpha Lowercase [onzvmqarzjxouyqtyojzhquzrhftft]
Alpha Uppercase [NXMBGEQNVLPGCQQBRJJDBMZXZFVEOR]
Alpha Numeric   [EJLFE6PGFF7JTGMWPGC1E985OI5A8U]
Any Printable   [p%%Ft~Gl)%Oss0W`E`C?:3Kkp(&dd\]
```

You need to choose which of these methods is right for your company. For purposes of demonstration, suppose you like the `ANY_PRINTABLE` and `ALPHA_NUMERIC` strings. There are a couple of nuances to note about the output generated by each. First, Oracle Database 12*c* does not permit passwords to start with numeric values. You can easily get around this by enclosing passwords in double quotes, which also makes passwords case sensitive alphanumeric with special characters, like this:

```
CREATE USER joe IDENTIFIED BY "6OENAZ9YYMXCFADMX9Z0TDPJEES6ZX";
```

Joe doesn't have to enclose his password in double quotes when he uses it. He can, but he doesn't have to.

The other nuance is that an apostrophe has been generated in the `ANY_PRINTABLE` output. There are some characters that you want to stay away from because Oracle Databases don't support them, such as the apostrophe, ampersand, double quote, and backtick. All of the other printable characters are fair game.

The following generates Jane's user account using `ANY_PRINTABLE` output:

```
CREATE USER jane IDENTIFIED BY "N%6qQp6~?I/HSDZR19X?_<!/z;[x)T";
```

One might ask, "How will Jane remember a password like that?" The simple answer is, "She probably won't." Fortunately, with the use of a password-management tool such as Password Safe, TK8 Safe, or Seahorse, she doesn't need to. You should strongly consider requiring all users to use a password-management tool. That way, they need to memorize only one password to access all of their passwords, and they won't be tempted to write down their passwords or use other unsecure methods to keep track of them. Be sure to train the users to take advantage of a significant passphrase to open their password-management utility, like:

```
"I go to work at 9:00 AM and get home by 6:00 PM"
"This is my VERY SECRET pass phrase that keeps me safe from H4cK0r$"
```

Now, you are ready to explore the fun stuff. Next, you will make a package called `DBSEC` and place a password generator in it as the first program. (The second program will be a password verification function, as covered in the next section.) It's a good idea to keep your security code in a package, not only for better maintenance, but also in case you decide to wrap it.

The following code block creates a password generator:

```
SQL> CREATE OR REPLACE FUNCTION random_password
  ( pv_length   INTEGER ) RETURN VARCHAR2 IS
    -- Declare local variables.
    lv_seed       VARCHAR2(60);
    lv_char       VARCHAR2(1);
    lv_password   VARCHAR2(30);
  BEGIN
    -- Assign values to the local variables.
    lv_seed := TO_CHAR( SYSTIMESTAMP );
    lv_seed := lv_seed || SYS_CONTEXT( 'USERENV', 'SID' );
    lv_seed := lv_seed || SYS_CONTEXT( 'USERENV', 'INSTANCE' );
    -- Generate a random seed value.
    dbms_random.seed( lv_seed );
    -- Generate random characters.
    FOR i IN 1..pv_length LOOP
      lv_char := dbms_random.string( 'p', 1 );
      -- Cleanup ", `, &, ', and white space.
      WHILE lv_char IN ( '"', '`', '&', ' ', '''' ) LOOP
        lv_char := dbms_random.string( 'p', 1 );
      END LOOP;
      -- Create the password one character at a time.
      lv_password := lv_password || lv_char;
    END LOOP;
    -- Return the password.
    RETURN lv_password;
  EXCEPTION
    WHEN OTHERS THEN RETURN 'NO PASSWORD';
  END random_password;
  /
```

Note that the preceding code incorporates the seed value identified in the previous discussion of the `STRING` function from the `DBMS_RANDOM` package. It also incorporates the stronger method of returning almost all printable characters. Test it like so:

```
SELECT   dbsec.random_password(30) AS my_password
FROM     dual;
```

This returns the following:

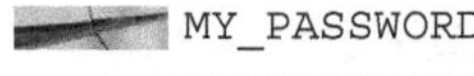

```
MY_PASSWORD
------------------------------
.k?L442\-rp#=dg3:+#Dn{b,,](xJS
```

You can use this function any time you want to generate a significantly strong password.

A Password Verification Function Now that you have a good password generator, you need a password verification function that checks the user name against the password. Oracle provides a password verification function, which you can find in the `utlpwdmg.sql` script, located in the `$ORACLE_HOME/RDBMS/ADMIN` directory. However, you may notice right away that the `utlpwdmg.sql` file contains only a basic password verification function. Therefore, I created a new password verification function, and it appears to improve on the one shipped by Oracle. The `encrypting_password.sql` file contains all the components to test how to build and deploy a password validation script."), identify in the preceding sentence where specifically to find the full code on the McGraw-Hill Education website, and delete the "Supporting Scripts" section at the end of the chapter.

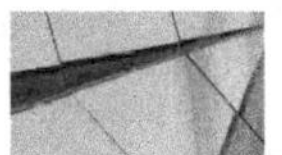

NOTE
Interestingly, Oracle's sample password function uses a complex set of loops to accomplish what the developer could have done with one call to the `EDIT_DISTANCE_SIMILARITY` function. Before you spend time planning and writing complex code, always make sure to check the built-in SQL and PL/SQL functions first to see if there is a nifty one-liner that suits your needs.

From a functional standpoint, there is no difference between my function and the one supplied by Oracle; however, my function will perform much better because it takes advantage of the `reverse` keyword in SQL so that there is no looping. If the password passes all of the tests, my function returns the Boolean value `TRUE`. This tells Oracle that the password is okay, and the Oracle database proceeds to alter the user password.

Voilà! You now have a password verifier that can actually help you with your security efforts. This isn't necessarily the end of your modifications, but implementing this last function would begin to harden access to your environment.

Listener Hardening

The security discipline is relatively new to database administrators. As such, this discussion doesn't expect you to know how to use a packet-sniffing tool such as Wireshark. However, you do need to know that, because default SQL communication between client and server is unencrypted, Wireshark and similar tools can be used to harvest sensitive DBA activity like `ALTER USER` *`username`* `IDENTIFIED BY` *`password`*`;` commands.

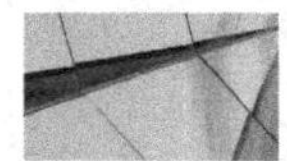

NOTE
The following example uses VNC (Virtual Network Computing) because it is convenient and free. VNC lets you see the desktop of a remote machine and control it with your local mouse and keyboard. VNC traffic typically is clear and can be sniffed. If you decide to use VNC in your workplace, make sure that you do so through an SSH tunnel.

The following example demonstrates why encrypting SQL*Net traffic is important:

1. Open a remote desktop connection to your server (VNC).
2. Download and install Wireshark.
3. Open Wireshark on Linux: *Applications* | *Internet* | *Wireshark*.
4. Click the `eth0` interface.
5. Add the filter `tcp.port == 1521 || udp.port == 1521`.
6. Connect to the database with your favorite SQL client (SQL Developer is used in this example).
7. Issue an `ALTER USER jane IDENTIFIED BY abc123;` command.
8. Look at the output sniffed via Wireshark, as shown in Figure A-6. As you can see, a system administrator on your database server can easily be *watching* your traffic.

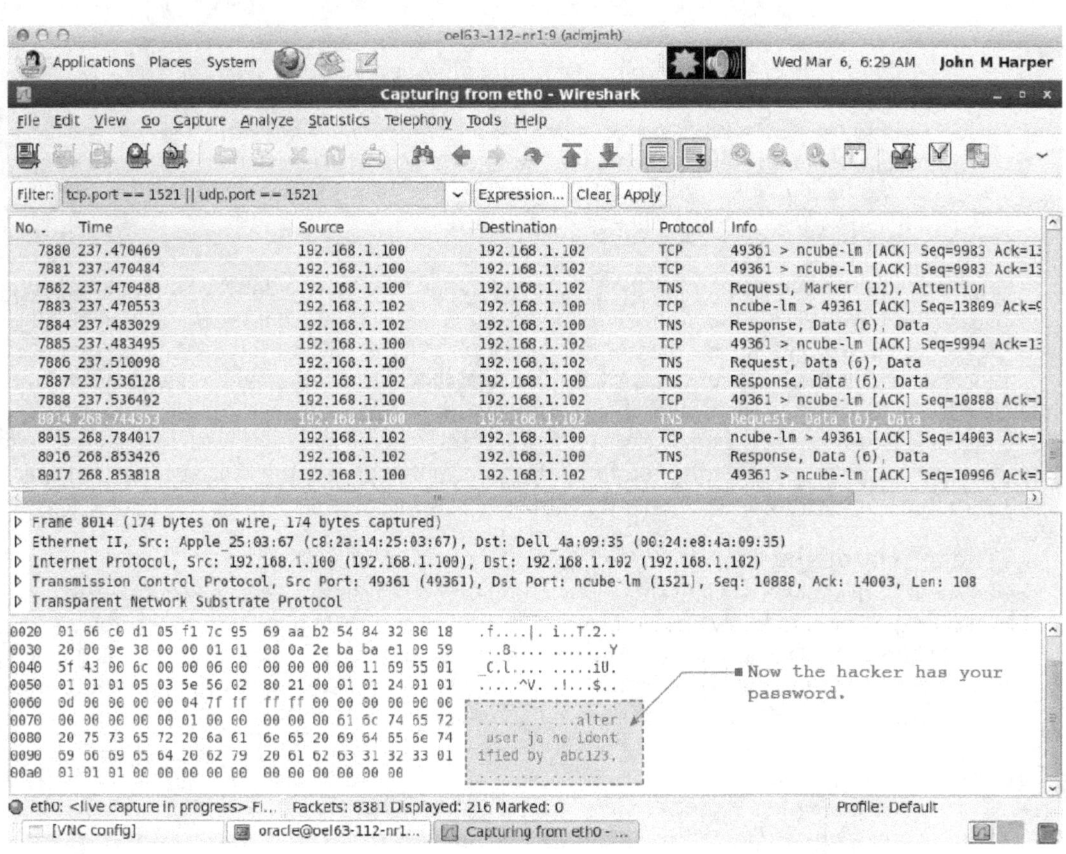

FIGURE A-6. *Exception scope and routing*

To encrypt your SQL*Net traffic to protect it against a packet-sniffing tool such as Wireshark, do the following:

1. Run the command `netmgr` from a Linux or Unix prompt to open *Oracle Net Manager* (make sure you're the `oracle` user and have environment variables set). The following illustration shows you how the Oracle Net Manager will look after you've launched it and accomplished steps 2 through 9.

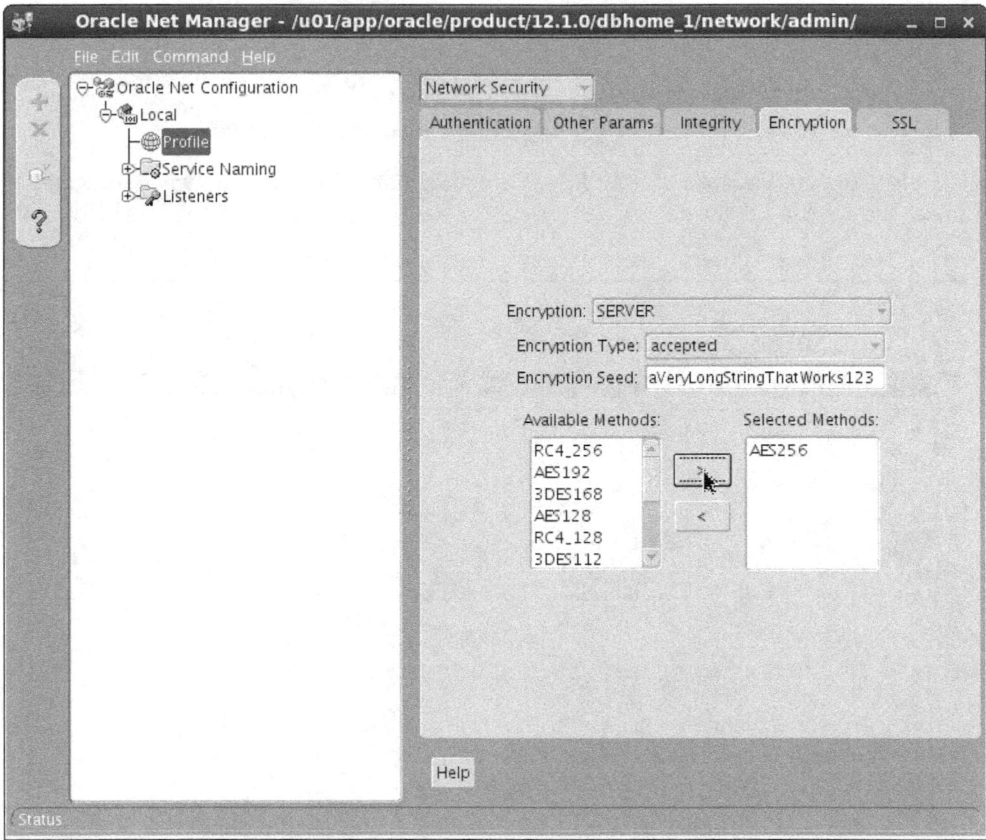

2. Click the *Profile* option in the left menu tree.
3. Click the *Network Security* option from the drop-down menu above the tabbed section.
4. Click the *Encryption* tab.
5. Click the *SERVER* selection in the *Encryption* drop-down list.
6. Click the *accepted* selection in the *Encryption Type* drop-down list.
7. Type a seed value in the *Encryption Seed* text box; you can have up to 256 characters.
8. Choose an encryption method from the *Available Methods* list, such as *AES256*, and click the *assign right* button to move your selected method into the *Select Methods* list.

9. Save the configuration: *File* | *Save Network Configuration*.
10. Look at the `sqlnet.ora` file.
11. Restart your SQL client.
12. Open Wireshark: *Applications* | *Internet* | *Wireshark*.
13. Click the `eth0` interface.
14. Add the filter `tcp.port == 1521 || udp.port == 1521`.
15. Connect to the database with your favorite SQL client (again, SQL Developer is used in this example).
16. Issue an `ALTER USER jane IDENTIFIED BY abc123;` command.
17. Look at the output sniffed via Wireshark, as shown in Figure A-7.

Just like that, you protect your SQL*Net traffic. Before you deploy Oracle Advanced Security, make sure you're licensed to use it.

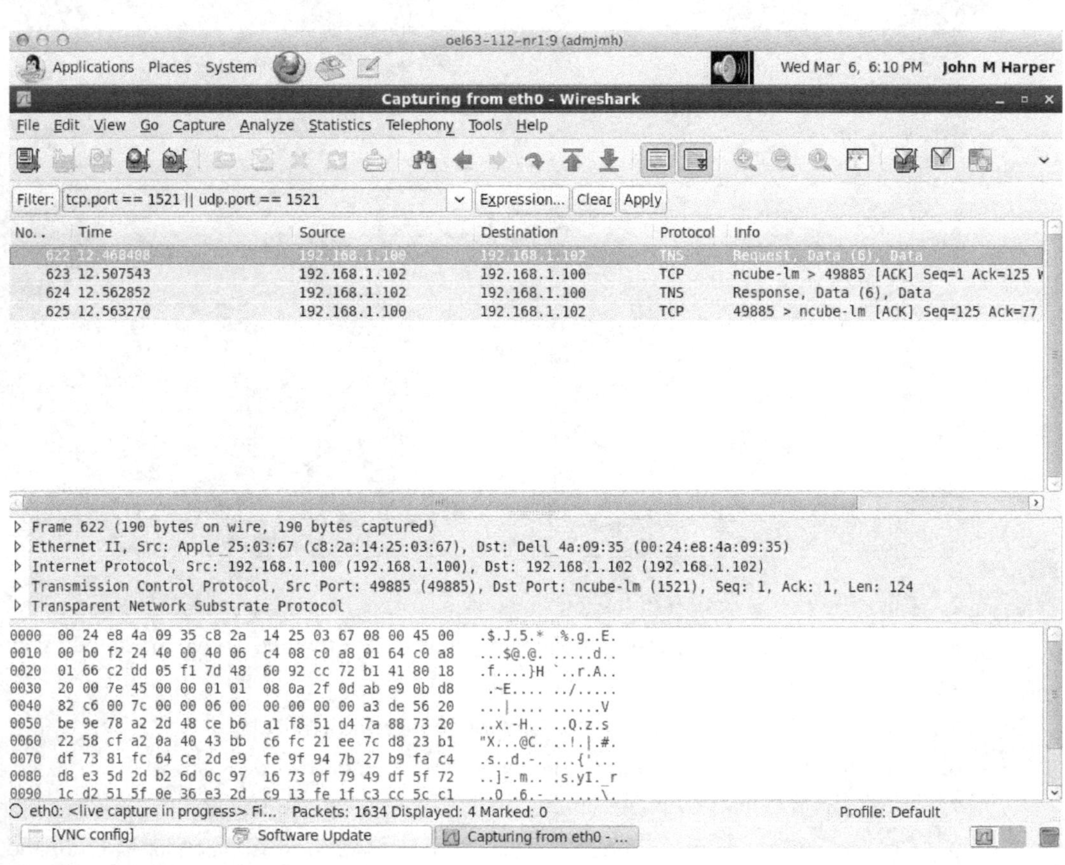

FIGURE A-7. *Wireshark packet capture after encryption*

Listener White Listing In addition to using encryption, you can modify the listener so that it either accepts or rejects connection requests. This is very easy to perform. Before you do so, make sure to obtain management approval, because there *will* be someone who complains that they can no longer connect to your database (which is a good thing, because you don't want any rogue connections anyway).

After obtaining buy-in, make the following modifications to your `sqlnet.ora` file:

```
TCP.VALIDNODE_CHECKING = YES
TCP.EXCLUDED_NODES = (192.168.1.110)
TCP.INVITED_NODES = (192.168.1.100, 192.168.1.102)
```

Then, restart your SQL client and connect to your Oracle instance.

Best practice states that you should use hostnames, not IP addresses, but it works either way. Also, make sure you add the server into the invited nodes.

To test these exclusions, set your machine IP address as an excluded node and then restart your SQL listener and attempt to connect to your Oracle instance. As a rule, you may get SQL Developer users who call to complain about an `ORA-17002` error (generated from Oracle's JDBC implementation).

While it may be helpful to add a host-based firewall on top of the preceding measures, they should put you well on your way to a more secure environment.

Remember that your security efforts are never a done deal. If you "set it and forget it," hackers will eventually penetrate your firewalls and steal your company's data. Vigilance is required. The company's data may well be its most valuable asset. If it is lost or breached, your company may cease to exist. It is imperative that you do all that you can to protect your company's data and adequately anticipate possible attacks.

Data Governance

The previous section discussed the technical aspects of hardening the database. You should now have the tools and understanding to put some of these practices in place to detect and prevent attacks against your databases. It's unlikely that you control or influence enough of your company's IT process to implement a complete security framework or security awareness program, but you can certainly advocate that one be implemented. Implementing data governance as a complete security framework trumps simply educating staff about the risks with a security awareness program.

Data governance is an emerging discipline in the IT industry. At present, data governance in many organizations means completely different things. The following sections discuss how you overcome resistance to, implement, and develop an ongoing culture of data governance.

Overcoming Resistance to Data Governance

Many companies resist data governance because they have an unspoken bias against security. The bias is often rooted in their employee perceptions that data governance restricts the employees' ability to exercise day-to-day discretion over their job responsibilities. Database administrators and database engineers (DBEs) resist data governance policies because such policies negatively impact metrics that drive DBA and DBE direct or variable compensation. For example, DBAs and DBEs may receive a year-end bonus for achieving greater throughput and machine optimization, but data governance policies may make such achievements impossible. DBAs and DBEs also see anything that impedes their ability to optimize the database server as an obstacle to overcome. These are a few reasons why DBAs and DBEs see data governance policies as a hindrance to their work. While they should value data governance policies as helpful to their charter of securing the data, they often perceive them as attempts to block normal access to the database server.

Security measures are always intended to block unauthorized access to data, not to block normal maintenance access to data. Security should hinder intruders so that they can't get to the data, but it should not overtly restrict normal business processes—such as tuning the database server. Unfortunately, security does erect barriers to normal and productive tasks. Overcoming resistance to these barriers is complicated because DBAs and DBEs keenly understand the following:

- Their business customers' demands for information that is highly available and easy to access
- Their performance metrics for salary increases and bonuses

Management may recognize the reasons for DBA and DBE resistance to implementing data governance. It's also widely known how often large, well-known software companies release to market products with known bugs and serious security vulnerabilities. Management also recognizes the pressure to implement these products quickly in their businesses. That pressure to implement newly released software can compromise a team's adherence to security policies that screen for vulnerabilities. Hackers waiting to exploit these vulnerabilities are elated when DBAs and DBEs fail to guard against these vulnerabilities.

Management's conundrum is simple and generally based on a risk management model that weighs four things:

- The metrics assigned to DBAs and DBEs support their internal customers' business requirements, and also support their management compensation plans.
- Bugs and security vulnerabilities threaten the viability of software solutions, and place at risk employee and management compensation pools.
- Senior management focuses on things managers can control and influence directly.
- Senior management's lack of focus on quality and assurance leaves *wiggle room* for lapses in quality, which may translate to security vulnerabilities in application software, networks, and database deployments.

Managers seldom remove performance metrics as a factor in DBA or DBE compensation because motivating DBAs and DBEs to achieve certain metrics helps the managers to ensure that their units meet performance targets that directly affect the managers' own compensation." The managers' risk assessment is a simple application of the principle of lost opportunity cost in economics. They must determine and weigh, "What is the lost opportunity cost of having a DBA or DBE fail against performance metrics?" and "What is the lost opportunity cost of having a DBA or DBE guarantee the security compliance of software before release?"

Management typically solves the conundrum when executive or senior management changes the subordinate unit's metrics to reflect that a *zero tolerance* policy. A zero tolerance policy means that addressing security vulnerabilities trumps all other productivity issues. That means the unit managers must alter DBA and DBE metrics to focus their efforts on eliminating security vulnerabilities. Once executive or senior management makes such a decision, companies or corporations gain the ability to implement an effective data governance program.

Implementing Data Governance

Data governance is the process of managing the proper use, control, access, quality, security, and retention of company hardware and software. This includes compliance with all licenses and fair use requirements.

Data Governance Unit A data governance unit acts much like an inspector general's office in a military or governmental organization. It is a central policy making and enforcement unit within a corporation, and it is managed outside of the normal chain-of-command. Day-to-day profit and loss responsibilities can't let business units opt in or out of the program. The benefits of effective data governance can only be achieved when you implement it across the organization. A data governance unit should exercise complete authority and control over all of the organization's data assets.

The best approach is to leverage an existing organizational unit to implement a new data governance program. This suggestion follows the recommendation of Robert Seiner, one of the pioneers in data governance. Using an existing organizational unit promotes a less-intrusive impact to a company or corporation. As a practical matter, data governance should report through your chief counsel's (or corporate law) office.

Data Governance Process Without getting too deep into the definitions and issues of data governance, this section describes the best practices necessary to make database security a reality in an organization. An organization lays the foundation for these best practices by ceding authority to a single entity to define, maintain, and audit compliance with corporate or company standards.

All departments must be held to the corporate standard and should periodically and spontaneously be measured. Measurements should include having a paid hacker try to exploit services that should be secured by compliance against corporate policy.

The governance process should adhere to a mission statement agreed upon by an executive committee that acts as the data governance board of directors. An executive commitment to data governance requires a long-range objective, such as: "All data stores shall be treated as confidential repositories and shall be secured against intruder access within two years."

Tactical implementation would occur by establishing short-range objectives, like:

- Define, approve, and implement a data classification scale, process, and initiative to identify all confidential data stores before next fiscal year.
- Define, approve, and implement a database security policy before the end of this fiscal year.
- Define, approve, and implement a process for updating database security policies against new threats and vulnerabilities by the end of each fiscal year.

Accomplishment of the short-range objectives leaves you with the need to define integrated business metrics for future operating years. By way of example, you may implement the following key measures for your database security policy:

- All security patches will be applied to all databases within one week of their availability.
- All databases will be deployed and administered in a secure area.
- All database audit logs will be reviewed daily by production, stage, test, and development DBAs.
- All database audit logs and daily activity will be collected and reported weekly to the stakeholder (or process holder).

Data Governance Compliance You need a neutral method for collecting statistics across the organization. The best collection systems employ objective metrics and collect data points from multiple systems. Companies should implement this type of approach consistently across all units within the organization.

Metrics should be reported to the unit, peer units, and stakeholders. Costs associated with implementing and managing data governance should become a cost of all Profit/loss units, and costs should be billed to individual cost centers on an accounting period-by-period basis.

Data Governance Reports Reports for compliance should be measured two ways. One should ensure the process stability and the other the process improvement. Process improvement should be measured by monitoring compliance against an annual unit goal. Data governance reports should ensure both process stability and process improvement.

Compliance and noncompliance with the company or corporate standard should be reported. Compliance should be rewarded by the compensation model, and, by extension, noncompliance should be punished by the compensation model and subject to potential disciplinary action.

Open access to metric information should be available to DBAs, DBEs, and their managers, but that access should be closely guarded. The data should measure actual performance against individual types of security vulnerabilities.

Data Governance Remediation The data governance unit should develop and deploy tools that enable individual DBAs and DBEs to evaluate and fix any security vulnerability. Failure during periodic metric collection should lead to the engagement of the data governance unit as a mentor in acquiring and maintaining database security skills.

Developing a Culture of Data Governance

Developing a culture of data requires teaching staff about security and explaining the costs and benefits of the corporate data governance program. Like any change management process, developing a culture of data may require an internal marketing campaign and an initial award system for early adopters of the new security standards.

Initial awards, such as payment in cash or kind, are one type of incentive to adopt new security standards. Over time, you can also use punishment/fear (such as a salary deduction for noncompliance) and competition (for example, by measuring compliance with data governance procedures among distinct internal groups).

The Chief Information Security Officer should be the person who is responsible for using the summary report information to motivate groups and to report compliance/noncompliance to executive management.

While changing an organization's general IT culture is a large and complex process, the return on investment is generally very positive. Likewise, it's imperative to secure the data from intrusive attacks, and failure to do so isn't an option.

SQL Tuning

SQL tuning is the process of examining how well a SQL statement runs and making necessary adjustments if it doesn't run well. You have little to do when the SQL statement runs well in very little time and sometimes much to do when the SQL statement doesn't perform well.

To demonstrate SQL tuning, this section works with a single query that has multiple joins—two inner joins and one outer join. While Oracle's cost-based optimization (CBO) constantly keeps track of the data so that CBO can enable optimal join patterns, the developer's understanding of the data often drives the approach to interaction and choice of indexes. Indexes often ensure optimal access to data, but sometimes they can work against optimal access.

SQL tuning may involve either optimizing queries or suboptimizing queries. Optimization typically is the goal for queries that will run in an online transaction processing (OLTP) or online analytical processing (OLAP) system. OLTP systems support business operations, such as finance, purchasing, order management, payroll, and human resources. OLAP systems are typically data warehouses.

Sometimes you may want to suboptimize query performance in OLTP systems to prevent delays in processing DML commands such as inserts, updates, and deletes. Query suboptimizing typically means you reduce the number or breadth of indexes. Every index that speeds a query slows `INSERT`, `UPDATE`, and `DELETE` statements because indexes require changes with every transaction that changes the data.

OLAP systems typically optimize queries regardless of transaction cost because the data is subject to very little change. Typically, the only DML statements in data warehouses are from their ETL (Extract, Transform, and Load) updates, which occur weekly, monthly, or quarterly.

Whether you're working in an OLTP environment or an OLAP environment, the first step to SQL tuning is to identify which SQL statements run most frequently. The following query lets you find the top ten most frequently running SQL statements in the Oracle Database 12*c* database server:

```
SQL> COLUMN sql_id        FORMAT A14        HEADING "SQL ID #"
SQL> COLUMN child_number  FORMAT 9999       HEADING "Child|Number"
SQL> COLUMN sql_text      FORMAT A30        HEADING "SQL Text"
SQL> COLUMN elapsed_time  FORMAT 9999999990 HEADING "Elapsed Time"
SQL> SELECT   sql_id
     ,        child_number
     ,        sql_text
     ,        elapsed_time
     FROM    (SELECT   sql_id
              ,        child_number
              ,        sql_text
              ,        elapsed_time
              ,        cpu_time
              ,        disk_reads
              ,        RANK() OVER
                      (ORDER BY elapsed_time DESC) AS elapsed_rank
              FROM     v$sql)
     WHERE    elapsed_rank <= 10;
```

You have two approaches to SQL tuning in an Oracle database: the old way and the new way. They're really not that different, but the new way, the `dbms_xplan` package, provides a richer set of analytical data for less work. The following sections show you how to use the old `EXPLAIN PLAN` approach and the new `dbms_xplan` package to analyze query performance.

EXPLAIN PLAN Statement

The `EXPLAIN PLAN` statement lets you analyze the performance of any SQL statement. The prototype for explaining a statement from the SQL*Plus command line is

```
EXPLAIN PLAN
SET STATEMENT_ID = '&input'
FOR sql_statement;
```

The `'&input'` is a substitution parameter when you set the `statement_id` value. (Substitution variables are explained in the "SQL*Plus Command-Line Interface" section, earlier in this appendix.) Using a substitution variable is generally the best approach unless you plan to remove the data that supports analysis after running each statement. A substitution variable eliminates the need to cleanup the `plan_table` each time. Substitution variables also let you use a different value for the unique `statement_id`, which ensures they won't conflict with each other. The `FOR` keyword precedes the `SELECT`, `INSERT`, `UPDATE`, or `DELETE` statement that you're analyzing.

Here's the statement we're working with in this section:

```
EXPLAIN PLAN
SET STATEMENT_ID = '&input'
FOR
SELECT   DISTINCT
         r.rental_id
,        c.contact_id
,        tu.check_out_date AS check_out_date
,        tu.return_date AS return_date
FROM     member m INNER JOIN contact c
ON       m.member_id = c.member_id INNER JOIN transaction_upload tu
ON       c.first_name = tu.first_name
AND      NVL(c.middle_name,'x') = NVL(tu.middle_name,'x')
AND      c.last_name = tu.last_name
AND      tu.account_number = m.account_number LEFT JOIN rental r
ON       c.contact_id = r.customer_id
AND      tu.check_out_date = r.check_out_date
AND      tu.return_date = r.return_date;
```

If you run the statement from the SQL*Plus command-line interface, it'll prompt you for the `input` value, or `statement_id` value. The example enters `query1` as the `statement_id` value and runs the `EXPLAIN PLAN` statement. The `EXPLAIN PLAN` statement generates several rows of data in the `plan_table` in the database instance.

DBMS_XPLAN Package

The `dbms_xplan` package lets you analyze the performance of statements. It returns the formatted output of operations, the tables accessed, the rows processed, the bytes managed, and the time taken to process the operation.

Table A-5 qualifies the `dbms_xplan` package's table access modes for internally managed tables. Beyond internally managed table access, you have `EXTERNAL TABLE ACCESS`, `RESULT CACHE`, and `MAT_VIEW REWRITE ACCESS`. Respectively, they manage row retrieval through external access, result cache retrieval, and queries written to take advantage of materialized views.

The three index operations provided by `dbms_xplan` are `AND-EQUAL`, `INDEX`, and `DOMAIN INDEX`. The `AND-EQUAL` operation combines results from one or more index scans. The `DOMAIN INDEX` operation looks up a domain index for use in a join operation. Table A-6 qualifies the six `INDEX` scan modes.

Are the Database Statistics Up to Date?

Some DBAs disable statistics, contrary to Oracle's guidance. So, you should make sure to update your statistics before you run an `EXPLAIN PLAN` statement; otherwise, you may tune the wrong statistics.

Table Access Mode	Description
FULL	Reads every row in the table
CLUSTER	Reads data via an index cluster key
HASH	Reads one or more rows in a table with a matching hash key
BY INDEX ROWID	Reads rows by specific index ROWID values
BY USER ROWID	Reads rows by using a ROWID value provided by a bind variable, literal value, or WHERE CURRENT OF CURSOR clause
BY GLOBAL INDEX ROWID	Reads rows by using a ROWID returned from a globally partitioned index
BY LOCAL INDEX ROWID	Reads rows by using a ROWID returned from a locally partitioned index
SAMPLE	Reads rows by using a ROWID returned from a SAMPLE clause

TABLE A-5. *SQL Tuning Internal Table Access Modes*

Bitmap operations are similar to index operations. dbms_xplan provides five BITMAP scan modes, which are listed and described in Table A-7.

dbms_xplan provides three join operations. A CONNECT BY operation performs a hierarchical self-join on the output from preceding steps in a DML statement. A MERGE JOIN operation performs a merge join on the output of preceding steps in a DML statement. A NESTED LOOPS operation performs nested loop lookup and comparison on the output from the preceding steps in a DML statement.

dbms_xplan also offers four hash join operations, OUTER (outer join), ANTI (antijoin), SEMI (semijoin), and CARTESIAN (Cartesian join). There are also *set*, *miscellaneous*, *partition*, and *aggregation* operations. You can find more information about all of these operations in the *Oracle Database Performance Tuning Guide 12*c *Release*.

Index Scan	Description
UNIQUE SCAN	Reads a unique index for a single row address—the ROWID value
RANGE SCAN	Reads an index for a range of values—returning multiple ROWID values
FULL SCAN	Reads every entry in the index through the key order
SKIP SCAN	Reads nonleading columns in the index key
FULL SCAN (MAX/MIN)	Reads an index for the highest or lowest value
FAST FULL SCAN	Reads every entry in an index by block order and, where possible, uses multiblock reads

TABLE A-6. *SQL Tuning INDEX Scan Modes*

Bitmap Scan	Description
CONVERSION	Converts ROWID values to bitmaps or bitmaps to ROWID
INDEX	Retrieves a value or range of values from the bitmap
MERGE	Merges multiple bitmaps
MINUS	Subtracts one bitmap from another
OR	Creates a bitwise OR of two bitmaps

TABLE A-7. *SQL Tuning BITMAP Scan Modes*

You access and format the data with the DISPLAY function of the dbms_xplan package, like this:

```
SELECT *
FROM   TABLE(dbms_xplan.display(NULL,'query1'));
```

It generates the following output (formatted and slightly truncated for the page):

```
PLAN_TABLE_OUTPUT
-------------------------------------------------------------------------------
Plan hash value: 3289798709
-------------------------------------------------------------------------------
| Id | Operation                        | Name                 | Rows  | Bytes |
-------------------------------------------------------------------------------
|   0 | SELECT STATEMENT                |                      |   229 | 24274 |
|   1 |  HASH UNIQUE                    |                      |   229 | 24274 |
|*  2 |   HASH JOIN OUTER               |                      |   229 | 24274 |
|   3 |    VIEW                         |                      |     4 |   248 |
|*  4 |     HASH JOIN                   |                      |     4 |   572 |
|*  5 |      HASH JOIN                  |                      |    15 |  1230 |
|   6 |       TABLE ACCESS FULL         | MEMBER               |     9 |   180 |
|   7 |       TABLE ACCESS FULL         | CONTACT              |    15 |   930 |
|   8 |      EXTERNAL TABLE ACCESS FULL| TRANSACTION_UPLOAD   |  8168 |   486K|
|   9 |    TABLE ACCESS FULL            | RENTAL               |  4689 |   201K|
-------------------------------------------------------------------------------
Predicate Information (identified by operation id):
---------------------------------------------------
   2 - access("TU"."RETURN_DATE"="R"."RETURN_DATE"(+) AND
              "TU"."CHECK_OUT_DATE"="R"."CHECK_OUT_DATE"(+) AND
              "C"."CONTACT_ID"="R"."CUSTOMER_ID"(+))
   4 - access("C"."FIRST_NAME"="TU"."FIRST_NAME" AND
              NVL("C"."MIDDLE_NAME",'x')=NVL("TU"."MIDDLE_NAME",'x') AND
              "C"."LAST_NAME"="TU"."LAST_NAME" AND
              "TU"."ACCOUNT_NUMBER"="M"."ACCOUNT_NUMBER")
   5 - access("C"."MEMBER_ID"="M"."MEMBER_ID")
Note
-----
   - dynamic sampling used for this statement
30 rows selected.
```

The Cost column from the output is truncated, but initially this statement has a cost value of 50. The immediate problem with this example is that the query accesses an external table, as indicated in Line 8. Line 8 also tells us that we're processing 486KB of data because of the external table read.

The biggest improvement we can make requires copying the data from the external table to an internal table. The following shows the execution plan and rows and bytes processed. Rerunning the output, the processing bytes decline from 486KB to 61 bytes. What you don't see is that the cost value drops from 50 to 34 by moving the data into an internal table.

```
PLAN_TABLE_OUTPUT
--------------------------------------------------------------------------------
Plan hash value: 3624831533
------------------------------------------------------------------------------
| Id  | Operation                        | Name              | Rows  | Bytes |
------------------------------------------------------------------------------
|   0 | SELECT STATEMENT                 |                   |   400 | 42400 |
|   1 |  HASH UNIQUE                     |                   |   400 | 42400 |
|*  2 |   HASH JOIN OUTER                |                   |   400 | 42400 |
|   3 |    VIEW                          |                   |     7 |   434 |
|   4 |     NESTED LOOPS                 |                   |     7 |  1001 |
|*  5 |      HASH JOIN                   |                   |    15 |  1230 |
|   6 |       TABLE ACCESS FULL          | MEMBER            |     9 |   180 |
|   7 |       TABLE ACCESS FULL          | CONTACT           |    15 |   930 |
|*  8 |      INDEX RANGE SCAN            | IMPORT_DATE_RANGE |     1 |    61 |
|   9 |    TABLE ACCESS FULL             | RENTAL            |  4689 |   201K|
------------------------------------------------------------------------------
Predicate Information (identified by operation id):
---------------------------------------------------
   2 - access("TU"."RETURN_DATE"="R"."RETURN_DATE"(+) AND
              "TU"."CHECK_OUT_DATE"="R"."CHECK_OUT_DATE"(+) AND
              "C"."CONTACT_ID"="R"."CUSTOMER_ID"(+))
   5 - access("C"."MEMBER_ID"="M"."MEMBER_ID")
   8 - access("TU"."ACCOUNT_NUMBER"="M"."ACCOUNT_NUMBER" AND
              "C"."LAST_NAME"="TU"."LAST_NAME" AND
              "C"."FIRST_NAME"="TU"."FIRST_NAME" AND
              NVL("C"."MIDDLE_NAME",'x')=NVL("MIDDLE_NAME",'x'))
Note
-----
   - dynamic sampling used for this statement
31 rows selected.
```

We've achieved some performance by working with an internal table. Now let's add three indexes to speed performance by changing the dynamics of how the database accesses the data:

```
SQL> CREATE UNIQUE INDEX natural_key_rental
  2  ON rental (rental_id, customer_id, check_out_date, return_date);
SQL> CREATE UNIQUE INDEX member_account
  2  ON member (member_id, account_number);
SQL> CREATE UNIQUE INDEX contact_member
  2  ON contact (contact_id, member_id, last_name, first_name
  3             ,NVL(middle_name,'x'));
```

Here's the modified execution plan:

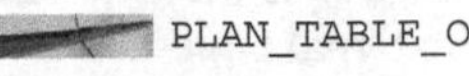

```
PLAN_TABLE_OUTPUT
--------------------------------------------------------------------------------
Plan hash value: 1185696375
--------------------------------------------------------------------------------
| Id  | Operation                 | Name                | Rows  | Bytes | Cost (%CPU)|
------------------------------------------------------------------------------------
|   0 | SELECT STATEMENT          |                     |   400 | 42400 |    28   (8)|
|   1 |  HASH UNIQUE              |                     |   400 | 42400 |    28   (8)|
|*  2 |   HASH JOIN OUTER         |                     |   400 | 42400 |    27   (4)|
|   3 |    VIEW                   |                     |     7 |   434 |    17   (0)|
|   4 |     NESTED LOOPS          |                     |     7 |  1001 |    17   (0)|
|   5 |      NESTED LOOPS         |                     |    15 |  1230 |     2   (0)|
|   6 |       INDEX FULL SCAN     | CONTACT_MEMBER      |    15 |   930 |     1   (0)|
|*  7 |       INDEX RANGE SCAN    | MEMBER_ACCOUNT      |     1 |    20 |     1   (0)|
|*  8 |      INDEX RANGE SCAN     | IMPORT_DATE_RANGE   |     1 |    61 |     1   (0)|
|   9 |    INDEX FAST FULL SCAN| NATURAL_KEY_RENTAL  |  4689 |   201K|     9   (0)|
------------------------------------------------------------------------------------
Predicate Information (identified by operation id):
---------------------------------------------------
   2 - access("TU"."RETURN_DATE"="R"."RETURN_DATE"(+) AND
              "TU"."CHECK_OUT_DATE"="R"."CHECK_OUT_DATE"(+) AND
              "C"."CONTACT_ID"="R"."CUSTOMER_ID"(+))
   7 - access("C"."MEMBER_ID"="M"."MEMBER_ID")
   8 - access("TU"."ACCOUNT_NUMBER"="M"."ACCOUNT_NUMBER" AND
              "C"."LAST_NAME"="TU"."LAST_NAME" AND
              "C"."FIRST_NAME"="TU"."FIRST_NAME" AND
              NVL("MIDDLE_NAME",'x')=NVL("MIDDLE_NAME",'x'))
Note
-----
   - dynamic sampling used for this statement
31 rows selected.
```

The execution plan shows us that we now have two nested loops with the outer hash join, which is as good as it gets with this little import example. You can also put SQL tuning hints into your queries to take advantage of certain join operations that optimize the DML statement.

SQL Tracing

Oracle provides the ability to trace SQL activities. SQL tracing involves two key steps:

- Begin tracing in a current session or in another session
- Generate meaningful information from a trace file using the `tkprof` tool

Refer to Appendix D for an easy way to obtain live stats on queries. It outlines how to snap live statistics within a session.

The next two subsections show you how to start (and stop) tracing and how to convert the proprietary tracing file into a readable output report.

Tracing Session Statements

You have a number of options for how you start tracing session data. For example, you can do any one of the following:

- Issue a command from your application code to trace the current session
- Issue a command to trace another session
- Leverage the DBMS_MONITOR package to specify sessions for automatic tracing
- Issue a command from a login trigger to trace the current session

You can enable session tracing with a SQL command or by calling one of the procedures in the DBMS_SESSION package. The DBMS_MONITOR package lets you enable tracing in another session.

Enable Tracing in the Current Session

The simplest way to start tracing in your current working session is to enter the following, which starts a basic trace:

```
ALTER SESSION SET SQL_TRACE=TRUE;
```

A basic trace captures SQL statement execution statistics and plans, but it doesn't capture bind variables or the time spent on events during the session. The following sets the trace file's identifier for a session:

```
ALTER SESSION SET trace_file_identifier=MySession;
```

You can check for a vast number of events in trace files. The most useful code (10053) lets you capture information about optimizer processing during query execution. The command to set this event is

```
ALTER SESSION SET EVENTS '10053 trace name context forever';
```

You can get more information by using the DBMS_SESSION package. The prototype for the DBMS_SESSION package is

```
DBMS_SESSION.SESSION_TRACE_ENABLE(
    waits       IN  BOOLEAN DEFAULT TRUE
  , binds       IN  BOOLEAN DEFAULT FALSE
  , plan_stat   IN  VARCHAR2 DEFAULT NULL);
```

You would call the DBMS_SESSION package to enable tracing with the following anonymous PL/SQL block:

```
BEGIN
  dbms_session.session_trace_enable( waits     => TRUE
                                   , binds     => FALSE
                                   , plan_stat => 'all_executions');
END;
/
```

While the trace is ongoing, you can use the following SELECT statement to find any active trace file for the current session:

```
SQL> SELECT   p.tracefile
  2  FROM     v$session s INNER JOIN v$process p
  3  ON       p.addr = s.paddr
  4  WHERE    s.audsid = USERENV('SESSIONID');
```

It returns

```
TRACEFILE
---------------------------------------------------------------
C:\APP\ORACLEDBA\diag\rdbms\orcl\orcl\trace\orcl_ora_4856.trc
```

Alternatively, you can simply browse the directory where the trace files are written. You can find that directory with the following query:

```
SELECT   value
FROM     v$parameter
WHERE    name = 'user_dump_dest';
```

It prints the following for an Oracle Database 12*c* database on Windows:

```
VALUE
---------------------------------------------
C:\app\oracledba\diag\rdbms\orcl\orcl\trace
```

The user_dump_dest directory is where the raw trace files are stored. The location of the physical directory may change, but the Oracle Database 12*c* database can always find it for you with the preceding query.

Disable Tracing in the Current Session

After you start the trace process, you can stop it with this command:

```
ALTER SESSION SET SQL_TRACE=FALSE;
```

Alternatively, you can stop it with this call to the DBMS_SESSION package in an anonymous block:

```
BEGIN
  dbms_session.session_trace_disable;
END;
/
```

Enable Tracing in Another Session

As mentioned previously, the DBMS_MONITOR package has the capability to start tracing in another session. The prototype for the SESSION_TRACE_ENABLE procedure is

```
DBMS_MONITOR.SESSION_TRACE_ENABLE(
    session_id  IN  BINARY_INTEGER DEFAULT NULL
  , serial_num  IN  BINARY_INTEGER DEFAULT NULL
```

```
, waits        IN   BOOLEAN DEFAULT TRUE
, binds        IN   BOOLEAN DEFAULT FALSE
, plan_stat    IN   VARCHAR2 DEFAULT NULL);
```

NOTE
The `PLAN_STAT` *parameter is only available from Oracle Database 11g forward.*

The following shows a call to the `SESSION_TRACE_ENABLE` procedure in the `DBMS_MONITOR` package:

```
SQL> BEGIN
  FOR i IN (SELECT   s.sid
            ,        s.serial#
            FROM     v$session s
            WHERE    UPPER(s.program) LIKE '%SQLPLUS%') LOOP
    dbms_monitor.session_trace_enable( session_id => i.sid
                                     , serial_num => i.serial#
                                     , waits      => FALSE
                                     , binds      => TRUE);
  END LOOP;
END;
```

You can also identify a specific SID and serial number. If you do so, you can enable tracing on only one other session.

Convert Raw Trace Files to Readable Trace Files

You use the `tkprof` utility to convert a raw trace file from the `user_dump_dest` directory into a readable trace file. The general prototype for the utility is

```
tkprof trace_file output_file explain=connection waits=key sort=(keys)
```

The prototype contains a trace file, an example of which (`orcl_ora_4856.trc`) appeared in the preceding "Enable Tracing in the Current Session" section. Raw trace files have a `.trc` file extension. The output file doesn't require a specific file extension, but the Oracle convention uses a `.prf` file extension. The `explain=` argument needs to be a *user_name/password* combination that applies to the schema where you captured the raw trace data. The `waits=` argument takes a *yes* or *no* string literal value. The `sort=` argument takes a parenthetical list of one to three sort keys delimited by commas, like (*key1*, *key2*, *key3*).

Each sort key has two parts. The first part sorts on parse, execute, or fetch operations, while the second part sorts on aspects of the statement, as qualified in Table A-8. The following sorts parse, fetch, and execute sorts by elapsed time:

```
tkprof orcl_ora_4856.trc output.prf explain=student/student waits=yes
sort=(prsela,fchela,exeela)
```

Sort Key	Part of Sort Key	Description
prs	1st	Sorts on values during parse calls
exe	1st	Sorts on values during execute calls
fch	1st	Sorts on values during fetch calls
cnt	2nd	Sorts on number of calls
cpu	2nd	Sorts on CPU consumption
ela	2nd	Sorts on elapsed time
dsk	2nd	Sorts on disk reads
qry	2nd	Sorts on consistent reads
cu	2nd	Sorts on current reads
mis	2nd	Sorts on library cache misses
row	2nd	Sorts on rows processed

TABLE A-8. *tkprof Sort Options*

There are several other `tkprof` options available, including the following:

- `aggregate=` Lets you report identical SQL statements once with summed statistics
- `table=` Lets you substitute a different table name for the `plan_table` default
- `print=` Takes a number that limits the number of SQL statements printed to the output file
- `sys=` Lets you provide a nonstring literal to suppress SQL statements executed by the `sys` user
- `record=` Lets you designate the name of the file to which all the SQL statements from the trace file are written
- `insert=` Lets you designate the name of the file to which the `tkprof` utility can write a script that lets you store and keep a record of the statements and their execution statistics

Summary

This appendix has given you a primer on the concepts of the Oracle 12c database, enabling you to work in both the SQL Developer and SQL*Plus command-line interfaces and to understand elements of user configuration, database constraints, database security, and SQL tuning and tracing.

APPENDIX B

SQL Primer

This primer supports the SQL `SELECT`, `INSERT`, `UPDATE`, and `DELETE` statements that exist throughout the book. This primer a critical resource to avoid you choosing to use PL/SQL to solve problems that are better solved with SQL. It's provided for you because all too often other developers resort to PL/SQL solutions when more effective SQL solutions are available but unknown. PL/SQL should help you solve those problems that can't be solved with SQL alone.

I've made an effort in this primer to highlight the SQL concepts and best practices that support key features of Oracle Database 12c. It seemed best to me to put complete discussions of SQL solutions in this primer rather than to try to intermingle them in the discussion of PL/SQL features. Throughout the book, I refer you to this primer to explore SQL alternatives or concepts. This SQL primer should help you write better PL/SQL programs because you'll know what's available in SQL.

As mentioned in Chapter 1 and Appendix A, the client-side software is a command-line console. The client submits requests to the server-side engine, which in turn sends results and acknowledgement of success or failure back to the client. These requests are written in SQL statements. SQL stands for Structured Query Language and was initially developed by IBM.

NOTE
IBM originally labeled its language Structured English Query Language *(SEQUEL), but SEQUEL as a name ran afoul of an existing trademark of a British company, so IBM shortened it to* SQL. *IBM engineers continued to use the pronunciation* sequel *rather than S-Q-L.*

Although SQL is often labeled as a nonprocedural programming language, that's *technically* inaccurate. Nonprocedural languages are typically event-driven languages, such as Java. Instead, *SQL is a set-based declarative language*. Declarative programming languages let developers state what a program should do without qualifying how it will accomplish this. Declarative languages are much like an automatic transmission in a car. High-level instructions map to detailed activities hidden from the driver, such as accelerating and decelerating without having to use a clutch to change gears.

Imperative languages change the state of variables and sets of variables for any assigned task. Internally, the Oracle Database 12c engine supports *imperative languages*. Like the throttle or gas pedal, SQL statements submit requests to a database engine. The engine receives the request, determines the sequence of actions required to accomplish the task, and performs the task. On a steep hill in San Francisco, I'd prefer an automatic transmission; and with a tight deadline for developing a program, I'd prefer SQL over any imperative language.

SQL lets you interact with data, but it also lets you define and configure data structures without dealing with the specific mechanics of operation. The SQL statement engine processes all SQL statements. All means *all*, with no exceptions. SQL statements are *events* and fall into several categories: *Data Definition Language (DDL)*, *Data Manipulation Language (DML)*, *Data Control Language (DCL)*, or *Transaction Control Language (TCL)*.

Although there are many variations of how you use SQL commands, only 16 basic commands exist. The DDL commands let you create and modify structures in the database via `CREATE`, `ALTER`, `DROP`, `RENAME`, `TRUNCATE`, and `COMMENT` statements. DML commands let you query, add, modify, or remove data in structures via `SELECT`, `INSERT`, `UPDATE`, and `DELETE` statements. These four DML statements deliver classic *CRUD* (create, read, update, and delete) functionality, depicted in Figure B-1 (CRUD corresponds, respectively, to `INSERT`, `SELECT`, `UPDATE`, and `DELETE`).

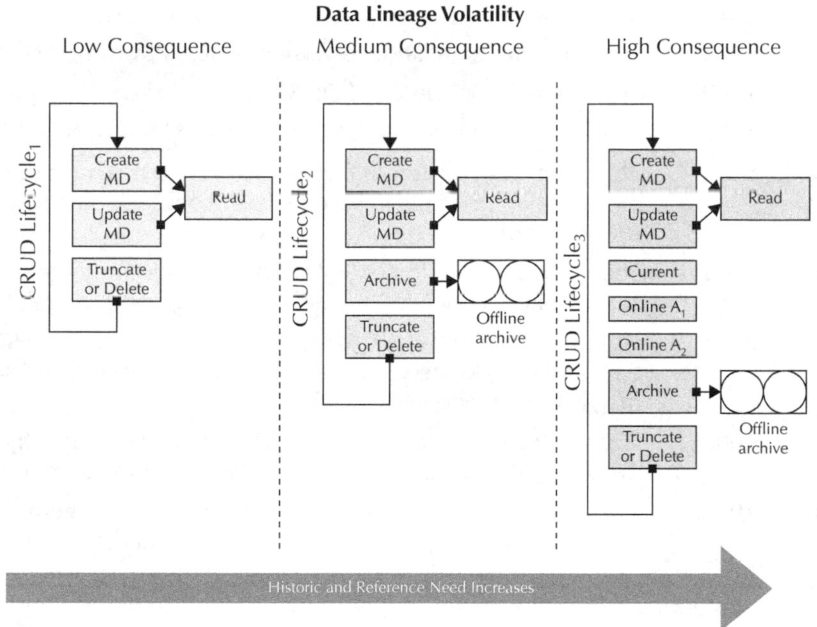

FIGURE B-1. *Typical CRUD lifecycles*

CRUD functionality actually has lifecycles that hold low, medium, or high consequences within application implementations. Consequences are determined by the volatility (or frequency of change) of transactions.

In the CRUD lifecycle, some data is more crucial to the business than other data. For this reason, many DBA teams create online archives of the data for rapid reference, if it is required. They store the data either in partitions or in separate tables labeled with a timestamp, like `SALES_JAN2013` for a data warehouse. These partitions or tables can be removed when they are no longer required. If the data is critical enough, DBAs create offline archives (called tape backups) of the data before it is removed from the transactional table. This ensures data constancy and keeps your transactional system speedy.

The DML family of commands also includes the hybrid `MERGE` statement, which lets you insert or update rows based on logic you embed in the statement. While you can tune `MERGE` statements, they aren't as efficient as ordinary `INSERT` statements because they insert or update data. Oracle also provides a multiple-table `INSERT` statement, `INSERT ALL`, in which you embed logic that determines which table should be the target for inserting each row of data.

When you transact across more than a single table, you use the TCL commands `SAVEPOINT`, `ROLLBACK`, and `COMMIT`. Lastly, the `GRANT` and `REVOKE` DCL commands let you grant and revoke privileges to act in the database.

Set-based declarative languages such as SQL don't accomplish all that databases need to do, which is why programmers write procedural programs and event-driven triggers in PL/SQL, write object-oriented solutions in event-driven languages like Java or C#, and write web development solutions using Perl, PHP, or Ruby.

Name	Year	Description
SQL-86	1986	This is the first standardized version of SQL. It was ratified by ISO in 1987.
SQL-89	1989	This is a minor revision of SQL-86.
SQL-92	1992	This is a major revision of SQL-89 and also known as SQL2.
SQL:1999	1999	This is a major revision of SQL-92 that added recursive queries, regular expression handling, database triggers, nonscalar data types, and object-oriented features.
SQL:2003	2003	This is a major revision of SQL:1999 that added auto-generated columns, standardized sequences, window functions, and XML-related functions.
SQL:2006	2006	This includes ISO/IEC 9075-14:2006, which defines how SQL can work with XML and XQuery. It also defines ways to import and store XML data in a relational model.
SQL:2008	2008	This legalizes the `ORDER BY` clause outside of cursor definitions and adds `INSTEAD OF` triggers and the `TRUNCATE` command to the standard.
SQL:2011	2011	This includes ISO/IEC 9075:2011, which revisited a number of elements but significantly improves support for temporal databases.

TABLE B-1. *ANSI SQL Standards*

SQL implementations differ for many reasons. They vary in their level of compliance with different ANSI standards. For example, Oracle SQL supports two semantic join models—one is the Oracle proprietary method and the other is compliant with ANSI SQL:2003. Table B-1 covers the SQL standards. By and large, Oracle Database complies with or surpasses more of the ANSI standards than any other database.

Like Oracle Database 11*g*, Oracle Database 12*c* is ANSI SQL:2003 compliant, except in the handling of parameters to PL/SQL (Oracle believes its approach is superior to the ANSI standards in this regard). It should be noted that many improvements and efficiencies in merging XML and XQuery have been made in the Oracle Database 12*c*. As to `INSTEAD OF` triggers and the `TRUNCATE` statement in the ANSI SQL:2008 standard, Oracle has had most of those features since the Oracle 7 database in 1993.

The appendix covers

- Oracle SQL data types
- Data Definition Language (DDL)
- Data Manipulation Language (DML)
- Transaction Control Language (TCL)
- Queries: `SELECT` statements
- Join Results

While the topics in this appendix are arranged for the beginner from start to finish, you should be able to use individual sections as independent references if you already have a foundation in SQL. *Head First SQL* by Lynn Beighley (O'Reilly, 2007) is a basic introduction to how SQL statements work. A more complete treatment of Oracle SQL is found in *Oracle Database 12*c *SQL* by Jason Price (Oracle Press, 2013). The comprehensive reference is the *Oracle Database SQL Reference 12c Release 1* manual, which has over 1,700 printed pages and is available online at http://otn.oracle.com.The following sections cover the SQL building blocks. You start with DDL statements because they build the tables, views, sequences, structures, and constraints. DML statements let you control how you insert, update, or delete data. TCL statements let you manage ACID-compliant transactions (combinations of insert, update, and/or delete statements) across two or more tables or views. Queries, or `SELECT` statements, let you access unfiltered or filter data, and joins let you combine data from different tables and views.

Oracle SQL Data Types

Oracle Database 12*c* supports *character, numeric, timestamp, binary, spatial, XML, user-defined,* and *row address* data types. These types are declared in SQL and may also be declared in PL/SQL. Table B-2 summarizes these SQL data types and qualifies two widely used data subtypes by groups. While the list is not comprehensive of all subtypes, which can be found in the *Oracle Database SQL Reference 12c Release 1* manual, it should cover the most frequently used data subtypes. Alternatively, you can look in the `dbms_types` package specification for the information found in Table B-2.

Data Type	Raw Code	Description
CHAR	96	The `CHAR` data type column stores fixed-length character data in bytes or characters. You can override the default by providing a formal *size* parameter. The `BYTE` or `CHAR` qualification is optional and will be applied from the `NLS_LENGTH_SEMANTICS` parameter by default. It has the following prototype: `CHAR [(size [BYTE | CHAR])]`
NCHAR	96	The `NCHAR` data type column stores fixed-length Unicode National Character data in bytes or characters. Unicode variables require 2 or 3 bytes, depending on the character set, which is an encoding schema. The `AL16UTF16` character set requires 2 bytes, and `UTF8` requires 3 bytes. You can override the default by providing a formal *size* parameter. It has the following prototype: `NCHAR [(size)]`
STRING	1	The `STRING` data type column is a subtype of `VARCHAR2` and stores variable-length strings in bytes or characters up to 32,767 bytes in length with a `MAX_STRING_SIZE` value of `EXTENDED`. If `BYTE` or `CHAR` is not specified, the type uses the `NLS_LENGTH_SEMANTICS` parameter defined for the database instance. You define a `VARCHAR2` data type by providing a required *size* parameter. It has the following prototype: `STRING [(size [BYTE | CHAR])]`

(continued)

TABLE B-2. *SQL Data Types*

Data Type	Raw Code	Description
VARCHAR	1	The VARCHAR data type column acts like a synonym for the VARCHAR2 data type. If you use it to define a column, Oracle implicitly converts it to a VARCHAR2 data type. It has the following prototype: `VARCHAR [(`*`size`*` [BYTE | CHAR])]`
VARCHAR2	1	The VARCHAR2 data type column stores variable-length strings in bytes or characters. If BYTE or CHAR is not specified, the type uses the NLS_LENGTH_SEMANTICS parameter defined for the database instance. This value is 2 bytes for AL16UTF16 and 3 bytes for UTF8. You define a VARCHAR2 data type by setting its maximum *size* parameter. The maximum size differs based on the value of the MAX_STRING_SIZE parameter. When the parameter is set to EXTENDED, a VARCHAR2 can be 32,767 bytes; it can be only 4,000 bytes long when the MAX_STRING_SIZE parameter is set to STANDARD. It has the following prototype: `VARCHAR2 [(`*`size`*` [BYTE | CHAR])]`
NVARCHAR2	1	The NVARCHAR2 data type is the Unicode equivalent of the VARCHAR2 data type. The size per character is determined by the Unicode setting for the database instance. You define an NVARCHAR2 data type by setting its maximum *size* parameter. It has the following prototype: `NVARCHAR2 (`*`size`*`)`
CLOB	112	The CLOB data type column stands for Character Large Object. CLOB columns store character strings up to 4GB in size. Variables with Unicode character sets are also supported up to the same maximum size. CLOB types are defined without any formal parameter for size. It has the following prototype: `CLOB`
NCLOB	112	The NCLOB data type column stands for Unicode National Character Large Object. NCLOB columns store character strings up to 4GB in size. Variables with Unicode character sets are also supported up to the same maximum size. NCLOB types are defined without any formal parameter for size. It has the following prototype: `NCLOB`
LONG	8	The LONG data type column is provided for backward compatibility and will soon become unavailable because the CLOB and NCLOB data types are its future replacement types. *(Note: Oracle recommends that you begin migrating LONG data types, but has announced no firm date for its deprecation.)* It contains a variable-length string up to 2GB of characters per row of data, which means you can have only one LONG data type in a table definition. You define a LONG without any formal parameter. It has the following prototype: `LONG`

TABLE B-2. *SQL Data Types*

Data Type	Raw Code	Description
`BINARY_FLOAT`	100	The `BINARY_FLOAT` is a 32-bit floating-point number data type that takes 4 bytes of storage. It is defined without a formal parameter. It has the following prototype: `BINARY_FLOAT`
`BINARY_DOUBLE`	101	The `BINARY_DOUBLE` is a 64-bit floating-point number data type that takes 8 bytes of storage. It is defined without a formal parameter. It has the following prototype: `BINARY_DOUBLE`
`FLOAT`	2	The `FLOAT` is a 126-position subtype of the `NUMBER` data type column. You can define it without a formal parameter or with a formal parameter of *size*. It has the following prototype: `FLOAT [(size)]`
`NUMBER`	2	The `NUMBER` is a 38-position numeric data type column. You can declare its precision (or size) and its scale (or number of digits to the right of the decimal point). You can define it without a formal parameter, with a single *precision* parameter, or with both *precision* and *scale* parameters. It has the following prototype: `NUMBER [(precision [, scale])]`
`DATE`	12	The `DATE` is a 7-byte column and represents a timestamp from 1 Jan 4712 B.C.E. to 31 Dec 9999 using a Gregorian calendar representation. The default format mask, `DD-MON-RR`, is set as a database parameter and found as the `NLS_DATE_FORMAT` parameter in the `V$PARAMETER` table. It has the following prototype: `DATE`
`INTERVAL YEAR`	182	The `INTERVAL YEAR` is a 5-byte column and represents a year and month, and the default display is `YYYY MM`. You can define it with or without a formal parameter of *year*. The `year_precision` is the number of digits in the `YEAR` datetime field, and it can be between 0 and 9 digits, and the default is 2 digits. The default limits of the year interval are –99 and 99. It has the following prototype: `INTERVAL YEAR [(year)] TO MONTH`

`INTERVAL DAY`	183	The `INTERVAL DAY` is an 11-byte representation of days, hours, minutes, and seconds in an interval. The default display is `DD HH:MI:SS`, or *days*, *hours*, *minutes*, and *seconds*. The `day_precision` is the maximum number of digits in the `DAY` datetime field, between 0 and 9 digits, and the default is 2 digits. The `factional_seconds` is the number of digits in the fractional part of the `SECOND` field. Accepted values are between 0 to 9 digits, and the default is 2 digits. It has the following prototype:
		`INTERVAL DAY [(day_precision)]`
		`TO SECOND [(fractional_seconds)]`

(continued)

TABLE B-2. *SQL Data Types*

Data Type	Raw Code	Description
TIMESTAMP	180	The TIMESTAMP is a 7- to 11-byte column and represents a date and time, and it includes fractional seconds when you override the default *seconds* parameter. The default *seconds* parameter returns seconds without any fractional equivalent. The fractions of *seconds* must be values between 0 and 9 and have a maximum display precision of microseconds. It has the following prototype: TIMESTAMP [(*seconds*)]
TIMESTAMP WITH TIME ZONE	231	The TIMESTAMP WITH TIME ZONE is a 13-byte column and represents a date and time including offset from UTC; it includes fractional seconds when you override the default *seconds* parameter. The default *seconds* parameter returns seconds without any fractional equivalent. The fractions of *seconds* must be values between 0 and 9 and have a maximum display precision of microseconds. It has the following prototype: TIMESTAMP [(*seconds*)] WITH TIME ZONE
BLOB	113	The BLOB data type column may contain any type of unstructured binary data up to a maximum size of 4GB. It has the following prototype: BLOB
BFILE	114	The BFILE data type column contains a reference to a file stored externally on a file system. The file must not exceed 4GB in size. It has the following prototype: BFILE
RAW	23	The RAW data type column is provided for backward compatibility and will soon become unavailable because the BLOB data type is its future replacement. *(Note: Oracle recommends that you begin migrating RAW data types, but has announced no firm date for the type's deprecation.)* It can contain a variable-length raw binary stream up to 2,000 bytes per row of data, which means you can only have one RAW data type in a table definition. It has the following prototype: RAW (*size*)
LONG RAW	24	The LONG RAW data type column is provided for backward compatibility and will soon become unavailable because the BLOB data type is its future replacement. *(Note: Oracle recommends that you begin migrating LONG RAW data types, but has announced no firm date for the type's deprecation.)* It can contain a variable-length raw binary stream up to 2GB bytes. It has the following prototype: LONG RAW

TABLE B-2. *SQL Data Types*

Data Type	Raw Code	Description
ROWID	69	The ROWID data type column contains a 10-byte representation of a Base 64 binary data representation retrieved as the ROWID pseudocolumn. The ROWID pseudocolumn maps to a physical block on the file system or raw partition. It has the following prototype: ROWID
UROWID	208	The UROWID data type column contains a maximum of 4,000 bytes, and it is the Base 64 binary data representation of the logical row in an index-organized table. The optional *size* parameter sets the size in bytes for the UROWID values. It has the following prototype: UROWID [(*size*)]
XMLType	112	The XMLType data type column contains a maximum of 4,000 bytes, and it is the Base 64 binary data representation of the logical row in an index-organized table. The optional *size* parameter sets the size in bytes for the XMLType values. It has the following prototype: XMLType [(*size*)]

TABLE B-2. *SQL Data Types*

Spatial data types and user-defined data types don't quite fit nicely into Table B-2. Spatial data types are Oracle-provided object types. User-defined SQL data types fall into three categories: object types (which may have methods), collections of a single column (or Attribute Data Types [ADTs] according to Oracle's documentation), and collections of object types (or user-defined types [UDTs]). This appendix shows you how to implement and evolve basic object types, and Chapter 11 shows you how to implement object types, subtypes, and their respective PL/SQL object bodies.

You can also find examples using these Oracle SQL data types in the *Oracle Database Application Developer's Guide – Fundamentals* and *Oracle Database Application Developer's Guide – Large Objects*. The most frequently used data types are the BLOB, BFILE, CLOB, DATE, FLOAT, NUMBER, STRING, TIMESTAMP, and VARCHAR2 data types. International implementations also use the TIMESTAMP WITH LOCAL TIME ZONE data type to regionalize Virtual Private Databases available in the Oracle Database 12*c* product family.

Data Definition Language (DDL)

The DDL commands let you *create*, *replace*, *alter*, *drop*, *rename*, and *truncate* database objects, permissions, and settings. You require a database instance before you can create, replace, alter, drop, rename, and truncate database objects. When you installed the Oracle database, the installation script created a clone of a sample database. Alternatively, the installation program could have used the CREATE command to build a database instance. After creating the database instance, you can then use the ALTER command to change settings for the instance or for given sessions. Sessions last the duration of a connection to the database instance.

The DDL section is organized into subsections and covers

- `CREATE` statement
- `ALTER` statement
- `RENAME` statement
- `DROP` statement
- `TRUNCATE` statement
- `COMMENT` statement

You will most frequently use DDL commands to manage tables, constraints, indexes, views, sequences, and user-defined types. This section works through applications that apply to these command uses.

CREATE Statement

The `CREATE` statement provides the DBA and Application DBA with the ability to create databases, tablespaces, and users. It also provides you with the ability to create tables, sequences and identity columns, constraints, indexes, views, functions, procedures, packages, object types, external tables, user-defined types, partitioned tables, and synonyms.

In this section of the appendix, you cover how to create users, privileges, tables, sequences, identity columns, nested collections, constraints, indexes, views, functions, procedures, packages, object types, external types, and synonyms. Understanding how to use these types of commands is important for all Oracle database programmers.

Users

Users are synonymous with *schemas* in an Oracle database, and sometimes schemas are labeled as *namespaces*. A *database* or *schema* is a private work area, but it is also a container of tables. Oracle Database 12*c* supports container databases (CDBs) and pluggable databases (PDBs). Container users are the common schemas, like `sys`, `system`, and so forth. However, you can create user-defined common users with a `c##` prefix, or local users for the pluggable databases. You define local users with the same user name convention used by prior releases of the Oracle database. User-defined common users shouldn't have tables and shouldn't serve administrative purposes across multiple or single pluggable databases. You should define local users when you want to create schemas to hold tables.

Users hold privileges to work in the database. Each database designates at least one default *superuser*. The superuser enjoys *all* privileges in the database. The Oracle database defines two superusers, `sys` and `system`, and follows the ANSI-SPARC architecture's three-tiered model. This architectural model divides the internal, conceptual, and external views of schemas or databases.

The *internal* view consists of the physical reality of how data is organized, which is specific to any DBMS. The internal view also contains the editable data catalog that maintains all the data about data, or *metadata*. This metadata contains all the definitions of users, databases, tables, indexes, constraints, sequences, data types, and views. Inside the internal view and with the proper credentials, a superuser can alter the contents of the data catalog with Data Manipulation Language (DML) statements. That means an authorized user could use an `INSERT`, `UPDATE`, or `DELETE` statement to change critical metadata outside the administrative barrier of system privileges and Data Definition Language (DDL) statements.

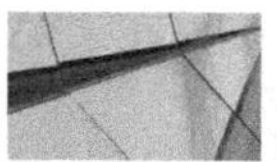

NOTE
Never use DML statements to change the data catalog values without the express instruction of Oracle Support.

The *conceptual* view consists of the community view of data. The *community view* is defined by the users with access privileges to the database, and it represents an administrator's view of data from the perspective of SQL. This view of data provides administrator-friendly views of data stored in the data catalog.

It isn't possible to change the contents of the metadata in the community view, except through DDL statements such as `ALTER`, `CREATE`, and `DROP` statements. Developers can use only these DDL statements against objects, or in the case of the `ALTER` statement, against system and database environment settings. These types of environment settings enable such things as database traces measuring behavior and performance. More on these types of DDL statements can be found in the *Oracle Database SQL Language Reference 12*c *Release*.

Oracle implements the concept of a community view as a collection of *striped views*. Striped views detect the user and allow them to see only things they have rights to access. These views typically start with `CDB_`, `DBA_`, `ALL_`, and `USER_` prefixes, and you access them as you would any other table or view through queries with a `SELECT` statement. The `ALL_` and `DBA_` prefixed views are accessible only to the Oracle superusers: `sys`, `system`, and user-defined accounts granted super privileges. Every user has access to the community view prefixed with `USER_`. Those views provide access to structures only in the user's schema or personal work area.

The *external* view consists of access to the user's schema or database, which is a private work area. Users typically have complete control over the resources of their schema or database, but in some advanced architectures, users can have restricted rights. In those models, the user may be able to perform only the following tasks:

- Create tables and sequences
- Create or replace stored program units
- Provide or rescind grants and synonyms
- Limit access to memory, disk space, or network connections

Oracle's `sys` and `system` users are synonymous with the two schemas for the internal and conceptual views, respectively. The differences between the definition of the internal view and the privileges conveyed when connecting as `sys` aren't immediately visible. You cannot change things in the `sys` schema when you connect as the `sys` user, unless you connect with the `/ as sysoper` (*system operator*) or `/ as sysdba` (*system DBA*) privilege. You have full privileges as the system DBA but only a subset of privileges as the system operator. Typically, the only thing you perform with either of these responsibilities is routine maintenance or granting of specialized privileges. Routine maintenance would include starting and stopping the database. Specialized privileges include granting a user wider privileges or revoking privileges already granted, and defining the internal Java permissions though the `dbms_java` package.

Although you can create new users and grant them privileges like the superuser, you shouldn't alter the predefined roles of the superusers. The next sections describe how you create users and grant privileges to or revoke privileges from a user.

Creating an Oracle User Creating a user is synonymous with creating a schema in an Oracle database. This section focuses on the aspects of authentication, profile, and account status for an Oracle database user.

The SQL prototype to create a user allows you to identify the user with a password, an external SSL-authenticated certificate name, or a globally identified user name based on a Lightweight Directory Access Protocol (LDAP) entry. The following syntax (similar to that in Appendix A) lets you create a PDB `student` user that is identified by a local database password:

```
CREATE USER student IDENTIFIED BY student;
```

Or, you can create a user-defined common user with this syntax:

```
CREATE USER c##plsql IDENTIFIED BY W0rk1ng2 CONTAINER=ALL;
```

Common users can also be restricted to a pluggable database by specifying it in the `CONTAINER` clause, like

```
CREATE USER c##plsql IDENTIFIED BY W0rk1ng2 CONTAINER=HR;
```

One alternative to a local user is an SSL-authenticated certificate name, which would look like this:

```
CREATE USER student IDENTIFIED EXTERNALLY AS 'certificate_name';
```

The LDAP alternative for a local user would look the same but use a different source:

```
CREATE USER student IDENTIFIED EXTERNALLY AS 'CN=miles,O=apple,C=us';
```

Oracle Password Rules and Recommendations

Oracle recommends that you comply with these rules when specifying a password:

- Contains at least one lowercase letter.
- Contains at least one uppercase letter.
- Contains at least one digit.
- Is at least eight characters in length.
- Uses the database character set, which can include the underscore (_), dollar sign ($), and pound sign (#) characters.
- Is enclosed with double-quotation marks if it contains special characters, including a number or symbol beginning the password.
- Should not be an actual word.

Likewise, you can't use the old educational passwords:

- The sys account password cannot be change_on_install (case insensitive).
- The `system` account password cannot be manager (case insensitive).
- The `sysman` account password cannot be sysman (case insensitive).
- The `dbsnmp` account password cannot be dbsnmp (case insensitive).
- If you choose to use the same password for all the accounts, then that password cannot be *change_on_install*, *manager*, *sysman*, or *dbsnmp* (case insensitive).

The certificate is an SSL (Secure Sockets Layer) file. It lets you encrypt your database credentials to support secure data communication.

Any of the three syntax methods can be used to create a private `student` work area, which is a schema. A number of other options are available for the default and temporary tablespaces of the work area, and quota syntax is available to limit the space authorized for a schema.

Another clause allows you to assign a profile to users when you create them. That clause generally follows any tablespace assignments and quota limits. An example that assumes default assignment of tablespaces and quota limits would look like this with a local password:

```
CREATE USER student IDENTIFIED BY student
PROFILE profile_name;
```

Profiles allow you to restrict the number of concurrent user sessions, amount of CPU per call, and so forth. Profiles also let you impose restrictions or overriding password functions. The latter allows you to enhance the base security provided by the Oracle database, like surrounding the castle gate with a moat.

You can also set a password as expired. With this setting, when the user signs on with a provided password, he or she will be prompted to change it immediately. This is the best practice for issuing user accounts. Accounts are unlocked by default, but sometimes an account should be locked. For example, you might need to create the schema as a reference for development purposes in another schema before planned use of the schema. These clauses generally follow all of those previously discussed. A sample `CREATE` statement with these clauses would look like this:

```
CREATE USER student IDENTIFIED BY student
PROFILE profile_name
PASSWORD EXPIRE
ACCOUNT LOCK;
```

You can use an `ALTER` statement to unlock the user account when the time comes to activate it. More details on that are provided in the "User" subsection of the "ALTER Statement" section.

Restricting access through the Oracle Transparent Network Substrate (TNS) is accomplished by configuring the Oracle networking stack. For example, you can configure the `sqlnet.ora` file to be used to restrict connections within a domain.

The following shows how to enable or exclude client machine access. The parameter lines go in to the `sqlnet.ora` file on the server.

```
tcp.validnode_checking = yes
tcp.invited_nodes = (192.168.0.91)
tcp.excluded_nodes = (192.168.0.129)
```

The first parameter allows you to check whether the IP address is authorized or not. The second line shows you how to authorize a client, and the third line shows you how to prohibit a client from connecting to the Oracle database server.

After the user connects to the database, you can provide fine-grain access control through SQL configuration. For example, you can restrict a user's access down to the column level by using the new invisible columns and `dbms_redact` package.

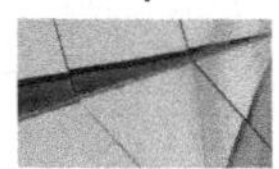

NOTE

You can find full documentation on Oracle networking in the Oracle Database Net Services Reference 12*c* Release.

This concludes the basics of setting up a new user account. You can explore more on the topic online in the *Oracle Database SQL Language Reference 12c Release*.

Granting Oracle Privileges

There are two types of security privileges. One type contains system privileges and the other contains object privileges. System privileges don't relate to a specific object or schema/database. Object privileges provide specific permissions to work with individual objects or schemas/databases.

System privileges allow wide-ranging actions and should be restricted to specific administrative user accounts. These administrative accounts are *common user* accounts in Oracle Database 12*c*, like `sys`, `system`, and any user-defined common account that starts with a `c##` prefix.

System privileges allow a common user to administer a system, create new privileges, change the behavior of existing privileges, change the behavior of system resources, or manipulate any type of object, such as tables, views, indexes, and so forth. DBAs have system privileges, and these privileges are often frequently provided to developers in small test systems. When developers package their code for integration testing and deployment, DBA system privileges run their code.

Object privileges grant specific access to a single user or set of users. These privileges often allow the user to manipulate data objects such as tables or views: a user can select, insert, update, or delete data. They also grant privileges to run or execute stored programs, such as stored functions, procedures, and, in object-relational databases, instantiable objects. Object privileges also are granted to the DBA during implementation, but they're key components of application architectures. They allow the application designer to segment sets of tables and programs into separate schemas. These schemas act like packages in object-oriented programming languages.

Both system and object privileges can be revoked by the grantor or other superuser. Any work the user does to the data while he or she had access to the system remains unaltered when privileges are revoked. Therefore, privileges should be granted only where appropriate and their use should be monitored.

The Oracle Database 12*c* database supports statements that let you grant and revoke privileges. These commands are colloquially called *Data Control Language (DCL)* statements.

DCL statements can grant privileges to container users, like DBA or user-defined common users. This is just the basic set of commands; you can find more in the *Oracle Database SQL Language Reference 12c Release*.

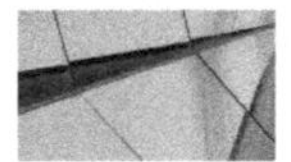

NOTE

`ANY` *is an optional keyword and provides wide-ranging permissions in Oracle. This privilege shouldn't be granted to anyone except a DBA or container user.*

The current section shows you how to grant and the subsequent section shows you how to revoke a system privilege in the Oracle Database 12*c* database.

Creating an account in an Oracle database doesn't automatically enable it for use. First you must grant basic permissions to use a local account (one reserved for a pluggable database). The `system` user or any common administrator account created with the `CREATE ANY USER` privilege should run these commands.

You should only extend those basic privileges that users require, as a rule. You also must manage the limits on access to physical space. You should note that privileges don't work when you create a user without a DEFAULT clause and a TEMPORARY TABLESPACE clause, unless you also grant UNLIMITED TABLESPACE as shown here:

```
GRANT create cluster, create indextype, create operator
,     create procedure, create sequence, create session
,     create table, create trigger, create type
,     create view, unlimited tablespace TO student;
```

This type of GRANT statement lets you create a user in a small, developer-only environment, but you shouldn't do this in a production database. It works because you avoid assigning default and temporary tablespaces by granting unlimited space rights. This is never a good thing to do, except on your laptop! Some might say that you shouldn't do it on your laptop either, but this is something for you to decide.

Common users must be granted permissions for each or all pluggable databases by a privileged superuser, like system. The following grants CONNECT and RESOURCE roles to a user-defined c##dba user across the CDB:

```
GRANT CONNECT, RESOURCE TO c##dba CONTAINER=ALL;
```

Omitting CONTAINER=ALL from the statement means the user has granted only privileges to the local CDB. For example, let's say that the system user connects to an hr container, like so:

```
C:\> sqlplus /nolog
sqlplus> connect c##plsql@hr
```

The system user enters the password and grants the privilege without the CONTAINER=ALL clause:

```
GRANT CONNECT, RESOURCE TO c##dba;
```

Then, the c##plsql user has only those permissions for the hr pluggable database.

Privileges and roles may be granted locally to users regardless of whether they are local or common grantees, grantors, or roles. Table B-3 qualifies local grants; you can find more in the *Oracle Database Concepts 12c Release* manual.

Privileges granted to common roles may be limited to the container where they were granted. Privileges granted to local roles are limited to the container where they were granted. Roles are groups of privileges. Refer to the *Oracle Database 12c DBA Handbook* for more information on roles.

Grantee	May Grant Locally	May Be Granted Locally	May Receive a Role or Privilege Granted Locally
Common User	Yes	No	Yes
Local User	Yes	No	Yes
Common Role	No	Yes (rules apply)	Yes
Local Role	No	Yes (rules apply)	Yes
Privilege	No	Yes	No

TABLE B-3. *Local Grants*

The ALTER statement also lets you assign a default tablespace and a temporary tablespace after a user is created. Both the CREATE and ALTER statements let you assign quotas to the default tablespace, but you can no longer assign a quota to the temporary tablespace. Any attempt to do so raises an error. This change became effective with Oracle Database 10*g*.

Most commercial databases define user profiles and assign them when creating new users. You can find out more about that in the *Oracle Database 12*c *DBA Handbook*.

NOTE
*Beginning with Oracle Database 10*g *Release 2, you can no longer assign a temporary tablespace quota.*

A sample grant of select privileges, typically made by a user for his or her own schema objects, would look like this:

```
GRANT SELECT ON some_tablename TO some_user;
```

Sometimes a user wants to grant privileges to another user with the privilege to extend that privilege to a third party. This is the infrequent pattern of grants reserved for setting up administrative users. You append a WITH GRANT OPTION clause to give another user the right to provide others with the privileges you've conveyed to them:

```
GRANT SELECT ON some_tablename TO some_user WITH GRANT OPTION;
```

Oracle also supports the concept of a *synonym*, which simplifies how another user can access your object. Without a synonym, the other user would need to put your user name and a dot (.) in front of the object before accessing it. The dot is called a *component selector*. A synonym creates an alias that maps the user name, component selector, and object name to a synonym (alias) name in the user's work area or schema.

You don't need to use a component selector on objects that you create in your schema. They're natively available to you. The sys superuser has access to every object in the Oracle Database 12*c* Server by simply addressing objects by their fully qualified location—schema name, component selector, and object name. This makes perfect sense when you recall that the user and schema names are synonymous.

You create a synonym like this:

```
CREATE SYNONYM some_tablename FOR some_user.some_tablename;
```

Typically, the local table name is the same as the table name in the other schema, but not always. You can also grant privileges on a table to a PUBLIC account, which gives all other users access to the table. Public synonyms also exist to simplify how those users access the table.

You would grant the SELECT privilege to the PUBLIC account with this syntax:

```
GRANT SELECT ON some_tablename TO PUBLIC;
```

After granting the privilege, you create a public synonym with this syntax:

```
CREATE PUBLIC SYNONYM some_tablename FOR some_user.some_tablename;
```

As a rule of thumb, use the PUBLIC account only when you're granting privileges to invoker rights stored programs. Appendix A discusses the default definer and invoker rights models. Chapter 8 shows you how to define stored programs that run under definer or invoker rights models.

Revoking Privileges

You can revoke any privilege from a user provided you or a peer superuser made the grant. Let's say you just finished reading the "ALTER Statement" section of this appendix and realized that you should remove the `UNLIMITED TABLESPACE` privilege from the `student` user. That command would look like this:

```
REVOKE unlimited tablespace FROM student;
```

The funny thing about this revocation is that it doesn't immediately disable a user from writing to the tablespace generally. That's because revocation only disallows the allocation of another extent to any table previously created by the user. An extent is a contiguous block of space inside a tablespace. Extents are added when an `INSERT` or `UPDATE` statement can't add anything more in the allocated space. The number of extents allocated to a table is a measure of the fragmentation of the table on disk. You can export table contents and the table definition and then re-create the table with a new storage clause to defragment storage.

You can revoke privileges from the `PUBLIC` account with the same type of syntax:

```
REVOKE SELECT ON some_tablename FROM PUBLIC;
```

When you revoke privileges that include a `WITH GRANT OPTION` clause, make sure you also revoke the granting option. There should be a routine process in place for validating the grants and privileges to ensure that they comply with your company's governance policy and appropriate laws, such as the Sarbanes-Oxley Act in the United States. You can find more about hardening in an application context in the Oracle Press book *Oracle E-Business Suite Security*.

Tables

Database tables are two-dimensional record structures that hold data. Grants of permissions to read and write data are most often made to tables. Sometimes grants restrict access to columns in tables.

Although databases contain tables, tables contain data organized by data types. A data type is the smallest container in this model. It defines what type of values can go into its container. Data values such as numbers, strings, or dates belong, respectively, in columns defined as numeric, variable-length string, and `DATE` data types. Data types that hold a single value are scalar data types (or, to borrow some lingo from Java, primitive data types).

Tables are seldom defined by a single column. They are typically defined by a set of columns. The set of columns that defines a table is a type of data structure. It is more complex than a single data type because it contains a set of ordered data types. The position of the elements and their data types define the structure of a table. The definition of this type of structure is formally a *record structure*, and the elements are fields of the data structure.

This record structure description can be considered the first dimension of a two-dimensional table. The rows in the table are the second dimension. Rows are organized as an unordered list because relational operations should perform against all rows regardless of their positional order.

Tables are defined by the DDL `CREATE TABLE` command. The command provides names for columns, data types, default values, and constraints. The column, data type, and default values must always be defined on the same line, but constraints can be defined two places. Defining a constraint on the same line as a table column is defining an inline constraint. This is the typical pattern for *column constraints*, such as a not null or single-column `PRIMARY KEY` column. You can opt to define column constraints after all columns are defined. When you do so, the constraints are out-of-line constraints. Sometimes constraints involve more than one column. Constraints that apply to two or more columns are *table constraints*.

Database Constraints

Assuming you are building a table for the first time as a structure where you will hold information, you need to determine whether the table will have database constraints. Database constraints are rules that define how you will allow users to *insert* and *update* rows or records in the table. Five database constraints are available in an Oracle database: *check, foreign key, not null, primary key,* and *unique*. Constraints restrict DML commands as follows:

- *Check* constraints check whether a column value meets criteria before allowing a value to be inserted or updated into a column. They check whether a value is between two numbers, a value is greater than two numbers, or a combination of logically related compound rules is met. Also, *not null* and *unique* constraints are specialized types of *check* constraints.
- *Foreign key* constraints check whether a column value is found in a list of values in a column designated as a *primary key* column in the same or a different table. *Foreign key* constraints are typically managed in the application programs, rather than as database constraints, because of their adverse impact on throughput.
- *Not null* constraints check whether a column value contains a value other than null.
- *Primary key* constraints identify a column as the *primary key* for a table and impose both a *not null* constraint and a *unique* constraint on the column. A *foreign key* can only reference a valid *primary key* column.
- *Unique* constraints check whether a column value will be unique among all rows in a table.

Database constraints are assigned during the creation of a table or by using the `ALTER` command after a table is created. You can include constraints in the `CREATE` statement by using *inline* or *out-of-line* constraints. While some maintain that this is a matter of preference, it is more often a matter of finding working examples. You should consider using *out-of-line* constraints because they're organized at the end of your table creation and can be grouped for increased readability. Unfortunately, only *inline* not null constraints are visible when you describe a table.

A not null constraint is always a column constraint. The ANSI SQL standard requires that all columns in tables be unconstrained by default. An unconstrained or *nullable column* is an optional column when you insert or update a row. A *not null column* is a mandatory column when you insert or update a row. The Oracle database adheres to this ANSI standard use. Note that Microsoft SQL Server doesn't adhere to the standard, because it makes all columns mandatory by default.

RDBMS implementations comprise five basic groups of data types: numbers, characters, date-time intervals, large objects, and Boolean data types. The Boolean data type was added in ANSI SQL:1999, and it includes three-valued logic: true, not true, and null. It adopts three-valued logic because the ANSI SQL-89 standard and later accept that any column can be a null allowed—or, simply put, a column can contain no value or be empty.

Although RDBMSs determine which data types they'll support, they also determine how they'll implement them. Some data types are scalar or primitive data types, and others are built on those primitive data types. Only Oracle (and PostgreSQL) supports building composite data types that can be implemented as nested tables.

Like previous versions of Oracle, Oracle Database 12*c* does not support a Boolean data type. The lack of a Boolean data type does sometimes cause problems, because standard comparison operators don't work with null values. Null values require the `IS` or `IS NOT` comparison operator, which is a reference operator rather than a value comparison operator. Table design and management should take into consideration the processing requirements to handle three-valued logic of pseudo-Boolean data types effectively.

NOTE
Oracle SQL does not support calling of functions with Boolean parameters or returns. Therefore, you must design them to return numbers (0 or 1) or character strings ('TRUE' or 'FALSE') when creating user-defined functions for use in SQL statements (see Chapter 7 of the Oracle Database SQL Language Reference 12c Release*).*

Oracle also supports cloning relational tables through a `CREATE` statement. The syntax to create a relational table from existing data is

```
CREATE TABLE target_table_name AS SELECT * FROM source_table_name;
```

This syntax replicates the structure of an existing table in a new table. It also clones, or copies, all the data from the source table to the target table. You can remove the cloned data if it's of no use by truncating the contents with this command:

```
TRUNCATE TABLE target_table_name;
```

You should know that the `TRUNCATE` statement doesn't work when an enabled foreign key constraint exists that references a column in the table. You must first disable or remove the foreign key constraint before performing table maintenance with the `TRUNCATE` statement.

While you can create a relational database table from existing data, as just shown in an example, you can't create an object table that way. You can only create an object table by using this type of definition:

```
CREATE TABLE target_table_name OF source_object_type;
```

Object tables appear like relational tables when you describe them. Object tables also let you insert data like you would with an `INSERT` statement into a relational table, while letting you insert object signatures of the base type or any subtype derived from the base type. More details on this can be found later in the "Object Data Type" subsection of this section.

When you incorporate a storage clause in a `CREATE` statement, this process allows you to disable constraints, move the table contents, drop the table, and re-create it with contiguous space. Naturally, you should drop the extra copy after re-creating the table.

Oracle Database 12*c* provides the ability to create tables with invisible columns. Invisible columns aren't displayed when you describe a table from the command line, but their definition can easily be found by querying the `CDB_`, `DBA_`, `ALL_`, or `USER_TAB_COLUMNS` views.

Oracle Database 12*c* provides two options when creating tables: create ordinary tables that persist from session to session, or create temporary tables that exist only during the duration of the session. As a rule, temporary tables are not liked by DBAs because they inherently fragment disks.

Can't Clone, Migrate the Data

While you can't clone object data into a new object table, you have two options that let you migrate the object data. One moves the data from an object table or object column into a standard relational structure, and the other moves the data into an existing object table using the same object type or a generalized object type. A generalized object type is a supertype of another type, and sometimes is referred to as a parent, grandparent, or antecedent node in a class hierarchy. Class hierarchies are simply inverted tree structures.

Migrate from Objects to a Relational Table The subsequent example code migrates an object type into a relational table by a pseudo-cloning operation, which is more or less what you might use in an ETL (Extract, Transform, and Load) process. We use a pseudo-cloning operation because we're cloning the data but not the exact structure, which is why we should call it migrating data. The example leverages object type examples from this appendix and Chapter 3. For reference, without reprinting the code examples, the `hobbit_t` data type is a subtype of the `base_t` object and contains information about hobbits (a make-believe people taken from Tolkien's *The Hobbit* or *The Lord of the Rings*). The statement migrates the data from an object type column into a relational table:

```
SQL> CREATE TABLE hobbit AS
  2    SELECT *
  3    FROM   TABLE(
  4             SELECT CAST(
  5                      COLLECT(
  6                        TREAT(log_object AS hobbit_t)) AS hobbit_c)
  7             FROM   log_base
  8             WHERE  log_object IS OF (hobbit_t)) t;
```

The foregoing statement is a fancy (or more appropriately, *a very complex*) approach that uses the power of SQL to accomplish a task that might too often be written in PL/SQL when it's inappropriate to do so. SQL is a better solution because this statement can be parallelized and run more efficiently than in a PL/SQL block. Check Appendix C for explanations of how to use the `TABLE`, `CAST`, `COLLECT`, and `TREAT` functions.

Migrate a Subtype Set into a Table of That Subtype The other alternative lets you migrate a `hobbit_t` subtype from a generalized `base_t` type composite table (a table with scalar and object type columns). The syntax is simpler than the previous example:

```
SQL> CREATE TABLE hobbit AS
  2    SELECT b.log_object AS little_folk
  3    FROM   log_base b
  4    WHERE  b.log_object IS OF (hobbit_t);
```

It creates a table of an object type, which differs substantially from an object table. The `hobbit` table has an object type structure rather than ordinary columns like an object table.

You could rewrite line 2 like this,

```
  2    SELECT   TREAT(log_object AS hobbit_t) AS little_folk
```

but it wouldn't do anything but add overhead because the WHERE predicate already guarantees selection of only hobbit_t rows. You would need the TREAT function when you drop the WHERE predicate because it would guarantee values are hobbit_t object types, hobbit_t subtypes, or null values. Alternatively, you would use the TREAT function together with the COLLECT function when gathering a set of object types into a collection of object types.

A description of the new hobbit table returns:

```
SQL> DESC hobbit
 Name                         Null?    Type
 ---------------------------- -------- ----------
 LITTLE_FOLK                           HOBBIT_T
```

You can no longer insert a list of values in this hobbit table like you would in any relational table. A table of an object type, like the hobbit table, requires that you only insert object type constructor calls, or what's known as a collapsed object signature. Check the "Object Data Type" section later in this appendix for details or consult the glossary for help with the terms.

You should make sure that you work with your DBA when you opt for temporary tables because the DBA might have created a special *locally managed* tablespace for temporary tables to minimize impacts on other tables.

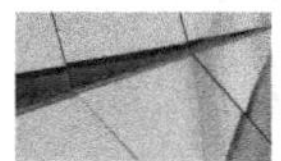

CAUTION
It's a bad idea to create temporary tables without consulting the DBA about them. This will ensure that you don't inadvertently fragment the production database.

The general and basic prototype for a relational table with the CREATE TABLE statement without storage clause options follows, with Oracle Database 12*c* features in bold:

```
CREATE [GLOBAL] [TEMPORARY] TABLE [schema_name.] table_name
( column_name NUMBER [GENERATED [{ALWAYS] | BY DEFAULT}] AS IDENTITY
  [{START WITH number | INCREMENT BY number | NOCACHE}]]
  [{DEFAULT expression | AS (virtual_expression)}]
  [[CONSTRAINT] constraint_name constraint_type]
, [column_name data_type [INVISIBLE]
  [{DEFAULT expression | AS (virtual_expression)}]
  [[CONSTRAINT] constraint_name constraint_type]
, [...]
, [CONSTRAINT constraint_name constraint_type(column_list)
  [REFERENCES table_name(column_list)]]
, [...]);
```

The INVISIBLE keyword must follow the data type in all cases, which means the DEFAULT expression, virtual expressions, and constraints must follow the INVISIBLE keyword.

The Invisible Column

Oracle Database 12*c* now provides you with the power to hide information easily by making a column invisible. All columns are visible by default. An invisible column doesn't display when you describe a table. Likewise, you can't provide a value for an invisible column in an `INSERT` statement's `VALUES` clause or subquery without providing the column's name explicitly in the column list. The column list overrides the data catalog's published definition, published column list, or default signature for an insert into a table.

You can use a hidden column as a partitioning key, as a virtual column, or as part of a column expression. You can't use invisible columns in external or temporary tables.

A small example helps visualize a hidden column:

```
SQL>  CREATE TABLE secret
  2  ( secret_id     NUMBER CONSTRAINT secret_pk PRIMARY KEY
  3  , description   VARCHAR2(20)
  4  , reality       VARCHAR2(20) INVISIBLE);
```

You can see here that only visible columns are displayed when you describe the table:

```
SQL> DESCRIBE secret
Name                    Null?    Type
 ---------------------- -------- ------------
 SECRET_ID              NOT NULL NUMBER
 DESCRIPTION                     VARCHAR2(20)
```

You can find the complete description of the table by querying the `CDB_`, `DBA_`, `ALL_`, or `USER_TAB_COLUMNS` views. Visible columns have a valid `COLUMN_ID` value, while invisible columns don't have a value. The `COLUMN_ID` value denotes a column's availability for use in its default position within a `VALUES` clause or a `SELECT` list of an embedded query. The following query against the `CDB_`, `DBA_`, `ALL_`, or `USER_TAB_COLS` administrative view lets you see both visible and invisible columns:

```
SQL> COLUMN table_name  FORMAT A15
SQL> COLUMN column_id   FORMAT 999
SQL> COLUMN column_name FORMAT A14
SQL> SELECT   table_name
  2  ,        column_id
  3  ,        column_name
  4  FROM     user_tab_cols
  5  WHERE    table_name = 'SECRET';

TABLE_NAME       COLUMN_ID COLUMN_NAME
--------------- ---------- --------------
SECRET                   1 SECRET_ID
SECRET                   2 DESCRIPTION
SECRET                     REALITY
```

A salary column is naturally a great candidate for an invisible column, but please remember that anybody with free reign in the schema can discover the invisible column and then explicitly display its values. You must also redact the information to protect it from prying eyes, which you do with the `dbms_redact` package.

You would create a table like this, where the ellipses represents columns and constraints:

```
CREATE TABLE table_name (...);
```

You create a temporary table by inserting one keyword, like so:

```
CREATE TEMPORARY TABLE table_name ( ... );
```

Temporary tables have several restrictions: they can't be partitioned, clustered, or index organized; can't hold foreign key constraints; can't contain columns of nested tables; can't specify LOB, tablespace, storage, or logging clauses; can't work with parallel `UPDATE`, `DELETE`, and `MERGE` statements; can't support distributed transactions and can't support invisible columns. There are also limitations with how you can use `SEGMENT` clause when creating a temporary table, which you can find qualified in the *Oracle Database Concepts 12c Release 1*.

Temporary tables should be configured as locally managed.

Figure B-2 shows you how the `CREATE TABLE` statement defines a permanent table with different types of column and table constraints. The figure is annotated to help you see available possibilities when you create tables.

Inline constraints are always single-column constraints, and they apply to the column defined on the same line. Out-of-line constraints are defined after the last column in a table. When an out-of-line constraint applies to a single column, it is a column constraint. A table constraint is an out-of-line constraint that applies to two or more columns defined in the table.

Inline column constraints

```
CREATE TABLE member
( member_id          NUMBER         CONSTRAINT pk_member_1 PRIMARY KEY
, member_type        NUMBER
, account_number     VARCHAR2(10)   CONSTRAINT nn_member_2 NOT NULL
, credit_card_number VARCHAR2(19)   CONSTRAINT nn_member_3 NOT NULL
, credit_card_type   NUMBER         CONSTRAINT nn_member_4 NOT NULL
, created_by         NUMBER         CONSTRAINT nn_member_5 NOT NULL
, creation_date      DATE           CONSTRAINT nn_member_6 NOT NULL
, last_updated_by    NUMBER         CONSTRAINT nn_member_7 NOT NULL
, last_update_date   DATE           CONSTRAINT nn_member_8 NOT NULL
, CONSTRAINT fk_member_1
  FOREIGN KEY(member_type)
  REFERENCES common_lookup(common_lookup_id)
, CONSTRAINT fk_member_2
  FOREIGN KEY(credit_card_type)
  REFERENCES common_lookup(common_lookup_id)
, CONSTRAINT fk_member_3
  FOREIGN KEY(created_by)
  REFERENCES system_user(system_user_id)
, CONSTRAINT fk_member_4
  FOREIGN KEY(last_updated_by)
  REFERENCES system_user(system_user_id));
```

Out-of-line constraint; when these constraints apply to more than one column, they're also table level

FIGURE B-2. *Oracle CREATE TABLE statement*

Case-Sensitive Table and Column Names

Oracle Database 10*g* introduced the quoted identifier delimiter. This lets you define case-sensitive table and column names in the database. The only problem with case-sensitive table and column names is that you can only query them with special handling. You must know the correct case and enclose case-sensitive table and column names inside two quoted identifiers—double-quotation symbols.

You can create tables with all case-sensitive column names, all case-insensitive column names, or a mix of both. The case of table and column names is found in the `USER_TAB_COLUMNS` view or, if you enjoy DBA privileges, the `ALL_TAB_COLUMNS` and `DBA_TAB_COLUMNS` views.

The following creates a table with a case-sensitive table name, two case-sensitive column names, and one case-insensitive column name:

```
CREATE TABLE "CaseSensitive"
( "CaseSensitiveId" NUMBER
, "CaseSensitive"   VARCHAR2(30)
,  case_insensitive VARCHAR2(30));
```

After you insert and commit the row, you can then query the record delimiting any case-sensitive column and table names inside double quotes (the quoted identifier). This query demonstrates the technique:

```
SELECT  "CaseSensitiveId"
,       "CaseSensitive"
,        case_insensitive
FROM    "CaseSensitive";
```

You can view the table definition by querying the `TABLE_NAME` and `COLUMN_NAME` columns from the `USER_TAB_COLUMNS` view. You would use the following syntax to query the database catalog view:

```
SELECT   table_name, column_name
FROM     user_tab_columns
WHERE    table_name = 'CaseSensitive';
```

You'll find that the stored definition is a mix of case sensitive and case insensitive, as shown here:

```
TABLE_NAME       COLUMN_NAME
---------------  ------------------
CaseSensitive    CASE_INSENSITIVE
CaseSensitive    CaseSensitive
CaseSensitive    CaseSensitiveId
```

Double quotes must delimit case-sensitive strings, and case-insensitive strings can be delimited by double quotes when you use uppercase text for their values.

Oracle's check constraint and generic primary key, unique, and foreign key constraints can apply to more than a single column, and that makes them possible out-of-line constraints. As a rule, when they address more than one column, they're out-of-line constraints because they can only be defined separately from individual columns.

The following shows you how to define a multiple column primary key:

```
SQL> CREATE TABLE essay
  2  ( essay_name    VARCHAR2(30)
  3  , essayist      VARCHAR2(30)
  4  , published     DATE
  5  , text          CLOB
  6  , CONSTRAINT essay_pk
  7    PRIMARY KEY (essay_name, essayist, published));
```

The foregoing table uses a three-column natural key as the primary key, and defines an out-of-line constraint that follows the column definitions of the table. Lines 6 and 7 show a composite (concatenated, or multiple column) primary key. While the `essay_pk` out-of-line constraint statement spans two lines for presentation convenience, you would generally write it on a single line. It's important to note that primary key constraints automatically create system-named unique constraints that can't be altered or dropped outside of altering or dropping the primary key constraint.

You can assign a primary key's unique index with the `USING INDEX` clause of the `ALTER` statement when you defer creating a primary key constraint until after the table is built. This approach is often used to associate the index with the table, but realistically it's managed by the scope of the primary key, and thus you should focus on managing the primary key constraint, not the indirect index.

While it's possible to use *natural keys* as the primary key, it's better to map natural keys to a surrogate key column (generated by a sequence) because any change to the natural key doesn't require changing join clauses, which typically depend on the surrogate key column.

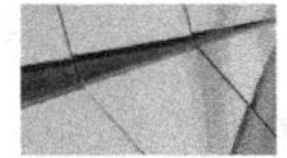

NOTE
Natural keys can be one or more columns that uniquely qualify all rows in a table.

For example, a `magazine` table would have three columns in a foreign key that points to the `essay` table's primary key, like

```
SQL> CREATE TABLE magazine
  2  ( magazine_name  VARCHAR2(30)
  3  , issue_date     DATE
  4  , essay_name     VARCHAR2(30)
  5  , essayist       VARCHAR2(30)
  6  , published      DATE
  7  , CONSTRAINT magazine_fk
  8    FOREIGN KEY (essay_name, essayist, published)
  9    REFERENCES essay (essay_name, essayist, published));
```

Like the earlier composite primary key, the composite foreign key definition runs over lines 7 to 9 to avoid wrapping in this text. You could just as easily put the entire foreign key constraint on a single line.

Adding a surrogate key to the `essay` table lets you define a single-column foreign key. You can define a single-column primary key to solve this problem with a surrogate key, which you see in the "Sequences" section later in this appendix.

Scalar Data Type Columns Oracle supports only four of the five data type groups in SQL: numbers, characters, date-time-intervals, and large objects. While a Boolean is available in Oracle's Procedural Language extension, PL/SQL, it isn't provided for as a data type in SQL. Your only alternative to a Boolean data type would be to implement a number data type that mimics a Boolean, as you'll see in the "Boolean" section a bit later.

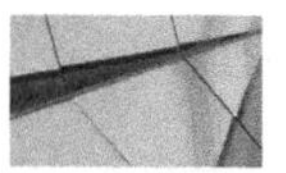

NOTE
Remember that a Boolean doesn't exist as a default type.

Oracle also supports ANSI-compliant data types that automatically map to native Oracle data types. Writing scripts in the ANSI standard data types makes your scripts more portable to other databases. Table B-4 shows you the data type mapping when you use the ANSI standard aliases. Some types don't exist in the Oracle ANSI set, such as `TEXT` for a character large object. Oracle uses `CLOB` for that data type.

You also have support for both virtual columns, which are created by concatenating or calculating values from other column values in the same row, and invisible columns. Virtual columns, which became available in Oracle Database 11*g*, let you include expressions in your table definition. Virtual columns can reference any other data columns in the same table.

As previously introduced, invisible columns became available in Oracle Database 12*c*. Invisible columns let you hide columns from blanket queries using the * (asterisk). Virtual columns

ANSI Data Type	Native Data Type	Physical Size
`BLOB`	`BLOB`	8 to 32 terabytes
`CHAR(n)`	`CHAR(n)`	2,000 bytes
`DATE`	`DATE`	Date and time to hundredths of a second
`DECIMAL(p,s)`	`NUMBER(p,s)`	1×10^{38}
`DOUBLE PRECISION`	`FLOAT(126)`	1×10^{26}
`FLOAT`	`FLOAT(126)`	1×10^{26}
`INT`	`NUMBER(38)`	1×10^{38}
`INTEGER`	`NUMBER(38)`	1×10^{38}
`NUMERIC(p,s)`	`NUMBER(p,s)`	1×10^{38}
`REAL`	`FLOAT(63)`	1×10^{63}
`SMALLINT`	`NUMBER(38)`	1×10^{38}
`TIMESTAMP`	`TIMESTAMP(6)`	Date and time to hundredths of a second
`VARCHAR(n)`	`VARCHAR2(n)`	4,000 or 32,767 bytes

TABLE B-4. *Oracle ANSI SQL Data Type Map*

are typically scalar values, and they're discussed later in this section. The discussion of invisible columns is the last subsection in this section.

The last subsection discusses how to implement nested tables. It highlights an advanced component of the Oracle database that leverages user-defined types (UDTs).

Number Data Type Numbers have four subgroups: three use proprietary Oracle math libraries—binary integers, PLS_INTEGER, and NUMBER data types. The new IEEE 754 variable data types use the operating system math libraries and are recommended when you want to do more than financial mathematics. For example, a cube root of 27 has mixed results in PL/SQL with the ** (double asterisks) exponential operator and a NUMBER data type, but it works perfectly with a BINARY_DOUBLE data type.

You can put whole numbers or decimal numbers in any of the numeric data types except the integer types—they only take integers.

Number data types allow you to qualify precision and scale. *Precision* is the total number of allowed digits. *Scale* is the number of allowed digits that follow the decimal point. This same concept applies to the DEC, DECIMAL, NUMERIC, BINARY_DOUBLE, and DOUBLE_PRECISION data types. For example, the following sets 12 as the maximum number of digits, with 2 digits on the right of the decimal point. You define the precision and scale for DECIMAL numbers inside parentheses and separated by a comma (rather than a period), like this:

```
SQL> CREATE TABLE sample_number
  2  (column_name  NUMBER(12,2));
```

You can inspect the table by describing it in a SQL*Plus session or by displaying it in SQL*Developer. Here's the SQL*Plus command:

```
DESCRIBE sample_number
```

It displays the following:

```
 Name                          Null?    Type
 ----------------------------- -------- --------------
 COLUMN_NAME                            NUMBER(12,2)
```

The preceding syntax creates a one-column table with a single numeric column. The column is optional because it doesn't have a column not null constraint, which would appear under the Null? title header. That means you could insert in the table a row that consists of only null values.

You can create a table with a mandatory column by adding a not null constraint on the column. The constraint can be added as an inline or out-of-line constraint. Here's the inline constraint syntax for a mandatory column with a system-generated constraint name:

```
SQL> CREATE TABLE sample_number
  2  (column_name NUMBER(12,2) NOT NULL);
```

As a matter of best practice, it is always better to name constraints. You would use a different syntax to create a table with a named not null constraint. Named constraints are much easier to find when you explore the Oracle Database 12*c* catalog. An example of the type of error raised without a constraint name appears later in this section for a check constraint. The syntax for a named constraint is as follows:

```
SQL> CREATE TABLE sample_number
  2  (column_name NUMBER(12,2) CONSTRAINT nn_sample1  NOT NULL);
```

The table with a not null constrained column looks like this:

```
Name                      Null?    Type
------------------------- -------- --------------
COLUMN_NAME               NOT NULL NUMBER(12,2)
```

Oracle Database 12*c* provides an alternative to a not null constraint because you can now specify a default value for a null-entered column, like

```
SQL> CREATE TABLE sample_number
  2  (column_name NUMBER(12,2) DEFAULT ON NULL 3.1416);
```

The new `DEFAULT ON NULL` clause ensures any null value will insert a four-decimal constant for Pi. Oracle Database 12*c* also lets you link sequences' `.nextval` and `.currval` pseudocolumns as default values in columns, which is covered in the "Sequences" section later in this appendix.

The table with a not null constraint requires a value, which means you can't insert a null value. While this appendix covers the `INSERT` statements later, you would insert a 12-digit number with two placeholders to the right of the decimal point like this:

```
SQL> INSERT INTO sample_number
  2  VALUES ( 1234567890.99 );
```

A different rule applies to the `BINARY_FLOAT` and `FLOAT` data types. They have only a precision value and no scale. You can assign scales dynamically, or the values to the right of the decimal point can vary. That's because the nature of a floating decimal point allows for dynamic values to the right of the decimal point.

You would define a floating data type like this:

```
SQL> CREATE TABLE sample_float
  2  (column_name FLOAT(12));
```

Inserting values follows this pattern:

```
SQL> INSERT INTO sample_float
  2  VALUES (12345678.0099);
```

Oracle doesn't natively support an unsigned integer (positive integers). By design, Oracle supports both positive and negative numbers in all numeric data types. You can create a numeric data type and then use a check constraint to implement the equivalent of an unsigned integer. The following table design shows that technique with an inline constraint:

```
SQL> CREATE TABLE unsigned_int
  2  ( column_name NUMBER(38,0) CHECK (column_name >= 0));
```

This column definition allows entry of only a zero or positive integer. The check constraint is entered as an inline constraint because it affects only a single column. Check constraints must be entered as out-of-line constraints when they work with multiple columns. Multiple-column constraints are table constraints. An exception is raised if you attempt to insert a negative integer, like this:

```
INSERT INTO unsigned_int VALUES (-1)
*
ERROR at line 1:
ORA-02290: check constraint (SCHEMA_NAME.SYS_C0020070) violated
```

This type of error message isn't as helpful as a named constraint, but you should know how to read it. The SCHEMA_NAME (synonymous with the user name) is the first element of the error, and the system-generated constraint name is the second element.

You can name check constraints in Oracle like this:

```
SQL> CREATE TABLE unsigned_int
  2  ( column_name NUMBER(38,0)
  3    CONSTRAINT ck unsiqned int 01 CHECK (column name >= 0));
```

Although the constraint drops down to line 3, there is no comma separating the definition of the column from the constraint. This means the constraint is an inline constraint, and it could be written on a single line outside the confines of the book's formatting. An out-of-line constraint in this example would differ only by having a comma in line 3, like this:

```
SQL> CREATE TABLE unsigned_int
  2  ( column_name NUMBER(38,0)
  3  , CONSTRAINT ck_unsigned_int_01 CHECK (column_name >= 0));
```

Then the same error is raised with this message:

```
INSERT INTO unsigned_int VALUES (-1)
*
ERROR at line 1:
ORA-02290: check constraint (STUDENT.CK_UNSIGNED_INT_01) violated
```

You also have a DEFAULT expression that lets you assign a default value. Modifying the unsigned_int table, the next example makes the default 0:

```
SQL> CREATE TABLE unsigned_int
  2  ( column_name NUMBER(38,0) DEFAULT 0
  3  , CONSTRAINT ck_unsigned_int_01 CHECK (column_name >= 0));
```

The DEFAULT expression can't contain any PL/SQL functions, references to other column values, the pseudocolumns LEVEL, PRIOR, and ROWNUM, or date constants that aren't fully qualified. You can eliminate the check constraint if you only want to guarantee that a null value can't be entered by appending the ON NULL to the DEFAULT expression, like

```
SQL> CREATE TABLE unsigned_int
  2  ( column_name NUMBER(38,0) DEFAULT ON NULL 0);
```

Although this looks simpler, it does provide a change in logic. Now it's impossible to insert a null value, and any attempt inserts a 0, but it's now possible to enter a negative number with an INSERT statement.

By incorporating the name of the table in the constraint name, you can immediately identify the violation without having to read the data catalog to associate it with a table and business rule.

DATE Data Type Dates and timestamps are DATE and TIMESTAMP data types respectively. Their implementation is through complex or real numbers. The integer value represents the date, and the decimal value implements time. The range of dates or timestamps is an *epoch*. An epoch is a set of possible dates and date-times that are valid in the database server.

The DATE data type in an Oracle database is a date-time value. As such, you can assign a date-time that is accurate to hundredths of a second. The default date format mask in an Oracle database is dd-mon-rr or dd-mon-yyyy. The rr stands for relative date, and the database server chooses whether the date belongs in the current or last century. The yyyy format mask requires that you explicitly assign the four-digit year to dates.

Here's the syntax to create a DATE column:

```
SQL> CREATE TABLE sample_date
  2  ( column_name DATE DEFAULT SYSDATE);
```

A DATE data type can be assigned a date-time that is equal to midnight by enclosing the date column in a TRUNC function. The TRUNC function shaves off any decimal value from the date-time value. The SYSDATE is a current date-time function available inside an Oracle database. You would define a date-only value as a default value with this syntax:

```
SQL> CREATE TABLE sample_date
  2  ( column_name DATE DEFAULT TRUNC(SYSDATE));
```

A more accurate timestamp and timestamps with local or general time zone are also available starting with the release of Oracle Database 11*g*. They're more accurate because they measure time beyond hundredths of a second. You would define a TIMESTAMP like this:

```
SQL> CREATE TABLE sample_timestamp
  2  ( column_name TIMESTAMP DEFAULT SYSTIMESTAMP);
```

You also have INTERVAL DAY TO SECOND and INTERVAL DAY TO MONTH data types. They measure intervening time (like the number of minutes or seconds between two timestamps), which is similar to measuring the difference between two decimal parts of DATE data types.

Character Data Type Character data types have several subgroups in an Oracle database. They can be summarized as fixed-length, long, Unicode, row identifiers, and variable-length strings. In all cases, character data types work very much alike. You specify how many characters you plan to store as the maximum number.

This is the syntax for a fixed-length string:

```
SQL> CREATE TABLE variable_string
  2  ( column_name  CHAR(20) CONSTRAINT nn_varstr_01 NOT NULL);
```

This variable-length string is the equivalent:

```
SQL> CREATE TABLE variable_string
  2  ( column_name  VARCHAR(20) CONSTRAINT nn_varstr_01 NOT NULL);
```

This definition allocates 20 bytes of space. An alternative syntax lets you define space by the number of characters, which supports Unicode strings. That syntax requires including a CHAR flag inside the parentheses. Here's the syntax for a fixed-length string:

```
SQL> CREATE TABLE variable_string
  2  ( column_name  CHAR(20 CHAR) CONSTRAINT nn_varstr_01 NOT NULL);
```

The variable-length equivalent is shown here:

```
SQL> CREATE TABLE variable_string
  2  ( column_name  VARCHAR(20 CHAR) CONSTRAINT nn_varstr_01 NOT NULL);
```

The Oracle database also includes national language character types. They are designed to store Unicode and different character sets in the same database. The syntax for NCHAR or NVARCHAR2 uses the same definition pattern. You specify the maximum size of the string in bytes or characters inside parentheses. CHAR should be used when you define Unicode columns.

The maximum size of a fixed-length CHAR variable is 2,000 bytes, and the maximum length of a VARCHAR2 is 4,000 or 32,767 bytes (that is when it's an Oracle Database 12*c* database). Whether its 4,000 or 32,767 bytes depends on the setting of the MAX_STRING_SIZE variable. Beyond that, you can implement a LONG data type, which is 32,767 (the positive portion of 2^{16}) bytes, but it's soon to be deprecated. The last and *best choice* for a very long string is a Character Large Object (CLOB), which has a maximum size of 8 terabytes when the block size is 8 kilobytes and 32 terabytes when the block size is 32 kilobytes. Oracle makes these large object types available through a built-in API, which you must use to work with these data types.

Large Strings You can define a table with a CLOB or NCLOB column similar to the following example, but it lacks a physical maximum size and a name for the storage clause. The physical size for a CLOB is set by the configuration of the database. As mentioned, the maximum size is set by the block size and is typically 8 terabytes. The Oracle database assigns a system-generated name, which can make calculating and maintaining its storage difficult for DBAs. This is true any time you leave something to an implicit behavior, such as naming a constraint or internal storage.

Failing to specify LOB storage can cause enormous problems, and you should generally always store LOB columns in a separate tablespace. This is doubly important when you forget to specify DEDUPLICATE while creating a LOB column. The DEDUPLICATE keyword instructs the database to eliminate duplicate copies of LOBs. Using a secure hash index to detect duplication, the database coalesces LOBs with identical content into a single copy, reducing storage consumption and simplifying storage management. You would define a generic CLOB column without a specific tablespace that allows duplicates like this:

```
SQL> CREATE TABLE clob_table
  2  ( column_id   NUMBER
  3  , column_name CLOB DEFAULT '');
```

The DEFAULT keyword assigns an empty string to the column_name column, which is equivalent to an INSERT or UPDATE statement putting a call to empty_clob in the column as its value. The DEFAULT value places the default value in a column only when the INSERT statement uses an overriding signature that excludes the column_name column, like so:

```
SQL> INSERT INTO clob_table (column_id) VALUES (1);
```

You can discover that storage clause by using the dbms_metadata package and the get_ddl function. The get_ddl function reads the data catalog and provides the complete syntax for creating the table. The easiest way to get this information is to run the command from the SQL*Plus prompt. You'll need to expand the default 80 characters of space allotted for displaying a LONG data type before you run the query. Also, you'll need to remember that Oracle stores all metadata strings in uppercase, which means the actual parameters (or arguments) to the get_ddl function must be in uppercase for it to work.

Here are the SQL*Plus and SQL commands:

```
-- Reset the display value for a large string.
SET LONG 300000
-- Query the data catalog for the full create statement.
SELECT dbms_metadata.get_ddl('TABLE', 'CLOB_TABLE') FROM dual;
```

Some liberty has been taken with reformatting the output to increase readability of it for this book, but this is what would be returned from the query:

```
CREATE TABLE "STUDENT"."CLOB_TABLE"
  ("COLUMN_NAME" CLOB DEFAULT '')
  PCTFREE 10 PCTUSED 40 INITRANS 1 MAXTRANS 255
  NOCOMPRESS NOLOGGING
  STORAGE(INITIAL 65536 NEXT 1048576 MINEXTENTS 1 MAXEXTENTS 2147483645
          PCTINCREASE 0 FREELISTS 1 FREELIST GROUPS 1 BUFFER_POOL DEFAULT)
  TABLESPACE "USERS"
  LOB ("COLUMN_NAME") STORE AS BASICFILE
  (TABLESPACE "USERS"
   ENABLE STORAGE IN ROW CHUNK 8192 RETENTION NOCACHE LOGGING
   STORAGE(INITIAL 65536 NEXT 1048576 MINEXTENTS 1 MAXEXTENTS 2147483645
          PCTINCREASE 0 FREELISTS 1 FREELIST GROUPS 1 BUFFER_POOL DEFAULT))
```

The better way to define a CLOB or BLOB column includes some explicit syntax and a name for the BASICFILE. A BASICFILE means that the CLOB isn't encrypted. The other option in this syntax creates an encrypted file with the SECUREFILE keyword. You should note that a SECUREFILE clause requires that you store the CLOB or BLOB column in a tablespace with automatic segment-space management. Secured files also provide you with the ability to encrypt and deduplicate data. Deduplication avoids creating two copies of a LOB in storage.

Finding and Fixing Duplicating LOBs

The Star Trek universe has a fictional animal known as a Tribble, which breeds until all food supplies are exhausted. That's all too close to what may happen when a DBA mismanages LOB storage: As the number of LOB indexes and LOB segments grow without user-defined STORAGE clause names, managing LOB storage becomes more difficult. This sidebar shows you how to find system-generated names and storage requirements for LOB columns and then shows you how to migrate and fix those columns.

I enjoyed Tom Kyte's example of how you can find and match a LOB index to LOB segment (*Expert Oracle Database Architecture: 9i and 10g Programming Techniques and Solutins*, p. 542). I've noticed variations of it posted in various locations. While it works well for sample schemas that have only one LOB, the following works for any number of LOBs in any schema. This simplifies working with system- and user-defined segment names. The first CASE statement ensures that joins between user-named segment names are possible. The second CASE statement ensures two things:

- Joins between system-generated segment names don't throw an error when matching unrelated system-generated return values found in the DBA_ or ALL_SEGEMENTS view.
- Joins between named segments are possible and don't throw an error.

Provided you have inserted data into a LOB column, you can run the following script from any schema with permissions to read the `DBA_SEGMENTS` view:

```
SQL> COL owner          FORMAT A5   HEADING "Owner"
SQL> COL TABLE_NAME     FORMAT A5   HEADING "Table|Name"
SQL> COL column_name    FORMAT A10  HEADING "Column|Name"
SQL> COL segment_name   FORMAT A26  HEADING "Segment Name"
SQL> COL segment_type   FORMAT A10  HEADING "Segment|Type"
SQL> COL bytes                      HEADING "Segment|Bytes"
SQL> SELECT   l.owner
  2  ,        l.table_name
  3  ,        l.column_name
  4  ,        s.segment_name
  5  ,        s.segment_type
  6  ,        s.bytes
  7  FROM     dba_lobs l
  8  ,        dba_segments s
  9  WHERE    REGEXP_SUBSTR(l.segment_name,'([[:alnum:]]|[[:punct:]])+'
 10  , CASE
 11      WHEN REGEXP_INSTR(s.segment_name,'[[:digit:]]',1) > 0
 12      THEN REGEXP_INSTR(s.segment_name,'[[:digit:]]',1)
 13      ELSE 1
 14    END) =
 15  REGEXP_SUBSTR(s.segment_name,'([[:alnum:]]|[[:punct:]])+'
 16  , CASE
 17      WHEN REGEXP_INSTR(s.segment_name,'[[:digit:]]',1) > 0
 18      THEN REGEXP_INSTR(s.segment_name,'[[:digit:]]',1)
 19      ELSE 1
 20    END)
 21  AND      l.TABLE_NAME = UPPER('&table_name')
 22  AND      l.owner = UPPER('&owner')
 23  ORDER BY l.column_name, s.segment_name;
```

Lines 21 and 22 force a SQL*Plus prompt for a table name and schema owner. The script then finds all storage for that table. It would return output like the following for an `item` table with two LOB columns:

```
Table  Column                                 Segment      Segment
Name   Name       Segment Name                Type           Bytes
------ ---------- -------------------------- ---------- ---------
PLSQL  ITEM_BLOB  SYS_IL0000074435C00007$$   LOBINDEX       65,536
PLSQL  ITEM_BLOB  SYS_LOB0000074435C00007$$  LOBSEGMENT  2,097,152
PLSQL  ITEM_DESC  SYS_IL0000074435C00006$$   LOBINDEX       65,536
PLSQL  ITEM_DESC  SYS_LOB0000074435C00006$$  LOBSEGMENT    720,896
```

Unfortunately, you can't simply modify a LOB column when it was configured incorrectly. You must create a temporary column, move the data from the original column to the temporary

(continued)

column, drop the original column, re-create the original column correctly, move the data back from the temporary column to the newly re-created column, and then drop the temporary column.

You can move the data and remove duplicates in a single `ALTER` statement to a `lob_temp` tablespace for LOB column storage. The following example creates a temporary `item_temp CLOB` column with a hash index that eliminates duplicate storage segments:

```
SQL> ALTER TABLE item ADD (item_temp CLOB)
    LOB (item_temp) STORE AS SECUREFILE item_temp
    (TABLESPACE lob_temp ENABLE STORAGE IN ROW CHUNK 32768
     PCTVERSION 10 NOCACHE NOLOGGING DEDUPLICATE
     STORAGE (INITIAL 1048576
              NEXT 1048576
              MINEXTENTS 1
              MAXEXTENTS 2147483645));
```

You may see that the LOB is stored in a `SECUREFILE` tablespace, which is the Oracle Database 12*c* default, and should be the default for most production databases. After creating the new column, you can transfer the data with the following `UPDATE` statement, which transfers the content of the `item_desc` column to the `item_temp` for every row in the table:

```
SQL> UPDATE item SET item_temp = item_desc;
```

After moving the data from the non-deduplicated original column to a deduplicated temporary column, you can drop the original column with this syntax:

```
SQL> ALTER TABLE item DROP COLUMN item_desc;
```

Next, you add back the original column with a user-defined LOB segment name, and deduplication enabled:

```
SQL> ALTER TABLE item ADD (item_desc CLOB)
    LOB (item_desc) STORE AS SECUREFILE item_desc
    (TABLESPACE lob_temp ENABLE STORAGE IN ROW CHUNK 32768
     PCTVERSION 10 NOCACHE NOLOGGING DEDUPLICATE
     STORAGE (INITIAL 1048576
              NEXT 1048576
              MINEXTENTS 1
              MAXEXTENTS 2147483645));
```

Lastly, you move the data from the temporary column to the new `item_desc` column and drop the `item_temp` column with the following two statements:

```
SQL> UPDATE item SET item_desc = item_temp;
SQL> ALTER TABLE item DROP COLUMN item_temp;
```

In the event of a table with two or more columns, you can repeat the process to fix all columns. It's best to only try to fix one column at a time.

The right way to use a CREATE TABLE statement with a LOB is to name the CLOB or BLOB file. This extra step makes your life easier later, as described in the "XMLTYPE Data Type" section a bit later.

Here's the syntax that assigns a user-defined SEGMENT_NAME at table creation:

```
SQL> CREATE TABLE sample_table
( column_name CLOB DEFAULT '')
LOB (column_name) STORE AS sample_table_clob
  (TABLESPACE users ENABLE STORAGE IN ROW CHUNK 32768
   PCTVERSION 10 NOCACHE NOLOGGING DEDUPLICATE
   STORAGE (INITIAL 1048576
            NEXT 1048576
            MINEXTENTS 1
            MAXEXTENTS 2147483645));
```

The additional four parameters in the storage clause will be appended by using the default values as noted in the output from preceding call to the get_ddl function of the dbms_metadata package. The company's DBA should provide guidelines on the STORAGE clause settings.

TIP
The default creates BLOB and CLOB storage with logging enabled. As a rule, these types should have logging turned off.

Boolean It is possible to mimic a Boolean data type in an Oracle database. To accomplish this, you define a number column and assign a table-level constraint on that column. The constraint would allow only a 0 (for false) or 1 (for true). The syntax to implement a column that performs like a Boolean data type is shown next:

```
SQL> CREATE TABLE sample_boolean
( column_name NUMBER
, CONSTRAINT boolean_values
  CHECK (column_name = 0 OR column_name = 1));
```

This type of column would allow only a null, 0, or 1 to be inserted into the table. Anything else would trigger a constraint violation error, like this:

```
INSERT INTO sample_boolean VALUES (2)
*
ERROR at line 1:
ORA-02290: check constraint (STUDENT.BOOLEAN_VALUES) violated
```

After dropping the original sample_boolean table, you can re-create it with the addition of a not null constraint. Now it implements two-valued logic, because it disallows the insertion of a null value.

```
SQL> CREATE TABLE sample_boolean
( column_name NUMBER CONSTRAINT no_null NOT NULL
, CONSTRAINT boolean_values
  CHECK (column_name = 0 OR column_name = 1));
```

You can also use other comparison operators such as greater than, less than, greater than or equal to, and so forth. It is also possible to use SQL *lookup operators* such as `IN`, `=ANY`, `=SOME`, or `=ALL`. You can find examples of lookup operators in the "Multiple-Row Subqueries" section later in this appendix.

Object Data Type Object types are an advanced element of the object-oriented portion of the Oracle Database 12*c* database, and they let you create UDTs. You can use them as the definition of the table's structure, as a column in a table's structure, or as a nested element in another object type. A table that's wholly based on an object type structure is also called an object table, whereas a table with an embedded object type is simply a table with a UDT column. This subsection shows you how to define and work with persistent object types, which are those object types found in the structure of database tables.

Object types have two parts: an object type and a body. The object type acts like a package specification by publishing the object type's declaration, and the object body implements the published object type by providing an implementation in PL/SQL. Chapter 11 discusses transient and persistent object types and shows you how to implement them. Transient object types exist solely in the scope of stored programs and object types, while persistent object types exist as columns of tables.

Collections of object types are described in the "Nested Collection Tables" section later in this appendix and in Chapter 11. You can also find more about creating object types in the "Object Types" subsection of this section in the appendix, and more about how you can evolve object types in the "Evolving an Object Type" section of this appendix.

Before we can explore how to declare and use object types, we need to define a basic object type. Limiting our discussion here to object types appears to be the best way to keep our discussion as simple as possible.

Here's the `base_t` object type declaration:

```
SQL> CREATE OR REPLACE
       TYPE base_t IS OBJECT
       ( obj_id     NUMBER
       , obj_name   VARCHAR2(30)
       , obj_ref    REF base_t)
       NOT FINAL;
     /
```

Interface Definition Language (IDL)

IDL is a specification language that describes software interfaces. IDL is meant to be a language-independent way of sharing values between programs. Oracle delivers IDL through PL/SQL in the form of the published specifications of stand-alone functions and procedures, package specifications, and object type definitions.

Most C and C++ programmers are familiar with IDL from the perspective of Remote Procedure Calls (RPCs), while Java programmers know them through Remote Method Invocation (RMI) calls. Publication of the prototype or signature for functions, procedures, or object constructors guarantees what's required when you call them in another programming language. PL/SQL also serves as that IDL framework, which is why you use PL/SQL functions and procedures to wrap Java libraries.

The base_t object type lacks an implementation, but you're able to construct instances of the object type by using the object's default constructor (at least you can in Oracle Database 11*g*). Oracle Database 12*c* now requires you to implement object bodies because Oracle has added many new features. The default constructor is a function that mirrors the list of columns by name and data type.

You can describe the base_t object type like you describe a table:

```
SQL> DESCRIBE base_t
 base_t is NOT FINAL
 Name                                      Null?    Type
 ----------------------------------------- -------- ---------------
 OBJ_ID                                             NUMBER
 OBJ_NAME                                           VARCHAR2(30)
 OBJ_REF                                            REF OF BASE_T
```

The third field (or attribute) is designed to hold a reference or a unique indexing value to an object view in the scope of the table. You can only populate the obj_ref column with a reference, and then you can only do it after you've created the row with an INSERT statement.

Shortly, we create a table that uses the base_t object type as the definition of the table's data structure. There are three options that present themselves to us when we define a table based on an object type:

- A table without a primary key
- A table with a primary key
- A table with a primary key that is also an object view key

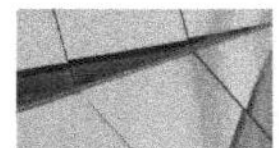

TIP
You can't set the obj_ref value when you designate another column as the object view's key.

You define a table based exclusively on the base_t object type without a primary key constraint with this syntax:

```
CREATE TABLE base OF base_t;
```

By default, all object tables and columns of object types are substitutable, which means you can insert or update them with a variable that matches the object type of an object table, or matches the object type of an object column. You can turn off default *substitutability* by appending the following clause when you create the object table:

```
SQL> CREATE TABLE base OF base_t
  2  NOT SUBSTITUTABLE AT ALL LEVELS;
```

Alternatively, you can turn off substitutability for a specific attribute with the following statement:

```
SQL> CREATE TABLE base OF base_t
  2  COLUMN object_id NOT SUBSTITUTABLE AT ALL LEVELS;
```

You must choose between table and column substitutability because you can't set both at the same time. If you change your mind about your choice of substitutability for an object column, you can't use the ALTER statement to change the configuration because there's no way to reset the table's substitutability after you create an object table.

You extend the definition to include a primary key constraint by adding the reference to one of the columns in the object type, like

```
CREATE TABLE base OF base_t
( obj_id  CONSTRAINT  base_pk  PRIMARY KEY );
```

The preceding table definition lets you later use the obj_ref column as a unique reference to the object view. This works because using the obj_id attribute as a primary key column doesn't conflict with the use of the obj_ref as a unique object reference.

The obj_id column becomes a primary key and object identifier when you change the base object table by adding the OBJECT IDENTIFIER IS PRIMARY KEY clause to the syntax:

```
SQL> CREATE TABLE base OF base_t
     ( obj_id  CONSTRAINT  base_pk  PRIMARY KEY )
       OBJECT IDENTIFIER IS PRIMARY KEY;
```

You can seed the object table with data by using the INSERT statement style shown next. Inside the VALUES clause you embed a call to the base_t object type constructor. As mentioned earlier, object type constructors share the object type's name and have a function signature that mirrors the object type's list of columns.

```
INSERT INTO base VALUES (base_t(1, 'Dwalin',NULL));
INSERT INTO base VALUES (base_t(2, 'Borfur',NULL));
INSERT INTO base VALUES (base_t(3, 'Gloin',NULL));
```

You may note that the NULL value is inserted into the object type's obj_ref field (or more formally, *attribute*). While you can use named notation, you can't exclude any field value from a constructor's function call.

Following is an example of named notation that inverts the obj_name and obj_ref columns to construct an instance of the base_t object type:

```
SQL> INSERT INTO base
     VALUES (base_t(obj_id => 8, obj_ref => NULL, obj_name => 'Thorin'));
```

A query against the object table would show you that there aren't any object references. You can populate null object references with the following UPDATE statement, or exclude the WHERE clause to populate and repopulate all object references:

```
SQL> UPDATE base b
     SET obj_ref = REF(b)
     WHERE obj_ref IS NULL;
```

The preceding UPDATE statement is one of the rare cases where you must use a table alias. If you attempted to exclude the table alias and refer to the physical table in the REF function, you would raise this exception:

```
SET obj_ref = REF(base)
                  *
ERROR at line 2:
ORA-00904: "BASE": invalid identifier
```

Another potential error occurs when the preceding UPDATE statement runs against a table created with the OBJECT IDENTIFIER IS PRIMARY KEY clause. The error occurs because the object identifier and reference compete to become the object view's unique identifier.

```
UPDATE   base b
         *
ERROR at line 1:
ORA-22979: cannot INSERT object view REF or user-defined REF
```

The competition between the object identifier and the reference leaves us with only one choice when we want to use the obj_id field as a primary key and the obj_ref as the object's unique identifier: avoid using the OBJECT IDENTIFIER IS PRIMARY KEY clause.

You also can create a table that uses both ordinary column data types and the same base_t object type as a column's data type. The following creates a child table that includes an object type column:

```
SQL> CREATE TABLE child
  2  ( child_id   NUMBER  CONSTRAINT child_pk PRIMARY KEY
  3  , base_ref   REF base_t SCOPE IS base
  4  , child_obj  base_t);
```

After creating the child table, it's helpful to see the definition by describing it:

```
SQL> desc child;
 Name                          Null?    Type
 ----------------------------- -------- ---------------
 CHILD_ID                      NOT NULL NUMBER
 BASE_REF                               REF OF BASE_T
 CHILD_OBJ                              BASE_T
```

The description of the child table shows that the base_ref column is a reference to a base_t object type. Although you can't see who owns the original reference by using the dbms_metadata package's get_ddl function, you can access the table description by setting two SQL*Plus environment variables—LONG and PAGESIZE. The LONG environment variable sets the display size of the CLOB data type returned by the get_ddl function call, and the PAGESIZE variable avoids inadvertent page breaks.

Here are the SQL*Plus commands and the query to see the table definition and identify the defining scope of the reference:

```
SQL> SET LONG 100000
SQL> SET PAGESIZE 999
SQL> SELECT dbms_metadata.get_ddl('TABLE','CHILD') AS TABLE_DEF
  2  FROM   dual;
```

It returns a table definition, which I've shortened here by removing the storage information:

```
TABLE_DEF
---------------------------------------------------------------
CREATE TABLE "STUDENT"."CHILD"
("CHILD_ID" NUMBER,
 "BASE_REF" REF "STUDENT"."BASE_T",
```

```
 "CHILD_OBJ" "STUDENT"."BASE_T",
 SCOPE FOR ("BASE_REF") IS "STUDENT"."BASE",
 CONSTRAINT "CHILD_PK" PRIMARY KEY ("CHILD_ID")
...
```

As you can see, the description of the `child` table shows that the scope for its `base_ref` column is the `base` table. The `child_obj` column therefore holds a copy of references from the `base` table and enables it to act like a foreign key reference.

The `child_id` primary key is an ordinary scalar data type and unrelated to the embedded object. You insert a row into the `child` table with the following statement:

```
SQL> INSERT INTO child
  2  SELECT 1, obj_ref, base_t(1, 'Gimli',b.obj_ref)
  3  FROM   base b
  4  WHERE  b.obj_name = 'Gloin';
```

The `SELECT` statement gets the `REF` value for the row where you've stored the values for Gloin, Gimli's father in Tolkien's *The Lord of the Rings*. The reference inside the object lets us join the row with Gloin from the `base` table to the row with Gimli in the `child` table. In this scenario, we use the `obj_ref` column value in the `base` table as a primary key and use the copied reference in the `base_ref` column of the `child` table as a foreign key. The join is a little more complex because you must use a table alias and dot notation to reach the relative objects to match in the base table row, as shown in the following query:

```
SQL> COLUMN father FORMAT A10
SQL> COLUMN son    FORMAT A10
SQL> SELECT   b.obj_name AS "Father"
  2  ,        c.child_obj.obj_name AS "Son"
  3  FROM     base b INNER JOIN child c
  4  ON       b.obj_ref = c.base_ref.obj_ref;
```

Line 2 uses a table alias to refer to its `child_obj` instances because it's required. You should take note of the join between the `base` and `child` tables. The `b.obj_ref` refers to a column of the object table, and it maps directly to an attribute (or field) of the object type. The other `obj_ref` isn't quite so easy to reach. You must refer to the `child` table alias, then to the `base_ref` object type column whose scope is the `base` table, and finally to the object type's `obj_ref` field. Oracle calls this type of dot notation chaining *inner capture*. You need to use inner capture mechanics because a reference to the object type column would lead to an unqualified name error.

Your query returns the following data:

```
Father     Son
---------- ----------
Gloin      Gimli
```

If you forget to use a table alias in a query like this, you raise an exception like

```
ON       b.obj_ref = base_ref.obj_ref
                     *
ERROR at line 4:
ORA-00904: "BASE_REF"."OBJ_REF": invalid identifier
```

The errors are returned from the end of the SELECT statements. That means you get the first error due to a missing table alias on line 4. If you provide an alias on line 3 and use it on line 4, preceding the base_ref column, the next exception thrown will be on line 2 because you also need to put the table alias before the child_obj.obj_name column.

Object types also let you subclass or extend the behavior of a data type. *Subclassing* means that you add fields (attributes) to the object and you can override methods of the parent class. The discussion of subtypes requires an understanding of methods and thus it is presented in Chapter 11.

The last thing you need to understand about object types is how to gather them up from rows into a collection. To accomplish this, you need one more preparation step. You need to create a collection of the base object type, like

```
CREATE OR REPLACE TYPE base_c IS TABLE OF base_t;
/
```

After creating the collection type of your UDT type, you need the CAST, COLLECT, and VALUE functions to transform your object data types into a collection type. The VALUE function lets you return the flattened object type definition, which is the name of the object type and a list of call parameters to construct an instance of the object type. The COLLECT function (you can find more on this function in Appendix C) assembles the object types into a generic collection. Lastly, the CAST function lets you transform the runtime collection into an already defined collection data type, where the object type is a schema-level object type.

Together, they work like this:

```
SELECT CAST(COLLECT(VALUE(b)) AS base_c) FROM base b;
```

The query returns a collection that you can assign to a collection variable. The following anonymous PL/SQL block collects and assigns the collection to a local variable:

```
SQL> DECLARE
  2    lv_collection  BASE_C;
  3  BEGIN
  4    /* Collect the object table into a collection variable
  5       and assign it to a collection variable. */
  6    SELECT  CAST(COLLECT(VALUE(b)) AS base_c)
  7    INTO    lv_collection
  8    FROM    base b;
  9
 10    /* Read through the collection of object types and print
 11       the attribute values. */
 12    FOR i IN 1..lv_collection.COUNT LOOP
 13      dbms_output.put('ID: ['||TO_CHAR(lv_collection(i).obj_id)||'] ');
 14      dbms_output.put_line('Name: ['||lv_collection(i).obj_name||']');
 15    END LOOP;
 16  END;
 17  /
```

Lines 6 through 8 hold the statement that converts a list of object types into a collection before assigning the result to a local collection variable. The SELECT-INTO statement lets you assign the result from the query directly to a collection variable.

NOTE
The `COLLECT` function only takes a `VALUE` function return while working with an object table, which is a table of an object type.

You can find out more about how you create object types and object type collections in the subsequent "Object Types" sections, and you can learn how to evolve (or change) data types wherever they appear in your database tables or stored programs in the "Evolving an Object Type" section later in this appendix.

BLOB Data Type The `BLOB` data type is very much like the `CLOB` data type. You can store a binary signature for an image or document inside a `BLOB` data type. The maximum size is 8 to 32 terabytes, and the behaviors and syntax mirror those for the `CLOB` data type. I won't repeat the syntax here since it is the same as for the `CLOB` data type already discussed.

XMLTYPE Data Type The `XMLTYPE` is a specialized form of a `CLOB` data type. You use it as the column data type, but then you provide a specialized storage clause that identifies its storage as a `CLOB` data type. This process follows the pattern that Oracle databases use consistently between subtypes and types.

Here's the syntax to create an `XMLTYPE` column:

```
SQL> CREATE TABLE item
  2  ( item_id          NUMBER CONSTRAINT pk_item PRIMARY KEY
  3  , item_title       VARCHAR2(30) CONSTRAINT nn_item_01 NOT NULL
  4  , item_description XMLTYPE)
  5  XMLTYPE item_description STORE AS CLOB item_desc_clob
  6  ( TABLESPACE some_tablespace_name
  7    STORAGE (INITIAL 819200 NEXT 819200 )
  8    CHUNK 8192 NOCACHE LOGGING);
```

The storage clause is highlighted in line 5 because a lot of the Oracle documentation simply instructs you to use the `STORE AS CLOB` clause. Unfortunately, that fails to provide a meaningful storage name for matching segments to LOBs in the data catalog. You join the `CDB_`, `DBA_`, `ALL_`, and `USER_LOBS` view to the equivalent `USER_SEGMENTS` view on the `SEGMENT_NAME` column value. The name of the `CLOB` in the storage clause facilitates that join. System-generated names can be matched, but that match requires a complex regular expression in the SQL syntax. It's better to provide a name and simplify the DBA's life upfront.

The use of XML inside the Oracle database continues to grow release by release. The XML Developer's Kit (XDK) for Oracle is complex and an awesome resource to delve into when you're going to use XML inside the Oracle database. I'd recommend you start by reading the *Oracle XML Developer's Kit Programmer's Guide 12c Release*.

Virtual Columns Virtual columns are sometimes known as *derived columns*, but Oracle has opted for *virtual*, and that's what might crop up on a certification exam. A virtual column lets you store a formula that joins strings from other columns in the same row together or a formula that calculates values—the functions are stored in the table, not the values.

Resolving LOB Storage with System-Generated Names

As previously discussed in the sidebar "Finding and Fixing Duplicating LOBs," Tom Kyte provided an example of how you find and match a LOB index to LOB segment in his *Expert Oracle Database Architecture* on page 542. Over the years, I've noticed variations of it posted in various locations. While it works well for sample schemas that have only one LOB, it fails when you have multiple LOBs and schemas.

Matching LOB index and LOB segment is tricky when you forget to give them user-defined names in the `STORAGE` clause. It's even more tricky when you have a mix of user-defined and system-assigned LOB index and LOB segment values. The following query works for any number of LOBs in any schema *because it's designed to work with administration privileges*. This simplifies working with system- and user-defined segment names.

```
COL owner         FORMAT A5   HEADING "Owner"
COL TABLE_NAME    FORMAT A5   HEADING "Table|Name"
COL column_name   FORMAT A10  HEADING "Column|Name"
COL segment_name  FORMAT A26  HEADING "Segment Name"
COL segment_type  FORMAT A10  HEADING "Segment|Type"
COL bytes                     HEADING "Segment|Bytes"
SQL> SELECT    l.owner
  2  ,         l.TABLE_NAME
  3  ,         l.column_name
  4  ,         s.segment_name
  5  ,         s.segment_type
  6  ,         s.bytes
  7  FROM      dba_lobs l
  8  ,         dba_segments s
  9  WHERE     REGEXP_SUBSTR(l.segment_name,'([[:alnum:]]|[[:punct:]])+'
 10  , CASE
 11      WHEN REGEXP_INSTR(s.segment_name,'[[:digit:]]',1) > 0
 12      THEN REGEXP_INSTR(s.segment_name,'[[:digit:]]',1)
 13      ELSE 1
 14    END) =
 15      REGEXP_SUBSTR(s.segment_name,'([[:alnum:]]|[[:punct:]])+'
 16      , CASE
 17          WHEN REGEXP_INSTR(s.segment_name,'[[:digit:]]',1) > 0
 18          THEN REGEXP_INSTR(s.segment_name,'[[:digit:]]',1)
 19          ELSE 1
 20        END)
 21  AND       l.TABLE_NAME = UPPER('&table_name')
 22  AND       l.owner = UPPER('&owner')
 23  ORDER BY l.column_name, s.segment_name;
```

The first `CASE` statement on lines 10 through 14 ensures that joins between user-named segments are possible. The second `CASE` statement on lines 15 through 20 ensures two things: joins between system-generated segment names don't throw an error when matching unrelated system-generated return values found in the `DBA_SEGMENTS` view, and joins

(continued)

between named segments are possible and don't throw an error. If you're new to regular expressions in the Oracle database, please check the regular expression primer in Appendix E.

With the SQL*Plus formatting, it displays something like the following:

```
Table  Column                                     Segment      Segment
Name   Name       Segment Name                    Type           Bytes
------ ---------- ------------------------- --------- ---------
PLSQL  ITEM_BLOB  SYS_IL0000074435C00007$$  LOBINDEX        65,536
PLSQL  ITEM_BLOB  SYS_LOB0000074435C00007$$ LOBSEGMENT 2,097,152
PLSQL  ITEM_DESC  SYS_IL0000074435C00006$$  LOBINDEX        65,536
PLSQL  ITEM_DESC  SYS_LOB0000074435C00006$$ LOBSEGMENT   720,896
```

This isn't a preferred solution, but it's the only solution when someone forgot to label the LOB storage clause correctly. You can avoid it by always naming the LOB storage area with the `STORE AS` clause when you create the table.

The following demonstrates the syntax to create a virtual column that concatenates strings:

```
SQL> CREATE TABLE employee
  2  ( employee_id NUMBER
  3  , first_name  VARCHAR2(20)
  4  , last_name   VARCHAR2(20)
  5  , full_name   VARCHAR2(40) AS (first_name || ' ' || last_name));
```

Line 5 is the virtual column. Instead of a column data type, two columns are joined together with white space in between.

The next example demonstrates a virtual column that uses math operations against values in other columns:

```
SQL> CREATE TABLE salary
  2  ( salary_id    NUMBER        CONSTRAINT pk_salary PRIMARY KEY
  3  , salary       NUMBER(15,2)  CONSTRAINT nn_salary_01 NOT NULL
  4  , bonus        NUMBER(15,2)
  5  , compensation NUMBER(15,2) AS (salary + bonus));
```

Line 5 in this example shows you how to use a math operation in a virtual column. Virtual columns are marked in the database catalog. You can display the `virtual_column` in the `CDB_`, `DBA_`, `ALL_`, or `USER_TAB_COLS` view or the `USER_TAB_COLUMNS` view to see if a column is virtual. Any column that has a `'YES'` entry is a virtual column. The formula for the virtual column is in the `data_default` column of the same view.

Invisible Columns Oracle Database 12*c* provides the ability to create invisible columns. Columns are visible by default and are shown when you describe a table, but when you define an invisible column, the `DESCRIBE` command can't display it. A `SELECT` statement with an `*` (asterisk) for all columns does not show invisible columns, but a `SELECT` statement that lists the invisible column explicitly does display the column and its values. That means invisible columns are less apparent but not secured.

NOTE
An `*` in a `SELECT` clause acts like a pointer to all columns of a table.

You secure access by redacting access to any column regardless of whether it is visible or invisible. Redacting a column hides it from all but those who are *white listed* (given explicit access) to see the column. Oracle Database 12*c* provides redaction through the `dbms_redact` package.

The following makes the `salary` and `compensation` columns of the `salary` table invisible, and it's worth noting that `salary` is an ordinary column and `compensation` is a virtual column and the result of an expression:

```
SQL> CREATE TABLE salary
  ( salary_id    NUMBER        CONSTRAINT pk_salary PRIMARY KEY
  , salary       NUMBER(15,2) INVISIBLE
    CONSTRAINT nn_salary_01 NOT NULL
  , bonus        NUMBER(15,2)
  , compensation NUMBER(15,2) INVISIBLE AS (salary + bonus));
```

Note that the `INVISIBLE` keyword must come immediately after the data type for a column definition (as mentioned earlier when discussing the prototype). If you forget that, and append the `INVISIBLE` keyword at the end of a column definition, Oracle Database 12*c* raises this (perhaps misleading) exception:

```
ERROR at line 4:
ORA-00907: missing right parenthesis
```

Describing the table shows you only the visible columns:

```
SQL> DESCRIBE salary
 Name                     Null?    Type
 --------------------- -------- ------------
 SALARY_ID                NOT NULL NUMBER
 BONUS                             NUMBER(15,2)
```

You can see why by querying the `USER_TAB_COLUMNS` view, like so:

```
SQL> COLUMN column_id      FORMAT 999
SQL> COLUMN hidden_column  FORMAT A4
SQL> COLUMN table_name     FORMAT A20
SQL> COLUMN column_name    FORMAT A20
SQL> SELECT   column_id
  ,        hidden_column AS "HIDE"
  ,        table_name
  ,        column_name
```

```
FROM      user_tab_columns
WHERE     table_name = 'SALARY';

COLUMN_ID HIDE TABLE_NAME                COLUMN_NAME
--------- ---- --------------------- --------------
        1 NO   SALARY                SALARY_ID
          YES  SALARY                SALARY
        2 NO   SALARY                BONUS
          YES  SALARY                COMPENSATION
```

The `salary` and `compensation` columns don't have `column_id` values, which is a characteristic of hidden columns. You also have a `YES` or `NO` value in the `hidden_column` column. Positional numbering of columns is now reported by the `internal_column_id` column, which is available in the `CDB_`, `DBA_`, `ALL_`, and `USER_TAB_COLS` views but not in the `ALL_` and `USER_TAB_COLUMNS` views. If you were wondering about the difference between the views ending in `_COLS` and those ending in `_COLUMNS`, so was I. After a bit of research, it appears the one ending in `_COLS` is intended for the DBA while the one ending in `_COLUMNS` is intended for database developers.

```
SQL> SELECT   column_id
,             internal_column_id
,             table_name
,             column_name
FROM          user_tab_cols
WHERE         table_name = 'SALARY'
ORDER BY internal_column_id;

COLUMN_ID INTERNAL_COLUMN_ID TABLE_NAME COLUMN_NAME
--------- ------------------ ---------- --------------
        1                  1 SALARY     SALARY_ID
                           2 SALARY     SALARY
        2                  3 SALARY     BONUS
                           4 SALARY     COMPENSATION
```

While coverage of the `INSERT` statement appears later in this appendix, the following `INSERT` statement is provided here to keep the flow of conversation smooth. Please note that you must provide an override signature (also known as the *column list* in Oracle documentation) to insert values into a table using an identity column.

```
SQL> INSERT INTO salary
( salary_id, salary, bonus )
VALUES
( salary_s.nextval, 100000, 5000 );
```

A query with the `*` in the `SELECT` clause yields only the results of visible columns:

```
SQL> SELECT * FROM salary;
 SALARY_ID      BONUS
---------- ----------
         1       5000
```

However, you can explicitly add the names of any hidden columns to the `SELECT` clause, and the query returns a complete set of column values, like

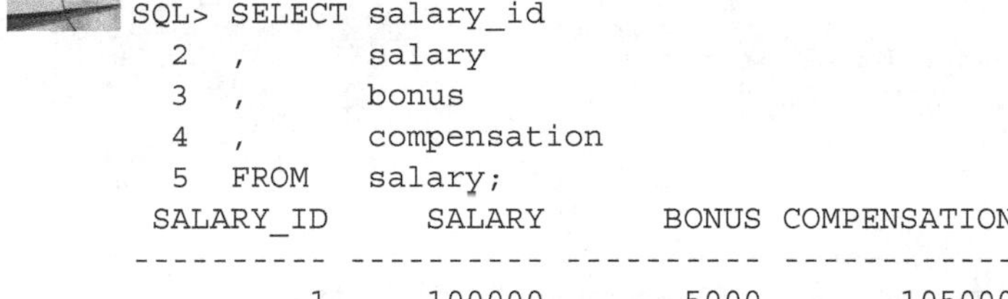

```
SQL> SELECT salary_id
  2  ,      salary
  3  ,      bonus
  4  ,      compensation
  5  FROM   salary;
 SALARY_ID     SALARY      BONUS COMPENSATION
---------- ---------- ---------- ------------
         1     100000       5000       105000
```

It's important to note that invisible columns are also invisible to an old friend of most PL/SQL developers—the `%ROWTYPE` attribute. You should avoid using the `%ROWTYPE` attribute to anchor directly against a table unless you can guarantee the table won't ever have an invisible column. A complete example in the "Dynamic Explicit Cursors" section of Chapter 5 shows how you should anchor against an explicit cursor that lists all desired (both mandatory and optional) columns.

TIP

You should always anchor PL/SQL structures to explicit cursors because the `SELECT` list lets you manage changes in the table's published description.

Naturally, the largest benefit of column invisibility is hiding the existence of columns from quick inspection of the database schema's objects. Wrapping columns with an object table function lets you return invisible column values without disclosing where they exist when you obfuscate the stored function, package body, or object type. You can read more about object table functions in Chapter 8 and read more about obfuscation in Appendix F.

NOTE

Any variable declared with a `%ROWTYPE` anchors to a table, view, or cursor, but an invisible column in a table makes a view or cursor a safer choice.

Sequences and Identity Columns

If you've used Oracle databases for years, you're knowledgeable about sequences and the fact that they act independently of tables that they may support. Until the Oracle Database 12*c* release, all you had to work with were separate sequences and `.nextval` and `.currval` pseudocolumns, unlike other databases that support identity columns. Oracle Database 12*c* now includes *identity* columns.

This section covers both the old and new approaches. Discussion of the old approach with sequences precedes that of the new identity columns because it appears that IT shops may take some time to adopt the new approach—and if history is any guide, that may be several years.

Sequences Oracle Database 11*g* and its predecessors don't support automatic numbering in tables through identity columns. It provides a separate `SEQUENCE` data structure for use in surrogate keys. Surrogate keys are artificial numbering sequence values that uniquely define rows. They're typically used in joins, because subsequent redefinition of a natural key doesn't invalidate their ability to support joins across tables. The "Indexes" section later in this appendix qualifies how to use surrogate key columns with the natural key to define row uniqueness and optimize joins.

The prototype for sequences is

```
CREATE SEQUENCE sequence_name [INCREMENT BY increment_value]
      [MINVALUE minimum | NOMINVALUE]
      [MAXVALUE maximum | NOMAXVALUE]
      [CACHE | NOCACHE]
      [ORDER | NOORDER]
```

A typical sequence holds a starting number, an incrementing unit, and a buffer cycling value. The naming convention is to use a table name and append `_S` to it. It should be noted that you should only use a sequence for one table.

Each time you call the sequence with a `sequence_name.nextval` statement, the value of the sequence increases by one (or whatever value was chosen as the `INCREMENT BY` value). This occurs until the system consumes the last sequence value in the buffer cycle. When the last value has been read from the buffer cache, a new cycle of values is provided to the instance. The default for the cycle or sequence buffer is a set of 20 number values.

You create a `SEQUENCE` structure with the default values, like this:

```
CREATE SEQUENCE sequence_name;
```

Sometimes application development requires preseeding (inserting before releasing an application to your customer base) rows in tables. Such inserts are done manually without the sequence value or with a sequence starting at the default `START WITH` value of 1. After preseeding the data, you drop the sequence to modify the `START WITH` value because Oracle doesn't provide an alternative to modifying it.

Preseeding generally inserts 10 to 100 rows of data, but after preseeding data, the `START WITH` value is often set at 1001. This leaves developers an additional 900 rows for additional post-implementation seeding of data. You create a sequence starting at that value like this:

```
CREATE SEQUENCE sequence_name START WITH 1001;
```

You also have the option of creating a sequence value that doesn't leave gaps by suppressing a buffered cache of values (not recommended). The syntax for that adds the `NOCACHE` keyword, as follows:

```
CREATE SEQUENCE sequence_name START WITH 1001 NOCACHE;
```

Suppressing the buffered cache of sequence values has a substantial negative impact on performance, so you are advised not to do it.

You use sequences by appending (with dot notation) two pseudocolumns to the sequence name: `.nextval` and `.currval`. The `.nextval` pseudocolumn *initializes* the sequence in a session and gets the *next value*, which is initially the `START WITH` value. After accessing the `.nextval` pseudocolumn, you get the *current value* by using the `.currval` pseudocolumn. You receive an `ORA-08002` error when attempting to access the `.currval` pseudocolumn before having called the `.nextval` pseudocolumn in a session. The error message says that you have tried to access a sequence *not defined* in the session, because `.nextval` *initializes* or *declares* the sequence in the session.

There are several ways to access sequences with the `.nextval` pseudocolumn. The basic starting point is querying the pseudo-table `dual`:

```
SELECT    sequence_s.nextval
FROM      dual;
```

Then, you can see the value again by querying

```
SELECT    sequence_s.currval
FROM      dual;
```

The number will be the same, provided you did not connect to another schema and/or reconnect to a SQL*Plus session. You can also use the `.nextval` and `.currval` pseudocolumns in the `VALUES` clause of an `INSERT` statement or inside a subquery feeding an `INSERT` statement. The "INSERT Statement" section later in this appendix demonstrates how to use sequences.

TIP
Sequences are part of your world in Oracle Database 12c when you implement user-defined types (UDTs), as qualified in Chapter 11, because they don't have identity attributes (or the equivalent of columns in object types).

Oracle requires that you couple sequences with database triggers to mimic automatic numbering *in releases of the database prior to 12c*. The "INSERT Statement" section later in this appendix shows you how to call the sequence to insert values, and Chapter 13 shows you how to write the necessary trigger that supports automatic numbering.

Identity Columns To Oracle-only developers, the identity operator may be revolutionary, but it's been around a long time in other databases. The good news is that Oracle now has an identity operator; the better news is that the identity sequence generator has options others databases don't have, like the `ALWAYS` and `BY DEFAULT` keywords.

The basic identity column typically uses `id` as its label, and Oracle supports that convention if you choose it. The following creates an identity column with the standard default values:

```
SQL> CREATE TABLE identity
  2  ( id NUMBER GENERATED AS IDENTITY );
```

If you were to try and insert a null into the table, you'd discover that `ALWAYS` is the sequence generator default value. That's why `ALWAYS` is an optional clause in the earlier statement prototype.

TIP
Using the table name with an `_ID` suffix as the identity column name is a better practice than simply using `ID` as the identity column name.

For example, this `INSERT` statement attempts to insert a null value:

```
SQL> INSERT INTO identity VALUES (null);
```

It fails and raises this exception:

```
ERROR at line 1:
ORA-32795: cannot insert into a generated always identity column
```

More or less, the preceding definition is equivalent to this:

```
SQL> CREATE TABLE identity
  2  ( id NUMBER GENERATED ALWAYS AS IDENTITY );
```

The present `identity` table example is as barebones as it gets because the default identity behavior is `ALWAYS`. `ALWAYS` means you can't manually enter an identity value in the `id` column, and since there are no other columns in the table, you can't enter a row. You can only insert rows into a table with an identity column when the table has two or more columns in it. Fortunately, most real-world tables have two or more columns.

Here's a new `identity` table with two columns:

```
SQL> CREATE TABLE identity
  2  ( id NUMBER GENERATED AS IDENTITY
  3  , text  VARCHAR2(10) CONSTRAINT identity_nn1 NOT NULL );
```

If you're coming from MySQL or Microsoft SQL Server, you might try something like this:

```
SQL> INSERT INTO identity VALUES ('One');
```

It fails with the following error:

```
ERROR at line 1:
ORA-00947: not enough values
```

You must use an override signature to insert into a table with an identity column. An override signature adds a *column list* between the table name and `VALUES` or subquery clauses. This column list can refer only to the `text` column because you can't submit into the `id` identity column any value that includes a null. You can try it for yourself if you want to, but you'll get an `ORA-32795` error.

The correct way to work with an `INSERT` statement to this type of table excludes the `id` identity column from the column list, like this:

```
SQL> INSERT INTO identity (text) VALUES ('One');
```

Why did Oracle choose `ALWAYS` as the default? The documentation doesn't indicate why, but let me venture a guess. If you use `BY DEFAULT` and enter a number higher than the current generated sequence value, you can duplicate a column value without a primary key or unique constraint and cause an insert into the table to fail when it has a primary key or unique constraint.

A small change to the `identity` table lets you test the preceding scenario, where the `id` identity column is a primary key column, which is typically the use of an identity column. An identity column is also typically a surrogate key column, or stand-in for the natural key. For reference, an identity column should always have a one-to-one mapping to the natural key in the same table. Likewise, it should never be used to make rows unique because you wouldn't be able to figure out what the natural key is!

Mapping Identity Columns to Sequences

Identity columns are helpful because they can eliminate the task of controlling sequence values for primary key columns. However, they are simply a link to a sequence that gets created with a system-generated name.

You can map a table to its sequence when you have access to the `obj$` and `idnseq$` administrative tables. Superuser accounts, like `sys` or `system`, have access to these. You can map the table to an internal sequence value with the following query:

```
SQL> COLUMN table_name    FORMAT A20
SQL> COLUMN sequence_name FORMAT A20
SQL> SELECT   o1.name AS "TABLE_NAME"
  ,        o2.name AS "SEQUENCE_NAME"
  FROM     sys.obj$ o1 INNER JOIN sys.idnseq$ s
  ON       o1.obj# = s.obj# INNER JOIN sys.obj$ o2
  ON       o2.obj# = s.seqobj#
  WHERE    o1.name = 'IDENTITY';
```

It returns the following information for an `identity` table:

```
TABLE_NAME           SEQUENCE_NAME
-------------------- ---------------
IDENTITY             ISEQ$$_91929
```

While this is a sequence, it's an indirect sequence. Like an indirect index created by a unique database constraint, you can't `DROP` or `RENAME` this indirect sequence. You can query information about it from the data catalog as shown here:

```
SQL> SELECT sequence_name
  FROM   dba_sequences
  WHERE  sequence_name = 'ISEQ$$_91929';
```

It returns

```
SEQUENCE_NAME
---------------
ISEQ$$_91929
```

As mentioned, any attempt to remove this indirectly created sequence with a

```
SQL> DROP SEQUENCE ISEQ$$_91929;
```

raises an exception that says

```
ERROR at line 1:
ORA-02289: sequence does not exist
```

Identity columns are simply reserved and internally managed sequences. They guarantee numeric ordering when bulk inserts don't use them, which avoids some of the problems that can occur with sequence values.

The following creates an `identity` table redefined with the `id` column renamed to the table name plus `_id` (a common convention in database application design) and an `identity_pk` primary key constraint. It demonstrates there's no magic to or restriction on an identity column name.

```
SQL> CREATE TABLE identity
  ( identity_id NUMBER GENERATED BY DEFAULT AS IDENTITY
    CONSTRAINT identity_pk PRIMARY KEY
  , text  VARCHAR2(10) CONSTRAINT identity_nn1 NOT NULL );
```

The use case (or test case) to prove the problem with using the `BY DEFAULT` option requires three `INSERT` statements, as follows:

```
SQL> INSERT INTO identity VALUES (2,'One');
SQL> INSERT INTO identity (text) VALUES ('Two');
SQL> INSERT INTO identity (text) VALUES ('Three');
```

The first `INSERT` statement inserts a row with an `identity_id` column value of 2. The second `INSERT` statement inserts a row with an `identity_id` column value of 1, because that's the first value from the sequence generator unless you add a `START WITH` clause and another integer value. The third `INSERT` statement attempts to insert a row with an `identity_id` column value of 2, because that's the next number in the sequence, but it fails with this error:

```
ERROR at line 1:
ORA-00001: unique constraint (STUDENT.IDENTITY_PK) violated
```

Assuming you choose `ALWAYS` over `BY DEFAULT`, sequences work well as surrogate keys. There is another role for identity columns, and that is to provide the value that you then consume as a foreign key value.

Let's examine a transaction between two tables using identity columns. The `unconstrained` table, created here, holds the primary key for itself and doesn't have a foreign key column to any other table, which makes it an independent table:

```
SQL> CREATE TABLE unconstrained
  ( unconstrained_id  NUMBER GENERATED AS IDENTITY
  , text              VARCHAR2(10)
  , CONSTRAINT unconstrained_pk PRIMARY KEY(unconstrained_id));
```

The `constrained` table, created next, holds a primary key column and a foreign key column that references the primary key column of the `unconstrained` table. The foreign key makes the `constrained` table a dependent table.

```
SQL> CREATE TABLE constrained
  ( constrained_id    NUMBER GENERATED AS IDENTITY
  , unconstrained_id  NUMBER
  , text              VARCHAR2(10)
  , CONSTRAINT constrained_fk FOREIGN KEY (unconstrained_id)
    REFERENCES unconstrained(unconstrained_id));
```

Using the `RETURNING INTO` clause of the `INSERT` statement, you return the automatically generated value of the `unconstrained` table's primary key, which comes from a hidden (or abstracted) sequence into a local variable. In this example, we'll use a SQL*Plus `seq_value` variable.

```
SQL> VARIABLE seq_value NUMBER
SQL> INSERT INTO unconstrained (text) VALUES ('One')
  2  RETURNING unconstrained_id INTO :seq_value;
```

Next, you use the local `:seq_value` variable as the foreign key value in an `INSERT` statement to the `constrained` table, like

```
SQL> INSERT INTO constrained (unconstrained_id, text)
  2  VALUES (:seq_value,'One');
```

This approach lets you pass an unknown and system-generated primary key value to the foreign key in a transaction context. It works the same way in scripting languages, like PHP, or in object-oriented programming languages, like Java.

If you're an experienced Oracle developer, you may notice that identity columns work like sequences. Unfortunately, rather than using the `.nextval` and `.currval` pseudocolumns, you should use the following clause with any table inserting an identity column value:

```
RETURNING column_value INTO local_variable
```

Therefore, I'd strongly recommend you opt for the `ALWAYS` default with identity columns and ensure that all identity columns are primary key constrained to guarantee unique constraint violations.

Nested Collection Types

This section shows you how to create single-level and multiple-level nested collections within tables. Oracle Database 11*g* supports nested table data types, but many other databases don't. Oracle documentation calls the nesting of tables within nested tables a *multilevel collection*.

Nested tables are tables within a column inside a row of another table. These are object types must be defined in SQL before they can become data types for columns in a table. The definition can be a one- or two-step process. It's a one-step process when you create an object type that is a collection of a scalar data type. It's a two-step process when you create an object type that contains a set of variables. The set of variables in this case becomes a *record structure*. Elements of record structures are *fields*. You create an object type (or record structure) as a schema-level object type and then you create a collection of the object type.

As an object relational database management system (ORDBMS), Oracle databases let you define object types. Object types have two roles in Oracle databases. One role is as a SQL data type, which you see in this chapter as a nested table. The other role acts like a traditional object type inside an object-oriented programming language (OOPL) such as Java, C#, or C++. Instantiable object types are advanced PL/SQL concepts. You can find a full description of how you can define and work with object types in Chapter 11.

Two possible syntaxes can be used for creating a collection of a scalar data type. One creates an array, which has a fixed size; the other creates a list, which has no fixed size. Oracle names these collections of scalar data types Attribute Data Types (ADTs).

The syntax to create a varray ADT is

```
SQL> CREATE OR REPLACE
  2    TYPE street_array IS VARRAY(3) OF VARCHAR2(30);
  3  /
```

Array or List?

The terms *array* and *list* both refer to a collection of the same type of data, which can be a scalar data type or a record structure. An array is a structure that has a fixed maximum number of elements that is uniquely indexed by a sequential set of numbers. A sequential set of numbers is also known as a *densely populated index*. Programmers iterate (move across arrays one by one) using sequential index values.

A list is like an array but different. A list has no maximum number of elements and can be indexed by a sequential or nonsequential index. A nonsequential set of numbers or strings acts like a sparsely populated index. Programmers must iterate through elements of the list by using an iterator to traverse the links between each element from the first until the last. This behavior is similar to a singly linked list in the C/C++ programming languages.

The elements in arrays or lists can be ordered or unordered. More often than not, arrays are ordered sets. Lists are more frequently unordered sets. The closest corollary to a database table is an unordered list.

The statement creates an array of no more than *three* 30-character variable-length strings. The forward slash (/) is required to execute the statement terminated by a semicolon. This is a case where the semicolon acts like a statement terminator, not an execution command. The forward slash executes the creation or replacement of a data type.

It's important to note that you can't change an existing data type when it has type dependents. *Type dependents* are any types, functions, procedures, packages, tables, or views (stored queries) that use the data type or a type that depends on its earlier definition.

You can then define a table that uses the `STREET_ARRAY` ADT as a column data type. The following defines an `address` table by using it to capture one to at most three street addresses for an address:

```
SQL> CREATE TABLE address
  ( address_id      NUMBER
  , street_address  STREET_ARRAY
  , city            VARCHAR2(30)
  , state           VARCHAR2(2)
  , postal_code     VARCHAR2(10));
```

Storage Considerations for Varrays

The size of a stored varray depends on the count and size of elements plus the overhead required to manage null elements. Oracle stores varrays as either raw values or LOBs.

Oracle decides how to store varray columns when they're defined by a `CREATE` statement. Oracle stores the varray inline as raw values or as a LOB when the cumulative size is less than 4,000 bytes, and stores the varray out-of-line as a LOB when the cumulative size is more than 4,000 bytes.

You don't require a special storage clause when you embed a varray ADT because the database allocates space on the basis of the number of items and required size of the base scalar data type.

Alternatively, you can create a list of 30 character variable-length strings with this:

```
SQL> CREATE OR REPLACE
       TYPE street_list IS TABLE OF VARCHAR2(30);
     /
```

You can then define a table that uses the UDT `street_list` as a column data type. Although a nested table ADT appears like the varray ADT, a nested table acts like a list, not an array. A list has no fixed size, which means that you can't create a table without designating a `NESTED TABLE STORAGE` clause.

The following defines an `address` table by using it to capture one to however many street addresses might be required by an address:

```
SQL> CREATE TABLE address
  2  ( address_id     NUMBER
  3  , street_address STREET_LIST
  4  , city           VARCHAR2(30)
  5  , state          VARCHAR2(2)
  6  , postal_code    VARCHAR2(10))
  7  NESTED TABLE street_address STORE AS street_table;
```

As mentioned, a nested table like the `street_list` ADT on line 3 requires you to add a `NESTED TABLE` clause to the `CREATE TABLE` statement. Line 7 defines a `street_table` storage name for the `street_address` column. The "INSERT Statement" section shows examples of how you insert into nested tables.

A question some ask is, "How do you create a nested table within a nested table?" Oracle's documentation labels nesting a table within a table as a *multilevel collection*. The most difficult part of nesting a table within a nested table is learning how to write the storage clause. Then, the storage clause syntax is straightforward.

The following extends the original design by changing the `address` table into an object type and then nesting it in an `employee` table. The first step in this example creates an `address_type`, like this:

```
SQL> CREATE OR REPLACE TYPE address_type AS OBJECT
     ( address_id     NUMBER
     , street_address STREET_LIST
     , city           VARCHAR2(30)
     , state          VARCHAR2(2)
     , postal_code    VARCHAR2(10));
     /
```

You create a list collection of the `address_type` with the following syntax:

```
SQL> CREATE OR REPLACE TYPE address_list AS TABLE OF address_type;
     /
```

The employee table holds a nested table of the address_type, which in turn holds a nested table of street_address, as shown next:

```
SQL> CREATE TABLE employee
  2  ( employee_id      NUMBER
  3  , first_name       VARCHAR2(20)
  4  , middle_name      VARCHAR2(20)
  5  , last_name        VARCHAR2(20)
  6  , home_address     ADDRESS_LIST)
  7  NESTED TABLE home_address STORE AS address_table
  8  (NESTED TABLE street_address STORE AS street_table);
```

Line 7 defines the nested table storage for the address_type, associated with the home_address column. The parentheses on line 8 indicate that the nested table for street_address is part of the previous nested table (or a multilevel collection). Embedding one table collection inside another is a form of type chaining, which becomes more noticeable when you unnest the data in a query. There's an internally managed link that connects the employee table with the nested home_address table and another link that connects the street_address table to the home_address column (or nested table).

It's also possible to construct the nested collection differently when you need to create the multilevel collection for access through the OCI collection functions. You can store the nested collection as a locator value by appending the RETURN AS LOCATOR clause, as shown:

```
SQL> CREATE TABLE employee
  2  ( employee_id      NUMBER
  3  , first_name       VARCHAR2(20)
  4  , middle_name      VARCHAR2(20)
  5  , last_name        VARCHAR2(20)
  6  , home_address     ADDRESS_LIST)
  7  NESTED TABLE home_address STORE AS address_table
  8  (NESTED TABLE street_address STORE AS street_table
  9   RETURN AS LOCATOR);
```

Line 9 designates that retrieving data from the nested table can use a locator reference, but you can also ignore the locator reference with a performance loss. Locator references allow you to recover the contents of nested tables more quickly, so they should be your choice when the nested collection has a large number of elements. You use a NESTED_TABLE_GET_REFS hint when writing a query that uses the locator references, which is shown in the "Unnesting Queries" section later in this appendix.

Although you've seen how to implement nested tables, they're complex and not very flexible to changing business requirements. Use them only when they meet a specific need that can't be met by normal primary-to-foreign key relationships. For more information on nested tables, check the *Oracle Database SQL Language Reference 12c Release*.

Constraints

Table constraints can apply to a single column or against multiple columns. That's because table constraints are defined by their position in the CREATE TABLE statement syntax. They occur after the last column definition. However, that really makes them out-of-line constraints. Table constraints apply against multiple columns or impose a unique constraint across rows.

The Nested Table Design Pattern

Nested tables are an advanced implementation made possible by the Oracle Object Relational Model (ORM). They provide an internal connection between tables that acts like an inner class in OOPLs.

Like inner classes in OOPLs, there's no way to go directly to the inner class. You must first go through the outer (or container) class. This type of relationship between tables in database design is known as an *ID-dependent relationship*. The only way to discover the ID is through the table holding the key to the nested tables.

If subsequent discovery of the business model identifies a use for nested table data, the design must be changed to open up access to the nested data. That means removing the nested table and making it an ordinary table connected by a primary-to-foreign key relationship. That type of change is typically expensive. Ordinary table primary-to-foreign key relationships are more flexible (and for the curious, their official label is *non–ID-dependent relationships*).

While seldom written as an out-of-line constraint, you can write a single-column primary key that way. The reason they're uncommon is that a single primary key constraint imposes both a not null constraint and a unique column constraint, and they're the only constraints that would displace an inline primary key. The syntax requires that you provide the column name as an argument to the constraint. You have two options, as with inline constraints: one uses a system-generated constraint name, and the other uses a user-defined constraint name.

Here's an out-of-line primary key constraint with a system-generated constraint name:

```
, PRIMARY KEY(system_user_id)
```

And here's the same constraint with a user-defined name:

```
, CONSTRAINT pk_system_user PRIMARY KEY(system_user_id)
```

A multiple-column primary key constraint would look like this:

```
, CONSTRAINT pk_contact PRIMARY KEY(first_name, last_name)
```

Check constraints often occur as out-of-line constraints because the columns involved can hold other inline constraints, such as a not null constraint. A check constraint with a system-generated constraint name looks like this:

```
, CHECK(salary > 0 AND salary < 50000)
```

Adding a user-defined name, the constraint looks like this:

```
, CONSTRAINT ck_employee_01 CHECK(salary > 0 AND salary < 50000)
```

A table constraint on multiple columns would look like the following:

```
, CONSTRAINT ck_employee_02 CHECK
  ((salary BETWEEN      0 AND  49999.99 AND employee_class = 'NON-EXEMPT')
OR (salary BETWEEN  50000 AND 249999.99 AND employee_class = 'EXEMPT')
OR (salary BETWEEN 250000 AND 999999.99 AND employee_class = 'EXECUTIVE'))
```

You create a unique constraint as an out-of-line constraint in two cases. The first case occurs when you've applied a not null inline constraint and you want to create a unique single-column constraint. The second is when you want to create a multiple-column unique constraint.

Here's the syntax for a single-column unique constraint:

```
, UNIQUE(common_lookup_id)
```

The multiple-column syntax isn't much different for a unique constraint. The only difference is a comma-delimited list of column names in lieu of a single column. This syntax example includes a user-defined constraint name:

```
, CONSTRAINT un_lookup
  UNIQUE(common_lookup_table, common_lookup_column, common_lookup_type)
```

The most popular table-level constraint is a FOREIGN KEY constraint. You must provide the FOREIGN KEY phrase in an out-of-line constraint, unlike the inline version that starts with the REFERENCES keyword. Here's an example of a FOREIGN KEY constraint without a user-defined constraint name:

```
, FOREIGN KEY(system_id) REFERENCES common_lookup(common_lookup_id)
```

The system_id column name identifies the column in the table that becomes constrained by the FOREIGN KEY. The REFERENCES clause identifies the table and column inside the parentheses where the constraint looks to find the list of primary key values.

You would add a CONSTRAINT keyword and a user-defined constraint name when you name a FOREIGN KEY constraint. The syntax would look like this:

```
, CONSTRAINT fk_system_01 FOREIGN KEY(system_id)
  REFERENCES common_lookup(common_lookup_id)
```

Like a unique constraint, you can provide a single-column reference or a comma-delimited list of columns. Single-column FOREIGN KEY constraints generally refer to surrogate keys that are generated values from a sequence. Multiple-column FOREIGN KEY values relate to the multiple-column (or composite) *natural key* of the table. Composite primary keys have a primary key constraint, and they also have an implicitly created unique constraint.

This concludes how you define constraints in the CREATE TABLE statement syntax. You also have the option of adding, dropping, disabling, or enabling constraints with the ALTER TABLE statement. The "Adding, Modifying, and Dropping Columns" section later in this appendix covers how you use the ALTER TABLE statement. The next section shows you the syntax to create partitioned tables.

Indexes

Indexes are separate data structures that provide alternate pathways to finding data. They can and do generally speed up the processing of queries and other DML commands, like the INSERT, UPDATE, MERGE, and DELETE statements. Indexes are also called *fast access paths*.

The Oracle Database 12c database maintains the integrity of indexes after you create them. The upside of indexes is that they can improve SQL statement performance. The downside is that they impose overhead on every INSERT, UPDATE, MERGE, and DELETE statement because the database maintains them by inserting, updating, or deleting items for each related change in the tables that the indexes support.

Indexes have two key properties—*usability* and *visibility*. Indexes are both usable and visible by default. That means they are visible to the Oracle Database 12*c* cost-based optimizer and usable when statements run against the tables they support.

You have the ability to make any index invisible, in which case queries and DML statements won't use the index because they won't see it. However, the cost-based optimizer still sees the index and maintains it with any DML statement change. That means making an index invisible isn't quite like making the index unusable or like dropping it temporarily. An invisible index becomes overhead and thus is typically a short-term solution to run a resource-intensive statement that behaves better without the index while avoiding the cost of rebuilding it after the statement runs.

It is also possible to make an index unusable, in which case it stops collecting information and becomes obsolete and the database drops its index segment. You rebuild the index when you change it back to a usable index.

Indexes work on the principal of a key. A key is typically a set of columns or expressions on which you can build an index, but it's possible that a key can be a single column. An index based on a set of columns is a composite, or concatenated, index.

Indexes can be unique or nonunique. You create a unique index anytime you constrain a column by assigning a primary key or unique constraint, but they're indirect indexes. You create a direct unique index on a single column with the following syntax against two nonunique columns:

```
CREATE INDEX common_lookup_nuidx
ON common_lookup (common_lookup_table);
```

You could convert this to a nonunique index on two columns by using this syntax:

```
CREATE INDEX common_lookup_nuidx
ON common_lookup (common_lookup_table, common_lookup_column);
```

Making the index unique is straightforward; you only need to add a unique keyword to the `CREATE INDEX` statement, like

```
CREATE UNIQUE INDEX common_lookup_nuidx
ON common_lookup ( common_lookup_table
                 , common_lookup_column
                 , common_lookup_type);
```

Most indexes use a B-tree (balanced tree). A B-tree is composed of three types of blocks—a *root branch block* for searching next-level blocks, *branch blocks* for searching other branch blocks, and *leaf blocks* that store pointers to row values. B-trees are balanced because all leaf-blocks are at the same level, which means the length of search is the same to any element in the tree. All branch blocks store the minimum key prefix required to make branching decisions through the B-tree.

There are six schemas for creating B-tree indexes and a couple of schemas for creating bitmap indexes. The B-tree schemas are described first, followed by a description of a single bitmap schema.

Index-Organized Tables Index-organized tables are stored in a variation of a B-tree index structure. The rows of an index-organized table are stored in an index defined by the primary key for the table. Each index entry in the B-tree also holds the values of non-key columns. Index-organized tables provide faster access to the table rows through the primary key, and the presence of non-key columns of the row foregoes additional data block I/O.

Reverse Key Indexes A reverse key index is a type of B-tree index that reverses the physical byte order of each index key while keeping columns in sequence. Reversing the key solves contention problems for leaf blocks in the right side of a B-tree index. Moreover, a reversal of the byte order distributes inserts across all leaf keys in the index.

Ascending and Descending Indexes Ascending indexes are the Oracle default, and they store character data by their binary values, store numeric data from smallest to largest number, and store dates from earliest to latest value. A descending index reverses the sort order.

You create a composite nonunique descending index by appending the DESC keyword to the creation statement:

```
CREATE INDEX common_lookup_nuidx
ON common_lookup (common_lookup_table, common_lookup_column) DESC;
```

Descending indexes are most useful when queries sort some columns in ascending order and other columns in descending order. The Oracle database searches key values to find and then use the associated ROWID values.

B-tree Cluster Indexes A B-tree cluster index is a table cluster that uses a cluster key to find data. You must create a cluster before you create the tables. The following shows how to create a cluster:

```
CREATE CLUSTER sales_records ( cost_center_id NUMBER(4)) SIZE 512;
```

The syntax to create the index is

```
CREATE INDEX sales_uidx ON CLUSTER sales_records;
```

Finally, you'd create the tables like this:

```
CREATE TABLE eastern_region ( <column_list> )
CLUSTER sales_records (cost_center_id);
CREATE TABLE western_region (<column_list>)
CLUSTER sales_records (cost_center_id);
```

This type of configuration ensures rows from both tables are written inside the same file block. The database then stores the rows in a heap and locates them with the index.

Function-based Indexes Function-based indexes are efficient for evaluating statements that contain functions in their WHERE clauses. The Oracle Database 12*c* database only uses the function-based index when queries use functions in the WHERE clause.

You create a function-based index with the following syntax:

```
CREATE INDEX employee_uidx
ON employee (salary + commission_percent, salary, commission_percent);
```

The function is triggered when a query includes a like arithmetic expression:

```
SELECT   employee_id
,        first_name
,        last_name
,       (salary + commission_percent) AS annual_salary
FROM     employee e
```

```
WHERE    (salary + commission_percent) > 100000
ORDER BY annual_salary DESC;
```

The optimizer can use an index range scan on a function-based index for queries with an expression in the WHERE clause. The range scan access path has better benefits when the WHERE clause has low selectivity. Selectivity is calculated by dividing cardinality by the number of records in a table. For example, a column with 75 distinct values and 5,000 records has a 1.5 percent selectivity.

Application Domain Indexes An application domain index is a customized index designed to support an application. Oracle Database 12*c* provides extensible indexing to do the following:

- Work with indexes on customized, complex data types such as documents, spatial data, images, video clips, and other unstructured data
- Make use of specialized indexing techniques

You use a cartridge to control the structure and content of a domain index. The database interacts with the application to build, maintain, and search the domain index.

Bitmap Indexes A bitmap index stores a bit array for each index key. Bitmap indexes are best suited to data warehousing systems where queries are ad hoc, and work against tables with low cardinality. Bitmapped indexes are expensive and ill suited to read-write tables with frequent changes to the data. Bitmaps work best with data that is either read-only or not subject to significant changes.

Views

Oracle supports ordinary views that are read-only or read-writeable. Here's the basic prototype for creating a view in Oracle:

```
CREATE [OR REPLACE] [[NO] FORCE] VIEW view_name
[( column_name [inline_constraint] [, ...]
[,CONSTRAINT constraint_name
  UNIQUE (column_name) RELY DISABLE NONVALIDATE]
[,CONSTRAINT constraint_name
  PRIMARY KEY (column_list) RELY DISABLE NONVALIDATE]
AS select_statement
[WITH {READ ONLY | CHECK OPTION}]
```

The OR REPLACE clause is very helpful because you don't have to drop the previous view before re-creating it with a new definition. Although NO FORCE is the default, FORCE tells the DBMS to create the view even when the query references things that aren't in the database. This is handy when you're doing a major upgrade because you can compile the views concurrently with scripts that change the definition of tables.

You can query the data catalog to find invalid views. This query returns a list of all invalid views in a user's schema:

```
SQL> SELECT   object_name
  2  ,        object_type
  3  ,        status
  4  FROM     user_objects
  5  WHERE    status = 'INVALID';
```

Read-writeable Views A read-writeable view exists when all columns are simply references to a single table, which occurs when a view typically stripes data. A striped view occurs when you implement a filter or virtual private databases (VPDs). Filters can be as simple as a `WHERE` clause statement that checks whether the current time is between a `start_date` and `end_date` column, which is known as *temporal striping* (striping to a time epoch, and nothing to do with time travel, *Star Trek: The Next Generation*, or the character "Q" from the same TV series).

You have two alternatives for VPDs—the schema-level security model or the user-level security model. The schema-level security model is based on a database user or schema, while the user-level security model requires you to use an access control list (ACL) and to filter authenticated users by using context information in the session metadata. An ACL is typically a table that lists individual users and their access privileges, and typically all users connect through the same Oracle database user account. Both require you to use the `dbms_rls` package to add, maintain, and remove security policies.

A temporally bound view is the simplest read-writeable view to illustrate, and it returns all columns for a range of rows stored in the table. You can compare the range of rows to the complete set of rows like a piece of pie from the whole pie, as shown in Figure B-3.

An example of a temporal view is

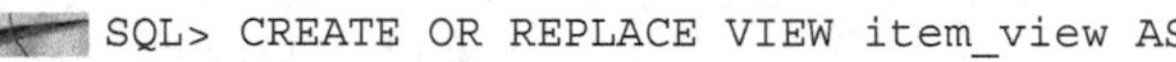

```
SQL> CREATE OR REPLACE VIEW item_view AS
  SELECT *
  FROM item i
  WHERE SYSDATE
    BETWEEN TRUNC(i.start_date) AND NVL(i.end_date,TRUNC(SYSDATE) + 1);
```

An important thing to note about the `BETWEEN` operator is that the lookup value and both the starting and ending values can't be null values. Since Oracle doesn't provide a `DATE` data type,

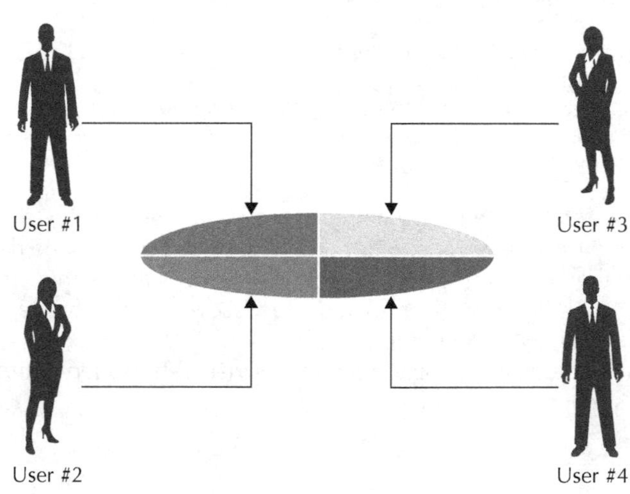

FIGURE B-3. *Virtual private databases*

you can create one by using the TRUNC function, which shaves off the hours and minutes of a date (the values to the right of the decimal point). You find tomorrow by simply adding 1 (or one day) to the truncated SYSDATE value, as shown in the preceding temporal view example.

Read-only Views A read-only view occurs when the query (SELECT statement) contains a subquery, collection expression, selectivity operator (DECODE function or CASE operator), or DISTINCT operator in the SELECT list; or when the query uses a join, set operator, aggregate function, or GROUP BY, ORDER BY, MODEL, CONNECT BY, or START WITH clause. The last two clauses are hybrid Oracle clauses that support recursive queries. You can't write to base rows when views perform these types of operations. However, you can deploy INSTEAD OF triggers in Oracle that unwind the logic of the query and let you write to the base rows.

The following is an example of a read-only view:

```
SQL> CREATE OR REPLACE VIEW employee_view
  2  ( employee_id
  3  , employee_name
  4  , employee_status
  5  , CONSTRAINT pk_employee
  6    PRIMARY KEY (employee_id) RELY DISABLE NOVALIDATE)
  7  AS
  8  SELECT    c.contact_id AS employee_id
  9  ,         c.last_name || ', ' || c.first_name ||
 10            CASE
 11              WHEN c.middle_name IS NULL
 12              THEN ' '
 13              ELSE ' '||c.middle_name
 14            END AS employee_name
 15  ,         CASE
 16              WHEN c.contact_type = common_lookup_id
 17              THEN 'Active'
 18              ELSE 'Inactive'
 19            END AS employee_status
 20  FROM      contact c INNER JOIN common_lookup cl
 21  ON        common_lookup_table = 'CONTACT'
 22  AND       common_lookup_column = 'CONTACT_TYPE'
 23  AND       common_lookup_type = 'EMPLOYEE';
```

Line 6 has a primary key constraint on employee_id, which maps inside the subquery to the primary key contact_id column for the contact table. The employee_name column is selectively concatenated from other columns in the contact table, and the employee_status column is fabricated through the combination of an INNER JOIN operator and a CASE operator. While this is intended as a read-only view, only the sales_tax and total columns are nonupdatable, as you can see in the CDB_, DBA_, ALL_ or USER_UPDATABLE_COLUMNS administrative view.

A read-write trigger can contain derived columns or expressions, but you cannot write to those specific columns. You can write through the transaction_view to the underlying transaction table through an INSTEAD OF trigger (see Chapter 13 for more details on INSTEAD OF triggers).

The following creates a view with two derived and nonupdatable columns:

```
SQL> CREATE OR REPLACE VIEW transaction_view AS
  2  SELECT   t.transaction_id AS id
  3  ,        t.transaction_account AS account
  4  ,        t.transaction_type AS purchase_type
  5  ,        t.transaction_date AS purchase_date
  6  ,        t.transaction_amount AS retail_amount
  7  ,        t.transaction_amount * .0875 AS sales_tax
  8  ,        t.transaction_amount * 1.0875 AS total
  9  ,        t.rental_id AS rental_id
 10  ,        t.payment_method_type AS payment_type
 11  ,        t.payment_account_number AS account_number
 12  ,        t.created_by
 13  ,        t.creation_date
 14  ,        t.last_updated_by
 15  ,        t.last_update_date
 16  FROM     transaction t;
```

Lines 7 and 8 contain results from a calculation based on column values multiplied by numeric constants. You can write to the base table through this view by providing an override signature that excludes the two derived columns. This appendix discusses the mechanics of using override signatures in the "INSERT Statement" section.

Object Table Function View Beyond an ordinary query, you can create a view that uses a PL/SQL object table function. An object table function returns a collection of an ADT or of a UDT. You can read more about ADTs and UDTs in the "Object Types" section later in this appendix. You can also find the UDT object structure and table of the UDT used in the object table function in the "Object Types" section.

You can create object table views to embed calls to autonomous functions or procedures that can record information about the user's credentials, time of access, and records viewed. This type of approach gives you the opportunity to create pseudo-triggers behind functional query views, and is quite handy when you need to ensure employee compliance with privacy rules, such as those contained in the U.S. Sarbanes-Oxley Act (SOX), Health Insurance Portability and Accountability Act (HIPPA), or Family Educational Rights and Privacy Act (FERPA).

The first step for this type of trigger requires creating a SQL UDT, like the one declared in the "Object Types" section later in this appendix. The second step requires creating a SQL collection of the UDT, which you'll also find in the "Object Types" section. The third step requires creating an autonomous procedure that can record who accessed what, and when. This is more or less a "who done it" audit without the private eye of fiction—the object table function and autonomous view replace the detective. That third step requires a logging table with a nested table for an unknown number of records and an autonomous procedure to insert the records.

Business Use Case

Object table function views enable you to capture who queries data and which data they query. They enable you to more fully comply with privacy rules by monitoring which records are accessed.

Here's the `CREATE` statement to build the table:

```
SQL> CREATE TABLE item_looked_up
  ( looked_up_id  NUMBER GENERATED ALWAYS AS IDENTITY
  , looked_up     ITEM_LOOKUP)
    NESTED TABLE looked_up STORE AS looked_up_table;
```

The `item_looked_up` table is narrowly scoped to keep this sample to as few moving parts as possible. If you create an *object type hierarchy*—a base type and subtypes (which are specializations of the base type)—there's no reason you couldn't write any type of object type data to the base type or generalized object type. An implementation of this type of architecture is in Chapter 11.

While the following autonomous transaction procedure writes only the data queried by the view, it could readily include session-level data to support a Virtual Private Database (VPD) implementation. The `PRAGMA` (a PL/SQL precompiler instruction) for an autonomous transaction and embedded commit are covered in the "DML-Enabled Pass-by-Value Functions" section of Chapter 8. You also can extend this logic to run an autonomous procedure.

```
SQL> CREATE OR REPLACE PROCEDURE log_item_lookup
  2  ( pv_item_lookup  ITEM_LOOKUP ) IS
  3
  4    -- Declare the procedure as an autonomous procedure.
  5    PRAGMA AUTONOMOUS_TRANSACTION;
  6  BEGIN
  7    INSERT INTO item_looked_up (looked_up)
  8    VALUES (pv_item_lookup);
  9    COMMIT;  -- Autonomous transactions require a commit.
 10  END;
 11  /
```

Line 5 declares a precompiler instruction that enables the `log_item_lookup` procedure to work within the scope of a query and to write data to the `item_looked_up` table in a separate session. The `COMMIT` statement on line 9 makes permanent the write to the log table.

NOTE
The embedded `INSERT` statement relies on an identity column, which is only available in Oracle Database 12c forward.

After creating the UDTs, logging table, and procedure, you create an object table function that returns a UDT collection like this:

```
SQL> CREATE OR REPLACE FUNCTION get_item_types RETURN item_lookup IS

    -- Declare a variable that uses the record structure.
    lv_counter      PLS_INTEGER := 1;

    -- Declare a variable that uses the record structure.
    lv_lookup_table  ITEM_LOOKUP := item_lookup();

    -- Declare static cursor structure.
```

```
10    CURSOR c IS
11      SELECT   cl.common_lookup_id AS lookup_id
12      ,        SUBSTR(cl.common_lookup_meaning,1,60) AS lookup_meaning
13      FROM     common_lookup cl
14      WHERE    cl.common_lookup_table = 'ITEM'
15      AND      cl.common_lookup_column = 'ITEM_TYPE'
16      AND      SYSDATE BETWEEN
17                 cl.start_date and NVL(cl.end_date,TRUNC(SYSDATE) + 1)
18      ORDER BY cl.common_lookup_meaning;
19
20  BEGIN
21
22    FOR i IN c LOOP
23      lv_lookup_table.EXTEND;
24
25      /* The assignment pattern for a SQL collection is
26         incompatible with the cursor return type, and you
27         must construct an instance of the object type before
28         assigning it to a collection. */
29      lv_lookup_table(lv_counter) := item_structure( i.lookup_id
30                                                   , i.lookup_meaning
31                                                   , user );
32
33      lv_counter := lv_counter + 1;
34    END LOOP;
35
36    /* Call an autonomous procedure to log the queried values. */
37    log_item_lookup(lv_lookup_table);
38
39    RETURN lv_lookup_table;
40  END;
41  /
```

A best practice is to use a SQL collection UDT when you want to store the value set in a table, which is what the call to `log_item_lookup` on line 36 does. You could use a PL/SQL UDT, but then you'd require a `CAST` operation inside the autonomous procedure.

```
SQL> CREATE OR REPLACE VIEW item_lookup_view AS
    SELECT *
    FROM   TABLE(get_item_types);
```

Lastly, we can use the following query to confirm that our embedded procedure works after we query the view:

```
SQL> SELECT   looked_up_id
  ,        log.id
  ,        log.lookup
  FROM     item_looked_up ilu CROSS JOIN TABLE(ilu.looked_up) log;
```

It returns the following data:

```
LOOKED_UP_ID         ID LOOKUP              USER_NAME
------------ ---------- ------------------- ---------
           1       1013 DVD: Full Screen    STUDENT
           1       1014 DVD: Wide Screen    STUDENT
           1       1017 DVD: XBOX           STUDENT
           1       1015 Nintendo GameCube   STUDENT
           1       1016 PlayStation2        STUDENT
```

The object table function isn't an updatable view. You would need to create an `INSTEAD OF` trigger when you wanted to write to the view. The object table function view does provide you with the ability to record the information seen by users when they query data from this type of view. Object table function views also provide an improved means of monitoring compliance against laws like the U.S. SOX, HIPPA, and FERPA statutes. Naturally, the `dbms_fga` package provides facilities to manage this type of information too.

Updatable Columns in a View A view's updatable columns are columns that map directly to a table's columns. All other columns are nonupdatable, which means virtual (or defined) columns, or columns used to group aggregated results. Views with both updatable and nonupdatable columns aren't read-writeable, and they require you to create `INSTEAD OF` triggers to manage writes to the view. You can read more about this in Chapter 13, which covers database triggers.

You can see which columns are updatable with the following query (formatted with SQL*Plus commands):

```
COLUMN column_name FORMAT A20
COLUMN updatable   FORMAT A9
SQL> SELECT   column_name
  2  ,        updatable
  3  FROM     user_updatable_columns
  4  WHERE    table_name = 'TRANSACTION_VIEW'
  5  AND      updatable = 'NO';
```

It would return the two derived columns:

```
COLUMN_NAME          UPDATABLE
-------------------- ---------
SALES_TAX            NO
TOTAL                NO
```

The `WITH CHECK OPTION` clause limits the rows that you can change with an `UPDATE` statement or delete from the table with a `DELETE FROM` statement. It does so by applying a rule that allows you to touch only those rows that you can see in the view.

If a view becomes invalid, you can query the `USER_DEPENDENCIES` concept view. It shows you which dependencies are missing. Replacing the dependencies allows the next DML against the view to work.

The following query finds dependencies for a view:

```
SQL> SELECT   name
  2  ,        referenced_owner||'.'||referenced_name AS reference
  3  ,        referenced_type
```

```
FROM      user_dependencies
WHERE     type = 'VIEW'
AND       name = 'view_name';
```

Views are powerful and complex. Although the views you've seen only store queries and rules, Oracle also supports materialized views, which are query results stored in the database. The results in materialized views are often not current with the moment and can be hours or even a day or more old. Materialized views are created when the cost of returning a result set is very high and places an inordinate load on the server during normal operational windows. Materialized views are often used in data marts and warehouses.

Functions, Procedures, and Packages

Functions, procedures, and packages, all of which are stored programs, are the principal subject of this book. Stored programs in Oracle are written in the PL/SQL programming language or other languages with PL/SQL wrappers. You can build libraries in C/C++, C#, or Java programming languages.

You use `CREATE OR REPLACE` syntax to build functions, procedures, and packages. Packages contain functions, procedures, and user-defined types. However, you can't use the `CREATE OR REPLACE` syntax when changing a function to a procedure or vice versa. The general prototype for a function is

```
CREATE OR REPLACE FUNCTION function_name;
```

The general prototype for a procedure is

```
CREATE OR REPLACE PROCEDURE procedure_name;
```

The general prototype for a package specification is

```
CREATE OR REPLACE PACKAGE package_name;
```

and this for a package body:

```
CREATE OR REPLACE PACKAGE BODY package_name;
```

It's important to note that the published list of functions and procedures in the specification must agree exactly with the implementations in the package body.

Stored programs cannot be renamed, but they can be dropped from the database and re-created under a new name. Let's look at a small example of the problem. We'll create a procedure that only prints *"Hello World!"*, and then we'll try to convert it to a function with a `CREATE OR REPLACE` clause. It will raise an exception when we try it because we can't replace a procedure with a function.

Here's the `hello_world` procedure:

```
SQL> CREATE OR REPLACE PROCEDURE hello_world IS
BEGIN
  dbms_output.put_line('Hello World!');
END;
/
```

Now, let's try to replace it with a function that uses the same name in the data catalog:

```
SQL> CREATE OR REPLACE FUNCTION hello_world RETURNS VARCHAR2 IS
     BEGIN
       RETURN 'Hello World!';
     END;
     /
```

It raises the following exception:

```
CREATE OR REPLACE FUNCTION hello_world RETURNS VARCHAR2 IS
*
ERROR at line 1:
ORA-00955: name is already used by an existing object
```

It requires that we drop the existing `hello_world` procedure before we attempt to create the `hello_world` function. That's one little trick that new PL/SQL programmers seem to encounter all too often.

You can find much more information about stored programs in Chapters 4, 8, and 9.

Object Types

While object types are largely a discussion for PL/SQL because their type body implementations are written in PL/SQL, object types may also be defined as SQL-level objects without an implementation. SQL-level objects are UDTs, and any UDT can be

- A set of positioning-related attributes grouped into an object type
  - Without user-defined constructors and member functions and procedures
  - With user-defined constructors and member functions and procedures
- An array or list of scalar data types, which are known as attribute data types (ADTs)
- A collection of UDT objects

A non-collection UDT object type without user-defined constructor functions or any member functions or procedures is more like a free-floating row of data, which is equivalent to a record structure in computer science. The fields of the record structure are more frequently known as *attributes* because that's what object-oriented analysis and design (OOAD) calls them. A collection of a single attribute scalar data type is called an Attribute Data Type (ADT).

ADTs and UDTs can be parameters, return types, or local variables in functions, procedures, and objects. Oracle Database 12*c* has promoted PL/SQL object types from their previous limitations within an exclusively PL/SQL scope. Although promoted, they haven't replaced SQL object types, which can also be the data type of a column in a table. How that column may evolve is described in the "Object Types" subsection of the "ALTER Statement" section later in this appendix.

Oracle Database 12*c* qualifies object types as either persistent or transient objects. Any parameter to a function or procedure, return data type of a function or procedure, or local variable in a named or unnamed block is a transient object. Transient objects are *short-lived* because their life span is constrained by the life time of the program unit using them. Persistent objects are *long-lived* because they are used inside a table as a column's data type, which is unlikely to change.

Business Use Case

UDTs enable you to create data structures and collections with a default constructor like table definitions create a default signature for `INSERT` statements—a positional signature by data type. You can also define methods for these object types as you would in any object-oriented programming language. UDT data types can be passed as object instances with data between SQL and PL/SQL stored programs, with one restriction. A UDT can't be read in a SQL `SELECT`-list unless you use the `COLLECT` built-in to put it in a varray or table collection before you use the `TABLE` built-in to read it into a query's result set, and since Oracle supports object type evolution, they can become general-purpose column data types.

The first step in using object types is to create the structure in SQL or PL/SQL. Since our object table function requires an object type, that's what we'll develop in this section.

Our `item_structure` example holds a surrogate key `id` column, a descriptive `lookup` text field, and a `user_name` column that will hold the schema name responsible for querying an object table function view. You can find PL/SQL implementation of the object table function view in the earlier section "Object Table Function View."

```
SQL> CREATE OR REPLACE
  2    TYPE item_structure IS OBJECT
  3    ( id          NUMBER
  4    , lookup      VARCHAR2(30)
  5    , user_name   VARCHAR2(30));
  6  /
```

You may notice that the preceding statement creates an object type by breaking up the syntax to illustrate the SQL and PL/SQL elements. The `CREATE OR REPLACE` on line 1 and the / (forward slash) are SQL elements, and the definitions on lines 2 through 4 are PL/SQL elements. More or less, the only difference between a PL/SQL record and a SQL object is the choice of `OBJECT` as a keyword after `IS` on line 2. A PL/SQL record structure uses `IS RECORD`. The design calls for inserting the current `USER` value into the `user_name` column.

As shown in the preceding "Object Types" section, you can describe the object type like you would a table from the SQL*Plus command line. For example, the following describes the `item_structure` object:

```
SQL> DESCRIBE item_structure
 Name                          Null?    Type
 ----------------------------- -------- --------------
 ID                                     NUMBER
 LOOKUP                                 VARCHAR2(30)
 USER_NAME                              VARCHAR2(30)
```

Chapter 11 covers object types and bodies with methods, but here we'll leave it as simply a structure to hold data. After creating the object type, you can create a collection of the object type with the following syntax:

```
SQL> CREATE OR REPLACE
    TYPE item_lookup IS TABLE OF item_structure;
  /
```

Like the preceding example, the syntax to create a collection of the structure has SQL and PL/SQL elements. Lines 1 and 3 are the SQL elements, and line 2 is the PL/SQL object type structure. A structure like this without an object body has a default constructor, and it follows the pattern of a table for an `INSERT` statement. You insert elements (or, in OOPL lingo, *attributes*) in the same positional order in which you defined them when you created the structure, with one exception: PL/SQL supports named notation that lets you mix up the order because you're labeling the parameters as you go.

Likewise, you can describe the `item_lookup` collection UDT:

```
SQL> DESCRIBE item_lookup
 item_lookup TABLE OF ITEM_STRUCTURE
 Name                      Null?    Type
 ---------------------- -------- --------------
 ID                                 NUMBER
 LOOKUP                             VARCHAR2(30)
 USER_NAME                          VARCHAR2(30)
```

You should notice that a description of the UDT collection includes a line that identifies that it is a `TABLE OF` another UDT type. The balance of the SQL*Plus `DESCRIBE` statement displays the base `item_structure` UDT.

You can see examples of using a UDT collection as a nested table in the preceding "Nested Collection Types" section. The alternative approach uses the object table inside a PL/SQL block, as discussed in the earlier "Object Table Function View" section.

External Tables

Oracle lets you define externally organized tables. Externally organized tables appear like ordinary tables in the database but are structures that read-only or read and write files from the operating system. Read-only files can be comma-separated value (CSV), tab-separated value (TSV), or position-specific files. Read and write files are stored in an Oracle Data Pump proprietary format. However, both of these file types are known as *flat files*.

Feature or Fluke in Oracle Database 11*g*?

While it fails to appear anywhere in the documentation, Oracle Database 11*g* provides the ability to insert into a base object type when you define only a base object type specification and specializations that extend the attribute list of the base object type. This means you don't need to implement object type bodies to accomplish overloading of a column using the base type.

Oracle Database 12*c* removes that behavior, and any attempt to overload an object column without implementing object type bodies raises the following exception:

```
ERROR at line 1:
ORA-04067: not executed, type body "STUDENT.ITYPE" does not exist
ORA-06508: PL/SQL: could not find program unit being called: "STUDENT.ITYPE"
ORA-06512: at line 1
```

Oracle Database 12*c* does allow you to overload a column of a base object type when you've implement the object type bodies with proper constructors.

Oracle SQL*Loader lets you read these flat files with a `SELECT` statement from what appear as standard tables. Like Oracle SQL*Loader, Oracle Data Pump lets you read with a `SELECT` statement, but Oracle Data Pump also lets you write with an `INSERT` statement. The write creates a proprietary formatted file, and the read extracts the data from the file.

Two key preparation steps are required whether you're working with externally organized read-only or read-write files. These steps help you create virtual directories and grant database privileges to read from and write to them. The first subsection shows you those preparation steps, and the next two show you how to work with read-only and read-write files.

Virtual Directories Virtual directories are structures in the Oracle database, and they're stored in the data catalog. They map virtual directory names to physical operating system directories. Virtual directories make a few assumptions, which can become critical fail points. For the database grants to work successfully, the physical directories must be accessible to the operating system user who installed the Oracle Server. That means the operating system user should have read and write privileges to the related physical directories.

As the `sys`, `system`, or authorized CDB administrator account, you create a virtual directory with the following syntax:

```
SQL> CREATE DIRECTORY upload AS 'C:\Data\Upload';
```

After you create the virtual directory, you must grant permissions to read from and write to the directory. This is true whether you're deploying a read-only file or a read-write file because both types of files typically write error, discard, and log files to the same directory.

```
SQL> GRANT READ, WRITE ON DIRECTORY upload TO importer;
```

After creating a virtual directory, you find the mapping of virtual directories to operating system directories in the `DBA_DIRECTORIES` view. Only a `sys` or `system` superuser can gain access to this conceptual view. Unlike many other administrative views, there is no `USER_DIRECTORIES` view.

For reference, virtual directories are also used for `BFILE` data types. Web developers need to know the list of virtual directories and their physical directories. They need that information to ensure their programs place the uploaded files where they belong.

Oracle SQL*Loader Files After the preparation steps, you can define an externally organized table that uses a read-only file. Line 6 sets the `TYPE` value as Oracle SQL*Loader and line 7 sets the `DEFAULT DIRECTORY` as the virtual directory name you created previously:

```
SQL> CREATE TABLE CHARACTER
  2  ( character_id NUMBER
  3  , first_name VARCHAR2(20)
  4  , last_name VARCHAR2(20))
  5    ORGANIZATION EXTERNAL
  6    ( TYPE oracle_loader
  7      DEFAULT DIRECTORY upload
  8      ACCESS PARAMETERS
  9      ( RECORDS DELIMITED BY NEWLINE CHARACTERSET US7ASCII
 10        BADFILE     'UPLOAD':'character.bad'
 11        DISCARDFILE 'UPLOAD':'character.dis'
 12        LOGFILE     'UPLOAD':'character.log'
 13        FIELDS TERMINATED BY ','
```

```
 14        OPTIONALLY ENCLOSED BY "'"
 15        MISSING FIELD VALUES ARE NULL )
 16      LOCATION ('character.csv'))
 17  REJECT LIMIT UNLIMITED;
```

Lines 10 through 12 set the virtual directory and log files for any read from the externally organized table. Logs are written with each `SELECT` statement against the `character` table when data fails to conform to the definition. After the log file setup, the delimiters define how to read the data in the external file. Line 13 sets the delimiter, `FIELD TERMINATED BY`, as a comma. Line 14 sets the optional delimiter, `OPTIONALLY ENCLOSED BY`, as a single quote mark or apostrophe—this is important when you have a comma in a string.

The character file reads a file that follows this format:

```
1,'Indiana','Jones'
2,'Ravenwood','Marion'
3,'Marcus','Brody'
4,'Rene','Belloq'
```

Sometimes, you don't want to use CSV files because you've received position-specific files. That's the case frequently when the information comes from mainframe exports. You can create a position-specific table with the following syntax:

```
SQL> CREATE TABLE grocery
  2  ( grocery_id  NUMBER
  3  , item_name   VARCHAR2(20)
  4  , item_amount NUMBER(4,2))
  5    ORGANIZATION EXTERNAL
  6    ( TYPE oracle_loader
  7      DEFAULT DIRECTORY upload
  8      ACCESS PARAMETERS
  9      ( RECORDS DELIMITED BY NEWLINE CHARACTERSET US7ASCII
 10        BADFILE 'UPLOAD':'grocery.bad'
 11        LOGFILE 'UPLOAD':'grocery.log'
 12        FIELDS
 13        MISSING FIELD VALUES ARE NULL
 14        ( grocery_id  CHAR(3)
 15        , item_name   CHAR(20)
 16        , item_amount CHAR(4)))
 17      LOCATION ('grocery.csv'))
 18  REJECT LIMIT UNLIMITED;
```

The major difference between the CSV-enabled table and a positionally organized external table is the source signature on lines 14 through 16. The `CHAR` data type specifies fixed-length strings, which can be implicitly cast to number data types. When a `SELECT` statement reads the external source, it casts the values from fixed-length strings to their designated numeric and variable-length string data types.

An alternative position-specific syntax replaces lines 14 through 16 with exact positional references, like this:

```
 14        ( grocery_id  POSITION(1:3)
 15        , item_name   POSITION(4:23)
 16        , item_amount POSITION(24:27)))
```

The casting issue works the same way because `POSITION(1:3)` expects to find a fixed-length string. The value in the flat file can be cast successfully only when it is a number.

The `grocery` table reads values from a flat file, like this:

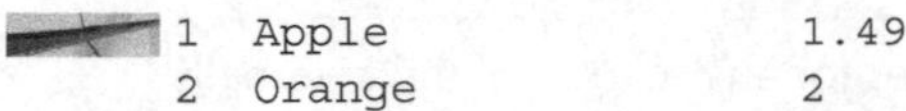

```
1  Apple                  1.49
2  Orange                 2
```

These are the preferred solutions when importing large amounts of data. Many data imports include values that belong in multiple tables. Import sources that include data for multiple tables are *composite* import files. Most import source files generally ignore or exclude surrogate key values because they'll change in the new database. Importing the data is important, but taking data from the externally managed table into the normalized business model can be tricky. The `MERGE` statement lets you import data, and, based on some logic, you can determine whether it's new or existing information. The `MERGE` statement then lets you insert new information or update rows of existing data.

Oracle Data Pump Files Oracle Data Pump lets you read and write data in a proprietary format. It is most often used for backup and recovery. You have import files for reading proprietary formatted files and export tables for saving data in a proprietary format.

The next example requires you to create a new `download` virtual directory and grant the directory read and write permissions. The following creates a table that exports data to an Oracle Data Pump–formatted file:

```
SQL> CREATE TABLE item_export
     ORGANIZATION EXTERNAL
     ( TYPE oracle_datapump
       DEFAULT DIRECTORY download
       LOCATION ('item_export.dmp')
     ) AS
     SELECT   item_id
     ,        item_barcode
     ,        item_type
     ,        item_title
     ,        item_subtitle
     ,        item_rating
     ,        item_rating_agency
     ,        item_release_date
     ,        created_by
     ,        creation_date
     ,        last_updated_by
     ,        last_update_date
     FROM   item;
```

The exporting process with externally organized tables has only one very noticeable problem, which is that it throws a nasty error when the file already exists, like so:

```
CREATE TABLE item_export
*
ERROR at line 1:
ORA-29913: error IN executing ODCIEXTTABLEOPEN callout
ORA-29400: DATA cartridge error
KUP-11012: file item_export.dmp IN C:\DATA\Download already EXISTS
```

My advice on this type of process is that you create an operating system script, a Java application, or a web solution that checks for the existence of the file before inserting data into the `item_export` table. Alternatively, you can create a set of utilities in Java libraries. You deploy the libraries inside the database and wrap them with PL/SQL function definitions. They can clean up the file system for you if you call them before you query the table.

NOTE
Java libraries work only in the Standard and Enterprise Editions of Oracle Database 12c.

Reversing the process and importing from the external file source isn't complex. There are a few modifications to the `CREATE TABLE` statement. Here's a sample:

```
SQL> CREATE TABLE item_import
( item_id              NUMBER
, item_barcode         VARCHAR2(20)
, item_type            NUMBER
, item_title           VARCHAR2(60)
, item_subtitle        VARCHAR2(60)
, item_rating          VARCHAR2(8)
, item_rating_agency   VARCHAR2(4)
, item_release_date    DATE
, created_by           NUMBER
, creation_date        DATE
, last_updated_by      NUMBER
, last_update_date     DATE)
ORGANIZATION EXTERNAL
( TYPE oracle_datapump
  DEFAULT DIRECTORY upload
  LOCATION ('item_export.dmp'));
```

Notice that the table definition mirrors the source file. This means you must know the source before you can define the external table `CREATE TABLE` statement.

Partitioned Tables

Partitioning is the process of breaking up a data source into a series of data sources. Partitioned tables are faster to access and transact against. Partitioning data becomes necessary as the amount of data grows in any table. It speeds the search to find rows and insert, update, or delete rows. Oracle Database 12*c* supports four types of table partitioning: list, range, hash, and composite partitioning.

List Partitioning A list partition works by identifying a column that contains a value, such as a `state` column in an `address` table. Partitioning clauses follow the list of columns and constraints.

A list partition could use a `state` column, like the following (the complete example is avoided to conserve space, and the three dots represent the balance of partitions not shown):

```
CREATE TABLE franchise
( franchise_id     NUMBER CONSTRAINT pk_franchise PRIMARY KEY
, franchise_name   VARCHAR(20)
, city             VARCHAR(20)
```

```
, state             VARCHAR(20))
PARTITION BY LIST(state)
( PARTITION offshore VALUES('Alaska', 'Hawaii')
, PARTITION west VALUES('California', 'Oregon', 'Washington')
, PARTITION desert VALUES ('Arizona','New Mexico')
, PARTITION rockies VALUES ('Colorado', 'Idaho', 'Montana', 'Wyoming')
, ... );
```

This can be used with other values such as ZIP codes with great effect, but the maintenance of list partitioning can be considered costly. Cost occurs when the list of values changes over time. Infrequent change means low cost, while frequent change means high cost. In the latter case, you should consider other partitioning strategies.

Range Partitioning Range partitioning is very helpful on any column that contains a continuous metric, such as dates or time. It works by stating a minimum set that is less than a certain value and then a group of sets of higher values until you reach the topmost set of values. This type of partition helps you improve performance by letting you search ranges rather than complete data sets.

A range example based on dates could look like this:

```
PARTITION BY RANGE(rental_date)
( PARTITION rental_jan2011
  VALUES LESS THAN TO_DATE('31-JAN-11','DD-MON-YY')
, PARTITION rental_feb2011
  VALUES LESS THAN TO_DATE('28-FEB-11','DD-MON-YY')
, PARTITION rental_mar2011
  VALUES LESS THAN TO_DATE('31-MAR-11','DD-MON-YY')
, ... );
```

The problem with this type of partitioning, however, is that the new months require constant management. Many North American businesses simply add partitions for all months in the year as an annual maintenance task during the holidays in November or December. Companies that opt for bigger range increments reap search and access benefits from range partitioning while minimizing ongoing maintenance expenses.

Hash Partitioning Hash partitioning is much easier to implement than list or range partitioning. Many DBAs favor it because it avoids the manual maintenance of list and range partitioning. Oracle Database 12*c* documentation recommends that you implement a hash for the following reasons:

- There is no concrete knowledge about how much data maps to a partitioning range.
- The sizes of partitions are unknown at the outset and difficult to balance as data is added to the database.
- A range partition might cluster data in an ineffective way.

This next statement creates eight partitions and stores them respectively in one of the eight tablespaces. The hash partition manages nodes and attempts to balance the distribution of rows across the rows.

```
PARTITION BY HASH(store)
PARTITIONS 8
STORE IN (tablespace1, tablespace2, tablespace3, tablespace4
         ,tablespace5, tablespace6, tablespace7, tablespace8);
```

As you can imagine, the maintenance for this type of partitioning is low. Some DBAs choose this method to get an initial sizing before adopting a list or range partitioning plan. Other DBAs report that partition pruning doesn't work as well with hash partitioning as it does with range partitioning, and they point to Oracle's cost-based optimizer (CBO) opting for full table scans when using hash partitioning.

Maximizing the physical resources of the machine ultimately rests with the DBAs who manage the system. Developers need to stand ready to assist DBAs with analysis and syntax support.

Composite Partitioning Composite partitioning requires a partition and subpartition. The composites are combinations of two types of partitioning—typically, list and range composite partitioning, or range and hash composite partitioning. Which of these you should choose depends on a few considerations. List and range composite partitioning is done for historical information and is well suited for data warehouses. This method lets you partition on unordered or unrelated column values.

A composite partition like this uses the range as the partition and the list as the subpartition, like the following:

```
PARTITION BY RANGE (rental_date)
 SUBPARTITION BY LIST (state)
 (PARTITION FQ1_1999 VALUES LESS THAN (TO_DATE('1-APR-2011','DD-MON-YYYY'))
  (SUBPARTITION offshore VALUES('Alaska', 'Hawaii')
  , SUBPARTITION west VALUES('California', 'Oregon', 'Washington')
  , SUBPARTITION desert VALUES ('Arizona','New Mexico')
  , SUBPARTITION rockies VALUES ('Colorado', 'Idaho', 'Montana', 'Wyoming')
  , ... )
,(PARTITION FQ2_1999 VALUES LESS THAN (TO_DATE('1-APR-2011','DD-MON-YYYY'))
  (SUBPARTITION offshore VALUES('Alaska', 'Hawaii')
  , SUBPARTITION west VALUES('California', 'Oregon', 'Washington')
  , SUBPARTITION desert VALUES ('Arizona','New Mexico')
  , SUBPARTITION rockies VALUES ('Colorado', 'Idaho', 'Montana', 'Wyoming')
  , ... )
, ... )
```

Range and hash composite partitioning is done for historical information when you also need to stripe data. *Striping* is the process of creating an attribute in a table that acts as a natural subtype or separator of data. Users typically view data sets of one subtype, which means organizing the data by stripes (subtypes) can speed access based on user access patterns.

A composite partition like this typically uses the range as the partition and the hash as the subpartition. The syntax for this type of partition is shown next:

```
PARTITION BY RANGE (rental_date)
 SUBPARTITION BY HASH(store)
  SUBPARTITIONS 8 STORE IN (tablespace1, tablespace2, tablespace3
                           ,tablespace4, tablespace5, tablespace6
                           ,tablespace7, tablespace8)
   ( PARTITION rental_jan2011
     VALUES LESS THAN TO_DATE('31-JAN-11','DD-MON-YY')
   , PARTITION rental_feb2011
     VALUES LESS THAN TO_DATE('28-FEB-11','DD-MON-YY')
   , PARTITION rental_mar2011
     VALUES LESS THAN TO_DATE('31-MAR-11','DD-MON-YY')
   , ... )
```

NOTE
Developers need to understand techniques, but DBAs often have major decision-making authority in partitioning. Partitioning effectively requires an understanding of the underlying choices made by DBAs in organizing the database.

Synonyms

Oracle supports the concept of a *synonym*, which simplifies how another user can access your objects after you've granted them privileges to select, insert, update, or delete data in a table, or to execute a stored program unit—function, procedure, package, or object type. Without a synonym, the other user would need to put your user name and a dot (`.`) in front of the object before accessing it. The dot is called a *component selector*. A synonym creates an alias that maps the user name, component selector, and object name to a synonym (alias) name in the user's work area or schema.

You don't need to use a component selector on objects that you create in your schema. They're natively available to you. The `sys` superuser has access to every object in the Oracle Database 12*c* Server by simply addressing objects by their fully qualified location—schema name, component selector, and object name. This makes perfect sense when you recall that the user and schema names are synonymous.

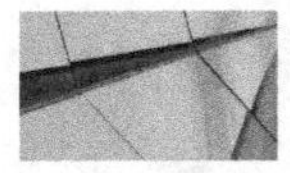

NOTE
*The Oracle Database 12*c *`SYS` user's visibility to columns within tables can be restricted by redacting access with the `dbms_redact` built-in package.*

You create a synonym like this:

```
CREATE SYNONYM some_tablename FOR some_user.some_tablename;
```

Typically, the local table name is the same as the table name in the other schema, but not always. You can also grant privileges on a table to a `PUBLIC` account in a CDB, which gives all other users access to the table. Public synonyms also exist to simplify how those users access the table. Alternatively, you can grant privileges on a table to a `PUBLIC` account in a PDB, which limits access to only the pluggable database.

NOTE
You can also restrict synonyms by designating them as `EDITIONABLE` or `NONEDITIONABLE` when you're using edition-based redefinition (EBR).

You would grant the `SELECT` privilege to the `PUBLIC` account with this syntax:

```
GRANT SELECT ON some_tablename TO PUBLIC;
```

After granting the privilege, you create a public synonym with this syntax:

```
CREATE PUBLIC SYNONYM some_tablename FOR some_user.some_tablename;
```

As a rule of thumb, use the PUBLIC account only when you're granting privileges to invoker rights stored programs. Appendix A shows you how to define and implement stored programs that run under definer or invoker rights models using synonyms.

ALTER Statement

This section focuses on how you can use the ALTER statement to change users, databases, tables, and indexes you've created in the database, and it explores how you can change your session to meet your needs in Oracle. The section is organized by the following topics:

- Users
- Tables
- Indexes
- Object Types

As explained earlier, users are synonymous with schemas in an Oracle database. Databases are private work areas, and changes to them remain until you remove or change a database again. Connections to your database management system are *sessions*, and a session lasts only for the duration of your connection to a database or schema. Any changes to a session are lost when you break the connection by logging out or by connecting as another user to another database. Tables are permanent structures unless you define them as temporary tables. Changes made to tables, like databases, last until you drop the table, undo the changes, or make new changes. As with tables, indexes exist as long as the table they reference exists, unless you drop or alter the table. Although users can modify index structures, content changes in the index occur only through changes in the referenced tables.

NOTE
User accounts don't technically own a schema until they've been granted a quota and the privilege to create tables.

The following sections discuss how you can the Oracle ALTER statement to alter users, tables, indexes, and object types. You'll learn what a developer needs to know to work with these structures in Oracle. You won't find an exhaustive listing of all the things you can do with or to databases, because entire books are written on that, but I've tried to give you the basics to effectively use the ALTER statement in an Oracle database.

Users

The user and schema are inseparable in an Oracle DBMS. They share the same names, and the user generally holds all definer privileges on the schema. That means you must change a user to change a schema or database. Commands that change the database are actually changing accounts on the Oracle server.

Oracle users typically don't have privileges that let them change their user or schema properties unless they've been granted superuser privileges. That means commands that change users or schemas are run typically by the system user. Dropping a user is a rare occasion in most Oracle databases, but changing properties of the user occurs routinely.

The prototype for the ALTER USER statement lets you change properties of a user, such as their role, profile, storage, password, and account status. The generic prototype for the ALTER USER statement is shown here:

```
ALTER USER user_name
[IDENTIFIED
{[BY current_password REPLACE new_password] |
 [EXTERNALLY AS 'certificate_name'] |
 [GLOBALLY AS 'directory_name']]}
[DEFAULT TABLESPACE tablespace_name]
[TEMPORARY TABLESPACE {tablespace_name | tablespace_group }]
[QUOTA {size_clause | UNLIMITED} ON tablespace_name]
[PROFILE profile_name]
[DEFAULT ROLE {role_name | ALL EXCEPT role_name | NONE}]
[PASSWORD EXPIRE]
[ACCOUNT {LOCK | UNLOCK}]
[{GRANT | REVOKE} CONNECT THROUGH
 {ENTERPRISE USERS |
  WITH {ROLE {role_name | ALL EXCEPT role_name} |
        NO ROLES} [AUTHENTICATION REQUIRED]}]
```

Using the ALTER USER statement, you can configure one of three different authentication types for a user: password, Secure Sockets Layer (SSL) certificate, and Lightweight Directory Access Protocol (LDAP) certificate. You also have the security options to expire a password (useful when terminating employees) and locking an account.

The other clauses let you change default or temporary tablespaces, or a quota, profile, role, or pass-through authentication, none of which occurs frequently. These changes are also seldom made by developers because doing so is the DBA's responsibility.

If a user loses a password, you could change a container database (CDB) user's password like this:

```
ALTER USER student IDENTIFIED BY P0lici3s;
```

Then you'd need to let the user know the new password and hope somebody doesn't crack it before the user logs in to change it.

Better yet, you can go one more step by expiring the password after changing it. An expired password prompts the user for a new password when he or she logs in. You expire a password like this:

```
ALTER USER student PASSWORD EXPIRE;
```

The user would try to connect like this,

```
sqlplus student/P0lici3s
```

and would then see the following messages and prompts at the command-line interface to SQL*Plus, where the user would enter a new password:

```
C:\data\oracle>sqlplus student/P0lici3s
SQL*Plus: Release 12.1.0.0.2 Beta on Tue Mar 19 22:38:33 2013
Copyright (c) 1982, 2012, Oracle.  All rights reserved.
Last Successful login time: Sun Mar 17 2013 00:01:54 -06:00
```

```
Connected to:
Oracle Database 12c Enterprise Edition Release 12.1.0.0.2 - 64bit Beta
With the Partitioning, OLAP, Advanced Analytics and Real Application Testing
ERROR:
ORA-28001: the password has expired

Changing password for P0lici3s
New password:
Retype new password:
Password changed
```

Assuming you've configured the database to use LDAP authentication and provided a wallet, you can also change a login to an LDAP validation, like this:

```
ALTER USER student IDENTIFIED GLOBALLY AS 'CN=miles,O=apple,C=US'
```

A user can change his/her password with the `ALTER USER` statement. The following syntax requires that the user know his/her current password:

```
ALTER USER student IDENTIFIED BY P0lici3s REPLACE Beatles1964;
```

The only problem with the preceding syntax is that it discloses the user's new password in plain text. Unfortunately, there's no way around that syntax limitation. More often than not, individual users remember their passwords and can change it like this:

```
SQL> password
Changing password for STUDENT
Old password:
New password:
Retype new password:
Password changed
```

The reason changes of tablespaces, roles, and profiles aren't done by developers is that they are managed by the superuser accounts. These superuser accounts are owned by DBAs who administer the physical resources of the database. Developers work closely with the system administrators to ensure that adequate disk space and processing resources are available for the database on any server.

A key DBA activity that you should know how to perform while working in your laptop development databases is locking and unlocking accounts, such as the oe sample or the legacy `scott` schemas. You would unlock the oe schema with this syntax:

```
ALTER USER student ACCOUNT UNLOCK;
```

Alternatively, you can open an account and change the password with a single command like this:

```
ALTER USER student ACCOUNT UNLOCK IDENTIFIED BY Backl0gs;
```

After you're done with a sample schema like these, you can lock them away by typing this:

```
ALTER USER student ACCOUNT LOCK;
```

You should never leave user schemas open (unlocked) when you're not actively using them. It's simply a best practice to lock unused schemas that you might need to reopen and likewise to drop obsolete schemas.

Tables

Table definitions and constraints change over time for many reasons. These changes occur because developers discover more information about the business model, which requires changes to table definitions. This section examines how you can add, modify, and remove columns or constraints; rename tables, columns, or constraints; and drop tables.

First, however, you need to understand how table definitions are stored in the data catalogs. When you understand the rules of these structures and how they're stored, you can appreciate why SQL is able to let you change so much, so easily.

Data Catalog Table Definitions The data catalog stores everything by the numbers, which happens to be through surrogate primary keys. The database also maintains a unique index on object names, which means that you can use a name only once per schema in an Oracle database. This list of unique values is known as the schema's *namespace*.

As discussed, Oracle maintains the data catalog in the `sys` schema and provides access to administrative views, which are prefaced by `CDB_`, `DBA_`, `ALL_`, and `USER_`. The `USER_` prefix is available to every schema for objects that a user owns. The `CDB_` prefix is for the new container database views. The `ALL_` and `DBA_` prefixes give you access to objects owned by others, and only superusers or administrative users have access privileges to these views.

Many developer tools can easily display information from the data catalog views, such as Oracle SQL Developer, Quest's Toad for Oracle, or Oracle CASE tools. Sometimes you need to explore a database for specific information, and the fastest way would be to launch a few quick queries against the data catalog. The catalog view that lets you explore column definitions, including for invisible columns, is the `USER_TAB_COLUMNS` view. The catalog view that lets you explore column definitions only for visible columns is the `USER_TAB_COLS` view. Another catalog `USER_TAB_COLS` view lets you explore only visible columns (short for table's columns).

The following query leverages some SQL*Plus formatting to let you find the definition of a specific table and display it in a single-page format:

```
SQL> COLUMN column_id FORMAT 999 HEADING "Column|ID #"
SQL> COLUMN table_name FORMAT A12 HEADING "Table Name"
SQL> COLUMN column_name FORMAT A18 HEADING "Column Name"
SQL> COLUMN data_type FORMAT A10 HEADING "Data Type"
SQL> COLUMN csize FORMAT 999 HEADING "Column|Size"
SQL> SELECT   utc.column_id
  2  ,        utc.table_name
  3  ,        utc.column_name
  4  ,        utc.data_type
  5  ,        NVL(utc.data_length,utc.data_precision) AS csize
  6  FROM     user_tab_columns utc
  7  WHERE    utc.table_name = 'CONTACT';
```

The table name is in uppercase because Oracle maintains metadata text in an uppercase string. You could replace line 7 with the following line that uses the `UPPER` function to promote the text case before comparison, if you prefer to type table names and other metadata values in lowercase or mixed case:

```
  7  WHERE    utc.table_name = UPPER('contact');
```

It displays the following:

```
Column                                                 Column
  ID # Table Name   Column Name        Data Type    Size
------ ------------ ------------------ ---------- ------
     1 CONTACT      CONTACT_ID         NUMBER         22
     2 CONTACT      MEMBER_ID          NUMBER         22
     3 CONTACT      CONTACT_TYPE       NUMBER         22
     4 CONTACT      FIRST_NAME         VARCHAR2       20
     5 CONTACT      MIDDLE_NAME        VARCHAR2       20
     6 CONTACT      LAST_NAME          VARCHAR2       20
     7 CONTACT      CREATED_BY         NUMBER         22
     8 CONTACT      CREATION_DATE      DATE            7
     9 CONTACT      LAST_UPDATED_BY    NUMBER         22
    10 CONTACT      LAST_UPDATE_DATE   DATE            7
```

The `column_id` value identifies the position of columns for `INSERT` statements. The ordered list is set when you define a table with the `CREATE TABLE` statement or is reset when you modify it with an `ALTER TABLE` statement. Columns keep the position location when you change the columns' name or data type. Columns lose their position when you remove them from a table's definition, and when you add them back, they appear at the end of the positional list of values. There's no way to shift their position in an Oracle database without dropping and re-creating the table.

Each column has a data type that defines its physical size. The foregoing example shows that `NUMBER` data types take up to 22 characters, the strings take 20 characters, and the dates take 7 characters. As you learned in Chapter 4, numbers can also have a specification (the values to the right of the decimal point) that fits within the maximum length (or precision) of the data type.

The `USER_CONSTRAINTS` and `USER_CONS_COLUMNS` views hold information about constraints. The `USER_CONSTRAINTS` view holds the descriptive information about the type of constraint, and the `USER_CONS_COLUMNS` view holds the list of columns participating in the constraint.

You would use a query like this to discover constraints and columns (formatting provided by the SQL*Plus commands):

```
SQL> COLUMN table_name FORMAT A12 HEADING "Table Name"
SQL> COLUMN constraint_name FORMAT A16 HEADING "Constraint|Name"
SQL> COLUMN position FORMAT A8 HEADING "Position"
SQL> COLUMN column_name FORMAT A18 HEADING "Column Name"
SQL> SELECT   ucc.table_name
     ,        ucc.constraint_name
     ,        uc.constraint_type ||':'|| ucc.position AS position
     ,        ucc.column_name
     FROM     user_constraints uc JOIN user_cons_columns ucc
     ON       uc.table_name = ucc.table_name
     AND      uc.constraint_name = ucc.constraint_name
     WHERE    ucc.table_name = 'CONTACT'
     ORDER BY ucc.constraint_name
     ,        ucc.position;
```

It would produce the following output:

```
                 Constraint
Table Name       Name                 Position Column Name
---------------- -------------------- -------- ------------------
CONTACT          PK_CONTACT_1         P:1      CONTACT_ID
CONTACT          UNIQUE_NAME          U:1      MEMBER_ID
CONTACT          UNIQUE_NAME          U:2      FIRST_NAME
CONTACT          UNIQUE_NAME          U:3      MIDDLE_NAME
CONTACT          UNIQUE_NAME          U:4      LAST_NAME
```

The first line of output reports a single-column primary key, which is most often a surrogate primary key. You can tell that because a `constraint_type` column value represents the code for a primary key constraint, as qualified in Table B-5. In the query, the position column is the concatenated result of the constraint type code and position number related to the column name. The remaining lines report a unique constraint that spans four columns, which is the natural key for the table. It's an imperfect third-normal form (3NF) key for the subject of the table, but it's an adequate natural key for our demonstration purposes.

The material in this section has described how you find definitions for tables and constraints. You'll find this information helpful when you need to change definitions or remove them from tables.

Adding, Modifying, and Dropping Columns Database tables should be designed to hold a single subject, and when they hold a single subject, they help you normalize information that supports business, research, or engineering processes. In the real world, requirements change, and eventually modifying a table becomes necessary. Some of these changes are relatively trivial, such as changing a column name or data type. Some changes are less trivial, such as when some descriptive item (column) is overlooked, a column isn't large enough to hold a large number or string, or a column of data needs to be renamed or moved to another column. You can make any of these changes using the `ALTER TABLE` statement.

More involved changes occur in three situations:

- When you must change a column's data type when it contains rows of data
- When you rename a column when existing SQL statements already use the older column
- When you shift the position of adjoining columns that share the same data type

Constraint Code	Constraint Meaning
`C`	Represents a check or not null constraint
`P`	Represents a primary key constraint
`R`	Represents a foreign key, which is really referential integrity between tables and is why an `R` is the code value
`U`	Represents a unique constraint

TABLE B-5. *Constraint Codes and Types*

When you need to change the data type of a column that contains data, you need to develop a data migration plan. Small-scale data migration might entail adding a new column, moving the contents from one column to the other, and then dropping the original column. Unless the database supports an implicit casting operation from the current to future data type, you will need a SQL statement to change the data type explicitly and put it into the new column.

Changing the name of a column in a table seems a trifling thing, but it's not insignificant when application software uses that column name in SQL statements. Any change to the column name will break the application software. You need to identify all dependent code artifacts and ensure that they're changed at the same time you make the changes to the column in the table. A full regression-testing plan needs to occur when columns are renamed in tables that support working application software. You can start by querying the ALL_, DBA_, or USER_DEPENDENCIES views that preserve dependencies about tables and stored program units.

Shifting the position of columns can have two different types of impacts. One potential impact is that you break INSERT statements that don't use a column list before the VALUES clause or subquery. This happens when the columns have different data types, because the INSERT statements will fail and raise errors. The other potential impact is much worse, because it produces corrupt data. This happens when you change the position of two columns that share the same data type. The change doesn't break INSERT statements in an easily detectable way, as did the other scenario, because it simply inverts the data into the wrong columns. The fix is the same as when you change the positions of columns that have different data types, but the fix depends on when you notice the problem and how much corrupt data you need to sanitize (fix).

Release Engineering

Release engineering is a component of software engineering, and it focuses on how you plan and control the creation and evolution of software—in other words, how you set, enforce, evaluate, and manage software standards. The more time you take to avoid problems, the less time you'll spend fixing them.

During the course of normal product release cycles, release engineers manage multiple code branches and dependency trees. Good release engineers invest proactively in software configuration management, because they know it helps identify where problems exist. In a proactive model, you examine process and software dependencies to identify and manage risk exposure. You take corrective action before the event occurs in this approach, which requires you to set and enforce standards that prevent errors.

For example, in a database-centric application, you would check the impact of table definition changes before making them. That's because those types of changes can destabilize your application software. You flag all code modules that depend on existing table and view definitions so you can have them changed concurrently as part of the project. Identifying errors before regression testing by quality and assurance teams is less expensive.

This type of good release engineering requires a code repository that tracks dependencies and prevents check-ins that would break other code modules. You need to understand the dependencies in your software process to create an effective process, and you need process automation to manage it. Like any good application that prevents a user from entering garbage data, release management should prevent dependency invalidation. Sometimes this means disallowing changes until you understand their full impacts.

These risks should be managed by your company's release engineering team and should be subject to careful software configuration management of your code repository. You can leverage the CDB_, ALL_, DBA_, and USER_DEPENDENCIES views to check on dependencies in your software.

The prototypes discussed in the next two sections qualify how you make these types of changes in Oracle Database 12*c*.

Column Maintenance The ALTER TABLE statement allows you to add columns or constraints, to modify properties of columns and constraints, and to drop columns or constraints. A number of DBA-type properties are excluded from the ALTER TABLE prototype, and the focus here is on those features that support relational tables.

Here's the basic prototype for the ALTER TABLE statement:

```
ALTER TABLE [schema_name.]table_name
[RENAME TO new_table_name]
[READ ONLY]
[READ WRITE]
[{NO PARALLEL | PARALLEL n}]
[ADD
  ({column_name data_type [SORT] [DEFAULT value] [ENCRYPT key] |
    virtual_column_name} data_type [GENERATED] [ALWAYS] AS (expression)}
  ,{column_name data_type [SORT] [DEFAULT value] [ENCRYPT key] |
    virtual_column_name} data_type [GENERATED] [ALWAYS] AS (expression)}
 [, ...])]
[MODIFY
  ({column_name data_type [SORT] [DEFAULT value] [ENCRYPT key] |
    virtual_column_name} data_type [GENERATED] [ALWAYS] AS (expression)}
  ,{column_name data_type [SORT] [DEFAULT value] [ENCRYPT key] |
    virtual_column_name} data_type [GENERATED] [ALWAYS] AS (expression)}
 [, ...])]
[DROP
  (column_name {CASCADE CONSTRAINTS | INVALIDATE} [CHECKPOINT n]
  ,column_name {CASCADE CONSTRAINTS | INVALIDATE} [CHECKPOINT n]
 [, ...])]
[ADD [CONSTRAINT constraint_name]
  {PRIMARY KEY (column_name [,column_name [, ...]) |
   UNIQUE (column_name [,column_name [, ...]) |
   CHECK (check_condition) |
   FOREIGN KEY (column_name [,column_name [, ...])
   REFERENCES table_name (column_name [,column_name [, ...])}]
[MODIFY data_type [SORT] [DEFAULT value] [ENCRYPT key] |
    virtual_column_name} data_type [GENERATED] [ALWAYS] AS (expression)}
 [, ...])]
[RENAME COLUMN old_column_name TO new_column_name]
[RENAME CONSTRAINT old_constraint_name TO new_constraint_name]
```

The following sections provide working examples that add, modify, rename, and drop columns and constraints. Notice that you don't add a not null constraint to a column, but you modify the property of an existing column.

Adding Columns and Constraints—This section shows you how to add columns and constraints. It also provides some guidance on when you can constrain a column as not null.

Here's how you add a new column to a table:

```
SQL> ALTER TABLE rental_item
  2    ADD (rental_item_price  NUMBER);
```

If the table contains no data, you could also add the column with a not null constraint, like this:

```
SQL> ALTER TABLE rental_item ADD
  2    (rental_item_price  NUMBER CONSTRAINT nn1_rental_item NOT NULL );
```

Adding a column with a not null constraint fails when rows are included in the table because when you add the column, its values are empty in all the table rows. The attempt would raise the following error message:

```
ALTER TABLE rental_item
            *
ERROR at line 1:
ORA-01758: table must be empty to add mandatory (NOT NULL) column
```

You can disable the constraint until you've entered any missing values and then you can re-enable the constraint. After you've added values to all rows of a nullable column, you can constrain the column to disallow null values. The syntax requires you to modify the column, like so:

```
SQL> ALTER TABLE rental_item MODIFY
  2   (rental_item_price  NUMBER CONSTRAINT nn1_rental_item NOT NULL );
```

You can also add more than one column at a time with the `ALTER TABLE` statement. The following would add two columns:

```
SQL> ALTER TABLE rental_item
  2    ADD (rental_item_price  NUMBER)
  3    ADD (rental_item_type   NUMBER);
```

Notice that no comma appears between the two `ADD` clauses.

That's it for columns. Now you'll see how to add the four constraints that work with the `ADD` clause: primay key, check, not null, unique, and foreign key. Note that you can raise errors with these statements when you already have data in a table and it fails to meet the rule of the constraint.

All the following examples work when tables are empty or conform to the constraint rules. After all, what would be the point of a database constraint that didn't constrain behaviors?

This example adds a primary key constraint to a surrogate key column. A primary key in this case restricts a single column's behavior. Here's the syntax:

```
SQL> ALTER TABLE calendar
  2    ADD PRIMARY KEY (calendar_id);
```

The alternative would be to add a primary key constraint on the natural key columns, like this:

```
SQL> ALTER TABLE calendar
  2    ADD PRIMARY KEY (month_name, start_date, end_date);
```

The check constraint is very powerful in Oracle, because it lets you enforce a single rule or a complex set of rules. In the following example, you add the column and then an out-of-line constraint on the new column:

```
SQL> ALTER TABLE calendar
      ADD (month_type VARCHAR2(1))
      ADD CONSTRAINT ck_month_type
      CHECK(month_type = 'S' AND month_shortname = 'FEB'
        OR  month_type = 'M' AND month_shortname IN ('APR','JUN','SEP')
        OR  month_type = 'L')
```

The check constraint verifies that a `month_type` value must correspond to a combination of its value and the value of the `month_shortname` column. Any month with less than 30 days holds an `S` (short), with 30 days holds an `M` (medium), and with 31 days holds an `L` (long).

The following unique constraint guarantees that no `start_date` and `end_date` combination can exist twice in a calendar table:

```
SQL> ALTER TABLE calendar
      ADD CONSTRAINT un_california UNIQUE (start_date, end_date);
```

A foreign key constraint works with surrogate or natural keys by referencing the table and column or columns that are in its primary key. The next example sets the two foreign keys in a translation table between the `rental` and `item` tables:

```
SQL> ALTER TABLE rental_item
      ADD CONSTRAINT fk_rental_id_1
          FOREIGN KEY (rental_id) REFERENCES rentals (rental_id)
      ADD CONSTRAINT fk_rental_id_2
          FOREIGN KEY (item_id) REFERENCES items (item_id);
```

The next example sets a foreign key on the natural key of the `contact` table, as shown earlier in this chapter. Foreign keys composed of more than one column are composite foreign keys (outside of Oracle documentation, these may also be labeled as compound keys). This references three natural columns and one foreign key column:

```
SQL> ALTER TABLE delegate
  ADD CONSTRAINT fk_natural_contact
      FOREIGN KEY ( member_id, first_name, middle_name, last_name )
      REFERENCES contact (member_id, first_name, middle_name, last_name);
```

NOTE

*Composite foreign keys are limited to no more than 32 columns in Oracle Database 12*c.

The key concept is that you can add both column- and table-level (that is, multiple column) constraints with the `ALTER TABLE` statement. As shown, you can also add the column and then the constraint that goes with it.

Modifying Columns and Constraints Oracle lets you change column names, data types, and constraints with the ALTER TABLE statement. Although column names and data types change routinely during major software upgrades, these changes can and do cause problems because existing code can depend on the type or names of columns and encounter failures when they change unexpectedly.

The following examples demonstrate what you're likely to encounter when working with modifying tables. The first example lets you change the name of a column:

```
SQL> ALTER TABLE calendar
  2     RENAME COLUMN calendar_name TO full_month_name;
```

It's also possible to make more than one change with a single ALTER statement, like

```
SQL> ALTER TABLE calendar
  2  ADD (month_name  VARCHAR2(9))
  3  ADD (short_name  VARCHAR2(3) CONSTRAINT calendar_nn1 NOT NULL);
```

The ALTER statement supports a superuser, or a common user who has been granted the ALTER ANY TABLE privilege to change the column name of another schema's table to change the column name of another schema's table when they have the ALTER ANY TABLE privilege. While you can make multiple changes to columns in a single ALTER statement, there's an exception to that rule when renaming multiple columns.

If you wanted to change the names of two or more columns in one ALTER STATEMENT, you would try something like this:

```
SQL> ALTER TABLE calendar
  2     RENAME COLUMN calendar_name TO full_month_name
  3     RENAME COLUMN calendar_short_name TO short_month_name;
```

but that would fail and raise an ORA-23290 error:

```
ALTER TABLE calendar
*
ERROR at line 1:
ORA-23290: This operation may not be combined with any other operation
```

The failure occurs because you can't combine a RENAME clause with any other clause in an ALTER TABLE statement. It's simply disallowed, with no further elaboration provided in the *Oracle Database Administrator's Guide 12*c *Release*.

Data type changes are straightforward when the table contains no data, but you can't change the type when data exists in the column. A quick example attempts to change a start_date column using a DATE data type to using a VARCHAR2 data type. The following syntax works when no data is included in the column but fails when data exists:

```
SQL> ALTER TABLE calendar
  2  MODIFY (start_date VARCHAR2(9));
```

With data in the column, it raises this error message:

```
MODIFY (start_date VARCHAR2(9))
        *
ERROR at line 2:
ORA-01439: column to be modified must be empty to change datatype
```

You would add a not null constraint to the `start_date` column with the following DML statement:

```
SQL> ALTER TABLE calendar
  2  MODIFY (start_date DATE NOT NULL );
```

The only problem with the foregoing statement is that it creates a not null constraint with a system-generated name. The best practice would assign the constraint a name, like so:

```
SQL> ALTER TABLE calendar
  2  MODIFY (start_date DATE CONSTRAINT nn_calendar_1 NOT NULL);
```

Now you know how to rename columns and change column data types. The next section shows you how to drop columns and constraints.

Dropping Columns and Constraints You drop columns from tables rarely, but the syntax is easy. You would drop the following `short_month_name` column from the `calendar` table with this:

```
SQL> ALTER TABLE calendar
  2  DROP COLUMN short_month_name;
```

You would encounter a problem dropping a column when the column is involved in a table constraint (a constraint across two or more columns). For example, attempting to drop a `middle_name` column from the `contact` table fails when the columns referenced by a multiple-column unique constraint. The statement would look like this:

```
SQL> ALTER TABLE contact
  2  DROP COLUMN middle_name;
```

It would raise the following error message:

```
DROP COLUMN middle_name
            *
ERROR at line 2:
ORA-12991: column is referenced in a multi-column constraint
```

Oracle Database 12*c* and its predecessors disallow you from dropping a column that's a member of a multiple-column unique constraint. You must drop the constraint before you drop the column and then create a new unique constraint across any remaining columns.

NOTE
Dropping columns when the table contains data can fragment the storage in physical files.

Dropping constraints is easy, because all you need to know is a constraint's name. The following drops the `unique_name` constraint from the `contact` table:

```
SQL> ALTER TABLE contact
  2  DROP CONSTRAINT unique_name;
```

This concludes the discussion about adding, modifying, and dropping columns and constraints in an Oracle database.

Indexes

Indexes are structures that hold search trees that help SQL statements find rows of interest faster. These search trees can be balanced trees (B-trees), hash maps, and other mapping data structures.

The following are some of the major reasons for fixing indexes in Oracle, all of which you perform with an `ALTER` statement:

- Rebuilding or coalescing an existing index
- Deallocating unused space or allocating new space
- Enabling and specifying the degree of parallelism for storing the index
- Changing storage parameters to improve index performance
- Enabling or disabling logging
- Enabling or disabling key compression
- Marking the index as unusable
- Making the index invisible
- Renaming the index
- Starting or stopping index usage monitoring

The next subsections review some basics of using indexes from a developer's perspective. Clearly, storage and parallel optimization belong to the DBAs, because they know the critical resources of CPUs, memory, and disk space.

Prototype and Usage of Indexes The Oracle `ALTER INDEX` statement lets you manage indexes, and the `DROP INDEX` statement lets you remove indexes. You can also use the `ALTER TABLE` statement to enable primary key column(s) to use indexes.

The prototype for the `ALTER INDEX` statement, minus the DBA options, is shown here:

```
ALTER INDEX [schema_name.]index_name [COMPILE] |
[{ENABLE | DISABLE}] |
[UNUSABLE] |
[REBUILD [{PARTITION partition_clause |
           SUBPARTITION subpartition_clause |
           [{REVERSE | NOREVERSE}]}] |
[{VISIBLE | INVISIBLE}] |
[RENAME TO new_index_name] |
[COALESCE] |
[{MONITORING | NOMONITORING} USAGE] |
```

The first thing developers want to do when they've discovered poor throughput in a query is disable the index to see what impact it has on their code. I'll show you how to do that, but it's generally better done by modifying the query so that it doesn't run the index by concatenating an empty string to a string or by adding a 0 to a number or date.

Enable and Disable Indexes You can enable an index as follows when necessary:

```
ALTER INDEX nk_rental_item ENABLE;
```

Or you can disable it:

```
ALTER INDEX nk_rental_item DISABLE;
```

Sometimes you want to mark an index to rebuild it. You do that with the `UNUSABLE` keyword:

```
ALTER INDEX nk_rental_item UNUSABLE;
```

Rebuild and Coalesce Indexes You can rebuild an index, provided it isn't partitioned, with this:

```
ALTER INDEX nk_rental_item REBUILD;
```

If you don't have the space to rebuild an index online, you can try offline rebuilding, or *coalescing* the index. Coalescing is like defragmenting a disk. When you coalesce an index, it reorganizes the data and maintains fully free blocks, which eliminates the cost of releasing and reallocating blocks. Many DBAs choose to coalesce indexes because of the speed, absence of locking, and minimal incremental disk space requirements.

This syntax coalesces an index:

```
ALTER INDEX nk_rental_item COALESCE;
```

Visible and Invisible Indexes The idea of visibility or invisibility might seem odd, but the `VISIBLE` and `INVISIBLE` keywords make an index visible or invisible to the cost-based optimizer for queries. DML statements, such as `INSERT`, `UPDATE`, and `DELETE` statements, maintain an invisible index, but queries don't use it. As a rule, from Oracle Database 11*g* forward, you want the optimizer to see indexes. You can discover whether an index is invisible by checking the `visibility` column in the `ALL_`, `DBA_`, or `USER_INDEXES` view.

TIP
Setting an index to `INVISIBLE` is without merit when the DBA has set the `OPTIMIZER_USE_INVISIBLE_INDEXES` parameter to true because it makes all invisible indexes visible.

You make an index visible with this:

```
ALTER INDEX nk_rental_item VISIBLE;
```

Rename Indexes Renaming an index is something to consider if you originally chose a poorly descriptive index name. Here's the syntax:

```
ALTER INDEX nk_rental_item RENAME TO naturalkey_rental_item;
```

Use Existing Indexes You can use the `ALTER TABLE` statement to let a table's primary key column use an existing index, like so:

```
ALTER TABLE rental_item ENABLE PRIMARY KEY USING nk_rental_item;
```

Don't forget that some views in the data catalog let you see the indexes you've already created.

Object Types

As a refresher, Oracle provides three types of object types—known as user-defined types (UDTs). Oracle provides three categories of user-defined SQL data types: object types (which may have methods), ADTs (collections of a single column), and UDTs (collections of object types).

This section discusses how you can modify an existing object type, even when the object type has dependent objects that use it. An object type with dependents means that after we built one user-defined type, we built another on top of it. This is similar to a child class inheriting from its parent class by adding new attributes (or fields) and methods. That creates a dependency, much like a foundation to a house (parent class) limits where load-bearing walls (child classes) can be built. Fortunately, Oracle 9*i* forward provides us with the capability to evolve data types even when they have objects built on top of them. Extending the house analogy, this capability enables us to do what builders can't do: build load-bearing walls where there isn't a concrete foundation because the concrete foundation magically extends itself beneath our walls.

As described in Chapter 11, object types may be transient objects or persistent objects. A transient object is one that lets our functions, procedures, packages, or object types use it. A transient object gets promoted to a permanent object when we use it as a column's data type in a table. Only a persistent object holds a unique identifier in the scope of the database instance that creates it.

This section describes how you modify object types rather than collections of object types, because collections are discrete forms of object types. The functionality of object types offers us greater flexibility and the set functionality of collections (check Chapter 6 for details on collections). Although, the negative side of the final functionality of collections is that we can't store collections of specializations (object types that build on top of other object types) in ordinary collections. We can, however, create object types that take an ordinary collection as a constructor parameter. That approach subsequently requires us to write an *accessor* method, a fancy term for *getter* method, to return a collection data type from our object type itself. This type of object acts like a tortoise shell that protects the collection from access without an explicit call to our getter method, which means encapsulating (hiding the details) of our code in the object.

The syntax for creating object types is provided earlier in this appendix in the "Object Type" subsection of the "CREATE Statement" section. However, I use a different object type in this section to show you how to evolve types. The base type in this example becomes a platform for us to build on, like a concrete foundation for a house. Base types have the least amount of information and the fewest methods to ensure they're more flexible to extension. You extend them by creating object types that build on top of them.

You have three options when evolving an object type:

- Adding or dropping an attribute (or field)
- Modifying the length, precision, or scale of an attribute
- Changing the finality of a type from `FINAL` to `NOT FINAL` or vice versa

To show you how to extend functionality, the example builds the minimum unit first and uses the `ALTER` statement to add attributes (equivalent to columns in a table) and methods to the object type.

The smallest possible object type that we can build in this case is

```
SQL> CREATE OR REPLACE
       TYPE base_t IS OBJECT
       ( obj_id  NUMBER )
       NOT FINAL;
     /
```

The `NOT FINAL` clause is a SQL-only syntax, and its presence pushes the semicolon that ends the block from line 3 to line 4. `NOT FINAL` means that you can build on top of this object type, which means it's *extensible* in object-oriented speak. You must explicitly define any objects that should be extensible by appending the `NOT FINAL` clause.

After defining the object type, you can describe it like you would a table:

```
SQL> DESCRIBE base_t
 Name                    Null?    Type
 ----------------------- -------- --------
 OBJ_ID                           NUMBER
```

An `obj_id` attribute by itself isn't too useful, so let's evolve it by adding an `obj_name` attribute to it. The `ALTER` statement syntax is

```
SQL> ALTER TYPE base_t
  2    ADD ATTRIBUTE ( obj_name  VARCHAR2(30))
  3    CASCADE INCLUDING TABLE DATA;

Type altered.
```

You should note that the `ALTER` statement worked, and that should mean our type has evolved. Unfortunately, as with Oracle 9*i*, 10*g*, and 11*g*, Oracle Database 12*c* returns an error when you try to `DESCRIBE` the altered object type in the same session context:

```
SQL> DESCRIBE base_t
ERROR:
ORA-22337: the type of accessed object has been evolved
```

Likewise, a query against the evolved type,

```
SQL> SELECT base_t(1,'Hello World!') FROM dual;
```

returns this error because the type was evolved during the current session:

```
ERROR:
ORA-22337: the type of accessed object has been evolved
```

While tedious and perhaps annoying to some during testing as you're making changes to object types, there's no easy work-around to the `ORA-22337` error. The problem occurs when you evolve any type because its very evolution makes the type unavailable to display during the same session (or connection) that made the change. You must disconnect from your current session and re-create another to avoid the error.

After you log off and reconnect to the server, you're able to `DESCRIBE` the evolved object type:

```
SQL> DESCRIBE base_t
 base_t is NOT FINAL
 Name                      Null?    Type
 ------------------------- -------- -------------
 OBJ_ID                             NUMBER
 OBJ_NAME                           VARCHAR2(30)
```

You can also query the object type, as shown here:

```
SQL> SELECT base_t(1,'Hello World!') FROM dual;
```

This produces the following results:

```
BASE_T(1,'BASE_T')(OBJ_ID, OBJ_NAME)
-------------------------------------------------
BASE_T(1, 'BASE_T')
```

You should note that the output from a query against a base type prints the flattened object—the object type name with the construction call parameters in parentheses—and, new in Oracle Database 12*c*, renders the object signature. The object signature is the formal parameter list for the default constructor. The default constructor exists for any object type until you define a constructor function and implement it in the object body.

Adding a constructor function is straightforward, but dropping one among several constructor functions isn't quite as simple. So, we're going to create one constructor function that we'll remove later, and create another constructor function that we'll keep. This is the one that we will drop:

```
SQL> ALTER TYPE base_t
      ADD
      CONSTRUCTOR FUNCTION base_t
      ( obj_id    NUMBER ) RETURN SELF AS RESULT
      CASCADE INCLUDING TABLE DATA;
   /
```

Here's how you add a constructor function that lets you set both of the columns in the `base_t` object type:

```
SQL> ALTER TYPE base_t
      ADD
      CONSTRUCTOR FUNCTION base_t
      ( obj_id    NUMBER
      , obj_name  VARCHAR2 ) RETURN SELF AS RESULT
      CASCADE INCLUDING TABLE DATA;
   /
```

You can also add a member function with the following syntax:

```
ALTER TYPE base_t
  ADD MEMBER FUNCTION to_string RETURN VARCHAR2
  CASCADE INCLUDING TABLE DATA;
```

Disconnecting and reconnecting to the database lets us `DESCRIBE` the object type:

```
SQL> desc base_t;
 base_t is NOT FINAL
 Name                       Null?    Type
 -------------------------- -------- -------------------
 OBJ_ID                              NUMBER
 OBJ_NAME                            VARCHAR2(30)
```

```
METHOD
------
 FINAL CONSTRUCTOR FUNCTION BASE_T RETURNS SELF AS RESULT
 Argument Name                  Type          In/Out Default?
 ------------------------------ ------------- ------ --------
 OBJ_ID                         NUMBER        IN

METHOD
------
 FINAL CONSTRUCTOR FUNCTION BASE_T RETURNS SELF AS RESULT
 Argument Name                  Type          In/Out Default?
 ------------------------------ ------------- ------ --------
 OBJ_ID                         NUMBER        IN
 OBJ_NAME                       VARCHAR2      IN

METHOD
------
 MEMBER FUNCTION TO_STRING RETURNS VARCHAR2
```

You can now drop the `base_t` constructor function that uses only an `obj_id` attribute. The syntax to drop the constructor function requires only a semicolon (`;`) or forward slash, but not both, similar to what you need to do when adding attributes, constructor functions, or member functions and procedures.

The syntax to drop a constructor function includes the parameter list to ensure that only one of the possibly many overloaded functions or procedures is dropped:

```
SQL> ALTER TYPE base_t
  2    DROP CONSTRUCTOR FUNCTION base_t ( obj_id NUMBER )
  3    RETURN SELF AS RESULT
  4    CASCADE INCLUDING TABLE DATA;
```

After dropping the constructor function, you will see that the `base_t` object type now has only one constructor function. Oracle Database 12*c* requires that you define an object body to use it. Here's a quick program that shows how to implement an object body:

```
CREATE OR REPLACE TYPE BODY base_t IS
  CONSTRUCTOR FUNCTION base_t
  ( obj_id NUMBER, obj_name VARCHAR2 )
  RETURN SELF AS RESULT IS
    BEGIN
      self.obj_id := obj_id;
      self.obj_name := obj_name;
      RETURN;
    END base_t;
  MEMBER FUNCTION to_string RETURN VARCHAR2 IS
    BEGIN
      RETURN '['||obj_id||']['||obj_name||']';
    END to_string;
END;
/
```

You can then query the object and return formatted output from the `to_string` method, like

```
SQL> SELECT
       TREAT(
         base_t( 1,'Sample BASE_T') AS base_t).to_string() AS "BASE_T"
     FROM   dual;
```

It would display the data as follows:

```
BASE_T
--------------------
[1][Sample BASE_T]
```

The `TREAT` function lets you instantiate an object instance in SQL. Once it is instantiated, you're able to use any of the nonstatic functions to manipulate data inside the object instance.

When altering or dropping attributes, you can limit changes to only transient dependent types. You do this by using the `NOT` operator before the `INCLUDING TABLE DATA` clause to the attribute change, like

```
SQL> ALTER TYPE base_t
  2    DROP ATTRIBUTE ( obj_unnecessary_field  VARCHAR2(30))
  3    CASCADE NOT INCLUDING TABLE DATA;

Type altered.
```

Line 3 tells the database to drop the `obj_unnecessary_field` attribute but to defer performing that action on object columns of that `base_t` object type or any of its dependent object types until they're accessed. This type of behavior is known as a *lazy compile*. Lazy compilation defers changes from the DDL event making the change to the first time the object is run after the change. While you can access the prior `obj_unnecessary_field` values, they cease to be available when you save the now modified object type.

You also have an `INVALIDATE` option that bypasses all the type and table checks when you drop a method. It lets you defer subtype changes until you access the respective type dependents. The default is `VALIDATE`, and it's rare that you should choose to defer type dependent validation.

Check Chapter 11 for more details on how you implement and work with object types and subtypes. I'd wager (but not gamble) more developers implement object types now that Oracle has significantly simplified the maintenance of user-defined object types by letting you evolve them throughout their usage in the database. Object types seem quite ready for primetime use in PL/SQL solutions if you're ready to adopt OOPL thinking.

RENAME Statement

The `RENAME` statement lets you rename database tables, synonyms, and views. You can't rename object types or change column names. The syntax to rename the supported object is

```
RENAME employee_view TO employee_v;
```

The `RENAME` statement can't be used by a common user to rename an object in another schema; for example,

```
SQL> RENAME student.calendar TO student.monthly_calendar;
```

raises the following exception:

```
RENAME student.calendar TO student.monthly_calendar
       *
ERROR at line 1:
ORA-01765: specifying owner's name of the table is not allowed
```

It's a useful command to illustrate that the database really keeps track of all objects by their object identifier, not by their name. Table, view, and synonym names are like aliases and are changeable without altering the underlying structure.

DROP Statement

Oracle provides you with the ability to drop users, tablespaces, tables, indexes, views, functions, procedures, packages, and object types.

DROP USER Statement

Dropping a user is a big step, and generally a developer only performs this task in a development database. The syntax is simple unless there are grants and privileges previously extended to other database users.

You drop a self-contained user (one without grants to others) with the following syntax:

```
DROP USER user_name;
```

You drop a user with grants to others with the `CASCADE` keyword, like

```
DROP USER user_name CASCADE;
```

You should note that when you drop the user, you remove the workspace allocated but not the space. That requires dropping a tablespace and its attached files.

DROP TABLESPACE Statement

Tablespaces are logical repositories that map to one or more physical data files. As covered earlier in the appendix, you have locally managed tablespaces and catalog managed tablespaces. You can drop a tablespace after you've taken it offline, as follows:

```
DROP TABLESPACE tablespace_name;
```

After you have dropped the tablespace, you need to remove the physical files from the operating system that were associated with the tablespace.

DROP TABLE Statement

You use the `DROP TABLE` statement to remove tables from the database. The `DROP TABLE` statement can fail when other tables or views have referential integrity (foreign key) dependencies on the table or view.

Oracle lets you drop only a single table with a `DROP TABLE` statement. You can drop tables when they contain data or when they're empty. This statement also drops global temporary tables. You can set aside referential integrity by using the `CASCADE CONSTRAINTS` clause.

The prototype for the `DROP TABLE` statement is shown here:

```
DROP TABLE [schema_name.]table_name [CASCADE CONSTRAINTS] [PURGE];
```

A DROP TABLE statement against a table that has foreign keys referencing it raises an exception:

```
DROP TABLE parent
           *
ERROR at line 1:
ORA-02449: unique/primary keys in table referenced by foreign keys
```

The CASCADE CONSTRAINTS clause removes dependencies from other tables, such as foreign key constraints that reference the table. It does not remove the data from the other table's previous foreign key column, which is important if you plan on re-creating the table and re-importing data. Any re-import of data would need to ensure that primary key values would map to existing foreign key values.

The PURGE keyword is optional for tables but is required when you're dropping a partitioned table. The PURGE keyword starts a series of subtransactions that drop all the partitions of the table. The first successful subtransaction marks the table as UNUSABLE in the data catalog. This flag in the data catalog ensures that only a DROP TABLE statement works against the remnants of the table. If you encounter a problem trying to access a table, you can query the status column value to see if it's unusable. The UNUSABLE column is in the CDB_, DBA_, ALL_, and USER_TABLES, administrative views and in the USER_PART_TABLES, USER_ALL_TABLES, USER_OBJECT_TABLES, and USER_OBJECTS administrative views.

DROP INDEX Statement

Indexes are sometimes dropped because they no longer apply or because the cost of dropping and re-creating them is less than the cost of altering it. You drop an index with the following syntax:

```
DROP INDEX index_name;
```

After dropping an obsolete index, it's always a good idea to verify the impact of removing an index by testing SQL statements that previously used the index.

DROP VIEW Statement

Dropping a view works much like dropping a table. The syntax is simple:

```
DROP VIEW view_name;
```

DROP FUNCTION Statement

Dropping a function also works much like dropping a table. The syntax is simple:

```
DROP FUNCTION function_name;
```

DROP PROCEDURE Statement

Dropping a procedure also works much like dropping a table. The syntax is simple:

```
DROP PROCEDURE procedure_name;
```

DROP PACKAGE Statement

Dropping a package has two variants. You can drop the package and package body, or only drop a package body. The syntax to drop both is

```
DROP PACKAGE package_name;
```

You can drop the implementation, which means all dependencies on the package specification aren't invalidated. This is convenient when you're making changes to the implementation of the package body without changing the specification. The syntax to drop only the package body is

```
DROP PACKAGE BODY package_name;
```

DROP TYPE Statement

Dropping an object type has two versions: one where the type has no dependents and another where the type has dependents. Oracle Database 12*c* has simplified dropping types by adding the `FORCE` keyword to the `DROP TYPE` statement.

You would drop a type without any type dependents with the following syntax:

```
DROP TYPE type_name;
```

You would drop a type with type dependents with the `FORCE` keyword, which in turn removes dependent types and columns from tables that use that type or any of its dependents. Therefore, you should be *absolutely* sure you understand the consequences before you attempt this command with the `FORCE` option.

```
DROP TYPE type_name FORCE;
```

For more on evolving object types, check the "Evolving an Object Type" section earlier in this appendix.

TRUNCATE Statement

The `TRUNCATE` statement gives you the ability to remove data from any table without writing changes to a redo log file, or any archive log file. The `TRUNCATE` statement deallocates all space previously used by the removed rows of a table in a dictionary-managed tablespace. The `TRUNCATE` statement leaves the `MINEXTENTS` storage parameter and resets the `NEXT` storage parameter to the size of the last extent removed from the segment where the data was stored. The `TRUNCATE` statement doesn't shrink the size of the tablespace, which is where the internal segments and extents that manage data are stored. You can find more on the logical storage structures or Oracle Database 12*c* in the *Oracle Database Concepts 12c* manual.

The `TRUNCATE` statement removes all data from the `item` table with the following:

```
TRUNCATE TABLE item;
```

You should use the `TRUNCATE` statement when you want to remove data without a recovery point. It is very fast and DBAs typically use it when they've already copied data somewhere else. The DBA then removes the data with the `TRUNCATE` statement and restructure the `STORAGE` clause of the table.

COMMENT Statement

The `COMMENT` statement provides you with the ability to place comments on tables, columns, operators, indextypes, materialized views, and mining models. The prototype for the `COMMENT` command is

```
COMMENT ON
{TABLE schema_name.{table_name | view_name}
|COLUMN schema_name.{table_name | view_name |
                    materialized_view_name}.column_name}
|OPERATOR schema_name.operator
|INDEXTYPE schema_name.indextype
|MATERIALIZED VIEW materialized_view_name
|MINING MODEL schema_name.model} IS 'comment';
```

You would add a comment to the `item` table with the following syntax:

```
SQL> COMMENT ON TABLE item
  2    IS 'Video Store Items.';
```

You add a comment to the `item_title` column of the `item` table with this:

```
SQL> COMMENT ON COLUMN
  2    item.item_title IS 'A Video Item Title.';
```

It's helpful to provide comments generally, but it's critical when the column or table has special meaning or purpose in the context of your data model. The same can be said for operators, index types, materialized views (like the periodicity of refresh), and mining models. I strongly recommend the use of comments to document your data models.

Data Manipulation Language (DML)

DML statements add data to, change data in, and remove data from tables. This section examines four DML statements—the `INSERT`, `UPDATE`, `DELETE`, and `MERGE` statements—and builds on concepts in the "Data Transactions" section of Appendix A. The `INSERT` statement adds new data, the `UPDATE` statement changes data, the `DELETE` statement removes data from the database, and the `MERGE` statement either adds new data or changes existing data.

As mentioned in the "Data Transactions" section of Appendix A, any `INSERT`, `UPDATE`, `MERGE`, or `DELETE` SQL statement that adds, updates, or deletes rows in a table locks rows in a table and hides the information until the change is committed or undone (that is, rolled back). This is the nature of ACID-compliant SQL statements. Locks prevent other sessions from making a change while a current session is working with the data. Locks also restrict other sessions from seeing any changes until they're made permanent. The database keeps two copies of rows that are undergoing change. One copy of the rows with pending changes is visible to the current session, while the other displays committed changes only.

ACID Compliant Transactions

ACID compliance relies on a two-phase commit (2PC) protocol and ensures that the current session is the only one that can see new inserts, updated column values, and the absence of deleted rows. Other sessions run by the same or different users can't see the changes until you commit them.

ACID Compliant INSERT Statements

The INSERT statement adds rows to existing tables and uses a 2PC protocol to implement ACID-compliant guarantees. The SQL INSERT statement is a DML statement that adds one or more rows to a table. Oracle supports a VALUES clause when adding a single-row, and support a subquery when adding one to many rows.

Figure B-4 shows a flow chart depicting an INSERT statement. The process of adding one or more rows to a table occurs during the first phase of an INSERT statement. Adding the rows exhibits both atomic and consistent properties. *Atomic* means all or nothing: it adds one or more rows and succeeds, or it doesn't add any rows and fails. *Consistent* means that the addition of rows is guaranteed whether the database engine adds them sequentially or concurrently in threads.

Concurrent behaviors happen when the database parallelizes DML statements. This is similar to the concept of threads as lightweight processes that work under the direction of a single process. The parallel actions of a single SQL statement delegate and manage work sent to separate threads. Oracle supports all ACID properties and implements threaded execution as parallel operations. All tables support parallelization.

After adding the rows to a table, the *isolation property* prevents any other session from seeing the new rows—that means another session started by the same user or by another user with access to the same table. The atomic, consistent, and isolation properties occur in the first phase of any

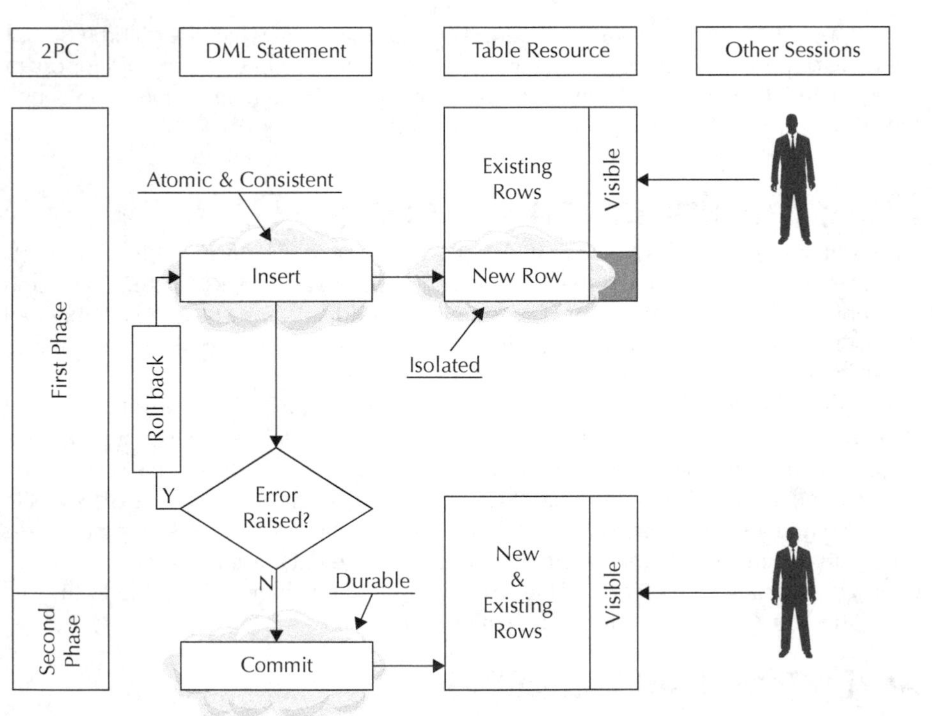

FIGURE B-4. *2PC INSERT statement*

INSERT statement. The durable property is exclusively part of the second phase of an INSERT statement, and rows become durable when the COMMIT statement ratifies the insertion of the new data.

ACID Compliant UPDATE Statements

An UPDATE statement changes column values in one-to-many rows. With a WHERE clause, you update only rows of interest, but if you forget the WHERE clause, an UPDATE statement would run against all rows in a table. Although you can update any column in a row, it's generally bad practice to update a primary or foreign key column because you can break referential integrity. You should only update *non-key data* in tables—that is, the data that doesn't make a row unique within a table.

Changes to column values are atomic when they work. For scalability reasons, the database implementation of updates to many rows is often concurrent, in threads through parallelization. This process can span multiple process threads and uses a transaction paradigm that coordinates changes across the threads. The entire UPDATE statement fails when any one thread fails.

Similar to the INSERT statement, UPDATE statement changes to column values are also hidden until they are made permanent with the application of the *isolation property*. The changes are hidden from other sessions, including sessions begun by the same database user.

It's possible that another session might attempt to lock or change data in a modified but uncommitted row. When this happens, the second DML statement encounters a lock and goes into a wait state until the row becomes available for changes. If you neglected to set a timeout value for the wait state, such as this clause, the FOR UPDATE clause waits until the target rows are unlocked:

```
WAIT n
```

As Figure B-5 shows, actual updates are first-phase commit elements. While an UPDATE statement changes data, it changes only the current session values until it is made permanent by a COMMIT statement. Like the INSERT statement, the atomic, consistent, and isolation properties of an UPDATE statement occur during the first phase of a 2PC process. Changes to column values are atomic when they work. Any column changes are hidden from other sessions until the UPDATE statement is made permanent by a COMMIT or ROLLBACK statement, which is an example of the *isolation property*.

Any changes to column values can be modified by an ON UPDATE trigger before a COMMIT statement. ON UPDATE triggers run inside the first phase of the 2PC process. A COMMIT or ROLLBACK statement ends the transaction scope of the UPDATE statement.

The Oracle database engine can dispatch changes to many threads when an UPDATE statement works against many rows. UPDATE statements are consistent when these changes work in a single thread-of-control or across multiple threads with the same results.

As with the INSERT statement, the atomic, consistent, and isolation properties occur during the first phase of any UPDATE statement, and the COMMIT statement is the sole activity of the second phase. Column value changes become durable only with the execution of a COMMIT statement.

ACID Compliant DELETE Statements

A DELETE statement removes rows from a table. Like an UPDATE statement, the absence of a WHERE clause in a DELETE statement deletes all rows in a table. Deleted rows remain visible outside of the transaction scope where it has been removed. However, any attempts to UPDATE those deleted rows are held in a pending status until they are committed or rolled back.

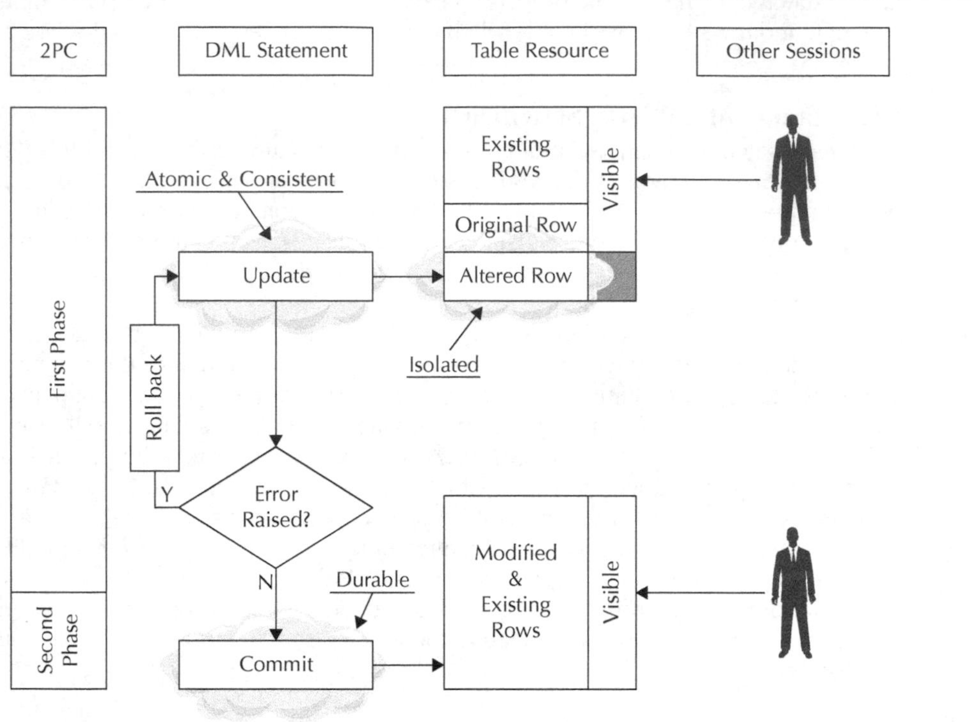

FIGURE B-5. *2PC UPDATE statement*

You delete rows when they're no longer useful. Deleting rows can be problematic when rows in another table have a dependency on the deleted rows. Consider, for example, a `customer` table that contains a list of cell phone contacts and an `address` table that contains the addresses for some but not all of the contacts. If you delete a row from the `customer` table that still has related rows in the `address` table, those `address` table rows are now *orphaned* and useless.

As a rule, you delete data from the most dependent table to the least dependent table, which is the opposite of the insertion process. Basically, you delete the child record before you delete the parent record. The parent record holds the primary key value, and the child record holds the foreign key value. You drop the foreign key value, which is a copy of the primary key, before you drop the primary key record. For example, you would insert a row in the `customer` table before you insert a row in the `address` table, and you delete rows from the `address` table before you delete rows in the `customer` table.

Figure B-6 shows the logic behind a `DELETE` statement. Like the `INSERT` and `UPDATE` statements, acid, consistency, and isolation properties of the ACID-compliant transaction are managed during the first phase of a 2PC. The durability property is managed by the `COMMIT` or `ROLLBACK` statement.

There's no discussion or diagrams for the `MERGE` statement because it does either an `INSERT` or `UPDATE` statement based on it's internal logic (shown in the "MERGE Statement" section later

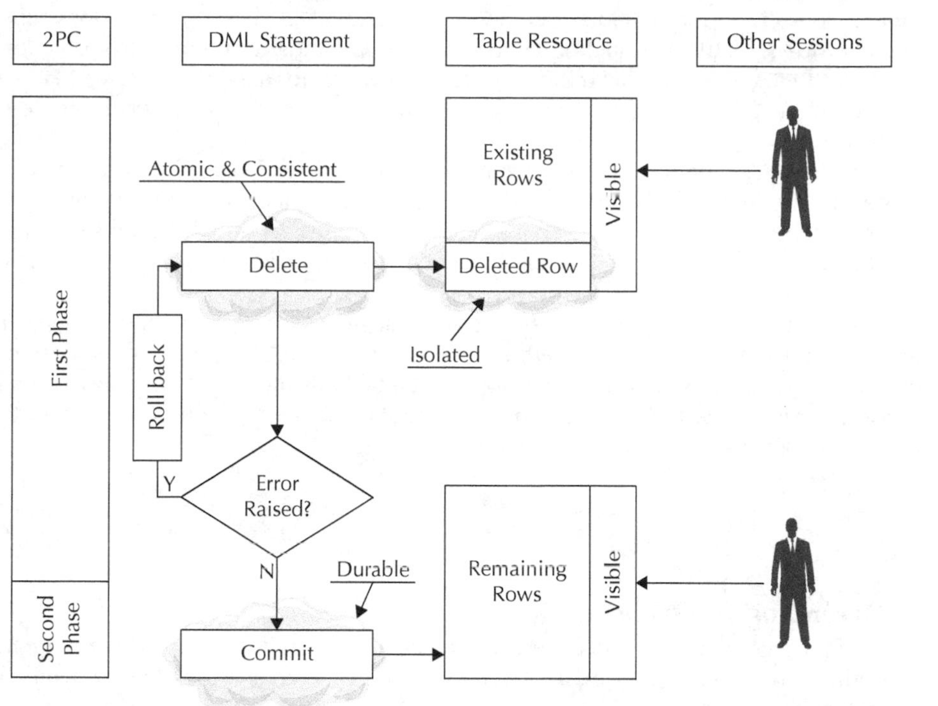

FIGURE B-6. *2PC DELETE statement*

in this appendix). That means a MERGE statement is ACID compliant like an INSERT or UPDATE statement.

The following subsections cover the INSERT, UPDATE, DELETE, and MERGE DML statements in more detail and provide real-world examples.

INSERT Statement

The INSERT statement lets you enter data into tables and views in two ways: via an INSERT statement with a VALUES clause and via an INSERT statement with a query. The VALUES clause takes a list of literal values (strings, numbers, and dates represented as strings), expression values (return values from functions), or variable values.

Query values are results from SELECT statements that are subqueries (covered earlier in this appendix). INSERT statements work with scalar, single-row, and multiple-row subqueries. The list of columns in the VALUES clause or SELECT clause of a query (a SELECT list) must map to the positional list of columns that defines the table. That list is found in the data dictionary or catalog. Alternatively to the list of columns from the data catalog, you can provide a named list of those columns. The named list *overrides* the positional (or *default*) order from the data catalog and must provide at least all mandatory columns in the table definition. Mandatory columns are those that are not null constrained.

Oracle databases differ from other databases in how they implement the INSERT statement. Oracle doesn't support multiple-row inserts with a VALUES clause. Oracle does support default and override signatures as qualified in the ANSI SQL standards. Oracle also provides a multiple-table INSERT statement. This section covers how you enter data with an INSERT statement that is based on a VALUES clause or a subquery result statement. It also covers multiple-table INSERT statements.

The INSERT statement has one significant limitation: its *default signature*. The default signature is the list of columns that defines the table in the data catalog. The list is defined by the position and data type of columns. The CREATE statement defines the initial default signature, and the ALTER statement can change the number, data types, or ordering of columns in the default signature.

The default prototype for an INSERT statement allows for an optional column list that overrides the default list of columns. Like methods in OOPLs, an INSERT statement without the optional column list constructs an instance (or row) of the table using the default constructor. The override constructor for a row is defined by any INSERT statement when you provide an optional column list. That's because it overrides the default constructor.

Overriding vs. Overloading

OOPLs have special vocabularies. You define a class in OOPLs by writing a program that outlines the rules for how to create an instance of a class and the methods available for any instance of that class.

Objects have special methods known as constructors that let you create instances. The default constructor generally has no formal parameters. When writing the code for a class, you can define constructors that override the default constructor's behavior. These user-defined constructors are known as *overriding* constructors. Objects also have methods that perform actions against the instance, and some of these methods are overloaded, which means a given method name supports different lists of formal parameters. This is known as *method overloading*.

The list of parameters in an overriding constructor is also known as the *overriding signature*, defined as something that serves to set apart or identify. The same logic makes the formal parameter list of any method a signature of that method.

The class is also known as an object *type*, which is a data type. A table in a database is an object type, because it contains a definition of what it can include. Every row is an instance of that object type.

As qualified in the introduction to this appendix, SQL is a set-based declarative language. Declarative languages hide the implementation details while providing a means for the developer to state what should happen. The default signature to enter a row of data is read from the data catalog and compared against the list of values in a VALUES clause or query. The INSERT statement's optional column list lets you override the default signature to enter a row of data, but the database checks to ensure that you conform to any not-null column-level constraints.

The generic prototype for an INSERT statement is confusing when it tries to capture both the VALUES clause and the result set from a query. Therefore, I've opted to provide two generic prototypes. The first uses the VALUES clause:

```
INSERT
INTO table_name
[( column1, column2, column3, ...)]
VALUES
( value1, value2, value3, ...);
```

Notice that the prototype for an INSERT statement with the result set from a query doesn't use the VALUES clause at all. A parsing error occurs when the VALUES clause and query both occur in an INSERT statement.

The second prototype uses a query and excludes the VALUES clause. The subquery may return one to many rows of data. The operative rule is that all columns in the query return the same number of rows of data, because query results should be rectangles—rectangles made up of one to many rows of columns. Here's the prototype for an INSERT statement that uses a query:

```
INSERT
INTO table_name
[( column1, column2, column3, ...)]
( SELECT value1, value2, value3, ... FROM table_name WHERE ...);
```

A query, or SELECT statement, returns a SELECT list. The SELECT list is the list of columns, and it's evaluated by position and data type. The SELECT list must match the definition of the table or the override signature provided.

Default signatures present a risk of data corruption through insertion anomalies, which occur when you enter bad data in tables. Mistakes transposing or misplacing values can occur more frequently with a default signature, because the underlying table structure can change. As a best practice, always use named notation by providing the optional list of values; this should help you avoid putting the right data in the wrong place.

TIP
Inserts should always rely on named notation to help you avoid adding data in the wrong columns.

The following subsections provide examples that use the default and override syntax for INSERT statements in Oracle databases. The subsections also cover multiple-table INSERT statements and a RETURNING INTO clause, which is an extension of the ANSI SQL standard. Oracle uses the RETURNING INTO clause to manage large objects, to return autogenerated identity column values, and to support some of the features of Oracle's dynamic SQL. Note that Oracle also supports a bulk INSERT statement, which is covered in Chapter 5 because it requires knowledge of PL/SQL.

Insert by Values

Inserting by the VALUES clause is the most common type of INSERT statement. It's most useful when interacting with single-row inserts. You typically use this type of INSERT statement when working with data entered through end-user web forms. In some cases, users can enter more than one row of data using a form, which occurs, for example, when a user places a meal order in a restaurant and the meal and drink are treated as order items. The restaurant order entry system would enter a single-row in the `order` table and two rows in the `order_item` table (one for the meal and the other for the drink). PL/SQL programmers usually handle the insertion of related rows typically inside a loop structure when they use dynamic `INSERT` statements. Dynamic inserts are typically performed using NDS (Native Dynamic SQL) statements.

Oracle supports only a single-row insert through the `VALUES` clause. Multiple-row inserts require an `INSERT` statement from a query.

The `VALUES` clause of an `INSERT` statement accepts scalar values, such as strings, numbers, and dates. It also accepts calls to arrays, lists, or user-defined object types, which are called *flattened objects*. Oracle supports `VARRAY` as arrays and nested tables as lists. They can both contain elements of a scalar data type or user-defined object type.

The following sections discuss how you use the `VALUES` clause with scalar data types, how you convert various data types, and how you use the `VALUES` clause with nested tables and user-defined object data types.

Inserting Scalar Data Types The basic syntax for an `INSERT` statement with a `VALUES` clause can include an optional *override signature* between the table name and `VALUES` keyword. With an override signature, you designate the column names and the order of entry for the `VALUES` clause elements. Without an override signature, the `INSERT` signature checks the definition of the table in the database catalog. The positional order of the column in the data catalog defines the positional, or default, signature for the `INSERT` statement. As shown previously, you can discover the structure of a table in Oracle with the `DESCRIBE` command issued at the SQL*Plus command line:

```
DESCRIBE table_name
```

You'll see the following after describing the `rental` table in SQL*Plus:

```
Name                                     Null?    Type
 --------------------------------------- -------- --------
 RENTAL_ID                               NOT NULL NUMBER
 CUSTOMER_ID                             NOT NULL NUMBER
 CHECK_OUT_DATE                          NOT NULL DATE
 RETURN_DATE                                      DATE
 CREATED_BY                              NOT NULL NUMBER
 CREATION_DATE                           NOT NULL DATE
 LAST_UPDATED_BY                         NOT NULL NUMBER
 LAST_UPDATE_DATE                        NOT NULL DATE
```

The `rental_id` column is a *surrogate key*, or an artificial numbering sequence. The combination of the `customer_id` and `check_out_date` columns serves as a *natural key* because a `DATE` data type is a date-time value. If it were only a date, the customer would be limited to a single entry for each day, and limiting customer rentals to one per day isn't a good business model.

The basic INSERT statement would require that you look up the next sequence value before using it. You should also look up the surrogate key column value that maps to the row where your unique customer is stored in the contact table. For this example, assume the following facts:

- Next sequence value is 1086
- Customer's surrogate key value is 1009
- Current date-time is represented by the value from the SYSDATE function
- Return date is the fifth date from today
- User adding and updating the row has a primary (surrogate) key value of 1
- Creation and last update date are the value returned from the SYSDATE function.

An INSERT statement must include a list of values that match the positional data types of the database catalog, or it must use an override signature for all mandatory columns.

You can now write the following INSERT statement, which relies on the default signature:

```
SQL> INSERT INTO rental
  2  VALUES
  3  ( 1086
  4  , 1009
  5  , SYSDATE
  6  , TRUNC(SYSDATE + 5)
  7  , 1
  8  , SYSDATE
  9  , 1
 10  , SYSDATE);
```

If you weren't using SYSDATE for the date-time value on line 5, you could manually enter a date-time with the following Oracle proprietary syntax:

```
  5  , TO_DATE('15-APR-2011 12:53:01','DD-MON-YYYY HH24:MI:SS')
```

The TO_DATE function is an Oracle-specific function. The generic conversion function would be the CAST function. The problem with a CAST function by itself is that it can't handle a format mask other than the database defaults ('DD-MON-RR' or 'DD-MON-YYYY'). For example, consider this syntax:

```
  5  , CAST('15-APR-2011 12:53:02' AS DATE)
```

It raises the following error:

```
  5  ,  CAST('15-APR-2011 12:53:02' AS DATE) FROM dual
        *
ERROR at line 1:
ORA-01830: date format picture ends before converting entire input string
```

You actually need to double cast this type of format mask when you want to store it as a DATE data type. The working syntax casts the date-time string as a TIMESTAMP data type before recasting the TIMESTAMP to a DATE, like

```
  5  ,  CAST(CAST('15-APR-2011 12:53:02' AS TIMESTAMP) AS DATE)
```

Before you could write the preceding `INSERT` statement, you would need to run some queries to find the values. You would secure the next value from a `rental_s1` sequence in an Oracle database with the following command:

```
SQL> SELECT   rental_s1.nextval FROM dual;
```

This assumes two things, because sequences are separate objects from tables. First, code from which the values in a table's surrogate key column come must appear in the correct sequence. Second, a sequence value is inserted only once into a table as a primary key value.

In place of a query that finds the next sequence value, you would simply use a call against the `.nextval` pseudocolumn in the `VALUES` clause. You would replace line 3 with this:

```
  3   ( rental_s1.nextval
```

The `.nextval` is a pseudocolumn, and it instantiates an instance of a sequence in the current session. After a call to a sequence with the `.nextval` pseudocolumn, you can also call back the prior sequence value with the `.currval` pseudocolumn.

NOTE

Sequences are separate objects from tables, and the code ensures that only the appropriate sequence maps to the correct table.

Assuming the following query would return a single-row, you can use the `contact_id` value as the `customer_id` value in the `rental` table:

```
SQL> SELECT   contact_id
     FROM     contact
     WHERE    last_name = 'Potter'
     AND      first_name = 'Harry';
```

Taking three steps like this is unnecessary, however, because you can call the next sequence value and find the valid `customer_id` value inside the `VALUES` clause of the `INSERT` statement. The following `INSERT` statement uses an override signature and calls for the next sequence value on line 11. It also uses a scalar subquery to look up the correct `customer_id` value with a scalar subquery on lines 12 through 15.

```
SQL> INSERT INTO rental
  2   ( rental_id
  3   , customer_id
  4   , check_out_date
  5   , return_date
  6   , created_by
  7   , creation_date
  8   , last_updated_by
  9   , last_update_date )
 10   VALUES
 11   ( rental_s1.nextval
 12   ,(SELECT    contact_id
 13     FROM      contact
 14     WHERE     last_name = 'Potter'
```

```
    AND      first_name = 'Harry')
  , SYSDATE
  , TRUNC(SYSDATE + 5)
  , 1
  , SYSDATE
  , 3
  , SYSDATE);
```

When a subquery returns two or more rows because the conditions in the `WHERE` clause failed to find and return a unique row, the `INSERT` statement would fail with the following message:

```
,(SELECT   contact_id
  *
ERROR at line 3:
ORA-01427: single-row subquery returns more than one row
```

In fact, the statement could fail when there are two or more "Harry Potter" names in the data set because three columns make up the natural key of the `contact` table. The third column is the `member_id`, and all three should be qualified inside a scalar subquery to guarantee that it returns only one row of data.

Handling Oracle's Large Objects—Oracle's large objects present a small problem when they're not null constrained in the table definition. You must insert empty object containers or references when you perform an `INSERT` statement.

Assume, for example, that you have the following three large object columns in a table:

```
 Name                              Null?    Type
 --------------------------------- -------- ------------------------
 ITEM_DESC                         NOT NULL CLOB
 ITEM_ICON                         NOT NULL BLOB
 ITEM_PHOTO                                 BINARY FILE LOB
```

The `item_desc` column uses a `CLOB` (Character Large Object) data type, and it is a required column; it could hold a lengthy description of a movie, for example. The `item_icon` column uses a `BLOB` (Binary Large Object) data type, and it is also a required column. It could hold a graphic image. The `item_photo` column uses a binary file (an externally managed file) but is fortunately null allowed or an optional column in any `INSERT` statement. It can hold a null or a reference to an external graphic image.

Oracle provides two functions that let you enter an empty large object, and both are covered in Appendix C:

```
empty_blob()
empty_clob()
```

Although you could insert a null value in the `item_photo` column, you can also enter a reference to an Oracle database virtual directory file. Here's the syntax to enter a valid `BFILE` name with the `BFILENAME` function call:

```
  , BFILENAME('VIRTUAL_DIRECTORY_NAME', 'file_name.png')
```

You can insert a large character or binary stream into BLOB and CLOB data types by using the stored procedures and functions available in the dbms_lob package. Chapter 13 covers the dbms_lob package.

You can use an empty_clob function or a string literal up to 32,767 bytes long in a VALUES clause. You must use the dbms_lob package when you insert a string that is longer than 32,767 bytes. That also changes the nature of the INSERT statement and requires that you append the RETURNING INTO clause. Here's the prototype for this Oracle proprietary syntax:

```
INSERT INTO some_table
[( column1, column2, column3, ...)]
VALUES
( value1, value2, value3, ...)
RETURNING column1 INTO local_variable;
```

The local_variable is a reference to a procedural programming language. It lets you insert a character stream into a target CLOB column or insert a binary stream into a BLOB column.

Capturing the Last Sequence Value—Sometimes you insert into a series of tables in the scope of a transaction. In this scenario, one table gets the new sequence value (with a call to sequence_name.nextval) and enters it as the surrogate primary key, and another table needs a copy of that primary key to enter into a foreign key column. While scalar subqueries can solve this problem, Oracle provides the .currval pseudocolumn for this purpose.

The steps to demonstrate this behavior require a parent table and a child table. The parent table is defined as follows:

```
Name                                      Null?    Type
----------------------------------------- -------- -------------
PARENT_ID                                 NOT NULL NUMBER
PARENT_NAME                                        VARCHAR2(10)
```

The parent_id column is the primary key for the parent table. You include the parent_id column in the child table. In the child table, the parent_id column holds a copy of a valid primary key column value as a foreign key to the parent table.

```
Name                                      Null?    Type
----------------------------------------- -------- -------------
CHILD_ID                                  NOT NULL NUMBER
PARENT_ID                                          NUMBER
PARENT_NAME                                        VARCHAR2(10)
```

DBA Heads-up on Large Object Storage

CLOB and BLOB columns are stored with the rest of a row when they're smaller than 4,000 bytes. Larger versions are stored out-of-line, which means they're placed in a contiguous space that is away from the rest of the related row.

DBAs often designate a special tablespace for the storage clauses of BLOB and CLOB columns. This extra step is beneficial, because large objects change less frequently and consume a lot of storage. They're also generally on different backup schedules than other transactional columns in a table.

After creating the two tables, you can manage inserts into them with the `.nextval` and `.currval` pseudocolumns. The sequence calls with the `.nextval` pseudocolumn insert primary key values, and the sequence calls with the `.currval` pseudocolumn insert foreign key values.

You would perform these two `INSERT` statements as a group:

```
SQL> INSERT INTO parent
  2  VALUES
  3  ( parent_s1.nextval
  4  ,'One Parent');

SQL> INSERT INTO child
  2  VALUES
  3  ( child_s1.nextval
  4  , parent_s1.currval
  5  ,'One Child');
```

The `.currval` pseudocolumn for any sequence fetches the value placed in memory by call to the `.nextval` pseudocolumn. Any attempt to call the `.currval` pseudocolumn before the `.nextval` pseudocolumn raises an `ORA-02289` exception. The text message for that error says the sequence doesn't exist, which actually means that it doesn't exist in the scope of the current session. Line 4 in the insert into the `child` table depends on line 3 in the insert into the `parent` table.

You can use comments in `INSERT` statements to map to columns in the table. For example, the following shows the technique for the `child` table from the preceding example:

```
SQL> INSERT INTO child
     VALUES
     ( child_s1.nextval      -- CHILD_ID
     , parent_s1.currval     -- PARENT_ID
     ,'One Child')           -- CHILD_NAME
     /
```

Comments on the lines of the `VALUES` clause identify the columns where the values are inserted. A semicolon doesn't execute this statement, because a trailing comment would trigger a runtime exception. You must use the semicolon or forward slash on the line below the last `VALUES` element to include the last comment.

TIP

A comment on the last line of any statement requires that you exclude the semicolon and place it or a forward slash on the next line.

Data Type Conversions Oracle supports a series of conversion functions that let you convert data types from one type to another. The generic SQL conversion function is `CAST`, which lets you convert the following data types:

- Convert from `BINARY_FLOAT` or `BINARY_DOUBLE` data type to `BINARY_FLOAT`, `BINARY_DOUBLE`, `CHAR`, `VARCHAR2`, `NUMBER`, `DATE`, `TIMESTAMP`, `NCHAR`, `NVARCHAR`.

- Convert from CHAR or VARCHAR2 data type to BINARY_FLOAT, BINARY_DOUBLE, CHAR, VARCHAR2, NUMBER, DATE, TIMESTAMP, DATE, TIMESTAMP, INTERVAL, RAW, ROWID, UROWID, NCHAR, NVARCHAR. Here's an example of converting a string literal date into a timestamp:

  ```
  CAST('14-FEB-2011' AS TIMESTAMP WITH LOCAL TIME ZONE)
  ```

  This example works because the date literal conforms to the default format mask for a date in an Oracle database. A nonconforming date literal would raise a conversion error. Many possibilities are available, because you can organize the valid elements of dates many ways. A nonconforming date literal should be converted by using the TO_DATE or TO_TIMESTAMP function, because each of these lets you specify an overriding date format mask value, such as this conversion to a DATE data type:

  ```
  TO_DATE('2011-02-14', 'YYYY-MM-DD')
  ```

  or this conversion to a TIMESTAMP data type:

  ```
  TO_TIMESTAMP('2011-02-14 18:11:28.1500', 'YYYY-MM-DD HH24:MI:SS.FF')
  ```

  Converting to an INTERVAL data type is covered in the next bullet because you first must extract a time property as a number. It's also possible that implicit casting of a numeric string can change the base data type to an integer for you. The method of implicit or explicit conversion depends on how you get the initial data value.
- Convert from NUMBER data type to BINARY_FLOAT, BINARY_DOUBLE, CHAR, VARCHAR2, NUMBER, DATE, TIMESTAMP, NCHAR, NVARCHAR. Interval conversions are a bit more complex, because you need more than one function to convert them. Typically, you pull the value from a DATE or TIMESTAMP data type and EXTRACT the element of time by identifying its type before converting that value to an INTERVAL type. The following provides an example:

  ```
  NUMTODSINTERVAL(EXTRACT(MINUTE FROM some_date), 'MINUTE')
  ```

  You will use this type of built-in function layering frequently in some situations. It's always a better approach to understand and use the built-in functions before you write your own stored functions.
- Convert from DATETIME or INTERVAL data type to CHAR, VARCHAR2, DATE, TIMESTAMP, DATE, TIMESTAMP, INTERVAL, NCHAR, NVARCHAR.
- Convert from RAW data type to CHAR, VARCHAR2, RAW, NCHAR, NVARCHAR.
- Convert from ROWID or UROWID data type to CHAR, VARCHAR2, ROWID, UROWID, NCHAR, NVARCHAR.

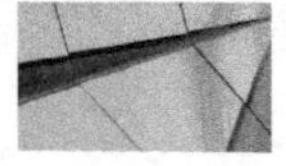

NOTE
You cannot cast a UROWID to a ROWID in the UROWID of an index-organized table.

- Convert from NCHAR or NVARCHAR2 data type to BINARY_FLOAT, BINARY_DOUBLE, NUMBER, NCHAR, NVARCHAR.

Inserting Arrays and Nested Tables The ability to insert arrays and nested tables in an Oracle database is an important feature made possible by the *object-relational* technology of the database. You can access these embedded structures only through the containing table, which makes them much like inner classes in object-oriented programming. From a database modeling perspective, they're ID-dependent data sets, because the only relationship is through the row of the containing table.

You can walk through a simple design and development by creating a collection of a scalar data type, a table that contains the data type, and then an `INSERT` statement to populate the table with data. You create the user-defined collection data type of a scalar data type by using this syntax:

```
CREATE TYPE number_array IS VARRAY(10) OF NUMBER;
```

A collection of scalar variables like the `number_array` is a specialized collection known as an Attribute Data Type (ADT). After you have the user-defined ADT collection type, create a table that uses it and a sequence for an automatic numbering column, like so:

```
SQL> CREATE TABLE sample_nester
     ( nester_id    NUMBER
     , array_column NUMBER_ARRAY);
SQL> CREATE SEQUENCE sample_nester_s1;
```

You enter values into the table by calling a collection constructor. Calls are made to the data type name, not the column name, like so:

```
SQL> INSERT INTO sample_nester
     VALUES
     ( sample_nester_s1.nextval
     , NUMBER_ARRAY(0,1,2,3,4,5,6,7,8,9));
```

Here are formatting instructions and an ordinary query against this table:

```
SQL> COLUMN array_column FORMAT A44
SQL> SELECT * from sample_nester;
```

It returns the following:

```
 NESTER_ID ARRAY_COLUMN
---------- --------------------------------------------
         1 NUMBER_ARRAY(0, 1, 2, 3, 4, 5, 6, 7, 8, 9)
```

The value in the `array_column` is a call to the user-defined ADT collection data type's constructor. This collection is a simple array of ten numbers. You can join the `nester_id` column against all ten elements in the collection with the following syntax:

```
SQL> SELECT nester_id
     ,      collection.column_value
     FROM   sample_nester CROSS JOIN TABLE(array_column) collection;
```

The `TABLE` function extracts the element of the collection into a SQL result set, which can then be treated like a normal set of rows from any table. Oracle always returns collections of base scalar data types into a `column_value` column, which is a hidden column for ADTs. The results from the sample query follow:

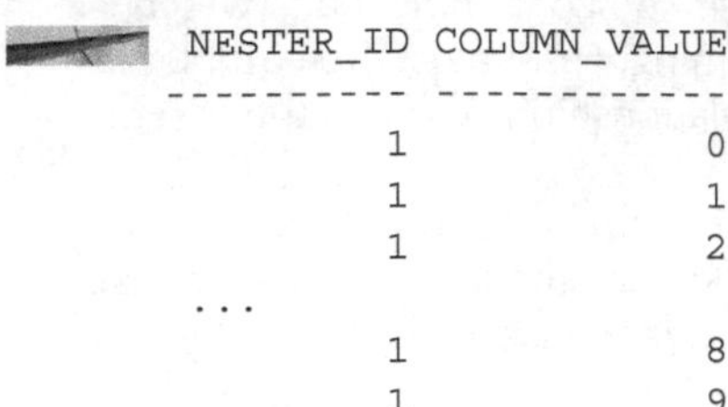

```
NESTER_ID COLUMN_VALUE
---------- ------------
         1            0
         1            1
         1            2
...
         1            8
         1            9
```

Here's a multilevel `INSERT` statement based on the `employee` table. The following inserts a single-row that contains an `address_list` collection of two instances of the `address_type` user-defined object type, which in turn holds a collection of a `street_list` nested table of variable-length strings:

```
SQL> INSERT INTO employee
  2  ( employee_id
  3  , first_name
  4  , last_name
  5  , home_address )
  6  VALUES
  7  ( employee_s1.nextval
  8  ,'Sam'
  9  ,'Yosemite'
 10  , address_list(
 11      address_type( 1
 12                  , street_list('1111 Broadway','Suite 322')
 13                  ,'Oakland'
 14                  ,'CA'
 15                  ,'94612')
 16    , address_type( 2
 17                  , street_list('1111 Broadway','Suite 525')
 18                  ,'Oakland'
 19                  ,'CA'
 20                  ,'94612')));
```

Lines 10 through 20 insert a nested table (list) of two `address_type` instances. The sequence numbers are manually entered because this type of design would always start elements with the nested table with a sequence value of 1. This is an implementation of an ID-dependent relationship. The nested table is accessible only through the row of a table, and as such, it acts only when connected with the containing row.

NOTE
Nested tables are complex to access and model. As mentioned earlier in this appendix, they also create type chaining, which presents maintenance headaches during major software releases. If you opt to use nested tables, you should have a good reason for adding the complexity.

The next `INSERT` statement inserts a second record in the `employee` table. It differs because there's no `street_address` instance value inserted for *Wile E Coyote* (he's too busy chasing the Road Runner). The omission of a `street_address` instance helps to demonstrate the difference between *unnesting queries* with or without collection instance values in the "Unnesting Queries" section later in this appendix.

```
SQL> INSERT INTO employee
  2  ( employee_id
  3  , first_name
  4  , middle_name
  5  , last_name
  6  , home_address )
  7  VALUES
  8  ( employee_s1.nextval
  9  ,'Wile'
 10  ,'E'
 11  ,'Coyote'
 12  , address_list(
 13      address_type( 1
 14                  , NULL
 15                  ,'Phoenix'
 16                  ,'AZ'
 17                  ,'85087')));
```

Line 14 enters a null instead of inserting an instance of the `street_list` data type. A null differs from an empty instance. An empty instance occurs when the object type's attributes (or fields) are all null. More or less, as qualified in Chapter 11, persistent object types have three possible states—null, empty, or constructed. Null instances require a special operation when you want to show the containing table or collection values matched against a null record. I've put that code in the "Unnesting Queries" section later in this appendix.

Multiple-Table Insert Statements

As mentioned earlier, Oracle SQL syntax provides you with the ability to perform multiple table inserts with the `INSERT` statement. A multiple-table `INSERT` statement can be useful when you receive an import source file that belongs in more than one table. There are some caveats with this type of multiple-table insert. There must be a one-to-one map between all the data in the same row. When you have a one-to-many relationship between columns in the single import source table, the `MERGE` statement is a better solution, as shown in Chapter 11.

The prototype for the multiple-table `INSERT` statement is

```
INSERT {ALL | FIRST}
 [WHEN comparison_clause THEN ]
  INSERT INTO table_name_1
  ( column_list )
  VALUES
  ( value_list )
[[WHEN comparison_cluase THEN ]
  INSERT INTO table_name_2
  ( column_list )
  VALUES
```

```
  ( value_list ) ]
 [ ... ]
 [ELSE
  INSERT INTO table_name_else
  ( column_list )
  VALUES
  ( value_list ) ]
 query_statement;
```

There are three ways to perform a multiple-table insert. One uses the ALL keyword but excludes the WHEN clauses. The second uses the ALL keyword while including the WHEN clauses. The last one uses the FIRST keyword instead of the ALL keyword and inserts so many rows to the first table before moving to the second, and so forth.

The multiple-table INSERT statement variations are discussed in the following subsections, but they're all supported by the following three tables and sequences.

The rank_index is the first table, and it contains a string for the military service, such as Army, Navy, Marines, or Air Force, with the accompanying abbreviated and full-titled ranks:

```
-- Create the rank_index table and sequence.
CREATE TABLE rank_index
( rank_id         NUMBER
, rank_service    VARCHAR2(10)
, rank_short_name VARCHAR2(4)
, rank_full_name  VARCHAR2(30));
CREATE SEQUENCE rank_index_s;
```

The soldier and sailor tables are target tables for the inserts from the multiple-table INSERT statement. They contain the rank and name of soldiers and sailors, respectively:

```
-- Create the soldier table and sequence.
CREATE TABLE soldier
( soldier_id    NUMBER
, soldier_rank  VARCHAR2(4)
, soldier_name  VARCHAR2(20));
CREATE SEQUENCE soldier_s;

-- Create the sailor table and sequence.
CREATE TABLE sailor
( sailor_id    NUMBER
, sailor_rank  VARCHAR2(4)
, sailor_name  VARCHAR2(20));
CREATE SEQUENCE sailor_s;
```

All the examples get their data from a SELECT statement that uses the dual pseudo-table and a fabricated result set. The INSERT ALL or INSERT FIRST statement inserts the data into one or both of the target tables. The tables are unconstrained because constraints aren't required for the examples.

Multiple-Table INSERT ALL Without WHEN Clauses The first example shows you how to insert into multiple tables without any qualifications. Values from each row returned by the query are inserted into the `soldier` and `sailor` tables. Unfiltered multiple-table `INSERT` statements put rows into all tables referenced by an `INTO` clause. In this regard, the `INSERT ALL` statement works like a *switch* statement with fall-through in C#, C++, or Java. (*Fall-through* is the principal that after meeting the condition of one `CASE` statement, all subsequent `CASE` statements are valid and their code blocks also run.)

```
SQL> INSERT ALL
     INTO soldier
     VALUES
     (soldier_s.nextval,service_rank,service_member_name)
     INTO sailor VALUES
     (sailor_s.nextval,service_rank,service_member_name)
     SELECT 'MSG' AS service_rank
     ,      'Ernest G. Bilko' AS service_member_name FROM dual
     UNION ALL
     SELECT 'CPO' AS service_rank
     ,      'David Vaught' AS service_member_name FROM dual;
```

This example has no `ELSE` block. This type of statement would also run the `ELSE` block and perform any `INSERT` statement found in it.

Queries against the target tables show you that both rows are inserted into both tables:

```
SQL> SELECT * FROM soldier;

SOLDIER_ID SOLD SOLDIER_NAME
---------- ---- --------------------
         1 MSG  Ernest G. Bilko
         2 CPO  David Vaught

SQL> SELECT * FROM sailor;

 SAILOR_ID SAIL SAILOR_NAME
---------- ---- --------------------
         1 MSG  Ernest G. Bilko
         2 CPO  David Vaught
```

This type of statement is useful when you want to put data from one row of a table or view into multiple tables. Unfiltered `INSERT ALL` statements don't let you choose among a set of tables (like a filtered `INSERT ALL` statement), and they're used less often than filtered statements.

Multiple-Table INSERT ALL with WHEN Clauses The multiple-table `INSERT ALL` statement also works with `WHEN` clauses that determine which table they'll insert into. The logic can include subqueries, as shown in this example:

```
SQL> INSERT ALL
     WHEN service_rank IN (SELECT rank_short_name
                           FROM   rank_index
                           WHERE  rank_service = 'ARMY') THEN
     INTO soldier
     VALUES
```

```
 7  (soldier_s.nextval,service_rank,service_member_name)
 8  WHEN service_rank IN (SELECT rank_short_name
 9                        FROM   rank_index
10                        WHERE  rank_service = 'NAVY') THEN
11  INTO sailor
12  VALUES
13  (sailor_s.nextval,service_rank,service_member_name)
14  SELECT 'MSG' AS service_rank
15  ,      'Ernest G. Bilko' AS service_member_name FROM dual
16  UNION ALL
17  SELECT 'CPO' AS service_rank
18  ,      'David Vaught' AS service_member_name FROM dual;
```

The `WHEN` clause on line 2 checks whether the service rank belongs in the Army. It inserts into the `soldier` table any row in which the query's `service_rank` value matches the subquery's `rank_short_name` value. The second `WHEN` clause does the same kind of evaluation against Navy ranks. Any rows that don't match one of the two criteria are discarded because there's no `ELSE` clause.

Queries against the target tables yield the following results:

```
SQL> SELECT * FROM soldier;

SOLDIER_ID SOLD SOLDIER_NAME
---------- ---- --------------------
         1 MSG  Ernest G. Bilko

SQL> SELECT * FROM sailor;

 SAILOR_ID SAIL SAILOR_NAME
---------- ---- --------------------
         2 CPO  David Vaught
```

The filtered `INSERT ALL` places rows from one source query into one or only the correct tables. This is the best practice, or at least the most frequently used version of the statement.

Multiple-Table INSERT FIRST with WHEN Clauses The `INSERT FIRST` statement works differently from the `INSERT ALL` statement. The `INSERT FIRST` statement inserts data into the first table only when it meets a `WHEN` clause condition. This means it performs like a switch statement in C#, C++, or Java where fall-through is disabled. For your reference (in case you don't write programs in those languages), you disable fall-through by putting a *break* statement in each `CASE` statement's code bock. The *break* statement signals completion and forces an exit from the switch statement. The `FIRST` keyword effectively does that for all `WHEN` clause statement blocks.

Here's an example using the concept of conscripts (draftees). The first conscript goes to the Army (line 2), the next four go to the Navy (line 6), and any others get to go home without serving in the military:

```
SQL> INSERT FIRST
  2  WHEN id < 2 THEN
  3  INTO soldier
  4  VALUES
```

```
(soldier_s.nextval,'PVT',draftee)
WHEN id BETWEEN 2 AND 5 THEN
INTO sailor
VALUES
(sailor_s.nextval,'SR',draftee)
SELECT 1 AS ID,'John Sanchez' AS draftee FROM dual
UNION ALL
SELECT 2 AS ID,'Michael Deegan' AS draftee
FROM dual
UNION ALL
SELECT 3 AS ID,'Jon Voight' AS draftee FROM dual;
```

You'll see in the result set that only two went into the Navy, so there weren't enough drafted today. The statement will need to be rewritten tomorrow for the new batch of draftees unless the rules change every day. The queries and results are

```
SQL> SELECT * FROM soldier;

SOLDIER_ID SOLD SOLDIER_NAME
---------- ---- --------------------
         1 PVT  John Sanchez

SQL> SELECT * FROM sailor;

 SAILOR_ID SAIL SAILOR_NAME
---------- ---- --------------------
         2 SR   Michael Deegan
         3 SR   Jon Voight
```

My suggestion is that the `INSERT FIRST` statement is probably suited to dynamic creation inside Native Dynamic SQL (NDS). You can see examples of NDS in Chapter 13.

UPDATE Statement

The `UPDATE` statement lets you change data in tables and views by resetting values in one or more columns. A single `UPDATE` statement can change one, many, or all rows in a table. The new values can come from literal values, variables, or correlated query results. *Correlation* is the matching of one set of data with another through join operations. This section discusses equijoin (equality value joins); later in this appendix we'll examine join options in detail in the "Join Results" section.

Oracle implements the basic `UPDATE` statement syntax in an ANSI-compliant way, but Oracle supports both a record update and a large object update (through the `dbms_lob` package). The large object update appends the `RETURNING INTO` clause to `UPDATE` statements.

This section covers how you do the following:

- Update by values and queries
- Update by correlated queries

An `UPDATE` statement's most important behavior is that it works against all rows in a table unless a `WHERE` clause or a correlated join limits the number of rows. This means you should always limit which rows should be changed by providing a WHERE clause or a correlated join. The list of columns in the SET clause of an UPDATE statement is the expression list.

Changes by the UPDATE statement are hidden until committed in an Oracle database, but are immediately visible in nontransactional databases. Oracle is always in transaction mode by default.

Generic Update by Values and Queries

Some UPDATE statements use date, numeric, or string literals in the SET subclause. The SET subclause can work with one to all columns in a table, but you should never update a primary surrogate key column. Any update of the externally known identifier column risks compromising the referential integrity of primary and foreign keys.

The generic UPDATE statement prototype with values resetting column values looks like this:

```
UPDATE some_table
SET    column_name = 'expression'
[,     column_name = 'expression' [, ...]
WHERE [NOT] column_name {{= | <> | > | >= | < | <=} |
                        [NOT] {{IN | EXISTS} | IS NULL}} 'expression'
[{AND | OR } [NOT] comparison_operation] [...];
```

The target table of an UPDATE statement can be a table or updateable view. An expression can be a numeric or string literal or the return value from a function or subquery. The function or subquery must return only a single-row of data that matches the data type of the assignment target. The right operand of the assignment may contain a different data type when its type can be implicitly cast to the column's data type, or explicitly cast to it with the CAST function. In the generic example, a subquery needs to return a single column and row (this type of subquery is a scalar subquery or SQL expression). Ellipses replace multiple listings in the SET and WHERE clauses.

The WHERE clause lets you evaluate truth or non-truth, which is the purpose of each comparison operation. The comparison operators in the prototype are broken into sets of related operators by using curly braces: first the math comparisons, then the set and correlation comparisons, and finally the null comparison. The AND, OR, and NOT are logical operators. The AND operator evaluates the truth of two comparisons or, with enclosing parentheses, the truth of sets of comparison operations. The OR operator evaluates the truth of one or the other comparison operator, and it employs short-circuit evaluation (the statement is true when the first comparison is true). The negation operator (NOT) checks whether a statement is false.

An actual UPDATE statement against an item table would look like this when you enter the actual movie name in lieu of a placeholder value:

```
SQL> UPDATE item
  2  SET    item_title = 'Pirates of the Caribbean: On Stranger Tides'
  3  ,      item_rating = 'PG-13'
  4  WHERE  item_title = 'Pirates of the Caribbean 4';
```

Variations to this syntax exist in Oracle, but this is the basic form for UPDATE statements. Specifics for how Oracle handles it are provided in the following section.

Oracle Update by Values and Queries

The biggest difference between Oracle and other databases is that Oracle allows you to reset record structures, not just columns. Recall from the discussion of tables earlier in this appendix that the definition of a table is equivalent to the definition of a record structure, and a record structure is a combination of two or more columns (or fields).

The prototype of an UPDATE statement for Oracle differs from the generic profile, as you can see:

```
UPDATE {some_table | TABLE(query_statement)}
 SET    {column_name = 'expression' | (column_list) = 'expression_list'}
[,      {column_name = 'expression' | (column_list) = 'expression_list'}
[, ...]]
 WHERE [NOT] {column_name | (column_list)}
                {{= | <> | > | >= | < | <=} |
                 [NOT] {IN | =ANY | =SOME | =ALL } |
                 [NOT] {IS NULL | IS SET} | [NOT] EXISTS} 'expression'
[{AND | OR } [NOT] comparison_operation] [...]
[RETURNING {column_name | (column_list)}
 INTO {local_variable | (variable_list)}];
```

Oracle extends the target of the UPDATE statement from a table or view (traditionally a named query inside the data catalog) to a result set. In Oracle's lexicon, the result set is formally an *aggregate result set*, which is a fancy way of saying that the result set acts like a normal query's return set in processing memory (inside the System Global Area, or SGA). The TABLE function makes this possible. (The TABLE function was previously known as the THE function—that's ancient history from Oracle 8*i*, although some error message have never been updated and still reflect this relic.)

Oracle also extends the behavior of assignment in the SET operator by allowing you to assign a record structure to another record structure. A (data) record structure in the SET operator is any list of two or more columns from the table definition, which is less than the complete data structure of the table or its definition in the data catalog. Ellipses replace continuing the list of possible elements in the SET and WHERE clauses.

The WHERE clause comparison operators are also expanded in an Oracle database. They're separated by curly braces, like the generic prototype, with math comparisons, set comparisons, null comparisons, and correlation. Set comparisons act as lookup operators, and correlation is explained in the "Update by Correlated Queries" section of this appendix.

The RETURNING INTO clause allows you to shift a reference to columns that you've updated but not committed into variables. Those variables are critical to how you update large objects in the database.

Here's an example of how you would use Oracle's record structure assignment operation in a SET clause:

```
SQL> UPDATE item
  SET    (item_title, item_rating) =
           (SELECT 'Pirates of the Caribbean: On Stranger Tides'
            ,      'PG-13'
            FROM   dual)
  WHERE  item_title = 'Pirates of the Caribbean 4';
```

The values reset the columns item_title and item_rating on all lines where item_title is "Pirates of the Caribbean 4." The subquery uses string literals inside a query against the dual table. This is straightforward and not much different from the comma-delimited SET clauses for each column. You might wonder why you should bother with implementing this twist on the other syntax. That's a great question! There's not much added value with date, numeric, or string literals from the pseudo-table `dual`; rather, the value occurs when the source is a row returned from a query. The record structure syntax allows you to assign a row's return values directly from a single-row subquery with multiple columns to a row of the target table.

Here's an example of an assignment from a subquery to record structure:

```
SQL> UPDATE item
     SET    (item_title, item_rating) =
              (SELECT   item_title, item_rating
               FROM     import_item ii
               WHERE    item_barcode = 'B004A8ZWUG')
     WHERE  item_title = 'Pirates of the Caribbean 4';
```

The `item_title` and `item_rating` values from the subquery are assigned to the equivalent columns in the `item` table when the `item_title` column holds the string literal value. The power of this type of assignment increases when you add correlation, because you can process sets of data in a single `UPDATE` statement. (That's covered in the "Update by Correlated Queries" section later in the chapter.)

Two specialized forms of `UPDATE` statements are included in the Oracle Database 12*c* database. One works with collections of object types, and the other works with scalar and large object types. The ability to use the result of the `TABLE` function inside an `UPDATE` statement lets you update nested tables (collections of object types). A `RETURNING INTO` clause supports scalar and large objects by returning the values or references from the `UPDATE` statement to the calling scope. The calling scope is the SQL*Plus session in the examples but could be an external program written in PL/SQL or C, C++, C#, or Java. This technique provides you with access to recently updated values without requerying the table, and in the case of large objects this technique allows you to read and write to large objects through a web application.

RETURNING INTO Clause You can append the `RETURNING INTO` clause to any `UPDATE` statement. The `RETURNING INTO` clause lets you retrieve updated column values into locally scoped variables. This lets you avoid requerying the columns after the `UPDATE` statement.

We can use a brief example to demonstrate this concept because even the shortest example can use session-level bind variables. The bind variables eliminate the need for a procedural programming language such as Java or PHP to demonstrate the concept. As Appendix A describes, SQL*Plus commands declare session-level bind variables. This example requires a pair of session-level variables to act as the target of the `RETURNING INTO` clause. You can declare these two bind variables with this syntax:

```
SQL> VARIABLE bv_title  VARCHAR2(60)
SQL> VARIABLE bv_rating VARCHAR2(60)
```

The following demonstrates an `UPDATE` statement that uses the `RETURNING INTO` phrase:

```
SQL> UPDATE item
     SET    (item_title,item_rating) =
              (SELECT 'Pirates of the Caribbean: On Stranger Tides'
               ,      'PG-13'
```

```
          FROM dual)
WHERE  item_title = 'Pirates of the Caribbean 4'
RETURNING item_title, item_rating INTO :bv_title, :bv_rating;
```

The values updated into the table are returned in the local variables. They can be displayed by using SQL*Plus formatting and a query:

```
COLUMN bv_title  FORMAT A44 HEADING ":bv_title"
COLUMN bv_rating FORMAT A12 HEADING ":bv_rating"
SELECT :bv_title AS bv_title, :bv_rating AS bv_rating FROM dual;
```

The `HEADING` value is enclosed in double quotes so that a colon can be used in the column titles. This returns the literal values from the query against the `dual` table:

```
:bv_title                                    :bv_rating
-------------------------------------------- ------------
Pirates of the Caribbean: On Stranger Tides  PG-13
```

Note that the `RETURNING INTO` phrase has several restrictions:

- It fails when updating more than a single-row.
- It fails when the expression list includes a primary key or other not null column when a `BEFORE UPDATE` trigger is defined on the table.
- It fails when the expression list includes a `LONG` data type.
- It fails when the `UPDATE` statement is parallel processing or working against a remote object.
- It is disallowed when updating a view that has an `INSTEAD OF` trigger.

Returning scalar, `BLOB`, or `CLOB` data types is the most effective way to leverage the `RETURNING INTO` phrase. The `RETURNING INTO` phrase is very advantageous in web applications. A web application would implement a stored procedure to start a transaction context and pass a reference for updating a `CLOB` column.

```
SQL> CREATE OR REPLACE PROCEDURE web_load_clob_from_file
  2  ( pv_item_id     IN      NUMBER
  3  , pv_descriptor IN OUT CLOB ) IS
  4  BEGIN
  5    -- A FOR UPDATE makes this a DML transaction.
  6    UPDATE    item
  7    SET       item_desc = empty_clob()
  8    WHERE     item_id = pv_item_id
  9    RETURNING item_desc INTO pv_descriptor;
 10  END web_load_clob_from_file;
 11  /
```

The `pv_descriptor` parameter in the procedure's signature on line 3 uses an `IN OUT` mode of operation, which is a *pass-by-reference* mechanism. It effectively enables sending a reference to the `CLOB` column out to the calling program. The `RETURNING INTO` clause assigns the reference to the parameter on line 9. With the reference, the external program can then update the `CLOB` column.

How to Write to a CLOB Column from PHP

Although this book isn't about how you write PHP to work with an Oracle database, an example using PHP can show you how to capture the handle from the `web_load_clob_from` file procedure.

The PHP function to write a large file to a `CLOB` column is

```
if ($c = @oci_connect(SCHEMA,PASSWD,TNS_ID)) {
  // Declare input variables.
  (isset($_POST['id']))    ? $id = (int) $_POST['id']  : $id = 1021;
  (isset($_POST['title'])) ? $title = $_POST['title'] : $title = "Harry #1";

  // Declare a PL/SQL statement and parse it.
  $stmt = "BEGIN web_load_clob_from_file(:id,:item_desc); END;";
  $s = oci_parse($c,$stmt);

  // Define a descriptor for a CLOB and variable for CLOB descriptor.
  $rlob = oci_new_descriptor($c,OCI_D_LOB);
  oci_define_by_name($s,':item_desc',$rlob,SQLT_CLOB);

  // Bind PHP variables to the OCI types.
  oci_bind_by_name($s,':id',$id);
  oci_bind_by_name($s,':item_desc',$rlob,-1,SQLT_CLOB);

  // Execute the PL/SQL statement.
  if (oci_execute($s,OCI_DEFAULT)) {
    $rlob->save($item_desc);
    oci_commit($c); }

  // Release statement resources and disconnect from database.
  oci_free_statement($s);
  oci_close($c); }
else {
    // Assign the OCI error and manage error.
    $errorMessage = oci_error();
    print htmlentities($errorMessage['message'])."<br />";
    die(); }
```

The four boldfaced lines make reading and writing to the `CLOB` column possible. The lines, respectively, define an anonymous PL/SQL block as a statement, create a socket, map the placeholder and the statement to the socket, and write the `CLOB` through the socket to the file.

If you're interested in learning more about PHP and the Oracle database, you can check *Oracle Database 10g Express Edition PHP Web Programming* (Oracle Press). The first 12 chapters cover PHP and the last 3 cover Oracle's OCI library. Alternatively, you can refer to the *Oracle Database 2 Day + PHP Developer's Guide 12c Release* on Oracle's website.

You can check Chapter 10 for the details on how to write this type of programming logic to support web applications and large objects in Oracle Database 12*c*.

Nested Table Updates Nested tables are lists, which are like arrays but without a maximum number of rows. As such, lists mimic database tables when they're defined by object types. Object types act like record data structures in an Oracle database. This is possible because Oracle is an object relational database.

The original SQL design didn't consider the concept of object types or collections of object types. This leaves Oracle with the responsibility to fit calls to these object types within SQL extensions. The interface is rather straightforward but has limitations as to what you can perform on nested tables and arrays through `INSERT` and `UPDATE` statements. You can insert or update complete nested tables, but you cannot replace only certain elements of the nested tables. PL/SQL lets you access and manipulate the elements of nested tables and arrays. Chapter 8 show you how to perform that type of change to an existing nested table.

NOTE
A collection of a scalar type is an ADT, while a collection of a SQL structure is a UDT.

This example revisits the `employee` table from earlier in this appendix. Here's the definition of the table:

```
Name                                      Null?    Type
----------------------------------------- -------- ------------------
EMPLOYEE_ID                                        NUMBER
FIRST_NAME                                         VARCHAR2(20)
MIDDLE_NAME                                        VARCHAR2(20)
LAST_NAME                                          VARCHAR2(20)
HOME_ADDRESS                                       ADDRESS_LIST
```

The `home_address` column is a UDT collection named `address_list`. To save flipping back to an earlier section of this appendix, the `address_list` UDT holds an `address_type` UDT (object type that acts like a record data structure), and the `address_type` UDT holds another nested table of a scalar variable. This means the table holds a multiple nested table.

You can also describe the `address_list` UDTs with the `DESCRIBE` command in SQL*Plus:

```
address_list TABLE OF ADDRESS_TYPE
Name                                      Null?    Type
----------------------------------------- -------- ------------------
ADDRESS_ID                                         NUMBER
STREET_ADDRESS                                     STREET_LIST
CITY                                               VARCHAR2(30)
STATE                                              VARCHAR2(2)
POSTAL_CODE                                        VARCHAR2(10)
```

This collection is a nested table. You can tell that because it says `TABLE OF`. An ADT or UDT array would print a `VARRAY(n) OF` phrase before the respective object structure's name. This example includes a nested `street_list` table collection, which is an ADT. You can describe it the same way and it shows the following:

```
street_list TABLE OF VARCHAR2(30)
```

As mentioned, this type of table structure is called *multiple table nesting*. It is inherently complex. This type of design also presents migration issues when you want to modify the UDTs. You must put the data some place, drop the table, and then add the UDTs in the reverse order of how you created them—at least until you arrive at the UDT that you want to change. After making the change, you'll need to re-create all data types and tables and migrate the data back into the new table.

When you perform an update, you need to replace the entire nested table element. You can read out what's there and identify where the change goes through PL/SQL or some other procedural language that leverages the Oracle Call Interface (OCI), Open Database Connectivity (ODBC), or Java Database Connectivity (JDBC). This assumes you've written the code logic to capture all existing data and dynamically construct an `UPDATE` statement. NDS lets you dynamically create these types of SQL statements. You can read about NDS in Chapter 13.

Earlier in this appendix, we inserted a row into the `employee` table. Here's how you would extract the information from the nested tables into an ordinary result set of scalar columns:

```
-- These SQL*Plus commands format the columns for display.
COLUMN employee_id FORMAT 999 HEADING "ID|EMP"
COLUMN full_name   FORMAT A16 HEADING "Full Name"
COLUMN address_id  FORMAT 999 HEADING "ID|UDT"
COLUMN st_address  FORMAT A16 HEADING "Street Address"
COLUMN city        FORMAT A8  HEADING "City"
COLUMN state       FORMAT A5  HEADING "State"
COLUMN postal_code FORMAT A5  HEADING "Zip|Code"

SQL> SELECT   e.employee_id
     ,        e.first_name || ' ' || e.last_name AS full_name
     ,        st.address_id
     ,        sa.column_value AS st_address
     ,        st.city
     ,        st.state
     ,        st.postal_code
     FROM     employee e CROSS JOIN
              TABLE(e.home_address) st CROSS JOIN
              TABLE(street_address) sa
     ORDER BY 2, 3, 4;
```

It uses the cross join to extract nested table material to the single containing row that holds it. In this process, the cross join makes copies of the content of the single-row for each row of the nested table. This example first unwinds `street_address` within `home_address` and then `home_address` within the container `employee` table. It returns four rows, because there are two rows in each of the nested tables and only one row in the sample table. Cross joins yield Cartesian products, which are the number of rows in one set times the number of rows in the other set, or in this case the multiplied product of rows in three sets (1 × 2 × 2 = 4). It renders the following output:

```
  ID                      ID                                   Zip
 EMP Full Name           UDT Street Address    City     State Code
---- ---------------- ---- ---------------- -------- ----- -----
   1 Sam Yosemite          1 1111 Broadway    Oakland  CA    94612
   1 Sam Yosemite          1 Suite 322        Oakland  CA    94612
   1 Sam Yosemite          2 1111 Broadway    Oakland  CA    94612
   1 Sam Yosemite          2 Suite 525        Oakland  CA    94612
```

Let's assume you want to change Suite 525 in the second row to Suite 521. The `UPDATE` statement would look like this when you replace the entire structure:

```
SQL> UPDATE employee e
  2  SET    e.home_address =
  3         address_list(
  4           address_type( 1
  5                       , street_list('1111 Broadway','Suite 322')
  6                       ,'Oakland'
  7                       ,'CA'
  8                       ,'94612')
  9         , address_type( 2
 10                       , street_list('1111 Broadway','Suite 521')
 11                       ,'Oakland'
 12                       ,'CA'
 13                       ,'94612'))
 14  WHERE  e.first_name = 'Sam'
 15  AND    e.last_name = 'Yosemite';
```

The syntax to replace the content of a UDT is to use the name of the data type as an object constructor and then provide a list. Lines 4 to 8 are highlighted to demonstrate the constructor for an `address_type` UDT. Lines 5 and 10 are separately highlighted to show the constructor for a `street_list` ADT. In the preceding statement, a comma-delimited list lets you construct nested tables. Of course, you probably want to nest only data that changes infrequently and that fails to merit its own table.

You can also replace only an element of the nested `address_type` UDT by using some complex `UPDATE` syntax. The `UPDATE` statement is complex because it uses a query to find a nested table in one row of the `employee` table. The `TABLE` function then casts the object collection into a SQL result set (formally, an aggregate result set). This type of result set may also be called an inline view, runtime table, derived table, or common table expression. The `UPDATE` statement lets you change the `city` value for the first element of the `address_type` UDT in the `address_list` collection:

```
SQL> UPDATE TABLE (SELECT e.home_address
                   FROM   employee e
                   WHERE  e.employee_id = 1) e
     SET   e.city = 'Fremont'
     WHERE e.address_id = 1;
```

Line 3 refers to a row in the `employee` table where the `employee_id` column value is equal to 1. Line 5 refers to the `home_address` object collection column's `address_id` column value where it is equal to 1. Unfortunately, although the city is correct for the address, *Suite 521* is wrong. It should be *Suite 522*. There is no way to replace only one element of a varray or nested table of a scalar data type in SQL by itself. An attempt would use the same cross-joining logic shown earlier in the query that unfolds nested tables, like so:

```
SQL> UPDATE TABLE(SELECT  addr.street_address
  2               FROM    employee e CROSS JOIN TABLE(e.home_address) addr
  3               WHERE   e.employee_id = 1
  4               AND     addr.address_id = 1)
  5  SET column_value = 'Suite 522'
  6  WHERE column_value = 'Suite 521';
```

Although the query returns the expected result set, the assignment in the `SET` clause fails. You can't make an assignment to the default `column_value` column returned by an unwound nested table of a scalar data type. It raises an `ORA-25015` error:

```
SET column_value = 'Suite 522'
    *
ERROR at line 5:
ORA-25015: cannot perform DML ON this nested TABLE VIEW COLUMN
```

The error documentation does not seem to explain why it doesn't work. Hazarding a guess, I think that collections of scalar data types, or ADTs, are handled differently than collections of UDTs. At least, there's a difference between them: scalar collections work in the result cache PL/SQL functions, while collections of UDTs don't.

The following lets you reset the city and replaces the nested address element by replacing the entire `street_list` instance:

```
SQL> UPDATE TABLE (SELECT e.home_address
  2                FROM   employee e
  3                WHERE  e.employee_id = 1) e
  4  SET   e.street_address = street_list('1111 Broadway','Suite 522')
  5  ,     e.city = 'Oakland'
  6  WHERE e.address_id = 1;
```

Line 4 stores a complete constructor of the scalar collection. It's not terribly difficult when only a few elements exist, but it becomes tedious with long lists. The alternative to an `UPDATE` statement like these is to use PL/SQL, which allows you to navigate the collections element-by-element and then process the individual list elements.

You have the option of writing PL/SQL functions that let you insert, update, or delete elements of ADT collection columns. A function to insert an element should check whether an empty or populated collection exists before adding one, and when the insert function finds a null value in the collection column, the function should initialize the collection before adding an element. An update function is the easiest way to update of a nested ADT column. That's true because you can guarantee an initialized collection inside the function before you try to append or change an element of an ADT column. This capability inside a function helps you manage the issues with potential null values. You should check the "PL/SQL to the Rescue of Updating an ADT Element" sidebar for more complete coverage of how to make it work. A delete element function should remove the element and leave a populated collection, or, in the case of having removed the last element, an empty collection. A separate function should let you remove an empty collection, at least if you approach the problem in a solid OOAD manner.

In general, with collections, you store nested tables, varrays, and object types the same way—with a call to their object type, which serves as a constructor method. You pass values inside the parentheses as actual parameters (also called arguments). The `TREAT` function lets you instantiate these in memory.

PL/SQL to the Rescue of Updating an ADT Element

PL/SQL can help remedy the `UPDATE` statement's inability to insert, update, or delete a value in an ADT, which is any varray or nested table collection of a scalar data type. You can develop a PL/SQL function that lets you insert, update, or replace elements in an ADT collection.

The following is an example of a function that succeeds when we focus on test cases with nested ADT values and forget the test cases for a null value in the ADT column. It updates an element in an *initialize collection* of the same `street_list` element shown in the "Nested Table Updates" section examples:

```
SQL> CREATE OR REPLACE FUNCTION update_collection
( old_element_collection  STREET_LIST
, old_element_value       VARCHAR2
, new_element_value       VARCHAR2 ) RETURN STREET_LIST IS

  -- Declare and initial a new counter.
  lv_counter  NUMBER := 1;

  -- Declare local return collection variable.
  lv_element_collection  STREET_LIST :=  street_list();

BEGIN
  FOR i IN 1..old_element_collection.COUNT LOOP
    IF NOT old_element_collection(i) = old_element_value THEN
      lv_element_collection.EXTEND;  -- Allocate space.
      lv_element_collection(lv_counter) := old_element_collection(i);
    ELSE
      lv_element_collection.EXTEND;  -- Allocate space.
      lv_element_collection(lv_counter) := new_element_value;
    END IF;
    lv_counter := lv_counter + 1;
  END LOOP;

  RETURN lv_element_collection;
END update_collection;
/
```

(continued)

This appears a sound solution because you can successfully replace a nested ADT value with it in the unnesting `UPDATE` statement, like

```
SQL> UPDATE TABLE (SELECT e.home_address
                   FROM   employee e
                   WHERE  e.employee_id = 1) e
     SET   e.street_address =
             update_collection(e.street_address, 'Suite 525','Suite 522')
     ,     e.city = 'Oakland'
     WHERE e.address_id = 1;
```

The preceding `UPDATE` statement works because the nested ADT column value is an initialized and populated collection. Unfortunately, when we change the `UPDATE` statement to work with the data set for our *Wile E Coyote* example (found in the "Inserting Arrays and Nested Tables" section earlier in the appendix), it fails with the following message:

```
SET   e.street_address =
        update_collection(e.street_address, 'Suite 525','Suite 522')
        *
ERROR at line 4:
ORA-06531: Reference to uninitialized collection
ORA-06512: at "STUDENT.UPDATE_COLLECTION", line 13
```

The failure occurs because the original `update_collection` function makes an unfortunate assumption—that all collections are initialized. We can rewrite the example to manage both uninitialized and initialized collections by checking whether the nested table column is null or not. The change is made in the following code:

```
SQL> CREATE OR REPLACE FUNCTION update_collection
  2  ( old_element_collection  STREET_LIST
  3  , old_element_value       VARCHAR2
  4  , new_element_value       VARCHAR2 ) RETURN STREET_LIST IS
...
 12  BEGIN
 13    IF old_element_collection IS NOT NULL THEN
 14      FOR i IN 1..old_element_collection.COUNT LOOP
...
 23      END LOOP;
 24    END IF;
 25
 26   RETURN lv_element_collection;
 27  END update_collection;
 28  /
```

Lines 13 and 24 enclose the replacement logic with a check for a null element in the object collection column. The check prevents an uninitialized collection error but it does replace the null value with an empty collection. It's attractive because it makes the function more cohesive and less subject to failure, but it changes the column's value from a null value to an initialized empty collection.

While that solution typically works for most business solutions, it may not work for all business problems. Assuming you leave the function with an inability to manage null values as the call parameter to the `old_element_collection` parameter, you could handle the logic in your `UPDATE` statement, like this with a `CASE` statement:

```
SQL> UPDATE TABLE (SELECT e.home_address
  2                FROM    employee e
  3                WHERE   e.employee_id = 2) e
  4  SET    e.street_address =
  5           CASE
  6             WHEN e.street_address IS NOT NULL THEN
  7               update_collection(e.street_address, 'value1','value2')
  8             ELSE
  9               NULL
 10           END
 11  ,      e.city = 'Phoenix'
 12  WHERE e.address_id = 1
```

Lines 4 through 10 show how to implement a `CASE` statement to handle the null condition, and I would argue it's the right approach. Writing a PL/SQL function to manage something that should be written in SQL is simply bad coding, and unfortunately, *overreaching solutions like that can give PL/SQL a bad rap because they're done too often*. The preceding `UPDATE` statement ensures you don't replace a null with an initialized collection.

While you can solve this with an Oracle proprietary `DECODE` statement, you shouldn't. If you haven't already, you should start moving your SQL code toward the generic ANSI components, like the `CASE` statement.

This sidebar has shown you how PL/SQL can bridge limits in SQL syntax, and that you can overuse PL/SQL when SQL solutions are available. As a rule of thumb, try to use SQL *where it works*, because it's generally faster in those cases.

NOTE
Chapter 11 shows you how to implement a basic object type, and it and the SQL statements that support it are discussed there.

Large Objects Large objects present complexity in Oracle because you need to load them by segments. After all, they can grow to 32 terabytes in size. The `BLOB` and the `CLOB` are the only two data types stored physically inside the database. The other large object type, the `BFILE`, is a locator that points to an external directory location (see the "External Tables" section earlier in the appendix) and filename. The first argument is a call to a virtual directory that you've created in the database, and the second argument is the relative filename.

An ordinary UPDATE statement handles changes to BFILE locators like this:

```
SET = bfilename('virtual_directory_name', 'relative_file_name')
```

The BLOB and CLOB data types require special handling. The most common need is to overwrite the column value. That's because these are binary or character streams and they're seldom simply edited.

The following illustration shows you how to update a BLOB column. BLOB columns larger than 4KB are stored out-of-line from the transactional table because they're infrequently changed and less frequently backed up. It is also common practice to change these columns by themselves, after any updates to the scalar columns of a table.

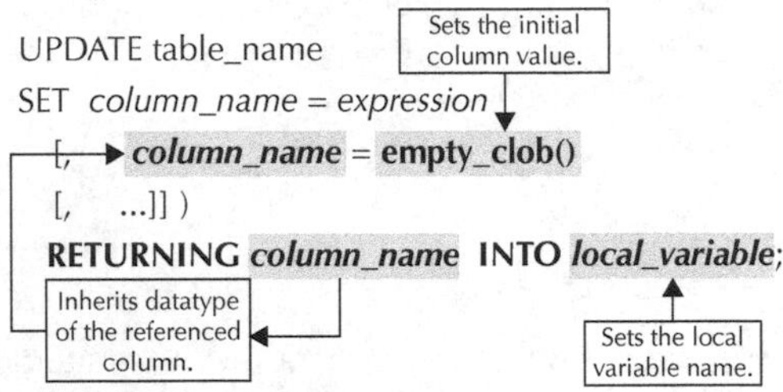

This prototype statement demonstrates the syntax if you were to update all columns at the same time. The first step of an update to a BLOB column is reinitialization, which occurs with an empty_blob function call. The second step maps the column name in a row to an external stream (receiving end), which uses the column name as an identifier. The third step assigns the stream (originating end) to a local program variable. Basically, this is a socket communication between a program and the database, and it lasts until all segments have been loaded into the column.

The local variable in this example can be a PL/SQL variable or any external OCI, ODBC, or JDBC programming language variable. The local variable data type must support a mapped relationship to the native Oracle data type.

The CLOB data type works the same way, and, as you can see in the next illustration, there's no SQL statement difference. Only the call to the empty_clob differs, but it's an important difference that you shouldn't overlook.

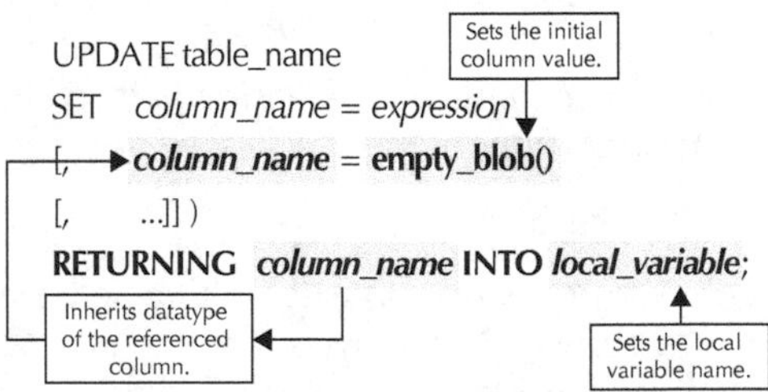

The XML_TYPE data types use the empty_clob function to clear the columns' contents. After all, XML_TYPE columns are specializations of the CLOB data type.

Update by Correlated Queries

A correlated query is a specialized subquery that contains a join to an outer query. An UPDATE statement can contain a correlated in the SET clause, which allows the UPDATE statement to change multiple rows with potentially different values.

```
SQL> UPDATE    rental_item ri
  2  SET       rental_item_type =
  3              (SELECT   cl.common_lookup_id
  4               FROM     common_lookup cl
  5               WHERE    cl.common_lookup_code =
  6                 (SELECT   TO_CHAR(r.return_date - r.check_out_date)
  7                  FROM     rental r
  8                  WHERE    r.rental_id = ri.rental_id));
```

Line 1 designates the rental_item table as the target of the UPDATE statement, and line 1 assigns a ri table alias to the rental_item table. Line 2 assigns the result of a correlated subquery to the rental_item_type column. Line 8 matches the rows to update in the rental_item table with the rental table based on matching the primary key value to the foreign key value. The rental_id column is the surrogate and primary key column of the rental table, while the rental_id column in the rental_item table is a foreign key column.

DELETE Statement

The DELETE statement lets you remove data from tables and views. There are two types of DELETE statements: one uses literal values or subquery comparisons in a WHERE clause; the other uses correlated results from a subquery. It is also possible to combine values or subquery results with correlated results in the WHERE clause. This section covers how you use both statements.

Like the UPDATE statement, a DELETE statement removes all rows found in a table unless you filter what you want to remove in a WHERE clause. A DELETE statement also writes redo logs, similar to INSERT and UPDATE statements, and supports bulk processing options inside Oracle's PL/SQL blocks.

The DELETE statement has a closely related cousin, the DDL TRUNCATE statement. DBAs often disable constraints, copy a table's contents to a temporary table, TRUNCATE or DROP the table, re-create the table with a new storage clause, and then INSERT the old records from the temporary table. The TRUNCATE statement doesn't log deletions; it simply removes the allocated storage space in a tablespace, which makes it much faster for routine DBA maintenance tasks.

NOTE

Earlier in this appendix you learned how to use the CREATE TABLE statement to clone a table.

The DELETE statement also works on nested tables in the Oracle database. Deleting nested tables without removing the row from the table is the exception rather than the rule for a DELETE statement, as you'll see in the next section.

The following two sections demonstrate the syntax for deleting rows by value matches and by correlation between two or more tables. Value matches can be literal values or ordinary subqueries. Correlation between two or more tables requires joins between tables.

Delete by Value Matches

This DELETE statement uses a table name and a WHERE clause that allows you to filter which rows you want to remove from a table. The WHERE clause works with date, numeric, and string literal values.

Here's the basic prototype for a DELETE statement:

```
DELETE FROM table_name
WHERE [NOT] column_name {{= | <> | > | >= | < | <=} |
                          [NOT] {{IN | EXISTS} | IS NULL}} 'expression'
[{AND | OR } [NOT] comparison_operation] [...];
```

An actual DELETE statement would look like this:

```
SQL> DELETE FROM item
  2  WHERE  item_title = 'Pirates of the Caribbean: On Stranger Tides'
  3  AND    item_rating = 'PG-13';
```

The first line sets the target table for the deletion operation. Lines 2 and 3 filter the rows to find those that will be deleted. All rows meeting those two criteria are removed from the table and immediately become invisible to the current user in transaction mode. As explained in Appendix A, in the two-phase commit (2PC) model, the first phase removes rows from the current user's view, and the second phase removes them from the system. Between the first and second phases, other users see the deleted rows and can make decisions based on their existence—unless you've locked them in the context of a transaction.

You should lock rows that are possibly subject to deletion before running DELETE statements. This is straightforward in a transactional database such as Oracle. You can use SQL cursors to lock rows when deletions run inside PL/SQL stored program units. You lock the rows in a SQL cursor by appending a FOR UPDATE clause. Regardless of your method of operation, failure to lock rows before deleting them can lead to insertion, update, or deletion anomalies. The anomalies can occur because other DML statements can make decisions on the unaltered rows, which are visible to other sessions before a COMMIT statement.

Transaction Management

The basis for a transaction doesn't require specialized steps in an Oracle database, because Oracle statements are natively transactional and use a 2PC process to insert, update, or delete rows in tables. However, you want to bracket more than a single INSERT, UPDATE, or DELETE statement in transaction logic. That means

1. Setting a SAVEPOINT before starting the transaction.
2. Firing the COMMIT only when all DML statements in the set of statements are successful.
3. Firing the ROLLBACK when any individual DML statement fails.

In the scope of the transaction, no other session can see the inserted values until the COMMIT statement ends the transaction and makes changes permanent. You could substitute DELETE statements for the INSERT statements, and no one would be able to see the deleted row until you have committed the changes.

In addition to using literal values in the `WHERE` clause, you can use ordinary subqueries. Ordinary subqueries aren't joined to the target table of the outer `DELETE` statement. These subqueries do have a restriction: they can return only a single-row when you use an equality comparison operator, such as the equal (=) operator. You can also use multiple-row subqueries, but they require a lookup operator. SQL has four lookup operators you can use: `IN`, `=ANY`, `=SOME`, and `=ALL`. The `IN`, `=ANY`, and `=SOME` operators behave similarly. They allow you to compare a column value in a row against a list of column values, and they return true if one value matches—this is like an `OR` logical operator in a procedural `IF` statement. The `=ALL` operator also allows you to compare a column value in a row against a list of column values, and it returns true when all values in the list match the single column value. The `=ALL` operator performs like an `AND` logical operator in a procedural `IF` statement. For reference, there is no standard *exclusive OR* operator in SQL.

Inside the `WHERE` clause, you can use `AND` or `OR` logical operators. The order of precedence requires that a group of logical comparisons connected by the `AND` logical operator be processed as a block before anything connected later by an `OR` logical operator.

Modifying the preceding example, let's add an `OR` logical comparison based on the release date. The following statement uses the default order of operation in the `WHERE` clause:

```
SQL> DELETE FROM item
WHERE  item_title = 'Pirates of the Caribbean: On Stranger Tides'
AND    item_rating = 'PG-13'
OR     TRUNC(item_release_date) < TRUNC(SYSDATE,'YY');
```

This removes all rows where the literal values match the `item_title` and `item_rating` or all rows where the `item_release_date` precedes the first day of the year. You must use parentheses to change the order of operation.

Let's say the business rule changes and now requires that the `item_title` match the literal value and that either the `item_rating` match the literal value or the `item_release_date` be less than the first day of the current year. A modified statement would look like this:

```
SQL> DELETE FROM item
  2  WHERE  item_title = 'Pirates of the Caribbean: On Stranger Tides'
  3  AND   (item_rating = 'PG-13'
  4  OR     TRUNC(item_release_date) < TRUNC(SYSDATE,'YY'));
```

The parentheses on lines 3 and 4 change the order of operation and remove only rows with matching `item_title` values and matches in other criteria.

Alternatives to values in the `WHERE` clause can be subqueries that return one or more column values. You can write a `DELETE` statement when the query returns only one row, like this:

```
SQL> DELETE FROM item
  2  WHERE (item_title,item_rating) =
  3          (SELECT 'Pirates of the Caribbean: On Stranger Tides'
  4           ,      'PG-13'
  5           FROM   dual);
```

Line 2 contains an equal (=) comparison operator that works only when a single-row is returned by the subquery. All queries from the `dual` pseudo-table return one row unless a `UNION` or `UNION ALL` set operator fabricates a multiple-row set.

The IN, =ANY, and =SOME lookup operators work when the subquery returns one or more rows. It's always best to use a lookup operator unless you want to raise an exception when the subquery returns more than one row. This type of exception signals when a prior business rule has been violated—the rule that the subquery supports.

The following demonstrates a DELETE statement with a lookup operator:

```
SQL> DELETE FROM item
     WHERE (item_title,item_rating) IN
             (SELECT 'Pirates of the Caribbean: On Stranger Tides'
             ,       'PG-13'
             FROM    error_item);
```

In addition to supporting the DELETE syntax variations demonstrated in this section, Oracle supports the use of a DELETE statement when you're working with nested table elements in rows of a table, as covered next.

Delete Nested Table Row Elements

As mentioned, nested tables are object relational database management system (ORDBMS) structures. The "Nested Collection Types" section earlier in this appendix showed you how to create and alter tables with nested tables. The "Inserting Arrays and Nested Tables" section showed you how to insert nested tables, and the "Nested Table Updates" section showed you how to update nested tables.

NOTE

You can only use an UPDATE *statement and a user-defined function to delete an element from an ADT column.*

The following example builds on the employee table introduced in "Nested Collection Types" section earlier in this appendix. The following data should be included in the table by the steps covered in the "Inserting Arrays and Nested Tables" section earlier in this appendix, but it won't be formatted like the following (which was reformatted to fit on the printed page):

```
  ID Full Name     Street Address Nested Table
---- ------------ ------------------------------------------------------
   1 Yosemite Sam  ADDRESS_LIST
                   ( ADDRESS_TYPE
                     (1,STREET_LIST(...),'Oakland','CA','94612')
                   , ADDRESS_TYPE
                     (2,STREET_LIST(...),'Oakland','CA','94612')
                   )
   2 Bugs Bunny    ADDRESS_LIST
                   ( ADDRESS_TYPE
                     (1,STREET_LIST(...),'Beverly Hills','CA','90210')
                   , ADDRESS_TYPE
                     (2,STREET_LIST(...),'Beverly Hills','CA','90210')
                   )
```

Previous DELETE statements would let you remove the row with *Yosemite Sam* or *Bugs Bunny* but not an element of the nested employee table. The DELETE statement applied against a view of the nested table would let you remove a row.

The following statement lets you remove a row element from the nested table:

```
DELETE FROM TABLE (SELECT e.home_address
                   FROM   employee e
                   WHERE  e.employee_id = 1) ha
WHERE  ha.address_id = 1;
```

This works only on a collection of user-defined object types. It doesn't work for nested tables built as collections of a scalar data type, such as a date, number, or string. You must replace the collection of a scalar data type with a new collection that doesn't include the undesired element. PL/SQL lets you read through and eliminate undesired elements from any nested table structure. While reading the records, you can capture all the records you want to keep, and then update the table's collection with the locally stored collection values.

After the preceding `DELETE` statement, you would hold the following in the `employee` table:

```
  ID Full Name     Street Address Nested Table
---- ------------- ------------------------------------------------------
   1 Yosemite Sam  ADDRESS_LIST
                   ( ADDRESS_TYPE
                     (2,STREET_LIST(...),'Oakland','CA','94612')
                   )
   2 Bugs Bunny    ADDRESS_LIST
                   ( ADDRESS_TYPE
                     (1,STREET_LIST(...),'Beverly Hills','CA','90210')
                   , ADDRESS_TYPE
                     (2,STREET_LIST(...),'Beverly Hills','CA','90210')
                   )
```

Notice that the first nested row has been removed from the nested table in the Yosemite Sam row. Maintenance on nested tables is possible when they are collections of object types, but it's not possible when they are collections of scalar variables.

Delete by Correlated Queries

Although deletions can remove one to many rows when the conditions of the `WHERE` clause are met, they can also work with joins between tables. Like the `UPDATE` statement, the `DELETE` statement supports correlated joins that allow you to work with multiple tables when deleting rows.

Correlated joins use the `EXISTS` keyword in the `WHERE` clause. The actual equality or inequality of the join is in the `WHERE` clause of the subquery. The subquery has scope access to the target table of the `DELETE` statement, which makes referencing it in the subquery possible.

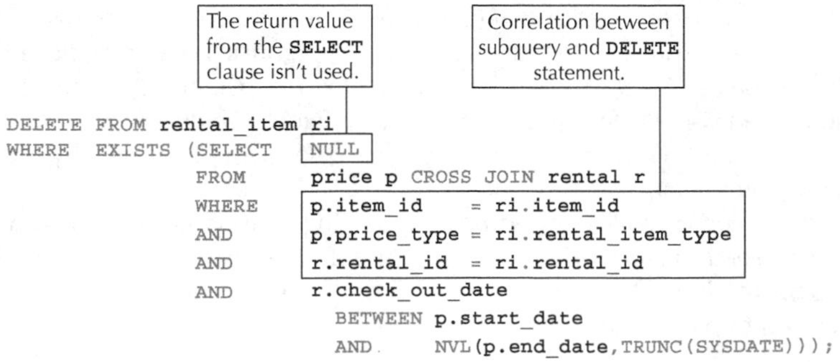

The return value from the **SELECT** clause isn't used.

Correlation between subquery and **DELETE** statement.

```
DELETE FROM rental_item ri
WHERE  EXISTS (SELECT NULL
               FROM   price p CROSS JOIN rental r
               WHERE  p.item_id    = ri.item_id
               AND    p.price_type = ri.rental_item_type
               AND    r.rental_id  = ri.rental_id
               AND    r.check_out_date
                        BETWEEN p.start_date
                        AND     NVL(p.end_date,TRUNC(SYSDATE)));
```

Correlated subqueries in the `WHERE` clause don't return a value, because the match occurs in the subquery's `WHERE` clause. That's why a `NULL` is frequently returned from correlated subqueries, but you can return anything you'd like. In the preceding example, two columns from the `price` table and one column from the `rental` table match three columns in the target table of the `DELETE FROM` statement. The three columns from the `rental_item` table are the natural key. Together they uniquely identify rows as the natural key. A match between the three columns guarantees unique row deletions.

MERGE Statement

Sometimes you need to insert new data and update existing data to relational tables during a bulk import of a physical file. You can accomplish this type of insert or update activity using a `MERGE` statement in Oracle.

Data import files often present interesting challenges because they frequently contain rows of data that belong in multiple tables (*denormalized data sets*). Import processes have to deal with this reality and discover the rules in order to break them up into normalized data sets. Only normalized data sets fit into the merge processes, because they work with single tables.

You need to understand why these files contain data from multiple tables. Although data modelers normalize information into single subject tables to avoid insertion, deletion, and update anomalies, analysts seldom use information in isolation because the data is useful to them only when it's been assembled into information. Analysts typically apply business rules against data from a set of related tables. This means that they get these denormalized records sets from a query. As qualified earlier in this appendix, queries let you assemble data into meaningful and actionable information, which makes the information as a whole greater than the sum of its data parts.

As developers of database-centric applications, we seldom have control over the origin of these files. Although it's not critical that we know where the files come from and why they're important, it can be helpful. Typically called *flat, loader*, or *batch import* files, these files are *import sources* that feed corrections and additions into our data repositories.

Import sources come from many places, such as from business staff who sanitize data (analyzing data against business rules and fixing it) or from other business partners. Business partners can be organizations within the corporation or company, or other companies with whom your company does business. The business staff sanitizing or exchanging data within the company are intra-company import sources.

Intra-company imports can come from other IT organizations or from finance departments without professional IT staff. Those coming from other IT organizations are considered *business-to-business (B2B)* exchanges, and they package their outgoing files as export files. These export files support order management systems or financial systems.

Professionally packaged export files are typically formatted in an agreed upon XML (eXtensible Markup Language) or EDI (Electronic Data Interchange) formats. Those coming from your company's internal finance, accounting, or operations departments are considered *consumer-to-business (C2B)* exchanges. That label works because the import files are typically comma-separated value (CSV) files from Microsoft Excel, which is what you would expect from a consumer (internal information consumer). These XML files are typically managed by procedural programming interfaces.

This section demonstrates importing and merging data based on CSV and XML files on an *ad hoc* basis. This section shows you how to use the `MERGE` statement with Oracle external tables as source files for the import source. You can flip back to the "External Tables" section if you need to recall how to set up external tables.

The MERGE statement in Oracle works similarly to the INSERT ALL statement presented earlier in this appendix. It merges data from a query into a *target table* based on criteria evaluated in the ON subclause. The query in the subclause can be described as the *source result set*. The result set is like a virtual table, and virtual tables can be composed of data from multiple tables or a subset of data from one table. The results from a query can be thought of as the *source table*. The MERGE and INSERT ALL statements are different in two ways: the WHEN clause is limited to two logical conditions, MATCHED and NOT MATCHED, and the MERGE statement works with only one target table.

The MERGE statement has the following prototype:

```
MERGE INTO table_name
USING (select_statement) query_alias
ON ( condition_match [ {AND | OR } condition_match [...]] )
WHEN MATCHED THEN
update_statement
WHEN NOT MATCHED THEN
insert_statement;
```

Merging data from a source table to a target table requires that you know the columns that define the natural key of the target table, and in some cases the natural keys of all tables collapsed into the import source file. It also requires an outer join based on the natural key held between the source and target tables, to ensure that it returns the relative complement of the target table. The relative complement would be all the rows found in the source table that aren't found in the target table. The set of rows in the relative complement exists only when you're adding new rows from an import source file.

External data sets seldom have a copy of surrogate keys, because those columns aren't useful to analysts working with the data. The absence of surrogate keys means that you need to use the natural keys to determine how to get parts of the import source into their respective normalized tables. An outer join based on the natural key in the source query always returns a null value as the surrogate key. This is helpful for two reasons: the lack of a surrogate key identifies new rows, and surrogate keys can be auto-generated by available sequences. You attempt a surrogate key match in the ON clause of a MERGE statement. New rows that fail to match are inserted, while those that match are updated. New rows are assigned new surrogate key values.

Although not all import source files contain new rows, most do. The following sections contain the steps necessary for importing or modifying data through bulk uploads. Bulk imports are frequently accomplished through the use of externally organized tables. As introduced earlier in this appendix, an externally organized table is a table that points to a flat file (often a CSV file) deployed on the operating system. External tables in Oracle require that a DBA set up virtual directories and grants.

Step 1: Create a Virtual Directory The process of creating a virtual directory was covered earlier in the appendix, but it's repeated here as a setup step for your convenience. You must create at least one virtual directory to use external tables. Creating virtual directories and granting privileges to read and write to them is reserved to the sys or system superuser. The following lets a superuser create an upload virtual directory and grant privileges to the student user to read and write to the directory:

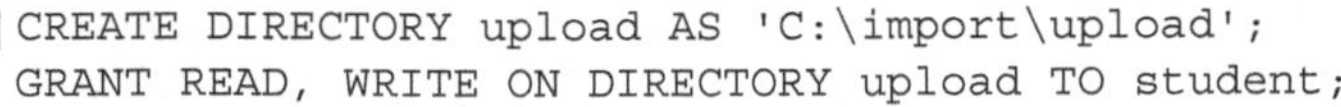

```
CREATE DIRECTORY upload AS 'C:\import\upload';
GRANT READ, WRITE ON DIRECTORY upload TO student;
```

In this example, both read and write privileges are granted to the `student` user because the file needs to read the import source file and write log files to the same directory. Reading and writing files from the same virtual directory isn't recommended as a best practice, however. You should create `badfile`, `discard`, and `log` virtual directories to hold their respective output files and then grant only read privilege to the `upload` directory. You should grant read and write privileges to the `badfile`, `discard`, and `log` virtual directories, especially if you're writing modules to let your business users confirm the upload of data.

Step 2: Position Your Physical CSV File After you create the `upload` virtual directory in the database, you need to create the physical directory in the file system of the server's operating system. Creating the physical directory after the virtual directory should help show you that a virtual directory's definition is independent of its physical directory. Virtual directories only store data that maps the virtual directory name to a physical directory, and they do not validate the existence of that location until you try to use it.

This example uses a `kingdom_import.csv` file that holds data for the `kingdom` and `knight` tables. The data in the file describe two epochs of the mythical kingdom of Narnia:

```
'Narnia',77600,'Peter the Magnificent','20-MAR-1272','19-JUN-1292',
'Narnia',77600,'Edmund the Just','20-MAR-1272','19-JUN-1292',
'Narnia',77600,'Susan the Gentle','20-MAR-1272','19-JUN-1292',
'Narnia',77600,'Lucy the Valiant','20-MAR-1272','19-JUN-1292',
'Narnia',42100,'Peter the Magnificent','12-APR-1531','31-MAY-1531',
'Narnia',42100,'Edmund the Just','12-APR-1531','31-MAY-1531',
'Narnia',42100,'Susan the Gentle','12-APR-1531','31-MAY-1531',
'Narnia',42100,'Lucy the Valiant','12-APR-1531','31-MAY-1531',
```

Notice that there are no surrogate key values in the data set. This means that the `MERGE` statement needs to provide them.

Step 3: Create Example Tables You should now connect to the `student` schema in the database. As the `student` user, create two internally defined tables, `kingdom` and `knight`, and then create one externally defined table, `kingdom_knight_import`. The `kingdom` table is the parent and the `knight` table is the child in this relationship. This means a column in the `knight` table holds a foreign key that references (points back to) a column in the `kingdom` table. The `kingdom_id` column is the primary key in the `kingdom` table, and the `kingdom_allegiance_id` column holds the copy of the primary key value as a foreign key in the `knight` table.

Here's the `CREATE TABLE` statement for the `kingdom` table:

```
SQL> CREATE TABLE kingdom
  2  ( kingdom_id     NUMBER
  3  , kingdom_name   VARCHAR2(20)
  4  , population     NUMBER);
```

And here is its sequence:

```
CREATE SEQUENCE kingdom_s1;
```

Here's the CREATE TABLE statement for the knight table:

```
SQL> CREATE TABLE knight
  ( knight_id               NUMBER
  , knight_name             VARCHAR2(24)
  , kingdom_allegiance_id NUMBER
  , allegiance_start_date DATE
  , allegiance_end_date   DATE);
```

Here is its sequence:

```
CREATE SEQUENCE knight_s1;
```

Here is the CREATE TABLE statement for the kingdom_knight_import table:

```
SQL> CREATE TABLE kingdom_knight_import
  ( kingdom_name            VARCHAR2(8)
  , population              NUMBER
  , knight_name             VARCHAR2(24)
  , allegiance_start_date DATE
  , allegiance_end_date   DATE)
    ORGANIZATION EXTERNAL
    ( TYPE oracle_loader
      DEFAULT DIRECTORY upload
      ACCESS PARAMETERS
      ( RECORDS DELIMITED BY NEWLINE CHARACTERSET US7ASCII
        BADFILE     'UPLOAD':'kingdom_import.bad'
        DISCARDFILE 'UPLOAD':'kingdom_import.dis'
        LOGFILE     'UPLOAD':'kingdom_import.log'
        FIELDS TERMINATED BY ','
        OPTIONALLY ENCLOSED BY "'"
        MISSING FIELD VALUES ARE NULL )
      LOCATION ('kingdom_import.csv'))
REJECT LIMIT UNLIMITED;
```

There is no sequence for an external table. Recall that there is also no surrogate key in the data set or the definition of this externally managed table. Likewise, you can't assign an identity column to an externally managed table.

Step 4: Test Configuration You should be able to query from the externally managed table after the first three steps have completed successfully. This query should return eight rows:

```
SQL> SELECT   kingdom_name AS kingdom
  ,         population
  ,         knight_name
  ,         TO_CHAR(allegiance_start_date,'DD-MON-YYYY') AS start_date
  ,         TO_CHAR(allegiance_end_date,'DD-MON-YYYY') AS end_date
  FROM      kingdom_knight_import;
```

You should get the following data set if it works:

```
KINGDOM  POPULATION KNIGHT_NAME            START_DATE  END_DATE
-------- ---------- ---------------------- ----------- -----------
Narnia        77600 Peter the Magnificent  20-MAR-1272 19-JUN-1292
Narnia        77600 Edmund the Just        20-MAR-1272 19-JUN-1292
Narnia        77600 Susan the Gentle       20-MAR-1272 19-JUN-1292
Narnia        77600 Lucy the Valiant       20-MAR-1272 19-JUN-1292
Narnia        42100 Peter the Magnificent  12-APR-1531 31-MAY-1531
Narnia        42100 Edmund the Just        12-APR-1531 31-MAY-1531
Narnia        42100 Susan the Gentle       12-APR-1531 31-MAY-1531
Narnia        42100 Lucy the Valiant       12-APR-1531 31-MAY-1531
```

An error like the following occurs if you failed in setting up the physical directory or file, the virtual directory, or the grant of permissions:

```
SELECT   kingdom_name
*
ERROR at line 1:
ORA-29913: error in executing ODCIEXTTABLEOPEN callout
ORA-29400: data cartridge error
KUP-04040: file kingdom_import.csv in UPLOAD not found
```

You need to fix whatever piece is broken before continuing.

CAUTION
Oracle assumes that any physical directory is on the local system disks. It is possible that you could run into the error shown in the example if the physical directory is a virtual directory itself.

Step 5: Merge the Import Source Merges work with one table at a time, and they must start with the least dependent table. The `kingdom` table is the one without dependencies and should be the first table in which data is included. In a real situation, the `MERGE` statements would be bundled into a stored procedure and wrapped in Transaction Control Language (TCL) commands to make sure both statements worked or failed. TCL would require a `SAVEPOINT` before the first `MERGE` statement and a `COMMIT` after the last `MERGE` statement, and the following should appear in an exception handler in the event one `MERGE` statement failed:

```
ROLLBACK TO savepoint_name;
```

The following `MERGE` statement reads data from the externally managed `kingdom_knight_import` table and performs a `LEFT JOIN` operation between a copy of the target and source tables:

```
SQL> MERGE INTO kingdom target
     USING
      (SELECT DISTINCT
               k.kingdom_id
       ,       kki.kingdom_name
```

```
 6      ,       kki.population
 7      FROM    kingdom_knight_import kki LEFT JOIN kingdom k
 8      ON      kki.kingdom_name = k.kingdom_name
 9      AND     kki.population = k.population) SOURCE
10    ON (target.kingdom_id = SOURCE.kingdom_id)
11    WHEN MATCHED THEN
12    UPDATE SET kingdom_name = SOURCE.kingdom_name
13    WHEN NOT MATCHED THEN
14    INSERT VALUES
15    ( kingdom_s1.nextval
16    , SOURCE.kingdom_name
17    , SOURCE.population);
```

The only time line 4 returns a `kingdom_id` value from the `kingdom` table is when the row already exists. The row can exist only when the natural key values match, which means the surrogate keys on line 10 also match. The `UPDATE` statement on line 12 doesn't change anything, because when line 10 matches, the `kingdom_name` column values also match on line 8. The `INSERT` statement on lines 14–17 runs when there is no match between the natural keys. Notice that the `INSERT` statement excludes a target table name, because it works with the target table of the `MERGE` statement. The source values in the `INSERT` statement come from the relative complement of the `kingdom` table, which is the `kingdom_knight_import` table. These are new rows from the import source file.

The merge should report the number of rows merged, which might exceed the number of new rows inserted into the table. You confirm the number of rows inserted with the following query:

```
SQL> SELECT * FROM kingdom;
```

It returns the following:

```
KINGDOM_ID KINGDOM_NAME         POPULATION
---------- -------------------- ----------
         1 Narnia                    42100
         2 Narnia                    77600
```

Note that the `ON` subclause should use the natural key, and the nested `UPDATE` statement must `SET` a column not found in the `ON` clause. Changing line 12 from `kingdom_name` to `kingdom_id` raises this error message:

```
  ON (target.kingdom_id = SOURCE.kingdom_id)
      *
ERROR at line 9:
ORA-38104: Columns referenced in the ON Clause cannot be updated:
"TARGET"."KINGDOM_ID"
```

The second `MERGE` statement can work only when there are matching rows in the `kingdom` table for new rows in the import source file. That's why it performs an `INNER JOIN` operation between the `kingdom` and `kingdom_knight_import` tables before it performs an outer join against the `knight` table.

Here is the second MERGE statement:

```
SQL> MERGE INTO knight target
  2  USING
  3   (SELECT kn.knight_id
  4    ,      k.kingdom_id
  5    ,      kki.knight_name
  6    ,      kki.allegiance_start_date
  7    ,      kki.allegiance_end_date
  8    FROM   kingdom_knight_import kki INNER JOIN kingdom k
  9    ON     kki.kingdom_name = k.kingdom_name
 10    AND    kki.population = k.population LEFT JOIN knight kn
 11    ON     k.kingdom_id = kn.kingdom_allegiance_id
 12    AND    kki.knight_name = kn.knight_name
 13    AND    kki.allegiance_start_date = kn.allegiance_start_date
 14    AND    kki.allegiance_end_date = kn.allegiance_end_date) source
 15  ON (target.knight_id = source.knight_id)
 16  WHEN MATCHED THEN
 17  UPDATE SET target.knight_name = source.knight_name
 18  WHEN NOT MATCHED THEN
 19  INSERT
 20  ( knight_id
 21  , knight_name
 22  , kingdom_allegiance_id
 23  , allegiance_start_date
 24  , allegiance_end_date)
 25  VALUES
 26  ( knight_s1.nextval
 27  , source.knight_name
 28  , source.kingdom_id
 29  , source.allegiance_start_date
 30  , source.allegiance_end_date);
```

Although it works like the last MERGE statement, the query that provides the source uses an INNER JOIN operator to confirm that a matching kingdom exists. It checks whether a new knight exists in the import source only when a valid kingdom for that knight exists. The matching criterion on line 15 is the surrogate key value of the knight table. This is the same rule as for the prior MERGE statement.

Lines 20–24 show an overriding signature for the INSERT statement. Other than the absence of a target table name, the INSERT statement works as it does on its own. A query for this data set requires a couple of SQL*Plus formatting commands to make it fit nicely here in the book, like so:

```
COLUMN knight_id   FORMAT 999 HEADING "Knight|ID #"
COLUMN knight_name FORMAT A22 HEADING "Knight Name"
COLUMN kingdom_allegiance_id FORMAT 999 HEADING "Allegiance|ID #"
COLUMN allegiance_start_date FORMAT A9 HEADING "Start|Date"
COLUMN allegiance_end_date FORMAT A9 HEADING "End|Date"
```

The query would be as follows:

```
SQL> SELECT * FROM knight;
```

The `knight` table should yield the following rows:

```
Knight                          Allegiance Start     End
  ID # Knight Name                    ID # Date      Date
------ --------------------- ---------- --------- ---------
     1 Peter the Magnificent          2 20-MAR-72 19-JUN-92
     2 Edmund the Just                2 20-MAR-72 19-JUN-92
     3 Susan the Gentle               2 20-MAR-72 19-JUN-92
     4 Lucy the Valiant               2 20-MAR-72 19-JUN-92
     5 Peter the Magnificent          1 12-APR-31 31-MAY-31
     6 Edmund the Just                1 12-APR-31 31-MAY-31
     7 Susan the Gentle               1 12-APR-31 31-MAY-31
     8 Lucy the Valiant               1 12-APR-31 31-MAY-31
```

At the end of this step, you see the results from the `kingdom` and `knight` tables. There should be two rows in the `kingdom` table for two epochs of Narnia and eight rows in the `knight` table for the two visits by the four Pevensie children, who become kings and queens in this mythical land (at least in the first two books).

A verification of the ability to merge data can be achieved by adding a single-row to the `kingdom_import.csv` file, which would give it this extra line for Caspian X:

```
'Narnia',40100,'Caspian X','31-MAY-1531','30-SEP-1601',
```

Rerunning the `MERGE` statements, you would see one row added to the previous two rows in the `kingdom` table and one row added to the previous eight rows in the `knight` table. The `UPDATE` clause of the statement assigns the existing `knight_id` surrogate key value back to the same column, which results in no net change.

Transaction Control Language (TCL)

Transaction Control Language (TCL) is the ability to guarantee an all-or-nothing approach when changing data in more than one table. Table B-6 covers the key commands involved in TCL to manage transactions.

A good programming practice is to set a `SAVEPOINT` statement before beginning a set of DML statements to change related data. Then, if you encounter a failure in one of the DML statements, you can use the `ROLLBACK` statement to undo the DML statements that completed. You use the `COMMIT` command to make the changes permanent when all changes have been made successfully.

The following shows an example of writing to two tables in the scope of a PL/SQL procedure:

```
SQL> CREATE OR REPLACE PROCEDURE tandem
  ( pv_parent_text  VARCHAR2
  , pv_child_text   VARCHAR2 ) IS

    -- Declare local variable to hold primary key for later use.
    lv_foreign_key  NUMBER;

  BEGIN
```

```

    -- Set savepoint.
    SAVEPOINT all_or_none;

    -- Insert into the first table.
    INSERT INTO unconstrained ( text )
    VALUES ( pv_parent_text )
    RETURNING unconstrained_id INTO lv_foreign_key;

    -- Insert into the second table.
    INSERT INTO constrained ( unconstrained_id, text )
    VALUES ( lv_foreign_key, pv_child_text );

    -- Commit the work.
    COMMIT;

  EXCEPTION
    WHEN OTHERS THEN
      ROLLBACK TO all_or_none;
  END;
  /
```

Statement	Description
COMMIT	The COMMIT statement makes permanent all DML changes to data up to that point in the user session. Once you commit data changes, they are *permanent* unless you perform some form of point-in-time database recovery. It has the following prototype: COMMIT
ROLLBACK	The ROLLBACK statement reverses changes to data that have not yet become permanent through being committed during a user session. The ROLLBACK makes sure all changes are undone from the most recent DML statement to the oldest one in the current user session, or since the last commit action. Alternatively, when a SAVEPOINT has been set during the user session, the ROLLBACK can undo transactions only since either that SAVEPOINT or the last commit. It has the following prototype: ROLLBACK [TO *savepoint_name*]
SAVEPOINT	The SAVEPOINT statement sets a point-in-time marker in a current user session. It enables the ROLLBACK command to only roll back all transactions after the SAVEPOINT is set. It has the following prototype: SAVEPOINT *savepoint_name*

TABLE B-6. *Transaction Control Language Statements*

The `tandem` procedure sets a `SAVEPOINT` on line 11 before inserting a row into the unconstrained and constrained tables. It commits the work on line 23 when both inserts happen and rolls back any insert to the first table if the insert fails to the second table. The `EXCEPTION` block captures the error and rolls back to the previous `SAVEPOINT`. You should note that the unconstrained and constrained tables use autogenerated identity columns, which means you must snag the current sequence value when inserting a new record. That's done by the `RETURNING INTO` clause on line 16. The `RETURNING INTO` clause transfers the current value of a column into the locally scoped `lv_foreign_key` variable.

Queries: SELECT Statements

A `SELECT` statement (query) reads differently from how it acts. In English, a *query* selects something from a table, or a set of tables, where certain conditions are true or untrue. Translating that English sentence into programming instructions is the beauty and complexity of SQL. Although English seems straightforward, queries work in a different event order. The event order also changes with different types of queries.

Queries can be divided into three basic types:

- Queries that return columns or results from columns
- Queries that aggregate, or queries that return columns or results from columns by adding, averaging, or counting between rows
- Queries that return columns or results selectively (filtered by conditional expressions such as *`IF` statements*), and these types of queries may or may not aggregate result sets

You can return column values or expressions in the `SELECT` list. Column values are straightforward, because they're the values in a column. Expressions aren't quite that simple. Expressions are the results from calculations. Some calculations involve columns and string literal values, such as concatenated results (strings joined together to make a big string), parsed results (substrings), or mathematical results of columns, literal values, and function returns. Mathematical results can be calculated on numeric or `DATE` data types and returned as function results from several built-in functions in both databases.

You can also be selective in your `SELECT` list, which means you can perform if-then-else logic in any column. The selectivity determines the resulting value in the final result set. Result sets are also formally called *aggregate results* because they've been assembled by `SELECT` statements.

Here's the basic prototype for a `SELECT` list:

```
SELECT {column_name | literal_value | expression } AS alias [,      {...}]]
WHERE [NOT] column_name {{= | <> | > | >= | < | <=} |
                              [NOT] {{IN | EXISTS} | IS NULL}} 'expression'
[{AND | OR } [NOT] comparison_operation] [...];
```

You can return three things as an element in the `SELECT` list: a column value from a table or view, a literal value, and an expression. The *column value* is easy to understand, because it's the value from the column—but what is its data type? A column returns the value in its native data type when you call the query from a procedural programming language, such as C, C#, C++,

Java, or PL/SQL, or as a subquery. Subqueries are queries within queries and are covered in the "Subqueries" section later in this appendix. A column returns a string when you call the query from SQL*Plus, and it is written to a console or a file. *Literal values* must have a column alias when you want to reuse the value in a procedural program or as a subquery result, and in those cases they are a string or a number. *Expressions* are more difficult because they're the result of processing operations, such as concatenation or calculation, or they return results from built-in or user-defined functions.

The `SELECT` list is determined by columns listed in the `SELECT` statement, which are determined by the columns available in the set of tables qualified by the `FROM` clause. The `FROM` clause requires that you query from the `dual` pseudo-table when returning a numeric or string literal value, or a return value from a function without referencing a table. While other databases, such as Microsoft SQL Server and MySQL, don't require the `dual` pseudo-table to query literals or function return values, Oracle does require it. The required and optional clauses of the `SELECT` statement are shown in Table B-7.

All `SELECT` statements are parsed and planned before they're run (or, more formally, *executed*). Figure B-7 shows you the SQL statement processing steps. Parsing includes a syntax check, a semantic check, and a shared pool check, all of which occur *before statement execution*. The syntax check verifies that the identifiers, which are literal values, punctuation, operators, object names, and keywords, are in the right order. The semantic check verifies that object names (such as table, column, function, procedure, package, and object type names) are valid in the data dictionary or catalog. The shared pool check looks to see if an exact match to the `SELECT` statement has already been placed in the Oracle Database 12c database instance's shared pool. Oracle reruns a matching query from the shared pool rather than optimizing and planning the statement's execution again.

The Oracle Database 12c cost-based optimizer examines various plans to run the statement and chooses the best query plan before statement execution. Unfortunately, that doesn't guarantee successful execution because it is possible to encounter a runtime failure.

The next three sections show you how the types of queries work. All examples use queries from a single table to let you focus on the differences between types.

Clause	Required	Description
`SELECT`	Yes	A list of literal values, columns, or function return values.
`FROM`	Yes	A list of tables or views from which you get the data.
`WHERE`	No	A list of filters that determines which rows to include in the result set.
`GROUP BY`	No	A list of nonaggregated values, columns, or function return values when one or more elements in the `SELECT` list are aggregated.
`HAVING`	No	A list of aggregation filters that filters the rows aggregated by the `GROUP BY` clause.
`ORDER BY`	No	A list of columns or expressions that determines how rows are sorted. The columns or expressions can be identified the column name, alias, or numeric position in the `SELECT` list.

TABLE B-7. *SELECT Statement Clauses*

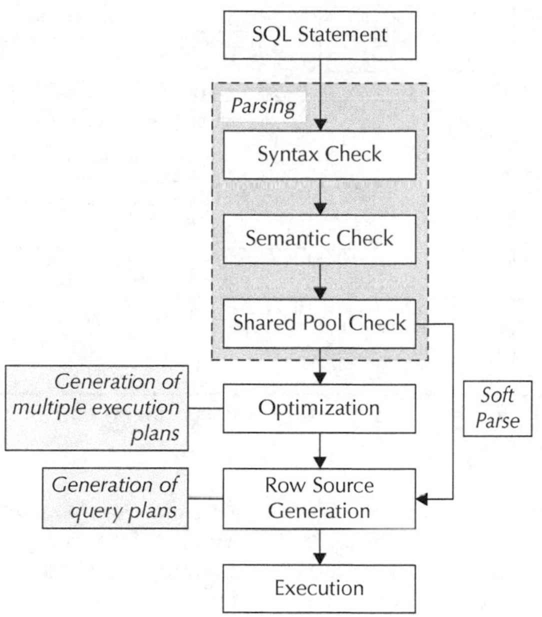

FIGURE B-7. *SQL statement processing steps*

Queries that Return Columns or Results from Columns

Figure B-8 shows how a query returns a result set of column values in the `SELECT` list. The figure shows how the elements are labeled and processed and helps you to visualize table aliases, column aliases, basic comparison operations, and the basic order of clauses within the `SELECT` statement.

The following list qualifies the ANSI SQL pattern for processing a single table query:

- It finds a table in the `FROM` clause.
- It *optionally* assigns a table alias as a runtime placeholder for the table name.
- It gets the table definition from the data catalog to know the valid column names, which isn't shown in the figure because it's a hidden behavior.
- If a table alias is present (and it is), it optionally maps the alias to the table's data catalog definition.
- It filters rows into the result set based on the value of columns in the `WHERE` clause.
- The list of columns in the `SELECT` clause filters the desired columns from the complete set of columns in a row.
- If an `ORDER BY` clause occurs in the query, rows are sorted by the designated columns.

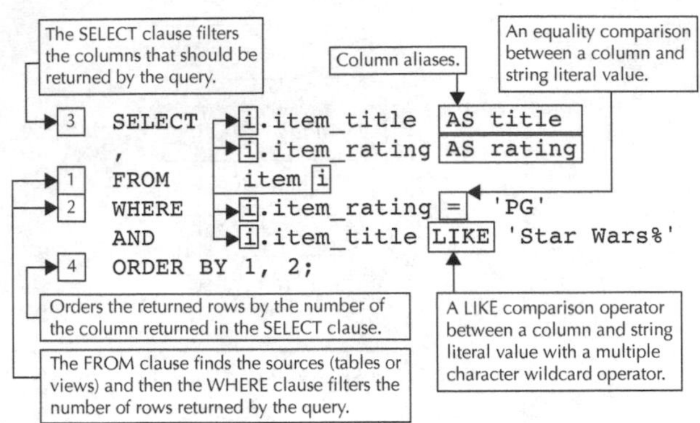

FIGURE B-8. *Queries that return columns or results from columns*

Figure B-8 also demonstrates table and column aliases. The table alias is generally unnecessary when writing a query against a single table. It is useful and necessary when you want to avoid typing complete table names to disambiguate column names that are the same in two or more tables. Because the `FROM` clause is read first, all references to the `item` table are mapped to `i` in the rest of the query. This means that a reference to `item.item_title` would not be found.

TIP
The `AS` keyword is optional when setting column aliases but ensures clarity that an alias follows it. Consistent use increases typing but decreases support costs.

Column aliases shorten the `item_title` and `item_rating` column names to *title* and *rating*, respectively. Aliases let you use shorter or more descriptive words for columns in a specific use case. Sometimes the shorter words aren't appropriate as column names because they're too general, such as *title*. The `AS` keyword is optional in Oracle and other databases, but I recommend that you use it, because the clarity can simplify maintenance of queries. Just note that `AS` works only with column aliases and would create a statement parsing error if you tried to use before a table alias.

NOTE
The `AS` keyword cannot precede a table alias; it can precede only a column alias.

In our example, we can modify the `SELECT` list to return an expression by concatenating a string literal of `'MPAA: '` (Motion Picture Association of America) to the `item_rating` column. Concatenating string is like gluing them together to form a big string. It would look like this in Oracle using a *piped concatenation*:

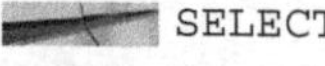

```
SELECT   i.item_title AS title
,        'MPAA: ' || i.item_rating AS rating
```

The two vertical bars (||) are *pipes*, and using them to glue strings together is known as *piped concatenation*. This would return results like these:

```
TITLE                      RATING
-------------------------- ----------
Star Wars I                MPAA: PG
Star Wars II               MPAA: PG
Star Wars II               MPAA: PG
```

In another context, you can perform math operations and string formatting. The following `SELECT` list retrieves a `transaction_date` column and a `transaction_amount` column from the `transaction` table:

```
SQL> SELECT   t.transaction_date
  2  ,        TO_CHAR(t.transaction_amount,'90.00') AS price
  3  ,        TO_CHAR(t.transaction_amount * .0875,'90.00') AS tax
  4  ,        TO_CHAR(t.transaction_amount * 1.0875,'90.00') AS total
  5  FROM     transaction t
  6  WHERE    t.transaction_date = '10-JAN-2009';
```

The `TO_CHAR` function formats the final number as a string. The `90.00` format mask instructs the display as follows: a `9` means display a number when present and display a white space when no number fits the placeholder; `0` means display a number when it is present and display a `0` when no number is present. Inside the `TO_CHAR` function on lines 3 and 4, the column value is multiplied by numeric literals that represent sales tax and price plus sales tax. It would produce output like so:

```
Date       Price  Tax    Total
---------  ------ ------ ------
10-JAN-09   9.00   0.79   9.79
10-JAN-09   3.00   0.26   3.26
10-JAN-09   6.00   0.53   6.53
```

The output is left-aligned, which means it's formatted as a number, because strings are displayed as right-aligned.

The `FROM` clause takes a single table or a comma-separated list of tables when writing queries in ANSI SQL-89 format. The `FROM` clause takes tables separated by join keywords and their join criterion or criteria in ANSI SQL-92 syntax.

The `WHERE` clause performs two types of comparisons. One is an equality comparison of two values, which can come from columns, literals, or expressions. The other is an inequality comparison, which can check when one value is found in another (such as a substring of a larger string); when one value is greater than, greater than or equal to, less than, or less than or equal to another; when one value isn't equal to another value; when one value is in a set of values; or when one value is between two other values. You can also state a negative comparison, such as `WHERE NOT`. The `WHERE NOT` comparison acts like a *not equal to* operation.

A specialized operator lets you limit the number of rows returned by a query. Oracle supports a `ROWNUM` pseudocolumn. You use `ROWNUM` to retrieve only the top five rows, like this:

```
WHERE rownum <= 6;
```

Regular Expression Alternatives

The Oracle database provide regular expression alternatives to the `LIKE` comparison operator. They aren't cross-portable, which makes the `LIKE` comparison operator the more generic or vendor-neutral approach.

Oracle Regular Expression Alternative Oracle provides a variation on that generic SQL `LIKE` comparison with the `REGEXP_LIKE` function. The last line of the query in Figure B-8 could use the following in an Oracle database:

```
AND       REGEXP_LIKE(i.item_title,'^Star Wars.*$');
```

Check Appendix E for more information on the regular expression functions provided by Oracle Database. Regular expressions are much better solutions than the older wildcard operators.

This is a handy tool when you've presorted the data and know where to cut off the return set. When you forget to sort, the results generally don't fit what you're looking for.

The data set in the table determines whether the query returns unique or nonunique data—that is, there could be multiple-rows with an `item_title` of "Star Wars: A New Hope," and they would be returned because they match the criteria in the `WHERE` clause. You can use the `DISTINCT` operator to suppress duplicates without altering the logic of the `WHERE` clause (see Figure B-9).

The next two subsections discuss subqueries and *inline views*, also known as *runtime* or *derived tables*.

Subqueries

Subqueries are any `SELECT` statement nested within another DML statement, such as `INSERT`, `UPDATE`, `DELETE`, and `SELECT` statements. Subqueries have been demonstrated in earlier in this appendix because they're very useful.

Guarantees a unique set of rows.

```
SELECT   DISTINCT
         i.item_title  AS title
,        i.item_rating AS rating
FROM     item i
WHERE    i.item_rating =  'PG'
AND      i.item_title LIKE 'Star Wars%'
ORDER BY 1, 2;
```

FIGURE B-9. *Query that returns distinct columns or results from columns*

Four types of basic subqueries can be used:

- **Scalar subqueries** Return only one column and one row of data
- **Single-row subqueries** Return one or more columns in one row of data
- **Multiple-row subqueries, ordinary subqueries, or subqueries** Return one or more columns in one or more rows of data
- **Correlated subqueries** Return nothing, but they effect a join between the outer DML statement and the correlated subquery

Another subquery can be used inside the FROM clause of a SELECT statement. This type of subquery is actually a *runtime view*, or *derived table*. It isn't technically a subquery. The following sections describe the uses and occurrences of subqueries in DML statements.

Scalar Subqueries Scalar subqueries return only one thing: one column from one row. They return a single value from a query. That's because scalar variables are numbers, dates, strings, and timestamps. Scalar data types are like primitive data types in the Java programming language.

Scalar subqueries are much like functions. You put comparative statements in the WHERE clause to find a single-row, similar to defining formal parameters in a function. Then you return a single column in the SELECT clause, which inherits its data type from the data catalog. The SELECT clause designates the return data type of a function just like the *return* keyword in procedural programming languages.

You can use scalar subqueries in the following places in DML statements:

- The VALUES clause of an INSERT statement
- The SELECT clause of a SELECT statement
- The SET clause of an UPDATE statement
- The WHERE clause of a SELECT, UPDATE, or DELETE statement

Single-Row Subqueries Single-row subqueries return one or more columns from a single-row. This is more or less like returning a record data type. You can apply the same analogy of comparative statements in the WHERE clause mapping to formal parameter definitions and the return type mapping to the list of columns in the SELECT clause. When you exclude the scalar behaviors of a single-row subquery, the following uses remain:

- The SET clause of an UPDATE statement
- The WHERE clause of a SELECT, UPDATE, or DELETE statement

Multiple-Row Subqueries Multiple-row subqueries are frequently called *ordinary subqueries*, or just *subqueries*. These subqueries return one to many columns and rows of data. That means they return result sets that mimic two-dimensional tables.

You can use multiple-row subqueries only in the WHERE clause of SELECT, UPDATE, or DELETE statements. You also must use a valid lookup comparison operator, such as the IN, =ANY, =SOME, or =ALL operator. These operators act like a chain of logical OR comparisons in a WHERE clause, because they look to see if the leftmost operand in the comparison is found in the list of possible values. The leftmost operand can be a single column or a record data type comprising two or more columns.

A couple of quick examples to qualify these behaviors might help. These examples use the `dual` pseudo-table to keep them bare bones. The list of values inside a set of parentheses is the same as the value set returned by a multiple-row subquery. Here's a standard use of a logical or lookup comparison that deals with a single column:

```
SELECT 'True Statement' FROM dual
WHERE  'Lancelot' IN ('Arthur','Galahad','Lancelot');
```

This is equivalent to the chaining of logical `OR` statements in the `WHERE` clause, like this:

```
SELECT 'True Statement' FROM dual
WHERE 'Lancelot' = 'Arthur'
OR    'Lancelot' = 'Galahad'
OR    'Lancelot' = 'Lancelot';
```

The syntax doesn't change much when you make the comparison of a record type to a list of record types. The only other change is the substitution of the `=ANY` lookup operator for the `IN` operator. As you can see, the lookup operators work the same way in this example:

```
SELECT 'True Statement' FROM dual
WHERE ('Harry Potter and the Chamber of Secrets','PG') =ANY
      (('Harry Potter and the Sorcerer's Stone','PG')
      ,('Harry Potter and the Chamber of Secrets','PG')
      ,('Harry Potter and the Prisoner of Azkaban','PG'));
```

which would work like this with a set of logical `OR` comparisons:

```
SELECT 'True Statement' FROM dual
WHERE (('Harry Potter and the Order of the Phoenix','PG-13') =
        ('Harry Potter and the Sorcerer's Stone','PG')
OR     ('Harry Potter and the Order of the Phoenix','PG-13') =
        ('Harry Potter and the Chamber of Secrets','PG')
OR     ('Harry Potter and the Order of the Phoenix','PG-13') =
        ('Harry Potter and the Prisoner of Azkaban','PG'));
```

The `=ALL` lookup operator is different because it checks whether a scalar or record data type is found in all instances of a list. This means it works on a logical `AND` comparison basis. This statement

```
SELECT 'True Statement' FROM dual
WHERE 'Lancelot' =ALL ('Lancelot','Lancelot','Lancelot');
```

is roughly equivalent to this:

```
SELECT 'True Statement' FROM dual
WHERE 'Lancelot' = 'Lancelot'
AND   'Lancelot' = 'Lancelot'
AND   'Lancelot' = 'Lancelot';
```

Although these examples use lists of literal values, you could substitute multiple-row subqueries. In many cases, this type of comparison is unnecessary because the same logic can be resolved through ordinary join statements.

The only problem with lookup comparison operators is that they don't easily extend the behavior of the LIKE comparison operator. Figure B-9 introduced a LIKE operator against a string literal with a wildcard operator. When the literal value is replaced by a subquery, the comparison no longer works when the query returns more than one row. It would fail with an ORA-01427 error in Oracle, which tells you a "single-row subquery returns more than one row."

You can fix this behavior by doing two things: substitute an IN, =ANY, or =SOME lookup comparison operator for the LIKE comparison operator, and use the SUBSTR function to make the comparison against exact matches. This allows you to match the substrings that should be the same. This particular match (shown in Figure B-10) starts at the first character, which is position 1, because characters in strings are 1-based, not 0-based, in databases, and use the first nine characters.

There are two natural wildcard characters in SQL. The multiple-character wildcard is the percent symbol (%) and the single-character wildcard is an underscore (_) character. The dot (.) is only a wildcard when used as part of a regular expression, which you can read about in Appendix E.

Oracle supports the SUBSTR function. The SUBSTR function is covered later in Appendix C.

Correlated Subqueries Correlated subqueries join the inside query to a value returned by each row in the outer query. As such, correlated subqueries act as function calls made for each row returned by the outer query. The rule of thumb on correlated subqueries requires that you join on uniquely indexed columns for optimal results. Ordinary subqueries typically outperform correlated subqueries when you can't join on uniquely indexed columns.

Correlated subqueries appear to return something when they're inside the SET clause of an UPDATE statement. As you saw earlier in the "UPDATE Statement" section, a multiple-row subquery actually returns values based on a match between the row being updated and a nested correlated subquery. The actual update is performed by a multiple-row subquery, not a correlated subquery. Correlated subqueries can't return values through the SELECT list; they can only match results in their WHERE clause.

```
SELECT    DISTINCT
          i.item_title  AS title
,         i.item_rating AS rating
FROM      item i
WHERE     i.item_rating =  'PG'
AND       SUBSTR(i.item_title,1,9) =SOME
           (SELECT   SUBSTR(ti.item_title,1,9)
            FROM     temp_item ti)
ORDER BY 1, 2;
```

A match using a combination of the SUBSTR function and a lookup comparison operator.

FIGURE B-10. *Wildcard comparison against multiple-row subquery*

You can use correlated subqueries in the following:

- The `SELECT` list
- The `WHERE` clause of a `SELECT`, `UPDATE`, or `DELETE` statement

The multiple-row subquery example extends the behavior depicted in Figure B-9. The multiple-row subquery runs once for the outer query and returns a list of values. The `IN`, `=ANY`, or `=SOME` lookup operator lets you perform a lookup to determine whether a variable is found in the list of values.

Although less efficient, a correlated subquery can be used to solve this type of problem. Oracle lets you perform it with the `REGEXP_LIKE` function, like this:

```
AND       EXISTS
 (SELECT NULL
  FROM    temp_item ti
  WHERE   REGEXP_LIKE(i.item_title,'^'||SUBSTR(ti.item_title,1,9)||'.+'));
```

In these correlated query examples, you see Oracle's piped concatenation model. The limitation of Oracle's `CONCAT` function dictates that you should use piped concatenation, which differs from other databases that use a recursive `CONCAT` function.

Inline Views

An inline view is a query inside the `FROM` clause of a query or inside a `WITH` clause. The `WITH` clause is newer and was introduced in the ANSI SQL-1999 standard. Inline views are also labeled a runtime or derived table, and Microsoft calls them Common Table Expressions (CTEs). Oracle Database 12*c* documentation also calls them global temporary tables.

The query in a `FROM` or `WITH` clause dynamically creates a view at runtime. It's possible that the same inline view can be used in multiple places within a large query. When an inline view appears in multiple places within a query, it is run multiple times. This is inefficient and unnecessary when the `WITH` clause is supported in the database. The `WITH` clause provides an inline view with a named reference, runs it only once, and lets you use the name reference in more than one place in the query.

Here's a sample of an inline view in the `FROM` clause:

```
SQL> SELECT   c.first_name||' '||c.last_name AS person
     ,        inline.street_address
     ,        inline.city
     ,        inline.state_province
     FROM     contact c INNER JOIN
             (SELECT   a.contact_id
              ,        sa.street_address
              ,        a.city
              ,        a.state_province
              FROM     address a INNER JOIN street_address sa
              ON       a.address_id = sa.address_id) inline
     ON       inline.contact_id = c.contact_id;
```

The inline view is on lines 6 through 11, and the join between the `i1` inline view and `contact` table is on line 12. The inline view must return the foreign key column in the `SELECT` list for it to be used later in the join on line 12. Failure to return the key column in the inline view would leave nothing to use in a join statement.

The preceding inline view can be refactored to work with a `WITH` clause, like this:

```
SQL> WITH inline AS
  2  (SELECT    a.contact_id
  3   ,         sa.street_address
  4   ,         a.city
  5   ,         a.state_province
  6   FROM      address a INNER JOIN street_address sa
  7   ON        a.address_id = sa.address_id)
  8  SELECT   c.first_name||' '||c.last_name AS person
  9  ,        inline.street_address
 10  ,        inline.city
 11  ,        inline.state_province
 12  FROM     contact c INNER JOIN inline inline
 13  ON       inline.contact_id = c.contact_id;
```

Line 12 references the inline name of the inline view, which is on lines 1 to 7. Line 12 identifies an `INNER JOIN` between the `contact` table and the inline view, and line 13 provides the criteria to match values between the table and the view. Large queries have a tendency to reuse inline views in multiple places, which isn't a good thing. Inline views must be run each time they're encountered in the query. The `WITH` clause fixes this performance nightmare because the query is run once, given a name, and then the result sets are usable anywhere else in the query. The `WITH` clause should always be your first choice for subqueries, especially when you have two or more copies in the statement.

It's also possible to have multiple inline views (or *global temporary tables*). You list them with a designated name in a comma-delimited list. The following code shows a `WITH` clause with two inline views:

```
SQL> WITH inline1 AS
       (SELECT    a.contact_id
        ,         sa.street_address
        ,         a.city
        ,         a.state_province
        FROM      address a INNER JOIN street_address sa
        ON        a.address_id = sa.address_id)
       , inline2 AS
       (SELECT  c.first_name || c.last_name AS person
        ,       i.street_address
        ,       i.city
        ,       i.state_province
        FROM    contact c INNER JOIN inline1 i
        ON      i.contact_id = c.contact_id)
     SELECT * FROM inline2;
```

Line 1 declares `inline1` as a runtime view, while lines 2 through 7 implement a query that joins both the `address` and `street_address` tables. Likewise, line 8 declares `inline2` as a runtime view, while lines 9 through 14 implement a join between the `contact` table and the `inline1` view. Line 15 holds a query based on the `inline2` runtime view. Oracle Database 12*c* provides the new `CROSS APPLY`, `OUTER APPLY`, and `LATERAL` joins, as qualified in Chapter 2. These new cross join operations let you rewrite the preceding `WITH` clause into a correlated query between two runtime views.

Oracle Database 12*c* introduces PL/SQL functions inside the `WITH` clause. The only catch comes when you try to run them, because they have embedded semicolons. Let's say you run the command from inside SQL*Plus. You would first disable the default SQL terminator, a semicolon (`;`), with this SQL*Plus command:

```
SET SQLTERMINATOR OFF
```

Then, you can create a local function in your `WITH` statement, like this:

```
SQL> COLUMN person FORMAT A18
SQL> WITH
  2    FUNCTION glue
  3    ( pv_first_name VARCHAR2
  4    , pv_last_name  VARCHAR2) RETURN VARCHAR2 IS
  5      lv_full_name  VARCHAR2(100);
  6    BEGIN
  7      lv_full_name := pv_first_name || ' ' || pv_last_name;
  8      RETURN lv_full_name;
  9    END;
 10    SELECT  glue(a.first_name,a.last_name) AS person
 11    FROM    actor a
 12  /
```

The function on lines 2 through 9 simply concatenates two strings with a single-character white space between them. The semicolons are treated as ordinary characters in the query since the default SQL terminator is disabled. You should also note that the SQL statement is run by the SQL*Plus forward slash and that the complete statement doesn't have a terminating semicolon on line 11.

In this simple example, the `actor` table contains two actors' names (from the *Iron Man* franchise), and the query returns

```
PERSON
------------------
Robert Downey
Gwyneth Paltrow
```

You will encounter some parsing difficulty running queries like this when you submit them through tools such as Oracle SQL Developer. The easiest fix to those problems is to wrap the query in a view, because calls through tools to SQL*Plus disallow changing the `SQLTERMINATOR` value. Only the interactive SQL*Plus mode lets you change the `SQLTERMINATOR` value. This means you can't write and run a dynamic `SELECT` statement with a `WITH` clause that has an embedded PL/SQL function. Embedding this type of query inside a view is your only feasible option to call them from your application software.

The following DDL statement creates a view based on an embedded PL/SQL function within a WITH statement:

```
SQL> CREATE OR REPLACE VIEW actor_v AS
  2  WITH
  3    FUNCTION glue
  4    ( pv_first_name VARCHAR2
  5    , pv_last_name  VARCHAR2) RETURN VARCHAR2 IS
  6    BEGIN
  7      RETURN pv_first_name || ' ' || pv_last_name;
  8    END;
  9    SELECT  glue(a.first_name,a.last_name) AS person
 10    FROM    actor a
 11  /
```

As you know, a view is nothing more than a stored query. The `actor_v` view shrinks the `glue` function by two lines. It removes the declaration of `lv_full_name` and replaces the assignment of the concatenated values with a direct return of the result on line 7.

If you want to run ordinary SQL commands with the default semicolon, you should reenable the default SQL terminator:

```
SET SQLTERMINATOR ON
```

The obvious benefit of the `WITH` clause is that it runs once and can be used multiple times in the scope of the query. Likewise, you can embed functions that have a local scope to a single query. Some ask, why use a `WITH` clause when you can use the global temporary table? Tom Kyte answered that in his *Ask Tom* column, stating more or less that *the optimizer can merge the `WITH` clause with the rest of the statement, while a global temporary table can't.*

Hierarchical Queries

You can use hierarchical queries to step through tree-like data stored in self-referencing tables, like those shown in Figure B-11 for organizations and organizational structures. The `org_structure` table in Figure B-11 contains two foreign keys (`org_parent_id` and `org_child_id`), both of which reference the `organization_id` column.

The topmost node, or *root* node, contains 0 as an `org_parent_id` because organizations start numbering at 1. You could also define the root node `org_parent_id` as a null value. Bottom nodes, or *leaf* nodes, are those organizations that appear as `org_child_id` but not as `org_parent_id`.

This section shows you four hierarchical query techniques:

- How to navigate a complete tree from the top down and order by siblings
- How to navigate from a leaf, or any intermediary, node up a tree to the root node and how to limit the depth of traversal
- How to find all leaf nodes and use the result to navigate several trees concurrently
- How to use `NOCYCLE` to identify rows that cause an `ORA-01436` error, which means the tree-linking relationship is broken

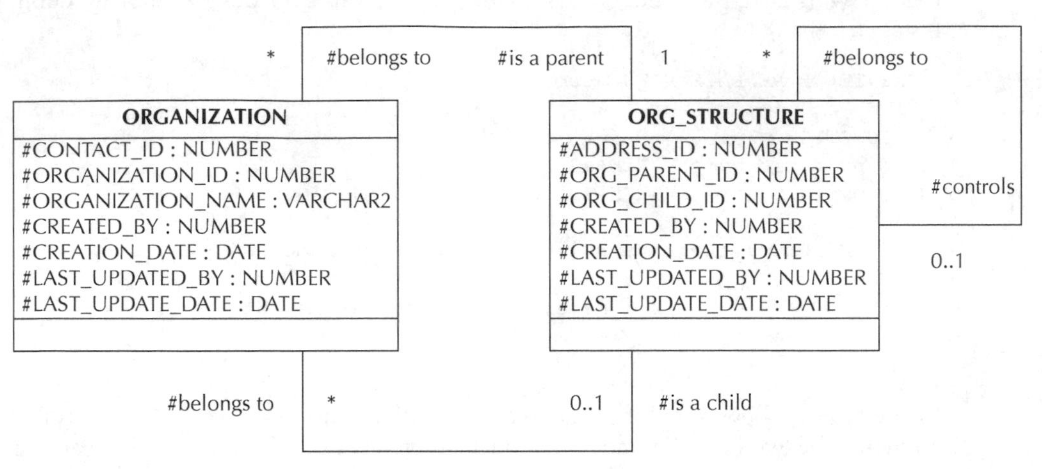

FIGURE B-11. *Flexible organization hierarchy*

As a quick caveat, the `START WITH` clause is technically optional. If you exclude it, all nodes are root nodes and the default depth is only two. So, practically, it's not optional for meaningful work.

Down the Tree

This query allows you to navigate down the tree from the root node. You navigate down the tree when the `PRIOR` keyword precedes the child or dependent node. The SQL*Plus formatting commands generate the output shown.

```
COL org_id FORMAT A12
COL org_name FORMAT A12

SELECT   LPAD(' ', 2*(LEVEL - 1)) || os.org_child_id AS org_id
,        o.organization_name org_name
FROM     organization o
,        org_structure os
WHERE    o.organization_id = os.org_child_id
START
WITH     os.org_parent_id = 0
CONNECT
BY PRIOR os.org_child_id = os.org_parent_id;
```

It produces the following output:

```
ORG_ID       ORG_NAME
------------ ------------
1            One
  2          Two
```

```
    5        Five
      11     Eleven
      12     Twelve
    6        Six
      13     Thirteen
      14     Fourteen
        20   Twenty
  3          Three
    7        Seven
      15     Fifteen
    8        Eight
      16     Sixteen
      17     Seventeen
  4          Four
    9        Nine
      18     Eighteen
      19     Nineteen
    10       Ten
```

If there were an offending row in the table that didn't have a connecting parent and child set of foreign keys, you'd raise an `ORA-01436` error. It means you can't `CONNECT BY PRIOR` because a row's values are nonconforming. You can enter a row to break the hierarchy provided that the `org_parent_id` and `org_child_id` have the same value. Then, this modified query will identify the offending row for you:

```
SELECT         LPAD(' ', 2*(LEVEL - 1)) || os.org_child_id AS org_id
,              o.organization_name org_name
FROM           organization o
,              org_structure os
WHERE          o.organization_id = os.org_child_id
START WITH     os.org_parent_id = 0
CONNECT BY
NOCYCLE PRIOR os.org_child_id = os.org_parent_id;
```

The next query changes the output because it orders by siblings. This means that the numeric ordering of the parent and child nodes is overridden.

```
SELECT   LPAD(' ', 2*(LEVEL - 1)) || os.org_child_id AS org_id
,        o.organization_name org_name
FROM     organization o
,        org_structure os
WHERE    o.organization_id = os.org_child_id
START
WITH     os.org_parent_id = 0
CONNECT
BY PRIOR os.org_child_id = os.org_parent_id
ORDER
SIBLINGS
BY       o.organization_name;
```

The sort now represents a tree in alphabetical ordering of the organization name:

```
ORG_ID       ORG_NAME
------------ ------------
1            One
  4          Four
    9        Nine
      18     Eighteen
      19     Nineteen
    10       Ten
  3          Three
    8        Eight
      17     Seventeen
      16     Sixteen
    7        Seven
      15     Fifteen
  2          Two
    5        Five
      11     Eleven
      12     Twelve
    6        Six
      14     Fourteen
        20   Twenty
      13     Thirteen
```

Up the Tree

The following query switches the position of the PRIOR keyword. It now precedes the parent node. This means that it will go up the tree. The START WITH clause in this case starts with an intermediary node.

```
SELECT   LPAD(' ', 2*(LEVEL - 1)) || os.org_child_id AS org_id
,        o.organization_name org_name
FROM     organization o
,        org_structure os
WHERE    o.organization_id = os.org_child_id
START
WITH     os.org_child_id = 6
CONNECT
BY       os.org_child_id = PRIOR os.org_parent_id;
```

The output is

```
ORG_ID       ORG_NAME
------------ ------------
6            Six
  2          Two
    1        One
```

Restricting the Depth of Search

This is another up-the-tree hierarchical query. It starts from the bottommost leaf node, which is at depth five from the root node. The query restricts upward navigation to three levels or the two immediate parents (or, if you prefer, parent and grandparent).

```
SELECT   LPAD(' ', 2*(LEVEL - 1)) || os.org_child_id AS org_id
,        o.organization_name org_name
FROM     organization o
,        org_structure os
WHERE    o.organization_id = os.org_child_id
AND      LEVEL <= 3
START
WITH     os.org_child_id = 20
CONNECT
BY       os.org_child_id = PRIOR os.org_parent_id;
```

The output is

```
ORG_ID       ORG_NAME
------------ ------------
20           Twenty
  14         Fourteen
    6        Six
```

Leaf Node Up

Traversing from a leaf node can start by inspecting which are leaf nodes first and then hard-coding a value in the `START WITH` clause. A better approach is to use a subquery to identify leaf nodes and then use a filter in the outer `WHERE` clause to limit the leaf nodes. The leaf nodes are plural in both of these solutions.

This solution works prior to Oracle Database 10*g* and continues to work through Oracle Database 12*c*:

```
SELECT   LPAD(' ', 2*(LEVEL - 1)) || os.org_child_id AS org_id
,        o.organization_name org_name
FROM     organization o
,        org_structure os
WHERE    o.organization_id = os.org_child_id
START
WITH     os.org_child_id IN (SELECT os1.org_child_id
FROM     org_structure os1 LEFT JOIN org_structure os2
ON       os2.org_parent_id = os1.org_child_id
MINUS
SELECT   os1.org_child_id
FROM     org_structure os1 JOIN org_structure os2
ON       os2.org_parent_id = os1.org_child_id)
CONNECT
BY       os.org_child_id = PRIOR os.org_parent_id;
```

The following solution uses the `connect_by_leaf` pseudocolumn (introduced in Oracle Database 10*g*) to replace the outer join minus the join in the subquery. It also uses the `ORDER SIBLINGS BY` clause to order the tree by the alphabetical `organization_name` column values.

```
SELECT   LPAD(' ', 2*(LEVEL - 1)) || os.org_child_id AS org_id
,        o.organization_name org_name
FROM     organization o
,        org_structure os
WHERE    o.organization_id = os.org_child_id
START
WITH     os.org_child_id IN (SELECT   org_child_id
FROM     org_structure
WHERE    CONNECT_BY_ISLEAF = 1
START
WITH     org_child_id = 1
CONNECT BY PRIOR org_child_id = org_parent_id)
CONNECT BY os.org_child_id = PRIOR os.org_parent_id
ORDER SIBLINGS BY o.organization_name;
```

The snapshot of output for the latter is

```
ORG_ID     ORG_NAME
---------- ----------
18         Eighteen
  9        Nine
    4      Four
      1    One
11         Eleven
  5        Five
    2      Two
      1    One
15         Fifteen
  7        Seven
    3      Three
      1    One

  ... content removed for readability ...

12         Twelve
  5        Five
    2      Two
      1    One
20         Twenty
  14       Fourteen
    6      Six
      2    Two
        1  One
```

I did leave out the `connect_by_root` and `sys_connect_by_path`. You can find the two missing functions in the *Oracle Database SQL Language Reference 12c Release 1*.

Queries that Aggregate

Aggregation means counting, adding, and grouping results of COUNT, SUM, AVERAGE, MIN, and MAX functions. Aggregation queries add one or two more clauses than those presented in Figure B-8. Figure B-12 shows the GROUP BY and HAVING clauses.

The GROUP BY clause must refer to all nonaggregated columns in the SELECT list, because they're not unique, and there's no sense in returning all the rows when you need only one row with the nonunique columns and the aggregated result. The GROUP BY clause instructs the database to do exactly that: return only distinct versions of nonunique columns with the aggregated result columns. As you can see in Figure B-12, the GROUP BY clause runs after the query has identified all rows and columns. The COUNT function takes an asterisk (*) as its single argument. The * represents an indirection operator that points to rows returned by the query. The * is equivalent to the ROWID pseudocolumn in Oracle. It counts rows whether a row contain any values or not.

NOTE
The asterisk (*) is one of the places where the concept of indirection and a pointer shows itself in databases.

After the database returns the aggregated result set, the HAVING clause filters the result set. In the example, it returns only those aggregated results that have two or more rows in the table. The ORDER BY clause then sorts the return set.

The following list qualifies the ANSI SQL pattern for processing a single table query with aggregation and a GROUP BY and HAVING clause:

1. It finds a table in the FROM clause.
2. It *optionally* assigns a table alias as a runtime placeholder for the table name.
3. It gets the table definition from the data catalog to determine the valid column names.

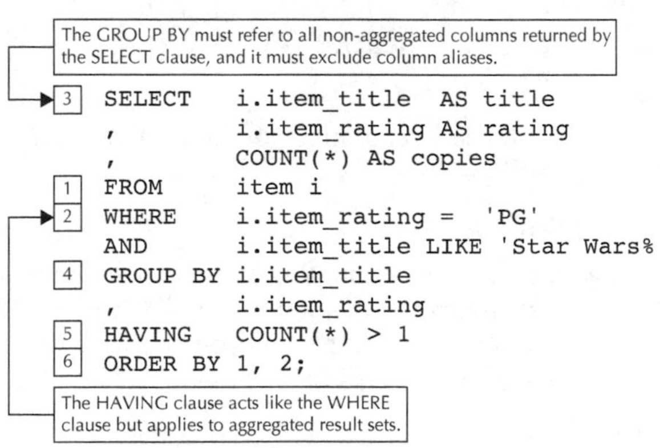

FIGURE B-12. *Order of operation on aggregate queries*

4. If a table alias is present (and it is), it optionally maps the alias to the table's data catalog definition.
5. It filters rows into the result set based on the value of columns in the `WHERE` clause.
6. The list of columns in the `SELECT` clause filters the desired columns from the complete set of columns in a row.
7. The aggregation function triggers a check for a `GROUP BY` clause when nonaggregated columns are returned in the `SELECT` list and then aggregates results.
8. The `HAVING` operator filters the result set from the aggregation or the `GROUP BY` aggregation.
9. If an `ORDER BY` clause occurs in the query, rows are sorted by the designated columns.

We'll work through the basic aggregation steps most developers use frequently. They cover the `COUNT`, `SUM`, `AVERAGE`, `MAX`, and `MIN` functions. The following discussions use two sets of ordinal and cardinal numbers (some values are not displayed to save space) that are stored in the `ordinal` table, like so:

```
        ID LIST_SET             LIST_NAME  LIST_VALUE
---------- -------------------- ---------- ----------
         1 Value Set A          Zero                0
         2 Value Set A          One                 1
         3 Value Set A          Two                 2
         4 Value Set A          Three               3
         5 Value Set A          Four                4
         6 Value Set A          Five                5
         7 Value Set A          Six                 6
         8 Value Set A          Seven               7
         9 Value Set A          Eight               8
        10 Value Set A          Nine                9
        11 Value Set A
        12 Value Set B          Zero                0
        13 Value Set B          One                 1
       ...
        21 Value Set B          Nine                9
        22 Value Set B
```

You've been exposed to the data set to help you understand how the aggregation functions work in the following subsections.

Aggregate Columns Only

The `COUNT` function has two behaviors: counting by reference and counting by value. They differ on how they treat null values. You count the number of physical rows when you count by reference, and you count the physical values when you count by value.

The count by reference example counts the number of rows in the `ordinal` table, like this:

```
SQL> SELECT COUNT(*) AS number_of_rows FROM ordinal;
```

It returns the following:

```
NUMBER_OF_ROWS
--------------
            22
```

The count by value example counts the values in the `list_value` column. The `list_value` column contains two null values. The column name is substituted for the asterisk, like this:

```
SQL> SELECT COUNT(list_value) AS number_of_values FROM ordinal;
```

It returns the following:

```
NUMBER_OF_VALUES
----------------
              20
```

The return set is two less than the number of rows because the `COUNT` function doesn't count null values. You can also count all values (which is the default performed in the preceding example) or distinct values only. Both approaches exclude null values.

The following query demonstrates counting using the default, an explicit `ALL`, and `DISTINCT` number of values found in the `list_name` and `list_value` columns:

```
SQL> SELECT COUNT(list_name) AS default_number
     ,      COUNT(ALL list_name) AS explicit_number
     ,      COUNT(DISTINCT list_value) AS distinct_number
     FROM   ordinal;
```

Here are the results:

```
DEFAULT_NUMBER EXPLICIT_NUMBER DISTINCT_NUMBER
-------------- --------------- ---------------
            20              20              10
```

Notice that the `COUNT` function returns the same number with or without the `ALL` keyword. That's because the default is `ALL`, which is provided when you don't use it. It also counts the occurrences of strings or numbers. When `ALL` is specified, you count each individual element, not just the unique set of elements. The `DISTINCT` keyword forces a unique sort of the data set before counting the results.

The `SUM`, `AVG`, `MAX`, and `MIN` functions work only with numbers. The following demonstrates the `SUM` and `AVG` functions against the `list_value` column:

```
SQL> SELECT SUM(ALL list_value) AS sum_all
     ,      SUM(DISTINCT list_value) AS sum_distinct
     ,      AVG(ALL list_value) AS avg_all
     ,      AVG(DISTINCT list_value) AS avg_distinct
     FROM   ordinal;
```

Here's the result set:

```
   SUM_ALL SUM_DISTINCT    AVG_ALL AVG_DISTINCT
---------- ------------ ---------- ------------
        90           45        4.5          4.5
```

The sum of two sets of the ordinal numbers is 90, and the sum of one set is 45. The average of all or the distinct set is naturally the same.

The next example runs the MAX and MIN functions:

```
SQL> SELECT MIN(ALL list_value) AS min_all
  ,       MIN(DISTINCT list_value) AS min_distinct
  ,       MAX(ALL list_value) AS max_all
  ,       MAX(DISTINCT list_value) AS max_distinct
  FROM    ordinal;
```

It produces these results:

```
   MIN_ALL MIN_DISTINCT    MAX_ALL MAX_DISTINCT
---------- ------------ ---------- ------------
         0            0          9            9
```

The minimum or maximum of two sets of the same group of numbers is always the same. The minimum is 0 and the maximum is 9 for ordinal numbers.

Aggregate and Nonaggregate Columns

The principal of returning aggregate and nonaggregate columns starts with understanding that you get only one row when you add a column of numbers. By extension, you get one row for every type of thing you count. A real-world example of that would be counting a bag of fruit. You separate the fruit into groups, such as apples, oranges, pears, and apricots. Then you count the number of each type of fruit.

The following counts the number of rows and values for each unique value in the `list_set` column:

```
SQL> SELECT   list_set AS grouping_by_column
  ,           COUNT(*)
  ,           COUNT(list_value)
  FROM        ordinal
  GROUP BY list_set;
```

And here are the results of this query:

```
GROUPING_BY_COLUMN     COUNT(*) COUNT(LIST_VALUE)
-------------------- ---------- -----------------
Value Set A                  11                10
Value Set B                  11                10
```

The results tells you that you have 11 rows in each group and only 10 values, which means each group has one row that contains a null value. You change the `SELECT` list and the `GROUP BY` clause when you want to identify the rows with the null values.

The following query returns a 0 when the value is null and returns a 1 otherwise:

```
SQL> SELECT   list_set AS grouping_by_not_null
     ,        list_name AS group_by_null_too
     ,        COUNT(*)
     ,        COUNT(list_value)
     FROM     ordinal
     WHERE    list_set = 'Value Set A'
     GROUP BY list_set
     ,        list_name;
```

And here are the results from the query:

```
GROUPING_BY_NOT_NULL GROUP   COUNT(*) COUNT(LIST_VALUE)
-------------------- ----- ---------- -----------------
Value Set A          Zero           1                 1
Value Set A          Five           1                 1
Value Set A          Three          1                 1
Value Set A          Four           1                 1
Value Set A          One            1                 1
Value Set A          Two            1                 1
Value Set A          Eight          1                 1
Value Set A          Nine           1                 1
Value Set A          Seven          1                 1
Value Set A          Six            1                 1
Value Set A                         1                 0
```

The only problem with the return set is that the cardinal numbers aren't in numeric order. That requires a special `ORDER BY` clause with a `CASE` statement. You could add the following to the last query to get them sorted into numeric order:

```
ORDER BY CASE
           WHEN list_name = 'Zero'  THEN 0
           WHEN list_name = 'One'   THEN 1
           WHEN list_name = 'Two'   THEN 2
           WHEN list_name = 'Three' THEN 3
           WHEN list_name = 'Four'  THEN 4
           WHEN list_name = 'Five'  THEN 5
           WHEN list_name = 'Six'   THEN 6
           WHEN list_name = 'Seven' THEN 7
           WHEN list_name = 'Eight' THEN 8
           WHEN list_name = 'Nine'  THEN 9
         END;
```

This type of `ORDER BY` clause lets you achieve numeric ordering without changing any of the data. Note that null values are always sorted last in an ascending sort and first in a descending sort.

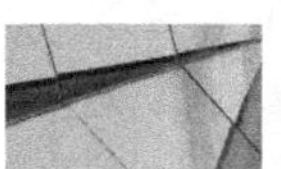

NOTE
Ascending sorts put nulls last while descending sorts put nulls first.

The following query demonstrates the `GROUP BY` for the `SUM`, `AVG`, `MAX`, and `MIN` functions:

```
SQL> SELECT    list_set AS grouping_by_not_null
  ,         SUM(list_value) AS ordinal_sum
  ,         AVG(list_value) AS ordinal_avg
  ,         MIN(list_value) AS ordinal_min
  ,         MAX(list_value) AS ordinal_max
  FROM      ordinal
  GROUP BY list_set;
```

It displays the following:

```
GROUPING_BY_NOT_NULL ORDINAL_SUM ORDINAL_AVG ORDINAL_MIN ORDINAL_MAX
-------------------- ----------- ----------- ----------- -----------
Value Set A                   45         4.5           0           9
Value Set B                   45         4.5           0           9
```

This returns the expected result set from the functions. They naturally match for each set of ordinal numbers. If you were to alter the data set, you could get different results.

Queries that Return Columns or Results Selectively

Queries that return columns or results selectively depend on conditional logic. Originally, SQL wasn't designed to contain any conditional logic. Oracle introduced conditional logic as an extension to the definition in the 1980s by implementing the `DECODE` function. The ANSI SQL definition added the `CASE` operator, which you saw illustrated in an `ORDER BY` clause in the preceding section.

You need to understand the different proprietary solutions and the `CASE` operator before you see an exhibit of selective aggregation. The following sections discuss the Oracle proprietary `DECODE` function and the `CASE` statement before discussing selective aggregation.

Oracle Proprietary DECODE Statement

The `DECODE` function allows you to perform if-then-else logic on equality matches. It doesn't support inequalities except as the else condition of an equality comparison. You can nest `DECODE` functions as call parameters to a `DECODE` function. The `DECODE` function is also not portable. As a best practice, avoid the `DECODE` function. As a reality check, millions of lines of code use the `DECODE` function, which makes its coverage essential and learning it unavoidable.

Here's the prototype for the `DECODE` function:

```
DECODE(expression, search, result
                [, search, result [, ... ]]
                [, default])
```

The function requires at least an expression or column return value, a search value, and a result before an optional default value. You can also add any number of pairs of search values and results before the optional default value.

Some SQL*Plus formatting is necessary to get a clean test in Oracle. You can check back to Appendix A for instructions on these formatting commands:

```
-- Set null to a visible string.
SET NULL "<Null>"
```

```
-- Set column formatting for an alphanumeric string.
COLUMN "Test 1" FORMAT A9
COLUMN "Test 2" FORMAT A9
COLUMN "Test 3" FORMAT A9
COLUMN "Test 4" FORMAT A9
COLUMN "Test 5" FORMAT A9
COLUMN "Test 6" FORMAT A9
COLUMN "Test 7" FORMAT A9
```

The following single test case covers the outcome possibilities of a DECODE function:

```
SQL> SELECT   DECODE('One','One','Equal') AS "Test 1"
     ,        DECODE('One','Two','Equal') AS "Test 2"
     ,        DECODE('One','One','Equal','Not Equal') AS "Test 3"
     ,        DECODE('One','Two','Equal','Not Equal') AS "Test 4"
     ,        DECODE('One','Two','Equal'
                           ,'Three','Equal') AS "Test 5"
     ,        DECODE('One','Two','Equal'
                           ,'Three','Equal','Not Equal') AS "Test 6"
     ,        DECODE('One','Two','Equal'
                           ,'Three','Equal'
                           ,'One','Equal','Not Equal') AS "Test 7"
     FROM     dual;
```

The query returns the following results:

```
Test 1    Test 2    Test 3    Test 4    Test 5    Test 6    Test 7
--------- --------- --------- --------- --------- --------- ---------
Equal     <Null>    Equal     Not Equal <Null>    Not Equal Equal
```

Tests 1 and 2 These tests use the DECODE function as an if-then block of code. The first call parameter to the DECODE function is what you're trying to match with the second call parameter. When they match, the third call parameter is returned. When they fail to match, the null value is returned.

TIP

The mnemonic for an if-then block is "three call parameters to the DECODE function."

This behavior is handy when you're counting success in a selective aggregation model, because the following would count only individuals who are single:

```
SQL> WITH inline AS
     (SELECT 'Single' AS marital_status FROM dual
      UNION ALL
      SELECT 'Single' AS marital_status FROM dual
      UNION ALL
      SELECT 'Married' AS marital_status FROM dual)
     SELECT COUNT(DECODE(inline.marital_status,'Single',1)) AS Single
     FROM   inline;
```

It returns the number of rows in the `single` column:

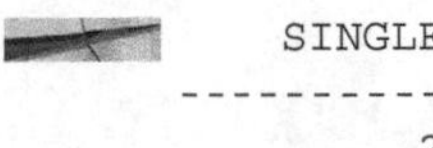

```
    SINGLE
----------
         2
```

This demonstrates that the `DECODE` function selectively counts results based on matches and nonmatches in the fabricated table of three rows. What it can't do is provide the count of nonmatches.

Tests 3 and 4 These tests use the `DECODE` function as an if-then-else block of code. The first, second, and third call parameters work like tests 1 and 2. The thing that's different with an `else` condition is that something meaningful is returned when the compared values fail to match.

TIP
The mnemonic for an if-then-else block is "four call parameters to the `DECODE` function."

This behavior is even better than the results from tests 1 and 2 for selective aggregation. It lets you count matches and nonmatches by using two columns instead of one in the `SELECT` list. You can count the number of rows in the `single` column and in the `married` column, like so:

```
SQL> WITH inline AS
  (SELECT 'Single' AS marital_status FROM dual
   UNION ALL
   SELECT 'Single' AS marital_status FROM dual
   UNION ALL
   SELECT 'Married' AS marital_status FROM dual)
  SELECT COUNT(DECODE(inline.marital_status,'Single',1)) AS Single
  ,      COUNT(DECODE(inline.marital_status,'Married',1)) AS Married
  FROM   inline;
```

The two columns now give us this more meaningful result:

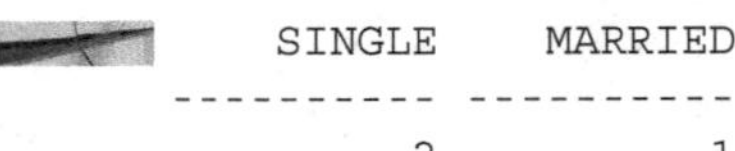

```
    SINGLE    MARRIED
---------- ----------
         2          1
```

This demonstrates that you can ask two sides of the same question by putting the results in separate columns. This is a form of SQL transformation.

Tests 5, 6, and 7 These tests use the `DECODE` function as if-then-elseif and if-then-elseif-else blocks of code. They act more or less like traditional switch statements, except Oracle doesn't support fall-through behavior. Fall-through behavior would return a result for the first and every subsequent `CASE` statement where the conditions were met.

The first, second, and third call parameters work like tests 1 through 4, but call parameters 4 and 5, 6 and 7, 8 and 9, and so forth would be cases. The lack of an even number of parameters means there's no default case. That means an odd number of parameters 5 and above makes a `DECODE` function into a switch statement without a default condition. Likewise, an even number of parameters 6 and above makes a `DECODE` function into a switch statement with a default condition.

TIP

The mnemonic for an if-then-elseif block is "five or any greater odd number of call parameters to the `DECODE` function," and the mnemonic for an if-then-elseif-else block is "six or any greater even number of call parameters to the `DECODE` function."

This behavior allows us to test more than just two cases. The downside is that it becomes verbose quickly. You can now count the number of rows in the `single` column, the `divorced` column, and the `married` column, like so:

```
SQL> WITH inline AS
    (SELECT 'Single' AS marital_status FROM dual
     UNION ALL
     SELECT 'Single' AS marital_status FROM dual
     UNION ALL
     SELECT 'Divorced' AS marital_status FROM dual
     UNION ALL
     SELECT 'Annulled' AS marital_status FROM dual
     UNION ALL
     SELECT 'Married' AS marital_status FROM dual)
    SELECT COUNT(DECODE(inline.marital_status,'Single',1)) AS Single
    ,      COUNT(DECODE(inline.marital_status,'Divorced',1)) AS Divorced
    ,      COUNT(DECODE(inline.marital_status,'Married',1)) AS Married
    FROM   inline;
```

The data set now has four classifications in the inline view but only three evaluations in the `SELECT` list. Any person whose marital status is annulled is excluded from your SQL report. The results would be the following:

```
    SINGLE   DIVORCED    MARRIED
---------- ---------- ----------
         2          1          1
```

You could capture the annulled marriages by some math operation, such as the following, with the `DECODE` function:

```
SELECT COUNT(DECODE(inline.marital_status,'Single',1)) AS Single
,      COUNT(DECODE(inline.marital_status,'Divorced',1)) AS Divorced
,      COUNT(DECODE(inline.marital_status,'Married',1)) AS Married
,      COUNT(inline.marital_status) -
        (COUNT(DECODE(inline.marital_status,'Single',1)) +
         COUNT(DECODE(inline.marital_status,'Divorced',1)) +
         COUNT(DECODE(inline.marital_status,'Married',1))) AS Other
FROM   inline
```

It would now give you this:

```
    SINGLE   DIVORCED    MARRIED      OTHER
---------- ---------- ---------- ----------
         2          1          1          1
```

This is the limit of what you can do with the DECODE function, which is why using the CASE operator is recommended.

ANSI SQL CASE Operator

The CASE operator is the most portable operator, and it allows for equality and inequality evaluation, range comparisons, and in-set comparisons. It also supports multiple CASE statements, such as a switch statement without fall-through characteristics. You can likewise use comparisons against subqueries and correlated subqueries.

In an Oracle database, the following query matches case-insensitive strings from the inline view against string literals for the primary colors on the color wheel:

```
SQL> SELECT   inline.color_name
     ,        CASE
                WHEN UPPER(inline.color_name) = 'BLUE' THEN
                  'Primary Color'
                WHEN UPPER(inline.color_name) = 'RED' THEN
                  'Primary Color'
                WHEN UPPER(inline.color_name) = 'YELLOW' THEN
                  'Primary Color'
                ELSE
                  'Not Primary Color'
              END AS color_type
     FROM    (SELECT 'Red' AS color_name FROM dual
              UNION ALL
              SELECT 'Blue' AS color_name FROM dual
              UNION ALL
              SELECT 'Purple' AS color_name FROM dual
              UNION ALL
              SELECT 'Green' AS color_name FROM dual
              UNION ALL
              SELECT 'Yellow' AS color_name FROM dual) inline
     ORDER BY 2 DESC, 1 ASC
```

The CASE operator includes several WHEN clauses that evaluate conditions and an ELSE clause that acts as the default catchall for the CASE operator. Note that END by itself terminates a CASE operator. If you were to put END CASE, the word CASE would become the column alias.

Although the sample evaluates only a single logical condition, each WHEN clause supports any number of AND or OR logical operators. Any comparison phrase can use the standard equality and inequality comparison operators; the IN, =ANY, =SOME, and =ALL lookup operators; and scalar, single-row, multiple-row, and correlated subqueries.

You would get the following results from the preceding query in Oracle—at least you would when you format the color_name column to an alphanumeric ten-character string in SQL*Plus (check Appendix A for syntax):

```
COLOR_NAME COLOR_TYPE
---------- -----------------
Blue       Primary Color
Red        Primary Color
Yellow     Primary Color
Green      Not Primary Color
Purple     Not Primary Color
```

There's a lot of power in using the `CASE` operator, but you need to understand the basics and experiment. For example, you can write a query with a `CASE` operator that returns whether or not an item is found in inventory, like this:

```
SELECT CASE
         WHEN 'Star Wars VII' IN (SELECT item_title FROM item)
         THEN 'In-stock'
         ELSE 'Out-of-stock'
       END AS yes_no_answer
FROM   dual;
```

The `CASE` operator also allows you to validate complex math or date math. The following subsection explains Oracle date math and provide a `CASE` statement that leverages date math in the Oracle Database 12*c*.

Oracle Date Math Oracle's date math is very straightforward. You simply add or subtract numbers from a date to get a date in the future or past, respectively. The only twist in the model is that the `DATE` data type is a date-time, not a date. You can shave off the hours and minutes of any day with the `TRUNC` function and make the date-time equivalent to midnight the morning of a date. This is the closest you have to a true `DATE` data type in an Oracle database.

The following example looks at yesterday, today, and tomorrow:

```
SQL> SELECT   SYSDATE - 1 AS yesterday
  2  ,        SYSDATE     AS today
  3  ,        SYSDATE + 1 AS tomorrow
  4  FROM     dual;
```

The results are deceiving because Oracle automatically prints them as dates, like so:

```
YESTERDAY TODAY     TOMORROW
--------- --------- ---------
19-JUN-11 20-JUN-11 21-JUN-11
```

If we convert the date-time values to strings with formatting instructions down to the second, you would see the full date-time stamp. This query uses the Oracle proprietary `TO_CHAR` function to do that:

```
SQL> SELECT   TO_CHAR(SYSDATE - 1,'DD-MON-YYYY HH24:MI:SS') AS Yesterday
  2  ,        TO_CHAR(SYSDATE    ,'DD-MON-YYYY HH24:MI:SS') AS Today
  3  ,        TO_CHAR(SYSDATE + 1,'DD-MON-YYYY HH24:MI:SS') AS Tomorrow
  4  FROM     dual;
```

It yields the following:

```
 YESTERDAY            TODAY                TOMORROW
-------------------- -------------------- --------------------
19-JUN-2011 22:59:45 20-JUN-2011 22:59:45 21-JUN-2011 22:59:45
```

You could use the TRUNC function to shave the decimal portion of time, which would give you 12 midnight in the morning of each day. The following query truncates the time from the SYSDATE value:

```
SQL> SELECT   TO_CHAR(TRUNC(SYSDATE)-1,'DD-MON-YYYY HH24:MI') AS Yesterday
  2  ,        TO_CHAR(TRUNC(SYSDATE)  ,'DD-MON-YYYY HH24:MI:SS') AS Today
  3  ,        TO_CHAR(TRUNC(SYSDATE)+1,'DD-MON-YYYY HH24:MI:SS') AS Tomorrow
  4  FROM     dual;
```

The results show that everything is now 12 midnight the morning of each day:

```
YESTERDAY         TODAY                TOMORROW
----------------- -------------------- --------------------
19-JUN-2011 00:00 20-JUN-2011 00:00:00 21-JUN-2011 00:00:00
```

This means any date plus an integer of 1 yields a day that is 24 hours in the future, and any date minus an integer of 1 yields a day that is 24 hours behind the current date-time value. The TRUNC function also lets you get the first day of a month or the first day of a year. It works like this:

```
SQL> SELECT   TRUNC(SYSDATE,'MM') AS first_day_of_month
  2  ,        TRUNC(SYSDATE,'YY') AS first_day_of_year
  3  FROM     dual;
```

Here are the results:

```
FIRST_DAY_OF_MONTH FIRST_DAY_OF_YEAR
------------------ ------------------
01-JUN-11          01-JAN-11
```

If you subtract two days, you get the number of days between them, like so:

```
SQL> SELECT TO_DATE('30-MAY-2011') - TO_DATE('14-FEB-2011') AS days
  2  FROM dual;
```

It would tell us the number of days between Valentine's Day and Memorial Day, as shown here:

```
      DAYS
----------
       105
```

Although you can subtract days, you can't add them. If you tried to add dates, the following error would be raised:

```
SELECT TO_DATE('30-MAY-2011') + TO_DATE('14-FEB-2011')
                              *
ERROR at line 1:
ORA-00975: date + date not allowed
```

Table B-8 provides a summary of additional built-in functions that can help when you're performing date math on an Oracle database. Although the table's not inclusive of timestamp functions, it covers those functions that work with dates. You can check the *Oracle Database SQL Language Reference 12*c *Release* or Appendix D for more information on key built-ins.

Date Function	Description

`ADD_MONTHS`	Lets you add or subtract months, like so:
	`SELECT ADD_MONTHS(SYSDATE, 3)`
	`FROM dual;`

`CAST`	Lets you convert a string that uses the Oracle default date format masks of `DD-MON-RR` or `DD-MON-YYYY` to a `DATE` data type. The example uses an `INSERT` statement to show the conversion:
	`INSERT INTO` *`some_table`*
	`VALUES`
	`(CAST('15-APR-11' AS DATE));`

`CURRENT_DATE`	Finds the current system date: `SELECT CURRENT_DATE FROM dual;`

`GREATEST`	Finds the most forward date in a set of dates. It works like this to find tomorrow:
	`SELECT GREATEST(SYSDATE,SYSDATE + 1)`
	`FROM dual;`

`EXTRACT`	Lets you extract the integer that represents a year, month, day, hour, minute, or second from a `DATE` data type. The following prototypes show you how to grab the day, month, or year from a `DATE` data type:
	`SELECT EXTRACT(DAY FROM SYSDATE) AS dd`
	`,      EXTRACT(MONTH FROM SYSDATE) AS mm`
	`,      EXTRACT(YEAR FROM SYSDATE) AS yy`
	`FROM dual;`

`LEAST`	Finds the most forward date in a set of dates. It works like this to find yesterday:
	`SELECT LEAST(SYSDATE -1,SYSDATE)`
	`FROM dual;`

`LAST_DAY`	Lets you find the last date of the month for any date, like so:
	`SELECT last_day(SYSDATE)`
	`FROM dual;`

`LEAST`	Finds the most forward date in a set of dates. It works like this to find yesterday:
	`SELECT LEAST(SYSDATE -1,SYSDATE)`
	`FROM dual;`

`MONTHS_BETWEEN`	Lets you find the decimal value between two dates. The function returns a positive number when the greater date is the first call parameter and returns a negative number when it's the second call parameter. Here's an example:
	`SELECT MONTHS_BETWEEN('25-DEC-11',SYSDATE)`
	`FROM dual;`

`NEXT_DAY`	Lets you find the date of the next day of the week, like so:
	`SELECT next_day(sysdate,'FRIDAY')`
	`FROM dual;`

(continued)

TABLE B-8. *Oracle Built-in Date Functions*

Date Function	Description
`ROUND`	Shaves off the decimal portion of a `DATE` when the current date-time is before noon. Alternatively, it adds the complement of the decimal to make the day midnight of the next day. Use it like this: `SELECT ROUND(SYSDATE) FROM dual;`
`SYSDATE`	Finds the current system date: `SELECT SYSDATE FROM dual;`

`TO_CHAR`	Lets you apply a format to a date, like so:
	`SELECT`
	`  TO_CHAR(SYSDATE,'DD-MON-YYYY HH24:MI:SS')`
	`FROM dual;`
	Supports the following format syntax:
	`DD` – Two-digit day
	`MM` – Two-digit month
	`MON` – Three-character month, based on `NLS_LANG` value
	`YY` – Two-digit year
	`YYYY` – Two-digit absolute year
	`RR` – Two-digit relative year
	`HH` – Two-digit hour, values 1 to 12
	`HH24` – Two-digit hour, values 0 to 23
	`MI` – Two-digit minutes, values 0 to 59
	`SS` – Two-digit seconds, values 0 to 59

`TO_DATE`	Converts a string to a `DATE` data type. Lets you convert to nonstandard `DATE` format masks, which come from external import sources. The default format masks of `DD-MON-RR` and `DD-MON-YYYY` also work with the `TO_DATE` function but can be cast to a `DATE` with the `CAST` function. The `TO_DATE` function would convert a Perl default format date string to a `DATE` with this syntax: `SELECT TO_DATE('2011-07-14','YYYY-MM-DD') FROM dual;`

TABLE B-8. *Oracle Built-in Date Functions*

The `EXTRACT` function lets you find an integer equivalent of a month, day, or year for any `DATE` data type. Blending the conditional `CASE` operator with the `EXTRACT` date function, you can write a statement that finds `transaction_amount` values for a given month. The following is such a statement:

```
SQL> SELECT  CASE
               WHEN EXTRACT(MONTH FROM transaction_date) = 1 AND
                    EXTRACT(YEAR FROM transaction_date) = 2011 THEN
                 transaction_amount
             END AS "January"
     FROM    transaction;
```

Lines 2 and 3 identify transaction amounts from a month and year, and only `transaction_amount` values for January 2011 would be returned by the query. However, it would also return null value rows for every other month and year present in the table. You need to filter the query with a `WHERE` clause to restrict it to the interested data. The `CASE` operator in a `SELECT` list works in tandem with the `WHERE` clause of a query.

Another approach could have you return a `Y` as an `active_flag` value when the `item_release_date` values are less than or equal to 30 days before today, and return an `N` when the values are greater than 30 days. You would write that `CASE` operator like this:

```
SQL> SELECT CASE
              WHEN (SYSDATE - i.release_date) <= 30 THEN 'Y'
              WHEN (SYSDATE - i.release_date) >  30 THEN 'N'
            END AS active_flag
     FROM   item i;
```

In conclusion, the `CASE` operator is more flexible than the `DECODE` function or `IF` function. The best practice is to write portable code with the `CASE` operator.

Selective Aggregation

Selective aggregation uses conditional logic, similar to the `DECODE` function, `IF` function, or `CASE` operator inside aggregation functions. The conditional decision-making of these if-then-else functions lets you filter what you count, sum, average, or take the maximum or minimum value of. Understanding this is the first step toward transforming data into useful data sets for accountants and other professional data analysts. The second step lets you transform aggregated rows into column values, which you accomplish through column aliases.

The next example demonstrates transforming rows of data into a financial report where the columns represent months, quarters, and year-to-date values and the rows represent account numbers charged for various expenses. The following query returns a column of data for the month of January 2011. Since all numbers are stored as positive values, a nested `CASE` operator evaluates the `transaction_type` column in the same row to determine whether to add or subtract the value. Debits are added and credits are subtracted, because this works with an asset account.

```
SQL> SELECT   t.transaction_account AS "Transaction"
     ,         LPAD(TO_CHAR
              (SUM
                (CASE
                   WHEN EXTRACT(MONTH FROM transaction_date) = 1 AND
                        EXTRACT(YEAR FROM transaction_date) = 2011 THEN
                     CASE
                       WHEN t.transaction_type = 'DEBIT' THEN
                         t.transaction_amount
                       ELSE
                         t.transaction_amount * -1
                     END
                 END),'99,999.00'),10,' ') AS "JAN"
     FROM     transaction t
     GROUP BY t.transaction_account;
```

You would see something like this when you expand beyond a single column, which has been limited to the first three months of the year and the first two rows of data:

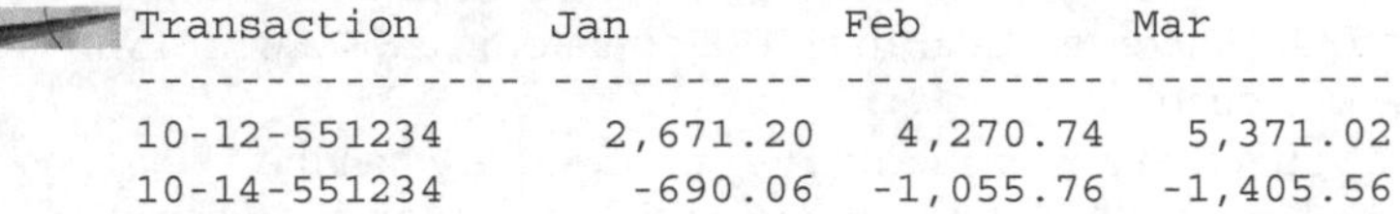

```
Transaction     Jan        Feb        Mar
--------------- ---------- ---------- ----------
10-12-551234      2,671.20   4,270.74   5,371.02
10-14-551234       -690.06  -1,055.76  -1,405.56
```

The value passed to the `SUM` function is all rows that meet the selectivity criteria. The criteria are the result of a `CASE` and nested `CASE` operator. The business result is the total expense grouped by the transaction account number. The `LPAD` function right-aligns the string returned by the `TO_CHAR` function, which formats the number always to have two decimal places, even when it's zero cents.

Line 5 could be replaced by the following to capture a first-quarter result:

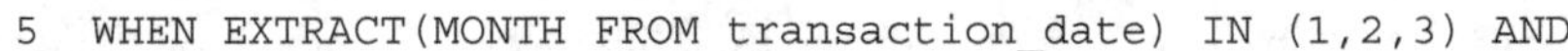

```
5  WHEN EXTRACT(MONTH FROM transaction_date) IN (1,2,3) AND
```

Moreover, you could generate a year-to-date report or year-end report for a completed year by eliminating the validation criterion for the month.

Join Results

You can join tables (logical structures that store physical data) or views (logical structures that store directions on how to find data stored in other views or tables) into larger result sets. Views can be subsets of tables, filtered to show only some columns and rows. Views can also be the result sets combined from two or more tables or views. You combine tables through join operations.

Although joins in procedural programming languages would involve an outer loop and an inner loop to read two sets into memory, SQL doesn't have loops. As a set-based declarative language, SQL operates like an automatic transmission that hides the clutch and gear-changing process. Imperative languages, on the other hand, are like standard transmissions. Imperative languages require the developer to master the nature of manually switching gears. Managing the clutch and gears would be equivalent to writing outer and inner loops and conditional logic to join the results from two sets into one. SQL joins hide the complexity by letting the developer state what he or she wants without specifying the implementation details.

You can perform several types of joins in SQL. They can be organized into an abstract Unified Modeling Language (UML) inheritance diagram, which is a hierarchy, as shown in Figure B-13. This type of hierarchy is also known as an inverted tree. The top of the hierarchy is the root node and the bottom nodes are the leaf nodes. The root node is the parent node and is not derivative of any other node. Nodes below the root (or parent) node are its child nodes. Leaf nodes aren't parents yet but may become so later; they are child nodes. Nodes between the root and leaf nodes are both parent and child nodes.

Inheritance trees indicate that the most generalized behaviors are in the root node and the most specialized behaviors are in child nodes. The inheritance tree tells us the following:

- A *cross join* is the most generalized behavior in joins, and it inherits nothing but implements the base behaviors for join operations in a set-based declarative language.
- An *inner join* is the *only* child of a cross join, and it inherits the behaviors of a cross join and provides some additional features (specialized behaviors) by extending the parent class's behaviors.

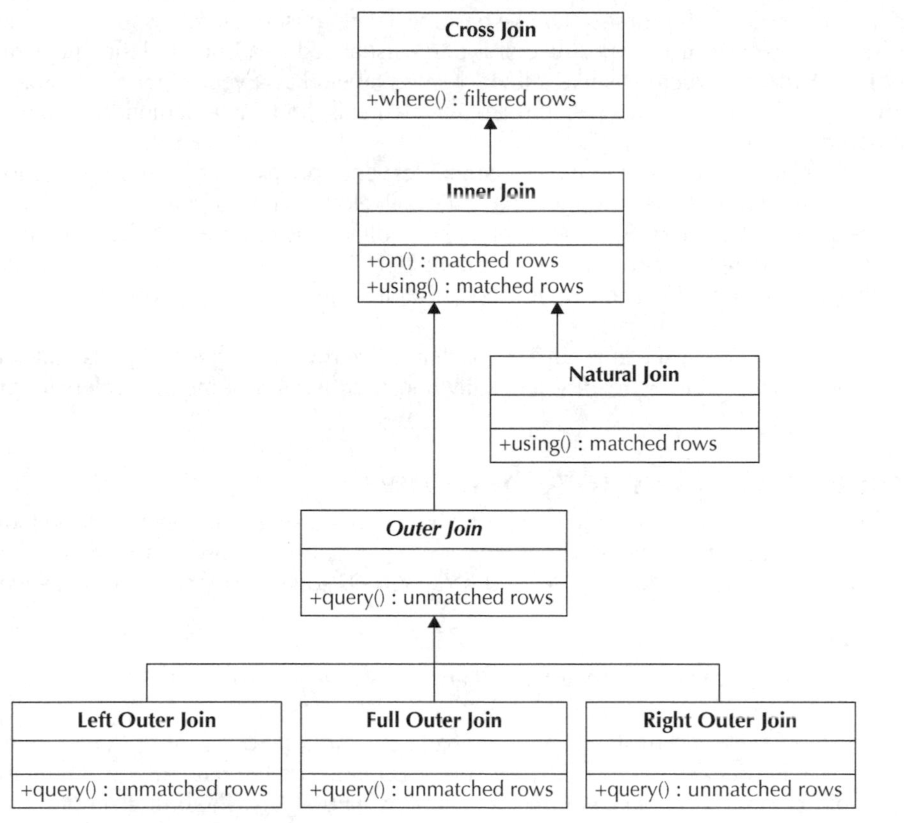

FIGURE B-13. *Join inheritance tree*

- A *natural join* is a child of an inner join, and it inherits and extends the parent class's behaviors. The natural join is also a leaf node, which means no other class extends its behaviors.
- An *outer join* is an abstract class, which means its implementations are available only to subclasses, but it does extend the behavior of the parent class. Through the parent class, it also extends the behavior of the root node or grandparent class.
- A *left join* is a concrete class that extends its abstract parent class and all other classes preceding its parent in the tree. It implements a left outer join behavior beyond the inherited inner join operations.
- A *full join* is a concrete class that extends its abstract parent class and all other classes preceding its parent in the tree. It implements a full outer join behavior beyond the inherited inner join operations.
- A *right join* is a concrete class that extends its abstract parent class and all other classes preceding its parent in the tree. It implements a right outer join behavior beyond the inherited inner join operations.

The subsections qualify what the various join types do. Each section uses Venn diagrams to depict the relationship of sets. Unlike basic sets with a list of elements, the rows in tables are vectors, or record structures. A vector is often visualized as a line, and the line is made up of points. A record structure is like a line when it's labeled as a vector but isn't composed of points. The points in a record data structure are the elements, and each element of a row belongs to a column in a table or view.

There are two types of joins between tables: one splices rows from one table together with rows from another table, and the other splices like collections together. The spliced rows become larger record structures. Splicing together two collections requires that both original collections have the same record structure or table definition. The cross, inner, natural, and outer joins work with splicing rows together. You use set operators to splice together collections of the same record structure.

The next two subsections cover joins that splice rows together and joins that splice collections together. They should be read sequentially because there are some dependencies between the two sections.

Joins that Splice Together Rows

Tables should contain all the information that defines a single subject when the tables are properly normalized. This section assumes you're working with normalized tables. You'll see the differences between ANSI SQL-89 and ANSI SQL-92 joins throughout the subsequent sections.

TIP

You should learn both ANSI SQL-89 and ANSI SQL-92 join semantics.

As a refresher, normalized tables typically contain a set of columns that uniquely defines every row in the table, and collectively these columns are the natural key of the table. Although possible but rare, a single column can define the natural key. The best example of that use case is a `vehicle` table with a `vin` (vehicle identification number) column. In the use case, you also add surrogate key columns, which are artificial numbers generated through sequences. Surrogate key columns don't define anything about the data, but they uniquely define rows of a table and should have a one-to-one relationship to the natural key of a table. Although the surrogate and natural keys are both candidates to become the primary key of a table, you should always select the surrogate key.

The primary key represents rows of the table externally, and you can copy it to another table as a foreign key. Matches between the primary and foreign key columns let you join tables into multiple-subject record structures. Joins between primary and foreign key values are known as *equijoins*, or joins based on an equality match between columns. Joins that don't match based on the equality of columns are *non-equijoins*, and they're filtered searches of a Cartesian product. The "Cross Join" section that follows explains these types of joins.

The natural key differs from a surrogate key because it represents the columns that you use to find a unique row in a table, and it contains descriptive values that define the unique subject of a normalized table. When you write a query against a single table, you use the natural key columns in the `WHERE` clause to find unique rows.

Cross joins are the most generalized form; outer joins are the most specialized.

Cross Join

A cross join in SQL produces a Cartesian product, which is the rows of one table matched against all the rows of another table. It is equivalent to a `FOR` loop reading one row from one collection and then a nested `FOR` loop appending all rows from another collection to copies of that one row. The operation is repeated for every row in the outer `FOR` loop.

A Venn diagram for a cross join is shown in the following illustration. The discrete math represents that one set is multiplied by the other. For example, a cross join between a `customer` table and an `address` table would return 32 rows when the `customer` table holds 4 rows and the `address` table holds 8 rows.

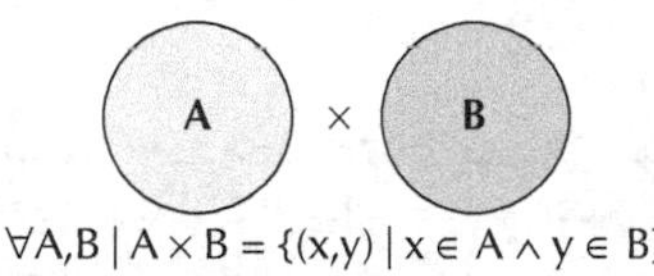

Cross joins are useful when you want to perform a non-equijoin match, such as looking up transaction amounts based on their transaction dates within a calendar month. In this case, you'd be filtering a Cartesian product to see when one column in a table holds a value between two columns in the other table. This is also known as a *filtered cross join* statement.

The difference between ANSI SQL-89 and ANSI SQL-92 syntax for a cross join is that the tables are comma-delimited in the `FROM` clause for ANSI SQL-89, whereas they're bridged by a `CROSS JOIN` operator in ANSI SQL-92.

ANSI SQL-89 Cross Join The following shows a filtered cross join between the `transaction` and `calendar` tables:

```
SQL> SELECT   c.month_short_name
  2  ,        t.transaction_amount
  3  FROM     calendar c, transaction t
  4  WHERE    t.transaction_date BETWEEN c.start_date AND c.end_date
  5  ORDER BY EXTRACT(MONTH FROM t.transaction_date);
```

Notice that the `FROM` clause on line 3 lists comma-delimited tables, and the `WHERE` clause on line 4 doesn't have an equality-based join between the primary and foreign key columns.

It would display the following type of result set:

```
Month
Name  Amount
----- ------
JAN    32.87
JAN    38.99
MAR     9.99
APR    43.19
```

A `GROUP BY` clause on a line 5 combined with a `SUM` aggregation formula on line 2 would return three rows of aggregated data, one row for each distinct month:

```
SQL> SELECT   c.month_short_name
  2  ,        SUM(t.transaction_amount)
  3  FROM     calendar c, transaction t
```

```
WHERE    t.transaction_date BETWEEN c.start_date AND c.end_date
GROUP BY c.month_short_name
ORDER BY EXTRACT(MONTH FROM t.transaction_date);
```

This type of cross join logic is extremely useful when you're creating financial statements with SQL queries. It filters results based on whether one table's column is between two columns of another table.

ANSI SQL-92 Cross Join Like the prior syntax example, this example shows a filtered cross join between the `transaction` and `calendar` tables:

```
SQL> SELECT   c.month_short_name
  2  ,        t.transaction_amount
  3  FROM     calendar c CROSS JOIN transaction t
  4  WHERE    t.transaction_date BETWEEN c.start_date AND c.end_date
  5  ORDER BY EXTRACT(MONTH FROM t.transaction_date);
```

It would return the same result set from the sample data found in the video store database (see the Introduction to the book for details). Notice that in lieu of the comma-delimited tables on line 3, two tables are separated by the `CROSS JOIN` operator.

You also can refactor this query to use the following syntax:

```
SELECT   c.month_short_name
,        t.transaction_amount
FROM     calendar c INNER JOIN transaction t
ON      (t.transaction_date BETWEEN c.start_date AND c.end_date)
ORDER BY EXTRACT(MONTH FROM t.transaction_date);
```

Although this appears to be an inner join operation, it actually runs as a filtered cross join. The `ON` subclause performs a range comparison that determines whether the `transaction_date` column value is found between two columns from the `calendar` table. Why is the last syntax important if it's misleading and does the same thing? Because Oracle has included this on the certification test recently. If you get the question on the Advanced SQL certification test, the answer is that it's an inner join.

Cross joins also let you add literal values to the rows of a table or to the rows of any other type of join between two or more tables. Adding a literal column to a table lets you perform calculations with the literal value against the other columns of the table.

Cartesian Product

A Cartesian product is the result of a cross join in SQL. The Cartesian product is named after René Descartes, who is known for penning the phrase, "*Cogito ergo sum*." Translated, it means, "I think therefore I am." He was also a 17th century mathematician who developed the theory of analytical geometry, which lays the foundation for calculus and many aspects of set theory. Set theory is a major foundational element for relational calculus and databases.

Unnesting Queries Oracle calls joins between a table containing nested tables and its nested tables *unnesting queries*. They work slightly differently than cross joins because they resolve instances of a nested table against the containing row or the instance found in a containing collection. The process works for both nested varrays and tables.

The following query uses two cross joins to get the rows from those values inserted earlier in the "Inserting Arrays and Nested Tables" section of this appendix. Unnesting tables requires a cross join against a table, and the `TABLE` function allows you to convert the nested table collection into a SQL result set that works in a join operation.

```
SQL> COLUMN id          FORMAT 999
SQL> COLUMN full_name   FORMAT A20
SQL> COLUMN street      FORMAT A20
SQL> COLUMN city_state  FORMAT A20
SQL> SELECT   e.employee_id
  2  ,        e.first_name
  3  ||       DECODE(e.middle_name,NULL,' ',' '||e.middle_name||' ')
  4  ||       e.last_name AS full_name
  5  ,        s.column_value AS street
  6  ,        n.city || ', ' || n.state AS city_state
  7  FROM     employee e CROSS JOIN TABLE(e.home_address) n
  8           CROSS JOIN TABLE(n.street_address) s;
```

Lines 7 and 8 unnest the query by comparing results between containing rows and instances of an ADT or UDT. The query displays

```
  ID FULL_NAME            STREET               CITY_STATE
---- -------------------- -------------------- -------------
   1 Sam Yosemite         1111 Broadway        Oakland, CA
   1 Sam Yosemite         Suite 322            Oakland, CA
   1 Sam Yosemite         1111 Broadway        Oakland, CA
   1 Sam Yosemite         Suite 525            Oakland, CA
```

Unfortunately, there's no join between the row containing *Wile E Coyote* because the join fails to find an instance in the result from the `TABLE` function. That's because the "Inserting Arrays and Nested Tables" section inserted a null value for the `street_address` column, and there isn't an instance to join.

We can fix the problem by making the unnesting work like an outer join, which is covered later in the "Outer Join" section of this appendix. Oracle implements the unnesting feature by using the `(+)` operator on any table where a null value may exist in a collection. That way the (+) operator works like it does in ANSI-89 syntax outer joins. It instructs the SQL statement to return values from the opposite side of the cross join when a null instance is found by the `TABLE` function.

Modifying the prior query, it now can return individuals without a `street_address` instance:

```
SQL> SELECT   e.employee_id AS id
  2  ,        e.first_name
  3  ||       DECODE(e.middle_name,NULL,' ',' '||e.middle_name||' ')
  4  ||       e.last_name AS full_name
  5  ,        s.column_value AS street
  6  ,        n.city || ', ' || n.state AS city_state
  7  FROM     employee e CROSS JOIN TABLE(e.home_address) n
  8           CROSS JOIN TABLE(n.street_address) (+) s;
```

The `(+)` operator now lets you find the missing row from the containing table, as you can see in the query results:

```
  ID FULL_NAME             STREET                CITY_STATE
---- --------------------- --------------------- -------------
   1 Sam Yosemite          1111 Broadway         Oakland, CA
   1 Sam Yosemite          Suite 322             Oakland, CA
   1 Sam Yosemite          1111 Broadway         Oakland, CA
   1 Sam Yosemite          Suite 525             Oakland, CA
   2 Wile E Coyote                               Phoenix, AZ
```

We can see from the results that the outer cross join principal of unnesting queries lets us see the missing *Wile E Coyote* row of the containing table and nested UDT. Clearly, there's no substitute for cross joins in unnesting queries, which makes cross joins an essential solution space for Oracle Database 12*c*.

You can also create a multilevel table structure like this to use locator references when querying data. You need to provide the `NESTED_TABLE_GET_REFS` hint to a `SELECT` statement when you want to use the locator references to find the data, like

```
SQL> COLUMN full_name       FORMAT A16
SQL> COLUMN street_address  FORMAT A16
SQL> COLUMN city_state      FORMAT A12
SQL> SELECT /*+ NESTED_TABLE_GET_REFS +*/
  2         e.first_name || ' ' || e.last_name AS full_name
  3  ,      s.column_value AS street_address
  4  ,      h.city || ', ' || h.state AS city_state
  5  FROM   employee2 e CROSS JOIN TABLE(e.home_address) h
  6         CROSS JOIN TABLE(h.street_address) (+) s;
```

Line 1 shows the use of the tuning hint. It's also a good idea to use locator references when the nested data set is large, and to avoid them when the data set it small.

Inner Join

An inner join in SQL produces an intersection between two tables. It lets you splice rows into one large row. It is equivalent to a `FOR` loop reading one row from one collection, then a nested `FOR` loop reading another row, and finally a conditional `IF` statement checking whether they match. When they match, you have an intersection, and only those rows are returned by an `INNER JOIN` operator.

The Venn diagram for an inner join is shown in the next illustration. The discrete math represents that one set intersects the other. For example, when you match a table with a primary key value and a foreign key value, you get only those rows that match both the primary and foreign key values.

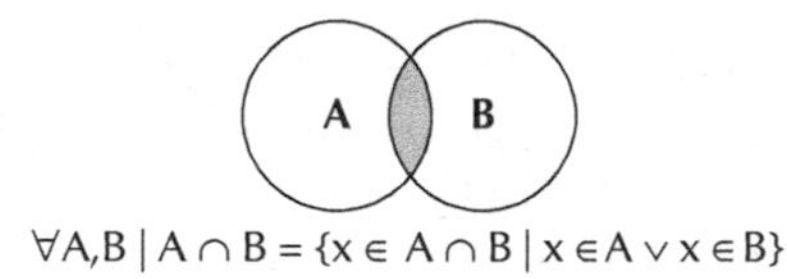

$$\forall A,B \mid A \cap B = \{x \in A \cap B \mid x \in A \vee x \in B\}$$

There are two key differences between ANSI SQL-89 and ANSI SQL-92 syntax for an inner join. One is that tables are comma-delimited in the `FROM` clause for ANSI SQL-89, and they're separated by the `INNER JOIN` operator in ANSI SQL-92. The other is that the join condition is in the `WHERE` clause in ANSI SQL-89 and is in the `FROM` clause in ANSI SQL-92. You use a `USING` clause when the primary and foreign key column(s) share the same column name, and you use the `ON` clause when they don't.

ANSI SQL-89 Inner Join The following shows you how to join the `member` and `contact` tables on their respective primary and foreign key columns. Notice that the tables are comma-delimited and that the join is performed in the `WHERE` clause.

```
SQL> SELECT   COUNT(*)
     FROM     member m, contact c
     WHERE    m.member_id = c.member_id;
```

The query returns the number of rows where the values in the two `member_id` columns match exactly. This is an equijoin (or equality value match) relationship.

For subsections, the parent table will always be on the left side of the operator and the child table will be on the right side. If you swap their locations, the results would likewise invert, because the left join of parent to child is the same as the right join of child to parent.

ANSI SQL-92 Inner Join Like the preceding example, this example shows you how to join the `member` and `contact` tables on their respective primary and foreign key columns. The `INNER JOIN` operator replaces the comma-delimited notation of the older syntax pattern.

Two subclause notations are available for joins: the `USING` subclause and the `ON` subclause. The `USING` subclause works when the column or columns have the same name. These operators are required in inner and outer joins but not with the `NATURAL JOIN` operator.

Here's the `USING` prototype:

```
FROM   table [alias] {LEFT | INNER | RIGHT | FULL} JOIN table [alias]
USING ( column [, column [, … ]])
```

You can provide as many columns as you need in the `USING` subclause. You should enter them as a comma-separated list. They are processed as though they were connected through a series of logical `AND` statements.

The `ON` prototype works when the columns have the same or different names. Here is its prototype:

```
FROM   table  [alias] {LEFT | INNER | RIGHT | FULL} JOIN table [alias]
   ON {table |[alias]}.column = {table | alias}.column
[ AND {table |[alias]}.column = {table | alias}.column
[ AND ... ]}
```

Notice that the following tables aren't comma-delimited. The `INNER JOIN` operator replaces the comma between tables. This join uses the `USING` subclause to match primary and foreign key columns that share the same name.

```
SQL> SELECT   m.account_number
     ,        c.last_name || ', ' || c.first_name AS customer_name
     FROM     member m INNER JOIN contact c USING(member_id);
```

You use the ON subclause when the column name or column names aren't the same. Here is an example of the ON subclause syntax:

```
SQL> SELECT   m.account_number
   ,          c.last_name || ', ' || c.first_name AS customer_name
   FROM       member m INNER JOIN contact c ON m.member_id = c.member_id;
```

Both of these queries return the number of rows where the values in the two member_id columns match exactly. Like the older syntax, that means they return the intersection between the two tables and a result set that potentially includes data from both tables.

Natural Join A natural join doesn't exist in the ANSI SQL-89 standard. It exists only in ANSI SQL-92 forward. The intent of a natural join is to provide the intersection between two sets. It's called a *natural* join because you don't have to provide the names of the primary or foreign key columns. The natural join checks the data catalog for matching column names with the same data type and then it creates the join condition implicitly for you:

```
SQL> SELECT   m.account_number
   ,          c.last_name || ', ' || c.first_name AS customer_name
   FROM       member m NATURAL JOIN contact c;
```

The only problem with a natural join occurs when columns share the same column name and data type but aren't the primary or foreign key results. A natural join will include them in the join condition. Attempting to match non-key columns that make up the who-audit columns excludes rows that should be returned. The who-audit is composed of the created_by, creation_date, last_updated_by, and last_update_date columns.

Outer Join

Outer joins allow you to return result sets that are found in the intersection and outside the intersection. Applying the paradigm of a parent table that holds a primary key and a child table that holds a foreign key, three relationships are possible when foreign key integrity is enforced by the API rather than database constraints:

- **Scenario 1** A row in the parent table matches one or more rows in the child table.
- **Scenario 2** A row in the parent table doesn't match any row in the child table.
- **Scenario 3** A row in the child table doesn't match any row in the parent table, which makes the row in the child table an orphan.

Any or all of the three scenarios can occur. Inner joins help us find the results for scenario 2, but outer joins help us find rows that meet the criteria of scenarios 1 and 3.

NOTE
The ANSI SQL-89 syntax has no provision for outer joins.

Oracle provided outer join syntax before it was defined by the ANSI SQL-92 definition. Oracle's syntax works with joins in the WHERE clause. You append a (+) on the column of a table in the join, and it indicates that you want the relative complement of that table. A relative complement contains everything not found in the original set.

For example, the following `SELECT` statement uses an Oracle proprietary outer join, and you would get all `account_number` values from the `member` table that had a contact or didn't have a contact. That's because any `member_id` values found in the `member` table that aren't found in the `contact` table are returned with the inner join result set.

```
SQL> SELECT    m.account_number
     FROM      member m, contact c
     WHERE     m.member_id = c.member_id(+);
```

If you change the `SELECT` list and switch the `(+)` from the `contact` table's column to the `member` table's `member_id` column, you would get any orphaned rows from the `contact` table. Here's the syntax to get orphaned contacts' names:

```
SQL> SELECT    c.last_name || ', ' || c.first_name AS customer_name
  2  FROM      member m, contact c
  3  WHERE     m.member_id(+) = c.member_id;
```

Line 3 has the change of the `(+)` from one side of the join to the other. As mentioned, the `(+)` symbol is included on a column of one table in a join and effectively points to its relative complement in the other table. Having positioned the `member` table on the left and the `contact` table on the right in the previous examples, when the `(+)` is pointing from a `contact` table's column, you get the equivalent of a left join. Switch the `(+)` to point from a column in the `member` table and you get the equivalent of a right join.

Oracle's proprietary syntax isn't portable to any other platform. It also doesn't support a full outer join behavior unless you combine results with a `UNION ALL` set operator, which is covered later in this appendix.

Left Outer Join A left join in SQL extends an inner join because it returns the intersection between two tables plus the right relative complement of the join. The right relative complement is everything in the table to the left of the join operation that's not found in the table on the right. The Venn diagram for a left join is shown next:

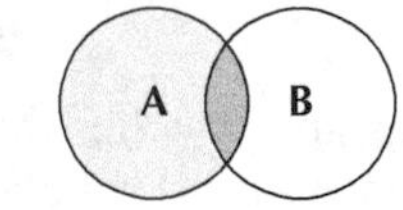

$$\forall A,B \mid A \cap B + A \setminus B = \{x \in A \wedge x \in B\} + \{y \in A \wedge y \neg\in B\}$$

A left join splices several rows into one large row, and it puts null values in the columns from the table on the right when nothing is found in those columns. Left joins use join conditions like those in the inner join section. The ANSI SQL-92 syntax supports a left join operation. That means join statements are in the `FROM` clause, not the `WHERE` clause, and you use either the `ON` or `USING` subclause to qualify the joining columns.

The following lets you find any `account_number` values in the `member` table, whether or not they have valid customer information in the `contact` table:

```
SQL> SELECT    m.account_number
     FROM      member m LEFT OUTER JOIN contact c
     ON        m.member_id = c.member_id;
```

The `LEFT OUTER JOIN` phrase is the fully qualified syntax, but the `OUTER` keyword is optional in Oracle database. If you were to reverse the relative positions of the `member` and `contact` tables, only the `account_number` values that meet the conditions of an `INNER JOIN` operator would be returned. That's because you would get the right relative complement of the `member` table, not the `contact` table. The right relative complement of the `member` table returns the data rows in the `contact` table that have foreign key values that don't resolve to primary key values in the `member` table. Naturally, this type of data set is possible only when you're not maintaining database-level foreign key constraints.

The more frequent use of a `LEFT JOIN` would be to look for orphaned customers to delete them from the database. In that use case, you'd write the statement like this:

```
SQL> SELECT   c.last_name || ', ' || c.first_name AS customer_name
  2  FROM     contact c LEFT JOIN member m
  3  ON       m.member_id = c.member_id;
```

Notice that the values in the `SELECT` list should come from the table that holds data, not from the table that may not contain data. Otherwise, you get a bunch of null values. The preceding query returns rows from the `contact` table that don't point back to a row in the `member` table, and such rows would be orphans. They are called orphans because their foreign key column values aren't found in the list of primary key column values. This can occur when there aren't foreign key constraints in the database.

Right Outer Join Like a right join, a left join in SQL extends an inner join. A right join returns the intersection between two tables, plus the left relative complement of the join. The left relative complement is everything in the table to the right of the join operation that's not found in the table on the left. This makes the right join a mirror image of the left join, as shown in the following Venn diagram.

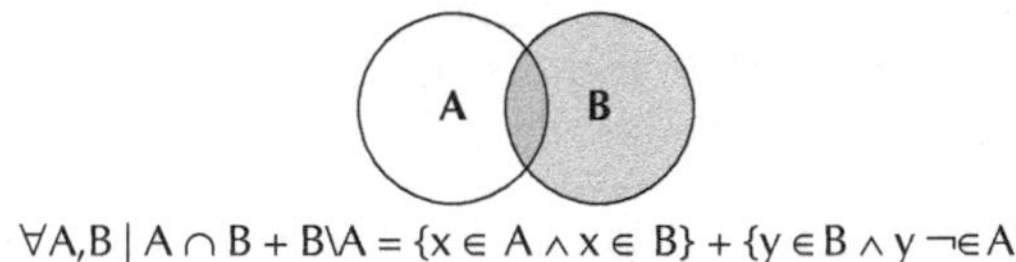

$$\forall A,B \mid A \cap B + B \setminus A = \{x \in A \wedge x \in B\} + \{y \in B \wedge y \neg\in A\}$$

A right join splices rows into one large row like the inner and left join. It puts null values in the columns from the table on the left when they don't match columns that exist in the table on the right. Right joins use join conditions like those in the inner and left join operations. That means they adhere to the ANSI SQL-92 syntax rules, and join statements are in the `FROM` clause, not the `WHERE` clause. You can choose to use the `ON` or `USING` subclause to qualify joining columns.

The first example, shown next, lets you find all customer names in the `contact` table—those names that have a valid foreign key value that matches a valid primary key value, and those that have an invalid foreign key value. Invalid foreign key values can exist only when you opt not to enforce database-level foreign key constraints. Rows holding invalid foreign key values are known as *orphaned* rows because the row with a valid primary key doesn't exist. This follows the paradigm that the parent holds the primary key and the child holds the foreign key (copy of the primary key).

This example returns all customer names from the `contact` table and really doesn't require a join operation at all:

```
SQL> SELECT   c.last_name || ', ' || c.first_name AS customer_name
  2  FROM     member m RIGHT JOIN contact c
  3  ON       m.member_id = c.member_id;
```

A more meaningful result would exclude all rows where the primary key value is missing. That's easy to do by adding a single filtering WHERE clause statement that says "return rows only where there's no valid primary key in the member table." Here's the example:

```
SQL> SELECT   c.last_name || ', ' || c.first_name AS customer_name
  2  FROM     member m RIGHT JOIN contact c
  3  ON       m.member_id = c.member_id
  4  WHERE    m.member id IS NULL;
```

Line 4 filters the return set so that it returns only the orphaned customer names. You would use that type of statement to delete orphan records, typically as a subquery in a DELETE FROM statement. Here's an example of such a statement:

```
SQL> DELETE FROM contact
WHERE  contact_id IN (SELECT   c.contact_id
                      FROM     member m RIGHT JOIN contact c
                      ON       m.member_id = c.member_id
                      WHERE    m.member_id IS NULL);
```

The right and left join semantics are very useful for cleaning up data when foreign key values have lost their matching primary key values. They help you find the relative complements of outer joins when you subtract the inner join rows.

Full Outer Join A full outer join provides the inner join results with the right and left relative complements of left and right joins, respectively. The combination of the two relative complements without the intersection is known as the *symmetric difference*. The Venn diagram for a full outer join is shown next:

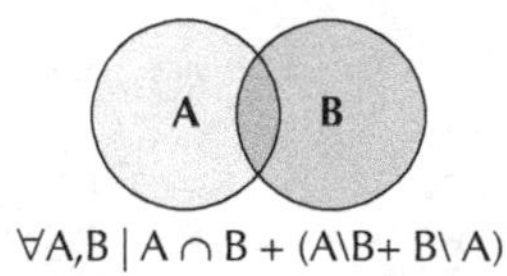

$\forall A,B \mid A \cap B + (A \setminus B + B \setminus A)$

Like the left and right joins, a full outer join splices rows into one large row, like the inner and left join. It puts null values in the columns from the table on the left and right. Assume the following FULL JOIN syntax (by the way, OUTER is an optional keyword and seldom used):

```
SQL> SELECT   m.account_number
,        c.last_name || ', ' || c.first_name AS customer_name
FROM     member m FULL JOIN contact c
ON       m.member_id = c.member_id;
```

This query's result set would return null values for the account_number when there isn't a foreign key using a primary key in the member table, and would return the customer_name when a foreign key value isn't found in the primary key list. This type of analysis is done when database-level foreign key constraints aren't maintained and the API failed to synchronize primary and foreign key values properly. You need to figure out which customers should be associated with a member, because a member row would never be written unless a contact row was also written. This kind of problem occurs more often than you might expect.

You would filter out the inner join by using the following syntax or the MINUS set operator (shown later):

```
SQL> SELECT   m.account_number
     ,        c.last_name || ', ' || c.first_name AS customer_name
     FROM     member m FULL JOIN contact c
     ON       m.member_id = c.member_id
     WHERE    m.member_id IS NOT NULL
     AND      c.member_id IS NOT NULL;
```

This wraps up joins. Next you'll see how to work with set operators. The next section builds on the examples in this section.

Joins that Splice Collections

Set operations often combine or filter row sets. That means they act as the glue that binds together two queries. The queries must return the same SELECT list, which means the column names and data types must match.

The basic prototype glues the top query to the bottom query. Both top and bottom queries can have their own GROUP BY or HAVING clauses, but only one ORDER BY clause can appear at the end. You can splice more than two queries by using other set operators in sequence. The value operations are performed top-down unless you use parentheses to group set operations. The default order of precedence splices the first query result set with the second, and they become a master set that in turn is spliced by another set operator with a subsequent query. Here's an example:

```
SELECT column_list
FROM some_table
[WHERE some_condition [{AND | OR } some_condition2 [ ...]]]
[GROUP BY column_list]
[HAVING aggregation_function]
VALID_SET_OPERATOR( INTERSECT | UNION | UNION ALL | MINUS )
SELECT column_list
FROM some_table
[WHERE some_condition [{AND | OR } some_condition2 [ ...]]]
[GROUP BY column_list]
[HAVING aggregation_function]
[ORDER BY column_list];
```

As qualified in the prototype, there are four set operators in SQL: INTERSECT, UNION, UNION ALL, and MINUS. The INTERSECT operator finds the intersection of two sets and returns a set of unique rows. The UNION set operator finds the unique set of rows and returns them. The UNION ALL set operator finds and returns an unsorted merge of all rows from both queries, which results in two copies of any like rows. The MINUS set operator removes the rows in the second query from the rows of the first query where they match.

The following sections discuss the set operators in more depth and provide examples and use cases for them. They're organized in what is the general frequency of use.

UNION

The `UNION` set operator acts like a union in set math and returns the unique things from two sets. This is a two-step process: first it gathers the rows into one set, then it sorts them and returns the unique set. The next illustration shows the Venn diagram for a `UNION` set operation, which looks exactly like a full outer join Venn diagram. The difference between the two is that a full outer join returns all the columns from two tables into one new and larger row, while the `UNION` set operator merges one set of rows with another uniquely.

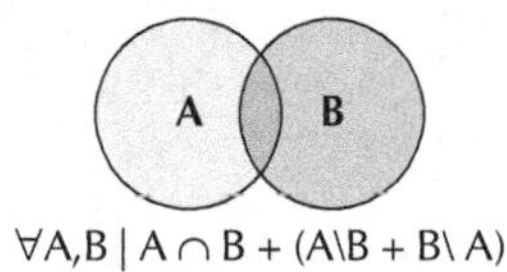

$\forall A,B \mid A \cap B + (A \setminus B + B \setminus A)$

The `UNION` set operator lets Oracle achieve a full outer join with its proprietary syntax. One query (A) gets the left join and the other query (B) gets the right join, and the `UNION` set operator sorts the nonunique row set and returns a unique set.

The code for an Oracle proprietary pseudo full outer join would look like this (pseudo because the combination of outer join and set operators is required):

```
SQL> SELECT   m.account_number
     ,        c.last_name || ', ' || c.first_name AS customer_name
     FROM     member m, contact c
     WHERE    m.member_id = c.member_id(+)
     UNION
     SELECT   m.account_number
     ,        c.last_name || ', ' || c.first_name AS customer_name
     FROM     member m, contact c
     WHERE    m.member_id(+) = c.member_id;
```

The first query returns a left join, which is the inner join between the columns and the right relative complement (those things in the left table not found in the right table). The second query returns the right join. The right join holds a copy of the left relative complement and a second copy of the inner join result set. The `UNION` set operator sorts the nonunique set and discards the second copy of the inner join.

This is more or less the use case for the `UNION` set operator. You use it when you can't guarantee that the queries return exclusive sets of rows.

UNION ALL

The `UNION ALL` set operator differs from the `UNION` set operator in one key way: it doesn't sort and eliminate duplicate rows. That's a benefit when you can guarantee that two queries return exclusive row sets because a sorting operation requires more computing resources. The following Venn diagram for a `UNION ALL` looks remarkably like the one for a `UNION`. The difference is seen in the discrete math below the illustration that indicates that it holds two copies of the intersection between the row sets.

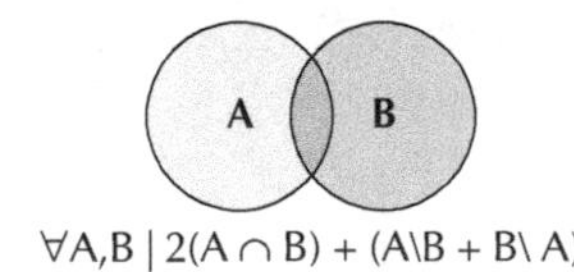

$\forall A,B \mid 2(A \cap B) + (A \setminus B + B \setminus A)$

The UNION ALL set operator is the preferred solution when you can guarantee that query one (A) and query two (B) return unique rows, which means there's no intersection. A symmetrical difference between two sets is the easiest way to demonstrate this set operator because it is the combined results of the left and right relative complements. This means it doesn't include the intersection between two row sets.

```
SQL> SELECT   m.account_number
     ,        c.last_name || ', ' || c.first_name AS customer_name
     FROM     member m LEFT JOIN contact c
     ON       m.member_id = c.member_id
     WHERE    m.member_id IS NOT NULL
     UNION ALL
     SELECT   m.account_number
     ,        c.last_name || ', ' || c.first_name AS customer_name
     FROM     member m RIGHT JOIN contact c
     ON       m.member_id = c.member_id
     WHERE    c.member_id IS NOT NULL;
```

The first query (A) is a left join that excludes the inner join set, and the second query (B) is a right join that excludes the inner join set. It returns only the symmetric difference between the two row sets.

INTERSECT

The INTERSECT set operator returns only the unique rows found in two queries. It's useful when you want to find rows that meet the criteria of two different queries. The following Venn diagram for the INTERSECT set operator is exactly like that for the inner join. The only difference is one joins row sets and the other joins column sets into larger column sets.

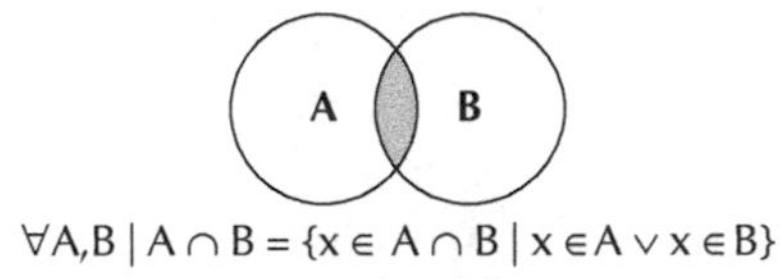

$\forall A,B \mid A \cap B = \{x \in A \cap B \mid x \in A \vee x \in B\}$

While it might look like a lot of work to get the unique set of rows with an INTERSECT set operator, you can verify that the inner join between the member and contact tables is the unique intersection of rows. The INTERSECT operator returns the rows that match between query one (A) and query two (B), which is the INNER JOIN between the two tables.

```
SQL> SELECT   m.account_number
     ,        c.last_name || ', ' || c.first_name AS customer_name
     FROM     member m LEFT JOIN contact c
     ON       m.member_id = c.member_id
     INTERSECT
     SELECT   m.account_number
     ,        c.last_name || ', ' || c.first_name AS customer_name
     FROM     member m RIGHT JOIN contact c
     ON       m.member_id = c.member_id;
```

It returns the same set of information as an `INNER JOIN` between the `member` and `contact` tables using the `member_id` column. The two relative complements are discarded because the collective values of all columns in the row differ.

MINUS

The `MINUS` set operator lets you subtract the matching rows of the second query from the first query. It allows you to find the symmetric difference between two sets or the relative complement of two sets. Although you can accomplish both of these tasks without set operators by checking whether the joining columns aren't null, sometimes it's a better fit to use set operators to solve this type of problem.

The following Venn diagram for the `MINUS` set operator is different from those for join statements because it excludes the intersection area. I was tempted to provide two examples in this section: one that subtracts the inner join from a full join, and another that subtracts the cross join from the same full join. The result would be the same row set, because the only row matches between a full join and an inner join are the intersection rows, which is also true for a full join and a cross join. That's because the possible nonjoins in a Cartesian product aren't found in a full join result set.

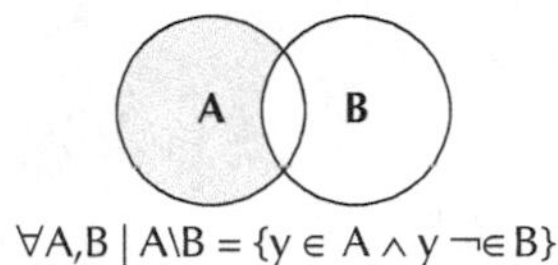

$\forall A,B \mid A \backslash B = \{y \in A \wedge y \neg\in B\}$

Here's the full join minus the cross join:

```
SQL> SELECT   m.account_number
     ,        c.last_name || ', ' || c.first_name AS customer_name
     FROM     member m FULL JOIN contact c
     ON       m.member_id = c.member_id
     WHERE    m.member_id IS NOT NULL
     MINUS
     SELECT   m.account_number
     ,        c.last_name || ', ' || c.first_name AS customer_name
     FROM     member m CROSS JOIN contact c;
```

You always subtract a cross join from a full join when you want the symmetrical difference because it is less expensive than subtracting an inner join.

Summary

This appendix has reviewed the Structured Query Language (SQL) and explained how and why basic SQL statements work. The coverage should enable you to work through the Oracle Database 12c examples in the book.

APPENDIX C

SQL Built-in Functions

Oracle Database 12*c* provides a number of built-in functions for working with character strings, dates, and numbers. It also provides you with data type conversion functions. This appendix covers these functions as well as SQL built-in functions that Oracle Database 12*c* provides for object reference and error management. Last, it includes a miscellaneous section that covers additional built-in functions that initialize large objects, perform advanced comparisons, and audit system environment variables.

Alphabetically indexed, the built-in functions are organized by type. Only a subset of all functions is listed in this appendix. These should be the more frequently used functions in your programs. Small example programs demonstrate how to use the built-in functions in PL/SQL.

- Character functions
- Data type conversion functions
- Date-time conversion functions
- Collection management functions
- Collection set operators
- Number functions
- Error handling functions
- Miscellaneous functions

The built-in functions are a library of utilities to help you solve problems. They are often an underutilized resource for many developers.

Character Functions

Character functions actually cover characters and strings. They are extremely useful when you want to concatenate, parse, replace, or sort characters and strings. Appendix E covers the regular expression functions that are also mentioned briefly in some of these descriptions.

ASCII Function

The `ASCII` function returns an ASCII encoding number for a character. The following sample evaluates the first character of the string:

```
SQL> DECLARE
       text VARCHAR2(10) := 'Hello';
     BEGIN
       IF ASCII(SUBSTR(text,1,1)) = 72 THEN
         dbms_output.put_line('The first character of the string is [H].');
       END IF;
     END;
     /
```

The ASCII-encoded English alphabet starts with an uppercase *A*, which has an ASCII value of 65. The lowercase letter *a* has a value of 97. Therefore, the uppercase *H* has a value of 72 as the eighth letter in the encoding sequence. The program prints

```
The first character of the string is [H].
```

This function can be used when you are searching strings for encoding matches. You'll find it useful when multiple encoding schemas have been used over time in the database.

ASCIISTR Function

The `ASCIISTR` function returns an ASCII encoding string for a character. The following sample evaluates the fourth character of the string, which is a French ê that is a Unicode character:

```
SQL> DECLARE
       text VARCHAR2(10) := 'forêt';
     BEGIN
       dbms_output.put_line(ASCIISTR(SUBSTR(text,4,1)));
     END;
     /
```

The circumflex-annotated ê renders as a `\xxxx` character stream because it is a Unicode character. The quartet following the backslash represents a UTF-16 code unit. The string printed is

```
\00EA
```

This is a convenient function to convert strings into ASCII values, which lets you check if they contain Unicode characters. Enclosing the source and result strings as arguments to regular expression functions lets you compare whether the result contains more backslashes than the source string. This comparison would identify Unicode characters in strings.

CHR Function

The `CHR` function returns the binary equivalent character for an ASCII integer in the database character set or national character set. The latter behavior requires that you use `USING NCHAR_CS`, as shown in the prototype:

```
CHR(n [USING NCHAR_CS])
```

The following demonstrates sending a line break in the midst of a string through the standard out procedure, `DBMS_OUTPUT.PUT_LINE`. This is a convenient way to force a line break in the midst of an output string.

```
SQL> DECLARE
       text1 VARCHAR2(10) := 'Title';
       text2 VARCHAR2(10) := 'Content';
     BEGIN
       dbms_output.put_line(text1||CHR(10)||text2);
     END;
     /
```

It prints

```
Title
Content
```

The `CHR` function also lets you embed extended characters into your programs. This is useful when they are constrained by ASCII encoding.

CONCAT Function

The `CONCAT` function concatenates two strings into one, and it is equivalent to using the concatenation operator (| |). The prototype is

```
CONCAT(string1, string2)
```

The `CONCAT` function implicitly adopts the broadest data type when the data types of the strings differ. This means that this function adheres to the traditional implicit casting model, which requires that no precision be lost.

The following demonstrates the `CONCAT` function:

```
SQL> DECLARE
       text1 VARCHAR2(10) := 'Hello ';
       text2 VARCHAR2(10) := 'There!';
     BEGIN
       dbms_output.put_line(CONCAT(text1,text2));
     END;
     /
```

It prints

```
Hello There!
```

This function really presents a syntax alternative to the standard concatenation operator. You should use it when it makes your code more readable.

INITCAP Function

The `INITCAP` function is very handy when you want to convert a string to title case. Title case is a convention where the first letter of every word is capitalized while all other letters are in lowercase. The function takes a string and returns a converted string.

The following demonstrates the function:

```
SQL> DECLARE
       text VARCHAR2(12) := 'hello world!';
     BEGIN
       dbms_output.put_line(INITCAP(text));
     END;
     /
```

It prints

```
Hello World!
```

This function would be handy if you were searching for Java source files in a database repository, provided they adhere to the title case convention. You could also use it if you were writing a parser for data entry, such as customer contact notes. There is also an `NLS_INITCAP` function that works with different character sets.

INSTR Function

The INSTR function lets you find the position where a substring starts in a string. You also can find the starting position by using INSTRB when the string is encoded in bytes, INSTRC when the string contains Unicode complete characters, or either INSTR2 or INSTR4 for backward compatibility with UCS-2 or UCS-4 code points, respectively.

UCS-2 provides backward compatibility similar to the backward compatibility of a UTF-16 character set, which is a variable-length character encoding standard. UCS-2 fails, however, to use surrogate pairs and is actually a fixed-length character encoding standard that uses 16 bits to store characters. UCS-4 is a fixed-length character encoding variant of UCS-2; it encodes in 32-bit chunks.

The prototype for the INSTR family of functions is

```
INSTR(target_string, search_string [, position [, occurrence ]])
```

You search the target string looking for the search string, like looking in a haystack for a pin. The *position* is 1 or the beginning of the string unless you specify another positive integer. You may provide *occurrence* only when you have provided a *position* value. The *occurrence* must also be a positive integer value. The regular expression REGEXP_INSTR function is a natural alternative to this function. Appendix E contains definitions of the regular expression functions.

All of the INSTR function variations work the same way: they take a string and calculate its length as a return value.

The following demonstrates the INSTR variation of the functions:

```
SQL> DECLARE
       text VARCHAR2(12) := 'Hello World!';
     BEGIN
       dbms_output.put_line('Start ['||INSTR(text,'World',1)||']');
     END;
     /
```

It prints

```
Start [7]
```

The INSTR functions are useful when you want to parse strings into substrings in a looping structure. INSTR and INSTRC are the safest with all character types except byte-allocated strings. Use INSTRB for byte strings.

LENGTH Function

The LENGTH function lets you calculate the length of a string by using character units. A variant, LENGTHB, calculates the length of a string in bytes, and LENGTHC uses Unicode complete characters. The LENGTH2 and LENGTH4 functions count using UCS-2 and UCS-4 code points, respectively.

UCS-2 provides backward compatibility like the UTF-16 character set, which is a variable-length character encoding standard. UCS-2 fails, however, to use surrogate pairs and is actually a fixed-length character encoding standard that uses 16 bits to store characters. UCS-4 is a fixed-length character encoding variant of UCS-2 that encodes in 32-bit chunks.

All of the LENGTH function variations work the same way: they take a string and calculate its length as a return value.

The following demonstrates the LENGTH variation of the functions:

```
SQL> DECLARE
    text VARCHAR2(12) := 'Hello World!';
  BEGIN
    dbms_output.put_line('Length ['||LENGTH(text)||']');
  END;
  /
```

It prints

```
Length [12]
```

The LENGTH functions are useful when you want to parse strings into substrings. You should probably stick to using LENGTH or LENGTHC when writing production code, and you should avoid LENGTHB because it counts only the number of bytes.

LOWER Function

The LOWER function lets you demote a string to match a lowercase string literal. There is also NLS_LOWER for Unicode strings. This is convenient when you don't know the case of stored data.

The following demonstrates the LOWER function:

```
SQL> DECLARE
    text VARCHAR2(12) := 'Hello World!';
  BEGIN
    dbms_output.put_line(LOWER(text));
  END;
  /
```

It prints

```
hello world!
```

This function and the UPPER function let you easily enter and match string literals against values of unknown case in database columns. There is no processing difference between demoting strings to lowercase and promoting strings to uppercase. You should pick one and use it consistently.

LPAD Function

The LPAD function lets you add a character one or more times at the beginning of a string. The prototype is

```
LPAD(output_string, output_length, padding_character)
```

The following demonstrates how you left-pad a string. The *output_length* sets the new length of the string and pads copies of the *padding_character* until the string reaches the new length. The number of padding characters is equal to the *output_length* minus the number of characters in the beginning *output_string*.

```
SQL> DECLARE
  output     VARCHAR2(10) := 'Wowie';
  whitespace VARCHAR2(1)  := ' ';
BEGIN
  dbms_output.put_line('['||LPAD(output,10,whitespace)||']');
END;
/
```

It prints

```
[     Wowie]
```

The square brackets ensure that padded white space prints, because the procedure DBMS_OUTPUT.PUT_LINE normally removes leading white space. Other characters are not impacted by the paring of strings before printing them.

LTRIM Function

The LTRIM function lets you remove a set of characters from the beginning of a string. The prototype is

```
LTRIM(base_string, set_of_values)
```

The LTRIM function imposes a limit on what is trimmed from a string. The set of values must contain all values from the beginning of the string to where you want to pare it. If any character in that stream is missing, the trimming stops at that point.

The following demonstrates the LTRIM function:

```
SQL> DECLARE
  comment VARCHAR2(12) := 'Wowie Howie!';
BEGIN
  dbms_output.put_line('['||LTRIM(comment,' eiwoWo')||']');
END;
/
```

The example contains all the characters to remove the first word plus an extra *o*. However, it cannot remove the second *o* because the *H* is not found in the set. So it removes only the first word and white space, printing

```
[Howie!]
```

A second *o* in the set of values is unnecessary because the function trims all instances of any character in the set, provided there is no intervening character that is not found in the set (such as *H* in this example).

This has shown you how to trim the leading part of a string. You can also trim the right side of a string with the RTRIM function, covered later in this appendix.

REPLACE Function

The REPLACE function lets you search and replace a substring in any CHAR, VARCHAR2, NCHAR, NVARCHAR2, CLOB, or NCLOB string. It returns the modified string. The prototype is

```
REPLACE(base_string, search_string, replace_string)
```

The following demonstrates how to use the function:

```
SQL> DECLARE
  base_string    VARCHAR2(40) := 'The Republican President said ...';
  search_string  VARCHAR2(40) := 'Republican';
  replace_string VARCHAR2(40) := 'Democratic';
BEGIN
  dbms_output.put_line(
    REPLACE(base_string,search_string,replace_string));
END;
/
```

It prints

```
The Democratic President said ...
```

The word "Democratic" has been substituted for the word "Republican." You should ensure that you're using uniform character sets for all actual parameters, because the `REPLACE` function is sensitive to character set.

REVERSE Function

The `REVERSE` function lets you reverse a string literal, like

```
SQL> COLUMN reverse FORMAT A10
SQL> SELECT REVERSE('String') AS "Reverse" FROM dual;
```

It returns

```
Reverse
---------
gnirtS
```

This is a handy function when you want to reverse a string because it avoids looping through the string and reordering it.

RPAD Function

Like the `LPAD` function, the `RPAD` function lets you add a character one or more times to a string. The difference is that `RPAD` adds the characters to the end of the string. The prototype is

```
RPAD(output_string, output_length, padding_character)
```

The following demonstrates right-padding a string:

```
SQL> DECLARE
  output     VARCHAR2(10) := 'Wowie';
  whitespace VARCHAR2(1)  := ' ';
BEGIN
  dbms_output.put_line('['||RPAD(output,10,whitespace)||']');
END;
/
```

It prints

```
[Wowie     ]
```

The square brackets highlight the padded white space. While the procedure DBMS_OUTPUT .PUT_LINE removes leading white space, it does not remove trailing white space.

RTRIM Function

The RTRIM function lets you remove a set of characters from the end of a string. The prototype is

```
RTRIM(base_string, set_of_values)
```

The RTRIM function imposes a limit on what is trimmed from a string. The set of values must contain all values from the end of the string to where you want to pare it. If any character in that stream is missing, the trimming stops at that point.

The following demonstrates the RTRIM function:

```
SQL> DECLARE
    comment VARCHAR2(12) := 'Wowie Howie!';
  BEGIN
    dbms_output.put_line('['||RTRIM(comment,' Howie!')||']');
  END;
  /
```

The example contains all the characters to remove the first word, but the characters "owie" are found twice in the string. Also, there is no intervening character not found in the set. Therefore, this function pares more than what you might expect, printing

```
[W]
```

This has shown you how to trim the trailing part of a string. It has also showed you that one character can be removed multiple times, provided there is no intervening character that is not found in the set of values.

You can also trim the left side of a string with the LTRIM function, covered earlier in this appendix. Trimming characters more than once also applies to the LTRIM function.

UPPER Function

The UPPER function lets you demote a string to match a lowercase string literal. There is also NLS_UPPER for Unicode strings. This is convenient when you don't know the case of stored data.

The following demonstrates the UPPER function:

```
SQL> DECLARE
    text VARCHAR2(12) := 'Hello World!';
  BEGIN
    dbms_output.put_line(UPPER(text));
  END;
  /
```

It prints

```
HELLO WORLD!
```

This function and the LOWER function let you easily enter and match string literals against values of unknown case in database columns. There is no processing difference between promoting strings to uppercase and demoting them to lowercase. You should pick one and use it consistently.

Data Type Conversion Functions

Data type conversion is simply casting, which is the process of taking a variable defined as one data type and changing it to another data type. Implicit casting makes the change for you automatically but only works when the rules are simple and well understood. Explicit casting lets you instruct the programming language how to assign one data type to another when the programming language has no rule that applies to how the data type can be converted implicitly, or without formal programming instructions.

Data type conversion is often done implicitly in PL/SQL. Unlike other strongly typed programming languages, PL/SQL does implicit conversions even when there is a potential loss of precision. For example, you can assign a complex number in a `NUMBER` data type to a `SIMPLE_INTEGER` data type and lose any values to the right of the decimal point. Chapter 2 provides an example of this type of implicit conversion.

The data type conversion functions are useful when you want to make a conversion that requires you to provide instructions. You have to manually convert strings to dates when strings don't adhere to default format mask conventions. Likewise, some specialized types require you to take specific actions before you can convert data.

The examples that follow focus on demonstrating how to use these functions. You'll notice that there are no conversions between user-defined object types and standard types. You should include conversion methods in your object type definitions.

CAST Function

The `CAST` function is very useful because it converts built-in data types to another built-in data type, or converts collection-typed variables to another collection-typed variable. The `CAST` function does have some limits; for instance, it uses only the default date conversion format mask, as discussed in Chapter 3. Unlike most functions, `CAST` works with all but the `LONG`, `LONG RAW`, `ROWID`, and `UROWID` built-in data types. `CAST` also limits how it casts data from `BLOB` and `CLOB` types into a `RAW` data type because it relies on an implicit database behavior. You raise an exception when `CAST` tries to convert a large object into a `RAW` type when it is too large to fit inside a `RAW` data type.

There are two prototypes: one for scalar built-in variables and another for collections. The scalar variable built-in prototype is

```
CAST(type1_variable_name AS type2_variable_name)
```

and the collection prototype is

```
CAST(MULTISET(subquery)) AS collection_type_variable_name)
```

The following program shows how to cast a date to a string:

```
SQL> DECLARE
       source DATE := TO_DATE('30-SEP-07');
       target VARCHAR2(24);
     BEGIN
       target := CAST(source AS VARCHAR2);
       dbms_output.put_line(target);
     END;
     /
```

This type of usage is exactly the same in both SQL and PL/SQL contexts, but the `MULTISET` context is restricted to SQL statements. If you attempt to use a `CAST` function with a `MULTISET` and subquery as a right operand, you raise a `PLS-00405` exception. However, you can embed these in SQL statements inside your PL/SQL blocks.

The `CAST` operation inside a query statement requires that you cast to a SQL data type, such as a collection of scalar variables. This leaves you with a choice between varrays and nested tables. You should use nested tables because they are easier to manage and don't require incremental conversion with the `TABLE` function call (see Chapter 6).

This creates a nested table of strings as a SQL data type:

```
SQL> CREATE OR REPLACE
    TYPE collection IS TABLE OF VARCHAR2(5);
  /
```

You should create a table or view because the `MULTISET` operator disallows queries that use set operators, like `INTERSECT`, `MINUS`, `UNION`, and `UNION ALL`. The `MULTISET` operator raises a `PLS-00605` exception when set operators are found in the subquery.

The following builds a sample table:

```
SQL> CREATE TABLE casting (num VARCHAR2(5));
```

Next, you can insert into the table the English ordinal numbers "one" to "nine" by using the table fabrication pattern:

```
SQL> INSERT INTO casting
  (SELECT 'One'   FROM dual UNION ALL
   SELECT 'Two'   FROM dual UNION ALL
   SELECT 'Three' FROM dual UNION ALL
   SELECT 'Four'  FROM dual UNION ALL
   SELECT 'Five'  FROM dual UNION ALL
   SELECT 'Six'   FROM dual UNION ALL
   SELECT 'Seven' FROM dual UNION ALL
   SELECT 'Eight' FROM dual UNION ALL
   SELECT 'Nine'  FROM dual);
```

The sample program demonstrates how to use the `CAST` and `MULTISET` functions together:

```
SQL> DECLARE
    counter NUMBER := 1;
  BEGIN
    FOR i IN (SELECT CAST(
                       MULTISET(
                         SELECT num
                         FROM   casting) AS COLLECTION) AS rs
              FROM   casting) LOOP
      dbms_output.put_line(i.rs(counter));
      counter := counter + 1;
    END LOOP;
  END;
  /
```

Table Fabrication

Sometimes you want to create data without building a temporary table. There are two alternatives to avoid building temporary tables that can fragment your database. One is to build runtime views, which are aliased queries inside the FROM clause. This approach works when the data can be queried from one or more real tables. The other approach leverages the UNION ALL set operator to join a series of related data. This approach, known as data or table fabrication, lets you build data in a query when it doesn't exist in your database.

The following uses table fabrication to multiply the number of returned rows:

```
SQL> SELECT   alias.counter
  2  FROM    (SELECT 1 AS counter FROM dual UNION ALL
  3            SELECT 2 AS counter FROM dual) alias;
```

It returns two rows because the runtime view contains two fabricated rows, and prints

```
COUNTER
-------
      1
      2
```

There are two caveats about table fabrication. You must ensure the list of SELECT clause columns return the same data type, and you must provide matching aliases for any literals or expressions in any column position. These are the same rules imposed by set operators in any query.

This prints the ordinal number words in a list. The CAST function returns a collection of items. Unfortunately, you also need to match a collection structure to the row structure of the query. You use this type of structure to return nested table contents from tables.

CONVERT Function

The CONVERT function converts a string from one character set to another. It has the following prototype:

```
CONVERT(string, destination_character_set, source_character_set)
```

Finding the Character Set of a Database Instance

You can log in as a privileged user, like system, and run the following query:

```
SELECT value$ FROM sys.props$ WHERE name = 'NLS_CHARACTERSET';
```

More often than not folks are disappointed when they look in the V$PARAMETER view for the character set. The V$PARAMETER view does contain most of the configuration values for the database instance. The miscellaneous section demonstrates how you can implement a function to read the character set in the EMPTY_BLOB function section.

The following demonstrates converting the French word forêt (forest in English) from the AL32UTF8 character set to the UTF-8 character set:

```
SQL> DECLARE
  text VARCHAR2(10) := 'forêt';
BEGIN
  dbms_output.put_line(CONVERT(text,'AL32UTF8','UTF8'));
END;
/
```

This prints the same forêt but it now takes 3 bytes of storage rather than 2 bytes. You will find this function handy when you work in multiple character sets.

TO_CHAR Function

The TO_CHAR function lets you do several types of conversion. You can convert CLOB, DATE, NCHAR, NCLOB, NUMBER, or TIMESTAMP data types to VARCHAR2 data types. This function is overloaded and has two prototypes. The prototype for string data types is

```
TO_CHAR({clob_type | nchar_type | nclob_type})
```

The alternative prototype for dates, numbers, and times is

```
TO_CHAR({date_type | timestamp_type | number_type}
        [, format_mask [, nls_param ]])
```

The following subsections demonstrate converting other types of strings to character strings, dates to characters strings, and numbers to character strings. The date and number subsections also have two examples each: one with the native National Language Support (NLS) character set of the instance, and one that overrides the instance default.

Converting a String to a Character String

The following demonstrates converting a CLOB data type to a CHAR data type:

```
SQL> DECLARE
  big_string CLOB := 'Not really that big, eh?';
BEGIN
  dbms_output.put_line(TO_CHAR(big_string));
END;
/
```

Converting a Date to a Character String

The TO_CHAR function takes two arguments, or call parameters: the date or date-time, and the format mask. The following demonstrates converting a DATE to a CHAR:

```
SQL> DECLARE
  today DATE := SYSDATE;
BEGIN
  dbms_output.put_line(TO_CHAR(today,'Mon DD, YYYY'));
END;
/
```

While your date will reflect the current system date, this prints the day this was written:

```
Sep 27, 2007
```

When you add the NLS_DATE_LANGUAGE parameter to the function, you can override the NLS setting for the database. The following resets the NLS_DATE_LANGUAGE parameter to French:

```
SQL> DECLARE
       today DATE := SYSDATE;
     BEGIN
       dbms_output.put_line(TO_CHAR(today,'Mon DD, YYYY'
                           ,'NLS_DATE_LANGUAGE = FRENCH'));
     END;
     /
```

This then prints the date in the French style, which adds a period after the abbreviation of the month, like

```
Sept. 27, 2007
```

Converting a Number to a Character String

Converting numbers to characters works much like converting dates to characters. The following illustrates converting a number to a formatted dollar amount in American English:

```
SQL> DECLARE
       amount NUMBER := 2.9;
     BEGIN
       dbms_output.put_line(TO_CHAR(amount,'$9,999.90'));
     END;
     /
```

The format mask prints a digit if one is found when there's a 9 and always print a 0 when there is no value. The format mask substitutes a 0 since there is no value in the hundredths placeholder, printing

```
$2.90
```

Adding the NLS parameter, you can now format the currency return in Euros:

```
SQL> DECLARE
       amount NUMBER := 2.9;
     BEGIN
       dbms_output.put_line(TO_CHAR(amount,'9,999.90L'
                           ,'nls_currency = EUR'));
     END;
     /
```

This prints

```
2.90EUR
```

This section has demonstrated how to use the TO_CHAR function to convert national language and large object strings to character strings and convert dates, timestamps, and numbers to character strings. The format masks only cover characters in those specific positions. You need to expand the format mask when dealing with larger numbers.

TO_CLOB Function

The TO_CLOB function lets you convert the NCLOB column data type or other character types to character large objects. You can convert CHAR, NCHAR, NVARCHAR2, and VARCHAR2 data types to NCLOB types.

The prototype for this is

```
TO_CLOB({char_type | nchar_type | nclob_type | nvarchar2_type | varchar2_type})
```

The following converts a string to CLOB and then uses TO_CHAR to reconvert for printing by the DBMS_OUTPUT.PUT_LINE procedure:

```
SQL> DECLARE
    initial_string VARCHAR2(2000) := 'Not really required. :-)';
  BEGIN
    dbms_output.put_line(TO_CHAR(TO_CLOB(initial_string)));
  END;
  /
```

This is a handy function when you're moving an array of strings into a CLOB variable. It also lets you move NLS large object columns into a standard format for your programs.

TO_DATE Function

The TO_DATE function lets you convert strings to dates. The prototype for this is

```
TO_DATE(string_type [, format_make [, nls_param ]])
```

The following program demonstrates converting a string through implicit conversion:

```
SQL> DECLARE
    target DATE;
  BEGIN
    target := '29-SEP-94';
    dbms_output.put_line(
      'Back to a string ['||TO_CHAR(target)||']');
  END;
  /
```

The implicit cast works because the default format mask for a date is DD-MON-RR or DD-MON-YYYY. When the string or source is not in that format, you must provide a format mask to cast the string into a date.

The next example explicitly casts a string by providing a format mask:

```
SQL> DECLARE
    target DATE;
  BEGIN
    target := TO_DATE('September 29, 1994 10:00 A.M.'
```

```
                         ,'Month DD, YYYY HH:MI A.M.');
    dbms_output.put_line(
      'Back to a string ['||TO_CHAR(target)||']');
  END;
  /
```

The A.M. formatting option is a mask available in some National Language Support (NLS) languages, like American English. It is not supported in French because the appropriate format mask in that language is AM. If you apply an unsupported format mask, you raise an `ORA-01855` exception.

The following example demonstrates overriding the default of language:

```
SQL> DECLARE
    target DATE;
  BEGIN
    target := TO_DATE('Septembre 29, 1994 10:00 AM'
                     ,'Month DD, YYYY HH:MI AM'
                     ,'NLS_DATE_LANGUAGE = French');
    dbms_output.put_line('Back to a string ['
    ||                    TO_CHAR(target
                                 ,'Month DD, YYYY HH:MI AM'
                                 ,'NLS_DATE_LANGUAGE = French')||']');
  END;
  /
```

The nature of converting to a date from a string is a virtual mirror to reversing the process, as should be clearly seen in the example. The `TO_DATE` function is frequently used in PL/SQL.

TO_LOB Function

The `TO_LOB` function lets you convert `LONG` or `LONG RAW` column data types to large objects. However, there are restrictions on how you can use this function. It can only be used to convert your `LONG` data types to large objects when used in an `INSERT` statement as a `SELECT` list element of a subquery.

The prototype for this is

```
TO_LOB({long_type | long_raw_type})
```

There are several steps to build a small test case to examine this function. You need to create `source` and `target` tables and seed the `source` table with data:

```
SQL> CREATE TABLE source
  ( source_id NUMBER
  , source    LONG);

SQL> INSERT INTO source
  VALUES
  ( 1, 'A not so long string');

CREATE TABLE target
( target_id NUMBER
, target    CLOB );
```

After you've done that, you can build an anonymous block to transfer the LONG column values to a CLOB column in the new table. The following demonstrates that along with a query of the moved contents:

```
SQL> DECLARE
       CURSOR c IS SELECT target_id, target FROM target;
     BEGIN
       INSERT INTO target
       SELECT source_id, TO_LOB(source) FROM source;
       FOR i IN c LOOP
         dbms_output.put_line('Clob value ['||TO_CHAR(i.target)||']');
       END LOOP;
     END;
     /
```

Alternative Migration Strategy for LONG and LONG RAW Columns

Beginning with Oracle Database 11*g*, you can use the TO_LOB function to migrate data. More often than not you don't want to move a large table to a new table and then rename it as part of a single column migration.

You can solve the problem by adding a CLOB column to the table and using the TO_LOB function in an UPDATE statement. Like the INSERT statement limitation, the TO_LOB function must be part of a SELECT list in a subquery. This type of movement from one column to another in the same row requires a correlated subquery. This is how you synchronize the two copies of the same table to work on the same row.

You would alter the source table with the following syntax:

```
SQL> ALTER TABLE source ADD (new_source CLOB);
```

Then, you migrate the data with the following UPDATE statement:

```
SQL> UPDATE source outer
     SET    outer.new_source =
              (SELECT TO_LOB(inner.source)
               FROM   source inner
               WHERE  outer.source_id = inner.source_id);
```

Cleanup is easy; drop the old column:

```
SQL> ALTER TABLE source DROP COLUMN source;
```

Then, you can rename the source column new_source, which will map to the original column. The command is

```
SQL> ALTER TABLE source RENAME COLUMN new_source TO source;
```

This works well after you've developed the new code that expects a CLOB, not a LONG or LONG RAW column. It has the advantage of not moving the balance of columns while migrating away from the obsolete data types.

This is a handy function for data migration. If this were a real CLOB value, you'd need to read chunks of the column inside a loop. The latter is best done with a combination of the LENGTH and SUBSTR (*substring*) functions.

TO_NCHAR Function

The TO_NCHAR function lets you do several types of conversion. You can convert CHAR, CLOB, DATE, NCLOB, NUMBER, or TIMESTAMP data types to NVARCHAR2 data types. This function is overloaded and has two prototypes. The prototype for string data types is

```
TO_NCHAR({clob_type | nchar_type | nclob_type})
```

The alternative prototype for dates, numbers, and times is

```
TO_NCHAR({date_type | timestamp_type | number_type}
        [, format_mask [, nls_param ]])
```

The examples in the TO_CHAR function description also work with the TO_NCHAR function. You can modify those to see how the TO_NCHAR function works.

TO_NCLOB Function

The TO_NCLOB function lets you convert the CLOB column data type or other character types to character large objects. You can convert CHAR, NCHAR, NVARCHAR2, and VARCHAR2 data types to CLOB types.

The prototype for this is

```
TO_NCLOB({clob_type | char_type | nchar_type | nvarchar2_type |
          varchar2_type})
```

The examples in the TO_NCLOB function description also work with the TO_NCLOB function. You can modify those to see how the TO_NCLOB function works.

TO_NUMBER Function

The TO_NUMBER function lets you convert an expression into a numeric value. The expression can be a BINARY_DOUBLE, CHAR, NCHAR, NVARCHAR2, or VARCHAR2 data type. You can also use the NLS_NUMERIC_CHARACTERS parameter or NLS_CURRENCY parameter for National Language Support (NLS).

The prototype for this is

```
TO_NUMBER(expression [, format_mask [, nls_param ]])
```

The example converts a formatted string to a number by using a format mask:

```
SQL> DECLARE
       source VARCHAR2(38) := '$9,999.90';
     BEGIN
       dbms_output.put_line(TO_NUMBER(source,'$9,999.99'));
     END;
     /
```

The program prints a number without a hundredth placeholder:

```
9999.9
```

You can also use NLS formatting like that shown in the TO_CHAR function examples, or use it this way:

```
SQL> DECLARE
       source VARCHAR2(38) := '9,999.90EUR';
     BEGIN
       dbms_output.put_line(
         TO_NUMBER(source,'9G999D99L','nls currency = EUR'));
     END;
     /
```

It also prints

```
9999.9
```

The G stands for comma, D for decimal point (or period), and L for string qualifying the currency format. There is no dollar symbol leading a currency expression when you use an ISO currency string such as USA, JPY, or EUR. The string provided as the value of nls_currency must also match the value in the original string.

Date-time Conversion Functions

Date-time functions let you perform key behaviors that support how you manage dates and date-time data types. These functions are also mentioned in Table B-8. The date math examples in Appendix B show you how some of them work.

ADD_MONTHS Function

The ADD_MONTHS function lets you work around the basic issues with the Gregorian irregular month length. Adding two months to January 15th of any year demonstrates the usefulness of this function, because it works whether it's leap year or not:

```
SQL> SELECT ADD_MONTHS(TO_DATE('15-JAN-2012'), 2) AS two_months
     FROM   dual;
```

It returns

```
TWO_MONTH
---------
15-MAR-12
```

Victory is achieved through the function whether February is 28 or 29 days.

CURRENT_DATE Function

The CURRENT_DATE function returns the same result as the SYSDATE function. You query the CURRENT_DATE function like this:

```
SQL> SELECT TO_CHAR(
       CURRENT_DATE,'DD-MON-YYYY HH24:MI:SS') AS DATE_ONLY
     FROM   dual;
```

It returns

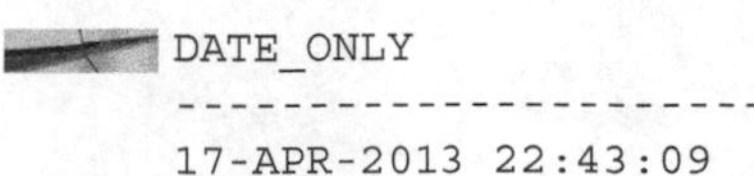

```
DATE_ONLY
----------------------
17-APR-2013 22:43:09
```

CURRENT_TIMESTAMP Function

The `CURRENT_TIMESTAMP` function returns the same result as the `SYSDATE` function. You query the `CURRENT_TIMESTAMP` function like this:

```
SQL> SELECT TO_CHAR(
  2    CURRENT_TIMESTAMP,'DD-MON-YYYY HH24:MI:SS') AS TIMESTAMP_ONLY
  2  FROM   dual;
```

It returns

```
DATE_ONLY
----------------------
17-APR-2013 22:43:09
```

DBTIMEZONE Function

The `DBTIMEZONE` function lets you find your time zone relative to the Coordinated Universal Time (UTC). An example is

```
SQL> SELECT DBTIMEZONE FROM dual;
```

It returns

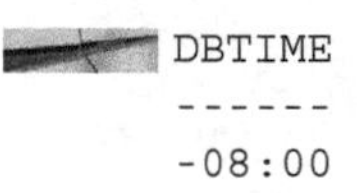

```
DBTIME
------
-08:00
```

EXTRACT Function

The `EXTRACT` function lets you find an integer equivalent of a month, day, or year for any date data type. It's handy when you want to identify transactions occurring on a day, in a month, in a year, or in a set of months or years.

The basic example for finding a day is

```
SQL> SELECT EXTRACT(DAY FROM TO_DATE('15-APR-2013')) AS day
  2  FROM   dual;
```

Naturally, the example returns

```
       DAY
----------
        15
```

You can substitute a case-insensitive `MONTH` or `YEAR` keyword before the `FROM` keyword to extract the month or year. The argument following the `FROM` keyword must be a `DATE` or date-time data type. That means converting a literal date to a timestamp would let you extract the hour, minute, or second from a timestamp, like this:

```
SQL> SELECT EXTRACT(HOUR FROM TO_TIMESTAMP('15-APR-2013')) AS hour
  2  FROM   dual;
```

This returns

```
      HOUR
----------
         0
```

While extracting a time element isn't generally too useful by itself, the foregoing example lets me qualify that the time element of any `DATE` data type is equal to zero, or `00:00:00` hours, minutes, and seconds. Moreover, a `DATE` data type in Oracle is a timestamp set to the first second of each day.

The `EXTRACT` function also lets you find ranges of days, months, or years in a `WHERE` predicate, like

```
SQL> SELECT SUM(transaction_amount)
  2  FROM   transaction
  3  WHERE  EXTRACT(MONTH FROM transaction_date) IN (1,2,3);
```

The `IN` operator is often called a *lookup operator* because it checks whether one thing matches one thing in a set. More or less, a lookup function compares a single value or variable against a list of values.

Combining the `EXTRACT` function and `CASE` statement enables you to transform data like a pivot function. The "Data Type Conversions" and "Oracle Date Math" sections of Appendix B shows you an example how to make this type of transformation in a SQL statement.

FROM_TZ Function

The `FROM_TZ` function converts a timestamp value and a time zone to a `TIMESTAMP WITH TIME ZONE` value.

The following demonstrates the `FROM_TZ` function:

```
SQL> SELECT FROM_TZ(
  2           TIMESTAMP '2012-04-15 08:00:00', '8:00') AS "Date-Time"
  3  FROM dual;
```

It returns

```
Date-Time
---------------------------------------------
15-APR-12 08.00.00.000000000 AM +08:00
```

LAST_DAY Function

The `LAST_DAY` function lets you find the last day of the current month. It's useful when you combine it with a date math trick to get the first day of the month.

The following is an example of the LAST_DAY function:

```
SQL> SELECT SYSDATE AS today
  2  ,      LAST_DAY(SYSDATE) AS last_day
  3  FROM   dual  1;
```

It returns

```
TODAY     LAST_DAY
--------- ---------
17-APR-13 30-APR-13
```

Adding 1 to the LAST_DAY function return yields the first day of the next month, like

```
SQL> SELECT SYSDATE AS today
  2  ,      LAST_DAY(SYSDATE) + 1 AS first_day
  3  FROM   dual;
```

It returns

```
TODAY     FIRST_DAY
--------- ---------
17-APR-13 01-MAY-13
```

LOCALTIMESTAMP Function

The LOCALTIMESTAMP function lets you see the local time, not the server time. Before you test this function on a local server, you should alter your session. You can do so with this command:

```
SQL> ALTER SESSION SET TIME_ZONE = '-8:00';
```

Now run the following query, which will show you an eight-hour difference between the two dates:

```
SQL> COLUMN current_timestamp FORMAT A36
SQL> COLUMN localtimestamp    FORMAT A30
SQL> SELECT CURRENT_TIMESTAMP
  2  ,      LOCALTIMESTAMP
  3  FROM   dual;
```

It shows the following results:

```
CURRENT_TIMESTAMP                    LOCALTIMESTAMP
------------------------------------ ------------------------------
17-APR-13 08.02.53.883000 PM -08:00  17-APR-13 08.02.53.883000 PM
```

MONTHS_BETWEEN Function

The MONTHS_BETWEEN function calculates the number of months and fractional equivalent between two dates. It works like this:

```
SQL> SELECT MONTHS_BETWEEN(
  2             TO_DATE('07-04-2012','MM-DD-YYYY')
```

```
            ,TO_DATE('01-01-2012','MM-DD-YYYY')) AS Interval
FROM   dual;
```

which produces the following result:

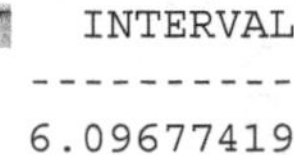

```
INTERVAL
----------
6.09677419
```

NEW_TIME Function

The `NEW_TIME` function lets you set a new date and time by using any of the arguments in Table C-1. The `NEW_TIME` function takes three parameters: a new date, a time zone to display, and a time zone to use with the supplied date.

You must set the `NLS_DATE_FORMAT` parameter to display 24-hour time. The return type is always a `DATE`, regardless of the data type of the supplied date.

The following changes the date to 11 o'clock, 11 minutes, and 11 seconds and displays the time in the Atlantic time zone for a Pacific time zone time value:

```
SQL> SELECT TO_CHAR(
            NEW_TIME(
              TO_DATE('15-APR-13 11:11:11','DD-MON-YYYY HH24:MI:SS')
                     ,'AST','PST')
                     ,'DD-MON-YYYY HH24:MI:SS') AS NEWDATE
FROM   dual;
```

It displays

```
NEWDATE
---------
15-APR-12
```

Standard Time	Daylight Time	Time Zone
AST	ADT	Atlantic
BST	BDT	Bering
CST	CDT	Central
EST	EDT	Eastern
GMT		Greenwich Mean Time
HST	HDT	Alaska-Hawaii
MST	MDT	Mountain
NST		Newfoundland
PST	PDT	Pacific
YST	YDT	Yukon

TABLE C-1. *Time Zone Keywords*

ROUND Function

The ROUND function has two roles. One works with dates and the other works with numbers. They require different mechanics, so it seemed appropriate to introduce both roles here. The explanation and example for the numbers role also appears in the "Number Functions" section in this appendix.

ROUND(date) Function

The ROUND function lets you trim time, days, months, and years from date-time data types. Let's examine shaving the time from a date-time data type, SYSDATE (it always returns the system clock value):

```
SQL> SELECT TO_CHAR(
           SYSDATE,'DD-MON-YYYY HH24:MI:SS') AS actual
  ,        TO_CHAR(
             ROUND(SYSDATE, 'DAY'),
             'DD-MON-YYYY HH24:MI:SS') AS trimmed
  FROM   dual;
```

It returns

```
ACTUAL               TRIMMED
-------------------- ----------------------
17-APR-2013 21:15:26 21-APR-2013 00:00:00
```

As you may notice, the rounding works for the time but yields an incorrect date. Unfortunately, this is the same result in Oracle Database 11*g* and 12*c*.

ROUND(number) Function

The ROUND function also lets you round a number to a whole number or a decimal equivalent. The following rounds 2.5 to a whole number:

```
SQL> SELECT ROUND(2.5,0) FROM dual;
```

You should note that the ROUND function rounds up at 2.5 and rounds down with anything less than 2.5. The ROUND function is important when preparing reports, especially financial reports. It's very useful when using Oracle's math libraries because some functions return incorrect values, like the POWER function (see its description later in this appendix).

SYSDATE Function

The SYSDATE function returns the current date-time value to the hundredth of a second. The easiest way to display the result is with the TO_CHAR(*date*) function, like

```
SQL> SELECT TO_CHAR(SYSDATE,'DD-MON-YYYY HH24:MI:SS') date_time
  FROM   dual;
```

It returns the current formatted date-time value:

```
DATE_TIME
----------------------
18-APR-2013 00:13:32
```

SYSTIMESTAMP Function

The `SYSTIMESTAMP` function returns the current time stamp for the system. Like other examples, the `TO_CHAR(`*`date`*`)` function provides formatting to view the time:

```
SQL> SELECT TO_CHAR(
                SYSTIMESTAMP
              ,'DD-MON-YYYY HH24:MI:SS') AS CURRENT_TIME
     FROM   dual;
```

It returns

```
CURRENT_TIME
----------------------
18-APR-2013 00:13:32
```

TO_CHAR(date) Function

The `TO_CHAR` function has more capabilities than simply a date conversion, which is why it's also covered in the "Data Type Conversion" section earlier in this appendix. While it didn't seem necessary to rewrite the `TO_CHAR` function section, it did seem advisable to put the content in both locations for quick reference and to provide the date- and date-time-specific format masks.

The `TO_CHAR` function takes two arguments, or call parameters: the date or date-time, and the format mask. The format masks for dates are as follows:

`DD`	Two-digit day
`MM`	Two-digit month
`MON`	Three-character month, based on `NLS_LANG` value
`YY`	Two-digit year
`YYYY`	Two-digit absolute year
`RR`	Two-digit relative year
`HH`	Two-digit hour, values 1 to 12
`HH24`	Two-digit hour, values 0 to 23
`MI`	Two-digit minutes, values 0 to 59
`SS`	Two-digit seconds, values 0 to 59

The following demonstrates converting a `DATE` to a `CHAR`:

```
SQL> DECLARE
       today DATE := SYSDATE;
     BEGIN
       dbms_output.put_line(TO_CHAR(today,'Mon DD, YYYY'));
     END;
     /
```

While your date will reflect the current system date, this prints the day this was written:

```
Sep 27, 2007
```

When you add the NLS_DATE_LANGUAGE parameter to the function, you can override the NLS setting for the database. The following resets the NLS_DATE_LANGUAGE parameter to French:

```
SQL> DECLARE
       today DATE := SYSDATE;
     BEGIN
       dbms_output.put_line(TO_CHAR(today,'Mon DD, YYYY'
                                     ,'NLS_DATE_LANGUAGE = FRENCH'));
     END;
     /
```

This then prints the date in the French style, which adds a period after the abbreviation of the month, like

```
Sept. 27, 2007
```

TO_DSINTERVAL Function

The TO_DSINTERVAL function converts a string literal (like the CHAR, VARCHAR2, NCHAR, or NVARCHAR2 data type) to an INTERVAL DAY TO SECOND data type. The SQL format is days, hours, minutes, and seconds, where all values use integers. The integer range is 0 to 999,999,999 for days, 0 to 23 for hours, and 0 to 59 for minutes and seconds.

The following example determines when a rental is over 10 days past due:

```
SQL> SELECT   r.rental_id
     FROM     rental r
     WHERE    r.check_out_date + TO_DSINTERVAL('10 00:00:00') <
                TRUNC(SYSDATE);
```

This returns all rentals checked out more than 10 days ago. The TO_DSINTERVAL function is most useful when you need to add a fractional time equivalent less than a day, where a day is simply an integer of 1.

TO_TIMESTAMP Function

The TO_TIMESTAMP function lets you convert a string expression into a timestamp. The prototype for this is

```
TO_TIMESTAMP(expression [, format_mask [, nls_param ]])
```

The example demonstrates a call to the TO_TIMESTAMP function:

```
SQL> DECLARE
       source TIMESTAMP := TO_TIMESTAMP('30-SEP-07 15:17:04'
                                       ,'DD-MON-YYYY HH24:MI:SS');
     BEGIN
       dbms_output.put_line(TO_CHAR(source
                           ,'Mon DD, YYYY HH:MI:SS AM'));
     END;
     /
```

This is similar to the behavior of the TO_DATE expression. It is useful to note that there is also the TO_TIMESTAMP_TZ function when you work with multiple time zones but there isn't any function to help you bridge between the two time zones. You simply have to build such comparisons into your application programming code logic by using the TO_TIMESTAMP_TZ function.

TO_TIMESTAMP_TZ Function

The TO_TIMESTAMP_TZ function lets you convert a string expression into a timestamp. The prototype for this is

```
TO_TIMESTAMP_TZ(expression [, format_mask [, nls_param ]])
```

The example demonstrates a call to the TO_TIMESTAMP_TZ function:

```
SQL> SQL> SELECT TO_TIMESTAMP_TZ(
                  '2013-09-11 15:17:04 -0100'
                 ,'YYYY-MM-DD HH24:MI:SS TZH TZM') AS TZTIME
     FROM   dual;
```

It returns

```
TZTIME
---------------------------------------------
11-SEP-13 03.17.04.000000000 PM -01:00
```

This is similar to the behavior of the TO_TIMESTAMP expression with the exception that the 24-hour clock supplies the TZH (time zone hour) value, or in this case PM. The 15 (hundred) hour value under a 24-hour clock converts to 3 PM on the local value, as you can see by examining the statement and return result.

Any attempt to use a 12-hour clock value and an alphabetic value for the time zone hour results in the following error:

```
SELECT TO_TIMESTAMP_TZ('2013-09-11 03:17:04 PM -0100'
                                  *
ERROR at line 1:
ORA-01858: a non-numeric character was found where a numeric was expected
```

For reference, there isn't a TO_TIMESTAMP_TZ function choice when you work with multiple time zones.

TO_YMINTERVAL Function

The TO_YMINTERVAL function is handy when you want to add time measured in years and months to an existing date-time data type.

The following sample adds two months to the rental_date column:

```
SQL> SELECT   SELECT   return_date AS "Base"
     ,        return_date + TO_YMINTERVAL('00-02') AS "Changed"
     FROM     rental;
```

It returns

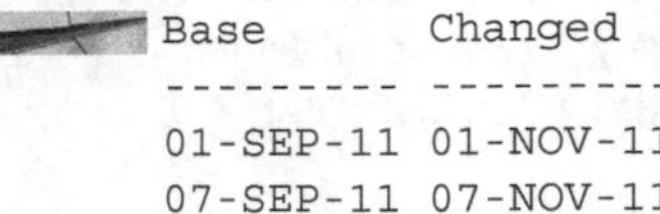

```
Base      Changed
--------- ---------
01-SEP-11 01-NOV-11
07-SEP-11 07-NOV-11
```

You return one year and four months in the future with the following:

```
SQL> SELECT   SELECT   return_date AS "Base"
  2  ,        return_date + TO_YMINTERVAL('01-04') AS "Changed"
  3  FROM     rental;
```

The key is that if you don't want to add years, provide a `00` for the year value to the left of the dash; likewise, when you don't want to add or subtract a month, use `00` to the right of the dash.

TRUNC(date) Function

The `TRUNC` function for dates is essential when you want to convert a date-time data type to a date. Oracle's date data types are all really date-time data types. The value to the left of the decimal point maps to a date in an epoch, while the value to the right of the decimal point maps to a decimal equivalent for any time in a day within an epoch.

The following example because an integer represents a day and a decimal represents a fraction of time during the day. The `TRUNC` function removes the fractional equivalent, leaving the integer representing 12 midnight of the day.

```
SQL> SELECT   TO_CHAR(dt.datetime
  2                    ,'DD-MON-YY HH24:MI:SS') AS "Date-Time"
  3  ,        TO_CHAR(TRUNC(dt.datetime)
  4                    ,'DD-MON-YY HH24:MI:SS') AS "Date"
  5  FROM    (SELECT SYSDATE AS datetime FROM dual) dt;
```

It returns

```
Date-Time            Date
-------------------- --------------------
12-MAY-13 12:14:10   12-MAY-13 00:00:00
```

As you can see from the output, a date rather than a date-time data type is only the whole number that maps to the epoch.

TZ_OFFSET Function

The `TZ_OFFSET` function lets you find the offset value for a time zone, like

```
SELECT TZ_OFFSET('US/Mountain') AS offset FROM dual;
```

It returns

```
OFFSET
-------
-06:00
```

This concludes the time management functions.

Collection Management Functions

Collection management functions operate on object tables (tables defined based on an object type), nested object type columns, and collections—of nested tables or varrays. They also work with collections in the scope of PL/SQL blocks.

This section works with object types and collections from Chapter 11 and Appendix B in various sections. While the collection management functions have some restrictions, they also have behaviors that you can exploit in SQL cursors. That's why we examine their behaviors where possible in SQL statements.

CARDINALITY Function

The `CARDINALITY` function counts the number of elements in a list and performs like the `COUNT` function for `SELECT` statements. The `CARDINALITY` function is also explained in the subsequent "Collection Set Operators" section. All of those examples use PL/SQL blocks, but here the `CARDINALITY` function works in a query:

```
SQL> SELECT CARDINALITY(
              CAST(
                COLLECT(VALUE(b)) AS base_c)) AS cardinality
     FROM   object_base b;
```

The `CARDINALITY` function counts the number of objects found in the `object_base` object table (a table of an object type). Actually, it would have been less expensive to find it with a `COUNT` function, and that's what I'd recommend.

COLLECT Function

The `COLLECT` function lets you gather a set of object types into a varray or nested table collection. As a rule you should use nested tables, simply because they're more flexible with no maximum limit on the number of elements.

You can use the `COLLECT` function with a persistent object only when it is defined as part of an object table. An object table is defined solely by an object type, and you can create an `object_base` object table of the `base_t` object type as follows:

```
SQL> CREATE TABLE object_base OF BASE_T;
```

Describing the table, you'd think it is an ordinary table because it outputs

```
SQL> DESCRIBE object_base
 Name                          Null?    Type
 ----------------------------- -------- -------------
 ID                                     NUMBER
 NAME                                   VARCHAR2(30)
```

A composite table is an alternative to an object table, and it's made up of both scalar and object type columns. The `COLLECT` function works differently with an object table than it does with a composite table, as you see in the examples; however, it supports both object tables and composite tables.

COLLECT Function in an Object Table

An object table lets you insert records using a relational VALUES clause, nested SELECT list that matches the object type definition, or an object type constructor. So, you can insert a record like this with a relational VALUES clause:

```
SQL> INSERT INTO object_base
  2  VALUES (base_t_s.nextval,'Tom Bombadil');
```

or like this with a base_t object type constructor:

```
SQL> INSERT INTO object_base
  2  VALUES (base_t(base_t_s.nextval,'Goldberry'));
```

The following query displays the inserted values as ordinary columns:

```
SQL> SELECT * FROM object_base;

  ID NAME
---- ------------------------------
   1 Tom Bombadil
   2 Goldberry
```

However, with the VALUE function, the query returns the details of collapsed objects (or, a call to an object type with parameters):

```
SQL> SELECT VALUE(b) FROM object_base b;

VALUE(B)(ID, NAME)
----------------------------------------
BASE_T(1, 'Tom Bombadil')
BASE_T(2, 'Goldberry')
```

You can COLLECT the object table's base_t object types with

```
SQL> SELECT COLLECT(VALUE(b)) AS collection
  2  FROM   object_base b;
```

A VALUE function requires a correlation variable, which is a table alias. You would raise an ORA-00904 error if you were to replace the table alias with a column name. Collecting a set of object types without specifying the type of collection generates a dynamically generated system collection, like

```
COLLECTION(ID, NAME)
------------------------------------------------------------
SYSTPyVBav+vfR/WgCSImjOW1Ig==(BASE_T(3, 'Tom Bombadil'), ...
```

You should actually provide the AS keyword and a valid collection type inside the call to the COLLECT function. When properly assigned to a collection data type from the data catalog, the COLLECT function returns a collection that you can pass as a call parameter to a PL/SQL function or procedure. Likewise, you can insert the collection into a column of a composite table.

This is an example of gathering the rows of an object table into a collection:

```
SQL> SELECT CAST(COLLECT(VALUE(b)) AS base_c) AS collection
  FROM   object_base b;
```

The COLLECT function converts the object types into a dynamic collection and then the CAST function converts the generic collection to a base_c collection object type. This is actually the closest Oracle comes to a full adapter pattern with native SQL and user-defined types (UDTs). The results are displayed in a collapsed collection, which extends the definition, as shown:

```
COLLECTION(ID, NAME)
----------------------------------------------------------------
BASE_C(BASE_T(3, 'Tom Bombadil'), BASE_T(4, 'Goldberry'))
```

You can use the CAST and COLLECT functions together to create interesting SELECT statements for reports. Moreover, you can also use those interesting SELECT statements as cursors in PL/SQL blocks. The result from the cursor can become a call parameter to another named PL/SQL block.

For example, let's create a print_elements procedure that has one formal parameter of a base_c collection data type:

```
SQL> CREATE OR REPLACE PROCEDURE print_elements
  2  ( pv_collection  BASE_C ) IS
  3    -- Declare a collection.
  4    lv_collection  BASE_C := base_c();
  5  BEGIN
  6    -- Check whether the collection is populated.
  7    IF pv_collection IS NOT EMPTY THEN
  8      lv_collection := pv_collection;
  9    END IF;
 10
 11    -- Read through the list and print values.
 12    FOR i IN 1..lv_collection.COUNT LOOP
 13      dbms_output.put_line(
 14        '['||lv_collection(i).id||']['||lv_collection(i).name||']');
 15    END LOOP;
 16  END;
 17  /
```

Line 2 shows the pv_collection formal parameter. Lines 7 through 9 check whether the collection isn't empty before assigning it to a local variable of the base_c collection type. You may be wondering why we didn't check for a null, especially if you've read the whole book or come to this part with a background in PL/SQL. The reason you don't need to check is that:

- If it's not empty, it's filled.
- If it's null, it's not empty.
- If it's empty, it's not handled because there's no ELSE block.

Finally, lines 13 and 14 print the results.

Next, let's use an anonymous block program to gather the rows into a collection and pass them to the `print_elements` procedure:

```
SQL> DECLARE
  2    -- Declare a cursor of a collection type.
  3    lv_collection  BASE_C;
  4  BEGIN
  5    -- Cursor to create a collection from rows of an object table.
  6    SELECT CAST(
  7             COLLECT(
  8               VALUE(b)) AS base_c) AS base_c
  9    INTO    lv_collection
 10    FROM    object_base b;
 11
 12    -- Pass the cursor variable to the procedure.
 13    print_elements(lv_collection);
 14  END;
 15  /
```

Line 3 declares an uninitialized collection. Line 9 assigns the results of the `SELECT-INTO` cursor to the `lv_collection` variable, which initializes it through a direct assignment of values. Sizing of the list occurs by an implicit evaluation of the number of elements in the collection. Line 13 calls the named PL/SQL block with the collection variable.

The `print_elements` procedure prints

```
[3] [Tom Bombadil]
[4] [Goldberry]
```

In all cases the `COLLECT` function is much faster than individually allocating space and assigning values to a collection within the scope of PL/SQL block. I recommend you use the `COLLECT` function to marshal object values into collections.

COLLECT Function with an Object Type Column

Object type columns exist as the sole or one of several column data types in composite tables. The `COLLECT` function works slightly differently with composite tables. Foremost, you can't use the `VALUE` function because there's no correlation variable for a column within a table.

Here's the definition of the `log_base` composite table:

```
SQL> CREATE TABLE log_base
     ( log_base_id  NUMBER
     , log_object   BASE_T);
```

It contains a scalar `log_base_id` column and a `base_t` object type column. Describing the table, you see

```
SQL> DESCRIBE log_base
 Name                        Null?    Type
 --------------------------- -------- --------
 LOG_BASE_ID                          NUMBER
 LOG_OBJECT                           BASE_T
```

Like object tables, object columns can store instances (really, collapsed object definitions) of their base type or any subtype of the base type. In this example, `base_t` is the base type and `hobbit_t` is a subtype. Querying the content of the table with the following `SELECT` statement lets you see that it holds different object types within the same object hierarchy:

```
SQL> SELECT log_object
  2  FROM   log_base;
```

The results are

```
LOG_OBJECT(ID, NAME)
----------------------------------------------------------------------
BASE_T(1, 'Tom Bombadil')
BASE_T(2, 'Goldberry')
HOBBIT_T(3, 'Bilbo Baggins', 'Bag End', 'Hobbiton', 'Westfarthing')
HOBBIT_T(4, 'Frodo Baggins', 'Bag End', 'Hobbiton', 'Westfarthing')
HOBBIT_T(5, 'Sam Gamgee', 'Hobbiton', 'Hobbiton', 'Westfarthing')
```

You can collect the data with or without casting it to an existing object collection type, but you should always cast to an object collection. You have the choice of using or excluding the table alias because it's an ordinary table alias in this context, rather than a correlation variable.

The following query collects object instances of the supertype and any subtype into a single collection result:

```
SQL> SELECT CAST(COLLECT(b.log_object) AS base_c) AS collection
  2  FROM   log_base b;
```

It returns the following collection, which mirrors the named collection from the prior section in this appendix (at least with a little manual formatting for the extra data):

```
COLLECTION(ID, NAME)
----------------------------------------------------------------------
BASE_C(BASE_T(1, 'Tom Bombadil'), BASE_T(2, 'Goldberry'),
HOBBIT_T(5, 'Bilbo Baggins', 'Bag End', 'Hobbiton', 'Westfarthing'),
HOBBIT_T(6, 'Frodo Baggins', 'Bag End', 'Hobbiton', 'Westfarthing'),
HOBBIT_T(7, 'Sam Gamgee', 'Hobbiton', 'Hobbiton', 'Westfarthing'))
```

Other than remembering that you don't need the correlation variable, this is virtually like how you work with object tables. The "Can't Clone, Migrate the Data" sidebar in Appendix B shows you how to translate object tables and object columns to relational data in the "Can't Clone, Migrate the Data" sidebar. Naturally, Chapter 11 covers the definition and implementation of object types in detail, and the "Object Types" section of Appendix B covers how you create, evolve, and drop them.

POWERMULTISET Function

Like the `COLLECT` function, `POWERMULTISET` collects instances of an object type into a collection. It takes a column name for a nested table and returns the object type and any nested object types (called *submultisets*) from the nested table.

The following example uses the employee table from the "Object Data Type" section of Appendix B, and it's important to note that this table doesn't share the definition of the employee tables found in Oracle's sample schemas.

```
SQL> SELECT CAST(
              POWERMULTISET(home_address) AS address_list_table)
     FROM   employee;
```

It returns the collection in a representation of collapsed objects with nested collapsed objects, like the results of the COLLECTION function.

POWERMULTISET_BY_CARDINALITY Function

The POWERMULTISET_BY_CARDINALITY function takes a nested table and a cardinality value as inputs, and returns a submultiset (nonempty subset) based on the cardinality. A cardinality of 1 indicates a unique cardinality.

Here's how you use the CAST function to convert the result of the POWERMULTISET_BY_CARDINALITY function into a table collection:

```
SQL> SELECT CAST(
              POWERMULTISET_BY_CARDINALITY(home_address,1)
                AS address_list_table)
     FROM   employee;
```

This returns similar output to that produced by the COLLECT and POWERMULTISET functions.

SET Function

The SET function is also a collection set operator, so I decided to provide the description and supporting example only in the following "Collection Set Operators" section.

Collection Set Operators

Oracle Database 12c delivers collection set operators. They act and function like SQL set operators in SELECT statements. The difference is that they are used in assignments between collections of matching signature types. They work only with varrays and nested tables because they require numeric index values.

You have to migrate associative arrays into varrays or nested tables before using set operators. Table C-2 describes the collection set operators.

Sets are displayed as comma-delimited lists of values. The following subsections qualify how to work with the set operators listed in Table C-2. The following code shows you how to format and print results from sets (varrays and nested tables) as a comma-delimited string:

```
SQL> CREATE OR REPLACE
       TYPE list IS TABLE OF NUMBER;
     /

SQL> CREATE OR REPLACE FUNCTION format_list(set_in LIST)
     RETURN VARCHAR2 IS
       retval VARCHAR2(2000);
```

Set Operator	Description
CARDINALITY	Counts the number of elements in a collection. It makes no attempt to count only unique elements, but you can combine it with the SET operator to count unique elements. The prototype is CARDINALITY(*collection*)
EMPTY	Acts as an operand, similar to checking whether a variable is null or is not null. The comparative syntax is *variable_name* IS [NOT] EMPTY
MULTISET	Lets you group rows from a return set into a collection. The prototype is *collection* MULTISET *sql_result_set*
MULTISET EXCEPT	Removes one set from another. It works like the SQL MINUS set operator. The prototype is *collection* MULTISET EXCEPT *collection*
MULTISET INTERSECT	Evaluates two sets and returns one set. The return set contains elements that were found in both original sets. It works like the SQL INTERSECT set operator. The prototype is *collection* MULTISET INTERSECT *collection*
MULTISET UNION	Evaluates two sets and returns one set. The return set contains all elements of both sets. Where duplicate elements are found, they are returned. It functions like the SQL UNION ALL set operator. You may use the DISTINCT operator to eliminate duplicates. The DISTINCT operator follows the MULTISET UNION operator rule. It functions like the SQL UNION operator. The prototype is *collection* MULTISET UNION *collection*
SET	Removes duplicates from a collection and thereby creates a set of unique values. It acts like a DISTINCT operator sorting out duplicates in a SQL statement. The operator prototype is SET(*collection*) You can also use the SET operator as an operand, similar to checking whether a variable is null or is not null. The comparative syntax is *variable_name* IS [NOT] A SET
SUBMULTISET	Identifies if a set is a subset of another set. It returns true when the left operand is a subset of the right operand. The true return can be misleading if you're looking for a proper subset, which contains at least one element less than the superset. The function returns true because any set is a subset of itself. There is no test for a proper subset without also using the CARDINALITY operator to compare whether the element counts of the two sets are unequal. The prototype is *collection* SUBMULTISET OF *collection*

TABLE C-2. *Set Operators for Collections*

```
BEGIN
  IF set_in IS NULL THEN
    dbms_output.put_line('Result: <Null>');
  ELSIF set_in IS EMPTY THEN
    dbms_output.put_line('Result: <Empty>');
  ELSE  -- Anything not null or empty.
    FOR i IN set_in.FIRST..set_in.LAST LOOP
      IF i = set_in.FIRST THEN
        IF set_in.COUNT = 1 THEN
          retval := '('||set_in(i)||')';
        ELSE
          retval := '('||set_in(i);
        END IF;
      ELSIF i <> set_in.LAST THEN
        retval := retval||', '||set_in(i);
      ELSE
        retval := retval||', '||set_in(i)||')';
      END IF;
    END LOOP;
  END IF;
  RETURN retval;
END format_list;
/
```

The `format_list` function works only with numeric indexes because collection set operators are limited to varrays and nested tables, which are indexed only by integers. The set operator examples all use this function to format output.

CARDINALITY Operator

The `CARDINALITY` operator lets count the elements in a collection. If there are unique elements, they are counted once for each copy in the collection. The following example shows you how to exclude matching elements:

```
SQL> DECLARE
  a LIST := list(1,2,3,3,4,4);
BEGIN
  dbms_output.put_line(CARDINALITY(a));
END;
/
```

The program prints the number 6 because there are four elements in the collection. You can count only the unique values by combining the `CARDINALITY` and `SET` operators, like this:

```
SQL> DECLARE
  a LIST := list(1,2,3,3,4,4);
BEGIN
  dbms_output.put_line(CARDINALITY(SET(a)));
END;
/
```

The program now prints the number 4 because there are four unique elements in the set derived from the six-element collection.

EMPTY Operator

The EMPTY operator is covered in the SET subsection.

MULTISET Operator

The MULTISET operator lets you gather a set of scalar variables into a collection within a SQL statement. To demonstrate how it works, we need to create a table and object type. For the object type, we'll reuse the street_list ADT (Attribute Data Type) from Appendix B:

```
SQL> CREATE OR REPLACE
       TYPE street_list IS TABLE OF VARCHAR2(30);
     /
```

Then, we create a table to hold the scalar strings:

```
SQL> CREATE TABLE street_multiset
     ( street_multiset_id  NUMBER
     , address_id          NUMBER
     , line_id             NUMBER
     , street_element      VARCHAR2(30));
```

Finally, we insert a couple of related rows:

```
SQL> INSERT INTO street_multiset VALUES ( 1, 1, 1,'1111 Broadway');
SQL> INSERT INTO street_multiset VALUES ( 2, 1, 2,'Suite 521');
```

The following MULTISET operator groups the two rows together into a street_list collection structure based on the shared address_id column:

```
SQL> SELECT CAST(
              MULTISET(
                SELECT street_element
                FROM   street_multiset
                WHERE address_id = 1) AS STREET_LIST) AS collection
     FROM   dual;
```

It displays

```
COLLECTION
-------------------------------------------
STREET_LIST('1111 Broadway', 'Suite 521')
```

The MULTISET operator groups scalar values into collections. The TABLE operator performs the opposite action, exploding object types into standard result sets—made of columns and rows.

The MULTISET operator can also work inside an UPDATE statement. For example, let's update the street_address column nested inside a home_address column of our employee table, which you can find in Appendix B. The UPDATE statement assembles the rows of a column value into a street_list ADT and then assigns them to the nested street_address column within the nested `home_address` column. See Appendix B for an explanation of unnesting queries.

```
SQL> UPDATE  TABLE(SELECT e.home_address
                  FROM   employee e
                  WHERE  e.employee_id = 1) e
     SET e.street_address =
          (SELECT   CAST(
                      MULTISET(
                        SELECT street_element
                        FROM   street_multiset
                        WHERE address_id = 1) AS STREET_LIST) AS collection
                    FROM     dual)
     WHERE e.address_id = 1;
```

This updates only the nested ADT value for a single row in our `employee` table where the primary key `address_id` column's value is 1.

MULTISET EXCEPT Operator

The `MULTISET EXCEPT` operator lets you find the elements remaining from the first set after removing any matching elements from the second set. The operator ignores any elements in the second set that are not found in the first set. The following example shows you how to exclude matching elements:

```
SQL> DECLARE
       a LIST := list(1,2,3,4);
       b LIST := list(4,5,6,7);
     BEGIN
       dbms_output.put_line(format_list(a MULTISET EXCEPT b));
     END;
     /
```

Only the element 4 exists in both sets. The operation therefore removes 4 from the first set. The following output is generated by the block:

```
(1, 2, 3)
```

MULTISET INTERSECT Operator

The `MULTISET INTERSECT` operator lets you find the intersection or matching values between two sets. The following example shows you how to create a set of the intersection between two sets:

```
SQL> DECLARE
       a LIST := list(1,2,3,4);
       b LIST := list(4,5,6,7);
     BEGIN
       dbms_output.put_line(format_list(a MULTISET INTERSECT b));
     END;
     /
```

Only one element from both sets matches, and that's the number 4. The following output is generated by the block:

```
(4)
```

This section has demonstrated how you can use set operators to create a set of the intersection between two sets.

MULTISET UNION Operator

The `MULTISET UNION` operator performs a `UNION ALL` operation on two collections. The following example demonstrates how to combine the sets into one set:

```
SQL> DECLARE
       a LIST := list(1,2,3,4);
       b LIST := list(4,5,6,7);
     BEGIN
       dbms_output.put_line(format_list(a MULTISET UNION b));
     END;
     /
```

The operation result of the `MULTISET UNION` is passed as an actual parameter to the `format_list` function. The function converts it into the string:

```
(1, 2, 3, 4, 4, 5, 6, 7)
```

You'll notice that both sets contain the integer 4, and the resulting set has two copies of it. You can eliminate the duplication and mimic a `UNION` operator by appending the `DISTINCT` operator, like

```
SQL> DECLARE
       a LIST := list(1,2,3,4);
       b LIST := list(4,5,6,7);
     BEGIN
       dbms_output.put_line(format_list(a MULTISET UNION DISTINCT b));
     END;
     /
```

Alternatively, you can take the result of the `MULTISET UNION DISTINCT` operation and pass it as an argument to the `SET` operator to eliminate duplicates. This shows that approach:

```
SQL> DECLARE
       a LIST := list(1,2,3,4);
       b LIST := list(4,5,6,7);
     BEGIN
       dbms_output.put_line(format_list(SET(a MULTISET UNION b)));
     END;
     /
```

Both the `DISTINCT` and `SET` operators produce the following output:

```
(1, 2, 3, 4, 5, 6, 7)
```

SET Operator

The SET operator acts on a single input, which is another set. It removes any duplicates from the set and returns a new set with unique values. The following example demonstrates how to pare a set into unique elements:

```
SQL> DECLARE
       a LIST := list(1,2,3,3,4,4,5,6,6,7);
     BEGIN
       dbms_output.put_line(format_list(SET(a)));
     END;
     /
```

The original set contains ten elements, but three are duplicated. The SET operator removes all duplicates and generates a new set with seven unique elements:

```
(1, 2, 3, 4, 5, 6, 7)
```

You can also use SET as an operand in comparison statements, like

```
SQL> DECLARE
       a LIST := list(1,2,3,4);
       b LIST := list(1,2,3,3,4,4);
       c LIST := list();
       FUNCTION isset (set_in LIST) RETURN VARCHAR2 IS
       BEGIN
         IF set_in IS A SET THEN
           IF set_in IS NOT EMPTY THEN
             RETURN 'Yes - a unique collection.';
           ELSE
             RETURN 'Yes - an empty collection.';
           END IF;
         ELSE
           RETURN 'No - a non-unique collection.';
         END IF;
       END isset;
     BEGIN
       dbms_output.put_line(isset(a));
       dbms_output.put_line(isset(b));
       dbms_output.put_line(isset(c));
     END;
     /
```

NOTE

Always remember to use empty parentheses when you build empty collections. If you forget the parentheses (a common mistake, because you don't need them to call some functions or procedures), you'll raise an ORA-00330 *error—invalid use of type name.*

The program returns

```
Yes - a unique collection.
No  - a non-unique collection.
Yes - an empty collection.
```

This anonymous block demonstrates that the `IS A SET` comparison returns true when the collection is either unique or empty. You must use the `IS EMPTY` comparison to capture empty collections, as done in the `format_set` function previously shown.

SUBMULTISET OF Operator

The `SUBMULTISET OF` operator acts on two inputs. The first input precedes the `SUBMULTISET OF` operator and the second follows the operator. The `SUBMULTISET OF` operator checks whether the leading set is a proper subset of the following set. That means that all members of the subset are found in the other set. The following example demonstrates how to evaluate a whether a collection is a subset of another set:

```
SQL> DECLARE
  2    a LIST := list(1,2,3,3,4,4,5);
  3    b LIST := list(3,4);
  4  BEGIN
  5    IF b SUBMULTISET OF a THEN
  6      dbms_output.put_line(format_list(b));
  7    ELSE
  8      dbms_output.put_line('Subset not found in set.');
  9    END IF;
 10  END;
 11  /
```

Line 5 checks whether set `b` is a subset of `a` and when it is a proper subset, it prints the formatted list. The `SUBMULTISET OF` operator finds that the subset is a valid subset and prints set `b`'s formatted members:

```
(3, 4)
```

Number Functions

The number built-in functions provide key typical mathematical functions. Aside from the trigonometric functions, you should find `FLOOR` and `CEIL` useful when you want to find a bottom and upper integer limit for a range of complex (fractional) numbers. Also, `ROUND` lets you round complex numbers to their nearest integer, and `TRUNC` lets you strip the values to the right of the decimal place.

You'll also find functions for modulo mathematics and exponentiation. Understanding what's available should increase your options while writing PL/SQL programs.

CEIL Function

The `CEIL` function lets you round any real number to the next higher integer. You can use it as follows:

```
SQL> DECLARE
       n NUMBER := 4.44;
     BEGIN
```

```
    dbms_output.put_line('Ceiling ['||CEIL(n)||']');
  END;
  /
```

It prints

```
Ceiling [5]
```

This is handy when you're trying to group things into whole units.

FLOOR Function

The FLOOR function lets you truncate any remaining fraction from a number, returning the whole integer value. You can use it as follows:

```
SQL> DECLARE
    n NUMBER := 4.44;
  BEGIN
    dbms_output.put_line('Flooring ['||FLOOR(n)||']');
  END;
  /
```

It prints

```
Flooring [4]
```

This is handy when you're trying to group things into whole units.

MOD Function

The MOD function lets you find the remainder of a division operation, like the REMAINDER function. It returns a 0 when there is no remainder and returns the integer of any remainder when one exists.

The prototype is

```
MOD(dividend, divisor)
```

You can use it as follows:

```
SQL> DECLARE
    n NUMBER := 16;
    m NUMBER := 3;
  BEGIN
    dbms_output.put_line('Mode ['||MOD(n,m)||']');
  END;
  /
```

It prints

```
Mode [1]
```

The MOD function uses the FLOOR function in the calculation. It is designed to work with positive integers. You will get nonclassical modulo arithmetic results when either number is negative. You should use the REMAINDER function for classic modulo results when either number has a negative value or the divisor is a real number.

Modulo Arithmetic

Modulo arithmetic is a system of integer math. It is designed on the principal that numbers wrap around, like a clock. An example is how 60 seconds becomes a minute, and then the seconds reset to 0. It comes from the work of Carl Friedrich Gauss and was first published in 1801.

The example does a bit of casting to demonstrate clock arithmetic by leveraging the system clock function, `SYSDATE`:

```
SQL> DECLARE
       c_time INTEGER;
       e_time INTEGER;
       n_time INTEGER;
       s_time INTEGER;
     BEGIN
       LOOP
         /* Use the MOD function. */
         s_time := MOD(TO_NUMBER(TO_CHAR(SYSDATE,'SS')),60);
         IF c_time IS NULL THEN
           c_time := s_time;
           e_time := s_time - 1;
           n_time := s_time;
           dbms_output.put_line(
             '['||TO_CHAR(SYSDATE,'MI:SS')||']['||s_time||']');
         ELSE
           n_time := s_time;
           IF n_time <> c_time THEN
             dbms_output.put_line(
               '['||TO_CHAR(SYSDATE,'MI:SS')||']['||s_time||']');
             c_time := n_time;
           END IF;
         END IF;
         IF c_time = e_time THEN
           EXIT;
         END IF;
       END LOOP;
     END;
     /
```

This prints 59 values. It starts with the current time and ends 59 seconds later with the 24-hour clock value and modulo integer result. The following displays the rows immediately before and after the wrapping between minutes:

```
[53:58][58]
[53:59][59]
[54:00][0]
[54:01][1]
[54:02][2]
```

Modulo arithmetic lets you time events to the minute or hour with a divisor of 60. You can time events to the half-minute by using a divisor of 30, or quarter-minute by using a divisor of 15. As you explore your application needs, it is likely that you'll have several occasions to use the `MOD` function.

POWER Function

The POWER function doubles for the exponential operator, **. It is really your preference whether you use the POWER function or the exponential operator, but you should pick one and stick with it. There's *power* in writing code consistently.

The prototype of the POWER function is

```
POWER(base_number, exponent)
```

The follow demonstrates cubing a number:

```
SQL> DECLARE
    n NUMBER := 3;
    m NUMBER := 3;
  BEGIN
    dbms_output.put_line('Cube of ['||n||'] is ['||POWER(n,m)||']');
  END;
  /
```

This prints

```
Cube of [3] is [27]
```

While the math libraries work well when you square or cube numbers, they do produce rounding errors when calculating cube roots, like the following:

```
SQL> DECLARE
    n NUMBER := 27;
    m NUMBER := 1/3;
  BEGIN
    dbms_output.put_line('Cube of ['||n||'] is ['||POWER(n,m)||']');
  END;
  /
```

This prints

```
Cube root of [27] is [2.9999999999999999999999999999999999998]
```

While it should print 3, it doesn't. The math error is not generally significant because you can use the ROUND function to get the whole number cube root, like

```
ROUND(POWER(n,m),0)
```

You get 3 when you change the data types from NUMBER to BINARY_DOUBLE because the latter uses the server's local math libraries. The same program written with a BINARY_DOUBLE data type prints

```
Cube root of [2.7E+001] is [3.0E+000]
```

You should consider using data types tied to the server math libraries when the data types are scientific in nature, like finding cube roots.

REMAINDER Function

The `REMAINDER` function lets you find the remainder of a division operation, like the `MOD` function. It returns a 0 when there is no remainder and returns the integer of any remainder when one exists.

The prototype is

```
REMAINDER(dividend, divisor)
```

The `REMAINDER` function behaves differently depending on whether the dividend and divisor are `NUMBER` data types or data types linked to the local math libraries, like `BINARY_FLOAT` and `BINARY_DOUBLE`. More or less, the results are slightly more meaningful with `BINARY_FLOAT` and `BINARY_DOUBLE` because you get a NaN (not a number) when the divisor is 0. You get a numeric or value error (`PLS-06502`) when the actual parameters are `NUMBER` data types.

You can use it as follows:

```
SQL> DECLARE
       n NUMBER := 16;
       m NUMBER := 3;
     BEGIN
       dbms_output.put_line('Remainder ['||REMAINDER(n,m)||']');
     END;
     /
```

It prints

```
Remainder [1]
```

The difference between the `REMAINDER` and `MOD` functions can best be shown by using a real number as the divisor. This program uses both functions:

```
SQL> DECLARE
       n NUMBER := 16;
       m NUMBER := 3.24;
     BEGIN
       dbms_output.put_line('Remainder ['||REMAINDER(n,m)||']');
       dbms_output.put_line('Remainder ['||MOD(n,m)||']');
     END;
     /
```

There are two perspectives on this problem. One divides the dividend by the divisor and returns either a positive integer as the remainder or 0. This works when the dividend and divisor are positive integers. The `MOD` function uses this method; when the divisor is 3.24 and the dividend is 4, there are four whole 3.24 values, or 12.96, in 16. The divisor minus the dividend times 4 yields a remainder of 3.04.

The other perspective approximates the least remainder of the division. This means that when the remainder is greater than half the dividend, it looks for the next whole division value. The remainder in this case is the difference between what the number is and what the next higher number would be without a remainder. The `REMAINDER` function uses the same divisor but finds the closest possible result, or the world as it should be. From this perspective, there should be five whole 3.24 values, or 16.2, in the *dividend*, which leaves a remainder of –0.2.

More likely than not, you'll use MOD more frequently than REMAINDER because application programming deals with reality. In rare cases, the other fits. You now know why the REMAINDER function works the way it does.

ROUND Function

The ROUND function has two roles. One works with dates and the other, described here, works with numbers. (For completeness, this definition also appears in the "Date-time Functions" section.) The ROUND function lets you round a number to a whole number or a decimal equivalent. The following rounds 2.5 to a whole number:

```
SQL> SELECT ROUND(2.5,0) FROM dual;
```

You should note that the ROUND function rounds up at 2.5 and rounds down with anything less than 2.5. The ROUND function is important when preparing reports, especially financial reports.

It's very useful when using Oracle's math libraries because some functions return incorrect values, like the POWER function (see its description a bit earlier in this appendix).

Error Reporting Functions

The error reporting functions only work in the exception block of PL/SQL program units. The SQLCODE function returns the code number for the error, like ORA-01422. The SQLERRM function returns the error code and a brief message. The messages are defined by language, and you should note that in some earlier Oracle Database releases, some language translations have had incomplete message files.

Chapter 7 covers exception handling and contains additional examples that you may find useful. These two sections summarize the utility of the SQLCODE and SQLERRM functions.

SQLCODE Function

The SQLCODE function returns the Oracle error number for standard exceptions and a 1 for user-defined exceptions. You can also raise a user-defined custom error and exception message by calling the RAISE_APPLICATION_ERROR function. This section demonstrates all three approaches.

The following program generates a standard exception:

```
SQL> DECLARE
  2    a NUMBER;
  3    b CHAR := 'A';
  4  BEGIN
  5    a := b;
  6  EXCEPTION
  7    WHEN others THEN
  8      dbms_output.put_line('SQLERRM ['||SQLERRM||']');
  9  END;
 10  /
```

It prints the following to console:

```
SQLERRM [ORA-06502: PL/SQL: numeric or value error: character to number ...
```

The next program generates a user-defined exception number:

```
SQL> DECLARE
       e EXCEPTION;
     BEGIN
       RAISE e;
     EXCEPTION
       WHEN others THEN
         dbms_output.put_line('SQLCODE ['||SQLCODE||']');
     END;
     /
```

It generates the following because user-defined exceptions always return `1`:

```
SQLCODE [1]
```

The `RAISE_APPLICATION_ERROR` function lets you define a user exception number and exception. The `SQLCODE` value works for user-defined exceptions exactly as it does for standard exceptions.

SQLERRM Function

The `SQLERRM` function mirrors the behaviors of the `SQLCODE` function with the exception of the value returned. `SQLERRM` returns the error code and a default message. The message files are read from a generic message file in the `$ORACLE_HOME/rdbms/mesg` directory. The message files are found in the `oraus.msg` file for American English exception messages. They are language-specific files when you install Oracle in a different language. You can also evaluate error messages in Linux or Unix by using the `oerr` utility.

You execute the `oerr` utility by providing the three-character error type and five-number error message, like

```
# oerr ora 01422
```

The `oerr` utility treats the three-character error type string as case insensitive. Unfortunately, it isn't available on the Windows operating system port of the database.

The `SQLERRM` function works the same for standard exceptions and user-defined exceptions. It reads the message file. The next program demonstrates raising a user-defined exception:

```
SQL> DECLARE
       e EXCEPTION;
     BEGIN
       RAISE e;
     EXCEPTION
       WHEN others THEN
         dbms_output.put_line('SQLERRM ['||SQLERRM||']');
     END;
     /
```

This program generates the following:

```
SQLERRM [User-Defined Exception]
```

You can use an `EXCEPTION_INIT PRAGMA` (a precompiler instruction) to map a user-defined exception to a standard Oracle exception. Using the `EXCEPTION_INIT` precompiler instruction is preferred to the standard exception message `User-Defined Exception`.

The next program demonstrates mapping a related standard exception message to a user-defined exception:

```
SQL> DECLARE
       e EXCEPTION;
       PRAGMA EXCEPTION_INIT(e,-01422);
     BEGIN
       RAISE e;
     EXCEPTION
       WHEN others THEN
         dbms_output.put_line('SQLERRM ['||SQLERRM||']');
     END;
     /
```

It prints the following output:

```
SQLERRM [ORA-01422: exact fetch returns more than requested number of rows]
```

You can use the `RAISE_APPLICATION_ERROR` function when you require a specialized error message. Unfortunately, this function limits you to an exception range between –20,001 and –21,999. If you use any number outside that range, you'll raise an `ORA-20000` exception.

The following demonstrates the `SQLERRM` result for a user-defined exception message:

```
SQL> BEGIN
       RAISE_APPLICATION_ERROR(
          -20001
         ,'An overriding user-defined error message.');
     EXCEPTION
       WHEN others THEN
         dbms_output.put_line('SQLERRM ['||SQLERRM||']');
     END;
     /
```

It raises the following to console:

```
SQLERRM [ORA-20001: An overriding user-defined error message.]
```

This section has demonstrated how you can use standard and user-defined exception messages. You've learned that you can *only return standard messages* unless you call the `RAISE_APPLICATION_ERROR` function.

Miscellaneous Functions

These miscellaneous functions initialize large objects, perform advanced comparisons, and audit system environment variables. They are very powerful features in the PL/SQL language.

The `BFILENAME`, `EMPTY_BLOB`, and `EMPTY_CLOB` functions initialize large objects. The `BFILENAME` function defines a data structure for an external file. `EMPTY_BLOB` and `EMPTY_CLOB` initialize `BLOB` and `CLOB` data types, respectively.

Advanced comparisons are conditional evaluations. They are performed by the COALESCE, DECODE, GREATEST, LEAST, NANVL, NULLIF, and NVL functions. COALESCE uses short-circuit analysis to find the first not-null value in a set. If all values in a set are null, COALESCE returns null. DECODE performs if-then-else and if-then-elseif-then-else logic. GREATEST finds the highest character, string, or number in a set of like data types. LEAST finds the lowest value in a set. NANVL substitutes a default number when *not a number* is returned but only applies to types using native operating system math libraries. NULLIF returns a null when its two actual parameters are equal. NVL substitutes another value when the first actual parameter is null; it requires both actual parameters to be the same data type.

The balance of the functions audit system environment variables. They are DUMP, NLS_CHARSET_DECL_LEN, NLS_CHARSET_ID, NLS_CHARSET_NAME, SYS_CONTEXT, SYS_GUID, UID, USER, USERENV, and VSIZE. The DUMP and VSIZE functions inspect the physical size of data types. Oracle's National Language Support (NLS) represents how Oracle databases manage different character sets. As discussed in the "Unicode Characters and Strings" section of Chapter 4, Oracle supports two Unicode character sets—AL32UTF16 and AL32UTF8. It also supports numerous other character sets. NLS is the umbrella term for all character sets. The NLS_CHARSET_DECL_LEN, NLS_CHARSET_ID, and NLS_CHARSET_NAME functions let you discover the physical storage details of NLS character sets. The remaining functions, SYS_CONTEXT, SYS_GUID, UID, USER, and USERENV, audit database session information.

This section covers the three functions for initializing large objects, the TREAT for instantiating a persistent object, the TABLE function for translating a collection to a result set, the seven functions for performing advanced comparisons, and four of the system environment functions: DUMP, SYS_CONTEXT, USERENV, and VSIZE. Rather than create separate nesting levels, these functions are simply presented alphabetically. The description of each qualifies its purpose in the PL/SQL language.

BFILENAME Function

The BFILENAME function is used to insert or update a reference to an externally stored binary large object. It takes two parameters: a virtual directory path and a filename. Unfortunately, it makes no effort to validate whether the virtual directory or file exists. This is because you may build the reference before creating the virtual directory mapping or placing the file in the target location. It returns a binary file locator.

The following prototype demonstrates that you call the function with two strings; the first is limited to 30 characters and the second to 4,000 characters:

```
BFILENAME('virtual_directory','physical_file')
```

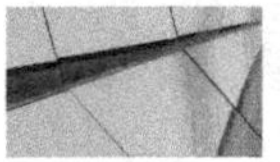

NOTE
Operating systems generally constrain the fully qualified path to a value smaller than 4,000 characters.

You can find the mapping of virtual directories to the external file system in the DBA_DIRECTORIES view. The view is available when you are the privileged user system or have been granted the DBA role privilege, which actually inherits the privilege through the SELECT_CATALOG_ROLE.

The following query lets you find the virtual directories and their physical server mapping:

```
SQL> SELECT   owner
  ,        directory_name
  ,        directory_path
  FROM     dba_directories;
```

All virtual directories are owned by the sys schema. You cannot access the contents from a cursor inside a stored program unit because the privilege exists through a role. Chapter 8 shows you how to query the contents of the table inside a stored procedure, which requires that the sys schema grant system the SELECT privilege on the DBA_DIRECTORIES view.

When you don't have the SELECT privilege, you are limited to using the dbms_lob package for access to the information inside a BFILE column. You can verify whether the file exists on the server by using the dbms_lob.fileexists function and get the physical size by using the dbms_lob.getlength function. The next program assumes you build the following table:

```
SQL> CREATE TABLE sample (sample_id NUMBER, sample_bfile BFILE);
```

and then insert a record into the table like this:

```
SQL> INSERT INTO sample
  VALUES (1, BFILENAME('VIRTUAL_DIRECTORY','file_name.ext'));
```

You can also use the BFILENAME function in the SET clause of an UPDATE statement to change either the virtual directory or filename. These external files are read-only data types, and you update data as part of maintenance programs that manipulate their location or names.

This program will now read the column and return a physical size for a file, or a message that the file was not found:

```
SQL> DECLARE
    file_locator BFILE;
  BEGIN
    SELECT   sample_bfile
    INTO     file_locator
    FROM     sample
    WHERE sample_id = 1;
    IF dbms_lob.fileexists(file_locator) = 1 THEN
      dbms_output.put_line(dbms_lob.getlength(file_locator));
    ELSE
      dbms_output.put_line('No file found.');
    END IF;
  END;
  /
```

The dbms_lob.fileexists function was built to work in both SQL and PL/SQL. Since SQL does not support a native Boolean data type, the function returns 1 when it finds a file and 0 when it fails.

The next program illustrates creating a binary file locator outside of a database column and then reading the locator to find the filename with the dbms_lob.filegetname function:

```
SQL> DECLARE
       alias    VARCHAR2(255);
       filename VARCHAR2(255);
     BEGIN
       dbms_lob.filegetname(
                   BFILENAME('virtual_dir','file_name.gif')
                  ,alias
                  ,filename);
       dbms_output.put_line(filename);
     END;
     /
```

It prints

```
file_name.gif
```

This section has demonstrated how to use the BFILENAME function. You will use it when you store files externally from the database. They must be no larger than the maximum file size supported by the operating system. They are typically files like .gif, .jpg, or .png image files, sound recording files, Flash components, and other media files.

COALESCE Function

The COALESCE function uses short-circuit analysis to find the first not-null value in a set. Short-circuit evaluation means that the function stops searching when a not-null value is returned. COALESCE returns null when all values evaluate as nulls.

The COALESCE prototype that works with scalar variables of the same data type is

```
COALESCE(arg1, arg2 [, arg3 [, arg(n+1)]])
```

The following demonstrates the function using a collection of strings:

```
SQL> DECLARE
       TYPE list IS TABLE OF VARCHAR2(5);
       ord LIST := list('One','','Three','','Five');
     BEGIN
       dbms_output.put_line(
         COALESCE(ord(1),ord(2),ord(3),ord(4),ord(5)));
     END;
     /
```

The function prints the first not-null element in the collection:

```
One
```

You can put a loop around the COALESCE function to perform the function repeatedly. Alternatively, you can use a FOR loop, nested IF statement, and NVL function call to print only not-null values. The two procedures consume roughly the same resources, but the latter may be clearer to most programmers.

DECODE Function

The `DECODE` function performs if-then-else and if-then-else-if-then-else logic in SQL statements. It is known as a pseudocolumn, and you can also use it inside your PL/SQL programs. The prototype for an if-then-else statement is

```
DECODE(evaluation_expression, comparison_expression
                             , true_expression, false_expression);
```

The alternate prototype for if-then-else-if-then-else is

```
DECODE(evaluation_expression, comparison_expression1, true_expression1
                             , comparison_expression2, true_expression2
                             , comparison_expression(n+1), true_expression(n+1)
                             , comparison false_expression);
```

The following illustrates an if-then-else `DECODE` function:

```
SQL> DECLARE
       a NUMBER := 94;
       b NUMBER := 96;
       c VARCHAR2(20);
     BEGIN
       SELECT DECODE(a,b,'Match.','Don''t match.')
       INTO c FROM dual;
       dbms_output.put_line(c);
     END;
     /
```

It prints the following because the numbers are unequal:

```
Don't match.
```

The following program shows the case logic of a multiple if-then-else statement:

```
SQL> DECLARE
       redsox   NUMBER := 96;
       yankees  NUMBER := 94;
       division NUMBER := 96;
       headline VARCHAR2(30);
     BEGIN
     SELECT DECODE(division,yankees,'Yankees clinch pennant.'
                           ,redsox,'Red Sox clinch pennant.'
                           ,'Tied Again!')
     INTO   headline
     FROM   dual;
       dbms_output.put_line(headline);
     END;
     /
```

While using static values, you should see the potential. Examine when you can resolve procedural questions in your SQL statements, and do it when it simplifies the program!

DUMP Function

The DUMP function examines the data type and real length of registered data types. It returns a value that is independent of the database or session character set. You can use the DUMP function only inside a SQL statement.

The following block demonstrates how to find the real size of a LONG RAW variable:

```
SQL> DECLARE
    buffer LONG RAW := HEXTORAW('42'||'41'||'44');
    detail VARCHAR2(100);
  BEGIN
    SELECT DUMP(buffer)
    INTO detail
    FROM dual;
      dbms_output.put_line(detail);
  END;
  /
```

It prints the data catalog number for a LONG RAW, the length of the data value, and the ASCII values of the original hexadecimal values:

```
Typ=23 Len=3: 66,65,68
```

You may not use this function too often, but when you're trying to figure out why something is broken and the error message and web hits are limited, it may be very helpful. It certainly helps when working with the dbms_lob package and raw streams, as covered in the next section.

EMPTY_BLOB Function

The EMPTY_BLOB function lets you initialize a database column with an empty BLOB data type. This is important because large objects have three possible states: null, empty, or populated. The dbms_lob package fails by raising an ORA-22275 exception when you attempt to work with a null BLOB column. The error is raised because there is no valid locator found in the column for null values.

The dbms_lob package fails by raising an ORA-01403 exception when you have an empty BLOB. This is more meaningful than the "invalid LOB locator" message that you'll receive when the column isn't initialized, and you can always append to an empty BLOB column. In some cases, using a default value during table creation may be a viable solution, but generally there are good reasons to leave a BLOB column null until you want to use it.

The next program assumes you build the following table:

```
SQL> CREATE TABLE sample (sample_id NUMBER, sample_blob BLOB);
```

and then insert into the table a record like this:

```
SQL> INSERT INTO sample (sample_id) VALUES (1);
```

You'll need to configure your database as noted in the proximate "Deploying a Character Set Function" sidebar. The following program demonstrates how to update a BLOB column in an existing row:

```
SQL> DECLARE
    amount BINARY_INTEGER := 100;
    buffer LONG RAW := HEXTORAW('43'||'44'||'5E');
```

```
  character_set VARCHAR2(12);
  offset INTEGER := 1;
  source BLOB;
  -- Convert character length to byte length.
  FUNCTION byte_length(n BINARY_INTEGER) RETURN BINARY_INTEGER IS
    al32utf8 BINARY_INTEGER := 2;
    utf8     BINARY_INTEGER := 3;
  BEGIN
    -- Find database instance character set.
    SELECT value
    INTO   character_set
    FROM   nls_database_parameters
    WHERE  parameter = 'NLS_CHARACTERSET';
    -- Branch sizing for Unicode.
    IF character_set = 'AL32UTF8' THEN
      RETURN n / al32utf8;
    ELSIF character_set = 'UTF8' THEN
      RETURN n / utf8;
    END IF;
  END byte_length;
BEGIN
  -- Change column value in existing row.
  UPDATE sample2
  SET    sample_blob = empty_blob()
  WHERE  sample_id = 1
  RETURNING sample_blob INTO source;
  -- Append to empty BLOB column.
  dbms_lob.writeappend(source,BYTE_LENGTH(LENGTH(buffer)),buffer);
  -- Read new content from column.
SELECT sample_blob INTO source FROM sample2 WHERE sample_id = 1;
  dbms_lob.read(source,amount,offset,buffer);
  dbms_output.put_line(buffer);
END;
/
```

The `UPDATE` statement uses the `RETURNING INTO` clause to create a transactional opening to the `BLOB` column. The `source` variable is the opening, and it lets you change the contents of the `BLOB` column. The target variable of the `RETURNING INTO` clause acts as an implicit bind variable that you can see by peeking into the SGA. The local `byte_length` function divides any Unicode character set length to arrive at the byte code length. You would need to modify that function when using other multibyte character sets. If you fail to convert the byte width of the `BLOB` variable, you raise an `ORA-21560` error. This happens because the `amount` parameter is larger than the actual number of bytes in the `buffer` parameter of the `dbms_lob.writeappend` function.

TIP

If you try to update a row that doesn't exist with the `dbms_lob.writeappend` procedure, you'll raise an `ORA-22275` exception, which indicates an invalid LOB locator is specified in the function call. This actually means there is no row where you can insert the LOB value.

You can also replace the `character_set` function and simplify the program by using the `VSIZE` function. `VSIZE` returns the size in bytes of expressions returned in SQL statements. The alternative local function would be

```
SQL> FUNCTION byte_length(n LONG RAW) RETURN BINARY_INTEGER IS
       realsize BINARY_INTEGER;
     BEGIN
       SELECT VSIZE(n) INTO realsize FROM dual;
         RETURN realsize;
     END byte_length;
```

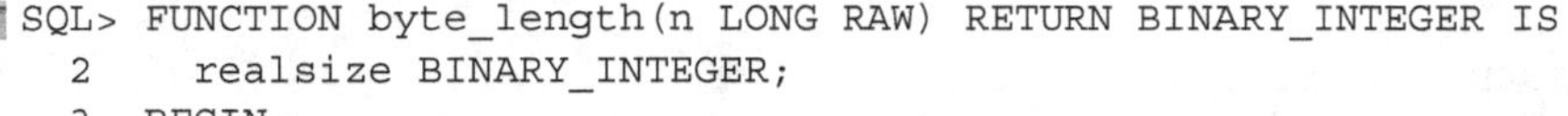

You can also change the call and eliminate the nested call to the `LENGTH` function, like

```
dbms_lob.writeappend(source,BYTE_LENGTH(buffer),buffer);
```

Clearly, this is simpler than dealing with the character sets. It also makes the case that you can leverage SQL-only built-in functions to do difficult things easily.

This section has demonstrated how to use the `EMPTY_BLOB` function in an `UPDATE` statement. You can also use it the same way in the `VALUES` clause of an `INSERT` statement, or as a default column value when creating a table or altering a table to include a `BLOB` column.

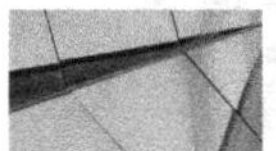

NOTE

The `dbms_lob` package also raises `ORA-06502` errors, typically without much explanation beyond pointing to line numbers that vary between releases. These errors are most often raised by passing a null value into one of the `IN` or `IN OUT` mode parameters of the `dbms_lob` functions or procedures.

Deploying a Character Set Function

As demonstrated in the update of a `BLOB` column, the user-defined `character_set` function lets you determine the character set of the database in a restricted privilege schema. This is critical when you need the real byte count for `BLOB`, `RAW`, or `LONG RAW` data types.

The first step requires that you connect as the privileged user `sys` as the `SYSDBA`. There you can grant privileges to the `sys.props$` table, like

```
GRANT SELECT ON props$ TO SYSTEM;
```

Then, you can compile the following function in the `system` schema (*don't forget to connect as the `system` user*):

```
SQL> CREATE OR REPLACE FUNCTION character_set RETURN VARCHAR2 IS
       -- Return variable.
       characterset VARCHAR2(20);
       -- Explicit cursors are always recommended.
       CURSOR c IS
         SELECT value$ FROM sys.props$ WHERE name = 'NLS_CHARACTERSET';
```

(continued)

```
BEGIN
  OPEN c;
  FETCH c INTO characterset;
  CLOSE c;
  RETURN characterset;
END character_set;
/
```

You grant execute privileges on this function to schemas that require access to the database character set. The following grants that privilege to the PLSQL schema:

```
SQL> GRANT EXECUTE ON character_set TO plsql;
```

After granting the privilege to the target schema, you should connect to the PLSQL schema and create a synonym or alias that points to the system.CHARACTER_SET function. You use the following syntax:

```
CREATE SYNONYM character_set FOR system.character_set;
```

This lets the local schema return the string representing the character set as an expression. This approach is what lets you update a BLOB column in a multibyte character set. It eliminates that nasty ORA-21560 error because the LENGTH function returns the number of bytes required by the character set, not raw storage. Using it properly, this function lets you deal with the real length of binary streams. You can also use the DUMP function to find the real length for byte streams.

EMPTY_CLOB Function

The EMPTY_CLOB function works like the EMPTY_BLOB function. It lets you initialize a database column with an empty CLOB data type. This is important because large objects have three possible states: null, empty, or populated. The dbms_lob package fails by raising an ORA-22275 exception when you attempt to work with a null CLOB column. The error is raised because there is no valid locator found in the column for null values.

The dbms_lob package fails by raising an ORA-01403 exception when you have an empty CLOB. This is more meaningful than the "invalid LOB locator" message that you'll receive when the column isn't initialized, and you can always append to an empty CLOB column. In some cases, using a default value during table creation may be a viable solution, but generally there are good reasons to leave a CLOB column null until you want to use it.

The next program assumes you build the following table:

```
SQL> CREATE TABLE sample (sample_id NUMBER, sample_clob CLOB);
```

and then insert into the table a record like this:

```
SQL> INSERT INTO sample (sample_id) VALUES (1);
```

The following demonstrates how to update a CLOB column in an existing row:

```
SQL> DECLARE
       amount BINARY_INTEGER := 100;
       buffer VARCHAR2(2000) := 'Something is better than nothing.';
       offset INTEGER := 1;
       source CLOB;
     BEGIN
       UPDATE sample
       SET    sample_clob = empty_clob()
       WHERE  sample_id = 1
       RETURNING sample_clob INTO source;
       -- Check that the source is empty.
       IF NVL(dbms_lob.getlength(source),0) = 0 THEN
         dbms_lob.writeappend(source,LENGTH(buffer),buffer);
       END IF;
       -- Read the first 2,000 characters of the CLOB.
       dbms_lob.read(source,amount,offset,buffer);
       dbms_output.put_line(buffer);
     END;
     /
```

This section has demonstrated how to use the EMPTY_CLOB function in an UPDATE statement. You can also use it the same way in the VALUES clause of an INSERT statement or as a default column value when creating a table or altering a table to include a CLOB column.

NOTE
An ORA-21560 exception is raised by the WRITEAPPEND procedure when the second actual parameter is a null value or 0.

GREATEST Function

The GREATEST function lets you check which of two values is the greatest. This works with scalar data types, like dates, numbers, and strings. The prototype is

```
GREATEST(variable1, variable2)
```

The GREATEST function requires that both actual parameters have the same data type, and it returns the least value in that data type. Comparing the number of winning games by the Boston Red Sox and New York Yankees for the 2007 season shows that 96 games wins the division pennant for the Boston Red Sox:

```
SQL> BEGIN
       dbms_output.put_line(GREATEST(96,94));
     END;
     /
```

Alternatively, you can compare two dates, such as the date that Sammy Sosa hit 600 career homeruns against the date that Alexander Rodriguez hit 500 career homeruns. The following program uses the TO_CHAR function to demonstrate that the return type is actually a date against which you can apply a format mask:

```
SQL> DECLARE
       rodriguez DATE := '04-AUG-07';
       sosa      DATE := '20-JUN-07';
     BEGIN
     dbms_output.put_line(
       TO_CHAR(GREATEST(rodriguez,sosa),'Mon DD, YYYY'));
     END;
     /
```

This prints the later date:

```
Aug 04, 2007
```

Although the previous examples are small, the string comparison highlights using the GREATEST function as a key element to implement a traditional descending bubble sort. The local swap procedure is quite simple as a pass-by-reference procedure, which leaves the array re-sorted upon successful completion of the program.

The bubble sort uses a set of nested loops, which lets you compare the first element against all elements in the collection, leaving the greatest element first—or in descending order:

```
SQL> DECLARE
       TYPE namelist IS TABLE OF VARCHAR2(12);
       names NAMELIST := namelist('Bonds','Aaron','Ruth','Mayes');
       -- Local swap procedure.
       PROCEDURE swap (a IN OUT VARCHAR2, b IN OUT VARCHAR2) IS
         c VARCHAR2(12);
       BEGIN
         c := b;
         b := a;
         a := c;
       END swap;
     BEGIN
       FOR i IN 1..names.COUNT LOOP
         FOR j IN 1..names.COUNT LOOP
           IF names(i) = GREATEST(names(i),names(j)) THEN
             swap(names(i),names(j));
           END IF;
         END LOOP;
       END LOOP;
       FOR i IN 1..names.COUNT LOOP
         dbms_output.put_line(names(i));
       END LOOP;
     END;
     /
```

The example prints the descending ordered surnames of the top four career homerun hitters:

```
Ruth
Mayes
Bonds
Aaron
```

You could also accomplish the same sorting by replacing the GREATEST comparison with the following line:

```
IF names(i) < names(j) THEN
```

You do need to watch the behavior of both Unicode and differing character sets when you do comparisons. The CONVERT function can help you ensure that comparisons are between like character sets.

These examples have demonstrated the versatility of the GREATEST function. They're revisited in the description of the LEAST function.

LEAST Function

The LEAST function lets you check which of two values is the least. This works with scalar data types, like dates, numbers, and strings. The prototype is

```
LEAST(variable1, variable2)
```

The LEAST function requires that both actual parameters have the same data type, and it returns the least value in that data type. Comparing the number of winning games by the Boston Red Sox and New York Yankees for the 2007 season shows that 94 games loses the division pennant for the New York Yankees:

```
SQL> BEGIN
       dbms_output.put_line(LEAST(96,94));
     END;
     /
```

Alternatively, you can compare two dates, such as the date that Sammy Sosa hit 600 career homeruns against the date that Alexander Rodriguez hit 500 career homeruns. The following program uses the TO_CHAR function to demonstrate that the return type is actually a date against which you can apply a format mask:

```
SQL> DECLARE
       rodriguez DATE := '04-AUG-07';
       sosa      DATE := '20-JUN-07';
     BEGIN
       dbms_output.put_line(
         TO_CHAR(LEAST(rodriguez,sosa),'Mon DD, YYYY'));
     END;
     /
```

This prints the earlier date:

```
Jun 20, 2007
```

Although the previous examples are small, the string comparison highlights using the LEAST function as a key element to implement a traditional bubble sort. The local swap procedure is quite simple as a pass-by-reference procedure, which leaves the array re-sorted upon successful completion of the program.

The bubble sort uses a set of nested loops, which lets you compare the first element against all elements in the collection, leaving the least element first—or an ascending alphabetical list:

```
SQL> DECLARE
       TYPE namelist IS TABLE OF VARCHAR2(12);
       names NAMELIST := namelist('Sarah','Joseph','Elise','Ian','Ariel'
                                 ,'Callie','Nathan','Spencer','Christianne');
       -- Local swap procedure.
       PROCEDURE swap (a IN OUT VARCHAR2, b IN OUT VARCHAR2) IS
         c VARCHAR2(12);
       BEGIN
         c := b;
         b := a;
         a := c;
       END swap;
     BEGIN
       FOR i IN 1..names.COUNT LOOP
         FOR j IN 1..names.COUNT LOOP
           IF names(i) = LEAST(names(i),names(j)) THEN
             swap(names(i),names(j));
           END IF;
         END LOOP;
       END LOOP;
       FOR i IN 1..names.COUNT LOOP
         dbms_output.put_line(names(i));
       END LOOP;
     END;
/
```

This reorders the names in the collection to an ascending alphabetical list:

```
Ariel
Callie
Christianne
Elise
Ian
Joseph
Nathan
Sarah
Spencer
```

You could also accomplish the same sorting by replacing the `LEAST` comparison with the following line:

```
IF names(i) < names(j) THEN
```

You do need to watch the behavior of both Unicode and differing character sets when you do comparisons. The `CONVERT` function can help you ensure that comparisons are between like character sets.

These examples have demonstrated the versatility of the `LEAST` function. They're revisited in the description of the `GREATEST` function.

NANVL Function

The NANVL function substitutes a default value when a BINARY_DOUBLE or BINARY_FLOAT is not a number (NaN). This allows trapping an operating system math library return value of NaN.

The prototype is

```
SQL> NANVL(evaluation_parameter, substitution_parameter)
```

The primary substitution value is 0, as illustrated in the following program:

```
SQL> DECLARE
       bad_number     BINARY_DOUBLE := 'NaN';
       default_number BINARY_DOUBLE := 0;
     BEGIN
       dbms_output.put_line(NANVL(bad_number,default_number));
     END;
     /
```

You can substitute a BINARY_FLOAT and it works the same way. This is a useful approach when performing math-intensive calculations.

NULLIF Function

The NULLIF function substitutes a null value when two actual parameters are found to be equal. This is equivalent to returning a null when two values match.

The prototype is

```
NULLIF(evaluation_parameter1, evaluation_parameter2)
```

The primary substitution value when two actual parameters are not found to be equal is the value of the first parameter to the NULLIF function, as illustrated in the following program:

```
SQL> DECLARE
       /* Returns a null */
       IF NULLIF(harry_potter,ron_weasley) IS NULL THEN
         dbms_output.put_line(
          'Same house? '||
          '['||NULLIF(harry_potter,ron_weasley)||']');
       END IF;
       /* Returns a string. */
       IF NULLIF(harry_potter,cedric_diggory) IS NOT NULL THEN
         dbms_output.put_line(
          'Different house? '||
          '['||NULLIF(harry_potter,cedric_diggory)||']');
       END IF;
     END;
     /
```

It prints

```
Same house? []

Different house? [Gryffindor]
```

The first IF statement calls the NULLIF function with two members of J.K. Rowling's Harry Potter series that share the same house. It returns a null because the house values are equal. The second IF statement returns the value of the first parameter because the houses differ, and it is checking whether the logical expression is not null. The is not null comparison lets you return a shared value from two variables. There are many opportunities to use this type of comparison, and now you know how to do it.

NVL Function

The NVL function substitutes a default value when the primary value is null. The prototype for the function is

```
NVL(evaluation_parameter, default_substitution_parameter)
```

The NVL function works well in conditional statements. It removes the possibility that comparison values are null. The following program demonstrates an NVL function:

```
SQL> DECLARE
       condition BOOLEAN;
     BEGIN
       IF NOT NVL(condition,FALSE) THEN
         dbms_output.put_line('It''s False!');
       END IF;
     END;
     /
```

The condition variable is not initialized and therefore is a null value. The conditional logic would fail if the NVL function was left out, because a null value is not true or false. The NVL function converts all null values to false, making the statement true and printing the result.

SYS_CONTEXT Function

The SYS_CONTEXT function returns information about the system environment or an environment you've established by using dbms_session.set_context. It replaces the USERENV legacy function and provides many more options using the USERENV context.

The prototype is

```
SYS_CONTEXT('context_namespace','parameter'[,'length'])
```

It raises an ORA-02003 exception when you submit an invalid parameter value, but only a null value if you submit a nonexistent context namespace. Table C-3 lists the valid parameters for the USERENV context, and Table C-4 lists the deprecated parameters for the same context. All calls to the SYS_CONTEXT function return a VARCHAR2 variable that has a default maximum length of 256 bytes. You can override the size of return strings by providing a valid integer value between 1 and 4,000

You call the SYS_CONTEXT function as follows:

```
SQL> BEGIN
       dbms_output.put_line(SYS_CONTEXT('USERENV','HOST'));
     END;
     /
```

It returns the server's hostname value as a 256-byte string.

Parameter	Return Value
ACTION	Identifies the position in the module. You use the dbms_application_info package to set the value.
AUDITED_CURSORID	Returns the cursor ID of the SQL statement that triggered an audit event. It is not a valid value when you're using fine-grain auditing, in which case it returns a null.
AUTHENTICATED_IDENTITY	Returns the authenticated identity in a format that differs by type of authentication, like Kerberos, SSL, password, OS, Radius, proxy, or SYSDBA/SYSOPER.
AUTHENTICATION_DATA	Contains the value used to authenticate the user, which may be an X.503 certificate.
AUTHENTICATION_METHOD	Returns the authenticated method, like Kerberos, SSL, password, OS, Radius, proxy, or background process.
BG_JOB_ID	Returns the current session identifier when established by a background database process.
CLIENT_IDENTIFIER	Returns an identifier set by calling the SET_IDENTIFIER procedure from the dbms_session package, the OCI_ATTR_CLIENT_IDENTIFIER attribute, or the setClientIdentifier method of the Java class Oracle.jdbc.OracleConnection.
CLIENT_INFO	Returns a 64-byte character string set by calling the SET_CLIENT_INFO procedure of the dbms_application_info package.
CURRENT_BIND	Returns bind variables or fine-grain auditing.
CURRENT_EDITION_NAME	Returns the edition in use by the current session.
CURRENT_EDITION_ID	Returns the identifier of the edition in use by the current session.
CURRENT_SCHEMA	Returns the current schema name, which you can change by calling the ALTER SESSION SET CURRENT_SCHEMA statement.
CURRENT_SCHEMAID	Returns the current schema identifier, which you can change by calling the ALTER SESSION SET CURRENT_SCHEMA statement.
CURRENT_SQL or CURRENT_SQL*n*	Returns the first 4KB of the current SQL statement that triggered fine-grain auditing. You use CURRENT_SQL*n* (where *n* is an integer) to get the next 4KB of the current SQL statement.
CURRENT_SQL_LENGTH	Returns the byte length of the SQL statement that triggered a fine-grain auditing event.
DB_DOMAIN	Returns the database initialization parameter of the same name when it is set.
DB_NAME	Returns the database initialization parameter of the same name when it is set.
DB_UNIQUE_NAME	Returns the database initialization parameter of the same name when it is set.

(continued)

TABLE C-3. *SYS_CONTEXT Predefined Parameters for the USERENV Namespace*

Parameter	Return Value
ENTRYID	Returns the current audit entry number. This sequence value is shared between regular and fine-grain auditing and cannot be used in distributed scope.
ENTERPRISE_IDENTITY	Returns the user's enterprise-wide identity, which is an OID value set as the DN value.
FG_JOB_ID	Returns the current session identifier when established by a foreground database process.
GLOBAL_CONTEXT_MEMORY	Returns the number being used in the SGA by the globally accessed context.
GLOBAL_UID	Returns the current session identifier when established by a background database process.
HOST	Returns the machine hostname value.
IDENTIFICATION_TYPE	Returns the method used to establish the current session, as follows: `LOCAL` when identified by password `EXTERNAL` when identified externally `GLOBAL SHARED` when identified globally `GLOBAL PRIVATE` when identified globally by *DN*
INSTANCE	Returns the identification number of the current instance.
INSTANCE_NAME	Returns the name of the current instance.
IP_ADDRESS	Returns the IP address for the server or virtual machine running the instance.
ISDBA	Returns true when the current user has DBA privileges and returns false when they do not.
LANG	Returns the ISO abbreviation for the language name.
LANGUAGE	Returns the language and territory currently in use and the character set separated by a period.
MODULE	Returns the application name set by the `SET_MODULE` procedure in the `dbms_application_info` package.
NETWORK_PROTOCOL	Returns network protocol value for a connection.
NLS_CALENDAR	Returns the current session's calendar.
NLS_CURRENCY	Returns the current session's currency.
NLS_DATE_FORMAT	Returns the current session's default date format.
NLS_DATE_LANGUAGE	Returns the current session's language for expressing dates.
NLS_SORT	Returns the current session's linguistic sort basis or the default `BINARY`.
NLS_TERRITORY	Returns the current session's territory.

TABLE C-3. *SYS_CONTEXT Predefined Parameters for the USERENV Namespace*

Parameter	Return Value
OS_USER	Returns the operating system user account that initiated the current database session.
POLICY_INVOKER	Returns the invoker of row-level security (RLS) policy function.
PROXY_ENTERPRISE_IDENTITY	Returns the Oracle Internet Directory *DN* when the proxy user is an enterprise user.
PROXY_GLOBAL_UID	Returns the global user identifier from the Oracle Internet Directory for Enterprise User Security (EUS) proxy users, or null for all other proxy users.
PROXY_USER	Returns the user name of the database user who opened the current session on behalf of the SESSION_USER.
PROXY_USERID	Returns the user identifier of the database user who opened the current session on behalf of the SESSION_USER.
SERVER_HOST	Returns the server hostname.
SERVICE_NAME	Returns the service hostname.
SESSION_EDITION_NAME	Returns the edition in use by the current session.
SESSION_EDITION_ID	Returns the edition identifier in use by the current session.
SESSION_USER	Returns the schema for Enterprise users, and the database user name by which the current session is authenticated.
SESSION_USERID	Returns the database user identifier by which the current session is authenticated.
SESSIONID	Returns the auditing session identifier.
SID	Returns the session number, which is different from the session identifier.
STATEMENTID	Returns the number of the SQL statement audited in a given session. This attribute cannot be used in distributed scope.
TERMINAL	Returns the server hostname.

TABLE C-3. *SYS_CONTEXT Predefined Parameters for the USERENV Namespace*

Parameter	Description
CURRENT_USER	Use the SESSION_USER parameter instead.
CURRENT_USERID	Use the SESSION_USERID parameter instead.
EXTERNAL_NAME	This parameter returned the name of the external user. You should use the AUTHENTICATED_IDENTITY or ENTERPRISE_IDENTITY parameter in lieu of EXTERNAL_NAME because they return superior information about the external user.

TABLE C-4. *SYS_CONTEXT Deprecated Parameters for the USERENV Namespace*

This section has demonstrated the SYS_CONTEXT function, which replaces the legacy USERENV function.

TABLE Function

The TABLE function lets you disassemble collections and object types into SQL result sets made up of rows of columns. The simplest example disassembles an ADT (Attribute Data Type) collection, which is a collection of a scalar data type, like a variable-length string (VARCHAR2).

The example presented next uses the street_list collection, qualified in the "Nested Table Updates" section of Appendix B. It is an unbounded list of values, and that makes it a list rather than an array because arrays are bound at runtime. The street_list data type is composed of a set of single variable-length strings, and the underlying data type is a list of VARCHAR2 variables.

A street_list column or PL/SQL variable would display as a collapsed object. Collapsed objects display the name of the object type, also known as the constructor function name, and a parameter list of call parameters to instantiate an instance of the object.

NOTE
You instantiate any object type in Oracle by calling it with the TREAT function from SQL or PL/SQL.

A simple query like the following would display information:

```
SQL> SELECT street_list('4000 Warner Blvd','Suite 701') AS list
  2  FROM   dual;
```

It displays

```
LIST
----------------------------------------------
STREET_LIST('4000 Warner Blvd', 'Suite 701')
```

Displaying information more meaningfully requires knowing how to pull the information out of the collection. The following query uses the TABLE function to do just that; it disassemble a collection of street address values:

```
SQL> SELECT *
  2  FROM   TABLE(street_list('4000 Warner Blvd','Suite 701'));
```

This query displays

```
COLUMN_VALUE
------------------
4000 Warner Blvd
Suite 701
```

Effectively, the TABLE function pivots the member elements of the ADT collections to rows in a result set. The column display COLUMN_VALUE is a hidden column that exists for all ADTs, or collections of scalar data types.

The TABLE function also decomposes a collapsed object into columns of data. The database stores a persistent address_type object type as a collapsed object. We can mimic querying 1 from a table by using the pseudo-table dual, like

```
SQL> SELECT address_type( 1
  2                     , NULL
  3                     ,'Phoenix'
  4                     ,'AZ'
  5                     ,'85087') AS home_address
  6  FROM   dual;
```

Line 2 uses a null in lieu of a nested street_list table to simplify how the TABLE function shows us a single-level object. (Another sample with a nested street_list column value is provided a bit later.) Line 5 assigns an alias for our address_type UDT name, and by using an alias we get the equivalent of what we would see if the alias were a column name for the object type.

The query returns the following:

```
ADDRESS_TYPE(ADDRESS_ID, STREET_ADDRESS, CITY, STATE, POSTAL_CODE)
------------------------------------------------------------------
ADDRESS_TYPE(1, NULL, 'Phoenix', 'AZ', '85087')
```

The TABLE function can't return a single UDT element because the TABLE function works only with collections. For example, the following attempt to query an address_type object type by itself:

```
SQL> SELECT OBJECT_VALUE
     FROM   TABLE(SELECT address_type( 1
                                     , NULL
                                     ,'Phoenix'
                                     ,'AZ'
                                     ,'85087')
                  FROM   dual);
```

fails with this message because the object isn't nested in a collection:

```
FROM   TABLE(SELECT address_type( 1
             *
ERROR at line 2:
ORA-22905: cannot access rows from a non-nested table item
```

The street_list ADT holds collections of our address_type UDT, and you can find the definition and discussion in the "Nested Table Updates" section of Appendix B. Let's refactor our prior example by nesting it within a street_list collection:

```
SQL> SELECT OBJECT_VALUE
     FROM   TABLE(
              address_list(
                address_type( 1
                            , NULL
                            ,'Phoenix'
                            ,'AZ'
                            ,'85087')));
```

This works because line 3 encloses the `address_type` UDT in an ADT collection. Collections generally have more than one element, but a collection can be a null collection, as shown next, or have only one element:

```
OBJECT_VALUE(ADDRESS_ID, STREET_ADDRESS, CITY, STATE, POSTAL_CODE)
------------------------------------------------------------------
ADDRESS_TYPE(1, NULL, 'Phoenix', 'AZ', '85087')
```

Line 1 sets the return type in the `SELECT` list as the hidden `object_value` column. The hidden `object_value` column holds a collapsed object type for each row found in the collection. Alternatively, you can return an implicit set of columns with the asterisk (`*`), or you can return an explicit set of columns by providing them in the `SELECT` list clause, like

```
SQL> SELECT address_id
  2  ,      city
  3  ,      state
  4  ,      postal_code
  5  FROM   TABLE(
  6           address_list(
  7             address_type( 1
  8                         , NULL
  9                         ,'Phoenix'
 10                         ,'AZ'
 11                         ,'85087')));
```

It explodes the parameter list from the collapsed object type into ordinary columns:

```
ADDRESS_ID CITY       ST POSTAL_CODE
---------- ---------- -- -----------
         1 Phoenix    AZ 85087
```

The implicit or explicit `SELECT` list of column values can't be passed as a call parameter to PL/SQL function, procedure, and object type methods, but a collection of objects can be passed as a call parameter to other PL/SQL subroutines. The column result set from a `SELECT` list can't be passed to another PL/SQL subroutine, and you need to know which columns are qualified in the `SELECT` list before you can format them.

TIP
The hidden `object_value` column is the only way to return a collection of object types.

Oracle lets you unnest queries whether the table is the implementation of an object type or a combination of scalar and object type columns. Appendix B contains an "Unnesting Queries" section that explains and demonstrates how you unnest queries by using a cross join and the `TABLE` function.

TREAT Function

The `TREAT` function lets you bring to life persistent object types. That is, the `TREAT` function lets you instantiate (wake up and place into memory) the collapsed object types stored in columns of tables. The following example leverages object types and bodies defined in Chapter 11, but for your convenience they are repeated here. You create a `map_comp` object type with the following syntax:

```
SQL> CREATE OR REPLACE TYPE map_comp IS OBJECT
( who VARCHAR2(20)
, CONSTRUCTOR FUNCTION map_comp
  (who VARCHAR2) RETURN SELF AS RESULT
, MAP MEMBER FUNCTION equals RETURN VARCHAR2 )
INSTANTIABLE NOT FINAL;
/
```

There's a lot packed into those six lines; please refer to the section "Comparing with the MAP Member Function" in Chapter 11 for the full explanation. Object types are like package specifications (covered in Chapter 9), and object bodies are like package bodies—they contain the code implementation of the object type.

You create a `map_comp` object body with the following syntax:

```
SQL> CREATE OR REPLACE TYPE BODY map_comp IS
  CONSTRUCTOR FUNCTION map_comp
  (who VARCHAR2) RETURN SELF AS RESULT IS
  BEGIN
    self.who := who;
    RETURN;
  END map_comp;
  MAP MEMBER FUNCTION equals RETURN VARCHAR2 IS
  BEGIN
    RETURN self.who;
  END equals;
END;
/
```

The object type's body has a number of advanced elements, please check the equivalent code and explanation in "Comparing with the MAP Member Function" section of Chapter 11.

Having shown you how to define and implement the object type, the balance of this section helps you understand how to read your stored objects from the database. It's also handy to remind you at this point that objects aren't stored in memory but rather are stored as collapsed objects. A collapsed object stores the name of the object's constructor and a list of call parameters. Object types are *transient* when they're in your code modules and *persistent* when they're defined in tables. Please refer back to the "Trick-or-Treating with Persistent Object Types" sidebar in Chapter 11 for a complete example of working with persistent object types.

The `TREAT` function works with object types or subclasses of object types, as explained in the section "Inheritance and Polymorphism" in Chapter 11.

USERENV Function

The `USERENV` function returns information about the system environment. It is a legacy function replaced by the `SYS_CONTEXT` function covered earlier in this section. Table C-5 lists the available parameters that you can call by using the `USERENV` function.

Parameter	Return type	Description of Return Value
CLIENT_INFO	VARCHAR2	The CLIENT_INFO parameter returns a string up to 64 bytes long. It contains one or more values set by using the built-in dbms_application_info package. You should note that this context column is used by third-party applications.
ENTRYID	NUMBER	The ENTRYID parameter is a sequence value shared between both regular and fine-grain audit records. You cannot use this attribute in distributed queries.
ISDBA	VARCHAR2	The ISDBA parameter returns an uppercase true or false based on whether the current user has DBA privileges.
LANG	VARCHAR2	The LANG parameter returns an uppercase string for the ISO language abbreviation.
LANGUAGE	VARCHAR2	The LANGUAGE parameter returns an uppercase string containing the language and territory, a dot, and the character set for the database. Here's an example of the output: AMERICAN_AMERICA.AL32UTF8
SESSIONID	NUMBER	The SESSIONID parameter returns the auditing session identifier and cannot be used in distributed transactions.
TERMINAL	VARCHAR2	The TERMINAL parameter returns the operating system identifier for the terminal running the current session. If you use it in a distributed environment SELECT statement, it returns the identifier for the local transaction. The parameter cannot be used by distributed INSERT, UPDATE, or DELETE statements.

TABLE C-5. *USERENV Function Parameters*

While you can use the USERENV function in SQL statements, the following demonstrates using the USERENV function in a PL/SQL block:

```
SQL> BEGIN
  2    dbms_output.put_line(USERENV('TERMINAL'));
  3  END;
  4  /
```

It prints the hostname for the machine, like

```
MCLAUGHLIN-DEV
```

The following sets the V$SESSION view CLIENT_INFO column:

```
SQL> CALL dbms_application_info.set_client_info('Restricted');
```

You can query the contents by using the USERENV function, and it returns the case-sensitive word Restricted. It is demonstrated in the following block:

```
SQL> BEGIN
       dbms_output.put_line(USERENV('CLIENT_INFO'));
     END;
     /
```

This section has shown you how to use the USERENV function. It is a legacy function that appears in Oracle Applications code and other third-party applications, but you should use the new SYS_CONTEXT function in your own code. SYS_CONTEXT provides you access to more information.

VSIZE Function

The VSIZE function examines the real length of registered data types, like the DUMP function. It returns a value that is independent of the database or session character set. You can use the VSIZE function only inside a SQL statement.

The following block demonstrates how to find the real size of a LONG RAW variable:

```
SQL> DECLARE
       buffer LONG RAW := HEXTORAW('42'||'41'||'44');
       detail VARCHAR2(100);
     BEGIN
       SELECT VSIZE(buffer) INTO detail FROM dual;
       dbms_output.put_line(detail);
     END;
     /
```

It prints the length of the data value:

```
3
```

You may not use this function too often, but when you're trying to figure out why something is broken and the error message and web hits are limited, it may be very helpful. It certainly helps when working with the dbms_lob package and raw streams, as covered in the EMPTY_BLOB function section.

Summary

This appendix has reviewed the key SQL built-in functions used throughout the book. It isn't exhaustive, and you're encouraged to explore Oracle's online documentation.

APPENDIX D

PL/SQL Built-in Packages and Types

Oracle's PL/SQL built-in packages and types are a treasure trove of premade programs, ready for you to use. I could fill volumes with example programs of how to take advantage of this rich feature set; instead, I encourage you to study the programs provided by Oracle in the *Oracle Database PL/SQL Packages and Types Reference 12c Release*. Doing so *will* save you hundreds of hours that you would otherwise spend attempting to create and maintain similar programs on your own. What's more, they are free to use when you license Oracle Database 12*c*. Imagine that…a free set of programs that helps you become more efficient and do your job more effectively, one that is constantly being improved and has Oracle's commitment to excellence—and its track record of *not* deprecating/removing them with every new release. One could only hope for that kind of service from other software vendors.

Oracle Database 11*g* and 12*c* New Packages

Oracle Database 11*g* introduced 90 packages and 4 types. Oracle increased this count substantially in Oracle Database 12*c*. I performed the following query against typical sandbox instances, comparing versions 11.2.0.3 and 12.0.0.1:

```
SQL> WITH count_pt AS
     (
     SELECT    do.owner
     ,         do.object_type
     ,         COUNT(*) AS Total
     FROM      dba_objects do
     WHERE     do.object_type in ('PACKAGE', 'TYPE')
     AND       do.owner not IN
                ( 'ADMJMH', 'FMIQ', 'HR'
                , 'OE', 'PM', 'ORACLE_OCM', 'IX' )
     GROUP BY do.owner
     ,         do.object_type )
     SELECT    *
     FROM      count_pt
     PIVOT    (MAX(total) AS GT
               FOR (do.object_type) IN
                 ( 'PACKAGE' AS packages, 'TYPE' AS types ))
     ORDER BY owner;
```

The results, summarized in Table D-1, are very interesting. For one, it appears that Oracle moved its Database Vault (`DVF` and `DVSYS`) product inside a typical release. It also moved its Label Security products inside. I see this as a strategic move on Oracle's part to secure its database technology.

Notice that Oracle Database 12*c* has an additional 194 packages and 286 types compared to 11*g*. Also note that there appears to be some movement of programs from one schema to the other, as represented by the negative deltas in the `DBSNMP`, `MDMSYS`, and `OLAPSYS` schemas.

11*g* Owner	Packages	Types	12*c* Owner	Packages	Types	Package Changes	Type Changes
APEX_030200	189	4	APEX_040200	263	6	74	2
CTXSYS	74	35	CTXSYS	77	32	3	–3
DBSNMP	4	8	DBSNMP	3	8	–1	0
			DVF	1		1	0
			DVSYS	36	30	36	30
EXFSYS	18	30	EXFSYS	18	30	0	0
			GSMADMIN_ INTERNAL	6	10	6	10
			LBACSYS	23	9	23	9
MDSYS	70	207	MDSYS	78	189	8	–18
OLAPSYS	45	7	OLAPSYS		2	–45	–5
ORDPLUGINS	5		ORDPLUGINS	5		0	0
ORDSYS	28	446	ORDSYS	30	446	2	0
SYS	633	1347	SYS	711	1618	78	271
SYSTEM	1	1	SYSTEM	1	1	0	0
WMSYS	22	18	WMSYS	23	15	1	–3
XDB	35	97	XDB	43	90	8	–7
	1124	**2200**		**1318**	**2486**	**194**	**286**

TABLE D-1. *Comparison of 11g and 12c Packages*

Bear in mind, these two test instances do not represent all of Oracle's offerings, and there are some product packages not loaded by default. They do, however, represent typical database installations with sample schemas. It would behoove you to take a close look at these packages. Carefully test them for vulnerabilities. You know your black-hat counterparts will. In fact, they will strive to exploit every vulnerability.

Notice that our sample database contains 1,318 packages and 2,486 types. Instead of boring you with the details of 3,804 objects, the following eight tables list only those packages and types that are documented in the *Database PL/SQL Packages and Types Reference 12*c *Release*. Each of the tables lists the name of the object, the technology affected, and if the object has been newly introduced or updated in Oracle Database 12*c*. An ellipsis following a name in the Package/Type column indicates there are several packages in a set of product packages.

Package	Technology	New	Update
DBMS_ADVANCED_REWRITE	Query rewrite		
DBMS_AW_STATS	OLAP statistics generation	X	
DBMS_CUBE	OLAP cube creation/management	X	
DBMS_CUBE_ADVISE	OLAP cube performance	X	
DBMS_DATA_MINING	Data Mining/Warehousing		X
DBMS_DATA_MINING_TRANSFORM	Data Mining/Warehousing Transformation		X
DBMS_DIMENSION	Validation of data dimensional relationships		
DBMS_LOGMNR...	LogMiner packages		
DBMS_MVIEW	Management of materialized views		X
DBMS_PREDICTIVE_ANALYTICS	Data mining prediction		X
DBMS_TRANSFORM	Interface to the Message Format Transformation		

TABLE D-2. *Data Warehousing Packages*

Table D-2 presents the first set of built-in objects, which are those related to data warehousing. You may have already used them if your job requires you to work with materialized views, ETL (extract, transform, and load), or data mining.

PL/SQL developers use the set of objects in Table D-3 to aid them in debugging, profiling, and error stack formatting. Commonly used packages are `dbms_output` and `dbms_pipe`.

Package	Technology	New	Update
DBMS_DEBUG	PL/SQL Debugger		
DEBUG_EXTPROC	Debug of external procedures		
DBMS_ERRLOG	Error logging for DML operations		
DBMS_HPROF	PL/SQL profiling	X	
DBMS_OUTPUT	Print output to screen		
DBMS_PIPE	Push messages to other sessions		
DBMS_PREPROCESSOR	Print/retrieve source of PL/SQL units		
DBMS_WARNING	PL/SQL error stack manipulation		
UTL_LMS	Format of error messages in different languages		

TABLE D-3. *Debug-Related Packages*

Package	Technology	New	Update
DBMS_AUTO_TASK_ADMIN	AUTOTASK controls	X	
DBMS_JOB	Job management		
DBMS_SCHEDULER	Job management		X

TABLE D-4. *Job Management Packages*

Oracle built the packages in Table D-4 to manage job control. You should be very familiar with them if your job includes database administration.

Table D-5 presents the security-related packages. You should know and use `dbms_assert` to validate input passed into procedures and functions. Hackers write *fuzzing* programs to determine which procedures and functions are vulnerable to SQL injection. In addition, you can greatly streamline your auditing efforts with `dbms_fga`.

Database professionals use Oracle Streams for data replication and warehouse loading. The feature set presented in Table D-6 is similar to that offered in other third-party ETL tools, with the exception that Oracle built *Streams* to interface directly with its RDBMS, which affords it extra performance benefits such as hot mining of redo logs to reduce latency.

The packages in Table D-7 help you to diagnose performance problems with your SQL and PL/SQL code.

Table D-8 lists all of the utility objects that Oracle documents in the *Database PL/SQL Packages and Types Reference 12*c *Release*. It is the largest grouping by far; however, a general understanding of these packages is essential, so it's worth your time to study it.

Package	Technology	New	Update
DBMS_ASSERT	Parameter input validation		
DBMS_DISTRIBUTED_TRUST_ADMIN	Management of Trusted Database List		
DBMS_FGA	Fine-grain auditing		

TABLE D-5. *Security-Related Packages*

Package	Technology	New	Update
DBMS_APPLY_ADM	Oracle Streams		X
DBMS_AQ...	Oracle Streams Advance Queuing		X
DBMS_CAPTURE_ADM	Oracle Streams Capture Processes		X
DBMS_FILE_GROUP	Management of file groups/versions		
DBMS_PROPAGATION_ADM	Management of Streams propagation		X
DBMS_STREAMS...	Management of Streams interfaces		X
UTL_SPADV	Oracle Streams statistical analyses		X

TABLE D-6. *Oracle Streams–Related Packages*

Package	Technology	New	UPD
DBMS_ADVISOR	Performance diagnostics		X
DBMS_IOT	Management of Index Organized Tables		
DBMS_MONITOR	Tracing and statistics gathering		
DBMS_OUTLN...	Management of stored outlines		X
DBMS_PCLXUTIL	Creation of partition-aware indexes		
DBMS_PROFILER	Profile interface for PL/SQL programs		
DBMS_RESOURCE_MANAGER...	Consumer group resource planning		X
DBMS_SPM	SQL Plan Management	X	
DBMS_SQLDIAG	SQL Diagnostics		
DBMS_SQLPA	SQL Performance Analyzer		
DBMS_SQLTUNE	SQL Tuning interface		X
DBMS_STATS...	View and manage performance statistics		X
DBMS_WORKLOAD...	Gathering of workload statistics	X	X

TABLE D-7. *Performance Packages*

Package	Technology	New	Update
APEX_CUSTOM_AUTH	Apex authentication	X	
APEX_APPLICATION	Apex application support	X	
CTX...	Oracle Text Analytics		
DBMS_ADDM	Automatic Diagnostic Monitor	X	
DBMS_AQIN	Secure access to Oracle JMS		
DMBS_ALERT	Programmatic notification of database events		
DBMS_APPLICATION_INFO	Code instrumentation and tracing		
DBMS_DG	Oracle Data Guard event notification	X	
DBMS_CDC_	Change Data Capture		X
DBMS_COMPARISON	Comparison and convergence of data objects	X	
DBMS_CRYPTO	Encryption		
DBMS_CONNECTION_POOL	Management of Database Resident Connection Pools	X	
DBMS_CQ_NOTIFICATION	Provides alerts to clients on DML or DDL modification		X
DBMS_DATAPUMP	Moving all or part of a database		X
DBMS_DB_VERSION	Determines RDBMS release		
DBMS_DDL	Returns DDL information about stored procedures		
DBMS_DESCRIBE	Returns information about stored procedures		
DBMS_DEFER...	Defers remote transactions		
DBMS_EPG	PL/SQL execution via HTTP		
DBMS_FILE_TRANSFER	Moving binary files between databases		
DBMS_FLASHBACK	Rolls back DML/DDL		X
DBMS_HM	Database Health Check	X	
DBMS_HS_PARALLEL	Heterogeneous Parallel Processing	X	
DBMS_HS_PASSTHROUGH	Pass-through processing to non-Oracle systems		X
DBMS_JAVA	Database functionality to Java		
DBMS_LDAP...	LDAP Query		
DBMS_LIBCACHE	Remote extraction of PL/SQL and SQL		
DBMS_LOB	Management of LOBs		X
DBMS_LOCK	Management of locks		

(continued)

TABLE D-8. *Utility Packages*

Package	Technology	New	Update
DBMS_METADATA	Data dictionary to XML metadata or creation		
DBMS_MGD_ID_UTL	Sets/gets: logging level, proxy, metadata	X	
DBMS_MGW...	Oracle Messaging Gateway services		X
DBMS_OBFUSCATION_TOOLKIT	Encryption		
DBMS_OFFLINE_OG	Advanced replication		
DBMS_RANDOM	Random data generation		
DBMS_RECTIFIER_DIFF	Detect and rectify data differences between replicated sites		
DBMS_REFRESH	Management of materialized view refresh groups		
DBMS_REPAIR	Detect and repair corrupt data blocks		
DBMS_REPCAT	Management of symmetric replication users/templates		
DBMS_REPUTIL	Management of shadow tables		
DBMS_RESULT_CACHE	Partial management of shared pool cache	X	
DBMS_RESUMABLE	Suspend/time out large running programs		
DBMS_RLMGR	Rules Manager API		X
DBMS_RLS	Fine-grain access control for virtual private databases		
DBMS_ROWID	Management of ROWID, including creation and retrieval		
DBMS_RULE...	Rules Manager API		X
DBMS_SERVER_ALERT	Alerts the DBA when thresholds of the DB server are met		X
DBMS_SERVICE	Management of DB services		
DBMS_SESSION	Alter session programmatically		X
DBMS_SHARED_POOL	Management of the shared pool memory space		
DBMS_SPACE...	Analysis of segment growth		X
DBMS_SQL	Dynamic PL/SQL and types		X
DBMS_STORAGE_MAP	Communication with FMON		
DBMS_TDB	RMAN Transportable Diagnostics for moving DBs		
DBMS_TRACE	Tracing and statistics gathering		X

TABLE D-8. *Utility Packages*

Package	Technology	New	Update
DBMS_TRANSACTION	Management interface to SQL transactions		
DBMS_TTS	Transportable tablespace management		
DBMS_TYPES	Built-in constants and types		
DBMS_UTILITY	Various utilities		X
DBMS_WM	Interface to the Oracle Database Workspace Manager		
DBMS_XA	Interface to the XA/Open interface	X	
HTF	Hypertext functions and procedures		
HTP	Hypertext functions and procedures		
ORD...	Management of Digital Imaging and Communications in Medicine (DICOM)		
OWA...	PL/SQL web applications		
SDO...	Spatial/mapping	X	
SEM...	Resource Description Framework and Web Ontology Language interface	X	
UTL_COLL	Determines whether or not collection items are locators		
UTL_COMPRESS	Data compression		
UTL_DBWS	Database web services		
UTL_ENCODE	Conversion of RAW to standard data		
UTL_FILE	Writing to OS files		
UTL_HTTP	Access to the Internet within PL/SQL		
UTL_I18N	Globalization support within PL/SQL		
UTL_INADDR	Internet addressing utilities		X
UTL_MAIL	E-mail utility		
UTL_NLA	Statistical analysis within varrays		
UTL_RAW	Raw data type manipulation		
UTL_RECOMP	Recompilation of invalid DB objects		X
UTL_REF	Support of reference-based operations and generic type methods		
UTL_SMTP	E-mail utility		X
UTL_TCP	TCP/IP utilities		X
UTL_URL	URL address character management		
WPG_DOCLOAD	Interface for downloading BLOBs and BFILEs		

TABLE D-8. *Utility Packages*

Package	Technology	New	UPD
`DBMS_CSX_ADMIN`	Moving XML tablespaces	X	
`DBMS_RESCONFIG`	XML listener configuration	X	
`DBMS_XDB...`	XML access control list and user management	X	X
`DBMS_XEVENT`	XML event management	X	
`DBMS_XML...`	XML object management and manipulation	X	X

TABLE D-9. *XML Packages*

Table D-9 represents Oracle efforts to support XML databases. Oracle is committed to providing XML functionality to its users.

Overall, Oracle provides an extensive built-in library of code to support its developer community. The features of this library, along with SQL functions, enable you to accomplish more with less code.

Examples of Package Use

The examples presented in this section demonstrate the use of four important built-in packages. The examples show how you can take advantage of Oracle's built-in packages and types, and should also help you to simplify your code. I introduce each of the following packages briefly and then show you how to use one aspect of it. The space limitations of this appendix make covering each built-in package in detail prohibitive—that would require a few thousand pages.

- `DBMS_APPLICATION_INFO`
- `DBMS_COMPARISON`
- `DBMS_CRYPTO`
- `DBMS_FGA`

DBMS_APPLICATION_INFO Example

Have you ever wanted to check the status of your program during a long-running process? There are several ways to find out a program's status, none of which is more efficient than using the `dbms_application_info` package. In fact, one of the most common methods of watching a long-running process is to place `COMMIT` statements inside loops.

I have one thing to say about using this method: never, ever do it. If you're using it now, stop doing so. I can think of nothing that will slow down your database more than superfluous commits at every row.

The following block creates a large table we can use to test various methods of progress sampling:

```
SQL> CREATE TABLE mongo_item AS
       SELECT   rownum item_id
       ,        item_barcode||'#'||rownum item_barcode
       ,        item_title
       ,        item_subtitle
```

```
  ,         item_desc
  FROM      item CROSS JOIN
           (SELECT * FROM dual CONNECT BY LEVEL <= 100000 );
```

Wow! That's 9,300,000 rows in 24.48 seconds. And this was done on older hardware that I scrounged up for my sandbox environment. Mind you, it is hardware that most of us would have thought unobtainable if asked five years ago, but nonetheless it is old. To date, I have never found a faster way of moving or modifying data than to use the `CREATE TABLE AS` (`CTAS`) method. I was lucky enough to have the opportunity last year to test these theories on an Exadata X-2 and on Fusion-IO cards. Using `CTAS` and the `dbms_scheduler` package, I pushed 13,000,000 rows/second on the X-2 and around 7 Gbps on the latest Fusion-IO hardware.

With these numbers in mind, the following example shows the bad practice of placing a `COMMIT` statement inside a loop. The following block updates 9,300,000 rows, issuing a commit every row:

```
SQL> DECLARE
       CURSOR c IS
         SELECT * FROM mongo_item;
     BEGIN
       FOR i IN c LOOP
         UPDATE mongo_item
         SET    item_desc = 'This is the slowest and nastiest thing you '
                          ||'can do to your database... just don''t do it.'
         WHERE CURRENT OF c;
         COMMIT;
       END LOOP;
     END;
     /
```

The interesting thing to note about this block is that it consumes vast amounts of CPU cycles while doing something that the `CTAS` method completes in less than 30 seconds. I took a screenshot of the *System-Gnome-Monitor* for you (see Figure D-1) to show you how much CPU this statement uses.

As you can see, this is a nasty bit of code. I see it as something like a life-sucking leach, but instead of sucking the life out of you, it sucks the life out of your database. As I mentioned, if you're doing this type of thing, you should stop!

I waited an excruciating 29 minutes and 23 seconds for the job to complete. Instead of completing 379,902 rows per second, like the `CTAS` method did, this block completed the operation at a rate of only 5,275 rows per second. It also chewed up three CPU cores for the duration of its runtime.

The next best method, other than `CTAS`, would be to update the table in bulk. We can view its progress during the update by using the `set_session_longops` procedure of the `dbms_application_info` package, like so:

```
SQL> DECLARE
       /* Declare an associative array indexed by an integer. */
       TYPE udt_rowid IS TABLE OF rowid INDEX BY PLS_INTEGER;

       /* Declare local variables. */
       lv_rowid      UDT_ROWID;
```

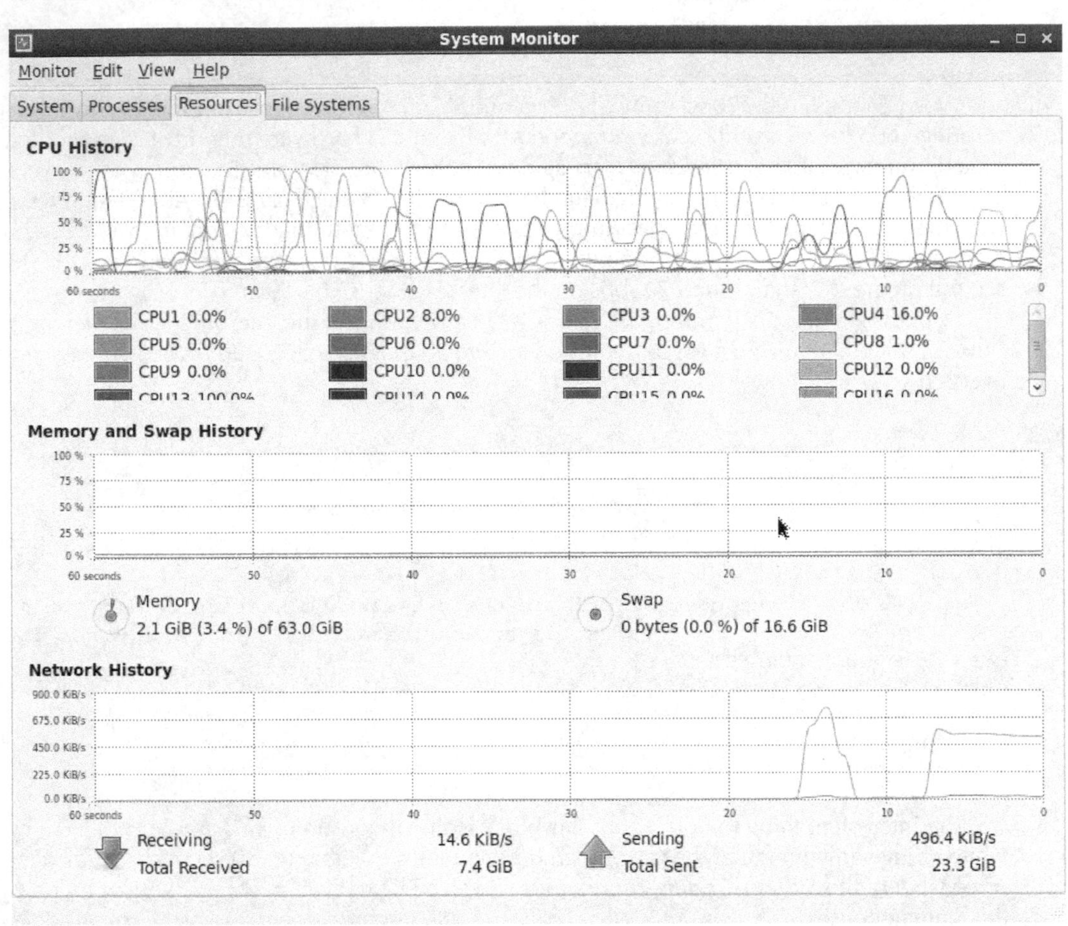

FIGURE D-1. *Slow-motion update*

```
  lv_rindex      BINARY_INTEGER;
  lv_slno        BINARY_INTEGER;
  lv_obj         BINARY_INTEGER;
  lv_totalwork   INTEGER;
  lv_sofar       INTEGER;

  /* Declare a cursor against a table. */
  CURSOR c IS
    SELECT ROWID rid
    FROM   mongo_item;
```

```
17 BEGIN
18   /* Initialize variables. */
19   lv_rindex    := dbms_application_info.set_session_longops_nohint;
20   lv_sofar     := 0;
21   lv_totalwork := 9300000;
22
23   /* Set module value. */
24   dbms_application_info.set_module(
25       module_name => 'ANONYMOUS Block'
26     , action_name => 'Update MONGO_ITEM.ITEM_DESC');
27
28   /* Open a cursor and fetch results. */
29   OPEN c;
30     LOOP
31       FETCH c BULK COLLECT INTO lv_rowid LIMIT 1000;
32
33       FORALL i IN 1..lv_rowid.COUNT
34         UPDATE mongo_item
35         SET    item_desc = 'Ah! This is much better.'
36         WHERE  rowid = lv_rowid(i);
37
38         lv_sofar := lv_sofar + 1000;
39
40         dbms_application_info.set_session_longops(
41           lv_rindex
42         , lv_slno
43         ,'updating rows'
44         , lv_obj
45         , 0
46         , lv_sofar
47         , lv_totalwork
48         ,'MONGO_ITEM'
49         ,'rows');
50
51         EXIT WHEN c%NOTFOUND;
52       END LOOP;
53       CLOSE c;  -- Release the cursor resource.
54       COMMIT;
55     END;
56 /
```

The `set_session_longops` procedure of the `dbms_application_info` package requires the variables from lines 4 through 8. They are input parameters and can't be omitted. We set several of these variables outside the bulk collect operation because they only need to be set once. Those set before the bulk collect are on lines 13 through 21. We also change the `lv_sofar` variable to properly alert the `set_session_longops` procedure of the `dbms_application_info` package. Notice that you should increase this variable at the same rate as you do the `LIMIT` clause.

Watching the progress of your query is easy. Just run the following query:

```
SQL> SELECT   opname
  ,        target_desc
  ,        sofar
  ,        totalwork
  ,        elapsed_seconds
  ,        message
  FROM     v$session_longops
  WHERE    target_desc = 'MONGO_ITEM';
```

It displays the following results:

```
OPNAME        TARGET_DESC SOFAR   TOTALWORK ELAPSED_SECONDS
------------- ----------- ------- --------- ---------------
updating rows MONGO_ITEM  9226000   9300000             551
```

The message portion of the results would wrap given the formatting of the book, so it's shown next on its own line:

```
MESSAGE
--------------------------------------------------------------------
updating rows: MONGO_ITEM 4173473632: 9226000 out of 9300000 rows done
```

Change the size of the `LIMIT` clause to determine the amount of work fetched per cycle. In this case, I tried several values, ranging from hundreds to tens of thousands, and found that very large and small sizes can be problematic. Also, notice in Figure D-2 that CPU usage is much more predictable.

I've provided this example not only to show how to use `set_session_longops` procedure of the `dbms_application_info` package but also to reiterate that a simple `MERGE` or `CTAS` will greatly outperform bulk collect methods. Moreover, I wish to restate that performing updates of this fashion serially (row by row) with commits inside the loop is just bad practice.

On the other hand, the following SQL statement completes the entire operation in 6.82 seconds:

```
SQL> CREATE TABLE new_mongo_item AS
    SELECT   item_id
    ,        item_barcode
    ,        item_title
    ,        item_subtitle
    ,       'This is the fastest method yet.' item_desc
    FROM     mongo_item;
```

Once completed, you merely need to issue a set of `rename` and `drop` commands, and your new `mongo_item` table is fully modified. What's more, the 6.82-second update happens to a secondary table, which does not affect online queries. Lastly, notice the overall CPU usage, as shown in Figure D-3.

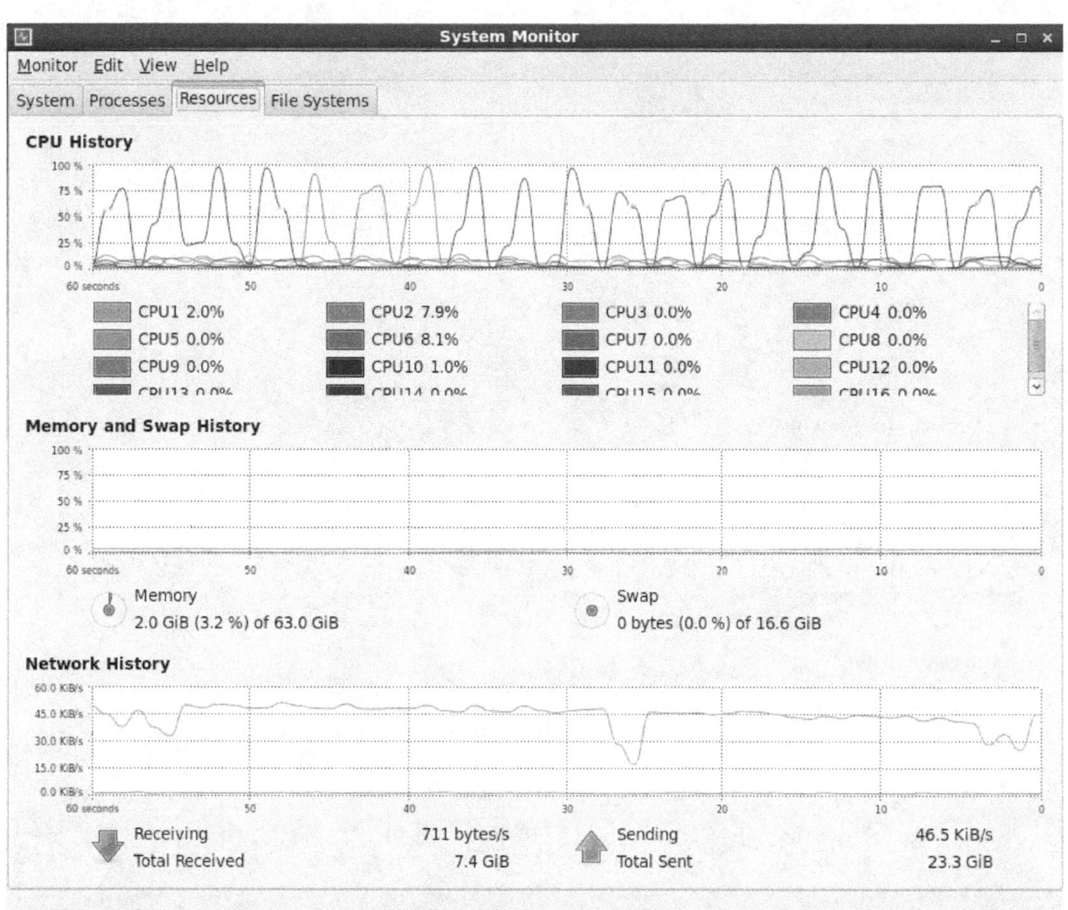

FIGURE D-2. *Bulk update*

There will be times when `CTAS` or `MERGE` statements won't fit your needs. When these cases come up, I suggest that you use bulk operations and `dbms_session_longops` instead of committing inside loops.

DBMS_COMPARISON

The following example demonstrates the power of `dbms_comparison`. Oracle wrote it with the intention of synchronizing shared tables that exist in distributed database systems.

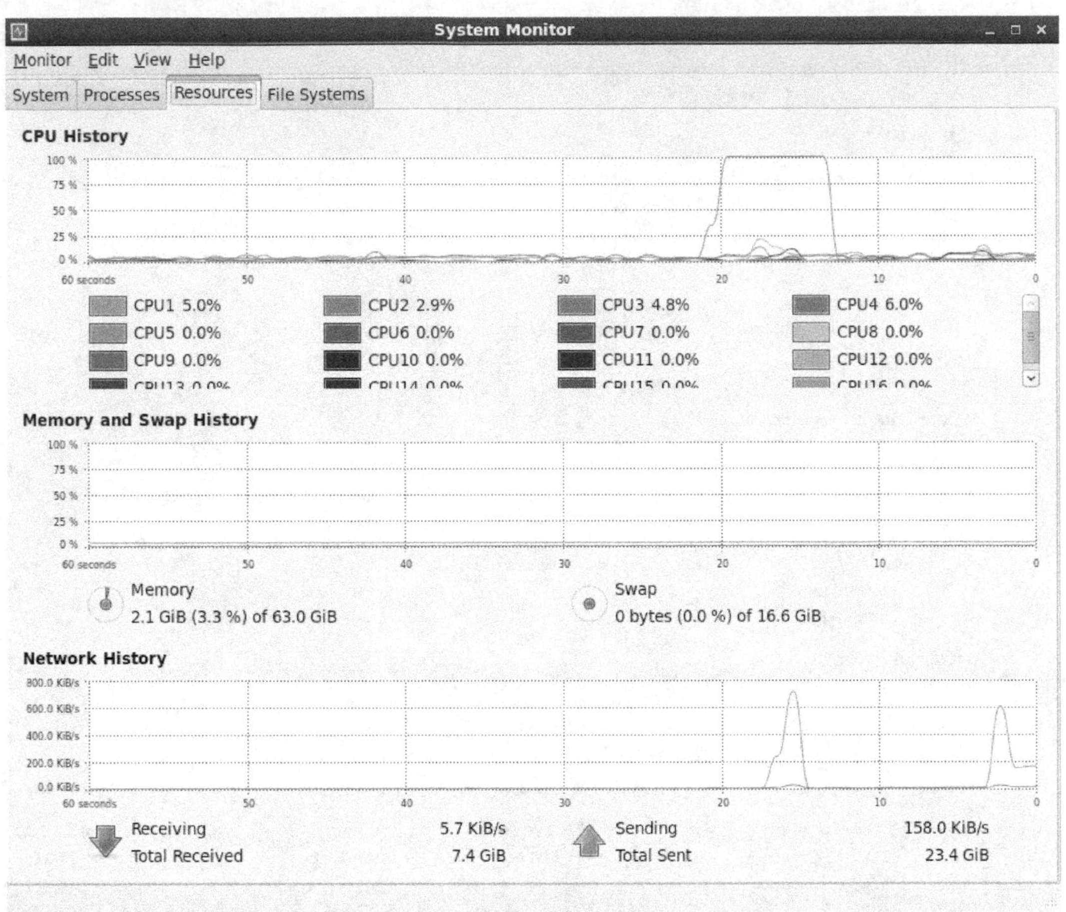

FIGURE D-3. *Updating via CTAS*

Briefing on Database Links

Database links have been around a while. They provide you with a unique ability to query remote databases as if they were internal to the database you are working on. If you have multiple Oracle databases within your intranet, database links can join them all together and make them appear as one.

A database link is nothing more than a stored SQL*Net connection. In fact, the Oracle instance issues a connection to a remote database just like you would through your SQL*Plus client, but it is completely transparent to you or your application.

Creating a database link is easy. You can do so statically or dynamically. Static connections store the connection credentials, while dynamic connections pass a token related to the user to the remote database based on the session user. Using dynamic linking is recommended because it is much more secure.

To create a link, you must have a connection defined in your `tnsnames.ora` file. For purposes of the following example, I simply copied the link that was in the `tnsnames.ora` file and renamed it. I did so to simulate a connection to a secondary database instead of spinning another instance. Even though the link is to itself, the Oracle database views it as a remote connection (as qualified in "Starting and Stopping the Oracle Database 12*c* Server" section of Appendix A):

```
VIDEO =
  (DESCRIPTION =
    (ADDRESS = (PROTOCOL = TCP)(HOST = mclaughlin12c)(PORT = 1521))
    (CONNECT_DATA =
      (SERVER = DEDICATED)
      (SERVICE_NAME = videodb)
    )
  )
```

Once you have created your definition, you can reference it within the Oracle instance. Creating a dynamic link is easy, but you need to enable a user to do so, or perform the operation as a privileged superuser. In the following example, the `video` PDB superuser has privileges to create a database link for the pluggable database.

You create a database link for a user in the PDB with the following syntax:

```
SQL> CREATE DATABASE LINK loopbackpdb
  2    CONNECT TO video IDENTIFIED BY video
  3    USING 'video';
```

You can test the link by selecting the credit card numbers from the `members` table, as follows:

```
SQL> SELECT credit_card_number
  2  FROM   member@video;

CREDIT_CARD_NUMBER
-------------------
1111-2222-3333-4444
2222-3333-4444-5555
  ...
```

As you can see, it is easy to create and use database links. They expand your ability to simultaneously and transparently query multiple databases within your organization.

To keep the use case small, I'm assuming that you're working on a single instance. That means you need to create a database link, which enables your database to act like two databases connected across the network. That's because the dbms_comparison packages assumes you're comparing two tables from different databases.

The dbms_comparison package is owned by the SYS user and is best run by using the SYSTEM user account. My second assumption is that you'll use the SYSTEM user, which means you'll need to configure a PDB and configure a pluggable user for that database. The scripts assume that you're using the videodb PDB, as configured in the introduction. While the videodb is the database, the ADMIN user for the PDB is videoadm. The scripts reference a generic video PDB account. You can access the copies of the tables through the PDB's ADMIN user and a database link. You can also read more about provisioning a PDB in Appendix A, if you're not up to speed on how that works.

The following creates a loopbackpdb database link between the same schema:

```
SQL> CREATE DATABASE LINK loopbackpdb
  2    CONNECT TO video IDENTIFIED BY "Video1"
  3    USING 'video';
```

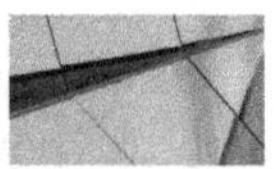

NOTE
Database links in PDBs must enclose case-sensitive passwords in double quotes.

The following blocks create two tables for demonstration purposes:

```
SQL> CREATE TABLE videoadm.member#1 AS
  2    SELECT * FROM video.member;

SQL> CREATE TABLE videoadm.member#2 AS
  2    SELECT * FROM video.member;
```

This statement alters the credit_card_number column to accept your update:

```
SQL> ALTER TABLE member#2
  2    MODIFY (credit_card_number  VARCHAR2(25));
```

You must create unique and not-null indexes for the dbms_comparison package. It uses them during the evaluation of rows. For this example, create a surrogate primary key on each of the member_id columns:

```
SQL> ALTER TABLE member#1
  2    ADD CONSTRAINT member#1_pk PRIMARY KEY (member_id);

SQL> ALTER TABLE member#2
  2    ADD CONSTRAINT member#2_pk PRIMARY KEY (member_id);
```

The next block updates the member#2 table:

```
SQL> UPDATE   video.member#2
  2     SET   credit_card_number = credit_card_number || '-123';
```

This queries the results of the UPDATE statement:

```
SQL> SELECT   m1.member_id AS "Member ID"
     ,        m1.credit_card_number AS "Credit Card #1"
     ,        m2.credit_card_number AS "Credit Card #2"
     FROM     video.member#1 m1
     ,        video.member#2 m2
     WHERE    m1.member_id = m2.member_id;
```

It displays the results of the UPDATE statement:

```
 Member ID Credit Card #1      Credit Card #2
---------- ------------------- ------------------------
      1001 1111-2222-3333-4444 1111-2222-3333-4444-123
      1002 2222-3333-4444-5555 2222-3333-4444-5555-123
...
```

Notice that the credit_card_number column values are different in the two tables. That would indicate that the tables have become unsynchronized, and in a distributed model that is something that a DBA must typically fix.

The next anonymous block creates and executes a comparison with the dbms_comparison package. Unfortunately, the dbms_comparison package isn't installed by default in the PDB system catalog. That means you need to install it manually. Connect as the ADMIN user for the PDB with SYSDBA responsibility and run the following two scripts:

```
SQL> @?/rdbms/admin/dbmscmp.sql
SQL> @?/rdbms/admin/prvtcmp.plb
```

You can DESCRIBE the dbms_comparison package to verify that it's successfully compiled and available to your SYSDBA role in the PDB. Each comparison requires a unique name. This sample uses COMPARE_NAME as the comparison name. It detects this difference and submits those differences to data dictionary tables.

```
SQL> DECLARE
       /* Declare local variables. */
       lv_compare_results  DBMS_COMPARISON.COMPARISON_TYPE;
       lv_difference       BOOLEAN;
     BEGIN
       /* Create the comparison. */
       dbms_comparison.create_comparison(comparison_name    => 'Compare_Name'
                                        ,schema_name        => 'video'
                                        ,object_name        => 'MEMBER#1'
                                        ,dblink_name        => 'loopbackpdb'
                                        ,remote_schema_name => 'video'
                                        ,remote_object_name => 'MEMBER#2');

       /* Check for a difference between the two tables. */
       lv_difference :=
         dbms_comparison.compare( 'Compare_Name'
                                , lv_compare_results
```

```
18                                , NULL
19                                , NULL
20                                , TRUE);
21
22    /* Print messages for not found and found. */
23    IF lv_difference THEN
24      dbms_output.put_line('None found.');
25    ELSE
26      dbms_output.put_line('Difference found.');
27    END IF;
28  END;
29  /
```

Line 3 declares a local variable using a package data type. Lines 7 through 12 call the `create_comparison` procedure of the `dbms_comparison` package. You must ensure that the `comparison_name` parameter is unique. A second attempt with the same name will fail because the names will conflict in the table where Oracle stores it. You also should observe that different table names are assigned to the `object_name` and `remote_object_name` parameters. The call to the `compare` function of the `dbms_comparison` package on lines 16 through 20 returns a Boolean value to the `lv_difference` variable on line 15.

If you forget that the `comparison_name` parameter must be unique, this error message will remind you of it:

```
DECLARE
*
ERROR at line 1:
ORA-23627: Comparison object "SYSTEM"."COMPARISON_NAME" already existed.
ORA-06512: at "SYS.DBMS_COMPARISON", line 5026
ORA-06512: at "SYS.DBMS_COMPARISON", line 454
ORA-06512: at line 7
```

You can use the `purge_comparison` or `drop_comparison` procedures to remove prior comparison data, like this:

```
SQL> BEGIN
       dbms_comparison.purge_comparison('COMPARE_NAME');
       dbms_comparison.drop_comparison('COMPARE_NAME');
     END;
     /
```

The following query returns some of the stored metadata that describes any comparison differences detected between the `member#1` and `member#2` tables:

```
COLUMN comparison_name  FORMAT A20
COLUMN status           FORMAT A6
SQL> SELECT  comparison_name
     ,       scan_id
     ,       status
     FROM    dba_comparison_row_dif;
```

The query returns any rows where differences occur:

```
COMPARISON_NAME         SCAN_ID STATUS
-------------------- ---------- ------
COMPARE_NAME                  2 DIF
COMPARE_NAME                  2 DIF
  ...
```

As you can see, Oracle assigned a `SCAN_ID` for each row that is different and assigned a status of `DIF` in the `STATUS` column. There are 19 data dictionary views, listed next, that display information about the changes at various view access levels. The access levels are `CDB_`, `DBA_`, `ALL_`, and `USER_`, but note that not all views enjoy all levels of access.

- CDB_, DBA_, USER_COMPARISON
- CDB_, DBA_, USER_COMPARISON_COLUMNS
- CDB_, DBA_, USER_COMPARISON_ROW_DIF
- CDB_, DBA_, USER_COMPARISON_SCAN
- CDB_, DBA_, ALL_, USER_COMPARISON_SCAN_SUMMARY
- CDB_, DBA_, USER_COMPARISON_SCAN_VALUES

The following code block uses the information from the view `dba_comparison_row_dif` to drive the resynchronization of data between the `member#1` and `member#2` tables:

```
SQL> DECLARE
       /* Declare local variables. */
       lv_compare_results  DBMS_COMPARISON.COMPARISON_TYPE;
       lv_counter          NUMBER := 0;
       lv_difference       BOOLEAN;
       lv_message          VARCHAR2(10);

       /* Declare switch back cursor. */
       CURSOR switch_back IS
         SELECT   comparison_name
         ,        scan_id
         ,        status
         FROM     dba_comparison_row_dif;

     BEGIN
       /* Read through the switch back. */
       FOR i IN switch_back LOOP
         dbms_comparison.converge
           ( comparison_name      => 'COMPARE_NAME'
           , scan_id              => i.scan_id
           , scan_info            => lv_compare_results
           , converge_options     => DBMS_COMPARISON.CMP_CONVERGE_LOCAL_WINS
           , perform_commit       => TRUE
           , local_converge_tag   => NULL
           , remote_converge_tag  => NULL);

         /* Recheck comparison. */
```

```
28      lv_difference := dbms_comparison.recheck( 'COMPARE_NAME'
29                                               , i.scan_id
30                                               , TRUE);
31
32      /* Check for a difference. */
33      IF lv_difference THEN
34        dbms_output.put_line('Scan ID ['||i.scan_id||'] is the same.');
35      ELSE
36        dbms_output.put_line('Scan ID ['||i.scan_id||'] is different.');
37        /* Increment counter when there's a difference. */
38        lv_counter := lv_counter + 1;
39      END IF;
40    END LOOP;
41
42    /* Purge and drop comparison. */
43    IF lv_counter > 1 THEN
44      dbms_comparison.purge_comparison('COMPARE_NAME');
45      dbms_comparison.drop_comparison('COMPARE_NAME');
46    END IF;
47  END;
48  /
```

Notice that line 33 checks the value of `lv_difference`. If it is false, the `lv_counter` variable is bumped up by one. Once the code completes its `FOR` loop, it evaluates the counter value, purges the comparison results from the data dictionary views, and drops the comparison.

The following requeries the `member#1` and `member#2` tables:

```
SQL> SELECT   m1.member_id AS "Member ID"
  2  ,        m1.credit_card_number AS "Credit Card #1"
  3  ,        m2.credit_card_number AS "Credit Card #2"
  4  FROM     video.member#1 m1
  5  ,        video.member#2 m2
  6  WHERE    m1.member_id = m2.member_id;
```

It prints column values that now agree in both tables:

```
Member ID Credit Card #1      Credit Card #2
---------- ------------------- ----------------------------
      1001 1111-2222-3333-4444 1111-2222-3333-4444
      1002 2222-3333-4444-5555 2222-3333-4444-5555
...
```

The creation of these programs without an Oracle built-in package would require much greater effort. This is one example where an Oracle PL/SQL built-in eliminates the need for you to figure out how to code a difference checker or maintain that code.

DBMS_CRYPTO

Sometimes you need to encrypt column values in such a way that even the `SYS` user can't access them. I created the following example to show how the `dbms_crypto` package can help you do this. It uses a user-defined type (UDT) and assumes you have a working knowledge of object types in Oracle Database 12*c*.

For reference, a good DBA would simply find this clear-text password in the SGA. A more secure approach might be to hide the encryption keyword in a one-column table or embed it as a position-specific substring in some string within a common lookup table column value. Alas, I don't have time to write something so elaborate.

The first step creates a masked UDT, which has only a single salary attribute or field. The code for the object type is

```
SQL> CREATE OR REPLACE TYPE masked IS OBJECT
  ( salary  RAW(1000)
  , CONSTRUCTOR FUNCTION masked RETURN SELF AS RESULT
  CONSTRUCTOR FUNCTION masked ( salary  NUMBER ) RETURN SELF AS RESULT
  , MEMBER FUNCTION get_raw_salary RETURN RAW
  , MEMBER FUNCTION get_salary ( KEY VARCHAR2 ) RETURN NUMBER
  , MEMBER FUNCTION to_string RETURN VARCHAR2
  , ORDER MEMBER FUNCTION equals ( object MASKED ) RETURN NUMBER )
  INSTANTIABLE FINAL;
  /
```

At the time of writing, Oracle Database 12*c* PDBs don't provision with the dbms_crypto package. That means you need to install it before you can compile the following object body. You must connect as the SYSDBA role for the PDB and run two files. The first file defines the specification and the second defines the package body.

These statements call the packages by referring to the $ORACLE_HOME or %ORACLE_HOME% environment variable:

```
SQL> @?/rdbms/admin/dbmsobtk.sql
SQL> @?/rdbms/admin/prvtobtk.plb
```

As the SYSDBA user for the PDB, you must grant the EXECUTE privilege on the dbms_crypto package to the target schema user. The command syntax is

```
SQL> GRANT EXECUTE ON dbms_crypto TO schema_name;
```

I was tempted to simply put the whole object body in the book, but it's 127 lines long when formatted for a standard page, so I settled for highlighting the encryption and decryption of data. The name of the script is use_dbms_crypto.sql, and you can find the code on the McGraw-Hill Professional website.

The masked CONSTRUCTOR FUNCTION encrypts the data. The code for the masked object type's constructor is

```
  CONSTRUCTOR FUNCTION masked ( salary NUMBER ) RETURN SELF AS RESULT IS

    /* Declare local variables for encryption. The object types hold
       object instances and object body variables. When you place them
       inside the methods it prevents their disclosure. */
    lv_key_string       VARCHAR2(4000)  := 'Encrypt Me!';
    lv_key              RAW(1000);
    lv_raw              RAW(1000);
    lv_encrypted_data   RAW(1000);

  BEGIN
```

```
26      /* Dynamic assignment. */
27      lv_raw := UTL_RAW.cast_from_number(NVL(salary,0));
28
29      /* Convert to a RAW 64-character key. */
30      lv_key := UTL_RAW.cast_to_raw(lv_key_string);
31      lv_key := RPAD(lv_key,64,'0');
32
33      /* Encrypt the salary before assigning it to the object type. */
34      lv_encrypted_data := DBMS_CRYPTO.ENCRYPT(
35                                   lv_raw
36                                 , dbms_crypto.ENCRYPT_AES256
37                                 + dbms_crypto.CHAIN_CBC
38                                 + dbms_crypto.PAD_PKCS5
39                                 , lv_key);
39      self.salary := lv_encrypted_data;
40
41      RETURN;
42    END masked;
```

Line 30 uses the `utl_raw` package to cast the string into a `RAW` data type. Line 31 pads the key to a length of 64 digits. The padding is required for the key value when you submit it as the fifth call parameter to the `dbms_crypto.encrypt` function. Lines 34 through 39 demonstrate a call to the `encrypt` function of the `dbms_crypto` package.

You decrypt the value with the `get_salary` function by calling it with the decryption key. While this is a trivial way to manage such an important encryption key, it's just for demonstration purposes of the `dbms_crypto` package. You would need to use a better approach in a real environment, but that's a topic for an advanced PL/SQL book.

The code for the function is

```
  MEMBER FUNCTION get_salary( key VARCHAR2 ) RETURN NUMBER IS

    /* Declare local variables for encryption. The object types hold
       object instances and object body variables. When you place them
       inside the methods it prevents their disclosure. */
    lv_key_string      VARCHAR2(4000)  := 'Encrypt Me!';
    lv_decrypted_data  RAW(4000);
    lv_key             RAW(1000);
    lv_return_value    NUMBER;

  BEGIN

    /* Verify key value matches local value before decrypting,
       substitute a zero value when the key doesn't match. */
    IF key = lv_key_string THEN
      lv_key := UTL_RAW.cast_to_raw(lv_key_string);
      lv_key := RPAD(lv_key,64,'0');
      lv_decrypted_data := DBMS_CRYPTO.DECRYPT(
                                   self.salary
                                 , dbms_crypto.ENCRYPT_AES256
                                 + dbms_crypto.CHAIN_CBC
```

```
70                                 + dbms_crypto.PAD_PKCS5
71                                 , lv_key);
73      lv_return_value := TO_NUMBER(
74                           TO_CHAR(
75                             UTL_RAW.cast_to_number(lv_decrypted_data)
76                           ,'9999990.00'));
77    ELSE
78      lv_return_value := 0;
79    END IF;
80
81    RETURN lv_return_value;
82  END get_salary;
```

Line 65 again pads the encryption key to a length of 64 characters before calling the decrypt function of the dbms_crypto package. That call is made on lines 66 through 71.

Once you verify that masked object type works, you need to wrap it, which obfuscates or hides the implementation details. You do that with the create_wrapped procedure of the dbms_ddl package. The syntax to wrap the logic is

```
BEGIN
  dbms_ddl.create_wrapped(procedure_logic);
END;
/
```

You can test the object implementation by creating a table that uses the object type as a column data type and inserting a couple of rows of data. That code would look like this:

```
SQL> CREATE TABLE sort_demo (salary MASKED);
SQL> INSERT INTO sort_demo VALUES (masked(82000.24));
SQL> INSERT INTO sort_demo VALUES (masked(61000.12));
SQL> INSERT INTO sort_demo VALUES (masked(93000.36));
```

The following PL/SQL block tests the code:

```
SQL> DECLARE
       o MASKED := masked(82000.12);
     BEGIN
       DBMS_OUTPUT.put_line('Override:  '||o.to_string());
       DBMS_OUTPUT.put_line('Decrypted: '||o.get_salary('Encrypt Me!'));
       DBMS_OUTPUT.put_line('Bad Key:   '||o.get_salary('Incorrect'));
     END;
     /
```

It outputs

```
Override:  Encrypted value
Decrypted: 82000.12
Bad Key:   0
```

The object type also provides sorting of the encrypted values, but that's a subject for Chapter 6. Download and test the code if you're curious.

DBMS_FGA

Setting up fine-grain auditing (FGA) is one of the easier methods available in Oracle's built-in library. To do so, you use the Oracle built-in package `dbms_fga` to create audit policies, as demonstrated in the next example.

This block executes the `DBMS_FGA.ADD_POLICY` procedure:

```
SQL> BEGIN
       DBMS_FGA.ADD_POLICY(
           object_schema      => 'VIDEO'
         , object_name        => 'PRICE'
         , policy_name        => 'AUDIT_PRICE_MODXML'
         , audit_condition    => 'VIDEO_STORE.PRICE.AMOUNT < 1'
         , audit_column       => 'AMOUNT'
         , handler_schema     =>  NULL
         , handler_module     =>  NULL
         , enable             =>  TRUE
         , statement_types    => 'INSERT, UPDATE'
         , audit_trail        =>  DBMS_FGA.XML + DBMS_FGA.EXTENDED
         , audit_column_opts =>  DBMS_FGA.ANY_COLUMNS);
     END;
     /
```

Observe that the entire setup spans only 15 lines of code. This is much easier than coding audit triggers. Oracle automatically logs an update of the `video.price` table in the data dictionary:

```
SQL> UPDATE   video.price
     SET      amount = .25
     WHERE    active_flag = 'Y'
     AND      rownum <= 5;
```

The update is recorded even if you issue a `ROLLBACK`:

```
SQL> ROLLBACK;
```

If you issue the following query, using an account with rights to the `V$XML_AUDIT_TRAIL` view, you can see the results of the audit:

```
SQL> SELECT   os_user
     ,        os_host
     ,        object_schema
     ,        object_name
     ,        policy_name
     ,        sql_bind
     ,        sql_text
     FROM     v$xml_audit_trail;
```

It produces the following output (which has been manually wrapped):

```
OS_USER    OS_HOST                OBJECT_SCHEMA     OBJECT_NAME
---------  ---------------------  ----------------  --------------
harperjm   WORKGROUP\HARPERJM-PC  VIDEO_STORE       PRICE
```

```
POLICY_NAME          SQL_BIND     SQL_TEXT
-------------------  -----------  ----------------------------------------------
AUDIT_PRICE_MODXML   (null)       UPDATE video_store.price SET amount = .25 ...
```

Notice that the audit policy captures user information and the SQL statement that violated your audit condition. Also, observe that you insert only one row, instead of many rows, for each record affected.

Case Study: Query Tool

This section shows a simple example of how you can combine built-in packages to create workable programs that benefit your organization. John Harper actually used this program to measure the runtime and statistics for business-critical reports. His IT department created service-level agreements with their business line-units that defined maximum runtimes for their ten most important queries, and we needed a way to track each query.

I've stripped out sections from the original program to keep the example short; a complete solution includes additional instrumentation, alerting, and log cleanup. All of these were completed in our actual package by using Oracle built-in functions.

We gave the following grants to the `VIDEO` PDB user:

```
SQL> GRANT SELECT ON v_$statname TO video;
SQL> GRANT SELECT ON v_$mystat TO video;
SQL> GRANT SELECT ON v_$latch TO video;
SQL> GRANT CREATE VIEW TO video;
```

We were required to grant these rights in order to create the `rts_session_stats` view shown next. We also created the following table to hold a roster of queries that we wanted to measure. This table acts like a driver to our measuring program:

```
SQL> CREATE TABLE rts_query
  ( report_id              INTEGER
  , report_name            VARCHAR2(50)
  , report_description     VARCHAR2(150)
  , view_name              VARCHAR2(65)
  , interval_text          VARCHAR2(30)
  , end_time               TIMESTAMP
  , max_duration           INTERVAL DAY(3) TO SECOND(2)
  , is_active_01_flag      INTEGER);
```

We inserted rows into this table with this syntax:

```
SQL> INSERT INTO rts_query
  VALUES
  ( 1
  ,'SALES_RIF_MONTHLY_GT_2012'
  ,'The gross total of rental revenue per month in 2012'
  ,'sales_rif_monthly_gt_2012'
  ,'FREQ=HOURLY;INTERVAL=3'
  , SYSDATE + 5
  ,'0 0:20:0.0'
  , 1);
```

Observe the `view_name` field in the foregoing `INSERT` statement. The `dbms_scheduler` package's `create_job` procedure has a `job_action` parameter that is limited to 4,000 bytes. This column lets you push either a SQL statement or a PL/SQL block into the procedure. The physical limit on the parameter isn't a big deal for standard reports, but some data warehousing queries exceed it. We actually found that about 60 percent of our data warehousing queries exceeded the 4,000-byte limit.

We create views to represent the underlying query, which ensures we fit within the 4,000-byte limit. Then, we simply reference the view, like so:

```
SQL> CREATE OR REPLACE VIEW sales_rif_monthly_gt_2012 AS
       SELECT    TO_CHAR(rental_date,'MON-YYYY') AS month_year
       ,         SUM(rental_price) AS monthly_gt
       FROM      rental_item_fact
       WHERE     rental_date BETWEEN '01-Jan-2012' AND '31-Dec-2012'
       GROUP BY TO_CHAR(rental_date,'MON-YYYY')
       ORDER BY TO_DATE(month_year,'MON-YYYY');
```

This view was built on a fictitious table named `rental_item_fact`. We populate that table with 20,000,000 rows to make our Oracle database server work a bit harder.

This task was easy because we used the built-in `dbms_random` package to generate realistic data. However, you may need to drop the `rental_item_fact` table first:

```
SQL> DROP TABLE rental_item_fact CASCADE CONSTRAINTS PURGE;

SQL> CREATE TABLE rental_item_fact
     ( contact_id       INTEGER
     , item_id          INTEGER
     , rental_id        INTEGER
     , rental_item_id   INTEGER
     , rental_type_id   INTEGER
     , rental_date      DATE
     , rental_price     NUMBER);
```

Having created the table, we use the `MERGE` statement to insert or update data:

```
SQL> MERGE
     INTO     rental_item_fact rif
     USING   (WITH iterator AS
               (SELECT   ROUND(dbms_random.value(1001,1007)) AS contact_id
                ,        ROUND(dbms_random.value(1001,1093)) AS item_id
                ,        ROUND(dbms_random.value(1037,1039)) AS price_type
                ,        TRUNC(SYSDATE - dbms_random.value(1,1095)) AS rental_date
                ,        level rental_id
                ,        level rental_item_id
                FROM     dual
                CONNECT BY LEVEL <= 20000000)
              SELECT   i.contact_id AS contact_id
              ,        i.item_id AS item_id
              ,        i.rental_id AS rental_id
              ,        i.rental_item_id AS rental_item_id
              ,        p.price_type AS rental_item_type_id
              ,        i.rental_date AS rental_date
              ,        p.amount AS rental_amount
              FROM     price p INNER JOIN iterator i
```

```
          ON       i.item_id = p.item_id
          AND      i.price_type = p.price_type
          WHERE    p.active_flag = 'Y') a
ON (rif.contact_id = a.contact_id AND
    rif.item_id = a.item_id AND
    rif.rental_id = a.rental_id AND
    rif.rental_item_id = a.rental_item_id AND
    rif.rental_type_id = a.rental_item_type_id)
WHEN NOT MATCHED THEN
INSERT
VALUES
( a.contact_id
 , a.item_id
, a.rental_id
, a.rental_item_id
, a.rental_item_type_id
, a.rental_date
, a.rental_amount);
```

The previous MERGE statement completed the 20,000,000-row insert in about 3 minutes. We find that merging is very fast and oftentimes preferred over procedural methods. The effectiveness of a MERGE statement increases when the table is highly parallelized.

Our last bit of setup before creating our logging package requires the creation of two tables and one view. The view is important because it exposes Oracle's automatic statistics gathering to our tool:

```
SQL> CREATE OR REPLACE FORCE VIEW VIDEO.RTS_SESSION_STATS AS
    SELECT   SYS_CONTEXT('USERENV','SID') sid
    ,       'STAT' stat_type
    ,        sn.name stat_name
    ,        m.value stat_value
    FROM     v$statname sn
    ,        v$mystat m
    WHERE    sn.statistic# = m.statistic#
    UNION ALL
    SELECT   SYS_CONTEXT('USERENV','SID') sid
    ,       'LATCH' stat_type
    ,        l.name stat_name
    ,        l.gets stat_value
    FROM     v$latch l
    UNION ALL
    SELECT   SYS_CONTEXT('USERENV','SID') sid
    ,       'TIME' stat_type
    ,       'Wall time' stat_name
    ,        TO_NUMBER(TO_CHAR(systimestamp,'DDMMYYYYHHMISS.FF9')) stat_value
    FROM  dual;
```

You can create a real-time statistics table with the following:

```
SQL> CREATE TABLE rts_stats_history
  ( report_id    INTEGER
  , job_name     VARCHAR2(30)
  , sid          INTEGER
  , stat_type    VARCHAR2(5)
  , stat_name    VARCHAR2(100)
  , stat_value   NUMBER
  , runtime      TIMESTAMP);
```

Notice that we added values from `v$mystat`, `v$statname`, `v$latch`, and some pseudocolumns created via the built-in `sys_context` and `systimestamp` functions. Latches are important because they represent the locking of memory structures during query operations. You will never be able to completely eliminate latching, but it is vital that you reduce these values as much as possible; otherwise, your applications will not scale well.

The last table we add before creating the package is a log table to store any errors that our program may encounter:

```
CREATE TABLE rts_log
(
  program          varchar2(65)
, error_message    clob
, update_ts        timestamp
);
```

The next step lets us create a package specification. The package includes a `printt` procedure for basic error logging, and a `snap` procedure for gathering point-in-time metrics. It also includes a procedure that runs our stored queries from the `rts_query` table.

The package specification is

```
SQL> CREATE OR REPLACE PACKAGE sql_stats AS
       -- -----------------------------------------------------------------
       --  ERROR HANDLING PROCEDURES
       -- -----------------------------------------------------------------
       PROCEDURE printt
       ( pi_program_name   IN VARCHAR2
       , pi_log_level      IN VARCHAR2
       , pi_status         IN NUMBER
       , pi_error_message  IN VARCHAR2);
       -- -----------------------------------------------------------------
       -- SNAP STATS BY SID
       -- -----------------------------------------------------------------
       PROCEDURE snap
       ( pi_sid IN NUMBER
       , pi_job IN VARCHAR2
       , pi_rpt IN VARCHAR2);
       -- -----------------------------------------------------------------
       -- RUN_QUERIES procedure.
       -- -----------------------------------------------------------------
       PROCEDURE run_queries;
     END sql_stats;
     /
```

I've opted to display the `sql_stats` package body in pieces to highlight how it works. The following is the package header and the first `printt` procedure:

```
SQL> CREATE OR REPLACE PACKAGE BODY sql_stats AS
     -- -------------------------------------------------------------------
     -- PRINTT
     -- -------------------------------------------------------------------
     PROCEDURE print
```

```
 6  ( pi_program_name   IN VARCHAR2
 7  , pi_log_level      IN VARCHAR2
 8  , pi_status         IN NUMBER
 9  , pi_error_message  IN VARCHAR2 ) IS
10    /* Make the procedure autonomous. */
11    PRAGMA AUTONOMOUS_TRANSACTION;
12  BEGIN
13    INSERT
14    INTO  rts_log
15    VALUES
16    ( pi_program_name
17    , TO_CHAR(gd_timestamp,'HH:MM:SS.FF MON DD, YYYY')||' ['
18    ||pi_log_level ||'] '
19    ||pi_program_name ||' '
20    ||pi_error_message
21    , systimestamp);
22    /* Commit write. */
23    COMMIT;
24  END printt;
```

The writes are set to be independent by the PRAGMA on line 11. They occur as resources become available.

The snap procedure in the following block simply selects the values stored in our RTS_SESSION_STATS view that we created previously:

```
25 -- ------------------------------------------------------------------
26 -- SNAP
27 -- ------------------------------------------------------------------
28 PROCEDURE snap
29 ( pi_sid IN NUMBER
30 , pi_job IN VARCHAR2
31 , pi_rpt IN VARCHAR2 ) IS
32 BEGIN
33   INSERT
34   INTO  rts_stats_history
35   SELECT  pi_rpt
36   ,       pi_job
37   ,       sid
38   ,       stat_type
39   ,       stat_name
40   ,       stat_value
41   ,       systimestamp runtime
42   FROM    rts_session_stats
43   WHERE   sid = pi_sid;
44   /* Commit the write to the history. */
45   COMMIT;
46 END snap;
```

That's it! Now, we have a way of determining how much resources are being used and how long each query takes. Our run_queries procedure in the next block simply creates a dynamic PL/SQL block and passes that block to the dbms_scheduler.create_job procedure. The nifty thing about the `run_queries` procedure is that a separate session is spun per query and the statistics gathering is specific to that session. It effectively isolates each query in its own session, as you can see:

```
-- ------------------------------------------------------------
-- RUN_SQL
-- ------------------------------------------------------------
  PROCEDURE run_queries IS
    lv_pls      VARCHAR2(4000);
    lv_rpt      VARCHAR2(30);
    lv_job      VARCHAR2(30);
    lv_vew      VARCHAR2(65);
  BEGIN
    SELECT   report_id
    ,        'RPT#'||report_id||'_'||to_char(sysdate,'SSMIHHDDMMYYYY') job_name
    ,        view_name
    INTO     lv_rpt
    ,        lv_job
    ,        lv_vew
    FROM     rts_query;

    lv_pls := 'DECLARE'||CHR(10)
           || '  lv_counter NUMBER;'||CHR(10)
           || '  lv_sid     NUMBER := SYS_CONTEXT(''USERENV'',''SID'');'||CHR(10)
           || 'BEGIN'||CHR(10)
           || '  sql_stats.snap(lv_sid,''$2'',$3); '||CHR(10)
           || '  SELECT COUNT(*)'|| CHR(10)
           || '  INTO lv_counter'|| CHR(10)
           || '  FROM $1; '|| CHR(10)
           || '  sql_stats.snap(lv_sid,''$2'',$3); '|| CHR(10)
           || 'END;';

    lv_pls := REGEXP_REPLACE(lv_pls,'\$1',lv_vew);
    lv_pls := REGEXP_REPLACE(lv_pls,'\$2',lv_job);
    lv_pls := REGEXP_REPLACE(lv_pls,'\$3',lv_rpt);

    DBMS_SCHEDULER.CREATE_JOB
    ( job_name     => l_job
    , job_type     => 'PLSQL_BLOCK'
    , job_action   => l_pls
    , enabled      => true
    , auto_drop    => true);
  END run_queries;
END sql_stats;
/
```

It was much more difficult to gather statistics in previous releases of Oracle Database (before 10*g*). You were required to enable tracing, mark the trace file for your test, trace the SQL, stop the trace, locate the trace file, and run the `tkprof` utility on the file to generate readable reports. Appendix A covers the basics of using the `tkprof` utility.

We run queries from the `rts_query` table by issuing the following command at a SQL*Plus prompt:

```
SQL> BEGIN
  2    video.sql_stats.run_queries;
  3  END;
  4  /
```

The following query returns results from the `dba_scheduler_job_run_details` view:

```
SQL> SELECT   owner
     ,        job_name
     ,        status
     ,        actual_start_date
     ,        run_duration
     ,        instance_id
     ,        cpu_used
     FROM     dba_scheduler_job_run_details
     WHERE    job_name LIKE 'RPT%';
```

It generates this output:

```
OWNER|JOB_NAME|STATUS|ACTUAL_START_DATE|RUN_DURATION|INSTANCE_ID|CPU_USED
----------------------------------------------------------------------------
VIDEO_STORE|RPT#1_23430311042013|SUCCEEDED|4/11/2013 3:43:23.681027 AM ...
VIDEO_STORE|RPT#1_14570412042013|SUCCEEDED|4/12/2013 4:57:14.824137 PM ...
```

You can see by this example that Oracle built-in packages greatly simplify and reduce the overall code you need to write in order to obtain simple statistics on queries.

Supporting Scripts

This section describes programs placed on the McGraw-Hill Professional website to support this appendix:

- The `use_dbms_comparison.sql` program contains small programs that support a complete example of how to use a built-in package to normalize data across two repositories. It supports the demonstration of the `dbms_comparison` PL/SQL built-in package.
- The `use_dbms_crypto.sql` program contains an object type and body that demonstrate encrypting and decrypting data. It supports the demonstration of the `dbms_crypto` PL/SQL built-in package.

Summary

This appendix introduced you to Oracle's extensive built-in library. It also illustrated how to use four of the Oracle built-in packages. You are encouraged to study the *Oracle Database PL/SQL Packages and Types Reference 12c Release*, which should be the first place you look when asked to implement a particular feature.

APPENDIX E

Regular Expression Primer

Regular expressions in Oracle Database 12*c* haven't changed from Oracle Database 11*g*. They enable you to perform powerful context searches in variable-length strings, like the `CHAR`, `CLOB`, `NCHAR`, `NCLOB`, `NVARCHAR2`, and `VARCHAR2` character data types. Regular expressions are strings that describe or match a set of strings. They provide a powerful set of pattern matching capabilities by combining character classes, collation classes, metacharacters, metasequences, and literals. Character classes are groups of possible characters at a point in the search. Collation classes are sets of characters and are treated like a range. Metacharacters are operators that specify search algorithms, and metasequences are operators created by two metacharacters or literals. Literals are characters, character sets, and words. Together, these let you search text by using patterns to match strings.

This appendix presents regular expressions in the following sections:

- Regular expression introduction
- Regular expression implementation

These sections explain what regular expressions are and how you can use them in your PL/SQL application code. Examples are provided that show you how to use regular expressions in both SQL and PL/SQL.

Regular Expression Introduction

Regular expressions enable you to conduct text searches based on common characteristics, such as case sensitivity, or based on approximate spelling. Some languages provide search functions to perform these operations, while others don't. Regular expressions are a major facility in scripting languages such as Perl and PHP. They provide pattern matching and flexibility when you search long strings for substrings or instances of substrings.

You build pattern matching expressions by combining character classes, collation classes, metacharacters, metasequences, and literals. These components are covered in the following subsections.

Character Classes

Character classes are groups or ranges of possible characters. They may appear at any point in your regular expression. Character classes are traditionally delimited by `[]` (*square brackets*). You use a "`-`" (*dash*) inside the square brackets to designate everything between two characters. The "`-`" in this context is a *character-class metacharacter*.

You use the ordinal numbers from 0 to 9 and upper- or lowercase letters `A` through `F` to designate hexadecimal values. The character class `[ABCDEFabcdef0123456789]` represents the group of possible characters found in hexadecimal characters. You can represent the same letter and number range sets by using the character class `[A-Fa-f0-9]`. There is no practical limit to the number of ranges that you can put in a character class.

The POSIX (Portable Operating System Interface) specification broadens the use of character classes by introducing the concept of portable character classes (which means portable across languages). Portable character classes are nested inside the basic [] as [::] (*square brackets with colons*). This means that the character class [A-Za-z] that represents all upper- and lowercase letters is equal to the [[:alpha:]] portable character class. You should note that the portable character classes are inside an additional set of square brackets. More or less, the portable character classes act like range aliases. The second set of square brackets delimits them as a character class. Unlike language-specific character classes, portable character classes map across languages and simplify globalizing search patterns. Table E-1 lists the POSIX portable character classes.

By themselves, character classes apply only to a single character or position of a string. When matched with the + *metacharacter* (which means one or more of the preceding characters or character classes), the expression may apply to more than a single character. Table E-2, later in this appendix, provides a list of available metacharacters.

To show you how range and portable character classes work, the following examples use two metacharacters, the ^ (*caret*) and $ (*dollar sign*). The caret represents the beginning of the string you're working with, and the dollar sign represents the end of the string. Moreover, they represent the beginning and ending of a line of text. (Table E-2 provides their formal definitions.) Using SQL statements with a `REGEXP_LIKE` function call in the `WHERE` clause is a simple way to present these examples. If you need further explanation about how the `REGEXP_LIKE` function works, flip to the "REGEXP_LIKE Function" section later in this appendix to check out the details. These examples use a two-character `A1` string and use range and portable character classes to match the string.

The first `REGEXP_LIKE` example compares the string literal against a range character class of the letters in the English alphabet, as shown in the following `SELECT` statement:

```
SQL> SELECT   i.column_name
  2  FROM     (SELECT 'A1' AS column_name FROM dual) i
  3  WHERE    REGEXP_LIKE(i.column_name,'^[A-Z]*$','i');
```

Portable Character Class	Description
`[:alnum:]`	All alphanumeric characters
`[:alpha:]`	All alphabetic characters
`[:cntrl:]`	All nonprintable control characters
`[:digit:]`	All numeric digits
`[:graph:]`	All `[:digit:]`, `[:lower:]`, `[:punct:]`, and `[:upper:]` portable character classes
`[:lower:]`	All lowercase alphabetic characters
`[:print:]`	All printable characters
`[:punct:]`	All punctuation characters
`[:space:]`	All nonprinting space characters
`[:upper:]`	All uppercase alphabetic characters
`[:xdigit:]`	All hexadecimal characters

TABLE E-1. *POSIX Portable Character Classes*

Line 2 fabricates a table of one column and row with a value of `A1`. The first call parameter is a two-character `A1` string, which is returned by the derived table in the `FROM` clause (see Appendix B for a discussion of derived tables). The action occurs in line 3.The second call parameter is a range character class for uppercase letters combined with a metacharacter (`*`) for one or more instances (see Table E-2). The third call parameter is an `i` character flag that instructs the function to perform a case-insensitive comparison. Naturally, the `SELECT` statement returns no rows because the first character is a number, not a letter.

NOTE
The difference between the `i` table alias on line 2 and the `i` character flag on line 3 in the example is important. The table alias is a valid identifier in the scope of the `SELECT` statement, while the character flag is a one-character string literal.

The next example changes the second parameter of the `REGEXP_LIKE` function from a range character class to a portable character class. Note that when you use a portable character class, you need to include it within another set of square brackets.

```
SQL> SELECT   i.column_name
  2  FROM    (SELECT 'A1' AS column_name FROM dual) i
  3  WHERE    REGEXP_LIKE(i.column_name,'^[[:alpha:]]*$','i');
```

The preceding `REGEXP_LIKE` function works like the one in the prior example, and likewise doesn't return any values because both characters aren't lowercase or uppercase letters.

Sticking with our little example, let's check for an alphanumeric value with a range character class first of uppercase, lowercase, and numeric characters:

```
SQL> SELECT   i.column_name
  2  FROM    (SELECT 'A1' AS column_name FROM dual) i
  3  WHERE    REGEXP_LIKE(i.column_name,'^[A-Za-z0-9]*$','i');
```

It returns the two-character `A1` string. Likewise, replacing the range character classes with a single portable character class and an extra set of square brackets works too. The following shows you the portable character-class logic:

```
SQL> SELECT   i.column_name
  2  FROM    (SELECT 'A1' AS column_name FROM dual) i
  3  WHERE    REGEXP_LIKE(i.column_name,'^[[:alnum:]]*$','i');
```

You can also deploy this in an anonymous block, like the following:

```
SQL> DECLARE
  2    lv_counter     NUMBER := 1;
  3    lv_source      VARCHAR2(12) := 'A1';
  4    lv_pattern_1   VARCHAR2(12) := '[[:alpha:]]';
  5    lv_return      BOOLEAN := TRUE;
  6  BEGIN
  7    -- Compare using standard character class ranges.
  8    FOR i IN 1..LENGTH(lv_source) LOOP
  9      IF NOT REGEXP_LIKE(
```

```
10          SUBSTR(lv_source,lv_counter,i),lv_pattern_1) THEN
11         lv_return := FALSE;
12       END IF;
13        -- Increment counter value.
14       lv_counter := lv_counter + 1;
15     END LOOP;
16
17     -- Print message when all characters are true.
18     IF NOT lv_return THEN
19       dbms_output.put_line(
20         'Not a character-only string ['||lv_source||'].');
21     END IF;
22   END;
23   /
```

The `IF` block on lines 9 through 12 runs for any nonalphabetic character and sets the `lv_return` variable to false. The `A1` string enters that `IF` block for the second character, and thereby prints the message set on lines 19 and 20:

```
Not a character-only string [A1].
```

The following change on line 4 from an alphabetic character class to an alphanumeric character class prevents the program from entering the `IF` block on lines 9 through 12:

```
  4     lv_pattern_1  VARCHAR2(12) := '[[:alnum:]]';
```

Changing the message on lines 19 and 20, like

```
19       dbms_output.put_line(
20         'An alpha-numeric string ['||lv_source||'].');
```

prints the following:

```
An alpha-numeric string [A1].
```

This section has demonstrated the basics of using range and portable character classes. You will revisit the concept later in the appendix in other program samples.

Collation Classes

The collation class is new to regular expressions. It was introduced by the POSIX regular expression standard and is designed to allow you to collate in languages that require a collating element. Collating elements may contain more than one character, whereas traditional regular expressions limit collating elements to single characters.

You define a collation class by using `[..]` (*square brackets with offsetting dots or periods*). An example drawn from the *Oracle Database Globalization Support Guide 12*c *Release* creates a collation element *inside* a character class: `[a-[.ch.]]`. This allows you to find whether a collating element is between `a` and `ch`. This is highly dependent on the `NLS_SORT` parameter and language implementation. The details are best left to another book on text retrieval.

Metacharacters

A metacharacter provides some mechanics for performing pattern matching. Some books and documents group character classes, intervals, and scope-limiting parentheses as metacharacters. This appendix takes a different tact. Character and collating classes are treated separately from other metacharacters. Both were covered earlier in the appendix. Table E-2 lists metacharacters.

Metacharacter	Name	Type	Description
`()`	parentheses	Delimiter	Act as a scope-of-comparison constraint. A common use is to choose between two alternatives with the | (or bar), like a `'t(o|oo)'` regular expression that finds a *to* or *too* in a string. *You create subexpressions when you enclose evaluation criteria in parentheses.* Failure to match parentheses in subexpressions raises an `ORA-12725` exception. This occurs because Oracle implements subexpressions only when they are inside parentheses. This differs from most implementations of regular expressions, and it also changes some syntax rules.
`{m}`	exact	Interval	Matches exactly *m* occurrences of the preceding subexpression or character.
`{m,}`	at least	Interval	Matches at least *m* occurrences of the preceding subexpression or character.
`{m,n}`	between	Interval	Matches at least *m* occurrences, but not more than *n* occurrences, of the preceding subexpression or character.
|	or bar	Logical	Acts as a logical `OR` operator and treats the characters to the left and right as operands in a matching operation. It returns a match when either operand is found. Alternatively, it can manage a logical `OR` relationship between sets of characters when they are inside ordinary parentheses. Parentheses act as scope delimiters, as noted in the *or bar* example earlier in the table.
.	dot	Matching	Matches any one character.
^	caret	Matching	Matches the beginning of a line in generalized regular expressions but represents the beginning of a multiple-line document unless you specify the `m` override flag for the `match_type_flag` parameter. (Refer to Table E-4 later in the appendix for more information about override flags.)

TABLE E-2. *POSIX Metacharacters*

Metacharacter	Name	Type	Description
$	dollar sign	Matching	Matches the end of a line in generalized regular expressions but represents the end of a multiple-line document unless you specify the `m` override flag for the `match_type_flag` parameter. (Refer to Table E-4 for more information about override flags.)
^	caret	Negation	Acts as a negation operator only when you use it inside a character class. Then, it is technically a character-class metacharacter. The following regular expression disallows any uppercase characters between `K` and `M`: `'[^K-M]'`
-	dash	Range	Acts as a range operator, but only when it is inside a character class. This limited context makes the dash a character-class metacharacter. See the earlier "Character Classes" section for more information on this metacharacter.
?	question mark	Repetition	Makes the preceding character optional in a matching solution. In other words, there may or may not be the preceding character in a string. The following regular expression checks for an American or British spelling using this metacharacter: `'colou?r'`
*	asterisk or star	Repetition	Matches any instance of zero to many characters. Functions like a combination of `.` and `?` for any character because it matches *any* character or *no* character.
+	plus	Repetition	Matches at least once or many times the preceding character. Returning to the earlier regular expression example of using parentheses to choose between two alternatives, `'t(o|oo)'`, which finds *to* or *too* in a string, you can rewrite it as the regular expression `'t(o|o+)'`, which works for *to*, *too*, or *tooooo*.

TABLE E-2. *POSIX Metacharacters*

As you've seen in this section, metacharacters have many uses. Unfortunately, not all of them can be shown in this primer. You will find broader examples combining these metacharacters into meaningful regular expressions in the "Regular Expression Implementation" later in this appendix.

Metasequences

Metasequences are characters combined with backslashes, like those in Table E-3. The backslash strips the special nature of other metacharacters, like parentheses or a `.` (dot). They also add metacharacteristics to ordinary characters like the < (*less than symbol*) or > (*greater than symbol*) in some programming languages.

NOTE
Oracle Database 11g and 12c don't support the \< (word beginning) *and* \> (word ending) *metasequences. This means you may need to leverage the* `LTRIM` *and* `RTRIM` *functions.*

Metasequence	Name	Type	Description
`\n`	backreference	POSIX	Matches the *n*th preceding subexpression. You raise an `ORA-12727` when the backreference exceeds the number of subexpressions. Oracle Database 12*c* requires you to enclose all subexpressions in parentheses.
`\d`	digit	Perl	Equal to the portable character class `[[:digit:]]`, matches any digit.
`\D`	nondigit	Perl	Equal to the portable character class `[^[:digit:]]`, matches any nondigit.
`\w`	word character	Perl	Equal to the portable character class `[[:alnum:]]`, matches any word character.
`\W`	nonword character	Perl	Equal to the portable character class `[^[:alnum:]]`, matches any nonword character.
`\s`	whitespace character	Perl	Equal to the portable character class `[[:space:]]`, matches any whitespace character.
`\S`	nonwhitespace character	Perl	Equal to the portable character class `[^[:space:]]`, matches any nonwhitespace character.
`\A`	beginning of string	Perl	Matches the beginning of a new string. It does not find the beginning of new lines when you enable multiple-line searches with the `match_type_flag` (covered in the "REGEXP_COUNT Function" section later in the appendix).
`\Z`	end of string	Perl	Matches the end of a new string. Like the `\A` metasequence, it does not find the end of lines when you enable multiple-line searches.
`\z`	end of string	Perl	Matches the end of a new string regardless of how you've set the `match_type_flag` value.

TABLE E-3. *Oracle Database 12c Supported POSIX and Perl Metasequences*

Oracle Database 11*g* and 12*c* don't support some popular regular expression metasequences. While Oracle has made no formal statement of how it plans to improve regular expressions, you can be certain that it will improve them.

Literals

Regular expression literal values are simply string literals, as discussed in Chapter 4. They may consist of one to many characters. Regular expressions can be explicit in providing the full text of a literal string, or they can use pattern matching sequences.

Regular Expression Implementation

PL/SQL and SQL began supporting these text search and comparison operations in Oracle Database 10*g*. Oracle Database 12*c* supports IEEE Portable Operating System Interface (POSIX) standard draft 1003.2/D11.2, and Unicode Regular Expression Guidelines of the Unicode Consortium. Oracle Database 11*g* extended matching capabilities for multilingual data beyond the POSIX standard. The Oracle Database 11g release also added support for the common PERL regular expression extensions that are not covered in and don't conflict with the POSIX standard.

Oracle Database 11*g* introduced a restricting subordinate expression to the `REGEXP_INSTR` (*regular expression in-string*) and `REGEXP_SUBSTR` (*regular expression substring*) functions, which were introduced in Oracle Database 10*g*. Oracle Database 11*g* also added the `REGEXP_COUNT` (*regular expression count*) function.

Oracle Database 11*g* and 12*c* support regular expressions against variable-length strings, like the `CHAR`, `CLOB`, `NCHAR`, `NCLOB`, `NVARCHAR2`, and `VARCHAR2` character data types. They do not support the `LONG` data type, which Oracle advises you should migrate to `CLOB` data types. After all, the `LONG` data type is provided only as a convenience for backward compatibility.

There are five regular expression functions in Oracle Database 12*c*: `REGEXP_COUNT`, `REGEXP_INSTR`, `REGEXP_LIKE`, `REGEXP_REPLACE`, and `REGEXP_SUBSTR`. The following subsections define them. Rather than summarize formal parameter definitions when they occur more than once, they're repeated in each function description. The exception is the `match_type_flag` value, which is covered once in the "REGEXP_COUNT Function" subsection. Hopefully, this choice makes the appendix an easier spot reference for you.

REGEXP_COUNT Function

The `REGEXP_COUNT` function is new as of Oracle Database 11*g*. It lets you count the number of times a specific pattern is found in a string. It has the prototype

```
REGEXP_COUNT(source_string, pattern [, start_position [, match_type_flag]])
```

The `source_string` can be any character expression, provided the data type is a `CHAR`, `CLOB`, `NCHAR`, `NCLOB`, `NVARCHAR2`, or `VARCHAR2`. You may recall from Chapter 8 that an expression can be a string literal or a function return value that meets the data type requirement. The character expression can also be a column value or a bind variable. For example, you could use `:new.column_name` as a `source_string` value in a database trigger. See Chapter 12 for more information on database triggers.

The `pattern` value can be any valid regular expression, but *the length must be less than or equal to 512 characters*. POSIX regular expressions are supported in Oracle Database 11*g* and 12*c*. You must prepend any apostrophe with a single quote because you pass the `pattern` value as an actual parameter into a function call. Alternatively, you can reset the quote identifier in your session. The "Back-Quoting in Oracle" sidebar of Appendix A shows you how to substitute another backquoting identifier for the default apostrophe.

The `start_position` value is an integer expression. The default value is 1. It is not uncommon to find a starting point inside the string by calling the `REGEXP_INSTR` function as an expression for this actual parameter.

The `match_type_flag` value is a text literal expression, typically a string literal. The string may contain either an `i` or a `c`, and one or more of the following: `n`, `m`, or `x`. Collectively, they override the default matching behavior. The default matching behavior performs as follows:

- It uses the `NLS_SORT` parameter and is *generally* case-sensitive matching. It is always case-sensitive matching (*by default*) when the `NLS_SORT` parameter is a Western European character set.
- It restricts the `.` (*dot* or *period*) so that it doesn't match a newline return.
- It treats the stings as a single line, which means the *caret* (`^`) and *dollar sign* (`$`) refer to the beginning and ending of the string, respectively.
- It matches whitespace characters against whitespace characters.

Table E-4 qualifies the override flags for the match_type_flag parameter. This table applies to all five of the regular expression functions

You might wonder why it was so important to add the `REGEXP_COUNT` function in Oracle Database 11*g*. The answer is quite straightforward. If you want to handle the occurrences of results individually rather than collectively, counting them lets you create a dynamic range `FOR` loop. Conversely, it eliminates the need for you to loop through a string counting the occurrences of a pattern match. The function typically solves the latter more frequently than the former.

Match Type Flag	Description
`i`	Sets the search to case-insensitive matching, overriding the `NLS_SORT` parameter where necessary.
`c`	Sets the search to case-sensitive matching, overriding the `NLS_SORT` parameter where necessary.
`n`	Enables the `.` (*dot* or *period*) to truly match any character, including a newline character.
`m`	Enables the search to recognize multiple lines inside a string. This ensures that the *caret* (`^`) and *dollar sign* (`$`) work as they normally do in scripting languages.
`x`	Sets the search to ignore whitespace characters.

TABLE E-4. *Possible Match Type Flag Values*

Sample Search String

The following is the sample search string for the example programs:

"The prologue, spoken by Galadriel, shows the Dark Lord Sauron forging the One Ring, which he can use to conquer the lands of Middle-earth through his enslavement of the bearers of the Rings of Power. The Rings of Power are powerful magical rings given to individuals from the races of Elves, Dwarves, and Men. A Last Alliance of Elves and Men is formed to counter Sauron and his forces at the foot of Mount Doom, but Sauron himself appears to kill Elendil, the king of the Mannish kingdom of Gondor. Just afterward, Isildur grabs his father's broken sword Narsil and slashes at Sauron's hand. The stroke cuts off Sauron's fingers, separating him from the Ring and vanquishing his army. However, because Sauron's life is bound in the Ring, he is not completely defeated until the Ring itself is destroyed. Isildur takes the Ring and succumbs to its temptation, refusing to destroy it, but he is later ambushed and killed by orcs and the Ring is lost in the river into which Isildur fell."

You can download the `regexp_in_clob.sql`.script from the McGraw-Hill Professional website to build the table and seed this string.

The examples for the `REGEXP_COUNT` and other regular expression functions are small and some rely on the paragraph found in the "Sample Search String" sidebar. Three examples are provided for `REGEXP_COUNT`; respectively, they count the number of title-case (*where only the first letter is capitalized*), lowercase, and case-insensitive "`the`" words in the sample string.

Title Case Count

The following query counts the number of the title-case "The" words followed by a whitespace character. The white space avoids counting any other words, like *Theory*, *They*, or *There*, found in the sample story.

```
SQL> SELECT REGEXP_COUNT(story_thread, 'The ') AS "Title Case"
  2  FROM   sample_regexp;
```

It returns an integer value of 3. There is also the possibility that with a different string, you could return an incorrect count if there was a word ending in a title case "`The`" followed by a space. Logic tells you that it is unlikely. You see how to address that possibility in the case-insensitive search example later in this section.

Lowercase Count

The next query counts the number of lowercase "`the`" words preceded and followed by a white space. As discussed, the white space avoids counting any words that begin with the pattern, like *theory*, *they*, or *there*. The white space before "`the`" rules out words that end in the pattern, like *routhe* (which means sorrow). Ironically, sorrow is what you might feel with regular expressions when you overlook a pattern matching possibility.

```
SQL> SELECT REGEXP_COUNT(story_thread, 'the ', 1, 'c') AS "Lowercase"
  2  FROM   sample_regexp;
```

It prints

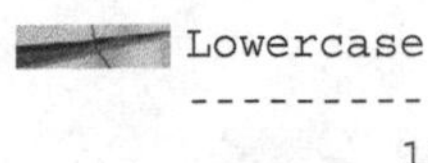

```
Lowercase
----------
        15
```

This function call uses the optional `start_position` and `match_type_flag` values to perform a case-sensitive search. The values provided as actual parameters are actually the default values.

You can reference these formal parameters earlier in this section. Table E-4 qualifies the valid list of values for these parameters. The case-sensitive search also requires that you enter the regular expression pattern in lowercase characters to find lowercase "`the`" words. This query returns an integer value of 15 from the sidebar string.

Case-Insensitive Count

The next query counts the number of the lowercase "`the`" words that start a line or are preceded or followed by a white space. As discussed in the prior sections, the trailing white space avoids counting any words that begin with the pattern but aren't the correct word, like *Theory*, *They*, or *There*. The leading white space prevents counting words that end in the pattern, like *routhe* (which means sorrow). The combination of leading and trailing characters surrounding "`the`" from inside the word "father" precludes counting it as a string.

Unfortunately, the leading white space also eliminates the first "`The`" word because it is preceded by a double quote. This is where patterns, subexpressions, and metacharacters solve a common searching problem. The next query looks for a case-insensitive "`the`" word that may be at the beginning of a line, immediately preceded by a double quote, or preceded by a white space. At the same time, the pattern will look for a "`the`" word that is followed by a dash, colon, comma, semicolon, or white space.

There are two approaches to solving this problem. One lets you accept the default matching behavior, and the other requires you to override the default matching behavior.

This one uses the default matching properties:

```
SQL> SELECT REGEXP_COUNT(
               story_thread
              ,'((^| +)|(["'']))(T|t)he(([-:,\.;])|( +|$))'
              ) AS "Case-insensitive"
     FROM   sample_regexp;
```

It accomplishes case-insensitive searches provided there are no capitals other than `T` in the "`the`" words. The pattern uses parentheses to create a subexpression. The subexpression checks for an uppercase `T` or lowercase `t`. This type of subexpression is sometimes labeled as an *alternation*, a regular expression term that means you choose between two alternatives.

The foregoing expression also uses two character classes. One qualifies a double or single quote (*please note that it is backquoted by an apostrophe because this is Oracle*). The other qualifies a dash, colon, comma, (*backquoted*) period, or semicolon. Both character classes are options inside subexpressions. The `((^| +)|(["'']))` subexpression says that either one or the other nested subexpression is true. The first nested subexpression condition is met when the first character is the beginning of a line or one or more white spaces. The second nested subexpression condition is met when the preceding string is a single or double quote.

The next `(([-:,\.;])|( +|$))` subexpression examines the trailing character. The first nested subexpression condition is met when the trailing character of the "`the`" word is a dash, colon, period, or semicolon. Alternatively, the other nested subexpression condition is met when the trailing characters are one or more white spaces or the end-of-line marker.

A simpler approach leverages the `match_type_flag` available as part of the function. As discussed in Table E-4, the "`i`" string designates case-insensitive searching. It has the following implementation:

```
SQL> SELECT REGEXP_COUNT(
              story_thread
             ,'((^| +)|(["'']))the(([-:,\.;])|( +|$))', 1, 'i'
             ) AS "Case-insensitive"
     FROM    sample_regexp;
```

Both of the preceding patterns yield a count of 18 words.

This section has demonstrated several approaches that show you how to use the `REGEXP_COUNT` function. The caveat is always the same whether it is PL/SQL, SQL, or regular expression programming: *know what you want, rule out what you don't, and look for the simplest way to find it.*

REGEXP_INSTR Function

The `REGEXP_INSTR` function was enhanced in Oracle Database 11*g* to enable the use of a restricting subordinate expression, and it retains the same capabilities in Oracle Database 12*c*. The `REGEXP_INSTR` function lets you find a position index value inside a string. You use it to find a starting point inside a string, and it is known as the regular expression in-string function.

The prototype for the function is

```
REGEXP_INSTR(source_string, pattern [, start_position [, occurrence
            [, return_option [, match_type_flag [, subexpression]]]]])
```

The new `subexpression` parameter lets you do priority searching on subexpressions. As qualified in the "Regular Expression Introduction" section, a subexpression matches the value on either the left or right of the | metacharacter. The | metacharacter acts like a logical `OR` operator. For example, you can use a pattern of `col(o|ou)r` when you want all those matching either *color* (American English) or *colour* (British English). The subexpression is the `(o|ou)`. If you read the introduction, you should know that you really don't require a subexpression in this case. You can accomplish the same thing with `colou?r` because the question mark (`?`) treats the character that precedes it as optional.

The `source_string` can be any character expression, provided the data type is a `CHAR`, `CLOB`, `NCHAR`, `NCLOB`, `NVARCHAR2`, or `VARCHAR2`. You may recall from Chapter 8 that an expression can be a string literal or a function return value that meets the data type requirement. The character expression can also be a column value or a bind variable. For example, you could use `:new.column_name` as a `source_string` value in a database trigger. See Chapter 12 for more information on database triggers.

The `pattern` value can be any valid regular expression, but *the length must be less than or equal to 512 characters*. POSIX regular expressions are supported in Oracle Database 11*g* forward. You must prepend any apostrophe with a single quote because you pass the `pattern` value as an actual parameter into a function call. Alternatively, you can reset the quote identifier in your session.

Single-Dimensional Character Array

A string is actually a single-dimensional character array. Oracle defines these character arrays by using the database character set. It also lets you override the default character set and build character arrays to your own specifications. This means that you could have an array of elements where each element is 1, 2, or 3 bytes, depending on how you configured it.

Whether stored in 1, 2, or 3 bytes, a string is really stored like an array. If you insert the word `Sample` into a variable or column using a fixed- or variable-length character data type, you actually store the following:

Index Value	Character Value
1	S
2	A
3	M
4	P
5	L
6	E

This index uses a 1-based numbering system to index the characters of your string. The index lets you find and parse strings.

The "Back-Quoting in Oracle" sidebar of Appendix A shows you how to substitute another backquoting identifier for the default apostrophe.

The `start_position` value is an integer expression. The default value is 1. It is not uncommon to find a starting point inside the string by calling the `REGEXP_INSTR` function as an expression for this actual parameter.

The `occurrence` value is an integer expression. The default value is 1. If you want another occurrence, you must provide a value. Override values typically have business rules that are too complex to predict here.

The `return_option` value is an integer expression. The default value is 0, which represents the position or index of *the beginning* of the first substring matched by the pattern. You can override this value by using a 1, which instructs the function to return *the character after* the substring that matches the pattern.

The `match_type_flag` value is a text literal expression, typically a string literal. The string may contain either an `i` or a `c`, and one or more of the following: `n`, `m`, or `x`. Collectively, they override the default matching behavior. Table E-4 in the previous section "REGEXP_COUNT Function" contains the default and overriding matching behaviors.

The `subexpression` value is 0 by default. This means that it returns only those values that match the complete set of subexpressions. You can override the subexpression with an integer value from 1 to 9. The function then returns all matches that meet that subexpression, whether or not they meet the other subexpressions.

The following example finds the starting and ending positions for the *first* occurrence of the proper noun Sauron in the sample story:

```
SQL> SELECT REGEXP_INSTR(story_thread,'sauron',1,1,0,'i') AS "Begin"
     ,      REGEXP_INSTR(story_thread,'sauron',1,1,1,'i') - 1 AS "End"
     FROM   sample_regexp;
```

This returns the following starting and ending values:

```
     Begin        End
---------- ----------
        56         61
```

This has demonstrated how to find starting and ending points in strings. Together these two values let you parse a substring from a string. The function becomes more useful as the complexity of your pattern search grows.

REGEXP_LIKE Function

The `REGEXP_LIKE` function lets you find a regular expression match inside a string. You use it in lieu of the old `LIKE` comparison operator.

The prototype for the function is

```
REGEXP_LIKE(source_string, pattern [, match_type_flag])
```

The `source_string` can be any character expression, provided the data type is a `CHAR`, `CLOB`, `NCHAR`, `NCLOB`, `NVARCHAR2`, or `VARCHAR2`. You may recall from Chapter 8 that an expression can be a string literal or a function return value that meets the data type requirement. The character expression can also be a column value or a bind variable. For example, you could use `:new.column_name` as a `source_string` value in a database trigger. See Chapter 12 for more information on database triggers.

The `pattern` value can be any valid regular expression, but *the length must be less than or equal to 512 characters*. POSIX regular expressions are supported in Oracle Database 11*g* forward. You must prepend any apostrophe with a single quote because you pass the `pattern` value as an actual parameter into a function call. Alternatively, you can reset the quote identifier in your session. The "Back-Quoting in Oracle" sidebar of Appendix A shows you how to substitute another backquoting identifier for the default apostrophe.

The `match_type_flag` value is a text literal expression, typically a string literal. The string may contain either an `i` or a `c`, and one or more of the following: `n`, `m`, or `x`. Collectively, they override the default matching behavior. Table E-4 in the earlier section "REGEXP_COUNT Function" contains the default and overriding matching behaviors.

In addition to the several examples illustrating range and portable character-class handling in the "Character Classes" section earlier in this appendix, the following example searches the sample string for a line beginning "a last alliance of elves and men":

```
SQL> SELECT sample_regexp_id
     FROM   sample_regexp
     WHERE  REGEXP_LIKE(
                story_thread
              ,'?a last alliance of elves and men?','i');
```

The effectiveness of this search is that you can apply it against a CHAR, CLOB, NCHAR, NCLOB, NVARCHAR2, or VARCHAR2 data type. The search is case insensitive and actually returns the row's primary key value. You should note that it uses ? (*question mark*) characters to make the white spaces before and after the string optional.

REGEXP_REPLACE Function

The REGEXP_REPLACE function lets you find and replace a substring inside of a string. The prototype for the function is

```
REGEXP_REPLACE(source_string, pattern , replace_string [, start_position
              [, occurrence [, match_type_flag]]])
```

The source_string can be any character expression, provided the data type is a CHAR, CLOB, NCHAR, NCLOB, NVARCHAR2, or VARCHAR2. You may recall from Chapter 8 that an expression can be a string literal or a function return value that meets the data type requirement. The character expression can also be a column value or a bind variable. For example, you could use :new.column_name as a source_string value in a database trigger. See Chapter 12 for more information on database triggers.

The pattern value can be any valid regular expression, but *the length must be less than or equal to 512 characters*. POSIX regular expressions are supported in Oracle Database 11*g* and 12*c*. You must prepend any apostrophe with a single quote because you pass the pattern value as an actual parameter into a function call. Alternatively, you can reset the quote identifier in your session. The "Back-Quoting in Oracle" sidebar of Appendix A shows you how to substitute another backquoting identifier for the default apostrophe.

The replace_string can be any character expression, provided the data type is a CHAR, CLOB, NCHAR, NCLOB, NVARCHAR2, or VARCHAR2. If the replace_string is a CLOB or NCLOB data type, then Oracle Database 12*c* truncates the string to 32KB.

The start_position value is an integer expression. The default value is 1. It is not uncommon to find a starting point inside the string by calling the REGEXP_INSTR function as an expression for this actual parameter.

The occurrence value is an integer expression. The default value is 1. If you want another occurrence, you must provide a value. Override values typically have business rules that are too complex to predict here.

The match_type_flag value is a text literal expression, typically a string literal. The string may contain either an i or a c, and one or more of the following: n, m, or x. Collectively, they override the default matching behavior. Table E-4 in the earlier section "REGEXP_COUNT Function" contains the default and overriding matching behaviors.

The following example replaces all occurrences of Sauron with Sauroman, which may disconcert some dedicated Tolkien fans. No sacrilege is intended to a great piece of fiction.

```
SQL> DECLARE
      lv_container   VARCHAR2(4000);
      lv_begin       NUMBER := 1;
      lv_end         NUMBER;
      -- Define a cursor to recover correct story thread.
      CURSOR c IS
        SELECT story_thread
        FROM   sample_regexp
```

```
 9     WHERE  REGEXP_LIKE(
10                story_thread,'a last alliance of elves and men','i');
11   BEGIN
12     OPEN c;
13     LOOP
14       FETCH c INTO lv_container;
15       EXIT WHEN c%NOTFOUND;
16       -- Count the number of instances of Sauron in the string.
17       lv_end := REGEXP_COUNT(lv_container,'Sauron',lv_begin,'i');
18
19       -- Replace all instances one at a time.
20       FOR i IN lv_begin..lv_end LOOP
21         lv_container := REGEXP_REPLACE(
22                           lv_container,'Sauron','Sauroman',lv_begin,1,'i');
23       END LOOP;
24       dbms_output.put_line(lv_container);
25     END LOOP;
26   END;
27   /
```

It prints the modified string:

```
"The prologue, spoken by Galadriel, shows the Dark Lord Sauroman forging the One
Ring, which he can use to conquer the lands of Middle-earth through his
enslavement of the bearers of the Rings of Power. The Rings of Power are
powerful magical rings given to individuals from the races of Elves, Dwarves,
and Men. A Last Alliance of Elves and Men is formed to counter Sauroman and his
forces at the foot of Mount Doom, but Sauroman himself appears to kill Elendil,
the king of the Mannish kingdom of Gondor. Just afterward, Isildur grabs his
father's broken sword Narsil and slashes at Sauroman's hand. The stroke cuts
off Sauroman's fingers, separating him from the Ring and vanquishing his army.
However, because Sauroman's life is bound in the Ring, he is not completely
defeated until the Ring itself is destroyed. Isildur takes the Ring and succumbs
to its temptation, refusing to destroy it, but he is later ambushed and killed
by orcs and the Ring is lost in the river into which Isildur fell."
```

A call to the `REGEXP_LIKE` function in the cursor looks for the correct row in the table. The call to the `REGEXP_COUNT` function on line 17 counts the number of times Sauron appears in the string. It does that by starting at the beginning of the `lv_container` string and looking through it for all instances of the literal word—*Sauron*. While not done in this case, the combination of subexpressions and nested subexpressions would let you check for alternatives.

The call to `REGEXP_REPLACE` on lines 21 and 22 replaces all occurrences of Sauron with Sauroman by reading the entire string each time through the loop and replacing the first instance of Sauron. After replacing the first occurrence, it returns the modified string to a new copy of the variable. The loop then performs the same operation until all instances are replaced.

REGEXP_SUBSTR Function

The `REGEXP_SUBSTR` function was enhanced in Oracle Database 11*g* to enable the use of a restricting subordinate expression, and it retains the same capabilities in Oracle Database 12*c*. The `REGEXP_SUBSTR` function lets you find a substring inside a string.

The prototype for the function is

```
REGEXP_SUBSTR(source_string, pattern [, start_position [, occurrence
          [, match_type_flag [, subexpression]]]]])
```

The new subexpression lets you do priority searching on subexpressions. A quick refresher of what this means is found in the "REGEXP_INSTR Function" section.

The `source_string` can be any character expression, provided the data type is a `CHAR`, `CLOB`, `NCHAR`, `NCLOB`, `NVARCHAR2`, or `VARCHAR2`. You may recall from Chapter 8 that an expression can be a string literal or a function return value that meets the data type requirement. The character expression can also be a column value or a bind variable. For example, you could use `:new.column_name` as a `source_string` value in a database trigger. See Chapter 12 for more information on database triggers.

The `pattern` value can be any valid regular expression, but *the length must be less than or equal to 512 characters*. POSIX regular expressions are supported in Oracle Database 11*g* and 12*c*. You must prepend any apostrophe with a single quote because you pass the `pattern` value as an actual parameter into a function call. Alternatively, you can reset the quote identifier in your session. The "Back-Quoting in Oracle" sidebar of Appendix A shows you how to substitute another backquoting identifier for the default apostrophe.

The `start_position` value is an integer expression. The default value is 1. It is not uncommon to find a starting point inside the string by calling the `REGEXP_INSTR` function as an expression for this actual parameter.

The `occurrence` value is an integer expression. The default value is 1. If you want another occurrence, you must provide a value. Override values typically have business rules that are too complex to predict here.

The `return_option` value is an integer expression. The default value is 0, which represents the position or index of *the beginning* of the first substring matched by the pattern. You can override this value by using a 1, which instructs the function to return *the character after* the substring that matches the pattern.

The `match_type_flag` value is a text literal expression, typically a string literal. The string may contain either an `i` or a `c`, and one or more of the following: `n`, `m`, or `x`. Collectively, they override the default matching behavior. Table E-4 in the earlier section "REGEXP_COUNT Function" contains the default and overriding matching behaviors.

The `subexpression` value is 0 by default. This means that it returns only those values that match the complete set of subexpressions. You can override the subexpression with an integer value from 1 to 9. The function then returns all matches that meet that subexpression, whether or not they meet the other subexpressions.

The `REGEXP_SUBSTR` function lets you find a substring inside a string. The following sample finds the first 50 complete words and punctuation beginning at position 53 in the data column:

```
SQL> SELECT LTRIM(REGEXP_SUBSTR(story_thread
               ,'((^| +)|(["'']))([[:alpha:]]+(([-:,\.'';])|( +|$))+\.?){1,7}'
               ,44,1,'i')) AS substring
     FROM sample_regexp
     WHERE  REGEXP_LIKE(story_thread,'a last alliance of elves and men','i');
```

It returns the following substring:

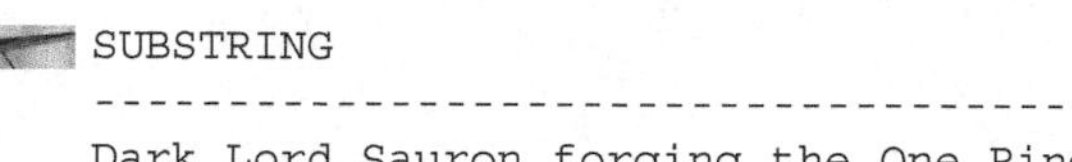

```
SUBSTRING
------------------------------------
Dark Lord Sauron forging the One Ring
```

The starting position is in the middle of the word prior to Dark. The interval captures the first seven whole words that start at or after position 44 in the `story_thread` column value. If you set the start point as 1 and the maximum interval value to a number greater than the number of words in the string, this pattern returns an entire string.

Like the prior patterns, this pattern uses a compound subexpression to check for (a) either a beginning line metacharacter or a white space, or (b) a quotation character at the beginning of the string. It then checks for an optional alphabetical string by using a POSIX portable character class. Finally, it uses another compound subexpression to check for (a) punctuation characters or (b) either a white space or end-of-line metacharacter.

Two search principals are demonstrated in the regular expression. First, the pattern uses a backquoted `.` (period) to find the beginning of another word before using the between interval metacharacter to repeat the matching behavior (check Table E-2 for more information on the between metacharacter). Second, the apostrophes are backquoted by other single quotes because the single quote is an identifier in an Oracle Database 12*c* database.

This section has presented the last regular expression function, `REGEXP_SUBSTR`, and has demonstrated how to capture a substring from a string using regular expressions. These features are nice for large character strings and are critical for quick pattern analysis of `CLOB` data types.

Supporting Scripts

This section describes programs placed on the McGraw-Hill Professional website to support this appendix:

- The `character_class.sql` program shows how alphabetic and alphanumeric values are managed in SQL and PL/SQL. It shows handling within `SELECT` statements and anonymous PL/SQL blocks. It uses the `REGEXP_LIKE` and `SUBSTR` functions.
- The `regexp_in_clob.sql` program shows all the examples that work with the passage describing *The Lord of the Rings*. It also creates and seeds the table used in the examples.

Summary

This appendix has explained regular expressions and shown you how to use regular expressions to search text. You also have learned why centralizing matching logic in the Oracle Database 12*c* database helps you avoid middle-tier string processing.

APPENDIX F

Wrapping PL/SQL Code Primer

Oracle Database 12*c* provides the capability to wrap your PL/SQL stored programs. Wrapping your code encapsulates the business logic of your applications from prying eyes by hiding (or *obfuscating*) the source code. It converts the clear text in the database to an unreadable stream of data. You can obfuscate the clear text by using the command-line `wrap` utility or by calling the `dbms_ddl` package's `create_wrapped` procedure or `WRAP` function.

You should wrap only the implementation details, which means you should wrap only functions, procedures, package bodies, and type bodies. This leaves the package specification and type specification as open text, enabling other developers to use your code. They won't know how your code performs the task, but they will know which actual parameters they can submit and what to expect back from functions or type methods. You should ensure that you comment the specification with any helpful information that will enable other developers to take advantage of wrapped code units, especially procedures because they don't define a direct return type like functions.

NOTE
Oracle Database 12c uses the internal DIANA (Descriptive Intermediate Attributed Notation for ADA) to obfuscate code. Using DIANA's structures to reverse-engineer and unwrap obfuscated code is difficult but not impossible.

The topics in this appendix are addressed in the following order:

- Limitations of wrapping PL/SQL
- Using the `wrap` command-line utility
- Using the `dbms_ddl` package to wrap PL/SQL
  - `WRAP` function
  - `CREATE_WRAPPED` procedure

Limitations of Wrapping PL/SQL

Generically wrapping PL/SQL code in the database has the following limitations:

- You cannot wrap the source code of a database trigger. However, you can reduce the logic to a single call to a wrapped stored function or procedure.
- Wrapping does not detect syntax or semantic errors, such as missing tables or views; in this respect, it differs from normal compilation. Wrapped code units manifest runtime errors for missing tables or views, like Native Dynamic SQL (NDS) statements.
- Wrapped code is only forward compatible for import into the database. This means that you can import wrapped modules built by an Oracle Database 10*g* or 11*g* database into a 12*c* database but not vice versa.

While it is difficult to decipher passwords in wrapped code, it isn't impossible. Oracle recommends that you don't embed passwords in wrapped program units. The exception to this rule occurs when you're using encryption and need to validate a password. An encrypted program can read an invisible and redacted column from a table or another *no parameter* procedure. The query or procedure may also use Virtual Private Database (VPD) striping to select the correct encrypted key.

There are specific errors generated by the method that you choose to wrap your code. The limitations are described in the next two subsections.

Limitations of the PL/SQL wrap Utility

The `wrap` utility is parsed by the PL/SQL compiler, not by the SQL*Plus compiler. This means that you cannot include SQL*Plus `DEFINE` notation inside wrapped program units. Also, most comments are removed when wrapped.

Limitations of the DBMS_DDL.WRAP Function

When you invoke `DBMS_SQL.PARSE` with a data type that is a `VARCHAR2A` or `VARCHAR2S` and the text exceeds 32,767 bytes, you must set the `LFFLG` parameter to false. If you fail to do so, `DBMS_SQL.PARSE` adds newline characters to the wrapped unit and corrupts it.

Using the wrap Command-Line Utility

The `wrap` command-line utility works with files. It wraps everything in the file, which is a critical point to understand. When you use the `wrap` utility, package specifications and type definitions should be in different physical files from their respective package bodies and type bodies. As discussed earlier, you should wrap only the implementation details, not the published specifications.

The prototype for the `wrap` utility is

```
wrap iname=input_file[{.sql |.ext}] [oname=output_file[{.plb |.ext}]
```

You can qualify the input and output files as relative or canonical filenames. Canonical filenames start at the root mount point in Linux or Unix and from a logical file system reference in Microsoft Windows. The default file extension is `.sql` for input files and `.plb` for output files. You do not need to provide either extension if you are prepared to accept the default values, but you must provide overriding values when they differ.

The following example works when the `wrap` command runs from the same directory as the input and output files:

```
wrap iname=input_file.sql oname=output_file.plb
```

After you wrap the files, you can then compile them into the database. The compilation process will not raise exceptions if table or view dependencies are missing, because no syntax, semantic, or dependency checking occurs during compilation of wrapped program units. They compile because the SQL DDL commands to `CREATE [OR REPLACE]` function, procedures, package specifications and bodies, and type definitions and bodies are scrambled into a form understood by the PL/SQL compiler.

The `CREATE [OR REPLACE] TRIGGER` statement and anonymous block `DECLARE`, `BEGIN`, and `END` keywords are not obfuscated. Comments inside the header declaration and C-style multiple-line comments, delimited by `/*` and `*/`, are also not obfuscated.

Using the DBMS_DDL Command-Line Utility

The `dbms_ddl` package contains an overloaded `WRAP` function and an overloaded `CREATE_WRAPPED` procedure. You can use either to create a wrapped stored programming unit. The subsections cover both.

WRAP Function

The `WRAP` function is an overloaded function that accepts a DDL statement as a single variable-length string of 32,767 or fewer bytes, a table of strings 256 bytes in length, or a table of strings 32,767 bytes in length. The `dbms_sql` package holds the definition of the data types for the 256- and 32,767-byte string collections.

The first prototype supports using a single input parameter:

```
DBMS_DDL.WRAP(ddl VARCHAR2) RETURN VARCHAR2
DBMS_DDL.WRAP(ddl DBMS_SQL.VARCHAR2S) RETURN VARCHAR2S
DBMS_DDL.WRAP(ddl DBMS_SQL.VARCHAR2A) RETURN VARCHAR2A
```

You can use this function to wrap a stored program unit as follows:

```
SQL> DECLARE
       source VARCHAR2(32767);
       result VARCHAR2(32767);
     BEGIN
       source := 'CREATE FUNCTION one RETURN NUMBER IS'||CHR(10)
              || 'BEGIN'||CHR(10)
              || '  RETURN 1;'||CHR(10)
              || 'END;';
       result := DBMS_DDL.WRAP(ddl => source);
       EXECUTE IMMEDIATE result;
     END;
     /
```

The program defines a DDL string, obfuscates it into the `result` variable, and then uses NDS to create the obfuscated function in the database. You can see the function specification by using the SQL*Plus `DESCRIBE` command:

```
SQL> DESCRIBE one
FUNCTION one RETURNS NUMBER
```

Any attempt to inspect its detailed operations will yield an obfuscated result. You can test this by querying the stored function implementation in the `text` column of the `user_source` table, like the following:

```
SQL> COLUMN text FORMAT A80 HEADING "Source Text"
SQL> SET PAGESIZE 49999
SQL> SELECT text FROM user_source WHERE name = 'ONE';
```

The following output is returned:

```
FUNCTION one wrapped
a000000
369
abcd
... et cetera ...
```

The function can be rewritten to use a table of strings, as follows:

```
SQL> DECLARE
  2    stmt    VARCHAR2(32767);
  3    source DBMS_SQL.VARCHAR2S;
  4    result DBMS_SQL.VARCHAR2S;
  5  BEGIN
  6    source(1)  := 'CREATE FUNCTION two RETURN NUMBER IS ';
  7    source(2)  := '   BEGIN RETURN 2;';
  8    source(3)  := 'END;';
  9    result := DBMS_DDL.WRAP(ddl => source
 10                           ,lb => 1
 11                           ,ub => source.COUNT);
 12    FOR i IN 1..result.COUNT LOOP
 13      stmt := stmt || result(i);
 14    END LOOP;
 15    EXECUTE IMMEDIATE ;
 16  END;
 17  /
```

Line 2 uses a 32,767-byte maximum size VARCHAR2 data type, while lines 3 and 4 qualify the 256-byte string collection from the dbms_sql package specification. If this wasn't a small function to wrap, you could overflow the stmt variable's maximum size with 128 full lines of program content in the source collection. Realistically, as a best practice, the stmt variable should use a CLOB data type to avoid any overflow of a variable type.

You also have the ability to define a much larger string size for the source and result variables—32,767 bytes. This simply requires changing the VARCHAR2S data type to a VARCHAR2A, like

```
  3    source DBMS_SQL.VARCHAR2A;
  4    result DBMS_SQL.VARCHAR2A;
```

Lines 9 through 11 call the dbms_ddl.wrap function. Developers should take note that the source variable must be defined as either the dbms_sql.varchar2s or dbms_sql .varchar2a data type. As mentioned, the former holds strings of up to 256 bytes, while the latter holds strings of up to 32,767 bytes. Any data type other than those defined in the dbms_sql package raises a PLS-00306 exception because the actual parameter wouldn't match the data type of the formal parameter.

Line 12 through 14 loop through the result collection data type and convert it to a simple string. This is required in Oracle Database 10*g* and 11*g* but not in 12*c*. Chapter 6 explains how PL/SQL and SQL variables are *implicitly* interchangeable from local PL/SQL blocks to SQL statements when the SQL statement is run from within the block where the PL/SQL variable is declared. The ability to assign a collection to a local CLOB variable appears restricted to this singular use case (only the return type from the dbms_ddl package's WRAP function works). Line 15 executes the wrapped statement.

A more effective way to write this sample program for Oracle Database 12*c* is

```
SQL> DECLARE
  2    stmt    CLOB;
  3    source DBMS_SQL.VARCHAR2A;
```

```
 4     result DBMS_SQL.VARCHAR2A;
 5   BEGIN
 6     source(1) := 'CREATE FUNCTION two RETURN NUMBER IS ';
 7     source(2) := '  BEGIN RETURN 2;';
 8     source(3) := 'END;';
 9     result := DBMS_DDL.WRAP(ddl => source
10                            ,lb => 1
11                            ,ub => source.COUNT);
12     SELECT   column_value
13     INTO     stmt
14     FROM     TABLE(result);
15     EXECUTE IMMEDIATE stmt;
16   END;
17   /
```

Line 2 defines the `stmt` variable as a `CLOB`, and lines 3 and 4 define the source and result variables as 32,767-byte PL/SQL collections. Lines 12 through 13 collect the result collection of a PL/SQL collection data type directly into a SQL result set that is assigned to a `CLOB` data type. Lastly, line 15 executes the contents of the `CLOB` and creates the `two` function as a wrapped program unit.

If you were to attempt the foregoing Oracle Database 12*c* syntax in Oracle Database 11*g* or earlier, you'd see this type of exception because PL/SQL data types couldn't be handled by SQL:

```
  FROM     TABLE(result);
                 *
ERROR at line 14:
ORA-06550: line 14, column 18:
PLS-00382: expression is of wrong type
ORA-06550: line 14, column 12:
PL/SQL: ORA-22905: cannot access rows from a non-nested table item
ORA-06550: line 12, column 3:
PL/SQL: SQL Statement ignored
```

The key errors are the `ORA-22905` and `PLS-00382`. The `PLS-00382` error occurs first and means you can't reference a PL/SQL collection as a call or actual parameter of the `TABLE` function (see Appendix C for more information on this change in behavior). The `ORA-22905` error is caused because the first error causes the function to return a null set from a collection.

You can see the function specification by using the SQL*Plus `DESCRIBE` command:

```
SQL> DESCRIBE two
FUNCTION two RETURNS NUMBER
```

You can also query the data dictionary to view the `two` function's source, like this:

```
SQL> SELECT text
  2  FROM   user_source
  3  WHERE  name = 'TWO';
```

It returns

```
TEXT
----------------------------------------------------------------
FUNCTION two wrapped
```

```
a000000
369
abcd
… et cetera …
```

SQL Scope Access in Oracle Database 12*c*

Oracle Database 12*c* makes some changes in SQL scope access within PL/SQL blocks. You can embed a locally defined PL/SQL collection inside a SQL statement, but you can't embed a call to a local function that returns a PL/SQL collection.

To examine how you leverage the changes in SQL scope access, you need to create a PL/SQL associative array, which can be done in a PL/SQL package. The following creates a bodiless package whose sole purpose is to define a PL/SQL associative array data type:

```
SQL> CREATE OR REPLACE PACKAGE type_defs IS
       TYPE plsql_table IS TABLE OF VARCHAR2(20)
         INDEX BY BINARY_INTEGER;
     END type_defs;
     /
```

Next, you define a schema-level function that returns a collection of the `plsql_table` data type defined in the `type_defs` PL/SQL package. The definition of the return type variable uses the package name, a dot (`.`), and a data type, like

```
SQL> CREATE OR REPLACE FUNCTION implicit_convert
  2    RETURN type_defs.plsql_table IS
  3    lv_index  NUMBER := 1;           -- Counter variable.
  4    lv_list   TYPE_DEFS.PLSQL_TABLE; -- Collection variable.
  5    CURSOR c IS SELECT person FROM honeymooners;
  6  BEGIN
  7    FOR i IN c LOOP
  8      lv_list(lv_index) := i.person;
  9      lv_index := lv_index + 1;
 10    END LOOP;
 11    RETURN lv_list;  -- Return locally scope PL/SQL collection.
 12  END;
 13  /
```

Line 4 declares a PL/SQL collection data type, and line 11 returns it from any call to the `implicit_convert` function.

The following code block tests the changes in SQL scope access by declaring a local `lv_list` variable of the PL/SQL associative array data type defined in the `type_defs` package:

```
SQL> DECLARE
       lv_list   TYPE_DEFS.PLSQL_TABLE; -- Local PL/SQL collection.
     BEGIN
```

(continued)

```
 4    lv_list := implicit_convert;      -- Assign collection values.
 5    FOR i IN (SELECT   column_value
 6              FROM     TABLE(lv_list)) LOOP
 7      dbms_output.put_line(i.column_value);
 8    END LOOP;
 9  END;
10  /
```

Line 2 declares a local PL/SQL collection, and line 4 populates the collection with the results from the `implicit_convert` function. Lines 5 and 6 show how you can use the local PL/SQL collection, an associative array, inside a `SELECT` statement by passing the local associative array as a call parameter to the `TABLE` function.

You raise a different error message when you attempt to put a call to the schema-level function inside the `TABLE` function, like

```
 5    FOR i IN (SELECT   column_value
 6              FROM     TABLE(implicit_convert) LOOP
```

It displays this type of error message:

```
           FROM     TABLE(implicit_convert)) LOOP
                          *
ERROR at line 6:
ORA-06550: line 6, column 28:
PLS-00382: expression is of wrong type
ORA-06550: line 6, column 22:
PL/SQL: ORA-22905: cannot access rows from a non-nested table item
```

SQL statements can use local variables with PL/SQL associative array data types, provided the SQL statement runs within the scope of a PL/SQL block. Calls to PL/SQL functions only work when the data type is a schema-level collection rather than a PL/SQL associative array.

This section has demonstrated how to use the `dbms_ddl.wrap` command. The next section shows you how to use the `create_wrapped` procedure.

CREATE_WRAPPED Procedure

The `create_wrapped` function is an overloaded function that accepts a DDL statement as a single variable-length string of 32,767 or fewer bytes, a table of strings 256 bytes in length, or a table of strings 32,767 bytes in length. You supply a lower and upper bound for the table of strings when the actual parameter is a table of strings. The lower bound is always 1, and the upper bound is the maximum number of rows in the collection of strings.

The prototypes support using a single input parameter or a table of strings:

```
DBMS_DDL.CREATE_WRAPPED(ddl VARCHAR2) RETURN VARCHAR2
DBMS_DDL.CREATE_WRAPPED(ddl DBMS_SQL.VARCHAR2S) RETURN VARCHAR2S
DBMS_DDL.CREATE_WRAPPED(ddl DBMS_SQL.VARCHAR2A) RETURN VARCHAR2A
```

You can use this anonymous block to test the wrapping procedure:

```
SQL> BEGIN
       dbms_ddl.create_wrapped(
         'CREATE OR REPLACE FUNCTION hello_world RETURN STRING AS '
         ||'BEGIN '
         ||'  RETURN ''Hello World!''; '
         ||'END;');
     END;
     /
```

After creating the `hello_world` function, you can query it by using the following SQL*Plus column formatting and query:

```
SQL> COLUMN message FORMAT A20 HEADING "Message"
SQL> SELECT hello_world AS message FROM dual;

Message
--------------------
Hello World!
```

You can describe the function to inspect its signature and return type:

```
SQL> DESCRIBE hello_world
FUNCTION hello_world RETURNS VARCHAR2
```

Any attempt to inspect its detailed operations will yield an obfuscated result. You can test this by querying the stored function implementation in the `text` column of the `user_source` table, like the following:

```
SQL> COLUMN text FORMAT A80 HEADING "Source Text"
SQL> SET PAGESIZE 49999
SQL> SELECT text FROM user_source WHERE name = 'HELLO_WORLD';
```

The following output is returned:

```
FUNCTION hello_world wrapped
a000000
369
abcd
… et cetera …
```

The procedure can be rewritten to use a table of strings, as follows:

```
DECLARE
  source DBMS_SQL.VARCHAR2S;
  stmt      VARCHAR2(4000);
BEGIN
  source(1) := 'CREATE FUNCTION hello_world2 RETURN VARCHAR2 IS ';
  source(2) := '  BEGIN RETURN 2;';
  source(3) := '  END;';
  DBMS_DDL.CREATE_WRAPPED(ddl => source, lb => 1, ub => source.COUNT);
END;
/
```

You don't have to use NDS to build the function when you call the `create_wrapped` procedure, because the `create_wrapped` procedure builds the stored program for you, unlike the `wrap` function, which only returns the wrapped string or table of strings.

Summary

This appendix has shown you how to hide the implementation details of your PL/SQL stored programming units. You've seen how to use the command-line `wrap` utility, and the built-in `create_wrapped` procedure and `wrap` function from the `dbms_ddl` package. You should remember to hide only the implementation details, not the package specifications and object type definitions.

APPENDIX G

PL/SQL Hierarchical Profiler Primer

The PL/SQL hierarchical profiler, introduced in Oracle Database 11*g*, enables you to capture the dynamic execution performance of your PL/SQL programs. It divides PL/SQL execution times into two parts: SQL statement execution times and PL/SQL program unit execution times.

A hierarchical profiler provides you with more insight than a nonhierarchical profiler. A nonhierarchical profiler only reports how much time a module consumed. A hierarchical profile tells you which program called what subroutine and how many times the subroutine was called. The PL/SQL hierarchical profiler stores results in a set of hierarchical profiler tables. It divides the data by subprogram units, including the relationship between calling and called subroutines, and it further subdivides execution time by the SQL statement versus PL/SQL execution segments.

This appendix describes the PL/SQL hierarchical profiler and demonstrates how to configure and use it. Coverage of the profiler is organized as follows:

- Configuring the schema
- Collecting profile data
- Understanding profiler output
- Using the `plshprof` command-line utility

The sections are organized sequentially, but you can jump directly to the information required provided the schema is configured.

Configuring the Schema

The first step to configure the PL/SQL hierarchical profiler is to build the tables in the `SYS` schema. You do this by connecting to the database as the privileged user.

In Oracle Database 12*c*, you no longer can directly connect as the `sysdba` privileged user from the command line. You must first connect to `sqlplus` without logging in to an account, like

```
# sqlplus /nolog
```

Once you're inside the `sqlplus` environment, you can connect as `sysdba` with the following command followed by a correct password:

```
Connect sys / as sysdba
Enter password:
Connected.
```

As the privileged user, you now build the supplemental data catalog tables required to support the PL/SQL hierarchical profiler. The following command runs the `dbmshptab.sql` script:

```
SQL> @?/rdbms/admin/dbmshptab.sql
```

The script should raise some exceptions for missing tables, which you can ignore. The PL/SQL hierarchical profiler uses the `dbms_hprof` package, which is invalid until you create the tables. Figure G-1 depicts the tables and their relationships, but you should remember that they're

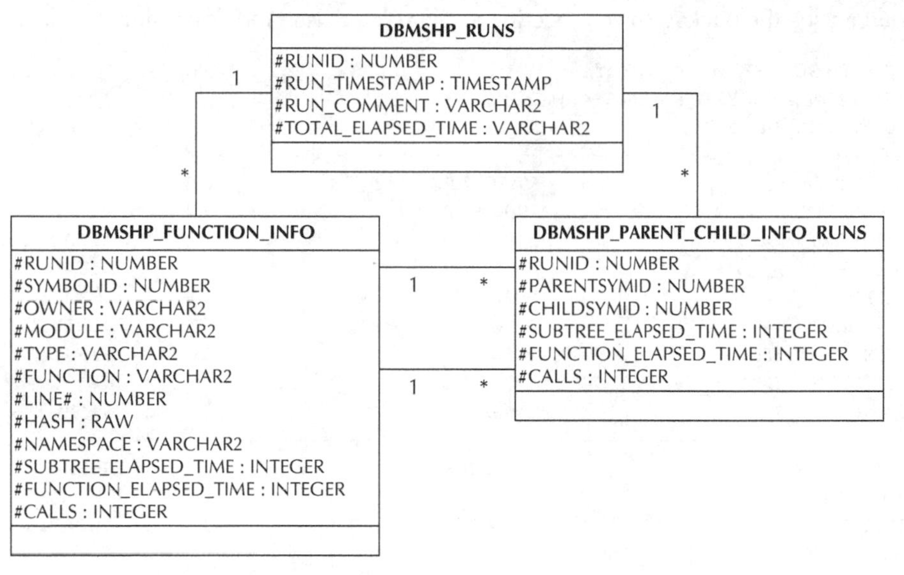

FIGURE G-1. *PL/SQL hierarchical profiler tables*

owned by `SYS` unless you grant `SELECT` permissions to development schemas or you rerun the `dbmshptab.sql` script against the target `video` schema.

If you don't rerun the script against the target `video` schema, you won't be able to analyze your output. Therefore, you should connect to the `video` schema and rerun this command:

```
SQL> @?/rdbms/admin/dbmshptab.sql
```

The "Understanding Profiler Data" section has more detail on the three tables that support the profiler. You need to understand this material if you want to build your own analytical modeling capability.

After creating the tables, you grant execute permission on the package to your target schema, create a profiler virtual directory, and grant read and write permissions on the directory to your target schema. This requirement exists because the hierarchical profiler runs as an *invoker rights* model (see Appendix A for a description of invoker rights). You execute these commands as `sysdba` when running in Linux or Unix (change `/tmp/` to `C:/Windows/Temp` on Windows):

```
GRANT EXECUTE ON dbms_hprof TO video;
CREATE OR REPLACE DIRECTORY profiler_dir AS '/tmp/';
GRANT READ, WRITE ON DIRECTORY profiler_dir TO video;
```

You do not need to create a synonym because the Oracle Database 12*c* database seeds a public synonym for the `dbms_hprof` package. This is also true for the `dbmshp_runnumber` sequence that is created when you build the PL/SQL hierarchical profiler repository. Verify that you can see the package by connecting as the `video` user and describing the package:

```
SQL> DESCRIBE dbms_hprof
FUNCTION ANALYZE RETURNS NUMBER
 Argument Name                  Type                    In/Out Default?
 ------------------------------ ----------------------- ------ --------
 LOCATION                       VARCHAR2                IN
 FILENAME                       VARCHAR2                IN
 SUMMARY_MODE                   BOOLEAN                 IN     DEFAULT
 TRACE                          VARCHAR2                IN     DEFAULT
 SKIP                           BINARY_INTEGER          IN     DEFAULT
 COLLECT                        BINARY_INTEGER          IN     DEFAULT
 RUN_COMMENT                    VARCHAR2                IN     DEFAULT
PROCEDURE START_PROFILING
 Argument Name                  Type                    In/Out Default?
 ------------------------------ ----------------------- ------ --------
 LOCATION                       VARCHAR2                IN     DEFAULT
 FILENAME                       VARCHAR2                IN     DEFAULT
 MAX_DEPTH                      BINARY_INTEGER          IN     DEFAULT
PROCEDURE STOP_PROFILING
```

The `dbms_hprof` package has two procedures for starting and stopping data collection, and one function for gathering and analyzing data. The next section explains how to use these methods.

Collecting Profiler Data

Collecting data from the PL/SQL hierarchical profiler requires that you configure the database, as covered in the prior section. Then, you must start the profiler, run your test, and stop the profiler. You stop it because running it constantly consumes unnecessary database resources.

In order to collect data from the profiler, you'll need to build a test case. This test case requires that you've run the video store code scripts found in the Introduction of this book. The `test_profiler.sql` script creates the code components, starts the profiler, runs the test, and stops the profiler. It will also verify that you got all the configuration steps correct, because it'll fail if it can't call the package methods or write a file to your `/tmp` (or `C:\Windows\Temp`) directory.

The first step in this test requires that you build a `glue_strings` function that will be called for every row of a cursor statement. The function definition follows:

```
SQL> CREATE OR REPLACE FUNCTION glue_strings
  (string1 VARCHAR2, string2 VARCHAR2) RETURN VARCHAR2 IS
    new_string VARCHAR2(2000);
  BEGIN
    IF string1 IS NOT NULL THEN
      IF string2 IS NOT NULL THEN
        new_string := string1 || ': ' || string2;
      ELSE
        new_string := string1;
      END IF;
    ELSE
      IF string2 IS NOT NULL THEN
```

```
        new_string := string2;
      END IF;
    END IF;
    RETURN new_string;
  END glue_strings;
  /
```

The function is designed to take two strings and concatenate them, provided neither of them is a null value. When one is a null value, the not-null value is returned. Naturally, a null is returned when both inputs are null because the `new_string` variable is declared, not defined, and all declared scalar variables are initialized with a null value by default.

The next component for the test is a `quantity_onhand` procedure. It takes two formal parameters by value and two by reference. Both `IN OUT` mode parameters are nested table collections (see Chapter 6 for details on collections).

The collections require you to define two user-defined Attribute Data Types (ADTs) in SQL. The first ADT collection is a table of variable-length strings with a maximum size of 2,000 characters, like

```
SQL> CREATE OR REPLACE
       TYPE varchar2_table IS TABLE OF VARCHAR2(2000);
     /
```

The second ADT collection is a table of numbers, like

```
SQL> CREATE OR REPLACE
       TYPE number_table IS TABLE OF NUMBER;
     /
```

Now that you've defined the two ADT collections (`varchar2_table` and `number_table`), you can define the `quantity_onhand` procedure, which uses the ADT collections as pass-by-reference formal parameters.

The `quantity_onhand` procedure is

```
SQL> CREATE OR REPLACE PROCEDURE quantity_onhand
     ( item_title         IN     VARCHAR2
     , item_rating_agency IN     VARCHAR2
     , item_titles        IN OUT VARCHAR2_TABLE
     , quantities         IN OUT NUMBER_TABLE) IS
       -- Define counter variable.
       counter            NUMBER := 1;
       -- Define dynamic cursor.
       CURSOR c
       ( item_title_in         VARCHAR2
       , item_rating_agency_in VARCHAR2) IS
         SELECT   glue_strings(item_title,item_subtitle) AS full_title
         ,        COUNT(*) AS quantity_on_hand
         FROM     item
         WHERE    REGEXP_LIKE(item_title,item_title_in)
         AND      item_rating_agency = item_rating_agency_in
         GROUP BY glue_strings(item_title,item_subtitle)
         ,        item_rating_agency;
```

```
BEGIN
  -- Read cursor and assign column values to parallel arrays.
  FOR i IN c (item_title,item_rating_agency) LOOP
    item_titles.EXTEND;
    item_titles(counter) := i.full_title;
    quantities.EXTEND;
    quantities(counter) := i.quantity_on_hand;
    counter := counter + 1;
  END LOOP;
END;
/
```

You assign *row-by-row* values to the nested table collections, but production systems would use a `BULK COLLECT` (as qualified in Chapter 3). The `counter` variable indexes the nested table collections because the `FOR` loop `i` variable is a pointer referencing the rows returned by the cursor. You raise a `PLS-00382` exception, which means the expression is the wrong type for an assignment.

Another alternative would involve using a system reference cursor, which you'd explicitly open inside the procedure. A system reference cursor example is not presented in the book, but one is provided on the publisher's website, named `profiler_test_script.sql`.

NOTE
When a system reference cursor replaces a set of parallel collections, the `IN OUT` mode `SYS_REFCURSOR` is passed back to the calling program as a pointer to the internal cursor work area.

As mentioned, the `glue_strings` function runs for all returned rows. The anonymous block program starts the profiler as the first action in the execution block, and it stops the profiler as the last action.

The following testing program runs the `quantity_onhand` procedure once:

```
SQL> DECLARE
  -- Input values.
  item_title          VARCHAR2(30) := 'Harry Potter';
  item_rating_agency  VARCHAR2(4)  := 'MPAA';
  -- Output values.
  full_title          VARCHAR2_TABLE := varchar2_table();
  rating_agency       NUMBER_TABLE := number_table();
BEGIN
  -- Start PL/SQL hierarchical profiler.
  dbms_hprof.start_profiling('PROFILER_DIR','harry.txt');

  -- Call reference cursor.
  quantity_onhand(item_title
                 ,item_rating_agency
                 ,full_title,rating_agency);

  -- Loop through parallel collections until all records are read.
  FOR i IN 1..full_title.COUNT LOOP
```

```
19       dbms_output.put(full_title(i));
20       dbms_output.put(rating_agency(i));
21     END LOOP;
22
23     -- Stop PL/SQL hierarchical profiler.
24     dbms_hprof.stop_profiling;
25   END;
26   /
```

Line 10 starts the hierarchical profiling and line 24 stops it. If everything is configured correctly, you will now find a `harry.txt` file in your `/tmp` directory. The file should have 20 lines and 547 bytes in it.

You can simply call a stored procedure or function between the `START_PROFILING` and `STOP_PROFILING` procedures as an alternative to testing anonymous block programs like the example. *At this point all the data is external to the database and in the raw output file.*

The next section will demonstrate how you interpret the profiler's output.

Understanding Profiler Data

There are three ways to interpret the PL/SQL profiler output. You can review the raw output file, analyze the data in the analysis tables, or create hierarchical queries of the analytical data. The next three subsections explore these data analysis tools.

Reading the Raw Output

The raw output is really designed to be read by the analyzer component of the PL/SQL hierarchical profiler. However, you can derive some information before you analyze it by leveraging the indicator codes from Table G-1. A small snapshot from the raw `harry.txt` file is

```
P#V PLSHPROF Internal Version 1.0
P#! PL/SQL Timer Started
P#C PLSQL."C##PLSQL"."QUANTITY_ONHAND"::7."QUANTITY_ONHAND"#a912f2026760fedf #1
P#X 13
P#C PLSQL."C##PLSQL"."QUANTITY_ONHAND"::7."QUANTITY_ONHAND.C"#28dc3402baeb2b0d #9
P#X 29
P#C SQL."C##PLSQL"."QUANTITY_ONHAND"::7."__static_sql_exec_line12" #12
P#X 315
P#R
P#X 2
P#R
P#X 11
P#C SQL."C##PLSQL"."QUANTITY_ONHAND"::7."__sql_fetch_line21" #21
P#X 277
P#R
P#X 20
P#R
P#C PLSQL."SYS"."DBMS_HPROF"::11."STOP_PROFILING"#980980e97e42f8ec #59
P#R
P#! PL/SQL Timer Stopped
```

Indicator	Description
P#C	Indicates a call to a subprogram, and it is known as a call event.
P#R	Indicates a return from a subprogram to a calling program, and it is known as a return event.
P#X	Indicates the elapsed time between the preceding and following events.
P#!	Indicates a comment in the analyzed file.

TABLE G-1. *Raw PL/SQL Hierarchical Profiler Data*

While you can discern what the lines do when you know the indicator codes, drawing out the relationship and statistic information from the raw data is harder than doing so from the analyzed data.

The PL/SQL hierarchical profiler tracks several operations as if they were functions with names and namespaces, as shown in Table G-2.

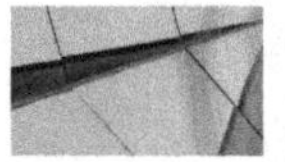

NOTE
This conclusion is drawn from testing that has produced gaps between parent and child keys in the `dbmshp_parent_child_info_runs` *table.*

The tracked operations show up as functions in your raw and filtered output, and they often bridge like a parent between a grandparent and grandchild.

Function Name	Tracked Operation	Namespace
`__anonymous_block`	Anonymous block PL/SQL execution	PL/SQL
`__dyn_sql_exec_line`*line#*	Dynamic SQL statement call made at a specific line number in a program	SQL
`__pkg_init`	Initialization code from a package specification or body	PL/SQL
`__plsql_vm`	PL/SQL virtual machine (VM) call	PL/SQL
`__sql_fetch_line`*line#*	SQL `FETCH` statement occurring at a designated line number in a program	SQL
`__static_sql_exec_line`*line#*	SQL statement happening at a specific line number in a program	SQL

TABLE G-2. *Operations Tracked by the PL/SQL Hierarchical Profiler*

Column Name	Data Type	Description
RUNID	NUMBER	A surrogate primary key generated from the dbmshp_profiler sequence.
RUN_TIMESTAMP	TIMESTAMP	Timestamp set when you run the dbms_hprof .analyze function.
RUN_COMMENT	VARCHAR2(2047)	User comment that you provide when calling the dbms_hprof.analyze function.
TOTAL_ELAPSED_TIME	INTEGER	The elapsed time for the analysis process called by the dbms_hprof.analyze function.

TABLE G-3. *DBMSHP_RUNS Table Columns*

Defining the PL/SQL Profiler Tables

The PL/SQL hierarchical profiler tables are created when you run the dbmshptab.sql script, which is found in the $ORACLE_HOME/rdbms/admin directory. It must be run against the SYS schema and any user schema where you want to collect profiler data. This is required because the dbms_hprof package uses invoker rights (you can read more about invoker rights in Appendix A).

Figure G-1, presented earlier in the appendix, shows the UML depiction of these tables and their relationships. Tables G-3, G-4, and G-5 list the column names, data types, and column descriptions for the analysis tables.

Column Name	Data Type	Description
RUNID	NUMBER	A foreign key from the dbmshp_runs table. The runid and symbolid columns define the composite primary key for the table.
SYMBOLID	NUMBER	The execution sequence ID value. The symbolid is unique when combined with the runid column value, and together they define a composite primary key for this table.
OWNER	VARCHAR2(32)	The owner of the module called.
MODULE	VARCHAR2(2047)	The module column contains a schema function, procedure, or package name such as dbms_lob, dbms_sql, or a user-defined package.
TYPE	VARCHAR2(32)	The module column defines the source of the module, such as a package, procedure, or function.

(continued)

TABLE G-4. *DBMSHP_FUNCTION_INFO Table Columns*

Column Name	Data Type	Description
FUNCTION	VARCHAR2(4000)	A subprogram name or operation (like those in Table G-1) tracked by the PL/SQL hierarchical profiler.
LINE#	NUMBER	The line number where the function is defined in the schema owner module.
HASH	RAW(32)	Hash code for the subprogram signature, which is unique for any run of the dbms_hprof.analyze function.
NAMESPACE	VARCHAR2(32)	Namespace of the subprogram, which can be either SQL or PL/SQL.
SUBTREE_ELAPSED_TIME	INTEGER	Elapsed time, in microseconds, for the subprogram, excluding time spent in descendant subprograms.
FUNCTION_ELAPSED_TIME	INTEGER	Elapsed time, in microseconds, for the subprogram, excluding time spent in descendant subprograms.
CALLS	INTEGER	The number of calls to a subprogram.

TABLE G-4. *DBMSHP_FUNCTION_INFO Table Columns*

Column Name	Data Type	Description
RUNID	NUMBER	A surrogate primary key generated from the dbmshp_profiler sequence.
PARENTSYMID	NUMBER	The execution sequence ID value. The parentsymid is unique when combined with the runid column value, and together they define a composite foreign key that maps to the dbmshp_function_info table runid and symbolid columns.
CHILDSYMID	NUMBER	The execution sequence id value. The childsymid is unique when combined with the runid column value, and together they define a composite foreign key that maps to the dbmshp_function_info table runid and symbolid columns.
SUBTREE_ELAPSED_TIME	INTEGER	Elapsed time, in microseconds, for the subprogram, excluding time spent in descendant subprograms.
FUNCTION_ELAPSED_TIME	INTEGER	Elapsed time, in microseconds, for the subprogram, excluding time spent in descendant subprograms.
CALLS	INTEGER	The number of calls to a child row that is identified by a composite key of runid and childsymid columns.

TABLE G-5. *DBMSHP_PARENT_CHILD_INFO_RUNS Table Columns*

The `dbmshp_runs` table contains information only about the execution of the `dbms_hprof.analyze` function. The `dbmshp_function_info` table contains information about executed functions, and the `dbmshp_parent_child_info` table has the hierarchical relationship between executed functions.

The `runid` column maps straight across to the `dbmshp_parent_child_info` table as the same column name. The `symbolid` column maps to both the `parentsymid` and `childsymid` columns. When you recursively join these structures, you should ensure you join the tables on the `symbolid` and `parentsymid` columns. The "Querying the Analyzed Data" section contains an example of this type of join.

This section has explained the three tables that show you how to interpret the PL/SQL profiler output, review the raw output file, and analyze the data. The analysis discussion has shown you how to create hierarchical queries that profile the analytical data.

Querying the Analyzed Data

A recursive query is the best way to get meaningful results. The following query captures the nesting of method names and uses SQL*Plus column formatting to organize the output:

```
SQL> COL method_name             FORMAT A30
SQL> COL function_name           FORMAT A24
SQL> COL subtree_elapsed_time    FORMAT 99.90 HEADING "Subtree|Elapsed|Time"
SQL> COL function_elapsed_time   FORMAT 99.90 HEADING "Function|Elapsed|Time"
SQL> COL calls                   FORMAT 99    HEADING "Calls"
SQL>
SQL> SELECT   RPAD(' ',level*2,' ')||dfi.owner||'.'||dfi.module AS method_name
     ,        dfi.function AS function_name
     ,       (dpci.subtree_elapsed_time/1000) AS subtree_elapsed_time
     ,       (dpci.function_elapsed_time/1000) AS function_elapsed_time
     ,        dpci.calls
     FROM     dbmshp_parent_child_info dpci
     ,        dbmshp_function_info dfi
     WHERE    dpci.runid = dfi.runid
     AND      dpci.parentsymid = dfi.symbolid
     AND      dpci.runid = 4
     CONNECT
     BY PRIOR dpci.childsymid = dpci.parentsymid  -- Child always connects.
     START
     WITH     dpci.parentsymid = 1;
```

This yields the following output:

```
                                                         Subtree Function
                                                         Elapsed  Elapsed
METHOD_NAME                    FUNCTION_NAME                Time     Time Calls
------------------------------ ------------------------ ------- -------- -----
  .                            __plsql_vm                   .04      .04    11
    PLSQL.GLUE_STRINGS         GLUE_STRINGS                 .00      .00     0
      PLSQL.QUANTITY_ONHAND    QUANTITY_ONHAND              .29      .05     1
        PLSQL.QUANTITY_ONHAND  QUANTITY_ONHAND.C            .24      .24     1
      PLSQL.QUANTITY_ONHAND    QUANTITY_ONHAND              .12      .03    11
        SYS.DBMS_OUTPUT        PUT_LINE                     .02      .02    11
        SYS.DBMS_OUTPUT        PUT_LINE                     .06      .05    11
```

```
      SYS.DBMS_OUTPUT          PUT                                    .02        .02       1
    PLSQL.QUANTITY_ONHAND      QUANTITY_ONHAND                       3.27       3.19       1

9 rows selected.
```

This subsection has demonstrated an approach to querying the PL/SQL profiler table data. It has also introduced the details of leveraging recursive SQL queries in Oracle Database 12*c*.

This section has shown you how to interpret the PL/SQL profiler output, review the raw output file, and analyze data. The analysis discussion has shown you how to create hierarchical queries that profile the analytical data. The next section demonstrates how to generate a web page report equivalent.

Using the plshprof Command-Line Utility

The `plshprof` command-line utility lets you generate simple HTML reports. You have the option of generating a report from one or two sets of analyzed data. You'll find the `plshprof` utility in the `$ORACLE_HOME/bin/` directory.

The `plshprof` utility has several command options that let you generate different report types. Table G-6 lists the available command-line options.

You can generate an output report in Linux or Unix by using the following syntax:

```
$ plshprof -output /tmp/magic /tmp/harry.txt
```

On Windows, you generate an output report like this:

```
plshprof -output C:\Users\mclaughlinm\Documents\magic C:\Windows\Temp
```

It echoes the following to the console when generating the file:

```
PLSHPROF: Oracle Database 12c Enterprise Edition Release 12.1.0.0.2 - 64bit Beta
[5 symbols processed]
[Report written to 'C:\Users\username\Documents\magic.html']
```

Option	**Description**	**Default**
`-collect` *`count`*	Collects the information for *`count`* calls. You should only use this in combination with the `-trace` *`symbol`* option.	`1`
`-output` *`filename`*	Sets the output filename. Don't include an extension; otherwise, you could end up with a strange filename, like `magic.htm.html`.	*`filename`*`.html` or `tracefile.html`
`-skip` *`count`*	Skips the first *`count`* calls. You should only use this in combination with the `-trace` *`symbol`* option.	`0`
`-summary`	Prints only the elapsed time.	None
`-trace` *`symbol`*	Specifies the function name of the tree root.	Not applicable

TABLE G-6. *plshprof Command-Line Options*

If you're an experienced Windows user, you're probably wondering whether the Documents folder is a typo, because the default is My Documents. Actually, before `plshprof` attempts to create the files, it will discover the absence of a Documents folder, create one, and then write the files.

This generates an index web page named `magic.html`. (By the way, the only thing "magic" about the filename is that it's the filename entered as a call argument to the `plshprof` utility.) You use this page to navigate to the other generated web reports:

```
magic.html      magic_2c.html   magic_2f.html   magic_2n.html
magic_fn.html   magic_md.html   magic_mf.html   magic _ms.html
magic_nsc.html  magic_nsf.html  magic_nsp.html  magic_pc.html
magic_tc.html   magic_td.html   magic_tf.html   magic_ts.html
```

The `magic.html` file in Figure G-2 demonstrates the list of reports produced by the `plshprof` utility. You can write a wrapper to read and store these into `CLOB` columns in the database or as external files accessible to your web server. Alternatively, you can simply generate them to the `/tmp` (or `C:\TEMP`) directory, browse them individually, and then remove them from the file system.

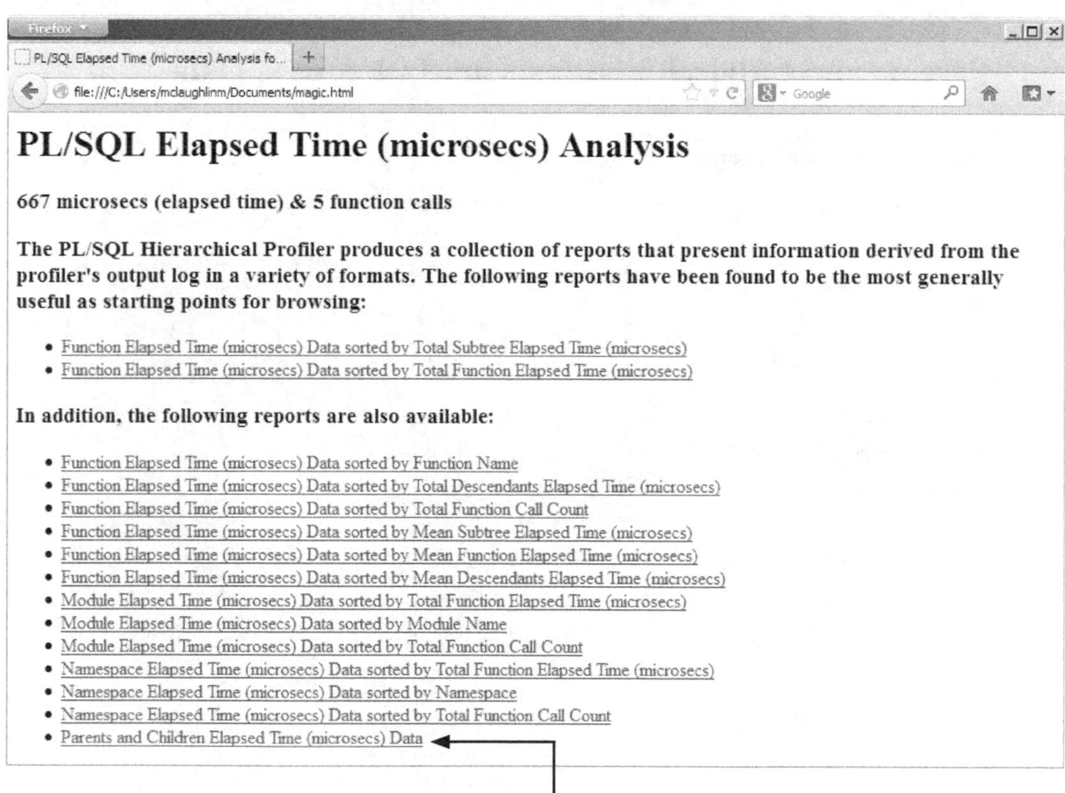

FIGURE G-2. *Sample plshprof index web page*

It important to note that the `-output` *file path can't have any white space in it or it fails*. Let's say you hadn't created a Documents folder under the user name and had tried to output the files to the My Documents folder. You would get the following error, which is consistent across Linux, Unix, and Windows:

```
plshprof -output 'C:\Users\username\My Documents\magic' C:\Windows\Temp\harry.txt
PLSHPROF: Oracle Database 12c Enterprise Edition Release 12.1.0.0.2 - 64bit Beta
ORA-44322: invalid file name 'Documents\magic''
```

Opening the *Parents and Children Elapsed Time (microsecs) Data* report (that's `magic_pc.html`) lets you see the hierarchical performance of your operations. Since these aren't stored in a directory accessible through a browser, you have to open them through the browser's menu. The report for the example in this appendix is shown in Figure G-3.

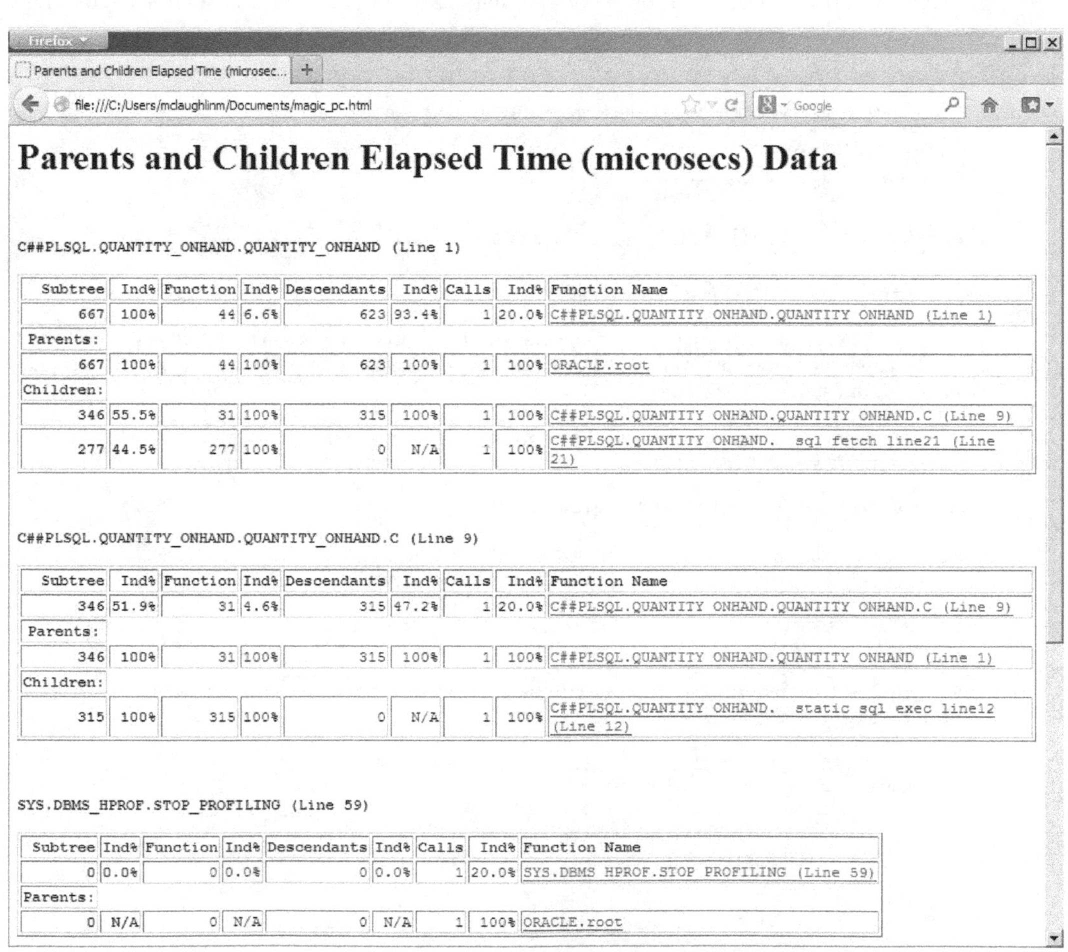

Parents and Children Elapsed Time (microsecs) Data

C##PLSQL.QUANTITY_ONHAND.QUANTITY_ONHAND (Line 1)

Subtree	Ind%	Function	Ind%	Descendants	Ind%	Calls	Ind%	Function Name
667	100%	44	6.6%	623	93.4%	1	20.0%	C##PLSQL.QUANTITY_ONHAND.QUANTITY_ONHAND (Line 1)
Parents:								
667	100%	44	100%	623	100%	1	100%	ORACLE.root
Children:								
346	55.5%	31	100%	315	100%	1	100%	C##PLSQL.QUANTITY_ONHAND.QUANTITY_ONHAND.C (Line 9)
277	44.5%	277	100%	0	N/A	1	100%	C##PLSQL.QUANTITY_ONHAND.__sql_fetch_line21 (Line 21)

C##PLSQL.QUANTITY_ONHAND.QUANTITY_ONHAND.C (Line 9)

Subtree	Ind%	Function	Ind%	Descendants	Ind%	Calls	Ind%	Function Name
346	51.9%	31	4.6%	315	47.2%	1	20.0%	C##PLSQL.QUANTITY_ONHAND.QUANTITY_ONHAND.C (Line 9)
Parents:								
346	100%	31	100%	315	100%	1	100%	C##PLSQL.QUANTITY_ONHAND.QUANTITY_ONHAND (Line 1)
Children:								
315	100%	315	100%	0	N/A	1	100%	C##PLSQL.QUANTITY_ONHAND.__static_sql_exec_line12 (Line 12)

SYS.DBMS_HPROF.STOP_PROFILING (Line 59)

Subtree	Ind%	Function	Ind%	Descendants	Ind%	Calls	Ind%	Function Name
0	0.0%	0	0.0%	0	0.0%	1	20.0%	SYS.DBMS_HPROF.STOP_PROFILING (Line 59)
Parents:								
0	N/A	0	N/A	0	N/A	1	100%	ORACLE.root

FIGURE G-3. *Parent and Child Elapsed Time Data report*

This section has demonstrated how to use the `plshprof` command-line utility. It generates a set of effective analysis tools that you should examine before attempting to write your own.

Supporting Scripts

This section describes programs placed on the McGraw-Hill Professional website to support this appendix:

- The `profiler_test_script.sql` program shows all the code that needs to be run in the `video` pluggable schema, or whichever schema you've decided to test in.

Summary

This appendix has explained what the PL/SQL hierarchical profiler does and has shown you how to configure and use it.

APPENDIX H

PL/SQL Reserved Words and Keywords

Certain identifiers or words are critical to building programming languages. PL/SQL divides those critical words into two groups: reserved words and keywords. They are listed in the data dictionary with each release and can be found in the `v$reserved_words` view.

Lexical symbols are also listed as reserved words in the view. They are covered in Chapter 3 and are not part of this appendix.

It appears that some reserved words, like `BEGIN` and `EXCEPTION`, are missing the '`Y`' in the `reserved` column of the `v$reserved_words` view. Other reserved words, like `ELSIF` and `OUT`, are completely missing from the view. Also, various editions of the *Oracle Database PL/SQL Language Reference* differ on the list elements and contents of the view; however, it appears Oracle Database 12*c* provides a comprehensive list in the `v$reserved_words` view.

Table H-1 lists reserved and keywords together alphabetically for reference.

Starts	Reserved Words and Keywords
A	A, ABORT, ABS, ACCESS, ACCESSED, ACCOUNT, ACL, ACOS, ACTION, ACTIONS, ACTIVATE, ACTIVE_COMPONENT, ACTIVE_DATA, ACTIVE_FUNCTION, ACTIVE_TAG, ACTIVITY, ADD, ADD_COLUMN, ADD_GROUP, ADD_MONTHS, ADJ_DATE, ADMIN, ADMINISTER, ADMINISTRATOR, ADVISE, ADVISOR, AFTER, ALIAS, ALL, ALLOCATE, ALLOW, ALL_ROWS, ALTER, ALWAYS, ANALYZE, ANCILLARY, AND, AND_EQUAL, ANOMALY, ANTIJOIN, ANY, ANYSCHEMA, APPEND, APPENDCHILDXML, APPEND_VALUES, APPLY, ARCHIVE, ARCHIVED, ARCHIVELOG, ARRAY, AS, ASC, ASCII, ASCIISTR, ASIN, ASSEMBLY, ASSIGN, ASSOCIATE, ASYNC, ASYNCHRONOUS, AT, ATAN, ATAN2, ATTRIBUTE, ATTRIBUTES, AUDIT, AUTHENTICATED, AUTHENTICATION, AUTHID, AUTHORIZATION, AUTO, AUTOALLOCATE, AUTOEXTEND, AUTOMATIC, AUTO_LOGIN, AUTO_REOPTIMIZE, AVAILABILITY, AVG
B	BACKGROUND, BACKUP, BASIC, BASICFILE, BATCH, BATCH_TABLE_ACCESS_BY_ROWID, BECOME, BEFORE, BEGIN, BEGINNING, BEGIN_OUTLINE_DATA, BEHALF, BEQUEATH, BETWEEN, BFILE, BFILENAME, BIGFILE, BINARY, BINARY_DOUBLE, BINARY_DOUBLE_INFINITY, BINARY_DOUBLE_NAN, BINARY_FLOAT, BINARY_FLOAT_INFINITY, BINARY_FLOAT_NAN, BINDING, BIND_AWARE, BIN_TO_NUM, BITAND, BITMAP, BITMAPS, BITMAP_AND, BITMAP_TREE, BITS, BLOB, BLOCK, BLOCKS, BLOCKSIZE, BLOCK_RANGE, BODY, BOTH, BOUND, BRANCH, BREADTH, BROADCAST, BUFFER, BUFFER_CACHE, BUFFER_POOL, BUILD, BULK, BY, BYPASS_RECURSIVE_CHECK, BYPASS_UJVC, BYTE
C	CACHE, CACHE_CB, CACHE_INSTANCES, CACHE_TEMP_TABLE, CALCULATED, CALL, CALLBACK, CANCEL, CARDINALITY, CASCADE, CASE, CAST, CATEGORY, CDB$DEFAULT, CDB$VIEW, CEIL, CELL_FLASH_CACHE, CERTIFICATE, CFILE, CHAINED, CHANGE, CHANGE_DUPKEY_ERROR_INDEX, CHAR, CHARACTER, CHARTOROWID, CHAR_CS, CHECK, CHECKPOINT, CHECK_ACL_REWRITE, CHILD, CHOOSE, CHR, CHUNK, CLASS, CLASSIFIER, CLEANUP, CLEAR, CLIENT, CLOB, CLONE, CLOSE, CLOSE_CACHED_OPEN_CURSORS, CLUSTER, CLUSTERING, CLUSTERING_FACTOR, CLUSTER_DETAILS, CLUSTER_DISTANCE, CLUSTER_ID, CLUSTER_PROBABILITY, CLUSTER_SET, COALESCE, COALESCE_SQ, COARSE, COLD, COLLECT, COLUMN, COLUMNAR, COLUMNS, COLUMN_AUTH_INDICATOR, COLUMN_STATS, COLUMN_VALUE, COMMENT, COMMIT, COMMITTED, COMPACT, COMPATIBILITY, COMPILE, COMPLETE, COMPLIANCE, COMPONENT, COMPONENTS, COMPOSE, COMPOSITE, COMPOSITE_LIMIT, COMPOUND, COMPRESS, COMPUTE, CONCAT, CONDITION, CONFIRM, CONFORMING, CONNECT, CONNECT_BY_CB_WHR_ONLY, CONNECT_BY_COMBINE_SW, CONNECT_BY_COST_BASED, CONNECT_BY_ELIM_DUPS, CONNECT_BY_FILTERING, CONNECT_BY_ISCYCLE, CONNECT_BY_ISLEAF, CONNECT_BY_ROOT, CONNECT_TIME, CONSIDER, CONSISTENT, CONST, CONSTANT, CONSTRAINT, CONSTRAINTS, CONTAINER, CONTAINER_DATA, CONTENT, CONTENTS, CONTEXT, CONTINUE, CONTROLFILE, CONVERT, CON_DBID_TO_ID, CON_GUID_TO_ID, CON_ID, CON_NAME_TO_ID, CON_UID_TO_ID, COOKIE, COPY, CORR, CORRUPTION, CORRUPT_XID, CORRUPT_XID_ALL, CORR_K, CORR_S, COS, COSH, COST, COST_XML_QUERY_REWRITE, COUNT, COVAR_POP, COVAR_SAMP, CO_AUTH_IND, CPU_COSTING, CPU_PER_CALL, CPU_PER_SESSION, CRASH, CREATE, CREATE_STORED_OUTLINES, CREATION, CREDENTIAL, CROSS, CROSSEDITION, CSCONVERT, CUBE, CUBE_AJ, CUBE_GB, CUBE_SJ, CUME_DIST, CUME_DISTM, CURRENT, CURRENTV, CURRENT_DATE, CURRENT_SCHEMA, CURRENT_TIME, CURRENT_TIMESTAMP, CURRENT_USER, CURSOR, CURSOR_SHARING_EXACT, CURSOR_SPECIFIC_SEGMENT, CV, CYCLE

TABLE H-1. *Reserved Word and Keyword List*

Starts	Reserved Words and Keywords
D	D, DANGLING, DATA, DATABASE, DATAFILE, DATAFILES, DATAMOVEMENT, DATAOBJNO, DATAOBJ_TO_PARTITION, DATAPUMP, DATA_SECURITY_REWRITE_LIMIT, DATE, DATE_MODE, DAY, DAYS, DBA, DBA_RECYCLEBIN, DBMS_STATS, DBTIMEZONE, DB_ROLE_CHANGE, DB_VERSION, DDL, DEALLOCATE, DEBUG, DEBUGGER, DEC, DECIMAL, DECLARE, DECODE, DECOMPOSE, DECORRELATE, DECR, DECREMENT, DECRYPT, DEDUPLICATE, DEFAULT, DEFAULTS, DEFERRABLE, DEFERRED, DEFINE, DEFINED, DEFINER, DEGREE, DELAY, DELETE, DELETEXML, DELETE_ALL, DEMAND, DENSE_RANK, DENSE_RANKM, DEPENDENT, DEPTH, DEQUEUE, DEREF, DEREF_NO_REWRITE, DESC, DESTROY, DETACHED, DETERMINES, DICTIONARY, DIMENSION, DIMENSIONS, DIRECTORY, DIRECT_LOAD, DIRECT_PATH, DISABLE, DISABLE_ALL, DISABLE_PARALLEL_DML, DISABLE_PRESET, DISABLE_RPKE, DISALLOW, DISASSOCIATE, DISCONNECT, DISK, DISKGROUP, DISKS, DISMOUNT, DISTINCT, DISTINGUISHED, DISTRIBUTED, DML, DML_UPDATE, DOCFIDELITY, DOCUMENT, DOMAIN_INDEX_FILTER, DOMAIN_INDEX_NO_SORT, DOMAIN_INDEX_SORT, DOUBLE, DOWNGRADE, DRIVING_SITE, DROP, DROP_COLUMN, DROP_GROUP, DST_UPGRADE_INSERT_CONV, DUMP, DV, DYNAMIC, DYNAMIC_SAMPLING, DYNAMIC_SAMPLING_EST_CDN
E	E, EACH, EDITION, EDITIONABLE, EDITIONING, EDITIONS, ELEMENT, ELIMINATE_JOIN, ELIMINATE_OBY, ELIMINATE_OUTER_JOIN, ELSE, EM, EMPTY, EMPTY_BLOB, EMPTY_CLOB, ENABLE, ENABLE_ALL, ENABLE_PARALLEL_DML, ENABLE_PRESET, ENCODING, ENCRYPT, ENCRYPTION, END, END_OUTLINE_DATA, ENFORCE, ENFORCED, ENQUEUE, ENTERPRISE, ENTITYESCAPING, ENTRY, ERROR, ERRORS, ERROR_ARGUMENT, ERROR_ON_OVERLAP_TIME, ESCAPE, ESTIMATE, EVAL, EVALNAME, EVALUATE, EVALUATION, EVENTS, EVERY, EXCEPT, EXCEPTIONS, EXCHANGE, EXCLUDE, EXCLUDING, EXCLUSIVE, EXECUTE, EXEMPT, EXISTING, EXISTS, EXISTSNODE, EXP, EXPAND_GSET_TO_UNION, EXPAND_TABLE, EXPIRE, EXPLAIN, EXPLOSION, EXPORT, EXPRESS, EXPR_CORR_CHECK, EXTENDS, EXTENT, EXTENTS, EXTERNAL, EXTERNALLY, EXTRA, EXTRACT, EXTRACTVALUE
F	FACILITY, FACT, FACTOR, FACTORIZE_JOIN, FAILED, FAILED_LOGIN_ATTEMPTS, FAILGROUP, FAILOVER, FAILURE, FALSE, FAMILY, FAR, FAST, FBTSCAN, FEATURE_DETAILS, FEATURE_ID, FEATURE_SET, FEATURE_VALUE, FETCH, FILE, FILESYSTEM_LIKE_LOGGING, FILE_NAME_CONVERT, FILTER, FINAL, FINE, FINISH, FIRST, FIRSTM, FIRST_ROWS, FIRST_VALUE, FIXED_VIEW_DATA, FLAGGER, FLASHBACK, FLASH_CACHE, FLOAT, FLOB, FLOOR, FLUSH, FOLDER, FOLLOWING, FOLLOWS, FOR, FORCE, FORCE_XML_QUERY_REWRITE, FOREIGN, FOREVER, FORWARD, FRAGMENT_NUMBER, FREELIST, FREELISTS, FREEPOOLS, FRESH, FROM, FROM_TZ, FULL, FULL_OUTER_JOIN_TO_OUTER, FUNCTION, FUNCTIONS
G	G, GATHER_OPTIMIZER_STATISTICS, GATHER_PLAN_STATISTICS, GBY_CONC_ROLLUP, GBY_PUSHDOWN, GENERATED, GET, GLOBAL, GLOBALLY, GLOBAL_NAME, GLOBAL_TOPIC_ENABLED, GRANT, GREATEST, GROUP, GROUPING, GROUPING_ID, GROUPS, GROUP_BY, GROUP_ID, GUARANTEE, GUARANTEED, GUARD
H	H, HASH, HASHKEYS, HASH_AJ, HASH_SJ, HAVING, HEADER, HEAP, HELP, HEXTORAW, HEXTOREF, HIDDEN, HIDE, HIERARCHY, HIGH, HINTSET_BEGIN, HINTSET_END, HOT, HOUR, HWM_BROKERED, HYBRID
I	ID, IDENTIFIED, IDENTIFIER, IDENTITY, IDGENERATORS, IDLE_TIME, IF, IGNORE, IGNORE_OPTIM_EMBEDDED_HINTS, IGNORE_ROW_ON_DUPKEY_INDEX, IGNORE_WHERE_CLAUSE, ILM, IMMEDIATE, IMPACT, IMPORT, IN, INACTIVE, INCLUDE, INCLUDE_VERSION, INCLUDING, INCR, INCREMENT, INCREMENTAL, INDENT, INDEX, INDEXED, INDEXES, INDEXING, INDEXTYPE, INDEXTYPES, INDEX_ASC, INDEX_COMBINE, INDEX_DESC, INDEX_FFS, INDEX_FILTER, INDEX_JOIN, INDEX_ROWS, INDEX_RRS, INDEX_RS, INDEX_RS_ASC, INDEX_RS_DESC, INDEX_SCAN, INDEX_SKIP_SCAN, INDEX_SS, INDEX_SS_ASC, INDEX_SS_DESC, INDEX_STATS, INDICATOR, INFINITE, INFORMATIONAL, INHERIT, INITCAP, INITIAL, INITIALIZED, INITIALLY, INITRANS, INLINE, INLINE_XMLTYPE_NT, INNER, INPLACE, INSERT, INSERTCHILDXML, INSERTCHILDXMLAFTER, INSERTCHILDXMLBEFORE, INSERTXMLAFTER, INSERTXMLBEFORE, INSTANCE, INSTANCES, INSTANTIABLE, INSTANTLY, INSTEAD, INSTR, INSTR2, INSTR4, INSTRB, INSTRC, INT, INTEGER, INTERLEAVED, INTERMEDIATE, INTERNAL_CONVERT, INTERNAL_USE, INTERPRETED, INTERSECT, INTERVAL, INTO, INVALIDATE, INVISIBLE, IN_MEMORY_METADATA, IN_XQUERY, IS, ISOLATION, ISOLATION_LEVEL, ITERATE, ITERATION_NUMBER
J	JAVA, JOB, JOIN
K	K, KEEP, KEEP_DUPLICATES, KERBEROS, KEY, KEYS, KEYSIZE, KEYSTORE, KEY_LENGTH, KILL
L	LABEL, LAG, LAST, LAST_DAY, LAST_VALUE, LATERAL, LAYER, LDAP_REGISTRATION, LDAP_REGISTRATION_ENABLED, LDAP_REG_SYNC_INTERVAL, LEAD, LEADING, LEAST, LEFT, LENGTH, LENGTH2, LENGTH4, LENGTHB, LENGTHC, LESS, LEVEL, LEVELS, LIBRARY, LIFE, LIFECYCLE, LIFETIME, LIKE, LIKE2, LIKE4, LIKEC, LIKE_EXPAND, LIMIT, LINEAR, LINK, LIST, LISTAGG, LN, LNNVL, LOAD, LOB, LOBNVL, LOBS, LOCAL, LOCALTIME, LOCALTIMESTAMP, LOCAL_INDEXES, LOCATION, LOCATOR, LOCK, LOCKED, LOG, LOGFILE, LOGFILES, LOGGING, LOGICAL, LOGICAL_READS_PER_CALL, LOGICAL_READS_PER_SESSION, LOGMINING, LOGOFF, LOGON, LOG_READ_ONLY_VIOLATIONS, LONG, LOW, LOWER, LPAD, LTRIM

(continued)

TABLE H-1. *Reserved Word and Keyword List*

Starts	Reserved Words and Keywords
M	M, MAIN, MAKE_REF, MANAGE, MANAGED, MANAGEMENT, MANAGER, MANUAL, MAPPING, MASTER, MATCH, MATCHED, MATCHES, MATCH_NUMBER, MATCH_RECOGNIZE, MATERIALIZE, MATERIALIZED, MAX, MAXARCHLOGS, MAXDATAFILES, MAXEXTENTS, MAXIMIZE, MAXINSTANCES, MAXLOGFILES, MAXLOGHISTORY, MAXLOGMEMBERS, MAXSIZE, MAXTRANS, MAXVALUE, MAX_SHARED_TEMP_SIZE, MEASURE, MEASURES, MEDIAN, MEDIUM, MEMBER, MEMORY, MERGE, MERGE$ACTIONS, MERGE_AJ, MERGE_CONST_ON, MERGE_SJ, METADATA, METHOD, MIGRATE, MIGRATION, MIN, MINEXTENTS, MINIMIZE, MINIMUM, MINING, MINUS, MINUS_NULL, MINUTE, MINVALUE, MIRROR, MIRRORCOLD, MIRRORHOT, MLSLABEL, MOD, MODE, MODEL, MODEL_COMPILE_SUBQUERY, MODEL_DONTVERIFY_UNIQUENESS, MODEL_DYNAMIC_SUBQUERY, MODEL_MIN_ANALYSIS, MODEL_NB, MODEL_NO_ANALYSIS, MODEL_PBY, MODEL_PUSH_REF, MODEL_SV, MODIFICATION, MODIFY, MODIFY_COLUMN_TYPE, MONITOR, MONITORING, MONTH, MONTHS, MONTHS_BETWEEN, MOUNT, MOUNTPATH, MOVE, MOVEMENT, MULTIDIMENSIONAL, MULTISET, MV_MERGE
N	NAME, NAMED, NAMESPACE, NAN, NANVL, NATIONAL, NATIVE, NATIVE_FULL_OUTER_JOIN, NATURAL, NAV, NCHAR, NCHAR_CS, NCHR, NCLOB, NEEDED, NEG, NESTED, NESTED_TABLE_FAST_INSERT, NESTED_TABLE_GET_REFS, NESTED_TABLE_ID, NESTED_TABLE_SET_REFS, NESTED_TABLE_SET_SETID, NETWORK, NEVER, NEW, NEW_TIME, NEXT, NEXT_DAY, NLJ_BATCHING, NLJ_INDEX_FILTER, NLJ_INDEX_SCAN, NLJ_PREFETCH, NLSSORT, NLS_CALENDAR, NLS_CHARACTERSET, NLS_CHARSET_DECL_LEN, NLS_CHARSET_ID, NLS_CHARSET_NAME, NLS_COMP, NLS_CURRENCY, NLS_DATE_FORMAT, NLS_DATE_LANGUAGE, NLS_INITCAP, NLS_ISO_CURRENCY, NLS_LANG, NLS_LANGUAGE, NLS_LENGTH_SEMANTICS, NLS_LOWER, NLS_NCHAR_CONV_EXCP, NLS_NUMERIC_CHARACTERS, NLS_SORT, NLS_SPECIAL_CHARS, NLS_TERRITORY, NLS_UPPER, NL_AJ, NL_SJ, NO, NOAPPEND, NOARCHIVELOG, NOAUDIT, NOCACHE, NOCOMPRESS, NOCOPY, NOCPU_COSTING, NOCYCLE, NODELAY, NOENTITYESCAPING, NOFORCE, NOGUARANTEE, NOKEEP, NOLOCAL, NOLOGGING, NOMAPPING, NOMAXVALUE, NOMINIMIZE, NOMINVALUE, NOMONITORING, NONBLOCKING, NONE, NONEDITIONABLE, NONSCHEMA, NOORDER, NOOVERRIDE, NOPARALLEL, NOPARALLEL_INDEX, NOPARTITION, NORELOCATE, NORELY, NOREPAIR, NORESETLOGS, NOREVERSE, NOREWRITE, NORMAL, NOROWDEPENDENCIES, NOSCHEMACHECK, NOSEGMENT, NOSORT, NOSTRICT, NOSWITCH, NOT, NOTHING, NOTIFICATION, NOVALIDATE, NOWAIT, NO_ACCESS, NO_AUTO_REOPTIMIZE, NO_BASETABLE_MULTIMV_REWRITE, NO_BATCH_TABLE_ACCESS_BY_ROWID, NO_BIND_AWARE, NO_BUFFER, NO_CARTESIAN, NO_CHECK_ACL_REWRITE, NO_CLUSTERING, NO_COALESCE_SQ, NO_CONNECT_BY_CB_WHR_ONLY, NO_CONNECT_BY_COMBINE_SW, NO_CONNECT_BY_COST_BASED, NO_CONNECT_BY_ELIM_DUPS, NO_CONNECT_BY_FILTERING, NO_COST_XML_QUERY_REWRITE, NO_CPU_COSTING, NO_DATA_SECURITY_REWRITE, NO_DECORRELATE, NO_DOMAIN_INDEX_FILTER, NO_DST_UPGRADE_INSERT_CONV, NO_ELIMINATE_JOIN, NO_ELIMINATE_OBY, NO_ELIMINATE_OUTER_JOIN, NO_EXPAND, NO_EXPAND_GSET_TO_UNION, NO_EXPAND_TABLE, NO_FACT, NO_FACTORIZE_JOIN, NO_FILTERING, NO_FULL_OUTER_JOIN_TO_OUTER, NO_GATHER_OPTIMIZER_STATISTICS, NO_GBY_PUSHDOWN, NO_INDEX, NO_INDEX_FFS, NO_INDEX_SS, NO_LOAD, NO_MERGE, NO_MODEL_PUSH_REF, NO_MONITOR, NO_MONITORING, NO_MULTIMV_REWRITE, NO_NATIVE_FULL_OUTER_JOIN, NO_NLJ_BATCHING, NO_NLJ_PREFETCH, NO_ORDER_ROLLUPS, NO_OUTER_JOIN_TO_ANTI, NO_OUTER_JOIN_TO_INNER, NO_PARALLEL, NO_PARALLEL_INDEX, NO_PARTIAL_COMMIT, NO_PARTIAL_JOIN, NO_PARTIAL_ROLLUP_PUSHDOWN, NO_PLACE_DISTINCT, NO_PLACE_GROUP_BY, NO_PQ_CONCURRENT_UNION, NO_PQ_MAP, NO_PQ_REPLICATE, NO_PQ_SKEW, NO_PRUNE_GSETS, NO_PULL_PRED, NO_PUSH_PRED, NO_PUSH_SUBQ, NO_PX_FAULT_TOLERANCE, NO_PX_JOIN_FILTER, NO_QKN_BUFF, NO_QUERY_TRANSFORMATION, NO_REF_CASCADE, NO_RESULT_CACHE, NO_REWRITE, NO_ROW_LEVEL_LOCKING, NO_SEMIJOIN, NO_SEMI_TO_INNER, NO_SET_TO_JOIN, NO_SQL_TRANSLATION, NO_SQL_TUNE, NO_STAR_TRANSFORMATION, NO_STATEMENT_QUEUING, NO_STATS_GSETS, NO_SUBQUERY_PRUNING, NO_SUBSTRB_PAD, NO_SWAP_JOIN_INPUTS, NO_TABLE_LOOKUP_BY_NL, NO_TEMP_TABLE, NO_TRANSFORM_DISTINCT_AGG, NO_UNNEST, NO_USE_CUBE, NO_USE_HASH, NO_USE_HASH_AGGREGATION, NO_USE_HASH_GBY_FOR_PUSHDOWN, NO_USE_INVISIBLE_INDEXES, NO_USE_MERGE, NO_USE_NL, NO_XDB_FASTPATH_INSERT, NO_XMLINDEX_REWRITE, NO_XMLINDEX_REWRITE_IN_SELECT, NO_XML_DML_REWRITE, NO_XML_QUERY_REWRITE, NO_ZONEMAP, NTH_VALUE, NTILE, NULL, NULLIF, NULLS, NUMBER, NUMERIC, NUMTODSINTERVAL, NUMTOYMINTERVAL, NUM_INDEX_KEYS, NVARCHAR2, NVL, NVL2
O	OBJECT, OBJECT2XML, OBJNO, OBJNO_REUSE, OCCURENCES, OF, OFF, OFFLINE, OFFSET, OID, OIDINDEX, OLAP, OLD, OLD_PUSH_PRED, OLS, OLTP, OMIT, ON, ONE, ONLINE, ONLY, OPAQUE, OPAQUE_TRANSFORM, OPAQUE_XCANONICAL, OPCODE, OPEN, OPERATIONS, OPERATOR, OPTIMAL, OPTIMIZER_FEATURES_ENABLE, OPTIMIZER_GOAL, OPTION, OPT_ESTIMATE, OPT_PARAM, OR, ORADEBUG, ORA_BRANCH, ORA_CHECK_ACL, ORA_CHECK_PRIVILEGE, ORA_CLUSTERING, ORA_DST_AFFECTED, ORA_DST_CONVERT, ORA_DST_ERROR, ORA_GET_ACLIDS, ORA_GET_PRIVILEGES, ORA_HASH, ORA_INVOKING_USER, ORA_INVOKING_USERID, ORA_INVOKING_XS_USER, ORA_INVOKING_XS_USER_GUID, ORA_RAWCOMPARE, ORA_RAWCONCAT, ORA_ROWSCN, ORA_ROWSCN_RAW, ORA_ROWVERSION, ORA_TABVERSION, ORA_WRITE_TIME, ORDER, ORDERED, ORDERED_PREDICATES, ORDINALITY, ORGANIZATION, OR_EXPAND, OR_PREDICATES, OTHER, OUTER, OUTER_JOIN_TO_ANTI, OUTER_JOIN_TO_INNER, OUTLINE, OUTLINE_LEAF, OUT_OF_LINE, OVER, OVERFLOW, OVERFLOW_NOMOVE, OVERLAPS, OWN, OWNER, OWNERSHIP

TABLE H-1. *Reserved Word and Keyword List*

Starts	Reserved Words and Keywords
P	P, PACKAGE, PACKAGES, PARALLEL, PARALLEL_INDEX, PARAM, PARAMETERS, PARENT, PARITY, PARTNUMINST, PARTIAL, PARTIALLY, PARTIAL_JOIN, PARTIAL_ROLLUP_PUSHDOWN, PARTITION, PARTITIONS, PARTITION_HASH, PARTITION_LIST, PARTITION_RANGE, PASSING, PASSWORD, PASSWORD_GRACE_TIME, PASSWORD_LIFE_TIME, PASSWORD_LOCK_TIME, PASSWORD_REUSE_MAX, PASSWORD_REUSE_TIME, PASSWORD_VERIFY_FUNCTION, PAST, PATCH, PATH, PATHS, PATH_PREFIX, PATTERN, PBL_HS_BEGIN, PBL_HS_END, PCTFREE, PCTINCREASE, PCTTHRESHOLD, PCTUSED, PCTVERSION, PENDING, PER, PERCENT, PERCENTILE_CONT, PERCENTILE_DISC, PERCENT_RANK, PERCENT_RANKM, PERFORMANCE, PERIOD, PERMANENT, PERMISSION, PERMUTE, PFILE, PHYSICAL, PIKEY, PIVOT, PIV_GB, PIV_SSF, PLACE_DISTINCT, PLACE_GROUP_BY, PLAN, PLSCOPE_SETTINGS, PLSQL_CCFLAGS, PLSQL_CODE_TYPE, PLSQL_DEBUG, PLSQL_OPTIMIZE_LEVEL, PLSQL_WARNINGS, PLUGGABLE, POINT, POLICY, POST_TRANSACTION, POWER, POWERMULTISET, POWERMULTISET_BY_CARDINALITY, PQ_CONCURRENT_UNION, PQ_DISTRIBUTE, PQ_DISTRIBUTE_WINDOW, PQ_FILTER, PQ_MAP, PQ_NOMAP, PQ_REPLICATE, PQ_SKEW, PREBUILT, PRECEDES, PRECEDING, PRECISION, PRECOMPUTE_SUBQUERY, PREDICATE_REORDERS, PREDICTION, PREDICTION_BOUNDS, PREDICTION_COST, PREDICTION_DETAILS, PREDICTION_PROBABILITY, PREDICTION_SET, PREPARE, PRESENT, PRESENTNNV, PRESENTV, PRESERVE, PRESERVE_OID, PREV, PREVIOUS, PRIMARY, PRIOR, PRIVATE, PRIVATE_SGA, PRIVILEGE, PRIVILEGED, PRIVILEGES, PROCEDURAL, PROCEDURE, PROCESS, PROFILE, PROGRAM, PROJECT, PROPAGATE, PROTECTED, PROTECTION, PROXY, PRUNING, PUBLIC, PULL_PRED, PURGE, PUSH_PRED, PUSH_SUBQ, PX_FAULT_TOLERANCE, PX_GRANULE, PX_JOIN_FILTER
Q	QB_NAME, QUERY, QUERY_BLOCK, QUEUE, QUEUE_CURR, QUEUE_ROWP, QUIESCE, QUORUM, QUOTA
R	RANDOM, RANDOM_LOCAL, RANGE, RANK, RANKM, RAPIDLY, RATIO_TO_REPORT, RAW, RAWTOHEX, RAWTONHEX, RBA, RBO_OUTLINE, RDBA, READ, READS, REAL, REALM, REBALANCE, REBUILD, RECORDS_PER_BLOCK, RECOVER, RECOVERABLE, RECOVERY, RECYCLE, RECYCLEBIN, REDACTION, REDEFINE, REDO, REDUCED, REDUNDANCY, REF, REFERENCE, REFERENCED, REFERENCES, REFERENCING, REFRESH, REFTOHEX, REF_CASCADE_CURSOR, REGEXP_COUNT, REGEXP_INSTR, REGEXP_LIKE, REGEXP_REPLACE, REGEXP_SUBSTR, REGISTER, REGR_AVGX, REGR_AVGY, REGR_COUNT, REGR_INTERCEPT, REGR_R2, REGR_SLOPE, REGR_SXX, REGR_SXY, REGR_SYY, REGULAR, REJECT, REKEY, RELATIONAL, RELOCATE, RELY, REMAINDER, REMOTE_MAPPED, REMOVE, RENAME, REPAIR, REPEAT, REPLACE, REPLICATION, REQUIRED, RESET, RESETLOGS, RESIZE, RESOLVE, RESOLVER, RESOURCE, RESPECT, RESTART, RESTORE, RESTORE_AS_INTERVALS, RESTRICT, RESTRICTED, RESTRICT_ALL_REF_CONS, RESULT_CACHE, RESUMABLE, RESUME, RETENTION, RETRY_ON_ROW_CHANGE, RETURN, RETURNING, REUSE, REVERSE, REVOKE, REWRITE, REWRITE_OR_ERROR, RIGHT, ROLE, ROLES, ROLESET, ROLLBACK, ROLLING, ROLLUP, ROUND, ROW, ROWDEPENDENCIES, ROWID, ROWIDTOCHAR, ROWIDTONCHAR, ROWID_MAPPING_TABLE, ROWNUM, ROWS, ROW_LENGTH, ROW_LEVEL_LOCKING, ROW_NUMBER, RPAD, RTRIM, RULE, RULES, RUNNING

(continued)

TABLE H-1. *Reserved Word and Keyword List*

Starts	Reserved Words and Keywords
S	SALT, SAMPLE, SAVEPOINT, SAVE_AS_INTERVALS, SB4, SCALE, SCALE_ROWS, SCAN, SCAN_INSTANCES, SCHEDULER, SCHEMA, SCHEMACHECK, SCN, SCN_ASCENDING, SCOPE, SCRUB, SDO_GEOM_MBR, SD_ALL, SD_INHIBIT, SD_SHOW, SEARCH, SECOND, SECRET, SECUREFILE, SECUREFILE_DBA, SECURITY, SEED, SEGMENT, SEG_BLOCK, SEG_FILE, SELECT, SELECTIVITY, SEMIJOIN, SEMIJOIN_DRIVER, SEMI_TO_INNER, SEQUENCE, SEQUENCED, SEQUENTIAL, SERIAL, SERIALIZABLE, SERVERERROR, SESSION, SESSIONS_PER_USER, SESSIONTIMEZONE, SESSIONTZNAME, SESSION_CACHED_CURSORS, SET, SETS, SETTINGS, SET_TO_JOIN, SEVERE, SHARE, SHARED, SHARED_POOL, SHARING, SHOW, SHRINK, SHUTDOWN, SIBLINGS, SID, SIGN, SIGNAL_COMPONENT, SIGNAL_FUNCTION, SIMPLE, SIN, SINGLE, SINGLETASK, SINH, SIZE, SKIP, SKIP_EXT_OPTIMIZER, SKIP_UNQ_UNUSABLE_IDX, SKIP_UNUSABLE_INDEXES, SMALLFILE, SMALLINT, SNAPSHOT, SOME, SORT, SOUNDEX, SOURCE, SOURCE_FILE_NAME_CONVERT, SPACE, SPECIFICATION, SPFILE, SPLIT, SPREADSHEET, SQL, SQLLDR, SQL_TRACE, SQL_TRANSLATION_PROFILE, SQRT, STALE, STANDALONE, STANDARD_HASH, STANDBY, STANDBY_MAX_DATA_DELAY, STAR, START, STARTUP, STAR_TRANSFORMATION, STATE, STATEMENT, STATEMENTS, STATEMENT_ID, STATEMENT_QUEUING, STATIC, STATISTICS, STATS_BINOMIAL_TEST, STATS_CROSSTAB, STATS_F_TEST, STATS_KS_TEST, STATS_MODE, STATS_MW_TEST, STATS_ONE_WAY_ANOVA, STATS_T_TEST_INDEP, STATS_T_TEST_INDEPU, STATS_T_TEST_ONE, STATS_T_TEST_PAIRED, STATS_WSR_TEST, STDDEV, STDDEV_POP, STDDEV_SAMP, STOP, STORAGE, STORE, STREAMS, STRICT, STRING, STRIP, STRIPE_COLUMNS, STRIPE_WIDTH, STRUCTURE, SUBMULTISET, SUBPARTITION, SUBPARTITIONS, SUBPARTITION_REL, SUBQUERIES, SUBQUERY_PRUNING, SUBSCRIBE, SUBSET, SUBSTITUTABLE, SUBSTR, SUBSTR2, SUBSTR4, SUBSTRB, SUBSTRC, SUCCESS, SUCCESSFUL, SUM, SUMMARY, SUPPLEMENTAL, SUSPEND, SWAP_JOIN_INPUTS, SWITCH, SWITCHOVER, SYNC, SYNCHRONOUS, SYNONYM, SYSASM, SYSAUX, SYSBACKUP, SYSDATE, SYSDBA, SYSDG, SYSGUID, SYSKM, SYSOPER, SYSTEM, SYSTEM_DEFINED, SYSTIMESTAMP, SYS_AUDIT, SYS_CHECKACL, SYS_CHECK_PRIVILEGE, SYS_CONNECT_BY_PATH, SYS_CONTEXT, SYS_DBURIGEN, SYS_DL_CURSOR, SYS_DM_RXFORM_CHR, SYS_DM_RXFORM_NUM, SYS_DOM_COMPARE, SYS_DST_PRIM2SEC, SYS_DST_SEC2PRIM, SYS_ET_BFILE_TO_RAW, SYS_ET_BLOB_TO_IMAGE, SYS_ET_IMAGE_TO_BLOB, SYS_ET_RAW_TO_BFILE, SYS_EXTPDTXT, SYS_EXTRACT_UTC, SYS_FBT_INSDEL, SYS_FILTER_ACLS, SYS_FNMATCHES, SYS_FNREPLACE, SYS_GETTOKENID, SYS_GETXTIVAL, SYS_GET_ACLIDS, SYS_GET_COL_ACLIDS, SYS_GET_PRIVILEGES, SYS_GUID, SYS_MAKEXML, SYS_MAKE_XMLNODEID, SYS_MKXMLATTR, SYS_MKXTI, SYS_OPTLOBPRBSC, SYS_OPTXICMP, SYS_OPTXQCASTASNQ, SYS_OP_ADT2BIN, SYS_OP_ADTCONS, SYS_OP_ALSCRVAL, SYS_OP_ATG, SYS_OP_BIN2ADT, SYS_OP_BITVEC, SYS_OP_BL2R, SYS_OP_BLOOM_FILTER, SYS_OP_BLOOM_FILTER_LIST, SYS_OP_C2C, SYS_OP_CAST, SYS_OP_CEG, SYS_OP_CL2C, SYS_OP_COMBINED_HASH, SYS_OP_COMP, SYS_OP_CONVERT, SYS_OP_COUNTCHG, SYS_OP_CSCONV, SYS_OP_CSCONVTEST, SYS_OP_CSR, SYS_OP_CSX_PATCH, SYS_OP_CYCLED_SEQ, SYS_OP_DECOMP, SYS_OP_DESCEND, SYS_OP_DISTINCT, SYS_OP_DRA, SYS_OP_DUMP, SYS_OP_DV_CHECK, SYS_OP_ENFORCE_NOT_NULL$, SYS_OP_EXTRACT, SYS_OP_GROUPING, SYS_OP_GUID, SYS_OP_HASH, SYS_OP_IIX, SYS_OP_ITR, SYS_OP_LBID, SYS_OP_LOBLOC2BLOB, SYS_OP_LOBLOC2CLOB, SYS_OP_LOBLOC2ID, SYS_OP_LOBLOC2NCLOB, SYS_OP_LOBLOC2TYP, SYS_OP_LSVI, SYS_OP_LVL, SYS_OP_MAKEOID, SYS_OP_MAP_NONNULL, SYS_OP_MSR, SYS_OP_NICOMBINE, SYS_OP_NIEXTRACT, SYS_OP_NII, SYS_OP_NIX, SYS_OP_NOEXPAND, SYS_OP_NTCIMG$, SYS_OP_NUMTORAW, SYS_OP_OIDVALUE, SYS_OP_OPNSIZE, SYS_OP_PAR, SYS_OP_PARGID, SYS_OP_PARGID_1, SYS_OP_PART_ID, SYS_OP_PAR_1, SYS_OP_PIVOT, SYS_OP_R2O, SYS_OP_RAWTONUM, SYS_OP_RDTM, SYS_OP_REF, SYS_OP_RMTD, SYS_OP_ROWIDTOOBJ, SYS_OP_RPB, SYS_OP_TOSETID, SYS_OP_TPR, SYS_OP_TRTB, SYS_OP_UNDESCEND, SYS_OP_VECAND, SYS_OP_VECBIT, SYS_OP_VECOR, SYS_OP_VECXOR, SYS_OP_VERSION, SYS_OP_VREF, SYS_OP_VVD, SYS_OP_XMLCONS_FOR_CSX, SYS_OP_XPTHATG, SYS_OP_XPTHIDX, SYS_OP_XPTHOP, SYS_OP_XTXT2SQLT, SYS_OP_ZONE_ID, SYS_ORDERKEY_DEPTH, SYS_ORDERKEY_MAXCHILD, SYS_ORDERKEY_PARENT, SYS_PARALLEL_TXN, SYS_PATHID_IS_ATTR, SYS_PATHID_IS_NMSPC, SYS_PATHID_LASTNAME, SYS_PATHID_LASTNMSPC, SYS_PATH_REVERSE, SYS_PXQEXTRACT, SYS_RAW_TO_XSID, SYS_RID_ORDER, SYS_ROW_DELTA, SYS_SC_2_XMLT, SYS_SYNRCIREDO, SYS_TYPEID, SYS_UMAKEXML, SYS_XMLANALYZE, SYS_XMLCONTAINS, SYS_XMLCONV, SYS_XMLEXNSURI, SYS_XMLGEN, SYS_XMLINSTR, SYS_XMLI_LOC_ISNODE, SYS_XMLI_LOC_ISTEXT, SYS_XMLLOCATOR_GETSVAL, SYS_XMLNODEID, SYS_XMLNODEID_GETCID, SYS_XMLNODEID_GETLOCATOR, SYS_XMLNODEID_GETOKEY, SYS_XMLNODEID_GETPATHID, SYS_XMLNODEID_GETPTRID, SYS_XMLNODEID_GETRID, SYS_XMLNODEID_GETSVAL, SYS_XMLNODEID_GETTID, SYS_XMLTRANSLATE, SYS_XMLTYPE2SQL, SYS_XMLT_2_SC, SYS_XQBASEURI, SYS_XQCASTABLEERRH, SYS_XQCODEP2STR, SYS_XQCODEPEQ, SYS_XQCON2SEQ, SYS_XQCONCAT, SYS_XQDELETE, SYS_XQDFLTCOLATION, SYS_XQDOC, SYS_XQDOCURI, SYS_XQDURDIV, SYS_XQED4URI, SYS_XQENDSWITH, SYS_XQERR, SYS_XQERRH, SYS_XQESHTMLURI, SYS_XQEXLOBVAL, SYS_XQEXSTWRP, SYS_XQEXTRACT, SYS_XQEXTRREF, SYS_XQEXVAL, SYS_XQFB2STR, SYS_XQFNBOOL, SYS_XQFNCMP, SYS_XQFNDATIM, SYS_XQFNLNAME, SYS_XQFNNM, SYS_XQFNNSURI, SYS_XQFNPREDTRUTH, SYS_XQFNQNM, SYS_XQFNROOT, SYS_XQFORMATNUM, SYS_XQFTCONTAIN, SYS_XQFUNCR, SYS_XQGETCONTENT, SYS_XQINDXOF, SYS_XQINSERT, SYS_XQINSPFX, SYS_XQIRI2URI, SYS_XQLANG, SYS_XQLLNMFRMQNM, SYS_XQMKNODEREF, SYS_XQNILLED, SYS_XQNODENAME, SYS_XQNORMSPACE, SYS_XQNORMUCODE, SYS_XQNSP4PFX, SYS_XQNSPFRMQNM, SYS_XQPFXFRMQNM, SYS_XQPOLYABS, SYS_XQPOLYADD, SYS_XQPOLYCEL, SYS_XQPOLYCST, SYS_XQPOLYCSTBL, SYS_XQPOLYDIV, SYS_XQPOLYFLR, SYS_XQPOLYMOD, SYS_XQPOLYMUL, SYS_XQPOLYRND, SYS_XQPOLYSQRT, SYS_XQPOLYSUB, SYS_XQPOLYUMUS, SYS_XQPOLYUPLS, SYS_XQPOLYVEQ, SYS_XQPOLYVGE, SYS_XQPOLYVGT, SYS_XQPOLYVLE, SYS_XQPOLYVLT, SYS_XQPOLYVNE, SYS_XQREF2VAL, SYS_XQRENAME, SYS_XQREPLACE, SYS_XQRESVURI, SYS_XQRNDHALF2EVN, SYS_XQRSLVQNM, SYS_XQRYENVPGET, SYS_XQRYVARGET, SYS_XQRYWRP, SYS_XQSEQ2CON, SYS_XQSEQ2CON4XC, SYS_XQSEQDEEPEQ, SYS_XQSEQINSB, SYS_XQSEQRM, SYS_XQSEQRVS, SYS_XQSEQSUB, SYS_XQSEQTYPMATCH, SYS_XQSTARTSWITH, SYS_XQSTATBURI, SYS_XQSTR2CODEP, SYS_XQSTRJOIN, SYS_XQSUBSTRAFT, SYS_XQSUBSTRBEF, SYS_XQTOKENIZE, SYS_XQTREATAS, SYS_XQXFORM, SYS_XQ_ASQLCNV, SYS_XQ_ATOMCNVCHK, SYS_XQ_NRNG, SYS_XQ_PKSQL2XML, SYS_XQ_UPKXML2SQL, SYS_XSID_TO_RAW, SYS_ZMAP_FILTER, SYS_ZMAP_REFRESH

TABLE H-1. *Reserved Word and Keyword List*

Starts	Reserved Words and Keywords
T	T, TABLE, TABLES, TABLESPACE, TABLESPACE_NO, TABLE_LOOKUP_BY_NL, TABLE_STATS, TABNO, TAG, TAN, TANH, TBLORIDX$PART$NUM, TEMPFILE, TEMPLATE, TEMPORARY, TEMP_TABLE, TEST, THAN, THE, THEN, THREAD, THROUGH, TIER, TIES, TIME, TIMEOUT, TIMES, TIMESTAMP, TIMEZONE_ABBR, TIMEZONE_HOUR, TIMEZONE_MINUTE, TIMEZONE_OFFSET, TIMEZONE_REGION, TIME_ZONE, TIV_GB, TIV_SSF, TO, TOPLEVEL, TO_ACLID, TO_BINARY_DOUBLE, TO_BINARY_FLOAT, TO_BLOB, TO_CHAR, TO_CLOB, TO_DATE, TO_DSINTERVAL, TO_LOB, TO_MULTI_BYTE, TO_NCHAR, TO_NCLOB, TO_NUMBER, TO_SINGLE_BYTE, TO_TIME, TO_TIMESTAMP, TO_TIMESTAMP_TZ, TO_TIME_TZ, TO_YMINTERVAL, TRACE, TRACING, TRACKING, TRAILING, TRANSACTION, TRANSFORM_DISTINCT_AGG, TRANSITION, TRANSITIONAL, TRANSLATE, TRANSLATION, TREAT, TRIGGER, TRIGGERS, TRIM, TRUE, TRUNC, TRUNCATE, TRUST, TRUSTED, TUNING, TX, TYPE, TYPES, TZ_OFFSET
U	U, UB2, UBA, UID, UNARCHIVED, UNBOUND, UNBOUNDED, UNDER, UNDO, UNDROP, UNIFORM, UNION, UNIQUE, UNISTR, UNLIMITED, UNLOAD, UNLOCK, UNMATCHED, UNNEST, UNPACKED, UNPIVOT, UNPLUG, UNPROTECTED, UNQUIESCE, UNRECOVERABLE, UNRESTRICTED, UNSUBSCRIBE, UNTIL, UNUSABLE, UNUSED, UPDATABLE, UPDATE, UPDATED, UPDATEXML, UPD_INDEXES, UPD_JOININDEX, UPGRADE, UPPER, UPSERT, UROWID, USABLE, USAGE, USE, USER, USERENV, USERGROUP, USERS, USER_DATA, USER_DEFINED, USER_RECYCLEBIN, USE_ANTI, USE_CONCAT, USE_CUBE, USE_HASH, USE_HASH_AGGREGATION, USE_HASH_GBY_FOR_PUSHDOWN, USE_HIDDEN_PARTITIONS, USE_INVISIBLE_INDEXES, USE_MERGE, USE_MERGE_CARTESIAN, USE_NL, USE_NL_WITH_INDEX, USE_PRIVATE_OUTLINES, USE_SEMI, USE_STORED_OUTLINES, USE_TTT_FOR_GSETS, USE_WEAK_NAME_RESL, USING, USING_NO_EXPAND
V	V1, V2, VALIDATE, VALIDATION, VALID_TIME_END, VALUE, VALUES, VARCHAR, VARCHAR2, VARIANCE, VARRAY, VARRAYS, VARYING, VAR_POP, VAR_SAMP, VECTOR_READ, VECTOR_READ_TRACE, VERIFIER, VERIFY, VERSION, VERSIONING, VERSIONS, VERSIONS_ENDSCN, VERSIONS_ENDTIME, VERSIONS_OPERATION, VERSIONS_STARTSCN, VERSIONS_STARTTIME, VERSIONS_XID, VIEW, VIOLATION, VIRTUAL, VISIBILITY, VISIBLE, VOLUME, VSIZE
W	WAIT, WALLET, WEEK, WEEKS, WELLFORMED, WHEN, WHENEVER, WHERE, WHITESPACE, WIDTH_BUCKET, WITH, WITHIN, WITHOUT, WORK, WRAPPED, WRITE
X	XDB_FASTPATH_INSERT, XID, XML, XML2OBJECT, XMLATTRIBUTES, XMLCAST, XMLCDATA, XMLCOLATTVAL, XMLCOMMENT, XMLCONCAT, XMLDIFF, XMLELEMENT, XMLEXISTS, XMLEXISTS2, XMLFOREST, XMLINDEX_REWRITE, XMLINDEX_REWRITE_IN_SELECT, XMLINDEX_SEL_IDX_TBL, XMLISNODE, XMLISVALID, XMLNAMESPACES, XMLPARSE, XMLPATCH, XMLPI, XMLQUERY, XMLQUERYVAL, XMLROOT, XMLSCHEMA, XMLSERIALIZE, XMLTABLE, XMLTRANSFORM, XMLTRANSFORMBLOB, XMLTYPE, XML_DML_RWT_STMT, XPATHTABLE, XS, XS_SYS_CONTEXT, X_DYN_PRUNE
Y	YEAR, YEARS, YES
Z	ZONE, ZONEMAP

TABLE H-1. *Reserved Word and Keyword List*

The following `reserved_key_word.sql` script lets you query and format the contents from the `v$reserved_words` view:

```
SQL> DECLARE
  -- Define and declare collections.
  TYPE alpha_key IS TABLE OF CHARACTER;
  TYPE list IS TABLE OF CLOB INDEX BY VARCHAR2(1);

  -- Declare a counter variable.
  lv_counter  NUMBER := 1;

  -- Define two collections.
  lv_reserved_word LIST;
  lv_key_word      LIST;

  -- Declare an initial associative array of keys.
  lv_code ALPHA_KEY := alpha_key('A','B','C','D','E','F','G','H'
                                ,'I','J','K','L','M','N','O','P'
                                ,'Q','R','S','T','U','V','W','X'
                                ,'Y','Z');
```

```

  -- Define cursor.
  CURSOR c IS
    SELECT   keyword
    ,        reserved
    ,        res_type
    ,        res_attr
    ,        res_semi
    FROM     v$reserved_words
    ORDER BY keyword;

  FUNCTION format_list (pv_list_in LIST) RETURN BOOLEAN IS
    -- Declare control variables.
    lv_counter  NUMBER := 1;
    lv_current  VARCHAR2(1);
    lv_element  CLOB;
    lv_status   BOOLEAN := TRUE;
  BEGIN
    -- Read through an alphabetically indexed collection.
    WHILE (lv_counter < pv_list_in.COUNT) LOOP
      IF lv_counter = 1 THEN
        lv_current := pv_list_in.FIRST;
        lv_element := pv_list_in(lv_current);
      ELSE
        IF pv_list_in.NEXT(lv_current) IS NOT NULL THEN
          lv_current := pv_list_in.NEXT(lv_current);
          lv_element := pv_list_in(lv_current);
        END IF;
      END IF;
      lv_counter := lv_counter + 1;
      dbms_output.put_line('['||lv_current||'] ['||lv_element||']');
    END LOOP;
    RETURN lv_status;
  END format_list;

BEGIN
  -- Initialize reserved word and keyword collections.
  FOR i IN 1..lv_code.LAST LOOP
    FOR j IN c LOOP
      IF lv_code(i) = UPPER(SUBSTR(j.keyword,1,1)) THEN
        IF NOT lv_reserved_word.EXISTS(lv_code(i)) THEN
          lv_reserved_word(lv_code(i)) := j.keyword;
        ELSE
          lv_reserved_word(lv_code(i)) :=
            lv_reserved_word(lv_code(i)) || ', ' || j.keyword;
        END IF;
      END IF;
    END LOOP;
  END LOOP;

```

```
  -- Initialize reserved word and keyword collections.
  FOR i IN 1..lv_code.LAST LOOP
    FOR j IN c LOOP
      IF lv_code(i) = UPPER(SUBSTR(j.keyword,1,1)) THEN
        IF NOT lv_reserved_word.EXISTS(lv_code(i)) THEN
          lv_reserved_word(lv_code(i)) := j.keyword;
        ELSE
          lv_reserved_word(lv_code(i)) :=
            lv_reserved_word(lv_code(i)) || ', ' || j.keyword;
        END IF;
      END IF;
    END LOOP;
  END LOOP;

  -- Print the list.
  IF format_list(lv_reserved_word) THEN
    NULL;
  END IF;
END;
/
```

Summary

The reserved word and keyword tables are alphabetized for you to browse them quickly. You can also recheck for changes with the `reserved_key_word.sql` script.

APPENDIX I

Mastery Check Answers

Chapter 1

True or False:

1. Relational Software, Inc. became Oracle Corporation.

   True. Software Development Laboratories (SDL) led to the formation of Relational Software, Inc. (RSI), which in turn led to the formation of Oracle Corporation.

2. Relational databases store information about how data is stored.

   True. Relational databases store information about how data is stored, and this type of information is called the data catalog or data dictionary.

3. Relational databases store data.

   True. Relational databases store data in tables.

4. SQL is an imperative language that lets you work in the Oracle database.

   False. SQL is a set-based declarative language that lets you work in the Oracle database.

5. The relational database model evolved from the object-relational database model.

   False. The object-relational database model evolved from the relational database model because object-oriented database models required too much memory to marshal objects.

6. PL/SQL is the procedural extension of SQL.

   True. PL/SQL is the Procedure Language/Structured Query Language.

7. PL/SQL is an imperative language that is both event-driven and object-oriented.

   True. PL/SQL is an imperative language that is both event-driven and object-oriented.

8. The Oracle database relies on an external Java Virtual Machine to run stored Java libraries.

   False. The Oracle internal JVM runs all stored Java libraries.

9. A two-tier model works between a browser and a database server.

   False. A two-tier model works between a SQL*Plus command-line interface (CLI) and the Oracle Database 12*c* database server.

10. A three-tier model is a specialized form of an *n*-tier model.

    True. A three-tier model is a specialized form of an *n*-tier model, where you have a browser, an Apache server, and a database server.

Multiple Choice:

11. Which of the following describes the roles of the Oracle listener? (Multiple answers possible)

    A. Listen for incoming client requests

    B. Send outgoing requests to client software

    C. Forward requests to the PL/SQL engine

    D. Forward requests to a SQL*Plus session

    E. Forward requests to the SQL engine

A and **D** are correct. The Oracle listener listens for incoming client requests and forwards requests to a SQL*Plus session. The actual SQL*Plus session is a different executable from the interactive one that you launch when working with Oracle Database 12*c*.

12. Which of the following converts a relational model to an object-relational model? (Multiple answers possible)

A. A data catalog

B. A set of tables

C. An object data type

D. An imperative language that lets you build native object types

E. A JVM inside the database

C, **D**, and **E** are correct. You require an object data type and an imperative language to create the objects. PL/SQL is that language, and the JVM runs the objects.

13. SQL*Plus provides which of the following? (Multiple answers possible)

A. An interactive mode

B. A call mode

C. A server mode

D. A client mode

E. All of the above

A, **B**, and **C** are correct. SQL*Plus supports an interactive mode, which is also known as the client software. Calls made by external programs run through a portion of SQL*Plus known as the call mode.

14. Which of the following is a capability of PL/SQL?

A. Call SQL

B. Implement object types

C. Wrap C-callable programs

D. Wrap Java programs

E. All of the above

E is correct. PL/SQL can call SQL, implement object types, wrap C-callable programs, and wrap Java programs.

15. Which of the following are types of SQL statements? (Multiple answers possible)

A. Data Definition Language (DDL) statements

B. Data Manipulation Language (DML) statements

C. Data Control Language (DCL) statements

D. Create, replace, update, and delete (CRUD) statements

E. Transaction Control Language (TCL) statements

A, **B**, **C**, and **E** are correct. DDL, DML, DCL, and TCL are valid types of SQL statements. CRUD is a description of functionality, not of the DML type of statements.

Chapter 2

True or False:

1. Valid-time (VT) indicates the point at which transactions commit.

   False. Valid-time (VT) indicates the point at which a business event occurs, and is unrelated to the transaction-time (TT).

2. It is possible to define a default column that uses the `.nextval` pseudocolumn for a sequence.

   True. Oracle Database 12*c* lets you define a default column that uses the `.nextval` pseudocolumn.

3. It is possible to define a default column that uses the `.currval` pseudocolumn for a sequence.

   True. Oracle Database 12*c* lets you define a default column that uses the `.currval` pseudocolumn.

4. The `.currval` pseudocolumn no longer has a dependency on a preceding `.nextval` pseudocolumn call in a session.

   False. Oracle Database 12*c* does not remove the session dependency that the `.currval` pseudocolumn has on the `.nextval` pseudocolumn.

5. Oracle Database 12*c* doesn't provide a means to prevent the entry of an explicit null in an `INSERT` statement, which means you can still override a `DEFAULT` column value.

   False. Oracle Database 12*c* does provide an `ON NULL` clause that prevents the insertion or update of an explicit null when a default value has been specified.

6. Identity columns let you automatically number the values of a surrogate key column.

   True. Oracle Database 12*c* lets you define an identity column in any table that uses an implicitly generated sequence.

7. `VARCHAR2`, `NVARCHAR2`, and `RAW` data types are now always 32,767 bytes in the Oracle Database 12*c* database.

   False. Oracle Database 12*c* provides a `max_string_size` parameter, which lets you set it to `EXTENDED` when you want `VARCHAR2`, `NVARCHAR2`, and `RAW` columns to hold 32,767 bytes. Data types remain capped at the prior maximum size when the `max_string_size` parameter is set to `STANDARD`.

8. A PL/SQL function can return a PL/SQL associative array directly into a SQL statement with the changes introduced in Oracle 12*c*.

   True. Oracle Database 12*c* lets you consume a PL/SQL associative array in a SQL statement when you meet three conditions. First, the data type must be defined in a PL/SQL package. Second, there must be a local variable that uses that data type. Third, the SQL statement must be embedded within the PL/SQL block.

9. Oracle Database 12*c* now supports top-n query results without an offset value.

   True. Oracle Database 12*c* lets you create top-n query with or without `OFFSET` values.

10. You can embed a PL/SQL function inside a query's WITH clause and call it from external programs.

    True. Oracle Database 12*c* lets you implement a PL/SQL function inside a WITH clause. Unfortunately, the semicolon required to terminate statements and blocks causes a conflict with the SQLTERMINATOR and limits your ability to reading the statement within a preconfigured SQL*Plus session. You must embed the query inside a view to call it from other program units.

Multiple Choice:

11. Which of the following keywords work when you define a view? (Multiple answers possible)
    - **A.** The AUTHID DEFINER keywords
    - **B.** The BEQUEATH INVOKER keywords
    - **C.** The AUTHID CURRENT_USER keywords
    - **D.** The BEQUEATH DEFINER keywords
    - **E.** All of the above

    B and **D** are correct. The BEQUEATH keyword may precede either the INVOKER keyword or DEFINER keyword. The AUTHID keyword may precede either DEFINER or CURRENT_USER but only for functions, procedures, packages, and object types.

12. Which of the following are correct about caching invoker rights functions? (Multiple answers possible)
    - **A.** A different result set exists for each invoker.
    - **B.** The same result set exists for each invoker.
    - **C.** A cached invoker rights function must be deterministic.
    - **D.** A cached invoker rights function may be non-deterministic.
    - **E.** All of the above.

    A and **D** are correct. Oracle Database 12*c* lets you create cached invoker rights functions. They implicitly use the current user to distinguish between cached result sets, and that means different results are kept for each invoker.

13. Which of the following support expanding the SQL text of LONG columns into CLOB columns when working with the CDB_, DBA_, ALL_, and USER_VIEWS in the Oracle Database 12*c* database? (Multiple answers possible)
    - **A.** You can use the to_lob built-in function to convert LONG data types to CLOB data types.
    - **B.** You can use the to_clob built-in function to convert LONG data types to CLOB data types.
    - **C.** You can use the dbms_sql package to convert LONG data types to VARCHAR2 data types.
    - **D.** You can use the length built-in function to discover the size of a LONG data type.
    - **E.** You can use the dbms_lob package to create a temporary CLOB data type.

C, **D**, and **E** are correct. While not an Oracle Database 12*c* feature, you need to convert views from their native `LONG` data type to a `CLOB` before you can use the new `expand_sql_text` procedure in the `dbms_utility` package. You convert a `LONG` to a `CLOB` through a three-step process unless you like to read all the characters one-by-one in a loop. If you read character by character in your `LONG` to `CLOB` procedure, you don't need to fetch the `LONG` data type into a local variable to size it before calling the conversion procedure. The first step gets the size of the `LONG` data value with the `LENGTH` built-in, which means you query the administrative view twice. The second step requires you to convert `LONG` to a `VARCHAR2` by using the result of the `LENGTH` built-in and the `define_column_long` procedure from the `dbms_sql` package. The third step uses the `VARCHAR2` as a call parameter to the `dbms_lob.write` procedure from the `dbms_lob` package to create a `CLOB` from the `VARCHAR2`.

14. Which of the following is true about which PL/SQL data types you can access in an embedded SQL statement? (Multiple answers possible)

    A. The PL/SQL data type must be declared in a package.

    B. The SQL statement needs to be embedded in the PL/SQL block where the type is defined.

    C. The PL/SQL data type must be locally defined.

    D. The PL/SQL data type may be a return from a PL/SQL function.

    E. All of the above.

    A, **B**, and **C** are correct. Oracle Database 12*c* lets you consume a PL/SQL associative array in a SQL statement when you meet three conditions. First, the data type must be defined in a PL/SQL package. Second, there must be a local variable that uses that data type. Third, the SQL statement must be embedded within the PL/SQL block.

15. Which of the following lets you access a surrogate primary key from an identity column for use in a subsequent `INSERT` statement as a foreign key value?

    A. `RETURN INTO`

    B. `RETURNING INTO`

    C. `.nextval`

    D. `.currval`

    E. None of the above

    B is correct. The `RETURNING INTO` clause lets you capture the value from an identity column.

Chapter 3

True or False:

1. A basic block in PL/SQL must have at least a null statement to compile.

   True. Any PL/SQL block must include at least one statement, like a `NULL;` statement. The `NULL;` statement is advantageous for testing whether the blocks of code are organized correctly before embedding logic.

2. The *elsif* statement lets you branch execution in an *if* statement.

   False. The *elsif* statement keyword lets you branch execution, not the `ELSEIF` keyword.

3. The `DECLARE` block is where you put all variable, cursor, and local function and procedure implementations.

   True. The `DECLARE` block is where you put all variable, cursor, and local function and procedure implementations.

4. An `EXCEPTION` block is where you put handling for errors raised in the declaration block of the same anonymous or named program unit.

   False. The `EXCEPTION` block is where you handle exceptions from the execution section, but it can't handle exceptions raised in the declaration block.

5. The colon and equal sign set (`:=`) is the only assignment operator in PL/SQL.

   False. The `:=` operator is the only right-to-left assignment operator in PL/SQL, but you can use the `SELECT-INTO` statement or `BULK COLLECT INTO` statement to perform left-to-right assignments.

6. You need to provide forward-referencing stubs for local functions or procedures to avoid a procedure or function "not declared in this scope" error.

   True. You need to provide forward-referencing stubs to avoid a forward reference.

7. Oracle supports both simple and searched *case* statements.

   True. You can implement a simple or searched *case* statement.

8. Oracle supports SQL and PL/SQL collections as parameter and return value data types.

   True. You can have a function that returns a SQL or PL/SQL collection. You must call functions that return a PL/SQL collection inside another PL/SQL program unit. Functions that return a SQL collection work in either SQL or PL/SQL.

9. Packages let you define overloaded functions and procedures.

   True. Oracle supports overloaded functions and procedures in packages, which is an object-oriented feature.

10. Database triggers run between the first phase of a DML statement and the `COMMIT` statement.

    True. Database triggers run between the first phase of a DML statement and the `COMMIT` statement. The `COMMIT` statement ends the transaction and is the second phase of a two-phase commit (2PC).

Multiple Choice:

11. Which parameter modes are supported in Oracle PL/SQL? (Multiple answers possible)

    A. `IN`

    B. `INOUT`

    C. `OUT`

    D. `IN OUT`

    E. All of the above

A, **C**, and **D** are correct. The `IN` mode works for pass-by-value parameters, and `IN OUT` and `OUT`-only mode work for pass-by-reference parameters. There isn't an INOUT mode.

12. Which of the following are valid loop structures in PL/SQL? (Multiple answers possible)
    - **A.** A simple loop
    - **B.** A `FOR` loop
    - **C.** A `WHILE` loop
    - **D.** An `UNTIL` loop
    - **E.** All of the above

    A, **B**, and **C** are correct. Oracle supports a range and cursor `FOR` loop, a `WHILE` loop, and a simple loop.
13. A simple *case* statement works with which of the following data types? (Multiple answers possible)
    - **A.** A `TEXT` data type
    - **B.** A `VARCHAR2` data type
    - **C.** A `NCHAR` data type
    - **D.** A `CHAR` data type
    - **E.** A `DATE` data type

    B, **C**, and **D** are correct. Oracle supports a `VARCHAR2`, `NCHAR`, or `CHAR` data type in a simple *case* statement.
14. Which of the following isn't a keyword in PL/SQL?
    - **A.** `RECORD`
    - **B.** `REVERSE`
    - **C.** `CURSOR`
    - **D.** `LIMIT`
    - **E.** `STRUCTURE`

    E is correct. Oracle doesn't support a `STRUCTURE` keyword. It does support the `RECORD`, `REVERSE`, `CURSOR`, and `LIMIT` keywords.
15. Which of the following isn't a cursor attribute?
    - **A.** `%FOUND`
    - **B.** `%ISOPEN`
    - **C.** `%TYPE`
    - **D.** `%NOTFOUND`
    - **E.** `%ROWCOUNT`

    C is correct. `%TYPE` is a column anchoring attribute, not a cursor attribute.

Chapter 4

True or False:

1. A declaration block begins with the function or procedure header, specification, or signature in a named block.

   True. A declaration block immediately follows the function or procedure header.

2. An execution block can contain a local named block.

   False. An execution block can't contain a local named block; local named blocks must be defined in the declaration block.

3. A declaration block can't contain an anonymous block.

   False. A declaration block can contain an anonymous block if the anonymous block is embedded in a named block.

4. An identifier is a lexical unit.

   True. An identifier is a lexical unit.

5. The colon and equal sign set (:=) is the only assignment operator in PL/SQL.

   False. The := operator is the only right-to-left assignment operator in PL/SQL, but you can use the `SELECT-INTO` statement or `BULK COLLECT INTO` statement to perform left-to-right assignments, as covered in Chapter 3.

6. The equal sign and greater than symbol set (=>) is an association operator.

   True. The equal sign and greater than symbol set (=>) is an association operator, and it's used for named notation.

7. PL/SQL lets you create subtypes of standard scalar variables.

   True. You can create subtypes of standard scalar variables with PL/SQL.

8. A record data type is a SQL data type.

   False. A record data type is a PL/SQL data type.

9. A system reference cursor is a PL/SQL-only data type.

   True. A system reference cursor is a PL/SQL-only data type.

10. The PL/SQL programming language supports arrays and lists as composite data types.

    True. PL/SQL supports array (varray) and list (table) collections, which are composite type variables.

Multiple Choice:

11. Lexical units are the basic building blocks in programming languages, and they can perform which of the following? (Multiple answers possible)

    A. A delimiter

    B. An identifier

    C. A literal

- **D.** A comment
- **E.** An anonymous block

A, **B**, **C**, and **D** are correct. Delimiters, identifiers, literals, and comments are lexical units.

12. Which of the following are valid symbol sets in PL/SQL? (Multiple answers possible)

- **A.** A colon and equal sign set (:=) assignment operator
- **B.** A guillemets or double angle bracket set (<< >>) as delimiters for labels
- **C.** A less than symbol and greater than symbol set (<>) as a comparison operator
- **D.** An exclamation mark and equal sign set (`!=`) as a comparison operator
- **E.** A opening curly brace and closing curly brace symbol set ({ }) as delimiters for an anonymous block

A, **B**, **C**, and **D** are correct. The colon and equal sign set (`:=`) performs an assignment; the guillemets or double angle bracket set (<< >>) is a label target for a `GOTO` statement; the less than symbol and greater than symbol set (<>) is a not equal comparison operator; and an exclamation mark and equal sign set (`!=`) is a not-equal comparison operator.

13. Which of the following are valid scalar data types in PL/SQL? (Multiple answers possible)

- **A.** A `TEXT` data type
- **B.** A `VARCHAR2` data type
- **C.** A `NCHAR` data type
- **D.** A `CHAR` data type
- **E.** A `DATE` data type

B, **C**, **D**, and **E** are correct. The `TEXT` data type isn't a valid data type in PL/SQL, but it is a valid data type in MySQL.

14. Which of the following data types are best suited for scientific calculations in PL/SQL? (Multiple answers possible)

- **A.** A `NUMBER` data type
- **B.** A `PLS_INTEGER` data type
- **C.** A `BINARY_DOUBLE` data type
- **D.** A `BINARY_FLOAT` data type
- **E.** A `BINARY_INTEGER` data type

C and **D** are correct. Only the IEEE-754 variables `BINARY_DOUBLE` and `BINARY_FLOAT` are considered scientific computing data types.

15. Which of the following are reasons for using a system reference cursor?

- **A.** A system reference cursor mimics a table collection
- **B.** An alternative when you want to query data in one program and use it in another
- **C.** A PL/SQL-only solution with the results of composite data type
- **D.** A SQL or PL/SQL solution with the results of a system reference cursor
- **E.** None of the above

B and **C** are correct. You use a system reference cursor when you want to query data in one program and use it in another. System reference cursors are also PL/SQL-only solutions with one exception that was covered in Chapter 2, and that's using an Implicit Record Set (IRS).

Chapter 5

True or False:

1. Conjunctive logic involves determining when two or more things are true at the same time.

   True. Conjunctive logic involves two or more comparisons joined by an `AND` keyword. Two or all of the comparisons must be true for a conjunctive statement to be true.
2. Inclusion logic involves determining when one or another thing is true at any time.

   True. Inclusion logic involves two or more comparisons joined by an `OR` keyword. At least one item must be found true, and when one is found true, short-circuit logic stops making any remaining comparisons.
3. Short-circuit logic occurs with inclusion logic.

   True. Inclusion logic uses short-circuit logic, which stops making comparisons once one item is found true.
4. Databases always rely on two-valued logic.

   False. Databases rely on three-valued logic because they must be capable of comparing a null value. That's why Oracle Database and other databases support the `IS [NOT] NULL` reference comparison operator.
5. A searched `CASE` statement may use a string or numeric selector.

   True. A searched `CASE` statement evaluates Boolean logic, or the result of comparison operations.
6. A simple `CASE` statement can use a numeric selector.

   True. A simple `CASE` statement evaluates a numeric value, and when it finds a match in one of the `WHEN` clauses, it exits the `CASE` statement.
7. Conditional compilation supports conditional compilation flags.

   True. Conditional compilation supports any number of compilation flags.
8. A `CONTINUE` statement lets you skip the balance of an iteration through a loop.

   True. The `CONTINUE` statement instructs the program to skip the balance of an iteration cycle and return to the top of the loop.
9. A `SELECT-INTO` statement is an example of an explicit cursor.

   False. A `SELECT-INTO` statement is an implicit cursor.
10. The `FORALL` statement lets you perform bulk `INSERT` statements.

    True. The `FORLL` statement is the key structure for performing bulk `INSERT` and `UPDATE` statements.

Multiple Choice:

11. A conditional statement applied against two operands can evaluate which of the following? (Multiple answers possible)

A. The truth of a comparison involving only not-null values

B. The non-truth (or falsity) of a comparison involving only not-null values

C. The truth of a comparison involving one or more null values

D. The non-truth (or falsity) of a comparison involving one or more null values

E. The truth of null values

A is correct. Comparison operations are three-valued logic comparisons unless you're checking for a null value. Checking for a null value is an evaluation of what a reference points to, not the value that it holds. Comparison operations between two operands only work when both operands hold not-null values.

12. Which of the following are *only* guard-on-entry loops? (Multiple answers possible)

A. A simple range loop

B. A range `FOR` loop

C. A `WHILE` loop

D. A `DO-UNTIL` loop

E. A `DO-WHILE` loop

A, **B**, and **C** are correct. A simple loop can be coded to guard on entry or exit. A range `FOR` loop guards on entry and exit, and a `WHILE` loop guards entry only. `DO-UNTIL` and `DO-WHILE` aren't loop structures in PL/SQL.

13. Which of the following guards entry and exit to the loop in PL/SQL? (Multiple answers possible)

A. A range `FOR` loop

B. A cursor `FOR` loop

C. A simple loop

D. A `DO-WHILE` loop

E. A `WHILE` loop

A and **B** are correct. The `FOR` loop guards entry and exit and manages them implicitly.

14. Which of the following are *only* guard-on-exit loops? (Multiple answers possible)

A. A simple cursor loop

B. A simple range loop

C. A cursor `FOR` loop

D. A `WHILE` loop

E. A range `FOR` loop

A and **B** are correct. Only the simple loop allows unfettered access, and allows you to guard on exit. That lets you run the logic once and exit regardless of any conditions before entering the loop.

15. Which of the following collections work best with a bulk delete operation on a well-defined (or normalized) table with a surrogate key for its single-column primary key? (Multiple answers possible)

    A. Parallel scalar collections

    B. A single scalar collection

    C. A single record collection

    D. All of the above

    E. None of the above

    B and **C** are correct. Bulk operations only work when there's one collection to traverse, and that means a single scalar or record collection.

Chapter 6

True or False:

1. SQL varray collections can only be used in a SQL context.

   False. You can use a varray collection in a SQL scope or a PL/SQL scope.

2. Table collections can be used in a SQL context or a PL/SQL context.

   True. You can use a table collection in a SQL scope or a PL/SQL scope.

3. Associative arrays can be used only in a PL/SQL context.

   True. You can only use a table collection in a PL/SQL scope.

4. A table collection can hold a record or object type as its a composite base data type.

   True. You can only use a table collection in a PL/SQL scope that refers to a composite record structure. There are limits on how you assign elements to the collection because object types and record structures aren't interchangeable.

5. A varray has a fixed number of elements when you define it.

   True. You define any varray (or *varying array*) with a maximum number of elements.

6. A varray or table of a scalar variable is an Attribute Data Type (ADT).

   True. A varray or table of a scalar variable is an ADT and returns a single `column_value` pseudocolumn when translated by the `TABLE` function in a query.

7. A varray or table of a composite data type is a user-defined type (UDT).

   True. A varray or table of a composite data type is a UDT and returns a list of column names that map to the user-defined object type when translated by the `TABLE` function in a query.

8. A `LIMIT` function from the Oracle Collection API only works with table collections.

   False. A `LIMIT` function from the Oracle Collection API only works with a varray (or varying array) data type.

9. A `BULK COLLECT` statement can work with a table collection of object types.

   False. A `BULK COLLECT` statement can only work with a table of scalar values or a table of PL/SQL record structures.

10. The `TABLE` function lets you consume a varray or table collection as an ordinary SQL result set.

    True. A `TABLE` function translates a collection into an aggregate result set, which is the form of any query's result set.

Multiple Choice:

11. Which of the following is a densely populated index in an Oracle varray or table collection? (Multiple answers possible)

    A. A sequence of negative integers without any gaps in the sequence of integers

    B. A sequence of positive integers starting at a number of your choosing without any gaps in the sequence of integers

    C. A sequence of positive integers starting at 1 without any gaps in the sequence

    D. A sequence of letters without any gaps in the sequence of integers

    E. A sequence of positive integers starting at 1 with some gaps in the sequence of integers

    B is correct. Only a sequence of integers without gaps and starting at 1 is considered densely populated.

12. Which of the following support string indexes? (Multiple answers possible)

    A. PL/SQL tables

    B. Table collections

    C. Varray collections

    D. Associative arrays

    E. Java ArrayList classes

    D is correct. Only associative arrays support string indexes.

13. Which of the following is a sparsely populated index in an Oracle varray or table collection? (Multiple answers possible)

    A. A sequence of negative integers without any gaps in the sequence of integers

    B. A sequence of positive integers starting at a number of your choosing without any gaps in the sequence of integers

    C. A sequence of positive integers starting at 1 without any gaps in the sequence

    D. A sequence of letters without any gaps in the sequence of integers

    E. A sequence of positive integers starting at 1 with some gaps in the sequence of integers

    D and **E** are correct. Letters implicitly have gaps even when they don't, because they're letters, not numbers, which makes them sparsely populated indexes. Any sequence of integers with gaps is sparsely populated.

14. Which of the following are boundary elements of collections? (Multiple answers possible)

    A. The index value returned by the `FIRST` function

    B. The index value returned by the `COUNT` function

    C. The index value returned by the `LIMIT` function

D. The index value returned by the `LAST` function

E. All of the above

A, **B**, and **D** are correct. The `FIRST` function returns the lowest boundary element. The `LAST` function returns the highest boundary element. The `COUNT` function also returns the highest boundary element (when the index is numeric) because collections use 1-based numbering.

15. Which of the following collections work in SQL and PL/SQL contexts? (Multiple answers possible)

    A. Varray collections of scalar data types

    B. Varray collections of record data types

    C. Table collections of scalar data types

    D. Table collections of object data types

    E. All of the above

    A, **C**, and **D** are correct. A varray or table collection can work in SQL and PL/SQL contexts when the base data type is a scalar or object data type.

Chapter 7

True or False:

1. Oracle PL/SQL programming requires you to understand how to capture and analyze both compile-time errors and runtime errors.

   True. You need to understand how to analyze and capture compile-time errors to make sure you can compile your code. You need to understand how to analyze and trap runtime errors.

2. A compile-time error may occur when you try to run an anonymous block program.

   True. Compile-time means the same thing for both anonymous block and named block programs. It's the time where the program is parsed and compiled into p-code. Any failure during parsing is a compile time error.

3. A runtime error may occur when you try to compile a stored procedure.

   False. A runtime error can only occur after you've successfully compiled a stored procedure. A compile-time error can occur when you try to create or replace a procedure.

4. A runtime error may occur when you call a stored procedure.

   True. A runtime error may occur when you call a stored procedure.

5. A `THROW` command raises a runtime exception.

   False. A `RAISE` statement or `RAISE_APPLICATION_ERROR` function call raises a runtime exception. A `THROW` command raises an exception in Java, not in PL/SQL.

6. It's possible to declare a user-defined exception variable with the same error code as a predefined exception.

   True. It's possible to declare a user-defined exception variable with the same error code as a predefined exception. You'll want to do so when you don't have a predefined exception to handle the error code.

7. A PRAGMA is a precompiler instruction or compiler directive.

   True. A PRAGMA is a compiler directive. Alternatively, a PRAGMA is also frequently referred to as a precompiler instruction.

8. An EXCEPTION_INIT complier directive lets you map a user-defined EXCEPTION variable to a message.

   False. While an EXCEPTION_INIT is a compiler directive, it maps a user-defined EXCEPTION variable and an error code number.

9. A RAISE_APPLICATION_ERROR function call lets you map only a user-defined error code to a custom error message.

   True. A RAISE_APPLICATION_ERROR function call does let you map a user-defined error code to a custom error message.

10. A call to the format_error_backtrace function from the utl_call_stack package creates a stack trace.

    False. The format_error_backtrace function doesn't belong to the utl_call_stack package. The format_error_backtrace function belongs to the dbms_utility package.

Multiple Choice:

11. Which of the following error codes belongs to a predefined exception? (Multiple answers possible)

    A. ORA-01402

    B. ORA-01722

    C. ORA-06548

    D. ORA-01422

    E. ORA-00001

    B, **C**, and **D** are correct. The ORA-01722 error belongs to the predefined INVALID_NUMBER exception, the ORA-06548 error belongs to the NO_DATA_NEEDED exception, and the ORA-01422 error belongs to the TOO_MANY_ROWS exception.

12. Which of the following is a predefined exception keyword? (Multiple answers possible)

    A. CURSOR_IS_OPEN

    B. INVALID_NUMBER

    C. LOGIN_DENIED

    D. NO_DATA_FOUND

    E. VALUE_INCORRECT

    B, **C**, and **D** are correct. The predefined INVALID_NUMBER predefined error belongs to an ORA-01722 error, the predefined LOGIN_DENIED predefined error belongs to an ORA-01017 error, and the predefined NO_DATA_FOUND predefined error belongs to an ORA-01403 error. CURSOR_IS_OPEN and VALUE_INCORRECT are invalid predefined exceptions.

13. Which of the following lets you raise an exception in PL/SQL? (Multiple answers possible)
    A. A `THROW e;` statement
    B. A `RAISE e;` statement
    C. A `THROW;` statement
    D. A `RAISE;` statement
    E. A `RAISE_APPLICATION_ERROR` function call

    B and **E** are correct. The `RAISE` statement requires a locally declared exception variable. A `RAISE_APPLICATION_ERROR` function call is also correct.
14. Which of the following are functions of the `utl_call_stack` package? (Multiple answers possible)
    A. The `backtrace_error` function
    B. The `backtrace_depth` function
    C. The `error_number` function
    D. The `subprogram_name` function
    E. The `error_depth` function

    B, **C**, and **E** are correct. The `backtrace_depth`, `error_number`, and `error_depth` functions are valid elements of the `utl_call_stack` package.
15. Which of the following displays an HTML-ready stack trace? (Multiple answers possible)
    A. The `utl_call_stack.current_edition` function
    B. The `dbms_utility.format_stack_trace` function
    C. The `dbms_utility.format_error_backtrace` function
    D. All of the above
    E. None of the above

    C is correct. The `format_error_backtrace` function is the only valid way to generate a HTML-ready stack trace.

Chapter 8

True or False:

1. A pass-by-value function takes parameters that are consumed completely and changed into some outcome-based value.

   True. The pass-by-value function takes parameter values and uses them to produce a result; the values are not returned individually.
2. An `INLINE` compiler directive lets you include a stand-alone module as part of your compiled program unit.

   True. The `INLINE` compiler directive lets you include other routines inside your program unit at compilation.

3. A pass-by-reference function takes literal values for any of the call parameters.

   False. A pass-by-reference function can take literal values for any pass-by-value or `IN` mode parameter, but it can't take a literal value for any pass-by-reference parameter—those are `IN OUT` or `OUT` mode parameters.

4. A pass-by-value procedure takes literal values for any of the call parameters.

   True. A pass-by-value procedure can be a string or numeric literal value.

5. The `RETURN` statement must always include a literal or variable for all pass-by-value and pass-by-reference functions.

   False. The `RETURN` statement takes a literal or variable in all but two cases: a pipelined table function and an object type. This chapter covers the `RETURN` statement in a pipelined table function.

6. You need to provide forward-referencing stubs for local functions or procedures to avoid a procedure or function "not declared in this scope" error.

   True. You should provide forward-referencing stubs to avoid a forward reference, which I interpret as you need to do it.

7. You can't assign an `IN` mode parameter a new value inside a stored function or procedure.

   True. You can't assign a value to an `IN` mode parameter.

8. You can't assign an `IN OUT` mode parameter a new value inside a stored function or procedure.

   False. You can assign a value to an `IN OUT` or `OUT` mode parameter.

9. You can't embed an `INSERT`, `UPDATE`, or `DELETE` statement in any function that you plan to call from a SQL `SELECT` statement.

   False. You can embed an `INSERT`, `UPDATE`, or `DELETE` statement and call it from a SQL `SELECT` statement when you designate it as an `AUTONOMOUS` function.

10. Some functions can only be called from within a PL/SQL scope.

    False. You can call a nonautonomous function with an embedded `INSERT`, `UPDATE`, or `DELETE` statement from a PL/SQL context. You can't call the same program from a SQL context.

Multiple Choice:

11. Which types of subroutines return a value at completion? (Multiple answers possible)

    A. A pass-by-value function

    B. A pass-by-value procedure

    C. A pass-by-reference function

    D. A pass-by-reference procedure

    E. All of the above

    A and **B** are correct. A pass-by-value or pass-by-reference function returns a variable.

12. Which of the following clauses are supported in PL/SQL? (Multiple answers possible)

    A. An `INLINE` clause

    B. A `PIPELINED` clause

    C. A `DETERMINISTIC` clause

    D. A `NONDETERMINISTIC` clause

    E. A `RESULT_CACHE` clause

    B, **C**, and **E** are correct. `PIPELINED`, `DETERMINISTIC`, and `RESULT_CACHE` are valid function clauses.

13. Which call notations are supported by the Oracle Database 12*c* database? (Multiple answers possible)

    A. Positional notation

    B. Named notation

    C. Mixed notation

    D. Object notation

    E. Exclusionary notation

    A, **B**, **C**, and **E** are correct. Positional, named, mixed, and exclusionary notation are supported. There isn't any such thing as object notation.

14. Which of the following isn't possible with a result cache function in the Oracle Database 12*c* database? (Multiple answers possible)

    A. A definer rights deterministic pass-by-value function

    B. An invoker rights deterministic pass-by-value function

    C. A definer rights nondeterministic pass-by-value function

    D. An invoker rights nondeterministic pass-by-value function

    E. A definer rights nondeterministic pass-by-reference function

    A, **B**, **C**, and **D** are correct. You can create result cached functions for any pass-by-value functions, as of Oracle Database 12*c*. Prior to Oracle Database 12*c*, you could not implement options B and D because invoker rights programs weren't supported.

15. Which of the following are specifically backward-compatible Oracle 8*i* Database compiler directives?

    A. `RESTRICT_ACCESS`

    B. `INLINE`

    C. `AUTONOMOUS`

    D. `DETERMINISTIC`

    E. `EXCEPTION_INIT`

    A is correct. Oracle supports only the `RESTRICT_ACCESS` compiler directive for Oracle 8*i* Database backward compatibility. The `AUTONOMOUS`, `EXCEPTION_INIT`, and `INLINE` compiler directives were introduced in prior releases but are also part of this release.

Chapter 9

True or False:

1. Package specifications can define only functions and procedures.

   False. While a package specification can define functions and procedures, it can also define variables and data types.

2. Package bodies can define variables, data types, functions, and procedures.

   True. Package bodies can define variables, data types, functions, and procedures but they're private to the package.

3. You define functions and procedures in package specifications and implement them in package bodies.

   True. Package specifications define functions and procedures, while package bodies implement them.

4. You define function stubs and provide their implementations in package bodies.

   True. You can define forward-referencing stubs, like package specifications, but they're only useful during the compilation of the package body. You must also provide the implementation for any package body function stubs or else compilation of the package body will fail.

5. A forward reference is required for any function or procedure to avoid inadvertent use before its implementation in the package body.

   False. Is this a hair splitter? No. You need to know that while *not required*, providing forward references for package-level functions and procedures *is highly advised*.

6. A grant of `EXECUTE` on a package lets a user in another schema run a definer rights package against the definer's local data.

   True. That's the purpose of granting the `EXECUTE` privilege to another user when they're going to run the definer rights package.

7. A `SYNONYM` provides an alias for a privilege.

   False. That's not the purpose of a `SYNONYM`. A `SYNONYM` provides an alias for a table, view, function, procedure, package, object type, or database link.

8. A package must contain all autonomous and non-autonomous functions and procedures.

   False. A package may contain one to many autonomous program units, but it may have a mix of autonomous and non-autonomous program units.

9. A package maintains a variable's value until it's aged out of the SGA or you issue a `FLUSH VARIABLE` *`variable_name`* statement.

   False. There's no such SQL statement. You have two alternatives. One is that you wait until the package ages out of the SGA. The other requires you to take action, like altering the package or changing the session.

10. You can query a serially reusable package from a `SELECT` statement.

    False. You can't query a serially reusable program from a `SELECT` statement.

Multiple Choice:

11. Which of the following is a `PRAGMA` (precompiler directive) reserved to packages? (Multiple answers possible)

A. `AUTONOMOUS_TRANSACTION`

B. `AUTO_TRANSACTION`

C. `SERIALLY REUSABLE`

D. `EXCEPTION_INIT`

E. `RESTRICT_REFERENCES`

C is correct. The `SERIALLY_REUSABLE` precompiler directive only works with packages.

12. Which of the following can be defined in a package specification? (Multiple answers possible)

A. An object type

B. A record type

C. A function

D. A procedure

E. An autonomous function

B, **C**, **D**, and **E** are correct. An object type is a SQL-only data type and can't be defined inside a package.

13. Which of the following is a publically accessible variable? (Multiple answers possible)

A. A variable declared in a function of a package

B. A variable declared in a procedure of a package

C. A variable declared in a package specification

D. A variable declared in a package body outside of a function or procedure

E. All of the above

C is correct. Only variables, data types, functions, and procedures defined in a package specification are publically accessible.

14. Which of the following support overloading? (Multiple answers possible)

A. Stand-alone functions

B. Stand-alone procedures

C. Functions declared in the package specification

D. Procedures declared in the package specification

E. Functions declared in the package body

C and **D** are correct. Only functions and procedures defined in the package specification are overloaded.

15. Which of the following guarantees variables are fresh each time you call a package? (Multiple answers possible)
    - **A.** A declaring variables in an autonomous function
    - **B.** A declaring variables in a local procedure
    - **C.** A declaring variables in a local function
    - **D.** A declaring variables outside a function or procedure in a package body
    - **E.** A declaring variables outside a function or procedure in a package specification

    A, **B**, and **C** are correct. Only variables defined as local variables are truly private. They are refreshed each time the function or procedure is called. Package specification and package body variables have values that persist until they age out of the SGA.

Chapter 10

True or False:

1. `CLOB` and `NCLOB` data types are object types and require explicit construction in a SQL context.

   True. `CLOB` and `NCLOB` data types are object types and require explicit construction in a SQL context.
2. `CLOB` and `NCLOB` data types are subclasses to a generic `LOB` class.

   False. `CLOB` and `NCLOB` data types are not subclasses to a generic `LOB` class.
3. The `BLOB` data type holds binary streams.

   True. The `BLOB` data type may hold binary streams but may also hold character streams. As a rule, `BLOB` data types hold only binary streams.
4. You can assign a string literal to a `CLOB` inside a `VALUES` clause of an `INSERT` statement.

   False. You can't assign a string literal to a `CLOB` or `NCLOB` inside a `VALUES` clause of an `INSERT` statement. You must push the string through a stored function that creates a temporary `CLOB` and returns a `CLOB` data type.
5. A stored function can convert a `LONG` data type to a `CLOB` data type.

   True. A stored function can convert a `LONG` data type to a `CLOB` data type, an example of which is provided in the sidebar "Converting a LONG to a CLOB."
6. The `empty_clob` function supports the `CLOB`, `NCLOB`, and `BLOB` data types.

   False. The `empty_clob` function supports the `CLOB` and `NCLOB` data types but not the `BLOB` data type. You must use the `empty_blob` function when you work with `BLOB` data types.
7. You can assign strings of hexadecimal values to `BLOB` variables in a PL/SQL context.

   True. You can assign hexadecimal values to a BLOB variable in either a SQL or PL/SQL context.

8. A BFILE depends on a virtual directory to find the external file.

   True. A locator for a BFILE is a combination of a virtual directory and a filename.

9. A SELECT-INTO statement can assign a string to a CLOB variable.

   True. A SELECT-INTO statement runs only inside a PL/SQL block, and it assigns a result from the SELECT-list into a local CLOB variable. This type of assignment is limited to the maximum size of a VARCHAR2, which is 32,767 bytes when the max_string_size parameter is set to EXTENDED.

10. A SELECT-INTO statement can assign a LONG column value to a CLOB variable.

    False. A SELECT-INTO statement can't assign a LONG column because it doesn't support the LONG data type. The TO_CHAR function doesn't accept a LONG call parameter either. That leaves you with the dbms_sql package as your only means to convert a LONG to a CLOB or NCLOB data type.

Multiple Choice:

11. Which of the following are pass-by-reference procedures in the dbms_lob package? (Multiple answers possible)

    A. lob_readonly

    B. write

    C. lob_readwrite

    D. writeappend

    E. isopen

    B and **D** are correct. The write and writeappend procedures of the dbms_lob package are pass-by-reference procedures. lob_readonly and lob_readwrite are package constants, and isopen is a function.

12. Which of the following are functions in the dbms_lob package? (Multiple answers possible)

    A. open

    B. isopen

    C. converttoblob

    D. unopened_file

    E. issecurefile

    B and **E** are correct. The isopen and issecurefile functions of the dbms_lob package are pass-by-reference functions. open and converttoblob are procedures of the dbms_lob package, and isopen is a function.

13. Which of the following are exceptions in the dbms_lob package? (Multiple answers possible)

    A. OPEN_TOOMANY

    B. NOPRIV_DIR

    C. NOEXIST_DIRECTORY

D. `UNINTIALIZED_BLOB`

E. `GETOPTIONS`

A and **C** are correct. `open_toomany` and `noexist_directory` are exceptions declared in the `dbms_lob` package. `nopriv_dir` and `uninitialized_blob` are not any part of the `dbms_lob` package. `getoptions` is a function in the `dbms_lob` package.

14. Which of the following are LOBs in an Oracle Database 12*c* database? (Multiple answers possible)

A. A `BLOB`

B. A `CLOB`

C. A `NCLOB`

D. A `BFILE`

E. All of the above

E is correct. The `BLOB`, `CLOB`, `NCLOB`, and `BFILE` are all valid large objects in the Oracle Database 12*c* database.

15. Which of the following are internally stored LOBs in Oracle Database 12*c*? (Multiple answers possible)

A. A `BLOB`

B. A `CLOB`

C. A `NCLOB`

D. A `BFILE`

E. All of the above

A, **B**, and **C** are correct. The `BLOB`, `CLOB`, and `NCLOB` are all valid large objects that are stored inside the Oracle Database 12*c* database. The `BFILE` only stores a locator and filename in the database; the physical file is stored outside the database as a file.

Chapter 11

True or False:

1. Object types are instantiable by default.

True. Object types are instantiable by default. You must provide the optional `NOT` to negate the default.

2. Object types are extensible by default.

True. Object types are extensible by default, you must provide the optional `NOT` to negate the default.

3. The *this* keyword references an instance of an object type inside an object body.

False. Oracle object bodies use `SELF` to reference the current instance of an object type.

4. You can have a `MAP` function and an `ORDER` function in the same object type.

False. Oracle only allows you to implement a `MAP` function or an `ORDER` function in the same object type. The `ORDER` function is the more OOPL-like one, and the preferred solution.

5. You can have a MAP procedure and an ORDER procedure in the same object type.

   False. Oracle only allows you to implement a MAP function or an ORDER function in the same object type. You can't implement a MAP procedure or an ORDER procedure in an object type.

6. CONSTRUCTOR functions require the name and data type to be the same as the attributes of the object type.

   True. Oracle CONSTRUCTOR functions require the name and data type to be the same as the attributes of the object type.

7. Getters always should be implemented as MEMBER procedures.

   False. Getters always should be implemented as MEMBER functions.

8. Setters always should be implemented as MEMBER procedures.

   True. Setters always should be implemented as MEMBER procedures.

9. The UNDER clause designates a superclass.

   False. The UNDER clause designates a subclass, subtype, or type dependent.

10. The OVERRIDING clause lets a subtype override a STATIC function or procedure.

    False. The OVERRIDING clause lets a subtype override a MEMBER function.

Multiple Choice:

11. Which of the following are keywords in object types? (Multiple answers possible)

    A. The MAP keyword

    B. The OVERRIDE keyword

    C. The OVERRIDING keyword

    D. The NONSTATIC keyword

    E. The MEMBER keyword

    A and **E** are correct. An object type may have one MAP function, and all instance-level functions and procedures are MEMBER methods.

12. Which of the following are valid types of functions in object types? (Multiple answers possible)

    A. An ORDER function

    B. An OVERRIDE function

    C. A MEMBER function

    D. An UNDER function

    E. A STATIC function

    A, **C**, and **E** are correct. The ORDER, MEMBER, and STATIC functions are supported.

13. Which of the following are valid types of procedures in object types? (Multiple answers possible)

    A. An ORDER procedure

    B. A MAP procedure

C. An UNDER procedure

D. A MEMBER procedure

E. A STATIC procedure

D and **E** are correct. The MEMBER and STATIC procedures are possible.

14. Which of the following require an instance of the object type? (Multiple answers possible)

    A. A STATIC function

    B. A STATIC procedure

    C. A CONSTRUCTOR function

    D. A MEMBER function

    E. A MEMBER procedure

    D and **E** are correct. The STATIC functions and procedures don't require an instance of the object type. All MEMBER functions and procedures are instance methods.

15. Which of the following can be a function return type (or normalized table with a surrogate key for its single-column primary key)? (Multiple answers possible)

    A. A VARCHAR2 data type

    B. A NUMBER data type

    C. A varray or table collection data type

    D. A RECORD data type

    E. An OBJECT data type

    A, **B**, **C**, and **E** are correct. All scalar and composite data types can be return values from object type functions and procedures except the PL/SQL-only RECORD data type.

Chapter 12

True or False:

1. Statement-level database triggers can change the new pseudo-record column values with the INSERT and UPDATE statements.

   False. Statement-level triggers can't access the pseudo-records because they run once per statement, not for each row touched by the transaction.

2. Oracle Database 12*c* supports triggers on Data Definition Language (DDL) statements.

   True. Oracle Database 12*c* supports DDL statement triggers.

3. Row-level database triggers can change the new pseudo-record column values with the INSERT and UPDATE statements.

   True. Row-level triggers can access the pseudo-records because they run once for each row touched by an INSERT or UPDATE statement.

4. Compound database triggers have four timing points.

   True. Oracle Database 12*c*'s compound database triggers have four timing points: BEFORE STATEMENT, BEFORE EACH ROW, AFTER EACH ROW, and AFTER STATEMENT.

5. Compound database triggers can implement a global exception handler.

   False. Compound database triggers can't implement a global exception handler. They can only implement exception handlers within the timing event blocks.

6. Event attribute functions are designed for use in triggers and non-trigger PL/SQL program units.

   False. Event attribute functions are designed for exclusive use in database triggers, and they have no context outside of database triggers.

7. You can implement event attribute functions in system event triggers.

   True. You can implement event attribute functions inside DDL triggers or system event triggers.

8. You can define a single DML trigger that fires for `INSERT`, `UPDATE`, or `DELETE` statements on the same table.

   True. Oracle supports triggers that work with an `INSERT`, `UPDATE`, or `DELETE` statement, or with two or three of the statements through the `OR` inclusion operators.

9. You can define a DDL trigger for a `MERGE` statement.

   False. The Oracle `MERGE` statement is a combination of an `INSERT` statement and an `UPDATE` statement. You use an `INSERT OR UPDATE` trigger to capture changes from a `MERGE` statement.

10. It's possible to define an autonomous trigger body.

    True. You can define an autonomous trigger body by using a precompiler directive, `PRAGMA AUTONOMOUS_TRANSACTION`.

Multiple Choice:

11. Which of the following types of database triggers work in an Oracle database? (Multiple answers possible)

    A. DDL triggers

    B. TCL triggers

    C. DML triggers

    D. `INSTEAD OF` triggers

    E. Compound triggers

    A, **C**, **D**, and **E** are correct. Oracle supports DDL, DML, `INSTEAD OF`, and compound triggers. There is no such thing as a TCL trigger.

12. Which of the following types of database triggers work with a nonupdatable view in an Oracle database? (Multiple answers possible)

    A. DDL triggers

    B. DML triggers

    C. System event triggers

    D. TCL triggers

    E. `INSTEAD OF` triggers

    E is correct. Only the `INSTEAD OF` trigger works with nonupdatable views.

13. You have `new` and `old` pseudo-record structures for which triggers in an Oracle database? (Multiple answers possible)

A. DML statement-level triggers

B. DDL row-level triggers

C. DDL statement-level triggers

D. DML row-level triggers

E. Compound triggers

D is correct. The Oracle database supports the `new` and `old` pseudo-record structures only in a DML row-level trigger.

14. Which of the following are event functions? (Multiple answers possible)

A. A `MERGING` function

B. An `INSERTING` function

C. An `UPDATING` function

D. A `DELETING` function

E. All of the above

B, **C**, and **D** are correct. The `INSERTING`, `UPDATING`, and `DELETING` event functions are the only event functions in Oracle Database 12*c*.

15. Oracle requires what syntax to access new column values from an `INSERT` or `UPDATE` statement in the code block? (Multiple answers possible)

A. `new.column_name`

B. `:new.column_name`

C. `old.column_name`

D. `:old.column_name`

E. None of the above

B is correct. Oracle can only access a `new` pseudo-record by using a bind variable, `:new`, from inside the trigger body. The reason is that the trigger body acts like a subshell and can gain access to the `new` pseudo-record structure's scope only by referring outside of its scope. The prefacing colon (signifying a bind variable) lets the program refer to the DML statement's scope.

Chapter 13

True or False:

1. NDS supports dynamic DDL statements with bind variables.

False. NDS doesn't support bind variables in dynamic DDL statements. You must use concatenation to create dynamic DDL statements.

2. NDS supports static DDL statements.

   True. NDS supports static DDL statements, but you're more likely to create statements by concatenating values into them.

3. NDS supports dynamic DML statements with bind variables.

   True. NDS supports dynamic DML statements with bind variables.

4. NDS supports dynamic `SELECT` statements with a known set of columns.

   True. NDS supports dynamic `SELECT` statements with a known set of columns in the `SELECT` list. It opens the dynamic statement into a system reference cursor.

5. NDS supports dynamic PL/SQL anonymous blocks.

   True. NDS supports dynamic PL/SQL anonymous blocks and it can pass `IN`-only, `IN OUT`, or `OUT`-only mode variables.

6. NDS supports string literals with an embedded colon (`:`).

   False. NDS doesn't support an embedded colon (`:`), and you have to use a `CHR(58)` to put one into the context of a dynamic statement.

7. NDS statements with an unknown number of inputs rely on the `dbms_sql` package.

   True. NDS statements with an unknown number of inputs rely on the `dbms_sql` package.

8. Without NDS, you must explicitly use the `dbms_sql` package to open a cursor.

   True. When you're not using NDS, you must explicitly open a cursor with the `dbms_sql` package.

9. With an unknown set of dynamic inputs, you must parse, execute, and fetch results with functions and procedures found in the `dbms_sql` package.

   True. You must parse, execute, and fetch results from the `dbms_sql` package to run dynamic statements with an unknown set of input parameters.

10. You only need to define columns and bind variables to retrieve `SELECT`-list values from a dynamic query with the `dbms_sql` package.

    False. You need to define columns and bind variables and map the column values to `SELECT`-list values.

Multiple Choice:

11. Which of the following are procedures in the `dbms_sql` package? (Multiple answers possible)

    A. `bind_array`

    B. `bind_variable`

    C. `fetch_rows`

    D. `is_open`

    E. `parse`

    A, **B**, and **E** are correct. `bind_array`, `bind_variable`, and `parse` are procedures. `fetch_rows` and `is_open` are functions.

12. Which of the following are functions in the `dbms_sql` package? (Multiple answers possible)

A. `bind_array`

B. `execute_and_fetch`

C. `fetch_rows`

D. `is_open`

E. `parse`

B, **C**, and **D** are correct. `execute_and_fetch`, `fetch_rows`, and `is_open` are functions. `bind_array` and `parse` are procedures.

13. Which of the following are package constants? (Multiple answers possible)

A. The `NATIVE` constant

B. The `V6` constant

C. The `V7` constant

D. The `V8` constant

E. All of the above

A, **B**, and **C** are correct. The `NATIVE`, `V6`, and `V7` are constants of the `dbms_sql` package. You should always use `NATIVE` from Oracle 7 forward.

14. Which of the following are `dbms_sql`-supported base scalar types for collections? (Multiple answers possible)

A. The `BLOB` data type

B. The `CLOB` data type

C. The `BINARY_DOUBLE` data type

D. The `BINARY_FLOAT` data type

E. The `TIMESTAMP` data type

A, **B**, **C**, **D**, and **E** are correct. All of the data types are supported base types of the `dbms_sql` Attribute Data Type (ADT) collections.

15. Which of the following `dbms_sql` functions or procedures execute a query? (Multiple answers possible)

A. The `parse_and_execute` procedure

B. The `parse_and_execute` function

C. The `execute` function

D. The `execute_and_fetch` function

E. The `execute_fetch_all` function

C and **D** are correct. `execute` and `execute_and_fetch` are the only functions that execute a dynamic query in the `dbms_sql` package.

Glossary

This glossary is intended to help you quickly reference and understand terminology that you encounter throughout this book. Many of these terms are defined in the book, but this glossary provides a central place to quickly look up a term. Some of these terms have varying meanings in mathematics and computer science; the definitions you'll find here are applicable in the context of database management systems and entity relationship diagramming for database instances.

0NF Acronym for *zero normal form*. A 0NF table is one whose normalization level is not normalized, which means that the collection of columns may result in nonunique rows and that any column may contain nonatomic values (composites of two or more values).

1NF Acronym for *first normal form*. A 1NF table is one whose columns hold only atomic values and whose rows are unique because the list of all columns guarantees unique rows.

2NF Acronym for *second normal form*. A 2NF table is one that meets 1NF rules and contains no partial dependency. A partial dependency exists when the table has a composite primary key (made up of two or more columns and chosen from possible candidate keys as a natural primary key) or when any non-key column in the table depends on only part of the composite primary key. The presence of a partial dependency in a table's design establishes it as a 1NF table. Moving a table from 1NF to 2NF typically requires that you divide the table into two tables, because the partial dependency indicates the initial table's design contains more than a single subject-fact or theme.

After removing the column from the composite natural primary key, you should check whether the natural key truly resolves uniqueness with the remaining columns. The remaining columns should describe uniqueness of the table's single subject-fact or theme. If they [the remaining columns] do, you have a good natural key for the table from a design perspective. While a valid natural key becomes a candidate key that you may select as the primary key, you should always add a surrogate key column as the primary key.

3NF Acronym for *third normal form*. A 3NF table is one that meets 2NF rules and contains no transitive dependency. A transitive dependency exists when the table has a non-key column that depends on another non-key column for context. The presence of a transitive dependency means the table is in 2NF. Moving a table with a transitive dependency from 2NF to 3NF requires removing the transitive dependency. Like the process of changing a table with a partial dependency, you remove both the dependent column and the column that it is dependent on. The column through which the transitive dependency exists should become the natural key of a new table, and the dependent column should become a non-key column in that new table. During early design, it is possible that more than one transitive dependency may exist. You should repeat the process for all transitive dependencies.

actual parameter list The call parameter list, or the arguments that you pass to the subroutine. Pass-by-value arguments can be literals or variables, while pass-by-reference arguments must be variables.

aggregate function A function that adds or calculates a single result for a set of values. When an aggregate function occurs in a `SELECT` statement, you must also provide a `GROUP BY` clause to instruct SQL to assign a single copy of nonaggregate result columns to each row of an aggregated result.

aggregate result set A SQL result set that has been aggregated through the use of an aggregation function. Most aggregate result sets hold a combination of aggregate and nonaggregate results. The nonaggregate result columns must be qualified in a `GROUP BY` clause because they become the determinant for the aggregation. More or less, SQL returns rectangular result sets that are determined by the number of columns across the X axis and the number of rows across the Y axis. The `GROUP BY` clause ensures that the many rows of repeating values are collected and represented as a single row value with the aggregated row.

anomaly A deviation from the common rule, type, arrangement, or form; or an incongruity or inconsistency.

array A collection of a specific set of things, which are typically unique. The things share one thing, the data type of the collection. Unlike a list, which has no limit, the number of elements in an array may grow over time only to the maximum number of elements specified when you defined the array's maximum size.

association operator An operator, represented by the symbol =>, that lets you perform named notation calls. Named notation lets you call a formal parameter list in an order of your choice by pairing the formal parameter name with the call value or variable.

association table A table designed to hold two or more foreign keys and enable resolving logical relationships into physical relationships. An association table is also called a *translation table*, and the terms are interchangeable.

attribute A specification that describes an object or element; in database modeling and theory, refers to a column in a table. *Attributes* (or column) describes elements in the row, where the row also can be called a tuple or object instance. (See the *column* definition for more details on the importance of attributes.) *Attributes* also applies to instance variables inside an object type, and they are interchangeably labeled as *fields*.

Attribute Data Type (ADT) A collection of scalar data types. ADT is a generic way of referring to a varray or nested table collection.

attribute domain The possible values that fit within an attribute. The domain of male and female represents the classic choices in a traditional gender column, while the domain of male, female, or other (third gender) represents the choices in a more modern gender column. The possible choices (or values) define the domain of the column, and you can restrict the domain values through database-level constraints.

balanced tree (B-tree) The most common type of database index, an ordered list of values divided into ranges. A key belongs to a range of rows, and the key lets the index find rows more quickly in any table than would a full table scan of the data.

branch block A component of a B-tree index. There are three types of branch blocks: a *root branch block* holds a list of index values from the leftmost branch-level block; a *branch-level block* holds a list of index values for the next level of blocks; and a *leaf block* holds a list of index values that points to values.

branch-level block A component of a B-tree index that isn't a root branch and holds a list of index values for the next level of blocks.

binary relationship A reciprocal set of relations between two things. In databases, the two things are tables, and the relation is between rows (or instances) of tables or views (where views are semipermanent result sets or temporary result sets). There are two physical binary relationships. The one-to-one and one-to-many binary relationships are physical relationships between two tables, or two rows in the same table for recursive relationships.

A *one-to-one binary relationship* between tables means one row in one table relates to one row in another table through a relationship. One row holding a primary key column qualifies as one half of the relationship, and a copy of the primary key column's value, a foreign key column, qualifies as the other half. In a one-to-one binary relationship, which row holds the primary key doesn't matter technically. However, if you choose the wrong one, changing it later when the relationship evolves to a one-to-many relationship can be expensive in both time and resources.

A *one-to-many binary relationship* between tables means one row holds a primary key column and another row holds multiple copies of the same primary key values as a foreign key column. In essence, the one-side donates a copy of itself to enable a join on the equality of values—an equijoin. Some references describe the primary to foreign key relationship as the one-side donating a copy to the many-side (albeit in rare cases the many-side can be the other one-side of the relationship).

It is also possible to have a recursive or self-referencing relationship between two copies of the same table. Such a relationship exists within a single table when it holds columns for both the primary key and the recursive foreign key. This lets any row match to one or more rows in the same table when you use table aliases in a join statement.

NOTE
A self-referencing relationship may resolve between two different rows or two copies of the same row.

There are also many-to-many relationships, but they're logical binary relationships because you can't implement a many-to-many relationship in a physical binary relationship. All many-to-many relationships require intermediary tables that hold copies of the respective primary keys in the same row. The row provides the mapping between the related rows of the two subject-fact or theme tables.

call parameter list The actual parameter list; *see* actual parameter list.

candidate key A unique key that you may choose as a primary key. Unique keys are one or more attributes (or elements) of a row that uniquely identify a tuple (or object instance).

Cartesian product The classic set theory term for a cross join operation, which is when one row from a set is joined with all rows of another set.

character classes Groups or ranges of characters. You can represent them by enumeration (listing them all explicitly) between square brackets or by using a dash character-class metacharacter between the starting and ending characters in a class. Enumeration looks like `[ABCDEabcde012345]`, and a range looks like `[A-Ea-e0-5]`. Character classes can also be represented as POSIX portable character classes, like `[:alnum:]` for alphanumeric characters, as qualified by the `NLS_LANG` environment variable.

Chen notation The first take at data modeling. It put relationships into diamond symbols and failed to capture minimum cardinality in relations.

Chen-Martin notation The second take at data modeling. It added the idea of minimum cardinality to the drawings but preserved the key binary relationships in the diamond.

collapsed object The name of the object type with a list of call parameters to the constructor function of the object type. It allows the Oracle database to store objects in a flattened mode when they're not used. The `TREAT` function lets you instantiate flattened objects into memory. Also known as a *flattened object*.

collection A set of variables of the same data or object type, with an index value or iterator that lets you navigate through the collection. When the index value is a sequentially numbered value the collection is densely populated, which means there are no numeric gaps. When the index value is a key (a number or string) the collection is sparsely populated, which means there may be numeric gaps between a numeric index values. A collection of elements has two implementations in an Oracle database. One is a varray that mirrors an array in an imperative programming language, and the other is a nested table that mimics a list. Collections may contain scalar data types, object types, or both.

column An alternative name for an attribute or element of a tuple, row, or object instance. It describes a vertical element in a two-dimensional table. It comes into the database lexicon from spreadsheets, where a column defines the vertical axis of data. A column also points to a single element of a data structure that is found in every tuple, row, or object instance.

Columns may or may not contain a value in any row. A column that allows a null value is an *optional column* and has a 0..1 cardinality, which means zero to one attribute (or element) per tuple, row, or object instance. A column that disallows a null value is a *mandatory column* and has a 1..1 cardinality. In a mandatory column, every row requires a not null value in the column or attribute. Databases let you allow or disallow a null value when you create or modify a table by assigning a column-level constraint.

column list A comma-delimited list of values. It may apply to the list of values in an override signature of an `INSERT` statement. It also may apply to a parameter list, which could be a formal parameter list or a call parameter list. The formal parameter list defines the parameters that support a function at call time. Call parameters are the values substituted for the formal parameter list when you call a function or procedure. Likewise, the column list that you submit to a `VALUES` clause is the list of call values to an `INSERT` statement.

component selector Represented by a period (`.`), glues references together, such as a schema and a table, a package and a function, or an object and a member function or field. *Dot notation* is the more common way to describe how a component selector works to bridge related parts.

composite (or compound) key A key that consists of two or more columns. A composite key may be applied to many different types of keys. The terms *composite* and *compound* allude to composite materials (such as fiberglass) and chemical compounds, respectively.

constructor A specialized function that returns an object instance.

data structure The definition of a type of data, such as a collection of elements. The elements can be a group of attributes such as integers, dates, or strings. The data structure can also become the base *user-defined type* (UDT) of a collection, where a collection is a set of rows characterized as a list or an array. This type of data structure can be the basis of a nested object instance.

default signature A data catalog's order and number of columns required for an `INSERT` statement. It is also the formal parameter list of a function or procedure.

delete anomaly An anomaly that occurs when the data model's design is flawed, allowing you to delete the wrong data. Like insertion and update anomalies, deletion anomalies occur when you fail to ensure that a table has a single thing, theme, or subject. A deletion anomaly generally occurs when non-unique keys fail to find the correct set of rows or a natural key fails to find a unique row.

densely populated index An index that has no gaps in a numeric sequence of numbers. Oracle implements the numbers as integers, and they use 1-based numbering in collections.

descriptor The term formerly used to describe a reference to the storage location of a `CLOB`, `NCLOB`, `BLOB`, or `BFILE` data type. It has been superseded by the term *locator*.

determinant The thing that decides meaning or context of another variable (see *functional dependency* for an example). A determinate may be part of a composite natural key or a single-column natural key. A single-column natural key (also called a candidate key) determines uniqueness in a table about a single thing, theme, or subject, and is a positive indicator of a good design. A determinate inside a composite natural key identifies a set of possible values that has context only with the determinate and indicates that the table is less than second normal form (2NF).

domain A set of related things, like the set of integers or the set of real numbers. For example, the set of real numbers is the domain of possible values in a column. It is also possible to apply *domain* to instances of a thing, theme, or subject. That makes the domain the set of possible unique rows in a table.

Domain can also apply to our knowledge of a subject, like algebra, biology, chemistry, or literature analysis. The sciences have rigorous definitions or boundaries, like biology's taxonomy of life, domain, kingdom, phylum, class, order, family, genus, and species. Literature analysis is not so easily classified and is arguably subject to interpretation. Most business problems can be classified as subject to interpretation, but sometimes they do follow clear-cut rules and definitions.

dot notation Using a dot or a period (`.`) to reference an element of a container, such as a table in a schema, a function in a package, or a member function or field in an object. It's the more common way to describe a component selector.

empty Describes an Oracle object type that holds only an empty copy of the object type. Its most common use is with the `empty_clob` and `empty_blob` function calls for initializing internally stored large objects.

entity A container, most often a table in a relational database.

entity-relationship model (ERM) A more common acryonym that replaces "ER model" by including "model" in the acronym.

entity-relationship (ER) model A graphical drawing that shows a collection of tables as symbols and identifies their connecting binary relationships through a series of lines.

equijoin A join between two tables or instances of one table based on the equality of values in the primary and foreign key columns.

field An attribute (or element) of a primitive or user-defined data type. A field is one element of a row and one instance of the column's data type. A field can have a fixed or variable size. The field descriptor belongs with the record descriptor for rows of a table.

file A repository of data. The data can be a set of binary or ASCII bytes representing information such as an image, program, or document.

file system Manages files, which are data repositories. Typically, file systems manage the storage, access, and retrieval of files.

flattened object *See* collapsed object.

foreign key One or a set of attributes (or elements) that maps to a primary key made up of one or a set of attributes (or elements). The primary key is typically in another table but can be in the same table as the foreign key. This type of relationship is a one-to-many binary relationship. The table holding the primary key is the one-side of the binary relationship, and the table holding the foreign key is the many-side of the binary relationship. A self-referencing one-to-many relationship exists when both the primary and foreign keys exist in the same table.

formal parameter list A list of parameters included in the definition of a stored program (such as a function, procedure, package function or procedure, or object method). It represents the position, data type, and any default values for the parameters, and whether they're pass-by-value or pass-by-reference parameters.

forward engineering The process of using a SQL script to create an ER model. *See also* entity-relationship (ER) model.

FROM clause Identifies the tables that will be used in a query or a `SELECT` statement.

function A subroutine that may have a parameter list of one or more formal parameters and a return type that maps to a SQL or PL/SQL data type. The formal parameters are inputs to the function, and, in some cases, outputs. Parameters have three modes of operation: as an input only, as an output only, or as both an input and an output. A function with input-only parameters is a pass-by-value function, while a function is a pass-by-reference function when at least one parameter acts as either an `OUT`-only mode parameter or an `IN OUT` mode parameter.

functional dependency A dependency that exists when an attribute or a set of attributes (or elements) depends on exactly one other unique attribute or set of attributes. For example, a movie rating of PG by the Motion Picture Association of America is an example of a functional dependency because the PG rating is wholly dependent on the rating body. This is shown as a functional dependency with the following notation:

Rating Agency → Rating

The expression says that the rating agency determines the rating. The variable on the left of this type of expression is called the determinant (the thing that decides meaning or context of the variable on the right). *See also* determinant.

GROUP BY clause Designates the nonaggregated columns in an aggregated result set from a query or a `SELECT` statement.

HAVING clause Filters an aggregated result set in a query or a `SELECT` statement.

HNF Acronym for *highest normal form*. HNF always the present normalization level the table, which means an unnormalized table's HNF is 0NF and so forth.

Information Engineering notation The formal name for the notation system developed by James Martin. It removed the diamond symbols used in Chen-Martin notation and put all notation along the relationship lines. The use of perpendicular lines, greater-than and less-than symbols, and zeros gave rise to a notation system that is easy to read and doesn't waste space when printed. MySQL Workbench uses the Information Engineering notation symbols.

initialized collection A varray or nested table that has been constructed with zero elements or one or more elements. An initialized collection with zero elements is called an empty collection, and an initialized collection with one or more elements is called a populated collection.

inner capture An Oracle-specific phrase that describes when a join is made between a field value of an object type column and either another column or a field value of another object type column. It describes a dot notation that goes one level deeper than the object type column itself. For example, the dot notation may connect things from the largest container to the leaf node scalar value, which means from a table name, through a column name, to a field.

insertion anomaly An anomaly that allows you to insert duplicate or incorrect data. An insertion anomaly typically occurs when your data model design fails to ensure that a table focuses on a single thing, theme, or subject. More often than not, it means that rows aren't unique if the table's highest normal form is first normal form (1NF), and that the primary key fails to *determine* the uniqueness of rows in second normal form (2NF).

instance A collection of databases managed by a database management system (DBMS). A MySQL Server instance is the set of databases it manages.

instantiate To promote an object from a collapsed object to an object instance in memory, thereby making it active.

key A unique or nonunique attribute or set of attributes that identifies rows in a table. A unique key identifies a unique row, while a nonunique key identifies one or more rows in a table.

Keys serve different purposes in tables. A key may identify the column or set of columns that uniquely qualifies a row, in which case the key is a candidate key to become the primary key.

leaf block A component of a B-tree index that holds a list of index values that point to actual values.

list A collection of a specific set of things, which are typically unique. The things share one thing, the data type of the collection. The number of elements in a list may grow over time because, unlike arrays, lists don't impose a limit on the number of elements in a collection.

locator A reference to the storage location of a `CLOB`, `NCLOB`, `BLOB`, or `BFILE` data type.

logical relationship A binary or n-ary relationship that has no physical implementation without an intermediary table. Logical relationships enable modeling patterns to accommodate real-world business problems. The logical relationship is always implemented by creating an association or translation table that maps the relationship between the two tables' primary keys. A mandatory column may have a 0..* (zero-to-many) cardinality when the column uses the MySQL SET data type.

mandatory column A column that requires a value when inserting a row or updating that specific column. It has a 1..1 cardinality during design and most often has a not null database constraint to guarantee the insertion or update of a valid value.

many-to-many binary relationship A nonspecific relationship between two tables where one row in one table may map to zero to many rows in the other, and vice versa. Naturally, you must resolve this type of logical binary relationship to a physical binary relationship. The one-to-many and one-to-one (infrequently implemented) relationships are the only physical binary relationships. You resolve the logical many-to-many binary relationship by creating a third table that holds the foreign key from both tables in the same row. The third table is typically called an association or translation table.

Martin notation *See* Information Engineering notation.

member A function or procedure inside an Oracle object type.

MEMBER OF A logical comparison operator that determines whether an element is a member of a collection, such as a varray or a nested table.

multilevel collection A collection held inside another collection. It's possible to implement multilevel collections as transient or persistent object types.

n-ary relationship A nonspecific relationship between three or more tables. Like the logical many-to-many binary relationship, an n-ary relationship doesn't have a physical implementation by itself. You map the three or more tables by using another table that holds foreign keys from all of the other tables in a single row. This intermediary table is typically known as an association or translation table. Typically, all of the original tables have a one-to-many relationship to the association table, and all relationships resolve through the association table.

name resolution A process whereby you at the top of a hierarchy and descend one level at a time. The hierarchy is typically an inverted tree of nodes. The starting point is the root node (or topmost node), nodes with dependent nodes are simply ordinary *nodes*, and leaf nodes are at the bottom of any branch of the inverted tree because the bottommost nodes don't have any child nodes. Such bottommost nodes are leaf nodes. An example would be starting at a schema and navigating down to a table or column within a table, or a field within an object type column.

natural key A unique key that identifies a row of data or instance of data. A natural key may be one or more attributes (or elements) that uniquely identify a tuple (a row) or object instance. Natural keys are typically a set of attributes that uniquely identifies each row in a table. A natural key is automatically a candidate key that you may choose as the table's primary key. All other columns in the table should enjoy a direct and full functional dependency on all attributes in the natural key.

A surrogate key varies only in one regard: it needs to map to one and only one natural key. A surrogate key should never be added to the natural key in order to achieve unique rows. This means the surrogate key plus the natural key should never become the natural key because otherwise the attributes that describe the table's single subject wouldn't do so uniquely.

NOTE
If you adopt a surrogate key for joins, the surrogate key plus the natural key should become a unique index to speed searches through the table.

nested table A collection of elements, where the elements can be scalar data types, object types, or collections of object types. A nested table acts like a doubly linked list in imperative programming languages. It has no limit, other than that imposed by the Oracle SGA, on the number of elements in the collection. The Oracle Collection API lets you navigate forward or backward through the list.

nested varray Like a nested table, a collection of elements where the elements can be scalar data types, object types, or collections of object types. Unlike a nested table, a nested varray has a fixed size and can't have more elements than that. A nested varray acts like a numerically indexed array in imperative programming languages. The Oracle Collection API lets you navigate forward or backward through it, and you can also access the limit of the maximum number of array elements.

nominated key The candidate key you choose to nominate as the primary key. At some point, the nominated key simply becomes the primary key. At that point, the nomination becomes history and nobody cares about it. The only subtle difference is that while most people use the term *nominated key* to indicate the candidate key they've tentatively chosen before making a final decision, some people substitute *nominated key* for *candidate key*. The latter usage should be discouraged.

nonempty subsets Nested tables, at any level of nesting, found in object tables or object columns. The official Oracle label for these is submultisets.

non-key An attribute (column) or set of attributes (columns) that contains a descriptive set of values that identifies unique rows as unique but provides a characteristic to a row of data. All non-key columns should have a full functional dependency on the natural key or primary key.

nonspecific relationship A logical or reciprocal set of relations between two things. Nonspecific relationships are many-to-many and n-ary relationships. Nonspecific relationships create situations where rows in two tables have no way to establish a relationship between the two tables, because one copy of the primary key can't be donated to the other row without breaking the many-to-many relationship pattern. Logical nonspecific relationships are thereby mapped through association or translation tables and decomposed into specific one-to-one or one-to-many binary relationships.

normalization The process of breaking a table or relation with more than one thing, theme, or subject into a set of tables. The goal of normalization is to have tables with one thing, theme, or subject so that they aren't susceptible to insertion, update, or delete anomalies.

object body In the context of a relational database, the implementation of an object type.

object column A column in a table that has an object type rather than a data type. The implementation of an object column is synonymous with the implementation of a persistent object type. Object columns may also contain other nested object types.

object instance A data structure or row of data inserted into an object type, which is like a hybrid table in an object-relational database management system (ORDBMS). Moreover, an object instance is a row in any table. The row contains purely attributes in a relational database.

object table A table defined by an object type. It supports inserts and updates directly to column values like a relational table, as well as inserts or updates with collapsed objects.

object table function A function that returns a collection of a composite data type, known as an object type.

object type In the context of a relational database, a data structure, or the definition of a table. Definitions of tables are stored in the database catalog and built upon pre-existing data types. Some databases support user-defined types (UDTs), which include attributes and methods. The pattern of a table is a generalization of a table, and rows are instances of an object type.

one-to-many binary relationship A physical relationship characterized by one table holding a primary key and the other table holding a foreign key. The primary key can be one or more attributes, and the foreign key is a copy of values from the primary key attribute(s). The one-side of the relationship holds the primary key, while the many-side holds one-to-many copies of the primary key as the foreign key. The tables resolve or map rows from one to the other by comparing the values of the primary and foreign key columns.

one-to-one binary relationship A physical relationship that you can implement in the database. It is also a specialized or subtype of a one-to-many relationship. One of the one-sides holds the primary key value(s) and the other one-side holds a copy of the primary key as the foreign key value. It is possible to choose either table as the one with the primary key, but if you choose incorrectly, the re-engineering cost is high because the one-side holding the single copy of the primary key as a foreign key should never become the table that holds the primary key in the relationship between the tables.

optional column A column that doesn't require a value when inserting a row or updating that specific column. It has a 0..1 (zero-to-one) cardinality during design and is typically unconstrained. An optional column may have a 0..* (zero-to-many) cardinality when the column uses the MySQL SET data type.

ORDER BY clause Designates how the rows are sorted by a `SELECT` statement.

override signature A form of named notation that allows you to provide call parameter lists in the order you choose. An override signature lets you provide a column list that overrides the data catalog's order and number of columns required for an `INSERT` statement. An override signature also lets you provide a named notation list of columns and values to a function or procedure.

parameter A placeholder variable defined as part of a function or procedure signature. A parameter is identified by its data type only, with one exception: parameters to object types are uniquely identified by their formal parameter name and data type.

parameter list A list of columns with individual modes of operation. Parameters can have an `IN`-only, `OUT`-only, or `IN OUT` mode of operation. Parameters with an `IN`-only mode of operation may also have a default value.

partial dependency A dependency that exists when the primary key is a composite key (aka compound key of two or more columns), and one or more non-key columns depend on less than all of the columns of the composite key primary key. Hence, the non-key column is partially dependent on the primary key.

object table function A function that returns a collection of a composite data type, known as an object type.

pipelined table function A function that returns a collection of records that is converted into a SQL object collection.

portable character classes Classes in which the ranges are represented by keywords described in Table E-1 in Appendix E. Classes are also known as POSIX keywords like `[:alpha:]` or `[:alnum:]` (alphabetic and alphanumeric ranges, respectively).

primary key A column or set of columns that is assigned a primary key constraint and uniquely identifies all rows in the table. A primary key may be a surrogate key, which is an artificial numbering schema, or a natural key made up of one to many columns of the table.

procedure A subroutine that may have a parameter list of one or more formal parameters but no return type. More or less, a procedure is a function that returns a void data type. Like functions, procedures have formal parameters as inputs, outputs, or both. A procedure with input-only parameters is a pass-by-value module, while a procedure with at least one `OUT`-only or `IN OUT` mode parameter is a pass-by-reference module.

range character classes Groups or ranges of characters. A range character class lets you represent a set of values by enumeration (listing them all explicitly) between square brackets or by using a dash character-class metacharacter between the starting and ending characters in a class. Enumeration looks like `[ABCDEabcde012345]`, and a range looks like `[A-Ea-e0-5]`.

record A row of data in a table, or an instance of a defined data structure (such as a table). The term *record* comes from file system technology, which predates database technology, so traditionally it meant only a horizontal element in a table composed of fields (in other words, a row or tuple). The latter meaning is specific to databases.

regular expression Any set of characters, numbers, classes, meta-sequences, and identifiers that let an engine discover an exact or like match in text. A *regular expression* are a grammar of special characters that let you make pattern matching clear and concise, at least once you understand how they work. You can find coverage on regular expressions in Appendix E.

result set A set of results returned by a SQL statement, formatted in rectangular shape. The rectangular shape is determined by the number of columns across the X axis and the number of rows across the Y axis.

reverse engineering The process of using an existing database to generate a SQL script capable of generating an entity relationship model. ER models are symbolic representations of how tables are connected in a relational database.

root branch block A component of a B-tree index that holds the list of all next-level or leaf-level blocks.

routine A subroutine, a stored program unit (a stored function or procedure), or a programming language function or method.

row An instance of an object where the object is a table or an instance of a data structure. Also, a horizontal element in a table. The term comes from a spreadsheet context, where *row* defines the horizontal axis of data. A row is also an instance of the data structure defined by a table definition, and the nested array of a structure inside an ordinary array.

SELECT list The comma-delimited list of columns in a `SELECT` statement.

SELF The keyword that represents a copy of the current object instance. It is equivalent to the *this* keyword in the Java programming language.

sparsely populated index An index that has gaps in a numeric sequence of numbers, or one that uses string index values. You must navigate across a sparsely populated index by using an iterator to move across the values in a collection.

specific relationship A reciprocal set of relations between two things where one row in a result set finds one row in another result set, or where one row in a result set finds many matches in another result set. These binary relationships are, respectively, one-to-one and one-to-many. Specific relationships have equijoin or non-equijoin resolution. Equijoin resolution matches values, like the process in a nested loop; non-equijoin resolution matches values through a range or inequality relationship. Equijoins typically have a primary key and a foreign key, and the one-side holds the primary key while the many-side holds the foreign key. In the specialized case of a one-to-one relationship, you must choose which table holds the primary key that becomes a functional dependency as a foreign key in the other.

subdomain A subset of related things. For example, negative, zero, and positive integers are subsets of the set of integers. The foregoing example describes the subdomain of possible values in a column based on the column's data type. *Subdomain* also describes a like set of rows in a table. The easiest example would be using a gender column to find the men or women in a set of people.

submultiset A nested table stored in a transient or persistent object. The submultiset may occur at any level deeper than the first. Also called a *nonempty subset*.

subroutine An alternate description for a routine. Like routines, subroutines are stored program units (stored functions or procedures) or programming language functions or methods.

super key A key that identifies a set of rows, such as a gender column that lets you identify males or females in your data model.

surrogate key A key that isn't related to the subject of the table and as an attribute provides no characteristic of the subject except uniqueness. Every surrogate key should map to one unique natural key. Using the natural key and surrogate key together to define uniqueness means the natural key isn't unique and therefore isn't a natural key.

symbol set A group of drawing symbols that lets you tell a story, such as a rectangle to depict a table and a line to depict a relationship between two tables. Unified Modeling Language is a common symbol set, and UML uses of two cardinal numbers separated by two dots to represent what would be otherwise a long hand (or wordy) description of cardinality. For example, you use a 0..* for a zero-to-many relationship and a 1..* for a one-to-many relationship. While a one-to-many relationship has no shorthand version, a zero-to-many relationship may be represented with an asterisk (*) or, in some tools, an infinity symbol (∞).

table A two-dimensional structure defined by the horizontal data structure that defines the list of column(s) as the X axis and the rows instances of the data structure as the Y axis.

TABLE function A function that lets you construct a SQL result set for join operations in SQL statements.

transitive dependency A dependency that exists when a column depends on another column before relying on the primary key of the table. It may exist in tables with three or more columns that are in second normal form. *See also* 2NF.

translation table A table that is designed to hold two or more foreign keys and that enables resolving logical relationships into physical relationships. A translation table is also known as an *association table*, and the terms are interchangeable.

tuple A row in a table. The term comes from relational algebra, where a column is an attribute and a row is a tuple.

unique key A column or set of columns that uniquely identifies a row of data.

uninitialized collection A collection that has been declared but not defined. A persistent object type (one used as a column data type in a table) is an uninitialized collection when a row contains a null value rather than a constructor signature. You define an empty collection by using a constructor signature of a type name followed by parentheses. A populated collection would include elements, which would be scalar values for an Attribute Data Type (ADT) and a object constructor for a user-defined type (UDT).

unnesting query A SELECT statement that requires creating table references to the object column collection with the TABLE function and then using cross joins. Cross joins resolve because the row that holds the object column collection is known through hidden internal columns. However, you must use a (+) on the object column collection when the potential exists that it may hold a null value, or uninitialized collection.

update anomaly An anomaly that occurs when the data model's design allows incorrect changes to data. Like insertion anomalies, update anomalies occur when you fail to ensure that a table has a single thing, theme, or subject. It generally occurs when nonunique keys fail to find the correct set of rows, but it also can occur when a natural key fails to find a unique row.

user-defined type (UDT) A data structure that typically groups a list of field values together into a record data structure. The default signature is position specific by the field list of columns, but Oracle does let you access them by named notation provided you initialize all of the field-list elements.

varray A collection of elements, where the elements can be scalar data types, object types, or collections of object types. A varray acts like an array in imperative programming languages. You define a varray with a specific maximum number of elements. The Oracle Collection API allows you to navigate the list forward and backward like a doubly linked list.

WHERE clause Filters nonaggregated results and returns the results from a query or a SELECT statement.

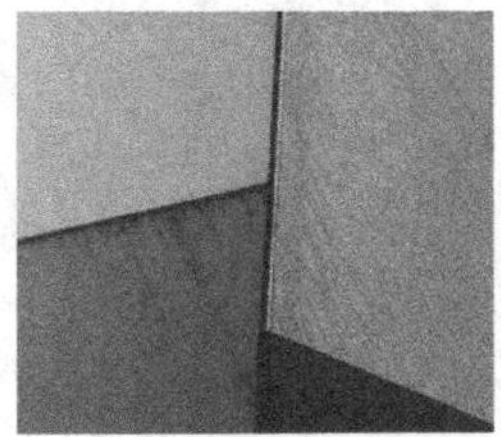

Index

Symbols

A

B

C

D

F

G

H

I

J

K

L

M

N

O

P

Q

R

S

T

U

V

W

X

Z

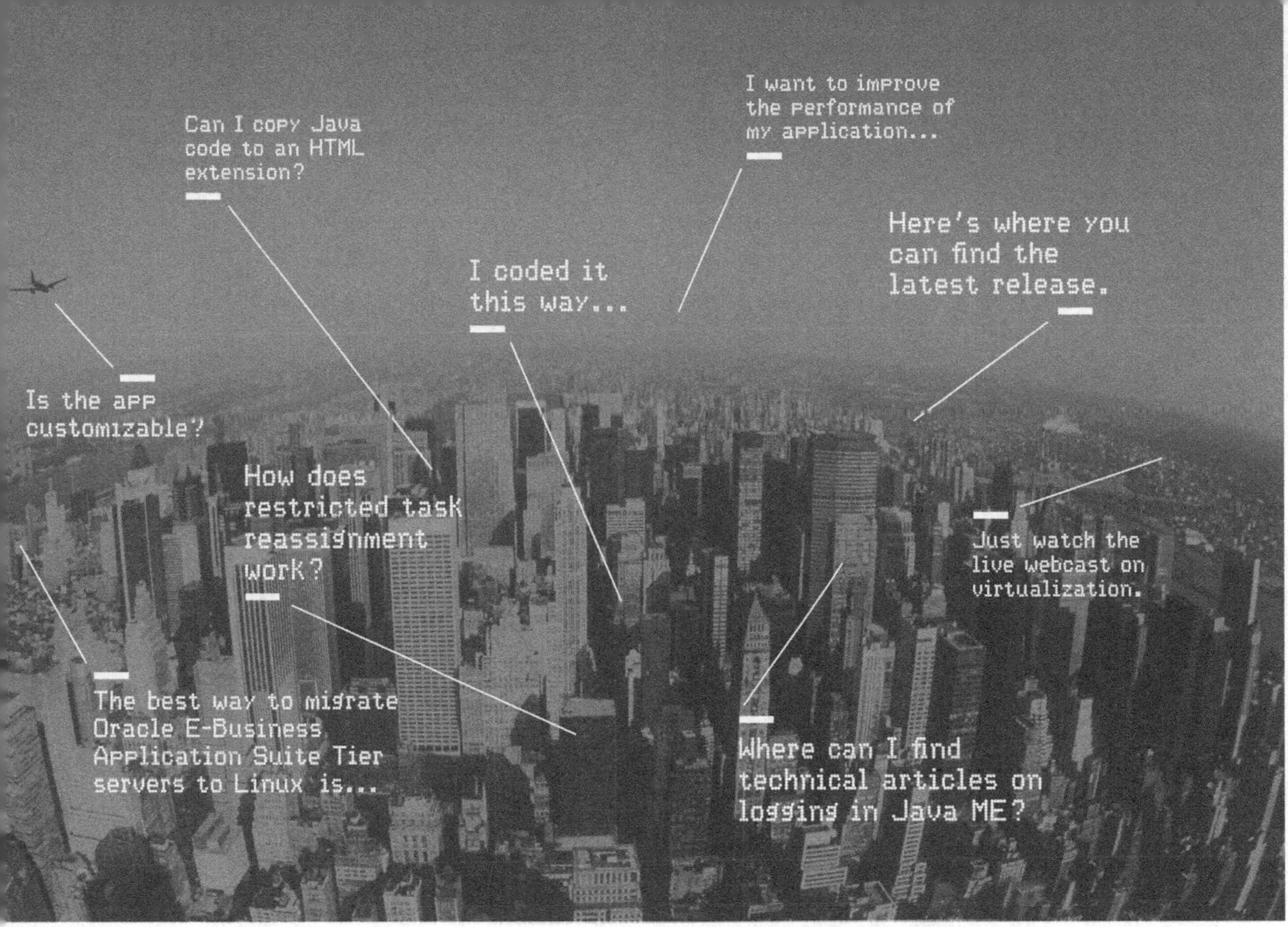